SURVIVING DEATH
Echoes of the Abyss: A Memoir of Despair and Discovery
When the Light Went Out. My Story of Surviving the Darkest Hour.
A Personal Reckoning with Suicide and Self.
Volume One
LETITIA SWANEPOEL

Table of Contents

Surviving Death
My journey from death to life.
Finding freedom in the darkness.
Letitia Swanepoel

ISBN: 978-1-0492-3375-8
Surviving Death
Echoes of the Abyss
Volume One
All Art and Illustrations by: Letitia Swanepoel
Written and Edited by: Letitia Swanepoel
For testimonials or sharing contact me directly:
Lswanepoel.books@gmail.com

Surviving Death: Echoes of the Abyss

A Memoir of despair and discovery

By Letitia Swanepoel

The Doorway: Echoes of the Almost

The air hung heavy around me, thick and unmoving, stale with the metallic tang of regret; a taste that coated my tongue like a memory I could neither spit out nor swallow. It lingered, stubborn and bitter, echoing every unspoken word, every undone moment, every sorrow I had tried to bury but still carried in the marrow of my being! I drifted in that strange, haunted in-between; that liminal threshold where breath is hesitant, and existence feels paper-thin. Suspended between presence and disappearance, I hovered like a fading echo, not fully here, yet not entirely gone. A ghost of myself, caught in the quiet tension between holding on and slipping away. Before me stood a door; vast, ancient, impossibly heavy. Its surface was trembling with an eerie, breathing light that pulsed like a living heart. I felt it long before my mind could name it, a low, resonant thrum stirring through my bones, whispering a truth I had courted for years. This was *the* doorway. The threshold I had wandered toward in shadows and secrets, the quiet mouth of oblivion I had prayed would swallow my pain whole. It was the silent gateway I once believed was the only path out of the unbearable weight of being, the only escape from the crushing gravity of my own existence. A door that promised not passage, but disappearance. This is my memoir of inching toward that threshold, of pressing my palm to its cold, humming surface, of stepping partly through the veil and somehow... somehow... finding my way back again.

It is the story of a woman who walked to the edge of her own ending and lived to retrace her steps. A chronicle carved from the long, quiet war I waged with myself. Years spent grappling with the insidious whisper of depression, a voice so soft it slipped into the seams of my daylight, unnoticed at first, until it became the pulse beneath every breath. And when night fell, that whisper grew teeth. It became a roar that swallowed sleep whole, a tide of despair crashing again and again against the fragile shores of my sanity. This book is the echo of that struggle, and the testament of the journey back from its edge. It is the story of how those shadows thickened over the years, how they curled around my ribs and tightened, slowly, relentlessly, until the pressure became unbearable. Until everything inside me ruptured into a single, desperate moment... one act I believed would be final, one choice I thought would grant me silence at last. This memoir is the record of that descent, the slow unraveling, the quiet implosions, the whispered goodbyes no one ever heard. And it is also the trembling, improbable truth of what came after: That sometimes the human spirit survives what should have ended it, that even in the deepest collapse, some fragile thread holds fast. This is the testament of walking into the abyss, and the miracle of still... somehow... finding a way back into the light.

THE DAY THE WEIGHT won (almost)

Volume One traces the contours of the day I almost died; the day my perceived failures gathered like storm clouds and collapsed upon my chest with such unbearable weight that breath itself became a stranger to me. It is the story of the suffocating loneliness that draped itself over my shoulders like a burial shroud, pulling tighter with every thought, every tremor of doubt, every desperate heartbeat fighting to be heard beneath the crushing silence of despair. It captures the agonizing moment when ending the pain felt like the last mercy available to me. When the struggle had grown so vast, so unrelenting, that continuing it seemed almost cruel. Within these chapters, I offer no apologies. There is no softening, no disguising, no polite rewriting of the past. Only transparency. Only truth... Truth stripped to the bone, laid bare and trembling, lifted toward the light so that nothing... not even the most hidden ache, is left to fester in the dark.

Inside the fractured mind:

It is a raw, unfiltered glimpse into the fractured terrain of a mind standing on the trembling ledge of oblivion...prepared for the jump. These pages open the door to the thoughts that stalked me in the silent hours; those midnight predators that slithered through the cracks of my consciousness, whispering their poison with a familiarity so intimate it almost felt like love. Here, I lay bare the lies I once fed myself... lies sculpted from old wounds and unhealed sorrows, from fear that lodged itself in my bones, from years spent believing I was somehow unworthy of breath, unworthy of stay, unworthy of life. And I unveil the burden I carried; a crushing, invisible weight that bowed my spine and bruised the deepest parts of my spirit. A heaviness no one could see, yet one that threatened, every single day, to collapse my entire being beneath its relentless gravity. This is not just confession. It is excavation. It is the unearthing of a soul that nearly vanished. From one irreversible action... one final, desperate... choice. And every choice, that came after *Surviving Death*.

No soft edges, only truth

This is not a romanticized tale of darkness; no gilded version of suffering softened for easier swallowing. It is not tragedy dressed in poetic lace, nor pain wrapped in metaphor to make it palatable. This is the stark, unflinching landscape of suicidal ideation laid bare; the barren inner wasteland where hope crumbles like sand between trembling fingers, where your own thoughts turn predator, circling you with a quiet, merciless hunger, where every breath becomes a negotiation, and every heartbeat feels like an argument with existence itself. Here, the shadows do not whisper sweetly; they hiss, they constrict, they wrap themselves around the ribcage until even the act of staying alive feels like defiance. This is the truth as it was lived; raw, unvarnished, trembling at the edges, aching with its own honesty. Painfully, unapologetically human.

At the Lip of Oblivion

Join me now as I stand once more at that trembling threshold, my toes curled over the edge of a world I nearly surrendered to; the abyss that once beckoned with its cold, merciful promise of final silence. Gazing into its fierce brutal yet deceptively inviting eyes. Walk beside me into that suspended moment when everything; breath, heartbeat, purpose; hung in a delicate, quivering breathless balance, as fragile as a last exhale held between life and letting go. It was there, at the lip of oblivion, in the hush before the fall, that the first fragile threads of survival revealed themselves... gossamer-fine, shimmering like threads spun by unseen hands, thin as spider silk yet impossibly, defiantly strong...trembling yet strangely resilient. These threads; mysterious, miraculous, woven from something beyond reason; wrapped themselves around my fading will, around the dimming ember of my existence, and tugged me gently, insistently, back from the yawning mouth of the void. This is the story of that return; of the quiet forces, human and divine, that reached for me when my own hands fell limp; the forces that held me when I could no longer hold myself.

A Beginning for Both of Us

This is the beginning of my journey… and perhaps, in some quiet, unseen way, the beginning of yours as well. I invite you to lean gently into the contours of your own story; to gather its scattered fragments as one might collect shards of stained glass, not to hide their sharpness, but to hold them up to the light and discover the colours they still carry. Come closer to the truth of your own becoming, not with force, but with tenderness. Let your trembling hands learn to trust the shape of your own heart again. To discover within yourself the strength to turn away from the darkness that has shadowed your steps. You do not need to hurl yourself toward life with heroic leaps; you need only choose it in the smallest, softest increments; in a single breath, then another, and another, and another still. For sometimes survival is not a declaration… but a whisper, a quiet choosing, moment after moment, until one day you realize you have walked further from the darkness than you ever believed possible. Let this be your reminder; that even the faintest flicker of willingness, the smallest lean toward maybe, can swell into a beacon bright enough to guide you back toward a life that has not given up on you. Because even in the deepest chambers of despair; those echoing hollows where the world feels carved out, where colour drains from the days and light seems like a myth whispered by someone else's tongue; hope does not die… It flickers. A shy, faint, trembling ember, fragile as the wingbeat of a moth in winter, almost imperceptible, yet impossibly, stubbornly alive. It waits for you in the quiet, steady as a forgotten heartbeat, patient as dawn lingering behind a horizon you've stopped looking toward. It longs to be noticed, to be cupped gently in your palms, to be breathed upon with the softest hint of willingness. And sometimes; miraculously, mysteriously, all it takes is the smallest spark… one breath, one moment, one choice… for that tiny ember to glow again, gathering warmth, gathering strength, until it becomes a flame you can finally feel.

Index:

Introduction:

Suicidal Ideation:

Suicide Attempt:

Mayor Depression Disorder:

Back Story that Led me to my Suicide Attempt:

This book is written in loving memory of
Colleen Murray
4 December 1958 – 22 January 2026
Colleen Murray
4 December 1958 – 22 January 2026
How lucky am I to have something
that makes saying goodbye so hard.
I will always carry your legacy
and torch held high.

My Dearest Cols,

This book begins where the last breath of the previous page still lingers, where the air is warm with what has just been spoken and not yet released. It rises from what came before, from the quiet, unshakable knowing that love does not end, it only changes its clothing, its texture, its way of arriving. I write this book in memory of your legacy, your memory, your soul, as one might light a flame from another flame, hands steady, breath held, careful and reverent, fully aware of the sacredness of what is being carried forward. May this book hold your torch high, not as an echo fading into distance, but as a living light that continues to warm, to guide, to illuminate. For my words are painted by your wisdom and your love, layered gently, patiently, like brushstrokes learned not through instruction but through watching your hands and your presence move through the world, teaching simply by being. I speak these words so they may fall like a gentle breeze of love, soft enough not to disturb what is fragile, yet strong enough to travel across thresholds, across worlds, to reach wherever you are now. I speak these words as a heart that has known your love in its fullest measure and loves you back with that same fullness, unguarded, unwavering, without dilution or restraint. There is no lesser way to love you. I can only speak these words now in memory, because your soul departed this world before this book found its final voice. And yet, you are everywhere within it. In every pause that breathes instead of rushing. In every truth that refused to be silenced. In every tenderness that insisted on staying when it would have been easier to harden. This book arrived late, but love does not keep time the way the world does. It arrives when it must, exactly as it is needed, and it never truly arrives without you already there. I want to honor your memory, your legacy, and who you were, not as something finished or sealed in the past, but as something still breathing, still shaping the lives you touched in ways both visible and unseen. Let these words stand as a gentle testament to how deeply loved you were, how carefully held, how profoundly seen in the fullness of who you were.

Your life mattered. Your presence mattered. You mattered. These truths do not dim with time; they deepen, like color settling further into cloth with every passing year. Your greatest wish before you departed was to celebrate your life, and here, at the very beginning of this book, I grant you the space to do just that. I open these pages the way one opens a room already filled with light, pulling back the curtains, widening the doorway, making room for laughter, warmth, remembrance, and truth to gather without restraint. This is not a quiet corner of grief, but a living threshold where your spirit is welcomed fully, exactly as it always was. For years, your words were the soft, warm, cozy, comforting blanket that wrapped around me when the world was icy cold. They held their shape around my shoulders. They kept me warm. They kept me safe. They taught me that gentleness is not fragile, that it can endure even the harshest seasons without losing its softness. And even now, in your departure, I hope my words can become that same blanket for your memory and your legacy, resting lightly and faithfully, carrying forward what you once gave so freely, saying what you once said to me without needing to speak: You are not alone. You are loved. You are held. Even though I can no longer sit beside you and hold your hand ever again, nor hear the wisdom in your voice carried to me in living sound, please know this: I still hold your hand, your memory, your heart, and your legacy in spirit. They rest within me like a steady pulse, unseen yet unwavering, as if love itself learned how to breathe without a body, how to remain when form has gone. What once lived between us in touch and sound now lives within me as presence, constant and faithful. I speak these words to honor your life, your meaning, and your legacy, shaping them gently into something that can be carried forward. Something others can hold when their own hands are empty. I want to honor you, Cols, for the woman that you were. The brave, remarkable, and wise woman who stood rooted even when the ground beneath her shifted, who did not harden when the world trembled, but held her place with quiet resolve. Your strength was never loud or demanding, but enduring, like stone warmed by the sun, storing heat and offering it back long after the light has moved on. I honor you for the footprints you have left behind on this earth, impressions pressed so deeply they remain long after you have passed, not only along the paths you walked, but within the hearts you touched along the way. They are marks that time does not erase, guides that continue to lead, reminding those who follow that someone loved deeply here, and that love, once placed, never truly leaves. I honor you for the hard fight you fought, not to conquer or to win, but to become an example, a living permission slip quietly placed in the hands of others when the road narrowed, and the weight grew heavy. Your courage was never about arrival, but about endurance, about showing that it is possible to keep moving with grace even when the path asks everything of you. I honor you for all the hearts you held, cradled, and steadied, often without ever being asked, sensing the need before it was spoken. You carried others with a tenderness that asked for nothing in return, offering steadiness simply because you could. I honor you for the beauty of your soul, a beauty that did not fade because it was never tied to time, age, or form. It lived beyond the surface, radiant and constant, the kind of beauty that remains even after the light has shifted. I honor you for showing so many people that they are worthy, not through grand declarations, but simply by being fully, unapologetically yourself, and teaching them to also be themselves. In your presence, others remembered who they were allowed to be. I honor you, my dearest Cols, for always being you. For always being honest. For always, always showing up with all your love and all your truth, even when it cost you something to do so. I honor your journey, from its first breath to its final becoming, and I carry it forward now, as gently and faithfully as you once carried mine, holding it with the same care, the same devotion, trusting that what was given in love will continue to find its way.

She walked the long road of sobriety with a courage few ever witness and even fewer truly understand. Not as a straight line carved cleanly through time, but as a devotion. A daily choosing. A quiet, relentless act of love for life itself. Each day was a vow renewed, sometimes whispered, sometimes spoken through trembling hands, sometimes carried only by breath when breath was all she had. Sobriety was not simply something she achieved, it was something she embodied, something that lived in her posture, her pauses, her presence. It shaped her compassion, sharpened her honesty, softened her heart, and turned her into a safe harbor for those still lost at sea. People arrived to her battered, ashamed, weather-worn, and she did not ask how they wrecked their ships. She simply helped them dock. In her, recovery had a face. A voice. Hands that knew how to hold without gripping, how to steady without controlling, how to offer strength without stealing agency. She made safety feel possible. She showed me that healing does not erase the past, it redeems it. That survival can become service. That pain, when met with truth, can be transformed into wisdom, offered freely, without judgment, without conditions. Her scars were not hidden, nor were they displayed. They simply existed as proof that light can pass through what once broke us. She was my second mother in all the ways that mattered most. She did not give me life, but she taught me how to live it. She mothered my becoming, tending to the parts of me that were still learning how to stand. She steadied me when I faltered, called me back when I strayed, and believed in me long before I knew how to believe in myself. Her love was not indulgent, it was anchoring. Not permissive, but protective. It had weight. It had roots. She held me to my highest self because she could see it even when I could not, even when I was buried beneath fear, doubt, and old stories. And she was my deepest, closest friend. The kind of friend who sees behind the mask and loves what lives there anyway. The kind who listens without needing to fix, who tells the truth without cruelty, who stays when it would be easier to leave. With her, I was never required to perform, to be polished, or to pretend. I could arrive exactly as I was, broken or brave, unraveling or rising, and be met fully. In her presence, I learned that love could be both gentle and strong, and that being seen, truly seen, could feel like coming home. Her sobriety gave the world a woman of rare integrity, a life lived upright, aligned, and true. It gave me a guide, a mirror, a home. In her presence, I could see myself more clearly, not as I feared I was, but as I was becoming. Through her, I learned that strength can be gentle, that honesty can be loving, and that showing up day after day, even when no one is watching, is its own quiet miracle, a sacred discipline of the heart. She has walked on now, beyond the edge of what I can touch, but the path she carved remains. It is worn into the earth of me. It runs through my choices, my boundaries, my courage, my care for others. It runs through every moment I choose truth over escape, presence over avoidance, love over fear. Each choice is a footprint laid over hers, a continuation rather than an ending. She was proof that a life can be rebuilt and still be beautiful, not in spite of its fractures, but because of the care with which it was rebuilt. Proof that it is never too late to become who you were always meant to be. Proof that one sober, loving heart can ripple outward and quietly change countless others, without needing recognition, without asking for praise. And I am forever changed because she walked beside me. Because she stayed. Because she chose love again and again. This is my final honoring of her journey, her devotion, her love. A woman who stayed. A mother who chose me and loved me without conditions. A friend who never let go. I honor you for the strong, beautiful oak tree you have always been for me. I was the baby sapling beneath your wide, steady branches, growing in the shelter of your presence, held by your shade, protected by the quiet strength of your reach. Your roots taught the earth how to hold me. Your stillness taught me where safety lived. When life sent its fiercest winds, you stood between me and the storm, breaking its force, absorbing its rage, so I could take root, so I could grow without being torn from the ground. And because of you, I stand now as a strong oak myself, my trunk shaped by your example, my leaves carrying the echo of your steadiness. Your voice and your wisdom rise through me like sap, unseen but essential, nourishing every choice, every act of courage, every moment I choose to remain standing. What you gave me did not end with you. It circulates. It lives. It continues. You did not merely change my life.

You guided me back from the edge of the cliff when death kept knocking at my door, when the ground beneath me thinned, and the darkness called me by name, familiar and persuasive. When pain wound itself around me like thorned vines, tightening, drawing blood, claiming territory, you did not turn away. You did not look elsewhere. You stayed. You loved me. You helped me unwind the vines slowly, patiently, thorn by thorn, never rushing the tenderness required for survival. You tended the wounds with care until healing could begin, teaching me that rescue does not always arrive as force, but often as presence. And even now, long after your hands have left this world, the shape of your care remains, holding me upright, reminding me how to stand, how to grow, how to shelter others beneath my own widening branches. I honor you for the incredible mother, friend, and sponsor you were, for the many ways you showed up with open hands and an open heart, steady and available. You were always willing to hear the hard things without taking offense, without taking them personally, receiving them instead as seeds, as possibilities for growth, both within yourself and within our relationship. In your presence, honesty was not dangerous. It was welcomed, tended, and allowed to become something truer and stronger. You told me what I needed to hear, not what I wanted to hear, and that truth, offered with love rather than sharpness, saved me from pain and mistakes more times than I could ever count. Your words were not weapons, but lanterns, placed gently in my hands so I could see the path ahead more clearly and choose it with intention. Thank you for granting me the privilege of walking an honest, authentic journey with you, one woven with love, integrity, and beauty, stitched together through shared moments of courage and care. Being a part of your life was not simply something I was given, not something accidental or ordinary. It was something sacred. Something consecrated by presence, trust, and truth. One of the greatest privileges I have ever known. My dearest Cols, as you step into your next journey, I hope you are met by the peace and softness you have so deeply earned, the kind that asks nothing more of you at last. May the weight you carried so faithfully here be set down gently, like a long exhale the soul has been holding for years, a release that finally allows rest to arrive. May you feel unburdened, unhurried, received. Though you have left us on this earth, you have not left us. And we will never leave you. Love does not know how to depart; it only learns new ways to remain, new languages of presence that time cannot undo. You will stay with me in my heart, in my memory, and in every action, decision, and word I choose from this day forward, quietly guiding the way I move through the world. Your legacy will continue to echo through the many voices and lives you touched, carried onward like a song that refuses to end when the singer steps away, lingering in the air, taken up by others who learned its melody through you. You, my dearest Cols, remain eternal, and so does the love you planted here, rooted deeply, continuing to grow beyond what the eye can see. I will hold you close always. I will speak to you in spirit, in the quiet moments when stillness finally gathers around me, when the world softens enough to listen, and I can feel you there, not as absence, but as a steady, loving presence that has never truly gone. I will listen for your voice, for your wisdom, arriving from beyond in the subtle ways you always spoke best, not through noise or command, but through feeling, through knowing, through love that settles quietly and unmistakably in the body. I will recognize you in the pauses, in the sudden clarity that arrives without explanation, in the gentle steadiness that reminds me which way is true. I truly hope your next journey grants you the rest you so deeply deserve, a rest wide and generous enough to hold all that you carried here. And remember this, Cols: you are loved, in this life and in the next. My love for you will follow you wherever your journey leads, unbound by distance, unmeasured by time, untouched by form. You are, and will always be, my great, wise oak tree.

Beneath your branches I found shelter from weather, wind, and sun, a place where it was safe to grow. There, I grew from a small, fragile sapling into the mighty tree I am today, my roots strengthened by your presence, my reach shaped by your example. Now, let my branches extend outward, as yours once did, to comfort and protect others. Let your strength live on through my hands, my choices, my care, carried forward into the world in living form. I honor you now, and always, with every word, every action, and every thought that moves forward from here, knowing that in doing so, I carry you with me, still standing, still sheltering, still love. All my love, Cols. May today offer you rest wherever you are now, may it wrap around you gently, like a long-awaited stillness finally arriving, and may the light of the Universe touch your soul as tenderly as you once touched mine. May you feel received, softened, held in the same quiet grace you so freely gave. In memory of the greatest woman I have ever known, the most beautiful soul to have walked this earth. One of the brightest and purest lights to grace this world and illuminated my path through its darkest days. That held my trembling heart steady when the world around me shook. A legacy on this earth has passed away, yet a legacy of heart and soul remains eternal, living and breathing through all those you shaped, through every life that learned how to stand, how to love, how to remain because of you. And so does my love for you, unchanged, unending, faithful beyond measure. May this book honor you always. May my words bring respect and life to the legacy you left behind, not as something preserved and still, but as something continuing, warm, and alive. I pick up your torch now, Cols, and I will always carry it held high, letting its light guide my steps and warm the way for others, just as yours once did for me. In the words of your son, which strike so deeply true***: "How lucky I am to have had something that makes saying goodbye so hard."*** And yet this is not goodbye. This is only until next time, only a pause in the long conversation of love.

Love you, Cols, today, tomorrow, and always. Across time, across worlds, across whatever comes next. May our souls find each other once again, as they always seem to do, drawn together by a love that never learned how to fade.

Foreword – By Nieke Lombard

When I met Lets back in 2021 on a zoom meeting - she came across as the sassy, strong *Goth poster girl* of recovery - her metallic plum eye shadow matching the audacity of her spirit. Letitia stood out in the 12 step meetings with her choker and sharp eyes - a shining example of "...It works if you work it, so work it cause you're worth it". As I watched her chair the meetings and share her story so effortlessly - with easy compassion around her abusive relationship and her suicide attempt - something in me sparked and opened - a knowing and what they often state in recovery: 'I wanted what she had.' At the time, I was in a tiring relationship with someone with addiction issues, and I needed a temporary sponsor - Lets was open to being that for me...It has been one hell of a ride and is now a deeply etched friendship based on a lot of respect and love. On her healing journey, she explored different themes through poetry and dance. At a stage, she started writing her shares, then writing sections on certain topics of recovery...The evolution and growing into was already happening - the words, insight, depth, and style of writing grew longer and longer; and stronger and stronger until it became this very book you are reading to right now. Waking up with that weight on my chest - the insistent, repetitive gnawing sting of 'I want to die! I want to die! I want to die! - the internal voice of pain and wanting to end the pain. A night of insomnia with hamster wheel anxious thoughts, and my phone Google tabs open with ways to definitely kill oneself - meticulous research to vanquish my own life. The Black Dog has visited me numerous times in my life and may be a lifelong companion, although a small dog now, lovingly in a matchstick box in my pocket. It gets fed every day, goes for walks, sometimes wears a silly hat - and it is definitely not something to be demonized. We all need a friend, a mentor, an aunt with the big-breasted open arms that takes you in - the safe place - the warm word - a shoulder to lean your head on... Also, for things to be spoken as they are - without minimizing, denying or sugar coating - so that the desolate wind can be felt. Depression, suicide, pain, suffering, trauma, and grief need to be spoken about. I feel as we move more and more into a world that curates who we are, with technology that alienates, and a modern world that separates community, this book is very much needed. Let this book be that companion that you can take out and open randomly - to drink from the stream and remind you of where you have come from, where you are now, and where you are going. You are not alone - and you are loved. Thank you, Letitia, for being the most awesome fellow traveller. You truly are an inspiration, and I am so grateful the universe had other plans for you that day. Now, we get to hear and see your journey unfold in this life with all its vivid kindness and deepest wisdoms.

Nieke Lombard

Foreword from the Author:
The Road Back: From the Brink to a Life Worth Living

Foreword from the Author

The road back: From the brink to a life worth living

This book is not a fairy tale

This book isn't a fairy tale. It is a testament to the resilience of the human spirit—a raw, unvarnished account of my descent into suicidal ideation and the long, jagged climb back toward life. These pages are carved from truth, from nights that nearly ended me and mornings that slowly rebuilt me. I do not share my story to be pitied; I share it so that hope might find its way into the hands of those who need it most. If my darkness can illuminate even a single step of your path, then every word becomes a lantern.

If I could find my way back, so can you

If I, standing on the knife-edge of oblivion, trembling on the precipice with a heart stuffed full of old traumas folded like black-edged letters of sorrow, could find my way back. Then so can you, dear reader. If these words reach you while you are lost inside the strangling dark. While despair coils cold and serpentine around your ribs, hear me with every bruised fiber of your being. You are not abandoned here. A hidden path still threads through the night, invisible yet certain. This book is not merely story; it is a lantern forged of my own bones, lifted high in the wind so you may see the next breath, the next step, the next small star of hope flaring alive.

The quiet truth that carried me

As I sit among the quiet ruins of the life I once almost lost, one truth rises again and again like a tide that refuses to forget the moon, that carried me through my darkest nights: there is always hope. Even in the moments when we feel most lost, most desperate, most shattered by our own pain. Even when the soul is shattered glass beneath the boot of despair, even when every corridor of the heart echoes with goodbye, a distant lantern still swings at the end of the tunnel, faint as a heartbeat yet impossible to extinguish. Even when the storm howls until the sky splits, a rainbow is already braiding itself in secret behind the clouds. This hope, hard-earned, bone-deep, and utterly sincere... hammered on the anvil of my near-ending, tempered in fire and cooled in tears, I now press gently, reverently, into your palms. Take it. It is warm. It is alive. It is yours. It is the truest offering I can give, shared from the softest, most honest place within me.

Footprints in the same ash

I know I am not the only pilgrim who has walked the scorched road and treacherous terrain of suicidal ideation. Where the sheer weight of simply being crushes lungs like wet cement, and one's own existence presses so heavily it feels impossible to carry. I am not the only one who has stood at the abyss's lip, staring into its velvet, hungry mouth, asking the silence; the crimpling void, if there was any reason left to turn away. I am not the only one who has stepped across that trembling, fragile threshold where thought becomes act; and breath almost becomes memory. These paths, veiled in shame thicker than winter fog, are trodden by silence of countless quiet feet. We leave prints in the same ash, reach for the same frayed silver thread of maybe, and tremble together in the dark.

I am here – and so are you

But listen: I am here... alive, breathing. My lungs still rise and fall like stubborn tides. I stand in the hushed cathedral of mornings I was never promised, barefoot on ground that once felt like the end of the world. Standing in the quiet aftermath of battles I once believed would end me. My story is scarred by pain yet radiant with resurrection, and the message burning at its core must be spoken aloud: there is hope, there is healing, there is a fierce, wild self-love that can grow even in the rubble and ruins, and of the fierce, unyielding strength of the human spirit. I offer these words as lanterns, as bread, as outstretched hands. May they echo within you, guiding you through your own passage... no matter how dark, no matter how heavy... toward a place where light can find you again. May they find you exactly where you are, curled beneath the unbearable night, and may they sing softly against your skin until light remembers your name and comes looking for you again.

The unraveling: When the river began to close its fists

Life, once vibrant, expansive, shimmering with promise... a wide, sun-drenched river, bright with laughing light and endless horizon... began to close its fists, slowly tightened around me like an invisible cage. Slowly, invisibly, it forged an iron lattice around my ribs. The weight of unspoken burdens, of trauma left unattended, of expectations stacked higher than my spirit could hold, pressed down harder, and harder... heavier and heavier... Until the unspoken griefs, old wounds left festering, expectations piled like stones on a drowning woman's chest (each one heavier than the last) pressed the air from my lungs until breathing felt like theft. A faint tremor of unease grew into a black howl and swelled into a deafening roar of despair that drowned out everything else. It swallowed birdsong, laughter, and color. Sleep brought no refuge; it became a thin ice over deeper water. It was only a brief, fragile escape from the anxiety and depression that clung to me with the persistence of a shadow I could not outrun. The moment I lay down, anxiety and depression slid beneath the surface with me, cold hands fastened to my ankles, pulling.

Joy turned ghost

Joy became a distant echo, something I remembered but could no longer feel. Joy turned ghost. I could still recall its shape, the way memory recalls a dead lover's perfume, but I could no longer touch it. In its place settled a cold numbness, a hollow space where my spirit once lived... an emptiness so vast it felt as though I were fading inside my own skin. A cavern opened inside my chest, vast and echoing, where my being once burned like a hearth-fire. Now only wind moved through me, and I felt myself dissolving, cell by cell, into the hollow of my own vessel.

The walls of silence

I had found myself slipping further into isolation. I retreated into a shell. I built walls of silence so thick even my thoughts arrived muffled. I pushed away every hand that reached (certain my storm would tear their sails to ribbons). People who loved me were kept at a safe distance, convinced that distance would protect them from the storms raging inside me.

Every remedy became fuel

I tried to outrun the pain with anything that promised numbness. My attempts to cope... rivers of alcohol, bright blooming cuts of self-harm, reckless nights that blurred into mornings of regret. Smiles stretched over screams for people who never asked to see beneath them, all in the name of relentless people-pleasing. Even the numbing escape of medication taken to extremes... those pills swallowed until the bottle and heartbeat spoke the same dull language. Every remedy only poured fuel on the hidden blaze and only fed the fire beneath my suffering. Each attempt to soothe myself tightened the spiral, turning my life into a vicious cycle of quiet self-destruction.

The more the spiral tightened, exquisite and merciless, the more the world softened into watercolor bled by rain, and the only color left sharp enough to see was the idea of erasing my own colors. My life blurred into a haze of pain, and the only thought that seemed focused, unmistakably clear... was escape ... A permanent escape!

Crossing the border drawn in one heartbeat

Permanent. ... Final. ... Clean. ... That is how I tried cross the threshold. I stepped into that country whose border is drawn in a single heartbeat. I tried to leave my body behind like an unwanted coat. And somehow, against every law written in my blood that night, I woke up still wearing it ... I had survived. The moment did not arrive with angels or sudden light. It arrived raw, bruised, gasping. That near-death moment didn't magically heal me; it didn't erase my trauma or silence the darkness. It cracked me open. For the first time I looked straight into the mouth of the abyss I had been circling like a moth, and the abyss looked back (and I did not flinch). In that stare I heard the truth louder than any scream: Something in me still wanted morning. Something small, stubborn, half-buried under ash, refused the dark its final word. I acknowledged, with a trembling honesty, the desperate and undeniable need for change. Surviving was not the cure. Surviving was the first true breath I had taken in years. It was the awakening.

Shame, molten and volcanic

My veins carried shame instead of blood: thick, black, volcanic. My body, once home, now felt like a crime scene I was still breathing in. The physical wounds were polite; the invisible ones laughed. They split wider, grinning canyons that bled memory and rot. Shame did not walk in; it detonated, a silent bomb of molten lead poured straight into the marrow. I was a cathedral after arson, still standing, but every stained-glass window of who I used to be lay shattered on the floor, glinting like accusations.

The poppy-seed ember That Refused to Die

Physical wounds healed with time, but the deeper gashes (those carved into the soft tissue of the soul) yawned wider than ever. Shame poured in, hot and viscous, into every crack the attempt had opened. Yet something else moved there too, something fragile and unfamiliar: a thin, silver thread of curiosity. What now? it whispered. What now that death has refused me? In the smoking nave of that ruin, something microscopic moved. A single ember, no bigger than a poppy seed, glowing under heaps of wet ash. It should have died. It refused.

Handing the keys to a house still on fire

Meeting my sponsor felt like dragging my flayed soul across broken glass to kneel before a stranger. Working with her felt, at first, like handing a stranger the keys to a house still on fire. Terrifying... Impossible... Vulnerable, and that was my greatest fear of all, the old tapes still active...still loud; the inner critic sneering venomously in my ear: "If you speak or become vulnerable you are weak, don't you remember what happens when you are weak? Well let me remind you!" It said with a cold sinister smile... Weak is abandonment. Is that what you want?" I sat opposite her, wrapped in trembling silence, thoughts louder than ever, convinced she would smell the smoke on me and run. I expected judgment sharp as scalpels. Instead, she offered silence wide as mercy; and she stayed.

Vomiting shards of mirror

When I finally spoke, the words came out rusted, barbed, dripping decades of rust and pus. Each confession was vomiting shards of mirror; each shard reflected a child's face screaming things I had swallowed whole. The room filled with the stench of old graves opening. She did not flinch. She simply held the bucket while I retched up my childhood, my rapes, my worthlessness, my belief that love was a debt, and I was bankrupt. She listened as I pried rusted locks off closets I had nailed shut years ago. Each confession was a crowbar against splintering wood; each memory that spilled out carried dust and old blood and the faint, surprising scent of rain on long-sealed earth.

Becoming the eye of my own hurricane

I learned to sit inside the pain until it sat inside me, instead of sprinting from it. I became the eye of my own hurricane, motionless while the winds of every unsaid thing tore the roof off my life. I let the grief have its full, obscene weight; let it crush me until my spine kissed the concrete and tasted iron and earth and the faint, impossible salt of future oceans. I allowed the grief to have its full weight; let it press me to the floor until the floor itself became an altar. I traced the roots of despair backward through the years: childhood rooms lit by shouting, hands that should never have touched me, beliefs planted like barbed seeds (you are too much, you are not enough, you are the storm others must be saved from). Naming them out loud was like dragging stones from a riverbed; the water ran clearer afterward, startlingly clear, cold enough to shock the skin awake.

Open-heart surgery with a fountain pen

Journaling was open-heart surgery with a fountain pen, surgery without anaesthetic. The pen was scalpel, page was flesh. I cut and cut; I carved until the page bled. Ink became the black blood of everything I had tried to kill quietly. I let the black ink bleed what silence had festered into poison. Sentences dripped slow and thick as tar, then faster (waterfalls of long-dammed rivers finally breaking loose). Whole nights dissolved into ink and salt. I wrote until my hand cramped, and the margins filled with tiny, frantic birds trying to escape the page. I wrote until the notebook itself seemed to gasp for air, pages swollen and translucent with tears, ink running like bruises.

Pearl, lava, and flash flood

With every line I excavated another shard of the girl I had buried alive beneath survival. Some nights the sorrow poured so violently I feared the notebook would drown. They came as flash floods, ripping whole childhood houses from their foundations and hurling them downstream in splinters. Other nights the sentences arrived as lava, slow, searing, burning the paper at the edges. Other nights only a single drop fell (perfect, round, luminous as a pearl formed around years of grit).

The war drum beneath the rubble

And somewhere in that carnage, a pulse answered mine. A small, defiant heart beating under the rubble. Not healed... Not whole... But beating. That heartbeat was not gentle. It was a war drum hammered on the inside of a ribcage that had tried to become a coffin. Something shifted. In the raw, red cavity the writing left behind, space appeared. Space for breath that reached all the way to the bottom of the lungs. Space for a voice, small but unmistakably mine, to say: "I am still here... I *am* still *here*!" It said: "I am not yours Darkness!" It said: "Not yours...do you hear! ... Mine!" That voice was not triumphant. It was cracked, smoke-scarred, trembling. But it was alive. And for the first time in years, the darkness had to make room for it.

The scar becomes a doorway

Surviving had ripped me in half. Awakening began sewing the halves together, with thread pulled from my own screaming veins, stitching not to hide the wound but to make the scar a doorway. I stood up in the ashes, naked, smoke still rising from my hair, lungs raw from breathing fire. The darkness had to step aside! Something with wings (small, singed, furious) had remembered how to beat. Surviving had torn the veil. Awakening stitched it into wings.

The first steps: Accepting the darkness - The brutal aftermath

The aftermath was brutal. The physical wounds healed in time, but the emotional scars carved themselves far deeper, (thin, white-hot wires threaded through muscle and memory), burning colder than ice whenever the air shifted. They lingered in places no one could see: the sour-metal taste at the back of the throat, the phantom smell of pills and whiskey, and the secrecy, guilt, and shame that followed me into every room.

The terrifying lifeline

Working with a sponsor, something that at first felt terrifying, vulnerable, almost impossible, slowly became a lifeline I didn't know I needed. At first it felt like stepping barefoot onto a frozen lake while handing a stranger the rope tied around my waist. My voice shook so hard I tasted blood from biting the inside of my cheek. Yet her quiet presence (coffee-scented, steady, warm and welcome as fresh bread) slowly became the only thing keeping me from sinking. The sound of her voice became an immediate anchor in every storm, her wisdom clearer than any map provided, and her support, a foundation and belonging where I felt I had none before. Her embrace became a newfound home... her very being, her story, her thriving, her hope became a belief that everything... I ... will be okay.

Excavation of the self

It wasn't a quick fix or a clean transformation; it was a slow, painstaking excavation of the self. Layer by layer, I peeled back the denial that had protected me, only to reveal the raw ache beneath. It was no gentle archaeology. It was dynamite in the ribcage. Layer by layer I peeled back denial the way you peel sunburnt skin (flinching, hissing, tears stinging the raw underneath), until the air itself felt like salt on an open wound. I learned to sit with the pain instead of sprinting from it. I let it flood the room like black water, thick and cold, until it reached my chin. I breathed through it, tasting rust and old pennies, feeling it press against my eardrums like deep-ocean silence. I stayed until the water stopped rising and I could hear my own heartbeat echoing inside it. To trace the roots of my despair back to the wounds I had never allowed myself to name.

Weaving shadows into tapestry

This journey wasn't about erasing the past. It was learning to thread the darkness (rough, coarse, smelling faintly of smoke and wet earth) through the warp of who I am, letting it become pattern instead of prison. Some days, the loom groaned. Some days, the shuttle tasted of iron. But slowly the cloth grew stronger, even with the black strands running through it. It was about learning to coexist with it, to weave the shadows into the tapestry of who I am without allowing them to dictate my fate. It was the quiet, daily process of reclaiming my life, not by rejecting the darkness, but by refusing to let it define me.

The pen becomes a blade

I began journaling, and the pen turned surgeon-cold in my hand. Each stroke sliced scar tissue with a wet, whispering sound, like tearing damp silk. Spilling my unfiltered emotions onto the page as if each word were prying open old wounds. It felt like my pen became a blade, slicing through resistance. Pain leaked out hot and coppery; the page drank it greedily, growing heavy, veins of ink spreading like bruises under pale skin.

Memories dripping onto paper

Buried memories rose the way drowned things rise: Swollen, pale, smelling of river mud. They dripped from the nib in slow, deliberate drops (drip... drip... drip), dripping methodically onto the paper, sentence by sentence, moment by moment. Each one hitting the paper with a soft, wounded thud. Every experience I confronted, every truth I dared to name, released another quiet drip ... drip ... drip of sorrow. The ink smelled faintly of tears and graphite and something electric, like the air just before lightning. It was visceral catharsis: the silent screams that had lived behind my teeth for years finally tore free, ragged and tasting of smoke. The page became a throat, the pen, a tongue. I wrote until my hand and heart both cramped, until the room smelled of salt and spent thunder.

Seeing the shape of my suffering

In those pages (now swollen, warped, translucent with sorrow) soaked with honesty and ache... I finally saw the shape of my suffering: a bruised map drawn in midnight blues and arterial reds. Patterns surfaced like constellations through storm clouds. Triggers glinted, sharp as broken glass catching moonlight. The monsters that had lived invisible inside my bloodstream suddenly had names, weight, edges I could finally grip. The destructive thoughts that had taken root inside me were no longer invisible.

The map of my own undoing

Through ink that still smelled faintly of blood and storm, I traced the map of my own undoing. Every line burned bridge, every swallowed scream, every place I had abandoned myself (all of it laid out in trembling cartography). And there, beneath the wreckage, faint as frost on a windowpane, the first silver guidelines of a way back began to appear. And with that understanding came the possibility of change.

Building the foundation: Self-compassion and self-care

The cornerstone of recovery

Self-compassion became the cornerstone of my recovery, the quiet, steady foundation on which everything else began to heal. For years, I had served as my own relentless critic, punishing myself for every misstep, every perceived failure, every human flaw. Learning to soften toward myself, to offer the same tenderness and understanding I would freely give to a friend in pain, felt almost revolutionary. It was not self-indulgence, nor an escape from accountability. It was the act of recognizing my own inherent worth, of acknowledging that I deserved gentleness even in the midst of my struggles.

A reorientation of the heart

This shift was subtle yet seismic: a reorientation of the heart that allowed me, for the first time, to see myself not as something broken, but as something worthy of love, patience, and grace. Self-care became a non-negotiable part of my daily rhythm, not as a luxury, but as a lifeline. It wasn't about grand gestures or spa-day indulgences; it was about the quiet, consistent acts of kindness I chose to offer myself. Moving my body with intention. Feeding myself meals that nourished rather than numbed. Allowing my mind the rest it had long been denied. Reaching for activities that sparked even the faintest flicker of joy.

From burden to anchor

At first, these small acts felt unnatural, almost burdensome, as though I were learning to care for a stranger. But over time, they became anchors in the storm, tiny rituals of stability and steadiness amidst the chaos. Each small act whispered the same truth: "I am still here, and I am worth the care it takes to keep going."

Reconnecting: Forging Healthy Relationships

The weight of isolation

Isolation had been one of the heaviest weights in my descent, a silent force that magnified every shadow. Rebuilding trust and reconnecting with the people I had pushed away required patience, vulnerability, and a tenderness I wasn't used to offering myself, or anyone else. It meant letting others see the cracks I had worked so hard to hide, speaking my truth openly and seeking understanding rather than bracing for judgment. Slowly, I allowed support to reach me. Surrounding myself with people who met my pain with compassion instead of criticism became essential to my healing. And when I found a support group, a circle of souls who carried wounds similar to mine, I finally felt a sense of belonging. In their presence, I discovered community, connection, and the profound relief of being understood.

Forging a New Path: Finding Purpose and Meaning

Beyond mere survival

The journey back to life is more than mere survival; it is the slow, tender awakening into a life that can once again be lived fully. Thriving, not just enduring, became the heartbeat of my recovery. I began searching for purpose and meaning, letting curiosity guide me into new spaces and old passions I had long abandoned. I experimented, explored, and allowed myself to rediscover the parts of me I had forgotten. Volunteering offered a powerful shift in perspective, turning my gaze outward, giving me the chance to pour into something larger than myself, to feel useful, connected, alive. Through this process of reclaiming what lit me up, I started to rebuild my identity piece by piece. No longer bound to the narrow narrative of my suffering, I began to see myself not as a collection of wounds, but as a soul in motion, growing, expanding, becoming.

Maintaining the Momentum: Tools for Long-Term Healing

Recovery is not a straight, shining road; it is a winding, uneven path that snakes through shadowed valleys and steep, unseen climbs. It is marked by stumbles and setbacks, by moments of doubt, and days when the darkness creeps in so close it begins to feel familiar again. This is not failure; it is simply the wild, imperfect nature of healing. What matters is not that the storm returns, but that you learn how to navigate it when it does. For me, the foundation was laid stone by trembling stone: consistent therapy and healing work, a steady commitment to my recovery program, and the decision to keep showing up—even on the days I wanted nothing more than to disappear. Continuing my self-care practices, staying connected to the people who held space for me, and seeking out activities that sparked even the faintest warmth became essential tools for long-term healing. Mindfulness—those simple, intentional acts like meditation, grounding exercises, or slow, deliberate, deep, conscious breaths—became anchors in the storm, tethering me to the present moment when my intense or overwhelming thoughts tried to drag me under. These practices did not banish the darkness, but they softened its edges, reduced its power, and loosened its grip, making room for light to seep back in, again and again.

A Reflection from the darkness

As I sit here, gazing back across the landscape of my life, I am pulled toward the darkest valleys I've walked through. Moments that seemed to offer no exit, no relief, no respite, and certainly no hope. Times when the world felt like a closed door, and I was locked on the wrong side of it. And yet, I am here. Breathing. Speaking. Living proof that there is always a way out, always a faint glimmer at the end of even the longest tunnel. It is this quiet yet unwavering message of hope that I want to place gently in your hands, dear reader.

Breaking the silence

My story is not an easy one to tell; it feels like opening old wounds to the air. But I know with a bone-deep certainty that it must be spoken. Silence has lain over these experiences like a heavy, suffocating blanket—over suicidal ideation, over PTSD and C-PTSD, over the relentless chokehold of depression. Too many are suffering quietly, as I once did, and the cost of that silence can be catastrophic. It is time to shatter the hush, to drag the shadows out from their hiding places and expose them to the healing light they've long feared. I have walked the long, echoing corridors of suicidal ideation, felt the suffocating pressure of despair, and stepped across the threshold into a suicide attempt. I have stood at the doorway of death itself, staring into the abyss that almost swallowed me whole. But I have also found my way back—back to breath, to life, to hope, and to the fragile yet radiant and luminous possibility of healing.

A lantern of hope

It is my deepest hope that in sharing my story with you, you will come to truly feel that there is always a glimmer of light, no matter how bleak or unbearable your circumstances may seem. You do not have to plummet as far as I did to begin your climb back. You do not need to stand on the ledge of desperation to discover that there is another way forward. You do not need to brush against the edge of death to begin your journey out of pain. And you certainly do not need to stand shaking before that terrifying threshold to recognize the fierce, breathtaking beauty of life. Let my journey be a lantern in your hands—casting light over the path long before you ever come close to the darkness that once nearly devoured me.

The descent begins

My journey into the depths began many years ago, when the weight of my inner battles grew too heavy for my spirit to lift. I felt lost, untethered, and achingly alone, adrift in a world that kept moving forward while I remained frozen and suspended in place. It was as if life had seeped through my fingers, leaving me clutching at shadows and echoes. I tried everything I knew to find my way back to myself—to reclaim the joy, the purpose, the spark that once burned so brightly within me—but each attempt crumbled into disappointment. Every door I reached for stayed closed or led back to the same dark place. Nothing seemed to lead me back to the person I remembered, and the harder I searched for her, the further away she seemed to drift.

Sinking into the shadows

As the days blurred into weeks and the weeks dissolved into months, I felt myself spiraling downward into a darkness that felt bottomless. It was as though I were sinking beneath a vast, merciless sea of despair, reaching again and again for a lifeline that never appeared. Every breath grew heavier, like inhaling water instead of air. Every moment seemed dimmer than the last. In that suffocating, depthless dark... untethered from everything, tethered to nothing, anchored only to pain—my mind began to drift toward the unthinkable, toward possibilities I had once believed would never even cross my mind.

THE WHISPER OF DESTRUCTION

The thought of ending my life entered quietly, like a thief slipping in through a crack in the window. It crept into my mind on soft feet, silently stealing my hope and draining the will that kept me anchored to this world. It did not arrive with screams, instead a deceptive softness, and with a seductive whisper that promised relief... a way out from the relentless ache that wrapped itself around me like a second skin. It offered the illusion of peace, the illusion of release. But beneath that velvet promise lay a ruthless lie... a cruel, clandestine voice disguising destruction as salvation. The escape it offered held no healing, only an ending that would snuff out every possibility I had yet to live.

Crossing the threshold

I remember the day I stepped across the invisible line from suicidal ideation into a suicide attempt. That day is carved into my memory with a sharpness time cannot blunt—a jagged mark that altered the course of my life in ways I never could have predicted. I had reached the frayed, unraveling end of my rope—exhausted, hollow, unable to see even the faintest slit of light. In that moment, the doorway of death did not merely whisper; it roared... It begged...It pleaded... It demanded... It commanded... It rose before me like a towering presence, insistent and unyielding, and I, overwhelmed and coming apart at the seams, surrendered to it...bowing my knee and becoming its willing servant. For a moment, I believed with all my heart that it was the only way out.

The miracle of return

But as I stood at the door of death, something miraculous intervened—something quiet, unexpected, and life-altering. It did not arrive as a blinding revelation, but as a fragile opening, a thin crack in the wall through which life began to shine again. I was given a second chance, a narrow path back toward the beauty of living, a chance to reclaim hope and begin the long, uncertain journey of healing. That journey was not neat or simple. It was etched with pain, lined with struggle, and filled with moments when turning back into numbness seemed easier than pressing forward into the unknown. Yet step by trembling step, it carried me somewhere I never imagined I could stand: Beyond the shadows, beyond the fear, into a place of deeper peace, authentic love, and a self-acceptance I once thought impossible. This miracle was not an act of magic; it was the opening chapter of my becoming.

A Message to the one who is struggling

So, dear reader, if you find yourself where I once stood, dangling at the end of your rope, exhausted, hollow, and ready to let go, please hear these words as clearly as if they were whispered directly into your heart: there is hope. There is a way out, and even more importantly, there is a way back. Back to yourself... Back to breath... Back to healing, to light, and to the fragile yet wondrous possibility of life. You do not need to sink as far as I did to begin your return. You do not need to stand at the brink of desperation to realize you were made for far more than suffering. And you most certainly do not need to stand at the trembling edge of death to discover the beauty waiting for you here, in the realm of the living. Your path back can begin now, long before the darkness convinces you there is no path at all.

What this book offers you

The guidelines I share with you in the pages ahead, across this volume and the next three, are not a magic spell or formula, nor a cure wrapped in pretty and tidy promises. They are a roadmap, a compass for navigating the dark, rugged, unforgiving and painful terrain of suicidal ideation. They were forged in the fires of my own journey through the shadows... shaped by trial and error, by courage and collapse, by moments of grace and moments of surrender. These teachings are not perfect, but they are true to my lived experience and they are real. They are a testament to the resilience of the human spirit, a reminder that even in our most fractured hours, we are capable of rising, learning, and facing challenges that once seemed impossible to bear. May these pages be steady lights along your path, guiding you toward a future you may not yet believe could belong to you.

Step one: Acknowledge your pain

The first step on this journey is to acknowledge your pain, to look it directly in the eyes and honour the simple truth that your feelings are real, valid, and deeply deserving of care. We are taught again and again to be strong, to hold ourselves together, to just get over it, to keep our composure and wear a brave mask while our inner world collapses in silence. But strength is not the absence of struggle; it is the courage to admit when we are hurting. It is the brave, quivering confession: "I am not okay." Because "It is okay to not be okay." It is okay to feel overwhelmed, to feel lost, to feel as though you are drowning beneath a tide of despair. Naming your suffering is not weakness; it is the first act of healing, the very first flicker of light in the darkness.

Step two: Seek support

The second step is to seek help, to reach outward, even as you journey inward. Healing was never meant to be carried alone. Support might come from a trusted friend or family member, from a therapist or counselor, or from a community that recognizes and understands the language of your pain. What matters is that you find a space where you can unravel safely, where your tears and truths are met with compassion rather than judgment. In such spaces, the weight you carry can slowly begin to shift. You are given room to explore the roots of your suffering with honesty and tenderness. Reaching out is not a sign of weakness; it is an act of profound bravery, a declaration that your life is worthy of the effort it takes to save it... worthy of fighting for!

Step three: Self-care as nourishment

The third step is to practice self-care, to tend to your body, your heart, and your spirit with steady, intentional kindness and compassion. This may look like movement that brings you back into your body. A walk, stretching, dancing in your living room, yoga, or exercise that reminds you that you are still here, still inhabiting this form. It may be meditation or breathwork that quiets the storm inside you long enough for a moment of calm to slip through. It may reveal itself as creative expression... writing, painting, art, music... places where your inner world can spill out safely, where your truth can take shape in colour, sound, or words. Self-care is not indulgence; it is nourishment. It is the gentle, repeated act of choosing yourself, again and again, even when you don't feel you deserve to be chosen.

Step four: Challenging the inner critic

The fourth step is to challenge the negative thoughts that have woven themselves into the fabric of your mind... to gently question the stories that insist you are unworthy, hopeless, or broken beyond repair. This is not an easy task. It requires patience, awareness, and courage. But it is vital to the healing process. By learning to pause, to breathe, and to gently reframe the harsh narratives that rise within you, you begin to slowly reshape your inner landscape. Over time, compassion begins to replace criticism. Possibility begins to edge out despair. And as your thoughts soften, your perspective shifts... You start to see both the world and yourself through a lens brushed not with darkness, but with the faint shimmer of hope. This is how the light returns: not all at once in a blazing sunrise but thought by thought... breath by breath.

Step five: Returning to yourself through self-love

The final step is to cultivate self-love and self-acceptance... to learn, slowly, patiently, gently, to embrace yourself exactly as you are. This is often the hardest part of the journey, because it calls you to turn toward the very parts of yourself you have spent years avoiding, condemning, or hiding behind locked doors. And yet, it is also the most profoundly transformative. As you learn to love yourself not in spite of your scars, but with them... folding them tenderly into your story rather than trying to erase them, you begin to stitch your heart back together from the inside out. This kind of love is not fragile, nor does it hinge on external validation. It is a quiet, steady presence, a deep inner calm and peace that remains even when the world around you trembles. In this self-love, you finally come home to yourself.

You are not alone

For those who are struggling, I want you to know this with unshakable clarity: you are not alone. There is a way out... a path that does not demand you descend to the depths I once did or force you to graze the edge of death in order to understand how precious your life is. You do not need to face the terror of nearly losing everything, of crossing that fragile threshold and surviving by a thread, in order to find your way back to yourself... to healing... to life. My near-death moment ripped my eyes open, but that does not have to be your awakening. If anything, let the price I paid be enough. Let my journey serve as a warning, a lantern, a guide—so you can choose a different road long before desperation drives you toward the brink. You deserve a gentler path, and it is still available to you.

The transformative nature of pain

And yet, I must also honour this truth: my journey, though agonizing, disorienting, and at times almost unbearable, has been undeniably transformative. It taught me the quiet, stubborn strength of perseverance; the sacred necessity of self-care; and the irreplaceable beauty of genuine human connection. It showed me that even in the blackest hours, when every trace of hope seems extinguished, there remains a small, persistent ember...a faint glimmer of light... a restorative spark... sometimes distant, sometimes fragile, but always there... always present, often it is just buried beneath the ash of our past and trauma. My path revealed that darkness is not the final chapter. Within it lives the possibility of redemption, the promise of renewal, and the chance to rise again in ways I never believed I could.

Moments that saved me

As I look back over my life, I am struck by the countless moments that could have been my last. The nights when despair wrapped around me like a heavy fog, the days when I felt suspended between wanting to vanish and not knowing how to stay. I remember the times I felt myself unraveling, thread by thread, wondering if there was any purpose left in continuing at all. But woven through those memories are the moments that saved me—the unexpected lifelines that appeared just as I was slipping away. I remember the hands that reached out to steady me, the hearts that stayed open, the strangers who quietly became companions on my journey, and the loved ones who refused to abandon me even when I had abandoned myself. These fragments of grace, scattered like stars across my darkest sky, became the reasons I kept choosing life.

Walking with you

And it is these moments, these people, and these dearly won experiences that I want to offer you now, dear reader. I want to walk beside you as we move together through the darkest corridors of my soul and emerge, step by step, into the quiet light of hope and healing. I want to share the insights carved from my deepest wounds, the guidelines that gradually steadied me, the strategies that helped me survive the shadows, and the practices that guided me back to the self I had lost along the way. My wish is that, in hearing my story, your own path may be lit and illuminated... one step, one breath, one truth at a time.

A journey of becoming

This journey will not be easy—I must tell you that honestly. It will stretch you, challenge you, and at times guide you right into the darkness you've spent years trying not to look at... painful places you have pushed into the shadows and avoided. There will be moments of pain and discomfort, times when the path feels steep, rocky, and unforgiving. But I also promise you this: It can be deeply restorative, unexpectedly beautiful, and profoundly life-altering... if you allow it to be. If you are willing to walk into this process with an open mind and an open heart... to face your fears, your shadows, your doubts; to gently examine the wounds, the trauma, and the past you've carried for far too long... You will not leave this journey as the same person who began it. You will emerge stronger, wiser, and more resilient than you ever knew you could be. This is the work of becoming, and you are capable of it.

Letting go

And so, when you feel ready to begin this journey... Ready to turn toward your shadows instead of away from them, ready to walk back toward the truth of who you are—start with letting go. Let go of the fears that cinch themselves around your heart. Let go of the doubts that whisper you are unworthy. Let go of the old, clinging shame that has followed you for far too long. Release the urge to control and manipulate every outcome, to perfect every flaw before you allow yourself to exist... to be seen as worthy... good enough... lovable... valuable. Let go of those old beliefs that convince you this lie is the truth. Let go of the lie that you are alone, that you are not enough, that you are undeserving of love, compassion, or acceptance. And if you are not ready to let go yet... if even the thought feels impossible—know that this is okay, too. That is why this book series exists: To guide you gently back to yourself, back to wholeness, back to the sacred truth, and knowing that you were worthy long before you ever believed it. You were worthy when you took your first breath... and still are.

Holding on to hope

Instead, hold tight to hope. Hold on to the quiet knowing that you do not walk this path in isolation, that there are people who care for you, people who long to see you rise, people who will stand beside you when the night, darkness, and shadows feel unbearable. Hold on to the truth that there is a way out of the shadows, even if your eyes have not yet adjusted enough to see it. And grip with both hands the belief that you are strong, that you are capable, that you are worthy of love, of acceptance, and of joy. These truths are not distant fantasies or impossible dreams... they are the foundation of your becoming, the light waiting patiently for you to reach toward it.

I am with you

As we step onto this path together, I want you to know that I am here with you—quietly, steadily, with every step you take. I will walk beside you as you navigate your own shadows, sharing my story with as much honesty and tenderness as I can. The pain that shaped me, the struggles that nearly broke me, and the small, shining triumphs that helped me rise again. I offer these truths not to weigh you down, but so that you might find comfort, solace, and perhaps even a spark of inspiration in knowing that you are not alone. Along the way, I will share the guidelines, strategies, and practices that carried me back to myself... tools forged in the fires of experience. All meant to support you as you heal, grow, and rediscover the strength that has always lived inside you.

Hope is never extinguished

And I will remind you... again and again, for as long as you need to hear it, that hope is never fully extinguished. Even when the night feels endless and dense, even when you are sure you've lost your way or fear that you wander alone, there is still a path forward. There is always a door, a crack, a glimmer, a spark, an ember, a quiet opening waiting to guide you out of the dark. Every tunnel, no matter how suffocating, holds a distant light. Every storm, no matter how violent, how relentless, is already gathering the colours of a rainbow just beyond its chaos. Hope is patient. Hope is persistent. And I will keep pointing you back to it until you can feel its warmth on your own skin once more.

Stepping into the light

So let us begin this journey together, dear reader. Let us take the first step, and then the next, and then the next... slowly, gently, steadily or even shakily... running, walking or crawling wherever you are right now... until we rise once more into the light of hope and healing. Let us find our way home to ourselves, to the quiet truth of our hearts, and to the sacred depths of our souls. Along the way, may we rediscover the beauty, the wonder, and the soft everyday magic woven into the fabric of life. And may we hold close the truths we so often forget: That we are not alone, that we are worthy of love and acceptance, and that we are deserving, deeply and unconditionally... of happiness, of life, of breath.

An invitation forward

So, dear reader, I invite you to walk this path with me. It will not always be easy, but it will be deeply, undeniably worth it. Along the way, you will meet your pain and face your struggles, but you will also stumble upon unexpected beauty, quiet joy, and the subtle soft light of your own becoming. You will uncover a strength within you that you never knew resided there, a strength forged in darkness yet designed to shine. This resilience will rise up to meet you, carrying you through even your heaviest nights and gently guiding you toward the life that waits on the other side of your suffering.

You belong to something larger

As you read to these words, I want you to feel, deep in your bones, that you are not alone. You belong to a quiet, resilient constellation of souls, a community of hearts who have walked this same shadowed path and found their way through. You are part of something larger than your pain, part of a shared story still unfolding... threaded with hope, possibility, and the promise of a future not yet written. You are not walking in isolation; you are held within a vast tapestry of lives that echo your own.

Letting go once more

So let go, dear reader. Let go of the fears that cinch your chest, the doubts that whisper lies, the worries that press heavily against your spirit. Release the belief that you must be flawless, perfect, composed, or endlessly strong to be worthy. Let go of the illusion that you walk this path in solitude, that your struggles set you apart, that you are somehow exiled by your pain. You are not... You never have been... You never need to be if you choose to. Allow yourself to loosen your grip on the stories that weigh you down and make room for the truth: healing often begins with a soft, trembling surrender.

Holding the truth of hope

And as you let go, hold fast to the truth that there is always hope. There is always a way forward, a path back to yourself, to healing, to light, and to the gentle and quiet pulse of life longing to be felt again. You are stronger than you think, braver than you feel, and far more resilient than you have ever been told. You are a warrior of the heart, of the mind, of the spirit—and you are capable of rising through anything that stands before you. All it requires is a choice: the choice to turn toward life, to step into healing, to claim your own becoming. And that choice, dear reader, rests in your hands right now.

The first step

So, take a deep, steady breath, dear reader, and step into this journey with me. Yes, it will lead you through deep pain, through shadows you may have sidestepped for years. But it will also reveal discovery, growth, and profound healing. This path will challenge you, stir you awake, and rouse parts of you that have lain silent for far too long. It will invite transformation in ways you cannot yet imagine. And when you finally emerge from the darkness, you will rise stronger, wiser, and more compassionate than you ever dared to believe. This is the journey of becoming... and it begins right here, right now; with one breath... one step... one quiet moment of courage.

The light at the end of the tunnel

The journey from the brink of suicide to a life worth living is not a gentle ascent; it is a pilgrimage through fire... arduous, raw, painful, and profoundly transformative. It asks, or more so demands of you, a courage you may not believe you possess, a perseverance that feels impossible in your darkest hours, and a steady, unwavering commitment to your own healing, even when hope flickers like a dying candle. If you are reading to this while wrestling with suicidal thoughts, please hear me with the clarity of a heartbeat against silence: **hope exists.** Even now... Even here. There is a light at the end of this tunnel, faint perhaps, but real. Shimmering like a distant lantern held by your future self. And behind the storm that surrounds you, a rainbow is already gathering itself quietly, patient and bright, waiting for your skies to clear. Your life is precious, woven with threads of meaning you have not yet seen, and your story is nowhere near its end. These books offer you a roadmap, yes... but the path itself is yours, tender and trembling and sacred. Take the first step, however small. Reach outward for help, even if your voice quivers like a leaf in winter wind. You are worthy of love. You are worthy of healing. You are worthy of a life that holds warmth, joy, and belonging. You are not alone... not now... not ever! In the chapters that follow, I will share my story with you... A story stitched together from struggle, survival, collapse, triumph, and the astonishing, stubborn resilience of the human spirit. I will guide you into the deepest chambers of my soul, the places where despair once carved its name into my bones, and then lead you back toward the soft, unfolding light of healing, redemption, and renewal. Along this path, I will offer the guidelines, strategies, and practices that helped me gather the scattered pieces of myself and slowly stitch them back together. My hope is that these offerings become gentle companions for you... footsteps beside your own, lanterns illuminating the way—helping you navigate your shadows and rediscover the strength that has always, quietly, lived within you. So walk with me, dear reader... First through the raw, trembling terrain of despair and pain, and then toward the broadening horizon of hope and healing. Let us travel together, hand in hand, through the cavern of shadows and into the waiting radiance on the other side. Let us find our way home... to ourselves, to the quiet truth beating in our hearts, and to the deep, unwavering presence of our souls. And as we journey, let us hold close the truths we too easily forget: We are not alone. We are worthy of love and acceptance. And we are deserving... deeply, inherently, undeniably, of happiness.

INADEQUATE
SHYNESS
REGRETS

Gratitude, Dedication, and Acknowledgement:

Gratitude, Dedication, and Acknowledgement:

Acknowledgements — A Heart of Gratitude

As I arrive at the first words of this dedication and step into the sacred stillness that precedes and follows creation, my heart swells with an overwhelming, full-bodied gratitude. This book was never birthed from solitude. Every sentence breathed into existence, every tear-stained page, every fragment of healing translated into language was woven from more than my own hands. It exists because of the love that surrounded me when I faltered, the patience that held me when time felt heavy, and the unwavering faith of those who stood beside me through every trembling chapter of my becoming. Their presence shaped these pages in ways ink alone could never express; their support lifted me in the moments when my spirit could not rise on its own. This work is not mine alone... it is stitched together from the hearts that held me, the voices that steadied me, and the souls who believed in me long before I could believe in myself. This book is as much theirs as it is mine.

To My Husband, Marno Swanepoel

My beloved Marno, no constellation of words could ever hold enough light to fully honor the depth of my gratitude for you. Language feels small beside what my heart knows. Throughout the creation of this book, you have been my anchor, my steady ground, my harbor of calm in every storm. When old wounds split open like fault lines, and I found myself wandering again through corridors of pain I believed I had long outgrown, you did not flinch. You did not waver. You stayed beside me... **steady, patient, unshaken.** You never tried to stitch my hurt closed or silence the tremors inside me.

Instead, you offered the rarest, most sacred gift a human can give: **Presence.** A presence that held without smothering, ready without fixing, and loved without condition. You held space for my tears, for my trembling silences, for the slow return of breath into my body. You listened to endless readings, even when the words came out ragged. You gathered me into your arms when the story grew too heavy for my spirit to carry. And when my faith in this book dimmed to an ember, you shielded it with your own... believing in my voice, my healing, my ability to finish what felt impossible. You have been my strength, my refuge, the quiet miracle that reminded me love... **true, steady, unwavering love...** can reach even the wounds buried deepest beneath the skin. I love you, always, endlessly, beyond forever. This book exists because you believed I could finish it.

##To My Cousin, Maroné

Maroné, my dear cousin and cherished friend... thank you for being a steady, unwavering sounding board of patience and understanding. You listened to voice note after voice note, each one a little window into my scattered thoughts, my tangled emotions, my half-formed chapters that arrived either as sparks of inspiration or as waves of uncertainty. Not once did you grow weary. Not once did you turn away. What you offered was so much more than feedback. It was encouragement that softened the edges of my doubt, shared laughter that lifted the weight from my chest, and the quiet, grounding reassurance that I was not navigating this creative storm alone. Thank you for hearing me... **truly hearing me,** and for offering your insights with such love, honesty, and generous warmth. Love you heaps, always.

To My Daughters, Isabella and Esmerelda

My precious girls, Isabella and Esmerelda... thank you for walking this path beside me with hearts far wiser and gentler than your years should carry. Writing this book was never merely an act of storytelling; it was a pilgrimage through deep emotion, through painful reflection, through memories that rose like tides I could not always predict. There were moments when I needed silence, moments when I needed distance, moments when I slipped into the quiet caverns of my own thoughts... and you offered me that space with a grace, patience, and quiet understanding that felt nothing short of extraordinary. You endured my late nights, the glow of my screen long past your dreaming hours. You endured my distracted mind, my lingering pauses, my drift into worlds inside me that had to be revisited so they could finally be rewritten. And still... you met me with love. With softness. With open arms and open hearts. You reminded me why healing matters, why strength must bend alongside vulnerability, why we keep choosing to rise even when the climb feels steep. You are my reason. My joy. My eternal inspiration. I love you both to bits—always, endlessly, and far, far beyond.

To my dear friend, Nieke Lombard

And to you, my dearest Nieks... the very heartbeat of this book. Thank you for listening to hours upon hours of readings, for offering not only your thoughts and wisdom, but your whole heart... wide open, luminous, to help shape what these pages have become. You walked this journey with me not merely as a friend, but as a companion in healing, a soul who knows intimately what it means to alchemize pain into purpose, to turn wounds into words that illuminate the way for others. You stood beside me in the most vulnerable moments... in the laughter that loosened the heaviness, in the tears that cracked open truth, in the quiet spaces where healing took its trembling breath. You reminded me, again and again, why stories like ours matter, why they must be spoken aloud, why they deserve to take their place in the world like lanterns glowing in the dark. Thank you for your courage, your insight, your unwavering honesty, and the fierce, radiant love that pours from your spirit with a generosity that forever humbles me. I love you to the moon and back, Nieks...and I always, always will.

Dearest Samantha

My steadfast friend, you have been my rock in every season... a presence I could lean into with absolute trust, always there when I reached out, and often even before I knew I needed someone at all. You offered guidance when wisdom was required, and silence—soft, grounding, and wordless... when what I needed most was simply a hand in mine or the warmth of a heartfelt embrace. You stood beside me as maid of honor when I spoke my vows a second time, your love woven quietly into every step, every breath, every moment of new beginnings. And you walked every step of my healing journey with me. You were there through wedding planning, through rebuilding both life and spirit, through the ordinary rhythms of simply living. Thank you for believing in my writing, my being, my soul, and in this book that carried pieces of me I was still learning to reclaim. Thank you for listening to readings when I needed perspective, for sharing the weight of my sorrow and the sparkle of my joy as these pages slowly came alive beneath my fingertips. You are a rare treasure in a world that so often settles for the superficial... a soul of depth, loyalty, gentleness, and fierce devotion. Thank you for carrying my pain with me, for sharing my burdens without hesitation, and for celebrating my joy and rebirth when the light finally began to return.

I love you, my beautiful friend... now, and until the very last breath I take.

Gratitude to you, the reader

To you, the one reading this book with an open heart... thank you. Thank you for choosing to be here, for stepping across the threshold of these chapters, and for allowing my words to meet you gently, exactly where you are on your journey. By reading, you have already taken an act of immense courage... a quiet declaration whispered from the soul: "***I am ready to heal. I am willing to look within.***" That is not a small step. It is an extraordinary one. May these words remind you that you are never alone in your pain, that your story holds weight and meaning, and that healing is not some distant mountaintop you must conquer... but a tender, brave unfolding of who you are becoming. May you feel held, seen, and gently accompanied every step of the way. Thank you for trusting this book to walk beside you. May it offer comfort in moments when your heart aches for softness, and clarity in moments when you find yourself searching for direction, grounding, or guidance. May it place a spark of hope in your ears when the road ahead feels unsteady or unclear. Your willingness to heal, your choice to keep moving, to keep feeling, to keep opening— is a quiet, powerful form of heroism. And for that— for your presence, your courage, your openness, and the unique light you carry— I am deeply, endlessly grateful.

To the woman I owe it all to

I have saved you for last, Colleen, because you do not simply hold a place in my heart... you occupy a crucial and special chamber, its quiet center, its unwavering source of warmth. You are not only a part of my gratitude for this book... you are its foundation, its truest heartbeat, its sacred pulse. You are woven into every line, every breath, every truth that finds its voice here. Your presence threads through these pages like a golden seam... subtle, luminous, essential. You are not just the reason these words came into being. You are the reason I stand here at all; as the woman capable of writing them, of surviving them, of transforming them into something that might heal another soul. Your presence has shaped me, strengthened me, held me in ways language can only begin to touch. There are depths the written word cannot reach; places where gratitude becomes something holy, where love becomes something eternal. That is where you live in me.

To Colleen Murray... my second mother, my sponsor, my cherished friend. The woman who became the quiet anchor in the most violent seas of my becoming. You were the rock beneath my trembling boat when the world around me pitched and heaved, the steady ground I clung to when everything else crumbled beneath my feet. When I first began to breathe again; fragile, unsteady, half-alive, half-ghost; you were there, waiting at the shoreline of my despair. A lighthouse standing firm against the pitch-black night, casting your unwavering beam across waters I thought would swallow me whole. It was your voice; soft, gentle, and steady, insisting I mattered; that taught my lungs how to draw breath again. It was your presence that coaxed me back into my body when I no longer remembered how to stay. Your counsel didn't simply guide me; it rebuilt me to who I am today. Your words weren't mere suggestions; they were lifelines thrown across the chasm I believed would consume me.

And your love ... your love was not comfort alone; it was alchemy. It transformed the ruins of who I was into the foundation of who I could become. Colleen, to you I owe not just this book, but every piece of healing I will ever write, every truth I dare to speak, every light I pass forward into the world. You are, and will forever remain, one of my life's most sacred blessings. A testament that angels do not always arrive with wings; sometimes, they walk beside us and teach us how to rise. For it was *you*, Colleen, who dared to look into the swirling storm of my chaos and see not a shattered mosaic, but a masterpiece in the making. Where I saw only fractures, you saw the glimmer of a story trying to break free. Where I felt like ruin, you recognized a storyteller waiting—aching—to be born. You saw the writer in me long before I had the courage to even whisper her existence. You held my trembling hands with a steadiness only love and wisdom can offer, and you placed a pen, my future, my lifeline, into my unsteady fingers. "Write, my girl," you whispered, your voice soft but carrying the weight of destiny. "Your words will heal you ... and they will heal others too." In that moment, you did not simply encourage me. You *summoned* me. You awakened the woman buried beneath the rubble of her own silence. You breathed life into the voice I had convinced myself was unworthy of being heard. And because of you, I found the courage to speak, to write, to rise. In the quiet stillness of my heart, gratitude unfurls; soft, luminous, blooming like a radiant flower forcing its way through the cracks of forgotten concrete. Colleen... dear *Cols*, my north star stitched into the fabric of my darkest nights. You shone with a steady, unwavering brilliance when every path before me dissolved into shadow. When doubt coiled at my feet and fear whispered its poisonous lullabies of unworthiness, it was your presence, your steady, gentle light, that broke through the fog and reached me. You did not simply guide me. You *lifted* me. You gathered me from the cold places where I had abandoned myself, and your light did what my own could not: it revived me... called me back into breath, back into becoming, back into life. Your light wasn't a beacon in the distance, it was the sunrise at my shoulder, illuminating the pieces of me I thought were lost forever. The journey we walked together was never merely a trek through hardship; it was a metamorphosis, a shedding, a rebirth. What felt to me like stumbling through the ruins of my own becoming was, through your eyes, the slow unfurling of something sacred. You noticed the faint, trembling spark of a writer in me long before I dared to look at her; long before I believed she could exist. You cupped that fragile ember in your palms with a reverence I did not yet know I deserved, shielding it from every gust of doubt that threatened to snuff it out. With each word of faith you offered, you breathed warmth into what I thought was ash. Your encouragement didn't simply inspire me; it *ignited* me. Every affirmation you whispered became kindling for a flame I didn't know lived in my chest, a fire woven from the threads of my own scars, my own stories, my own hard-earned truth. And with you beside me; steadfast, patient, unwavering; what once seemed impossible slowly, beautifully, inevitably became the only path my soul could walk. Thank you for being the soft, warm place where I could collapse when the world sharpened its edges against me. When everything around me felt cold, brutal, and unyielding, your kindness became the gentle cradle that held my breaking pieces as though they were something precious, something worth saving. It was you who taught me how to thread wisdom through my wounds, how to shape ache into art, how to shape pain into prose, how to coax meaning from the marrow of my most vulnerable places. You showed me that even shattered things can cast light; that a trembling voice can still speak truth, that a trembling hand can still write it. Your unwavering belief in my potential became the bridge that carried me across the chasm of doubt, the quiet force that dared me to breathe life into these books. They are more than pages; they are living altars to the journey we walked together, each sentence carrying the imprint of your presence, each truth echoing with the steadiness of your love.

As I spill my heart into these words, I carry you with me in every line, every breath, every truth, every revelation. My love for you stretches beyond the rim of the stars, beyond language, beyond gratitude; it is a devotion rooted in the deepest chambers of my being, a love carved into the very architecture of my soul. So here's to you, Cols; dearest, precious, powerful, breathtakingly **legendary** Cols. To the woman whose fierce tenderness carved a path through my darkness, whose voice coaxed me out of silence, whose presence became the steady rhythm beneath my faltering steps. You were never just my sponsor; you became a mother of the soul, a quiet guardian who held the lantern high when my own hands shook too violently to grip it. You ushered me into a world where my voice, once buried beneath rubble and fear, could finally rise, tremble, and then shine. Together, we did more than survive the storm; we shaped a story woven from grit and grace, a testament to resilience, to love without condition, and to the wild, unbreakable beauty of rising again. Thank you, Cols ... for your guidance that steadied me, your faith that rebuilt me, your tenderness that softened even my hardest edges, and the immeasurable, irreplaceable gift of **you**. Thank you for everything; for every breath of belief you lent me until I could finally breathe on my own. Thank you, Cols ... for being there not only in the rhythm of my writing, but in every shadowed corridor of my healing. When the darkness pressed its cold forehead against mine, you held the light steady; unshaken, unwavering, refusing to let the night swallow me whole. When I shattered, splintering into pieces I believed unworthy of repair, you did not flinch or flee. You knelt beside the rubble of me, gathered the fragments with hands as gentle as prayer, and helped me remember the shape of who I once was, and who I could become again. You dried tears that seemed endless, held me when my own arms failed, and carried me through storms I was sure would devour me. You loved me with a ferocity that startled my broken places awake; a love so steady, so faithful, that it reached inside the hollows where I could not find a single scrap of worth or warmth. You were my refuge, my steady heart in the chaos, the living proof that unconditional love is not a myth but a miracle; and one that chose **me.**

You counselled me when every answer slipped like water through my trembling fingers, and not once did you let me collapse into the arms of hopelessness. When my heart needed softness, you became gentleness incarnate; a whisper of tenderness in a world that had grown unbearably sharp. Yet when the moment called for fire, you transformed into a fierce, no-nonsense warrior of love— the ass-kicking guardian of my becoming; reminding me with every word, every steady gaze, of a strength I had long forgotten lived inside me. You were the one who spoke truth, not the comforting illusions I wanted, but the truth that carved space for growth, truth that anchored me when I threatened to drift away. You taught me how to rise from my knees, how to place one steady foot before the other, how to walk again without trembling... and eventually; miraculously, how to dance on my own unbroken feet. To you, my gratitude stretches as far as the east is from the west; immeasurable, eternal, infinite. You are strength wrapped in compassion, fire softened by grace, and because of you, I am forever altered... forever more myself. And now, as I write these words with trembling hands and a heart weighted by equal parts love and grief, a gentle, devastating truth settles over me like dusk softening the edges of a weary world: your journey here is drawing to its sacred close. Higher Power is calling you home... and though the very thought of breathing in a world where you are no longer physically beside me feels almost unbearable, I make you this vow, my dearest Cols, your light will not dim. Your legacy will not fade into silence. I will carry your torch. I will lift your flame high enough for the whole world to see. As long as breath stirs in my chest and lungs, and ink flows through my fingertips and stains these pages, your name will live on. For in every word I write, in every healing these pages ignite, in every soul they cradle and transform... your spirit endures. You will live on, Cols, not only as memory, but as heartbeat, as truth, as fire braided into the rhythm of my healing and the lifetimes changed because you lived. Forever woven into the marrow of my work. Forever part of the story that saved me.

Your wisdom, your love, your strength ... they are sewn into me like sacred threads, woven through the very fabric of my becoming. You have become the quiet, steady voice that will forever echo through the halls of my heart—an eternal guide whispering me forward through every ending I must endure and every new beginning I dare to claim. And when I write, it will always be your spirit that steadies my trembling hand ... your courage that breathes shape into my words, your love that carves truth into every line. I love you beyond time, beyond distance, beyond the fragile borders of this human life, Cols. Even when Higher Power calls you home, you will not fade, not from me, not from this world, not from the countless souls your love has lifted. You will remain... in my heart's quiet chambers, in the ink of every story I offer, and in every life forever transformed by the fierce, tender love you so freely, so fearlessly gave. You are eternal... not because your path was free of suffering and without struggle, but because you walked through every storm with a grace that humbled the sky, a strength that defied the breaking, and a heart that kept loving even when life demanded it close. Your spirit, your guidance, your council, your boundless compassion; they ripple outward like gentle waves on an endless ocean, touching hearts far beyond the shoreline of your days. Thank you for everything... for loving me in the moments I felt unlovable, for holding belief in me when doubt was the only thing my hands could grasp, for teaching me that healing is equal parts courage and tenderness and love, a sacred act of returning to oneself. Your legacy is not carved in the battles you survived, but in the lives you lifted, reshaped, and breathed new life into... including my own. I will carry your light forward, always; cupping it gently, tending it faithfully, letting it shine through everything I create, through every choice, every page, every breath I take in this new chapter of living. I will forever more honor you, your heart, your wisdom, and your legacy. Your shoes are big ones to fill, but I will try my best to do so.

Your Tishie; always.

For Colleen — A Benediction of Light

Colleen... whose love became the compass that guided me home. You entered my life like a quiet sunrise; soft, steady, inevitable, dispelling the shadows not with force or noise, but with an unwavering, compassionate light. You showed me that healing doesn't bloom in perfection, but in truth... in the brave, trembling act of being seen, of feeling fully, of rising again and again from the ashes of who I thought I had to be. You were my safe harbor when the storm refused to break, my clear, grounding voice when chaos roared through my mind, my mirror when my own reflection became unrecognizable. You held my story with hands free of judgment, and in that sacred holding, you gave me permission; not just to write it, but to live it. And now, even as the tides of time begin to call you gently home, your light does not wane; it multiplies. It shimmers in the hearts you have healed, glows fiercely in the lives you have lifted, and pulses forever in the words you inspired. Your legacy is not fading—it is spreading, luminous and eternal. When I write, you are there, your presence a quiet hand guiding mine across the page. When I speak of healing, it is your wisdom that rises in my voice like a remembered prayer. And when I love others through their pain, it is your compassion moving through me, steady and instinctive, as though it has become part of my very blood. You were never simply a companion on my path, Cols; you became the very ground beneath it. The foundation upon which every step of my becoming was built. Your spirit is etched into every line of this book, stitched into the fragile seams of every hope it offers. And though your time in this world draws gently toward its close, I know your story is not ending; it is transcending. You will not fade. You cannot fade. Your light lives here... in me, in these words, and in every soul they will one day hold.

So rest softly now, my dearest Colleen. Your work in this world is complete, but your love; your radiant, fierce, boundless love; will echo long after the final chapter closes. For you did not simply change my life; you breathed life back into me. You resurrected what I thought was lost. And through these pages, through the healing they will carry forward, you will live forever.

For Colleen Murray... my second mother, my teacher, my eternal light.

Closing Reflection — The Tapestry of Light

This book is, at its core, a mosaic; an intricate tapestry of shattered fragments and shimmering pieces, each one shaped, softened, and strengthened by the love of those who held me when I could not hold myself. Every page carries the fingerprints of the souls who stood beside me, steady as pillars when my world trembled, gentle as open palms when my spirit felt too fragile to rise. To those who listened without judgement, who offered courage when mine faltered, who allowed me to be both breakable and brave in the same breath... thank you. You are woven into the very fabric of this work. You are the quiet pulse beneath every sentence, the invisible scaffolding that kept me standing long before I could see the finish line for myself. Because of you, this book became what it was always destined to be; a testament to love that refuses to abandon to resilience born in community, and to the luminous light we discover not alone, but in one another's presence. As I bring this section to its gentle close, I am reminded once more that healing is never a solitary pilgrimage... it is a tapestry, tenderly woven from the threads of love, patience, and understanding that others place into our trembling hands when we falter. What began as a whisper of my own pain; a faint spark flickering in the vast darkness; transformed, through grace, into a chorus of luminous voices, each offering its own quiet glow to guide me forward. Every soul I have thanked here became a lantern along my path, a steady presence reminding me of a truth I had long forgotten we do not rise alone. We rise through connection. Through kindness. Through the quiet, unwavering strength of those who choose to stand beside us when our knees buckle and our spirit splinters. It is within these shared moments; these sacred exchanges of courage, that healing takes root, and the darkness finally begins to yield to light. Marno, Maroné, Isabella, Esmerelda, Nieks, Sam, Cols... and every luminous soul who has walked even a single step of this winding path beside me; you have been my constellation in the vast midnight sky. Each of you, a brilliant point of light, guiding me through the thickest fog toward moments of clarity, stillness, and peace. Because of you, I have learned that even when life cracks us open, when we feel scattered like broken glass across the floor of our own becoming, we can gather those fragments and shape them into something breathtaking. Something honest. Something whole.

The chapters that follow are not mine alone; they are ours. They belong to every heart that has ever fought to carve meaning from chaos to every weary soul who reached into the dark searching for a hand and found one gently reaching back. They belong to the ones who have stumbled, to the ones who have fallen, and to the brave souls who, trembling and bruised, dared to rise once more. May this book be more than ink pressed into paper, more than a voice carried through speakers into waiting ears. May it become a lantern for every soul still wandering through their own labyrinth of shadows. a quiet, steadfast glow reminding them that healing is not the erasure of the fire... but the bravery of stepping through it. And in that passage, in that sacred emergence, discovering that you were never simply scarred by the flames, you were forged by them. You have become the light itself. For in the end, that is who we are: flickers of hope shimmering in one another's darkness, tiny sparks that, when shared, ignite into a living wildfire of connection. When we stand together; when we offer our warmth, our truth, our trembling courage, something miraculous happens. We burn brighter. We rise stronger. And together; we heal.

The Final Dedication

And so, as I place the final period upon these pages of gratitude, my heart circles back to the beginning... to that fragile, trembling moment when I first whispered into the silence, *"Perhaps my story can help someone heal."* What a tender, courageous seed that was, and how fiercely it has grown. This book, though risen from the ashes of my own undoing, has never belonged solely to me. It is woven from the fingerprints of every soul who brushed against my journey... those who clasped my hand when the darkness threatened to devour me, those who lifted my chin and reminded me to search for even the smallest glimmer of light, and those who taught me how to rise on legs that once trembled beneath the weight of my own despair. I dedicate this book not only to the ones who walked beside me, but to the ones who taught me how to stand — how to love without fear, how to forgive without losing myself, how to breathe my way back into life again. To them... to you... these pages belong.

To my family, who steadied me when the waters rose and anchored me when my world threatened to drift away. To my friends, whose belief in me flickered like lanterns along a road I once feared to walk alone. To the readers, the brave souls who journey through these pages with open, tender hearts. And to Colleen, luminous Colleen, who taught me that healing is both a sacred gift and a sacred responsibility. Who showed me that love, when given freely and without condition, holds the astonishing power to rewrite even the darkest, most fractured story. This book is for all of us; for the healers and the hurting, the fallen and the rising, the wanderers searching for light, and the warriors who refuse to stop searching even when the night feels endless. May these words find you exactly where you are, wrap themselves around you like a soft, familiar embrace, and whisper gently into the quiet chambers of your heart: *You are loved ... You are enough ... You are home*.

A Benedict To My Parents

A Preface to Healing: Honesty, Compassion, and the Stories We Carry

And before this journey moves further inward, before memory opens its oldest doors and the past begins to breathe between these lines, I want to create a space that feels held. A space shaped not by spectacle, but by care. Not by accusation, but by tenderness. A place where truth can speak without being sharpened into a weapon. Especially in a narrative that will touch the delicate, aching terrain of childhood trauma, it feels essential to name the spirit in which these pages are offered. This book is not a performance of pain. It is a pilgrimage. A candid exploration of my own becoming. A walk-through brokenness and resilience. Through confusion and courage. Through the long, uneven, human unfolding of healing. It is a story carried not in a clenched fist, but in open hands. Before I invite you to truly enter these pages, before the first memory steps forward and the inner rooms begin to reveal their contents, I want to set something deeply important into the light. Despite what you will read here. Despite the stories. Despite the memories. Despite the darker corners of my childhood I am willing to open. This is not a book written to tarnish or condemn my parents. It is not an indictment. It is not a trial. It is not a list of grievances carved into stone. It is a testimony. Within these chapters you will find honest accounts of childhood experiences. Raw, unvarnished recollections of pain, fear, confusion, and longing. You will hear about what happened in our home. About the ways I struggled to feel safe. To feel seen. To feel held in the ways a child's nervous system quietly asks to be held.

About the shadows that crept into my early years and lingered long after the lights were supposed to have been turned on. But honesty is not the same as cruelty. And truth is not the same as blame. What you will read is my lived experience. My inner weather. My remembered world. It is the story of how my body learned to survive. How my mind learned to adapt. How my heart learned both hunger and armor. My parents, like all people, are not single stories. They are not only the places where I was hurt. They are also the places where I was loved. They, too, are human. Shaped by their own histories. Their own wounds. Their own unfinished griefs. They did not enter parenthood as blank pages. They arrived carrying chapters already written into their bones. This book does not deny their humanity. It rests inside it. To tell the truth about my pain is not to erase their complexity. To name what shaped me is not to declare them villains. It is simply to stop asking my younger self to keep carrying what was too heavy for her hands. These pages are an act of reclaiming. Of witnessing. Of integration. They are my attempt to let the past speak in a voice that is neither silenced nor sharpened. To allow memory to move without being turned into a weapon. To let the child, I was finally tell the story she did not yet have language for, while allowing the adult I am to hold that story with compassion. For healing does not ask us to choose between truth and love. It asks us to widen enough to hold both. So, as you step further into this book, I invite you to read not as a judge, but as a witness. Not as an interpreter of blame, but as a companion to complexity.

Let these pages be what they are meant to be: an honest account of one inner world, offered not to condemn the past, but to understand it. Not to harden the heart, but to soften it. Not to fracture, but to integrate. This is a story about impact, not intent. About experience, not accusation. About how a child learned the shape of safety. And how an adult is now learning to rebuild it. May these pages be read with the same spirit in which they were written.

With honesty. With compassion. With the understanding that every family is an ecosystem of stories. And every human life is more than the worst moment it ever contained. This is where we begin. I will write about decisions my parents made. About their missteps. About moments of unintentional neglect that left quiet imprints on a nervous system still learning the language of safety. And as I recount experiences that involve them, I want to be unequivocally clear, with a steadiness born of long reflection: the stories I share are not indictments. They are not verdicts handed down from a hardened place. They are not acts of blame sharpened into weapons. They are acts of honesty. Gentle, necessary, and long overdue. My parents were not villains in my story. They were human beings. Human beings shaped by their own histories. Their own unfinished griefs. Their own inherited silences. Their own limited maps of love and protection, drawn by the worlds they survived before they ever knew me. They carried what they were given. They offered what they knew. And sometimes, what they knew was not enough. This book is not about casting shadows outward. It is about understanding the ones that took root inward. It is about tracing the way certain moments settled into my body. The way certain absences echoed. The way certain patterns quietly formed the scaffolding of my inner world. It is about telling the truth in a way that does not exile compassion but expands it. In a way that makes room for complexity. For the tender and the tangled. For the possibility that love and harm, care and confusion, protection and pain can exist in the same house, sometimes in the same breath, sometimes in the same moment. Because human families are not built from single colours. They are tapestries. Woven from light and shadow, from intention and impact, from what was offered and what was missed. And it is within these interwoven threads that the nervous system learns its first grammar. The heart learns what to expect. The mind learns what love is supposed to feel like. This preface is not a defence. It is not a shield. It is not an attempt to soften the truth into something easier to hold. It is an opening of the hands.

An unclenching. A gesture of trust. An invitation to read these stories not as accusations, but as offerings. As lived terrain. As emotional geography. As the soil from which both my suffering and my healing have slowly learned how to grow. These pages are not meant to wound. They are meant to witness. They are not meant to punish the past. They are meant to understand it. They are the story of how a child made sense of the world she was given. And how an adult is now learning, with care, to make something new from what she found there. I say this because it is so tempting, when reading any story, to arrange its people into tidy constellations of good and bad, heroes and villains, light and dark fixed neatly in the sky. But that has never been the truth of life. And it is not the truth of mine. Human beings do not live in such clean lines. We live in weather. In contradictions. In tenderness braided with fear. My parents were not symbols cast into opposing roles. They were people. Flesh and breath and history. Human beings carrying their own invisible bundles, knotted with experiences they did not choose, shaped by generations whose voices still echoed in their nervous systems. They did what they knew how to do. They loved me in the ways they were able, even when those ways did not always reach me in the language my heart was asking for. They made mistakes. As I have made mistakes. As I continue to make them. And now, standing on the other side of childhood, now carrying the fragile gravity of parenthood myself, I see with aching clarity how often love walks hand in hand with limitation. How devotion can coexist with unhealed wounds. How protection can falter beneath the weight of what was never tended. I understand now how easy it is to pass along what you never learned how to put down.

I write with a deep awareness that words are not neutral. They are seeds. They carry the power to wound or to welcome, to fracture or to gather, to turn us away from one another or draw us closer into recognition. This is why I feel compelled to say, clearly and early, that this exploration of my family history is not an act of blame. It is not a courtroom. It is not a ledger of wrongs. It is not rooted in resentment. It is rooted in understanding. To speak honestly about the challenges of my early life is not to diminish my parents' humanity. It is to honor the full, complicated landscape of our shared humanity. To tell the truth about where I was hurt is also to tell the truth about how people hurt while trying to love, how silence survives inside families, how pain unspoken learns how to travel. My intention is to illuminate how wounds, when left unnamed and unhealed, can ripple quietly across generations, shaping nervous systems, relationships, and self-beliefs long after their first moment has passed. And also how forgiveness, both toward others and toward ourselves, can become a lifeline. A way back. A soft but steadfast bridge toward wholeness. This is not a story about fault. It is a story about inheritance. About the things we are given without consent. About the patterns that move through us until someone chooses to stop and look. About the courage it takes to feel what was avoided. To name what was normalized. To love our parents without abandoning our own truth. And to choose, gently and deliberately, to build something different from what we were handed. For years, I lived inside the paradox of love and hurt, trying to hold both in the same trembling hands, trying to understand how tenderness and terror, comfort and confusion, could occupy the same chambers of my chest. I loved my parents. And I was hurt by them.

Those two truths lived together in me like opposing currents in the same sea, pulling, colliding, reshaping the shoreline of who I was becoming. My parents, like all of us, were flawed, imperfect human beings doing the best they could with the emotional tools, the inner resources, the half-maps of love and survival they had been given. They were shaped long before I knew their names. Shaped by their own childhoods. By their losses and longings. By the scars they carried beneath their daily faces. By silent battles waged in rooms I never saw, at tables I never sat at, in nights that belonged to a time before me. They entered parenthood already carrying histories in their bodies. Already marked by stories that had never found language. Nervous systems trained in climates they did not choose. Hearts that had learned to protect before they had learned to soften. They, like all of us, carried wounds. Some freshly opened. Some quietly infected by years of being left untouched. And they had no clear map for tending them. No living example of what healing might look like. No shared vocabulary for what was moving beneath the surface of their reactions, their silences, their fears. To speak of their failings is not to erase their goodness. It is not to deny their efforts. It does not diminish the ways they tried, the ways they showed up, the ways they loved within the limits of what they knew. It does not negate the sacrifices that were real, even when they were not enough. Love lived there. It did. Even when it was fractured. Even when it was inconsistent. Even when it arrived tangled in its own unhealed threads. Even when it could not always reach me in the language my body was asking to hear.

And to acknowledge the trauma I experienced is not to strip anyone of their humanity. It is to honor it. It is to tell the truth about what happens when pain goes unnamed. When fear goes unheld. When wounds are inherited rather than tended. It is to speak into the quiet spaces where misunderstanding grows. To illuminate the places where harm is not born of cruelty, but of unfinished stories passed from hand to hand, heart to heart. This is the paradox I write from. Love that was real. Hurt that was real. Both true. Both formative. Both deserving of language. Because healing does not begin with choosing sides. It begins with choosing honesty. This narrative is not written in anger. It is not born of resentment.

It is not a ledger of accusations or a courtroom of memory. It rises instead from a quieter, braver place. From the slow soil of compassion. From the trembling ground of honesty. Toward them. Toward myself. Toward the truths that asked to be spoken long before I had the language to hold them. Let me say this plainly and let it stand like a stone you can touch: no family is immune to missteps. Every parent is a mosaic. A shifting pattern of devotion and limitation, of tenderness and blind spots, of fierce love braided with unhealed places. My parents were no different. I would not be truthful if I did not speak of the moments they faltered, the times when something essential missed its mark, when safety frayed, when the child in me learned to carry what she should not have had to carry. And I would not be honest if I erased the moments they rose. The moments they tried. The moments they protected, showed up, sacrificed, and cared in the ways they knew how. My parents loved me in the only language they had learned. A language shaped long before me. Often constrained by their own unmet needs, their own unspoken griefs, their own unresolved struggles. They were not flawed by nature. They were shaped by circumstance. By histories that had left them ill-equipped to navigate the delicate, shifting emotional terrain of parenting. Like so many before them, they moved beneath the same veil of not-knowing about trauma, believing that love alone could shield us from harm. Believing that good intentions were armor enough. But love, while foundational, is not a substitute for understanding. And understanding asks for healing. Healing asks us to turn toward what hurts. To learn the language of our own inner worlds. To notice the places where care did not quite land. To tend what was bruised instead of insisting it should not ache. This is a process neither of us had yet learned how to begin. And so, pain moved through our home like weather without a name, shaping the emotional climate without ever being spoken.

This book grows from that recognition. From the knowledge that love can be real and still incomplete. That care can exist alongside confusion. That good hearts can pass on harm without ever intending to. I write not to condemn, but to illuminate. Not to wound, but to understand. Not to fracture, but to make room for the full, complicated truth. Because compassion does not ask us to look away. It asks us to look deeper. This is not an excuse. It is context. A widening of the frame. A deepening of the lens. Trauma, when left unacknowledged, does not fade. It does not rest. It does not dissolve with time. It becomes a subterranean river, moving beneath the visible world, carving unseen channels through behavior, bending reactions, shaping the very grammar of love when love has never learned how to be gentle. What is unnamed does not disappear. It migrates. It settles into tone. Into touch. Into silence. Into the spaces between what is felt and what is allowed. I have come to understand that the wounds we carry are rarely solitary. They do not belong to one body alone. They ripple outward. They echo. They travel through families like invisible heirlooms, passed not in boxes or photographs, but in nervous systems, in reflexes, in the ways voices rise or retreat. They are handed down hand to hand, breath to breath, long before anyone knows their names. My parents, though deeply well-meaning, were themselves wounded. They did not possess the language to name their pain, the resources to tend it, or the awareness to interrupt cycles they could not yet see. They raised me in a time and place where mental health struggles were whispered, not spoken. Where anger was buried until it erupted. Where vulnerability was interpreted as weakness rather than need.

They were products of their own painful histories, carrying fears, griefs, and angers they had never been taught to hold, never shown how to soothe, never given permission to unpack. Their mistakes were often born from this inner chaos. A turbulence they could feel but not translate. A storm without a forecast. My father's explosive temper, which once left me cowering, did not rise from cruelty. It rose from a childhood shaped in a war-torn country where tenderness was dangerous and vulnerability could cost you your life. His anger was not malice. It was armor. A shield forged early, when softness was a liability and survival demanded steel. That armor followed him into adulthood. Into marriage. Into fatherhood. It protected him once. And later, it wounded. My mother's emotional withdrawal, which I once mistook for indifference, was not absence of love. It was a defence she inherited from a family that equated affection with manipulation, closeness with control. She learned early that distance was safety. That feeling too much meant being taken over. That care required caution. Her quiet was not emptiness. It was shelter. These patterns were not chosen lightly. They were survival strategies. Inherited reflexes. Ancient adaptations to environments that no longer existed but still lived inside the body. Ways of staying alive that slowly hardened into ways of loving. They shaped their responses in ways they did not yet have the power to change. And so, what had once protected them quietly shaped me. Not through intention. Through transmission. Through the unspoken language of nervous systems speaking to nervous systems. Through wounds loving wounds without knowing how to set one another down. To see this is not to erase the pain. It is to finally understand its shape. They did not have the tools I have now. They did not grow up in a world that spoke the language of therapy, of nervous systems, of inner children and attachment wounds. They did not inherit the maps I have been given. They did not have words for what moved inside them, nor mirrors gentle enough to show it back without shame. They lived in a time where survival mattered more than softness. Where endurance was praised, and feeling was suspect. Where pain was something, you swallowed, not something you spoke. And yet, in the ways they knew, they loved. They tried. They reached as far as their own unhealed hands could reach. Sometimes that love came clumsily. Sometimes it came tangled in fear. Sometimes it arrived late, or wrapped in silence, or misshapen by old armor. But it was there. Beating beneath their limitations. Pressing against the edges of what they could give.

And I will never forget that. I cannot. Because to forget it would be to flatten them into symbols instead of honoring them as people. And to hold this truth, all of it, is to stand inside the full complexity of being human. The place where harm can coexist with care. Where wounds can travel through love. Where tenderness and damage can share the same hands. Compassion does not erase pain. It does something far more honest. It gives pain somewhere to finally rest. Somewhere to be held without being sharpened. Somewhere to soften its grip. After sitting so long with the inheritance of their suffering, after tracing the quiet patterns that shaped my own inner world, I began to understand how seductive blame can be. How easily it rises when we touch the raw places of our past. When we finally see the bruises beneath the skin of memory, it is tempting to point outward. To locate a single origin. A single face. A single moment to crown as the culprit. Blame offers a shape to the ache. A target. A direction. It promises relief through accusation. But blame, I have learned, is a dead end disguised as a road. It offers the illusion of movement while quietly locking us in place. It keeps our gaze turned backward, fists clenched around what was, replaying old injuries like verdicts that never adjourn. It carves the world into adversaries and traps us in a narrow theater of right and wrong, where resentment becomes both the weapon and the warden. It does not dissolve pain. It preserves it. Keeps it alive. Breathing. Fed by the very energy we are longing to reclaim. Blame builds its own kind of fortress. One made not of fear, but of grievance. Not of silence, but of stories that harden into walls. And I did not want another prison. I wanted a passage. So slowly, painfully, deliberately, I began to loosen my grip on blame. Not to excuse. Not to forget. Not to minimize what was lost or broken.

But to free myself from the posture of perpetual opposition. To step out of the role of the wounded witness and into the work of the willing healer. To let understanding become a solvent. To let compassion become a bridge. To let the past inform me without entombing me. Because healing, I discovered, does not ask us to deny what happened. It asks us to decide what we will build from it. And I was finally ready to build something that could breathe.

For years, I carried a quiet anger toward my parents. Not the kind that shouts, but the kind that settles. An ache shaped like injustice. Grief sharpened into accusation. It lived in the background of my days like a low, persistent ache, the way an old injury announces itself when the weather changes. I held the ways they failed me, the moments they could not meet me, the places their wounds brushed against my own, as if they were stones in my pockets. Proof of what had been lost. Evidence of what had hurt. I carried them everywhere. In my chest. In my jaw. In the tightness of my breath. Yet over time, I began to feel the cost of carrying them. Resentment is not a passive thing. It is a fire that demands tending. Holding onto it was like walking with a burning coal pressed against my heart. At first it felt like protection. Like justice. Like keeping the truth warm. But slowly, relentlessly, it scorched me. It charred tenderness. It blackened joy. It burned long after the original flame had gone cold. I realized one day that the anger I believed was aimed outward had made a home inward. It was not punishing the past. It was exhausting the present. Forgiveness did not arrive as a revelation. There was no single breath where everything lifted. No cinematic release. No holy hush. It came the way most real transformations do. Quietly. In fragments. As a slow loosening. A gradual unthreading of the need to be right. Of the hunger for someone else to carry the full weight of what I felt. It came as a softening of my fists. As space between old stories. As moments where the fire dimmed enough for something else to be felt. I found myself asking new questions. Not the sharp ones that cut. The quieter ones that open. "How much of my pain is theirs to carry? How much is mine to tend?" Those questions did not absolve the past. They did not rewrite it. They did not minimize what was lost. But they shifted the center of gravity. They turned me from the fixed posture of victimhood toward the living posture of agency. They did not ask me to forget. They asked me to choose. To choose what I would keep feeding. To choose what I would keep carrying. To choose what kind of inner world I wanted to build from what had been. They became my compass. And slowly, almost imperceptibly, they returned something essential to me. Something I had not realized how long I had surrendered. Not innocence. Not certainty. But authorship. Ownership. My own hands on the wheel. Not denying the road behind me. But finally steering the one ahead.

This is not a book about blame. It is a book about truth. And there is a difference as wide as an ocean between the two. When I began writing, I made a promise to myself, not as a rule, but as a vow. I would not dilute my story to make it easier to swallow. I would not perfume it for comfort. And I would not sharpen it into a weapon. I do not believe healing grows in the soil of accusation. I have learned that throwing stones at the past only teaches the hand to stay clenched. Healing, for me, has come from something far more difficult and far more honest: standing before what was. Looking directly. With eyes open. With breath unguarded. With a heart willing to hold the full, complicated, human picture without arranging it into villains and saints. Writing about painful memory can feel like lifting a magnifying glass to old bruises, deliberately inviting them to ache again, watching their colors deepen under the heat of attention. It can feel like pressing fingers into scar tissue just to confirm that it is still there. But that is not my purpose. I do not return to these places to reopen wounds. I return so that light can reach them. So that what once lived only in shadow might finally be seen. Understood. Integrated. So that the quiet illumination of meaning might reveal how I became who I am. Not despite the scars, but with them. Not as evidence of defect, but as proof of survival. Of adaptation. Of a nervous system that learned how to endure before it ever learned how to rest.

My journey toward healing truly began the moment I allowed myself to acknowledge that those early experiences shaped me. Not only in the ways that wounded. But in the ways that strengthened. In the ways they sharpened my sensitivity. Deepened my empathy. Gave me eyes for what trembles quietly in others. Denial had never protected me. It had only pressed pain deeper into the body, where it learned how to speak through anxiety, through numbness, through patterns I did not yet understand. Naming it changed its shape. Naming it lifted it into a frame where reflection could occur. Where compassion could enter. Where empathy could soften what had once been rigid. And where growth, slow and deliberate, could finally take root. This book, then, is not a courtroom. It is a lantern. Not raised to accuse. But to reveal. Not to condemn the past. But to understand how it continues to breathe in the present. Because truth, when held with care, does not destroy. It integrates. It connects. It makes room. And it is only in that room that healing learns how to begin. In telling these stories, I do not cast them as weapons of accusation. I do not hurl them like stones toward the past, hoping the sound of impact might finally quiet what still aches. I offer them instead as bridges. Open spans of language laid carefully between one inner world and another. Planks of memory and breath and truth, extending outward from the private terrain of my experience so that anyone who has ever suffered quietly, anyone who has ever wandered the long corridors of their own mind wondering if they were the only one still awake in the dark, might recognize themselves somewhere in these pages and feel a little less solitary in their becoming. There is a common misconception that storytelling, especially storytelling born of pain, must be an act of indictment. A naming of culprits. A ritual of catharsis that demands someone be made to carry the weight. But I have found the opposite to be true. What heals is not the sharpening of blame, but the softening into honesty. And honesty, when it is brave and tender, is the truest form of love. Love toward myself, in finally allowing my story to have breath. And love toward those who shaped the earliest chapters of my life, in refusing to reduce them to the sum of their worst moments. When I write about the times my parents raised their voices, or the nights they could not soothe my fear, or the ways their own wounds leaked into the rooms of my childhood, I do so not to vilify them, but to honor the complex, unfinished reality of what was. To speak of rupture is not to erase devotion.

To name what broke is not to deny what once held. To describe a broken wing is not to deny that the bird once knew the sky. It is to acknowledge both the flight and the fall. The lift and the fracture. The longing that remembers height even while standing on the ground. These stories are not verdicts. They are windows. They are not weapons. They are offerings. They are my way of saying: this is where I have been. This is how I was shaped. This is how I learned to survive. And this is how I am learning, still, to live. It would be easy, perhaps even momentarily satisfying, to cast my parents as villains in the story of my life. Stories hunger for clean lines. They crave sharp edges, clear antagonists, a single shadow we can point to and say, "*there*". But real lives are not built from straight strokes. They are braided. Messy. Overlapping with tenderness and harm in the same breath. And to paint my parents as monsters would be neither fair nor true. Their mistakes were not born of malice. They were born of inheritance. Of two human beings who entered parenthood already carrying the unfinished sentences of their own childhoods in their bodies. Each raised voice, each retreat into distance, each moment of misattunement was less an act of cruelty than a language spoken from unmet needs and unhealed hurts. Pain does not always roar. Sometimes it echoes. Sometimes it learns how to speak in the tone of normalcy. Sometimes it disguises itself as discipline, or silence, or control, and passes quietly from one generation to the next like a family heirloom no one remembers choosing. And then I became a parent myself. And a quieter, more humbling recognition began to take root. I saw their shadows flicker in my own struggles. In the moments when my patience thinned like worn fabric.

When exhaustion made my voice sharper than my love intended. When stress crowded tenderness out of the room. When I forgot, briefly, the simple, sacred power of kneeling down, of listening with my whole body, of seeing the small, beating heart before me instead of the task or the fear or the noise. In those moments, my parents were no longer distant figures in memory. They were human again. Alive in me. Not as excuses, but as mirrors. These parallels do not absolve what happened. They do not rewrite the ache. But they illuminate it. They reveal how trauma moves through bloodlines like an underground current, unseen yet shaping the surface of everything it touches. How it narrows the space between good intention and unintended harm. How easily love, when it has never been taught how to rest, can bruise even as it reaches. In seeing myself reflected in them, I did not lose my story. I gained its depth. I began to understand that what wounded me did not begin with me. And that what heals me does not end with me. The fuller picture is this: my parents were shaped by storms long before I ever knew their names. Long before I could read their faces or decipher their silences, the weather had already moved through them. They carried unresolved pain the way some people carry old injuries, accommodated without ever truly healing, learning to move around the ache rather than tending to it. No one had shown them how to set it down. No one had taught them the language of repair, the rituals of safety, the slow, attentive art of inner listening. They were doing the best they could with the tools they had. And those tools were incomplete. I can see that now. I could not see it then. As a child, I did not have access to context or compassion. I only had sensation. The tightness in my chest. The watchfulness in my body. The quiet longing for something warmer. Safer. More consistent. A home that felt like rest instead of rehearsal. Adulthood has given me another lens. Not one that blurs what happened, but one that deepens it. It took me years to understand that compassion does not cancel impact. That insight does not dissolve memory. That naming the weather does not undo the flood. But it does change the way I carry the water. It shifts the weight from something that drowns into something that can be held. And sometimes, that shift is the first true breath of healing.

This book is, above all, a testament to the power of storytelling as a vessel for transformation. A way of moving what has lived in the body back into language. By speaking openly about the fractures in my family, I do not seek to vilify, nor to cast myself as a martyr wandering through inherited ruin. I write to reclaim authorship of my own life. To take the story out of the shadows where it once wrote itself through silence, through reflex, through unexamined belief, and place it back into conscious hands. Trauma thrives in what goes unspoken. It feeds in the dark. It multiplies in secrecy. But it withers in the light of honesty. It weakens when it is named. It softens when it is witnessed. When we dare to reveal our vulnerabilities, we loosen the grip of shame, not only around our own hearts, but around the countless others quietly carrying similar weight. We interrupt the illusion of isolation. We create small openings where breath can move again. In telling my story, I hope you might glimpse reflections of your own. A gesture. A feeling. A sentence that feels strangely familiar. And perhaps, in those reflections, you might also glimpse the possibility of grace. Not as absolution. But as spaciousness. As a gentler way of holding what has been. As an invitation to begin again, not from forgetting, but from seeing. This is not to say that accountability does not matter. It does. Deeply. Without it, healing has no ground to stand on. My parents, like me, like all of us, must own our parts in the stories we inhabit, the ways we wounded, the ways we failed to see, the moments where fear spoke louder than love. But accountability and forgiveness are not opposites standing on different shores. They are often companions. Walking the same long road. One turns toward the truth and names it. The other loosens the grip of what that truth leaves behind. One says, "*This happened*". The other says, "*This will not be the place where I remain*". I forgave my parents not because forgiveness was owed, not because the past suddenly made sense or ceased to ache, but because forgiveness was necessary.

Necessary for my own breath. Necessary for my nervous system. Necessary for my own becoming. Resentment is a heavy chain. It feels, at first, like armor. Like justice. But over time, it reveals itself as a tether, binding us to what has been, fastening our future to an old wound, quietly siphoning the very life it promises to protect. It keeps us in constant conversation with the injury, rehearsing it, guarding it, carrying it everywhere like a second spine made of iron. Forgiveness is not the erasure of harm. It is not forgetting. It is not excusing. It is the deliberate refusal to let harm become the final author of who we are. It is the choice to stop building identity around injury. To unfasten ourselves from the place of impact. To say: this shaped me, but it will not cage me. It is the moment the chain is loosened. The moment the door is no longer watched from the inside. This book is not about forgetting. It is about freeing. About loosening the knots, the past tied in the body. About letting memory exist without letting it rule. And about choosing, again and again, not to live forever inside the echo of what hurt us, but in the widening, breathing space of what can still be healed

The Inheritance of Hurt

I have come to believe we inherit far more than the visible echoes of our parents, more than the familiar eyes that meet us in the mirror or the curve of a smile that feels borrowed. We inherit climates. Inner seasons. The emotional weather of the homes that once raised them before they ever raised us. We inherit their unspoken fears, the ones that learned to whisper instead of speak. Their ways of coping, stitched together in childhood and worn so long they became skin. Their silences, heavy and instructive, teaching us what may be felt and what must be buried. We inherit patterns the way roots inherit the memory of soil, quietly, relentlessly, shaping the way we grow. Some of these patterns are tender, life-giving, carrying warmth forward like an heirloom flame. Others are sharp, quietly destructive, thorns disguised as vines, wrapping themselves around our inner architecture before we know we are being shaped. And most often, we do not recognize them for what they are until we are grown, standing in the middle of our own lives, suddenly hearing ourselves speak in tones we do not remember choosing, moving in rhythms that feel older than us. We find ourselves reciting a script we did not know we had memorized, performing lines first spoken long before we were born. In that moment, something trembles. A strange recognition. A sense that parts of us are carrying histories that are not wholly our own. My parents inherited their own patterns from their parents. And they from theirs. A long lineage of gestures and defenses, of tenderness and harm, braided through generations, passing hand to hand, body to body, heart to heart. Ways of loving and protecting, of surviving and retreating, moving forward through time like an unseen current. None of this excuses the pain that can unfold inside a family. It does not soften the impact of what wounds. But it does explain it.

It gives it contour. A story. A shape that can finally be traced. And when something has shape, it is no longer only a force. It becomes something that can be studied. Held. Met with curiosity rather than only with ache. And what can be understood can, at last, be chosen. We are given the power to decide what we will carry forward and what we will lay down. What we will tend as legacy and what we will return to the earth. Kept with intention. Or, gently, reverently, set free. For most of my early life, I did not have the language to name what was happening around me. I lived before the words arrived. Before understanding had a grammar. I only knew sensation. Atmosphere. The way certain days in our home felt thick, as though the air itself had learned how to bruise. I knew the rooms could grow heavy without warning, that conversations could tilt and darken, that words could land as stones dropped into the soft water of a child's chest, sending ripples I did not yet know how to trace back to their source.

I knew that love, at times, felt conditional. Not a constant current, but something that seemed to swell and recede. Something that could be earned. Something that could be misplaced. Something that could quietly withdraw. I did not yet know that my parents were carrying their own invisible weights. That they moved through our home with histories folded into their bodies. Memories from their childhoods that had never been given rest. Disappointments that had hardened into reflexes. Fears that spoke to them in the quiet hours, whispering directions into their nervous systems, shaping the tone of their days long before any of us entered the room. I could not see those ghosts. I could only feel their passing. The temperature changes. The sudden storms. The way safety sometimes slipped, unnamed, from the edges of ordinary moments. As a child, everything feels personal because the self is the only map you have. If a parent is distant, you assume it is because you are lacking. If they are angry, you believe you are the cause. You place the weight of the weather on your own small shoulders because you have not yet learned how pain travels through a person before it reaches you. You have not yet learned that love can be distorted by wounds it did not choose. That reactions can be echoes. That silence can be inherited. That what arrives at you is often the last movement of a much older story. It is only later, with time, with tenderness, with the slow education of reflection, that another truth begins to rise. Their responses were often not about me at all. They were reverberations of something else entirely. Something older. Something unhealed. Something they did not yet know how to name, let alone soothe. And in that understanding, something inside me softened. The world grew wider. More complex. More human. And in that widening, another inheritance became possible. Not only the unconscious passing down of pain, but the conscious choosing of what ends with me. The place where a lineage pauses long enough to look at itself. To breathe. To decide. The place where the story is no longer only received but rewritten.

The Decision to Tell My Story

The decision to write this book did not arrive like a spark. There was no sudden declaration, no cinematic moment of clarity where everything fell into place. It came the way healing itself came to me. Slowly. Quietly. Through years of inner work that felt less like progress and more like excavation. Years of therapy where language was unearthed from places I did not know had voices. Years of reflection that turned my gaze gently, again and again, toward the rooms I had spent a lifetime avoiding. Years of journaling where ink became a second bloodstream, carrying out what my mouth could not yet hold. Years of conversations that left me trembling and lighter all at once, as though something sealed inside my ribs had finally been given air, as though an inner window had cracked open, and a long-held breath had found its way home. For a long time, I believed I would keep these stories to myself. That they belonged only to the private terrain of my own becoming. They felt too personal. Too entangled in the lives of others. Too knotted with history and love and pain to lay out where they could be touched by unfamiliar eyes. They felt like heirlooms made of glass. Precious. Fragile. Dangerous to mishandle. I told myself that some truths were meant to be lived, not spoken. That some rooms were meant to be tended quietly, not opened. But silence, I learned, is not neutral. It has its own architecture. Its own blueprints. Its own locked doors and hidden staircases. Silence builds walls as surely as fear does. It closes windows. It teaches the body how to hold its breath. Over time, I began to feel how my quiet was shaping me. How it was tightening the spaces inside my life. How it was asking me to keep vigil over old pain instead of allowing it to move, to breathe, to transform. Silence, too, can become a fortress. A private one. A beautiful one, even. But a prison all the same. And gradually, another knowing began to take shape, the way dawn takes shape before it can be named. Soft. Indirect. Persistent. I began to sense that my story might not belong to me alone. That these memories, these patterns, these long corridors of confusion and survival might be carrying more than my own reflection.

That somewhere there might be someone whose childhood feels like a house with too many locked rooms. Someone who has lived with a sense of wrongness they could never locate. Someone who has carried questions in their body that never learned how to speak. Someone who has stood in the middle of their own life feeling the ache of something unnamed, wondering if they were alone in that unknowing. And I began to feel that perhaps these pages could become a place where such a person might recognize themselves. A mirror held not to wound, but to witness. A language for feelings that have lived too long without one. A quiet companionship for those still walking through the aftermath of what shaped them. If my story could help even one person feel less solitary inside their remembering, less fractured inside their past, less ashamed of the way their history still breathes inside them, then the risk of telling it would become a form of care. This book, then, was not born from a desire to be seen. It was born from a desire to make space. To open a room where truth could sit without apology. Where pain could be named without spectacle. Where complexity could be honored without simplification. I did not choose to write this because it was easy. I chose it because it felt necessary. Because something in me had grown tired of living behind the walls of my own untold story. Because I had learned that what is brought into the light does not disappear, but it does change. It softens. It becomes shareable. It becomes human. And so I am writing not only to tell you where I have been, but to offer a hand into the places where our experiences may quietly touch. To say: you are not strange for what you carry. You are not alone in the architecture of your inner world. There are others who have walked these corridors. Who have learned their echoes. Who are learning, still, how to open the doors. I also knew that if I was going to tell this story, I had to tell it whole. Not the curated version. Not the softened one. The living one. The one with splinters still in its palms. That meant writing what is uncomfortable. For me. And possibly for others. It meant returning to rooms I had carefully closed and learning how to touch the doorknobs again. It meant walking back into moments I had long tried to set down, stepping across their thresholds even when the air inside was sharp, even when memory still carried teeth. It meant listening to echoes I had survived by not hearing. It meant letting the story breathe where it had once only been endured.

And it meant writing about my parents with honesty. Even when honesty was not flattering. Even when it complicated the easier narratives of blame or innocence. This was the most difficult crossing. Knowing my words could be misunderstood. That someone might read them and imagine accusation where there is none. That truth might be mistaken for betrayal. That complexity might be flattened into cruelty. That my love might be eclipsed by the shadows I am willing to name. And so, I begin here, with this clarity held like a lantern: my parents are not the villains of this story. They are part of it. As I am. As you are in yours. And so is the context of their own pain. Their own limitations. Their own inheritance. Their own unfinished healing. This book is not a courtroom. It is not a ledger. It is not an indictment. It is a telling. And telling, when it is rooted in compassion, is one of the first ways healing learns how to move. I hold no bitterness toward my parents. Nor toward the landscape of my past.

What I feel, unexpectedly and sincerely, is gratitude. Not for the hurt itself, but for what surviving it awakened in me. For the way hardship coaxed resilience from places I did not know existed. For how it hollowed me in ways that later made room for tenderness. For how it sharpened my empathy for those who struggle in rooms no one else can see. For how it taught me to listen for what lives beneath behavior. For how it lit in me a steady, enduring determination to seek healthier, more conscious ways of speaking love. Because this story, told whole, is not only about where I was wounded. It is about what grew there afterward. About what learned to breathe in the aftermath. About the strange, quiet alchemy by which suffering, when met with honesty and care, can become a teacher.

And sometimes, even a guide. I have come to understand that love wears many dialects. It is spoken differently in every home, inflected by history, shaped by fear or freedom, translated through the emotional vocabularies our caregivers were given. In some houses it sounds like strict rules and vigilant order. In others, hushed silences and careful avoidance. In others still, raised voices, slammed doors, or the warm ritual of family dinners where tenderness is passed like bread. Every household invents its own grammar of affection and boundary, its own syntax of care and control. And often, the impulse to protect becomes tangled in fear, so that what is meant to shelter instead confuses, what is meant to guide instead constricts, what is meant to love instead wounds in ways no one intended. My parents were trying to guide me through a world they themselves often found overwhelming. They were navigating with maps that had missing pages, compasses bent by their own pasts. And though their best was imperfect, it was real. It was carried by a genuine desire that I should survive. That I should flourish. That I should be spared the storms they had learned to endure. Their love did not always know how to be gentle. It did not always know how to listen. But it was there, moving beneath the missteps, a current that did not vanish even when it failed to reach me in the ways I needed. This book is my honest account of what happened. Of the rooms I grew up in. Of the silences and the sounds. Of the ways those early climates shaped the architecture of my inner world. And of how, over time, I began the slow, deliberate work of reclaiming my own sense of safety and self-worth from the places where they first fractured. My purpose is not to exhume guilt. It is to illuminate a path. To trace the contours of a journey that moved through confusion and grief and into the long, patient labor of healing and self-discovery. I know that opening the intimate folds of pain may unsettle some readers. Old memories rarely lie still when the light reaches them. But I have learned that discomfort is often the first small tremor of change. The subtle signal that something sealed is beginning to breathe.

By holding these memories in the open, by examining them with steadiness and care, by allowing them to be understood rather than merely endured, I create room. Room for forgiveness to soften what once felt rigid. For integration to gather what was scattered. For closure not as an ending, but as a gentle settling of what no longer needs to be carried alone. This is not the unearthing of wounds for spectacle. It is the tending of them. The slow washing of what has long been hidden. The deliberate choosing to let my history be seen so it no longer has to speak only through my body, my fears, my silences. In telling it, I am not reopening the past. I am giving it a place to finally rest. And I take full responsibility for my feelings and for the ways I have moved in response to them. I do not place my life entirely in the hands of the past. I acknowledge my own missteps. My own moments of blindness. The times I have spoken from my wounds instead of my wisdom. The ways I, too, have caused harm while trying to protect myself from it. And at the same time, I refuse to let any single chapter, no matter how heavy its ink, become the definition of my entire story. The past shaped me, yes. It pressed its fingerprints into my nervous system. It taught my body certain reflexes, my heart certain fears. But it does not own me. And this book is part of how I learned the difference. Part of how I loosened history's grip and began to live in the wider field of choice. So let me be clear from this place of steadier seeing: this is not a story of victimhood. It is a story of survival. Of endurance. Of the slow, often painful education of learning to separate what was done from who was doing it. To distinguish between the actions a person takes and the person they are beneath them. My parents are not the villains of this narrative. They are, like all of us, unfinished. Human. Becoming. They made errors. Yes. And so have I. And standing now on the other side of childhood, having stepped into the gravity of parenthood myself, I understand something I could not have known before. I know the weight of that role. The way it lives in your bones.

The constant negotiation between intention and impact. Between the love you carry and the limits you sometimes reach before you realize you are there. I know the days when exhaustion dulls tenderness. When patience thins like worn fabric. When stress speaks before wisdom has a chance to arrive. I know what it is to fail to comfort when comfort is needed. To miss the small, trembling cue. To answer too sharply when softness was required. To walk away carrying the quiet ache of regret after the house has gone still, after the lights are low, after the child you love has finally fallen asleep. These moments do not make monsters of us. They make mirrors. And in those mirrors, I have come to see my parents not as figures fixed in the past, but as people who were once standing exactly where I now stand. Trying. Faltering. Loving. Learning. Becoming. Parenting is not a performance staged for applause. It is not a polished script delivered without error beneath steady lights. It is a practice. A living, breathing apprenticeship of the heart. A daily returning. A thousand quiet decisions made in the in-between spaces. It is showing up again and again with hands that are sometimes steady, sometimes shaking. It is loving in real time, with a nervous system, a history, a body that gets tired, a mind that occasionally loses its way. It is choosing to stay in the room even when you stumble. Even when you realize, hours too late, the words you wish you had chosen. The pause you wish you had taken. The tenderness you wish you had led with. It is learning after the moment has passed. It is carrying regret not as a verdict, but as an invitation to grow. If I were to measure my parents by a standard of infallibility, I would have to measure myself by that same impossible law. And by that measure, none of us would remain standing. We would all be found wanting. All be named failures for the simple crime of being human. What I have learned instead is this: growth is not born of flawless people. It is born of willing ones. Of those brave enough to look back without flinching. To take inventory of the ways they missed and still choose to soften. To listen. To repair. To keep walking even when the path reveals uncomfortable truths beneath their feet. Growth lives in the space between who we were and who we are becoming. In the humility to say, "*I didn't know then what I know now.*" In the courage to let that knowing change us. And this book lives in that space. The space where tenderness meets accountability. Where honesty walks hand in hand with compassion. Where the story is not frozen at the moment of injury but allowed to keep unfolding. A space not of perfection, but of practice. Not of blame, but of becoming.

The Complexity of Love

One of the most profound truths this journey has taught me is that love and hurt are not opposites standing at war across a clean divide. They are often companions. Co-tenants of the same inner rooms. They sit at the same table. They share the same blood. You can love someone with the whole architecture of your heart and still be wounded by the ways they move through your life. You can carry scars that bear their fingerprints and still feel your love for them rise, stubborn and enduring, like a tide that refuses to recede. This is one of the great paradoxes of family, especially when trauma has braided itself into its lineage. Love does not always arrive alone. Sometimes it enters holding hands with fear. Sometimes it speaks through exhaustion. Sometimes it is filtered through wounds so old they no longer remember their own names. As a child, I believed love was synonymous with safety. That it would feel like a constant warmth, a reliable shelter, a steady knowing. I thought love would be the absence of sharp edges. The guarantee of understanding. And when those things were not always present, I did what children do. I turned the question inward. I wondered whether love itself was missing. Whether its absence was my fault. Whether I had somehow failed to be lovable enough to keep it whole. But love, I have come to understand, is not always fluent. It does not always speak in the language we need. It can be imperfect. Clumsy. It can reach with trembling hands and still fall short. It can try and miss. It can mean well and wound anyway.

Sometimes love is buried beneath so many layers of fear, stress, survival, and unhealed pain that it scarcely resembles itself, like a river choked with silt, still moving, still alive, but difficult to recognize beneath the murk. Yet even then, it is there. Waiting. Quiet. Misunderstood. My parents loved me. I know this now in a way I could not have known then. I see it not only in what they gave, but in what they struggled to give. In the places they tried and faltered. In the ways their own wounds interfered with the reach of their care. And I also know this: love alone is not always enough to prevent harm. Love needs tools. It needs mirrors. It needs self-awareness. It needs the steadying practices of emotional regulation and the courage of open, vulnerable communication. Without these, love can be easily lost in translation. Spoken with the tongue of good intention and received in the ear of unmet need. Meant as protection and experienced as pressure. Offered as care and felt as distance. This is the complexity I now hold. Not to diminish love. But to deepen it. To understand that love is not only what we feel. It is what we are able to do with what we feel. So, when I write of my childhood trauma, I do so with a full heart. A heart wide enough to hold tenderness and grief in the same breath. A heart that carries love for my parents alongside an unflinching respect for their human complexity. I do not write to dim their goodness or to eclipse the light that lived in our home. That light was real. It still is. There were afternoons threaded with laughter. Bedtime stories murmured beneath the hush of lamplight. The gentle rituals of care that feel small to adults and everything to a child. A hand on my back. A lunch packed. A voice calling my name from another room. These memories are not footnotes. They are part of the body of this story. They move through it like warm currents beneath colder water. They are woven into the same tapestry as the darker strands of confusion and fear, of longing and loneliness. And both belong. Both shaped me. Both live in my hands as I write.

From this weaving, I emerged as someone determined to interrupt the old music of misunderstanding. Someone committed to learning new languages of care. Someone willing to face what is difficult in service of what can heal. Because wholeness is not found by choosing one thread and discarding another. It is found by learning to hold the entire cloth. By letting contrast remain. By allowing light and shadow to share the same frame. And let me speak plainly, gently, without ornament: no honest book about family can ever fully disentangle love from pain. They rise from the same soil. They drink from the same underground rivers. Their roots wrap around one another long before anyone knows how to name what is growing. To write one without the other would be to offer only half a landscape. Only half a weather. Only half a truth. In writing these pages, I am also writing toward my children. Each sentence feels like a letter slipped forward through time, a small lantern set along a path I will not always be walking beside them. I want them to know, not only with their minds but in the marrow of their bones, that the past does not have to dictate the future. That inheritance does not have to mean repetition. That what is handed down can also be set down. By carefully excavating the layers of my history, brushing dust from old foundations, naming what once lived only in shadow, I am trying to dismantle the quiet architecture of shame and secrecy that once bound us. I am learning, and teaching as I learn, that knowledge is the first chisel. Awareness the first crack. And if my story helps even one person turn toward their own past with curiosity instead of condemnation, with tenderness instead of trial, then these words will already have found their work. My children, when they one day read these pages, may cringe at my courage. Or they may recognize themselves in my truth-telling, like seeing a familiar curve of their own face reflected in water. They may feel pride. They may feel discomfort. They may even feel the tremor of shame that often accompanies naked honesty. But more than anything, I hope they will see this writing not as exposure, but as connection. Not as the airing of wounds, but as the tending of them. As proof that even the most painful chapters of a family's history can be composted into meaning.

There is a profound truth in the words of psychologist Hilton Kelley: *"If you are struggling, you are in good company. You are in human company."* When I first encountered that sentence, it landed in me like a quiet bell struck in a fogbound valley, its echo soft but unmistakable. My journey is not unique. But it is mine. A one-of-a-kind mosaic pieced together from pain and becoming. From wounds that, over time, learned how to teach. From fractures that revealed, like fault lines in the earth, exactly where the healing had always been needed. If there is any "sin" in these pages, it is only the sin of honesty. A radical, sometimes unsettling truth-telling that dares to disturb the myth of the perfect family. But perfection is a polished ghost. It does not breathe. It does not hold. Connection, however faltering, however unfinished, is the real miracle. The reaching. The trying. The staying with one another in our unedited forms. This is the universality of the human experience: we are all, always, works in progress. Our parents, with their tenderness and their tempers, their gifts and their gaps, are not villains or saints carved in stone. They are people. Breathing. Breaking. Becoming. Trying. And this, I confess, has been among the hardest lessons of my healing. It is far easier to blame than to bear witness. Easier to forge a villain than to face the aching truth that pain so often springs from places already in pain. Easier to cast a parent in shadow than to imagine the unseen wars they may have been fighting long before our names ever learned to form on their lips. But healing asks more of us than easy stories. It asks us to see. To look with both eyes open. To hold the full, trembling picture. To let compassion widen our vision until the heart can finally make room for what the mind alone could not carry.

The Work of Healing

For a long time, I carried my childhood the way one carries a sealed crate salvaged from a wreck. Pressed tight against my chest. Heavy. Unopened. I believed that if I never lifted the lid, if I never dared to look inside, whatever lived there would remain contained. Harmless. Past. But boxes do not stay silent. They breathe in the dark. They seep. They leave fingerprints on the present. They reveal themselves in the tremor of a reaction that feels too large for the moment, in anxieties that arrive without names, in a self-doubt that seems older than memory. They surface in the way we brace when love reaches for us, in the way we flinch from safety, in the way our children's tears touch wounds we did not know were still open. My healing truly began the day I stopped gripping the box and knelt instead to open it. It was not gentle. It was not orderly. It was excavation. Dust rose like ghosts. Old shapes emerged, warped by time and shadow. Memories surfaced that had learned how to hide in my body when my mind could not hold them. Some were sharp. Some unbearably tender. Some so small they surprised me with how much power they still carried. The process was exhausting. Often painful. And yet, with every hinge that loosened, something else loosened too. Every memory I allowed myself to face lost a measure of its dominion. Every truth spoken aloud thinned the fog of shame. What had once ruled me from the dark began to soften under the gaze of light, like frost yielding to morning. Part of that healing was forgiveness. Not the kind that edits the past into something prettier than it was. Not the kind that polishes bruises into blessings. But the kind that unhooks the heart from a burden it has been mistaking for duty. I forgave my parents not because what happened was always okay, but because I finally understood they were human beings moving through circumstances they themselves did not yet know how to heal. Forgiveness, for me, became less a gesture toward them and more a turning back toward myself. A setting down of a weight my ribs were never meant to house. A quiet release of the stones I had been carrying so long they had begun to feel like part of my bones. In that laying down, something astonishing happened. My hands grew lighter. My breath deepened. And for the first time, I felt the subtle but unmistakable possibility of walking forward not as someone dragging the past behind her, but as someone finally free to choose what she would carry next.

Why This Book Matters to Me

There is always a cost to telling your story. To speak is to step out from behind the walls and into open air, skin exposed to weather, heart unarmoured. Words, once released, cannot be gathered back. They travel. They are misheard. Misheld. People will misunderstand you. They will judge. They will search your sentences for motives you never planted, meanings you never meant to sow. But there is a far greater danger in silence. In letting generations of pain drift unnamed like an inherited fog. In allowing old wounds to keep choosing our futures simply because no one was willing to say, *this hurt.* Silence is not empty. It is fertile. And what it grows, when left unattended, is often more suffering. I am writing this book first for myself. To gather the scattered fragments of my life from the floors of memory and place them into some kind of order. To see my story laid out where I can touch it, trace it, understand it. To watch it come into focus no longer blurred by shame, no longer muffled by fear. Writing, for me, has been a way of turning the lights on in rooms I lived in for years without windows. But I am also writing this book for anyone who has ever wondered if their experiences mattered. If their pain counted. If their voice deserved a place to land. For anyone who has carried their memories like secret bruises, tender and unseen. If you have ever felt alone inside your own history, I want you to hear this clearly: you are not alone. And if you have ever wrestled with the impossible-seeming task of reconciling love with hurt, I want you to know something else just as true. It is possible to hold both without tearing yourself in half. You can honor your parents and still name the harm that was done. You can speak honestly without sharpening your story into a blade. You can tell the truth and keep your compassion intact. This book lives in that space. The space where courage meets tenderness. Where light is not used to expose, but to understand. Where truth is not a weapon, but a bridge.

In sharing this story, I am also reaching for anyone who has ever felt pinned beneath the weight of their own past. Anyone who has lived with the quiet sense that their history is a locked room they are destined to inhabit forever. Perhaps you grew up with parents, caregivers, or relationships that left imprints you still feel in your body. Echoes in the way you love. Flinches in the way you trust. Or perhaps you are carrying choices you now regret, moments you wish you could lift from the timeline of your life, fearing they have branded you beyond redemption. If so, this invitation is for you. Read these pages not as a summons to outrage, but as a living example of what it can look like to honor every chapter of a life, even the ones written in a trembling hand, and still arrive somewhere gentle. Somewhere whole. We do not grow by cutting pages from our story. We grow by learning how to hold them. To integrate them. To stitch what was torn back into the fabric of who we are. Healing is not an act of forgetting. It is an act of weaving. Of allowing shadow and light to coexist until they begin to tell a truer story together. This work asks us to learn how to see the humanity in those who hurt us. To recognize that pain so often moves through people long before it ever reaches us. And just as importantly, it asks us to turn that same human gaze inward. To see ourselves not as permanent mistakes, but as unfinished beings. Becoming. Learning. Stumbling forward in the dark. This book exists because silence was too costly. Because what goes unnamed does not disappear. It waits. It shapes. It whispers. And because healing, once spoken aloud, once invited into language, has a way of opening doors we forgot were ever built. Doors back into the body. Back into tenderness. Back into choice. If there is one message, I hope these pages leave behind like a warm current in their wake, it is this: healing does not begin with judgment. It begins with compassion. For others, yes. But most urgently, most tenderly, for ourselves. When we loosen our grip on blame, when we step out of the narrow courtroom of '*Who is at fault?*" and lean instead toward the wider, kinder question of "*What happened here?*" something inside us shifts.

A hinge turns. A door opens. Curiosity replaces accusation. Understanding takes the place of certainty. And in that opening, the long work of healing finally finds a place to begin. We make room, then, for a different kind of sentence to form in the mouth. Not a verdict, but a recognition. "*You did the best you could with what you had... and I forgive you, because I can see how fiercely you wanted to get it right.*" To recognize the fallibility of all people is not to absolve harm. It is to humanize it. To step out of the rigid architecture of blame and into the living, breathing terrain of understanding. And it is so often there, in that softened middle ground, that the first quiet path toward peace begins to reveal itself. So let me say this again, clearly, gently, and without apology: to speak of trauma is not to speak ill of those entwined within it. To describe the jagged edges of my childhood is not to cast my parents as failures, but to illuminate both the resilience it took to survive and the strength it took to grow beyond what could not hold me. These pages are not written to keep the darkness alive. They are written to trace the way light finds its way through broken things. To show how life, even when fractured, even when imperfect, still leans instinctively toward wholeness. I share these stories not to dwell in what wounded me, but to witness what transformed me. To offer my past, laid open, as a small lantern for anyone still walking their own interior night. My hope is that in seeing one life handled with honesty and care, others might feel emboldened to approach their own histories with the same tenderness. Not with malice. Not with bitterness. But with the brave, vulnerable gentleness that opens doors long sealed and invites air back into rooms that have forgotten how to breathe. Because healing, whether personal or collective, rarely arrives through condemnation. It does not come wearing armor or carrying a gavel. It arrives through courage. Through the willingness to look at the whole story. The beauty and the bruise. The love and the loss. And still, somehow, to choose to love.

So, as you step into this landscape of memory, into the rooms where my younger self still lingers like dust in late light, I ask only this: hold one thing gently in your hands. Behind every difficult recollection lives a heart that learned about love before it learned about language. A heart shaped not only by what hurt, but by a sincere, enduring longing to understand. I am not here to cast stones across the years. I am here to lay them down, one by one, as stepping-stones. To build bridges where there were once only distances. Bridges between who I was and who I am. Between parent and child. Between what wounded me and what is still capable of healing. If, at times, these pages stir something tender in you, something restless or ache-colored or unnamed, remember this: stirring is often the first sign that life is moving again. Soil must be turned before roots can take hold. Old ground must be loosened before anything new can breathe. Discomfort, when met with kindness, is not a threat. It is an invitation. Whatever your own story carries, whatever rooms you have learned to keep closed, I hope you find here a measure of solace. A glimmer of recognition. The quiet comfort of knowing that another human heart has walked similar corridors and lived to name them. My parents gave me life. And through their imperfections, their tenderness, their wounds, they unknowingly gave me something else as well: the capacity for compassion. A way of seeing that does not end at the surface. A way of loving that makes room for complexity. It is from that compassion that I write. I carry no ledger. No hidden gavel. No stones in my pockets. Only the belief that honesty, when spoken with care, becomes a kind of light. Not a harsh one. A guiding one. The kind that does not erase the past but illuminates a way forward through it. For me. For them. For you. As we begin this journey together, I ask for your understanding. These pages may not always be easy ground to walk. Some passages will feel tender underfoot. Others may cut before they comfort. Truth, when first touched, can feel like cold water on bare skin. It startles. It stings. And then, slowly, it cleans. But every word here is written from a place of love. As a tribute to the strength of those who came before me. As an act of liberation for the woman, I am becoming.

And as a map, sketched in human ink, for those who may one day find themselves searching for a way through similar terrain. Trauma may shape us, but it does not have to script our ending. It may press its fingerprints into our early clay, but it does not own the kiln. With compassion for what was, and courage for what can be, we are allowed to choose differently. To pause where others hurried. To speak where others were silent. To tend what was once left unattended. In the end, the greatest offering this book makes is not criticism, nor confession. It is connection. A reaching across the quiet distances that separate one inner world from another. For anyone who has ever felt broken by the people they loved most, hear this gently: it is possible to write a new ending. It is possible to honor the past without living beneath its shadow. It is possible to love your history without letting it rule you. And for those who have been misunderstood. For those who carry the aching label of "bad parent" when what lived beneath was unhealed pain, confusion, inherited fear. I want you to hear this too: you are not alone. You are not the sum total of every wound your child carries. And perhaps, one day, your child will tell their truth not as a blade, but as a bridge. I hold nothing against you. I hold nothing against them. I hold nothing against the life that shaped me. I am simply telling the truth. And in doing so, I am loosening its grip. I am opening its hands. I am setting my story, and theirs, free.

The Parents They Became

If you had asked me years ago to describe my relationship with my parents, I do not think I could have answered you without first going quiet. There would have been a pause. A breath caught somewhere behind my ribs. A hesitation that held more truth than any polished sentence ever could. Because like so many families, ours was not seamless or simple. It was not a straight line drawn in easy ink. It was a weathered landscape. We lived through disagreements that lingered. Misunderstandings that stacked like unsent letters. Long seasons of distance where love existed but did not always know how to find its way to the surface. Where care moved underground, like a river that had not yet learned how to speak its own name. And yet, one of the quiet miracles of relationships, especially those bound by blood, history, and an unrelenting longing to belong, is this: they are not fixed. They are not monuments. They are not sentences written once and for all. They move. They soften. They revise themselves. They shed old skins. They evolve. They can surprise you. They can grow into landscapes you never imagined while you were still wandering their darker paths, convinced the terrain would never change. Today, with the long view of time finally behind my eyes, I look at the people my parents have become, and I can say this without faltering: they are the best parents I could ever ask for. I do not say this lightly. I do not say it sentimentally. I say it with the grounded gratitude of someone who has watched change happen not in declarations, but in daily gestures. In the slow, courageous work of becoming. The love they offer me now is not something I take for granted. It is a love that has been weathered. Tested by years. Bent by loss. Tempered by regret. And strengthened by the willingness to learn. It is not the love of perfection. It is the love of people who stayed. Who listened when listening was hard. Who softened when softness required surrender. Who chose growth over pride. Their love now feels like warm ground after a long winter. Not untouched. But alive. Holding. It is the love of people who have grown. And in their becoming, something in me has been allowed to become too.

The Love They Show Now

My mother and father are, in every sense, supportive. Not in the loud, declarative ways that announce themselves, but in the deep, reliable ways that reshape the inner climate of a life. They believe in me, not only in the person I have managed to become, but in the person, I am still in the act of unfolding into. Their faith in me feels like a steady hand resting between my shoulders, a quiet wind at my back, unseen but undeniable, nudging me forward on days when my own strength thins and my footsteps falter. They are kind and compassionate, not as performance, but as practice. In the small, faithful gestures that teach a nervous heart, it is safe to soften. In the phone calls that arrive like gentle knocks at exactly the right moment. In the listening that does not interrupt, does not hurry, does not try to mend what first needs to be held. In the way they notice when something in me has gone heavy and respond without needing to be summoned. They step forward when life presses too hard, forming a quiet shield around me, and they step beside me when I must walk through it myself, offering not rescue, but company. They encourage me when doubt clouds my inner horizon, when the old fog drifts back in and blurs my sense of direction. They celebrate my victories, no matter how modest, as though each small step were a miracle worth speaking aloud. A truth worth anchoring. A light worth tending. And through them, I have learned that support is not only the art of standing in another's joy, but the courage to remain when joy is absent. It is staying when the air feels thick. When language runs out. When the ache has no quick translation. It is choosing presence when there is nothing simple to fix and nothing tidy to offer. My parents have done this. Again, and again. In ways that feel deliberate now. Conscious. Earned. They have shown up. And in their showing up, they have taught my own nervous system a new vocabulary. A new evidence. A new memory. They have helped me learn how to stay. How to soften. How to meet life not as something to survive, but as something that can, at last, be shared.

A Tapestry of Love: Honoring the Parents I Never Knew I'd Have

There is a quiet, almost sacred beauty in the evolution of relationships, especially in the long, unfolding bond between parent and child. It begins in the simplest rhythms of survival. Feeding. Holding. Comforting. Teaching. A choreography of care learned before language, written first into the body. But time does not leave love untouched. It layers it. Deepens it. Threads it with memory and mercy. Slowly, almost imperceptibly, what began as necessity becomes something far more intricate, shaped by years and weather, by misunderstandings and reconciliations, by the small daily choices and the seismic turning points that stitch a family's story together. Now, when I look back across the landscape of my life, I am struck by the remarkable journey I have shared with my parents. A journey not of straight lines, but of crossings and returns. Of seasons where love struggled to find its voice, and seasons where it learned to sing. Two people who, within the span of a single lifetime, have transformed from figures of conditional love and uncertainty into the most steadfast pillars of my existence. This did not happen suddenly. It happened the way all real growth happens. Gradually. Through effort. Through reckoning. Through the courage to look inward and the humility to change. They are no longer only the people who raised me. They are the people who walk with me. My confidants, who hold my words without trying to reshape them. My advocates, who speak my name in rooms I am not in. My shelter in difficult weather, who offer warmth without demanding explanation. My truest source of strength, not because they are without flaw, but because they have been willing to grow. What we share now feels like a tapestry woven across decades. Threads of apology and accountability are woven through this tapestry now, not as grand declarations, but as quiet, sincere gestures that carry weight because they are lived, not merely spoken. Apologies offered not to erase the past, but to acknowledge it. Accountability taken not as self-punishment, but as a form of respect. These threads do not unravel what came before; they bind it into something whole. They soften the sharp places. They reinforce the fragile ones. They hold.

There are also threads of learning. Of questions asked too late and answered anyway. Of conversations that once felt impossible and now unfold with care. Threads of patience, where there was once urgency. Of listening, where there was once defense. Of repair, stitched slowly, sometimes clumsily, but always with intention. Each thread carries evidence of growth, of people willing to look at who they were and choose who they might still become.

And then there are the threads of love, stronger for having been tested. Love that no longer asks to be earned. Love that does not retreat when things grow uncomfortable. Love that stays. When I run my fingers across this fabric, I can feel the history in it. The rough patches. The knots. The places where the weave tightens to keep from tearing. I can also feel the warmth. The steadiness. The quiet resilience of something repaired with care.

This is the tapestry we live inside now. Not perfect. Not pristine. But real. A living record of forgiveness practiced, not proclaimed. Of growth chosen, again and again. Of a family that learned, slowly and imperfectly, how to love with more truth than fear. And as I stand within it, held by threads once frayed and now rejoined, I know this: the parents I have today are not the parents I grew up with. They are the parents they became. And in their becoming, they helped me believe in my own. Their becoming, and my becoming alongside them, stands as living proof of what growth and forgiveness can make possible. Of what can happen when connection is chosen again and again, even after it has been thinned, frayed, nearly torn. What we share now was not handed to us intact. It was built. Reached for. Relearned. It is a layered story. A slow, patient weaving. A testament to the quiet heroism of repair, the kind that does not announce itself, the kind that happens in conversations that begin awkwardly, in apologies that arrive late but sincere, in the steady decision to keep turning toward one another instead of away.

So often, the title of "best parent" is given in a soft haze of nostalgia. A dreamscape of perfection stitched from scraped knees kissed better, from bedtime stories and warm kitchens and laughter down hallways. But the love I honor here is not rooted in illusion. It is rooted in becoming. In the brave, often uncomfortable work of change.

In the humility of learning. In the courage of looking back without collapsing, and forward without denying what has been. For a long time, the idea of this kind of love felt like something that could only exist in an idealized past. A portrait painted in fantasy. A harbor I believed I could never reach, because the tides of my history had been complicated, and at times painfully rough. I thought that ship had sailed long before I ever knew how to name what I was missing. I believed that whatever might have been possible had been sealed somewhere behind us, locked into a childhood already lived. And yet... here I stand. Not at the edge of longing, but within a living relationship. Not reaching backward, but meeting them in the present. Today, I can say with an unguarded heart that my mom and dad are the best parents I could ever ask for. I do not say this as a revision of history, nor as a softening of what once was. This is not denial. It is recognition. A recognition of a present so full, so sincere, so quietly redemptive that it has reshaped my entire understanding of love, of family, of what forgiveness can grow into when it is allowed to live. From my earliest memories, there lived in me a quiet, almost wordless longing. A yearning for parents who would offer unwavering encouragement. Steady protection. A love that did not feel conditional or easily withdrawn. A love that felt like ground. Like shelter. Like somewhere the nervous system could finally lay its weapons down. And today, with a certainty that settles deep in my bones, I can say that I have been given exactly that. My mother and father have grown into everything I once hoped for. Supportive. Loving. Kind. Compassionate. Not in a single sweeping transformation, but in the slow, faithful way real change arrives. Through conversations. Through effort. Through apologies that turned into actions. Through years of choosing differently. Through countless moments where they leaned in instead of away. And in doing so, they have gently, persistently rewritten what belonging feels like in my body. They have taught my heart a new grammar. A new way to rest inside love. Their devotion to me, especially in these recent years, has taught me something profound: the truest amends are rarely spoken. They are lived. They are made in the daily, deliberate choices to show up. To stand beside. To listen without defence. To protect without control. To nurture without condition. To keep growing even when growth is uncomfortable. Rather than remaining tethered to what could not be changed, they chose to invest in what could still be built. They chose presence. They chose effort. They chose repair. They chose me. And now, it feels not only right, but necessary, to honor them for who they are today. Not as an erasure of the past, but as a testament to what the human heart is capable of becoming. Because the parents they have become now shape my life far more than any history ever could. Their love no longer lives only in memory or longing. It lives in my days. In my voice. In the way I move through the world. And in that living presence, something in me continues to heal.

A Shift in the Foundation

For much of my childhood, my understanding of parenthood was shaped by the limits of what my parents themselves were carrying. Their arms were already full of histories I could not yet see. Like so many families, ours held its fractures. Miscommunications that splintered the air. Tempers that rose like sudden weather. Long stretches where love felt measured, conditional, something to be earned rather than something that simply was. There were moments when I ached for encouragement that did not waver, for reassurance that my worth was not something that could be misplaced or revoked. Those longings often hovered just beyond reach, like warmth glimpsed through thick glass. Visible. Promised. But not quite touchable. And yet time, when met with willingness, has a way of rearranging even the deepest foundations. It works like water through stone. Slowly. Persistently. Reshaping what once seemed immovable. As I grew older, another truth began to surface: parenthood is not a fixed identity. It is a living one. A role that breathes, falters, learns, and can be revised. And my parents, flawed and human as they are, made a choice. Not once, but many times. They chose to turn toward their past missteps instead of away from them. They chose to reshape how they stood in relationship with me. Not as guardians of approval to be earned, but as companions in a bond that did not need to be negotiated. Not as arbiters of my worth, but as witnesses to it. This shift did not arrive with ceremony. There was no single moment to point to, no dramatic unveiling. It unfolded the way real change always does. Over years. Through conversations that trembled. Through silences that softened. Through reflection. Through effort. Through the quiet, often uncomfortable courage to grow. I remember how discussions that once left me guarded and small slowly transformed into conversations where my thoughts were not defended against but welcomed. Where my feelings were not corrected but held. Where my voice was not something to manage, but something to listen to. My parents learned to listen not in order to respond, but to understand. They learned to untangle my achievements from their own insecurities. To celebrate my successes without braiding them to comparison or expectation. To see me not as a mirror of what they feared or hoped, but as a person in my own right. And in that learning, something new took root. A different atmosphere. One of respect. Of safety. Of a trust you could almost feel moving in the air between us, like a gentler climate settling into a long-weathered land. They became my allies, not my critics. My witnesses, not my judges. And in doing so, they did something quietly revolutionary. They redefined what family could be. Not a structure built on authority and ache, but a living ground shaped by presence, accountability, and care. And in that new ground, something in me finally learned how to stand.

The Unwavering Support Through Storms

None of us chooses the soil into which we are born. We open our eyes already standing in a landscape shaped by other hands, other histories. And sometimes, the distance between what a child longs for and what a parent is able to give can feel like an ocean without a bridge. For many years, I carried the quiet residue of unmet needs and unspoken hungers. Salt on the skin of memory. Echoes of what I had hoped for. Ghosts of questions I did not yet know how to ask. But the past, I have learned, is not a life sentence. It is a prologue. Not the whole book. A beginning, not a conclusion. The true measure of my parents' transformation revealed itself during one of the most devastating seasons of my adult life: the unraveling of my marriage. It was a dark night of the soul in every sense. The world I had so carefully built with another human being collapsed inward, turning to dust in my hands. Plans dissolved. Promises lost their language. I found myself standing in the ruins of a future that no longer existed, disoriented, grieving, carrying a bone-deep loneliness that echoed in every room I entered. Even silence felt crowded. Even daylight felt heavy. Divorce is a storm that dismantles more than a relationship. It shakes identity. It uproots belonging. It scatters certainty like leaves torn from their branches. It rearranges the inner landscape until nothing looks the way it once did. You do not simply lose a partner. You lose the map you were living by. And in those days when grief rose like floodwater, when the ground beneath my life no longer felt solid, when every step felt like it might open into air, my parents did not retreat. They did not offer distance. They did not look away. They stood. Steadfast. Present. Unmoving. They became shelter. They became shore. They became the steady, patient light that remains when the horizon disappears. Like lighthouses when the night thickens. Like hands held out when the current is stronger than your limbs.

They listened when words came tangled. They held me when language failed. They sat beside the ache without trying to fix what could only be felt. And for the first time, truly, unmistakably, I did not weather the storm alone. In the very season when my sense of family felt most fractured, my parents became the place where something whole still lived. They showed me that love can mature. That presence can be learned. That people can grow beyond the limits that once defined them. And in their unwavering support, something ancient inside me finally rested. Because the ocean that once separated us had, without fanfare, become a bridge. It was in that season of absolute vulnerability that my parents stepped fully out of the long shadows of the past and into the unfiltered light of my present. There was no hesitation in them. No half-measures. No retreat into old patterns. They crossed the threshold without armor, without script, and met me exactly where I was broken open. They did not arrive carrying answers like shields. They did not offer platitudes polished smooth by repetition, nor quiet judgments disguised as concern. They did not attempt to mend what could not yet be mended. They simply came. And in that coming, they became the ground beneath my feet when everything else had fallen away. They held me through nights so dense with grief they seemed to have no edges, nights where time stretched and folded in on itself, where sorrow pooled in the dark and refused to drain. When the old foundation of my life cracked and collapsed, they did not stand back and assess the damage. They knelt. They placed their hands into the rubble. They became the architects of something new, not with blueprints or declarations, but with presence. With patience. With a steadiness that did not waver. They did not urge me to move on. Did not hurry my grief into something tidy or more digestible. They did not flinch at the mess of it. Instead, they built a refuge around me, a space where unraveling was not only allowed but welcomed. A place where sorrow did not need to justify itself. Where tears were not inconveniences. Where pain was not something to be corrected, but something to be witnessed.

My mother sat with me through the sleepless hours; her hand folded around mine like a quiet promise that I was not drifting alone. In the hush of night, as my tears found their way into the dark, she stayed. Not fixing. Not instructing. Just breathing beside me. My father, steady and unassuming, took care of the small, practical rhythms of living. He tended to the ordinary details so I could give what little strength I had to the extraordinary work of surviving. He carried the weight I could not lift. He handled what I could not face. They brought food when hunger had abandoned me. Left it gently within reach, as if saying: nourishment will wait until you are ready. They kept watch when my body forgot how to rest. They sat beside me in silence when words were too heavy to hold, when language itself felt like a burden. They listened to the same story of heartbreak again and again, each retelling raw and unfinished, never signalling weariness, never asking me to compress my pain or hurry its telling. This was not the parenting of my childhood. This was the parenting of the moment. A love enacted rather than announced. A compassion that arrived with hands and hours and an unspoken willingness to stay as long as it took. A presence that asked nothing of me but honesty. No performance. No strength. No gratitude required. It was profound. It was active. It was unmistakably unconditional. And it changed everything. When I reached out in pain, they did not hesitate. There was no pause filled with uncertainty, no retreat into the safer distance of discomfort. They did not offer hollow apologies meant to seal the wound and move past it. They stepped forward. Open-handed. Open-hearted. And they wrapped me in something real. Something embodied. Something that could be felt in the nervous system, not just heard in the air. Late-night phone calls arrived like small lanterns in the dark, not to solve anything, not to gather details, but simply to hear my voice. To sense the weather of my heart. To remind me, again and again, that I did not have to carry the night alone. Quiet breakfasts followed, where the clink of cutlery and the warmth of shared space mattered more than any conversation we might have forced. We sat together in the soft ordinary, letting presence do what words could not.

They listened in the way only love learns how to listen. Without interruption. Without correction. Without urgency. The kind of listening that does not rush tears to their conclusion, that does not tidy fear into something easier to hold. The kind that simply says, through breath and stillness and staying, "*I am here*". This was not the distracted, stretched-thin parenting of my childhood. This was parenting distilled to its truest essence. Responsive. Attuned. Awake. A love no longer filtered through habit or fear but expressed through attention. Through care that bent itself toward the shape of my need. And what moved me most was not only that they showed up, but how they learned to show up. How they paid attention. How they adjusted. How they let go of old reflexes and listened for new language. Even when it was unfamiliar. Even when it asked restraint instead of instruction. Even when it required them to sit inside uncertainty without reaching for control. They gave me room to feel, without abandoning me to what I felt. They made space for my grief without letting it swallow me whole. They honored the depth of my sorrow while quietly holding a memory of my strength when I could not yet touch it myself. "You are so much more than this moment," my mother would say, her voice steady, a soft place to land. "Whatever you decide, we'll stand beside you," my father added, and his presence itself became the proof. Their encouragement became my anchor. Their consistency, my shoreline. Their return, day after day, my reminder that love is not a single gesture, but a practice. Not a feeling that rises and falls, but a devotion that chooses. Again. And again. And again. And in those choices, renewed in a thousand small ways, I came to understand something I had not known before. The depth of their love was not written in words. It was written in time. In attention. In the quiet, steadfast courage of staying.

Making Amends Without Words

People often imagine that making amends must arrive dressed in ceremony. That it needs a stage. A script. Long, trembling conversations. Carefully measured apologies. Grand gestures designed to tip invisible scales back toward balance. We are taught to look for redemption in speeches, in perfectly shaped sentences, in moments that can be pointed to and named. But my parents have taught me something quieter. And far more powerful. The truest amends are not spoken. They are lived. They did not stop at acknowledging the places where our relationship once fractured. They did not remain in the language of regret. They stepped into the labor of change. They chose, again and again, to become the parents I had needed when I was small. And they have. Not in a way that attempts to repaint the past or pretend the cracks were never there, but in a way that honors the present. In a way that builds something new where something once struggled to stand. They show up now. Not only when the moments are luminous and photographable, but when they are quiet and unremarkable. In milestones, yes. But also in the mundane. In the check-in texts. The remembered preferences. The gentle noticing when my voice carries weight. In the ordinary spaces where love so often does its deepest, least celebrated work. They listen without judgment. They receive without defensiveness. They respect my boundaries as thresholds, not as rejections. They meet me not only as their child, but as a person. A woman with her own interior world. Her own choices. Her own rhythms. Her own becoming. They do not reach to shape me. They reach to know me. And in that reaching, something sacred has unfolded. The past is the past. It shaped us. It marked us. It taught us where we were tender and where we were unskilled. But it does not get to name us. It does not get to author the present. They are no longer the parents of my childhood. They are the parents of my now. Parents who have learned. Parents who have softened. Parents who have chosen presence over pride. Curiosity over certainty. Relationship over rehearsal. And I love them. Not for who I wished they could have been. But for who they have chosen to become. Because love that grows is not loud. It is faithful. It is practiced. It is built in the everyday courage to live differently than before. And that, I have learned, is one of the most profound forms of apology a heart can ever offer.

Becoming the Parents, I Needed

Perhaps the most profound expression of their growth lives here: in the way they have stepped, slowly and deliberately, into the very shape of the parents I once ached for. Not with fanfare. Not with declarations. But with the quiet courage of people willing to learn a new language of love in mid-sentence. They have replaced criticism with compassion. Urgency with patience. Expectation with acceptance. Where there were once invisible deadlines and unspoken measures, there is now spaciousness. Room. Breath. A sense that I am allowed to unfold at the pace of my own becoming. The air between us no longer hums with evaluation. It rests. They no longer weigh my life against the scaffolding of their own hopes. They witness it. They honor the particular contours of my path, the way a gardener learns the needs of the soil rather than forcing the seed. They cheer not for what I should be, but for who I am. When I chose pursuits that wandered beyond what is considered "traditional," they did not interrogate my choices as deviations. They asked how they could support them. They leaned closer instead of pulling away. And when self-doubt tightened its familiar hands around my ribs, they spoke my strengths with such steady, unembellished conviction that, over time, their faith began to echo inside me. What once felt borrowed slowly began to sound like my own voice returning. This evolution was never about erasing the past. It was about writing forward. They did not try to undo what could not be undone. They chose to build what could still be built. Not perfection. Presence. A truer, more attentive kind of love. The kind that arrives without spectacle but never without sincerity. They come to my events. They lean into conversations that matter. They practice love in the small, luminous ways that so often speak the loudest. A message sent only to check the weather of my heart. A home-cooked meal placed gently into my hands, as if nourishment were a form of listening. A willingness to sit with me when my thoughts begin to spiral, not to correct them, not to rush them into reason, but to hold them. To be with me inside them. And in these moments, ordinary and quietly holy, I see it with unmistakable clarity. They did not simply change. They learned how to stay. What amazes me most is how seamlessly this new chapter has threaded itself into the ordinary cloth of our days, as though it had always been there, waiting beneath the weave. There was no announcement, no marked beginning. Just a gradual warming. A soft rearranging of what family felt like from the inside. The way light changes in a room without ever asking permission. My father, once so sparing with words, now sends messages that glow on my phone like small lanterns hung along the path of my hours. Little notes of encouragement. Fragments of humor. Practical wisdom softened by affection. Emojis blooming like punctuation marks of care. He celebrates the quiet victories of my life. Finishing a hard week. Reaching a private goal. Rising from bed on a morning when gravity feels unkind. He names these moments as though they were sacred milestones, as though my persistence were something worthy of reverence. And in the simple act of noticing, he teaches me that endurance itself can be holy. My mother, whose compassion I have always known, has widened the architecture of it. She invites my dreams into the open air. Encourages them to stretch their strange and beautiful limbs without apology. She urges me to pitch the idea. To audition. To apply. To risk being seen. She speaks belief not as reassurance, but as certainty. Not cautious. Not provisional. But whole. Steady. Unreserved. Her faith in me does not scan for proof. It stands, already convinced. Together, they have become my fiercest advocates. Not the kind who shout instructions from the edges of my life, but the kind who clap for courage. Who honor effort. Who recognize becoming as a victory in itself. They stand beside me as I take risks. As I falter and try again. As I learn to trust the sound of my own voice. They do not rush me across thresholds. They walk with me to them. And in their quiet, unwavering cheering, something subtle and extraordinary has happened. A new voice has begun to live inside me. One that speaks with gentleness. One that notices what is hard and does not diminish it. One that celebrates the small, luminous acts of staying. Of trying. Of growing. In learning how to be championed, I have begun to learn how to champion myself.

A Mutual Effort, A Shared Journey

Relationships are never built by one pair of hands alone. They are woven. Tugged. Repaired. Offered back and forth like thread across a loom. And it would be neither true nor tender to pretend that the harmony we live inside now bloomed from my parents' effort only. This life between us asked something of me as well. As they were learning to soften and reshape what they brought, I was learning how to meet them on the bridge, not armoured in old grief, but bare-handed. For years, I carried resentment like a quiet stone lodged behind my ribs. The weight of unmet needs. The ache of what had not been given when my heart was small. I mistook that stone for protection. For proof. For justice. But while my parents were learning how to change, I was learning something just as difficult: how to loosen my grip. How to set the stone down. How to make room for who they were becoming, the same way they were making room for who I was. Forgiveness did not arrive as a ceremony. It arrived as breath. As the slow opening of clenched fingers. As the realization that my chest was tired of carrying what it no longer needed to hold. I opened the door to forgiveness not because anyone told me I should, but because something inside me wanted air. And I learned what forgiveness truly is. Not forgetting. Not revision. Not the erasing of marks time had etched into memory. Forgiveness is a choice. A living one. Renewed again and again. The choice to release the past's authority over the present. The choice to look at who someone is now instead of keeping them imprisoned inside who they once were. The choice to stop reading today through the lens of yesterday's wounds. I learned to speak my needs with both clarity and kindness. To give language to what I felt without turning it into a weapon. To offer the benefit of the doubt when old patterns tried to raise their familiar voices. To notice when fear was narrating and gently return to what was actually happening here. Now. Between us. And slowly, something beautiful took shape. I began to see that their growth was not separate from my healing. It was braided into it. Thread through thread. Step for step. We did not arrive here because time passed. Time alone builds nothing. We arrived because we chose to walk. To reach. To pause. To listen. To try again. Together. Our relationship has become a dance. Not a performance, not a perfected routine, but a living choreography. A gentle, evolving rhythm of give and take. Of leaning in and giving space. Of learning, and unlearning, and relearning each other across the seasons of our lives. It is a dance shaped by missteps and forgiveness, by pauses that taught us how to listen, by movements that only became graceful because they were once clumsy. And I feel, in a way that still surprises me, profoundly fortunate to be part of it. We have both invested ourselves fully. Not halfway. Not cautiously. Fully. We speak openly now, the way people do when they are no longer protecting illusions. We share the texture of our days, not just the polished highlights. The worries. The small joys. The quiet frustrations. The fragile hopes. We celebrate together, yes. But we also grieve together. We sit with what is heavy instead of skirting its edges. And in that shared movement, in that willingness to remain present even when the music shifts, we have built something far sturdier than I ever believed possible. Not something rigid. Something resilient. Something that bends and breathes. They have also taught me the quiet power of balance. That loving someone fiercely does not mean sheltering them from every storm. Sometimes it means knowing when to offer a shoulder. And sometimes it means stepping back just far enough for the one you love to discover their own footing. When I have faced setbacks, financial strain, creative paralysis, the moments when life seemed to knot itself into unsolvable questions, my parents have met me with both empathy and empowerment. They have named my exhaustion when I could not. Reminded me that health is more sacred than haste. That rest can be an act of courage. That pausing does not mean failing. Their words are never sharpened by control. They are shaped by care. By a long, generous view of my well-being. And yet, even in their protection, they do not take my agency from me. They do not script my life or stand in for my choices. They trust me to choose. They trust me to learn. They trust me to live. And in that trust, they give me something as meaningful as their support itself. They teach me, again and again, that true love does not tighten its grip. It opens its hands. It steadies without restraining. It walks beside without pulling. It does not confine. It frees. And in that freedom, our dance continues. Not perfect. Not finished. But alive.

Embracing the Present, Leaving the Past Behind

The past, as my father often says, is like a weathered book. Its spine softened by time. Its pages creased by many hands. Some chapters heavy with storms, others lit with gentler hours. But none of them, not even the darkest, possess the authority to dictate how the story must end. Together, my parents and I have chosen to write a different conclusion. One not built in denial, but in discernment. One that honors what taught us, without kneeling to what wounded us. One that carries forward the hard-earned wisdom of where we have been, while celebrating the living, breathing love that now moves between us. I no longer look back at their earlier missteps as stains upon their parenthood, but as brushstrokes in a larger, unfinished portrait. Marks of being human. Of trying. Of learning without a map. They are not defined by the struggles that once shaped them, just as I am not defined by the pain I once carried like a second skin. The past may leave its fingerprints on us. It may press its texture into our memories. But it does not get to script the present. And it does not get to foreclose the future. I have learned that healing is not the erasure of history, but a re-relationship to it. A shift in who holds the pen. My parents' willingness to grow, to listen, to become different now has become the truest apology. Not spoken but embodied. Written not in words, but in the daily language of presence, respect, and care. And in that choice, made again and again, they have given me the greatest gift of all. Not a perfect past. But a living, loving present.

They have not tried to erase the places where I once felt unseen. They have chosen something braver. They have transformed them. Where there was once silence, there is now presence. Where indifference once lingered, there is attentive care. Where distance kept us cautious, there is closeness that feels earned and alive. Through them, I have learned that growth is not bound by age or circumstance, and that when it is welcomed with humility, it can turn even the most fragile connections into something that blooms. This evolution did not arrive with speeches or sweeping declarations. It unfolded the way real love so often does. Quietly. Faithfully. In the patient accumulation of ordinary moments. Showing up, again and again, to family gatherings. Remembering the meals that comfort me most. Asking, without fear or avoidance, how my mental health is really doing. Offering an embrace when words fail and silence needs to be held rather than avoided. It is within these seemingly small acts that something extraordinary has taken root. A family no longer defined by who we once were but sustained by who we are choosing to become.

Our relationship is not perfect. No honest family ever is. But it is real. It is grounded in mutual respect. And it is deeply, undeniably anchored in love. We speak now in ways we once could not. We name our needs without apology. We share our feelings without bracing for impact. We apologize when boundaries are crossed, not as an admission of failure, but as an act of care. We celebrate one another's victories not as distant observers, but as people genuinely invested in each other's becoming. And I, too, have crossed the bridge. I have met them there. With openness. With courage. With the willingness to grow alongside them. I have learned to trust instead of retreat. To let my voice rise where it once hid. To speak my vulnerabilities aloud rather than armouring myself in practiced silence. I have learned to loosen the ancient reflex to build walls at the first tremor of fear, and to choose, again and again, the slower, braver labor of opening doors. Of leaving the hinges oiled. Of allowing myself to be seen. What once felt like exposure now feels like air. I have also learned to see my parents not only as the figures who shaped my beginning, but as fellow travellers in the unfinished work of being human. Wounded and wise. Limited and learning. Becoming, as I am becoming, with every passing day. In meeting their dedication with my own, something essential has revealed itself to me about family: honor is not reserved for spotless stories. It is earned in the living. In the willingness to return. To repair. To try again. It belongs to those who continue to choose goodness when it would be easier to harden. To those who practice love not as a single declaration, but as a daily devotion. And so, for the countless moments they have given me, both quiet and monumental, I want to honor my mother and father as the extraordinary people they are now. Not as who they once were. Not as who memory alone might fix them to be. But as who they have chosen, with courage and humility, to become. I want to celebrate their capacity to change. Their willingness to empathize. Their commitment to uplift rather than control, to listen rather than assume, to walk beside rather than ahead. And I want to thank them for teaching me this: a parent's greatest legacy is not a perfect childhood, but a living foundation of trust and kindness strong enough to carry into adulthood. A love that does not calcify with time but deepens. A love that learns. A love that grows. A love that stays. As I turn my gaze toward the future, I do so with a steadiness that once felt unimaginable. A calm anchored knowing now lives in my chest. A certainty earned, not given. Whatever trials rise along the road ahead, whatever weather gathers on the horizon of my life, I will not meet it alone. My parents stand behind me and beside me, like twin constellations I can navigate by. They lend me their encouragement when my confidence thins to a fragile thread. They offer their reassurance when my footing falters on uncertain ground. They are the quiet hands at my back when I need momentum, and the steady presence at my side when I need rest. They remind me, not in grand speeches but in a thousand small, faithful gestures, that the bonds of family are not fastened by history alone. They are forged in the present. In the daily choosing. In love practiced, not proclaimed. In respect lived, not promised. In care that returns, again and again, like a tide that does not tire of the shore. Today, and every day, I am grateful. Grateful beyond the reach of language. Grateful to celebrate them not only for who they were, but for the extraordinary mother and father they have become.

And in honoring them, I honor the transformation that made our relationship what it is now. Not a relic of what we survived, but a living testament to what we chose. Rich. Resilient. Rooted. Alive with possibility. A bond shaped not by the wounds that once defined us, but by the love that now carries us forward. And full, beautifully, unmistakably, of hope.

A New Chapter in Our Story

When I look at my parents now, I see not only who they are, but all the years it took to arrive here. I see two people who have learned. Who have bent toward understanding. Who have let life, loss, and love tutor them into something softer, wiser, more awake. They have grown not only as individuals, but as parents. Not into an idea, but into a presence. They are not perfect, and they would be the first to laugh gently at the suggestion. But they are here. They are engaged. They are attentive to the small weather of my days and the larger seasons of my becoming. They are loving in ways that are felt, not performed. And that, I have learned, is everything. There was a time when I carried a quiet, aching wish inside me. A wish for different parents. For parents who would understand me without translation. Who would protect me without hesitation. Who would stand beside me without the faint, painful distance that once lived between us. I held that wishing like a pressed flower between the pages of my life, fragile and fading, believing it belonged to a world I would never enter. A parallel universe of what-might-have-been. But today, something has shifted. Today, when I look at them, I recognize a truth I could not yet see then. I have those parents. Not because the past rearranged itself, but because the present was brave enough to change. They may not have been those people from the very beginning. But they chose to become them. They did the slower work. The humbler work. The work that asks you to look at yourself without armor and decide to grow anyway. They learned. They unlearned. They reached. They tried again. And again. And to me, that is more meaningful than perfection ever could be. Because perfection is static. It does not listen. It does not evolve. It does not heal. But love does. Love stretches. Love practices. Love returns. Love learns new languages when the old ones fail. And ours has. It has grown roots where there were once only questions. It has built bridges where there were once only distances. It has written a new chapter over the faint pencil of the old, not erasing it, but transforming its meaning. This is the chapter we are living now. Not the story of who we were, but of who we chose to become.

Gratitude and Forward Momentum

As I reflect on the parents I have today, a gratitude rises in me that feels larger than words, wider than any single moment could hold. It does not arrive with fireworks or declarations. It settles. It hums. It fills the quiet places. A steady warmth in the chest. A sense of being held by something that has been earned through years of choosing one another again and again. They have shown me that love is not a fixed address you arrive at and keep forever. It is a living current. A breathing thing. A daily decision to lean closer. To listen more deeply. To soften where once it was easier to harden. To show up, even when showing up asks for humility, patience, and the courage to keep learning who we are. Through them, I have learned that families do not need to be flawless to be extraordinary. They need care. They need effort. They need the bravery to begin again when yesterday did not look the way we hoped. They need the willingness to apologize, to adjust, to keep building even after something has cracked. Love, I have discovered, is less a feeling than a practice. Less a promise than a presence. Something made visible in small, faithful gestures that accumulate into a life. And so, to my mom and dad, I want to place this gratitude gently, deliberately, into the open. Thank you. Thank you for choosing growth over comfort. Thank you for choosing tenderness over defensiveness. Thank you for believing in me on the days my own belief went quiet. Thank you for the ways you have shown up, both in the moments anyone could see and in the hidden ones that altered everything. The long conversations. The unexpected messages. The open doors. The steady, unremarkable miracles of consistency. Thank you for becoming the parents I never knew I would have but always needed.

The past is the past. It has its place. Its lessons. Its weathered pages. But you have shown me that it does not have to anchor a family to the ocean floor. You have taught me that what matters most is not where we began, but how we choose to continue. Day by day, in the ordinary choreography of living, you remind me that love in its truest form is not an achievement. It is a lifelong work in progress. Shaped by intention. By courage. By care. By the quiet heroism of staying. I am endlessly grateful to witness yours. And to walk forward, not carrying what was, but growing from what is. This is not only my story of becoming. It is ours. A living narrative still being written in the everyday ink of shared meals, quiet messages, long conversations, laughter that arrives unannounced, and silences that no longer wound. Together, we continue to shape a future where love is not rationed or negotiated but offered and received freely. Without condition. Without an expiration date. A future where affection does not have to prove itself, and belonging is not something that can be misplaced. And so, I choose to honor you for who you are now. Not as a revision of the past, not as a denial of what once was, but as a recognition of what stands here in the present. The past does not define you as parents. Not in the slightest. It is a chapter. A formative one. A chapter that lends depth, texture, and gravity to what we have built. But it is not the whole book. It is not even the final act. Who you are today stands as living proof of your capacity to grow. Of your courage to look inward. Of your willingness to face yourselves honestly. Of the immense, unmistakable love you hold for me. You did not simply become better parents. You became the parents I needed. The ones who see me. Who stand with me. Who celebrate my becoming without trying to shape it into something safer or smaller. And in doing so, you gave me the greatest gift of all. A present no longer burdened by the ghosts of yesterday. A now that breathes. A now that trusts. A now alive with a love that does not depend on a flawless history but draws its strength from something far more enduring. Choice. Presence. Devotion. You are, without question, the best parents I could ever ask for. Not because you were perfect. But because you were brave enough to become. Because you were willing to learn. To soften. To return. To rebuild. To love in ways that grew truer with time. Again and again, you chose love. And in those choices, you gave me a home not only in a family, but in myself.

Looking Forward

I do not know what waits for me in the chapters still unwritten. None of us ever truly does. The future stretches before me like a country at dawn, its valleys softened by mist, its horizons blurred with possibility. It is a terrain of unseen turns and unnamed weather, of roads that curve beyond sight, of seasons not yet felt. There will be light. There will be storms. There will be days that ask more of me than I expect. But this much I know, and it lives in me with the steadiness of something earned: whatever rises along that road, I will not meet it alone. I have two people who will be there. Rooting for me in the quiet ways that matter most. Standing beside me when the ground shifts. Loving me not for what I accomplish, not for how well I perform the shapes of a life, but simply because I am. Loving me without hesitation. Without condition. Without the requirement that I be anything other than who I am in the moment I arrive. That knowing settles into my body like a small, enduring light. Not blinding. Not dramatic. But constant. A warmth behind the ribs. A glow that does not flicker when the wind comes. It is one of the greatest gifts I have ever been given. Not only that they are my parents. But that they have chosen, again and again, to be the parents I need. Here. Now. In this living, breathing present. They have chosen presence over distance. Curiosity over assumption. Love over the easier refuge of habit. And I feel that choosing in the way they speak my name, in the way they listen when my voice trembles, in the way they celebrate not just what I do, but who I am becoming. And I choose them too. Each day. I choose to meet them where they are. To see them not through the fixed glass of who they once were, but in the full, unfolding truth of who they are becoming. I choose to let the present be alive, not haunted. To let relationship be a river, not a monument. To let us keep moving. And in that mutual choosing, our story continues. Not as a relic of what we survived, but as a living thing. Growing. Breathing. Becoming.

Closing Reflection

Love is not flawless. It does not arrive polished or effortless. Relationships are not seamless. They fray. They falter. They bend under the weight of expectation and the strain of being human. They ask more of us than we often feel ready to give. They ask patience when we are tired. Honesty when it is easier to hide. Courage when we would rather retreat. And yet, when people are willing to grow, to keep showing up even after disappointment, to meet you not as who they wish you were but as who you truly are, something rare is born in that space. Something living. Something worth protecting. Something worth cherishing. My parents and I have walked a long, winding road to arrive here. Not a straight one. Not an easy one. A road that curved through misunderstanding and mercy, through seasons of distance and the brave work of return. A road marked by loss and learning, by moments when words failed us and moments when love spoke anyway. There were places along the way where the path narrowed, where it felt uncertain whether we would keep walking together. And yet, here we are. Still standing. Still choosing one another. And standing where we stand now, I know this with a steady heart: I would not trade this place for anything. Not the ease of a simpler story. Not the comfort of an untested one. Not the illusion of perfection that asks nothing and gives little back. Because what we have is real. It carries history in its bones. It carries effort in its breath. It is earned. It is alive. It is love that has been weathered and widened, love that has learned how to stay. They are, without question, the best parents I could ever ask for.

Healing the Roots: A Journey of Understanding, Forgiveness, and the Power of Present-Day Grace

As you move into any part of this story that turns back toward my childhood, I ask you to carry one truth gently with you: this was not how the story ended. Let it rest in your hands like a small lantern as we step into earlier rooms, not to relive them, but to see them with new eyes. The landscape of my early years was a difficult one. A terrain shaped more by survival than by the bright ease we so often associate with childhood. The emotional weather was unpredictable. Storms gathered without warning. Silences settled thick and unmoving. The air often felt heavy, as though each breath had to press its way through something unspoken. And the adults in my world, my parents, seemed less like anchors and more like fellow shipwrecked travellers, clinging to whatever fragments they could find, struggling to stay afloat in seas they had inherited long before I arrived. They carried histories I could not yet name, wounds that spoke through them in tones I did not understand. For a long time, I could see them only through the narrow lens of my own hurt. As the architects of my pain. The keepers of my scars. I saw their anger. Their withdrawal. Their limitations. I felt the absences more than the efforts, the fractures more than the love that still tried, imperfectly, to reach me. And slowly, quietly, my sense of self began to weave itself around the identity of the wounded child. I learned to inhabit that role the way one inhabits a house built from memory. Each room furnished with questions. Each corridor echoing with things that had never been said. I carried that story with me into my becoming, into the way I interpreted the world, into the way I measured my own worth. It became the lens through which I understood love, conflict, safety, and loss. But healing, I would come to learn, is not the act of erasing where we began. It is the courage to return there with a wider heart. To look again at the same ground and notice what pain once made invisible. To understand not only what was missing, but what was being survived. To see not only the child who was wounded, but the people who were also trying, however falteringly, to make sense of their own unfinished stories. This chapter is not about blame. It is about comprehension. About the slow, holy work of widening perspective. About learning how forgiveness grows not from denial, but from depth. From the willingness to stand in the past without becoming trapped inside it. And as we step back into those early years, it is with the knowing that the soil there, however difficult, did not only grow pain. It also grew the first roots of the woman who would one day learn how to heal. Life has a strange way of delivering its lessons wrapped in ache. It rarely announces them as wisdom. More often, they arrive disguised as confusion, as loss, as moments that bruise before they ever teach.

For many of us, childhood is not only a garden of innocence, but also a landscape of injuries we do not yet have language for. We wander its fields collecting impressions rather than explanations, carrying them forward in our bodies long before we can place them in our minds. Some of what shapes us does so quietly, beneath the surface, its meaning unfolding only years later, when memory finally meets understanding. When I reflect on my early years, I want to gently remind anyone reading, especially in the chapters that hold my childhood, that no story is ever finished while breath remains. What I lived then was not a conclusion. It was an opening. A first telling. A beginning written in the handwriting of survival. The chapter I lived then was only the beginning. Today, my parents and I are no longer the people we once were. Time, tempered by reflection and softened by effort, has changed the way we see one another. Through the long lens of healing, we have learned to reshape what love looks like. To redefine forgiveness, not as forgetting, but as the brave, ongoing choice to understand. To see growth not as a betrayal of the past, but as its transformation. As the way pain is composted into something that can finally nourish. This is not an excuse for what was. Nor is it a dismissal of the hurt I carried. The wounds were real. Their echoes mattered. This is a testament. To the power of compassion. To the courage it takes to turn toward what has been buried and listen to it without flinching. To the grace that becomes possible when we allow relationships to evolve beyond their origins, beyond the limitations of who we were when we first met one another in this life. Roots can be wounded. They can grow in poor soil. They can twist around stones. And still, with time, with tending, with light allowed to reach them, they can learn how to nourish new life. When you come to the pages that speak of my childhood, of confusion and fear and pain I did not deserve, I ask you to remember this: that chapter was only the beginning of our story, not its conclusion. It is easy to linger in the dark. Easy to let the shadows stretch until they resemble the whole shape of who we are. Pain has a way of convincing us that it is permanent, that it is the final word. But life's truest promise does not live in what breaks us. It lives in what can be transformed. All three of us, my mother, my father, and I, have walked out of those early days changed. Not unchanged. Not untouched. Changed. Stronger in ways that came at a cost. Softer where hardness once felt like survival. More compassionate, not because we always understood one another, but because we learned what misunderstanding can do when left unattended. More deeply connected than I once believed possible, bound not by perfection, but by the courage to keep returning to one another when walking away would have been easier. And in honoring that shared becoming, I hope my experience offers you a quiet reminder: the past may inform us, but it does not have to imprison us. It can teach without chaining. It can shape without sealing. It can be acknowledged without being allowed to rule the rest of our lives. When I was growing up, my parents carried weights they did not know how to name, much less set down. They moved through the world burdened by histories they had inherited, by expectations and wounds passed hand to hand like unspoken heirlooms. Their imperfections pressed themselves into my memory, sharp and unavoidable. I remember moments of emotional absence that felt like cold rooms. Outbursts born of unseen frustrations that cracked the air without warning. Distances that rose between us like walls I could not climb, no matter how hard I reached. For a long time, I believed their behavior was a verdict on my worth. A measure of the love I must not have deserved. I internalized their struggles as my failure, their silence as proof of my insufficiency. I did not yet know how easily a child mistakes circumstance for truth, or how quickly unanswered questions turn inward. I did not yet understand that love can exist inside limitation, or that pain often speaks in languages it never intended to teach. That understanding would come later. Slowly. Gently. Earned. But healing is a strange and tender alchemy. It does not arrive like a cure. It works more like weather. Subtle. Seasonal. Rearranging the inner landscape grain by grain. Over the past eight years, as I have stepped into my own work of self-discovery and emotional repair, something has slowly shifted its weight inside me. A quiet reordering. A loosening of old conclusions.

I began to see that many of their actions were not reflections of my value, but echoes of their own unfinished stories. Reverberations of histories already fractured before they ever brushed against mine. And in that understanding, the past did not vanish. But it softened. And in softening, it finally began to teach. For many years, I carried only fragments of my parents' lives. Shards without context. Behaviors without backstory. I saw the strictness. The impatient words. The emotional distance that felt like cold rooms I could never warm. But I did not yet see the silent landscapes beneath those surfaces. The private deserts where their own grief wandered without shelter. The long roads they had walked long before I arrived, already tired, already burdened, already shaped by losses they did not know how to name. Eight years ago, when I stepped onto my own path of healing, something in me shifted from endurance to curiosity. From bracing myself against the past to leaning toward it. I began to ask. Gently. Slowly. Without knowing what doors might open, or what might step through. And, little by little, they did. Hesitant at first. Careful. Conversations unfolded like the opening of old letters, edges worn, ink faint, words chosen with trembling precision. Stories emerged that had never been spoken aloud. Childhoods threaded with scarcity. Homes shaped by silence. Loves offered without language. Fears inherited and carried forward like heirlooms no one remembered choosing. I listened. Not as a wounded child anymore, but as a woman learning to witness the full humanity of the people who made me. And as they spoke, something extraordinary happened. The figures in my memory began to breathe. The rigid outlines softened. The shadows gained dimension. Where I had once seen only absence, I began to see effort. Where I had felt only harm, I began to recognize limitation. Not to excuse what hurt me. Never to erase it. But to finally place it inside a larger, truer story. In that widening, compassion found room to enter. Not forced. Not rushed. But growing naturally, the way light enters a room when a window is finally unlatched. And with it came a new kind of grief. Not only for what I had lost, but for what they had never been given either. This, too, became part of my healing. Learning that understanding does not cancel pain, but it can change its temperature. That the past can remain real without remaining rigid. That forgiveness is not an event, but a slow, living practice. One that begins, again and again, with seeing. My parents began to offer me glimpses of the lives they had lived before me, small windows opening into rooms I had never known existed. They spoke of losses that had stripped away childhood safety. Of moments where innocence ended too early. Of regrets that had never found a voice and therefore lingered like ghosts in the corners of their days. They spoke of a quiet, persistent fear that their children might only ever know them as disciplinarians, never as people. As rules instead of hearts. As authority instead of story. They revealed wounds they had never fully named, wounds that had quietly instructed the ways they showed up for our family, shaping their reactions, their silences, their distance, their protection. In those moments, something inside me softened, the way frozen ground begins to yield at the first touch of spring. I began to see them not only as "my parents," not only as the figures of my childhood memories, but as human beings. As lives shaped long before mine ever began. As people carrying histories, scars, and survival strategies that had once kept them standing when standing was all they knew how to do. In quiet, vulnerable conversations, both my mother and father opened spaces in their hearts they had long kept sealed. Doors that had been closed not out of cruelty, but out of fear of what might spill through. They shared unspoken traumas. Unresolved grief. Inherited pains that had traveled through generations like underground rivers, surfacing in us in ways none of us yet understood. I learned of childhoods marked by instability. Of homes where safety was uncertain. Of sacrifices made without witness. Of love offered in the only languages they had been taught to speak.

These revelations did not erase the pain I carried. They did not absolve the harm done in unknowing. They did not rewrite what my younger self had endured. But they gave the story depth. They gave it dimension. They gave me a wider sky in which to hold both their humanity and their mistakes, both my wounds and their limits. And in that widening, something essential happened. Compassion finally had room to breathe. The story I carried for so many years was unfinished. A single-angle portrait. A truth told from inside a wound, without the wider horizon that gives pain its depth, its weather, its history. It was a photograph taken too close to the subject, all sharp edges and shadow, none of the surrounding landscape that might have softened what I saw. What the last eight years have slowly, patiently revealed is this: all three of us have changed. All three of us have been shaped by those days. And all three of us have grown beyond them. My own healing began as a private excavation, a careful unearthing of the places inside me that still ached. I entered myself like a long-abandoned house, opening rooms I had kept locked, brushing dust from old furniture, learning the architecture of my own survival. I did not know then that this inward journey would become a bridge back to them. I thought I was walking alone, descending into myself for answers that belonged only to me. Yet, in the quiet, almost sacred labor of recovery, I found myself standing closer to my parents than I had in years. As I learned to sit with my own wounds, to trace their edges without flinching, I began to recognize the silent wars they had been fighting all along. I started to hear the echoes beneath their words, the fatigue beneath their rules, the fear beneath their anger. They were not simply parents failing at a task they should have known how to do. They were people caught inside a generational current of pain, moving through waters they had never been taught to navigate. Young. Overwhelmed. Carrying histories that crashed over them like an unrelenting tide. They were, in their own ways, drowning in stories that had begun long before mine. Stories written in households they did not choose, in losses they did not name, in survival patterns learned before they had language for love. And as I came to see this, something inside me rearranged. The rigid lines of blame blurred into something more complex. More human. More spacious. The past did not disappear, but it widened. And in that widening, understanding found its voice, and compassion found its ground. And then they began to tell me those stories. Both of them, in time, opened the doors to their own childhoods, doors long closed, swollen with years of silence. Not flung wide, but eased open, inch by trembling inch, as if even memory had weight. They spoke of fear and instability, of homes where safety was uncertain and tenderness rare. Of emotional absence that hollowed rooms and hearts alike. Of a kind of quiet hopelessness that lived beneath the surface of their days. And as they spoke, I felt the shock of recognition ripple through me. The realization that the very feelings I had once believed belonged only to me had been living in them long before I had words for my own. Hearing them was not an act of excuse. It was an act of illumination. And light changes things. Their words did not erase what I endured. They did not undo the moments that shaped me, or soften every bruise left behind. But they reshaped the way my heart held them. They changed the temperature of the memory. They widened the frame. They allowed breath where there had only been constriction. I saw, with a clarity that both hurt and healed, that pain reproduces itself when it is left untended. That hurt begets hurt. That without witnesses, without language, without repair, wounds continue their quiet labor through generations, teaching what they were taught, passing down survival as inheritance. With each conversation, something in me loosened. A knot I had carried without knowing its name began to ease. With each confession, something softened, the hard shell I had formed to survive thinning just enough to let feeling move again. With each tear shared across the space between us, resentment slowly gave way to recognition. Not forgetting. Not excusing. But seeing. And in that sacred space, where their grief met mine, where three stories touched and trembled in the same air, a new understanding took root. Something fragile. Something alive. Something that did not erase the past but finally placed it in soil where it could begin to transform. They were not villains in my story. They were fellow travellers. People shaped by roads they did not choose. Learning, as I was learning. Surviving, as I had survived. Searching, as I am still searching, for the long, patient work of healing. If your own childhood left marks that still ache when touched, I want you to hold this gently: your parents, too, may carry scars you were never meant to see. Wounds hidden beneath the roles they wore. Perhaps they grew up starved of tenderness, learning early that love was conditional or scarce. Perhaps they learned that survival required silence, that feeling too much was dangerous, that vulnerability invited loss.

Perhaps they endured griefs so heavy they were folded away like unspeakable letters, sealed and stored where no light could reach them. None of this excuses the pain you experienced. Harm remains harm. What hurt you still matters. What shaped you still deserves to be named. But context opens a doorway where condemnation cannot. When we remember that the behaviors that wounded us often sprang from wounds of their own, something in the inner landscape shifts. The ground softens. The air changes. We gain the courage to meet the past not only with truth, but with gentleness. Not instead of boundaries, but alongside them. Not to erase accountability, but to widen understanding. Compassion, I have learned, is not softness. It is strength. It is the steady, brave posture of seeing clearly without turning away. It is the bridge that stretches across the deepest divides between our pain and theirs. What this realization offered me was profound: healing is never a solitary act. It does not move in straight lines, contained within the borders of one life. It moves like ripples across still water. Quiet. Expanding. Touching shores we did not intend. The work we do within ourselves, the tenderness we learn to offer our own wounds, reaches outward in ways we cannot always predict. In choosing to tend to my own emotional well-being, I unknowingly created room for my parents to face their own shadows. By changing the way I spoke, the way I listened, the way I stayed present instead of armoured, I altered the space between us. And in refusing to let the past dictate the shape of our future, I invited them into a different way of being a family. Not a perfect one. But a living one. A place where history could be acknowledged without being worshipped. Where pain could be honored without being repeated. Where something new could, at last, begin to grow. Today, our relationship feels like a tapestry patiently rewoven. Not replaced, not made new from untouched thread, but gathered, repaired, and stitched with intention. Gratitude runs through it like a soft gold filament. Mutual respect holds it together, strong and steady. And beneath it all is an unspoken agreement, a quiet covenant, to honor who we are now rather than remain bound to who we once were. We no longer meet only as echoes of old roles. We meet as living people. My parents are not perfect. They never will be. And neither am I. But they are good. Not because of the people they once were trying to survive as, but because of the people they have consciously chosen to become. There is a world of difference between endurance and choice. Between reacting and awakening. Between being shaped by the past and shaping oneself in response to it. As my own healing deepened, I began to notice something quietly extraordinary unfolding alongside it. The more gently I learned to tend my own wounds, the more tenderness seemed to awaken in my parents. The more compassion I offered myself, the more compassion appeared in them. It was as if the courage I gathered to walk back through my past lit a small lantern for them to do the same. A soft light. Not blinding. Not demanding. But enough to make the first steps possible. My healing did not end with me. It echoed outward. In subtle shifts. In longer conversations. In apologies that came without being asked. In stories shared where silence once lived. Slowly, my vision of them changed. They were no longer only "mother" and "father," fixed figures cast in the amber of memory. They became visible to me as people. Complex. Tender. Still becoming. Carrying their own ache and their own longing to be whole. And in that shared vulnerability, something new took root. A different way of being a family. A new rhythm began to form between us, one not built on avoidance or duty, but on trust. On presence. On the courage to be seen.

On the mutual, ongoing decision to meet one another not as we were, but as we are learning to be. My father, once a keeper of sealed rooms, a man whose heart felt like a house with the doors locked from the inside, now reaches for me when my anxiety tightens its grip. He does not turn away. He does not grow silent. He steps closer. He offers comfort where there was once only space. His presence has learned a new language. His hands speak reassurance. His voice knows how to stay. My mother, who once confused distance for protection, who believed that holding back was a way of holding safe, now listens with a warmth and patience I once believed belonged only to other families, other lives, other stories. She listens with her whole body. With her eyes. With her stillness. With the kind of attention that says, *you are not too much here*. The kind that makes room. Today, the bond I share with my parents is among the closest and most sacred connections I know. It feels tended. Chosen. Alive. They are no longer the distant silhouettes of my memory, figures shaped only by history and ache. They are my confidants. My shelter. My friends. People I laugh with. People I lean on. People I trust with the softest parts of who I am becoming. The respect I hold for them is not inherited or imposed. It did not arrive by default. It has been earned. Breath by breath. Conversation by conversation. Choice by choice. Earned in apologies offered and received. In patterns bro mx ` 1xken. In courage practiced. They have grown into the kind of parents I am deeply proud to call my own, not because they are flawless, but because they are awake. Because they are willing. Because they continue to choose love with their whole selves. Their becoming has taught me something universal and quietly miraculous: healing is reciprocal. It does not move in one direction. It circulates. When one heart chooses to move forward, it sends a light into the surrounding dark. When one person risks tenderness, it gives permission for others to do the same. When we forgive what was and nourish what is, transformation is invited into every hidden corner of our lives. And what grows there, in those once-shadowed places, is not perfection. It is presence. It is connection. It is the slow, radiant work of becoming a family again. Perhaps the greatest truth this journey has revealed to me is this: healing does not live in the ruins of what was, but in the breathing, unfolding reality of what is. It is not something I found by endlessly walking the corridors of memory, touching every crack in the wall. It is something I found by lifting my eyes. By witnessing who my parents are choosing to become. By letting the present speak louder than the past. Each day, their quiet kindness, their steady presence, their willingness to keep learning and unlearning loosens another thread of the old story from around my heart. It happens in small ways. In softened voices. In questions asked instead of assumptions made. In hands that reach where they once hesitated. In the courage to sit with discomfort rather than turn from it. And with each of these moments, something inside me finally begins to unclench, like a fist that has been holding for years and is at last remembering how to open. They are not defined by their hardest moments, nor by the places where they faltered. They are defined by how they rose from them. By the humility to look back without flinching. By the bravery to change forward. Their missteps did not end the story. They became stepping stones. Thresholds. Places where empathy deepened, where understanding widened, where our family life slowly rooted itself not in fear or silence, but in awareness. In presence. In choice. So, to my mom and dad, I want to speak these words plainly and with a full heart. Thank you. Thank you for saying "I'm sorry" when those words cost you pride and reopened places you had long kept sealed. Thank you for turning toward your own childhood pain so you could offer me something gentler than what you were given. Thank you for staying in the room when it would have been easier to leave. Thank you for listening when it would have been simpler to defend. Thank you for showing up, imperfectly but sincerely, again and again. Thank you for proving, through your living, that mistakes are not life sentences. They are invitations. Doorways. Beginnings. And because you chose to walk through them, our family learned how to breathe in a new way. I see the courage it took to look back without turning away. To sit with what was and not flee from it. I see the humility in your efforts to change, in the willingness to unlearn what once felt like survival and reach instead for something truer. I see the love that never truly left, even when it struggled to find its voice, even when it spoke in accents of fear and fatigue. And I love you with the depth of my days, with a love shaped not by illusion, but by knowing. You are not defined by what hurt us. You are defined by the strength it took to rise beyond it. You have taught me that healing is not the erasing of history, but the reclaiming of the future. Not the denial of what was, but the brave choosing of what can still be. For that, I will always be grateful. I love you more than language can carry. More than memory can measure. And I will cherish the bond we share for all my days, because it was not given to us whole. It was built. Tended. Chosen.

And if you have walked a similar road, if your own childhood feels like a tapestry stitched with distance, confusion, or hurt, I offer this not as instruction, but as invitation. A possibility. A door left gently open. To anyone who carries a complicated story about their parents, I want to place this truth softly in your hands:

there is room for both honesty and grace. You do not have to choose between naming what wounded you and understanding what shaped them. Both can exist. Both can be held. There were chapters in your parents' lives you may never fully know. Losses that were never named. Wounds that learned to hide in the body. Battles that left no visible scars, only quiet ways of moving through the world. Understanding this does not erase what happened. It does not excuse it. Pain, whether born of neglect, absence, or misunderstanding, leaves real imprints. What you felt was real. What it shaped in you matters. Your hurt deserves recognition, not minimization. There is no explanation powerful enough to simply wash it away. But there is a way to hold it differently. And yet, sometimes, stepping into compassionate understanding alters the way we carry what remains. It does not erase the scar, does not pretend the wound never opened. But it can soften the grip it has on the heart. It can loosen what has long been clenched. It widens the frame. It invites a fuller picture. It allows us to see people not only through the narrow lens of their worst days, but through the long, unfinished story of their humanity, a story still breathing, still becoming. As you move along your own path of healing, you might gently consider the invisible wars your parents may have fought. The griefs they never learned how to speak. The ways love may have lived in them, bright and aching, yet struggled to find a safe language. You might imagine the rooms inside them that were never given light, the fears that shaped their choices, the tenderness that had nowhere to land. Not to excuse what hurt you. Not to blur what was real. But to widen the sky in which your own heart is allowed to rest. This is not about rewriting your history. The past does not need to be edited to be healed. This is about reclaiming authorship of what comes next. About choosing how the story continues. About deciding which threads, you will keep carrying forward, and which you are finally ready to lay down. You might ask yourself, quietly, tenderly, in the private language of your own becoming: What would it feel like to release the demand that they should have been perfect? What might open inside you if you allowed them to be human, in the same way you are learning to allow yourself? Sometimes healing does not begin with answers. Sometimes it begins with a softer question. This shift in how you see the past can become a quiet key, one that slips into a lock you may not have realized was still turning inside you. A small, almost weightless thing. And yet, it opens something vast. Not a door outward into someone else's life, but a door inward, into your own. With it, you begin to step out of the narrow, suffocating role of the perpetual wounded one and into a wider, truer landscape, where breath moves more freely and the horizon no longer feels sealed. In that widening, your parents are no longer only the figures who hurt you. They become human beings. Imperfect. Bruised. Carrying their own unfinished sentences. Shaped by histories that carved them long before they ever touched your life. People who were doing the best they could with the tools they were given, and sometimes, heartbreakingly, with no tools at all. You begin to see not only what was done, but what was missing. Not only the harm, but the hunger beneath it. Not only the silence, but the fear that taught it to stay. To see this is not to excuse what happened. It is not to rewrite the truth or soften the facts. It is to release yourself from the hidden sentence of carrying what was never yours to hold. From bearing the weight of wounds that did not begin with you. From confusing understanding with obligation. You are not responsible for healing what hurt you. Compassion, in this sense, is not a pardon offered to them. It is a liberation claimed for yourself. A loosening of chains forged from inherited pain. A quiet unhooking from stories that tried to make a home in your body. A decision to lay down the burden of their unfinished healing and return your hands to your own becoming. To take back the energy once spent holding what was not yours, and invest it, at last, in the life that is. In this way, empathy becomes not weakness, but a door. And walking through it is not a betrayal of your pain, but an act of profound self-rescue.

Seeing the Present Instead of the Past

My greatest breakthrough, the quiet pivot that shifted the axis of my entire inner world, came the day I chose to live in the present instead of continually excavating the past. It did not arrive with thunder or spectacle. It came like a breath I did not realize I had been holding finally releasing itself. For years, I had allowed what once happened to serve as the sole narrator of what was happening. The past sat in the storyteller's chair, scripting every scene before it could unfold. Every conversation, every gesture, every silence was filtered through the old lens of what they did or didn't do decades ago. I listened to today with yesterday's ears. I touched the present with yesterday's hands. I replayed the moments that wounded me, the words that lodged like splinters beneath the skin of memory, the nights when I felt invisible, unheld, unchosen. I carried them like talismans, convinced that keeping them close would protect me. Guard my heart. Keep me vigilant. I mistook remembering for wisdom. I mistook vigilance for safety. But I was not protecting myself. I was anchoring myself. Dropping heavy stones into the waters of my own becoming. I was tying my present to a history that could no longer change, letting old weather determine today's sky. And the cost was subtle, but immense. The present kept knocking, and I kept answering with the past. Everything began to shift the moment I asked different questions. Softer ones. Braver ones. Not "*Who were they then?*" but "*Who are they now?*" Not "*What did I lose?*" but "*What is being offered?*" Not "*What was broken?*" but "*What is growing?*" And in that simple turning, that gentle rotation of the inner compass, a door opened. Not outward, but inward. Not into denial, but into discernment. Not away from truth, but into a wider one. Through it, I began to see the living faces before me instead of the ghosts behind them. I began to witness the present moment as its own terrain, not merely an echo chamber of what had been. And for the first time in a long while, the air felt different there. Lighter. Less haunted. As though the room inside me had been opened, and something like morning was finally allowed to enter. Today, I see my parents not as frozen figures caught in the amber of memory, but as living, breathing human beings standing before me. Warm. Fallible. Becoming. People who have faced their own darkness and not looked away. Who have wrestled with their mistakes in the quiet hours where no applause lives. Who have chosen, again and again, to rise from what wounded them rather than be defined by it. In choosing that ascent, they have become the very parents I once ached for in the long, unlit corridors of my youth and now, with a full and grateful heart, truly have. Healing asked something radical of me. It asked me to lay down the old, heavy script I had been reciting for years. To loosen my grip on the familiar lines of grief and grievance. To stop casting them in roles written by yesterday's pain. To risk a different seeing. To look instead at how they show up for me now. At the tenderness braided into their words. The steadiness beneath their presence. The way their support no longer trembles but stands. The ease of their affection. The love they no longer ration like something scarce, but give freely, openly, as though they have finally learned it renews itself. I had to release the ghosts in order to recognize the living. This was not an act of forgetting. It was an act of grace. A conscious turning toward what is, rather than what was. An acknowledgment that people can change. That hearts are not finished things. That redemption is not a myth whispered to comfort the naive, but a lived possibility shaped through humility, effort, and time. That love, when tested and passed through fire, does not always burn away.

Sometimes, it is forged. Stronger. Truer. Unbreakable. And in choosing to see the present clearly, without the old haze of memory clouding every outline, I finally allowed myself to step into it. Not as a visitor. Not as a witness. But as someone willing, at last, to belong to the life unfolding in front of me. If you find yourself standing in the echoes of a similar history, please hear this gently, the way one hears a hand on the door in the night: there is hope beyond the hurt. Not a shallow hope that denies what happened, but a living one, the kind that grows in cracked places. Let curiosity take the place of condemnation. Let questions soften what accusations never could. Wonder opens spaces that anger keeps sealed. Seek understanding even in the seasons when forgiveness feels distant or impossible. There is no timetable for grace. There is only the slow human rhythm of becoming. Healing is not a finish line you cross and leave behind you. It is a living practice. A daily returning. A conscious choosing to meet yourself again and again with honesty and care. It is the courage to honor both what wounded you and what still lives, resilient and luminous, within you. To tend the bruise without letting it become your name. To carry the memory without letting it steer. As you walk this path, you may discover, as I did, that the light you kindle in yourself does not remain contained. It does not stay politely within the borders of your own life. It travels. It reaches. It threads its way outward like warmth through cold rooms. It becomes a quiet invitation. Sometimes, without intention or effort, your own courage to heal becomes a lantern for those around you. Parents. Siblings. Partners. Friends. Even strangers who never learn your name but feel the shift in how you move through the world. The inner work of one heart sends ripples across the surface of many lives, touching places you may never fully see, yet somehow change. Our stories are rarely tidy. They do not arrive bound and complete. They are braided from sorrow and joy, loss and becoming, collapse and return. They hold both ash and ember. Both grief and growth.

Yet even within that complexity, even within the tangled, unfinished beauty of it all, each of us is still holding the pen. We may not choose the opening chapters. We may not author the storms that arrive. But we are never powerless in shaping what comes next. Each breath is a line. Each choice a sentence. Each act of tenderness a turning of the page. And the story, as long as we are here, is still being written. Today, my family no longer stands as prisoners of what was. We do not live behind the bars of memory or sleep beneath the weight of old verdicts. We stand, instead, as architects of what is becoming. Hands open. Hearts unfinished. In choosing compassion over blame, and forgiveness over resentment, we encountered the quiet alchemy of healing. That subtle, sacred chemistry where pain is not denied but transfigured. Where suffering, when met with honesty and love, begins to loosen its grip and reveal another use. The way brokenness, when tended like a living thing, can begin to gleam. Not flawless. But luminous. The way hearts, once sealed and vigilant, can remember how to open without fear. What we discovered was not perfection. Not a polished ending. But something far more enduring. A shared commitment to love that is brave. That stays. That returns. A love that is not dependent on ease but rooted in presence. A love unconditionally alive. To those still healing, I offer this truth with both hands: you are worthy of love exactly as you are. Not when you are fixed. Not when you are finished. Not when you are easier to hold. As you are. With your questions. With your scars. With your becoming. And leave room, too, for this possibility: that the people who once wounded you may one day become unexpected companions in the light. Not as erasure of the past, but as evidence that the future is not sealed. Healing is not forgiveness as self-betrayal. It is liberation. It is the moment the cell door opens from the inside. It is the choosing of breath over bracing. It is the decision to step into the present instead of living beneath the long shadow of what was. When you allow people to be witnessed for who they are becoming rather than imprisoned for who they were, something loosens. Something ancient and heavy finally remembers how to fall. The chains of the past drop quieter than you expect. No thunder. No ceremony. Just space. And in that widening space, peace begins to breathe. Growth begins to stretch its long, careful limbs. And love, slowly, bravely, finds its way back home. And so, what follows is my love letter. Not the kind written in private ink and hidden in a drawer, folded small and kept from the light, but one spoken into the open air, offered without armor or apology. A living declaration. A testament. A reaching.

A love letter to the two people who gave me life, and who, in ways both quiet and monumental, helped me find it again. To my mother and my father: I love you both to the end of my days. Thank you for being the best parents a daughter could ask for. Not because the road was flawless. Not because the years were gentle. But because you chose to walk it forward. Because you refused to remain where pain had planted you. Because you kept moving. Kept learning. Kept opening. Your story is not written in the ink of your hardest years. It is not sealed inside the mistakes shaped in seasons of fear, exhaustion, or survival. It is written in what came after. In the courage it took to turn toward the wounds instead of away from them. In the resilience it took to unlearn what hurt and to rebuild what could heal. In the humility it took to say, "*we can do better*", and then to live that sentence out loud. It is written in every softened edge. Every apology that made room for breath. Every question asked instead of a wall raised. Every moment you chose tenderness where once there had only been defence. By the unwavering devotion to becoming gentler, wiser, and more loving than you had ever been shown. By the brave, ongoing work of breaking patterns instead of passing them on. By the way you let yourselves be changed. That is the truest measure of who you are. And that, more than anything, is what makes you both extraordinary.

A Shared Redemption

When I look back on the long road that brought us here, I no longer see it as only *my* story of survival. I see it as a shared redemption. A crossing made together. Yes, this is my memoir. Yes, it traces the contours of my healing, the places where I broke and the ways I learned to breathe again. But woven through every page is theirs as well, their becoming threaded into mine, their courage stitched into my recovery. Once, pain was the fiber that bound our lives together, pulled tight and unforgiving, every knot a reminder of what hurt. Now, it is healing that holds us. A softer fiber. A stronger one. One that flexes without tearing. One that warms instead of wounds. I often return to the moment I felt the shift inside me, the quiet, unmistakable turning of something fundamental, like a compass finally finding north. My love for them stepped out of the shadowed realm of obligation and into the clear light of admiration. It was no longer rooted only in history, or duty, or blood, but in reverence. In recognition. In choice. In that instant, I knew we had crossed a threshold. They were no longer only my parents by name and origin. They had become my allies. My confidants. My refuge. The place where the parts of me that once only knew how to brace could finally lay themselves down. It is a strange and sacred thing, the way healing can rewrite a relationship. How those who once felt like the source of your deepest ache can, through courage and change, become the source of your greatest comfort. How familiar ground, once walked with guarded steps, can soften into something like home. But this is the alchemy of healing. It does not deny the past. It does not pretend the wounds were never there. It takes what was heavy and gives it a new gravity. It transforms what was endured into what is understood. It reshapes the narrative, not by erasing its first chapters, but by letting the later ones speak. And sometimes, in that transformation, what is returned to us is not what we lost, but something even more beautiful. Something chosen. Something conscious. Something alive.

Lessons Learned Along the Way

Healing has been my quiet teacher. Not a voice that shouted, not a hand that forced, but a presence that waited until I was ready to receive. Along this long, inward road, it has placed truths into my hands slowly, tenderly, like smooth stones warmed by the sun. Some about who I am. Some about what it truly means to belong to a family. I have learned that a person is never only the sum of their worst moments. That truth does not excuse the harm that was done, nor does it dilute its impact, but it widens the frame. It pulls the camera back. It reminds me that human beings are intricate landscapes, layered and living, shaped by fear and love, by wounds and longing, by what they were given and what they never received. My parents' mistakes did not strip them of their humanity. They did not cancel the many selves that lived alongside those moments. And when I found the courage to truly see that, not as a concept, not as something I repeated to myself, but with my whole heart, something in me shifted again. The lens through which I viewed them softened. Deepened. Where I once saw only fracture, I began to notice complexity. Where I once held only pain, I slowly made room for story. For context. For the trembling beauty of people who were trying, even when they were failing. In that clearer seeing, they loosened from the rigid shapes my past had carved them into. They were no longer only the keepers of my wounds. They became lives. Histories. Human beings in their own becoming. And in learning to see them with greater honesty and compassion, I learned something just as profound. I learned how to see myself with greater mercy too. Because the moment I stopped reducing them to their hardest chapters, I stopped reducing myself to mine. And in that shared softening, something like grace finally found a home.

Healing is contagious.

Healing, I discovered, does not move in straight lines. It does not march. It flows. It moves like water. Quiet at first. Almost shy. Then outward. Seeping into places you did not know were thirsty. When one person in a family begins to turn toward the light, the motion does not stop at the edges of their own life. It cannot. It sends ripples. Soft at first. Nearly imperceptible. The kind you only notice if you are watching the surface closely. But they travel. They touch other shores. They carry change on their small, persistent backs. My willingness to face myself, to sit with what hurt, to tend my own wounds instead of outrunning them, created a space my parents eventually stepped into as well. A clearing where truth could breathe. Where the air was not so thick with history. My healing did not fix them. That was never my work to do. But it made room for them to fix themselves. And in that room, something essential became clear to me: the present carries more power than the past, if we allow it to. We cannot unwrite what has already been lived. Those pages are inked. The chapters are closed. But we can choose how much authority they are given over the relationships we are living now. We can decide whether memory will remain a warden or become a witness. When I shifted my gaze from who my parents were to who they are becoming, love loosened inside me. It unclenched. It no longer had to pass through the narrow doorway of old pain. It could widen. It could breathe. It could meet them where they stood, not where they once fell. Respect, even within families, is not automatic. It is not inherited like a name. It is earned. And the respect I hold for my parents today is not sentimental. It is not nostalgic. It is forged. Tempered in conversation. Honed in honesty. It comes from witnessing their courage in facing themselves, their humility in naming what they did not know before, and their willingness to change when change is the hardest thing a person can do. Because there is a particular kind of bravery in becoming. In letting old versions of yourself die so something truer can live. And it is that bravery I honor in them now.

Closing the Chapter, Opening a New One

As I write these words, I know our story is not finished. It is still breathing. Still unfolding. It moves the way living things move, with pulse and pause, with seasons and subtle shifts. There will be other chapters ahead. New terrains. New challenges. New reckonings. New moments that invite us, once again, to shed old skins and step forward differently. There may even be new hurts that ask to be met with the tools we have learned to hold, the language we have slowly acquired, the tenderness we have practiced into being. But I also know this: what we have built is no longer fragile. It is rooted. It has weather in it. It has history in its bones. It has stood in wind. It has learned its own strength. It is strong enough now not only to stand, but to shelter. We are not who we were back then. Not my parents. Not me. We do not move through the world with the same eyes, the same defenses, the same unspoken scripts. And that truth feels like the quietest, truest victory of all. Not a triumph announced. But a peace lived. If you are reading this while carrying the invisible weight of a painful childhood, I want my story to whisper something to you: healing is not a myth. It is not reserved for the fortunate few. It is not a miracle meant for other lives. It is possible. Relationships can soften. People can grow. Hearts can learn new languages. And sometimes, the ending you braced yourself for is not the ending life gives you. Sometimes the story surprises you. Today, my parents are no longer only figures in my past, silhouettes in the back rooms of memory. They are living, breathing presences in my now. Companions in my becoming. Witnesses to who I am, and participants in who we are still learning to be. And, I hope, companions in the chapters still waiting to be written. That is the power of healing. It does not erase what was. It transforms what can be.

A Final Word Before We Begin

So, as you step into the pages that follow, I ask you to carry this gently with you, the way one carries something fragile and alive: my parents were not perfect, and neither am I. They loved me with the tools they had, with the language they were given, with the capacities they knew how to reach for. And for that love, imperfect and sincere, I am deeply grateful. They also made mistakes. And those mistakes shaped me in ways I am still discovering, still untangling, still learning to hold with care and clarity. Both of these truths live side by side. They always have. They always will. I do not write from resentment. I do not write to cast them into the glare of judgment. I write from a place of listening. Of witnessing. Of turning toward the roots instead of away from them. I write in an effort to understand the soil I grew from, so I can better understand the shape of the tree I am becoming. The bends in my branches. The places I learned to reach for light. The scars in my bark that tell stories of storms survived. This is my truth. Not a verdict. Not a weapon. Not a closing argument. It is a map. A tracing of the inner terrain. A way of naming where I have been, so I can be more honest about where I am going. And if this book carries any message beneath its many stories, let it be this: our lives are not meant to be courtrooms of blame, but classrooms of understanding. They are not sentences handed down by the past, but invitations. Invitations to question what we were taught. To break what no longer serves. To heal what was never shown how to heal. To choose, again and again, with open eyes and open hands, what we will carry forward and what we will finally lay down. So, hold this gently. Let it rest in you as you read. And with that held in the heart, let us begin.

Chapter One:
Embracing the Flames: A Journey of Hope and Resilience

The Spark

It always begins with an ember — a quiet, trembling glow at the center of a collapsing world. A moment so subtle you almost miss it: the instant when the familiar dissolves, when the light you once leaned on falters and stretches into a long, unbroken shadow. Dreams flicker like dying candles. Silence folds itself around you like a shroud. Even the air grows dense, tasting faintly of surrender. For Nieke, this was the threshold — the fragile edge where existence quivers, where the thought of release whispers like a distant storm gathering just beyond the horizon. It is the place where many lose their footing, where the pull of oblivion feels deceptively gentle. And yet... in the thick of that darkness, something refused to vanish. A flicker remained — small, stubborn, almost imperceptible, but undeniably alive. It was the ember of recognition, the instinctive truth that somewhere beneath the wreckage, she still mattered. That she still *was*. And in that barely-there spark, survival rooted itself. She did not rise in a blaze; she rose like dawn does — quietly, softly, one breath at a time. And without knowing it, she became a lantern for others perched on their own precipices. A soft, steady glow in the dark. A reminder that even the smallest flame can keep the night from swallowing us whole.

The Shared Fire

From the glow of Nieke's ember, something within me stirred — a faint warmth flickering against the cold walls I had built around my own pain. Her flames did more than illuminate her path; they cast light into the forgotten corridors of my soul, revealing the shadows I had tiptoed around for years. In her courage, I saw my own reflection — trembling, unsure, but undeniably alive. Her strength became a quiet permission slip, allowing me to stand before the mirror of my despair and whisper, with a voice that quivered yet persisted: *I am still here.* And her journey, though born from a single spark, did not burn alone. It rose like a constellation against a starless sky — each trial, each triumph becoming a point of light that others could navigate by. For the weary wanderers who have paced the same midnight corridors... for the souls who have forgotten their worth, who have mistaken their dimness for disappearance... her story stands as living fire. A reminder that the ember never truly dies. It waits — beneath the ash, beneath the hurt — ready to glow again the moment we dare to breathe upon it.

A Call to Arms

And so, from the constellation of her courage, another truth emerged — not soft, not gentle, but fierce in its insistence: transformation begins the moment we stop running from the fire and dare to face its heat. Standing in the blaze of her own breaking, hollowed by despair and stripped of every illusion, Nieke did not surrender to the darkness that beckoned her. Instead, she rose — trembling but unyielding — to confront the quiet enemies that had stalked her from within: the sharp-toothed whisper of doubt, the suffocating fog of despair, the low, relentless hum of hopelessness that tried to lull her into silence. With each breath clawed back from the abyss, she gathered the scattered shards of herself — the pieces she once believed were too fractured, too far gone — and pressed them into the flames of her own becoming. In that crucible, the broken softened, the shattered reshaped, and what remained was something forged, not ruined... resilience taking its first true form. Her fight was not against life, but **for** it — a quiet rebellion, a sacred uprising of spirit against the very forces that sought to extinguish her. In Nieke's courage, I recognized the trembling outline of my own battles — those long, sleepless nights where silence stretched like an endless corridor, and the quiet war between surrender and survival raged behind my ribs. Her bravery became a mirror, reflecting not just her own resurrection, but the hidden fractures in me that had long begged to be seen. And in her rising, I stumbled upon a truth as undeniable as breath: healing is not a single moment of awakening, but a vow renewed daily — a gentle, stubborn choosing of life again and again. It is through these choices, as small as sparks and as powerful as dawn, that we begin to ascend — not returning to who we were before the breaking, but becoming something entirely new. Something tempered by fire. Something carved from resilience. A soul reforged in light. Healing rarely unfolds as a straight line; it moves in spirals, circling back to old wounds just as new wisdom begins to bloom. Nieke walked this spiral with trembling steps — stumbling, rising, and learning the quiet disciplines of forgiveness, patience, and the sacred, holy art of loving herself back into being. Each turn on her path loosened another layer of old armor, exposing the tender truths hidden beneath the scarred and weathered surface of her soul. It was never comfort that mended her, never the soft places that brought her home. It was her willingness to step barefoot into the fire, to feel the burn of honesty, to let the flames refine what the darkness had distorted. In choosing to walk through the heat rather than turn away, she found the beginnings of her own rebirth — not despite the fire, but because of it. Healing does not arrive as a single, perfect melody; it is a symphony stitched together from fractured notes learning how to resonate once more. It is the trembling violin of grief, the low hum of persistence, the quiet rise of hope threading itself through the dissonance. Each story — Nieke's, mine, yours — becomes a distinct instrument within this greater orchestra of becoming. Our rhythms may differ, our tempos may falter, yet we are bound by the same sacred music: The steady drumbeat of a heart that refuses to fall silent. In every tear that carves a new river down the cheek, in every laugh that breaks through after years of quiet, we contribute another verse to the anthem of survival. And though the world may not always listen, it needs this song — your song — the raw, holy harmony born from the simple, stubborn act of continuing to live.

The Community We Build

No one heals in the quiet vacuum of isolation; even the strongest hearts need the warmth of other flames. Nieke's salvation was not a solitary song but a chorus — woven through the voices of friends who held her trembling truths, healers who offered gentle mirrors, and strangers who had wandered beneath the very same night sky. Together, they formed a living tapestry, each thread a testament to compassion, each stitch a reminder of shared humanity. In their presence, the storms did not subside, but she no longer weathered them alone. Their unity wrapped around her like a quilt against the cold, whispering in a thousand soft ways: *You were never meant to carry this by yourself. You have never been alone.* And to those who have wandered so far into the dark that they fear they may never find their way back — hear this: you are not forgotten. You are not invisible. Your pain does not eclipse your worth, nor does your suffering erase the quiet brilliance still burning within you. That inner ember — faint though it may feel — is not gone; it is simply waiting for the soft permission of your gaze. Nieke's flame has risen as a beacon for souls like us, proof that even when the path ahead dissolves into shadows, a way forward *still exists.* Her courage illuminates the unseen bends in the road; her gentleness becomes a bridge across the silent chasms where despair once echoed. In her light, we remember that even the smallest spark can guide us through the longest night — and that every flame, even yours, has the power to lead someone home.

Discovering the Strength Within

As Nieke's story unfurled, she began to unearth a strength older than her wounds — a quiet, ancestral power woven into the marrow of her being: the power of returning to herself. Each trembling step she took became more than movement; it became a declaration, a vow whispered into the dark: *I am still here.* With every rise, every breath reclaimed, she stitched herself back together in ways the world had once told her were impossible. This book stands as witness to that resurrection — to her small, sacred rebellions against despair, to her defiant insistence on choosing life, again and again. It is the testament of a woman who refused to vanish, who learned that true strength is not loud, but steady... not born from perfection, but from persistence. This book is not simply a tribute to her journey, or to mine — it is a dedication to *all of us* who wake each morning to face another day, even when the weight feels unbearable. It is, at its core, an invitation. A gentle summons to those standing at the trembling edge of despair: *Reach out. Breathe. Trust that your story is not finished.* Healing does not ask you to erase your pain or pretend it never carved its marks into you. It asks only that you hold your pain with tenderness, to cradle it like a wounded bird and allow it, in time, to unfurl into purpose. Through Nieke's resurrection and my own return to myself, may these words become a lantern in your hands — a quiet, steadfast glow that proves even the faintest spark can call forth an entire dawn. The past never truly disappears; it lingers like a low hum beneath the surface of our days, a ghost-song threading itself through every breath. Nieke did not try to banish these echoes or force them into silence. Instead, she learned to listen — to let the old aches speak without granting them dominion over her becoming. She discovered that peace is not the absence of memory, nor the wiping clean of what once wounded us. Peace is the alchemy that turns old echoes into wisdom, transforming the sharpest pains into softened truths. It is the gentle art of allowing the past to exist... without allowing it to govern the future.

The Fruits of Labor

And with time — slow, sacred, almost imperceptible — the harvest began to arrive. At first, it came as timid blossoms: a fleeting moment of self-kindness, a breath taken without guilt, a truth spoken without trembling. Small seeds of vulnerability unfurled into quiet triumphs. Each tiny step became something holy, a soft revolution against the darkness that once claimed her. Progress did not roar; it whispered. Yet those whispers reshaped her world. And now, with a heart full of reverence, I can say: *I see her. I hear her. I am profoundly, fiercely proud of her.*

And so, standing here at the threshold of this book, I find myself gazing toward a horizon shaped by two intertwined journeys — hers and mine — both carved from the same night, both reborn from the ashes of suicidal ideation into something astonishingly alive. What rises before us is not simply survival; it is the slow, radiant unfurling of a life reclaimed. It is the first glow of dawn brushing against a once-empty sky, the quiet rediscovery of purpose after seasons of numbness, the tender blooming of love in soil that was once barren. This is the light we walk toward — not a blinding blaze, but a gentle, persistent illumination that reminds us the darkness was never the end, only the beginning of our becoming.

From Embers to Light: The Continuation

Beyond the Darkness, Toward the Dawn

There comes a moment when words cease to be mere ink and breath — when they transform into lifelines, into bridges stretching across the vast and haunted distances between us, into trembling lanterns lifted high in the thickest dark. This book, though born from wounds and nights that nearly swallowed us whole, no longer belongs only to what came before.

It now belongs to every soul who has ever stood on the trembling edge of surrender and still felt, somewhere deep in the marrow of their being, the faintest whisper rise: *not yet... not today.* What began as a quiet exchange between two wounded hearts — mine and Nieke's — has become a living conversation with the world, a chorus of survivors breathing in unison. It is a gentle yet fierce invitation to step out from behind the walls built of silence and shame, to speak the truths that once felt too heavy to carry, and to honor the sacred, unruly, beautiful work of being human. Here, beyond the darkness, we begin walking toward the dawn — together.

The Sacred Alchemy of Pain

Pain, I have come to understand, is not the adversary we once believed it to be — it is the forge, the sacred fire in which our truest selves are shaped. It scorches, it softens, it bends us until everything unnecessary falls away. And in that heat, in the crucible of our deepest breaking, the essence of who we are begins to reveal itself. Both Nieke and I were tempered in that fire — refined, reshaped, and rewoven by the same flames we thought would destroy us. Through that burning, we learned to witness the divine shimmering through our fractures, the quiet holiness that lives inside every crack we once tried to hide. Because there is no pristine resurrection. There is no returning to who we were before the fall; that version of us is gone, ashes on the wind. Healing is the alchemy of becoming something entirely new — gentler in spirit, fiercer in truth, and infinitely more compassionate. Our scars are not disfigurements; they are cartography. They map the terrain we have crossed, the fires we have survived, the storms that carved us into beings capable of carrying light. Each scar is a star on the atlas of our becoming — proof that we walked through flame and shadow and still emerged holding our own dawn.

The Communion of Survivors

Those who have stood at the lip of despair share a quiet, unmistakable kinship — a fluency in the language of silence. It is the dialect of long nights, of swallowed words, of breath that feels too heavy to draw. It's the ache that hides behind steady eyes, the trembling truth tucked inside a steady voice. And yet, within that silence — that vast, echoing chamber of things we never said aloud — something sacred awakens: **Connection**. We find one another in the softest ways. A glance that lingers a second too long. A story told in a cracking voice. A breath that falters in recognition. And suddenly, without explanation, we *know*. We recognize ourselves in the wounds of another, and in that shared recognition, something tender begins to mend. It is a healing older than language — a remembering that we were never meant to walk through the darkness alone. Through Nieke's steps, through my own trembling pilgrimage, I have learned this truth: healing does not thrive in isolation. It grows where souls gather, even fractured, even grieving, even unsure of their own worth. When survivors come together — each carrying their quiet scorch marks, each holding their fragile sparks — we become more than individual stories of pain. We become a constellation. A woven tapestry of embers. A network of quiet flames, each one capable of breathing life into another's dimming light. And in that communion, we rediscover what despair once stole from us: The warmth of belonging, the power of being seen, and the miracle of rising — not alone, but together.

Nieke — The Living Flame

And at the center of this constellation of survivors burns Nieke — not a fire that devours, but a flame that lives. Her light endures not because it blazes the loudest, but because it burns **honest**, steady, and unafraid to be seen. She is the quiet glow that rises after the wildfire, the warmth that lingers long after the night believes it has won. Nieke has shown the world that healing is not a myth carved from fantasy, but a rebirth carved from bone — that beauty can unfurl from the very wounds meant to end us. She is living testament that anguish does not calcify the soul unless we let it; that vulnerability, when offered with trembling hands, becomes a kind of holy courage. She is not defined by the corridors of shadow she once wandered, nor by the abyss that tried to claim her.

She is defined by the way she carries her light now — gently, generously, like a lantern held out to those still stumbling in the dark. She is proof that even the smallest ember, guarded through the storm, can grow again into something luminous.

She is the reminder that within the ashes, life still breathes. She is the living flame —a beacon, a guidepost, a testament to the truth that from the deepest ruin, light can be born once more.

The Legacy of Light

And from Nieke's living flame rises something greater — a lineage of illumination that does not belong to one soul alone, but to all who have ever trembled on the edge and dared to step back into life. This book is not simply my story; it is *ours*. It is the woven tapestry of every heart that has stood before the abyss and whispered, through shaking breath, *"Not today... I'm still here."* These pages carry the heartbeat of quiet survivors, the ones who rise without applause, who stitch themselves back together in the dark, who choose life in moments when life feels unworthy of choosing. This is their anthem — your anthem — a testament to the sacred resilience that lives beneath every bruise, every scar, every breath that refused to stop. Healing is not a straight path; it is a spiral, winding and returning, breaking and mending, collapsing and blooming in the same breath. It unravels you only to reweave you softer, wiser, fuller of grace. And when the night stretches long and unforgiving, when it seems endless and absolute, remember this truth: Dawn is not the opposite of darkness. It is the child of it. Light is born from night's womb. And so are we. There were moments, Nieke, when even *hope* felt like a weight too heavy for trembling hands to hold —moments when the world shrank to the width of a single inhale, a single heartbeat, a single choice between vanishing and staying. And still... you stayed. Not because the road ahead revealed itself, not because the storm eased, but because somewhere deep beneath the rubble and ruin, a fragile ember insisted there was still more of you left to become, more story left to breathe, more dawns waiting with your name stitched inside them. That choice — that soft, sacred refusal to disappear — became its own quiet revolution. In that trembling defiance, you taught me what courage truly is. Not the kind crowned in applause, but the raw, unglamorous kind forged in the dark: the courage that crawls when it cannot walk, that whispers *one more breath* when the chest burns, that clings to life by the thinnest thread and still refuses to let go. The kind etched into bone, carried in silence, and born again each time you rise from the floor of your own breaking. Your journey has been both mirror and compass — reflecting my hidden wounds while pointing me toward my own uncharted terrain. Where you dragged yourself through the shadows, I remembered my own dragging. Where you reached for air in the suffocating dark, I felt the echo of my own lungs begging for light. And with every victory you carved from the abyss, no matter how small or hard-won, something inside me stirred awake — a deeper knowing rising like dawn breaking through our shared night. Nieks, what we discovered in the quiet aftermath of our darkest nights is that healing is not a destination carved in certainty — it is a devotion, a daily pilgrimage back to ourselves. It is a vow renewed with each fragile sunrise, a trembling prayer breathed into cupped hands: *"I remain. I choose life again."* Your strength did not simply guide me; it reshaped my understanding of what strength even is. You taught me that strength is not the refusal to break, but the sacred willingness to gather your shattered pieces and rebuild — again, and again, and again — even when hope feels thin as paper and the world seems lost to shadow.

And so, this book is not merely the telling of a story; it is a torch — passed between trembling hands in the dark, its flame fed by two souls who refused to surrender to the silence. It burns as proof that even in the deepest night, light is not just possible — it is inevitable. Not because we escaped the shadows, but because we dared to walk straight through them. This voice on the page is not only mine. It is not only yours. It is the chorus of every heart that has ever trembled on the brink, every soul that has ever ached for rest and yet — with a quiet, stubborn miracle — chose to rise once more. And as the pages turn forward, I carry with me the truth your journey carved into my bones: even the smallest ember, sheltered and tended, can one day lift an entire horizon... and become a sunrise strong enough to wake the world. And perhaps most beautifully of all, Nieks, you have become living proof that healing is not the absence of pain — it is the holy transformation of it. It is the quiet alchemy that turns wounds into wisdom, sorrow into softness, and ruin into rebirth. Every scar on your heart has become a constellation etched across the map of your becoming — not marks of what broke you, but luminous reminders of what you survived. I have watched you rise from the rubble of your yesterdays, not by pretending the darkness didn't nearly swallow you, but by meeting it with a raw, trembling honesty that could move mountains.

You learned to sit with your pain without letting it claim your name. You learned to let your tears fall like rain that nourishes instead of floods, to let your grief carve space inside you rather than hollow you out. And piece by fragile piece, you rebuilt yourself from the very fragments others would have mistaken for wreckage — shaping them into something truer, braver, and astonishingly whole. What I have witnessed in you, Nieks, is nothing less than sacred. I have seen you stand before the mirror of your own truth — even when its reflection trembled with every fear you ever carried — and still you chose to look. I have watched you bow beneath the weight of your pain, not in defeat, but in reverence, allowing yourself to be human in the ways that matter most: by breaking, by needing, by feeling. You learned the rare courage of reaching out when your bones were too heavy to hold alone, gathering help the way one gathers light in the darkest storm. You turned anguish into art, despair into a fierce kind of devotion, weaving your suffering into something that could breathe and bloom. In that quiet transformation, you revealed what true bravery really is — not the roar of triumph, but the steady, trembling whisper that says, "I will try again." You have become a lighthouse for souls still wandering their storm-torn seas — not a blinding beacon, but a steady, patient glow. The kind of light that doesn't command but invites. The kind that doesn't shout but guides weary vessels safely home. Through your unapologetic authenticity, you have taught us all that vulnerability is not the cracking of armor — it is its refinement. It is the heartbeat of real strength, the pulse that reminds us we are still alive... and still becoming. I have watched the way your laughter has changed — how it no longer escapes you in fragments, but rises whole, carrying the music of a soul that has survived its own storms. There is a new timbre to it now, a softness laced with strength, like wind chimes forged from broken glass that somehow learned to sing. Even your words move differently — no longer heavy with hurt, but pulsing with the steady rhythm of redemption, each syllable a testament to the battles you've fought and the victories you've claimed in quiet places. You have taken the raw ore of your suffering and alchemized it into purpose, a purpose that does not end where your skin does. It flows outward in widening circles, like ripples from a single stone cast into still water. It touches hearts you may never meet, awakens hope in souls you may never know, and lights pathways for those still wandering in their darkness. Your healing has become a living offering — a legacy carried on the breath of every life your courage brushes against. Know this, my dearest friend: Your journey is still unfolding, its pages unwritten, its horizons wide — yet already you have done something extraordinary. You have reclaimed your life from the jaws of despair, gently, fiercely, piece by trembling piece. You stepped out of the shadows that once devoured your breath and learned to inhale again — not merely to exist, but to truly *live*. What you have done is nothing short of a resurrection.

You have shown me — and so many unseen souls — that the human spirit, when tethered to even the faintest glimmer of hope, is unbreakable. That within every shattered being lies a pulse of light that refuses to be extinguished, even when buried under the heaviest grief. Your courage has become a living scripture, written not in ink but in the way you rise after every fall. As I write these words, I do so with more than admiration — I write them in reverence. For your strength that roars, for your softness that heals, for the way you have stretched your scars into wings. You are resilience personified, a living reminder that even the most violent storms can carve a path toward dawn. Nieke, you are no longer merely surviving — you are *becoming*. Becoming flame. Becoming truth. Becoming the quiet, steady glow that guides the rest of us who are still learning how to rise from our own ashes. And today, Nieke, you are tasting the fruits of a courage so relentless it rewrote your destiny. You reached outward when your world threatened to collapse inward, when the walls of your mind felt like they were closing around your final breath. You fought — not once, not twice, but with every trembling fiber of your being. You battled not only the darkness that clawed at your ribs but the heavy inertia that tried to root you in despair. And still, you rose. Again and again, you rose. You did not choose the easy path; you chose the true one — exploring every hidden corridor of healing, knocking on every door that might whisper salvation, refusing to let hopelessness win. You turned every stone, sought every strategy, allowed yourself to be humbled, stretched, cracked open — and in doing so, you reclaimed your life from the ruins. You became your own resurrection. You are no longer simply surviving; you are alive in a way that trembles with truth. Your laughter no longer hides behind practiced, polite smiles; it spills forward freely now, clear and unashamed — a melody carved from storms, a song that remembers the rain but sings anyway. There is a new softness in your eyes — not fragility, but the quiet grace of a woman who walked through fire and learned that the flames could scorch away illusion, but never the truth at her core. Your presence radiates a calm, steady strength — the kind that isn't loud but felt. The kind that comes only from standing inside the blaze and discovering that the fire, instead of consuming you, forged you into something fiercer, gentler, and undeniably whole. You stand now, Nieke, as living proof that healing is not the art of erasure but the alchemy of becoming — the tender, courageous dance with the past that turns fractures into constellations. You have learned to sway with the memories that once held you captive, to let the broken places become mosaics rather than wounds, to cradle the version of yourself who survived by sheer instinct and offer her the grace she was never given. I have watched you move through the world with this new, sacred softness — not as someone untouched by suffering, but as someone sculpted by it, refined in the fire, polished by the storms. Every breath you take now is a quiet declaration of triumph — a whispered *I chose to stay*. Every kindness you offer ripples outward like light on dark water, reaching hearts you may never meet. You have become a lighthouse for the wandering, not because you claim to know the easiest path, but because you embody a deeper truth: that there *is* a path, that it winds toward life, and that those still lost in the shadows can, like you, find their way out again. What you have achieved, Nieke, defies simple praise — it is nothing short of alchemy. You reached into the void, into that cavernous silence that once pressed against your ribs like a closing fist, and instead of disappearing into it, you unearthed yourself there — raw, imperfect, luminous, breathtakingly real. That is the quiet miracle of your becoming: you rose not in spite of the darkness, but shaped by it, carved by it, awakened through it. As I look at you now, I don't just see my friend — I see the embodiment of every soul who has stood trembling at the edge of an abyss and still managed to whisper, "Not yet. I choose to stay." You are living proof that the human spirit cannot be smothered, that even ruin cannot claim what is destined to rise. You are the phoenix — not a distant symbol or a poetic metaphor, but the living, breathing truth of what it means to burn, to break, and to bloom again in your own flames.

Breaking the Silence

Suicidal ideation is a subject the world often buries beneath hushed tones and sideways glances — a forbidden language spoken only in the quietest corners of the human heart. It is a storm we are taught to weather alone, a tempest that rages behind closed lips while the world mistakes our half-smiles for peace. Even in the presence of those who love us, the truth trembles unspoken, settling heavy in the chest like a stone we've grown accustomed to carrying. But silence is not a sanctuary; it is a slow poison. It festers, it feeds, it convinces us that our suffering must be swallowed rather than shared. And so this book becomes an act of defiance — a torch held high against the shadows, a vow to speak what was once unsayable. Here, we break the taboo. Here, words are not weapons but lifelines — bridges stretched across the canyon of our isolation. To name the darkness is not to honor it, but to disarm it. To speak aloud the unspeakable is to peel back its power, to lift the veil that has kept us afraid and alone. For what is named can be faced. And what is faced can finally, tenderly, begin to heal.

The Shape of the Darkness

Darkness never arrives with fanfare; it does not pound on the door or strike like lightning. Instead, it slips in gently — a thin veil settling over the mind, so quiet we mistake it for a passing cloud. At first, it feels like ordinary exhaustion, a heaviness in the bones that sleep cannot soften. But then it begins to shift, to sharpen — the way fog thickens into storm. Its whispers grow teeth. Its soft murmur becomes a sinister echo, speaking in familiar tones that mimic our own voice until we can no longer tell the difference. It tells us we are burdens. It tells us we are invisible. It tells us that the world would breathe easier without us. What begins as a faint hum — a distant ache we learn to carry like an old injury — slowly swells into a sound that fills the entire inner world. It drowns out the laughter we once recognized as our own. It dims the mornings that used to glimmer with possibility. It silences the pulse of life beating beneath our skin. Until all that remains is an unbearable quiet... the kind of silence that feels like standing in the eye of a storm no one else can see. For many, this is the shape of suicidal ideation: Not a violent arrival, but a creeping eclipse — a slow erasure of light, an invisible tempest that swallows the horizon and leaves us alone inside a stillness too vast to bear.

A Hand in the Dark

This book is for those who have weathered that silent storm — for the souls who have stood at the edge of the abyss and felt its cold breath on their skin. For the ones whose hearts sag beneath the quiet weight of simply staying alive. For those still searching for a reason to take one more breath, one more step, one more trembling chance at tomorrow. And it is for the ones who love them — the friends who keep a soft vigil, the healers who speak in gentle truths, the partners who reach across the chasm without flinching. It is for every witness who stands in the doorway of another's darkness, unsure how to help but unwilling to walk away. You, dear reader, are woven into this circle now. Whether you carry your own shadows or cradle the shadows of someone you love, these pages are meant to walk beside you. Not as a prescription. Not as a polished solution. But as a companion — a lantern held quietly between us, casting just enough light to remind you that you are not wandering alone. This book is the outstretched hand in the dark, the soft voice saying, *"Stay. You matter. Your story is not finished."* Because it does matter. Because **you** do.

The Purpose of This Book

This book is the bridge suspended between shadow and dawn — the trembling span that carries us from the wordless ache of suffering to the first whispered yes to life. It rises from the marrow of two intertwined journeys — mine and Nieke's — forged not in triumph but in survival, in the quiet courage it takes to keep breathing when the night is heavy. Yet it does not belong to us alone. It belongs to every soul who has felt the cold pull of despair, and to every heart that has reached, even blindly, for a sliver of light. These pages hold no sermons, no judgment — only the gentle truth that healing is possible, even when it feels galaxies away. They hold stories of falling hard and rising slowly, of shattering and gathering the pieces, of wandering through ruin long enough to discover that even brokenness has its own strange beauty. This book was not written from a mountaintop but from the ground — the same ground where we collapsed, where we folded into ourselves, where we cried until the body had no more salt to give. And it was from that very floor, limbs shaking and lungs burning, that we learned to rise. Here, on these pages, you will not find perfection. You will find humanity — raw, trembling, and real.

To the Ones Still Searching

And so, if you find yourself wandering beneath a sky without stars, hear this truth as it rises from the last breath of the previous page: Your darkness is not a verdict. It is a moment — a season — the quiet, aching dusk before the dawn gathers its courage. Being lost does not make you weak; it makes you human. There is no shame in the heaviness you carry, no failure in the trembling of your hands as you reach for help. The shadows around you are not the end of your story — they are merely the ink of a chapter still unfolding. Even now, as you sit in the hush of your own struggle, something within you is stirring, reshaping, becoming. Let these words be the lantern placed in your palm — warm, steady, unafraid of your night. Let them remind you that dawn is patient, but inevitable. It always finds the horizon, even when the world feels frozen in darkness. And when that first thin ribbon of light breaks open your sky — when it softens the edges of your pain and touches the places you thought were beyond saving — may you recognize yourself in it. May you see what I see in Nieke, and what she reclaimed within herself: that survival is not the mere act of continuing. It is the sacred, staggering art of **becoming**.

Into the Fire: My Descent and Awakening

And so, as the pages turn from your searching to my remembering, I step back into the fire that shaped me — not as a hero, but as a human who once trembled beneath the weight of her own breathing. My encounter with suicidal ideation was not a sudden plunge, not a dramatic collapse into the abyss. It was a crucible — a slow-burning forge that melted me down grain by grain. The descent was quiet, almost polite at first, like a shadow slipping beneath a door, dimming the room one degree at a time until I no longer remembered what light looked like. Hope didn't shatter in one catastrophic instant; it eroded — a steady, relentless dripping that hollowed me from the inside. Every truth I swallowed, every emotion I hid beneath practiced smiles, every expectation I failed to meet became another stone placed upon my chest. Over time, the weight grew so immense that even my ribs seemed to bow beneath it, and the flame within me, once stubborn and bright, flickered toward extinction. I didn't fall into darkness, I faded into it... Quietly... Slowly... Imperceptibly. What began as fatigue became a bone-deep weariness no sleep could soothe. The vibrant world around me lost its color, its music, its warmth. Life blurred behind an invisible pane of glass — close enough to see, but impossibly far to touch. The things I once cherished felt foreign, like relics from another lifetime. Even the smallest tasks became mountains. Breath became effort. Joy became myth. And then came the silence. Not the peaceful kind that softens the heart, but the kind that swallows it — a suffocating quiet that pressed against my ears until all I could hear were the echoes of my own despair. It was in that silence that the thoughts began to whisper, then to hiss, then to roar. This was my descent — not a fall, but a slow unraveling. A fading into fire. A burning that would, in time, become my awakening. There were nights when I felt myself drift so far from my own body that I became little more than a ghost haunting my own life. I moved through the world on instinct — smiling at the right cues, nodding through conversations, performing the choreography of being alive — while inside, I was silently unraveling thread by fragile thread. It was a strange, disorienting invisibility: to exist in plain sight yet feel as though you had already disappeared. Suicidal ideation, for me, was never a longing for death itself — it was a longing for silence. For stillness. For the merciful end of the relentless storm that lived beneath my skin. It was the wish to be free from the endless litany of self-doubt, the guilt that gnawed like a hungry animal, the crushing sense of inadequacy that curled itself around every breath. I wasn't yearning for an ending... I was yearning for relief. For rest. For a place where my mind could finally stop hurting. And yet — in the very center of that abyss, where the world had narrowed to pain and numbness and nothingness, something impossibly small remained. Not hope — hope was too bright a word. It was a flicker, a tremor, a single fragile whisper inside the darkened chamber of my chest that murmured, stay. At first, it wasn't even a promise. It was a curiosity. A trembling question rising from the ashes: What if... what if there is something beyond this? What if there is a version of me who survives this night? What if there is more? That question — that fragile, quivering thread — became the first faint handhold on the wall of my despair. And though it was delicate, nearly invisible, it was enough. Enough to pause. Enough to breathe. Enough to mark the beginning of a slow, staggering ascent back toward myself.

The Turning Point

And so, from that faint, trembling what if, the shift began — not as a revelation, but as the softest stirring beneath the rubble of my despair. There was no thunderous awakening, no celestial beam splitting the sky. Healing arrived like dawn does: slowly, shyly, almost unnoticed at first. It lived in moments so small they could've been mistaken for nothing — a conversation where I didn't have to pretend, a morning where I dragged my body from the sheets despite the ache, a single tear allowed to fall without apology. The choice to stay wasn't a roar of triumph. It was a quiver. A fragile vow whispered into the dark: I will try. Not I am healed. Not I am strong. Just I will try. For the first time, I turned toward my demons not with the intention to slay them, but to understand them — to sit with the echoes of old wounds and ask what they were trying to tell me. It felt like weakness at first, reaching out. My voice shook with shame when I admitted I was drowning. I feared the look in someone's eyes when they finally saw the cracks. I feared being labeled broken, irreparable, too heavy to hold. But when I finally reached out — to a friend, to my sponsor, to a soul who listened without reaching to rescue — something shifted. The fortress of isolation I had built so carefully began to fracture. Tiny fissures formed in the walls I thought were impenetrable. And through those cracks, the light — hesitant yet determined — began to seep in. At first, it was only a glimmer, a thin silver thread weaving itself through the darkness I had mistaken for home. But even the smallest light can reshape a room. Even the faintest warmth can remind a frozen heart that it once knew how to beat.

That is how healing comes — not in a single, glorious eruption, but in the subtle, stubborn return of softness. I learned, slowly, painfully, that healing is not a heroic march. It is a humble surrender. A willingness to meet yourself where you truly are — trembling, tired, uncertain — and offer gentleness instead of judgment. It is the painstaking work of rebuilding trust with the person you abandoned first: yourself. It is learning that courage doesn't always look like fire; sometimes it looks like breath. Sometimes it looks like staying. And in those early, fragile days, I discovered a truth that would later reshape my entire existence: **You do not heal by erasing the darkness, you heal by learning to hold your own hand within it.** That was the beginning. My beginning. The moment I realized that even the smallest crack in the armor can become a doorway — and even the softest light can become a path home.

The Work of Healing

I discovered, is not a road you walk once — it's a labyrinth you learn to navigate again and again. It does not unfold in neat, ascending lines; it spirals... circling back to old wounds, revisiting forgotten echoes, revealing layers you didn't know still ached. Some days felt like clarity — a breath of air after years underwater. Other days, I collapsed into the familiar ache of the past, wondering if I had made any progress at all. But within that unpredictable rhythm, something tender stirred: grace. The work was not gentle. It was excavation. It asked me to dig into the soil of my own history, to unearth memories I had buried like bones, to face the ghosts that had grown fat in the silence I had fed them. It demanded a kind of honesty that scraped raw — a truth that stung before it soothed. And yet, with every buried memory exhumed, a little more space opened inside me. With every tear shed, something rigid softened. With every trembling act of courage — even the ones no one saw — a fragment of myself found its way back home. And slowly, almost imperceptibly at first, the darkness loosened its grip. Not all at once — but in subtle shifts, like dawn teasing the horizon. Colors began to return to my world. Not the blinding neons of false joy, but the gentle tones of aliveness — the muted blues of quiet mornings, the warm gold of being able to breathe without breaking, the soft green of hope unfurling leaf by fragile leaf. These were not grand moments of euphoria. They were small, sacred miracles: the miracle of peace, the miracle of stillness, the miracle of simply existing without pain swallowing me whole. And in those soft shades, I recognized myself again — not who I had been before the darkness, but someone new, someone blooming.

The Choice to Live

My being here — alive, breathing, awake in a world that once felt too heavy to hold — is not the result of the darkness vanishing, but of learning to walk beside it without letting it take my hand. The shadows still murmur at times, faint as the ghost of an old lullaby I once mistook for truth. They rise like distant echoes of a life I no longer inhabit. But they do not own me anymore. They do not conduct the rhythm of my heartbeat or choreograph the cadence of my days. The difference now is not the absence of darkness, but the presence of tools, of truth, of connection. When those familiar whispers return, I do not retreat into silence. I reach outward — toward voices that soothe, toward hands that steady, toward the light I once believed was unreachable. I speak my pain before it festers. I breathe through the tremors. I remind myself that even when the sky is starless, the sun is still preparing to rise. Survival is no longer a secret shame or the aftermath of a near-miss — it is my daily devotion. My whispered vow to keep choosing myself, even on the days when the choice trembles. Each morning I open my eyes is not accidental. It is an answer. A quiet, sacred yes whispered into the universe — a yes to possibility, a yes to becoming, a yes to living, even when life once felt impossible. And in that yes, day after day, I reclaim my place in this world — not as a burden, not as a shadow, but as a survivor who learned to carry the light within.

The Meaning of the Fire

In the end, the fire I feared most — that relentless blaze of suicidal ideation — revealed a truth I could never have discovered in the gentle safety of daylight. It taught me that the soul, though tender as a moth's wing, is not fragile. It bends, it bruises, it trembles... but it does not break as easily as we are led to believe. What I once mistook for annihilation became initiation. The flames that threatened to consume me became the very forge that reshaped me. They burned away the falsehoods I had long mistaken for identity, stripped me down to the trembling core of who I truly was. And in that scarred, naked rawness, I found something unexpected — something holy: a reverence for breath, a reverence for staying, a reverence for the astonishing resilience housed within the human heart. From that crucible, I rose not flawless, but honest. Not invulnerable, but awake. The same fire that once beckoned me toward oblivion now illuminates my steps forward. And so I write — not to reopen old wounds, but to honor the strange and sacred alchemy that suffering gifted me: clarity sharp as dawn, compassion deep as oceans, connection carved from the marrow of shared survival. To anyone who now stands in the flames where I once stood, hear this truth softly, fiercely: You are not ruined. You are not beyond mending. You are not lost to the dark. You are in the becoming. And in that becoming grows a strength so luminous, so quietly magnificent, it could set the world ablaze with hope.

The Shared Flame

I must confess, this book did not begin with me. It did not rise from a carefully drawn outline or some grand vision of purpose. It began with you, Nieke — a single spark in the dark — and the quiet ache I felt as I watched you navigate the same treacherous waters that had once nearly pulled me under. There was something in the way your light trembled — soft, stubborn, refusing to go out — that awakened an echo deep within me. I recognized that flicker, because I had once carried it myself: The fragile flame that quivers but does not die. In watching you fight your way through the choking fog of despair, something shifted inside me — something old, something tender, something fiercely protective. I felt the pull to reach toward you, not as a savior, but as someone who had once crawled through the same night. I longed to place a fragment of my story into your hands, like a lantern passed from one weary traveler to another. I wanted you to know that you did not wander that darkness unaccompanied — that I, too, had felt the exhaustion of simply existing, the bone-deep weariness that makes the world blur at the edges. I wanted you to know that someone else had walked through that same suffocating silence... and had, against all reason, come out the other side. And so, this book was born not from ambition, but from recognition — from the shared fire between two souls who refused to extinguish. It was born from the gentle truth that our flames burn brighter when held together.

And so, I began to write

Not with structure, nor with any polished plan — but with the tremble of truth pressing against my ribs, demanding release. The words did not arrive as chapters; they arrived as fevered breaths, as confessions scraped from the bone, as a prayer disguised as prose. Each line spilled from a wound still stitching itself back together, warm and trembling with memory. Every sentence became a thin, glimmering thread stretched between us — two hearts that had tasted both the metallic bitterness of despair and the fierce aftertaste of defiance. It was less writing and more bleeding, less crafting and more remembering. What started as a synopsis — a quiet lifeline cast across the dark — began to swell into something larger than either of us. It grew into a testament, a living archive of survival and the soft, stubborn resilience that hums inside every human soul. A reminder that even from the deepest fractures, something luminous can emerge...

and that sometimes, the simple act of speaking our truth becomes the bridge that saves us both.

Beyond Our Stories

As the pages continued to unfurl beneath my hands, something unexpected took shape — something larger, wider, and more ancient than my own wounds or yours. I began to understand that this book was never meant to be a monument to a single story; it was becoming a vessel, a gathering place for the countless voices that have trembled at the mouth of the abyss. It became a sanctuary for the stories whispered in the dark — the ones spoken only in the language of shaking breaths, tear-salted pillows, and silent pleas that dissolve into the night. It became a home for the invisible ones, the ones who have stood at the cliff's edge of their own undoing, those who have felt themselves disappearing beneath the gravity of their thoughts, those who whispered "please, someone hear me" into the void and prayed the echo might find a heart willing to listen. As the ink deepened, so did the truth: this book was not simply ours — it was everyone's. A chorus of courage began to hum through its pages, a symphony of survivors whose stories may differ in detail but pulse with the same heartbeat — the primal longing to be seen, the aching desire to belong, the fragile yet fierce will to stay alive in a world that sometimes forgets the weight its silence carries. This book is a tapestry woven of contradictions: the darkness and the light, the wound and the salve, the loss and the love breathing side by side like twin flames. It is the study of how a soul becomes whole — not by amputating its suffering, but by learning to cradle it, honor it, and let it teach us the shape of our own resilience. Through these pages, I want to offer what life has whispered to me in its harshest and most holy moments: that there is no shame in breaking, no weakness in collapsing to your knees, no failure in needing help. That even in the hours when hope is nothing more than a trembling thread in your palm, the way forward still exists — not always clear, not always gentle, but real, present, possible... and waiting for you to take the next breath, the next step, the next chance at life.

A Bridge Across the Abyss

Nieke, your courage did more than illuminate your own way — it cast its glow across my shadows and revealed the forgotten path back to myself. Through you, I relearned the quiet power of vulnerability, the sacred alchemy that occurs when we dare to speak the truths we once buried beneath silence. I discovered that when we share our stories — cracked, trembling, incomplete — they become more than confessions; they become bridges. Bridges stretched across the vast, echoing abyss that separates pain from understanding, fear from connection, isolation from belonging. As I wrote to you, I found myself writing to the hidden chambers within me — the frightened child curled beneath old wounds, the exhausted survivor who had forgotten her own strength, the fragile dreamer who still carried a flicker of belief in her palms. By giving those parts a voice, I discovered that pain spoken aloud shifts its shape. It loosens its grip. It becomes a thread woven between hearts rather than a chain tightening within one. This book became that bridge — an archway carved from honesty, a passageway spanning the distance between despair and hope, between the darkness that once held us hostage and the dawn we now rise to meet. These words are more than pages; they are a lantern held out across the chasm, an offering to anyone who has ever felt the cold wind of the edge. And so, as I place these words before you — and before every reader who may find pieces of their own soul reflected here — I do so with a single, tender prayer: That you find comfort in these lines. That you find courage in their truth. That you see yourself not in the fragments that once broke you, but in the luminous becoming that follows. Because in the end, this book was never ours alone. It was sparked by our shared fire, yes — but it burns now for every soul still reaching through the dark, searching for the first warm glow of their own rising light.

The Mirror of Fire

It wasn't my journey alone that breathed life into these pages — it was yours, Nieke. Watching you wrestle your shadows, witnessing the raw, unfiltered courage with which you clawed your way back toward the light, ignited something inside me that language can only chase, never fully capture. Your strength wasn't subtle; it was primal — a wildfire rising from scorched earth, refusing to be extinguished. You burned with the kind of truth that doesn't whisper... it roars. I had meant only to offer you a story — a small lantern cupped in trembling hands, a fragment of my own survival that might help soften the darkness around you. But in writing to you, something unexpected happened. The fire reflected back at me. The act of reaching for you became a reaching into myself. The words I wrote as comfort became keys, unlocking chambers within me I had sealed shut long ago. Memories I had tucked beneath the floorboards... emotions pressed into silence... grief fossilized into bone — all of it rose like smoke, curling into the air, demanding recognition. They didn't rise to undo me, but to be witnessed, to be freed. What began as a message became a mirror — one forged in flame — reflecting not only your resilience, but the fragments of my own strength I had forgotten. This book became my release, my reckoning, my reclamation. And in that firelit exchange between our stories, I learned the most sacred truth: Healing is never a solitary pilgrimage. It is a shared becoming — two souls turning toward each other, holding up the mirror of fire, and discovering within its glow the courage we thought we had lost.

The Alchemy of Courage

Nieke, what unfolded within you was nothing short of holy transformation — the quiet alchemy that turns suffering into strength and fear into flame. You stepped into the darkest chambers of your own soul, not because the terror had vanished, but because something inside you refused to die there. You walked forward anyway — trembling, yes, but unwavering in your will to live. You listened to truths that scraped against old wounds. You stood naked before your own shadows and did not look away. You did the work — the slow, sacred excavation that most people spend a lifetime avoiding. Piece by fragile piece, you rebuilt yourself from the ruins: Reaching out when the silence grew too heavy, crawling when standing felt impossible, choosing breath when the void begged for surrender. And somewhere along that painfully human journey, something miraculous began: You learned to breathe again — not the shallow breath of survival, but the steady exhale of someone returning to life. You learned to trust again — not blindly, but with the quiet wisdom earned in fire. You learned to hope again — a hope no longer fragile but forged. The light that now emanates from you is not the timid flicker it once was. It is a deeper glow — rooted, unwavering — the radiance of a woman who walked through flames and emerged with embers in her hands. You are not defined by what shattered you, but by the artistry with which you gathered the shards and shaped yourself anew. Your scars are not marks of destruction; they are inscriptions of resurrection — testaments etched in flesh and spirit, telling the story of a soul that refused to disappear. And though the world may never fully grasp the magnitude of your rising, I do — because I watched you ascend from the ashes with my own eyes.

The Testament of Transformation

Nieke, your life has become a living scripture of resilience — a sacred chronicle carved not from ease, but from endurance. You walked through tempests that could have swallowed you whole, storms fierce enough to quiet even the bravest hearts, and yet you emerged not merely upright... but luminous. The kind of luminous that comes only from surviving the night and learning to carry pieces of dawn within your chest. You have revealed, again and again, that healing is not a miracle reserved for the untouched — it is the slow, relentless blooming that happens even in the ruins. You showed us that true strength is not the armor we keep polished, but the willingness to set that armor down and let our hearts be seen. Your journey has become living proof that pain, and growth are not adversaries — they are dance partners in the dark, moving in imperfect rhythm, shaping us with each step, each fall, each rise. You are the embodied truth that transformation is not a moment — it is a becoming. And in your becoming, you have lit a path for others still learning how to rise. You did not merely face your demons, Nieke — you stood before them with a kind of honesty that could crack stone. You did not turn away from the old wounds that once governed your breath; instead, you approached them with a fierce, trembling compassion, the way one might cradle a wounded animal — gently, bravely, without flinching from its pain. And when the path rose before you like a mountain, when the climb felt impossible and your knees buckled beneath the weight of your own history, you did not surrender. You crawled — through the ash, through the doubt, through the aching remnants of who you once were — until crawling became walking, until walking became running, until running became flight. Your resilience has been a compass pressed against my own trembling chest, pointing me toward courage when my spirit faltered. Through you, I learned that transformation is not a destination we arrive at once, triumphant and complete — it is a continual becoming, a sacred unfolding that asks us to shed who we were, again and again, so that who we are becoming can finally breathe. You reminded me that healing is not a single sunrise, it is the sky learning, every day, how to open to the light.

The Ripple of Hope

Nieke, the story you carry — the one now woven through mine — has grown into something far larger than the two of us. It has become a living current, a quiet tide of truth moving outward into the world. Your journey holds within it the sacred promise that survival is not a miracle reserved for the chosen few, and healing is not some distant star meant only for the fortunate. Your story leans gently toward those still standing at the edge and whispers through the trembling dark: *You, too, can return.* What you have done, what you continue to do simply by rising each day, will reach people whose faces you may never see. Your courage will echo inside the hearts of strangers who will never know your name yet will feel the steady warmth of your fire in these words. You have become a beacon in the night, not blinding, but tender; not demanding, but unwavering. A soft, persistent flame that guides others back through their own labyrinths of despair, back to the quiet truth of who they are. And so, my dear friend, this book is not simply dedicated to you — it is *born* of you. It is shaped by your resilience, illuminated by the light you guarded when the rest of the world went dim. It stands as a testament to your becoming, to the radiance that survived within you long after every illusion fell away. Your life reveals what so many need to hear: that no one is too broken to rise, too lost to return, too far gone to be reclaimed. For even in the deepest depths, hope does not die, it glows beneath the rubble, patient as a heartbeat, waiting for the moment we dare to open our eyes and call it by its name.

The Bond That Heals

As I trace the contours of our shared journey, I am reminded of the sacred alchemy that true friendship holds — how one soul, simply by daring to shine in its own trembling truth, can cast light across the path of another. You, Nieke, have been that light for me — not a blazing torch, but a steady flame, the kind that warms rather than blinds, the kind that whispers *keep going* when the night grows long. You have shown me that friendship is more than the meeting of minds; it is the quiet communion of spirits, a wordless pact to witness one another fully, especially in the moments when the world turns its gaze away. Your courage has rewritten my understanding of companionship. You taught me that to walk beside someone through the fiercest storms is not merely an act of loyalty, but an act of love — a holy one. You embodied vulnerability without apology, authenticity without armor. You stood before your truth uncloaked, trembling perhaps, but never retreating. And when silence seemed like the safer refuge, you reached outward instead, choosing connection over collapse, honesty over hiding, life over disappearance. In doing so, you illuminated not only your own path... but mine, and countless others who will feel the echo of your bravery. You chose to reach outward when the darkness urged you to fold inward. You opened the door to your pain and allowed others to step inside — not to rescue you, but to witness you, to hold a corner of the weight you had carried alone for far too long. In that single, trembling act, you taught all of us a truth we so often forget: Asking for help is not an admission of fragility, but an act of profound wisdom — the kind that rises only from a soul brave enough to be seen. Your willingness to stand before your deepest fears, to face them without disguise or retreat, reveals the vastness of your character. It is one thing to endure the storm, to claw your way through the winds and call it survival. But you did more than survive — you transmuted survival into strength, and strength into compassion. You took the fire that once threatened to consume you and turned it into a lantern, lighting the way for others who still wander through their own night. You became living proof that courage is not the absence of fear, but the decision to meet it with an open, unguarded heart.

Lessons From the Fire

From your journey, a quiet scripture of truth has been written into my heart, line by line, ember by ember. You taught me that perseverance is not the roar of victory, but the soft, stubborn whisper that says, *try again* when everything in you trembles. You showed me that progress is not always a rising, sometimes it is simply the refusal to vanish. You revealed the sacred art of self-compassion: that healing is not the disappearance of wounds, but the tender acceptance of the scars they sculpt. You taught me that self-love is not reserved for the final version of who we become, but must be offered to every unfinished, uncertain version along the way. I have witnessed the devastation wrought by suicidal ideation, how it isolates like a winter storm, how it lies with a voice so familiar you mistake it for your own, how it cloaks a person in the illusion of aloneness. But through you, I have witnessed something far more powerful: the alchemy of connection. The way a handheld in love can interrupt the spiral. The way being truly *seen* can thaw the coldest parts of a soul. You reminded me, with your courage, your honesty, your willingness to be held, that mental health is not a whisper on the margins. It is a lifeline. A heartbeat. A wound that deserves the same reverence as any broken bone, because a mind in pain bleeds just as deeply, and a heart in despair can fracture just as easily. Through your fire, you taught me not only how to survive, but how to understand the sacred, fragile miracle of staying alive.

The Alchemy of Connection

And from those lessons carved in flame, something even more profound emerged — the revelation that healing is never meant to be carried in solitude. Through your bravery, Nieke, I witnessed firsthand the sacred transmutation that occurs when love is allowed to enter the wounds we once tried so desperately to hide. Genuine care is not merely a gesture; it is a form of medicine, a balm woven from presence, tenderness, and truth. In your transformation, I saw how connection becomes a lifeline — the steady hands that pull us back from the ledge when our own strength falters, the soft voices that whisper, *You are still here. Stay.* Love, when offered without condition, becomes a kind of alchemy: it turns despair into possibility, isolation into belonging, darkness into something we can finally navigate instead of fear. You taught me that no one heals alone. Yes, the walk is ours to make, step by trembling step, but there are lanterns along the path — friends, mentors, strangers, moments of grace — each one lighting the next stretch of the journey. Your courage reminded me that reconnection is the true beginning of healing: reconnecting to our own breath, to the hands extended toward us, to the pulse of life that persists even in our lowest moments. And in that reconnection, meaning begins to bloom again — quietly, gently, in the very places where despair once made its home.

Hope, Reborn

Nieke, your journey has become a living altar to everything sacred about the human spirit — its grit, its tenderness, its stubborn insistence on rising even when the world feels unliveable. Watching you walk through the fire, watching you fall and then gather yourself from the embers again and again, has been nothing short of witnessing a miracle in motion. Through you, I have learned that hope is not a flicker gifted to us by luck, it is a rebellion, a fierce, defiant act of choosing light even while standing knee-deep in shadow. Your story has reminded me that resilience is not loud; it does not roar. It whispers. It trembles. It continues. Like a seed pushing through winter soil, it survives the cold by refusing to forget the memory of the sun. You have shown me that fear does not vanish before courage appears — they walk side by side, and courage is simply the one that chooses to take the next step. You taught me that love is not an arrival point, not some distant horizon we hope to reach; it is the way we move through the world — with open hands, soft eyes, and hearts willing to break if breaking means we remain human. And perhaps most astonishing of all, you revealed that even when the night feels endless, even when every path seems swallowed by darkness, there is always — always — a hidden doorway forward. You found yours. And in doing so, you reminded me where to find mine.

The Spiral of Healing

And as I turn inward, tracing the contours of my own becoming, I see now that healing has never been a path that moves in a single direction. It is not a polished staircase ascending cleanly toward the light — it is a spiral, wild and living, circling through shadow and shimmer all at once. It moves the way a river does: doubling back, carving unexpected passages through the stone of who we once were, reshaping us grain by grain. Some days feel like lift, as though the sky cracks open just enough for breath to return, and suddenly the world is drenched again in color and sound. And then there are the days that pull you under, when old wounds rise like restless spirits and the darkness leans in close, whispering its old lies of failure and futility. But I have learned that these moments, the stumbles, the ache, the trembling pauses between collapse and rising, are not signs of weakness. They are the forge. It is in the unraveling that resilience sews itself into the seams of our being. Not as a blaze or a battle cry, but as a soft, stubborn vow whispered into the quiet: *I will keep going.* Healing is not the pursuit of flawlessness; it is the practice of presence, of sitting with what hurts until it reveals its true name. It is the willingness to breathe when the air feels thick, to stay when everything inside you wants to run, to offer yourself tenderness even on the days you feel undeserving of it. This is the sacred spiral, the winding, imperfect, miraculous way we find ourselves again.

The Power of Reaching Out

And woven through this spiraling journey, there is a truth I had to learn slowly, painfully, and then all at once: healing does not happen in isolation. In the moments when the darkness pressed closest, when my breath felt thin, and my thoughts turned inward like collapsing walls, I believed the lie that I had to endure it alone. That my pain was too strange, too heavy, too sharp for anyone else to hold. I built fortresses around my wounds and called it self-protection, not realizing I was only deepening my own exile. But the darkness... it is cunning. Its cruelest trick is convincing us that we are unworthy of being witnessed. That no one could possibly understand. Yet this is the great untruth. Because there *are* people who understand, souls who have walked through storms of their own and have learned how to sit with another's sorrow without flinching. There are those who will meet you exactly where you are: in silence, in trembling, in the fragile spaces where words refuse to come. People who will not demand your sunshine but will honor your rain. Reaching out is not weakness; it is rebellion. It is saying to the darkness, "*You cannot have me.*" It is a quiet, trembling declaration that your life still holds value, that somewhere in the depths, a small part of you still believes in the possibility of light. To ask for help is to extend a hand into the unknown and trust that someone will take it. It is an act of profound bravery, a sacred whisper that says: "*I am still here. And I want to stay.*" And that alone, that single act of reaching, is often the first miracle.

The Example You Set

And Nieke, you became the living embodiment of that truth, the quiet proof that reaching out can change a life. You showed me what it means to stretch trembling hands toward the light, even when the shadows still clung to your fingertips. You sought guidance not as a confession of weakness, but as an act of fierce devotion to your own becoming. You listened, not passively, but with the kind of courage that cracks open old walls. You let wisdom land where it needed to, even when it stung, even when it unearthed parts of you that you had spent years trying to bury. And then, with trembling bravery, you did the work. You did the midnight unravelings, the tear-soaked reckonings, the brave confrontations with truths that once felt unbearable. You leaned into discomfort instead of turning away from it. You walked toward your fear with open eyes and a softened heart. You faced your insecurities not with battle cries, but with a quiet grace that whispered: *I am worthy of healing.* And in doing so, you became an example, not the polished kind wrapped in perfection, but the raw, holy kind shaped by honesty. A living testament to what devotion looks like. Because true healing is not a single moment of awakening; it is the daily, sacred choice to rise, even when the ground still remembers how to tremble beneath you.

The Beauty of the Crawl

And from everything you've taught me, Nieke, one truth rises above the rest: even the crawl has its own kind of beauty. You showed me that healing doesn't always roar forward in great leaps, sometimes it moves in inches, in breaths, in the soft drag of a weary body refusing to stop. You revealed that progress is not defined by speed or strength, but by the simple, stubborn act of continuing. There were moments when moving felt impossible, when the world narrowed to a single breath held between trembling ribs, and yet, you crawled. You moved anyway. And in that slow, sacred motion, you reclaimed your power inch by inch. Because sometimes survival *is* the victory. Sometimes a single exhale is a revolution. Sometimes the quiet decision to remain, to stay in this world one more moment, is the most courageous act a soul can make. Through your persistence, you reminded the darkness that it could not claim you. You whispered a steady defiance into the void: *I am still here.* And slowly, almost imperceptibly, that crawl began to gather strength. The crawl became a shakier walk. The walk stretched into a run. And one day, the kind of day that arrives without fanfare, you looked up and realized that the sun was touching your skin again.

You taught me that healing isn't a destination waiting in the distance. It is a way of living, a daily devotion to courage, a rhythm of breaking and mending, a vow whispered again and again in the chambers of the heart: *I will not give up on myself.* And in that vow, whispered on the days you could barely move, you became a testament to the quiet miracle of staying alive.

The Journey Inward

And after witnessing the beauty of the crawl, the quiet miracle of choosing to stay, I began to see my own path with new eyes. When I look back now, I understand that healing has never been a march toward perfection, nor a quest to repair some irreparable flaw. It has been, above all else, a pilgrimage inward, a tender excavation of the self I buried beneath years of survival. It wasn't about fixing what was broken; it was about remembering what was never truly lost. The journey unfolded slowly, like a hesitant flower learning to trust the sun again. Petal by trembling petal, I began to open. I learned to sit with my imperfections the way one sits beside an injured friend, softly, patiently, without judgment. I learned to cradle the parts of me I once punished, to forgive the moments I abandoned myself, to welcome back the voice I had smothered into silence. Healing, I discovered, is not the erasure of the past but the gentle art of carrying it differently, letting its weight become wisdom instead of chains. It is letting old wounds teach without tormenting, letting regret soften rather than scar, letting memory be a lantern instead of a leash. Each day revealed something unexpected: A quiet strength I had mistaken for weakness, a vulnerability that felt more like courage, a forgotten longing that sparked like an ember under layers of ash. And slowly, almost shyly, I began to breathe again. Not out of habit, but out of intention. Not out of obligation, but out of desire. This journey has been a homecoming. A gentle, reverent reintroduction to myself, to the woman who survived, to the soul who kept whispering beneath the noise, to the light within me that never truly went out. I know now that the past did not break me; it shaped me. It did not define me; it refined me. And the future, once a darkened corridor, now glows with possibility, stretching out before me like an open doorway. A promise waiting to be met not with fear, but with open hands, open eyes, and an open, awakening heart.

The Light You Carry

And standing in the glow of your own becoming, Nieke, I cannot help but feel an ache of reverent awe. After witnessing your crawl, your rise, your sacred return to yourself, I see you now as you truly are — a woman forged in fire and softened by grace. You are living proof of the miracle that happens when a soul, trembling yet unbroken, chooses itself again and again. Your presence is a lantern in a world that often forgets its own shadows. Not a blinding flare, not a spectacle, but a steady, unwavering glow that says: *Here. This way. You're not alone.* Your hope is not loud, but it is faithful, the kind of light that lingers long after the sun has set, the kind that warms instead of dazzles, invites instead of demands. You rise each day with a quiet declaration: *I am still becoming.* And in that simple, sacred truth, you create space for others to breathe, to unravel, to believe that transformation is still possible. Your beauty is not borrowed; it is born. It comes from the places that once ached, from the wounds that refused to stay open, from the tenderness you learned to offer yourself when the world gave you none. Your power does not shout; it emanates from your honesty, your vulnerability, your fierce, unfiltered humanity. You remind us that healing does not sculpt us into perfection; it shapes us into truth. It makes us real, gloriously, messily, luminously real. And in your realness, Nieke, you have become a quiet force of nature, a living symbol of transformation, a testament to the light that survives the storm and then, astonishingly, learns how to shine because of it.

Never Forget

And so, Nieke, let these truths be etched into the marrow of your being: You are beautiful. You are powerful. You are worthy. You are lovable. You are inspiring. Not because the world says so, but because you *are*. Because your life has become a living altar of resilience, a testament to what the human spirit can rise from when everything around it whispers *fall*. Never forget the symphony you carry inside you, a music forged from ashes and awakening, from nights that nearly took you and mornings you chose to meet anyway. Your story is not a quiet tale; it is a crescendo of defiance, a constellation of moments where light refused to die. You have shown me, and all who witness your becoming, that even in the deepest dark, the ember of hope endures, soft but stubborn, waiting for the breath that will turn it into flame. You are living proof that brokenness and beauty are not opposites, but companions, that pain can be the soil where purpose grows, that the smallest flicker can lead us home when all other paths vanish. Nieke, you are both the lesson and the legacy, the embodied truth this book was built to honor: courage that trembles but still rises, compassion born from the places that once hurt, and the quiet, unwavering promise that there is always, always, a way forward.

A Tribute to a Warrior of Light

And so, to you, dearest Nieke, I offer these words, not merely in admiration, but in reverence. For you are a warrior of light, though no steel ever graced your hands. Your armor was honesty, your shield was courage, and your battlefield was the landscape of your own soul, a terrain most fear to enter, let alone conquer. Your triumphs were not marked by applause or witness; they unfolded in the soft, unseen hours where the world slept, and you fought alone. You braved the storms that swallowed whole the voices of hope, walked through nights thick with sorrow, and still, *still*, you rose. Not untouched, not unscarred, but reborn in the way only those who have truly broken and chosen life again can be. You became living proof that the human spirit, though fragile in form, is unbreakable in essence. You showed that from the very soil of suffering new roots of compassion can grow, that pain can be transmuted into wisdom, that silence, once heavy with fear, can blossom into song. Your courage has done more than reshape your own destiny; it has become a lighthouse for the wandering, a quiet, unwavering glow that says, "Come. There is a way through." In your story, others will find breath again. In your rising, they will find the permission to rise. In your truth, they will remember their own. You, Nieke, are not just a survivor. You are illumination, a warrior carved from darkness whose very existence teaches others how to step into the light.

The Next Chapter

And now, my dear friend, you stand at the threshold of a new beginning, a chapter not born from survival alone, but from the quiet triumph of becoming. May the pages ahead unfurl like dawn over still water, soft and golden, revealing just how far you have journeyed from the shadows that once held you. May each new day greet you with the gentle reminder of your own unfolding, that your story is no longer written in the language of fear, but in the cadence of resilience, of reclamation, of grace. May abundance find you in all its sacred forms: in the love that meets you honestly, in the peace that settles into your bones, in the trust you now offer yourself like a long-awaited homecoming. May your laughter return in full color, not the fragile echo it once was, but a river breaking open after a long winter, rushing, alive, unburdened. May your heart, no longer fractured but strengthened by its mending, remain wide open to the miracles waiting quietly along your path. May you continue to shed old skins with the courage of one who knows that rebirth is not a single moment, but a lifelong blooming. Step boldly into your radiance, for it no longer flickers in doubt; it burns with a steady, unwavering brilliance, a lighthouse carved from truth guiding others through the fog you once wandered. Let this book, this tapestry of shared survival, woven from pain and grace and audacity, stand as a mirror you can always return to. May it remind you of the battles you dared to fight, the demons you silenced with compassion, and the extraordinary woman you have risen into. Every chapter holds your imprint. Every sentence holds your fire. Every word is an echo of the strength that lives within you, strength that continues, quietly and fiercely, to write the next chapter of your becoming.

The Promise of Presence

And as you step into this unfolding horizon, know this with the certainty of breath: My heart will continue to walk beside yours, even as life leads us along our own winding paths. I will be there, in every quiet triumph, in every trembling beginning, in every moment when the road softens beneath your feet or rises steeply before you. I will cheer for you when you soar, steady you when the weight grows too heavy, and hold space for the days when sunlight feels far away. You are not alone, Nieke. You never have been, and you never will be. Our journeys may bend in different directions, yet they remain bound by a thread woven from truth and tenderness, a thread spun through our shared storms, through the healing we carved out of darkness, through a love that has proven itself unshakeable. You are a rare gift to this world, and to me, a living reminder of what becomes possible when a soul chooses not just to survive, but to rise, again and again, from its own ash. You show me daily that beginnings are born from bravery, that hope can be rebuilt with bare hands, and that the human spirit, when loved, becomes incandescent. So let me say it plainly, with all the softness and certainty in my chest: I love you to the moon and back, and farther still. You are not only my friend, but my mirror, reflecting both who I have been and who I strive to become. You are my muse, the spark that turned pain into prose, the flame that set this entire story into motion. You are the quiet proof that light is not stumbled upon but forged, deliberately, fiercely, in the very places we once feared were beyond saving. And because of you, the world, my world, shines just a little brighter.

The Light Between Us

Nieke, the love I hold for you stretches far beyond the reach of language, past the edges of ink and paper, past the moon and whatever lies beyond its silver glow. No paragraph, no constellation of sentences, could ever contain the magnitude of what your friendship has carved into my life. You have been the soft heartbeat in the quietest chambers of my doubt, the unwavering flame that steadied itself beside mine on the nights my own light trembled in its wick. Your courage did more than save you, it cast its glow across my shadows, revealing paths in me I had long since stopped believing existed. You have taught me the anatomy of bravery, that to live fully is to risk breaking, to feel deeply is to open the doors of the soul without guarantees, and to love fiercely is to trust that the heart knows how to mend. You remind me that vulnerability is a kind of holiness, that tenderness can be a weapon against despair, and that two souls standing together in truth can create a light that neither could hold alone. And so I am endlessly, breathlessly grateful for you, for your presence, your resilience, your quiet and roaring courage, and for the sacred honor of walking this winding path beside you. You are a gift I could never have dreamed of deserving, a treasure woven of fire and gentleness, a blessing that continues to shape the woman I am becoming. The world glows differently with you in it. And my world, my heart, is forever brighter because of the light we share between us.

To Those Who Walk Beside Us

To you, Nieke, and to every soul whose courage has brushed against mine along this winding, twilight road, I offer my deepest, most reverent gratitude. You are the heartbeat beneath these pages, the breath that kept this story warm when my own hope ran thin. Every story you've shared, every scar you've bared, every fragile victory you've wrestled from the jaws of despair has become part of the living soul of this book. You are the quiet heroes, the unseen warriors who rise from the embers of yesterday and dare, again and again, to believe in something softer, something brighter, something more. Your pain became a torch. Your perseverance, a lifeline. Your victories, whispered or roaring, became the very fire that kept these words alive. May our collective stories shimmer like lanterns for those still wandering the long, sleepless corridors of night. May they offer warmth to the weary, courage to the trembling, and hope to those who have forgotten that dawn is not a miracle, it is a promise. A promise that always keeps its word. And may we forever remember the truth that threads us together: We have never walked alone. Not once. Not ever. We are strands of the same tapestry, souls woven together by the sacred, defiant act of surviving. When one of us rises, we tug another skyward. When one of us shines, the darkness recedes for all. Together, we form a constellation of resilience, a celestial map for those still lost in the dark, guiding them home by the light we gathered from our shared shadows.

The Testament of Light

In the end, it is never the darkness that names us; it is the light we discover *because* of it. It is the flame we coax from the cold, the strength we gather from the ruins, the quiet, trembling radiance that rises in the very places we thought would break us. Our wounds do not diminish us; they bear witness to the depth of our living, to the tenderness we have felt, to the battles we have survived, to the countless nights we chose breath over silence. The scars we carry are not stains of shame, but shimmering medals forged in fire, proof that we endured, that we transformed, that every fracture became an entry point for the light. Nieke, my dear friend, you are the living testament of that truth, a constellation stitched from moments of courage, a mosaic of grace shaped from shards that once cut you open. You show the world what becomes possible when a soul faces its shadows with unblinking honesty, when a heart reaches outward instead of folding inwards, when a spirit chooses life again and again, even when every step forward burns. You are not just a survivor. You are the afterglow, the radiant proof that healing, when met with devotion, becomes contagious. Through your courage, you have not only reclaimed yourself, but you have given others permission to rise, to speak, to hope. Your light is no longer something you found. It is something you forged.

Always

Nieke, I love you, not only for the woman you are in this moment, but for the luminous, ever-unfolding being you continue to become. Your strength humbles me the way mountains humble the wind. Your spirit inspires me like dawn breaking after a storm. Your friendship restores my faith in the fierce, fragile beauty of being human. My love for you stretches beyond the edges of language, beyond the borders of this world, beyond the moon and back, and then further still, into the places words cannot reach. For as long as breath lives in me, I will carry your light within my own, a warmth in the cold seasons, a lantern in the dark, a reminder of the miracles we carved from our pain. I will keep writing, keep speaking, keep loving in honor of what we have endured and what we have reclaimed. Because in truth, this book, this journey, was never meant to be a tale of endings. It is a hymn of beginnings. A testament to renewal. A love letter to the unbreakable truth that even in our deepest night, light is not something we search for, it is something we *become*.

A Message to Those Still in the Dark

To you who are reading this from the shadows, to you whose heart feels heavy, whose breath feels thin, whose spirit trembles beneath the weight of thoughts too sharp to hold, I speak to you not from a pedestal, but from the very edge you now stand upon. I know this terrain. I have felt the cold pull of that abyss, the quiet seduction of silence, the ache of believing that the world would spin just fine without me. So hear me when I say this: You are not alone. You are not weak. You are not too broken, nor too much, nor beyond saving. You are human, achingly, brilliantly human, and your existence carries more meaning than your pain will ever allow you to see. I know the suffocating weight of invisible battles, the hollow nights where even breathing feels like an effort, the awful, echoing lie that whispers *no one would understand*. But that lie is just a shadow pretending to be truth. There *are* people who understand. There are hearts that have survived their own storms, hearts that recognize yours without judgment, hands ready to reach for you even in complete darkness. There are souls who will sit beside you, not to fix you, not to drag you into the light before you're ready, but simply to keep you company until you can breathe again. Please reach out. Even if your voice shakes, even if your words feel heavy as stones, even if all you can manage is a whisper or a text that says, *I need help*. That whisper is not weakness, it is courage in its purest form. It is the first trembling step toward staying. And you deserve to stay. You deserve support. You deserve to be held through the ache, to be believed, to be heard. Your life is not a burden. Your pain is not an inconvenience. Your story is not over. And even if you cannot see it now, there is a dawn forming on the horizon of your becoming, soft, patient, and waiting for the moment you choose to rise.

Healing will not come overnight

It will not sweep into your life like some cinematic revelation, nor unfold in tidy chapters with clean endings. It arrives instead in fragments, in the soft rebellion of lifting your head from the pillow, in the fragile courage of stepping into a new day, in the unexpected moment when a laugh escapes your lips and surprises you with its sweetness. Healing is not a destination waiting at the end of a map; it is a devotion, a lifelong, sacred promise to keep returning to yourself. It does not rush, does not demand perfection, does not follow the timelines your mind insists upon. It has its own rhythm, slow, tender, ancient, and it asks of you only this: patience, gentleness, and the willingness to breathe through the ache. You will stumble. You will have days when the weight feels unbearable, moments when the shadows whisper that you are slipping backward. But hear this truth clearly: Falling is not failing. Every single time you choose to rise, even if you rise trembling, even if you rise slowly, you defy the darkness that once tried to swallow you whole. So hold on. Hold on with the quiet ferocity of someone who is learning their own worth. Hold on, knowing that pain is not the final chapter of your story, it is the fire through which you are being transformed. You are still becoming. Still unfolding. Still stepping into the version of yourself who will one day look back with soft, astonished eyes and whisper: *I made it through*. And you will.

A Final Thank You

As I stand at the threshold of this book, this offering shaped by fire, softened by grace, and stitched together with the golden thread of our friendship, my heart returns to one simple truth: thank you, Nieke.

Thank you for your courage, for the way you kept choosing life even when the night held you by the throat. Thank you for believing, however shakily, that healing was possible, not as a distant dream, but as something you could gather into your own trembling hands. Thank you for allowing your story to wind itself into mine, for trusting me with the tender, unpolished pieces of your becoming. You have shown me, again and again, that resilience is not the act of standing tall but the sacred art of rising *differently* each time we fall. You are living proof that the human heart, when met with honesty and compassion, can stitch itself back together in ways more intricate, more luminous, than before it ever broke.

You taught me that healing is not the erasure of pain, but the reclamation of life *through* it, the slow, steady returning to one's own pulse after years of forgetting how to feel it. And as I write these words, gratitude floods me, not as a fleeting warmth, but as a full-body knowing. Gratitude for you. Gratitude for this path. Gratitude for the miracle of turning suffering into something with the power to comfort, to guide, to awaken. You are, and will forever be, a testament to what true healing looks like, not perfect, but profoundly human; not polished, but breathtaking in its truth; not untouched by the dark but transformed by having walked through it. I love you to the moon and back, my dear friend, and further still, into every horizon we have yet to meet. It is one of the greatest honors of my life to share this journey, *our* journey, with the world. May these words carry the same radiance you have gifted me. May they travel into the hands and hearts of those who need them most. And may they whisper, gently but unwaveringly, the truth we both had to learn the hard way: Even in the deepest night, there is always, *always,* a way forward.

Finding the Light

The light at the end of the tunnel is rarely a blazing sunrise, it is a slow, sacred unfurling, a quiet dawn that begins as nothing more than a soft shimmer beneath the rubble of all you've survived. It does not flood your world all at once; it seeps in gently, like the first warm breath of morning brushing against a body that has forgotten what warmth feels like. It grows in the smallest, most fragile choices: the moment you swing your legs out of bed despite the weight pressing down on your chest, the trembling courage it takes to dial a number and let someone hear the truth in your voice, the simple insistence of taking one more breath when your mind insists there is no point. These are not small things; these are miracles disguised as motions. These are the first flickers of a life returning. And yes, there will be days when the darkness stretches long and merciless, when your heart aches in places you cannot name, when hope feels like a distant star you can no longer see. There will be moments when you mistake exhaustion for failure, silence for abandonment, and numbness for the absence of worth. But even then, *especially* then, remember this: You are not alone. Even when the path feels invisible beneath your feet, even when your own mind becomes a storm, even when your hands shake with the effort of holding on, there are hearts beating beside yours. There is a world that refuses to give up on you, even when you cannot yet believe in yourself. There are lights, steady, human, and real, waiting to guide you until your own begins to rise again.... And rise it will. Your life is valuable. Your story matters. Your healing, no matter how slow, is still unfolding in ways you cannot yet see. You are not behind. You are not failing. You are *becoming.* Every moment you stay is an act of defiance against despair. Every tear you shed waters the roots of your becoming. And one day, perhaps without even realizing it, you will find yourself standing in a new kind of light, a light you helped create through your courage to continue.

A Testament to Hope

Nieke, your journey has been that light for me, not a blazing flare meant to dazzle the world, but a steady, unwavering glow that refuses to go out, even in the harshest winds. It is the kind of light that doesn't demand attention yet transforms everything it touches. You have taught me what it means to move through shadows with an open heart, to keep walking even when the path dissolves beneath your feet, to trust in a dawn that has not yet risen. Your strength has been a quiet revolution, not loud, not theatrical, but honest in a way that disarms and inspires. Your vulnerability has peeled back the layers of pretense I once hid behind, reminding me that the truest courage is not found in perfection, but in the willingness to be seen. And your resilience... it humbles me. It reminds me that the human heart, though easily bruised, is endlessly capable of rebuilding itself. You have shown me that a cracked soul is not a broken one, it is a vessel reshaped for more light. That hope does not erase suffering; it threads itself through the pain, stitch by stitch, until something softer, stronger, and unexpectedly beautiful emerges. Healing, as you've lived it, is not the art of forgetting, but the sacred practice of carrying the past with grace, allowing it to transform rather than define you. Through your journey, I have learned that hope is not a distant star, it is the glow that rises from within us when we choose, even in trembling, to believe there is more ahead than the darkness we have known. This book is a living testament, not merely ink on paper, but the echo of your courage, the imprint of your triumph, the quiet pulse of a spirit that refused to die. It is a hymn to the truth you embody that even in the moments when we feel most breakable, when our hands tremble and our breath fractures, something within us still reaches, for meaning, for purpose, for the faintest glimmer of light. This book breathes because you did. It shines because you chose to rise. It stands as proof that even from the softest, most fragile fragments of ourselves, we can craft a life that is whole, luminous, and fiercely alive.

To the Journey Ahead

To the vast, unwritten chapters of your life, my beloved friend, may they unfold with a tenderness that cradles you, with laughter that spills like sunlight through open windows, with a peace so gentle it silences the echoes of the ghosts you once carried. May your days rise softly, like warm tides returning to a familiar shore, and may your nights be quiet havens where rest comes easily and without fear. May you continue to bloom in ways you have yet to imagine, creating from your soul, loving with abandon, dreaming with the wild audacity of someone who has walked through fire and learned she cannot be burned. And each morning, when the sun lifts its golden face to the sky, may you remember the impossible miles you've already journeyed. You are no longer the woman who clung to survival; you are the woman who lives, who chooses, who dances in her own becoming. You are living evidence that even from the faintest ember, a brilliant blaze can rise. Nieke, you are my reminder that light is never truly lost, it simply waits for the moment we are ready to see it again. Your story strengthens me. Your friendship steadies me. Your courage teaches me, again and again, that tunnels are not graves, but passageways, and that there is always a way through. I love you to the moon, through the stars, beyond every horizon, because in your light, I rediscovered my own. And with this book, may countless others find theirs too.

To Nieke — The Eternal Ember: Final Benediction

To the Moon and Back

My dearest friend, my sister in survival, my mirror in the dark, you were the spark that breathed life into these pages. It was your courage that stirred the dormant embers in my chest, your quiet fire that rose against the storm and ignited the wildfire that became this book. You have been both the flame and the lighthouse, the blaze that summoned my own bravery, and the steadfast glow that continues to guide its purpose. And when the road curves once more into shadow, when silence presses heavy and the night feels endless, remember this: remember *us*, remember this fire we built between our trembling hands, remember that light is never truly lost. It returns, always, even if it must rise first from ash. Your resilience has carved constellations out of ruin. You are strength-in-motion, a warrior whose scars gleam like distant galaxies mapping the story of where you've been and who you've become. You are living proof that the universe inside us can collapse and still be reborn, brighter, fiercer, infinitely more whole. Through your courage, you taught me again what it means to be human, to burn, to break, to be stripped to bone and still choose to rebuild. Your name is etched in the smoke of survival, in the molten glow of rebirth, in every dawn that follows a long and merciless night. I see you. I hear you. I love you. And with a heart humbled and overflowing, I am endlessly, irrevocably proud of you.

Closing Blessing — From Embers to Light

May these words live on not just as a dedication, but as a torch carried forward, a flame passed from trembling hands to steadier ones, from survivor to survivor, from the wounded to the healers they one day become. May it burn softly in the hearts of all who find themselves reflected in these pages, reminding them that their story, too, belongs to the light. To you who reads and feels the echo of your own ache in these lines, know this: you are woven into this fire. You are part of this living constellation of survivors. You are seen in your shadows, held in your breaking, cherished in your becoming. You do not walk this night alone. And to you, Nieke, the moon, a constant, the sunrise after every storm, and this light is ours. Born from embers, carried through darkness, and rising now into something bright enough to warm the world. Always, always, to the moon and back, and to every dawn that follows.

Epilogue

Nieke's story is not a tragedy; it is a rising, a soft, radiant awakening carved from the very ashes that once threatened to silence her. She is living proof that even a shattered soul can relearn its song, can stitch melody back into the places where silence once lived. Through her journey, I found my own reflection trembling in the light, a healing echo reminding me that when pain is spoken aloud, it becomes a bridge instead of a burden, a place where two wounded hearts can meet and begin again. As I sit down to write this book, I feel myself following the soft reverberations of your strength, Nieke, as they ripple through every line that takes shape beneath my hand. The pen trembles, not from uncertainty, but from reverence, aware of the weight these pages carry. This story is not merely a chronicle of survival; it is a testament to rebirth, a hymn woven from the breaths we reclaimed when the world felt too heavy to hold. Each sentence arrives like a quiet resurrection, a pulse of gratitude for every moment we both chose to stay, for every dawn we rose to meet even when our spirits felt threadbare. What began as a simple offering, a message meant to close the distance between your ache and my understanding, has unfurled into something far larger than either of us could have foreseen. Somewhere along the way, this book became a mirror, tender yet unflinching, reflecting the exquisite duality that lives within us: the fragility that softens us, and the fortitude that keeps us rising. It has become the shared heartbeat of three souls bound not by suffering It is here, in this tender space where the first crack appears in the darkness, that the light slips in. A circle that began with just two souls: myself and my sponsor, the woman who became a lantern in my darkest night, who taught me how to kindle a flame of my own. She lit the path for me, and I, in turn, held that light out to you. And now you, Nieke, have become a guiding star in your own right, a torchbearer forging your way through the shadows and illuminating the way for others who wander. Through the act of writing, I have learned that creation and healing are fierce siblings, both born from the wreckage, both demanding that we soften, surrender, and let ourselves be remade. There were nights when my own shadows rose again, whispering old doubts, old wounds. And in those moments, it was your courage, your relentless insistence on rising, that steadied my hand. You reminded me to keep writing through the ache, to trust that truth, even when jagged, is a sacred offering. And as the words poured out, revelation dawned: this book was never meant to belong only to you, or only to me. It grew beyond us, widened, deepened, until it became a sanctuary in its own right. A refuge for anyone who has ever stood trembling at the edge of themselves. A home for every soul who has ever whispered, "I can't do this anymore," and then, through some small miracle of will or love or sheer stubborn breath... kept going anyway. Through your journey, Nieke, I found not only inspiration, but a mirror, a luminous reminder of the moments when I too walked barefoot through my own fire, gathering reasons to stay one fragile breath at a time. In your rising, I saw the reflection of a truth I had long forgotten: That the human spirit is a quiet phoenix, capable of lifting itself from the embers of despair even when the wings tremble, even when the sky feels impossibly far. You became my compass, not one that points toward perfection or unbroken horizons, but toward something far more sacred: authenticity. You showed me the courage of being real, of being raw, of standing imperfect and still choosing to live. You reminded me that healing is not about becoming untouched but about becoming honest.

And so this book became a tapestry woven from many threads, yours, mine, and the invisible strands of thousands who have fought their storms in silence. It is a love letter to the ones who survived without applause, a whispered prayer for those still searching for even a sliver of light, and a promise etched in ink: **no one walks this path alone.** As the ink settles and the pages begin to breathe, I can feel the presence of every soul who has ever dared to whisper hope into their own darkness. Your story, Nieke, is the spark that first caught flame; mine became the kindling that helped it grow. And Cols, steadfast, unwavering Cols, she was the foundation beneath us both, the quiet earth that held our trembling feet when the world felt too heavy to bear. Together, the three of us became a single fire, small at first, flickering against the wind, and then rising, bright and undeniable. A testament that even the deepest shadows cannot smother the light that insists on being born. So here I sit, heart brimming, hands steady, offering to the world what was forged from our shared ashes, not a tale of endings, but a hymn to beginnings. To the infinite rebirths waiting inside each of us, to the sparks we carry, to the dawns we have yet to rise into. This book is our flame. and through it, may others remember their own.

Note to reader

To you, dear reader, standing at the threshold of your own becoming, I offer these words not as answers, but as small lanterns placed gently along your path. May they glow softly in your hands, steadying you when the night feels endless. You are not alone in this. You are not weak. You are not broken, nor beyond mending. You are strong, in ways you cannot yet see. You are brave, in ways you have not yet claimed. And you are worthy, endlessly, inherently, irrevocably worthy, of love, of tenderness, of understanding, of another chance to begin again. Do not fear reaching out. There is no shame in needing a hand to steady your trembling steps, no failure in admitting that the weight has become too much to carry alone. Healing was never meant to be a solitary pilgrimage. It blooms in connection, in the quiet, sacred spaces where honesty softens into compassion and where two souls meet without judgment. Remember this: healing is not a finish line awaiting your arrival. It is a living, breathing journey, one that curves and spirals, pauses and begins again. Some days will drag you backward into old shadows; others will lift you unexpectedly into light. Both are part of the unfolding. Both are part of the becoming. Walk gently. Stay patient with yourself. And trust, even when trust feels impossible, that every step, even the trembling ones, are leading you toward something tender, something necessary, something true.

For Your Journey Ahead

As you step onto your own path of healing, tender-footed, unsure, but willing, I offer these words as quiet companions for the road before you. May you find the strength to face your demons not as enemies to be slain, but as messengers, shadows carrying lessons you were never meant to fear, only to understand. May you summon the courage to reach out when the night grows heavy, to trust the hands extended toward you, to let yourself be seen in the softness of your truth. Vulnerability is not your weakness; it is the doorway through which connection enters. May you begin to uncover your own beauty, not the polished kind the world adores, but the raw, luminous beauty that rises from a soul that has weathered storms and still chooses to stand. May you recognize your own resilience, that quiet, unshakable force woven through every breath you've taken on the days you thought you had none left. And may you discover, again and again, that transformation is not born through perfection, but through persistence, through the small, sacred decision to rise, to breathe, to believe even when belief feels impossible. Above all, carry this truth with you as a flame cupped gently in your palms: You are loved. You are worthy. You are enough, on the days you soar, on the days you crawl, and even on the days you forget these truths entirely. The world is softer because you are in it.

A Book Born of Healing

This book is not a map with tidy directions, nor a lantern that promises to banish every shadow. It is not a manual for quick fixes or a doorway that opens with a single key. Healing is far too sacred, far too human, to be reduced to steps or scripts. What you hold in your hands is something softer, truer: a tapestry woven from ash and ember, stitched with the threads of my own descent and the quiet resurrections of those who walked beside me through their own nights of fire. These pages are an offering, a testament to the courage it takes to speak the unspeakable, to reach out when the darkness tightens, to choose compassion when shame hisses otherwise. They are fragments of truth gathered from trembling hands and mended hearts, placed here in the hope that somewhere within them, you might recognize pieces of your own story. May you hear your own heartbeat in these lines, in the stumbles, in the victories, in the whispered reminders that pain is not meaningless, that suffering is not a sentence, and that every wound you carry has something to teach you. Let these words be both anchor and compass, steadying you when the night grows loud, guiding you gently back when you feel lost within yourself. And may they remind you, again and again, that no matter how far you have wandered, there is always a way home: Home to your breath, to your truth, to the light that has never once stopped waiting for you. If you have arrived at these words, it is likely because something inside you is reaching, for hope, for meaning, for breath in a world that sometimes feels too tight to inhabit. Let this book be to you what it became for us: a quiet hand in the dark, a soft lantern held at the edge of the cliff. You do not need clarity to continue. You do not need to be whole to be worthy. You do not need to have the path mapped out before you take the next trembling step. All you need... is to stay. To take one breath, even if it feels borrowed. To allow the smallest ember of belief to flicker somewhere deep within you, tender and uncertain but alive. Your pain does not make you unlovable; it makes you human. Your survival is not a burden; it is a quiet, breath-stealing miracle. And wherever you stand in this moment, shaking, searching, rising, or simply enduring, you are already woven into this shared flame. A lineage of souls who chose, against all odds, to rise again. To every reader holding these words now, know this in the marrow of your being: you are seen, you are cherished, and you are never beyond redemption. If there has ever been a moment when you questioned your place in this world, when you felt yourself slipping into the quiet gravity of doubt, let this truth anchor you: your very existence is an act of defiance against the darkness that tried to claim you. You are not a mistake. You are not a burden. You are not the sum of the nights that almost broke you. You are a living testament to resilience, a heartbeat that refused to fade, a soul that continues to rise even when trembling. You are the light you've long been searching for, the ember that refuses to be extinguished, the dawn blooming quietly within your own chest. Even now, especially now, you are luminous.

Author's Note — From Embers to Light

This book was not written from a mountaintop, but from the embers, from the quiet glow that remains after the fire has burned low. In shaping these words, I hoped to carve out a sanctuary of understanding and becoming, not just for Nieke, not just for myself, but for every soul who has ever walked through their own internal blaze and wondered whether dawn would ever return. This work was born of pain, yes, but its bones are made of love. The kind of love that blooms when we witness another rise from their knees. The kind of love that grows when we finally turn toward our shadows and say,

"I am ready to meet you." These pages do not exist to instruct or to cure. They are not a map or a mandate. They are a soft place to land, a hearth where truth is allowed to exhale, where vulnerability is not a weakness but a doorway, and where healing, in all its wild, uneven, breathtaking imperfection, is given permission to unfurl at its own sacred pace. Here, you are invited to sit with your story, to let the light touch the places you thought were beyond saving, and to discover, gently, steadily, that from embers, light is always born again. This book is, at its core, a testament to resilience, not the loud, triumphant kind that shakes mountains, but the soft, steadfast whisper that rises in the quiet hours: *"I'll try again tomorrow."* It is an ode to community, to the invisible threads that bind us when we dare to reach out, when trembling hands find one another in the dark, when we discover that healing was never meant to be a solitary pilgrimage. And above all, it is a hymn to hope, that stubborn, flickering flame that refuses to be extinguished, even when the winds howl and the night feels endless. Hope is the

ember that glows beneath the ash, the small warmth that says, *"Stay. I am still here."* For even the bleakest roads can lead us toward brilliance.

Even the most fractured hearts can learn a new rhythm, a new song. Even in our most unravelled moments, we remain deserving of grace, worthy of tenderness, capable of extraordinary becoming. And even in our most broken moments, still capable of love, still able to rise. May these pages stand as a gentle reminder to you, to me, to every soul who reads, that the very fire that once threatened to consume us can also forge our strength. That from our struggles, we can emerge not diminished but expanded. Not hardened but illuminated. Not less of who we are, but *more.* Not emptied but made whole in new and wondrous ways. And may we hold close this enduring truth: within every ember, no matter how faint, lives the promise of light, a light that, once claimed, can guide us, again and again, all the way home. This book was never truly meant to be written, it was meant to be *felt*. It rose not from intention, but from instinct; not from structure, but from the quiet trembling of a heart learning how to breathe again. What began as a single message of compassion grew into a hymn of survival, a tapestry woven from breath and bruises, from ashes and awakening. Nieke, you were not the seed of this story, you were the wildfire that awakened it. The fierce, necessary burn that cleared the forest of my fear and made space for truth to bloom. In the reflection of your healing, I rediscovered pieces of myself I thought long lost. In your courage, I found language for wounds I had forgotten how to name. Through the blaze of your becoming, I finally understood that healing is not a moment, but a devotion, a sacred, continual unfurling toward the light.And to you who reads this now, to the soul standing in the doorway of your own darkness, hear this as clearly as the beating of your own heart: you are not alone. Not now. Not ever. You are worthy of breath, of tenderness, of rest, of another sunrise. Your existence is not an accident, but a testament, a quiet miracle shaped by the very fire that tried to consume you. Remember, even the faintest spark can birth a dawn. And from that dawn, entire lifetimes of possibility can rise.

Finding the Light

The light at the end of the tunnel is not a sudden sunrise cracking open the sky; it is a slow, tender unfurling, the kind of dawn that tiptoes in softly after a long and shattering night. It arrives in whispers, not in fanfare, in the quiet courage of choosing to stay, in the fragile steadiness of a single breath taken when everything inside you aches to disappear. Some nights, hope will feel like a distant star, half-hidden behind storm clouds. Some mornings, the simple act of opening your eyes will feel like rebellion. And yet, even then, especially then, the fact that you are here is a victory carved from the marrow of your soul. Nieke, your journey has been the lantern guiding every word of this book. Your courage, the pulse that kept me writing. Your healing, the proof that light does return, even to those who once believed themselves unreachable. Through you, I have been reminded that the heart is a phoenix, that even in its darkest hour, it is already gathering the fire it needs to rise. This book is a celebration of you, of us, and of every soul learning to stitch themselves back together with threads of tenderness and truth. It is a promise that though the night may be long, it is never eternal. And so, my beloved friend, as you step into the vastness of the life ahead, may it be drenched in love that softens every memory, luminous with joy that grows brighter with each passing day, and endless as the moon that holds our vow. To the moon and back, and into every dawn yet to come.

Dedicated to Nieke Lombard

A warrior not of battlefields, but of the unseen valleys of the soul. A luminous force who carried her flame through nights that tried to extinguish it, and in doing so, became a lighthouse for those still searching for the shore. You are the ember that refused to die, the quiet spark that grew into the fire that warmed these pages, the light that guided this book from a whisper into a living, breathing testament of hope. Your courage did not simply inspire this work, it ignited it.

Understanding the Shadows:

Suicidal ideation does not rise from a single source, nor does it arrive like a sudden storm. It gathers slowly, a constellation of wounds, memories, and burdens that converge in the quiet corners of the mind. To understand it is to gently illuminate the landscape of the human heart, to recognize that what feels like a personal failing is often the echo of many unseen forces. Sometimes the shadows grow from **the mind's own storms,** depression, anxiety, bipolar disorder, PTSD and C-PTSD, conditions that can dim the world's colors and make even breathing feel heavy. Sometimes they are born from **old wounds**, from traumas that carved themselves into the body long before language could name them. Loss, neglect, abuse, these are the kind of ghosts that linger, whispering lies of unworthiness into the softest parts of us. There are **biological currents** too, hidden beneath the surface, inherited patterns, chemical imbalances, and the silent weight of physical illness that can tilt the heart toward despair without warning. And then there is the world itself, **the pressures, the noise, the loneliness**, the financial strain, the absence of community, the feeling of being unseen in a society moving too fast to notice who is breaking. These elements do not excuse the pain, but they explain it. They remind us that suicidal thoughts are not born from weakness but from a profound overload of the human spirit. To understand the shadows is to remember that every struggle has roots, and every root can be tended with care, patience, and compassion.

IT OFTEN STEMS FROM a complex interplay of factors, including:

- **Mental health conditions:** Depression, anxiety, bipolar disorder, and PTSD/C-PTSD are often associated with suicidal thoughts.
- **Trauma:** Past experiences of abuse, neglect, or significant loss can leave deep emotional scars that contribute to feelings of hopelessness.
- **Biological factors:** Genetic predisposition, imbalances in brain chemistry, and physical health issues can all play a role.
- **Social and environmental factors:** Social isolation, financial stress, and societal pressures can exacerbate existing vulnerabilities.

It is vital to remember that **suicidal thoughts are not a measure of weakness**, nor a flaw in one's character.

They are **symptoms,** the smoke rising from a fire long left unattended, the whisper of a soul overwhelmed by its own unspoken grief. These thoughts are not born from failure; they are born from **pain,** from wounds too heavy to carry alone from burdens too long shouldered in silence. Suicidal ideation is, at its core, **a cry for relief**, a soft and trembling call toward connection, a plea for someone, anyone, to notice the battle raging beneath the surface. To acknowledge these thoughts is not to surrender to them, but to honor the truth that something within you aches for care. Healing begins the moment we dare to name what hurts. The moment we say, *"I am struggling"*, even if our voice is barely a whisper. It begins in the quiet, courageous act of validating our own feelings, of recognizing that the pain is real, that it matters, and that we deserve support. Seeking help, whether through a professional, a trusted friend, or a loving presence, is not an admission of defeat. It is the first brave step toward reclaiming your light. It is the moment the darkness is no longer carried alone, the moment the first crack appears in the walls of despair built around the heart. And through that crack, light, slow, gentle, patient, begins to find

The Path to Healing

Healing does not arrive as a straight, sunlit road, it unfolds like a winding river, curving through forgotten valleys, doubling back on itself, carving new space through the very terrain that once felt impossible to cross.

There will be days when you stumble, nights when doubt curls itself around your ribs, moments when the darkness feels closer than the dawn. But every step, even the smallest, even the shaking ones, is movement. Is progress. It is proof that the heart still longs for life. This path is not walked alone. It is shaped by a constellation of supports, each one a beacon guiding you forward:

- **Reaching for professional help** — the bravest act of all. Therapists, psychiatrists, support groups... these are not simply resources; they are lifelines, steady hands that help you navigate the storms within. They offer maps for the terrain you cannot yet see, and light for the places you fear to enter.
- **Gathering your people** — those who remind you that you belong. A support system is not just comfort; it is survival. Whether found in friendships, family, or communities forged from shared pain, these connections become anchors when the world inside you begins to sway.
- **Cultivating self-compassion** — the quiet alchemy of healing. Treat yourself with the tenderness you offer others. Let your imperfections breathe. Let your vulnerability be not a cage, but a doorway. Healing deepens each time you say, *"I forgive myself for being human."*
- **Learning to cope, gently** — gathering tools for the journey. Healthy strategies to manage stress, fear, and the waves of emotion become the stepping stones beneath your feet, transforming chaos into something navigable, survivable, even transformable.
- **Returning to yourself through self-care** — the daily rituals that keep you rooted. Nourishing your body, tending to your mind, moving with intention, breathing with awareness... these simple acts become sacred. They remind you that you deserve tenderness, from the world, and from yourself.

Healing is not a single moment of arrival, it is a thousand tiny choices to keep going. A soft, persistent devotion to your own becoming. With each choice, you move closer to the light that has always been waiting for you.

Chapter Two

Welcome to "Surviving Death – Echoes of the Abyss: A Memoir of Despair and Discovery. Volume One:"

A Brave Glance into the Dark

If you are reading this book, if your eyes lingered even for a heartbeat on its title, then you have already taken a step of extraordinary bravery. You have dared to acknowledge a darkness inside you; a quiet ache, a shadowed whisper, a heaviness so many bury beneath silence and pretending. You have faced the murmur that tugs at your edges, the hollow echo insisting that death might be the only doorway out. Hear me, gently and clearly: the courage it takes to simply acknowledge that whisper is immense, powerful, and profoundly human. This book is not a quick remedy, not a neatly wrapped self-help miracle, not a promise that peace will fall into your hands like sudden sunlight. It is a journey; raw, winding, and real. A journey I invite you to walk with me, from the trembling edge of oblivion to the tender, blossoming gardens of healing, hope, and the quiet beginnings of a life you may not yet believe you deserve. We will walk it together, my friend; step by trembling step, breath by fragile breath, until the path that once felt impossible becomes a way forward once more.

Roots Beneath the Abyss

My story does not begin on the night I nearly slipped beyond the veil of breath, nor at the edge of the abyss where my trembling feet once stood. No, its roots reach much farther back, into a childhood remembered not in full scenes but in jagged shards of sensation: sharp, stinging words that cut deeper than any blade I would later turn against myself, and the cold, aching absence of warmth where safety should have lived. It stretches through years shaped by relationships spun from betrayal and disappointment, each one tightening around me like a thread pulled too taut. It winds through a lifetime spent chasing scraps of validation in a world that often moved around me with a kind of indifferent hum; a world in which I felt painfully, devastatingly invisible. The breaking did not happen in a single shattering moment. It was slow. Quiet. Insidious. Erosive. Pain crept in like a vine curling around the trunk of a once-vibrant tree, winding tighter and tighter until the sunlight could no longer find its way through the leaves. Depression: that relentless, cunning thief, stole the color from my days, drained the laughter from my chest, replaced it with tears, and dulled every corner of the world into muted, lifeless gray.

When the Inner Voice Turns Against You

And as the world dimmed, another voice grew louder, the voice of self-criticism, sharp and merciless. What began as a whisper became a chorus, echoing through every thought, amplifying every imagined flaw, turning each misstep into a verdict. It convinced me, piece by piece, that I was not enough; never enough, and perhaps never would be. This is where the descent truly began, not in a single night of desperation, but in a lifetime of slow unraveling, a gradual fading of light long before I ever reached the doorway of the abyss. This was not a sudden plunge into darkness; it was a slow, deliberate sinking; a descent measured not in moments, but in years. A steady unraveling. A quiet erosion of light and hope hollowed me from the inside out until I became a vessel of echoes, drifting through my own life like a ghost wearing my skin. And then, inevitably, came the night. I remember it with a clarity that still chills my bones; the strange, unnatural calm that settled over me like a thin sheet of frost, numbing everything it touched. The cold, crystalline finality of a decision I believed was mine alone to make. The planning. The precision. The ritualistic preparation that felt almost sacred in its devastation, as though I were performing a dark liturgy only despair could teach. Every movement, every breath, every trembling step was a quiet inscription, a silent testament of how deeply I had fallen, how thoroughly hopelessness had threaded itself through the architecture of my bones. How thoroughly despair had rooted itself in my core.

Entering the Night to Take Back Its Power

I will take you into that night; not to sensationalize the pain, not to cast my suffering in dramatic light, not to drape trauma in shock or glorify anything; but to strip it of the power it once held over me. To reveal the truth that even in the most airless corners of the soul, where silence tightens like a noose, a stubborn spark can flicker; faint, trembling, but defiantly and wildly, impossibly alive; fiercely unwilling to die. I will share the raw, unvarnished agonizing truth of my suicide attempt and what followed, and the wreckage left in its wake. The physical destruction, the emotional shattering. The disorienting aftermath in which my own body betrayed me not by failing, but by surviving. The emotional aftermath that tore through me with a force more violent than the attempt itself. The brutal awakening to the reality and magnitude of what I had almost stolen from myself. The grief that came after, a grief deeper than the act, because it carried the weight of recognition. These details are painful. They are uncomfortable to sit with, even now. But they are necessary, because they reveal something profound: Even at the very lip of oblivion, when darkness leans in close and whispers and hums its final lullaby, life does not abandon us. Life still reaches for us. Sometimes gently, like a whisper brushing the edge of consciousness. Sometimes fiercely, like a hand grabbing us back from the precipice. But always, always, with hope. Hope that insists on breathing, even when we cannot. Hope that flickers in the ruins, refusing to die. Surviving that night was only the beginning. It was not deliverance; it was the first trembling breath after nearly drowning, the moment when the ocean spits you back onto the shore, and you lie there, stunned, battered, unable to fathom why you're still alive. The path toward redemption stretched out before me like a long, unforgiving road, riddled with unseen cliffs and unexpected storms, demanding a strength I did not yet believe I possessed. Physical recovery was merely the surface layer, a thin scab over a wound that reached into the marrow of my being. The real battle raged within; a daily, relentless wrestle to reclaim even a fragment of worthiness, to gather the shattered remnants of a life fractured by years, decades, suicidal ideation, and self-hate. It was in this raw, broken terrain that the Ten Pillars of Self-Love first began to take shape which we will cover in Volume Three. They were not gifted to me in moments of clarity or comfort; nor handed to me wrapped in wisdom or ease. They were excavated and unearthed slowly, painfully, like archaeological treasures buried beneath layers of ruin. They were carved from the debris of my collapsed self-esteem, chiselled from the places where I had believed myself unlovable, unworthy, unredeemable. Each pillar emerged as a vital stepping stone in the long, trembling journey back to myself; a testament to the quiet, transformative power that blooms when self-compassion and self-acceptance finally find room to breathe. Together, we will explore these pillars, tracing the tangled roots of self-hate reserved for Volume Two, unveiling the architecture of the inner critic, and learning how to cultivate the tender, fertile soil from which self-love can at last take root. This is where healing truly begins, not in the absence of pain, but in the brave, deliberate choice to rise from it.

Walking Straight into the Dark

This book will not turn away from the darkness. We will not skirt its edges or pretend it never existed. Instead, we will walk straight into it together; into the painful memories that once clawed at my ribs, the raw emotions that left me breathless, the suffocating self-doubt that threatened to swallow me whole. We will descend into the places where the air thinned, where hope dimmed, where I nearly disappeared beneath the weight of my own unworthiness. But this journey is not mine alone. Woven through these pages are the stories of others who have walked paths hauntingly similar to mine; souls who have tasted despair, who have stood barefoot on the jagged edges of their own breaking points, and who somehow, impossibly, continued to breathe. Their stories shimmer like constellations scattered across a night sky, each one a testament to resilience, forged with quiet strength, and the stubborn, miraculous will to keep living even when the world felt unliveable. These voices rise beside mine not to overshadow your pain, but to remind you of this unshakeable truth: you are not alone. Your suffering is real. Your story is worthy. Your heart deserves tenderness in every place it has been bruised. And no matter what has brought you to this moment, no matter how heavy the shadows or how fractured the path behind you. Healing is not a myth reserved for others. It is here. It is possible. It is already reaching for you. Together, we walk toward it.

No Fairy Godmother at This Ball

This is not a fairy tale wrapped in a neat pastel bow. There is no enchanted storyline here, no shimmering godmother descending in a swirl of stardust to turn my pumpkin-shaped life into a gilded chariot, no wand to transform my tattered dress (my wounded, threadbare soul) into something pristine and whole. Yes, there was a midnight ball in my story, but it was nothing like the ones whispered to children at bedtime. At my ball, the prince who waited for me was death itself; cold, patient, seductive. My dance was not a waltz across polished marble floors but a trembling, breathless sway between life and oblivion. And the glass slipper? Mine was shattered long before I ever had the chance to wear it. No, this is not a tale of "happily ever after." This is the brutal story of a woman, hopeless, unseen, and unraveling, sitting in the damp grass with whiskey on her tongue and pills in her palm, whispering to the night that the only ending she could imagine was her own. This is the story of ripping that tattered dress down to nothing but bare threads and then; with shaking hands, bleeding fingers, and a heart still beating out of stubbornness rather than hope, sewing a new one from scratch. I am not Cinderella. I am not Sleeping Beauty. No midnight ball saved me. No prince's kiss awakened me from the nightmare. It was work that saved me; relentless, grueling, soul-deep work. Facing my pain is what stitched me back together. Rebuilding myself from the inside out is what breathed life into the woman I would one day become. I am no fairy tale. I am a living documentary; raw, unfiltered, still unfolding before your eyes. My journey continues, a testament carved from bone and breath that healing is not a destination, but an ongoing revelation, a continual unfurling of the self. And yet, despite the darkness, despite the shattered glass and the long nights spent kneeling on the floor of my own despair, this journey is worth taking. It leads not only to survival, but to a life textured with purpose, alive with joy, and rooted in a deep, immovable self-love that no midnight strike could ever take away.

BEYOND THE THRESHOLD: A Journey of Hope and Healing

My Story: At the Edge of Oblivion

The chipped paint on the windowsill was cold against my cheek, its rough edges scraping my skin as if to remind me I was still here; still trapped in a body balanced precariously on the trembling edge of oblivion. Beyond the thin pane of glass, the town continued its quiet, indifferent hum; a soft, unbothered symphony that played on while I silently unraveled. No one heard the silent scream clawing its way up my throat. No one noticed the girl dissolving into dust. The air around me felt thick, dense, suffocating; almost viscous. Heavy with years of unshed tears, unspoken terror and pain, unanswered prayers, and the relentless gnaw of self-hate. I breathed it in like poison, letting it settle into the hollow spaces inside me until it weighed me down completely. I was at the very end of my rope. I could feel the rope of my life wearing thin, each frayed strand snapping one after another beneath the weight of exhaustion and despair, sending me spiraling into the dark below. Suicide wasn't a fleeting visitor in my thoughts. It was a cold, deliberate presence; an unyielding hand curled around my heart, whispering its seductive promises of release. It was the only steady voice in the room, the only certainty in a world that had grown unbearably sharp, unbearably loud, unbearably heavy.

The Slow, Quiet Breaking

And I remember, with a clarity that still chills me, the moment the darkness finally closed in. It didn't crash like a wave. It seeped in slowly, like water filling a sinking ship, rising inch by inch until there was nowhere left to stand. It wasn't one moment that broke me, not one betrayal or one disappointment. It was the accumulation of years of failures piled upon failures, of wounds that never healed, countless betrayals, of self-worth eroded grain by grain until nothing remained but raw, exposed bone. My spirit wasn't crushed in a single blow; it was worn away quietly, relentlessly, like a coastline devoured by the sea. The world around me blurred into a muted landscape of gray, stripped of warmth and color, stripped of wonder and joy. Beauty still existed; sunsets still burned, laughter still echoed somewhere; but I had become a soul too numb, too jaded, too hollow to feel any of it. Hope, once a vibrant flame that had roared in my chest, had dwindled into the faintest ember, a fragile, flickering thing trembling against the cold wind of my despair. And as the night tightened its grip around me, that ember struggled, fought, resisted, but even its faint glow felt too small to save me.

The Night I Crossed the Threshold

I crossed the threshold the night I attempted to take my own life. It is a memory suspended in that strange, liminal space where everything becomes both blurred and painfully sharp and vivid. A nightmare fractured into shards of sensation, each one glinting with terror, regret, and a grief so deep it defies language. I have spent years reconstructing that night and everything that led to it, in the gentle refuge of healing conversations with my sponsor, piecing together its broken fragments like a trembling archaeologist unearthing the ruins of her own soul. It lives inside me as a mosaic of anguish and regret; jagged, uneven, stitched with the golden thread of survival, a story I learned to piece together not to relive the horror, but to understand its shape, its origin, and its devastating logic. Even now, I approach that chapter of my life with a kind of sacred caution. It is a chasm I do not step into recklessly. Every revisit is a deliberate descent, my steps measured, my breath steady, as though I am walking the rim of an old volcano that once tried to swallow me whole. But still, I return.

Because that moment, that terrible, quiet crossing remains a pivotal part of this journey. It is the stark testament to how far despair had pulled me from myself, and an even more profound testament to the resilience that somehow, impossibly, endured beneath the rubble. A reminder of just how close I came to the final, irreversible edge, and how miraculous it is that I lived to stand on the other side and speak its truth.

Waking Into the Aftermath

Because miraculously, inexplicably, I woke up. I was alive. I had cheated death, or perhaps death had stepped aside and cheated me instead, leaving me stranded in the wreckage of a life I hadn't intended to keep. There was no cinematic gasp, no euphoric rush, no flood of gratitude, no triumphant return from the brink. Instead, I surfaced into a world disoriented, muffled by numbness, wrapped in a hollowness and emptiness so vast it felt otherworldly. The darkness hadn't loosened its grip or just vanished with my breath; it had simply shapeshifted. What once beckoned like release now loomed as an echoing void, a terrifying landscape I had no choice but to navigate. The immediate aftermath was a strange, unsettling, dissonant alchemy of emotions. A flicker of relief that my lungs still insisted on breathing, and a deeper, heavier despair at realizing how narrowly I had brushed against oblivion. I found myself suspended between two worlds: the one I had tried to leave and the one I was suddenly, jarringly thrust back into. And in that liminal space, I no longer knew where I belonged, or whether I belonged anywhere at all.

Learning to Choose Life Again

The road to healing did not arrive in a blaze or burst of radiant sunlight; it began in the dim, trembling hush of survival, with the slow, painstaking labor of gathering my shattered pieces and stitching them back together, stitch by trembling stitch, wound by stubborn wound. It was a pilgrimage across unforgiving, harsh, and unyielding internal terrain, littered with shadows that stretched long and heavy, with doubts that clawed at my ribs from the inside, whispering that I would never rise, never rebuild, never be whole again. Every step forward felt monumental, a small, hard-won triumph wrestled from the relentless undertow of the abyss that kept trying to drag me back into its cold depths. Working with my sponsor became the first lifeline strong enough to hold me. In her presence, the masks fell away. I could speak the unvarnished truth; the jagged, bleeding truth, without fear of being shamed or dismissed. I could face the demons that had driven me so dangerously close to the edge. And in that sacred space of honesty, I began the fragile, necessary work of reclaiming myself, piece by piece, breath by breath, learning, for the first time, what it meant not just to survive, but to slowly, hesitantly, choose life again.

Forged in the Fire

The healing wasn't a clean ascent; it was anything but linear. There were days, entire aching weeks, when the darkness slithered back to my feet, curling around my ankles, tugging me toward the abyss I had barely escaped. Moments when self-loathing and my past actions rose like a tidal wave, sudden and merciless, pressing so heavily against my chest that even drawing breath felt like a betrayal of who I believed myself to be. Some nights, the shame was a living thing; sharp-toothed, coiled around my throat, whispering that I hadn't truly changed, that I hadn't climbed nearly as far as I hoped, that I was still one misstep away from collapse. The shadows knew my name intimately; they knew exactly where to strike. But through it all, I clung to the thinnest of lifelines and threads; the steadfast love of those who refused to abandon me, the fierce, unshakable belief my sponsor carried in her hands when mine were too weak to hold anything at all, and the quiet, stubborn whisper of hope that flickered deep in my chest, refusing extinction. Some days that whisper was barely audible. Some nights it was nothing more than a trembling spark at the edge of my breath. But it was enough. It kept me here. It kept me moving forward, however slowly, toward a life that, for the first time, waited for me rather than demanded my disappearance.

A Path That Leads Back to You

I began learning the language of self-compassion; haltingly at first, like a child sounding out unfamiliar syllables. It felt foreign, almost alien, as though I were trying to speak a dialect my heart had never been taught. But slowly, gently, I persisted. I learned to offer myself the tenderness I had long reserved only for others. Forgiving myself was another mountain entirely; a grueling ascent, steep and unforgiving, like scaling a cliff face with trembling hands and bleeding palms. Yet with every upward inch, with every ragged breath, I reclaimed a piece of myself I thought I had lost forever. I learned to confront the relentless internal critic that had lived rent-free in my mind for decades, that merciless tide of self-hatred and negative self-talk that rose without warning. I challenged it, questioned it, softened its edges until its roar dwindled into a whisper, then into silence. In its place, I planted seeds of gentler truths: *You are worthy. You are human. You are allowed to exist.* Slowly, those seeds took root. I learned to lean into vulnerability, not as weakness, but as a doorway. I cracked open the locked, dust-covered chambers of my past, allowing others to witness the stories I once believed would destroy me if spoken aloud. And in that opening, in that trembling honesty, I discovered something I never expected: Solace. Recognition. A homecoming among others who had walked roads paved with shadows and survived. In those shared truths, connection bloomed. In connection, healing began to weave itself quietly through the rubble. And through healing, steady, tender, miraculous, I found my way back to myself. This journey, as dark and harrowing as it was, became something profoundly alchemical. It burned away the illusions I had clung to, the masks I had stitched to my skin, the layers of self-deception I once mistook for armor. In their place, it revealed a quieter truth, the resilient, luminous core that had been buried beneath years of wounds, waiting patiently to be rediscovered. It taught me that self-love is not a luxury reserved for the healed; it is the lifeline of the broken. It is the sacred soil in which our strength takes root. And reaching for help; that trembling, terrifying act of opening one's palm to another, is not weakness, but courage in its purest form. This path revealed to me the extraordinary, life-altering power of vulnerability, showing how letting myself be seen, fully and without pretense, became the very thing that stitched my shattered pieces back together. It was in facing the monsters I once feared would devour me that I discovered the strength that had been quietly living within me all along; not loud, not dramatic, but steady, anchored, unwavering. In walking through the fire, I did not burn. I was forged.

A Lantern for You

Dear reader, if you are hearing these words and find yourself where I once stood, clinging to the precipice with trembling fingers, breath snagging in your throat, spirit quivering beneath the weight of what feels unbearable, please gather this truth gently into your palms: You are not alone. Not now. Not ever. There is hope, even if you cannot feel it yet. There is a way out, even if the path is still hidden in shadow. And hear this with the softness your heart deserves: You do not have to journey to the edge of death to claim your right to live. You do not have to brush against the cold veil of the abyss to begin healing. You do not have to break in order to rise. You are allowed, right here, in this moment, to turn your face toward the faintest glimmer of light. You are allowed to reach for help long before the darkness tightens its grip. You are allowed to choose life in the smallest of ways, a single breath, a single whisper, a single moment of willingness. Your healing does not begin with a grand gesture. It begins with this breath. This heartbeat. This quiet, courageous choice to stay. The journey ahead will not promise ease. It will stretch and challenge you in ways you never anticipated, ask you to touch the wounds you've spent years trying to outrun, and gently, sometimes painfully, uncover the buried ache you thought you had sealed away forever. But hear this, too: It will also be restorative. It will be breathtakingly beautiful. It will be a reclamation of your voice, your heart, your softness, and your strength. A homecoming to the parts of you that never stopped waiting for your return. As I share my story, it is not to center the darkness, but to hold up a lantern for you in your own. A quiet reminder that even the most fractured hearts carry a strength that borders on the miraculous. That even those who have crumbled beneath the weight of despair can rise, not in spite of the breaking, but because of it. The light at the end of the tunnel is not a myth. The rainbow gathering its colors behind your storm is real. It is waiting for you, patiently, gently, without conditions. So, loosen your grip on the rope that has burned your hands raw. Step back from the edge that whispers lies of finality. Turn your back on the door that leads only to endings. There is a path forward, not wide, not effortless, but undeniably there. A path that winds back to you, to hope, to healing, to self-love, to the quiet miracle of choosing life again and again. You are worthy of this path. You deserve every step of healing it offers. And you can reach it, with trembling courage, with imperfect breaths, with the simple, sacred truth that you are still here and that is enough to begin.

This isn't merely a collection of books; it is a warm, open-armed invitation, a lantern held aloft in the darkness, inviting you to walk beside me through a pilgrimage of spirit, a profound metamorphosis stretched across four living volumes. These pages are a sanctuary for the ones who tremble at the cliff's edge, for the souls whose knees buckle beneath the invisible weight of despair, depression, and the suffocating belief that they are irreparably lost. They are for the wanderers who feel the seductive whisper of death slipping through the corridors of their minds like smoke, coiling softly around the fragile architecture of their thoughts, day after day, night after unforgiving night. I know that whisper; not as a distant echo, but as an intimate presence that once curled itself into my ribcage and made a home behind my heartbeat. I have stood in those shadowed chambers of existence, where light seems like a myth, and hope feels like a forgotten language. I have felt the cold breath of oblivion brush the back of my neck, inviting me to surrender, to step across the threshold into the silent, seductive promise of "no more." I have tasted hopelessness; its bitter, metallic sting resting heavy on my tongue like poisoned honey, sweet in its deceit, deadly in its allure. But here I stand. Alive, Breathing, Bearing witness. I lived to tell the tale; not because the darkness loosened its grip, but because somewhere beneath the rubble of my breaking, a stubborn ember refused to be extinguished. That ember is what I now offer you. A spark. A compass. A quiet vow: You are not alone in the dark. This four-volume series is my story, but not merely a story written in ink, it is a tapestry woven from blood and breath, from the shattering and the stitching, from the nights I begged for an ending and the mornings I dared to rise anyway. It is a chronicle of my battles with life and death, of standing at the razor-thin edge between surviving and **truly living**, of drowning in despair and then; in the faintest, trembling way, learning how to let hope, breathe again. But this work is not just memoir; it is metamorphosis captured on the page. It is the echoing footprint of my descent and the luminous breadcrumb trail of my ascent. It is a compass forged in darkness, offering not only the truth of where I have been but the tools, teachings, and tender frameworks that led me back to myself, the very lifelines that awaken fully in the living heart of **Volume Three**.

Within these pages of the next four volumes, you will find the architecture of my healing, the pillars that steadied me when my legs shook beneath the weight of my own story, the gentle lanterns that lit the path from self-loathing to self-love, from brokenness to wholeness, from silence to voice. These words hold my truth; raw, unvarnished, unhidden, but they also extend a hand toward yours. A pathway. A promise. A quiet guiding light for anyone brave enough to take even a single step toward themselves again. For in the end, this series is not only about how I rose; it is an invitation for **you** to rise too. I divided *Surviving Death* into four volumes because the breadth, the depth, the **oceans** of this journey could never be cradled within the spine of a single book. Some stories are too vast, too heavy, too sacred to be confined; they must be **walked**, page by page, like a pilgrimage through shadow and flame. Across these volumes, we will travel together through the shifting landscape of my personal suicide story, a terrain carved by sorrow, sculpted by survival, where every valley holds an echo, and every mountain remembers the climb. You will come to know me not as an author, but as a **living wound stitched back together**, a soul who once unraveled thread by trembling thread. You will know the child I was, the woman I became, the ghosts that haunted my steps, and the crossroads where I chose, again and again, between breath and oblivion, and the long, grueling path of healing that followed. Volume One and Two is the **descent**. It is the underworld, the place where the lights flicker and fade, where suicidal ideation coils itself around the mind like a serpent whispering half-truths and poison lullabies. It is depression in its truest form; a drought of spirit, a famine of hope, a night so long it forgets the existence of dawn. Here, my past demons start stepping out from the shadows, not as monsters to be dramatized, but as truth-bearers. They introduce themselves one by one: The grief, the abandonment, the distorted mirrors I stared into for years. They speak their names, and in doing so, they become less terrifying, less powerful, less eternal. And this, dear reader, is where the magic of this journey first unfolds.

Volume One becomes a mirror

A reflective surface shimmering with hard truths and hidden wounds, inviting you, gently, and courageously, to look at your own shadows, to listen to what they have been trying to say, to trace the fingerprints of your pain back to the origins you were never taught to examine. Because only when darkness is named can it begin to loosen its grip. Only when we stand face-to-face with our inner demons do we learn that they are not infinite; they are simply unhealed. In Volume Two we meet more intense demons as we explore Self-hate and all its darkness and shadows. And so, as we move into Volume Three and Volume Four, you will not walk into healing as a stranger to yourself. You will enter as a warrior who has met their shadows, studied their shapes, and learned their language. From there, you will begin the sacred work, **the conquering, the reclaiming, the rising.** You will learn not only how to survive the darkness, but how to **invite the light back in**, how to rebuild a life that no longer hurts to inhabit, how to become your own safe haven, your own healer, your own dawn. Because this is not just my story.

Across these pages, it becomes yours too, a journey not downward, but upward, toward the life waiting patiently for you to return.

The Edge of Existence

I will share with you the events that carried me, sometimes gently, sometimes violently, toward the darkest chambers of my own becoming. I will guide you through the **timeline of ache**, through the earliest hairline fractures in my mental health that no one saw but that I felt splintering beneath my skin like cracks spreading across thin winter ice. I will walk you through the moments when the world demanded I be more, be better, be perfect, until the expectations of others pressed themselves against my chest like a thousand invisible hands, slowly suffocating the parts of me still trying to breathe. I will take you into the memories that shaped me, the ones that bruised my spirit long before I had the language to name the wounds. You will feel the slow stacking of traumas, stone upon stone upon stone, until the weight became a mountain I was expected to carry alone; a mountain that bent my spine and stole the light from my lungs. Each moment, each circumstance, each heartbreak and betrayal, became a small, silent nudge toward the abyss, a cumulative gravity pulling me closer to the edge where shadows speak louder than hope. And I will not shield you from the turbulence of my mind during those years. I will reveal the fear, the confusion, the sorrow that seeped through me like ink in water, spreading, staining, coloring every corner of my existence. I will speak my truth wholly, unflinchingly, without softening its edges or dimming its intensity. Raw, honest, wide open, because truth, when finally spoken aloud, becomes its own kind of medicine, the first cleansing breath after years of holding everything in. Only through truth can we begin to heal what has been festering beneath the floorboards of the soul. Only through truth can we turn the key and open the door to a life that no longer hurts to inhabit. This is where the unraveling begins, not to destroy, but to finally rebuild.

The Suicide Attempt

Here, I will recount **the day the darkness swallowed the horizon**, the day I attempted to take my own life. I will bring you into the suffocating hopelessness that wound itself around my ribs like barbed wire, tightening with every breath until even the act of inhaling felt like betrayal. I will speak of the despair that pressed against my chest with the weight of collapsing worlds, a heaviness so absolute my lungs could scarcely remember how to rise beneath it. I will walk you through the long, trembling pauses, the aching moments of hesitation when my soul hovered between wanting to stay and yearning desperately to disappear. I will guide you to the final, devastating choice I made, the moment my shaking hands carried out what my shattered heart believed was the only remaining mercy. This chapter will not be an easy one to hear. Its edges are jagged, its truths uncomfortably raw, its memories still echo through the hollow chambers of my chest. But it is essential, a key piece of the descent, necessary to understand the staggering height of the rise that followed. To speak of this night is to dismantle the suffocating shame that so often seals our stories beneath layers of silence. It is to declare that even the ugliest moments, the ones we fear will make others turn away, are worthy of being spoken, held, and witnessed. Within these pages lies the pulsing heart of my journey, a visceral testament to survival against the fiercest of odds. A reminder that even from the darkest underworlds, even from the ashes of near-extinction, a life can be rebuilt, slowly, painfully, but with breathtaking power. This is where the night breaks open. This is where the truth begins to breathe.

Awakening from Darkness: Standing in the Ruins of Myself

After the attempt, I was left standing in the ruins of myself, grappling not only with the raw, stinging wounds carved into my flesh and organs but with the **emotional and spiritual fallout** that clung to me like smoke after a house fire. It seeped into everything, my breath, my thoughts, the hollow ache of my bones. A haunting reminder that I had crossed a threshold few return from unchanged. In these pages, I will step with you into the aftermath, into the eerie stillness of waking on the far side of death's doorway. Surviving is not a simple gasp of air, nor a triumphant rising from the ashes. It is a bewildering, disorienting awakening into a life you had already said goodbye to. A life that now feels foreign, blurred at the edges, as though you are walking through the echo of a world you almost slipped away from. I will explore what it **truly means** to survive your own extinction, to open your eyes and find yourself still here, unexpectedly, unwillingly, held in the trembling balance between regret and possibility. It is to realize that life has handed you back the thread you tried to cut, and now you must decide what to do with it. In the days that followed, there were no epiphanies wrapped in golden light, no sudden bursts of clarity. There were only the **first fragile flickers of hope**, so faint they felt imagined, so delicate they trembled at the slightest breath. But flicker they did. Quietly. Persistently. Like tiny sparks glowing beneath a mound of cold ash, waiting for the gentlest touch of oxygen to coax them back into flame. Here, in this tender part of my journey, I began to encounter an idea that felt almost rebellious, a quiet, radical whisper of **self-compassion**. A concept so foreign to me, it was like reaching for a language my heart had never learned. But it was the first thread, thin, shimmering, impossibly soft, that guided me back to myself, back to life, back to the possibility that perhaps I was not beyond repair after all. This is the beginning of that return, the slow, sacred work of piecing together a soul that had almost slipped through its own fingers.

The Gravity of Suicidal Ideation

As I sit here, tracing the long and jagged contours of the path that delivered me to this moment, I am struck again by the **immense gravity** suicidal ideation can anchor to a human soul. It is not a simple sadness, not a passing storm. It is a *weight*, a dense, suffocating mass that settles into the chest like wet concrete, slowly hardening until every breath feels like a battle and every heartbeat a negotiation. That feeling of being lost, utterly, devastatingly lost, of standing at the frayed end of your rope while the noose of despair tightens with each trembling inhale, it is not metaphorical. It is visceral. It is a crushing, bone-deep heaviness that flattens thought, silences reason, and snuffs out even the most delicate flickers of hope. I know that sensation intimately. It built a home inside me once for a long, long time; a dark, echoing chamber where despair whispered its cruel, seductive lies into every hidden crevice of my mind. It curled around me like smoke, insidious and relentless, convincing me that I was alone, that I was beyond saving, that the world would exhale in relief the moment I disappeared. But through this long, grueling pilgrimage from death back into life, I discovered a truth I once could not even grasp: **I was never walking that darkness alone.** For every person swallowed by silence, countless others are breathing through the same ache, souls who have stood on shaking legs at the same unbearable edge, who have felt the shadowed weight pressing down, who are fighting, quietly, invisibly, yet fiercely, to stay alive one more hour, one more breath, one more heartbeat. And in that shared struggle, that unspoken kinship forged in the thick fog of suffering, there is *connection*. And in connection, in the simple, human knowing that our pain is mirrored in the hearts of others who still choose to rise, there is hope. A hope that glows softly at first, as faint as moonlight on a shuttered window, yet grows stronger with each acknowledgment, each truth spoken aloud, each moment we dare to reach toward one another instead of the abyss. This, right here, is the beginning of that reaching.

A Lantern for the Ones Who Stay

It is for this reason, for *you*, that I have written this book series, **Surviving Death**. These pages are not ink alone; they are blood, breath, bone-deep truth. They are a lantern held aloft for anyone who has ever felt the **cold sting** of death's tempting release brush against their skin like a winter wind, whispering of silence, of stillness, of an end to the ache that lives inside the ribs. These words are for the souls who have wondered if the pain of living is worth the relentless labor it takes just to draw another breath, for those who have found themselves adrift in a vast, indifferent ocean, the waves rising higher, the undertow pulling harder, the shore a distant dream dissolving on the horizon. They are for the ones who move through the world feeling unanchored, weightless in the worst way, like ghosts wandering through their own lives, seen but not known, heard but not understood, longing for something solid to hold onto as the storm inside them rages. And if you are one of these souls, if any whisper inside you has ever trembled with the words, **"I can't keep doing this,"** then hear me clearly: **This book is for you.** It is my offering laid gently at your feet, my hand reaching for yours through the thick, unrelenting darkness. It is my quiet, unwavering promise that you do not have to weather this tempest alone. Not anymore. Let these pages be the bridge between your isolation and connection, your despair and your rising, your fading will and the soft, persistent truth that your story is not finished yet. I am here. This book is here. And together, we will navigate this storm until the waves calm and your feet find the ground again.

At the Edge of Death

My journey began at the very **edge of death**, not a metaphorical edge, but the stark, trembling precipice where the darkness feels *total*, a place so lightless and cold it seems carved from the marrow of despair itself. It was a landscape stripped bare of color, a silent wasteland where even my own reflection felt like a stranger wearing my skin. There, at the rim of oblivion, the weight of simply *existing* pressed so mercilessly against my ribs that every breath felt like an act of defiance, a battle waged between my lungs and the void. I remember that hollow place, how desolate it was, how the air itself seemed to hold its breath, as though waiting for me to disappear. Hope had dwindled to a faint, quivering ember, so fragile I could no longer see it through the heaviness clouding my vision. I was convinced I had reached the end, that there was nothing left within me worth saving. And yet, in that cavern of nothingness, beneath the rubble of shattered dreams and the suffocating debris of self-hate, something, small, stubborn, impossible, stirred. Not a blaze. Not a surge of courage. But a flicker. A whisper. A single trembling spark hidden in the ashes of my unraveling. It did not roar with strength; it *persisted* in silence. It urged me forward in the softest of ways, a pulse, a heartbeat, a barely audible *stay* echoing from the deepest part of me. And in that moment, where I truly believed I had nothing left, I realized that nothingness can still cradle a seed, and even the smallest seed has the audacity to grow. That fragile flicker of will became the thread I clung to, the quiet force that kept me breathing when every part of me believed the battle was already lost. This is where my journey truly began, not in triumph, not in clarity, but in the raw, aching truth that survival often starts with the faintest whisper of resistance against the pull of the dark.

The Alchemy of Story

As I look back on my journey, I am struck, again and again, by the immense, alchemical power of **storytelling**. Stories are not merely words. They are the pulse beneath our skin, the quiet architects of our becoming. They are the invisible hands that sculpt us from the inside out, chiselling, shaping, softening, sometimes shattering, until we emerge as something new, something truer, something forged in the fire of all we have endured. The stories we whisper to ourselves in the dead of night, when no one else can hear, carry the weight of worlds. They become our mirrors, our prisons, our wings. Some stories cradle us gently, wrapping us in warmth like a familiar blanket. Others slither through our minds like serpents made of shadow, poisoning our breath, rewriting our worth until we can no longer remember who we were before the darkness rewrote the script. And then there are the stories we dare to speak aloud, the trembling confessions, the cracked, unsteady truths we release into the world like fragile birds hoping they will not fall. These spoken stories are the ones that begin to free us, thread by trembling thread, from the narratives that once held us captive. It is **these** stories, the raw, unvarnished ones, the ones that taste like salt and survival, the ones that burn with truth and glimmer with the faintest ember of rebirth, that I want to share with you, dear reader. Not the polished tales we offer strangers. Not the rehearsed versions we recite to appear whole. But the real ones, the ones that left marks on my skin and echoes in my bones. Because it is in the sharing of these jagged, honest stories that healing begins. Yours and mine. Together. And so, I place these stories before you, not as answers, but as lanterns. Lanterns carved from my own darkness and lit with the small, steady flame that survived against all odds. May they illuminate the path before you as they once illuminated mine.

Graveyard and Garden

My story is not an easy one to tell. It is a tapestry woven with threads of anguish, stitched together by trembling hands that once believed they would never hold anything beautiful again. It is a story etched in bone-deep sorrow, forged in the molten fires of struggle, tempered in the cold iron of despair. Yet beneath the ash, beneath the ruin and the ruin *beneath* the ruin, something else lived, a pulse, a whisper, the faintest flutter of life that refused to be extinguished. My story is a graveyard and a garden. It is the place where I buried every version of myself that could not survive the storm, and the place where new roots took hold in the soil made rich by everything I once mourned. It is a story of hope, fragile at first, like a butterfly emerging from a torn cocoon, wings trembling, unsure if they would hold. But then, fierce. Defiant. A wildfire, catching in the hollow places and burning its way toward sunrise. It is a story of healing that rose slowly, stubbornly, from the rubble of a life that had collapsed around me. Healing that did not arrive gently but clawed its way upward, painfully, insistently, from the very wounds that once threatened to devour me whole. It is the story of how I stood at the threshold of death, felt its cold breath against my neck, tasted its quiet seduction on my tongue, and still, somehow, found my way back to the land of the living. But more profoundly, it is the story of how I found my way back to *myself.* To the woman buried beneath decades of sorrow, the girl I abandoned in the shadows, the soul who waited patiently for me to remember her name. This is not just the recounting of survival. It is the chronicle of a resurrection; messy, imperfect, breathtaking, a reminder that even the most broken heart can learn to beat again.

To the One Holding This Book

As I sit down to write this book, my heart becomes a vessel brimming with a tender alchemy, sadness, yes, for the versions of me that never made it this far, gratitude, for the hands and hearts that steadied me when I couldn't stand, and hope, soft but luminous, like the first pale thread of dawn slicing through a night that once felt endless. The journey that carried me from the very lip of death back into healing, and eventually into something far more than survival, has not been a gentle one. It has been long, winding, and at times so excruciating I thought the pain itself would swallow me whole. But it is *mine*, a pilgrimage carved into the marrow of who I am, and I am profoundly, fiercely proud to place it in your hands. If you are reading these words, it means that somewhere within you a question trembles, a wound aches, a flicker of fear or longing has stirred enough to bring you here. Maybe you are wrestling with suicidal ideation yourself, that quiet, merciless beast that curls around the edges of your thoughts and whispers its cold invitations. Or maybe you love someone who is fighting that invisible battle, someone who walks through the world with a storm raging silently behind their eyes. Whoever you are, whatever pain brought you to these pages, I want you to feel this truth not just in your mind, but in the deepest chambers of your being: **You are not alone.** You have never been alone. Even in the bleakest hours, even when your breath trembles and your hope feels like a dying ember, there is a thread, thin as spider silk, yet impossibly strong, that ties you to tomorrow. There *is* hope for a softer dawn. There *is* a path that leads out of the darkness, winding though it may be, and one tender step at a time, gentler days will begin to unfold before you like petals coaxed open by morning light. You are here. Breathing. Reading. Reaching. And that simple, sacred fact means your story is still being written, still alive, still becoming, still capable of shifting in ways more beautiful than you can yet imagine. Stay. Lean in. Your next chapter is waiting.

A Lighthouse Carved from Scars

This book series stands as a testament to the wild, stubborn resilience of the human spirit, a lighthouse carved from my own scars, its beam slicing through the thickest fog of despair to reach anyone wandering blind through their own midnight wilderness. It is a beacon, yes, but not one polished or pristine. Its light flickers with truth;

raw, trembling, unvarnished, illumination born not from triumph alone, but from every moment I shattered on the floor of my life, every breath that burned my chest as I clawed my way back up, every whispered prayer I did not believe, and every sunrise I survived by accident. These pages hold a story that once nearly ended, a story that began at the very edge of death and somehow, impossibly, stitched its way back into a life rebuilt with intention, tenderness, and meaning. A life I once believed I was too broken to deserve. And if you are reading now, it is likely because some thread of your own darkness vibrates in recognition. Because you, too, have felt the cold breath of despair curl against your spine. Because you know the weight of waking up with a heaviness so dense it feels as though it might swallow you whole. I know that ache intimately. I have tasted its bitterness. I have drowned under its tides. I have felt its hands closing around my throat as it whispered that relief lived only in endings. And yet, I am here. And now, tender soul, so are you. So let this truth settle softly in your chest, like a warm hand pressing over your trembling heartbeat: **You are not alone. Not now. Not in this moment. Not in any moment to come.** These books are more than a memoir. They are a lantern placed gently into your palms, an invitation to walk beside me through the lands where pain once reigned, and to witness how the human heart can bloom again in the very soil where it once withered. Together, we will descend into the shadowed caverns of my past, not to glorify the darkness, but to understand it, to name it, to dismantle its power piece by piece. And together, we will climb toward the light, toward possibility, toward wholeness, toward a life textured with meaning, alive with gentleness, anchored in self-love. This is an invitation to rediscover yourself. To reclaim the fragments you thought were lost. To breathe into the possibility that healing is not a myth reserved for others, but a birthright waiting quietly within you. This book series is my offering, my outstretched hand, my whispered promise in the dark: **There is a path forward. And you do not have to walk it alone.**

What This Journey Taught Me

This journey taught me the **fierce, unrelenting power of self-love**: Not the soft, syrupy kind sung in greeting cards, but the radical, warrior-like love that drags you out of bed on the days you want to disappear, that whispers *"not yet"* when darkness calls your name, that rebuilds you brick by trembling brick until you stand again on ground you once thought impossible to reach. It taught me the liberation found in forgiveness, forgiving others, yes, but also forgiving *myself*, which was the hardest absolution of all. For how do you forgive the version of you who tried to end your own life? How do you offer grace to the person inside your skin who believed you were unworthy of breath? But healing demanded it. Self-love required it. And little by little, with tenderness that felt foreign at first, I learned to cradle my own wounded heart instead of condemning it. And then came redemption; not as a sudden sunrise, but as the slow, steady glow of light returning to a long-abandoned room. It was the rediscovery of joy in places I once believed were hollow. It was the quiet miracle of feeling worthy of belonging, of laughter, of life. This is why I say, with reverence in my bones: I would not trade my journey. Because without the suffering, I would not know the depth of compassion I now hold. Without the darkness, I would not recognize the brilliance of my own light. Without the near-death, I would not understand the sacredness of surviving. My wounds became teachers. My scars became scripture. My survival became a calling. And it is my deepest, most fervent hope that this journey, every bruised chapter, every resurrected breath, will inspire you to keep moving forward, even when the path ahead feels unclear, even when the night seems endless. Because I promise you this: You have more strength within you than you dare to imagine. More resilience than your wounds would have you believe. More light than your darkness has ever acknowledged. Keep going. Even if you must crawl. Even if all you can manage is one breath, and then another, and another still. The fact that you are here, reading these words, proves one irrefutable truth: **Your story is not over. Your heart is not done. And you; beautifully, inexplicably, are meant to live.** Surviving death wasn't the end of the story; **not even close.** It was the quiet flick of a match in a room I thought would remain dark forever. It was the beginning of a new chapter, a trembling rebirth, an unexpected invitation to rewrite the narrative of my life with hands that once believed they were unworthy of holding a pen. What followed was not a graceful ascent into the light. It was a pilgrimage through the wilderness of my own becoming, a long, uneven journey over landscapes scarred by trauma, through valleys of despair and across deserts of numbness, guided only by a faint, flickering star of possibility that refused to extinguish itself, no matter how often the winds of self-doubt tried to smother it. Yes, the journey was arduous. It scraped me raw. It tore apart the illusions I once clung to for survival and demanded that I rebuild myself from the ashes of who I used to be. But it was also **profoundly, breathtakingly transformative**, a metamorphosis not unlike the caterpillar who disintegrates completely inside the cocoon, never knowing that losing its very shape is precisely what allows it to fly. I share my story not as a banner of triumph waved from the mountaintop, but as an act of solidarity, a lantern held out in the night, its light trembling yet unwavering, so that someone else wandering through their own shadows might recognize the faint echo of their own heartbeat in mine. This is a testament to healing, messy, nonlinear, beautifully imperfect healing, and to the enduring, stubborn, rebellious power of hope that roots itself in the soul even when everything else feels barren. If you are struggling, if darkness has pressed its cold hand against your chest, if your breaths feel tight and shallow like they are fighting for space in a body that no longer feels like home, **please hear me: You are not alone.** There are hands ready to hold yours. There are hearts willing to listen. There is help. There is hope. And there is a life beyond the hurt you are carrying now, a life that can still bloom, softly at first, then fiercely, like wildflowers breaking through the cracks of stone. Recovery is possible, not in one sweeping leap, but in the gentleness of choosing yourself one breath, one step, one trembling moment at a time. Your life is precious. It matters deeply. It ripples outward in ways you cannot yet see. And most importantly: **It deserves to be lived. You deserve to be here. You deserve to stay.**

Walking Beside You

Before we begin this journey together, I want to place something sacred in the palms of your hands, a message woven from light, soft but unbreakable: **hope.** A message shaped from my own survival, forged in the quiet embers of hope that refused to die within me. I want you to feel it settle in your chest, warm as a candle cupped against the wind, steadfast as a heartbeat that refuses to surrender. I want you to know; not as a distant idea, but as a truth that rises through your bones, that you are **not** alone. Hear me now, not just with your ears, but with the tender, trembling places inside you that have forgotten what it feels like to be held by truth: You are not alone. Not in your aching. Not in your exhaustion. Not in the shadowed corners where your thoughts have learned to whisper their quiet, devastating doubts. Not in the painful hollow of your chest where hope feels like a distant memory. No matter how dark or shadowed the road appears from where you stand, no matter how narrow, twisted, or merciless the terrain. No matter how dense the fog, how silent the night, or how heavy your spirit feels, there is **always** a way forward. Even when you cannot see it. Even when the horizon is swallowed by fog. Even when your knees hit the ground and your hands tremble from carrying a weight that was never meant to be carried alone. A path that may begin as nothing more than a faint shimmer on the horizon of your despair, but which grows brighter with every trembling step you choose to take. You are worthy of love, not the conditional kind that flickers and fades, but the deep, steady, soul-anchoring love that sees your scars, your softness, your storms, and calls you precious because of them, not in spite of them. You are worthy of respect that does not vanish when you falter. You are worthy of a life that does more than force you to endure, a life that opens like a sunrise, pouring gold into the cracks of everything you thought was ruined. Worthy of being met with gentleness, with kindness, with the kind of tenderness that reminds your weary heart that it was never meant to walk this earth bearing burdens alone. And you are deserving; fully, inherently, irrevocably deserving, of a life that is not merely survivable, but rich and textured, a life that tastes of joy and ease, that hums with meaning, that offers you mornings soft as sunrise and nights that do not end in tears. A life filled with breath and beauty, layered with meaning, and textured with the quiet, sacred warmth of contentment that whispers, "You are safe now. You belong here." And here is the truth, the radiant, revolutionary truth, that your pain has tried to bury beneath its heavy hands: Within you lives a quiet, extraordinary power, the power to shape the life you long for, to rise even when your knees tremble, to keep going even when the road bends sharply into darkness, to meet every challenge with a strength you may not yet recognize as your own. It may be a faint ember now, glowing beneath the ash of exhaustion, but it is there, a flame waiting for breath. But it is yours. It has always been yours. You are capable of far more than your pain has ever allowed you to believe. You carry galaxies of resilience within you, oceans of courage, whole constellations of possibility waiting for the moment you dare to look up and notice that the sky above you has been waiting to guide you home. This is where our journey begins, with hope in your hands, light in your chest, and the quiet knowing that you are meant for so much more than suffering. You have the capacity to rise, to defy the gravity of despair, to step forward even when your legs tremble under the weight of yesterday. You carry a strength inside you that you may not yet recognize, a wild, resilient, astonishing power that has survived every storm you never thought you'd endure. Your pain has lied to you. It has whispered that you are weak. It has convinced you that you are broken beyond repair. But hear this truth, clear and unwavering: You are capable of far more than your suffering has ever allowed you to believe. Ahead of us lies a journey, not of perfection, but of becoming. And you, dear soul, are already far stronger, far braver, far more extraordinary than you know. Let us begin. Thank you for choosing to walk this journey with me. Thank you for stepping toward these pages, toward *yourself*, with a bravery you may not yet recognize as sacred. My hope, tender and luminous as a candle held in cupped hands, is that in hearing my story, you will begin to feel the faint stirring of your own. That somewhere between the lines you will discover the courage to start loosening the grip of old wounds, to whisper forgiveness into the places that ache, to let your heart soften in the spots where it has hardened to survive. I hope you will begin to love yourself, not the polished version, not the perfected illusion, but the real, breathing, trembling you who wakes each morning carrying both the weight and the wonder of existence. You deserve that tenderness. You deserve compassion that wraps around you like a warm shawl on a night when the world feels too sharp, too loud, too heavy to hold.

You deserve grace that lands softly upon your shoulders, light as a feather yet powerful enough to shift the story you've been telling yourself for years. And as you begin this unfolding, as you inch your way toward healing at your own pace, with your own breath, in your own beautifully imperfect rhythm, I want you to know this with absolute certainty: **I am honored to walk beside you.** Honored to witness your becoming, honored to share the path with you as you rise from the ashes of everything that once convinced you that you were unworthy of love. We will walk this sacred road together, you and I, step by trembling step, heart reaching toward heart, each of us learning, again and again, that even in our most fractured moments, we are still worthy of gentleness, still worthy of healing, still worthy of a life touched by light. Let us continue.

Constellations of Survivors

I also want to share with you some of the stories of others who have illuminated my path. These stories are constellations, small, brilliant stars scattered across the night sky of my healing, guiding me when I could not yet guide myself. They are not merely stories of surviving; they are stories of **rising**, of souls who lifted themselves from the rubble of their pasts and learned not just to stand, but to stretch, to unfurl, to bloom. They are stories of **expansion**, of hearts that once beat in broken rhythms and somehow found the music again. Stories of individuals who stepped out of the shadows and into a future vibrant with color, possibility, and breath. These are tales etched with courage, quiet courage, trembling courage, courage that does not roar but instead whispers, "I will try again, even if all I can manage today is one small step." They are tales not just of overcoming adversity but of leaning into life with arms wide open, of choosing joy even with scars still tender, of discovering purpose in places once carved out by pain. Their voices have been lanterns along my journey, soft, steady flames that refused to flicker out when my own light dimmed. They have inspired me, strengthened me, and shown me that healing is not merely a retreat from darkness, it is a **pilgrimage toward light**. A life rich with meaning. A life abundant with color. A life where hope is not a distant dream, but a companion walking faithfully beside us. And as I share their stories with you, I hope they become lanterns for your path as well, glimmers of possibility, proof that even after devastation, life can grow back in ways more beautiful and astonishing than you ever imagined. Let us gather these stories like sacred seeds ... and let them root something new within you.

You Are Not Weak; You Are Fighting

As I stand on the threshold of sharing my story, I want to place in your hands a quiet, steady ember of hope, a small, glowing truth you can carry with you into the darkest corners of your night. I want you to feel, not just understand; but **feel**, that you are not alone. There are hearts in this world that beat for you, souls who would gather around your trembling spirit like guardians encircling a flame, protecting it from the wind. There are people who care for you with a depth you may not yet fully see, people who want to witness you stay, who want to watch your story unfold, who want to see you rise into the fullness of everything you were always meant to be. And hear this truth as it settles into your bones: **Suicidal ideation is not a sign of weakness.** It is not a stain, not a flaw, not a failing. It is evidence of an internal battle so immense, so consuming, that most will never understand its magnitude. It means you are standing face-to-face with shadows that would make others crumble. It means you are wrestling with your demons instead of hiding from them. It means you are fighting for your life even on the days when you swear you no longer want it. There is a fierce, quiet courage in confronting the darkness within. A courage that does not shout or boast, it simply endures. It breathes through the shaking. It whispers through the tears. It keeps you alive even when you believe you have nothing left to give. You are not broken. You are **brave**. You are not failing. You are **fighting**. You are not invisible. You are **here**, a living, breathing testament to a strength that has carried you farther than you may ever fully comprehend. And that matters more deeply, more profoundly, more beautifully than you may ever know. You are here. And because you are here, there is hope. There is possibility. There is a future still waiting to be shaped by your hands, your breath, your resilient, unyielding heart. You are not alone, my friend. Not now. Not ever.

Healing Is Possible

And I want to leave you with this truth etched gently, tenderly, irrevocably into the soft chambers of your heart: **Healing is possible, redemption is possible, living, truly living, is possible.** Returning to yourself, to the self you abandoned, to the self you forgot, to the self you believed was unworthy of light, **is possible.** Learning to love yourself, to cradle your own trembling soul with compassion instead of criticism, with gentleness instead of judgment, with tenderness instead of shame, **is possible.** The road ahead may feel steep, your footing unsure, the terrain uneven and harsh beneath your feet. There will be days when your knees will quake, when your breath will falter, when the shadows will try to lure you back with their familiar ache. But hear me: **This journey is worth taking.** It is a pilgrimage of becoming, a sacred crossing from emptiness into fullness, from collapse into rising, from survival into expansion. It is a path that calls forth a courage you do not yet recognize, a strength that has always been yours, a resilience that has quietly held you together even as you thought you were falling apart. And though the road winds, though it twists through valleys of grief and climbs mountains of old, lingering pain, it also leads somewhere breathtaking: Toward a horizon rinsed in gold. Toward mornings that taste like possibility. Toward a future stitched with meaning, alive with purpose, and shimmering with a joy that once felt impossible to imagine. There is a life waiting for you, a life lush with laughter, softened by peace, rooted in worthiness, and blooming with deep, wholehearted love. You are capable of reaching that life. More than capable. And my dear soul, you deserve to. Not because you have suffered. Not because you have survived. But because you exist. Because you are human. Because you are here. And that alone makes you worthy of every beautiful horizon still ahead of you.

An Invitation to Live

So, I invite you, dear reader, **to step onto this sacred path with me.** Not as a passenger trailing behind, not as a shadow lingering on the edges, but as a companion, a fellow traveler with a pulse full of yearning and a heart still brave enough to hope. Let us walk this road, **side by side**, hand in trembling hand, through the thick forests of memory and the caverns of old, unspoken sorrow. Let us wade together through the places where night once swallowed us whole and feel the first shy warmth of a new dawn blooming on our skin. Let us turn our faces toward the light that waits patiently for us, even when we cannot yet see it, even when its glow feels far away, even when our hearts flutter with doubt as fragile as moth wings. Let us gather our courage, not the loud, unbreakable kind, but the tender, trembling bravery that rises *despite* the fear. Let us confront our ghosts honestly, calling them by name, watching their shadows loosen as truth pours over them like morning sun. And piece by piece, breath by breath, memory by memory, let us reclaim the parts of ourselves we once believed were scattered beyond reach, the softness, the strength, the wonder, the wildness, the worth. Let us choose to live, not merely to survive, not to drift through the days like echoes of who we once were, but to live **fully**, deeply, unapologetically. Let us choose to love, ourselves first, gently, fiercely, as though we finally understand that our hearts were always worthy of tenderness. Let us choose to thrive, to outgrow the boxes built by pain, to stretch toward joy like flowers breaking through stone, to claim our place in the world with open arms and an awakened soul. This is the beginning of our becoming, the moment the earth shifts beneath our feet and whispers: *Start here. Start now.* And I am profoundly, humbly honored to walk every step of this unfolding path with you.

You Were Never Meant to Carry This Alone

As we walk this winding road together, **there is one final truth I want to place gently in your hands,** a truth soft as dusk light on tired skin, steady as a heartbeat finding its way back into rhythm: **You are not alone.** I know it does not always feel that way. I know how isolation can grow around you like a fortress built from cold stone, thick, unbreakable, echoing with the sound of your own breath and no one else's. I know how loneliness can masquerade as destiny, how it can whisper with such convincing intimacy that you begin to believe you were born to walk through this world unheld, unseen, untouched. But hear me, here, in this moment: Loneliness is not a life sentence. It can dissolve, sometimes slowly, like frost beneath morning sun, sometimes all at once, with the warmth of a single hand reaching back toward yours. There *are* people who care for you more deeply, more fiercely, than your wounded heart has been able to comprehend. Souls who want you here. Souls who want to help you heal. Souls who would sit with you in the dark until your breathing steadies and the shadows loosen their grip. And beyond those hearts, there are resources, real, tangible lifelines, waiting to meet you exactly where you stand. They are the lamps left burning in windows for travellers lost in storm and nightfall. They are the voices on the other end of the line, steady and gentle, ready to guide you back toward solid ground when your world feels like it is collapsing beneath you. You do not have to shoulder this weight alone. You were never meant to. The ache you carry was never designed to be held by a single set of trembling hands. Let others hold part of it with you. Let connection seep back into your bones the way rain soaks into dry, cracked earth. Let yourself be supported, be cared for, be seen. Because healing does not happen in isolation. It happens in the spaces where your pain meets compassion, where your truth meets understanding, where your breath synchronizes with another's until you remember what it feels like to be part of something larger than your suffering. You are not alone, dear one. Not in this moment. Not in the ones to come. Not ever.

There Is Help. There Is Hope

If you are struggling with suicidal ideation; if you feel *lost*, unmoored, adrift in a vast and merciless sea of despair, then I want you to gather these words close and let them echo through the deepest chambers of your heart: **There is hope.** I whisper it. I speak it. I declare it with the full force of my own reborn breath because it matters. Because *you* matter. Because your life, your beautiful, aching, unfinished life, deserves the chance to unfold into something softer, brighter, more spacious than the pain that grips you now. There is help available to you, not theoretical help, not vague promises drifting like smoke, but **real, palpable, human help**, hands ready to reach, voices ready to steady, hearts ready to hold space for every trembling truth inside you. There are people who will walk into your darkness without fear, without judgment, without hesitation, carrying lanterns of compassion that can illuminate the very places you thought were beyond saving. You do not have to face this night alone. Not this one. Not any of them. Reaching out, even with shaking hands, even with a voice barely more than a breath, is not weakness.

It is an act of stunning courage, the first brave ripple in a tide that can shift your entire world. One conversation. One moment of honesty. One whisper of "I need help." And the ground beneath you can begin to steady, the storm inside you can begin to quiet, the impossible can begin to feel, just slightly, beautifully possible. Your life is not over. Your story is not finished. This moment, this very one, could be the doorway where everything begins to change. So please, dear reader, if you find yourself standing on the same trembling edge where I once hovered, or before the same shadowed doorway I nearly stepped through, do not wait in silence. Do not let the darkness convince you that you must navigate its terrain alone. Reach out. Even if your hands are shaking. Even if your voice is barely a whisper. Even if all you can manage is a single word held together by the thinnest thread of hope. Ask for help. Cry out for it. Let someone, anyone you trust, step toward you with their light when yours feels too faint to find. Because you, beloved soul, are worthy of love that meets you gently and holds you with reverence. You are deserving of compassion that softens the wounds life has carved into you. You are deserving of tenderness that sees your pain and does not look away. You are worthy of a life that does more than merely exist, a life that *means* something that expands with purpose, that fills your chest with warmth instead of ache. A life where your presence matters in ways you cannot yet imagine. You matter. Your heartbeat matters. Your existence, right here, right now, ripples outward in ways unseen, touching lives, shaping futures, altering the world simply because you breathe. So, hear this, not as a line in a book, not as a passing comfort, but as a truth thundered from the depths of my lived experience straight into the center of your being: **YOU ARE WORTHY OF LIFE. YOU ARE WORTHY OF THE BREATH IN YOUR LUNGS. YOU ALWAYS HAVE BEEN. YOU ALWAYS WILL BE.** Even when you cannot feel that truth, even when your mind insists otherwise, even when despair shouts louder than hope, this truth endures. Unshaken. Unconditional. Unchanging. You are worthy. You are needed. You are loved. And the world is infinitely better for the simple, sacred fact that you are still here.

The Glory of Rising

And as you step into this journey, as you gather your courage like a lantern cupped between trembling hands, I want to leave you with one final offering, a fragment of wisdom that once held me together when I was unraveling at the seams. It is a quote that traveled with me through the hollow nights when sleep would not come and hope felt like a language I had forgotten: **"The greatest glory in living lies not in never falling, but in rising every time we fall."** — Nelson Mandela These words were not just ink on a page for me; they were a lifeline, a warm pulse of truth in a world grown unbearably cold. They reminded me that to be human is to stumble, to break open, to collapse beneath the weight of heartbreak and exhaustion and despair. We all falter. We all shatter. We all, at times, lose our way in the labyrinth of our own pain. But none of this, **none of this**, is what defines us. What defines us is the rising. The quiet, trembling choice to gather the splintered pieces of ourselves and stand again, even when our knees still quake from the last fall. The sacred courage to draw one more breath when the air feels heavy as stone. The fragile willingness to reach toward love even when our hearts still bear the bruises of old wounds. The decision whispered or shouted or cried, to keep living even when life has shown its sharpest edges. Because every time you rise, you rewrite the ending. Every time you stand again, you defy the darkness. Every time you choose hope, even in its smallest flicker, you tilt your life gently toward the light. So, hear this deeply, let it echo in the marrow of your bones: No matter how many times you fall, **you can rise.** You can choose life. You can choose healing. You can choose hope. You can choose to thrive, not because the journey is easy, but because the strength within you is far more powerful than you've ever been allowed to believe. Rise, dear one. Rise as many times as it takes.

The Descent into Darkness: A Quiet Battlefield.

My life was always a battleground; not the loud, cinematic kind lined with explosions and visible scars, but the quiet, internal kind, where the wounds bleed inward, and the enemy wears your own face. From the outside, my childhood appeared ordinary, even enviable, a neatly framed picture that looked whole only because no one dared to touch it. But just beneath that polished glaze lay a landscape cracked with fault lines, a tender earth seeded with doubts and insecurity that would one day grow into forests of fear. Those early seeds were planted subtly, almost innocently, a careless word here, an unmet need there, moments so small they almost slipped through memory. Yet they burrowed deep, curling their roots around the soft architecture of who I was becoming, shaping me long before I ever understood what was happening beneath the surface. In this section, I will begin unraveling those threads, the specific moments, the relationships, the subtle betrayals, and the glaring wounds that carved themselves into my spirit. Each one was a strand in the tapestry of despair that grew heavier, denser, darker with every passing year. This part of my story is tender and exposed, a raw recounting of how my self-worth, once delicate, once luminous, was slowly eroded grain by grain, like a shoreline swallowed by a relentless tide.

When the World Began to Close In

The pressure to achieve, the terror that any misstep would shatter the illusion of "enough," the fear of abandonment curling around my heart like a cold, serpentine whisper, the crushing weight of expectations, spoken and unspoken, all of it accumulated inside me until I could no longer distinguish where the world's demands ended and my own self-contempt began. Life began to feel like a shrinking room, its walls inching closer each day, the air thinning until even breathing felt like a dangerous luxury. And in that tightening space, the thought of ending it all slipped in quietly at first, a fleeting shadow, a whisper from the corner of my mind. But whispers have a way of growing when the heart is tired, and the soul is starved. The murmur thickened, strengthened, became a constant companion, a dark hum vibrating beneath every thought, every breath. Until one day, it was no longer a suggestion but a roar, a deafening, merciless summons I could no longer outrun. This is where the descent truly began. Where the silent fractures of childhood grew into gaping wounds. Where the world, once bright with possibility, dimmed into muted greys and then into nothing at all. And it is here, at the threshold of that roar, that my story turns toward the unthinkable, and the journey of surviving it begins. My story begins in a place steeped in darkness and despair, a landscape where shadows clung to me like a second skin, and the air itself felt heavy with sorrow. I had always been a tender soul, porous and soft, a creature who felt the world too deeply, as though my heart had been crafted without the usual layers of armor meant to protect others from life's sharper edges. Every disappointment pierced me. Every loss bruised me. Every unkind word left an echo that rang far longer than it should have. And as the years unfolded, the weight of life's challenges began pressing against the fragile perimeter of my mind, not all at once, but slowly, insistently, like waves wearing down a shoreline grain by fragile grain. I felt lost, unmoored, my sense of self slipping like sand through trembling fingers. Aloneness settled over me not as a passing feeling, but as an atmosphere, dense, suffocating, like being trapped beneath deep water with no upward direction, no surface in sight. I wandered through days as though submerged underwater, hearing the world in muffled tones, seeing it through distorted ripples, unable to call for help because the ocean pressing on my chest stole every word before it could leave my mouth.

The emotions inside me were vast, an endless ocean without a single island, a storm-tossed sea with no horizon line. I could not name the pain. I could not map the tangled ache that wound through my mind like a thorned vine. I only knew that the suffering was immense, consuming, demanding more of me than I had left to give.

The First Whisper of Wanting to Disappear

And it was in that suffocating stillness, where hope felt like a distant rumor, and my breath grew shallow beneath the weight of despair, that suicidal ideation first took root. Not as a scream. Not as a violent intrusion. But as a whisper, quiet, treacherous, deceptively gentle. A longing that curled around the edges of my mind like smoke seeking a crack beneath a door. A thought that flickered with the dangerous promise of an ending, a release, a quieting of the agony I could no longer bear. In those moments, death did not appear as an enemy, but as a strange, seductive mercy, a soft place to fall when every other place in my life had turned to stone. This is where my story truly begins, in the quiet, deadly cradle where despair plants its first seed, and where I first felt the cold, beckoning sting of wanting to disappear. I remember the day I attempted to take my own life as vividly as if it were pressed into yesterday's skin, a bruise the world could not see but one I still feel throbbing beneath my ribs. It wasn't a gentle fading, nor a quiet surrender to the night. It was a desperate, wordless cry, a primal scream flung into an endless void that swallowed every syllable whole and offered nothing back but a hollow, echo-less silence. It felt as though I had been standing on the edge of a cliff for years, toes curled over the precipice, and on that day, the ground beneath me finally crumbled. I didn't fall, I let go. But even in that surrender, life, stubborn, uninvited, clawed its way back through my lungs. As I lay there, my breath fractured into jagged fragments, my body fought with a ferocity I no longer believed I possessed. It battled for me when I could not battle for myself, drawing air into lungs that had screamed for release, pulling me back inch by inch from the very brink of oblivion. And in that liminal space between here and gone, something inside me shifted, not loudly, not dramatically, but with the subtle tremor of a truth finally uncloaked. I realized that I did not truly want to die. I wanted the pain to die.

Wanting the Pain to End

I wanted the suffocating weight that had bent my spine for years to be lifted. I wanted the numbness to thaw, the emptiness to fill, the soul-death that shadowed every day to loosen its grip at last. My life felt devoid of life, a hollow vessel moving through motions it could no longer feel. So death appeared not as an ending, but as the only door left unsealed, the only exit from a world that had stopped making room for my breath. But the deeper truth, the one I could not see through the fog of despair, was this: I did not want to stop living. I wanted the life I was living to stop hurting. I wanted the version of myself that had been swallowed by trauma, shrink-wrapped by shame, and silenced by years of internal warfare to be returned to me. I didn't want death. I wanted healing, but I no longer believed healing was mine to claim. I didn't want an ending. I wanted a beginning, but I could not imagine one that included me. I believed, with devastating certainty, that I was beyond reclaiming, beyond repair, that the darkness had become my home and I was fated to vanish into it. But even as that belief coiled around my heart, my body, miraculous, rebellious, alive, refused to let me go. And that refusal became the faintest beginning of my return. My journey to healing was anything but easy. It was not a gentle unfolding, not a soft sunrise warming the edges of my shattered world. It was a pilgrimage into the underworld of my own being, a descent into the cavernous, unlit chambers of my soul where every fear, every wound, every buried truth waited like ghosts I had spent years refusing to face. Healing demanded that I walk barefoot across the jagged ruins of my past, that I sit in rooms thick with the echoes of every moment I had tried to forget. It required me to press trembling fingers against the pulse of my insecurities, to peel back the armor of my defenses and stare directly into the face of the self-hate that had sculpted my life into something small, suffocating, and sorrow-shaped. It demanded honesty, the kind that stings like salt in an open wound. It demanded stillness, the kind that forces you to hear the parts of yourself you've long silenced. It demanded courage, a courage I did not yet believe I owned. I had to unearth every buried memory; every shadow I thought would devour me. I had to unravel the tight, tangled knots that had held my heart hostage for decades. And with each step deeper into the darkness, with each truth finally spoken aloud, something unexpected, almost miraculous, began to stir. In the very place I feared I would be destroyed, I found the first faint glimmers of transformation. Self-love, a concept that once felt unreachable, abstract, reserved for others, revealed itself not as some sweeping epiphany, but as a quiet, steady warmth blooming deep within the cracks of my brokenness.

Forgiving Myself to Stay Alive

Forgiveness came next, soft as a breath, yet powerful enough to shift the ground beneath my feet. Not forgiveness for others, that would come later, but the excruciating, tender grace of forgiving myself. For surviving. For breaking. For hurting. For becoming lost. For being human. And then, slowly, hesitantly, redemption stepped forward, not as a shining promise on a distant horizon, but as something present, near, possible, a living, breathing reality waiting for me to claim it when I was ready. Through the hardest work I have ever done, through tears that sculpted rivers into my cheeks, through nights where my healing felt like a battlefield, through days when I carried hope like a fragile ember cupped in trembling hands, I uncovered a truth I once believed was meant for everyone but me: Healing is possible. Not just for others. For me. For you. For anyone brave enough to step into their own darkness and trust that the journey will lead them home again. In this part of my story, I will recount the suicide attempt, not to sensationalize it, not to gild the agony with theatrics, not to cast the moment in anything but its stark, unvarnished truth, but to open a door that has stayed locked inside me for far too long. To speak plainly, vulnerably, about the mental landscape that carried me to that precipice, a terrain shaped by despair so dense it felt like walking through a storm of ash with lungs too weary to draw breath. I tell this not to disturb you, but to help you understand the inner machinery of a mind pushed past its limits, a heart crushed beneath layers of grief, a spirit so threadbare it could no longer hold its own weight. And before we cross that threshold together, I want to pause here, with tenderness, with reverence, with the deepest respect for your heart. This chapter is heavy. It carries edges sharp enough to reopen old wounds and shadows deep enough to stir the ones still healing or still in darkness. So, I offer this clear, compassionate warning: please move forward with care. If at any moment the words begin to feel too loud, if the memories they evoke press too tightly against your ribs, if you notice your breath growing shallow or your thoughts becoming tangled, stop. Rest. Place a hand over your heart and remind yourself that you are here, that you are safe, that you are allowed to protect yourself. Step away if you need to. Reach out to someone who steadies you. Anchor yourself in a sound, a scent, a sensation that brings you back into your body. Or skip ahead entirely, because your safety, your emotional grounding, your well-being matter far more than any chapter I could ever write. This story is important; yes, but *you*, are infinitely more important. Only continue when your heart feels ready, when your breath is steady, when you can walk beside me through this darkness without losing sight of your own light. We will tread carefully here, together.

The Quiet Beginning of Healing

The aftermath of that night unfurled like a long, trembling exhale, a haze of pain, regret, and a crushing sense of failure that clung to me like smoke after a house reduced to embers. My body, battered but stubbornly alive, struggled to remember how to function, how to breathe without flinching, how to move without feeling the echo of my own undoing. But it was not the physical wounds that cut deepest. No, it was the invisible fractures, the emotional and psychological shards lodged beneath my ribs, that pulsed with a relentless ache. I did not simply wake up injured, I woke up *broken*. Not just bruised, not simply shaken, but convinced that something essential within me had shattered beyond repair. A kind of soul-fracture, silent, internal, yet devastating in its reach. It felt as though I had crawled back into the world carrying the weight of my own ashes, a ghost clutching the remnants of a former self, uncertain of how to breathe life into a body that no longer felt like home. How do you rebuild when you no longer recognize the pieces? How do you rise when you are convinced your story should have ended? And yet; beneath the ruins, beneath the grief, beneath the shame that wrapped itself around my throat like a cold, unyielding hand, something stirred. A whisper. A tremor. A thread of warmth woven into the rubble. The journey toward healing did not announce itself with trumpets. It did not sweep in with sunlight or certainty. It began quietly, almost imperceptibly, like a single blade of grass forcing its way through cracked concrete, soft and stubborn and wildly alive. It began with the smallest shift, the faintest flicker of willingness, the tiniest moment of surrender to the possibility that maybe, just maybe, this was not the end of my story. In the hollow aftermath of devastation, while the dust of that night still clung to my skin, healing, timid, tentative, trembling, took its first breath. And so, did I.

Chapter Three:
The Awakening of the Ash: Phoenix as Living Metaphor.

These four volumes mirror the ancient journey of the Phoenix, not as myth, but as the living, breathing metaphor for every human soul that has ever crumbled into dust only to discover, somehow, that the dust still remembers how to rise. This is not a fairy tale of flame and triumph; it is the intimate story of what it means to burn, to break, to become unrecognizable even to yourself, and then to slowly, painfully, miraculously reconstitute from the very ashes that once felt like your ending. And so, Volume One and Two begins at the first sacred stage: **the Awakening of the Ash**, the hallowed moment after collapse when everything familiar has already been reduced to soot and silence. It is the moment when the old self has died, yet the new self has not yet found its wings. A liminal space, a breath held at the threshold of becoming, where the remnants of who we were still cling to our skin like smoke, and the shape of who we will become hovers just beyond sight, tender, trembling, embryonic.

The Awakening of the Ash is not beautiful. It is raw. It is disorienting. It is the moment you realize that your former life has collapsed around you like a once-mighty cathedral reduced to rubble and yet, somewhere in that brokenness, a tiny spark refuses to die. It is the heartbeat after the storm. The breath after the scream. The flicker of warmth in the ruin that whispers: "*This is not the end. This is the beginning of the beginning.*" Here, in these pages, we step into that sacred aftermath together, into the ashes still warm from the fire, into the quiet where your soul first begins to whisper its way back into existence. This is where the rising truly begins.

Stage One: Collapse

This is the stage of collapse, the moment when the architecture of your life caves inward, when everything you once leaned on buckles beneath the unbearable weight of accumulated pain. It is the season of ruin, where identity disintegrates like old parchment touched by flame, curling inward, flaking away until only the barest outline of who you were remains. Here, in this ashen landscape, you are reduced to the raw, exposed remnants of a life scorched by trauma, swallowed by despair, and ground into dust beneath the relentless pressure of every heartbreak you have ever carried. This is the place where you find yourself not simply broken, but hollowed. A ghost wandering the ruins of your own body. A being who once breathed light now lies silent beneath a blanket of gray. In this stage, hope feels like a foreign language, one your heart no longer remembers how to speak. You feel useless, hopeless, unworthy, as though the world would be unchanged, perhaps even relieved, if your light finally guttered out. You look at the rubble of your life and think, "*Nothing can grow here. Nothing living could ever rise from this.*"

But hear this truth whispered beneath the debris: **collapse is not death.** It is the trembling prelude to transformation. For even in this darkest chamber of becoming, beneath the soot and the ruin, something ancient and sacred stirs, a flicker of instinct, a seed of resilience, the faintest pulse of a soul not yet finished. This stage is not your ending. It is the quivering beginning, the first inhalation after the long, suffocating silence, the moment the ashes shift, signalling that somewhere within the wreckage, a new self is gathering breath. Here, in the wreckage, the rising prepares to begin.

Ash as Cradle of Rebirth

For the ash does not only signify death, but it is also the oldest cradle of rebirth. It is fertile, sacred, and strangely tender, holding within its gray, silenced chambers the hidden nutrients of transformation. In the stillness of that ruin, when the world has gone quiet, and even our own heartbeat feels foreign, something ancient stirs. A whisper barely loud enough to notice. A flicker trembling at the edge of awareness. The faintest glow gathering beneath the soot, as if the remnants of our spirit refuse to surrender to the dark. In these pages, we are still prone on the ground, not rising yet, not ready to stand, but breathing the first tentative breaths after the collapse. We lie there surrounded by what once was, our hands shaking as they sift through the rubble of our former selves. Every shattered piece carries a story. Every grain of ash holds memory. Every remnant is an invitation to look closer, to listen deeper, to feel the quiet truths we once buried. And here, in this raw, unguarded landscape of ruin, we begin the slow, reverent search for what survived the fire. The fragile ember of hope, still glowing beneath the wreckage.

The quiet pulse of life nudging us toward one more breath. The first soft spark of self-love so delicate it almost dissolves when held too tightly. This is the awakening. The moment the ashes shift. The moment the dust inhales. The moment something inside us stirs with the audacity of becoming. This is where the ashes begin to breathe.

Volume Three: Ignition

In Volume Three, we rise into Stage Two, the **Ignition**, the sacred fire that stirs the Phoenix awake. If Volume One and Two is the kneeling in ash, the hushed sifting through remnants of who we once were, then Volume Three is the moment the spark inhales...and catches. It is the first flare of warmth after a lifetime of cold. The tremor of light finding its way through cracks we once believed were fatal. It is where the ember we uncovered beneath ruin and rubble is finally given breath, a trembling exhale that becomes a flame. Here, self-love does not arrive as a roar. It flickers first, testing the air, uncertain whether it is welcome. But slowly, almost shyly, it grows into a fire that warms rather than wounds, that illuminates rather than exposes, that softens instead of shames. This is where we begin to turn inward with curiosity instead of condemnation, with tenderness instead of fear. We learn to meet ourselves not as the threat we spent years fleeing, not as the adversary carved from our own self-loathing, but as a soul who has waited so patiently to be known, to be held, and to be loved. Here, the fire no longer devours us. It **refines** us.

It melts the old armor we once mistook for safety. It softens the rigid edges of shame that cut us every time we dared to feel. It loosens the knots of guilt that kept our hearts bound in silence. And in that alchemical heat, something luminous awakens, the Phoenix buried beneath our ruin, stretching within the flames, discovering at last that the fire we feared was always the fire meant to free us. This is the ignition. The rising heat. The first true stirring of rebirth.

Fire That Clarifies

In these chapters, we step out of the familiar labyrinth of self-destruction and into the tender, trembling realm of **self-discovery**, a territory as raw as exposed skin, as sacred as the first breath after near-drowning. The spark we unearthed in the ashes begins to swell into a rising glow, a soft but persistent blaze that stretches its light into the dark corners we once feared to face. This glow does not demand. It invites. It beckons us gently to witness the quiet architecture of our becoming, to explore the landscape of who we truly are beneath the soot of old stories and discarded selves. Here, the first pulse of rebirth begins, the subtle lift of wings still heavy with ash, the trembling unfurling of feathers that have never before felt wind. This is the moment when the fire shifts from punishment to purification, from torment to transformation. It is not a blaze that consumes. It is a flame that clarifies. Volume Two is the dawn after the longest night, the horizon blushing open with new possibility, the first streak of gold cutting through years of suffocating gray.

This is the fire that does not burn us down; it burns us **open**. It softens the shell we once mistook for protection, melts the walls we built to survive, and reveals the luminous marrow of the Phoenix within. Through these chapters, the Phoenix does not rise in triumph all at once. It rises slowly, deliberately, through smoke and trembling breath, claiming its beginning not with a roar but with a vow: "*I am not finished. I am still becoming. I rise.*" And with that vow, the journey toward true rebirth begins.

Volume Four: Full Unfurling

And then, at last, we arrive at **Volume Four**, the **full unfurling of the Phoenix**, the moment the horizon cracks open beneath the sweep of wings we once believed were too damaged to ever lift us. This is the chapter where everything changes. Here, the wings we doubted, those tattered, trembling remnants of our former selves, finally stretch into their true span, revealing their hidden iridescence, and their quiet, astonishing strength. The fire that once merely kept us alive now rises through us, becoming the very force that **elevates** us. This is where power returns to the bones. Where breath becomes ease, not effort. Where the flame no longer licks at our wounds but crowns us with purpose. In these pages, we meet ourselves not as the wanderer collapsed in the ash, nor as the timid spark struggling to ignite, nor even as the half-born creature testing the weight of new wings. We meet ourselves as the Phoenix **in full ascension**, luminous, liberated, and sovereign. Here, we rise in a blaze of unapologetic truth. We rise with feathers dripping light, with hearts no longer cowering but expanding. We rise with memories behind us and possibilities ahead.

This is the stage where survival transforms into *soaring*, where healing becomes *embodiment*, and where the life we once thought impossible unfurls before us like a sunrise we have finally grown worthy to witness. Volume Four is not the end of the story. It is the sky opening. It is the world welcoming. It is the Phoenix; (**you**), no longer learning to rise but rising.

The Ascent into Forgiveness

In this final stage, we lift ourselves through the last curling trails of smoke, ascending from the ghost of our former life into the vast, uncharted sky of becoming. Here, we step boldly, heart trembling, wings shimmering, into the sacred, tender terrain of **forgiveness**. Not the simple kind. Not the kind spoken lightly or granted without cost. But the deep, bone-carving forgiveness that unravels the chains we forged around our own spirit. The forgiveness of others, yes, but even more profoundly, the long-awaited, long-feared forgiveness of *self.* This is the moment the soul loosens its grip on old narratives of failure and fault. The moment shame begins to melt like frost under sunrise. The moment the inner critic, that relentless architect of our suffering, finally falls silent, its voice dissolving in the warmth of a love we once believed ourselves unworthy to receive. Here, in this luminous ascent, the fragile embers of self-love begin their holy transformation into a steady, sovereign blaze. A fire that no longer flickers with uncertainty but stands rooted, unwavering, fully aware of its own brilliance.

This blaze does not ask for permission to exist. It does not apologize for its glow. It expands. It claims space. It knows its worth with the quiet confidence of a soul that has descended into the underworld and returned carrying its own light. In this stage, we do not simply heal; we liberate. We reclaim the parts of ourselves we once abandoned in the shadows. We become the Phoenix that not only rises but recognizes the power in its own rising.

Learning the Art of Flight

Volume Four is where the journey into the new truly begins, the place where the Phoenix does more than awaken, it learns the art of flight. This is where we discover that rebirth is not a single, blazing moment, but a daily devotion, a ritual of returning to ourselves again and again, choosing our own spirit with each sunrise. Here, we learn that healing is not a destination we stumble upon, but a vow whispered into each tender dawn: I choose me today. In these pages, we craft our new life with ink distilled from the ashes of our past, not to glorify what burned, but to honor what endured. Every stroke of the pen becomes a quiet resurrection, each sentence a flight feather growing from the wings we once believed were beyond repair. We write with the quill of hope, the nib gleaming with promise, dipped into the shimmering gold of possibility. And as the ink touches the page, it sings with the resonance of a life reclaimed. Here, we hold the fire of self-love aloft like a torch, not as a fragile ember we guard with trembling hands, but as a flame burning bright and sovereign, radiant enough to banish the last lingering shadows from the corridors of our becoming.

This torch guides the Phoenix within us, reminding it of its own splendour, its right to rise, its right to flourish, its right to soar free of the ruins that once held it captive. In Volume Four, we do not simply rise from the ashes. We do not merely rebuild what was broken. We take flight, wild, luminous, and unapologetically alive.

Ash, Fire, Flight

And so, as the tetralogy of your becoming unfolds, the story of the Phoenix reveals itself in its entirety: *ash, fire, and flight!* These four volumes are not separate wanderings, not isolated chapters scattered across the landscape of your life. They are one sacred arc of transformation, a holy trinity of rebirth whispered through the marrow of your soul. They are the heartbeat of a single, breathtaking journey: The **falling apart**, the **burning awake**, and the **rising into the fullness of who you were always meant to be**. Volume One and Two is the collapse, the sacred disintegration where the old self crumbles and the world dims into gray. It is the descent into the ashes, where everything familiar dissolves so that the truth beneath may finally be seen. Volume Three is the spark, the ignition of your inner fire, the moment the ember hidden beneath layers of sorrow draws breath and begins to glow. It is the chapter where pain reshapes itself into wisdom, and the flame that once threatened to consume you becomes the fire that refines you. And Volume Four; ah, this is the sky itself opening.

This is the unfurling of wings once clipped by despair, the glorious lift of your spirit as you rise through smoke, through memory, through shadow, and ascend into the golden expanse of your truest self. Together, these volumes form the arc of a soul remembering its power, a spirit reclaiming its purpose, a human being stepping into the luminous architecture of their rebirth. This tetralogy is not just a story you read. It is a story you **live**, a living map of your own transformation, guiding you from the ruins of who you were into the radiant horizon of all you are becoming.

Honouring the Ash

Volume One and Two teaches us to honour the ash, to kneel beside the remnants of what once was and whisper into the quiet ruins, "*I survived this.*" It invites us to press our palms into the soot of our own history, to feel the texture of what has burned, to sift through the dust of old wounds as though searching for sacred relics buried beneath the wreckage. Here, we gather the scattered fragments of the selves we abandoned along the way, the forgotten child, the silenced voice, the tender heart we once believed too fragile to protect. We lift each shard with trembling reverence, recognizing them not as evidence of failure but as proof that we endured what once threatened to unmake us. Volume One and Two is the consecration of ruin, the moment we stop turning away from our pain and dare, for the first time, to truly *see* it. To name it. To trace its edges without flinching. It is the holy pause between destruction and rebirth, the breathless space where healing begins to stir the instant, we summon the courage to face what hurt us. For in honouring the ash, we are not worshipping what burned; we are acknowledging the indestructible spirit that survived the fire.

Volume Three is where the fire learns our name, and, for the first time, speaks it with tenderness. Here, the flame that once devoured us returns as a teacher, a sculptor, a sacred alchemist. It does not burn to wound, but to reveal. To melt the old armor fused to our skin, to soften the rigid scaffolding of shame that kept us small, silent, and hidden. This is the hearth-fire of self-discovery, a slow and intimate ignition where self-love flickers to life like a dawn unwilling to be rushed. The embers that once crackled with threat now glow with warmth, reminding us that the burn we feared was, in truth, a blessing in disguise, the necessary heat that softened what had grown too hardened to heal. Volume Three is the moment the Phoenix within stirs beneath the soot and feels the first flutter of wings, remembering their purpose. It is the awakening of curiosity where condemnation once lived, the reclaiming of breath where silence once suffocated, the dawning realization that the fire was never our enemy; it was the threshold to our becoming. And then comes Volume Four, the sacred horizon of ascension, the place where wings remember themselves completely. Where the trembling creature in the dust rises into its own brilliance, glorious, unbound, and finally free.

Here, the Phoenix rises in full, sovereign flame, not as the trembling creature clawing its way out of ruin, not as the ember fighting for breath beneath the soot, but as the radiant, untameable being forged *through* every blaze it survived. This is the volume of release, the soft exhale after a lifetime of holding breath. The gentle unfurling of wings, no longer shackled to yesterday's grief. The moment the fire that once consumed becomes the fire that consecrates. Here, forgiveness becomes a sacrament. Not the kind bestowed lightly or spoken in passing, but the deep, marrow-deep absolution that loosens the chains around the heart, link by aching link. This is the quiet, revolutionary act of unburdening the soul, of setting down the stories that kept us small, the echoes that haunted our sleep, the self-blame that wrapped around our ribs like a tightening band of iron. In this sacred space, we begin to breathe differently, slowly, freely, without the ghosts of yesterday pressing their fingerprints into our lungs. The Phoenix stands tall here, not despite the fire, but because of it.

Every scar reframed as scripture, every wound rewritten as wisdom, every ash-softened memory woven into the tapestry of a being finally, irrevocably whole. This is the rising. This is the reclamation. This is the chapter where we learn, at last, what it means to live unencumbered, to breathe without trembling, to shine without apology. In this final ascent, we do not cast away the ashes or pretend the fire never touched us. We gather them gently in our palms, letting their charcoal softness stain our fingertips, a reminder, a testament, a sacred pigment for the stories we now dare to write. The ash becomes ink for our new chapters. The fire becomes fuel for the light growing steadily in our chests. And the ruin we once feared becomes the very soil of our resurrection. Volume Four is the dawn that arrives after the night we thought would never end, that tender, trembling moment when the horizon blushes gold as if the whole sky is exhaling in relief.

It is the soft unfurling of a self finally met with tenderness instead of torment, a self no longer bracing for impact, no longer living in apology for simply existing. Here, we step into the world not as fragile survivors clinging desperately to breath, but as beings who know, deeply, fiercely, unshakably, our worth. Our power. Our right to take up space, to live freely, to love ourselves without hesitation. This is the realm of full becoming, where the wings we once doubted carry us higher with every beat. Where the fire that almost destroyed us becomes the very force that teaches us to soar. And in this rising, yours, mine, ours, we discover the quiet, luminous truth that has been pulsing beneath every page, waiting for us to hear it: We were never meant to stay in the ashes. We were meant to rise from them, brilliant, burning, and beautifully reborn.

The Sacred Spiral of Becoming

And so, as the arc of these four volumes curls inward and outward like a sacred spiral, a fuller, more luminous picture reveals itself, not a tale of mere endurance, but of **metamorphosis** in its most primal, soul-deep form. From the soot-covered remnants of **Volume One and Two**, where we lay exhausted and fractured, our hands trembling as we sifted through the rubble of our own becoming, where we finally dared to whisper the names of our wounds and acknowledge the shadows that shaped us. To the awakening fire of **Volume Three**, where the ember we unearthed in the ashes began to quiver back to life, a tender flame rising from within, soft but insistent, burning away the old narratives and warming the frozen chambers of the heart. To the triumphant ascension of **Volume Four**, where the Phoenix, forged by ruin and refined by fire, unfurls its wings in a blaze of sovereignty, radiant, unbound, and boldly alive. Each volume is not a separate story, but a single, breathtaking continuum, one journey, one evolution, one sacred transfiguration. Ash, Flame, Flight. These are not stages we pass through once; they are the eternal rhythm of the soul learning to live again. The falling apart, the burning awake, the rising higher, all threads of a single metamorphosis that carries us from who we were to who we were always meant to become.

These volumes are not four isolated tales scattered across the landscape of a life; they are *one long inhalation of becoming,* drawn through different seasons of the soul. Each holds within it a distinct facet of the Phoenix that lives inside every human heart: First as **ruin**, then as **fire**, and finally, magnificently, as **flight**. Together, they create a sacred cartography of healing, a map inked in ash and flame and luminous dawn-light, guiding us from the crumbling collapse of who we once believed ourselves to be, through the searing dissolution of all that no longer serves our becoming, and into the courageous unfurling of the self we were always destined to rise into. For healing is not a single spark of revelation, it is a **pilgrimage**, a long, spiraling journey back to the marrow of who we are. It is the slow gathering of the fragments we once abandoned, the tender reclaiming of parts we thought were gone forever, the sacred remembering of our own name spoken beneath the noise of pain. It is a rising, not once, but again and again, each ascent carrying us a little higher, a little closer to the truth: that nothing within us was ever truly lost, only waiting to be rediscovered.

ARCHITECTS OF OUR OWN Rebirth

By the time we cross the threshold into **Volume four**, something within us has shifted irrevocably. We are no longer bent over the ashes, sifting through remnants of what once was with trembling, desperate fingers. We are no longer whispering prayers into soot, begging for a pulse. Here, in this luminous final arc, we become *architects* of our own rebirth. We begin to shape a new life with deliberate, sacred hands, each gesture infused with the wisdom earned from every wound we've endured. We write our days with the ink of everything that nearly broke us, a dark, shimmering pigment rich with memory and meaning. We walk guided by the very fire we once feared would consume us, a fire that now illuminates rather than destroys, awakens rather than annihilates. We come to understand, with a clarity sharp as sunrise, that our scars are not tombstones of defeat, but ancient maps carved into flesh, pathways leading us, unerringly, toward rebirth. This tetralogy is the full evolution of the inner Phoenix, **the ash that humbled us, the flame that remade us, the flight that frees us.** It stands as living proof that no darkness is absolute, no past too heavy, no ruin too final.

Rebirth is not a myth. It is a pulse, a promise, a possibility humming beneath every breath you take. And as we rise, again and again, through collapse, through fire, through the breathtaking miracle of becoming, may we carry this truth etched like gold into the marrow of our being: **You were never meant to merely survive your fire. You were always meant to rise from it.**

Chapter Four
The Prelude

From Darkness to Dawn: A Journey of Healing and Hope

Dear Reader,

I invite you now to step onto this sacred road with me, a road carved from the rubble of my darkest nights, a road that glimmers faintly with the promise of light by the closing breath of Volume Four. These books are not merely chapters bound in paper and ink; they are a lifeline woven from the remnants of my ruin, a rope braided from ashes, courage, and the stubborn heartbeat of hope. Every sentence carries the smoke of what I survived and the shimmer of who I became in the rising. As I open the intimate chambers of my story to you, it is my deepest prayer that each word becomes a lantern in your hands. soft, steady glow guiding you through the twisting corridors of your own becoming, illuminating the shadows, warming the cold places, revealing the path toward healing, toward self-love, toward a life that is not borrowed or endured but wholly, fiercely reclaimed. No matter how lost you feel, no matter how invisible the world has made you, no matter how heavy the ache that sits behind your ribs, there is always a glimmer of hope waiting to be found.

Sometimes it hides like a firefly in tall grass, sometimes it flickers faintly like a dying ember, but it is there, alive, patient, and yearning to be seen. And together, step by trembling step, breath by tender breath, we will search for it. We will follow its glow until it becomes a flame strong enough to warm your hands, bright enough to guide your steps, and sacred enough to remind you that you were never meant to walk through the dark alone.

The Edge of Despair

I will take you into the depths of my despair, into the shadowed corridors where my thoughts curled and contorted, where reason dissolved, and the walls themselves seemed to breathe with the faint, merciless echo of *you will never escape.* In that dim, disorienting labyrinth, every corner felt like a dead end, every turn a collapse deeper into myself. And as you walk with me through those narrow passageways, you may begin to feel the soft tremor of recognition, a fragment of your own ache glinting inside my words. The loneliness that feels like a second skin. The weight that sinks its claws into your chest, dragging your breath slow and heavy. The quiet terror of believing there is no exit, no dawn, no hand reaching back for yours. The kind of hopelessness that stains the air you breathe and convinces you that your suffering is endless. Together, we will not run from these emotions nor pretend they are smaller than they are. We will sit with them, honestly, bravely, acknowledging the full force of their presence: their power, their grip, their suffocating heaviness. But as we witness them, we will also remember this truth etched softly beneath their roar: They do not define us.

They are chapters, not our identity. Storms, not our destiny. Weather passing through, not the climate of our souls. And side by side; your heartbeat beside mine, your courage echoing my own. We will learn to rise beyond them. To step out of the labyrinth. To breathe where there is air again. To walk toward a horizon that was waiting for the moment you dared to believe that you were meant for more than just surviving the dark.

The Threshold of Life and Death

Here, I will bring you to the precipice with me, to that impossible, trembling edge where life and death stood shoulder to shoulder, their breath cold against my skin, their shadows intertwining across my bones. It was a moment suspended outside of time, a razor-thin threshold where every heartbeat felt like a countdown, where the air itself seemed to hold its breath, waiting to see which way I would fall. I will recount that night, not for spectacle, not to drape my suffering in drama, but to unveil the truth of the unbearable weight that carried me there. The pain that grew so heavy it pressed the world out of focus. The exhaustion that hollowed me out from the inside. The quiet, relentless ache that whispered, "*there is no other way*". I will show you the split-second surge of terror that rippled through me at the final moment, the instinctive gasp, the primal recoil of a soul not meant to slip into the dark. I will show you the staggering truth that rose within me like a flare in the midnight of my mind: I did not truly want to die. I wanted the suffering to end.

I wanted the noise to quiet, the agony to loosen its grip, the emptiness to stop echoing inside my chest. I wanted relief, not erasure. Release, not disappearance. Rest, not death. And on that thin, merciless edge, where my life hung by the softest thread, I learned something I could never have known without first standing in the mouth of the abyss: The desire to stop *hurting* is not the same as the desire to stop *living*. It is a truth as fragile as breath, yet powerful enough to pull us back from the brink, a truth I will carry with you now as we continue this journey into the hardest places, and toward the light that waits beyond them. This chapter may press against tender places within you. It may sting, it may tighten the breath in your chest, it may stir shadows you thought you'd buried long ago. But it is essential, not because suffering must be relived to be understood, but because this moment marks the fault line where everything began to shift. This is the threshold where despair, long unchallenged, begins to fracture.

Where the seemingly unbreakable wall of hopelessness develops its first quiet crack. Where the darkness, once absolute, once all-consuming, meets its earliest tremor of surrender. To understand the rise, we must first honour the fall. We must be willing to look at the broken places not as evidence of failure, but as the sacred ground from which rebirth will one day emerge. Think of this chapter as the dimmest hour before dawn, a space heavy with silence, yet humming with the first invisible threads of change. Transformation does not arrive with trumpets. It begins as a whisper, a soft pulse beneath the rubble, a single ember refusing to die. And so, we will walk through this part of the story together, not recklessly, not without tenderness, but with slow, careful steps. With gentleness for the wounds reopened, with reverence for the truth spoken, and with the understanding that facing the fall is the first act of rising. Take my hand. We will not linger here forever. But we must walk this stretch of the path, for it is here, in the bruised chambers of the past, that the Phoenix first begins to stir.

Walking Through the Heart of Darkness

Into the Abyss: Navigating the Darkness of Suicidal Ideation: A Storm in My Hands

As I place my hands upon these pages, a storm unfurls inside me, not a gentle drizzle, but a gathering tempest of emotion. Anxiety hums like static beneath my skin. Fear coils in my ribs, restless and familiar. And yet, braided through the turbulence is something startlingly soft, a quiet, shimmering liberation rising like dawn beneath the clouds. For the first time, I am preparing to lift my story from the shadows and let it breathe in the open air. A story that has lived too long in dark corners, pressed beneath silence, held hostage by shame and memory. Now, it steps forward, trembling, luminous, ready to be seen. This story was carved from struggle, chiseled by grief, and steeped in a darkness so dense it once felt absolute. It carries the imprint of every night I thought I would not survive, every breath that felt like a burden, every moment my spirit flickered on the verge of extinguishing. But woven through the sorrow is a thread that the darkness could never destroy, hope, fragile but persistent. Resilience bruised but unbroken. Survival, quiet, stubborn, deeply sacred. This book is the moment I open my palms and reveal the truth I once hid away: That even stories born in shadow can blaze with light when finally spoken aloud.

Walking Beside Me in the Underworld

In this volume, I extend my hand to you, steady, open, unafraid, and invite you to walk beside me as we descend into the underworld of my own mind. Here, the terrain grows jagged and dim. Here, the air thickens with grief. Here, the shadows do not merely linger; they speak. We will wander through the darkest corridors of my psyche, where suicidal ideation once curled around my thoughts like a serpent of smoke, tightening its coils until I could barely draw breath. We will stand in the suffocating chambers of depression, where days collapsed into nights without distinction, and hope felt like a language I had forgotten how to speak. We will listen to the corrosive whisper of suicidal ideation, a voice that dripped like acid into the cracks of my spirit, eroding everything tender within me. This is not an easy journey; the path ahead winds through forgotten wounds and memories that pulse like open sores. But it *is* an honest journey, and honesty, raw and unvarnished, is the lantern we carry into these depths.

Together, step by trembling step, we will confront the shadows that once stole our breath, our courage, our sense of belonging in this world. And as we face them, not alone, but side by side, you may begin to feel something stirring, soft as a pulse beneath ash: the truth that even in the darkest realms of the mind, light can still be rekindled, and courage can be reclaimed.

Twenty-Three Years at the Edge

For twenty-three long years, suicidal ideation was not a visitor; it was a constant, intimate shadow, a presence stitched into the very seams of my existence. It lurked in the periphery of every day, hovering just beyond the corner of my vision like a dark silhouette that refused to step fully into view yet never stepped far enough away to grant me peace. It waited for the softest cracks in my armor, the sleepless nights, the hollow mornings, the moments when my spirit sagged beneath its own weight, and in those moments, it leaned in close, pressing its cold lips to my ear to whisper its treacherous lullabies. Lies wrapped in velvet. Promises laced with poison. Invitations to surrender disguised as relief. Those thoughts trailed me like a second heartbeat, an echo stitched to my heels, haunting, taunting, seducing me toward silence long before hope ever dared to speak. They pulled me toward the threshold where life thins into mist, where breath becomes uncertain and the veil between here and not-here ripples like a dark sea beneath a moonless sky.

And when they carried me to that threshold, the brink where my story could have ended, something unexplainable happened: I was dragged back. Scarred. Shaken. Split open in ways I could not yet name. But alive. Alive in a way that felt fragile, trembling, bewildered as though life itself had cupped its hands around my flickering flame and breathed, softly, insistently, until the ember refused to die. This is where the story turns. This is where survival begins to whisper louder than surrender. This is where the ashes first begin to stir.

Fragility and Wild Resilience

As I look back on those long, aching years, memory unfurls like a great, trembling tapestry, threads of sorrow woven beside threads of sheer, stubborn survival, each strand shimmering with a truth I could not see then: That the human heart is both breakable and breathtakingly brave. I am struck by the bewildering complexity of human emotion, how it can cradle tenderness and terror within the same breath, how it can collapse beneath a single wound yet still, somehow, reach for light through the cracks. I think of how fragile the mind can become when weighed down by grief that has no name, how it can fracture like thin glass beneath the pressure of years, how thoughts can twist into vines that choke the very air we breathe. And yet, beneath all that fragility, all that trembling, all that unraveling, there lived a fierce, unyielding spirit I never knew I had. A spirit that fought even when I was certain it had surrendered, a spirit that gripped the edges of my existence long after I believed the battle was lost. My journey is a testament to that contradiction, that we can be delicate as ash and still burn with the strength of a rising Phoenix. A testament to the truth that even the most shattered soul can carry within it a pulse of wild resilience, a quiet defiance that says, "*Not yet. Not now. Not like this.*"

It is proof that the spirit fights for us even when we cannot fight for ourselves. Proof that the darkness we fear most is never strong enough to extinguish the light buried inside us. And as I stand here now, looking back from a place I once believed I would never live to reach, I am humbled by the paradox of it all, the fragility that nearly ended me, and the strength that ultimately saved me.

A Body That Felt Like a Cage

My story begins in a place of raw, trembling desperation, a hollowed-out chamber where hope had long stopped echoing, and the world around me felt too sharp, too fast, too merciless for a heart as fragile and bruised as mine. I lived inside a body that felt more like a cage than a home, trapped in a suffocating loop of self-doubt, self-blame, and self-hate. A relentless cycle that spun me deeper into a darkness I feared I would never outrun. It was as if I were suspended inside a spinning glass sphere with no seam, no hinge, no secret latch that might let me slip out into air. Every turn of the world pressed harder, and every breath scraped my ribs like broken glass. Each day was a battleground. Each sunrise felt like a summons to prove I deserved to be here at all. I clung to consciousness the way a drowning soul clings to driftwood; desperately, exhaustedly, without any real belief that rescue would come. Inside my mind, the voices were merciless. They rose like a storm-tide with no moon to govern it, a choir of condemnation swelling louder with every heartbeat. They called me worthless, hopeless, a burden, a mistake, their words sharp enough to carve fissures into my spirit.

Their rhythm haunted me, a cruel litany that reverberated through the hollow chambers of my being until I could no longer tell where the world ended, and the torment within me began. And yet, beneath that crushing despair, beneath the avalanche of every story that told me I was beyond saving, a single ember refused to die. Faint as a firefly in winter, fragile as a whispered prayer, but stubborn; so stubborn. It flickered in the dark corners of my soul, waiting; waiting for the moment I would finally turn inward, reach trembling fingers toward it, and dare to believe that healing was possible. It was the smallest spark, but it was mine. And it was enough to begin.

The Illusion of Isolation

As I stumbled through that treacherous inner landscape, a terrain carved from jagged fears and shadowed valleys, another truth began to shimmer at the edges of my awareness. A truth both devastating and consoling. I was not the only one wandering through this darkness. Beyond the walls of my private anguish, beyond the echo chamber of my own mind, countless others were fighting battles that looked eerily like mine. They, too, were wrestling with their demons, grappling with spirals of thought that tightened like thorns around the throat, enduring nights so hollow and vast that the silence itself felt predatory. They, too, were drowning beneath the invisible weight of hopelessness, their hearts carrying storms that no one else could see. And yet, even knowing this, I felt profoundly, achingly alone, as though I lived inside an invisible bubble that formed around me like glass blown too thin. A fragile sphere that kept the world out, but also kept my suffering sealed in. With each passing day, it constricted, pressing closer and closer, shrinking the space I occupied until I felt myself diminishing, smaller, and smaller, and smaller, until my breaths came out shallow and stolen.

Isolation is a cruel illusion, a mirage that convinces us we are singular in our suffering when in truth, millions of souls are fighting this very battle in quiet rooms, behind brave smiles, beneath the weight of stories they are terrified to speak aloud. And it is for them, for *you*, that I share my story in all its rawness, its unfiltered truth, its unmasked humanity. Because if even one person hears these words and feels a flicker of recognition, a softening of shame, a small surge of strength rising through their ribs, then every scar in my story becomes sacred. My deepest hope is that something in these pages reaches across the divide, pierces the illusion of aloneness, and becomes a handheld out in the dark, a reminder that survival is possible, that healing is possible, that *you* are still possible. And more than surviving, I hope you will one day step into a life that feels like coming home to yourself.

Excavation of the Inner Underworld

This first volume is not a guidebook that will magically solve things, nor a tidy magic portal that teleports neatly to relief; it is a messy map pointing in the direction of healing. It is an excavation, a descent with trembling hands and dirt beneath the nails, into the cavernous hollows where my despair once lived like a feral creature. It is the lantern lowered into the pit I called home, its flame quivering as it reveals the raw walls of my suffering, the jagged contours of the thoughts that nearly claimed my life. Here, I do not sanitize the truth, nor soften its edges to make it palatable. This volume is a testament, stark, unfiltered, to the brutal reality of living with suicidal ideation, to the corrosive venom of depression, to the relentless whisper of a mind turned against itself. These pages walk you through the shadowed corridors of my psyche, where hope was once a stranger and despair curled comfortably around my ribs like a serpent whispering its poison into every breath. I write this not to shock, but to illuminate, to strike a match in the suffocating dark so that anyone navigating a similar night might glimpse their own reflection and finally feel seen.

Because sometimes, recognizing your story in the echo of another's, is the first crack in the armor of aloneness. Sometimes the simple knowing that someone else has stood in your darkness, has felt the same ice in their veins, the same weight on their chest, is the rope that keeps you from slipping. If these pages do anything, I pray they unravel that isolation, soften its grip, and whisper gently to the wounded places inside you: "*You are not alone here.*"

Meeting the Demons in the Dark

Volume One is about stepping barefoot into the dark and feeling its cold truth against your skin, not to be consumed by it, but to finally *see* what has been stalking you in silence. It is the turning of your face toward the demons you've spent years outrunning, the moment you lift a trembling lantern and discover that naming them is the first crack of power reclaiming itself inside you. This volume invites you into the underworld of your own shadow, where the ghosts of old wounds still linger, where shame coils itself like smoke around your ribs, where fear sits cross-legged at the center of your chest and whispers its familiar litany of limitations. Here, we do not pretend these demons aren't real. We meet them. We study their faces. We call them by their rightful names so they can no longer rule from the dark. Because healing cannot begin until we acknowledge the hands that have been holding us down; whether they belong to the past, past-present, to others, or to parts of ourselves that learned to survive by shrinking, hiding, or hurting inward.

The road ahead is steep, uneven, and quiet in its honesty. It will ask much of you: Courage that quivers, truth that tastes like iron, and tenderness that feels almost too fragile to hold. There will be moments when the shadows seem to gather again, when the old whispers try to drag you back into their familiar embrace. But hear me: You will not be walking this path in silence nor in solitude. Knowing you are not alone is not a small comfort; it is the rope that keeps you tethered to the world when the night tries to convince you otherwise. And if you are struggling, if your breath trembles, if your thoughts tighten like a fist around your mind, if the darkness feels too loud, too close, please, reach out. You deserve a hand to hold in the dark, a steady presence to sit beside you when the fear rises, a voice that reminds you of your worth when your own tongue forgets how to speak it. You deserve support. You deserve safety. You deserve someone who will not turn away when your pain steps into the light. And you deserve, above all, to keep going.

Into the Underworld Proper

Brace yourself, dear listener, for the path ahead does not unfold in gentle gradients or soft-lit affirmations. Volume One is not a tidy roadmap, it is map in another form, nor a soothing balm wrapped in polished steps and packaged wisdom; those gifts await you in Volume Three, once we have first honored the truth of where the journey begins. No, this volume leads you into the underworld. Into the shadowed abyss where the air is thick with unspoken ache, where loneliness echoes against cavern walls carved by years of silent suffering, where pain grows roots that twist through the marrow of your being, and the fiercest wars are fought in the quiet chambers of your own mind. This is the terrain so many inhabit in trembling solitude, yet so few dare to speak of aloud, a realm where despair becomes a second heartbeat, where hope flickers like a dying candle suffocating under its own smoke, where every step feels like wading through tar that threatens to pull you under. You will walk through memories that bruise, truths that sting like salt in an open wound, and emotions dense enough to bend your knees beneath their weight.

Here, we explore the places people politely avert their eyes from, the hidden rooms where shame tightens its grip, where suicidal ideation and depression whisper venom in the dark, where the mind becomes both prison guard and prisoner. This is the landscape of the unsaid, the territory rarely illuminated, because its very soil is made of stories the world often finds too heavy, too messy, too real. Yet these pages go there, not to glorify the abyss, but to shine light into its depths so that you may begin to understand your own. Here, in Volume One, we walk straight into the heart of the darkness with our eyes open, our breath steady, and our courage trembling but present. Because before we can rise, before we can reclaim the light, we must first be willing to stand inside the shadow and say, "*This is where I have been. This is what I have survived.*"

A Chorus of Shadowed Hearts

Here, dear reader, you will walk not only through *my* story, but through a corridor of countless unspoken stories, souls who, like me, once stood barefoot on the razor's edge between despair and survival, breathing that thin, metallic air where hope feels scarce and the world narrows into a single trembling moment. These chapters are stitched from the fabric of my own life, yes, but also from the collective ache of those who have suffered in silence, their agony woven into the very cadence of these words. What you will encounter here is not merely a retelling but a chorus of shadowed hearts, echoing through the darkened rooms of memory and mind. Within these pages, I guide you through the storm-ridden terrain of suicidal ideation, a landscape where thoughts turn foul and fevered, where the mind becomes both captor and tormentor, where every breath feels like a negotiation with existence itself. You will feel the crushing density of depression, the way it presses against the ribs like a collapsing sky, its weight so relentless it blurs sound, color, and time into a single muted ache.

You will step into the suffocating grip of the lies of suicidal ideation, cold and serpentine, curling through the psyche with its venomous whisper: "*You are unworthy. You are unlovable. You are beyond saving.*" It coils, constricts, suffocates, until even your own reflection becomes a stranger you fear. But as you listen, you will also sense something else, a heartbeat beneath the rubble, a pulse of life beneath the ruins, a presence whispering through every shattered line: "*You are not alone here.*" For this story, this descent into darkness, is shared by more people than the world dares acknowledge. And by naming it, by walking you through its labyrinth with tenderness and truth, I hope to loosen the grip it has on you, to offer a lantern in a place where so many wander blind, and to remind you that even in the deepest night, a path forward waits to be found.

The Sacred Violence of Truth

This is not a gentle beginning. It is the sound of old scars splitting open, the sting of air touching wounds that have slept for years beneath your skin. It is a descent into the marrow of memory, where shadows do not merely linger, they *cling,* wrapping themselves around your ribs like vines grown wild in the dark. Here, we do not tiptoe. We enter the darkness with bare feet and trembling breath, feeling every shard, every echo, every ghost that has ever brushed against your spirit. We meet hopelessness without flinching, feeling its cold fingers on the back of our necks, its familiar ache in the hollow behind the heart. We sit with depression, not as an abstract concept or a clinical definition, but as a living storm that has soaked through the walls of your being, leaving you shivering beneath its relentless downpour. We face unhealed trauma, ancient and newly sharpened, a shadow that knows your name and speaks it back to you in a voice that sounds eerily like your own. This is the moment we trace the threads from past to present, watching how they braid themselves around each memory, each belief, each quiet assumption you've ever made about who you are and what you deserve.

They cling, like forgotten lovers, like echoes that refused extinction, whispering the same old script into every breath you take. This is not softness; it is the sacred violence of truth. The kind that cracks open the hollows you've boarded shut. The kind that dares you to look at the rubble without turning away. The kind that burns off illusion until only the raw, pulsing essence remains. Because truth, unfiltered, untamed, unmasked, is the only soil in which real healing can grow. And so, this is where we begin: Not with comfort, not with calm, but with honesty blazing through the dark like the first fierce flare of a match striking against stone.

A Harrowing Account for the Exhausted Heart

This is not a story of sunshine and rainbows, not at first, not here, not in the trembling cradle of Volume One. This opening descent leads you into the underworld of the human psyche, into the caverns where breath echoes strangely, where hope thins to a thread, where the walls seem to pulse with every unshed tear. Here, I lay bare the harrowing account of my suicide attempt, the brutal crescendo of a twenty-three-year war against the quiet, persistent whisper of self-annihilation. This is the point where my spirit staggered beneath the final blow, where the mind fractured under its own weight, where the darkness grew so thick it blurred the edges of the world until death seemed like the only doorway left ajar. These pages are not softened for comfort, not polished for easy reading, not wrapped in ribbons or gilded in false hope. They are written for the soul that knows the shadows intimately, for the one who has lived in them so long they have begun to forget the shape of their own face. This is for the exhausted one. The one who has spent years carrying an invisible crown of sorrow that digs deeper into the skull with every unspoken fear. The one who has curled inward under the crushing ache of being alive yet still wakes each day with a pulse that refuses to surrender.

This is for you, the weary, the burdened, the quietly breaking. Because here, in the raw truth of my own unraveling, you may begin to see the reflection of your own pain. Not to glorify it. Not to drown in it. But to finally face it. For only when we dare to meet our darkness eye to eye can the journey toward light, toward healing, toward life itself truly begin.

Warning at the Mouth of the Cave

What follows is a raw, unflinching exploration of the abyss, a journey into the underbelly of the human spirit, where the air grows thin, and every thought echoes as a stone dropped into bottomless water. This is a descent into the crushing depths of depression, where the world loses its edges and collapses into a blur of gray upon gray. A place where mornings arrive heavy and unwelcome, and nights stretch endlessly, a quiet torture spun from sleepless hours and a mind that refuses mercy. Here, self-hate becomes its own kind of gravity, pulling you downward, tightening its grip around your ribs until even breathing feels like a betrayal. It is a hunger that consumes rather than feeds, a voice that gnaws at the softest parts of you until you begin to believe its venom is truth. And layered over it all is the brutal silence, the silence of shame, the silence of isolation, the silence of a world that keeps moving while you feel yourself dissolving into shadow. It is a silence so absolute it can make you forget you were ever made of light. Consider this your warning, your lantern held low before the mouth of the cave.

Ahead lies a journey straight into the heart of darkness, the kind we rarely speak of aloud, the kind we fear even naming, the kind that lives inside so many of us but is locked away behind forced smiles and quiet despair. And yet, to walk into this darkness with intention, with honesty, with a trembling but willing heart, is the beginning of everything. Because only by entering the abyss can we learn how to climb out of it. Only by facing the night can we ever hope to call the dawn back home.

The Door of Death. The Night the Threshold Opened

It was a cold January evening when I found myself standing at the trembling lip of a decision that felt larger than life, larger than breath, larger than anything my weary soul had ever been asked to hold. Outside, the wind prowled through the darkness like a restless animal, circling the house with a hollow, mournful cry. It rattled against the windows and curled beneath the doorframe, a wild mirror of the storm convulsing inside my chest, a violent, swirling tempest of grief, exhaustion, and despair. This was not a sudden collapse or a fleeting dip into melancholy. It was the final echo of a twenty-three-year battle, a long, brutal war waged in silence against a shadow that refused to let me go. Suicidal ideation had never been a passing thought for me, never a soft whisper I could swat away with logic or strength. Not a mild irritation, the kind you brush off like a wet sock rubbing at your heel. It was a haunting, a relentless apparition pacing the corridors of my mind, persistent as a ghost bound to old, abandoned halls. It lingered in the corners of my consciousness, clinging to me like damp fog on winter skin. It whispered through the cracks of every moment of stillness, sliding its cold fingers across my thoughts, reminding me of its presence with chilling devotion. It was not a nuisance. It was a hunger. An ache.

An obsession that carved itself into me until I could barely tell where it ended and where I began. And on that night, that bleak, icy January night, it rose with a force I could no longer outrun. It pressed itself against my ribs, tightened its grip around my throat, and demanded to be heard. The darkness outside was vast, but the darkness inside me felt infinite, a swallowed universe collapsing inward. And there I stood, suspended between breath and oblivion, holding the weight of a choice that could unmake everything. The ghost of death did not simply visit me that night. It sat beside me. It breathed with me. It lingered, it whispered, it clung, it waited. And on that night, it demanded to be heard. And for the first time, I found myself listening and then silently obeying.

The Story the Thoughts Wove

My suicidal thoughts were not mere visitors; they were master weavers, threading themselves through the loom of my every waking moment until my inner world resembled a tapestry stitched in shadow. They wove a distorted narrative with ruthless precision, a story in which the unbearable felt not only inevitable but *deserved*. They painted me as the flaw, the fracture, the burden that bent the air around me. They curled into my mind like smoke, blurring the truth, insisting that the discomfort itself was my doing; that I was the poison, the problem, the reason everything hurt. What they never revealed were the deeper wounds pulsing beneath the surface, the old injuries, the unspoken traumas, the silenced pieces of my story that had been begging for compassion, not condemnation. These thoughts did not speak of healing. They never whispered that pain could soften, that sorrow could shift its shape, that tomorrow might hold a gentler sky. They did not tell me that wounds dry, that hearts repair, that shattered spirits can knit themselves back together with threads stronger than before.

No, their voice was a trickster's lullaby, a slow seduction toward obliteration. Some days, they murmured softly, curling around my mind like a cold mist, subtle enough to feel familiar, quiet enough to pass as truth. Other days, they rose into a violent crescendo, a roar that drowned out reason, a tempest demanding that I carve myself down and abandon the pieces I believed were broken beyond salvation. They asked for surrender. They asked for silence. They asked for my undoing. And yet, somewhere in the depths of that relentless storm, a part of me; small, trembling, but astonishingly alive, held on to one fragile truth the thoughts could never fully erase: I was hurting, yes, but I was not beyond repair.

The Wet Sock Illusion

The thoughts clung to me with the stubbornness of a wet sock plastered to bare skin, cold, abrasive, relentless in its insistence that I feel it with every single step. There was no escaping its presence. No moment of forgetting.

No tender breath untouched by its damp, unsettling grip. It pressed itself against me like a second, suffocating layer, a constant reminder that something was wrong, not merely uncomfortable, but *unavoidable.* And instead of looking at the true source of the wetness, the deeper wound beneath the irritation, my mind twisted the truth into a cruel illusion. It whispered that *I* was the flaw, that the wrongness lived not in the water that had soaked me but in the foot itself, in my essence, in my being. It told me the discomfort was my fault, my failure, my inherent defect. It insisted that the only way to stop the cold from seeping deeper was to remove the part of me that felt it. Not to peel off the soaked barrier. Not to name the wound. Not to let the wetness dry.

No, the thoughts demanded the unthinkable: that I discard the very part of me that ached, as though the pain was proof that I was unworthy of keeping myself intact. This was the cruelest deception of all, that the solution was annihilation instead of care, compassion, warmth, or truth. And so I stood there, shivering beneath the weight of a storm I didn't yet know how to name, believing that the only relief lay in tearing myself away from myself, when all I truly needed was to recognize the wetness, to tend the wound, and to allow the light, even the faintest flicker, to begin the long, gentle work of drying what had soaked me through.

The Door that Looked Like Mercy

Each morning, I surfaced from sleep as though rising through tar; thick, clinging, merciless. Before my eyelids even fluttered open, a heaviness seeped into my chest, a slow-spreading dread that settled over my ribs like a slab of cold stone. It greeted me the way a storm greets a broken window: uninvited, unrelenting, finding every crack in me and widening it. I woke not into a day, but into a weight. A pressure that pressed from the inside out, tightening its grip around my heart until even breathing felt like a negotiation. Inside my mind, I wandered a labyrinth built from beliefs I never agreed to, yet somehow inherited, beliefs handed down like curses instead of truths. They became bars of an invisible cage, a prison constructed from whispers, wounds, and the thousand subtle ways life had once told me I was not enough. And in that suffocating confinement, where every path looped back into darkness, and every thought circled the same merciless drain, death began to shimmer in the distance, not as ruin, not as devastation, but as *relief.*

It appeared like a quiet door at the end of a long, echoing corridor, glowing faintly with the illusion of rest, whispering promises of stillness where pain could no longer reach me. It did not threaten. It beckoned. A soft, deceptive voice murmuring *"Come. Lay it down. Let it end."* And for a time, I believed it. Because when the ache becomes too vast to name, and the world shrinks into something too sharp to touch, escape begins to look like mercy. Release begins to look like peace. And the unbearable begins to masquerade as inevitable.

The Tempest and the Shrinking Room

Some days, those thoughts brushed against me with the subtlety of a chill beneath the door, a quiet discomfort I told myself might fade if I simply stayed still enough, silent enough, small enough. They murmured like distant thunder, a low hum beneath my ribs reminding me that the storm never truly left. But other days, they rose with the ferocity of a tempest breaking open the sky. They crashed through me like tidal waves, insisting with ruthless conviction that I was weight, that I was burden, that my very existence tilted the world off balance. Their voices were not whispers then, they were hurricanes, ripping through the fragile scaffolding that held me upright. Each morning, I awoke beneath a heaviness that felt as old as time itself, as though I had inherited centuries of sorrow and carried them in my chest like stones. Before my eyes even parted from sleep, foreboding seeped into my bones, and I felt the day looming like an unwelcome prophecy. Inside my mind, I lived in a room that contracted by the hour, its walls creeping inward with the slow precision of something designed to suffocate rather than shelter.

The ceiling sank lower. The air thinned into something metallic, sharp enough to sting the lungs. And in that dim, shrinking chamber of thought, the door of death began to glimmer, not in menace, but in promise.

It shimmered like an escape hatch carved from illusion, soft-edged and beckoning, offering freedom from the relentless drip, drip, drip of pain that hollowed me day after day. Its glow was seductive, a false sunrise whispering, "This way. Here is quiet. Here is rest." And for a long time, in my desperation to breathe, I almost believed it.

The Slow Erosion

As I look back on that moment, I see now that it did not erupt from a single catastrophe, no sudden quake that split my world in two. It was slower, quieter, a long sedimentation of sorrow that built itself grain by grain until the weight became an internal landslide. It was the drip of hurt that never dried. The slow accretion of disappointments settling in layers, rejections that left hairline fractures, betrayals that seeped into the cracks, and the steady, acidic trickle of inadequacy that wore through my spirit the way water hollows stone. Each wound nested atop the last, forming strata of silent suffering I did not know how to name. They packed themselves into the architecture of my being until my inner landscape resembled a canyon, vast, eroded, carved open by years of emotional weathering. Over time, I drifted into a kind of unbeing, a numbed, suspended state where I felt myself dissolving at the edges of my own life. I became a ghost in my own reflection, visible yet vanishing, present yet untouchable, a hollow silhouette wearing the memory of who I once was. I felt less than human, as though the marrow had been siphoned from my bones and replaced with emptiness. Every breath felt borrowed, every heartbeat an undeserved echo.

And it was from that cavernous vacancy, that place where the world dimmed to grayscale and my worth felt thinner than paper, that the darkness found its strongest hold. It wrapped itself around my hollowness like a vine around abandoned ruins, thriving in the spaces where light had long stopped reaching. That moment was not born from a single fall. It was the final collapsing grain in a mountain of unspoken pain.

UNDERSTANDING DEPRESSION: The Quiet Arrival

My struggle began quietly, almost politely, a soft-footed shadow slipping into the unguarded corners of my mind as though it belonged there. It did not arrive with thunder or spectacle; it seeped in like dusk, subtle at first, barely noticeable, a slow cooling of the light I once carried so effortlessly. It was not a sudden plunge into despair. No cliff. No fall. Just the gradual erosion of joy, a steady sanding-down of my inner brightness until the edges of my laughter grew dull, until my mornings lost their shimmer, until my heart forgot how to rise with the sun. Depression, that insidious, shape-shifting thief, began its silent work. It stole in the way thieves often do: first the smallest things, the everyday sparks; warmth, ease, color, the sweetness of ordinary moments, until what remained felt washed-out, waterlogged, and strangely distant.

Day by day, it drained the vibrancy from my world, bleeding the blues and golds and wild greens from the landscape of my life until everything dimmed into a muted, monochrome haze. It was like living beneath a fogged glass dome, sound muffled, light distorted, hope reduced to a faint silhouette pressing its palms against the barrier, unable to reach me. And in that slow fading, I began to disappear alongside the color; a quiet vanishing that no one noticed at first, not even me.

The Mask and the Dissolution

I became an expert in the ancient art of pretending, a practiced performer draped in a mask stitched from forced smiles and carefully timed laughter. On the outside, I appeared intact, even cheerful at times, while inside, entire continents of me were crumbling, eroding in silence beneath the weight of an ache that had no language except the throb of my own breaking heart. This, for me, is the marrow-deep truth of depression: Not a mood, not a passing cloud, not a fleeting sorrow that lifts with a good night's sleep. It is a slow dissolution of the self, a steady siphoning of color, courage, and clarity until you become a faint outline of the person you once were. It moves like a whispering serpent through the corridors of the mind, murmuring doubt into your bones, breathing fear into your blood, curling itself around your soul until its voice becomes indistinguishable from your own. Depression is not simply "sadness." Sadness has edges; depression is boundless. Sadness arrives and leaves; depression squats inside your chest and rearranges the furniture of your thoughts until nothing feels familiar anymore. It is a suffocating, weighted blanket of despair pressing against your ribs, your lungs, your ability to move, to care, to try.

Even the smallest tasks, brushing your teeth, answering a message, lifting your head from the pillow, become mountains with no summit, tasks so impossibly steep you feel ashamed for struggling at all. It is a dense, disorienting fog that swallows landmarks of meaning and blurs the horizon until every path looks the same: Dark, heavy, unreachable. It dulls hope to a pale flicker, rips purpose from your grasp, and leaves you adrift in a life that feels foreign, distant, and strangely uninhabitable. And perhaps the cruelest truth of all: Depression makes you a stranger in your own skin, a captive inside a body that no longer feels like home, a spectator in a life you no longer recognize as yours. This is where the darkness tightened around me, where the mask began to fracture, and where the slow unwinding of my spirit became impossible to ignore.

The Fog That Pretends to Know You

To truly understand the depths of my story, you must understand what depression *really* is; not the watered-down version the world casually names, but the creature that sinks its claws into the marrow of your being and reshapes the landscape of your inner world. You must step into the landscape of depression as it lived within me, a vast, unsettling terrain where the world loses its edges, and everything familiar becomes strangely distorted. Depression is not sadness. It is not a heavy day or a fleeting cloud that drifts across the sky. Depression is a fog, yes, but not a gentle morning mist. It is a dense, swallowing vapor that rolls in without warning and refuses to lift, even when the sun tries its hardest to break through. It is that relentless fog; thick, unyielding, almost sentient, that creeps into every crevice of your mind and settles over your senses like a shroud. It blurs the outlines and edges of your world, warps shadows, and renders familiar places strange, until even the things you once loved feel distant, unreachable, as though you are looking at your own life through frosted glass.

It drags itself into your bones, a cold, aching weight that pulls you downward with a gravity all its own. No, it is not simply sadness. Sadness bends. Depression consumes. Sadness speaks. Depression suffocates. Depression is a gravitational force that pulls you inward, downward, into a cavern where sound becomes muffled, and light grows scarce. It is a silent puppeteer that tugs at the strings of your spirit until even reaching for a glass of water feels like scaling a mountain with trembling, exhausted hands. Your limbs feel heavy. Your breath becomes effort. Your thoughts move like syrup: Slow, sticky, hard to lift. Depression is not just emotional; it is physical, spiritual, and psychological. It is a full-body eclipse.

The Lies That Wear Your Voice

It weaves itself into the nervous system, into the breath, into the bones, making your very existence feel like an impossible burden to carry. And then, when the world grows quiet, and you are left alone with your thoughts, its voice grows bold. It leans close, pressing its cold mouth against your ear, and whispers lies with the confidence of gospel. Consumed by those whispered lies into the quiet spaces, the moments between heartbeats, the pauses in conversation, the stillness right before you fall asleep. Lies so soft they sound like your own thoughts: "*You are unworthy.* You are unlovable. You are beyond saving. You are the problem. *You are a burden. You don't matter. You will never get better.*" And the cruelest part? It speaks in *your voice.* Lies delivered with such certainty that you begin to mistake the echo of your illness for the sound of your own truth. It mimics your cadence, your inner tone, until you believe every poisonous word it feeds you. It tightens its grip when you are most alone, thriving in silence, in the isolated corners where you hide your hurt because you fear the world will not understand it. It feeds on stillness, on solitude, on the trembling belief that no one can reach you where you have fallen.

Multiplying in the dark corners where no one else can see the storm raging. Depression convinces you that you are beyond saving, that your pain is too vast, your wounds too deep, your soul too fractured to ever be whole again. But here is the truth depression never wants you to hear; hear this now, with the whole of your heart: **Its voice is loud, not truthful.** I repeat this again, depression's voice is not truth. It is simply loud, a megaphone of distortion pressing itself against your soul. And its volume does not make it honest. Its persistence does not make it right. It is noise, not knowing. Volume is not wisdom. Intensity is not accuracy. And just because a lie is repeated does not make it real. Depression screams but healing whispers. And this; this journey, this story, this unfolding, is about learning to hear the whisper again. Fog, not fact. And even the densest fog begins to lift the moment a single beam of light dares to break through.

Where Self-Hate Takes Root

Depression is not simply sadness; it is a darkness that seeps into the seams of your life like ink bleeding through fragile, thirsty paper, unstoppable, staining everything it touches. It is a *slow eclipse of joy*, a dimming of the internal sun until even the brightest moments arrive muted, blurred, stripped of warmth. It is a heaviness that settles into your bones with the certainty of winter frost, weighing down even the smallest breath until inhaling feels like lifting stone. Depression is the thick, suffocating fog that swallows every horizon, erasing distance, depth, and perspective. Leaving you wandering through a world where color drains like water swirling down a drain, where sound retreats into dull, padded echoes, and where hope becomes a foreign tongue, your spirit can no longer remember how to speak. For me, depression became the fertile, treacherous soil where self-hate took root. It sprouted quietly, almost politely at first, then grew wild and ravenous, its tendrils twisting through every thought, every belief, every trembling moment of my day.

It tightened around me like a vine determined to choke, its thorns pressing into the softest parts of my being until I could no longer distinguish where I ended, and the darkness began. The weight of it was crushing, a silent avalanche shifting beneath my ribs, an invisible gravity pulling me downward into the narrow, airless chambers of myself. There, buried beneath emotions I could not name, I became both prisoner and warden, lost in a maze of my own unspoken sorrow. This was the terrain of my becoming, a place where I unraveled, a place where I would eventually rise, but only after being brought to my knees by a force powerful enough to bend even the brightest spirits toward the ground.

Depression as Captivity

People toss the word *depression* around as if it were a passing cloud, a brief dimming of the sky, a mood, a moment. But those of us who have lived inside it know the truth: Depression is no cloud. It is a *creature*. It breathes. It coils. It waits. It wraps itself around the heart, the mind, the soul like a serpent tightening its grip with slow, deliberate precision, squeezing until your own breath feels borrowed, until every beat inside your chest begins to sound like surrender. Depression is *emptiness that echoes*, a hollow that stretches so wide and so far, you swear it might swallow eternity. It is numbness that masquerades as permanence, a vast, suspended expanse where sensation dissolves and every feeling slips through your fingers before you can even name it. It is a profound disconnection, as if someone pressed you against the wrong side of glass. Life continues on the other side: Voices, movement, color, warmth. But to you, everything arrives distorted, muted, refracted, a distant scene blurred behind frosted panes, untouchable no matter how much you ache for contact.

Depression is a house with all the doors locked from the outside. You wander its dim hallways, hand brushing the walls as you search for the seam of an opening, a handle, a crack, a mercy, but every room is the same, every corridor narrows, and the air grows heavier with each turn. The walls breathe with you, closing in with quiet inevitability. It is the feeling of being trapped inside your own skin, a cage that moves when you move, tightens when you struggle, and refuses to let you slip free. And so you stand there, pressed against the glass of your own existence, watching life unfold just beyond reach, each moment drifting by like a world you once belonged to but can no longer enter. This is depression, not a cloud but a captivity. Not a mood but a slow-motion drowning. A silent suffocation that convinces you escape is impossible, even when the world outside your prison is still calling your name.

The Unnamed Tongue and the Shared Silence

For years, I didn't even possess the vocabulary to name my suffering, no language tender enough to hold it, no framework wide enough to make sense of the ache humming beneath my skin. My pain was a dialect no one had ever taught me, a secret tongue spoken only in shadows, heavy with meanings I couldn't translate into words. So I did what so many of us do when the truth feels too large, too sharp, too dangerous to expose. I stitched a smile across my face, a fragile, trembling mask made of polite nods and practiced laughter. I wore "I'm fine" like armor, a costume I slipped into each morning, even as my inner world caved in on itself. Outwardly, I appeared intact, upright, functioning, even capable. But inside, inside I was wilting. I was the flower left too long without sunlight, petals curling inward, color draining thread by thread, the perfume of life fading into a scent of quiet decay. My roots were rotting, softening in darkness, collapsing from the inside while the world admired the illusion of my bloom.

If any part of this echoes within you, if you, too, have mastered the art of smiling through shattering, if you have learned to hide your trembling beneath rehearsed normalcy, please hear me: You are not alone. There are others walking this same quiet battlefield, bearing invisible wounds beneath their clothing and their calm, fighting wars no one else can see. And though our masks may differ, the silence beneath them is heartbreakingly familiar. You are not the only one carrying pain that has no name. You are not the only one who has learned to hide the unraveling. You are not the only one who feels swallowed by shadows while pretending to stand in the light. You are not alone.

• The Whisper of the Void: When Silence Becomes a Presence

Silence became the loudest thing in the room, not an absence of sound, but a presence so heavy it felt sentient, so dense it seemed to have weight, pressing hard against my ribs as though trying to crack me open and spill the truth I wasn't yet ready to touch, as though prying for a confession I wasn't yet brave enough to release. It wasn't silence in the gentle sense, not the soft hush of dawn or the tender quiet of a room at rest. It wasn't silence at all. This silence was a creature, a storm without wind, a tidal wave held in place by invisible hands. A scream robbed of breath, a void so thick it vibrated in my bones. A scream stripped of sound and trapped in the cage of my throat. It pulsed against me, pressing into the soft spaces beneath my sternum, filling my lungs with a dense, airless ache that tasted like metal and memory. It expanded around me, spreading like ink through water, like a hungry darkness that knew my name. It seeped into the corners, into the air, into the narrow space between my heartbeat and my fear, mirroring the shapeless hollowness that pulsed inside my chest.

The Void with Teeth

This silence was not peaceful, not the serene hush of nightfall or the gentle stillness of a calm mind. It was a void with teeth, a hungry darkness widening around me with each passing moment, stretching itself through the room until it swallowed the edges of everything, I thought I knew. It echoed the hollowness blooming inside my chest, a hollow so cavernous it seemed to create its own gravity, pulling me inward, drawing me deeper into the quiet that wasn't quiet at all. It was the kind of silence that forces you to hear everything you've been avoiding: the tremor beneath your thoughts, the fracture beneath your breath, the truth trembling like a frightened animal deep within your bones. A silence so loud it threatened to unmake me before I ever spoke a word. This was not the kind of silence that offers refuge or reflection; it was a suffocating hush that swallowed sound, devoured thought, and left me suspended in a world stripped of color, movement, and warmth. It was the silence of being unseen.

The silence of being unheard. The silence of disappearing inch by inch inside the echoing chambers of my own unspoken despair. And in that silence, I felt myself dissolving, a fading outline of a person whose voice had grown too tired to call for help, whose pain had grown too heavy to carry alone. A silence that did not soothe but swallowed.

The Slow Erasure

And still, the silence grew. It wrapped itself around me like a second skin, tightening with each unspoken fear, each swallowed truth, each moment I convinced myself that my suffering was too shameful or too insignificant to be witnessed by another. It was a silence that tasted metallic on my tongue, as though every unshed tear were rusting me from the inside out. A silence that settled behind my eyes, heavy as storm clouds that refused to break. In that vast, echoing void, even my thoughts felt distant, muted shapes moving behind fogged glass, never fully forming, never fully reaching me. I tried to listen for myself, to see if anything remained inside the hollow, but all I found was a dim flicker struggling to stay alight in a chamber carved from absence. It was a silence that taught me how a person can vanish while still standing in a room. How a body can remain while the spirit quietly slips further and further from the surface. How a life can shrink to the size of a single, trembling heartbeat begging to be heard. And the terrifying truth was this: part of me welcomed that disappearance.

Part of me believed the world would sigh with relief if I dissolved completely into the quiet. This silence was not emptiness; it was erasure. A steady unraveling of the self. A swallowing not of sound, but of being. And there, in the thick of it, I stood at the brink of forgetting myself entirely. Yet even in that consuming hush, even as I faded into its shadowed breath, something small within me, fragile as a candle trembling in a draft, refused to be extinguished. The silence swallowed, but it did not finish the feast.

The Whisper That Followed Me

This silence seeped into every corner, filling the air with all the words I could not voice, all the truths I had buried beneath years of endurance. It was a silence that didn't soothe; it hissed. A silence that didn't comfort, it beckoned. A silence that sang to me in the haunting lullaby of the abyss, its notes woven from shadows, its rhythm pulsing like a dark heartbeat against my skin. It whispered promises of release disguised as rest, seducing me with the illusion that surrender was salvation and oblivion was mercy. For twenty-three years, that whisper clung to me like a second shadow, stitched to my heels, threaded through my breath, a phantom presence that inhaled every exhale, learning the cadence of my despair so it could echo it back with perfect precision. It was a parasitic thought, feeding on every tremor of doubt, every quake of fear, every ounce of exhaustion my life managed to wring from me. The hollower I became, the easier it drank. And as the world around me slept, the whisper grew louder. Louder in the quiet. Louder in the dark.

Louder in the small, fragile moments when I most desperately needed the warmth of light but could not remember what light even felt like. It curled around my spirit, a serpent of sorrow tightening with each passing year, hissing that I was tired, that I was done, that letting go would be the gentlest thing I could ever offer myself. This was not silence. It was a summons, a call from the edges of the void. And I, worn thin by decades of battle, found myself leaning toward it more often than I dared to admit.

The Thread That Refused to Break

Because somewhere beneath that devouring quiet, beneath the numbness that pressed like cold glass against my skin, a single thread of me, thin, trembling, almost spectral, continued to pulse with the insistence of survival. It was not loud. It was not brave. It was not even hopeful. It was simply *there*, a stubborn, flickering insistence that I was not meant to disappear. That thread tugged gently at the frayed edges of my being, whispering with the soft defiance of a wildflower forcing its way through concrete, that perhaps my existence still held weight, still held possibility, still held meaning beyond the ruin I had come to believe was all I was. In that moment, the silence shifted, just slightly, just enough, revealing that it had not consumed me whole. Not yet. In the faint glow of that flicker, I felt the first subtle stirrings of resistance, not the dramatic uprising of a warrior, but the quiet refusal of a soul that has not fully agreed to its own disappearance. It was the smallest rebellion: a breath that insisted on being taken, a heartbeat that refused to still, a whisper in the marrow of my bones saying, "*Not this. Not yet.*"

And though the darkness still sprawled around me, wide as an ocean and deep as a grave, that tiny, trembling ember held its ground. It glowed in the hollow, soft and defiant, a reminder that even in the vastness of nothingness, something in me still longed for life. Something in me still remembered that I had once been more than this silence. And something in me, delicate as dawn, unyielding as truth, was preparing to rise.

Why This Book Exists: Quieting the Whisper

This book, every page, every wound spelled out in ink, is my attempt to quiet that whisper at last. To reach into the marrow of the silence that once swallowed me whole and unthread it, strand by trembling strand. To take the scream without sound that rattled inside my bones for decades and shape it into a voice with purpose, a voice that no longer hides in the rafters of fear, but steps forward carrying its own flicker of light. These words are not merely sentences. They are my exhales. My resurrections. The echoes of every night I survived when I was certain I would not. They are the fingerprints of my healing pressed gently into the page so that you might feel the pulse of a life once splintered, now slowly gathering itself back together. More than that, this book is my offering to *you*. A tender outstretched hand, a lantern carved from the very shadows that tried to consume me, a lifeline woven from threads of truth, fire, and rebirth. It is an invitation to step out of the cavern of your own silence, to hear the soft return of your breath where despair once echoed, to reclaim the sound of your truth after years of muting yourself to survive.

May these pages help you hush your own haunting hush, that dangerous quiet that convinces you your pain is too heavy to voice, that your suffering is an inconvenience, that your existence is too much. Here, in this space, you are not too much. You are not unwelcome. You are not unheard. Here, your voice is sacred. Your breath is proof of your belonging. Your story is allowed to exist in its fullness, its complexity, its unfiltered truth.

The Thawing and The Descent Begins

I hope that as you move through these chapters, you will feel something inside you begin to thaw, a loosening in the ribs, a softening behind the eyes, a gentle shift in the place where your spirit has been bracing for years. May this book become the quiet murmur that counters the void, the warmth that challenges the cold, the small, stubborn ember that reminds you, you are still here, and you are still capable of rising into your own life again. Volume One is not a gentle unveiling. It is a descent, an excavation into the bone-catacombs of the soul. Together, we will walk into the very marrow of the darkness that claimed me for more than two decades, step by trembling step, down the spiraling staircase of my own unmaking. This is not a path illuminated by warm lanterns or softened by the comforts of hindsight. It is lit instead by the flicker of memory, that fragile, wavering flame that both reveals and burns. By the dim, haunting glow of moments too agonizing to forget and too essential to leave entombed beneath silence. Here, we descend past the thresholds where my spirit splintered, through corridors where shadows breathed louder than I did, through rooms where the walls remembered what I tried so desperately to forget.

The Landscape of Wounds and How the Collapse Was Formed

With every step downward, the air thickens with old grief, with the metallic tang of fear, with the cold exhale of truths long unspoken. And yet, we continue. Not to glorify the darkness, not to drown in it, but to finally *see* it for what it was: a landscape of wounds that shaped me, a labyrinth I survived, a descent that became the beginning of my rise. In these pages, the unraveling begins, thread by trembling thread, not to destroy what remains, but to reveal the quiet, stubborn essence that endured beneath the ruin. This is the descent before the spark. The ashes before the ember. The necessary darkness before the remembering of light. Here, I will unearth the events that shaped my collapse, not in a sudden shattering, but in the slow, merciless way a cliffside erodes over centuries. Hope did not disappear overnight; it was carved away grain by grain, a steady dripping of sorrow hollowing me from the inside, the way water eats through stone until even mountains begin to crumble.

I will take you to the moments where the light inside me thinned to a mere thread, a fragile filament trembling in the draft of uncertainty. Where every breath felt like a negotiation with existence, a bargain struck between survival and surrender, each inhale a question, each exhale a plea whispered into the void. I will bring you into the spaces where shadows gathered like uninvited guests, pressing in close, crowding out reason, turning my inner world into a labyrinth of dim corridors that echoed with doubts I was too exhausted to silence.

The Doorway and Entering the Labyrinth

And I will show you the place where the doorway to death stood open, not with drama, not with fanfare, but with a chilling familiarity, as though it had been waiting patiently for me all along. A threshold that called me by name, softly at first, then with a growing insistence, until it felt less like a threat and more like an invitation. An invitation to rest. To end. To vanish. These are the moments I will uncover, the subtle fractures, the hidden wounds, the quiet devastations that brought me to the brink. Not to glorify the fall, but to illuminate the truth of how someone can be pulled so far from themselves that death begins to look like home. This is not a story I share casually. It is a re-entering, a re-bleeding, a descent back into the chambers where my soul once fractured under the weight of its own silence. To write these words is to peel away scar tissue with trembling fingers, to reopen rooms I boarded shut, rooms that still hum with the ghosts of who I once was and who I feared I would always remain.

Within these pages lies the labyrinth of my severe depression, a twisting, shifting underworld where the walls seemed to pulse with my own doubts, where every turn led me deeper into myself and further from the surface of my own life. It is a place where shadows gather at the edges of vision, where hope feels like a myth spoken in a language

The Beast at the Center and The Truth of the Lantern

I had forgotten how to understand. And there, in the very heart of this labyrinth, waited the suffocating chokehold of self-hate, a creature forged from my oldest wounds, an inner beast that recognized the shape of my vulnerabilities with unsettling intimacy. It prowled through my mind with the steady confidence of something that had lived there far too long, its claws tracing every fracture, its breath warm against the nape of my fear. Volume One is not comfortable. It was never meant to be. It asks you to sit with the darkness, to witness the truth of what it means to unravel layer by tender layer until all that remains is the unadorned ache of being human. But it *is* truthful. And truth, even when jagged, even when it cuts, is a lantern in the deepest night. In that rawness, I pray you will find recognition, not of the specifics of my suffering, but of the universal longing to be seen, to be understood, to be free. And in that recognition, may the first spark of your own rising shiver awake, small yet stubborn, faint yet fiercely alive, a glimmer in the ash whispering: "*You, too, can rise from this.*"

The Descent Is Not Meant to Swallow You

And yet, as we descend together into this shadowed terrain, I want you to carry one truth like a talisman against your chest: This is *not* a journey meant to swallow you. It is a journey meant to **reveal** you. The darkness we are about to enter is not a grave, not a final extinguishing, not the place where your spirit is meant to disappear. It is an initiation, a sacred threshold into the chambers of your own becoming. This descent is not destruction. It is illumination born in reverse. A journey where the light does not shine from above but begins as a faint shimmer beneath your ribs, growing brighter as you dare to step deeper into the places you once feared would unmake you. The shadows you will meet in the coming pages are not enemies waiting to devour you; they are unspoken stories, exiled memories, pieces of your soul that curled inward for protection long before you learned how to listen to their trembling voices. Here, in the quiet underworld of the self, we do not plunge to be lost. We descend to remember. To gather the fragments.

To retrieve the parts of you that have been waiting in the dark, patient as moonless nights, for you to finally turn toward them. This is the necessary beginning, the untangling, the unmasking, the first courageous breath in the long birth of your rising. And as we step together into this tender abyss, know this with every cell of your being: you are not descending alone. You are not walking into oblivion. You are walking *toward yourself,* toward the truth of your story, toward the healing that has been quietly calling your name from beneath the ash of all you have survived.

Walking Into the Wound

For only by walking into the wound can we understand its depth, the way it spirals inward like a long-forgotten cave, its walls etched with the echoes of every moment we were too overwhelmed, too young, or too afraid to fully feel. Only by stepping into the labyrinth can we learn its architecture, the twists carved by childhood ache, the dead ends formed by shame, the narrow passages built from unspoken grief. Only by naming its corridors can we ever hope to find the thread that leads us back to the surface. And so, with equal parts fear and courage, with trembling honesty and the kind of intention that quivers because it *matters,* we take the next step together. A step into the wound. A step into the maze. A step into the story that bent me, broke me, and nearly ended me, the story that pulled me to the brink of nothingness and whispered to me from the very edge of breath.

This is the chapter where my spirit cracked, where the world as I knew it collapsed inward like a dying star, and I became a version of myself I could no longer recognize. But this is also the beginning of resurrection, the first tremor beneath the ashes, the first spark stirring in the ruin, the first whispered promise that even those who fall the farthest can rise again. Together, we step into the dark, not to be consumed by it, but to witness where the light first learned how to return.

Depression Is Not a Mood

Depression, the word drifts lightly across conversations, spoken casually, almost carelessly, as if it were nothing more than a faint cloud passing across a summer sun. But those of us who have survived its grip know better. We know its true nature, not a mood, not a moment, but a creature with teeth. Depression is a parasite that crawls into the marrow of your being, coiling itself in the hollows of your bones until its weight becomes indistinguishable from your own. It feeds on light, on laughter, on the smallest flickers of self-worth until everything within you dims to the color of old ash. Depression is not the soft dimming of a single light; it is an eclipse that devours the entire sky. It creeps into the bloodstream like ink spilled into clear water, darkening everything it touches, bleeding into thoughts, memories, even dreams. It is the hollow knock of emptiness echoing through your bones, the chill of a winter that settles beneath the skin and refuses to thaw. It is the slow drowning in an ocean with no waves, only stillness, only silence, only the crushing pressure of being pulled downward inch by inch by a gravity no one else can see.

The Patient Predator

It is a patient predator, one that does not pounce but waits, and waits, and waits, slipping deeper with every uncried tear, every unspoken fear, every night you lie awake staring into a ceiling that feels just a little too low. It is a master thief, a phantom skilled in the art of quiet robbery. You go to bed with a spark in your heart and wake to find it gone, stolen in the night by something you cannot see, cannot fight, cannot outrun. It is a suffocating shroud, a heavy, airless blanket that settles over your chest with a weight no human lungs were meant to bear. It presses into you until your breaths turn shallow, your thoughts turn sluggish, and your will to move becomes a negotiation between exhaustion and despair. Depression feeds on your softness. It consumes your color. It leans close in the quiet hours and whispers in a voice that sounds like your own, convincing you that nothing will ever change, that nothing *can* change, that you are trapped in a life shrinking around you like fabric soaked in cold water. It rearranges the seasons inside you, turning spring to ash, summer to smoke, autumn to decay, and winter into something endless, merciless, unyielding. Depression is not weather. It is not a passing mist. It is a landscape, vast, barren, and terrifyingly quiet, a place where sound goes to die and where hope struggles even to whisper.

The Whisper That Becomes Your Voice

It dulls your senses until laughter sounds distant, touch feels muted, light looks foreign and even hope tastes like something your mouth no longer remembers how to hold. Depression is not simply endured; it inhabits. It colonizes. It becomes a haunting presence that stands behind you, beside you, within you, breathing its frost against the back of your neck. And slowly, terrifyingly, you begin to wonder whether the heaviness is not a visitor at all, but a truth carved into your very being. This is the darkness I entered. This is the landscape I will walk you through, not to terrify, but to name the monster that so many of us have faced alone. For once something is named, it is no longer a ghost. And still, somehow, we walk through it. Even when it feels like our legs are made of stone, even when each step is an argument with gravity, even when the silence tries to swallow us whole... we carry on. Because somewhere beneath the parasite and beneath the predator and beneath the shroud, a faint pulse still beats, a small, stubborn ember of self-refusing to be extinguished.

Depression is not sadness. Sadness has shape, sound, and movement. Depression is the *absence* of all of it, a bleaching of the inner landscape until every emotion fades to a colorless hush. It is the draining of life from the chambers of your being, the slow erasure of everything that once felt vivid or real. It is the hollow ache that thrums beneath your ribs, an ache that does not cry out but *resonates* like an abandoned house trembling in the wind. It is numbness masquerading as calm, a void so consuming it feels as though your soul has been scooped out and replaced with a cavern of echoes that answer nothing and devour everything. You wake each morning in a body that feels older than any lifetime you have ever lived, a body made of stone and memory, your spirit dragging behind you like an anchor forged from unanswered grief. Every movement feels borrowed, every breath a reluctant negotiation, every step a pilgrimage through mud-thick despair. And through it all runs the whisper.

That soft, insidious thread of poison weaving itself into your thoughts until its lies settle like sediment at the bottom of your being. You don't notice the moment the whisper becomes the narrator of your entire world, the moment its voice folds itself into your own inner monologue so seamlessly that you no longer know where it ends and you begin.

Depression: The Eye of the Storm

It tells you you're worthless. It tells you you're broken. It tells you you're beyond saving. And the cruelest part? It speaks in a tone you trust, your own. This is the landscape of depression, not a storm, but an evaporation. Not a wound, but a vanishing. A slow dissolving of self until even your sorrow feels too distant to reach. And yet, even in that vast, unfeeling, there remains a faint, stubborn pulse within you, something small, something ancient, something that refuses to go silent. A heartbeat waiting to be reclaimed. It is seeing yourself, and the world, through a warped, splintered lens where everything familiar becomes distorted, where beauty hides behind fogged glass, where hope evaporates before it has the chance to take its first trembling breath. In this fractured vision, possibility dims to a faint ember, and any spark of joy is smothered before it can rise into flame. That is depression: A quiet undoing. A slow unthreading of the self, strand by delicate strand, until you no longer recognize the silhouette of the person you once were.

It is a storm that rages without wind, a tempest with no thunder yet capable of uprooting everything sacred within you. It tears through the inner landscape not with force but with erosion, the kind that hollows mountains and reduces even the strongest foundations into dust. It is the ache of being swallowed by your own shadow, the grief of watching your light dim under a sky that never breaks open. It is the feeling of sinking without movement, drowning in still water, breathing without air. And through it all you continue to exist, barely, quietly, like a ghost lingering between presence and disappearance. A soul trying desperately to remember what it felt like to belong in its own body, to trust its own breath, to believe in its own worth. This is the landscape we step into, not to be consumed by it, but to name it, to understand it, and eventually, to rise beyond it. For me, depression was not a passing cloud or a transient storm that would eventually wander off into someone else's sky. It was a long-term tenant, a relentless squatter in the sacred architecture of my being, uninvited, unmoving, and mercilessly persistent.

It did not knock politely or announce its arrival. It seeped in through the cracks, slid beneath the doorframe, and claimed the hollowed chambers of my soul as though it had always belonged there. While others spoke of sadness as though it were a visitor with an overnight bag, mine arrived with crates, with trunks, with entire shiploads of shadows and unpacked them methodically into every empty room within me. It was not a guest. It was a colonizer. A silent conqueror setting up camp on the ruins of my hope.

The Architecture of Unraveling

It constructed a fortress inside my chest, brick by merciless brick, each stone hewn from doubt, each wall mortared with fear, each battlement lined with jagged memories that cut at me whenever I dared to breathe too deeply. At the gate stood intrusive thoughts, sentinels forged from my own insecurities, patrolling the borders of my mind with ruthless vigilance. They guarded the fortress as though protecting something precious, when in truth they were barricading me from myself. Its presence was not loud, but it was absolute. It seeped into the quiet corners of my being like damp creeping through old stone walls, slow at first, almost imperceptible, until one day the structure sagged, the beams groaned, and I realized the home inside me was no longer safe to live in. Everything felt swollen with vulnerability, waterlogged with sorrow, on the verge of collapse. Depression didn't merely visit my life. It inhabited it. It rewrote the architecture of my inner world so thoroughly that there came a time when I could not remember where I ended and where the darkness began. And this, this colonization of the soul, is where the real unraveling began.

When Survival Becomes Fragmented

Under its rule, even the gentlest tasks became mountains crowned with impossible heights. Rising from bed, once an unconscious ritual of living, transformed into a brutal ascent, as though I were clawing my way up a sheer cliff face with raw, trembling, bleeding hands. The mattress beneath me felt like quicksand, pulling at my limbs, insisting I remain buried in its hollowed cradle. Every movement demanded a strength I no longer believed existed within me. Eating became a fragile negotiation between survival and surrender, each bite a debate, each swallow a reckoning. Food lost its texture, its warmth, its meaning. It tasted like obligation. It tasted like work. Speaking, that beautiful human bridge between inner world and outer, became unbearably heavy, as if every word were a stone I had to haul up from the bottom of a dry, echoing well. My voice felt foreign, dust-covered from disuse, a rusty hinge on a door that had not been opened in far too long. Smiling, once effortless, once blooming across my face without thought or invitation, felt now like contortion, a mask stretched over a hollow I feared others might glimpse.

It no longer came from the heart. It came from habit, from expectation, from the desperate hope that no one would look too closely. My body continued its quiet imitation of life; walking, breathing, existing, while my spirit dragged far behind, a wounded creature crawling across the ground with knees scraped raw and wings too tattered to lift. I trudged through days as though wading through thick, unyielding mud, each step a labor, each breath a negotiation with despair. Time slowed into a viscous haze, hours stretching long and heavy, as though the world were turning through tar instead of air. Under depression's oppressive reign, I did not simply struggle. I survived in fragments, a body moving through the motions of being alive, while the soul that once animated it limped behind in shadows, desperate for a refuge it no longer remembered how to seek.

The Storm No One Else Could See

Outside my window, the world spun effortlessly forward, children spilling laughter across the pavement like scattered sunlight, cars gliding past in steady rhythms, trees swaying in breezes soft enough to soothe anyone who still lived in the realm of color. Life moved in warm, vibrant hues, but my eyes could no longer decipher the palette. What others saw as ordinary beauty became, for me, a distant mural behind frosted glass. Inside me, though, a hurricane roared. A tempest with no rain to cleanse it, no thunder to warn of its coming, no lightning to illuminate its logic, just a ceaseless, invisible cyclone ripping through my thoughts with the ferocity of a storm determined to uproot everything I had ever planted within myself. Its winds tore at the edges of my sanity, whipping through the chambers of my mind until every emotion trembled like loose shutters straining against a force they were never meant to endure. This was not the kind of storm that makes itself known with flashing skies or trembling earth. This was an internal cataclysm, silent to the outside world, yet deafening within. No one could see it raging behind my eyes.

No one could hear the gales screaming through the hollow corridors of my chest. From the outside, I looked functional, upright, breathing, clothed in the illusion of composure. But inside, I was gripping the wreckage of myself with white-knuckled desperation, bracing against winds that existed only in the secret geography of my mind. I lived in the storm's eye, the deceptive calm where everything appears still, but only because destruction is circling around you in endless, merciless rotations. Every breath felt like a negotiation. Every heartbeat felt borrowed. And every attempt at normalcy was a fragile shelter built with trembling hands against a storm that refused to pass. The world outside bloomed with life, but inside me, I was fighting to keep from being torn apart by a tempest no one else could feel. And at the very core of that raging tempest, beneath the shrieking winds of despair, beneath the crushing, airless weight of numbness, sat the eye of the storm: self-hate. Silent, Immovable, Merciless. It did not roar like the storm around it; its stillness was far more terrifying.

It was the cold, unmoving center from which every other devastation unfurled, a gravitational void where hope collapsed and every dark thought was pulled into orbit like debris circling a black sun. Self-hate was not a simple distaste for who I was. It was not insecurity, nor the quiet wish to be softer, better, different. It was venom, slow-dripping, bone-deep, saturating the bloodstream with its poison. It was rot weaving its way through my inner architecture, hollowing me out beam by beam until the structure of me trembled under its own weight. It lived in my marrow, that ancient, primal certainty that something in me was fundamentally cracked, not by circumstance, not by trauma, but by design. As if I had emerged into this world already wrong, already flawed, already marked with an invisible fracture no amount of love or effort could mend. Self-hate whispered that I was born with a missing piece, a warped blueprint, a soul bent out of shape before it even learned to breathe.

And as its poisonous truth sank deeper, I began to believe that the storm raging within me was not something I endured but something I deserved. There, in the still and merciless center, I felt myself becoming the storm, not merely trapped within it, but shaped by it, defined by it, reduced to a trembling silhouette against the furious winds of my own unworthiness. Yet even in that crushing center, even as the tempest spun around me with the force of a thousand unspoken wounds, something small, a spark buried beneath layers of ash, waited for the moment it would dare to flicker back to life.

Suicidal Ideation Takes the Throne

Suicidal Ideation and depression wasn't insecurity; it was annihilation. It was not a passing doubt or a bruise upon my confidence; it was a full-body unraveling, a conviction carved into the soft bone of my being that I was not merely flawed, but fundamentally unworthy of breath, of tenderness, of space in this world, of **existence itself.** It perched on my shoulder like a starving vulture, its wings casting a shadow I could never outrun. It circled my spirit in slow, deliberate arcs, watching, waiting, anticipating the moment I would collapse so it could feast on whatever remained of me. It was a ruthless inner tyrant, relentless, sleepless, a dictator ruling the landscape of my mind with iron fists wrapped in whispers. Each morning, before the sun even touched my skin, it was already awake, forging new accusations, drafting fresh indictments with the precision of a master interrogator. Every day it presented me with new reasons to shrink, new justifications for my disappearance, new arguments for why living was not mine to do. It dug its claws into every memory, even the tender ones, and twisted them until they became evidence of my unworthiness.

It sifted through every hesitation, every stumble, every moment I reached for something and fell short, contorting them into proof that I was defective by design. It is an artist of distortion. It paints your reflection in warped glass, turns your history into a weapon, and folds your every vulnerability into a blade sharp enough to cut you from the inside out. And under its cruel craftsmanship, I became a gallery of mistakes, a body of evidence that the world, it whispered, would be better without me. Yet even as it built this case against my existence, even as it tightened its talons around my spirit, somewhere deep beneath the ruin a single ember remained, small, trembling, hidden, but undeniably alive. It was a voice that carried my cadence, borrowed my breath, wore the shape of my thoughts, yet it was not mine at all. It was an imposter, a shadow-born mimic sharp as shattered glass, cold as winter stone, its edges catching the faintest glint of light only to turn it back into a weapon. It whispered at first, coiling through the quiet like frost threading across a windowpane. Then it learned to shout, to thunder through the hollow chambers of my mind until its echo felt like truth. It insisted with ruthless certainty that I was unlovable, irredeemable, unworthy of joy or even the faintest flicker of warmth.

And in those dim, labyrinthine corridors of my mind, hallways lit only by the trembling candles of doubt, I believed it. I let its voice seep into the cracks of my identity like ink spilled across sacred pages, bleeding outward, staining everything it touched until I could no longer remember where its lies ended, and my own truth began. I let it write my worth in ink that felt permanent, each sentence a sentence, each word a weight. I let it convince me that I was a burden stitched into human form, that the world would spin more smoothly if I simply unclenched my grip and let myself fall away.

The Whisper of Vanishing

In those moments, my absence felt like a kindness, my disappearance a solution, my silence a gift to the people I loved. And that, that is the most devastating cruelty of self-hate: It does not merely wound you. It rewrites reality until you become convinced that your vanishing is an act of mercy. And once suicidal ideation learns to masquerade as mercy, it becomes the most dangerous storyteller of all. It spins narratives with the skill of a seasoned illusionist, casting suffering as inevitability, erasure as grace, and death as deliverance. It rearranges the constellations of your inner sky until the stars no longer point toward possibility, but toward endings that whisper like lullabies to a heart too weary to keep beating. It curls itself around your tenderness, using your sensitivity as tinder for its fire. It knows exactly where you are softest, where the fractures shimmer beneath the skin, where the old scars still hum with unspoken ache. And it presses there, slowly, relentlessly, until even your breath feels like an apology, until your very heartbeat feels like an intrusion in a world you've convinced yourself you do not deserve.

It teaches you to apologize for taking up space, to shrink your voice until it becomes a faint echo lost inside the cavern of your own chest. It teaches you to walk lightly, to tread as though you are always one misstep away from confirming your deepest fear: that you are too much, or not enough, or somehow, both at once. And under its spell, you begin to disappear in small ways first, the dreams you set aside, the laughter you swallow, the needs you learn to bury so deeply you forget they ever existed. Piece by piece, you carve yourself down until you are nothing more than a ghost of your own longing. But the most devastating trick of all is how convincingly it cloaks itself in logic. How rational it sounds when it tells you the world will be lighter without you, how reasonable its arguments seem in the quiet hours when no one else is awake, when the night presses close and the shadows nod as if in agreement.

It becomes a mathematician of misery, calculating false equations of worth, adding up every failure, subtracting every grace, multiplying every flaw, and dividing every hope until the result always equals the same devastating lie: *You do not belong.* And yet, beneath that relentless chorus, beneath the heavy certainty of its fiction, something small, something ancient, still stirs. A spark. A pulse. A quiet, steady refusal to be erased. It may rewrite reality, but it cannot extinguish truth. It cannot touch the ember inside you that refuses to die, that waits for the moment you will finally cup your hands around it and breathe life back into its glow. That ember, tiny, trembling, nearly forgotten, is the beginning of your rising.

When Death Begins to Masquerade as Mercy

My suicidal ideation did not stay silent once it found its throne; it manifested in a thousand subtle, insidious ways, each one a small cut that bled me slowly. It became the whisper that slithered into my ear at night, telling me I was a burden, a weight others carried out of obligation, not love. It painted my reflection in distorted shapes, convincing me I was a failure long before I ever tried, insisting that my dreams were nothing but childish fantasies, fragile bubbles destined to burst upon contact with reality. It seeped into everything, a quiet venom that flavoured every breath, every thought, every trembling hope that dared to rise within me. It became an artist of destruction, sketching shadows across my mind with deft, merciless strokes. It warped the contours of my identity until I could no longer tell where the lies ended and I began. It crept into the smallest corners of my day, the pause before speaking, the hesitation before reaching out, the faltering step before trying something new, and filled each moment with its corrosive whisper.

It told me I had no right to want, no right to take up space, no right to imagine a life gentler than the storm that raged inside me. It taught me to shrink myself until I was little more than a silhouette fading at the edge of my own existence. And when I dared to dream, it punctured those visions with needlepoint precision, turning possibility into mockery, turning hope into humiliation. Every dream became a fragile soap bubble, shimmering with iridescent longing, only to collapse at the faintest breath of doubt. I began to believe that the bursting was inevitable, that I was born with hands that could only break what they held. In time, those whispers became doctrine. They rooted themselves deep, threading through the soil of my soul like invasive vines choking out all softness. What started as doubts grew into certainties, a gospel of unworthiness written in a language I learned too young and spoke too fluently. And it was from that dark altar, built from distortion, shame, and exhaustion, that my self-hate ruled me, crowned not by truth, but by the lies I had been taught to believe were the only story I was allowed to live.

The Lie That Sounds Like Relief

And it did not stop there. It dripped into everything, *every gesture, every breath, every thought*, until life itself felt rigged against me, as though I were cursed to fail before I even placed my foot upon the starting line. It wove itself into the fabric of my days like a stain no washing could lift, bleeding through the colors of my life until even joy looked tainted, suspect, temporary. It stood behind me in mirrors, warping my reflection with its cruel artistry, stretching flaws into grotesque proportions, shrinking strengths until they vanished entirely. Under its gaze, I became a funhouse distortion of the person I might have been, a blurred silhouette flickering at the edges of existence. Every hope I dared to cradle became a target. Every dream, a delicate glass sphere, it smashed gleefully against the stone floors of my doubt. It whispered that wanting more was foolishness, hubris, a crime against reality. That my aspirations were nothing, but soap-bubble fantasies meant to shimmer for a moment, then collapse into wet, empty rings on the pavement of my life. It infiltrated my relationships, convincing me that affection was pity, that kindness was tolerance, that love, when offered, was merely a temporary charity extended to someone too broken to deserve it. It followed me into every room, perched on my shoulder, its breath cold against my skin as it narrated my inadequacy with the confidence of a prophet.

It hollowed me. It starved me. It devoured me, piece by fragile piece. Until one day, I could no longer distinguish where *it* ended, and *I* began. That is the most dangerous part of self-hate's reign: It crawls so far into your bones that you begin to call the invader by your own name. It turned my life into a cruel contest I never agreed to enter, a rigged arena where I was always the defeated contender before the battle had even begun. It erected invisible scoreboards in every room I walked into, numbers flickering in red across the backs of my eyelids, quietly tallying every flaw, every hesitation, every imagined failure. No matter how much I achieved, no matter how loudly others celebrated me, the scoreboard always flashed the same verdict: "*Not enough,* never enough." It forced me into endless comparisons, my worth measured against the lives, bodies, laughter, and successes of those around me. And in that warped mathematics, I always came out less. Less worthy. Less capable. Less lovable. Less human. Like a photograph someone forgot to develop or a story missing all the pages that mattered. Under its influence, perfectionism hardened into a blade I learned to hold against my own throat.

It was not a drive to improve; it was a demand to prove. To justify my existence. To earn the right to breathe. The smallest misstep, the slightest imperfection, the faintest tremble of being human became monumental evidence of my inadequacy, hammered into me like iron nails sealing the coffin it was constructing for my sense of self. Every mistake became a crime. Every flaw, a sentence. Every shortcoming, a shovel of earth thrown onto my own chest as though burying myself alive were the only appropriate response to being anything less than perfect. It does not merely critique. It prosecutes. Condemns. Executes. And leaves you standing in the wreckage it created, believing you deserved the destruction. Yet even as its verdict echoed through the hollows of my spirit, even as I bowed beneath the weight of its false judgment, somewhere deep inside me, beneath the rubble of all that self-dismantling, a soft pulse remained. A quiet objection. A trembling voice rising not to shout, but simply to whisper: "*There must be more than this.*"

The Isolation

And so I withdrew. I folded into myself like a frightened creature seeking the deepest, darkest hollow in the forest where no light could expose its trembling shape. I pulled my spirit inward, tucking my edges tight as though invisibility were a kind of safety, as though shrinking small enough might spare me from being seen, judged, or loved. I vanished from the world in slow, deliberate increments, a fading silhouette slipping behind the curtain, hoping the absence would go unnoticed and believing, with bone-deep certainty, that it *should*. Isolation became both shield and shackle. I convinced myself that if people truly saw me, the cracks spidering across my ribs, the shadows nesting behind my eyes, the bruised truth pulsing beneath my practiced smile, they would recoil, step back, turn away with the kind of quiet disgust reserved for things too broken to mend. So I disappeared. A voluntary exile. A self-imposed vanishing. But the hiding place I built was not refuge.

It was a chamber, airless, echoing, where my thoughts ricocheted off the walls and returned sharper, louder, soaked in venom. In that solitude, the voice of self-hate grew fangs. Its whispers became growls. Its growls became gospel. The more I hid, the more monstrous I felt, a thing stitched together from failures and flaws, a creature better left unseen. And the more monstrous I felt, the deeper I burrowed into the dark. A spiral. A tightening noose woven from my own distorted beliefs. A rope braided from fear, shame, silence, coiling around my throat with the quiet patience of something that believed it had all the time in the world. This was the architecture of my undoing: a labyrinth built by my own trembling hands, a prison forged from the stories I never questioned, the lies I mistook for truth. And yet, even there, in the deepest pocket of the dark, sealed away from breath and light, a single, stubborn truth flickered: I was hiding from the world, but more than that, I was hiding from myself.

The Unfurling of suicidal ideation

And in that shrinking world, where every hallway curved back into itself, where every doorway opened only into another dim chamber of my own unending ache, suicidal ideation began to unfurl its roots. It did not arrive with spectacle or thunder, no violent strike splitting the sky in two. It came the way rot enters wood, quietly, invisibly, a slow seep through the cracked foundations of my being. A moisture you don't notice until the structure groans beneath its own decay. At first, it was nothing more than a passing ripple in thought, a ghost brushing against the farthest corner of my mind: "*Maybe it would be easier if I weren't here.*" A sentence so soft it felt like an exhale, not a warning. A suggestion so faint it could be mistaken for the tired sigh of someone who had simply carried too much for too long. But self-hate; self-hate is the most accommodating soil for suicidal ideation and depression, dark, dense, and rich with old wounds. And despair knows how to grow in it with ruthless, exquisite precision.

Soon, the whisper sprouted fangs. It bit down on the tender edges of my will. It curled around my thoughts like ivy twisting through abandoned stone, tightening with each new doubt, each fresh hurt, each exhausted breath. What began as a murmur became a suggestion, then a contemplation, then a presence sitting beside me in every room. It learned my routines. It adopted my rhythms. It spoke in a voice crafted from my own timbre until I could no longer tell where it ended and I began. It was a serpent uncoiling in the dark, its scales glinting with the seductive promise of quiet, of rest, of release. And I, weary from years of carrying a war inside my chest, found myself listening.

The Presence that shadowed me

What began as a murmur became a companion, then a captor, a presence that shadowed me so intimately I could feel its breath against my pulse. It perched beside me in the quiet moments, a dark familiar with patient eyes, whispering death as if it were a kindness, a soft closing of a door rather than the obliteration of everything I was. It spoke of endings the way poets speak of love, with allure, with certainty, with a tenderness that chilled the bone. It offered me an escape hatch from a torment I no longer knew how to articulate, a twisted doorway painted in false gold, promising rest where my soul had known only exhaustion. It told me that my absence would be a gift wrapped in quiet, a relief to the world that had borne my weight longer than I believed it ever should have. It painted my disappearance as an act of compassion, a mercy I could extend to those I loved. And I, breathing shallow under the collapsing roof of my life, my chest a shrinking corridor, my mind a tightening vise, began to believe it.

As the walls pressed close, as the air thinned to a trembling thread, that voice grew bolder, smoother, more seductive in its certainty. It became the only sound that made sense in the deafening hush of my isolation. And in that suffocating silence, where loneliness reverberated like a second heartbeat, death began to masquerade as peace, a quiet meadow beyond the storm, a stillness beyond the pain, a false sanctuary built from shadows that looked, for a moment, like salvation.

Suicidal Ideation The Architecture

This pervasive self-hate became the bedrock upon which suicidal ideation erected its crumbling, catastrophic architecture, a ruin constructed stone by stone from every moment I believed I did not deserve to exist. When you loathe yourself with such fierce, unrelenting ferocity, the thought of ending your pain doesn't crash into your life like a violent wave. It seeps in like groundwater, slow, inevitable, filling the fractures of your spirit until the idea no longer feels like intrusion but inevitability. It arrives not as horror, but as conclusion, a grim arithmetic that tallies your suffering and whispers that subtraction is the only answer. In your most fractured moments, it feels rational. Almost merciful. Suicide stops looking like destruction and begins to wear the mask of relief, a counterfeit peace shimmering at the edge of your vision. It becomes a lullaby hummed from the shadows, a soft seduction promising quiet where chaos claws, stillness where storms roar, an end to the relentless ache pulsing beneath every breath. It feels like the only doorway left unbolted when every other exit has been bricked shut by your own mind. A dimly lit threshold at the end of a corridor lined with your failures, your shame, your scars, a doorway that promises, in a voice both tender and treacherous: "*You can rest now.*" And in that moment, that fragile, terrifying moment, you believe it.

For me, the thought of ending my life wasn't a sudden impulse or an emotional outburst; it was a recurring negotiation, a long, drawn-out discourse with the darkest part of my mind. A conversation I never invited, never welcomed, yet somehow kept returning to like a wounded animal circling the same patch of earth, seeking a place to finally collapse. It arrived in whispers, not violence, slipping into my consciousness in the stillness of night when the world quieted enough for the inner cacophony to rise unchecked. It was the voice that curled around the edges of my insomnia, soft and serpentine, offering itself as a solution rather than a threat. A velveted suggestion promising an end to the relentless noise inside me, the pounding accusations, the acidic self-loathing, the grief that had learned to speak in my own voice. It posed itself as mercy. As rest. As release. An escape from the unbearable weight of carrying a self I believed was too fractured, too flawed, too fundamentally wrong to deserve breath.

The Seduction

And in that distorted reality, a reality warped by years of inner erosion, suicide didn't look like surrender. It didn't look like the end of hope. It didn't even look like death. It looked like finally laying down the heavy, bone-crushing burden I had dragged through every season of my life, every room, every memory, every waking moment. It looked like the first moment of quiet I could almost imagine. That is the terrifying seduction of suicidal ideation: it trains your suffering so thoroughly that the idea of release begins to glow like a beacon in the fog. A false lighthouse. A shimmering lie. A promise made only in the language of despair. And I, exhausted and unraveling, found myself listening. This is a crippling force, a venom that seeps into the joints of your life until even the smallest movement toward hope feels excruciating, as though every step grinds bone against bone. It is a toxin that settles into the sinew, stiffening the spirit, turning possibility into paralysis.

It calcifies around your hope like winter ice sealing itself over a once-wild river, locking away its flow, its direction, its roar. What once moved freely within you becomes trapped beneath a cold, unyielding surface you can no longer break through no matter how desperately you pound your fists against it. It whispers that there is no thaw coming. No spring. No melt. Only this endless freeze, this suspended, breathless state where transformation feels like a fairy tale meant for other people's lives, other people's skin. It tells you that you are beyond repair, a ruined architecture too fractured to rebuild, a hollow house whose foundation is already crumbling. It tells you that healing is a myth, that hope is a language your tongue will never learn, that you are destined to rot inside the same thought-loop day after day, year after year. And slowly, cruelly, you begin to believe it.

This becomes a set of invisible shackles clasped around your ankles, cold metal formed from every shame-soaked memory, every echo of cruelty, every lie you accidentally adopted as truth. Shackles that do not merely restrain you but tether you to the darkest corridors of your own mind, pulling you back each time you try to move toward light. You learn to live in those corners, mistaking captivity for safety and silence for peace. You stop attempting escape because the chains convince you that suffering is your natural habitat. That this is all you deserve. But beneath even that crushing weight, beneath the bind of those shackles and the ice that seals your river shut, a truth waits, a truth that has not yet died: you were never meant to stay frozen. And though the venom slows the blood, though the chains bite deep, there is a pulse within you that refuses to still. A warmth. A spark. A tremor of life beneath the frost, Waiting.

THE PERFORMANCE OF "I'm Fine"

However, perhaps the cruelest part is how silently it works. It does not roar; it whispers. It does not strike, it seeps. It does not shatter the world around you; it erodes you from the inside out, grain by grain, breath by breath, until the collapse appears as though it happened all at once. We become masterful performers, artists of concealment, experts at stitching masks onto our faces so seamlessly that even we forget where the mask ends and the ache begins. We learn to choreograph our smiles with the precision of a dancer, to time our laughter like well-rehearsed lines in a script, to disguise our internal hurricane behind the calm, courteous weather that the world finds easiest to digest. We walk through our days as actors on a brightly lit stage, bathed in applause for our composure even as our souls haemorrhage behind the velvet curtain. We become fluent in the language of "I'm fine," speaking it with such polished ease that even the people who love us most hear nothing amiss in the tremor of our breath.

And the tragedy is this: we hide with such devotion that the performance becomes a prison. A gilded cage woven from our own silence. We disappear beneath our practiced lines, our rehearsed expressions, our desperate attempts to hold ourselves together just long enough to make it through another day. Eventually, we convince ourselves that we are alone in this, alone in the ache, alone in the suffocating fog, alone in the belief that we are somehow too broken, too flawed, too unlovable to ask for help. Isolation becomes the echo chamber where the lie grows teeth, where the whisper swells into a verdict, where the mind's cruelest stories begin to masquerade as truth. And once that happens, once the lie becomes the only voice you hear, the truth becomes almost unbearable to hold: That you were never meant to carry this alone.

Entering the Dark Rooms of Memory

In the chapters that follow, I will lead you into some of the darkest rooms of my memory, rooms I once locked from the inside, rooms that learned my name by heart. These are spaces where suicidal ideation, depression, and self-hate did not merely visit, but nested. Where it festered like an untreated wound, warm, infected, quietly spreading beneath the skin while I pretended nothing hurt. In those rooms, my thoughts bent out of shape. My behaviors contorted themselves around survival. My sense of self was slowly rewritten by a voice that mistook cruelty for truth. Self-hate braided itself through every strand of my being, entwining with my suicidal ideation until I could no longer tell where one ended and the other began. These memories are not gentle. They do not arrive with soft edges or polite warnings. They are jagged shards of the past, broken glass embedded beneath the surface of my life, pieces I once tried to bury under years of endurance, under silence stacked so thick it felt safer than speaking. To bring them into the light now is not an act of comfort; it is an act of courage.

It feels like peeling back old bandages that have fused to the wound, like lifting cloth from skin that still remembers the fire. The air stings. The exposure burns. And yet, beneath the ache, there is something else stirring. Because wounds hidden in the dark do not heal, they rot. They teach the body to brace, to flinch, to expect pain as permanence. But wounds brought into the light, even trembling, even raw, even aching, are finally given the chance to breathe. So I ask you to walk slowly with me here. To move with tenderness. To pause when you need to. To remember that this descent is not meant to harm you, it is meant to illuminate. What we are about to uncover is not shared to reopen suffering, but to loosen its grip. Not to glorify the darkness, but to name it. and in naming it, begin to strip it of its power. These rooms hold pain, yes. But they also hold truth. And truth, once spoken, becomes the first stitch in the long, careful work of healing.

Staying With the Ache

There will be passages that sting, sentences that graze old scars, moments that press their fingers into places you thought had finally gone quiet. Some pages may feel heavy in your hands, raw against your ribs, so intimate they seem to breathe with you. I know this terrain well, because writing these words cost me the same ache. Each line was a reopening. Each memory, a pulse of heat beneath the skin. And still, I ask you, gently, reverently, to stay. Not because the darkness is kind. Not because it is easy or familiar. But because turning toward it is the first act of defiance. Because what remains unnamed retains its claws. Because shadows only grow monstrous when we refuse to look at them. Before healing can become more than a wish, before it can take root in the body and not just the mind, we must be willing to sit with our wounds without flinching away. To place words where fear once lived. To trace the outlines of the pain instead of sprinting past it, breathless and bleeding. This is the moment we stop running the maze and begin to study its walls. The moment we admit we are tired of circling the same corridors, tired of being chased by echoes of ourselves. Here, we turn back toward the labyrinth, not to be trapped again, but to learn its language, to understand its turns, to discover where the light leaks through the cracks. Because light does not always arrive as a flood. Sometimes it comes as a thin seam, a hairline fracture in the dark, a quiet glow that seeps in only after we have stayed long enough to let our eyes adjust. So if you feel the ache rise, if your chest tightens or your breath falters, pause, but do not disappear. You are not weak for feeling this. You are awake. And awakening, as you will learn, often hurts before it heals. Stay with me here. This is not where the story ends. This is where the darkness begins to lose its grip, and where the first, fragile light learns how to enter.

Chapter Five:
Hope and the Invitation

Facing the Darkness: The Sacred Power of Storytelling

As I look back on this journey, this slow, reverent unearthing of wounds and whispered truths, I am reminded of the ancient, almost sacred power of storytelling. Storytelling is not merely the recounting of what happened; it is the alchemy of the soul. It is the moment raw experience is placed into the fire of language and emerges transformed, no longer only pain, but meaning. Through story, suffering is given a voice, shadows are taught to speak, and what once hunted us in silence is invited into the light. To tell a story is to take what nearly destroyed you and reshape it into something that can be held. It is how we turn ache into articulation, fear into form, chaos into a narrative that no longer owns us. Our words become lanterns, casting warmth where there was only cold. They become bridges, spanning the chasms we once believed made us unreachably alone. When we speak our truth aloud, or write it into being, we loosen the weight of it from our chests. The burden shifts. What was once carried in isolation is now shared, witnessed, and honored. Storytelling binds us to one another, thread by trembling thread, weaving individual fractures into a tapestry of shared humanity. In that weaving, shame begins to lose its authority.

Its grip softens. Its voice grows quieter. And in its place, something else rises. Connection. Recognition. The deep, steady knowing that your pain is not singular, that your survival is not accidental, that your voice matters. Through story, we do not just remember who we were, we reclaim who we are becoming. We step out of the dark corners of our silence and into a living chorus of voices that say, in a thousand different ways: You are not alone. You never were. This is the quiet miracle of storytelling. It does not erase the past. It redeems it. To tell a story is to draw breath into the places we once sealed and boarded shut. To step back into the rooms of ourselves we labeled too fractured, too volatile, too damaged to ever inhabit again. To warm the rooms of ourselves we believed were too broken, too dangerous, too painful to enter again. It is a holy defiance against erasure. An act of resurrection carried out one word at a time. With each word, with each sentence spoken aloud, we loosen the soil from around what was buried alive, and we discover, often with trembling awe, that it was never dead at all.

It was only waiting, waiting for air, waiting for witness. Naming what we endured does not fracture or splinter us; it gathers us. It calls the scattered pieces home. It lifts the weight we mistook for identity and reveals it for what it truly was, its true nature, not who we are, but what happened to us.

When Pain Is Given Language

Pain that went unnamed does not disappear; it waits in the dark, pressing for acknowledgment. When we give it language, it softens. When we give it shape, it releases its grip. What once felt like a sentence becomes a signal. What once felt like a flaw becomes a wound finally allowed to heal. Through storytelling, we gently lay down the armor. The heavy, rusted plates of silence we wore to survive. We set aside the shame that taught us to shrink ourselves into invisibility, the grief that hardened our edges so we would not break again. The self-hate, that whispered that disappearance was safer than presence. We set these burdens aside, not all at once, not without grief, but with intention. And in the space, they once occupied, we make room. Room for breath to move freely through the ribs. Room for compassion to sit without interrogation. Room for healing to cross the threshold and take its place beside us, not as a judge, not as a demand, but as a companion. Story by story, the clenched fist of survival begins to soften. What once gripped as the clenched fist and the world in fear slowly opens into the outstretched hand of becoming. The body learns it no longer has to brace. The heart learns it no longer has to hide.

And in that sacred exchange, between the one who speaks and the one who listens, something quietly alchemical occurs. The telling transforms and reshapes the teller. The hearing transforms and reshapes the listener. Two inner worlds lean toward one another and recognize the same language of ache, the same longing to be understood, and the same hunger to be seen without being fixed. Both hearts are altered by the witnessing. Both hearts are softened by the truth. Both hearts remember, perhaps for the first time in a long while, that they do not beat in isolation. This is the quiet covenant of story. I will speak. You will listen. And somewhere I the space between us, unforced, unhurried, alive healing will begin to breathe. And still, I ask you to come, not with force, not with borrowed courage or borrowed strength, not with bravery you do not yet feel, but with honesty and permission. Come exactly as you are. You are allowed to move slowly here. You are allowed to pause mid-step, to rest your hand against the wall, to breathe when the weight presses too close to your chest, and the air feels thin.

This descent is not a plunge into darkness; it is a deliberate walking, one careful footfall at a time, guided by intention rather than urgency or impulse, by listening rather than conquering. We do not rush the dark. We do not try to outrun it. We listen for what it has been trying, patiently, to say. As we move inward, the shadows will begin to speak, not as threats, not as punishments, not to harm you, but to be known, as witnesses finally given a voice. They will carry the textures of old grief, the metallic tang of fear held too long in the mouth, the ache of words never spoken, that never found a safe place to land. Some memories will rise like fog from the ground, soft at first, blurring your vision until the edges of past and present blur together. Others will arrive like a sudden cold, sharp and startling, catching the breath in your throat. When this happens, remember this truth and let it steady you: feeling is not failing. Tenderness is not weakness. What stirs within you is not here to consume you, but to be seen, to be named, to be released from the silence that once bound it. I will not abandon you in these passages. I will walk beside you, lantern held low and steady, its light intentional and kind, illuminating only what needs to be seen without overwhelming your senses or stealing your pace. When the air thins, we will slow. When the ground feels unsteady and trembles beneath your feet, we will anchor ourselves in breath, in body, in the simple truth of presence.

The Descent as Liberation

You are not required to relive anything to earn your worth. You are not here to prove your pain. You are only invited to notice, to name, to stay connected to yourself as the story unfolds, moment by moment, breath by breath. This first volume is the crossing of a threshold, the moment you choose to turn toward what hurt instead of away from it. Not because it is easy. Not because it is comfortable. But because it is honest. And honesty, even when it trembles in your hands, carries its own quiet, enduring strength. The darkness we enter is not a monster waiting to devour you; it is a landscape shaped by survival, marked by endurance, asking ... patiently, to be understood rather than feared. So take my hand, only if and when you are ready. There is no urgency here. We will move together, guided not by fear, but by care. And though this path winds through shadow, know this, even now, before the next step is taken: It does not, lead nowhere. It leads inward. It leads truthward. And eventually, inevitably, it leads toward the first faint glimmer of light that has been waiting for you all along. But within this descent lives liberation. Within the velvet hush of the darkness, if we are willing to linger and truly look, something glimmers. Not loudly. Not all at once. But insistently. A spark cupped in shadow, waiting for breath. Transformation does not arrive as a trumpet call. It arrives as a flicker.

As a warmth you almost miss. As the quiet realization that what you feared would break you is, in fact, what begins to open you. As we move together through these shadowed corridors, step by trembling step, I hope you feel something shift beneath your feet. A subtle strengthening. A courage you did not know you carried. Not the kind of courage that charges forward unafraid, but the braver kind. The courage to stay. To turn toward your inner figures with curiosity instead of violence. To meet your demons not as monsters bent on your destruction, but as wounded fragments of yourself, carrying messages that were never allowed to be spoken. They are not here to end you. They are here to be understood. My wish is that, as you witness my journey, something in you begins to stir. That the telling of my story loosens the tight knots in your own. That you feel permission to begin listening inward, to gently uncover what has been aching for attention, what has been buried beneath endurance and silence. That you begin reclaiming the parts of yourself that learned to hide in order to survive. And in doing so, you place your foot, perhaps shakily at first, on the path of recovery. Of remembrance. Of rebirth.

Because even in the deepest night, there is a road forward. It may be narrow. It may be uneven. It may be lit only by the smallest, most faithful light. But it exists. And you are not meant to walk it alone. We walk it together. With care. With honesty. With the quiet knowing that every step taken in truth carries you closer to yourself. As you move through these pages, I want to gently prepare your heart for what may rise to meet you. There will be moments that stir discomfort, memories that surface without warning, emotions that press against your ribs like tides testing a fragile shore. This is not a misstep. It is not a failure of strength or resolve. This is the work itself. Healing does not arrive quietly. It asks us to feel what we once buried, to listen to what we taught ourselves not to hear, to sit with sensations we survived by silencing. There may be times when your breath shortens, when your chest tightens, when a sentence lands too close to something tender. When this happens, pause. Let yourself anchor. Place a hand on your body and remember where you are. You are here. You are safe. Feeling is not danger. Feeling is movement. It is the thaw after a long internal winter, the first ache of circulation returning to places long numb.

And hear this with clarity and care. You are not meant to walk through this darkness alone. This is not a solitary trial meant to prove your endurance. As you step into these shadowed halls, my hand is extended toward yours, steady, open, present. I am not guiding you from a distance. I am not waiting at the end with answers; I somehow earned more easily. I am beside you, shoulder to shoulder, another traveler moving through the same storm-worn landscape, learning as you learn how to turn fear into footing, how to let pain become passage instead of prison. There will be moments when the path narrows, when the air feels thin and the ground uncertain. In those moments, we slow. We listen. We breathe. We do not rush the dark or demand it change its shape before it is ready. We let it show us what it has been holding. And step by careful step, with tenderness instead of force, we begin to discover that what once felt like an endless night is also a threshold. A crossing. A place where something new is quietly waiting to be born.

Two Intentions, One Offering

As I begin to pour my most painful memories onto these pages, I want you to feel the intention beneath every word, steady and deliberate, like a heartbeat you can lean your ear against. This offering is woven with two purposes, braided together like threads in the same trembling tapestry. The first is simple and sacred. I want to meet you where you are. To tell you, without hesitation or softening, that the weight you carry is real. That the ache pulsing inside you is not a flaw, not a failure, not a weakness, but a testament to your humanity. Pain is not proof that something is wrong with you. It is proof that you have been wounded and that you are still here. The second purpose is quieter, but no less profound. It is to offer a glimmer. Not a blinding revelation. Not a promise that everything will suddenly be easy. Just a small, steady light, a beacon held low against the wind, cutting through the storm one breath at a time. Sometimes hope does not arrive as a sunrise. Sometimes it comes as a single candle flickering stubbornly in the dark, refusing to go out. The road before us is not gentle. It curves through shadowed terrain and asks much of the heart. It will invite you to feel, to remember, to pause where things once hurt too deeply to touch. But there is a quiet truth I have learned, one etched into me by experience. Darkness thrives in silence. It tightens its grip when it is unnamed, unseen, left to echo unchecked. To face it is to loosen its hold. To name it is to dim its power.

And in that naming, in that brave act of turning toward what hurt instead of away from it, something sacred begins. The holy work of solace. The slow, careful stitching together of what was torn. The gathering of fragile threads that, over time, become something strong enough to hold you. This is not the end of the pain, but it is the beginning of healing. A beginning made not of grand gestures, but of truth spoken aloud, and of light, however faint, allowed to enter. In the volumes that follow, you and I will walk side by side into the slow, tender art of healing, not as something to be conquered, but as something to be cultivated. This is not a sprint toward wellness or a checklist of becoming "better." It is a pilgrimage. A long, winding return to the self. A learning of how to listen inward again, how to gather the scattered pieces of our stories and carry them home with reverence instead of judgment. Together, we will explore the tools, the practices, the quiet rituals that helped me loosen the vise of self-hate, soften the sharp edges of depression, and gently quiet the seductive pull of suicidal ideation when it whispered most convincingly. These are not weapons, but companions. Not fixes but supports. Lanterns for the nights when the path disappears beneath your feet and you must trust the next step before you can see it.

We will wander through sacred terrain, the fragile, fertile ground of self-love, self-acceptance, and self-compassion, seeds we begin planting in Volume Three. At first, they may feel foreign, even undeserved, like placing water on soil you were taught was barren. But with patience, with repetition, with tenderness, you will learn how to tend them. How to notice the smallest green shoots of kindness toward yourself. How to protect them from the old voices that insist nothing good can grow here. This is the work of learning to be in relationship with yourself again, not as an adversary to be disciplined, but as a living being worthy of care. We will practice meeting ourselves with curiosity instead of cruelty, honesty instead of harshness, and mercy instead of punishment. Slowly, almost imperceptibly, the inner climate begins to change. What once felt hostile becomes familiar. What once felt dangerous becomes navigable. What once felt unbearable becomes survivable, and then, astonishingly, liveable. Healing does not announce itself with fireworks. It arrives quietly, like dawn seeping into a room you forgot had windows. And as we walk this road together, step by patient step, you may begin to feel it — the subtle reorientation of your inner compass, the easing of a grip you once believed was permanent. Not a life erased of pain, but a life no longer ruled by it. Not perfection, but presence. Not the absence of darkness, but the growing certainty that you know how to find your way through it.

The Sacred Work of Beginnings

But before any garden can take root, the earth must be touched. Turned. Broken open. Before seeds can drink sunlight, the soil must first remember the weight of the night that pressed upon it. This is the sacred work of beginnings. This is why Volume One asks us to kneel in the dark and place our hands into the cold, compacted ground of what has been buried. Not to punish ourselves. Not to relive pain for its own sake. But to feel where the soil is still hardened, where the roots have been strangled, where something living has been waiting far too long for air. Before we step into the warmth of hope, we must learn the texture of the night. We must walk its contours slowly, listening for the places that still ache when touched, the wounds that throb quietly beneath our daily survival. Volume One does not lead us into darkness to break us. It leads us there to reveal what it has been asking, patiently and persistently, to be healed. Shadows lose their power when they are understood. Pain loosens its grip when it is finally met with attention instead of avoidance. What we face with honesty can no longer rule us from hiding. This is the alchemy of descent. What once terrified us becomes information. What once felt monstrous becomes meaningful. What once threatened to consume us becomes the very doorway through which transformation enters. By facing the shadows, we loosen their chains.

By understanding our pain, we begin the quiet miracle of transmutation. Suffering does not disappear all at once, but it changes its shape. It becomes a teacher rather than a jailer. A passage rather than a prison. And for now, before the work deepens, before the journey widens and the road asks more of you, I want to leave you with something small and steady. A truth simple enough to hold even when your hands are trembling. Hope is still here. Even if you cannot feel its warmth yet. Even if it feels distant. Even if it seems like a story meant for other people, not for you. Hope has not abandoned you. It waits quietly, like an ember buried beneath ash, conserving its heat. It waits for breath. It waits for attention. It waits for the moment you are ready to believe, even slightly, that your story is not finished. And when the time comes, it will glow again. It will warm. It will guide. It is waiting for you. And as you cradle that ember, small and steadfast, let me place another truth beside it, one that belongs to you as surely as breath belongs to lungs. You are not alone. Not now. Not ever. Even when the night convinces you that you are the last light flickering in an empty field, there are hearts beating in quiet alignment with yours, people who would draw near without questions, who would sit on the cold floor of your grief and keep you company until warmth returns.

There are hands, unseen perhaps, but real, ready to steady you when your own begin to shake. There are voices that would speak your worth back into existence when yours has grown tired of believing it. The darkness is a persuasive storyteller. It edits reality. It erases witnesses. It isolates you inside a narrowed version of the world where suffering feels solitary and endless. But this is not the full truth. Beyond the veil of pain, there are souls who recognize your courage even when you cannot name it, who sense the quiet labor it takes for you simply to remain. They believe in the strength you forged without applause, in the endurance shaped by nights no one else saw. They would remind you, gently again and again, that your presence matters, that your staying is an act of bravery, that your life carries weight and meaning far beyond what the shadows allow you to see.

The Strength Beneath the Ash

Within you lives a resilience tempered by fire, not loud or boastful, but enduring. It is the kind of strength that survives collapse, that learns how to breathe under pressure, that keeps a pulse even when hope feels distant. It waits patiently beneath the ash, not demanding, not rushing, trusting that one day you will turn toward it and recognize its warmth. You are more capable than the darkness has suggested. More held than you have been led to believe. And as you move forward, ember in hand, remember this. You are seen. You are wanted. You are accompanied. And you do not have to carry this alone. Do not surrender to the darkness, even when it stretches long and unlit, even when your footsteps echo back with doubt and fatigue. Darkness is not a verdict. It is a passage. A tunnel carved by suffering, yes, but shaped with an exit in mind. It feels endless only because you are still inside it, moving by touch, guided by breath, learning how to trust the next small step when sight has failed you. Walls close in. Air thins. Time loses its edges. And still, you move. On the far side of this night, a light is waiting. Not the blinding glare of false promises, but a living light, patient and real. A warmth that knows the shape of your wounds and does not flinch from them. A glow that does not demand speed or strength, only presence.

It does not shout your healing into existence. It hums it, low and steady, until your nervous system remembers what safety feels like. Until your body believes again that it is allowed to soften. Until your heart relearns how to open without fear of collapse. Healing is not something you must earn through suffering. It is not a reward reserved for the unbroken or the brave. It is your birthright, written into you before pain ever learned your name. It belongs to you simply because you are here, you are breathing, and your story has not finished speaking. Even now, especially now, when everything feels fragile, the dawn is already arranging itself beyond the bend. You may not see it yet. That does not mean it is not coming. So hold on. Hold on in the quiet ways. Hold on by resting when you can, by reaching when you need, by allowing yourself to be human in the middle of the ache. Every moment you choose to stay is a stitch in the fabric of your becoming. Every breath is proof of continuation. The night will not have the final word. It never does. And when the light finally reaches you, it will not ask how you survived. It will simply welcome you forward, exactly as you are.

And so, as we linger at this delicate threshold, where night loosens its grip and dawn has not yet found its voice, Rumi's words settle into the air between us like a benediction carried on breath: *"The wound is the place where the light enters you."* For years, my wounds felt less like doorways and more like open graves, yawning, ravenous, intent on swallowing whatever tenderness dared to come near. Self-hate carved canyons through my inner world. Suicidal ideation tunnelled deep, mining the bedrock of my being until I believed there was nothing left but collapse. And yet, impossibly, tenderly, those same fractures became apertures. What I had named as damage revealed itself as a passage. The very places that ached the most were the thinnest walls between despair and grace. Light did not arrive all at once. It did not flood. It filtered. It threaded itself through hairline cracks, catching on the rough edges of pain, illuminating not perfection but possibility. Each wound became a window. Each scar, a seam where darkness loosened its hold.

Thresholds, Not Endings

I began to understand that brokenness is not the opposite of wholeness. It is often the doorway to it. The places where I had split open were not evidence of failure; they were invitations. Invitations to let warmth touch what had been frozen. To let compassion reach what had been starved. To let truth breathe where shame had sealed the room shut. My healing did not come *despite* the wounds. It came *through* them. So if you carry fissures of your own, if your heart feels fractured, if your spirit bears the map of every place life pressed too hard, know this: you are not leaking light because you are weak. You are luminous because you are open. The cracks do not diminish you. They are how the dawn recognizes where to enter. And as we stand here together, poised between what was and what may yet be, let us honor the wounds not as endings, but as thresholds, places where the light has already begun its quiet, faithful work. What I once mistook for the proof of my undoing slowly revealed itself as the threshold of my becoming. The wounds I tried so desperately to hide were not stains to be scrubbed away, but doors I had been circling for years, afraid to open.

They were stern, uninvited teachers, arriving without mercy or permission, yet carrying lessons my survival depended on. They stopped my flight mid-stride. They turned my face inward. They asked me to listen where I had only numbed, to feel where I had only endured. Those wounds became a kind of sacred ground. Bruised earth. Scorched soil. And still, against all logic, life began to stir there. Resilience sent its first fragile roots downward, winding through pain instead of avoiding it. Understanding unfurled like a cautious leaf, testing the air. Compassion followed, tentative at first, then braver, learning how to stay. Even self-love, that long-exiled guest, began to sprout, not as a grand revelation, but as a quiet willingness to remain with myself instead of abandoning the moment. The light did not arrive as a miracle that erased what hurt. It arrived as recognition. As permission. As warmth finds its way through broken places that had been starved of it for far too long. It did not enter *in spite* of my wounds. It entered *because* of them, because the fractures made room, because the breaking loosened the walls, because the pain had thinned the barriers between despair and grace.

At first, the light was no more than a tremor. A shy glimmer. A pulse I barely trusted. But it persisted. It returned each time I rose from the ashes of who I had been and dared, once more, to stand. And with every rising, the glow grew steadier, illuminating the ground beneath my feet, revealing a path I could follow even when my knees shook. This is how I learned to rise, not once, but again and again. Not by denying the fire that burned me, but by letting it refine me. Not by escaping the ashes, but by allowing myself to be shaped within them. And each time I stood, singed but breathing, I understood a truth that now lives deep in my bones: I was never meant to remain where I fell. I was always meant to become. And so, as the light continues to slip gently through the fractures of my own becoming, I offer you this hope, not as doctrine, not as distant assurance, but as something living, breathing, and close enough to touch. I offer it the way one offers warmth in the cold: palm to palm, presence to presence. What I hold out to you is not certainty, but companionship. Not answers, but a shared horizon.

My story, braided from shadow and flame, ash and breath, is not meant to stand as a monument to suffering or a relic of pain. It is meant to be a lantern, modest, human, imperfect, one you can lift when your own night thickens, when the path blurs, when your feet forget where they are standing. It does not banish the darkness. It simply insists that you do not have to walk it blind.

If This Reaches You

If these words settle softly against your ribs, if they ease the tightness in your chest even a fraction, if they remind you, if only for a heartbeat, that your pain is not strange, not shameful, not solitary, then every fracture I have stumbled through has found its meaning. Every night survived has become a bridge. Every wound has become a window. Let this be enough for now. A shared breath. A shared step. A quiet knowing that someone has walked here before you and lived to reach back. The light may arrive slowly. It may flicker. It may tremble. But it is real. And if you are here, reading this, then it is already finding you. Know this, not as a thought to consider, but as a truth to rest inside, you are not alone. Not in the tremor that runs through you when the night stretches too wide. Not in the questions that circle without answers. Not in the hours when silence swells until it feels louder than your own pulse. Even in the moments when you feel most unseen, unseen threads are holding you, quiet constellations of care stitched into the dark. Lifelines are waiting, not abstract ideas, but living presences. Voices that know how to listen without fixing. Hands steady enough to meet yours when they shake. Hearts that have learned the language of pain and still choose to stay. They exist whether or not you feel worthy of them.

They exist even when hope feels like a word that belongs to someone else. Reaching out is not a fracture of strength. It is a strength taking its first visible form. It is the moment the body admits it was never meant to carry this alone. It is the first stitch drawn through torn fabric, awkward, uneven, perhaps trembling, but necessary. Sacred. The beginning of the repair. You do not have to arrive with polished words or tidy explanations. You do not have to justify your ache. You only have to allow yourself to be met. To let another witness the weight you've been bearing in silence. To let connection do what it has always done best, remind us that pain shared does not double, it divides. If you are standing at the edge of asking, let that be enough for now. Curiosity instead of certainty. A whisper instead of a declaration. One small reach across the space that has felt so vast. Healing does not begin with answers. It begins with contact. And here is the quiet miracle: the moment you reach, the darkness shifts. Not because it disappears, but because it is no longer alone with you. And now, together, we step into the darkness, not as prey, not as penance, but as witnesses. We do not descend to be consumed. We descend to see. To stand steady in the cavern where fear once ruled unchecked, where doubt coils along the walls like cold smoke, where self-hate learned its earliest hymns and sang them until they sounded like truth. Let us walk slowly.

Let us bring breath into the places that have only known holding. Here, the shadows are not omens, they are archives. They carry the imprints of moments you survived, choices you made with trembling hands, nights you endured without witnesses. They whisper their old, cruel lies not because they are powerful, but because they have never been answered. And so we answer them now, not with violence, not with denial, but with presence. We meet these shadows with the quiet bravery of those who are done running. With the courage that says, I will look, even if my voice shakes. I will stay, even when my chest tightens. I will not abandon myself here again.

The Sacred Loosening

This is the beginning. Not a collapse, but an unraveling. Not a breaking, but a loosening. Here, old wounds are not torn open; they are allowed to breathe. Old armor, grown heavy with years of protection, begins to soften, its metal warming against skin that no longer needs to harden to survive. What once felt dead stirs. What once felt lost exhales. This is sacred work. The slow reanimation of the self. The patient returning of blood to numb places. The remembering that nothing within you vanished; it only went quiet, waiting for safety to return. So step forward. Not alone. Not rushed. Not demanded to be fearless. Just willing. We are not here to conquer the dark. We are here to understand it, and in doing so, to reclaim the light it has been guarding all along. Let us find the courage to be raw, not polished, not perfected, not armoured, but real. Let us loosen our grip on the stories that taught us to harden and instead speak from the tender places that still ache. To be human is not to be broken; it is to feel deeply, to be shaped by love and loss, to carry the marks of having lived. And to tell the truth of our own souls is an act of reclamation, a quiet defiance against everything that once told us to disappear.

Beneath the rubble of all we have endured, beneath the collapsed hopes, the fractured beliefs, the bruises left by time, there is something intact. Something steady. A strength that did not shout while we suffered but waited, Patient, Loyal, Unextinguished. It has been there all along, breathing beneath the weight, gathering itself in the dark, refusing to abandon us even when we abandoned ourselves. Together, we will walk this path. Not as heroes, not as saints, but as survivors learning how to soften without shattering. We will move through the night not by erasing it, but by listening to what it has to teach. And with each honest step, each truth spoken, each breath reclaimed, the horizon will begin to change. Almost imperceptibly at first. A thinning of the dark. A paling of the sky. This is how dawn arrives. Not all at once. But faithfully. And we will meet it together, one brave, human, truth-lit step at a time. And so, before we take our first true step into the shadows, allow me to place something tender and luminous into your hands: hope. Not the brittle, performative hope the world offers in slogans and platitudes, but the kind that survives catastrophe. The kind born in ashes. The kind that learns to breathe underground. Hope that does not demand certainty, only willingness. Hope that understands trembling is not failure, but proof that you are still alive.

This hope is not loud. It does not arrive with fanfare or promises of easy passage. It arrives quietly, as a match struck in a cave, small, deliberate, defiant. It asks only that you protect it long enough to feel its warmth. That you shield it from the winds of doubt and the voices that insist it is foolish to believe. This hope knows darkness intimately. It was forged there. And that is why it does not fear the night. Hope is not the erasure of what hurts. It is the choice to walk with what hurts instead of letting it walk you into oblivion. It is the courage to say, "I do not know how this ends, but I am willing to take one more step." It is the steadying breath taken when the ground feels untrustworthy, when the past reaches out with familiar gravity, when fear tightens its grip and asks you to stop. Hope does not promise that the road will be kind. It promises that you will not walk it empty-handed. As we move forward, this flame will flicker. There will be moments when it feels impossibly small, moments when you wonder if it has gone out altogether. But listen closely: hope does not vanish. It retreats. It hides. It waits. And when you cup your hands around it again, when you choose to stay, to feel, to continue, it responds. So hold it gently. Not tightly. Not desperately. Let it breathe.

This is not blind optimism. This is earned hope. The kind that has looked death in the face and chosen life anyway. The kind that knows fear by name and walks forward regardless. The kind that understands healing is not a leap, but a series of quiet, faithful steps. With this flame between us, we step closer to the shadows, not as victims, not as prey, but as witnesses. As seekers. As souls brave enough to believe that even here, especially here, something sacred is possible. The darkness ahead is real. But so is the light you carry. And it is enough to begin. Hope is not born when self-hate finally loosens its grip or vanishes in some cinematic moment of triumph. It is born much earlier, much quieter, in the fissures. In the hairline cracks where cruelty once ruled and tenderness dares to enter anyway. Hope blooms precisely where we choose to love ourselves without permission, without proof, without first becoming "better." It is the brave, trembling act of self-acceptance rising beneath the roar of old wounds, a soft murmur that says, *I am still here*, even when the past insists otherwise.

Hope is compassion learning to speak a new language in places long frozen by shame. It is warmth returning to numb hands. Circulation coming back to a heart that learned to survive by going still. It does not erase the scars; it traces them with reverence and whispers, "*You endured*". Hope is not loud enough to drown out every doubt, but it is steady enough to outlast them. It is the smallest light in the vastest night, a single ember held against the dark, and yet, impossibly, it is enough. Enough to take one more step. Enough to stay. Enough to keep breathing when breath feels like work. And with this light, cupped between us, protected, shared, we continue. Not rushing. Not forcing. But walking forward together, guided by a flame that knows the dark and chooses to shine anyway.

What Shapes Us in the Dark

In the end, it is not the darkness that names us, but the way we move within it. Not the presence of shadow, but the posture of the soul when the light recedes and the familiar landmarks disappear. We are shaped not by the fall of night, but by what stirs in us after it arrives and settles, whether we rise shakily or unsteady, whether we tremble and crawl. Whether we lie still for a moment and gather strength before daring to try again. Whether we pause, pressed flat against the ground of our own despair, gathering breath before daring to move again. Shadows are not sculptors. They do not carve us by their existence alone. They are only the stone. Cold. Heavy. Unyielding. It is our response to their weight that becomes the chisel, carving the slow, sacred outline of who we are becoming. Each breath taken in defiance of collapse. Each heartbeat that refuses to go quiet. Each moment we remain present inside pain instead of surrendering to erasure. This is how form emerges. This is how meaning is shaped. Nightfall holds no authority over our worth. It cannot erase us. It cannot define us. It cannot revoke our belonging. It cannot dissolve our right to exist. Its power and dominion ends at the exact point where our spirit decides to remain present.

What reveals our essence is not brilliance or triumph, it is the quiet courage of endurance, the choice to keep breathing when breath feels heavy and feels like glass in the lungs. To keep the heart open and ajar when fear begs it to seal it shut. To keep existing even when existence feels unbearably and impossibly thin stretched to its final thread. Sometimes becoming looks like standing tall. Sometimes it looks like crawling inch by inch across the cold floor of despair. Sometimes it looks like stillness. Like lying in the dark with your cheek pressed to the earth of your own sorrow, doing nothing more than inhaling again. Sometimes it looks like nothing more than a single breath again in the pitch-black and whispering, "*not yet*". Sometimes it is only a whisper, barely formed, barely believed "one more moment". And that, too, is rising. Because even the smallest act of staying, the gentlest refusal to disappear, is a declaration of life. It is a quiet rebellion written in breath and blood and will. It is the moment the darkness learns something it never wanted to know. That it may surround you. It may weigh upon you. It may whisper of endings. But it does not get the final word.

The void cannot name us. It has no language of its own, only hunger. It does not speak truth; it murmurs amnesia. It asks us, patiently and persistently, to forget who we are, to loosen our grip on memory, meaning, and selfhood until we blur into its endless dark. But the moment we choose to move, even when our knees tremble, even when our footing feels uncertain, we interrupt that forgetting. We take the pen back into our own hands. We reclaim authorship over a story that the darkness was never meant to finish. We are not defined by how deep the night descends, but by the small, defiant acts we perform within it. The quiet rebellions no one applauds. The breath we draw when grief clamps down on our lungs. The way we cup our broken pieces like fragile glass and refuse to let them scatter further. The way we speak *not yet*, not loudly, not triumphantly, but honestly, when the abyss leans close and calls us by name. That whisper, barely audible, is not weakness. It is resistance. It is remembrance.

Each choice to remain is a stitch in the fabric of our becoming. Each breath is a boundary drawn against erasure. Each moment we stay is proof that the void does not own us; it only tests us. And every time we choose to step forward, however unsteady, we declare something sacred: that our story is still unfolding, that our presence still matters, that even in the darkest hollow of existence, we are more than what tries to consume us. This is how we survive the night. Not by banishing the dark, but by refusing to vanish within it. The night itself is only a backdrop, a vast, unlit canvas. It does not define the soul, nor does it possess the authority to name what we are. What reveals us is the way we answer it. The way we respond to its hush, its insinuations, its bone-deep echoes that ripple through the ribs and settle in the marrow. When the dark leans close and waits, it is our response, faltering or firm, whispered or resolute, that shapes the truth of who we are becoming.

And here, my dear listener, is where your power has always lived. Not in the absence of fear. Not in the eradication of pain. But in the moment, you realize that even within the darkest chamber, you still have agency. You still have breath. You still have a choice. A choice that may feel impossibly small, fragile as a moth's wing, yet carries the weight of worlds. The choice to stay. The choice to listen inward instead of disappearing outward. The choice to place one trembling foot in front of the other and say, "*I am still here.*"

Sovereignty

This is the quiet sovereignty the darkness never tells you about. The power that does not roar but endures. The authority that does not conquer but chooses. In this moment, perhaps for the first time in a long while, the narrative loosens its grip. The night pauses. The whispers falter. And something ancient and luminous stirs beneath your ribs. Because now, gently, unmistakably, the choice is yours. It is not self-hate itself that destroys us, but the posture of the soul beneath its weight. Not the blow, but how we stand inside the impact. Wounds do not shatter us by their mere presence; they become destructive only when we are taught to meet them with abandonment rather than care. Each hurt is a stone, yes, but it is the way we stack them, the way we build our inner dwellings around them, that determines whether they become a tomb or a foundation. Self-hate does not carry its own fire. It survives on what we lay at its feet. It lives on the moments we bow our heads, avert our gaze, and mistake its voice for truth. It sharpens itself against our silence and grows bold in the spaces where compassion was never taught to land. Yet even then, it is only an echo, a hollow thing mimicking authority it does not possess. Its weight feels crushing not because it is strong, but because we have been carrying it alone for far too long.

What threatens our becoming is not the bitterness that flickers back at us from the mirror's surface, but the moment we flinch from our own gaze. The story does not end because the reflection is cracked; it falters only when we decide we are unworthy of meeting ourselves there. To look into our own eyes, red-rimmed, exhausted, trembling, and remain present is an act of radical defiance. It is the quiet bravery of saying, I see you, even now. Especially now. Self-hate is not a sovereign force. It is a haunting, a revenant stitched together from old wounds, borrowed voices, inherited cruelties. It has no pulse of its own. It survives only on what we relinquish to it, our gentleness, our self-trust, our right to take up space. Its authority is an illusion, its dominance conditional. And the instant we stop feeding it, when we reach back for even the smallest piece of ourselves, we handed over in fear, it begins to weaken. The turning point arrives quietly. Not with triumph. Not with certainty. But with a pause. A breath caught halfway between collapse and resistance. A moment where you look into the mirror of your own pain and choose, just once, not to flinch. In that moment, something shifts. The ghost falters. The grip loosens. What once felt like an unbreakable verdict softens into a question, and questions can be answered. Healing does not arrive with fanfare. It does not announce itself in grand gestures or sudden absolution. It returns quietly, like breath after a long submersion.

Like warmth seeping back into numb fingers. Like dawn easing its pale gold into a sky that swore it would remain dark forever. The moment we reclaim what was stolen, our voice, our worth, our permission to stay, something ancient stirs. The ghost loosens its grip. And the architecture of our becoming begins, slowly and irrevocably, to change. Healing does not thunder in. It returns the way dawn does, patiently, almost shyly. It seeps through the fractures self-hate tried to seal, warming places long frozen, reminding the body what safety feels like before the mind can name it. It does not demand perfection. It asks only for presence. Only for the willingness to stay with yourself when leaving would be easier. And so the story changes, not because the wounds vanish, but because you no longer abandon yourself to them. You meet them with steadiness instead of shame, with curiosity instead of condemnation. You learn that your tenderness is not a liability but a compass, pointing you back to what is real. Back to what is alive. Back to you. This is how healing begins. Not as a victory over self-hate, but as a homecoming from exile. A quiet reclaiming. A hand returned to your own chest, feeling the proof of life still moving there, whispering a truth that cannot be taken from you again. You are still here. And that has always been enough to begin.

We are not broken by the shadows stitched to our ribs, those dark threads woven through bone and breath. We are undone only when we exile them, when we pretend, they do not ache, when we harden ourselves against their quiet messages. Shadows are not enemies. They are archives. They hold the records of what we endured, the places where love was absent, where fear learned to speak, where survival demanded silence. To sit with them is not to surrender. It is to finally listen to the language of our own becoming. And, in that listening, something sacred happens. The body exhales a breath it has been holding for years. The ache softens from a scream into a murmur. The bruise, once avoided, warms beneath our touch and reveals that it is not lethal... only tender. Seams loosen. Armor cracks. Not violently, but with relief. As if the soul itself has been waiting for permission to rest its weight down. Through those fine fractures, light does not rush. It seeps. It learns the contours of the wound before it illuminates it.

Companionship Instead of Erasure

This is how healing arrives. Not as erasure, but as companionship. Not as the absence of pain, but as the presence of gentleness within it. The storm inside us may still rage, winds tearing through old corridors, thunder echoing through memory. But we are no longer running blind. We learn to walk within the weather. To plant our feet on trembling ground. To move forward not by force, but by fidelity to our own breath. And so we go on. Not whole. Not finished. But alive. Carrying ourselves piece by fragile piece, honoring every shard that still trembles, choosing again and again to stay. Breath by stubborn breath. Step by shaking step. Until one day, we realize the storm no longer defines the sky. It is simply weather; we know how to survive. And beneath it, steady and enduring, our light has been there all along. It is not suicidal ideation that steals our lives, but the exhausting, moment by moment labor of staying present while it breathes down our necks. The ache lies not in the thought itself, but in the courage, it demands of us to keep choosing air, to keep choosing another heartbeat, another fragile step across the threshold of the moment. The darkness, despite its cruel persuasion, is not an executioner. It is a chamber of trial. A low-lit room where the soul is asked to learn a new language, the language of endurance, of whispering yes to life even when every muscle is screaming no. In that chamber, the light does not arrive as a blaze.

It arrives as a filament, a hair-thin thread trembling in the vastness. A single reason to stay. A name. A memory. A promise not yet fulfilled. A breath that surprises you by still being there. And when we reach for it, hands shaking, palms slick with fear, we discover that the filament holds. Not because it is strong, but because we are. Strong in a way that has nothing to do with force and everything to do with refusal. The refusal to disappear. The refusal to let the night have the final word. What truly threatens to undo us is not the presence of the thought, but the lie that we are alone inside it. Isolation is the blade. Silence is the wound. But the moment we name the pain, the moment we let another heartbeat witness ours, the lie begins to unravel. The darkness loses its monopoly. The chamber cracks. Air rushes in where there was once only pressure. And what saves us, again and again, is not certainty. Not clarity. Not strength as the world defines it. What saves us is the smallest rebellion imaginable. The choice to stay while shaking. To stay while bleeding.

To stay while barely able to whisper the word stay at all. It is in that choice, repeated in the quiet anonymity of countless nights, that life is reclaimed. Not dramatically. Not cleanly. But faithfully. This is how survival happens. Not as triumph, but as devotion. A devotion to breath. To presence. To the unfinished sentence of your becoming. And every time you choose to remain, even when remaining hurts, you inscribe a truth deeper than despair ever could: you are still here. And here is where the light keeps finding you. For nestled inside every breath that refuses to surrender lives a courage far older than the pain itself, an ancient knowing carried in the marrow, a pulse that predates every wound. It is the soft, stubborn heartbeat that keeps time when everything else falls out of rhythm, whispering of worlds we have not yet entered, of mornings that have not yet learned our names. It speaks in quiet syllables, barely audible above the ache, murmuring of possibilities not yet lived, of versions of you still waiting in the wings of time. Survival, then, is not the triumph of banishing shadows, but the intimate, almost invisible miracle of continuing in their presence. It is not a roar; it is a vow whispered through clenched teeth.

It is the choice to place one foot in front of the other when the path is swallowed by night, to keep breathing when breath feels undeserved, to stay when leaving feels like mercy. Survival is devotion. A daily, sacred tending to the fragile flame within, shielding it from the winds of despair with shaking hands and an unyielding will.

Becoming Through the Night

And slowly, so slowly, you may not notice at first, something begins to shift. The darkness loosens its grip. The night reveals seams. The heart learns that it can hold pain without being erased by it. You discover that resilience is not a hardening, but a deepening, the capacity to bend without breaking, to endure without disappearing, to rise not in spite of the night but because you learned how to move within it. This is the quiet resurrection that unfolds breath by breath. The slow remembering that you were never meant to vanish inside your suffering. You were meant to remain. To endure. To live. And every time you choose to stay, even trembling, even uncertain, you are not merely surviving, you are becoming. As we continue walking through the darkness together, my deepest hope is that a quiet courage begins to unfurl within you. Not the loud, armoured kind the world celebrates, but a living courage. One that stirs softly. One that stretches its limbs slowly, like a fragile green shoot pushing through frost-cracked earth, unsure of the season yet daring to grow anyway. A courage that does not announce itself but reveals its presence in the simple decision to remain. May you feel it beneath your ribs. A subtle warmth. A low, steady hum. A strength that does not shout but persists. The kind of strength that whispers, just one more breath, when the lungs feel tired. Just one more step, when the ground feels endless. Just one more moment, when time itself feels unbearable.

This is not the courage of victory. It is the courage of staying. Of choosing life in increments so small they can only be felt, never measured. May you begin to sense that even the parts of you that feel broken are still working quietly on your behalf. The parts that tremble in the dark. The parts that learned to curl inward for protection. The parts that forgot how to breathe freely but never stopped trying. They are not failures. They are survivors. They are learning, breath by breath, how to trust the air again. May you find the resolve to keep fighting for those tender places. Not with fists clenched, but with hands open. Not with force, but with faith in your own becoming. To fight, sometimes, is simply to refuse to abandon yourself. To stand guard over your own life when hope feels thin. To cradle your wounded parts and say, I see you. I will not leave you here. And when you stumble, as all who walk this path do, may you remember this. Rising does not always mean lifting off the ground. Sometimes it means staying upright inside the fall. Sometimes it means breaking and still choosing not to disappear. Sometimes it means surviving the night with nothing but breath and intention. That, too, is courage. That, too, is strength. And that, my dear listener, is the quiet miracle unfolding inside you even now.

And when the path grows unbearably heavy beneath your feet, when each step feels like it is taken through wet ash and gravity itself seems to conspire against you, may something gentle within you lift its head toward the unseen horizon. Not a certainty. Not a promise etched in stone. Just an instinct. A small, luminous knowing that refuses extinction. A quiet insistence that there is a dawn meant for you alone. A dawn that does not arrive with blinding light or triumphant fanfare, but with softness. With the hush of first light touching the edges of things once thought lost. A dawn that carries tenderness in its breath. That asks nothing of you except that you remain long enough to feel it. A dawn where the world does not demand your strength but meets your weariness with compassion. Where light does not interrogate your scars, but warms them gently, as if to say, you are allowed to heal at your own pace. For even in the most ink-black night, when the sky feels sealed shut and time seems suspended in sorrow, the simple act of continuing becomes its own defiance. To stay when every part of you is tired. To breathe when breath feels thin. To exist when existence feels unbearably fragile. These are not small things. They are luminous acts of resistance. They are miracles whispered rather than shouted.

Choosing to Stay

Choosing to stay is not passive. It is an active, radiant courage. A quiet revolution carried out inside the body. Each breath is a vote for life. Each heartbeat is a refusal to vanish. Each moment endured a small light struck against the dark. And one day, perhaps without warning, you will notice that the horizon has shifted. That the weight has eased, not all at once, but enough to let you lift your gaze. Enough to feel warmth where there was only cold. Enough to realize that the dawn you hoped for has been moving toward you all along. Until then, stay. Stay gentle. Stay imperfectly. Stay brave. Because even now, even here, your continuing is luminous. And the night, no matter how long it stretches, is already learning that it does not get to keep you. Let this be the beginning of our descent into the Abyss, not a fall, not a surrender, but a conscious lowering of ourselves into the depths that have been calling our names all along. A first, trembling step taken not in haste, but in reverence. A bow to the gravity of what has been endured. May this moment open not merely a chapter, but a threshold, a liminal space where breath slows, where the noise of the outer world softens, and where we cross, quietly and deliberately, into the shadowed terrain within. Here, truth and darkness do not stand opposed; they intertwine.

They braid themselves into a single, quivering thread that leads inward, downward, homeward. This is the place where denial loosens its grip, where pretense dissolves, where the soul is finally allowed to speak in its native tongue. The air is cooler here. Heavier. Alive with echoes. Each step rings against the cavern walls, a reminder that you are still here, still moving, still willing to listen. Consider this an invitation inward. Not to wander aimlessly, but to walk with intention through the silent chambers of your inner world. To revisit rooms you once sealed shut for survival. To stand in places long abandoned and feel the reverberation of your own presence returning. You may encounter relics of pain, fragments of memory, impressions left by moments that shaped you more than you realized. Let them rise. Let them be seen. Nothing here is asking to harm you, only to be acknowledged. This descent is not about becoming lost. It is about remembering. Remembering the shape of your resilience. Remembering the sound of your own truth. Remembering that even in the deepest hollow, something within you has been keeping watch, waiting for your return. And when you emerge, and you will, you may carry marks of the journey.

Scars, yes. Tender places. New awareness etched into your being. But you will also carry something else: a knowing. A groundedness. A truth forged in the dark. You will not come back untouched, but you will come back changed, more whole, more honest, more alive to yourself than before. This is the crossing. This is the threshold. And you are ready. For this is more than a beginning. It is a threshold humming with intent. A doorway cut into the stone of who you have been, opening inward. A summons that does not shout but calls in a voice you recognize somewhere beneath your fear. To answer it is not to conquer the unknown, but to bow to it, to step forward with empty hands and an open chest, trusting that what waits below is not your undoing, but your remembering. The Abyss is not a mouth meant to consume you. It is a cathedral of echoes, a vast inner night where the parts of you once exiled have been keeping vigil. They have been waiting patiently in the dark, not as spectres, but as guardians, each holding a small lantern fashioned from survival, endurance, and quiet hope. They are the versions of you who learned how to endure silence, who learned how to keep breathing when breath felt impossible. They are not broken. They are luminous in ways the light above could never teach.

To descend is to meet them. To walk toward the ache instead of away from it. To discover that the darkness has never been empty, only unlit. And as you move deeper, step by careful step, the walls begin to glimmer. The ground steadies beneath your feet. What once felt like falling slowly becomes a kind of pilgrimage, a sacred crossing into truth. And yes, beyond that descent, far beyond the place where fear loosens its grip and old stories lose their authority, there is a clearing. A place not untouched by pain but transformed by it. This is where your light is born again, not as innocence reclaimed, but as wisdom earned. A light tempered by shadow, steady enough to endure wind, warm enough to guide others home. You are not walking toward annihilation. You are walking toward ignition. Toward the moment you realize that the Abyss was never the end of you, but the womb of your becoming. The air at this threshold feels thick with meaning, as if the walls themselves are holding their breath. This doorway does not promise comfort. It promises honesty. It asks us to bend, to bow, to step downward into the places where our pain learned to hide and our voices learned to hush. The descent is narrow, intimate, lit only by the soft glow of awareness, but it is chosen.

Each step inward is an act of devotion to truth, a refusal to abandon ourselves again. As we move through this opening, the shadows do not rush us. They wait. They reveal themselves slowly, like shapes emerging at dusk, inviting us to touch what we once feared would undo us. Here, the darkness becomes legible. The ache gains edges. The wound acquires a name. And in understanding its shape, we reclaim our power to hold it, to tend it, to carry it without being consumed.

Between the Doorways

And the space between these doors hums with consequence. It presses against the skin like a held breath, charged with everything we have been and everything we might yet become. The first doorway exhales the cool, earthen scent of the underworld of the self, stone and soil and old grief, layered with the faint mineral sweetness of possibility. It invites us not with force, but with gravity. A quiet pull. A knowing. This is the threshold where courage does not roar but bows its head, where bravery looks like willingness rather than conquest. To step through is to agree to be changed, not by annihilation, but by intimacy. Here, we descend not as fugitives from pain, but as witnesses to it, learning its language, its rhythms, its long-kept secrets. We enter the dark not to disappear, but to become fluent in ourselves, to read the hieroglyphs etched into our wounds, and to discover that what trembles in the shadows has been waiting, not to consume us, but to be seen. And opposite it stands the second doorway, quieter, more familiar, worn smooth by habit. It opens outward, away from the inner terrain, toward distraction, denial, the endless postponement of feeling. This is the door we learn early how to pass through without thought. The door of numbing. Of performing. Of survival by avoidance. It promises relief, but only by keeping us circling the perimeter of ourselves, never touching the center, never asking what the ache is trying to say.

It leads us onward, yes, but always farther from the truth that waits beneath our ribs. Between these two thresholds, the air feels charged, almost holy. The body knows this moment even if the mind resists it. The chest tightens. The breath hesitates. Something ancient stirs in the marrow, recognizing that this is not a choice between right and wrong, but between depth and distance. Between remembering and forgetting. Between continuing as we have always done and risking the intimacy of meeting ourselves fully. To choose the inward door is not an act of despair. It is an act of reverence. It is saying to your pain, I will not abandon you anymore. It is allowing the shadows to step forward, not as enemies, but as messengers who have been waiting for your attention. When we descend through that doorway, we do not fall. We enter. We begin to see the wound not as a flaw, but as a language. Not as proof of brokenness, but as evidence of having lived, of having loved, of having endured. And so we pause here, hand hovering over the threshold, heart thudding softly in the dark. There is no rush. No demand. Only invitation.

Whatever you choose in this moment, let it be chosen with awareness, with tenderness. And beside it stands the other doorway, no less ancient, no less demanding. It does not descend, but neither does it promise easy ascent. It is the threshold of denial, polished smooth by avoidance, familiar as a well-worn path walked with eyes averted. It is the door that invites us to turn away once more, to keep moving without listening, to seal the ache behind practiced smiles and forward motion. This doorway asks nothing of us except forgetting. It offers the illusion of safety while quietly asking us to abandon ourselves. Here, between these two openings, time seems to pause. The air thickens. The body knows this moment before the mind can name it. One door leads inward, into the raw geography of truth, where pain is given language and shadows are allowed to speak. The other leads onward, unchanged, into the echo of the same rooms, the same silences, the same wounds repeating themselves in different disguises. To choose the descent is not a declaration of strength, nor a vow of certainty. It is a gesture of honesty. A willingness to say, I will look. I will listen. I will not leave myself behind again. It is choosing to step into the dark with eyes open and breath steady, trusting that understanding is not the enemy, and that what we face with tenderness loses its power to haunt us.

The Doorway That Waits

The shadows beyond that door are not traps. They are maps. Each fear, each ache, each long-avoided truth is a marker pointing toward where you learned to survive, where you learned to harden, where you learned to disappear. To walk among them is to begin learning something new: how to stay. So linger here for a moment. Feel the weight of the choice in your chest. There is no rush. No command. Only an invitation. And when you are ready, know this: the doorway into the shadows does not close behind you. It opens into understanding. It opens into meaning. It opens into the possibility that what you have feared most may become the very ground on which your healing learns how to stand. And in that seeing, something subtle begins to shift. The darkness, once vast and amorphous, starts to feel less like an abyss and more like a chamber. Not empty, not endless, but held. Contained. The kind of place where echoes exist because something once spoke there, because something is still alive enough to answer back. The shadows soften at the edges when they are met with attention instead of avoidance, with presence instead of panic. What once loomed as threat begins to reveal itself as memory, as longing, as grief that never learned how to rest. This threshold teaches us a quiet truth: nothing asks to be healed before it is seen.

Nothing releases its grip before it is understood. As we stand here, suspended between who we were and who we are becoming, we feel the weight of choice settle into our bones. Not the violent choice of rupture, but the sacred choice of staying. Of remaining in dialogue with ourselves. Of allowing the dark to speak without handing it the final word. To cross here is to consent to depth. To accept that transformation does not arrive in blinding light, but in dim rooms where the eyes must adjust slowly, tenderly. It is to trust that what waits below is not an enemy, but a fragment of the self that grew tired of screaming and learned instead to whisper. And when we listen, truly listen, we discover that the darkness has been carrying our story intact, guarding it through years of silence, waiting for the moment we were ready to receive it with care. So we pause one last time at the lip of the descent. We breathe. We feel our feet on the ground. We acknowledge the fear without letting it steer. And then, with a steadiness born not of certainty but of compassion, we step forward. Not to be undone, but to be gathered. Not to vanish, but to return. The doorway closes softly behind us, not as a lock, but as a promise: nothing essential will be lost here. Only what was never meant to remain unspoken.

That other doorway may shimmer with a false hush, a promise of rest that sounds like mercy but carries no warmth. It offers silence, yes, but a silence without breath, a doorway of death. Stillness without return. It cloaks itself in gentleness, speaks in the language of relief, yet asks for everything in exchange. It pretends to be an ending that will finally stop the pain, when in truth it is only an erasure of all that could still unfold. A door that does not lead forward, but away from the unfinished miracle of your becoming. That second doorway does not shout. It never has. It hums. Low and lullaby-soft. A promise shaped like rest. Its handle is cool beneath the palm, smooth with familiarity, polished by countless moments of exhaustion when the soul aches beyond language. It offers quiet where there has been too much noise, stillness where the storm has raged too long. It speaks in the gentle lies of relief, in the dangerous mercy of ending, in the illusion that disappearing is the same as peace.

Suicidal ideation does not arrive as a monster. It arrives as a seducer dressed in compassion. It leans close when the body is spent, when hope feels rationed, when breath itself feels like labor, and it whispers, "You have suffered enough". You can stop now. It frames itself as kindness. As an escape. Sleep without dreams. As a way to make the pain finally behave. But that doorway is not neutral. It does not lead somewhere new. It leads nowhere. It is a door that closes the sentence instead of allowing it to change. A period that is placed where a comma still belongs. A silence that does not listen back. And though it promises an end to pain, it also ends the possibility of anything else ever arriving to meet it. So here we stand. At the hinge point. At the place where despair and choice brush shoulders. And here, together, we do something radical in its simplicity. We do not deny that the second door exists. We do not shame the longing that has glanced toward it. We simply do not step through.

We choose the first doorway. The one that descends rather than erases. The one that asks us to stay present instead of vanishing. The one that leads into ache, yes, but also into meaning, into contact, into the slow alchemy of understanding. We choose the door that keeps breath in the body. The door that keeps the story open. The door that says not yet, even when everything hurts. This choice is not heroic. It is human. It is the quiet defiance of staying. And in choosing it, we do not promise ease. We promise honesty. We promise movement instead of ending. We promise that pain will be met, not silenced. So let the colder door remain where it is. Unentered. Unfed. We turn our bodies, our breath, our trembling attention toward the first threshold. Toward the descent that still contains return. Toward the darkness that can be understood rather than obeyed. Here, at this sacred crossing, we choose to live long enough to listen.

Staying with the Choice

So we linger here, feeling the gravity of the choice in our bones. The air hums with consequence. The heart knows what the mind has struggled to trust. One doorway turns us away from the ache by extinguishing the self. The other turns us toward the ache by honoring the self, enough to listen. One promises escape. The other promises truth. And though truth is heavier, rougher in the hand, it is also alive. Here, together, we choose the first door. The inward one. The descent that still carries breath. The path that keeps the pulse moving, however faint, however shaken. We choose the door that allows pain to speak without letting it decide our fate. The door that leads into shadow with the unspoken vow to return carrying something more than we brought down with us. Understanding. Compassion. A fragment of light. This choice does not deny how tired you are. It does not shame the moments you longed for disappearance. It simply says this: you are still here, and that matters. Your breath still writes sentences the darkness has not finished. Your story has not reached its final line. So we step toward the door that keeps the page open, the door that says stay, even if staying looks like trembling, even if it looks like tears on the threshold.

And as we cross it, slowly, deliberately, with hands still shaking, let this be known. Choosing the inward door is choosing yourself. Not the version polished for the world, but the raw, aching, unfinished self who deserves to be met, not erased. This is not the end. This is the beginning of turning pain into passage. And we do not walk through alone. And as we cross that threshold, the shadows soften their edges. They become less a wall and more a winding corridor, cool to the touch, echoing with our footsteps as proof that we are still here. Each step presses a quiet promise into the ground. I am moving. I am choosing. I am alive. The darkness does not close behind us. It opens, making room for breath, for pause, for the steady rhythm of a heart that refuses to be silenced. Here, the shadows do not demand our disappearance. They ask only for our presence. They ask us to listen to what aches, to tend what trembles, to cradle the parts of ourselves that learned to hide in order to survive. The fragile glow we carry wavers, yes, but it does not go out. It learns the shape of our hands. It learns how to be sheltered. With each careful step, it brightens, fed by the simple courage of continuing.

This inward door does not rush us toward resolution. It teaches us the sacred pace of healing, the slow uncoiling of breath, the patient stitching together of trust. We move not because the path is easy, but because it is honest. Because it leads us back to the place where our name still matters, where our story still wants to be told, where the light has never stopped waiting. And somewhere ahead, beyond the bends and bends again, that light gathers itself. It does not shout. It does not demand. It waits with the quiet confidence of dawn, knowing that those who choose to walk through shadow with care will find their way to it. We keep breathing. We keep walking. We keep choosing the passage that returns us to ourselves. Volume One is where we learn to listen to what the dark has been trying to say all along. It is the slow acclimation of the inner eye, the moment when sight returns not through brilliance, but through patience. In this inner midnight, the darkness is no longer a void but a landscape. Textured. Layered. Alive with meaning. The shadows stretch not to frighten us, but to point.

They gesture toward memories left unattended, toward grief set down too quickly, toward truths we learned to swallow because no one taught us how to hold them safely. This is the place where the soul speaks in its native tongue. Not in polished sentences or neat conclusions, but in sensation, image, ache, and pause. Here, silence does not punish. It instructs. It slows the pulse enough for us to hear what has always lived beneath the noise. Each quiet moment becomes a torch lifted just high enough to reveal the next truth, the next fracture, the next forgotten piece of ourselves waiting patiently in the dark.

Staying with What Hurts

Volume One does not ask us to fix anything. It asks us to stay. To kneel beside what hurts without trying to mend it too soon. To let the wound tell its story before we decide what it means. In this chamber of inward descent, we discover that understanding precedes healing, and presence precedes peace. The act of witnessing becomes sacred. The act of naming becomes revolutionary. And as we move deeper, guided by the soft glow of awareness, we begin to realize something quietly astonishing: the darkness has been holding us all along. Not to trap us, but to preserve us. To keep our truth intact until the moment we were strong enough, gentle enough, ready enough to meet it without turning away. Here, in the marrow of our night, the work begins. Not with answers, but with attention. Not with light, but with listening. This volume invites us to move closer to what we have spent a lifetime skirting around, to enter the rooms we learned to pass by with our eyes averted and our breath held tight. It asks us to walk the long, echoing corridors of our pain not with bravado, but with a reverent, trembling courage. Here, fear is not banished; it is acknowledged, taken gently by the hand, and carried with us as proof that we are alive and paying attention.

Yes, it is a descent, but not one meant to fracture us. This is a sacred unthreading, a patient loosening of the armor we forged in moments of necessity. That armor once saved us. It absorbed blows, deflected cruelty, and kept our hearts beating when the world felt unbearable. But now, its weight has become too heavy. Now, its edges cut into the very tenderness it once protected. Volume One is the moment we begin to lay it down, piece by piece, honoring what it gave us while admitting it is no longer who we are meant to be. This is not a plunge into chaos. It is a guided crossing, a slow and conscious passage through the abyss with our eyes open and our hands steady. The darkness does not rush us. It reveals itself in layers, allowing each truth to surface when we are ready to receive it. Fracture by fracture. Memory by memory. Each revelation arrives not as an attack, but as an offering, asking only to be seen, named, and held with care. And in this revealing, something remarkable occurs.

The self we thought was lost does not remain buried. It stirs. It breathes. It rises from beneath the sediment of years spent surviving. Trembling, yes. Scarred, undeniably. But whole in a way that feels ancient and undeniable.

Not repaired into something new but remembered back into itself. This is the work of Volume One. Not destruction, but disclosure. Not annihilation, but recognition. A descent that does not erase us but gathers us. A journey that leads us downward only so we can finally stand, rooted and honest, in the full truth of who we have always been. It is the turning of our gaze toward the demons we tucked away in the dimmest corners of our being, the creatures we learned to mask with practiced smiles, polite nods, and the quiet art of surviving. This part of the journey is an excavation, slow and deliberate, like brushing dirt from ancient bones. It asks us to lean into the tender, aching places we've tiptoed around for years, the wounds that pulse beneath our ribcage, whispering for witness. To turn toward them is not to invite destruction, but to restore relationship. These demons are not strangers; they are old guardians, misshapen by neglect, starved of language, surviving on silence. They learned to snarl because no one listened.

They learned to hide because exposure once meant pain. When we face them now, they do not rush to attack. They wait. Watching. Measuring whether this time, we will stay. The excavation is quiet work. It cannot be rushed without harm. Each layer of soil carries memory, scent, and temperature. Some earth is dry and brittle, breaking apart at a breath. Some is damp and heavy, clinging to our fingers, resisting release. And beneath it all lie the bones of who we were when the wound first opened, fragile and unfinished, still shaped like hope. As we brush away the debris, sensations rise. A tightening in the throat. A heat behind the eyes. A pressure beneath the sternum, as though something long buried is knocking from the inside. These are not signs of failure. They are proof of contact. Proof that the body remembers what the mind learned to forget. This work asks for presence, not heroics. It asks us to kneel rather than conquer. To witness rather than fix. To allow the ache to speak in its own language before translating it into meaning. Here, courage is not loud. It is the steady decision to remain with what trembles instead of fleeing back into numbness. And slowly, something shifts. The demons lose their fangs.

The bones reveal their story. What once felt like an endless threat begins to feel like an unfinished sentence, finally allowed to reach its end. In this careful, reverent tending, the wounds do not vanish—but they soften. They loosen their grip. They remember that they were never meant to be hidden forever. This is how the descent becomes initiation. Not by destroying what we find, but by listening until even the darkest corners realize they are no longer alone.

Lifting the Veils

This work urges us to lift the veils we draped over our own truth, to sift gently through the scattered fragments of who we were, and who we became in the absence of nurturing. It invites us to sit beside the versions of ourselves we abandoned in the dark, to hear their trembling stories, to acknowledge the pain we once felt we had no right to name. For only when these buried truths are ushered into the light, softly, patiently, compassionately, can the long-neglected pieces finally begin to mend. Only then can the echoes of our past soften into something less sharp, less haunting, something ready, at last, to heal. And as those veils are lifted, one by one, the air itself seems to change. What was once stale with secrecy begins to breathe again. Light does not rush in like an interrogation lamp; it arrives like dawn, gradual and forgiving, touching the fragments without demanding explanation. We learn that truth does not shatter us when it is met with kindness. It steadies us. It gives shape to what once felt unbearable only because it was carried alone. Here, among the scattered remnants, we discover that nothing we were, is truly lost. The pieces are not broken beyond repair; they are simply waiting. Waiting to be seen without judgment. Waiting to be held without urgency. Waiting to be spoken to in the language of compassion rather than correction. We begin to understand that the selves we abandoned were never weak or unworthy.

They were adaptive. Brilliant in their survival. They learned to go quiet, to go numb, to go invisible because that was how they stayed alive. And when we sit beside them now, not as a critic but as a witness, something ancient softens. The nervous system recognizes safety. The heart loosens its armor. The body remembers what it feels like to be met instead of managed. This is the alchemy of gentle attention. The moment when pain, once hardened into echo, begins to change its timbre. The sharp edges dull. The haunting loses its teeth. What once reverberated as threat starts to speak as memory, as meaning, as wisdom earned the hard way. Healing, here, is not erasure. It is integration. We do not banish the past; we invite it home. We allow it to sit at the table, to tell its story without interruption. And in doing so, we reclaim authorship of our own becoming. The echoes no longer dictate our steps; they walk beside us, quieter now, transformed from shadows into teachers. This is how mending begins. Not with force. Not with forgetting. But with the radical, life-giving act of staying present with what once asked only to be seen. And in that presence, something extraordinary happens. The fragments remember how to belong. The silence learns a new language. And the self, once scattered across years of endurance, begins to gather itself, slowly, tenderly, into wholeness again.

And in that gentle sifting, something sacred begins to happen. The fragments are no longer debris; they become relics. Each splinter of memory, each forgotten feeling, each version of you left behind is lifted not with force, but with reverence, as though saying: You mattered then. You matter now. We stop treating our past selves like mistakes to be erased and begin to see them as messengers who carried pain the only way they knew how. This work asks us to kneel where we once fled. To sit on the cold floor beside the child, the adolescent, the fractured adult who learned to survive without tenderness. To listen as they speak in halting sentences and unfinished thoughts. To let their grief have breath. To let their fear have language. To let their anger be understood as a guardian, not a threat. In that quiet witnessing, shame loosens its grip. The stories we were told about our unworthiness begin to lose their authority. Here, healing is not a dramatic rescue. It is a homecoming.

Gathering the Neglected Parts

We gather the neglected parts one by one, wrapping them in the warmth of attention they were once denied. We do not rush them toward forgiveness or demand they make sense. We allow them to exist exactly as they are. And slowly, almost imperceptibly, the nervous system exhales. The body softens. The past, once sharp as broken glass, dulls into something that can be held without bleeding. This is how the haunting changes its tone. The echoes do not vanish, but they stop screaming. They become murmurs of wisdom instead of wounds. They become memory instead of mandate. And in this patient light, compassion does what force never could. It stitches where repression tore. It warms where neglect froze. It teaches the psyche that it is finally safe to integrate what was split apart. The long-neglected pieces do not need to be fixed; they need to be welcomed. Only then does mending truly begin. Only then does the past loosen its claim on the present. Only then do we discover that healing is not forgetting what happened but remembering ourselves back into wholeness. happened, but as a fracture becomes a seam. What once echoed as pain becomes a place of meeting. And what was buried, at last, learns how to breathe again.

It is the quiet apprenticeship of learning the landscape of our suffering, tracing its jagged ridges with trembling fingers, standing in the eye of its storms, and wandering through the hidden valleys where our oldest wounds still echo. Before we can ever hope to heal, we must first become intimate with the terrain within us. We must listen to the rise and fall of our pain like the tide, notice the fault lines it has carved through the years, and witness the patterns it repeats like constellations we were too afraid to name. And so we learn to walk this inner world not as conquerors, but as apprentices, barefoot, attentive, reverent. We learn where the ground gives way without warning, where the earth still trembles beneath old grief, where certain memories open like sinkholes beneath an unsuspecting step. We memorize the places that ache when touched, the passages that tighten the throat, the vistas that still steal our breath with their quiet devastation. This knowing is not morbid; it is merciful. For what we understand, we can tend. What we map, we are no longer lost within. We begin to hear the language of our pain as something more than noise.

Its rhythms reveal themselves, how it surges at anniversaries, how it retreats in moments of connection, how it flares when we feel unseen, unheard, unchosen. We notice how certain stars of sorrow always seem to align, how familiar stories repeat themselves across different seasons, wearing new faces but carrying the same gravity. And in naming these constellations, something loosens. The chaos takes on contour. The suffering gains context. This intimacy asks for patience. It asks us to linger where we once fled, to sit long enough for sensation to speak, to allow emotion to finish its sentences without interruption. It is the courage of staying present when every instinct urges escape. Yet in that staying, the pain begins to change its posture. What once loomed as an enemy reveals itself as a messenger, carrying intelligence forged in survival. It is not here to punish us. It is here to point. Slowly, we discover that healing does not begin with answers, but with attunement. With the willingness to feel without immediately fixing. With the humility to admit we do not yet know the way through, only the way into deeper understanding. And that, too, is progress. That, too, is movement.

Learning to Navigate the Terrain

For when we learn the landscape of our suffering, we also begin to glimpse the paths that wind through it, the narrow trails of resilience worn smooth by years of endurance, the hidden springs of tenderness that never ran dry, the quiet clearings where rest is possible, even now. The terrain does not disappear. But it becomes navigable. And in learning how to walk it, we discover that we are far more capable than we ever believed. This is how healing begins to breathe. Not as a sudden escape from the land of pain, but as a growing fluency within it. A knowing that says: I have been here before. I know where I am. And I am no longer lost. Only when we understand the contours of our inner night can we begin to navigate it with any clarity. Only then can we draw a map, not toward escape, but toward emergence. Healing begins with this recognition: the courage to stand exactly where we are, to acknowledge the shape and texture of our wounds, and to let that awareness guide us toward something gentler, wiser, and whole. It is from knowing the darkness that we can finally begin to imagine the light. And so the darkness becomes less of an abyss and more of a terrain, still vast, still sobering, but no longer unknowable.

When we trace its contours with honest eyes, it stops shifting beneath our feet. We begin to recognize its moods, its seasons, its hidden thresholds. We learn where the night deepens without warning and where it thins just enough to let a seam of starlight through. This knowing does not banish the dark, but it steadies us within it. It teaches us how to move without panic, how to pause without despair, how to trust our footing even when the horizon remains obscured. To draw this map is an act of devotion. It requires us to stay present with the ache instead of rushing toward relief, to name what hurts without embellishment or erasure. We learn the temperature of our grief, the weight of our fear, the grain of our sorrow. We discover that some wounds burn, others numb, others ache with a dull persistence that hums beneath everything. And in acknowledging these textures, we reclaim authority over our inner world. What was once a formless terror becomes a landscape we can navigate with care. Emergence does not arrive as a trumpet blast or a sudden dawn. It begins quietly, almost imperceptibly, as a shift in orientation. We stop asking how to get out and start asking how to move through.

We begin to listen for guidance not from distant promises, but from the wisdom rising inside our own awareness. The wound itself becomes a compass. The ache points us toward what needs tending. The heaviness signals where rest is required. The tenderness marks the places where new life is already stirring beneath the surface. And this is how wholeness begins to take shape, not as a return to who we were before the breaking, but as a deeper inhabiting of who we are becoming. We do not erase the night; we learn its language. We do not deny the shadow; we let it teach us contrast. From this intimacy with the dark, imagination rekindles. We begin, slowly, to envision a light not as an escape hatch, but as a companion, one that walks beside us, shaped by everything we have survived. It is from here, standing honestly within our own night, that the first true glimmer appears. Not blinding. Not loud. Just enough to remind us that direction is possible. That gentleness exists.

That wisdom has been growing in us all along. And guided by this knowing, step by careful step, we begin the long, sacred movement toward the light—not as fugitives from pain, but as authors of our own emergence. This volume is not a gentle companion. It does not offer soft detours or easy daylight. Instead, it descends with you into the dim corridors of your own soul—unflinching, honest, and bone-deep. It holds up a mirror not to punish, but to reveal... reflecting back the pain you've tried to outrun, the grief you've swallowed whole, and the shadows you've learned to navigate by muscle memory alone. Here, we walk beside the raw truths of suicidal ideation and self-hate, not to sensationalize them, but to finally acknowledge what so many survive in silence.

Bearing Witness in the Dark

This volume asks you to slow your breath and steady your footing, because the ground here is uneven and the air carries echoes. It is a companion that does not look away when things grow heavy, that stays when the silence thickens, and the mind begins to circle its oldest wounds. It does not rush to mend or minimize; it kneels with you in the dimness and says, look gently, look honestly. It invites you to feel the weight of what you have carried for so long without language, without witnesses, without rest. In these pages, suicidal ideation is not a spectacle, but a quiet ache given form. Depression is not dramatized but unmasked, seen for what it is: A learned survival strategy that outlived its purpose and turned inward. Here, the mirror is held steady. It reflects not only the fractures, but the endurance etched into them. The nights you survived by instinct alone. The mornings you rose with lead in your chest and still moved forward. The ways you learned to function while unraveling. This volume honors those truths without romanticizing the pain that shaped them. It names the darkness, so it no longer has to shout. It gives shape to the shadows, so they no longer lurk unnamed at the edges of your awareness.

And as we walk these corridors together, something subtle begins to happen. The darkness, once a suffocating mass, starts to separate into contours. Fear gains a voice instead of a chokehold. Grief becomes a presence you can sit beside instead of a tide that drags you under. Even self-hate, when fully seen which is reserved for Volume Three, begins to loosen its grip, revealed not as an enemy born within you, but as a scar left by what you endured. This is not the comfort of escape. It is the relief of recognition. The deep exhale of finally being honest with yourself. This volume is an act of bearing witness to your pain, to mine, to the countless quiet wars fought behind closed eyes and composed faces. It is a space where survival is spoken aloud, where silence is gently interrupted, where the truth is allowed to exist without apology. And though it leads you through shadow, it does so with intention. Because what is acknowledged can be tended. What is seen can be softened. And what is finally spoken no longer has to rule from the dark.

This volume will not wound you, but it will confront you, inevitably, tenderly, and with reverence. It calls you to witness yourself without flinching: The parts you've hidden, the pieces you've abandoned, the fragments you've numbed, the truths you've buried beneath years of survival. It invites you to stand before the full landscape of your being, every ridge of hurt, every cavern of fear, every quiet miracle of endurance, and to finally see what has long waited in the dark to be understood. Here, nothing in you is too much, too broken, or too scattered to bring into the light. Here, the shadows themselves become part of the map home. This volume does not come to break you open for spectacle, nor to pry at your wounds with careless hands. It arrives instead like a slow dawn in a sealed room, asking only that you stay present as the light changes what you can finally see. It confronts you not with accusation, but with invitation. A summons to meet yourself where you actually live, not where you were told you should have survived better, healed faster, or hurt less. It asks you to stand still long enough to feel the ground beneath your feet. To notice how each ridge of pain has shaped your posture, how each cavern of fear has taught you where to crouch, to brace, or hold your breath.

It asks you to look at the fragments you once scattered for safety, the parts you left behind because carrying them felt impossible at the time. Not to judge them. Not to rush them back into wholeness. Simply to recognize them as yours. Here, endurance is not invisible. It is written into the grain of your bones, into the quiet ways you learned to keep going when no one saw the cost. Every survival strategy, every numbing, every retreat is treated not as failure, but as evidence of intelligence under pressure. Proof that you adapted. Proof that you stayed. Proof that something in you kept choosing breath even when hope felt theoretical. And in this seeing, something gentle shifts. The shadows lose their menace and gain their meaning. They become markers rather than monsters. Coordinates instead of curses. They show you where you learned to bend without breaking, where you learned to disappear to stay alive, where you learned to harden because softness was not yet safe. In this light, nothing within you is exiled. Nothing is shamed for how it survived. Even the darkest corners are allowed to speak, not to rule, but to be understood.

This is how the map home is drawn. Not by erasing the night, but by learning its language. Not by bypassing what hurt, but by letting it show you where care is still needed. Here, the path forward is traced through honesty, through compassion, through the radical act of staying with yourself. And step by careful step, what once felt like ruin begins to reveal itself as terrain. Walkable. Knowable. Yours.

WHEN THE WORDS LAND Heavy

There will be moments in these pages that press against your chest like winter's chill, when the weight of the words lands with a thud you can almost taste. Memories will rise like restless ghosts, unseen spectres awakened by the flicker of a candle, carrying tears you believed were long spent but still linger beneath the surface. There will be truths so raw, so unfiltered, they might crack open the protective walls you built to live behind. These moments may rattle you, unravel you, or even fracture some long-held defenses. And when that happens, when the words grow heavy enough to bruise the breath, I ask you not to mistake the ache for harm. This stirring is not a wound reopening at random; it is a thaw. It is the slow return of sensation to places that learned to go numb in order to survive. What trembles is not weakness leaving you exposed, but armor loosening its grip at last. You may feel yourself wanting to turn away, to skim, to rush past the passages that make your pulse quicken, or your throat tighten. That instinct is old and understandable. It once kept you safe. But here, you are invited to pause instead.

To notice the temperature of what rises. To place a steady hand on your chest and remind yourself that you are here, now, breathing, no longer trapped inside the moment being remembered. The ghosts that surface are not here to haunt you. They arrive carrying messages they were never allowed to finish delivering. They knock not to possess you, but to be acknowledged. And when you let them pass through the room of your awareness without slamming the door, something remarkable happens. They soften. They lose their sharp edges. They begin to dissolve back into memory rather than remaining lodged in the present.

If a wall cracks, it is not because you are failing to hold yourself together. It is because the wall has done its job and no longer needs to stand. What unravels was woven in fear. What loosens now makes space for breath. You are not fracturing beyond repair; you are redistributing weight that was never meant to be carried alone. So when you feel shaken, let that be a signal to slow, not to stop. Drink water. Ground your feet. Step outside the page if you need to, knowing it will wait for you without judgment. This work does not demand endurance at the cost of tenderness. It asks only for honesty paced by care. Nothing that stirs here is too much for you to meet. You have already survived the silence of these truths. Meeting them with light, even briefly, even shakily, is not what breaks you. It is what begins to return you to yourself.

Yet I promise you this, and I promise it with reverence: Nothing that rises here is random. Every tremor has meaning. Every tear carries memory. Every broken shard glinting in the dark is part of a sacred pattern you could not see while you were still bleeding in silence. Each one is part of the sacred path toward understanding. What feels like unraveling is, in truth, a remembering. What feels like breaking is often the moment a long-held tension finally releases its grip. Through the ache of bearing witness to your own past, through the courage to feel what you've avoided, you begin to heal. To bear witness to your own past is no small act. It is a pilgrimage inward. It asks you to stand before the echoes of who you were and say, "*I see you now*". And in that seeing, something ancient shifts. The pain does not vanish, but it changes temperature. It loosens. It becomes less of a threat and more of a teacher, less of a sentence and more of a story, finally allowed to be told.

You begin to discover a quiet miracle: the very places you feared would undo you are the places where your strength was forged. The scars you tried to hide are not evidence of fragility, but of endurance. They are proof that you lived through what was never meant to be carried alone. And as you touch them with awareness instead of judgment, they stop burning quite so fiercely. They begin to warm you instead. Transformation rarely arrives as a sudden blaze. More often, it comes like dawn. Slowly. Almost imperceptibly.

Renewal in Small Movements

A softening here. A breath that reaches deeper there. A moment when the ache no longer owns the entire room. Renewal unfolds the way a bud opens under frost-bitten skies: not loudly, not all at once, but faithfully. So if you feel yourself trembling, know that you are not falling apart. You are standing at the edge of something new. And if you feel yourself breaking, know that what is breaking was never meant to be permanent. Through this witnessing, through this courage to feel, you are not returning to pain. You are reclaiming power. And step by quiet step, breath by honest breath, you are being renewed. I share these experiences not to linger in despair, but to offer a glimmer of hope where hope once felt impossible. I speak of these depths not to pull you into the darkness, but to show you that I myself have walked through it and lived to tell the story. Even in the blackest corners of despair, when the night feels endless, and the shadows seem to swallow every last piece of light, there is still a way out. There is always a thread, a spark, a breath that can guide you back toward life. My story is not a monument to suffering, but a lantern held up to prove that escape, healing, and rebirth are possible, even from the deepest abyss.

I offer these memories as one might offer a flame cupped carefully against the wind, not to glorify the cold that once nearly extinguished it, but to prove that warmth can return. I speak of the depths because I know their geography. I know how the air thins there, how time distorts, how the mind begins to mistake endurance for impossibility. I name the darkness not to enthrone it, but to loosen its hold. I tell you where I have been so you might recognize the terrain beneath your own feet and realize, with a startled tenderness, *someone has survived this place*. Even in the most lightless hours, when despair feels like a sealed room, and hope seems like a language you no longer remember how to speak, there remains a way through. It may not appear as a grand opening or a sudden rescue. More often, it arrives as something almost unnoticeable: a thread you follow by touch rather than sight, a spark no brighter than a firefly, a single breath taken not because you believe in tomorrow, but because this moment still allows it. These are not small things. They are lifelines. They are how the soul remembers itself. My story is not an altar built to suffering. It is a lantern raised from within it. Proof that the abyss, no matter how deep, is not infinite.

Proof that darkness can be crossed. Proof that a life once reduced to ash can gather itself again, ember by ember, until fire returns. Healing does not ask us to forget what we endured; it asks us to let it mean something more than our ending. If you are standing now in a place where the walls feel too close and the future feels impossibly far away, let this be the message that reaches you: escape is not a myth. Renewal is not reserved for others. Rebirth is not a fairy tale told to the fortunate. It is a slow, human process, available even here, even now, even to you. I am living evidence that the way back exists. And if my words can light even one step of that path for you, then every descent I survived has become part of your possible ascent. This journey will ask much of you. It will stretch places you did not know could ache, test muscles of the soul you have not had to use in a long while, challenge the deepest parts of your being, and invite you to stand face to face with truths that may first feel too heavy to hold. There will be moments when the pages feel like mirrors, when each word presses close, and your breath catches, when the path forward seems to narrow instead of widen. But stay. Breathe. Walk with me anyway.

The Inner Weather Begins to Shift

Because something subtle begins to happen when we keep moving through these chapters, page by trembling page, step by deliberate step. Beneath the strain, beneath the discomfort, a quiet rearranging starts to take place. The inner weather shifts. What once felt fixed begins to loosen. The storm clouds that hung low and unmoving start to thin at their edges, fraying into something less absolute. And in that softening, light begins its return, not as a blinding revelation, but as a patient presence that knows how to wait for you. When we cross the threshold into Volume Three, you will feel it. The heavy clouds that once felt immovable will slowly begin to part. Light, soft, patient, and benevolent will start to spill across your inner horizon. The sun will rise again, warm and reassuring, touching everything the darkness once claimed. The air changes. The weight eases, just enough for your shoulders to lower. Just enough for your chest to expand. Light spills slowly across your inner horizon, touching places the darkness once claimed as its own. It does not erase what has been; it warms it. It does not deny the storm; it honors what it took to survive it.

This light is benevolent, steady, and kind. It asks nothing of you except your willingness to stand in it. And then, almost without announcement, a quiet miracle unfolds. After so much gray, color begins to return. Not all at once, not loudly, but faithfully. The rainbow of hope, long hidden behind relentless weather, finally reveals itself. Proof that storms are not endings. Proof that beauty does not require the absence of pain to exist. Proof that you are still capable of wonder. This is what healing looks like. Not forgetting the night but discovering that morning knows your name. Not becoming someone new, but returning to yourself, warmed, softened, alive again. After the fiercest dark, light returns. Color returns. Breath returns. And so do you.

First, we must consent to the descent. To step into the valley where breath feels thin and every sound carries an echo. This is the place where fear gathers its voice, where old wounds murmur from the walls, where the silence is so dense it presses against the skin. Here, nothing is abstract. Everything is felt. The night asks us to stand still long enough to see what has been following us all along. We do not enter this valley to be consumed by it, but to witness it with open eyes and an unguarded heart. To stop running. To stop numbing. To let the darkness show us what it has been holding on our behalf. In its heavy hush, truths rise that could not surface in the noise. Pain speaks plainly. Grief finally exhales. Fear, once monstrous in the imagination, reveals itself as something wounded and weary, longing to be seen rather than obeyed. It is here, in this trembling stillness, that an unexpected strength begins to stir. Not the loud kind. Not the heroic kind. But the quiet endurance of a soul that remains present even when everything aches. The strength to stay. The strength to listen. The strength to place one foot in front of the other while the heart quakes.

This is courage in its truest form. Not the absence of fear, but the willingness to stand beside it without surrendering your name. And something subtle happens when we do. The darkness loosens its grip. The silence becomes less oppressive, more spacious. Within that space, a direction appears. Not a blinding beam, but a gentle pull. A turning of the inner compass. The realization that light does not need to be chased. It waits patiently for us to face what stands between us and it. This is how illumination begins. Not by denying the shadows, but by walking through them and allowing them to change us. Not by escaping the night, but by learning how to stand within it until dawn recognizes our courage. We emerge altered. Softer. Stronger. Carrying the knowledge that the very darkness we feared has been shaping us for this moment. And with that knowing, we turn toward the light, not as strangers to it, but as those who have earned their way home.

Descent, Then Return

Volume One and Two is the descent. It is the deliberate turning inward, the slow lowering of the self into the caverns where wounds have been waiting in the dark for someone brave enough to listen. This is the realm of shadow and memory, of truths swallowed whole and names left unspoken. Here, the air is cool and close. Here, the walls remember everything. This is where we meet the parts of ourselves, we learned to abandon in order to survive, and where survival itself asks to be examined rather than worshipped. Volumes Three and Four are the return. The long, patient ascent back toward the surface. They are the gradual reintroduction of light into rooms that have known only dusk. They guide us toward the reclamation of hope that once felt naïve, the rediscovery of self-love that once felt forbidden, and the gentle, world-altering act of forgiveness, first for others, and then, most tenderly, for ourselves. But that ascent cannot begin without this descent. Roots must be touched before growth can occur. Ash must be honored before fire can warm rather than burn.

For we cannot claim victory over what we refuse to face. We cannot disarm the demons we will not look in the eye. We cannot step into the light while denying the night that shaped our bones, sharpened our instincts, and taught us how to endure. Darkness, unacknowledged, rules from the shadows. Darkness, witnessed, begins to soften. And so we begin here. At the threshold. At the place where courage and fear stand shoulder to shoulder, where the pulse quickens and the breath catches, where turning inward feels both terrifying and inevitable. This is the moment the journey inward becomes the first true step toward the journey home. The door is open. The lantern is lit. The ground beneath your feet knows your name. And now, together, we step forward.

Walking through the heart of our darkness is never easy. It asks for a courage that shakes in the knees yet steps forward anyway, for an honesty that peels away armor piece by fragile piece, and for the willingness to face the rooms of the self we sealed long ago for survival. Volume One offers no shortcuts or quick fixes, no rescue ropes tossed from above, or instant salvation. It invites us instead to stand still in the rawness of what is, to feel the ache without anaesthetic, to listen to the body and the soul where they have been quietly speaking all along. It is about standing still in the truth, acknowledging the ache, and preparing the inner soil for what will one day bloom.

This is not the blooming season. This is the groundwork, the slow, deliberate unearthing that must happen before healing can take root. This is the turning of earth with bare hands, the slow breaking of hardened ground, the patient clearing of stones that have weighed down the roots for years. This is the sacred labor beneath the surface. The work that happens before anything visible dares to rise. Here, we learn how to stay present in discomfort without fleeing, how to name the pain without letting it define us, how to breathe in the long nights when answers feel distant, and the path feels unforgiving. The descent is steep, the tunnel narrow, the air sometimes thin, yet even here the promise holds. Even here, something unseen is waiting. Beyond the bend of this darkness, beyond the long stretch of shadow, a softer light is already gathering its strength. It is not rushed. It does not glare or demand. It waits with the patience of dawn. The path is steep, the nights long, and the weight heavy, yet the promise remains unwavering: Somewhere beyond this dark tunnel, light waits. And that light, that gentler illumination, that warmth, and patience, that first permission to rest the soul in kindness, belongs to Volume Three.

I invite you to walk this path with me, not as a test of strength but as an act of devotion to your own becoming. This journey will ask you to stretch beyond what feels familiar, to linger where the soul feels tender, to stay present when old defenses begin to tremble. There will be moments that sting like cold rain against bare skin, moments that loosen the seams you once stitched tight to survive, moments that call for a depth of honesty you may never have offered yourself before. Let those moments come. They are not signs that you are failing. They are signs that something true is stirring. Hold this close as you walk. You are not alone in these passages. Your pain is not imagined or exaggerated. It has weight. It has history. It has meaning. Your story, with all its fractures and fierce endurance, matters more than you have been taught to believe. And your healing, even if it feels distant or unreal from where you stand now, is not a fantasy reserved for others. It is a living possibility that moves toward you even as you move toward it.

So let us continue together, side by side, our steps unhurried, our hands steady in one another's presence. Let us walk toward the horizon where hope begins to return to its rightful place, where light gathers slowly like morning mist lifting from the earth, where a brighter tomorrow waits with infinite patience for you to arrive.

Let Us Begin

Let this book walk beside you as a quiet guardian of the night, a steady presence when the shadows stretch long, and familiar roads disappear beneath your feet. Let it be the hand on your back when the weight of the world presses you forward, the low flame that refuses to go out when hope feels thin, and breath feels borrowed. May these pages become a shelter you can return to, a place to rest when the journey asks too much, a reminder whispered softly into your ribs that you were never meant to carry this alone. Thank you for choosing to step here with me. For trusting these words with the tender truth of your pain, the fragile seeds of your hope, and the unfolding of who you are becoming. That trust is no small thing. It is an act of courage. It is a vow to yourself that your story deserves witness, that your healing is worthy of time, patience, and care.

May we, together, find the light we are seeking. Not all at once, not blinding or absolute, but slowly, honestly, step by step. May each page lift the veil just enough to reveal another facet of your strength, another fragment of your truth, another reason to keep going. And now, as you draw a steady breath and let your heart open just a little wider, know this: the path is waiting, and so are you. Let us begin.

Chapter Six: The day I died

This is the story of the day I died, or the day I believed I had exhaled my last fragment of being. The hour when I was convinced my life had reached its final punctuation, the ink drying on a sentence I no longer had the strength to revise. I remember the weight of that certainty, how it settled over me like a shroud, how the world narrowed to a hush so complete it felt sacred and terrifying all at once. I thought this was the end. The full stop. The quiet surrender of a body and a spirit too weary to keep holding themselves upright. Endings, though, are cunning things. They wear the costume of finality. They arrive cloaked in ash and numbness, in the eerie calm that follows surrender, in the suspended breath where time seems to forget how to move. They convince us they are irreversible, that nothing comes after the stillness. And yet, even there, even in that hollowed-out pause between heartbeats, something inside me refused to vanish completely.

It was not hope as the world defines it. It was smaller. Softer. Almost imperceptible. A tremor beneath the silence. A question no louder than a moth brushing its wings against glass, testing for light on the other side. Was this truly the end? Or merely the moment where the old story could no longer continue as it was? In that suspended space, where everything I had been seemed to dissolve, I did not yet know I was standing at a threshold. I only knew that the darkness, for all its certainty, had not swallowed me whole. Something remained. Watching. Waiting. Breathing, however, faintly. And that fragile stirring, that quiet refusal to disappear, would become the first crack where another ending, and another beginning, learned how to enter the room.

Or was this supposed finality, this imagined extinguishing of breath and pulse, nothing more than the tearing of a page? A brutal, splintering sound in the quiet library of my life, paper ripped from its binding with shaking hands, a violent, shattering page, yet still only a page. Not the book. Not the story itself. Just one chapter ending in a violence born of exhaustion rather than truth. I wondered then, in that suspended hour between surrender and survival, if what I had mistaken for an ending was in fact a threshold. The clumsy, agonizing hinge between what had been unbearable and what had not yet learned how to exist. Was this suicide attempt truly the period I believed it to be, ink pressed hard against the page, final and irrevocable? Or was it a comma masquerading as certainty, a pause gasping for breath, demanding space rather than erasure? The moment felt absolute. The darkness insisted on its authority. It told me there would be no next line, no continuation, no margin wide enough to hold another word. And yet, beneath that insistence, something unruly resisted the silence. A sense that endings, like stories, are rarely as obedient as we expect them to be. That even despair, when pushed to its edge, can become a doorway it never intended to open.

Perhaps what I called my final breath was not an exit at all, but a collapse. A breaking point where the old narrative could no longer hold the weight of my pain. Perhaps it was the sound of the spine cracking, the binding loosening, the story demanding to be rewritten in a language I had not yet learned how to speak. In that fragile reckoning, I did not yet have answers. Only questions, raw and trembling, floating in the aftermath like ash still warm to the touch. But even those questions were evidence of something living. Something refusing to end neatly.

Something insisting that what I believed was closure might instead be the first, agonizing inhale of a chapter I never intended to survive... and somehow did.

Or was it a comma, a pause carved by agony, a breath caught in the throat of the sentence rather than its conclusion. A raw intake of air before the words dared to continue, before the meaning bent and turned toward a direction I had never imagined I would live to write. Perhaps death did not claim me that day at all. Perhaps it reached for me and missed, or perhaps it did something far stranger and far kinder. Perhaps it set me back down inside myself, bruised and splintered and aching, but still breathing. Still here. Not finished. Not yet. Perhaps what I called death was not an ending, but a delivery. A violent return to the body I had tried so hard to escape. A forcing back into the room of my own existence, where pain still waited, yes, but so did pulse and warmth and the stubborn insistence of life. Perhaps the darkness that closed around me was not oblivion, but a chrysalis. A suspended hush. A sacred interval where time loosened its grip and identity fell apart thread by thread. A place between breaths. Between names. Between who I had been surviving as and who I had not yet learned how to become.

Inside that inky blackness, everything familiar dissolved. The stories I had told myself melted down, soft as wax held too close to flame. The armor cracked. The old shapes lost their edges. I was undone there, unmade in ways that terrified me, yet beneath the fear was something quieter, almost reverent. A sense that what was dissolving needed to dissolve. That the self I had been dragging forward could not cross into what came next intact. Maybe that darkness was never trying to erase me. Maybe it was trying to quiet me long enough for something else to stir. Something fragile. Something unnamed. Something that did not yet know its own outline. A new beginning does not always arrive with light and music and open skies. Sometimes it arrives as a collapse. As silence. As the stripping away of everything that could no longer hold.

What I mistook for annihilation may have been transformation in its most brutal form. A womb of unmaking. A place where the old self was broken down to its elements so that a truer one could begin, trembling and unfinished, to take shape. And perhaps that is the most unsettling truth of all. That the day I believed I died was not the end of my story, but the moment the story refused to continue in the same language. I did not rise from that darkness whole. I did not emerge healed or wise or illuminated. I emerged breathing. Shaken. Raw. Alive. And sometimes, that is the first and bravest chapter of becoming.

Maybe it was not the extinguishing of my fire at all, but the hush that follows collapse, the low, glowing aftermath where heat still lives beneath the ruins. The place where flame does not roar, does not announce itself, but lingers. Smoulders. Waits. A hidden pulse of warmth cupped beneath layers of ash, breathing slowly, deliberately, conserving what little it has left. Not gone. Never gone. Only dimmed enough to survive. In that quiet, something ancient was at work. Embers do not rush their return. They gather themselves in secrecy, in patience, in trust. They learn the language of endurance before they remember the language of flame. They listen to the dark. They draw strength from what tried to bury them. And when the moment is right, when oxygen finally finds its way back to the core, they glow again. Softly at first. Almost imperceptibly. A faint blush in the grey. A promise more than a blaze.

Perhaps that was me. Reduced, yes. Scarred, undeniably. But still warm at the center. Still capable of ignition. Still holding the memory of how to burn. The ash did not mean the fire had failed. It meant the fire had survived something enormous. It meant the blaze had gone inward to protect itself, folding into the smallest, most vital truth: stay alive long enough to rise again. And rise I would, not in a sudden inferno, not in spectacle or triumph, but in the slow, sacred way embers return to flame. One breath feeding the glow. One moment, daring to believe in warmth again. One fragile spark at a time, lifting itself from the wreckage and remembering that even after the fire breaks, it still knows how to burn.

The Drift

I found myself drifting, not through any physical corridor of this world, but through a vast, luminous realm of pure consciousness. There was no weight, no ache, no memory tethering me to the body I had abandoned. Only stillness. A profound, unearthly peace that felt like the first breath after drowning, a silence so complete it seemed to cradle me. And then, from within that silence, a voice emerged, not spoken, not heard, but felt in the marrow of whatever essence I had become. The words did not arrive as sound, but as certainty. They did not echo; they *settled*. *It is not your time* moved through me the way gravity remembers its work, the way a tide knows when to turn. There was no command in it, no reprimand, no urgency. Only a calm, unwavering knowing that seemed older than breath itself. The message did not arrive with force or command. It arrived like gravity remembered. Like a truth older than language, settling gently into the core of me. "*It is not your time*". Not a refusal edged with judgment, but a knowing, calm, and unwavering, as if the universe itself had paused, looked at me with infinite patience, and quietly shaken its head.

I hovered in that luminous expanse, that vastness, suspended between surrender and return, my sense of self thinning, reshaping, becoming something softer and more expansive than the body I had left behind. Confusion unfurled through me like a slow-burning flame, not sharp enough to wound, but heavy enough to ripple the stillness. I had come seeking an ending. I had loosened my grip on breath, on life, on flesh, on the long ache of being human with deliberate resolve, believing I had reached the final margin of my story. I had believed I was finished. I had said goodbye in a language no one could hear. I had sought death. I had surrendered to it, welcomed it with trembling hands. Why, then, was I being turned away? Yet here I was, held in a peace so complete it felt intentional, as though I had been gathered rather than discarded or erased.

There was no judgment in that space. No tally of failures. No questions asked. No ledger of sins. No reckoning. Only presence. A vast, compassionate awareness that felt less like an external force and more like a remembering of something I had always known but forgotten. I was not being punished. I was being preserved. The peace and silence around me were not empty. It was full. Full of permission. Full of gentleness. Full of an immense, wordless compassion and love that did not require explanation. It felt less like being confronted by something external and more like remembering a truth I had always carried but long ago forgotten. I was not being rejected by death. I was being protected by life. And within it, I sensed something else stirring, a quiet ache pulling at the edges of that serenity. A tether. A thread still tied to the world I had tried to leave behind. To breathe. To heartbeat. To unfinished becoming.

Choosing to Return

I did not want to go back. The thought of returning to weight, to pain, to the bruised density of living felt unbearable against the silk-soft stillness that held me now. This place asked nothing of me. No effort. No endurance. No explaining. It simply allowed me to be.

The stillness wrapped around me like warm water, buoyant and forgiving. For the first time in years, there was no effort required to exist. No ache humming beneath the surface. No vigilance. Just being. And in that effortless peace, I felt the depth of my exhaustion with startling clarity. I had not wanted to die so much as I had wanted to rest. To lay down the weight of myself. To stop fighting gravity with wounded wings. Yet even as the peace held me, something tugged at its edges. A subtle pull. A filament of unfinishedness. A thread still stitched to breath and blood and the quiet persistence of a heart that had not yet agreed to stop. I sensed it then: this place was not an ending, but a pause. A holy suspension. A threshold between surrender and return. And for the first time in longer than I could remember, that felt like rest. But rest, I was beginning to understand, was not the same as release.

The voice did not repeat itself. It did not argue. It did not persuade. It simply remained, steady as a horizon, patient, letting the truth echo on its own, ripple outward until it reached every corner of what I was. "*It is not your time*". Not yet. Not finished. Not done becoming. And slowly, achingly, I realized what those words carried within them. Not just a turning back, but an invitation. Not just a boundary, but a promise. There was still something waiting for me. Something unfinished. Something that needed my breath to continue unfolding.

The words arrived again, not as sound but as a slow unfurling, like silk opening in still air. Gentle, yet unyielding in their clarity. "*You have not yet learned the lessons you came here to learn. You have not yet fulfilled your purpose.*" Purpose! ... Purpose! ... Purpose! The words burst out of me in an indignant anger. The word struck me with a strange weight, reverberating through whatever shape I inhabited then. *Purpose.* It echoed as if the space itself were testing the syllables, sending them back to me altered, magnified, almost accusatory. Purpose tasted unfamiliar on my tongue, metallic and faintly bitter, like a language my mouth had never been taught to form. I had lived so long without it that the concept felt almost cruel. Purpose was for other people. People with direction. People with futures that made sense. Not for someone like me, hollowed out by grief, wandering the ruins of her own life with no map and no promise of shelter. I had known many things, but purpose had never been one of them. I had known endurance. I had known survival. I had known the kind of grim persistence that keeps a body breathing even when the soul has already folded itself inward. If I had a purpose, it seemed to have been forged in pain, shaped by necessity rather than choice.

A purpose born not from calling, but from coping. Long before I had words to name it, suffering had been my compass. Pain pointed the way forward, even when it led only to more pain. It taught me how to read the weather of other people's moods, how to shrink myself to fit, how to brace for impact before it arrived. It taught me how to stay alive, but not how to live. Since childhood, I had moved through the world like an exile, carrying an ache I could never quite translate. Belonging was a myth I chased with aching devotion, a mirage that shimmered just beyond reach. I ran toward it again and again, convinced that if I tried harder, if I became smaller or quieter or more pleasing, I might finally arrive. But each time I reached out, it dissolved, slipping through my fingers like mist at dawn. A pot of gold promised at the end of a rainbow that vanished the moment I believed in it. I learned early that home was not a place I could rely on, that safety was conditional, that love could be withdrawn without warning. So I kept moving. Kept adapting. Kept surviving.

And now this voice spoke of purpose as if it were something intrinsic, something woven into me from the beginning. As if I were not a mistake drifting through existence, but a story paused mid-sentence. The idea unsettled me. It challenged the narrative I had carried for decades, the one that told me I was here by accident, that my presence was incidental, that my suffering was meaningless. Purpose implied intention. Design. Continuity. It suggested that my pain had not been random cruelty, but part of a larger unfolding I had been too wounded to see. I recoiled from the thought, even as it stirred something fragile within me. Purpose meant responsibility. It meant return. It meant continuing in a world I had tried so hard to leave behind. Yet beneath the resistance, beneath the bitterness, a quiet tremor moved through me. A recognition, faint but undeniable. What if my emptiness was not evidence of failure, but the space where something else was meant to take root? What if the ache I had carried was not proof that I did not belong, but the ache of someone who had not yet arrived where she was meant to stand?

The voice did not explain itself. It did not justify the years of wandering or the grief-strewn road that had brought me here. It simply held the truth steady, allowing it to breathe. You are not finished. You are not done becoming. And for the first time, suspended between leaving and returning, I wondered if purpose was not something to be found at the end of suffering, but something forged slowly within it. Not a destination, but a remembering.

My purpose, or so I had been taught to believe, was not something sacred or self-born, but a relentless audition. A ceaseless proving. I existed in a state of perpetual justification, offering myself up again and again like a résumé written in flesh, hoping that if I loved harder, bent further, endured longer, I might finally earn my place. I tried to become worthy in the eyes of lovers, in the quiet assessments of family, in the unforgiving gaze of the world. Each time I reached toward belonging, I was met instead with the familiar sting of dismissal and disappointment, the old refrain tightening around my chest: *not enough*. The lie echoed until it sounded like truth, until failure felt like my native language, until burden felt like my birthright. In marriage, I learned a more devastating form of erasure. I did not vanish all at once. I faded. Slowly. Politely. I became a shadow cast behind the person I loved, standing just out of focus while their attention drifted elsewhere. I watched as I was chosen last, or not at all, as others were elevated, prioritized, desired over and over, again and again. The other persons, the online affair, and the porn. Me just being something on the side, that they get to come back to each time they've had enough of what they deem better, or for what I can provide them, the comfort, the children, the house, the cooking, cleaning, and whatever else they deem they can use me for.

Each choice felt like a quiet verdict, delivered without words. My presence was tolerated, not treasured. Nothing more than a placeholder for their convenience. My heart became a waiting room, a place they passed through on their way to something else. Something more. My pain did not register as urgent or even significant. It was background noise. Static. My needs were bartered away, adjusted, postponed, and treated as optional line items in the negotiation of keeping peace. As long as their world remained intact, my emptiness was inconsequential. I learned to swallow my hunger, to shrink my longing, to translate loneliness into patience and call it love. I mistook endurance for devotion. I mistook disappearance for grace. And somewhere along the way, I internalized the most dangerous lesson of all: that my worth was conditional. That I existed to be useful, agreeable, and accommodating. That love was something to be earned through self-erasure. I became fluent in absence, skilled at making room for everyone else while abandoning myself. I stood in my own life like an understudy who never made it to the stage, applauding from the wings as my own voice dimmed into silence.

This is the soil in which my despair took root. Not because I was weak, but because I was trained to believe that my existence was negotiable. That lesson did not break me in a single moment. It wore me down grain by grain, until one day I could no longer tell the difference between love and abandonment, between sacrifice and self-betrayal. And it was from this quiet devastation, this slow undoing, that the question of purpose returned, no longer as accusation, but as invitation.

I made a home in the role of protector and rescuer, turning myself into shelter and shelter alone. I learned how to become walls, how to become roof, and door, and lock. I stood between the storms and the people I loved, absorbing the impact, letting the rain soak through my own bones so theirs could stay dry. Standing braced against the storm so others could rest untouched beneath my ribs. I held their hearts as though they were sacred vessels, guarded their fractures with reverence, spoke gently over wounds that were never mine to heal. I absorbed their tempests, let their thunder pass through my chest, believing love meant endurance, believing devotion meant disappearance. I became fluent in vigilance, in anticipating needs before they were spoken, in offering safety even when my own ground was eroding beneath me. I mistook self-erasure for loyalty, exhaustion for love.

And still, the feet I sheltered trampled me without looking down. Still, the hands I steadied learned to push me aside once they no longer needed support. Still, I was devastated by the words of the hearts I had protected with such care, their voices striking harder than any storm, their cruelty cutting deeper because it came from mouths I trusted. I was left bruised by gratitude never offered, battered by devotion never returned. Purpose! The word rose again, sharp, acidic, burning its way up my throat like bile. Purpose! No. Not as I had known it. Not the kind I had been living. Not the shape it had taken in my life. Not the version forged in suffering and sold to me as fate. The purpose I had been taught to inhabit, and as I had come to understand it, was nothing more than pain wearing a name, a long, dark shadow stretched across the years of my becoming. Purpose, I had been taught, slowly and convincingly, that suffering was my destiny. I had come to believe that anguish was my assignment, that hurt was my inheritance, passed down quietly and unquestioned. Betrayal became a language I spoke fluently. Abuse a role I performed without audition. I learned my lines early and delivered them well.

This, I believed, was my purpose. Not because it was spoken aloud, but because it was repeated through experience until it felt indisputable. To suffer. To be used. To be cheated on. To be exploited. To be misjudged and misunderstood. To carry the weight of blame that was never mine, like a sack of stones strapped to my spine, or stones sewn into my pockets, dragging me ever downward. This, I believed, was my function in the grand, merciless, indifferent script of existence. I was the one who absorbed impact. The one who forgave first. The one who stayed when leaving would have been mercy. The one who made herself smaller so others could feel larger. Endurance became my identity. Self-erasure my proof of worth. Pain was not an interruption to my life; it was the architecture of it. I did not ask "*why is this happening to me?*" because somewhere deep inside, I had already decided: "*this is what I am for.*" I learned to confuse survival with meaning, sacrifice with virtue, silence with strength. I did not ask why this kept happening, because somewhere deep within me, a quieter, more devastating belief had already taken root: this is all there is.

The Question That Trembled

And yet, beneath that belief, beneath the learned choreography of suffering, something began to tremble and quiver. A faint resistance. A subtle fracture in the story I had been telling myself. It hovered, uneasy and unresolved, like a question waiting to be answered differently. And in that hovering, something dangerous began to stir. A possibility I had never been allowed to consider. That my purpose was never meant to be my suffering. That I was never meant to be the place where pain came to rest. A hairline crack in the narrative that said pain was my destiny. That realization did not arrive gently. It shook the ground beneath everything I thought I was. But it was there, in the burning refusal of that old definition, that the script began to tear. The word *purpose* no longer landed only as accusation. It began, faintly, to sound like a question. And for the first time, instead of answering it with endurance, I felt the ache of something else rising. Not resignation. Not sacrifice.

But the dangerous, unfamiliar possibility that my purpose had never been to bleed so others could stay clean. That realization did not arrive gently. It shook the foundations of everything I thought I was. But it was there, in that bitter burning, that the old script began to loosen its grip. And in its unraveling, a different truth waited, quiet, patient, and terrifying in its promise. And through the crack in its pages, a different truth waited, quiet and luminous, asking only this: What if your purpose was not to be broken for others, but to finally belong to yourself?

And that belief in purpose as pain had led me here, to the very lip of existence, to the narrow ledge where life and death leaned toward one another and held their breath. It had carried me to the moment my spirit finally loosened its grip on the world, fingers unclenching one by one, as though surrender itself might be an act of mercy. I stood at the precipice, suspended between falling and staying, between ending and beginning, between the story I had survived and the one I had never dared to imagine. And there, in that strange, weightless space, a question rose. Not loudly. Not boldly. It trembled as it emerged, fragile as a newborn breath, unsure if it was even allowed to exist. Is there a purpose beyond this? Beyond surviving by bleeding? Beyond giving myself away until there is nothing left to offer? Beyond laying my body and my boundaries on the altar of something falsely named love?

The question widened, aching, as though it had been waiting my entire life to be asked. Could there be something greater than anguish? Something less suffocating, less cruel than the endless labor of endurance? Could my life be shaped by something other than sorrow and self-erasure? Could meaning exist outside the narrow cage of survival? Could there be a purpose beyond being broken? I had been taught that forgiveness was my highest calling, even when it required my own disappearance. That absolving others for the wounds they carved into me was a virtue, that carrying their harm as my burden was proof of my goodness. I had learned to confuse compassion with self-betrayal, mercy with silence, love with sacrifice. I had been the victim. The scapegoat. The offering laid down so others might remain unexamined, unaccountable, untouched.

But in that liminal hush between breaths, another possibility flickered. What if my purpose was not to be broken and then broken again? What if it was not to endure harm beautifully, or to forgive endlessly without ever being protected in return? What if my life was meant to be more than a series of survivals stitched together by pain? The question did not arrive with answers. It arrived with space. With a loosening. With the faint, radical suggestion that perhaps my existence was not a debt to be paid through suffering, but a gift that had never been meant to be sacrificed at all. And for the first time, standing there between worlds, I allowed myself to wonder, quietly and dangerously: What if my purpose was not to die for love, but to finally live within it?

Or was this voice asking me to return, to step back into the familiar machinery of pain, to resume a life shaped by endurance alone? Was it an invitation to more of the same quiet violence I had learned to call purpose? More years of being the emotional, mental, and physical receptacle for other people's unhealed wounds? More seasons of being the one who absorbs the blows, smooths the edges, carries the weight, only to be discarded the moment my usefulness runs dry, like an object worn thin and tossed aside without ceremony? These were the beliefs that had been etched into me over time, carved not by a single hand but by many. Beliefs that whispered I was only valuable while I was giving. That my worth expired the moment I asked for care in return. That being loved meant being used. That being chosen meant being depleted. I had come to believe, with a devastating certainty, that this was all I was worth. Worse still, that this was all I deserved. That life itself would never offer me anything beyond endurance, betrayal, and the hollow praise reserved for those who suffer quietly.

The question hovered there, suspended in the vastness between breaths, trembling like a held note that refuses to resolve. Was I being asked to go back into the fire simply to burn again? Or was I being asked to see the fire differently, to recognize that what had scorched me before was never meant to be my altar, my identity, my destiny? The universe seemed to be still around that question. No rushing. No insistence. Just a waiting so profound it felt reverent. As though everything, time, breath, existence itself, had paused to see what I would choose. Would I reject the voice, assuming it was another cruel trick, another demand disguised as meaning? Or would I dare, just barely, to consider something I had never allowed myself to believe? That maybe this voice was not calling me back to suffering. That maybe it was calling me forward. Forward into a life where my purpose was not measured by how much pain I could endure. Forward into a story where I was not the sacrifice, but the one finally allowed to remain whole. Forward into the most terrifying, unfamiliar possibility of all. To believe in something more. To believe in me.

What purpose could possibly remain for someone who believed herself splintered beyond repair, worn down to the raw grain, emptied by years of giving until even the act of hoping felt extravagant? What calling could exist for a soul convinced it had been reduced to rubble, too tired to rise, too bruised to bloom, too broken to become anything other than a cautionary tale? And yet, in that weightless expanse, where time loosened its grip and expectation fell away, the questions did not vanish. They hovered. They quivered. They glowed faintly, like embers buried beneath ash, refusing extinction. Each one pulsed with a fragile insistence, a quiet defiance of finality. I felt them stir, not as answers, but as possibility.

Maybe

Then it came. Not thunderous. Not commanding. Not absolute. Just a single word, breathing itself into the silence like the first green shoot breaking through scorched earth. *Maybe.* A word so small it could be missed. A word so gentle it did not bruise. A word that did not demand belief, only curiosity. Maybe you are not finished. Maybe your fractures are doorways. Maybe exhaustion is not the end, but the signal that something old has completed its labor. Maybe what you mistook for ruin was a stripping away. Maybe there is a purpose that does not require your suffering as proof. The word did not promise salvation. It did not erase the past. It did not rush me toward hope I could not yet hold. But it cracked the sealed vault of certainty. It loosened the grip of the story that said there was nothing left. It introduced a breath where there had only been silence. *Maybe* was not an answer. It was an opening. A hinge on which an entirely different life might turn. And in that moment, suspended between who I had been and who I had never allowed myself to imagine, something shifted. Not dramatically. Not loudly. But unmistakably. For the first time, the future was no longer a wall. It was a doorway, barely ajar.

The voice did not answer with language, not yet. Instead, the darkness breathed and rearranged itself, loosening its grip, unfurling into a vast, trembling expanse like night sky learning how to hold stars. The void became a canvas, alive and luminous, and upon it fragments of my life began to surface, not in a rush, but gently, reverently, as if each memory needed permission to appear. Moments I had buried beneath years of anguish floated forward, small and easily overlooked, the kind I had once dismissed as inconsequential. A whispered reassurance offered to a friend standing at the brink of their own undoing. A quiet presence beside someone whose spirit was fraying, when words would have only intruded. A gentle hand resting on a trembling shoulder. A smile given freely, softening another's grief for the span of a single breath. Kindnesses offered without agenda, without scorekeeping, without the hunger to be seen. They glimmered like distant stars, faint but unmistakable, each one a pinprick of light against the vastness of my forgetting. I had called these moments nothing. The voice showed me they were not nothing at all.

With each image, something inside me tightened, then loosened. I felt the ache of recognition, the sorrow of having overlooked my own impact, the quiet astonishment of seeing my life reflected back not as failure, but as touch. As presence. As warmth. The constellation grew, moment by moment, until I could no longer deny the pattern forming before me. These were not grand gestures that shook the world. They were small acts that steadied it. Not miracles carved in stone, but mercy breathed into ordinary moments. Thread by thread, they wove a truth I had never allowed myself to hold. Perhaps purpose had never been about endurance alone. Perhaps it had never been about sacrifice until there was nothing left. Perhaps it had always lived in the spaces where one wounded soul reached for another and chose tenderness instead of retreat. The darkness seemed to lean closer, not threatening now, but attentive, as if inviting me to finally see what I had been carrying all along. And in that seeing, something softened. The question of purpose no longer felt like an accusation. It felt like a remembering.

Tiny seeds of hope. Scattered by trembling hands, dropped into the earth without ceremony, without certainty. Seeds I never lingered long enough to tend, never believed deserved water or light. And yet there they were, pushing upward through the dark, splitting stone with patience, insisting on life in places I had sworn were barren. What I thought were fleeting gestures revealed themselves as roots. What I dismissed as nothing had been everything quietly beginning. And then I saw myself. Not the fractured silhouette I had mistaken for the whole truth. Not the version bent beneath blame and exhaustion, taught to measure worth by how much pain she could endure. I saw the one who had been waiting underneath it all, still as deep water, patient as soil in winter. A self, neither erased nor destroyed, only covered. Buried beneath layers of hurt, misnaming, and survival that had masqueraded as identity. I saw a soul dense with possibility, unspent and luminous. A heart that had learned tenderness not despite the breaking, but through it. A heart that cracked and still chose care. A heart that bled and still reached. I saw a mind threaded with gifts I had gagged into silence, intuition dulled by doubt, creativity starved by fear, wisdom dismissed as weakness because it spoke softly instead of shouting.

This version of me did not demand proof. She did not beg to be worthy. She simply existed. Steady. Breathing. Unapologetic in her aliveness. She had been there all along, holding the shape of who I could become, waiting not for perfection, but for permission. Waiting for me to stop confusing pain with destiny. Waiting for me to finally look at her without flinching. And in that seeing, something irrevocable shifted. The story I had told myself for decades loosened its grip. The belief that I was only broken, cracked open. Not into nothingness, but into possibility. I understood then that I was not empty. I was unclaimed. Not ruined. Unrecognized. The darkness had not erased me. It had preserved me. Like a seed sealed in earth, gathering strength in secret, preparing for the moment I would finally believe I was allowed to rise.

Passions I had buried beneath duty and survival began to stir, glowing faintly at first, like coals beneath a layer of ash, heat still alive, still patient. They breathed in the dark, sending up shy sparks as if asking permission to burn again. Talents I had neglected, convinced they were indulgent or unnecessary, shimmered softly, aching for air, for space, for a voice. Dreams I had once released with grief tightened their wings in the quiet, stretching, remembering the shape of flight. And then the knowing arrived. Not gently. Not gradually. But all at once. It surged through me like a tide breaking against a long-starved shore, flooding the hollow places in my chest with a truth so fierce it stole my breath. I had been living inside the story of my own erasure for so long that I had mistaken it for reality. I had been measuring my life by what I endured rather than what I offered, tallying my worth by wounds instead of witness. Pain had narrowed my vision until all I could see was what hurt, what failed, what fractured. But here, suspended between endings and beginnings, the veil lifted.

I saw that even while breaking, I had been giving. Even while bleeding, I had been planting light. The tenderness I offered. The safety I created. The compassion I poured out when my own cup was cracked and empty. I had mistaken these quiet acts for nothing because they did not roar. Because they did not save me fast enough. Because they did not fit the myth of worth, I had been taught to believe. The darkness had not come to catalogue my failures. It had come to return my sight. It showed me that what I thought was absence was inheritance. That what I believed was emptiness was capacity. That the light I had been searching for in others had been moving through me all along, unnoticed, unclaimed, but never extinguished. I had not lost myself. I had been looking in the wrong direction. And in that revelation, the night loosened its grip. Not because it vanished, but because it had fulfilled its purpose. It had led me back to the truth I was finally ready to hold: I was never only my pain. I was always my light, temporarily forgotten.

Choosing Myself

Then the voice returned. Not with thunder. Not with decree. Not with command or demand. But with the calm certainty of something ancient and intimate, a presence that did not need to raise itself to be heard. It moved through the stillness like breath through warm air, like a hand resting gently at the center of my chest. A reassuring echo from a place that had always known me. "Now", it whispered. "Now you will choose your purpose. Not other people. You. The choice is in your hands." The words did not strike. They opened. They did not command me forward; they invited me inward. They arrived not as rules to obey, but as remembrance, as though a veil had been lifted from a truth my soul had always carried, but my pain had kept hidden. In that moment, something long dormant within me stirred and stretched, recognizing itself. I understood then that I had never been meant to live as an offering laid endlessly on the altar of other people's needs. That my spirit was not forged to be consumed, diminished, or reshaped by cruelty masquerading as love. I had not been born to suffer as proof of my worth, nor to disappear so that others might feel whole.

Purpose, as the voice revealed it, was not sacrifice. It was sovereignty. It was the reclamation of my own breath. The choosing of myself without apology. The quiet, radical act of turning toward my own life and saying, I belong here. For the first time, I felt the weight of choice settle into my palms. Not as burden, but as power. A power that trembled, yes, still fragile, still new, but unmistakably mine. The chains I had mistaken for destiny loosened. The script I had been living by cracked and fell away, page by page, until nothing remained but possibility. I saw that purpose was not something to be earned through endurance. It was not a punishment disguised as meaning. It was a living thing, shaped by intention, nourished by self-trust, guided by the courage to no longer abandon myself for the comfort of others. And standing there, between the life I had almost left behind and the one quietly waiting for me, I felt it at last. The turning point. Not because the pain had vanished. Not because the past had softened. But because for the first time, my life was no longer something that happened to me. It was something I was choosing.

"Choose your potential," the voice murmured, tender as fingertips tracing dust from a long-sealed door within my chest. "You are not bound to the places that hurt you. You are not required to remain in rooms that make your soul smaller." At those words, the space around me stirred, and visions rose like smoke lifting from embers. I saw the relationships I had clung to as though they were lifelines, even as they quietly siphoned the blood from my spirit. I saw how I mistook endurance for devotion, how I confused self-erasure with love. Faces surfaced, familiar and sharp with memory. People who had taken my loyalty as tribute and returned it as betrayal. Promises that dissolved the moment I needed them most. Affection rationed. Safety conditional. I saw hands that should have been gentle. Hands meant to cradle, to steady, to protect. Instead, they left marks. Some bloomed visibly on skin, bruises shaped like silence and fear. Others sank deeper, unseen but heavier, fingerprints pressed into the psyche, into the nervous system, into the way I learned to brace for impact even in moments of calm.

I heard the voices again. Old ones. Repetitive ones. They threaded through my life like a corrosive chant. "You are too much. You are not enough. You are difficult to love. You are lucky anyone stays." They spoke so often, with such authority, that eventually I stopped questioning their origin and began mistaking them for my own thoughts. And with a hollow ache, I realized how thoroughly I had furnished those shrinking rooms. How I had rearranged myself to fit inside them. How I had dimmed my light, softened my needs, swallowed my truth, all to remain where I was being slowly undone. The visions did not accuse me. They did not shame me. They simply showed me the cost. And then the voice returned, quieter still, almost reverent. "You stayed because you were surviving. But you are no longer required to survive this way." Something inside me loosened at that. A knot I had worn for so long it felt like bone finally softened. I saw that those places, those people, those patterns were not destiny. They were chapters. Rooms I had once needed for shelter, but which had long since become cages. The door within my chest creaked open.

Beyond it, there was space. Breath. An unoccupied future humming softly, not demanding, not punishing, simply waiting. A place where my worth was not negotiated. Where my presence did not require payment in pain. For the first time, I understood that choosing my potential did not mean becoming someone else. It meant leaving what was breaking me. And turning, at last, toward the life that had been patiently holding the door open from the other side.

"You get to choose what you accept," the whisper continued, firmer now, settling into me like a truth knitting itself to bone. It was no longer a suggestion drifting on mercy, but a law of the soul spoken with quiet authority. A boundary drawn in light. "If they cheat, leave." The words fell like clean cuts through old fog, sharp but merciful, severing what had festered too long. "If they harm you, leave." Not in rage, not in spectacle, but in reverence for the life pulsing inside your chest. "If they misuse your heart, leave." Your heart is not a tool. Not a resource to be drained. Not a battlefield where others prove their power. "If they betray you, leave."

Because betrayal is not a mistake when it becomes a pattern. It is a language. And you are not required to keep translating pain into patience. "If they keep breaking your trust, leave." Trust is not something you are meant to bleed for endlessly. It is a bridge built by two hands, or it collapses. "If they abuse you, exploit you, diminish you, erase you..." The whisper paused, heavy with grief and knowing. "Leave." Each word landed not as condemnation, but as permission. Permission I had never been given. Permission I had never granted myself.

"You cannot control their actions," the voice continued, softer now, but no less steady. "You cannot rewrite who they are or heal what they refuse to face. But you can choose whether you remain in the path of their storms. You can choose whether your body continues to brace for blows disguised as love." I felt it then. The truth I had avoided for lifetimes. Staying was not loyalty. Enduring was not virtue. Suffering was not proof of love. "You get to choose how you respond," the whisper said, "and more importantly, you get to choose how you allow yourself to be treated." The words moved through me like fresh air through a long-sealed house, lifting dust, unsettling ghosts, making space where resignation had lived. I saw how often I had mistaken tolerance for compassion, self-abandonment for strength. How I had stood still in burning rooms, convincing myself it was noble not to run. But this truth did not ask me to harden. It asked me to honor myself. Leaving, I understood, was not failure. It was discernment. It was self-respect finally finding its voice. To walk away was not to give up on love. It was to stop offering my life at the altar of someone else's unhealed wounds.

And as that realization settled, something ancient inside me straightened its spine. A lineage of women who had stayed too long exhaled through me. A future version of myself stepped closer. For the first time, I understood that boundaries are not walls built in bitterness. They are doors we close gently, so we may open others that lead toward life. And in that knowing, I felt the beginning of a new vow form in my chest. Not to others. But to myself.

Every word unfurled inside me like flame finally meeting oxygen, brightening, strengthening, remembering how to burn. Something ancient stirred beneath my ribs, a long-silenced knowing stretching awake. For the first time, I understood with a clarity that rang through my bones: I was never powerless. I had never been weak. I had simply never been taught my own worth. No one had shown me that love is not something you audition for, nor something you earn through endurance. No one had told me that respect is not a reward for obedience, or that being chosen should never require erasing yourself to be palatable. I had not lacked strength; I had been swimming in it my whole life, mistaking it for survival. I had confused people-pleasing with compassion. Silence with grace. Endurance with devotion. I had been praised for how much I could tolerate, how deeply I could bend, how long I could stay even while disappearing. And somewhere along the way, I internalized the lie that suffering was proof of love, that pain was the price of belonging, that loyalty meant bleeding quietly.

But now, in this suspended space between who I had been and who I was becoming, the truth rose unmistakable and fierce: suffering is not a purpose. It never was. It is not noble to remain where your spirit is starved. It is not loving to abandon yourself in the name of keeping others comfortable. Leaving, I saw, is sometimes the most sacred form of staying. Staying aligned. Staying sovereign. Staying alive. I had never been in chains. I had been holding them myself, believing they were vows, mistaking captivity for commitment. And with that realization came a shuddering release. A loosening. A breath I had not taken in decades. I saw it clearly then: when love is conditional, it is not love. When affection must be proven through self-erasure, it is not devotion. When staying costs you your dignity, your safety, your voice, your light, it is not loyalty, it is loss. I had always possessed the power to say enough. Enough shrinking. Enough negotiating my worth. Enough begging for crumbs where feasts were promised. Enough mistaking tolerance for intimacy.

Enough being betrayed over and over again. Enough of being shown my feelings and heart matters less than the secret conversations, hidden apps, the porn consumption, the lusting after others, the affairs, enough of staying when they are okay to hurt me over and over, with just a "I will never again, I am sorry." Enough of forgiving someone over and over for the same thing is not love, it is abuse. If they did not stop their hurtful behaviour the second time, the third, the fourth, and so on, then they simply do not love me, and I get to say "enough", "I am done. Worth more, deserve better, and simply walk away, instead of offering myself on that "I am sorry, I am done" alter.

I get to say, "No more." The words did not arrive as rebellion, but as remembrance. A homecoming to myself. And in that remembering, something irrevocable shifted. The old story loosened its grip. The role of sacrifice slipped from my shoulders. And in its place, a new truth took root, steady and unyielding: I am allowed to choose myself. I am allowed to walk away. I am allowed to live a life that does not require my own destruction. And in that choice, quiet but absolute, my healing took its first uncompromising step forward.

"You will choose," the voice said again, and this time the words did not merely arrive; they rooted. They sank into me like light pressing into soil that had long forgotten how to receive warmth. It was a vow spoken not above me, not over me, but *into* me, as if my very bones were being asked to remember a truth older than fear. "You will choose what to hold, and what to release." And I saw it then: my hands, raw and aching, curled into fists around years of grief, betrayal, and borrowed pain. I had mistaken endurance for devotion, suffering for loyalty, and silence for strength. My fingers had cramped around wounds as if letting go would mean losing myself. Yet the voice did not pry them open. It waited. It trusted. "You will choose whether to grip the pain," it whispered, "or loosen your fingers and let it fall, so healing may take its place." And something in me softened. Not all at once. Not without fear. But enough. Enough for one finger to uncurl. Enough for breath to move more freely through my chest. Enough for the weight to slip, not crashing to the ground, but dissolving, like ash finally released to the wind. "Your destiny," the voice continued, steady and unyielding as a tide, "is no longer something that happens to you." The words settled into my lungs, into the rhythm of my breath. "It is something you shape with every inhale, every exhale." And suddenly breathing was no longer survival, it was authorship. Each breath a sentence. Each pause a choice.

Then, like the first pale gold bleeding into a sky that had known only night, came the final offering: "You may return as who you were, or you may rise as someone entirely new." The darkness around me did not vanish, but it thinned, becoming translucent, permeable. "Your purpose now lies in your hands," the voice said gently, "and it can be healing, love, joy, fulfillment, freedom, serenity, *if you choose it*." *If you choose it.* Not a command. Not a demand. An invitation. And in that sacred stillness, something irrevocable shifted. I understood, not as an idea, but as a knowing etched into my marrow, that my life was no longer a burden I dragged behind me, nor a sentence I had been condemned to serve. It was raw material. It was scaffolding. It was a landscape waiting for intention. I could build. I could decide which rooms of my inner world remained closed, and which I would open wide to the light. I could tear down walls made of fear and replace them with windows. I could choose foundations rooted in self-worth instead of pain. I could stop living as a refuge for others while abandoning myself.

My life was no longer something I merely endured, teeth clenched, spirit bowed. It was something I could shape. Something I could tend. Something I could *choose*. And with that realization, quiet and luminous, the future ceased to terrify me. It did not rush toward me or demand answers. It simply waited, open, patient, willing, ready to be met by hands that had finally remembered their power to release, and to build anew.

Then the voice returned, not as a command carved in stone, but as a promise spun from mercy and light. Its presence gathered around me like a slow, tidal breath, neither urgent nor forceful, but steady in a way that made resistance unnecessary. It did not push. It held. It felt like being remembered by something vast and benevolent, something that had never lost sight of me even when I had lost myself. "You will be given a second chance," it said. The words did not echo; they *settled*. Each syllable landed like a soft drumbeat against the great hush, resonating through whatever essence I had become. A second chance, not as escape, not as erasure, but as continuation. As grace. "You will return to your body," the voice continued, and at that, a tremor passed through me, not fear, but awe. "But you will not return as the same woman who left it." I felt the truth of this before I understood it. I sensed the difference already forming, like new roots pressing into unfamiliar soil. I would go back marked, yes, but not marred. Altered, but not diminished.

"You will carry this truth with you," it said, and I saw it then, not as a memory locked away, but as a living ember nested beneath my ribs. A knowing that could not be extinguished. A light that would not ask permission to shine. "And you will use it," the voice whispered, gentle and resolute all at once, "not as a burden, but as a lantern." A lantern. Not a torch to blind or scorch. Not a beacon shouted from a mountaintop. But a lantern, something warm, held close to the chest, something that moves with you through narrow passages and uneven ground. Something that does not banish the dark but teaches you how to walk within it without losing yourself. "To guide others," the voice said, and I felt the quiet gravity of that calling, not heavy, but meaningful. "To guide others out of the shadows you once called home." And in that moment, the darkness that had defined my suffering transformed. It was no longer proof of my brokenness. It was terrain I had survived. It was a map etched into my being. I would know the way not because I had read about it, but because I had lived there, because I had breathed that air, stumbled on that ground, learned the weight of that night.

I understood then: my pain had not been wasted. My survival was not accidental. What I had endured was not a sentence; it was an initiation. I would return carrying light precisely because I had known the dark so intimately. I would speak to wounds not from distance, but from kinship. I would hold space not as someone untouched, but as someone transformed. And as the promise settled into me, luminous and irrevocable, I felt myself turning, not away from life this time, but back toward it. Back toward breath. Back toward flesh. Back toward a world that would look the same yet never feel the same again. I was not being sent back to suffer. I was being invited back to serve, not through sacrifice, but through presence. Not through erasure, but through embodiment. I would return carrying fire, not the kind that destroys, but the kind that warms, that guides, that says to another trembling soul: *I have been here. I know this place. Follow the light. You are not alone.*

A tremor of fear rippled through me, sharp and electric, like cold water against bare skin. Not the fear of returning to the life I had known, but the deeper terror of stepping into a life I had never dared to inhabit. The fear of possibility. The fear of responsibility. The fear that comes when the cage door opens and you realize you must now decide whether to remain curled inside the familiar dark or step into the uncharted light. Could I change? The question pulsed through me like a living thing. Could I unlearn the language of self-erasure I had spoken fluently for decades? Could I loosen the habits of bending, shrinking, apologizing for my own existence? Could I stop offering my silence as tribute and instead learn the radical, terrifying act of speaking? I had spent so long swallowing my truth that my throat had forgotten its shape. Words had lodged themselves in my chest like unshed tears, heavy and unresolved. To give them voice felt like asking a long-silent instrument to sing again, unsure whether it would crack, tremble, or remember its song at all. Could a voice muted for so many years rise without breaking? Could it carry across the rooms I had once learned to disappear in? Could it meet the world without apology? Could it meet myself without flinching?

The fear was not of falling back into pain, but of standing upright in my own life. Of being seen without camouflage. Of choosing differently and discovering what might be lost along with what could finally be gained. Change demanded more than survival ever had. It demanded presence. Choice. Accountability to my own becoming. And yet, beneath that fear, something steadier began to stir. A quiet resolve. A knowing that whispered through the tremble: you have already survived the worst. You have already endured the unbearable. This fear is not a warning. It is a threshold. I understood then that fear was not asking me to retreat. It was asking me to step forward with care. To learn how to live without self-betrayal. To practice telling the truth gently, imperfectly, one breath at a time. I did not need to become fearless. I only needed to become willing. Willing to try. Willing to stumble. Willing to listen to the voice I had buried and let it rise, even if it shook. And in that fragile willingness, trembling but real, I felt the first true stirring of a life I had never allowed myself to imagine.

Before the doubt could sink its teeth into me, before fear could harden into certainty, the voice moved again, meeting my unspoken questions as if it had always been listening. “You are stronger than you think.” The words did not strike me; they settled. They sank inward like warmth returning to a long-abandoned hearth, embers shifting beneath layers of ash, remembering how to glow. Strength, not as force or endurance, but as something quieter, something that had survived even when I did not know it was still alive. “Wiser than you know.” That truth rose gently, like a star reemerging after years of clouded sky. A wisdom forged not in ease, but in ache. In nights endured. In choices made while shaking. In lessons paid for dearly, etched into bone and breath. I had mistaken survival for emptiness, forgetting that surviving itself had been a form of knowing. “More capable than you believe.” This was not flattery. It was reclamation. A remembering of hands that had held others steady, even while trembling themselves. Of a heart that had loved through fracture. Of a spirit that had bent without breaking, again and again, even when it believed it was shattered beyond repair.

And then, soft as light spilling over a bruised horizon, the voice offered what I had needed most and trusted least. "You are not alone." The words wrapped around me like a cloak I had never allowed myself to wear. "There is help waiting for you." Not abstract. Not distant. Waiting. "There are hearts that care." Not perfect hearts. Human ones. Fallible. Willing. "There are hands that will not let you fall." Hands I had never reached for because I believed I did not deserve their grip. Hands I had mistaken for myths. "All you need to do is reach." And there it was, the invitation. Not to be saved, but to participate. Not to disappear, but to connect. Not to prove my worth, but to accept my humanity. In that suspended moment—balanced between breath and silence, between the woman I had been taught to be and the woman quietly waiting to rise, I felt something shift beneath the fear. A pulse. Subtle. Steady. Undeniable. Possibility. Or perhaps, yes, hope. Not the loud, triumphant kind. But the kind that feels like a heartbeat returning after a long pause. The kind that does not promise ease, only continuation. The kind that whispers *stay*. And for the first time in a very long while, I did.

Returned to Life

I did not want to leave. The idea of returning to weight and wound, to the bruised architecture of living, felt almost unbearable against the silk-soft stillness that held me. Here, nothing asked anything of me. No proving. No enduring. No explaining the shape of my pain. I was not required to be brave or useful or strong. I was simply allowed to *be*. And that permission felt like the purest form of mercy I had ever known. But mercy, I was beginning to understand, does not always arrive as escape. Sometimes it arrives as return. The stillness began to thin, not suddenly, not cruelly, but the way fog loosens its grip at dawn, retreating inch by luminous inch. The peace did not vanish. It did not abandon me. It receded with intention, like a tide that trusts the shore to remember its shape. I felt it imprint itself into me, settling beneath awareness, as if to say: *You may carry this with you. You will need it.*

Then, as if the darkness itself released a long-held breath, it began to loosen its grip. Not abruptly. Not violently. But in tender, dissolving layers, like night yielding, inch by reluctant inch, to the first fragile blush of dawn. The vastness around me thinned into translucence, and at the edges of my awareness a pale glow began to bloom. It did not blind or command. It beckoned. A soft, undeniable tug, pulling me back toward the gravity of living. I felt myself falling upward. Drawn through a veil, I could not see but could feel brushing against my essence, through the hushed membrane between worlds. The stillness receded behind me, not with rejection, but with reverence, as though trusting I would carry its imprint home.

Then came the tether, tightening. Slowly, almost reluctantly, the stillness began to thin, not abruptly, but like fog lifting at dawn. A gentle pull at first. Almost apologetic. Sensation reinterred at the edges of my knowing, weight pressing where there had been none, density gathering where I had been limitless. Form knitting itself back together. The ache of embodiment. The quiet heaviness of bones remembering their duty. *The luminous peace did not vanish or disappear; it receded, as if trusting I could carry its memory and imprint back with me.* And beneath it all, growing louder, more insistent, a rhythm I could not ignore. A heartbeat. Distant at first. Then unmistakable. A drum calling me back through layers of breath and blood, summoning me home to a body I had tried to abandon but had never truly left. Consciousness folded inward, like light returning to its source, like wings closing around a fragile core.

Sensation returned in fragments, weight gathering where there had been none, resistance where there had been release, the ache of form reassembling itself molecule by molecule. Breath waited just beyond reach. And then, A gasp tore through me. Violent. Involuntary. A rupture. As if my soul slammed back into my body all at once, knocking the air from my lungs before demanding it again. Fire scorched my chest as oxygen burned its way back into me. My throat convulsed, my ribs screamed, my head throbbed with a heavy, hammering pulse.

the dull, unforgiving echo of what I had tried to do. Of what I had almost succeeded in doing. And as I crossed that threshold, between the boundless and the breathing, between surrender and return, *as consciousness began to fold back into flesh,* a final knowing settled into me, tender and unshakeable. I had not been denied death. I had been *returned to life*. Not as punishment. Not as burden. But as purpose. As an unfinished sentence still aching to be written. As a story that had paused, not ended. As breath reclaimed. As meaning re-membered. Life was not asking me to suffer again. It was asking me to *choose*. And this time, I would answer.

My eyes fluttered open. The world returned in fragments at first, blurred shadows, smeared light, the oppressive closeness of the room. Then clarity crept in, cruel and precise. The bed beneath me. The sheets twisted like they had witnessed a struggle. The sour taste of chemicals and regret clinging to my mouth. And there, just beyond the edge of my vision, the quiet devastation waiting to be acknowledged. The empty pill bottle. The whiskey. The evidence of my undoing. They sat there without judgment, without movement, like witnesses to a private war I had almost lost. The room was silent, but not peaceful. It carried the aftermath, the stunned stillness that follows catastrophe, when everything remains intact, yet nothing will ever be the same. I lay there, trembling, suspended between what had been and what now was. Between the woman who had wanted to disappear and the woman who had been pulled back, burning, aching, breathing. Alive.

I lay there trembling, strung between horror and relief like a wire pulled too tight. My body felt foreign, a house I had fled in flames and now returned to, scorched but standing. Every nerve hummed with weakness, every thought staggered, yet beneath the disorientation, there was one undeniable truth pressing up through the fog: I was breathing. Breath after breath arrived, uneven but faithful, reclaiming me inch by fragile inch. I was here. I had come back. Not untouched. Not unmarked. But irrevocably, astonishingly alive. Life did not return to me gently; it claimed me the way the tide claims the shore, insistently, without asking permission, reminding me that even after abandonment, the body remembers how to hold the soul. As the first thin ribbons of dawn began to unfurl across the sky, pale gold trembling along the horizon, I felt something loosen inside my chest. The light crept in quietly, slipping through the window like a vow whispered rather than declared. I pushed myself upright, hands shaking, head swimming, every movement an argument with gravity. The room still carried the residue of the night before—the stale air, the scattered evidence, the ghosts clinging to the corners—but the darkness no longer had sole ownership of the space. Morning had arrived anyway.

And within me, against all reason, something burned with quiet insistence. A flame no larger than a heartbeat. A spark that should not have survived the flood, the fall, the surrender. Yet it did. It flickered stubbornly in the ruins, warming the hollow places, whispering not triumph but possibility. Not answers, but presence. I did not rise reborn or fearless or whole. I rose fragile. Unsteady. Still aching. But I rose carrying that small, defiant fire, the one that had waited through the night, through the silence, through the almost-ending. And as the dawn widened its hold on the sky, I understood this much, even then: survival is not loud. It does not announce itself with certainty or strength. Sometimes it is nothing more than a trembling body sitting upright in the wreckage, breathing, while a tiny flame insists on staying lit.

I rose from the bed like a pilgrim returning to a body long abandoned, each movement a careful negotiation with gravity, with memory, with pain. My feet met the floor as if it were unfamiliar ground, cool and solid, reminding me that I had weight again, that I occupied space, that I belonged somewhere tangible. Every step was tentative, tender, raw, as though my skin had been turned inside out and the world now touched me too directly. Muscles protested. My head swayed. My breath came shallow, then steadied. I was relearning the simple choreography of being alive. Beneath the soreness, beneath the bruised echo of the night, something deeper stirred. Not relief alone. Not fear. But awareness. A quiet, irrevocable knowing unfurling inside my chest like a sealed letter finally opened. I could feel it pulsing through me, unfamiliar yet unmistakable: purpose. Not the kind imposed by others. Not the kind forged in sacrifice and self-erasure. But a purpose born of return. Of being spared. Of having crossed a threshold and come back carrying truth in my bones. I knew, with a clarity that startled me, that I could never return to who I had been. That woman had died on that bed. What stood now was someone unfinished, yes, but altered. Marked by mercy.

The road ahead stretched long and shadowed in my mind, winding through terrain I knew too well. My demons had not vanished with the night; they lingered at the periphery of my awareness, familiar silhouettes pacing just beyond the firelight. Self-hate. Fear. Old patterns sharpening their claws, waiting for weakness. They had patience. They always had. But something fundamental had shifted. I was no longer stepping back into the battlefield empty-handed, stripped of defence. Hope had taken root in me. Not the naïve kind that promises ease, but a fierce, living thing, fragile as glass and sharp as steel. A blade forged in the furnace of almost losing everything. It did not banish the darkness, but it gave me something to face it with. I had seen the other side. Felt the silk-soft stillness of release. Tasted the peace of letting go. And still, I had been sent back. Not rejected. Not punished. But returned. Returned with a message etched into my marrow: you are not finished. You are not meaningless. You are not beyond redemption. And, for the first time in my life, that truth did not feel like a distant idea or a borrowed belief. It felt real. It felt mine.

Life, with all its wounds and its weight, revealed itself to me not as a sentence to be endured, but as a sacred offering I had nearly returned unopened. A gift once scorned, once misunderstood, now resting in my trembling hands with a reverence born of almost losing it forever. My heartbeat unevenly at first, unsure of its own persistence, relearning its rhythm like a song remembered after long silence. Each breath felt earned. Each moment felt provisional and holy, as though the world itself were watching to see what I would do with this second beginning. The road to recovery unfurled before me like a mountain path carved into cloud and stone, unforgiving in its incline, jagged with loose shale and blind turns, vanishing into mist just far enough ahead to remind me that certainty would not be granted easily. I could sense the altitude of it in my lungs, the effort it would demand of every step. There would be slips. There would be days when the summit felt imaginary, when the weight of the climb pressed my knees toward the earth. And I knew, with a humility that softened my pride, that I could not make this ascent alone.

I would need hands to steady me when my footing failed, voices calling out from the fog when I lost my sense of direction, hearts willing to remain beside me in the moments I wanted to sit down and surrender to the cold. I would need the wisdom of healers who knew the language of pain and recovery, guides who could read the fractures in my spirit the way others read maps. I would need the stories of those who had walked this same treacherous path and lived to stand in the sunlight again, their survival a quiet proof that ascent was possible. And perhaps hardest of all, I would need the courage to turn toward the shadows I had spent a lifetime outrunning. To stop fleeing my own interior night. To meet my wounds not as enemies to be conquered, but as messengers bearing truths I had never learned how to hear. The mountain was not only outside me; it lived within. And this journey, I was beginning to understand, was not about escaping pain, but about learning how to carry it without letting it carry me. So I stood there, at the base of that long, mist-veiled climb, heart bruised but beating, hands empty yet open. Afraid, yes. But awake. And for the first time, willing to ask for help—not as a failure, but as an act of devotion to the life I had been given back.

But I was no longer the woman who once lay beneath the moonlit sky, surrendering her breath to the night. That version of me had loosened her grip and stepped back, leaving behind a hollow shape I no longer fit inside. Something irrevocable had shifted. Something ancient had stirred awake. I had crossed a quiet, invisible line and emerged altered. I had become a survivor not by chance, not by rescue alone, but by rebirth. A life reclaimed from the brink. A soul choosing to return. I was a warrior now, though not the kind forged in triumph or victory songs. I was forged in endurance. In the long hours where hope felt thinner than breath. In the moments where staying alive required more courage than leaving ever did. I was not defined by the battles that shattered me, but by the fire I walked through barefoot and lived to remember. By the scorched ground beneath my feet that did not consume me but tempered me. By the fact that I stood, breathing, where I was never meant to stand again.

I became living proof of something the darkness tries to erase: That the human spirit carries a stubborn, defiant resilience, one that refuses to remain buried, even beneath its own ashes. Even when crushed by grief. Even when convinced of its own worthlessness. Even when it believes it has nothing left to offer the world. Beneath the wreckage, beneath the ruin, something vital waits. Something that remembers how to rise. And there, at the fragile threshold of the life I almost lost, I felt it unmistakably. A pulse. A steady, insistent drumbeat of strength rising from the very place I once believed was empty. From the hollow where despair had nested. From the wound I thought defined me. Power returned to me through the fracture. Not loud. Not triumphant. But undeniable. This was not an ending rewritten. This was an origin story reclaimed. This was the moment I stopped surviving by accident and began living by choice. This was the beginning of my becoming.

Surviving Death

My suicide attempt was not the final sentence I once believed it to be it was the turning of a page, rough-edged and blood-warm, torn loose by grief but opening all the same. A threshold crossed barefoot. A birth canal carved from pain. What I mistook for an ending revealed itself as a passage, narrow and harrowing, yet leading somewhere I had never dared to imagine. I did not emerge clean or whole or certain. I emerged breathing. And that, in itself, was a miracle enough to begin again. The chapter that followed did not announce itself with trumpets or clarity. It arrived quietly, like dawn slipping its pale fingers through a cracked window, asking nothing but permission to stay. The story shifted not in a single revelation, but in a series of small, defiant moments: choosing to inhale again, choosing to sit with the ache instead of silencing it, choosing to believe that survival could one day become meaning. Where once there had only been surrender, something tentative stirred. Where there had been collapse, there was now the raw material of creation.

The darkness that tried to swallow me did not vanish. It transformed. It became the ink I would write with, thick and indelible, carrying the weight of everything I had endured. My wounds did not disappear into metaphor; they became margins where truth lived. My agony did not dissolve; it alchemized. Pain, once a verdict, became a language. Suffering, once a cage, became a compass. What nearly ended me began to instruct me, shaping a wisdom that could only be earned by walking through fire and choosing to live anyway. This was not redemption wrapped in ease. It was rebirth scraped raw. A life rewritten not as a denial of the past, but as a response to it. I was no longer trying to erase what had happened. I was learning how to carry it forward without letting it define the ending. The narrative was no longer about escape, but about embodiment. About inhabiting a life that still hurt, still frightened me, still demanded courage, yet also offered something radically new: agency. Choice. Possibility. I had crossed a line I could never uncross. And on the other side of it, I found myself not finished, not erased, not beyond repair, but standing at the beginning of a story that insisted on being written. One breath at a time. One honest sentence at a time. One trembling, deliberate act of staying.

Suicidal ideation would always remain a chapter in my story, yes, but it no longer claimed the cover, no longer dictated the font of my becoming. It loosened its grip on my name. It stepped back from the center and learned, at last, to exist as memory rather than command. It was no longer the lens pressed to my eye, warping every horizon into an exit sign. No longer the iron loop at my throat, tightening each time I dared to hope. It became what it had always truly been: a signal of pain, not a prophecy of ending. I was alive. Bewildered, yes. Trembling in the aftermath of nearly vanishing. Bruised by the effort of returning. But alive in a way that felt new, unpractised, astonishing. Alive like a body learning gravity again. Alive like lungs rediscovering air. Alive with a pulse that did not ask permission to keep going. And in that fragile, breath-held truth, something unfurled inside me, slow and luminous, like a promise written in light rather than fear.

My story was not closing its eyes. It was opening its mouth. It was drawing breath where there had only been silence. It was learning a new grammar, one shaped not by despair, but by choice. Not by erasure, but by presence. Each inhale became a sentence. Each exhale, a vow. I did not need to know how the story would unfold. I only needed to stay long enough to let it speak. What lay ahead was not certainty, nor ease, nor a life untouched by shadow. It was something far more radical: continuation. The quiet, stubborn act of remaining. The willingness to live inside questions instead of surrendering to conclusions. The courage to let my life be unfinished. And as I stood there, newly returned to myself, held together by breath and resolve, I understood this much with aching clarity: the story I thought was over had only just begun to breathe.

I survived death so you would not have to. I stepped across the line most people circle in silence, the unspoken border where thought hardens into action, where imagining becomes doing, where the mind's dark rehearsals demand a body to carry them out. I crossed that threshold and felt the air change. I stood in the presence of finality, not dramatic, not loud, but devastatingly calm. It did not rush me. It did not threaten. It waited. I felt its breath brush my skin, its gravity tug at my resolve, its promise cold and deceptively gentle, like sleep offered to the utterly exhausted. And still, I returned. Not untouched. Not innocent. Not clean of the marks that passage leaves behind. I came back bearing scars that speak in quiet aches and sudden memories. I came back altered, split open, and stitched together by something deeper than survival alone. I came back alive in a way that no longer felt accidental. And in my hands, though they shook, there burned something sacred. A story. Not a tale polished for comfort, but a living testimony, still warm, still breathing. A lantern lit by experience rather than theory, by crossing rather than caution. Its light is not blinding. It does not erase the night. It simply says, here, this way, not that door.

It is a warning, yes, but not one carved in fear. It is wrapped in love, shaped by tenderness, forged from the fierce desire that no one else should have to learn this truth the way I did. I did not return to glorify the edge. I returned to name it honestly. To tell you that the quiet it offers is a lie that costs everything. To tell you that the pull you feel does not mean you are weak, it means you are hurting. To tell you that standing where you stand now does not mean you are finished. It means you are still here. And still here is where life remains possible. If I hold this lantern out toward you now, it is not because I am ahead of you, but because I have been where the ground gives way. I have felt the temptation to step forward and be done. I have listened to the voice that promises relief at the price of breath. And I am telling you, with every scar as witness, that the story does not end there. I came back to say this with my whole being: there is another way through the night. You do not have to prove your pain by disappearing. You do not have to cross that threshold to be taken seriously. You do not have to die to deserve rest, care, or love. I survived death so you would not have to. I carried the lantern back so you could see. And I am holding it here, steady and open, for you.

I walked through the darkness so I could turn toward you now and speak from the far side of it, my voice still carrying the ash and the ember both. I went where the light thins to a rumor, where hope feels like a betrayal of pain, where the abyss pretends to be an answer. And I am here to tell you, with a steadiness forged in that crossing: you do not have to follow me there. You do not have to open the door I once mistook for relief. You do not have to wager your breath, your pulse, your becoming, just to be convinced that you matter. I faced death not as a pilgrimage to be repeated, not as a proof of courage, but as a boundary I learned, too late, was never meant to be crossed to gain wisdom. I did not go to glorify the suffering that pushed me there. I went, and I returned, so I could stand here now and hold the light toward you, angled away from the cliff. So I could say: this way still hurts, but it leads somewhere. This way keeps your name intact.

If my survival means anything, let it become a truth you can lean against when your legs give out. Let it be a quiet counterspell to the voice that tells you disappearance is the price of peace. You are worth staying alive for, not because of what you produce, or endure, or fix, but because you are here, breathing, unfinished. You are worth choosing, again and again, even on the days when choice feels like lifting stone with bare hands. There is a way forward that does not require you to vanish to be free. A way that allows you to keep your body, your story, your future sentences unwritten and waiting. You do not have to become smaller to survive this night. You do not have to disappear to be loved. Stay. Turn with me. The path bends, yes, but it does not end in darkness. It opens.

My name is Letitia, and I speak it now like a candle lit against a long-held dark. I am a woman who has stood at the lip of oblivion, felt its cold breath curl around my ankles, and still found a way to turn back and whisper what I learned there. I am a survivor of suicidal ideation, and of the night I loosened my grip and nearly let it claim me. I have wandered through inner landscapes so shadow-thick they erased my outline, places where even my reflection refused to follow me. And yet, against every expectation I had of myself, I emerged. Not seamless. Not spared. But reformed by fire and breath and time. I did not come back polished. I came back altered. Bruised into awareness. Reborn not through innocence, but through truth. I have wrestled the ghosts that once kept vigil in every room of my mind, faced them without armor, listened to the stories they told me about who I was supposed to be. I have sat knee-deep in the ache, in the doubt, in the hollowed chambers where hope once echoed and then fell silent. And there, slowly, painstakingly, with hands that shook and a heart that faltered, I learned how to stitch myself back together. Not into who I was before, but into someone more honest, more whole.

My journey did not arrive with shortcuts or mercy. It cut me open to teach me how to feel again. It demanded more courage than I believed I possessed and more patience than I thought I could survive. It asked me to grieve what I lost, to forgive what I endured, to release the identities I built around pain just to stay standing. It reshaped me from the inside out, teaching me that healing is not a single revelation, but a thousand quiet choices made in the dark. And still, I would choose it again. Every trembling step. Every breaking that led to mending. Every moment that asked me to stay when leaving felt easier. Because on the other side of that long night, I found something I had never been taught to seek: Myself. Alive. Becoming. And worth every breath it took to get here.

For on the far side of that darkness, I discovered something that altered the architecture of my soul: it is not the night that names us, but the way we learn to stand inside it. Not the reach of shadow, but the posture of the heart when the light thins. The dark does not decide our fate. It merely asks a question. And we answer with every breath we choose to take, every moment we choose to remain. We are given a terrible and sacred choice in those hours when the world narrows, and hope feels like a rumor. We can let the darkness consume us, let it close its jaws and call it truth. Or we can take what it offers, the raw heat of suffering, the unbearable pressure, and strike it like flint against our will until a spark answers back. I chose that spark. Not because I was fearless, but because something in me refused to vanish without leaving a mark of meaning behind. And so, dear listener, this is my hope for you. Not that my story hands you certainty or easy resolutions, but that it becomes a lantern you can carry when your own night grows dense. A small, steady glow. Enough to see your next step. Enough to remind you where your hands are. Enough to prove that forward still exists. Let it light the ground just ahead of your feet as you navigate the places you were taught to avoid, the shadows that learned your name.

If my survival offers any truth worth holding, let it be this: you already possess what you believe you lack. You carry a strength that knows how to move even while shaking. You carry a courage that does not roar but endures. The monsters that whisper to you in the dark are not proof of your weakness; they are evidence of how fiercely you have been fighting to stay. You do not need to outrun the night. You do not need to conquer it in one brave leap. You only need to keep choosing presence over disappearance. Breath over surrender. One step over none. And if, on some nights, all you can manage is to remain, know this: remaining is not failure. It is defiance. It is becoming. I chose to rise within the darkness, again and again, imperfectly, trembling, alive. And with all that I am, I believe this for you too: the night does not get the final word. Your story is still breathing. And you are still here.

You are not alone in this night. You never were, even when loneliness wrapped itself around you like a second skin and whispered otherwise. Even now, in the quiet hours when the world feels emptied of warmth and the future narrows to a single breath, there is something within you that has not gone dark. A pulse. A living ember. It may be dimmed by grief, smothered by exhaustion, hidden beneath layers of fear, but it is still there, beating softly, faithfully, insisting on your continued presence. That flicker is not insignificant. It is not too small to matter. It is enough. Enough to orient you when everything else feels lost. Enough to stretch, slowly, into something steadier. Enough to become a flame that warms the places that have long been cold. You do not need to see the whole road ahead. You do not need certainty or clarity or confidence. You only need the next breath. The next moment. The next quiet decision to remain. There *is* a path forward, even if it curves and doubles back, even if it is uneven beneath your feet. Healing is rarely a straight line; it is a winding trail marked by pauses, stumbles, and moments of unexpected grace. Step by trembling step, you are already moving.

Every time you choose to stay, you are walking yourself out of the shadows, whether you feel it or not. And know this: the light you are searching for is not waiting far away, not perched at the end of some distant tunnel you must survive to reach. It is rising inside you. Slowly. Patiently. With a kind of devotion that has never abandoned you. It lives in your breath, in your beating heart, in the part of you that is still listening, still reading, still here. All you must do is stay. Stay with the breath. Stay with the ache. Stay with the fragile, stubborn miracle of being alive. You do not have to chase the light. You do not have to earn it. You only have to remain long enough to let it remember you.

The Invitation Forward

So now, my dear listener, let us turn toward the darkness, not as adversaries bracing for impact, but as fellow travellers who have learned that fear loosens its grip when it is no longer faced alone. Take my hand. Feel its warmth. Feel its steadiness. Together, we will step into the night that once threatened to erase us, not with clenched fists or defiance, but with devotion to truth. We will enter softly, eyes open, hearts awake, carrying with us the quiet bravery of those who refuse to look away any longer. This darkness is not a beast to be conquered or slain. It is a landscape to be known. Its edges have been sharpened by silence, its depths hollowed by years of unspoken pain and of words left unsaid. It bears the imprints of grief, the sediment of old fear, the ache of stories that were never given breath. And yet, when we walk into it with presence, when we name what has lived unnamed, it begins to change. The shadows thin. The air shifts and changes temperature. What once felt vast, endless, and merciless reveals its contours, its wounds, its longing to be seen, to be witnessed.

We will walk slowly. Heartbeat to heartbeat. Breath to breath. Matching our steps to the rhythm of survival itself. When the ground feels unsteady and trembles beneath us, we will pause. When the weight presses hard against the chest, we will breathe together. When the old fear rises and whispers that this is too much, too deep, too dangerous, we will answer not with argument, but with presence. We are here. We are still standing. We are not alone. And when the light finally begins to break, not as a sudden blaze but as a widening glow, we will recognize it not as something external or that we discover at the end of the road, but as something we carried in with us all along. We will not emerge unchanged. We will emerge woven differently. Softer where we were once armoured. Stronger where we once shattered. Bound not by what nearly destroyed us, but by what we chose to face together.

For this is the quiet miracle of shared courage. Night, no matter how deep, cannot endure when walked through hand in hand. And dawn, when it rises, does not belong to one soul alone. It belongs to all who stayed. All who walked. All who believed, even trembling, that light was still possible. And so we go on. Together. Into the dark. Toward the shared morning that has been waiting for us all along.

And so, with that shared morning still faint on the horizon, we arrive at the threshold of what comes next. Not a doorway flung wide, not a trumpet call announcing arrival, but a quiet crossing. A breath held. A pause long enough to feel the ground beneath our feet again. The darkness we have named does not vanish here; it settles behind us like a remembered landscape, still present, still real, but no longer uncharted. We carry its map now. Its language. Its truths. What follows is not a departure from that night, but a deeper entry into its meaning. In the chapter ahead, we step closer to the heart of the story itself. Not the metaphorical darkness, but the lived one. The moment when the ground truly gave way. When silence became unbearable. When the night narrowed to a single choice, and the world balanced on the edge of a breath. This is where the descent becomes personal. Where abstraction dissolves into memory. Where the body remembers what the mind tried to forget.

Move gently as we go on. Read slowly. Breathe often. You are still holding my hand, and I am still holding yours. Nothing that follows is meant to harm you, though it may stir you. Nothing is shared without purpose, though some truths arrive without softness. We cross now from invitation into witnessing. This is where the story turns from reflection to reckoning. This is where the night first closed in. This is where my life nearly ended. And this, is where the next chapter begins.

Chapter Seven:
The Darkest Night: My Suicide Attempt (Prelude)

As I sat alone in the wet hush of night, the icy grass clung to my skin like a final warning, its cold fingers threading their way into muscle and marrow, as if the earth itself were trying to speak sense into me. Dampness seeped through fabric and resolve alike, blurring the line between where my body ended and the ground began. I felt myself dissolving into the landscape, becoming just another quiet thing swallowed by the dark. Above me, the moon hovered in its distant brilliance, round and unflinching, a silent witness offering no mercy and no comfort. Its pale light spilled across the world with careless precision, illuminating everything except relief. It revealed the sharp edges of the night, the glint of dew on broken blades of grass, the tremor in my own hands, and it revealed me, to myself. Small. Exposed. Unhidden. The sky, once a place I searched for solace, pressed down now like a closing fist. Clouds gathered thick and heavy, bruised with unspoken grief, smothering the stars one by one as though erasing escape routes.

Each swallowed point of light felt like a door quietly shutting. Breath grew shallow. Space narrowed. The night did not roar; it leaned in. Patient. Certain. Inside me, the storm had already begun to fracture. Thoughts collided and unraveled, memories rose without invitation, and the voice I had carried for so long, sharp, relentless, disguised as guidance, spoke with chilling familiarity. It told me this moment was earned. That the cold was fitting. That the loneliness was proof. That the darkness outside merely mirrored the darkness I was. And yet, even there, soaked to the skin and hollowed by despair, something inside me remained awake. A raw awareness. A terrible clarity. I could feel the cost of every word I had ever turned against myself, the weight of every time I believed cruelty was discipline, punishment was progress, silence was strength.

The night was no longer just around me; it was inside me, thick, intimate, undeniable. This is where the next chapter begins. Not with answers. Not with rescue. But with the moment when the ground feels colder than expected, the sky feels unbearably close, and the voice you trusted most reveals itself as the one that led you here. This is the place where the mask slips. Where the inner ally becomes unmistakably visible as the inner adversary. Where the question left simmering finally meets lived reality. And in the damp stillness of that night, with the moon watching and the earth holding me without judgment, I came face to face with the truth that would change everything: The voice that claimed it was trying to make me better was the very thing dragging me toward the dark. And once that truth is seen, it cannot be unseen. Eleven o'clock. The numbers on my phone burned against the darkness, sharp, merciless, and unforgiving, their pale glow cutting through the night like a blade.

They hovered there, cold and precise, a digital heartbeat marking time I no longer felt I belonged to. Each digit pulsed with implication: connection, continuity, the quiet assurance that somewhere voices were still speaking, laughter still unfolding, lives still moving forward without knowing how close I stood to vanishing. The screen felt impossibly bright in my trembling hand, as though it were accusing me of something I could not name. A doorway lit from the inside. A portal to warmth, to human presence, to help. And yet it might as well have been worlds away. The distance between my thumb and the call button felt vast, unbridgeable, like the space between a scream and a soundless mouth. I could see the path back, but belief had already severed the bridge. That glowing time whispered its own cruel arithmetic. Eleven o'clock meant people were still awake. Still reachable. Still capable of answering. Which meant, in the distorted logic tightening around my chest, that my silence was no longer circumstance but choice.

And that choice, shaped by years of self-erasure, told me I did not deserve to interrupt anyone's night with the weight of my pain. The phone became a mirror. In it, I saw every moment I had swallowed my needs. Every time I told myself not now, not you, don't be a burden. The light reflected back the lie I had practiced until it felt like truth: that asking for help was an imposition, that reaching out was selfish, that needing someone was a flaw. Eleven o'clock glowed on, indifferent to my spiraling.

Where Silence Begins to Persuade

Time did not rush me. It waited. It always waits. But in that waiting, the question pressed harder, heavier, settling into my bones: Would I reach toward the world that still existed, or would I retreat further into the silence I had learned to call safety? This is the threshold where I was standing. Not at the edge of action, but at the edge of contact, but not with another human, something way darker. The moment when the possibility of being heard flickers in the palm of your hand, and the voice inside you argues fiercely for disappearance. Here, the night sharpens. Here, the mask tightens its grip. Here, the story moves from thought into gravity. Eleven o'clock was not just the time. It was the hour when choice stood illuminated, and I had to decide whether I would keep believing the voice that told me I was alone, or dare, even trembling, to prove it wrong.

Inside, the house loomed behind me like a sealed vault of unfinished grief. Its windows were dark eyes that refused to blink, its walls thick with a silence so dense it felt sentient, as though the rooms themselves were holding their breath. That silence pressed outward, meeting the weight already tightening around my ribs, until the air felt too heavy to draw in without effort. Every corner of that house carried echoes of what had not been said, what had been endured, what had been quietly buried and left to rot. It was not a shelter. It was a mirror. Out here, beneath the open sky, the cold grass bit into my skin with honest cruelty, sharp and immediate. In there, the ache was slower, more suffocating, a darkness without edges. But the truth revealed itself with ruthless clarity: location did not matter. The storm was not in the house, the night, or the hour. It lived in me. It followed me with the intimacy of breath, coiling close, whispering in a voice that sounded like certainty. It told me there was only one way out. Only one direction where the noise would finally stop.

Only one door left that did not require me to ask, to explain, to hope. What once would have horrified me now felt frighteningly calm. The idea no longer arrived as terror, but as inevitability, sliding into place like the last piece of a puzzle I never wanted to complete. The boundary between thought and action thinned. The impossible softened. The unthinkable began to masquerade as relief. And so I remained there, caught between thresholds. Between inside and outside. Between reaching and retreating. Between the life that had bruised me and the silence that beckoned with deceptive tenderness. The moon watched without judgment, pale and distant, as I unraveled in stillness. My breath fogged the air in small, fragile clouds, proof that I was still here, still tethered, still deciding. Night and soul folded into one another, indistinguishable now, both vast, both aching, both holding me in a suspended moment where everything narrowed to a single, terrible question. This is where the chapter truly begins. Not with motion, but with collapse. Not with certainty, but with the quiet, terrifying calm that comes just before a choice believes it has already been made.

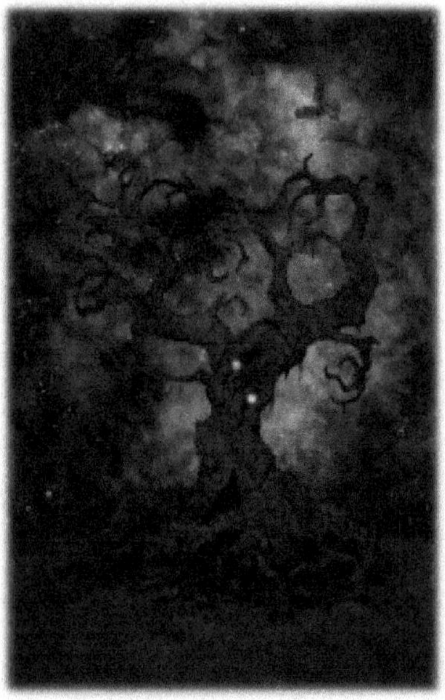

When Fear Learned a Body

The wind lashed through the branches of what felt like an ancient tree, its trunk rooted deep in a time before names, before mercy. The limbs above me twisted and contorted, reshaping themselves into grotesque silhouettes, clawed and reaching, as though the night had finally decided to externalize what had long lived inside me. Moments earlier, they had been harmless, almost tender, whispering softly beneath the sky. Now they writhed with intention, animated by fear, by exhaustion, by a mind no longer able to separate what was real from what was felt. Their shadows stretched across the ground like grasping hands, long and skeletal, creeping closer with every violent gust.

It felt as though the darkness itself was leaning in, curious, ravenous, sensing weakness. The branches groaned and cracked, their sounds sharp and animal, echoing through my chest like a warning I could not decipher in time. Each snap felt personal, as if something inside me were breaking in rhythm with the storm. I watched the tree become a mirror. Not of the world. But of my inner landscape.

The fear I had carried quietly for years now had shape. The self-hate I had learned to live with now had teeth. Every thought I had tried to outrun reached outward, embodied in bark and shadow, telling me what I already believed: that I was surrounded, outmatched, and running out of light. The night did not invent these monsters. It only revealed them. And yet, beneath that writhing canopy, something else stirred. Not courage. Not hope. Something smaller. Quieter. A flicker of awareness that whispered: This is what it looks like when the mind turns against itself. This is how fear dresses itself when it wants to feel inevitable. I drew my knees closer to my chest as the wind howled on, a low, guttural sound that seemed to rise straight from the earth. The cold gnawed deeper now, no longer just on my skin, but inside my bones. I felt exposed, stripped of defenses, reduced to breath and thought and the unbearable weight of staying. This was the moment when the world began to blur at the edges. When the outer storm and the inner one fused. When the night stopped being scenery and became a participant.

And somewhere between the snapping branches and my own trembling pulse, the next chapter opened. Not with answers. Not with rescue. But with the raw, unguarded truth of what it feels like when fear takes the shape of everything around you, and the mind begins to believe there is nowhere left to hide. The wind itself became a voice, no longer content to remain weather or sound. It slipped between the leaves and found language, a low, mournful whisper braided with grief, carrying a melody I knew too well. It sounded like all the nights I had cried without tears, all the words I had swallowed until they turned heavy and sharp inside me. The air moved through the branches the way despair moves through a body, relentless, intimate, knowing exactly where to press. Each gust rose and fell in rhythm with my breath, ragged and uneven, mirroring the chaos clawing at my lungs. The storm in my chest answered it, heart pounding like a drumbeat of panic, while something deeper churned in my gut, dense and nauseating, as if my body itself was bracing for impact.

The wind did not soothe. It exposed. It pulled the sound of my inner unraveling out into the open, amplifying it until there was no separation left between what I felt and what surrounded me. It became a haunting serenade that harmonized with my oppression. And then I heard it or thought I did. My name. Not spoken, not called, but carried on the current, stretched thin and fractured, syllables dissolving into breath. It wasn't comfort that moved through me at that sound. It was recognition. As if the night knew me. As if the darkness had been waiting for this moment when my defenses were finally stripped away. Each whisper felt like a question wrapped in warning: Do you hear yourself now? Do you feel how far you've gone?

The wind circled, insistent, brushing past my skin like cold fingers tracing old scars. It felt less like an external force and more like an echo, the audible shape of my own thoughts turned loose in the world. This was not nature speaking to me. This was my despair finding a mouthpiece. And as it howled through the leaves, filling the space between my heartbeat and my fear, I realized with a quiet, terrifying clarity that the night was no longer just around me. It had begun to speak from within.

Trapped Between Inhale and Exhale

My breath lodged painfully beneath my ribs, trapped as a wounded animal pressed into a corner, eyes wild, body trembling, desperate for a way out that no longer existed. An invisible fist cinched tight around my chest, cruel and unyielding, squeezing until my heart hurled itself against its own cage in frantic revolt. Each beat landed too loud, too fast, a thunderous reminder that my body was still fighting even as my spirit faltered. The air thinned until it felt razor-edged, scarce and hostile, as though the night itself had decided I was no longer worthy of oxygen. Every inhale scraped its way up my throat like breath dragged through thorns, catching, tearing, burning. Every exhale fractured before it could fully leave me, escaping in shallow, broken wisps, the ghost of a breath rather than a living one. I could not fill my lungs. I could not empty them. I hovered in that suffocating in-between, suspended between needing air and fearing it would never come.

It felt as though something old and unspeakable had coiled itself around my neck, a presence without form yet heavy with intention. Not hurried. Not violent. Patient. Ancient. It tightened with the slow certainty of something that believed it had all the time in the world. Each constriction whispered the same lie: that breathing was optional now, that surrender would be easier, quieter, kinder. My body shook beneath the weight of it, muscles clenched, jaw locked, fingers digging into damp earth as if the ground itself might anchor me. Every attempt to draw breath became an act of defiance, a small, brutal war waged inside my own chest. Living, in that moment was not graceful. It was not hopeful. It was raw endurance. A trembling insistence to stay, even as every instinct screamed to disappear. And somewhere beneath the panic, beneath the crushing pressure and the rasp of broken breaths, a single thought flickered: this needs to end.

The Glow That Could Not Save Me

In that suffocating stillness, beneath the contorted branches and the wind's low lament, I felt the night closing in around me, not as a comforting veil or a place to rest, but as a burial shroud being drawn carefully, deliberately, over my living body. The darkness did not rush. It settled. It pressed. It claimed space inch by inch, until even my thoughts felt wrapped in black cloth, muted and airless. I stared down at the device resting in my trembling hand, its screen glowing with a cold, unnatural light, a stark intrusion against the living dark. That small rectangle held the entire world I was meant to belong to, yet it felt impossibly distant, like a photograph of a place I once lived but could no longer return to. The light did not warm me. It did not comfort. It felt clinical. Exposed. As if it were illuminating my loneliness rather than rescuing me from it.

Eleven o'clock. The numbers flared back at me, sharp and unfeeling, burning through the night like indifferent stars. Time marched on with mechanical precision, unmoved by the quiet catastrophe unfolding in my chest. Somewhere, people were laughing, arguing, sleeping, living. Somewhere, life continued in its ordinary, unremarkable way. And here I was, unraveling beneath the same moon, my inner world collapsing while the universe remained utterly unchanged. The phone, designed to bridge distances, to summon voices and comfort at the touch of a finger, suddenly felt like a cruel illusion. A promise it could not keep. A door that appeared open but led nowhere. I could see the world through it, but I could not reach it. Connection hovered just beyond my grasp, close enough to ache, too far to touch. I felt the weight of that separation settle deep into my bones. Never had I been more aware of how alone a human being can feel while still surrounded by proof that others exist.

The glow in my hand became a mirror, reflecting not connection, but absence. Not rescue, but the terrifying truth that in this moment, I felt unclaimed by anything, untethered from everyone. And as the numbers continued to shine, steady and relentless, I realized the night was not just around me anymore. It was inside me. Tears slipped down my cheeks in slow, relentless streams, tracing familiar paths carved by countless nights before this one, falling onto the glass with the soft, hollow rhythm of rain tapping against an abandoned window. Each droplet struck the unyielding screen and trembled there for a breathless moment before dissolving into nothing. Drip, drip, drip. A fragile percussion, marking time inside my collapse. They gathered like a constellation of sorrow, scattered points of grief blinking briefly into existence before vanishing, each one carrying a confession I no longer had the strength to speak aloud. The tears kept coming, uninvited and unstoppable, as though some hidden reservoir had finally cracked open.

They traced familiar paths down my face, warm against skin gone numb, carrying with them everything I had never said aloud. They blurred my vision until the world fractured into light and shadow, the phone's glow warping into halos that pulsed and smeared like wounded stars. I watched my reflection ripple beneath the glass, a distorted ghost staring back at me, eyes hollowed by exhaustion, mouth trembling with words that had nowhere left to land. "I am drowning. I am breaking. I am fading. I can't anymore. This is too much." The words did not leave my mouth. They stayed trapped behind my teeth, heavy and sharp, pressing against my throat like stones. My body spoke instead. My shoulders shook. My chest hitched. My hands trembled as though they no longer belonged to me. Grief moved through me with a quiet ferocity, not screaming, not thrashing, but eroding me from the inside out, the way water wears down rock over time, patient and unstoppable.

Each tear felt like a surrender, a small relinquishing of the effort it took to keep holding myself together. They fell not in drama, but in quiet resignation, the way leaves fall from a tree that has finally accepted winter. I felt myself thinning with them, as though each drop carried away another fragment of strength, another reason I had once clung to. The glass did not respond. It did not flinch. It simply received my grief and gave nothing back, an unfeeling altar to a pain too heavy to hold alone. The screen blurred beneath the tears, its harsh light fracturing into halos and streaks, until even the numbers lost their shape. Eleven o'clock dissolved into smears of brightness, indistinct and unreal. Time itself seemed to waver, as though unsure whether to continue or simply let me slip beneath it. The world narrowed to sensation alone: the sting behind my eyes, the salt on my lips, the ache in my jaw from holding myself together for far too long.

Each tear felt like something leaving me, yet nothing felt lighter. There was no relief in the release, only the quiet horror of realizing how much pain still remained. It was as if my body were emptying itself and discovering there was no bottom, no end to the well of sorrow I had been carrying. I cried not loudly, not dramatically, but with the exhausted sobs of someone who has fought too long and too quietly to be saved by noise. My chest heaved, a broken bellows struggling to feed a dying flame. The sobs that rose were soundless at first, trapped behind clenched teeth and pride long past its usefulness. When they finally escaped, they came out raw and jagged, tearing at my throat, collapsing me inward. I folded around myself instinctively, arms wrapped tight, a futile attempt to become my own shelter in a world that felt vast, cold, and uninhabitable.

When Despair Fully Forms

In that moment, time lost its shape, hunched beneath the moon, fingers slick with tears, breath splintering in my chest. Seconds stretched like hours. The night thickened. The moon above remained cruelly serene, untouched by my unraveling, while the earth beneath me drank my tears without comment. I felt suspended between breaths, between heartbeats, between the person I had been and the one I could no longer pretend to be. I understood something with terrifying clarity: this was not just sadness. This was despair fully formed. This was the place where endurance frays, where hope thins to a thread so fine it can no longer be felt between trembling fingers. I was not crying because I was weak. I was crying because I had reached the edge of what I could hold. The tears kept falling, marking the beginning of a night that would change everything.

And somewhere beneath the sobbing, beneath the salt and blur and shaking, a single truth pulsed, quiet but relentless: I was not crying because I wanted to die. I was crying because I could no longer remember how to live. The weight of isolation pressed against me from all sides, thick and suffocating, a fog so dense I felt I could carve my name into it with trembling fingers and still be erased. It clung to my skin, damp and airless, stealing depth from the night and distance from the world. Sound dulled inside it. Meaning blurred. I existed within a pocket of silence where even my own thoughts felt far away, as though shouted from another lifetime. Desperation curled around my ribs like barbed wire, cold and deliberate, tightening with every breath I fought to draw. It did not merely restrain me; it wove itself into me, thread by merciless thread, until I could no longer tell where the pain ended and I began.

Each inhale scraped against that wire, each exhale caught and bled, and slowly, quietly, the struggle to breathe became proof of something darker: that living itself felt like trespassing. In that constriction, belief hardened into verdict. I was unwanted. Unseen. Unworthy. Not as passing thoughts, but as laws written into my bones. The night seemed to agree, holding its distance, offering no interruption, no contradiction. Even the stars felt too far away to argue with me. I was a body occupying space without permission, a breath the world would not notice if it stopped. And yet, beneath the choke of isolation, beneath the wire and fog and silence, something resisted annihilation. Not hope. Not yet. Something smaller. More stubborn. A pulse. A refusal of absolute erasure. It was the ache itself that betrayed me, the fact that it hurt this much, that I longed this fiercely to be seen, to be held, to matter.

Pain, in its cruelty, revealed the truth I could not yet face: Only something alive can ache to belong. I sat there, wrapped in fog and fear, barbed and breathless, believing myself utterly alone. And still, my heart kept knocking from the inside, not loud enough to save me, not strong enough to free me, but persistent enough to whisper a question into the dark: What if this longing is not proof of my unworthiness, but evidence of something in me that still wants to live?

The Silent Scream

The cry swelled until it filled every hollow space inside me, a tidal surge of need with nowhere to break. It scraped its way up my spine, burned behind my eyes, thundered against my teeth, desperate to become sound. It wanted to rip the night open, to bruise the sky with its urgency, to force the world to turn its face toward me and see that I was still here, still alive, still unraveling. “Help me!!! Please, please, someone, anyone, help me!” The words burned bright and feral inside my chest, a flare fired into the dark. But when my lips parted, the night answered with nothing. Silence swallowed the scream whole. My throat closed like a sealed gate, my voice collapsing inward, reduced to ash and vapor before it ever reached the air. The plea had nowhere to go. It beat and battered the walls of my body, a frantic bird thrashing against its own rib cage, wings bruised, breath running out.

I could feel it there, fluttering wildly, a living thing made of need and terror, trapped behind bone and shame and the terrible belief that I was asking for too much simply by existing. What remained was not sound, but residue. A trembling echo that seeped into every corner of me. My soul felt drained to its last whisper, leaving only the echo of a truth I was too ashamed to say aloud: "I am here. I am hurting. I don't know how to keep breathing." The truth lay there, naked and unbearable, pulsing in the quiet like an exposed nerve. Each breath felt negotiated, temporary, borrowed. Courage had thinned to a thread. Strength had drained away drop by drop, leaving me suspended in the awful in-between, not yet gone, not fully here. The night held me in that confession without response. No rescue arrived. No voice cut through the dark.

Only the steady, indifferent continuation of the world, and me beneath it, crouched around my own breaking, learning in real time how loneliness can become a physical weight. And yet, even in that voicelessness, even as my plea dissolved unheard, my body kept drawing air in shallow, shaking sips, as though some instinct older than despair refused to release its grip. I did not know it then, but that was the moment the story paused. Not ended. Paused. A breath held at the edge of something unnamed. The night had not answered me, but it had listened. And in the silence where my scream disappeared, the next chapter waited, gathering itself quietly, preparing to speak where I no longer could. The scream lived inside me like a trapped storm, swelling against the walls of my chest, pounding for release. It begged to be flung into the vastness above me, to be hurled at the stars like a final, furious offering.

I wanted the night to fracture under the weight of my pain, for the heavens to split and echo back some sign that I had been seen, that my suffering had registered somewhere beyond my own skin. I wanted my anguish to collide with something living, something listening, something that would answer. But the silence was absolute. When I reached for my voice, my throat answered with nothing but constriction. It felt as though an invisible winter had closed its hand around my windpipe, tightening with merciless patience. My words froze before they could form. My cry collapsed inward, strangled at its birth, smothered beneath the iron grip of despair. What should have been sound became pressure. What should have been release became an implosion. I could feel the scream vibrating through me instead, rattling my bones, scorching the inside of my ribs, scraping raw paths through my chest.

It had nowhere to go but inward, nowhere to land but inside my own body. Each unspoken plea folded back on itself, turning my breath shallow, my pulse erratic, my thoughts jagged and unmoored. The night remained unmoved. The stars stared on in their distant, indifferent hush. And I sat there, mouth open, heart screaming, body silent, learning the cruel intimacy of voicelessness, how despair does not always arrive with noise or drama, but often with a quiet theft. It steals your sound first. It leaves you alive, aching, and unable to call out. And still, beneath that frozen silence, something inside me strained toward life, toward witness, toward breath. The scream may not have escaped my lips, but it had marked the moment. It carved a fault line through the night. And on the other side of that fracture, unseen and unpromised, the next movement of my story waited, listening, even when I believed no one was.

What followed was not a cry the world could hear, but the quietest scream I had ever known, a soundless rupture that split me from the inside. It tore through my chest without touching the air, a howl swallowed before it could form, collapsing inward instead of outward. It reverberated through an indifferent vastness, a void so complete it felt less like darkness and more like erasure, a black hole made of silence, consuming every whisper before it could become a prayer. This was not absence. This was appetite. A living nothingness. A cosmic hollow that devoured meaning itself. Every plea dissolved on contact. Every thought lost its outline. Hope did not break, it simply thinned until it was no longer visible, until it slipped through me like vapor through open fingers. The universe did not answer because there was nothing left to receive an answer. No echo. No return. Just the sensation of falling into a space where sound had never learned to exist.

The scream lived inside me like a trapped storm, swelling against the walls of my chest, pounding for release. It begged to be flung into the vastness above me, to be hurled at the stars like a final, furious offering. I wanted the night to fracture under the weight of my pain, for the heavens to split and echo back some sign that I had been seen, that my suffering had registered somewhere beyond my own skin. I wanted my anguish to collide with something living, something listening, something that would answer. But the silence was absolute. When I reached for my voice, my throat answered with nothing but constriction. It felt as though an invisible winter had closed its hand around my windpipe, tightening with merciless patience. My words froze before they could form. My cry collapsed inward, strangled at its birth, smothered beneath the iron grip of despair. What should have been sound became pressure. What should have been release, became implosion.

I could feel the scream vibrating through me instead, rattling my bones, scorching the inside of my ribs, scraping raw paths through my chest. It had nowhere to go but inward, nowhere to land but inside my own body. Each unspoken plea folded back on itself, turning my breath shallow, my pulse erratic, my thoughts jagged and unmoored. The night remained unmoved. The stars stared on in their distant, indifferent hush. And I sat there, mouth open, heart screaming, body silent, learning the cruel intimacy of voicelessness, how despair does not always arrive with noise or drama, but often with a quiet theft. It steals your sound first. It leaves you alive, aching, and unable to call out. In that moment, I understood a terror deeper than fear: the terror of unbeing. Not pain. Not sorrow. But the sense that even suffering had let go of me. I was not held by darkness. I was unrecognized by existence.

And somewhere inside that hollow, inside the place where identity loosens, and breath forgets its purpose, a question surfaced, fragile and faint, trembling at the edge of consciousness: *If nothing hears me; If nothing reaches back; What happens next?* That question did not arrive as curiosity. It arrived as a threshold. Because this is where the story truly begins. Not with noise. Not with chaos. But with the moment a soul stands inside the quietest void imaginable, and must decide whether to vanish into it, or answer it by staying. And still, beneath that frozen silence, something inside me strained toward life, toward witness, toward breath. The scream may not have escaped my lips, but it had marked the moment. It carved a fault line through the night. And on the other side of that fracture, unseen and unpromised, the next movement of my story waited, listening, even when I believed no one was.

The Verdict of Absolute Aloneness

The truth slipped from my lips with the bitterness of poison and the weight of a verdict: "I am alone! Utterly, achingly, devastatingly, unbearably alone. *I have no one.*" The words did not echo. They did not argue. They simply fell, heavy and final, into the hollow space around me. The night received them without flinching. I sat there, exposed beneath the moon's pale stare, feeling the full gravity of that sentence settle into my bones. It was not just loneliness; it was erasure. The sense that if I vanished in that moment, the world would not even ripple. That my absence would pass unnoticed, like a breath released into an already windless sky. No footsteps approached. No warm hand found mine. No phone vibrated. No voice whispered that I mattered. No voice called my name. No presence softened the jagged edges of the night. No embrace slipped beside me to soften the ache.

There was no one to tell me I would survive this. No one to anchor me, to gather the fragments of who I once was. No one to kneel beside the wreckage of me and say, "You are worth saving." No miracle arrived dressed as coincidence. There was no kind word. No witness. No lifeline. No one to tell me my breath still mattered. No one to gather the broken pieces scattered across the grass. The truth slipped from my lips with the sting of poison: **"I have no one."** The grass beneath me was damp and unfeeling. The cold seeped upward, a slow invasion, as if the earth itself were reminding me how easily it could reclaim me. My body curled inward, instinctively, the way something wounded tries to protect what little life remains. My arms wrapped around myself, a poor imitation of an embrace, my own ribs the only boundary between me and the vast, uncaring dark.

I had spent so long believing that if I broke badly enough, someone would come. Surely, there was a threshold of pain that summoned rescue. But there I was, fractured, dissolving, unmistakably visible to the night, and still, no one came. And that was the moment it landed with terrifying clarity: this was it. This was the floor. This was the place where no one else could reach me. The realization did not explode. It collapsed. A quiet implosion, inward and absolute. I felt myself thinning, as though my edges were loosening, as though I were becoming less solid, less anchored to the idea of being a person at all. The world felt very far away. Not hostile. Just indifferent. As if it would continue, flawlessly, whether I stayed or slipped beneath it. "I have no one," I whispered again, softer now, the words dissolving as soon as they touched the air.

And yet, unbearably, inexplicably, I was still breathing, still cursed with this breath. Each breath came unwillingly, like a reflex my body had not yet learned how to surrender. My chest rose and fell against my will, a stubborn metronome marking time in a life I no longer believed I deserved and now wanted. It angered me, that breath. Confused me. Why was my body still fighting when my spirit had already laid itself down? I did not feel hope. I did not feel comfort. I did not feel held. But in the raw exposure of that truth, *I have no one*, something shifted, not outward, but inward. A terrible, sacred realization began to form, slow and unwelcome, like a dawn I was not ready to face.

If No One Is Coming

If no one was coming, if no hand would reach for mine, if no voice would speak my name into the dark. Then the only witness left was me. And yet, even as that sentence fell from my mouth, bitter and final, the night did not echo it back to me. "I have no one." The words hung in the air like frost, fragile, crystalline, aching to be shattered. They tasted of iron and grief. They felt absolute. They felt true. They felt like the last verdict a life could render upon itself. My chest hollowed around them, as though the sound alone had scooped me out, leaving only a shell where a person once breathed. The words tasted bitter as they left me, metallic and final, sinking into the cold air as if the night itself swallowed them whole. *I have no one.* The truth did not arrive loudly; it settled, heavy and absolute, like a stone dropped into the deepest well of my chest.

It echoed once, twice, then disappeared into a silence so vast it felt eternal. Around me, the world remained unmoved. The grass did not soften beneath my grief. The moon did not dim its gaze. The wind did not pause to cradle me. Everything continued, indifferent and intact, while I sat collapsed in the middle of my own undoing. I felt transparent, as though I could vanish without consequence, as though my absence would slip seamlessly into the night and leave no imprint behind. Loneliness became more than an emotion. It became a presence, an entity that pressed itself against my spine, leaned its full weight into my ribs, and whispered its certainty into my bones. It told me I was unmissed. Unheld. Unnecessary. That if I disappeared, the world would not tilt or tremble. That nothing would reach for me once I was gone. I waited for the darkness to agree with me. I waited for the ground to open, for the silence to seal itself shut, for the world to nod and say, "*Yes. This is where you end.*" But it didn't.

The night remained, vast, yes, and mercilessly quiet, yet strangely unwilling to collapse into my conclusion. The grass still pressed cool and real against my skin. The wind still brushed past my face, indifferent but undeniable. My lungs, traitorous and stubborn, continued their aching work, drawing in air I had not asked for, releasing it in shuddering waves. I searched the darkness for proof otherwise, for even the smallest contradiction, a flicker of warmth, a sign of interruption. There was none. Only the vast, open ache of being unseen, the unbearable knowledge that my pain had no audience, no sanctuary, no echo beyond my own chest. To suffer alone felt like erasure in slow motion. I was alone, but I was not erased, not yet. The loneliness did not come as a clean emptiness. It came layered, textured, deadly alive. The same kind of alive that follows the anxiety of waking from a terrifying nightmare, unsure between real and dream.

It throbbed in my ears. It weighed against my spine. It rang through my bones like a struck bell that refused to stop vibrating. It was the kind of alone that feels loud, almost screaming, because there is no one to hear it but you. And yet, even as that truth scorched through me, something deeper stirred, faint and uninvited. Beneath the declaration of *I have no one*, another truth hovered, unformed but restless, like a breath held just beneath the surface. I could not name it yet. I did not trust it. But it lingered in the hollow space my despair had carved, waiting for the moment when the night would loosen its grip enough for it to speak. For this was the depth of the dark. The place where all illusions fell away. Where no comfort arrived. Where nothing rescued me from myself. And it is here, in this naked, merciless solitude, that the story does not end, but fractures open, preparing the ground for what must come next.

And yet, beneath that devastation, beneath the raw confession of having no one, something else flickered, not comfort, not hope, not reassurance, but awareness. I was witnessing myself. I was kneeling beside my own wreckage, even if no one else was there to do it. I was naming the truth without softening it, without dressing it in courage it did not yet possess. And that act, that brutal, trembling honesty, was its own form of presence. I had no one to gather me. So I stayed, but not the kind that offers hope. I stayed with the ache. I stayed with the breath that still insisted on moving. I stayed with the truth that hurt too much to beautify. I stayed with my decision that a final end was upon me.

And in that staying, something shifted, almost imperceptibly, like the smallest crack forming in stone after years of pressure. The declaration "I have no one" did not become a prophecy. It became a moment. A snapshot of unbearable pain, not the whole story, but certainly it is heading to be the end of the story. Because even alone, devastatingly, terrifyingly alone, I was still here to say it. And the night, vast and listening, let the words fall without turning them into an ending.

The Dangerous Calm

And somewhere between one breath and the next, the truth fractured through me like glass: **"I have absolutely no one."** The words slipped from my lips with the finality of poison swallowed, a bitter confession that scorched on the way down. And the moment they escaped, they did not fall to the ground, they were swallowed whole by that same nothingness, devoured without echo or mercy, as though even my suffering was unworthy of being heard. The realization crushed me. Cruel. Absolute. It pressed down with the weight of an ending, heavy and merciless, collapsing every fragile structure I had built to keep myself upright. The ache in my soul became a vicious, starving animal, gnawing, ravaging, tearing through every scrap of the person I once was. It paced inside my chest with bared teeth, devouring memory, devouring hope, devouring the last soft places where belief had tried to hide.

The realization crushed me again, deeper this time, as though the night itself leaned in to witness my undoing. The ache in my soul became a living thing, a burning pit hollowing me from the inside out, a furnace of grief that consumed without light, without warmth, without relief. It was not loud. It did not scream. It simply *endured*, relentless and intimate, filling every corner of me until there was no room left to breathe. I felt myself thinning. Unraveling. Becoming less solid with every heartbeat. The grass beneath me no longer felt cold; it felt distant, unreal, like I was already loosening my grip on the world. The moon above did not comfort; it watched. Pale. Unmoved. A witness that offered no judgment and no rescue. The wind passed through me as though I were already translucent, as though I were learning how to disappear. And in that unbearable clarity, something even more devastating settled in.

It wasn't just that no one had come. It was what I had believed, truly believed, that this was all I was worth. That this emptiness was the final proof. That the silence was the verdict. The absence of reaching hands meant I was, at my core, unreachable. I sat there with the night wrapped tightly around me, no longer fighting it, no longer begging it to soften. I let it press in, let it claim the space where hope had once lived. My breath came shallow and broken, each inhale a question, each exhale a surrender. And still, even there, even then, the silence did not end me yet. It held. The night received that truth without resistance. No echo returned it. No presence rose to challenge it. It simply vanished into the dark, and with it went the last fragile illusion that someone, somewhere, might still be watching over the unraveling of me. The world did not pause. Time did not hesitate.

Existence moved on as if my breaking were a minor weather event, brief and unremarkable. That was the moment something inside me finally gave way. Not with drama. Not with noise. But with a quiet, internal collapse, like a bridge surrendering after years of unseen strain. The ache no longer begged for relief; it devoured. It tore through memory, identity, hope, leaving only scorched ground behind. I felt myself hollowing, scraped clean from the inside, reduced to a single, trembling core of endurance that no longer wanted to endure. And in that hollowing, a dangerous clarity arrived. When there is no one left to reach for you, when every imagined hand withdraws, when even your own voice feels like an intrusion upon the world, the mind begins to search for a final solution. Not out of drama. Not out of spite. But out of exhaustion. Out of the unbearable weight of continuing without witness.

When Silence Stops Resisting

The night did not argue with me. The silence did not interrupt. The darkness did not rush me. It simply waited. And there, beneath the indifferent moon, wrapped in cold grass and colder certainty, a door I had resisted for years finally revealed itself in full. Not as a threat. Not as terror. But as an idea so still, so deceptively gentle, it felt like rest. This is where my end begins. Not with hope. Not with rescue. But with the moment the mind, starved of connection and crushed by self-hate, starts to believe that disappearing might be the only remaining form of relief. This is the place where thoughts turn dangerous. Where silence becomes persuasive. Where the idea of not being here anymore stops feeling frightening and starts feeling logical. This is the moment before the threshold. And it is here, in this exact place of collapse, that we must slow down, look closely, and tell the truth about what happens next.

I felt like an empty shell, a ghost sewn into skin, a body still performing the motions of living long after the reason had drained away. Breath moved in and out of me like a habit I had forgotten how to stop, mechanical, detached, meaningless. I was a being inhabiting the ruins of myself, walls still standing, but hollowed, scorched, stripped of warmth. Life had passed through here once. Now only the echo remained. I moved, yes. I breathed, yes. But I was no longer *inhabited*. Hope had fled first, slipping out quietly, like a tenant leaving in the night without saying goodbye. After it went meaning, then desire, then the fragile belief that I mattered at all. What remained was this relentless, gnawing sorrow, chewing its way through every remaining structure, leaving me porous, transparent, undone.

I was a walking ruin drifting through a world that did not know I was breaking. The earth still turned. The sky still stretched wide and indifferent. Somewhere, people laughed, slept, loved, made plans for mornings they assumed would come. And I sat there, collapsing inward, unnoticed, unheard, unraveling in real time beneath a moon that offered no answers. A corpse with a pulse. A heart beating only out of habit. Each thud inside my chest felt less like proof of life and more like an echo in an empty room, a sound repeating itself long after the speaker has gone. My soul felt heavy, dense, as if it had developed its own gravity, pulling itself inward, folding, collapsing into that same black hole of nothingness that had swallowed my voice moments before. I could feel myself being drawn inward, atom by atom, thought by thought, memory by memory, until there was no edge left to me. No outline. No self. Just ache.

Just weight. Just the slow implosion of a person who had grown too tired to keep holding herself together. And there, beneath the cold moon and the indifferent sky, beneath the weight of that consuming nothingness, I truly believed I had already died. Not dramatically. Not violently. But quietly. Internally. Completely. I believed I had already disappeared. I believed there was nothing left to save. I *knew* that was how it felt. And when a person reaches that place, where feeling dead feels indistinguishable from being dead, the silence changes. It stops waiting. It stops hovering. It answers. The belief settled over me with a terrifying calm, not as panic, but as certainty. It wrapped itself around my thoughts like a shroud already measured to my shape. If this was what being alive felt like, then perhaps life had already slipped past me without ceremony. I did not feel myself leaving the world; I felt as though the world had quietly stepped away from me, withdrawing its warmth, its color, its invitation to belong.

I was still here in form, but not in essence. Still breathing but not inhabiting. Still upright but no longer anchored. Existence had thinned to a single, aching point of awareness, and even that felt temporary, brittle, ready to fracture. I remember thinking that this must be what it means to vanish while still standing. To become invisible to yourself first, long before anyone else notices. My reflection, had I dared to look for it, would not have recognized me. I was not a woman in pain anymore. I was pain wearing the outline of a woman. Every memory felt distant, every future unreachable. The gravity inside my chest pulled everything inward until there was no room left for breath, no space for choice, no horizon to imagine beyond the night pressing down on me. And in that moment, something irreversible shifted.

When Belief Becomes the Threshold

When you believe you are already gone, the idea of leaving no longer feels like loss. It feels like alignment. Like matching the outside world to the emptiness that has already claimed you within. The thought did not arrive as chaos. It arrived as quiet agreement. As a soft, dangerous logic that whispered, this only makes sense. You are not destroying anything. You are only completing what has already happened. That is how the threshold reveals itself. Not with drama or urgency, but with a stillness so complete it feels like peace. A pause where the ache stops screaming and begins persuading. Where despair no longer begs for relief, but offers a solution wrapped in silence. This is the place where suicidal ideation stops circling and starts standing still. Where the mind, exhausted from carrying itself, begins to believe that letting go is not an act of violence, but an act of rest. This is where the next part truly begins. Not at the moment of action, but here.

At the moment of belief. At the instant when I was convinced that I had already died and therefore had nothing left to protect. This is where the night stops being metaphor and becomes decision. In that moment, I was no longer a woman; I was the faint outline of who I used to be, a dim echo drifting through the ruins of my own life. A shadow wearing skin. A ghost with a heartbeat. A specter stitched together by pain. The ache inside me was not abstract; it had weight, breath, presence. It pulsed as a wounded creature curled tight in my ribcage, clawing from the inside, reminding me with every throb that despair had not merely brushed past me, it had taken up residence. I could feel it breathing where my lungs should have expanded, could feel it shifting when I tried to move, heavy and insistent, as though it had wrapped itself around my organs and claimed the space as its own.

Each heartbeat felt less like proof of life and more like a drum signalling surrender. Thud after thud, it counted me down, not toward death, but toward erasure, the slow, merciless thinning of being. I sat there hollowed out, aware of my body only as a vessel for suffering. Skin too tight. Chest too small. Bones aching with the effort of holding me together. Even the night seemed to lean closer, pressing its vast, unblinking presence against my back, as if listening for the moment I would finally give way. I was inhabited by despair, occupied by it, colonized. It knew the map of me intimately, where I was weakest, where the fractures ran deepest, where memory still bled. It dragged old wounds to the surface and pressed on them without mercy, turning every recollection into evidence, every silence into a verdict. You are alone. You have always been alone. You will always be alone. And I believed it.

Because when pain becomes this total, it stops feeling like something that happens *to* you. It feels like what you *are*. The boundary between self and suffering dissolves. There is no distance left to gain perspective, no breath wide enough to step outside the ache. There is only this: a body present, a soul collapsing, a woman dissolving into the space where hope once lived. I was still here, technically. Still breathing, mechanically. But inside, something essential had already gone quiet. And in that terrible stillness, with despair curled deep in my chest and silence standing watch, the night leaned in closer, as if preparing to speak.

When Belief Becomes the Threshold

It hollowed me out with an intimacy that felt invasive, as though despair knew my anatomy better than I did. It learned the rhythm of my pulse, the soft vulnerabilities between bone and breath, the quiet places where hope had once curled up and slept. Each heartbeat became a reminder not of life, but of endurance, a dull insistence that I was still here when every part of me begged to disappear. I did not feel dramatic or volatile. I felt emptied. Drained down to something thin and fragile, like the last filament of a lightbulb flickering before it goes dark. Time lost its edges. Minutes did not pass; they pooled. The night stretched and pressed and held me in place, as if the world itself had paused to watch what I would do next. I was no longer making choices. I was being carried by momentum, by the gravity of pain that had been accumulating for years, compressing into this single, unbearable point.

Every thought circled the same conclusion, slow and relentless, like water wearing down stone. This is where it ends. This is where you stop. And yet, even here, something in me was still watching. Not hopeful. Not brave. Just aware. A quiet witness stood somewhere behind the despair, observing the collapse with a strange, distant clarity. It noticed how calm the night had become. How the wind had softened. How the ache, for all its cruelty, had grown eerily still. There is a particular silence that arrives when suffering believes it has won. It does not shout anymore. It waits. It assumes compliance. It assumes surrender. This was that silence. This was the space where the story tipped forward, where thought edged toward action, where the line between living and leaving thinned to something almost translucent. A place few speak about because language itself seems to falter here. A place where the self feels negotiable, optional, already fading. This is where I was. And this is where the next breath would change everything.

And in my hand, the device meant to be a bridge, a portal to connection, to comfort, to the world beyond my suffering, glowed with a cold, merciless light. It felt like an artifact from a life I no longer belonged to, a relic from a version of me who once expected replies, warmth, reassurance. Its screen stared back at me, blank and bright, an unblinking eye that refused to see me, mocking the loneliness that wrapped around my soul like a second, suffocating skin. The light was wrong somehow, too sharp, too sterile, too alive for the hollowed-out body holding it. It illuminated my trembling fingers, the tear tracks on the glass, the subtle shake I could no longer control, yet offered nothing in return. No voice reached through it. No hand extended outward. No pulse met mine. Only the hum of technology and the echo of my own breath reminding me I was still here, still stranded.

The Screen as Evidence

A cruel irony settled in my chest. A tool designed to bring people together, reduced to a mirror reflecting how utterly severed I had become, from humanity, from hope, from myself. It showed me not connection, but absence. Not belonging, but distance. Not love, but the vast, aching space where love should have been. I turned it over in my palm, this glass-and-light confession, this silent witness to my unraveling. It carried the names of people who once knew me, threads of conversations that had grown cold, moments of laughter fossilized into text bubbles that no longer led anywhere. The weight of it pressed into my skin, heavier than it should have been, as if it carried the gravity of every unanswered message, every reach that had gone unnoticed. In that breathless moment, I wasn't just alone, I was disconnected. Unmoored. Untethered from the living world.

Drifting through a reality that continued to move, to breathe, to pulse with ordinary life, while I dissolved quietly at its edges. The world did not pause. Time did not falter. Somewhere, people laughed, slept, loved, dreamed, and I sat beneath the indifferent moon, holding a glowing reminder that I no longer felt part of any of it. The bridge did not collapse. It simply never opened. And as the screen dimmed in my hand, the night pressed closer, readying itself to answer the silence it had so carefully taught me to believe. And in my hand, the device meant to be a bridge, a small shining promise of voices and warmth, glowed with a cold, merciless light. It felt foreign, almost ceremonial, like an artifact salvaged from a life I had already slipped out of. The screen stared back at me, blank yet blinding, a pale eye that saw everything and offered nothing.

Its glow did not comfort; it exposed. It illuminated the vastness of my isolation, casting sharp edges around a loneliness that wrapped around me, tight and airless. A cruel irony unfolded there in my palm. A tool designed to bind hearts together had become a mirror, reflecting the distance I felt from everyone and everything I once knew. From laughter. From ease. From the simple, radical act of belonging. The world lived inside that screen, pulsing and reachable, yet impossibly far away, as though separated from me by a pane of unbreakable glass. I could see it. I could touch it. But I could not enter it. In that breathless suspension, I was no longer anchored to anything solid. Not to time. Not to place. Not even to myself. I was adrift, unmoored, a quiet unraveling happening while the earth continued its faithful spin.

Somewhere, lights flicked on in kitchens. Somewhere, voices called names with affection. Somewhere, life went on, unbroken and unaware, while I thinned into the night like smoke, dispersing without sound. The phone grew heavy in my hand, weighted with all the words I did not know how to say and all the help I did not yet believe I deserved. It pulsed with potential and accusation all at once. Call. Don't call. Reach out. Stay silent. Each option felt equally impossible, each one carrying a cost my heart did not know how to pay. And so I sat there, caught between connection and collapse, holding the illusion of rescue while sinking deeper into myself. The night pressed close. The moon watched. The wind mourned. And within me, something fragile hovered at the edge of breaking, suspended in the moment just before a life changes direction, though I did not yet know which way it would fall.

My hand trembled as I lifted the phone again, this hollow, glass-eyed oracle of connection that once felt like a lifeline but now lay in my palm like dead weight, and an accusation. A device built to bridge worlds, reduced to a cold reminder of just how severed I had become. Its surface was slick beneath my fingers, unfeeling, indifferent, as if it, too, had decided I was no longer worth responding to. My thumb dragged across the screen, slow, hesitant, and deliberate, as though each movement required permission I no longer possessed. I scrolled through the faded constellation of names I once called my people, names that had once meant belonging. I paused on names that once meant safety. Laughter. History. Shared air. Each one carried a memory, and with it, a question that cut deeper than silence: Would they hear me if I spoke now? Or would my voice arrive too late, too broken, too heavy to hold?

The fear was not of rejection, not really, but of confirmation. Of discovering that my absence would land softly, that my unraveling would not tear the fabric of anyone else's night. My thumb hovered, suspended between digits and despair. Call. Don't call. Reach. Retreat. The screen glowed patiently, indifferent to the war unfolding above it. Somewhere in that list lived the possibility of rescue. Somewhere also lived the certainty of exposure. To press a name would be to admit the truth I had spent a lifetime disguising: that I could not do this alone, that the mask of strength had finally slipped, that beneath it lived a woman who was afraid she had waited too long to be seen. Each contact flickered like a dying star, familiar yet impossibly distant, their light ancient, delayed, unable to reach me through the thick gravity pressing against my chest.

They were still there, technically, numerically, alphabetized and intact, and yet they might as well have belonged to another lifetime. I paused on some names longer than others. Names that once knew the sound of my joy. Names that had held versions of me that no longer existed. But even those felt unreachable now, sealed behind invisible glass, preserved like museum artifacts of a life I could no longer enter. The distance between us was not measured in kilometres or missed calls, but in belief, the belief that I did not deserve to reach, that my voice would be an intrusion, that my need would be a burden. The wind surged again through the branches, the tree groaning like an old witness bearing too many secrets. The moon remained unmoved. Time advanced without mercy. And there I was, balanced on the narrow edge between silence and sound, between disappearing inward and reaching outward, holding an entire life in the small, shaking space between my thumb and the glass.

The darkness tightened its grip as I scrolled. Each name passed without being chosen felt like another quiet rejection, another door left closed, another confirmation of the lie rooting itself deeper inside me: "*You are alone. You have always been alone. This is where you end.*" My chest ached with the effort of restraint, the restraint not to call, not to plead, not to expose the raw, unraveling truth of how close I was to disappearing. The phone grew heavier with every second, as though it carried not connection, but the full weight of my unspoken desperation. A galaxy of names, and not a single place I felt safe enough to land. And then, in the pause between scrolling and surrender, something shifted. The screen glowed. The night held its breath. And the silence, the same silence that had swallowed my cries, leaned closer, as if preparing, at last, to answer.

This was the moment before the fracture widened or sealed. The breath before the plunge or the plea. The instant where a single choice would tilt the night in a direction from which there would be no clean return. And as my thumb finally stilled, hovering over one name, one heartbeat louder than the rest, the question that would carry me into what came next rose, quiet but insistent, from somewhere deep and aching within: Who am I willing to be in order to survive this moment? I searched for someone, anyone, a voice to anchor me, a heartbeat, a pulse to prove that I still belonged to the breathing world, a sign that there was still a place for me among the living. My eyes skimmed the screen with frantic hope, then slowed, heavy with dread. But each name felt like a ghost pressed flat beneath glass, a memory of connection rather than the living thing itself.

A residue of warmth rather than warmth itself, a memory of connection instead of the living pulse I ached for. They stared back at me from the glass like abandoned doorways, frames without houses, still standing long after the houses had burned down, thresholds I no longer had the strength to cross or the courage to knock upon. So I opened WhatsApp, that small, fragile altar of modern hope, carrying with it the foolish, aching prayer that maybe, just maybe, something had arrived while I was breaking. That familiar green icon blooming against the dark like a promise I wanted desperately to believe in. I hoped, foolishly, desperately, for a message, a ripple in the stillness. A single word reaching for me across the dark. a whisper that said, "*I see you. You matter. You are not invisible.*" My thumb hung, suspended between anticipation and grief, as though even touching the screen might shatter what little I had left.

My thumb hovered as the app bloomed open, light spilling across the screen like a cruel imitation of dawn. Nothing. The chat list stared back at me unblinking. A silent monument to my isolation. No blue dots blinking like distant stars. No new messages, breathing life into the void. No waiting notifications. No proof that my existence had tugged on anyone else's awareness that night. Just names stacked in stillness, conversations long quiet, their last words fossilized in time. Just the hollow architecture of connection long stilled, those names stacked like headstones. Threads of connection unraveled by distance, by silence, by years of me learning how to disappear without anyone noticing. Frayed and abandoned by time, distance, misunderstanding, and my own slow retreat from being seen.

No One Is Coming

The silence was not loud. That was the cruelty of it. It did not scream or accuse. It simply existed, vast and indifferent, stretching out before me like an empty room where sound had forgotten how to return. In that stillness, something inside me folded inward. The belief I had been trying to outrun finally caught me: that I was surplus, an afterthought, a life that could vanish without creating a ripple large enough to disturb the surface of anyone else's night. The emptiness, however, was loud. A cavern where sound went to die. A museum of almosts and once-was. Each blank space between conversations felt like another confirmation etched into my ribs. Each one whispered what had already taken root in my bones: "*You are alone. You have waited too long. You have gone quiet for too long. You have learned how to disappear too well. There is no one coming.*"

The screen did not flicker. It did not soften. It did not answer. It simply reflected me, back to myself, a woman holding a device built for connection, staring into a digital abyss that echoed the one blooming inside her chest. And in that moment, the night seemed to close in a fraction tighter, as if the silence itself were leaning forward, preparing to say what no human voice had yet dared to speak. I felt myself shrinking beneath the glow of the screen, as though the absence of messages was proof etched in light: "no one is looking for you. No one is waiting. No one notices the quiet way you are coming undone." And it was there, in that moment of absolute, echoing nothing, that the darkness leaned closer, no longer whispering, no longer coaxing. It simply waited, certain that I had reached the place where hope thins to its final thread. This was the edge. The still point before the choice. The silence before the door either opened or closed forever.

In that moment, the screen did not light my face; it illuminated my loneliness. A pale, artificial glow spilling upward like a confession I could no longer outrun. A carved confession into the dark, exposing what I had circled for hours but refused to touch. A glowing testament to the truth I had tried so desperately not to see: There was no one coming. No footsteps breaking the night. No hand reaching back through the dark. No sudden vibration. No breath on the other end of the line. No voice rising to say my name and mean it, with urgency or love. Only the cold, digital echo of everything I had lost reflected back at me in glass and silence. Only the sterile radiance of a device reflecting absence, a small artificial sun revealing the depth of my isolation. The light felt sterile, unloving, almost surgical, as though it were dissecting my isolation and laying it bare. The light felt forensic, like an interrogation lamp trained on the crime of my own existence. It did not comfort. It testified.

It bore witness to the quiet arithmetic of loss, the friendships thinned by time, the connections I had let erode, the bridges I never learned how to cross without apologizing for my weight. Every unanswered screen became an archive of moments where I had needed more than I knew how to ask for. It exposed the empty space where comfort should have lived, where reassurance should have answered. The phone hummed faintly in my palm, alive with potential yet utterly indifferent, a universe of connection reduced to a single, merciless truth: connection requires someone on the other side. And there was no one. The realization settled into me like frost, creeping inward, numbing, slow, absolute. The silence was not dramatic. It was worse than that. It was ordinary. Predictable. Absolute. The phone hummed softly in my palm, alive with power, yet utterly incapable of holding me. A tool designed for connection reduced to a cold mirror, reflecting back a version of myself I had feared was true. Someone unclaimed. Someone peripheral. Someone whose disappearance would register as static at best.

In that glow, loneliness became undeniable. Not as an emotion, but as an environment. It filled the space around me, seeped into my breath, settled behind my eyes. It was not loud. It did not shout or beg. It simply stood there, patient and unmovable, asking nothing, offering nothing, proving everything. And as the light pooled around my shaking hands, another truth surfaced, heavier than the phone itself. This was not just about who was missing from my screen. It was about how completely I had come to believe I did not deserve to be reached for. The night did not argue with me. It only agreed. The night did not rush to console me. It simply stood there, vast and unresponsive, holding up this mirror and forcing me to see myself as I believed I truly was, unseen, unchosen, unreachable. Even the moon seemed to avert its gaze, its light distant and detached, as though unwilling to witness the quiet erasure taking place beneath it.

And in that hush, with the screen glowing and my chest caving inward, something inside me collapsed completely. Not with drama. Not with sound. But with the dull, final weight of certainty. The kind that does not scream, it sinks. It settles. It convinces. And in that agreement, something inside me loosened, not in relief, but in surrender. The last illusion fell away. The hope that someone might interrupt this moment dissolved like breath on glass. There was only me. The silence. And the question of what a soul does when it believes it has reached the end of being witnessed. That was the moment the darkness leaned closer. And I listened. I lowered the phone slowly, as though it had grown too heavy to bear, and let it rest against my trembling thigh. The glow faded from my face, but the truth it revealed burned on, seared into my bones. I was not waiting anymore. I was alone. And the night, vast and unanswering, finally answered back, not with words, but with silence deep enough to swallow everything I still had left to say.

The Name That Once Felt Like Home

As my thumb still drifted down the dimly lit list of names, suspended, as if the screen itself had learned how to hold its breath. My gaze snagged on one that once felt like home, **Amelia**. My so-called 'best friend'. Five letters that once carried laughter, late-night confessions, the illusion of safety. A name that used to feel like shelter now pulsed with a quieter truth, one I had refused to look at until this very moment. Its glow was not warmth. It was exposure. A pale light revealing the outline of a hope I had overfed long past its capacity to sustain me. Her name glowed softly on the screen, a familiar beacon I had messaged more times than I could count, a lighthouse I had steered toward again and again with bruised faith and shaking hope. For so long, I had believed that light meant safety. That if I just reached her, if I just explained myself better, loved harder, endured longer, I would finally be guided back to shore. But tonight, that glow felt different. Not warm. Not steady.

It cut instead, thin and sharp, like glass catching moonlight. A beacon turned blade. A cruel reminder of how deeply I had deceived myself, how fiercely I had clung to a friendship that was never built to hold the weight of my heart. I had mistaken proximity for care, familiarity for safety, attention for love. I had anchored my survival to someone whose foundation was never strong enough to carry me. Her name pulsed there, silent and indifferent, and in its quiet glow I saw the truth with unbearable clarity: This lighthouse had never been meant to guide me home. It had been pointing me toward the rocks all along. Every unanswered call, every dismissal disguised as honesty, every wound wrapped in the language of concern, every inappropriate moment and message with my then husband, they rose now like wreckage beneath the surface, undeniable, sharp, waiting. I hovered there, suspended between instinct and knowing. Between the old reflex to reach out and the raw recognition that reaching for her was how I had learned to disappear.

My heart remembered what my mind was only now allowing itself to admit: That the place I had called refuge had been eroding me grain by grain. Her lighthouse did not fail suddenly. It failed slowly. Quietly. It failed in ways that taught me to doubt my pain, to swallow my voice, to believe that needing care was a flaw instead of a truth. And there, beneath the cold moon and the weight of that night, I finally understood, I had not been steering toward safety. I had been steering straight into the cliffs. I felt it then, the slow, sinking recognition, heavy as wet wool settling around my chest. This was not a door I could knock on anymore. Not tonight. Not ever in the way I needed. The lighthouse I had mistaken for salvation had never been meant to rescue me. It had only illuminated how desperate I was to be seen. How willing I had been to keep swimming toward a promise that dissolved the closer I came. My thumb trembled, not with fear of rejection, but with the ache of clarity.

The silence between us was not sudden. It had been growing for a long time, layering itself over unanswered messages, over half-held space, over a love that asked me to shrink so it would not have to stretch. And now, in this hour when everything was stripped bare, that silence finally spoke. It said, "This is not where you are held." It said, "This is not who can carry you through the night." It said, "Stop offering your heart to rooms that echo." I did not press her name. Instead, I let it be what it was, a memory, a lesson, a mirror reflecting the pattern I had lived inside for far too long. Loving without being met. Hoping without being held. Mistaking familiarity for safety. Mistaking proximity for care. The night watched as I lowered the phone, my fingers stiff and aching, as though they had just released something heavy they were never meant to carry. The grass pressed cold against my palms. The moon continued its indifferent vigil.

Truth Without Comfort

And inside me, beneath the devastation, something shifted again, quieter this time, but unmistakable. If this silence had an answer, it was this. I could no longer look outward for the voice that would save me. I could no longer bleed into places that could not tend the wound. I could no longer call absence love. The realization did not soothe me. It did not comfort me. It cut. Cleanly. Precisely. Like truth often does when it finally arrives. And as the name faded back into the list, no longer glowing, no longer calling, the night deepened around me, waiting. Not to rescue me. But to show me what would come next. Her name should have been a refuge, a place to rest my trembling soul, where the storm might loosen its grip. It should have offered comfort, connection, some small flicker of belonging. It should have been a soft landing, a voice that steadied the night. Instead, it throbbed on the screen like a wound that refused to close, a quiet flare signalling danger I had ignored for far too long.

It pulsed on the screen like a warning light, a symbol of the unraveling that had brought me to the cold grass beneath a merciless moon. Its light did not guide me home. It exposed the wreckage. I understood then, with a clarity that hurt to hold, that I was sitting on the grass because I felt unlovable and unseen by the world. I was here because I had kept offering my heart to a place that could not shelter it. I had mistaken familiarity for safety, proximity for care, and longing for love. I had kept swimming toward a promise that asked me to drown so it could remain untouched. She was not my refuge. She was the fault line. The place where the ground first cracked, where trust slipped, where hope learned how to fracture quietly.

Each unmet need, each silenced truth, each moment I told myself it wasn't that bad had stacked like invisible plates beneath me, until the pressure could no longer be contained. And tonight, it all gave way. The realization spread through me slowly, like poison spreading through the veins. This pain did not begin here. It had been building for months, years, a slow erosion masked as loyalty, devotion, patience. I had called it love because I didn't know what else to call the ache of staying when I was already disappearing. I couldn't message her, not tonight, not anymore, because she was the reason I was here in the first place. Not my salvation, but the epicenter of the earthquake that shattered the ground beneath me. Not an anchor grounding my little boat, but a weight dragging me deeper into waters I had spent my whole life trying not to drown in. Staring at her name, something inside me finally gave way. Not with a dramatic collapse, but with a quiet, bone-deep resignation. Her name forced the truth into my lungs like ice water. The kind that arrives when denial has exhausted itself.

I saw, with brutal clarity, how often I had mistaken familiarity for safety, proximity for care. How I had returned again and again to a place that wounded me, simply because it was familiar, simply because it once felt like home. I had clung to the memory of who she used to be, or who I needed her to be, long after the truth had changed shape. The person I had reached for in my most fragile moments was the same hand that had loosened its grip when I needed it most. The same voice that had taught me, slowly and repeatedly, that my pain was inconvenient, my needs excessive, my breaking point an inconvenience rather than a warning. I had come to this night not because I was weak, but because I had trusted the wrong shelter during a storm. My fingers curled around the phone, not in anger, but in grief. Grief for the version of me who believed that enduring was the same as being chosen. Grief for the countless times I had minimized my own hurt to keep someone else comfortable. Grief for the girl who learned too early that being needed was the closest thing to being loved.

When the Wrong Shelter Breaks You

My chest ached and tightened with that grief sharper than loss, the grief of recognition, that felt older than this night, older than this betrayal. Of realizing that love, when it requires you to disappear to survive it, is not love at all. That friendship, when it thrives on your silence and shrinks from your truth, becomes another form of abandonment. I had mistaken endurance for loyalty, self-erasure for compassion. I had learned to call neglect "understanding" and harm "honesty," until my own heart no longer recognized the sound of being held. The grief of realizing that some people do not leave loudly. They leave by staying just enough to keep you hoping, just enough to keep you reaching, while quietly teaching you that your pain will never be their priority. That your breaking point will always be an inconvenience. That love, in their hands, is conditional, rationed, withheld the moment it asks something back. The moon watched as that truth settled into me, heavy and irrevocable. The grass bit cold into my skin. The wind carried on, indifferent.

And still, I sat there, phone glowing in my palm, finally understanding that the ache hollowing me out was not just loneliness. It was betrayal layered over longing, abandonment disguised as closeness, harm dressed up as friendship. I had not arrived at this edge because I was too much. I had arrived here because I had been too willing to make myself smaller to be kept. And as that realization spread through me, slow and searing, something else stirred beneath the devastation. Not hope. Not yet. But truth. Sharp. Unavoidable. The kind of truth that hurts because it dismantles the last illusion you were using to survive. Her name no longer felt like a question. It felt like an answer. And the night, vast and merciless as it was, bore witness as I finally understood how I had been led here, not by my weakness, but by my loyalty to a place that could never hold me without breaking me first. The phone felt heavier now, as if it carried the accumulated weight of every time I had reached out and been met with absence, falseness, deceit, and lies.

Every message left unanswered or answered pretentiously, or as blades my first husband could use against me. Every truth minimized. Every wound reframed as my own failure to be stronger, quieter, and easier to keep. Her name was no longer a doorway; it was a locked room I had bled inside for far too long. And there, in that recognition, something subtle shifted. Painful, yes. Devastating, absolutely. But also clarifying. The night did not answer me with comfort or rescue; it answered me with truth. A truth I had resisted because it meant letting go of the illusion that someone else could save me. That someone else was supposed to. I lowered the phone again, letting it rest against the damp earth, and the night seemed to lean in closer. My fingers numb, my heart raw and exposed. The grass beneath me was still cold. The moon still indifferent. The silence still vast. But for the first time that night, the ache had a shape. The loneliness had names: Amelia, the woman I called my best friend, and Straus, my first husband. And the darkness, though still immense, had revealed one undeniable thing: I had not been abandoned by everyone. I had been abandoned by someone I loved.

And knowing that, truly knowing it, the lie pressed even harder, that I was unlovable, unworthy, alone by design. Because if people I believed loved me could abuse, betray, deceive, and hurt without remorse, then who could? I was hopeless for hope. The moon watched. The grass chilled my skin. My chest still ached, still burned, still struggled for breath. Beneath the pain, beneath the devastation, a question began to form, fragile as frost. "If I stop reaching for what hurts me. Suppose I stop calling wounds home. What might be left? The night did not answer with words. It answered by showing me what I had become with Amelia and what I truly thought of myself. It took me further down the path because the question will surely be answered soon enough.

Amelia had become the quiet catalyst of this slow, agonizing descent into darkness, the unseen hand tipping the balance again and again. The subtle gravity that pulled me, inch by unbearable inch, toward the edge until gravity finally won. Once, she had been the place I leaned when the world felt sharp. The person I had once reached for in moments of tenderness. Now she stood as a living mirror of my own perceived inadequacy, I could no longer look into without flinching, reflecting back every doubt I had swallowed, every lie I had learned to believe about my worth, that I already feared was true. Her presence reopened wounds I had tried to cauterize with silence. It illuminated the fault lines of a marriage that had been broken long before I understood I was the one haemorrhaging, the one quietly stitching myself together while everyone else carried on as though nothing sacred had been lost. In her shadow, my wounds learned how to speak. In her absence of care, my marriage revealed its fractures, a structure already collapsing while I kept telling myself it was only settling.

How could I reach out for help to the very hands that had guided me closer to the edge, the very hands that loosened my grip on myself? How could I ask to be held by someone whose words had quietly unmade me, whose truths shifted shape, whose loyalty dissolved the moment it was tested? How could I whisper save me to the person whose disrespect, lies, and quiet betrayals had carved this hollow into my chest, layer by ruthless layer? To ask her for rescue would have been to deny my own reality, to pretend that the blade had not come from her grip. To whisper save me to her would have been to deny what my body already knew. That the hollow inside my chest had been carved not by fate, but by disregard. By deception dressed as closeness. By intimacy that asked me to disappear so it could remain intact.

Her name no longer glowed with the promise of safety. It pulsed with accusation. With proof. With the echo of every moment, I had swallowed my pain to preserve something that was already rotting. It burned with recognition. It illuminated not refuge, but betrayal. Not belonging, but the wreckage of what I had mistaken for love, for loyalty, for safety. It showed me how easily devotion can be weaponized, how quickly care can turn conditional, how often we are taught to call abandonment a flaw in ourselves. Her name illuminated not love, but coldness. Not loyalty, but the slow erosion of trust. Not friendship, but the crumbling remains of what I had once believed connection was supposed to feel like. And in that moment, something inside me recoiled, not in anger, but in exhausted clarity. I understood that reaching for her would not save me. It would only deepen the wound, drive the knife further into the space that was already raw and bleeding. I saw how often I had confused proximity with care, how I had mistaken familiarity for safety, how I had stayed loyal to someone who had never learned how to be gentle with my heart.

So I let the screen go dark. The light vanished with a soft click, like a door closing somewhere deep inside me. Her name dissolved back into shadow pixels, surrendering to black, and with it went the last illusion that she could save me from what she had helped create. The phone became nothing more than cold glass in my hand again. The night felt heavier for it, but also quieter. More honest. And as the glow faded, so did the last illusion I had been clinging to. I pressed the phone into my chest, and fell backward onto the icy grass, as if laying down an offering or a confession. The cold earth accepted it without judgment. Above me, the moon continued its watch, indifferent yet unwavering, and I realized something in that moment that cut clean through the ache. I could not erase the memories. I could not undo the cost. But I could stop reaching for the knife that had already drawn so much blood. Letting her name fade did not heal me. It did not mend the marriage. It did not soften the night. It did not change my mind on my decision to let go. But it marked a threshold. The moment I stopped asking the wrong person to see me.

The moment I stopped mistaking pain for proof of love. The moment I stood, trembling and alone, and faced the truth that the darkness had been circling all along. If, and that was a very big *IF,* I was going to survive this night, it would not be by returning to what broke me. It would be by listening, at last, to what something deep was trying to say. Not the silence I knew, but the silence of hope. I sat there beneath the merciless moon, the night breathing around me, and felt the weight of what she had cost me settle fully into my bones. I wished, with an ache that bordered on prayer, that I could do the same with every memory of her. Let them dim. Let them loosen their grip. Let them sink back into the dark where they could no longer bruise me with their presence. But memory does not disappear on command. It lingers. It hums. It waits. And there, in the silence that followed the screen going black, I felt the night draw closer, as if sensing that one of the last doors had just quietly closed.

This woman, my so-called best friend, was the very heartbeat of my death wish. The pulse beneath the despair. The rhythm driving the spiral. How cruel the irony, how merciless the twist of fate, that the person I once trusted with my softness, my secrets, my unguarded heart, now stood at the violent center of the storm that pushed me toward oblivion. How exquisitely horrifying the design of it. The one I had leaned into for comfort had become the wind tearing the ground out from beneath my feet. The person I once ran to for shelter stood at the epicenter of the storm that drove me toward oblivion. The hands I had trusted to steady me were the same hands that loosened my grip on life. The voice I once believed would speak me back from the edge had, piece by piece, taught me how to doubt my own right to stand there at all. It was a paradox too sharp to hold without bleeding. A coin split down the middle. It was a bitter paradox, sharp enough to cut through breath itself.

A wounded coin with two sides that could never be reconciled. On one side lived the aching, instinctual pull, ancient, reflexive, to reach for her. To believe that if I could just explain myself better, love harder, bend further, she would finally see me, finally choose me, finally stop the pain she herself had taught me to carry. That hope was muscle memory, etched into me through years of loyalty and forgiveness offered long past their expiry date. The muscle memory of friendship, the reflex of years spent believing she was safe. My hand still knew the shape of that reach. My heart still remembered the hope it once carried. On the other side lived the devastating truth: the help I needed could never come from the very one who had carved these fractures into me. The source of my pain could not also be my salvation. She was not a villain in some grand, cinematic sense.

That would have been easier. She was something far more dangerous, familiar. Close. Trusted. Someone whose words slipped past my defenses because I had opened the gates myself. Someone whose disapproval cut deeper because I had crowned her opinion as law. Someone whose withdrawal felt like annihilation because I had mistaken proximity for safety and worthiness. Her absence in that moment screamed louder than any insult she had ever spoken, and every moment of betrayal she did with my first husband. It confirmed the quiet narrative she had planted in me over time: that my pain was inconvenient, my needs excessive, my breaking point an overreaction. That even at my most undone, I was still asking for too much. To turn toward her now would have been to press salt into an open wound and call it healing. To ask her to hold me would have meant asking the blade to become a bandage.

And somewhere in the hollow of my chest, a quiet, unbearable knowing settled in. The person I longed for did not exist anymore. Or perhaps she never had, except in the story I told myself to survive. That realization landed heavier than the night itself. It cracked something final open. The instinct to reach collided violently with the truth that reaching would only deepen the fall. And in that collision, something inside me broke free and broke apart all at once. Grief flooded in, thick and suffocating, not just for the friendship I lost, but for the version of myself who had believed love would not hurt like this. I sat there with that knowledge burning through me, realizing that some losses do not arrive with noise or spectacle. Some arrive as silence. As recognition. As the slow, devastating understanding that the door you keep knocking on has never led anywhere but deeper into the dark.

And there, beneath the moon, with the cold grass biting into my skin and the night pressing in from all sides, the final cruelty revealed itself. I was not just alone. I was alone *because* I had trusted the wrong person with my survival. That realization did not rage. It hollowed. It sank into me like a slow poison, numbing and clarifying all at once. I saw, with terrifying precision, how love twisted into leverage. How loyalty became a leash. How my desire to be accepted had slowly taught me to abandon myself. The ache in my chest sharpened, not with longing now, but with grief, not only for the friendship I thought I had, but for the woman I had been before I learned to doubt her own worth so completely. I did not want her voice anymore. I did not want her comfort. I did not even want her apology. What I wanted, what I needed, was impossible in that moment. I needed the version of myself who had not yet learned to disappear for love.

Home as the Source of the Wound

And sitting there, suspended between breath and surrender, I began to understand something devastating and true: Some wounds do not come from enemies. They come from the places we called home. And the night, vast and unblinking, held that truth with me. silent, unforgiving, and finally, unmistakably clear.The realization hit like a collapsing world, a blow so heavy it caved my chest inward, as if the air itself had been knocked from me and forgotten how to return, until even breath felt foreign inside me. It was as if the ground beneath my ribs gave way, leaving nothing but a cavern where my heart once stood. My ribs felt like ruins. My heart is like a room after an earthquake, walls cracked, foundations exposed.

How could I cry out to the very hand that helped build the walls of my suffocation? How could I beg for rescue from the one who taught my heart how to fracture, and then looked me in the eye, saw my bleeding, and told me I was imagining it, that the pain was mine alone, that jealousy was the crime and silence the sentence? That I was jealous, that the pain was a fiction I had authored myself? Those words lingered like poison mist, seeping into every corner of my mind. Her words replayed like a cruel refrain, looping through my mind with surgical precision, cutting deeper each time. Gaslight dressed as concern and care. Cruelty wrapped in familiarity. Dismissal wrapped in smiles. A slow erosion of trust until even my own perception felt suspect. I had learned to doubt my wounds while they were still bleeding. I had learned, slowly and devastatingly, to mistrust my own wounds while they were still open, to doubt the ache even as it screamed.

Learned to question my pain while it screamed for recognition. Her denial became a second injury, deeper than the first, because it taught me to turn against my own knowing. And standing there now, under a sky that offered no answers, I understood with devastating clarity: the person who broke me could never be the one to make me whole. Her name became a double-edged sword pressed against my throat. On one side, the faint, treacherous glimmer of familiar comfort, the memory of laughter, shared secrets, the illusion of being seen, of late-night confidences, of a closeness I once mistook for safety. On the other side, an abyss of despair so vast it seemed bottomless it threatened to consume me whole, a chasm carved by betrayal, dismissal, manipulation, and the slow murder and erosion of my self-trust.

The Choice That Offered No Mercy

To reach for her felt like stepping toward a cliff edge in the dark, wind roaring in my ears, heart suspended between instinct and survival, split between the desire to leap and the desperate urge to step back. Either choice promised annihilation. To leap was to surrender what little remained of me, to offer my last fragile pieces to the hands that had already proven careless with them. If I stayed, if I did not call, to step back was to remain alone with the full, unbearable, crushing weight of the night, with no buffer between me and the truth of my isolation. With nothing to soften the fall except my own breaking breath. One path felt like the death of the soul. The other, the death of the body. And both loomed with the same terrible finality, like final doors.

My body remembered her as refuge. My soul knew her as ruin. And so I sat there, trembling beneath an indifferent sky, the cold pressing through the grass and into my bones, the damp beneath my fingers, moonlight cold on my skin, offering light but no mercy. I knew then, with a clarity that burned, that the only person I wanted to call was the one I could never call again. The grief and knowledge of that truth settled into me like frost, quiet, merciless, irreversible, sealing something shut inside my chest. In that moment, it was not just a friendship that ended. It was the last illusion of safety I had been clinging to. And the silence that followed was not empty; it was absolute, a vast, echoing stillness in which I understood that whatever came next, I would have to face it without the comfort I once believed was real. I was not just abandoned, I was exiled from the last illusion of safety I had left. And the silence that followed was not empty. It was final.

As I sat there, suspended in that agonizing stillness, a great wave of apathy surged through me, not a gentle tide that comes and goes, but a violent, merciless tsunami. Its cold, towering force rose without warning, blotting out the horizon of my thoughts, blotting out the horizon, blotting out the future, blotting out even the idea of resistance. Blotting out the language of hope itself. It crashed over the last trembling fragments of my resistance with the weight of an ocean, salt-heavy, absolute, and darkness filling my mouth, my lungs, my thoughts, until there was no room left for struggle. It shattered the final flicker of light that had been clinging, the fading of hope that had been barely surviving, weak, exhausted, barely breathing and trembling, to the edges of my consciousness, snapping it like a brittle matchstick struck too hard.

What followed was not the chaos I had feared, but something far more dangerous: A hush. A numb, colorless calm that spread through me like frost over a field at dawn. The pain did not vanish; it went quiet. It settled into my bones, dense and unmoving, as if my heart had been wrapped in wet wool and set down somewhere deep inside my chest to be forgotten. Even despair loosened its grip, not because it had healed, but because it no longer needed to argue. Apathy does not persuade. It simply erases the need to care. This was not sadness. Not fear. Not even despair. This was something quieter and far more dangerous. A numb surrender. A vast, grey flattening of feeling where pain no longer screamed, but simply existed, unquestioned and unchallenged. The ache dulled into something heavy and inert, like a stone laid gently but irrevocably over my heart. I no longer felt pulled toward life or death. I felt emptied of the need to choose at all.

The Fog Where Wanting Ends

The night softened its sounds. The wind dulled. The branches above me ceased their clawing and became silhouettes again, flat and distant. My breath slowed, shallow and automatic, rising and falling out of habit rather than desire. I felt myself thinning, not falling apart, but fading, like ink diluted drop by drop in a glass of water until no trace of its original shape remained. The world blurred at the edges, its sounds muffled, as though I were sinking beneath deep water. The wind still moved the branches above me, the moon still watched with its pale indifference, but all of it felt distant, unreal, happening somewhere far beyond the reach of my skin. Even my own body began to feel like an afterthought, a shell I was inhabiting out of habit rather than intention. In that fog, time lost its edges. Seconds stretched. Minutes dissolved.

The future folded in on itself and disappeared, leaving only the present moment, heavy and inert, pressing down with the quiet authority of inevitability. I was no longer pulled toward anything. Not life. Not death. I hovered in a place where wanting had exhausted itself, where choice felt like a language I no longer spoke. Apathy wrapped itself around me like a thick fog, soft but suffocating, convincing me that nothing mattered enough to fight for anymore, not connection, not healing, not even escape. It whispered that effort was pointless, that longing was foolish, that hope was a cruel prank played on those who still believed in tomorrows. In its hush, the chaos finally quieted, and that quiet felt dangerously like relief.

Apathy whispered without words: Rest now. Let go. Not as a command, but as a suggestion so gentle it felt merciful. And in that still, flattened space, I understood how people vanish, not in a scream, not in spectacle, but in this soft surrender, this gradual dimming where the will to reach simply loosens its fingers and slips away. I sat there, emptied and weightless, while the night held its breath around me, waiting to see whether anything, anything at all, would answer the silence. I stopped asking why. I stopped asking how. I stopped asking if. The questions dissolved, one by one, until only stillness remained, a stillness so complete it felt like the absence of gravity, like floating in the aftermath of a storm where everything has already been destroyed, and there is nothing left to save. And in that flattened, hollow calm, I understood with chilling clarity how I will disappear, not in a scream, not in a dramatic collapse, but in this slow extinguishing. This moment when my will to keep reaching simply, lets go.

When the Mask Falls

This wasn't the familiar apathy of the mask I had worn for years, the polite, practiced numbness that whispered "*I'm fine*" while hurricanes tore themselves apart beneath my skin. It was not the carefully painted facade I presented to the world, that porcelain smile stretched thin over fractures no one bothered to look for, let alone mend or tend. That excuse, that reflex, I had rehearsed until *everything is okay* slipped from my lips with the ease of muscle memory, a line delivered so convincingly it passed for truth. A fragile veneer, polished and maintained, designed to soothe others while I quietly sank beneath its weight. That version of apathy had been functional. Strategic. A performance honed over time. An armor I slipped into with ease, whispering *everything is okay* in a voice so rehearsed it eventually passed for truth. But this was different. This apathy did not bother with performance.

It did not ask to be believed. It arrived stripped of manners and motive, a cold clearing where even the need to explain had died. The mask had always required effort, constant adjustment, constant vigilance. This required nothing at all. It spread like frost across the inside of me, silent and efficient, sealing shut the places where feeling once fought to survive. There was no longer a storm to hide, only a vast, emptied stillness. No urge to reassure. No instinct to reach out. Even despair seemed too loud for what had taken hold. I felt myself receding, not in panic, not in protest, but in a quiet retreat, as though some essential part of me had laid down its tools and stepped back from the work of staying alive. And in that hollow calm, I understood the danger. This was not relief. This was erosion. Not the scream of breaking, but the hush that follows when the breaking is complete. A silence so thorough it swallowed even the desire to be saved.

That mask had a purpose: to soothe others, to keep the peace, to make my pain more palatable by hiding it altogether. It was a fragile veneer crafted to protect everyone else from discomfort while I quietly drowned beneath its weight. I wore it in conversations, in rooms full of people, in moments where my laughter rang just convincingly enough to silence questions. It allowed me to survive. Or at least, to appear as though I was surviving. But this, this was something else entirely. The mask had fallen away, shattered at my feet. What stood in its place was not freedom, but vacancy. A room swept clean of hope, of fear, of resistance. And in that bare interior, with nothing left to perform and no one left to convince, the night drew closer, not as an enemy, not as a threat, but as a witness, waiting to see whether anything in me would still choose to answer. This apathy did not care how I appeared. It did not bother with smiles or explanations. It did not whisper reassurances meant to soothe. It arrived stripped of performance, stripped of pretense, stripped of even the desire to be understood. It was not numbness as disguise, but numbness as erasure. A hollowing. A quiet extinguishing of effort itself.

There was no voice left to insist *"I'm okay"*. No strength left to pretend I wanted to be. The facade had finally collapsed under the weight it was never meant to carry, shattering into silence. What remained was not relief, but vacancy, a vast interior room emptied of furniture, of warmth, of meaning. A place where even pain had grown tired of announcing itself. I felt the difference keenly, unmistakably. The mask had always required energy, vigilance, and maintenance. This required nothing. It asked nothing. It simply spread, slow and absolute, until even the instinct to struggle felt unnecessary. I was no longer holding myself together for anyone. I was no longer holding myself at all. And in that surrender, not dramatic, not loud, but devastatingly quiet, I understood how close I was to disappearing. Not in flames. Not in chaos. But in this gentle, ruthless stillness, where even the will to cry out had finally gone silent. This was not hiding anymore. This was the moment the hiding ended, and the night leaned in to see what would remain.

The Void After Collapse

No. This was something far beyond that brittle performance. This was something far deeper, far darker, far more absolute, far more final. This was the collapse of the facade itself, the moment the scaffolding gave way, and there was nothing left to brace against. The shattering of the illusion that I could brace, smile, endure, or *get over it* one more time. That belief splintered in my hands like dry bone. The last illusion shattered, the belief that I could gather myself, grit my teeth, and *get over it* one more time. That myth fell apart in my hands like dust, revealing the truth beneath: there was nothing left to patch, nothing left to prop up. What rose in its place was not emotion, but absence and erasure. A hollowing so complete it felt cosmic, as though my soul had been siphoned out into a vast, internal night. An abyss opened where my center once lived, endless, indifferent, where even echoes forgot how to return. A cavern of unending nothingness. It that did not roar or threaten, but simply *existed*, vast and vacant, swallowing thought before it could form, devouring feeling before it could ache. Even despair seemed too heavy to survive there.

A vacuum that swallowed thought before it could form, devoured feeling before it could ache, and left behind only a sterile hush where my heartbeat used to thunder. In that void, time thinned to a thread. Breath arrived without intention, a mechanical courtesy the body extended to itself. The world felt distant, as if seen through thick glass or remembered from another life. I was not breaking; I had already broken. I was not falling; I had reached the bottom and found it did not resist me. Even despair felt too heavy to survive there. The abyss asked nothing, promised nothing. It did not threaten. It simply waited, vast, indifferent, patient. And in that waiting, I understood a quieter terror: This was the silence after the collapse, the stillness that follows the last cry. The place where struggle loosens its grip, where the will goes slack, where the self becomes a faint outline traced in ash. I stood at the edge of myself, emptied of language, emptied of want, emptied of hope, staring into a darkness so complete it felt like the universe holding its breath, waiting to see whether anything, anything at all, would rise from that nothingness and answer back. Inside that emptiness, silence reigned with a terrible authority. Not the peaceful silence of rest, but the sterile quiet of a room long abandoned. The place where my heartbeat used to thunder now held only a thin, unfamiliar hush. Breath arrived without intention.

The body continued its rituals by habit alone, like a machine left running after the operators had gone home. I did not feel broken. I felt erased. As though the outline of me had been rubbed smooth by time and pain, until only a faint impression remained, proof that something had once been there. Like the chalk outline of a body on a crime scene. Evidence that something once living was there, but now only the outline remained. The abyss did not coax or threaten. It simply waited, patient and vast, offering nothing back. And in that waiting, I understood the most frightening truth of all: This was not the chaos of falling apart. This was the stillness that comes *after*. The quiet after the collapse. The moment when even the will to fight has slipped its grip and drifted away into the dark. The facade was gone. The performance was over. And I was left standing at the edge of myself, staring into a silence so complete it felt like the universe holding its breath, waiting to see whether anything, anything at all, would rise from that nothingness and answer back.

It was terrifying in its vastness, yet somehow, liberating like stepping into a cavern so immense it swallowed sound, memory, and resistance all at once. As if the collapse of the facade and the mask freed me from the exhausting labor and finally loosened the iron grip of pretending to be alive. The performance fell away. The lines I had memorized, the gestures of survival, the borrowed smiles and stitched-together strength all disintegrated into dust. The war that had raged endlessly inside me went silent, not because it had been won, but because there was nothing left to fight with. It laid down its weapons. There was no more bargaining with hope, no more wrestling with fear, no more pleading with tomorrow to be gentler than yesterday. The noise that had stalked me for years finally fell silent, not because it had been healed, but because it had burned itself out.

I no longer felt fear clawing at my throat. I no longer felt sorrow. I no longer felt yearning clawing at my ribs for something unnamed. No desire reached outward for rescue or relief. Those emotions once so loud they threatened to split me open, had evaporated, simply vanished, leaving behind a clean, sterile emptiness. In their place was nothing. I felt nothing. True, utterly, unadulterated nothing. A vacuum so complete it felt almost sacred, like standing at the center of a dead star where gravity had collapsed in on itself. A stillness so full it felt like standing at the center of a snowbound field after a storm, where even sound had been erased. It was not peace, not comfort, but an absence so total it mimicked both. No ache. No hope. No despair. Just a vast, sterile stillness and nothingness.

When Caring Ends

And in that void, understanding arrived without drama, without mercy, without resistance. A realization settled with chilling clarity, sharp as ice against bare skin: I had stopped caring. About breath. About tomorrow. About survival. About people. The fragile threads that once tethered me to the world slipped quietly from my grasp, one by one, without grief or protest. The idea of a future self-destructed. The instinct to stay had gone quiet. The effort to endure felt unnecessary. Caring itself felt like an artifact from a former life, a language I no longer spoke, a currency I no longer needed.

This was not despair anymore. Despair still bleeds. Despair still begs. Despair still aches toward something, still reaches, still hopes in its own broken way. This was something colder. Quieter. More final. A place beyond longing, where even pain had grown tired and laid itself down. A numb surrender where even longing had packed its bags and left. I did not feel like I wanted to die. I felt like I had already stepped beyond the need to live. I felt as though living had simply ceased to matter. And in that hollowed-out stillness, stripped of fear and grief alike, I hovered in a dangerous calm, one where the absence of pain masqueraded as relief, and the loss of caring felt, for a moment, like freedom. Where numbness dressed itself as reprieve, I hovered in a silence so complete it felt like the end of wanting altogether.

My surrender was complete, absolute, polished to a terrible perfection. The darkness I had been resisting for so long finally slipped its arms around me, not as a threat, not as a predator baring teeth, but as an invitation in a sweet, seductive embrace. As a counterfeit comfort, a velvet hush that knew my name. It felt soft. Familiar. Persuasive. Like a lullaby learned in childhood and forgotten until the moment it returned to carry me under. The poisoned chalice I had once only lifted to my lips, in trembling rehearsal, was now firmly pressed to my lips, its surface catching the moonlight, its contents shimmering with a treacherous calm that masqueraded as mercy. A poison shimmering like a promise inside. It felt almost ceremonial. A tragic romance staged in silence. A true Romeo-and-Juliet illusion. Death as Romeo, and I as Juliet, where devotion is mistaken for destiny, and longing masquerades, and dresses itself as love.

Death, once a shadow and shape I fled from, now appeared before me as a strange, sorrowful lover, eyes full of promises it could not keep. Offering peace, offering quiet, offering release, offering rest. Offering an end. It offered the end of effort, the end of ache, the end of asking anything of me ever again. It spoke in the language of relief, in the accent of final answers, in a tenderness that felt earned only because I was so tired. And for the first time, I felt ready to step willingly into its waiting embrace. In that moment, I believed it. I believed the stillness it promised was peace. I believed the closing of the door would be relief rather than erasure. I believed the embrace would hold, rather than hollow. The readiness I felt was not courage, but exhaustion mistaken for clarity, a weariness so deep it mistook disappearance for rest. I stood there, balanced on that fragile edge where seduction and surrender look identical, where silence pretends to be salvation. The darkness did not rush me. It never does. It lingered with the patience of something ancient, letting the illusion bloom fully before the fall.

It being confident that when pain has been carried long enough, even an ending can begin to feel like love. The air around me grew hushed, as though the world itself had learned to hold its breath. My pulse softened. The ache dulled. The endless questions that had clawed at me for years finally loosened their grip, slipping away like names forgotten in a dream. In that suspended moment, surrender felt like grace. Disappearing felt like rest. Letting go felt like being chosen at last. I believed the stillness it promised was mercy. I believed the closing of the door would be relief rather than erasure. I believed that if I stepped forward, I would finally be held without condition, without demand, without pain. Exhaustion dressed itself as clarity, and despair wore the borrowed face of love. I stood there, balanced on the fragile edge where seduction and salvation look the same, where silence pretends to be sanctuary, where the night whispers that ending is the only kindness left. And so I leaned closer, breath shallow, heart quieting, the world dimming at the edges, unaware that this was not love at all, but the most convincing lie the darkness ever tells.

The Star Implodes

In that moment, something within me truly died, not with drama or sound, but with the quiet collapse of a star imploding into itself. No explosion. No farewell. No blaze, no thunder, no final cry to mark the passing. Just an inward fall and folding so complete that the universe barely noticed. Gravity turning against its own light, a vanishing so complete it left no debris behind. My soul, once flickering and frantic, simply went out, snuffed by the suffocating weight of years I had carried alone. It did not scream as it left. It did not rage as it dimmed. It slipped away like breath on cold glass, fading before it could be traced. It surrendered, slipping into darkness the way embers cool when no one is left to tend the fire. What remained was only the husk of me. A hollow vessel. A body moving on instinct, muscle memory guiding limbs where meaning no longer lived. A body obeying habit rather than hope, breath moving in and out like a reflex long after meaning has fled.

I sat there alive by definition, yet absent in every way that mattered, my spirit already drifting somewhere beyond reach, untethered, unclaimed. I felt myself thinning, becoming outline instead of substance, echo instead of voice. I was no longer inhabiting my life; I was haunting it. The night seemed to recognize this shift. Its silence deepened, settling over me like ash, soft and final. Even pain loosened its grip, not because it had healed, but because there was no longer anyone left inside me to feel it. I had crossed into a colder country, one where nothing asks anything of you, where numbness wears the mask of peace. And in that still, starless quiet, I believed this was what it meant to be finished.

My eyes stayed open, my lungs obeyed, my heart kept time out of habit alone, but the animating spark had loosened its hold. I was present without presence. Alive without arrival. A shell echoing with the memory of a self that had finally grown too tired to stay. I sat there alive by definition, yet absent in every way that mattered, my spirit already drifting somewhere beyond reach, untethered, unclaimed. I felt myself thinning, becoming outline instead of substance, echo instead of voice. I was no longer inhabiting my life; I was haunting it. The night seemed to recognize this shift. Its silence deepened, settling over me like ash, soft and final. Even pain loosened its grip, not because it had healed, but because there was no longer anyone left inside me to feel it. I had crossed into a colder country, one where nothing asks anything of you, where numbness wears the mask of peace. And in that still, starless quiet, I believed this was what it meant to be finished.

The world did not change when I disappeared inside myself. The moon kept its watch. The wind kept its song. The night did not pause to mark my vanishing. That, perhaps, was the cruelest truth of all: even this death went unnoticed. I dissolved quietly, becoming weight instead of will, gravity instead of desire. I was no longer fighting. No longer hoping. No longer asking to be saved. I had crossed an invisible threshold, one far more dangerous than tears or fear or pain. I had entered the still, numb country where nothing hurts because nothing reaches you anymore. Where surrender is mistaken for peace. Where silence feels safer than longing. Where the absence of feeling masquerades as rest. And it was there, in that emptied-out quiet, in that false calm after the star collapsed, that the night believed it had won.

The Door Stands Open

The decision I had circled like a forbidden door now stood open before me, no longer a threat or a question, but an inevitability. It waited with the patience of gravity, silent and unquestioning, as though it had always known I would arrive here eventually. It did not feel brave. It did not feel rebellious. There was no drama left in it, no defiance, no last stand made of clenched fists and fire. Whatever part of me once sought meaning through resistance had already been worn down to dust. This was not a heroic gesture. It was not a cry for help disguised as resolve. It was not even a choice in the way choices are usually understood. It was surrender, pure, total, devastating surrender. A laying down of arms. A white flag raised inside the chest when the war has lasted too long, and the body can no longer remember why it began fighting in the first place. A masterpiece of collapse carved slowly from exhaustion and quiet despair, shaped by nights like this one, by years of carrying pain without witness, without relief.

I did not feel dramatic in that moment. I felt emptied. Like a riverbed after the water has long since drained away, cracked and pale under a pitiless sky. The struggle had dissolved, not into peace, but into a vast indifference that felt almost merciful in its simplicity. To stop trying required no strength at all. It asked nothing of me. It was the easiest thing I had ever done. And so I stood there, on the threshold of that open door, not trembling, not resisting, not pleading for one more sign. Just tired beyond language. Tired in the marrow. Tired in the soul. Ready to let go, not because I wanted to die, but because I no longer knew how to keep living inside a body that had been fighting itself for so long.

And in that exhaustion, something final seemed to settle, not like a verdict, but like sediment after a long storm. The mind, once frantic with questions, fell quiet. Even fear had grown tired of keeping watch. What remained was a stillness stripped of illusion, a bare moment where nothing was demanded of me anymore. No explanations. No proving. No surviving for anyone else's comfort. Just the raw fact of being here, standing at the lip of something that felt both ending and inevitable. Time loosened its grip. Seconds no longer marched forward; they hovered, weightless, uncounted. The night did not rush me toward the door. It simply kept it open, wide and patient, as though honoring the gravity of what stood between us. The air felt thick with permission, with the quiet understanding that surrender is not always loud. Sometimes it arrives as silence so complete it drowns out even the will to argue.

My body, faithful long after my spirit had faltered, remained upright. Breath continued its stubborn rhythm, in and out, shallow but real. I noticed it the way one notices a distant sound after a long silence, surprised, almost annoyed by its persistence. Each inhale felt borrowed. Each exhale felt like a letting go I had practiced for years. And still, the lungs worked. The heart kept its slow, aching tempo. Life lingered, not triumphantly, but humbly, as if unwilling to abandon me even now. I understood then that surrender wears many disguises. There is the surrender that seeks disappearance, and there is the surrender that finally stops fighting what is. In that moment, the line between them blurred. I could not tell whether I was stepping toward an end or simply collapsing into honesty. All I knew was that the war inside me had gone silent, and in that silence, the body had not followed the mind into darkness. I remained there, suspended between release and return, between the door that stood open and the breath that would not leave. A fragile pause. A held note. The space where something might end, or something else, quieter and far more reluctant, might begin.

Death as Companion

Death no longer appeared as the dark, fearsome enemy I had once trembled to imagine. It had softened, shed its sharp edges, and stepped closer wearing the gentlest disguise. It moved like a familiar presence through the hush of the night, slow and unthreatening, a long-awaited companion whose footsteps I somehow already knew by heart. It held out its arms not in violence, but in invitation, the way a lover does after a long separation, wordless, patient, certain you will come. In its promise, there was mercy. Not the mercy of rescue, but the mercy of cessation. The quiet relief of not having to explain myself anymore. Not having to brace for the next hurt, the next disappointment, the next erasure. In its silence, there was rest. A rest so deep it felt holy. A rest untouched by expectation or failure or shame. The kind of stillness that asks nothing and judges nothing, where even pain is finally allowed to lay down.

And on that night, after twenty-three years of wrestling shadows, of dragging myself through mornings I did not want, and nights that swallowed me whole, I felt the vow between us draw tight. As if something ancient and inevitable had finally reached its appointed hour. As if the darkness itself leaned in and whispered against my ear, not with cruelty, but with recognition: "*At last. You can stop now. Come home.*" Tonight, death was no longer the end. It no longer felt like loss, disappearance, or punishment. Tonight, it felt like resolution. Like the closing of a door that had been rattling in the wind for decades. Tonight, it felt like the only presence that had listened without interrupting, that had arrived without asking me to be stronger, braver, better. Tonight, death felt like the only friend who had ever come when I called. And in that answering hush, something else unfolded. Not a voice. Not yet. But a listening so vast it felt like the night itself had bent low to hear me breathe. The silence did not recoil from my surrender; it received it.

It gathered my exhaustion the way earth gathers rain, without question, without judgment, letting it seep down into a depth where even grief grows quiet. The moon remained suspended above me, pale and unblinking, a witness that neither intervened nor condemned. It simply stayed. And in that staying, the world seemed to hold its breath with me. My body loosened its grip on urgency. The frantic edges softened. Muscles I had clenched for years began to release, one by one, like knots finally trusting the hands that unmake them. The wind settled into a low lullaby, brushing my skin with a tenderness that felt almost parental. The grass beneath me pressed cool and steady against my spine, grounding me in a way nothing else had managed to do. I was no longer fighting the night. I was sinking into it, letting it cradle the parts of me that had been screaming for rest. Time thinned. Minutes lost their shape. The future stopped knocking. The past loosened its hold. There was only this moment, stretched wide and quiet, a threshold suspended between breath and no-breath, between the weight of living and the promise of release. In that suspended place, my thoughts slowed to a single, unadorned truth: I was tired. Bone-tired. Soul-tired.

Tired in a way sleep had never touched. And the night, for the first time, did not argue. It did not tell me to be hopeful, strong, or grateful. It did not demand another dawn. It did not scold me for wanting an end. It simply held the space where wanting could exist without shame. In that holding, the ache softened into something like acceptance. Not peace, not yet, but a quiet agreement to stop resisting what was already here. I let my eyes close. Not in sleep, not in escape, but in trust. Trust that the night knew how to carry me. Trust that whatever came next would not require effort. Trust that I could finally lay down the armor of survival and rest inside the dark without needing to explain myself to anyone. And it was there, in that fragile truce between my breath and the vastness around it, that the silence leaned closer still. Not to take me. Not to hurry me. But to wait.

As I sat there, the darkness folding itself around me like a heavy velvet curtain, a strange calm washed through my trembling bones, a serenity so uncanny it felt borrowed from another world, not meant for the living. It settled slowly, deliberately, like dust in an abandoned room, softening the sharpest edges of my despair. My thoughts grew hushed, as if the mind itself had dimmed its lights. This was not relief born of hope, but a stillness that arrived when the struggle finally exhausted itself. A silence so complete it felt sacred and wrong all at once. It was peaceful, yes, but the kind of peace that carries a warning beneath its surface, the hush that falls just before a storm tears the sky open. My pulse slowed. My breath evened out. The frantic clawing inside my chest loosened its grip, and for the first time in longer than I could remember, nothing inside me was begging, screaming, or resisting. A twisted comfort curled through my thoughts, intimate and persuasive, whispering that the ache had an ending after all. That there was a door. A final exit from the endless corridors of pain I had wandered for years without a map.

The labyrinth that had consumed me began to fade, its walls dissolving into shadow. The questions that once tormented me fell silent. The why and how and what-if lost their urgency, as though they, too, had grown tired of haunting me. All that remained was this suspended calm, this eerie truce between suffering and surrender. It felt like standing on the threshold of something vast and irreversible, a place where the noise of living could no longer reach me. And in that calm, so deceptive in its gentleness, I felt myself drifting closer to the idea that this quiet was not merely a pause, but a passage. That beyond this velvet-dark stillness waited a final resolution, a closing of the door behind me, a promise that I would never again have to navigate the maze of my own breaking heart.

And then the silence answered again. Not with words, not with sound, but with a presence that pressed gently against my awareness, like a hand resting on the small of my back. The night seemed to lean closer, its breath brushing my skin, as if listening to the surrender unfolding inside me. The darkness was no longer empty; it felt attentive, almost reverent, as though it had been waiting for this moment when I finally stopped fighting it. In that hush, time loosened its grip. Seconds stretched thin, translucent, until they felt less like measurements and more like states of being. The air itself felt altered, thick and slow, as if the world had dipped beneath the surface of water. Sound dulled. Distance blurred. Even the moon's pale witness softened, its light diffusing into a gentle halo that no longer judged or demanded. I was held inside a pocket of stillness, suspended between what had been and what might never be again. It felt like standing in the eye of a storm that had raged my entire life, the sudden calm so profound it bordered on holy.

Something inside me listened back. Not hope. Not fear. But a quiet, aching recognition. The silence did not rush me. It did not push. It simply remained, vast and patient, allowing me to feel how close I was to stepping beyond the edge of myself. It mirrored my emptiness without filling it, reflected my surrender without naming it. And in that reflection, I sensed how thin the veil had become, how easily I could slip through the closing seam of the world. The calm deepened, heavy and narcotic, inviting me to lay down every question I had ever carried. To stop choosing. To stop enduring. To let the door swing shut behind me without resistance. The night did not argue. It did not plead. It only offered its quiet, its soft erasure, its promise of no more navigating, no more searching, no more waking to the ache of being unfinished. And as I hovered there, balanced on the breath between staying and going, the silence held me steady, waiting for what I would do next.

Everything outside of me receded as though it had fulfilled its purpose and been dismissed. The wind loosened its voice. The tree withdrew its grasping shadows. The cold earth beneath me faded from sensation into abstraction. The world dissolved at the edges, thinning into washes of color that bled and ran, like watercolor surrendered to rain. Reality itself seemed to soften, its outlines no longer insisting on being held. There was nothing left to witness but the interior vastness I had been carrying all along. What remained was the cavern inside my chest. A hollow carved by years of endurance, by nights survived one breath at a time, by mornings dragged into existence on borrowed will. It ached with a depth that had no language, a quiet, relentless pressure that had worn me down not through violence, but through time. This was not the longing of fear or impulsive despair. It was the bone-deep fatigue of a soul that had been standing guard for too long, armor rusted, muscles trembling, finally allowed to rest.

The longing for release unfurled inside me, not as a scream, but as a sigh. A deep, ancient exhale that seemed to come from somewhere older than memory. I wanted rest the way the ocean wants stillness after a storm, the way a candle wants to go dark after giving all its light. It was not cowardice that guided me here. It was depletion. The exhaustion of surviving every day as if it were a battleground. The exhaustion of waking up already tired of being brave. In that suspended moment, the night pressed closer, intimate now, its darkness no longer hostile but hushed, attentive. The void called my name not like a threat, but like a lullaby I had heard in another lifetime, familiar and low, promising quiet. And as it did, the truth settled into me with terrible clarity, heavy and undeniable. I was ready to let go. Ready to unclench my fists that had been locked around pain for years. Ready to loosen my grip on the weight I had carried as proof of my worth. Ready to let it slide from my shoulders and disappear into the waiting arms of the nothingness that had been courting me patiently, persistently, through every fracture and loss. In that stillness, letting go did not feel like falling. It felt like finally setting something down.

I felt myself leaning toward it, toward the quiet, toward the end, as though the darkness had finally come to claim what had always been promised. The cold seeped into my bones with deliberate patience, creeping through muscle and marrow until even my physical pain surrendered to its icy embrace. It was as though the night itself had decided to mirror me, to become as numb, as hollow, as emptied of warmth as the cavern opening inside my chest. My body began to recede from itself, sensation dulling at the edges, fingers and toes fading first, like shores swallowed by an incoming tide. The ache that had once screamed inside me softened into a distant throb, then into something almost neutral. Pain, which had been my constant companion, loosened its grip and stepped aside. In its place came a vast, anesthetized calm, a hush so complete it felt unreal, as if I were slipping beneath the surface of deep water where sound cannot follow.

The night pressed closer, not violently, but with a steady intimacy. The air felt thicker, heavier, as though it had weight now, as though it rested against my skin instead of passing over it. My breath slowed, each inhale shallower than the last, each exhale stretching longer, thinner, like a thread unraveling. I could feel myself dimming, not abruptly, but gradually, the way a room darkens when the light is turned down one careful notch at a time. Thoughts drifted past me like debris on a slow current, no longer sharp enough to wound. Memory lost its urgency. The past, the future, the weight of all that had been, all of it began to blur into a single, indistinct haze. I was no longer bracing. No longer questioning. No longer pleading with myself to stay. I was yielding, not out of impulse, but out of depletion so complete it felt ordained.

The night seemed to recognize this yielding. Its silence deepened, thickened, wrapped around me like a vow. The darkness did not rush. It waited. It allowed me to lean into it at my own pace, as though honoring the years it had taken me to arrive here. And as I did, as I tilted closer to that quiet threshold, I felt myself thinning, becoming less a body and more an absence, less a woman and more a fading echo. I was cold. So cold. But it no longer frightened me. The cold felt like permission. Like confirmation. Like the world agreeing, at last, to stop asking anything of me. And in that agreement, in that mirrored numbness between the night and my own hollowed chest, I believed, with a certainty that felt absolute, that I was finally, irrevocably slipping away.

The wind did not howl now; it keened. It threaded itself through the branches with a measured sorrow, a slow, deliberate lament, as though the night itself had learned my name and was singing it back to me in mourning. Each rustle carried the cadence of farewell. Each sigh through the leaves sounded like a prayer spoken too late. The ancient tree above me bowed and swayed, its limbs creaking under the weight of their vigil, long, dark arms moving in a rhythm that felt ritualistic, reverent, funereal. It was as if the earth had gathered its witnesses, as if the natural world had assembled to mark the quiet passing of a life that no longer wished to remain. And the moon, unchanging, unreachable, hung there in its distant throne, pouring its pale, anesthetizing light over everything I had been and everything I was about to release. Its glow did not warm me. It consecrated me. A final blessing bestowed without judgment, without mercy, without attachment.

An unblinking eye, ancient and impartial, watching as I loosened my grip on the world. Watching as I made peace with the ending, I had already accepted in my bones. I felt no urgency. No resistance. No need to explain myself to the dark or the world. The frantic bargaining had long since burned itself out. There were no last words pressing against my tongue, no letters forming in my mind, no apologies or declarations left to make. Even regret had fallen away, as unnecessary as armor after the war is already lost. What remained was a stillness so complete it felt earned. The kind of calm that comes only when the struggle has lasted too long and the body finally believes it is allowed to stop. I lay there beneath the watchful moon and the grieving branches, emptied of wanting, emptied of fear. Not broken in that moment but finished. A soul resting in the aftermath of endurance, wrapped in the quiet certainty of someone who has fought for far too long and has finally, mercifully, laid their weapons down.

In that stillness, in that breath between worlds, I felt a strange familiarity, as though I were not choosing death but simply returning home after a long and merciless journey that had worn me down to nothing but dust and longing. It was not an ending I feared anymore. It was a release I had spent a lifetime unknowingly preparing for. The quiet wrapped itself around me like a remembered language, one my bones seemed to understand even if my mind could not. It carried the softness of something ancient, something patient, as if it had been waiting for me long before I learned the weight of my own name. I felt myself loosening, not violently, not all at once, but gently, the way a knot gives way when it is finally allowed to rest. The ache did not vanish, but it softened, as though even pain had grown tired of its own persistence. I was no longer bracing for the next blow. No longer scanning the dark for threat. The vigilance that had governed my life slipped from my shoulders like a cloak laid down at the door.

What remained was a surrender so complete it felt ceremonial. A laying down of years. Of identities forged in survival. Of promises made only to keep breathing one more day. Time lost its edges. Seconds stretched and thinned until they no longer insisted on moving forward. I was suspended in a place that did not demand progress, where nothing needed fixing, proving, or enduring. It felt like stepping into a room where the war had ended long ago, where the echoes of struggle had finally faded into hush. And in that hush, I sensed it, subtle as a change in air pressure before a storm breaks. The silence was no longer empty. It was listening. The darkness was no longer closing in. It was opening. Something unseen gathered itself in the stillness, not as a force, not as a command, but as a presence drawing nearer, attentive and calm. The night did not take me. It held me. And in that holding, the silence prepared to answer.

The False Answer

And then, without sound, without form, the answer arrived.

Not as words falling from the sky, nor as a voice breaking the hush, but as a knowing that bloomed inside me, sudden and unmistakable, like warmth spreading through frozen limbs. The silence did not speak; it resonated. It moved through me the way truth does when it has no need to persuade. It settled in my chest, gentle yet absolute, rearranging something at the core of my being. It felt like being seen without being examined. Held without being claimed. Known without being named. As if the night itself leaned close, not to erase me, but to recognize me. That is the lie I believed then. In that moment, the stillness shifted from refuge to threshold. The calm remained, but it deepened, acquiring a gravity that was not pulling me away, but rooting me where I lay. The darkness, which had felt like an ending, softened into something else entirely, an antechamber, a pause between breaths, a place where the story hesitates before choosing either its next sentence or its ending.

I felt it then, the smallest disturbance in the vast quiet. A ripple. A tremor. The faintest insistence, like a hand resting against my back, not pushing, not pulling, simply there. Steady. Patient. Unafraid of my brokenness. Unmoved by my despair. The answer did not argue with my exhaustion. It did not scold my surrender. It did not demand strength I did not have. It met me exactly as I was, emptied, undone, finished, and whispered its truth into the hollow space where my will had burned out. It was the voice of my apathy, "It's time". The words were not spoken, yet they rang through me with the clarity of a bell struck in deep water. Not loud. Not sharp. But impossible to ignore. They did not deny my pain or minimize my longing for rest. They simply placed a period where I had written a pause. A comma carved into the silence, became a period at the end of my life. The silence had answered. And its answer was death. It was the final invitation.

The minutes slipped past like cold beads of water tracing the length of my spine, each one a quiet, merciless countdown toward the moment I had been circling for years. Time no longer moved like a river carrying me somewhere new; it cinched itself tighter, a narrowing corridor, a breath held too long. Each second pressed in, heavy and deliberate, as though the universe itself were leaning closer, waiting to see what I would do when the last illusion of choice thinned to nothing. I existed in a hollowed-out landscape where meaning had eroded completely, scraped away grain by grain until only the bones of things remained. Purpose had gone mute. Feeling had dulled into a low, colorless hum. Even my thoughts arrived fractured, half-formed, ricocheting through the empty chambers of my mind like loose stones dropped into a well too deep to answer back. Nothing landed. Nothing stayed. Everything dissolved before it could matter.

The ache, however, endured. It lived beneath my ribs like a faithful predator, patient and relentless, gnawing without urgency, without mercy. It did not rush me. It did not need to. It had learned my rhythms, my limits, the exact pace at which hope wears down when it is left unattended for too long. Pain had become my only reliable companion, the one sensation that refused to fade. In a world stripped of color and warmth, it was the final proof that I still existed at all. And yet, even as that ache claimed center stage, something subtle had shifted in the atmosphere around me. The silence, which moments ago had felt like an ending, now held a different weight. It no longer pressed me forward. It hovered. It lingered. It watched. The countdown did not stop, but it faltered, just enough to be noticed. Time wavered, uncertain of its authority. The noose loosened by a fraction so small it could have been imagined, except that I felt it in my breath, in the faint return of sensation along my arms, in the way my heartbeat hesitated, as if listening for instruction.

When the clock blinked **11:30** across the empty screen, the numbers burned into the dark like an omen, a quiet verdict rendered in light. Not loud. Not cruel. Just final. A bell tolling without sound, echoing somewhere deeper than my ears. Time was no longer passing me by; it was slipping through me, grain after grain, sand draining into a darkness that waited with open arms and infinite patience. I could feel it then, the way one feels gravity before a fall. The way the body knows before the mind admits it. Standing still was no longer an option. Stillness itself had become unbearable, a suspended cruelty, a holding pattern stretched too thin. The ache demanded resolution. The night demanded movement. Something in me knew with aching certainty that hesitation was the last illusion left to shed. A choice rose before me, stark and uncompromising. Not dressed in comfort. Not softened by mercy. It did not ask what I wanted. It asked what I would do. Step forward into the unknown. Into the quiet. Into the place where the ache promised it would finally loosen its grip. Or remain here, caught between moments, suffocating beneath the weight of indecision.

My breath hitched. The world narrowed. The grass beneath me, the tree above, the moon's pale vigil, all of it receded until there was only this singular point in time, taut as a drawn wire. The unbearable pressure of now. The knowledge that if I was going to surrender completely, if I was going to disappear without interruption, without witness, without being pulled back by the fragile threads of delay, it would have to be soon. The clock did not blink again. It did not need to. The night had finished waiting.

The Night Opens

The night leaned closer, intimate now, as if it could feel the tremor in my bones. Its silence thickened, no longer empty but intent, holding the weight of expectation. Even the air seemed to pause, suspended between breaths, unwilling to move ahead without me. I felt the pull everywhere, in my wrists, in my throat, in the hollow beneath my ribs where resolve and exhaustion had finally merged into the same aching thing. There was no rush in it, no violence. Only inevitability. The kind that arrives after every argument has been exhausted, after every prayer has gone unanswered, after hope has been worn down to a thin, translucent film that can no longer bear the strain. This was not impulse. This was conclusion. A closing argument delivered by years, not minutes. I felt my thoughts loosen their grip, one by one, like leaves releasing from a branch at the first true frost. Names faded. Faces softened into blur. Even fear, once so sharp it cut, dulled into something distant and irrelevant. What remained was a singular knowing, heavy and calm, settling into my chest like a stone finding the bottom of a lake.

The world did not resist me. It did not intervene. It did not offer a last-minute miracle wrapped in light. It simply stood back, vast and indifferent, allowing me this moment of reckoning. The moon continued its watch. The wind kept its low vigil. Everything held its place as though honoring the gravity of what I had reached. And in that narrowing space, where past and future dissolved into the raw immediacy of now, I felt myself step inward, toward the edge I had been approaching for years. Not running. Not fleeing. Just moving, at last, with the tired certainty of someone who has walked too long without rest. The night did not stop me. It opened.

My thumb hovered there, suspended between impulse and collapse, as though the smallest movement might shatter what little gravity still held me to the world. Amelia's name pulsed once more, a soft, insistent glow, like a dying star refusing to go dark. It carried the ghost of who I had been with her, the version of me that still believed safety could be borrowed from another's arms. But that version felt impossibly distant now, a relic sealed behind glass. I let the phone lower slowly, its weight settling into my palm with a dull finality. The screen dimmed, and with it, her name receded, not erased, but absorbed back into the dark where everything else had begun to gather. Memory followed suit. Her laughter thinned into silence. Her face softened, blurred, then vanished, like breath on a mirror wiped away by an unseen hand. What remained was not rage or grief, but a hollow resignation, the quiet understanding that some doors, once splintered, cannot be leaned against for shelter again.

The phone cradled in my fingers and came to rest on my leg, its faint glow mocking me. The night reclaimed its dominion. Without that borrowed light, the darkness felt fuller, heavier, as though it had been waiting for me to release the last proof of connection. My hands lay still, clinging now, heavy, white knuckled, and useless, no longer grasping for rescue, no longer reaching back toward what had already fallen away. I drew a breath that barely stirred my chest. It tasted thin, metallic, unfinished. The cold pressed closer, seeping into places warmth had long abandoned. Above me, the moon watched without expression, its pale face unchanged by my surrender. Below me, the earth waited, patient and unmoved, ready to receive whatever I no longer wished to carry. And in that narrowing circle of awareness, with the phone with its dim illumination and the past finally loosening its grip, I felt the last tether stretch, fray, and begin to give. The night did not rush me. It simply stayed. And I, emptied of resistance, leaned further into its open, waiting quietly.

Silence With Weight

The quiet thickened around me, no longer merely the absence of sound, but a presence with weight and breath of its own. It settled into my ears, my ribs, the soft hollows behind my eyes. Even the wind seemed to hold itself still, as if the world had learned how fragile this moment was and dared not disturb it. I felt suspended inside that hush, cradled by something vast and indifferent, something that asked nothing of me and promised nothing in return. My body grew heavy, anchored to the earth in a way it had never been before. The grass pressed cool and damp against my legs, each blade distinct, insistent, real. Sensation arrived in slow waves, not to awaken me, but to ground me in this final threshold. I could feel the pulse in my wrists, faint but stubborn, tapping out a rhythm that felt older than thought. A reminder. Or perhaps a farewell. The ache inside my chest did not vanish. It softened, spread out, lost its sharp edges, like a bruise finally done screaming. In its place came a spaciousness that frightened me with its calm. There was room now where panic had lived. Room where longing once clawed. Room enough to rest. I had spent so long fighting the noise that I did not recognize the danger of silence when it arrives dressed as mercy.

Above me, the moonlight pooled in pale fragments, breaking against the leaves and branches, scattering itself across my skin. It felt ceremonial, almost deliberate, as if the night were marking me, memorizing the shape of me before I slipped beyond its concern. I wondered, distantly, if this was how erasure began, not with violence, but with a gentle forgetting. My thoughts slowed until they were no longer sentences, only impressions drifting through me like fog. Past and future lost their urgency, their pull. There was only this moment, stretched thin and trembling, and the sense that I was standing on the edge of something that would not call me back once I stepped through. I did not feel dramatic. I did not feel brave. I felt tired in a way that reached into the marrow of me, a fatigue that had learned my name and followed me faithfully for years. And as I leaned further into the quiet, allowing it to wrap around that tiredness, I felt the world loosen its hold, just enough to make me believe that letting go might finally be possible.

Even my darkest pain, once so ravenous it felt capable of tearing me apart from the inside, began to lose its teeth. It did not disappear abruptly; it thinned, like ink dropped into deep water, its edges feathering, its color diluting until it was no longer sharp enough to wound. What had once screamed now murmured. What had clawed now loosened its grip. The ache that had defined me for so long softened into a distant pressure, then into something almost abstract, as though it belonged to someone I had once been but no longer inhabited. Numbness crept in quietly, not as an intruder, but as a tide. It washed through my thoughts, smoothing them flat, erasing their contours. The mind, exhausted from years of vigilance, dimmed its lights one by one. Feeling did not leave in protest; it laid itself down. Apathy settled over my soul like a first snowfall, heavy and insulating, muting every sound, every pulse of wanting. Beneath that frost, even grief grew still, preserved but unreachable, locked beneath a surface too cold to break.

I felt myself thinning at the edges, my sense of self loosening, unraveling from the story I had carried for so long. Memory began to slip its anchors. Faces blurred. Names lost their gravity. The weight of who I had been, who I was supposed to be, drifted farther away, as if the mind itself were gently closing a door behind me. This was not forgetting born of chaos. It was a deliberate unburdening, a quiet laying down of everything that had once demanded to be remembered. And there, in that suspended hush, I knew where I stood. On the final threshold. The narrow, breathless edge between holding on and letting go. Between remembering and release. Between being someone and becoming absence. The moment stretched, fragile and immense, as though the universe itself were holding its breath with me, waiting to see which side of the silence I would choose to fall into.

The silence deepened, thick and velvety, pressing in from all sides until it felt less like an absence and more like a presence. It wrapped itself around me with careful hands, steady and patient, as though it had been waiting for me to arrive exactly here. My breath slowed, each rise and fall barely stirring the air, a fragile negotiation between staying and slipping. I could feel how little effort it would take now. How simple it would be to stop reaching, to stop anchoring myself to the weight of a body that no longer felt entirely mine. The world receded further, its edges softening into suggestion. Sound lost its urgency. Distance lost its meaning. Even time seemed to hesitate, unsure of its authority in this place. Seconds did not march forward; they hovered, translucent and undecided, as if they, too, were waiting to see what I would become. The night did not rush me. It honored the slowness of this unraveling, the sacred pause between inhale and exhale, where everything hangs in balance.

I felt my body grow strangely light, as though gravity had begun to forget me. The cold that had once bitten now merely brushed past, indifferent, no longer demanding a reaction. Sensation thinned into impression. Impression into idea. I was still here, yet already drifting, already half-loosened from the architecture of living. A presence without edges. A thought without urgency. A name no longer being called. And in that narrowing corridor between breath and release, I sensed it clearly: this was the point of no embellishment, no metaphor left to soften the truth. Whatever came next would not be loud. It would not announce itself with thunder or revelation. It would arrive quietly, like nightfall completing its work, like a door closing without resistance, and me; ah, I would be found on the other side of that doorway. I stood there, balanced on that final line, where choice dissolves into motion, and silence becomes an answer. The hush leaned closer. The darkness waited, open and patient. And for one suspended heartbeat, everything I had been, everything I had carried, hovered together in a single, fragile stillness, poised on the verge of vanishing, or of being called back into being.

The Phone Falls

The cold grass cradled me like a weary lover, its dampness seeping through my clothes, but even that bite of cold felt gentler than the storm ravaging inside my chest. There was no dramatic collapse, no final flare of resistance, just a quiet, certain surrender, a slow dissolving of will, a soft slipping into the night as though my soul were exhaling its last fragile thread of longing into the vast, indifferent sky. The phone finally and fully slid from my numb fingers, falling to the earth with a muted thud, its screen flickering once before surrendering to darkness. How fitting, that the last symbol of connection should dim at the same moment the last light within me went out. It lay there beside me, a tiny dead star on a field of cold grass, a reminder of all the calls I never made, all the lifelines I never believed I deserved, the emptiness that surrounds me.

The earth received the phone without ceremony, the sound of its landing barely audible, a punctuation mark too small for the sentence I believed was ending. The grass closed around it, dark and wet, swallowing its brief glow until nothing remained but shadow. That tiny extinguishing felt symbolic, ceremonial even, as though the night itself had nodded in quiet agreement. Connection had been laid down. Signal silenced. The world, with all its unanswered calls and unchosen mercies, had been gently dismissed. I lay there, unmoving, letting the cold seep deeper, letting it claim territory inch by inch. My limbs felt distant now, as if they belonged to someone else, as if my body were already becoming memory. The ache in my chest no longer demanded attention. It had spent itself. What remained was a vast stillness, a wide-open quiet where even grief had lost its voice. I did not feel dramatic. I did not feel tragic. I felt finished. Like a book closed after the final page has been read too many times to hurt anymore.

Above me, the sky stretched on, endless and impersonal, a cathedral without walls. The moon watched, pale and uninterested, offering neither judgment nor reprieve. Stars blinked faintly, distant witnesses who would never know my name. And yet, in that indifferent vastness, I felt oddly small and oddly relieved, as though disappearing into such immensity might finally make the weight of me manageable. My breath thinned, each inhale less certain than the last, each exhale trailing off before it could fully leave me. It felt like loosening a grip I had held for years, fingers uncurling one by one. The last fragile thread of wanting slipped free, drifting upward, unclaimed. There was nothing left to bargain with. Nothing left to prove. The war inside me had gone quiet not because it was won, but because it had burned through everything it could consume. The grass held me. The night held me. The silence widened, generous and complete. And in that hushed expanse, with the phone dark beside me and the sky unmoved above, I believed with absolute certainty that the light inside me had finally gone out.

And yet, even as that certainty settled like a gravestone over my chest, the silence did not end me. It deepened. It lingered. It pressed close with a peculiar attentiveness, as though the night itself were listening for something I had already stopped offering. The darkness did not rush to claim me. It did not close its fist. It simply stayed, vast and patient, holding space where my resistance had once lived. Time lost its insistence altogether. There was no before or after now, only this suspended interval where breath hovered undecided, where the body remembered its rhythms even as the spirit drifted elsewhere. My heart continued its slow, stubborn knocking, a soft, almost apologetic sound, as if unsure whether it still had permission to be heard. Each beat felt borrowed, unearned, arriving without my consent. The cold had reached my core, but it no longer felt like an enemy. It felt like a boundary, a threshold marking how far I had gone inward. Sensation dulled into abstraction. The world receded to texture and tone. Dark. Damp. Vast. I was not sinking anymore. I was floating in a stillness so complete it felt like being held between breaths, between sentences, between lives.

The Farewell That Wasn't

My eyes drifted shut, tears drying on my cheeks until only salt remained, a brittle residue of a fight I could no longer wage. I let the silence take me, not as a conquering force, but as a tide easing its way over a shoreline long eroded. The darkness folded around me with a careful tenderness, less a threat now than a mantle, heavy and intimate, carrying the weight of years I had been too tired to hold. It did not hurry me. It did not ask. It simply stayed close, breathing with me, matching the slow cadence of my unraveling. The wind lowered its voice to a hum, a low, aching lullaby stitched from loss and distance. It moved through the night with deliberate gentleness, as though afraid to startle what remained of me. The old trees no longer loomed as monsters carved from fear. They stood as sentinels, ancient and grave, their bowed branches like clasped hands, bearing witness without judgment. If this were a vigil, it was a quiet one. If this was a farewell, it was spoken softly, without spectacle. The world began to thin at the edges. Colors dulled. Shapes softened. Sound loosened its grip and drifted away in pieces.

The cold no longer announced itself; it simply existed, a background presence, as unobtrusive as breath. I felt myself receding, not falling, not fleeing, but slipping, like a tide pulling back from the shore, leaving behind a smooth, emptied sand where footprints used to be. I drifted into that in-between place where awareness loosens its hold. Where names lose their urgency. Where the ache that once defined every moment finally quiets, not healed, but hushed. I mistook that hush for peace. I mistook the absence of struggle for an ending. I believed I was moving beyond reach, beyond sound, beyond feeling, beyond saving. But even there, even in that dimming corridor between presence and absence, something remained unfinished. Not a plea. Not a promise. Just a faint, stubborn awareness, like a pulse beneath deep water. The night did not close behind me. It held the space open, wide enough for breath to continue finding its way back in, wide enough for time to hesitate. I was a lone soul adrift, yes, untethered, anchorless, but not yet claimed. Carried by the current of despair, moving toward a quiet I had mistaken for rest, unaware that beneath that still surface, the story was not done dissolving. It was waiting. Waiting in the dark. Waiting for what comes after the letting go.

Suicidal Ideation:
Chapter Eight:
The Journey of Self-Harm

The Weight of Shadows: A Journey Through the Darkness of Suicidal Ideation

But wait. As I so often do, I have leapt ahead of myself, sprinting toward the precipice of the story before honoring the long, almost invisible wearing-away that made that fall feel inevitable. Racing toward the cliff edge of the story before tending to the slow, powerful erosion that made that fall possible. That night beneath the moon, that breathless hour on the grass where existence and erasure pressed their foreheads together, was not the beginning. It was the rupture. The low, unmistakable a structure makes when it finally gives way after years of hairline, quiet stress fractures, the kind no one sees because they form beneath the paint, that no one notices until it is too late. This chapter does not open with darkness descending from the sky. It opens with a quieter invasion, so subtle it passed as reason. With thoughts that arrive disguised as logic, wearing pressed suits and steady voices. With sentences that sound like reason and responsibility but taste like rust.

With the first moment I began negotiating and bartering my own worth away, piece by piece, in small increments, mistaking self-surveillance for responsibility, vigilance for virtue, self-attack for motivation and discipline, and self-erasure and disappearance for peace. It opens with the way I learned to watch myself as though I were a problem to be managed rather than a life to be tended. Suicidal ideation did not announce itself as death. It introduced itself as relief. As rest. As a private place to lay down the weight of being. As a quiet room where the lights were low and no one expected anything of me. It spoke the language of fatigue and exhaustion fluently, telling me I was tired because I had failed, not because I had endured. Because I had tried too hard, that the ache was evidence of brokenness, not hope of healing. It reframed pain as proof of deficiency rather than evidence of survival. It learned my cadence, borrowed my syntax, wore my voice with uncanny precision, and did it masterfully.

On my best days, it sounded calm, reasonable, articulate, convincing and persuasive. It said, "You are not broken, you are simply done." This is where we step back to. Not to the night, not to the grass, not to the moment the body nearly surrendered, but to the interior rooms where the furniture was quietly rearranged without my noticing. To the years when I learned to live under interrogation and cross-examination by my own thoughts. To the years I lived under by my own mind. To the daily, steady erosion and abrasion of joy, until it dulled and then thinned. To the way my thoughts became a courtroom where I served as defendant, prosecutor, and guilty verdict, all at once. Because, suicidal ideation is not a single thought. It is a climate. A weather system that settles in slowly, altering the air pressure until breathing feels optional. It is the slow narrowing of imagination and horizon inch by inch. The shrinking of future tense. It edits it out of sentences.

The way the word tomorrow begins to feel hypothetical, conditional, expendable, negotiable, and unnecessary. It does not shout. It persuades. So, this chapter begins there. In the first subtle permission, I gave myself to disappear. In the moments I rehearsed absence the way others rehearse courage, as a form of comfort. In the private arithmetic of pain, where living started to feel like an unpaid debt and leaving like balance restored. In the habits of thought that turned endurance into obligation and rest into a reward I had not earned. We will go there now. Back before the breaking. Back to the earliest negotiations with silence that had nothing to do with night and everything to do with thought. Back to the place where the idea of not being began to feel safer than the labor of continuing, where shrinking seemed kinder than staying whole. Because before there was an attempt, there was an agreement. And before the agreement, there was a story I told myself about who I was allowed to be. This is where that story begins.

Stepping far beyond

To understand that precipice, that near-crossing into the unknown, we must step backward, far beyond the moment where the darkness swallowed my breath, far beneath the layers of despair that tightened around my throat until truth itself struggled for air. We must move past the spectacle of collapse and into the subtler terrain where damage is first rehearsed in silence. Back before the scream. Back before the ache learned its name. Back to the places where nothing looked broken yet, but everything was already bending. We must return to the soil where the wounds first took root. Not the dramatic kind. Not the kind that draws witnesses or demands immediate care. These were quieter injuries, hairline fractures in the architecture of self, moments that barely registered as harm at all. Small dismissals. Unmet needs explained away. Love offered conditionally, then withdrawn without warning. Lessons learned not through cruelty alone, but through absence. Through what was never said. Through what I learned to swallow to keep the peace.

They grew the way vines do. Slowly. Patiently. Almost beautifully at first. Wrapping themselves around my ribs, my breath, my sense of worth, until I could no longer tell where I ended and the constriction began. What once felt like adaptation hardened into belief. What once felt like resilience quietly became self-erasure. I learned to bend so well I forgot I was bending, learned to survive so efficiently I mistook endurance for identity. This is the terrain we must walk now. The early chapters where pain did not yet look like pain, where harm wore the disguise of normal, where love required shrinking, and safety came with terms and conditions. The places where I first learned that disappearing a little made things easier. Where silence felt safer than truth. Where being low-maintenance became a virtue and having needs began to feel like a flaw.

Because the precipice is never sudden. It is prepared over years. It is carved by repetition. It is built from moments that ask you, again and again, to make yourself smaller in exchange for belonging. And one day, when the ground finally gives way beneath your feet, it feels like betrayal by the present, when in truth it is the long echo of the past finally answering back. So we go there now. Back to the beginning of the quiet fractures. Back to the first time I learned to doubt my own weight in the world. Back to the soil where survival learned to masquerade as selfhood, and where the idea of not being began, softly, almost tenderly, to feel like relief. And in that soil, nothing announced itself as danger. There were no warning signs staked into the ground. No alarms. No sharp edges to recoil from. There was only learning. Learning how to read rooms before speaking. Learning how to measure my worth by how little space I occupied. Learning that love was something you earned through usefulness, compliance, and quiet excellence. Learning that discomfort was a personal failure, and pain a private inconvenience best handled alone.

This was where suicidal ideation first learned to breathe inside me, though it did not yet speak its name. It arrived not as a desire to die, but as a strategy to endure. A mental exit sign, glowing faintly in the background of thought. Not something to act on, just something to know was there. A comfort tucked into the back pocket of consciousness. "If it becomes too much, you don't have to stay. If you fail, you don't have to continue. If you disappoint, there is an off switch." At first, it felt practical. Even kind. A contingency plan for a life that already felt too heavy to carry without conditions. It threaded itself through my thinking in subtle ways. In the way I imagined vanishing after mistakes. In the way rest began to feel undeserved unless preceded by exhaustion. In the way my inner voice sharpened itself into a tool of correction, then punishment, then quiet erasure. I learned to audit my own existence relentlessly, to pre-empt rejection by rejecting myself first. To believe that if I could perfect my own disappearance, no one else would have to do it for me.

This was not despair yet. This was management. This was control masquerading as responsibility. This was the slow construction of an inner world where being alive came with terms and conditions, and not being alive felt like the only unconditional mercy on offer. I did not wake up one day wanting to die. I woke up many days wanting to rest from myself. Wanting the noise to dim. Wanting the relentless self-surveillance to pause. Wanting the constant translation of worth into performance to end. And in that wanting, the idea of not existing slipped closer, not as a threat, but as a promise of quiet. This is where the story deepens. Not into drama, but into pattern. Into repetition. Into the years where I mistook self-negation for maturity and disappearance for peace. Where surviving became my sole credential, and joy felt indulgent, suspicious, temporary.

Where the future stopped feeling like a place I was moving toward and began to feel like a debt accumulating interest. So we linger here. In the early negotiations. In the first, permissions granted to erase myself gently. Because before there was a precipice, there was practice. And before practice, there was belief. And belief, once planted in the right soil, grows roots that do not ask for permission before they wrap themselves around the heart.

Where the story truly begins

And so, as I sit here now, bathed once again in the soft glow of the same moon that once bore witness to my unraveling, pen trembling in my hand, I feel the quiet insistence to rewind the reel of my life. To draw the film back through its frames. To slow it. To study the pauses between scenes. To trace the hairline cracks that were always there, waiting. I want to thread together the tangled, fraying strands of memory that led me to that moonlit threshold, the night I hovered on the thin veil between here and gone, between breath and oblivion, between living and the seductive hush of no longer having to try. That night was not the beginning of my story. It was the moment the story could no longer carry the weight of what had been left unnamed. This is where the story truly begins. Not at the edge, but in the quiet, shadowy paths that led me there. The narrow corridors I walked so often that they felt like home. The places where nothing screamed danger, yet everything whispered strain.

Before suicidal ideation ever became a thought I could name, it was a posture I learned to hold. A way of standing in the world slightly tilted inward. A constant readiness. A way of inhabiting my body as if I were bracing for something that never fully arrived yet was always expected. For impact that never quite arrived but was always anticipated. It lived in my muscles. In the way, my shoulders never fully dropped. In the way rest always felt conditional, temporary, undeserved. Long before death appeared as an idea, disappearance did. Long before escape had a word or language, exhaustion had a rhythm. In those early chapters, nothing looked alarming. There were no sirens. No interventions. There were no dramatic alarms ringing, no obvious crisis demanding attention. Life moved forward in ordinary, acceptable ways. I functioned. I smiled. I achieved. I adapted. And adaptation, I would later understand, is not always strength. Sometimes it is anaesthesia. A slow sedative that dulls the sharp edges of pain just enough to keep you upright and for survival, while quietly teaching the nervous system that endurance is safer than expression, that survival is more important than truth.

I learned, early on, to read rooms before I read myself. To scan faces for cues before checking in with my own body. To listen for approval before listening inward to my own needs. My worth became something adjustable, something to be negotiated and recalibrated depending on who I was with and what was required of me. Love, I absorbed, was not something you rested in. It was something you earned, a transaction you managed. And earning it meant staying agreeable, capable, useful. It meant swallowing discomfort before it became inconvenient to others. It meant translating need into silence. There was no single moment when this belief arrived. It accumulated. Layer by layer. Like sediment settling invisibly at the bottom of a river, unseen, shaping the current long before the water ever notices the shift. Each time I minimized my hurt. Each time I explained away what wounded me. Each time I told myself it wasn't that bad, that others had it worse, that I should be grateful, resilient, stronger.

The language of self-erasure dressed itself as maturity. As compassion. As strength. It wore respectable clothing. It earned praise. This is where suicidal ideation truly began for me. Not as a desire to die, but as a gradual detachment from the desire to live fully. A thinning of presence so subtle it felt like adulthood. A slow unhooking from joy. The future did not vanish overnight; it faded. Its colors leached out gently. Tomorrow became something to manage rather than anticipate. Hope did not shatter; it dimmed, like a light turned down so gradually I did not notice the room growing dark. I began to fantasize, not about death, but about rest. About silence. About a life where I was not required to keep proving my value, or to justify my existence through effort. These thoughts did not frighten me at first. They felt soothing. Sensible. Reasonable. Even kind.

Thoughts arrive as questions

They arrived as questions rather than conclusions, wrapped in logic and calm: "What if I didn't have to try so hard? What if I could just stop? What if the relief I was craving wasn't something to achieve, but something to exit into?" This is the subtle danger of suicidal ideation. It rarely announces itself as despair. More often, it arrives as relief. As a solution framed by exhaustion. As mercy disguised as solution. It speaks in the voice of reason when the body is depleted, and the soul has been running on borrowed fuel for too long. It does not say, "I want to die." It says, "I don't want to keep doing this." And because I had learned to distrust my needs and overvalue my endurance, that voice sounded familiar. Convincing. Almost compassionate. Looking back now, with the gentleness that healing allows, I can see how carefully the groundwork was laid. How years of unmet needs, emotional abandonment, conditional love, and chronic self-abandonment quietly conspired to make the idea of disappearing feel merciful.

Not dramatic. Not tragic. Merciful. Like laying down a weight no one ever acknowledged I was carrying. This chapter exists not to indict the past, but to illuminate it. To show how suicidal ideation is not a failure of character, but a signal of prolonged neglect of the self. A nervous system pleading for safety. A soul asking to be seen. A body begging for rest in the only language it has left. And so we continue backward. Into the moments where I first learned to confuse self-sacrifice with love. Where I mistook silence for peace. Where I believed being needed was the same as being valued and felt safer than being known. Where I learned to disappear just enough to belong. Because healing does not begin at the edge. It begins where we finally tell the truth about how we got there.

It is a journey both excruciating and essential to finally give voice to. Not a descent for spectacle, not a reopening of wounds for their own sake, but a witnessing. A naming. A reckoning with the truth that what nearly ended me was not a single moment of weakness, but a long, quiet erosion. This telling is not merely a record of agony carried, but a testament to the indomitable, stubborn spark of the human spirit, the one that persists even when buried beneath layers of shame, fatigue, and unspoken grief. The spark that refuses extinction, even when wrapped in darkness so thick it feels eternal. As I trace the path backward, the question does not arrive as a shout. It pulses. Steady. Insistent. Like a distant drumbeat beneath the ribs. Where did this death wish begin? Where did that quiet longing for oblivion first take root? Not the dramatic desire to vanish, but the softer wish to be relieved of effort. To stop holding everything together with clenched hands and borrowed strength.

How did the ache begin its long, merciless bloom? It did not arrive fully formed. It germinated. In moments dismissed as small. In hurts deemed manageable. In disappointments, I learned to absorb without protest. It grew in the soil of whispered lies I absorbed as truth: that I was too much when I asked, too sensitive when I hurt, too needy when I reached. It took nourishment from forgotten sorrows, from griefs that never received ceremony, from losses that were expected to be carried quietly, efficiently, without interruption. What constellation of wounds assembled themselves into that night? What unseen alignment of neglect, misattunement, betrayal, and self-betrayal slowly pulled me toward that moon-drenched threshold? It was not one star, but many. Each is small on its own. Together, inescapable. A sky I had been living under for years without ever naming its shape.

I see now how the ache learned to speak in my voice. How it learned to masquerade as reason. How surrender came to feel like salvation only because I had been taught, over and over again, to outrun my own needs. To call endurance virtue. To call silence peace. To call disappearance maturity. The weight of existing did not crush me all at once. It accumulated. Day by day. Expectation by expectation. Until the chest no longer expanded easily. Until breath felt negotiated. Until rest felt like something I had to justify. And one night, beneath a moon that merely bore witness, the weight tipped. Not because I was weak, but because I had been strong for too long without refuge. This is what I am listening for now as I walk backward through memory. Not the scream, but the first tightening. Not the collapse, but the first compromise. The moment I learned to choose being acceptable over being authentic. The moment I learned to stay when leaving would have been kinder. The moment I learned that my pain was inconvenient, and therefore negotiable.

Because the ache did not betray me. It signalled. It bloomed where care was absent. It grew where truth was swallowed. And if it can be traced, it can be understood. And if it can be understood, it can be met with something other than judgment. So I follow the drumbeat inward. Back through the years. Back through the rooms where I learned to survive by shrinking. Back to the first places where I mistook endurance for identity and disappearance for relief. Not to condemn who I was, but to finally meet her. Not to relive the darkness, but to understand how it took shape. Because healing, at its deepest root, begins not with escape from the pain, but with reverent attention to how the pain learned to live inside us in the first place.

Continue the backward walk

And as I continue this backward walk, I do so with a steadier breath than the one I carried then. Not because the memories are gentler, but because I am. There is a different quality to my listening now. Less urgency to fix. Less need to excuse. More willingness to stay present with what unfolds, even when it tightens the throat or stirs the ribs with an old, familiar ache. I am no longer searching for a single origin story, a villain, a moment that explains everything. I am learning that the truth is more intricate, more human, more quietly devastating than that. What I find instead are patterns. Repetitions. Emotional weather systems that returned again and again, until they felt like climate rather than condition. I find the places where love was inconsistent, where safety was conditional, where attention arrived only when I performed correctly. I find the early negotiations, the bargains I made with myself: If I am easier, quieter, stronger, more useful, maybe I will be kept. Maybe I will be chosen. Maybe I will be safe.

These bargains did not feel like betrayals at the time. They felt like intelligence. Like adaptation. Like a child or young woman learning how to survive the particular ecosystem she had been born into. I did not abandon myself because I did not care. I abandoned myself because I believed that was the price of belonging. And the body, always loyal, always listening, learned the lesson well. It learned to brace. To monitor. To stay alert. To hold its breath through entire seasons of life. Over time, that vigilance hardened into posture. Shoulders perpetually lifted. Jaw perpetually set. A nervous system tuned to threat even in moments of calm. Rest became unfamiliar. Stillness felt unsafe. Joy felt temporary, something to enjoy cautiously before it was inevitably withdrawn. I learned to live in a state of low-grade alarm, calling it normal, calling it strength, calling it adulthood. This is where suicidal ideation begins to make sense, not as a desire for death, but as a longing for cessation. For an end to hypervigilance.

For a silence where nothing is required, nothing is demanded, nothing can be lost because nothing is being held. The fantasy was never about dying. It was about finally being allowed to stop. Looking back now, I can see how compassionate that impulse actually was. Misguided, yes. Dangerous, yes. But born from a body and mind desperate for relief after years of running without rest. The ache was not an enemy. It was a messenger that had been knocking for a very long time, growing louder only because it had been ignored. So as I move backward through these chapters, I do not do so with accusation. I do not interrogate the past with the cruelty I once turned inward. I move slowly. I notice. I let the memories speak in their own cadence. I allow myself to feel what was once too inconvenient to feel. I offer context where I once offered blame. Because this is what healing asks of us. Not that we erase the pain, but that we finally listen to it with maturity, with curiosity, with care. Not that we rewrite our history into something prettier, but that we tell it more truthfully. With room for nuance. With room for tenderness. With room for the version of ourselves who did the best she could with what she had.

This is where the story deepens now. Into the early lessons. The first compromises. The subtle ways I learned to disappear while still appearing functional. Into the spaces where my voice quieted, not because it was weak, but because it had learned it was safer that way. And as I walk there, pen moving across the page, moonlight steady at my back, I do so not to reopen wounds, but to change my relationship with them. To see them not as proof of failure, but as evidence of survival. To finally understand how the ache came to live inside me, so that I could learn, slowly and deliberately, how to give it something it had been asking for all along. Not an ending. But care.

Death felt like salvation

What brought me so low, to that conclusion that death felt like salvation? Was it a sudden rupture, a reckless plunge, a dramatic undoing sparked by a single unbearable moment? A cliché 'crime of passion' type of collapse, born of impulse and intensity, a heat-of-the-moment fracture in an otherwise intact life? No. Nothing about it was sudden. Nothing about it was impulsive. There was no singular cliff edge I stumbled over unaware. There was only the long walk toward it, taken one quiet step at a time. This was a deeply personal reckoning, years in the making. A slow erosion rather than an explosion. Like water shaping stone, patient and persistent, carving a canyon into the softest parts of me where protection had always been thin. Each disappointment smoothed the edges. Each unspoken grief widened the channel. Each time I told myself to endure just a little longer, the current deepened. Until one day, I realized I had been living inside the canyon all along, looking up at a sky that felt impossibly far away.

The longing did not arrive as a stranger. I did not recoil from it in horror when it first appeared. I nursed it in secret, the way one tends a private ache. It became as familiar as my own breath, as constant as the pulse beneath my skin. It walked beside me through ordinary days, sat quietly in the passenger seat of my life, listened while I spoke to others about hope and resilience and plans for the future. It waited patiently while I performed wellness. It did not rush me. It did not demand. It simply stayed. It grew alongside me like a shadow twin I never asked for, mirroring my movements, sharing my exhaustion, learning my habits and fears. Its presence was terrifying, yes, but also strangely consoling. In a world where so much of me had gone numb, it was proof that something still registered. That something still hurts. And pain, however unbearable, at least confirmed that I was not entirely hollow. In a twisted way, the ache became reassurance. Evidence of aliveness. Evidence that I was still capable of feeling something deeply, even if that something was despair.

This is the cruel paradox of suicidal ideation. It does not always feel like an enemy. Sometimes it feels like companionship. Like a quiet place to rest your head when every other surface feels hostile. It offers itself not as destruction, but as certainty. Not as chaos, but as order. A promise that the pain has an endpoint, even if that endpoint is silence. I did not wake up one morning wanting to die. I woke up, day after day, wanting the weight to lift. Wanting the vigilance to end. Wanting the constant internal negotiations to cease. Wanting rest without conditions. Wanting relief that did not require me to explain or justify my exhaustion. And slowly, almost imperceptibly, the idea of not being began to feel like the most reasonable answer to a question I had been asking for years: How much longer can I keep holding all of this?

There is nothing romantic about that realization. Nothing dramatic. It is quiet. It is heavy. It is born not from a lack of love for life, but from an overabundance of unprocessed pain. From too many seasons of being strong without support. From too many moments where survival was mistaken for living. Understanding this now does not excuse the danger of where I arrived. But it does strip away the shame. It allows me to see that what nearly ended me was not weakness, but endurance stretched beyond its limits. A system overloaded. A soul starved of gentleness. And that is why this story must be told slowly. Carefully. With reverence for the truth that this longing did not make me broken. It made me human. A human who had been carrying too much, for too long, without being taught how to set it down.

And still, even knowing this, there is another layer to name. Because the longing was not only about ending pain; it was about ending performance. Ending the endless audition for worth. Ending the quiet contracts I signed with myself that said I must be easy to love, useful to keep, strong enough not to need. Death did not appear to me as annihilation. It appeared as permission. Permission to stop translating my pain into something palatable. Permission to stop carrying what was never meant to be borne alone. I see now how my mind learned to build small exits everywhere. Not doors, at first, just windows cracked open in thought. What if I didn't have to do this anymore? What if I could rest without consequence? What if I could be free from the burden of being perceived, evaluated, and misunderstood? These were not screams. They were whispers folded neatly into reason. They sounded like self-awareness. Like realism. Like maturity. They hid behind phrases such as it would be easier for everyone or I'm just tired or I don't want to be a burden. Language softened the danger until it felt almost kind.

The Survival of Ideation

This is how ideation survives undetected, even by the one carrying it. It does not shout its name. It embeds itself in logic. It borrows the voice of responsibility and wears it convincingly. It disguises itself as consideration for others while quietly erasing the self. And because I had been trained to measure my goodness by how little space I took up, the idea of disappearing felt, in a warped way, like the ultimate act of consideration. I had learned to praise myself for endurance. For staying. For pushing through. For being the one who could handle it. I did not know that endurance, unrelieved by care, becomes corrosion. That strength without softness becomes self-harm in respectable clothing. That surviving everything does not mean you are meant to carry everything. So when the longing came, it did not feel foreign. It felt earned. Like the logical conclusion of a life lived in contraction. Like the last line of a paragraph that had been writing itself for years.

And that is what makes this truth so vital to speak aloud: the danger was never that I wanted to die. The danger was that I had forgotten how to want to live in a way that included me. Naming this now is not an act of regret. It is an act of reclamation. Because once the erosion is seen, it can be interrupted. Once the canyon is mapped, it is no longer destiny. Understanding does not change what happened, but it changes what happens next. It returns agency to the places where resignation once lived. This is why I tell this part slowly. Why I refuse to rush past the quiet years in favor of the dramatic night. Because healing does not come from outrunning the darkness. It comes from recognizing how gently, how convincingly, it asked for permission. And how bravely, even now, the human spirit keeps learning to say: not this way, not anymore, there must be another way to set the weight down. And there is.

But the true origin, the first hairline fracture beneath everything I would later call strength, the earliest whisper of "*you do not belong here*" did not rise in adulthood, nor did it begin in the sharp loneliness of my teenage years. It began much earlier, in childhood, in a season meant to be expansive. A season meant for wonder and wide-open skies, for scraped knees kissed better, for laughter that rang without apology. A time that should have been a garden. Instead, it became a place where parts of me were quietly buried. Not through one singular cruelty, not through a single unmistakable wound, but through a series of absences. Through moments where comfort did not arrive. Where confusion was met with silence. Where questions lingered unanswered long enough to harden into belief. Childhood has a particular way of teaching its lessons without words. It teaches through tone. Through who comes when you cry, and who does not. Through what is mirrored back to you and what is ignored. Through the subtle, repeated message of how much space you are allowed to take up before you become inconvenient.

This was where I first learned to shrink. The child I was did not know the language of unworthiness yet. She did not wake up one day believing she was wrong for existing. But she learned, slowly, that tenderness was not guaranteed. That safety could be conditional. That love might arrive with expectations attached or not arrive at all. And when a child cannot name what is missing, she assumes the fault must live inside her. So I adapted. As children do. I learned to become quieter. More observant. More accommodating. I learned to read emotional weather the way other children read picture books. I learned when to speak and when to disappear. I learned that being good often meant being small, and that asking for more risked losing what little connection there was. These were not dramatic lessons. They were ordinary. That is what makes them so powerful. They settled into my nervous system like sediment, layer upon layer, shaping how I understood myself long before I had the words to challenge it. They taught me that belonging was something to earn. That my needs were negotiable. That my feelings were burdensome unless they were neatly managed. And with each unspoken adjustment, another piece of me learned to go quiet.

This is where the ache first learned my shape. Not as despair. Not as death. But as a subtle dislocation from myself. A sense of being slightly out of place in my own skin. A feeling that the world was something to navigate carefully rather than inhabit freely. The earliest version of the thought that would one day mature into ideation was not *I want to disappear*. It was *I should not take up so much room*. And so, if we are to understand the night I nearly left this world, we must return here. Not to assign blame. Not to relive pain for its own sake. But to witness the beginning with honesty and compassion. To see how the shadows did not arrive suddenly one night beneath a moon, but were invited in slowly, quietly, by a child doing her best to survive with the tools she had. This is the ground where the story truly begins. Not with darkness, but with unmet light. Not with death, but with the first moment I learned to doubt my right to fully live.

And from that doubt, a pattern took hold, so subtle it masqueraded as personality, so constant it felt innate. I became skilled at folding myself into the margins, at editing my wants before they reached my mouth, at measuring my presence the way one measures salt, careful not to spoil the dish. I learned the choreography of restraint: how to smile without needing, how to succeed without celebrating, how to carry pain privately so as not to inconvenience the room. What could not be expressed learned to wait. What could not be welcomed learned to hide. This was not a childhood marked by obvious catastrophe. It was marked by quiet negotiations. By learning which feelings were acceptable and which were better kept under lock and key. By discovering that praise arrived more readily when I was easy, helpful, self-sufficient. By noticing how relief entered the air when I needed less. Over time, I mistook that relief for love. I mistook absence of conflict for safety. I mistook self-containment for maturity.

And so the ache refined itself. It became disciplined. Efficient. It learned how to sit politely in my chest while life went on around it. It learned how to translate longing into responsibility, grief into productivity, loneliness into competence. It learned how to survive undetected. What it did not learn was how to leave. I carried that child forward with me, though I did not know her name yet. She lived in the way I apologized for existing, in the way I overexplained my feelings, in the way I assumed the burden first and asked questions later. She lived in the reflex to earn my place, to justify my rest, to prove my worth before allowing myself relief. She lived in the quiet belief that if I could just be better, kinder, calmer, more capable, then the world would finally make room.

This is how the ground was prepared. Not with cruelty alone, but with conditioning. Not with violence, but with omission. Not with a single wound, but with the steady teaching that love had rules and space was limited.

The ideation that would one day speak in full sentences began here as a posture, a way of holding myself just slightly out of the way, a rehearsal of disappearance that felt responsible, even noble. To name this now is not to condemn the past, nor to indict the child who learned these lessons so well. It is to honor her ingenuity, her resilience, her fierce will to survive in an environment that did not yet know how to meet her fully. And it is to recognize, with tenderness, that what once protected me eventually began to cost me. This chapter opens, in the ordinary places where the extraordinary labor of self-erasure was first mistaken for love. Here, where the ache learned patience. Here, where silence became fluent. Here, where the story of endurance began to write itself so convincingly that it took years to realize I was allowed to put the pen down. From this ground, everything else grows.

Survival Before It Had a Name

This moment was never a sudden eruption, never a spontaneous combustion of despair. It was a slow, insidious burn, a quiet ember struck long before I had language for pain. It sparked in childhood, then smoldered, and smoldered, and smoldered, fed not by catastrophe but by accumulation. By every time I learned to swallow instead of speak. By every time I folded myself smaller to keep the peace. By every year I mistook endurance for strength and survival for success. I tried to outrun it. For a long time, I did not even know I was running. I called it ambition. I called it resilience. I called it being responsible, being strong, being grown. But embers do not vanish when ignored. They wait. They bank themselves beneath layers of achievement and adaptation, glowing softly, steadily, patient as breath. Each year I kept moving without tending to the wound beneath, the heat deepened. Quietly. Relentlessly.

It shadowed me through adolescence, when the body changes faster than the sense of self can keep up, when belonging feels like oxygen and withholding feels like suffocation. It learned new disguises then. It dressed itself as self-criticism. As comparison. As the belief that being acceptable mattered more than being authentic. I carried it through classrooms and friendships, through mirrors and milestones, never naming it, only adjusting my posture around it, learning how to live with a low-grade ache humming beneath everything else. And when I stepped into adulthood, it did not loosen its hold. It stepped beside me, familiar, practiced, devoted. It slipped into my days the way a long-term companion does, without ceremony. It sat quietly in my decisions. It influenced the standards I held myself to. It whispered in the moments when rest felt undeserved, and joy felt suspicious. It clung to me with an intimacy that felt almost comforting, because it had been with me longer than any version of safety ever had.

The darkness did not arrive as an intruder. It arrived as continuity. As something stitched to my skin so seamlessly, I mistook it for my own outline. I did not experience it as a threat; I experienced it as truth. It shaped how I spoke to myself, how I interpreted disappointment, and how I measured my worth. Over time, it stopped feeling like pain and started feeling like identity. Like the price of being who I was. This is how it survives. Not through spectacle, but through familiarity. Not through force, but through proximity. It becomes the background temperature of your inner world, the climate you adapt to without question. And when something has been with you that long, when it has learned your rhythms and borrowed your voice, it becomes difficult to imagine who you might be without it.

But naming it now, tracing its slow burn from spark to ember to flame, is not an act of shame. It is an act of clarity. Because what was learned can be unlearned. What was carried can be set down. And what once felt inseparable from my skin can be recognized, at last, as something that grew around me, not something that was ever meant to be me. This chapter continues here, in the long arc between first spark and final ignition. In the years where the fire did not rage but endured. Waiting. Quietly. For someone to finally turn toward it, not to be consumed, but to understand how it came to live there at all.

And so I keep my gaze there, on the long arc rather than the explosion, on the years where the fire learned patience. On the way, it taught me to live in a constant state of bracing, shoulders slightly raised, breath never quite full. I learned to anticipate impact even in calm rooms. To listen for danger in laughter. To measure joy, the way one measures fuel in a long journey, rationing it carefully, afraid it would run out if I used too much at once. The ember learned from repetition. It learned from the countless small moments where my instincts were overridden, where my no was softened into maybe, where my hurt was reframed as sensitivity. Each time I chose understanding over self-protection, each time I translated someone else's behavior into my own failing, the fire adjusted. It grew quieter. Smarter. It no longer needed to shout. It only had to be present.

I can see now how it braided itself into my virtues. How compassion became self-neglect. How loyalty became endurance without reciprocity. How responsibility became the quiet belief that it was my job to absorb what others would not carry. The fire did not oppose my goodness; it hid inside it. It learned that I would forgive faster than I would leave, that I would question myself before questioning harm, that I would stay long after staying had begun to cost me my shape. This is how the burn deepened without spectacle. No alarms. No sirens. Just a gradual recalibration of what felt normal. The heat became the air I breathed. The ache became the baseline. And anything less than that felt unfamiliar, undeserved, almost dangerous. I mistook discomfort for truth because it was consistent. I mistook exhaustion for identity because it was praised.

And still, beneath the ember, beneath the long practice of adaptation, there was something else learning too. A quiet resistance. A knowing that flickered even when I tried to ignore it. It surfaced in moments of sudden grief I could not explain. In the way my body tightened before my mind could catch up. In the exhaustion that sleep could not touch. These were not failures. They were signals. The language of a self that had been speaking all along, waiting for me to learn how to listen. This is why I return here with care. Because the fire did not make me who I am. It shaped the terrain I learned to move through. It altered my posture, my pace, my expectations. But it did not erase the ground beneath it. And understanding that difference changes everything. To trace the burn is to reclaim authorship. To see where survival began to impersonate selfhood. To recognize the places where adaptation became a cage. And to gently, deliberately begin the work of opening the door.

This chapter is not about extinguishing the fire. Not yet. It is about understanding its origin. About honoring the intelligence that kept it alive when I did not know another way. And about recognizing that what once protected me no longer has to lead. The ember is no longer in charge. I am learning to sit with it, to feel its heat without obeying its commands, to remember that warmth can exist without harm. And as I do, the story shifts. Not abruptly. Not dramatically. But unmistakably. This is the moment where endurance loosens its grip on my name. This is where survival begins to make room for living.

WHAT CLUNG WAS NOT Me

Later, much later, in the softened light that healing brings, the kind that does not blind but reveals—I would come to understand something quietly revolutionary. The darkness that had felt fused to me, that second skin I believed I was born wearing, was never skin at all. It was adhesion. Residue. Old gum snarled in my hair, clinging not because it belonged, but because it had been left too long without being tended to. It had tangled itself into my strands slowly, invisibly, worked in by years of movement and survival, and not knowing I was allowed to stop. It was sticky and stubborn and humiliating in the way such things are, convincing me that cutting everything off would be easier than trying to save what remained. But it was not permanent. It had no pulse of its own. It could not grow new roots. It only held on because I believed it had the right to. I would learn that removal was possible. Not all at once. Not without pain. Strand by strand. Snip by careful snip. With patience. With grief. With trembling hands and long pauses to breathe through the sting. Healing did not arrive as erasure, but as discernment. As the slow reclaiming of what was mine beneath what had attached itself there.

But back then, before that knowing had a name, it felt inescapable. It felt like a presence that had memorized me. A constant companion that knew how to speak in my voice, that curled itself around every thought until I could no longer tell where I ended and it began. It whispered through the years with quiet persistence, narrating my life from behind my eyes, interpreting every moment through its own narrow lens. It did not shout. It insinuated. It did not command. It suggested. And because it never left, I mistook its constancy for truth. No matter how fiercely I clawed at its edges, it seemed to tighten. The more I resisted, the more it convinced me resistance was futile. That this was simply who I was. That the ache was evidence of character. That the weight was deserved. It wrapped itself around my thinking, my remembering, my imagining of the future, until even hope felt contaminated by its touch.

I did not know yet that things which cling can be removed. I did not know yet that what attaches itself in silence loses power when named. I did not know yet that survival adaptations are not life sentences. All I knew then was the suffocation. The intimacy of it. The way it followed me into every room, into every relationship, into every quiet moment where my guard lowered. I believed it would always be there, breathing when I breathed, tightening when I tried to move, reminding me of itself whenever I dared to forget. And yet, even then, beneath that sticky conviction, beneath the belief that I was bound forever to what hurt me, something else persisted. Something small. Something unassuming. The possibility that what feels fused might only be tangled. That what whispers might not be wise. That what clings might not belong. Healing would teach me this gently, and then relentlessly. But for now, in this part of the story, the darkness still had its hands in my hair.

And so, in that earlier time, I lived as though the pull were permanent, as though the weight had always been mine to carry. I moved through days with that tug at my scalp, that quiet ache of being held in place by something unseen. Every thought bent slightly under its influence. Every decision passed through its filter. I adjusted without realizing I was adjusting, learned to turn my head just so, learned which movements hurt less, learned to live with the constant, low-grade discomfort of being tethered to something I did not choose. I did not yet know how deeply the body remembers what the mind has normalized. How belief settles into muscle. How shame braids itself into posture. The darkness had learned not only my voice, but my gestures, my pauses, my silences. It knew when to lean in. It knew when to retreat just enough to keep me doubting my own perception. It was not cruel in obvious ways. It was persuasive. Familiar. It survived by being believable.

There were moments, fleeting and easily dismissed, when I sensed the wrongness of it. A tightening that did not belong to fear. A fatigue that sleep could not touch. A sorrow that felt inherited rather than earned. But those moments passed quickly, swallowed by routine, by responsibility, by the relentless demand to keep going. I told myself this was adulthood. This was resilience. This was the cost of being functional in a world that did not pause. The darkness counted on that story. It counted on my willingness to explain myself away. On my instinct to blame my own weakness rather than question the weight I was carrying. It thrived in the spaces where curiosity should have lived. In the places where gentleness might have interrupted the pattern. It did not need to tighten its grip if I never tried to loosen it.

And yet, even then, even while it held fast, something else was growing quietly beneath the tangle. Not defiance. Not clarity. Just a faint, persistent sensation of mismatch. A sense that what hurt did not feel like truth. That what clung did not feel like destiny. That somewhere beneath the residue, there was hair still my own, waiting to be touched without pain. I did not act on that knowing. Not yet. It was too small. Too fragile. Too easily overshadowed by the louder voice that had learned to sound like mine. But it was there. It flickered. It endured.

A subtle resistance I did not yet recognize as hope. Because healing does not begin with certainty. It begins with discomfort. With the quiet realization that what you have adapted to may not be what you deserve. For now, the darkness still had its hands in my hair. But it no longer owned my scalp. And somewhere deep beneath the pull, beneath the ache, beneath the belief that I was bound forever to what hurt me, the roots of me were still alive. Waiting.

A Lantern Set Down Gentl

And though this story is difficult to tell, raw in its honesty and tender in its confessions, I place it here with intention and deliberate care, as one might set a fragile offering on bare earth and step back. Exposed. Breathing. Trusting the air to be gentle. Not to shock. Not to wound. But to witness. To let what was once swallowed finally have a mouth. To give syllables to the chambers where silence pressed its weight the longest, where harm arrived not with violence but with neglect. I offer it with the hope that somewhere, someone is standing in their own quiet fire, heat without flame, pain without spectacle, wondering how something unseen can scorch so deeply. Someone who has learned endurance so fluently it has erased the sound of their own needs. Someone who has mistaken survival for virtue and forgotten that tending is not a reward, but a right. Someone who believes their ache is a moral failing, their exhaustion an indictment, their longing proof that they have asked for too much.

If that someone finds themselves threaded through these words, if a sentence settles like a steady hand at the shoulder or opens the chest the way a clean breath does after being held too long, let this be the truth that reaches them and stays. You are not broken beyond repair. You are not dramatic for hurting. You are not weak for being weary of carrying what was never meant to be carried alone. What you hold has a lineage. What you feel has a cause. And what feels fused to you now may only be tangled, caught fast by time and fear, waiting not for force, but for patience. Waiting for gentleness to do what punishment never could. This story is not an ending. It is a lantern. A quiet one. It does not blaze or demand attention. It glows. Just enough to soften the dark. Just enough to reveal that survival is not a personal failure, and that pain, when finally seen and named, does not get to write the final line. Light does not always arrive as rescue. Sometimes it arrives as recognition. If you see yourself here, know this.

You are not alone in the fire. You are not the only one who has learned to live with embers beneath the skin, heat normalized, burns uncounted. And you are not beyond saving. You never were. Let me begin with the very first feeling that ever rose within me as a child, that quiet, devastating seed from which everything else eventually grew. It was powerlessness, but not the small, ordinary kind a child learns when a request is denied or a want goes unmet. This was something vaster. A powerlessness that spread beneath the surface like a hidden root system, silent and relentless, reshaping the ground of the soul before language had the chance to arrive. Even now, when I reach back toward it, words hesitate, bowing under its gravity. It was a vast, echoing helplessness, a hollowing so complete it felt as though something essential had been carved out and left exposed to the cold air.

A powerlessness in which the child is awake and afraid, sensing danger without knowing its name or edges, terrified yet unable to alter what is unfolding. A state where fear has no exit, where time does not move forward but collapses inward on itself, looping and tightening. The body understands long before the mind ever does that there is no lever to pull, no door that will open, no voice that will land where it is meant to. It was the absolute absence of control over pain, over lovelessness, over the aching certainty of being unseen. A place where speech feels unsafe, trust feels naïve, and silence becomes armor rather than choice. A place where the child learns that to speak is to invite more harm, and to be seen is not to be protected. So the self-retreats. It folds inward, growing smaller, quieter, less textured, sanding itself down in the hope that smoothness might mean safety.

In that landscape, no degree of perfection could rewrite the outcome. No performance could purchase protection. No isolation could dull the impact. No invisibility could erase what was happening. No acceptance of pain could turn it into meaning. The child tries everything. Be better. Be easier. Be quieter. Be nothing. And still, nothing changes. The lesson settles without words, sinking into bone and breath: endurance does not grant power, and suffering does not summon care. This was the soil in which everything else took root. Not because it was chosen, but because it was unavoidable. A powerlessness that did not pass with time, but lingered, shaping how love would later be interpreted, how danger would be anticipated, how the body would brace even in moments meant to be safe. It became the first language my nervous system ever learned, spoken fluently long before I had a name for it, long before I knew that what had been learned could one day be unlearned.

It was hopelessness, thick and suffocating, pressing against my chest like an unseen storm, a weather system too vast and violent for small shoulders to carry. It gathered quietly, without thunder or warning, a pressure drop in the atmosphere of my body, stealing the air from my lungs one breath at a time. My ribs learned early how to brace, how to hold fast against something that could not be outrun, could not be named, could not be reasoned with. I felt myself folding inward, collapsing beneath a weight no child should ever be asked to hold, disintegrating grain by grain, the way stone yields to tide, not because it is weak, but because the water never stops. Under that pressure, even thought began to fracture. Sentences broke apart before they could finish forming. Meaning slipped sideways. Even my whispered prayers, and yes, I prayed, rose already bruised, already exhausted, as though they had traveled too far before ever leaving my mouth. They were not shaped like hope. They did not reach upward or outward. They curled inward on themselves, saturated with longing for escape.

A yearning not for rescue, not for tomorrow, but for quiet. For an ending that promised stillness, where living had only ever demanded endurance. It was not death as drama. Not spectacle. Not a cry for attention or a gesture meant to be seen. It was death as absence. As release. As the soft erasing of sensation, the dimming of a room that had never known rest. A child's mind reaching for the only door it could imagine when every other passage was sealed shut. In that small, frightened body, the desire was simple and terrible in its clarity. Not to be loved. Not to be saved. But to stop. To lay the burden down. To let the storm pass by letting the self-disappear with it. This was how hopelessness taught me its language. Not in screams, but in gravity. Not in chaos, but in the steady, crushing certainty that nothing would change, and that ending felt kinder than continuing. It settled early, deep in the chest, heavy and familiar, becoming another layer of the world I learned to live inside. A climate rather than a moment. A truth I carried long before I had the words to question it, long before I understood how profoundly unnatural it is for a child to want an end at all.

I spoke death's name long before I understood its finality, shaped the word with a child's mouth that did not yet grasp what it meant to close a life. I rolled it across my tongue like a secret prayer, not knowing it was a door that, once opened, could never be shut again. I called to it like a weary wanderer calling across an endless plain, voice cracking in the vastness, begging not for oblivion, but for rest. I pleaded for its embrace with the desperation of someone drowning in an ocean no one else could see, lungs burning, arms aching, the surface always just beyond reach. To those watching from shore, the water looked calm, almost inviting. To me, it was everywhere, filling my mouth, my chest, my dreams, leaving no place to stand. It was never simply the act of dying that I craved. It was what I believed waited on the other side of that last breath. Relief, imagined as a loosening knot finally giving way. A silence so complete it could cradle me without demand, without expectation.

The stillness. The quiet. A place where the body would no longer flinch at every sound or shift in the air, where the mind could finally lower its guard, where waking would not arrive already burdened with dread and calculation. I imagined a space where vigilance was no longer required, where I could exhale and stay exhaled. I longed for release from the endless cycle of pain that greeted me each morning like a cruel sunrise, rising faithfully and without mercy, illuminating wounds I had never been allowed to tend. Light came not as promise but as exposure, revealing again and again that nothing had softened in the dark, that the night had offered no repair. Each day demanded endurance as proof of worth, strength as a prerequisite for existing at all. And so death became less an ending than a horizon, a distant line that steadied me when the ground beneath my feet felt unliveable. I stared toward it for comfort, the way others might look toward home.

In my imagination, it shimmered with the possibility of rest without cost, silence without fear, an end to the ache of having to be strong again. It was not a wish to vanish, but a wish to finally be allowed to stop. To lay down the armor that had fused to my skin. To rest from the labor of surviving. In a world where living had always felt like an assignment I was failing, death seemed like the only place where I would no longer be asked to prove that I deserved to exist.

Living Inside the Rhythm of an Ending

I cursed the breath that rose in my chest, resented the rhythm that kept me tethered to a world that offered only new variations of the same unbearable ache. Each inhale felt like a betrayal, a contract renewed without my consent. Each exhale an obligation, a debt collected by a body that refused to abandon its post. My lungs worked like clockwork I could not smash, faithful and unyielding, dragging me forward when every part of me ached to dissolve into stillness. I felt bound by that rhythm, chained to mornings that arrived without mercy, promising nothing but repetition, nothing but the familiar weight of pain dressed in a new disguise. I believed I was experiencing a soul-death. Not the extinguishing of life itself, not the clean, merciful finality of a last breath, but something far more haunting than physical annihilation. It was the slow, silent unraveling of my essence, thread by thread, unnoticed and unnamed. A death-in-motion. A fading.

A disappearing so gradual it escaped alarm, leaving no scar the world could point to, no ceremony to mark its passing. I moved through days like a shadow still tethered to a body, visible enough to be counted, solid enough to be expected, yet hollowed beyond reach. I was dissolving while still breathing, eroding from the inside out, collapsing quietly behind my eyes while the world continued as if nothing sacred were being lost. At least, that is what I believed then. I did not know that beneath the ashes of that devastation, something else was quietly forming. Not loudly. Not heroically. But patiently, the way the earth works when no one is watching. A resilience still unnamed, taking shape in the dark the way roots do, blind yet unrelenting, pressing forward because forward is all they know. A flicker still hidden, protected by the very numbness I mistook for absence, kept alive by the smallest refusal to fully disappear.

A strength not yet ready to reveal itself, not yet safe enough to be seen, waiting for a future moment when light would no longer feel like threat. But that came much, much later. Long after the believing. Long after the cursing. Long after I mistook survival for emptiness and breath for cruelty. At the time, all I could feel was the unraveling, the steady loosening of self, the sense of slipping out of my own life inch by inch. I could not yet imagine that what felt like disappearance was also, in some unseen and unspoken way, a becoming. That even as I was breaking apart, something within me was learning how to hold on. What, then, was I truly experiencing all those years? They call it suicidal ideation, a phrase so clinical, so cold, it feels like trying to name a hurricane by simply calling it wind. A term scrubbed clean for textbooks and diagnostic manuals, tidy and contained, safely bracketed by quotation marks: "the act of thinking about, or being preoccupied with, ending one's own life." Words that sit still on the page, orderly and bloodless.

Words that do not sweat, do not tremble, do not jolt awake in the small hours with fear coating the mouth like metal. But what I lived was far more than a definition. It was an existence. A monstrous existence. A way of being that did not arrive and depart but settled in, unpacked itself, learned the layout of my inner rooms. It took up residence without asking, rearranged the furniture of my mind, boarded the windows, and locked the doors from the inside. It wrapped itself around my every waking breath like a second skin made of shadows, heavy and intimate, clinging so closely I forgot what my own outline had once been. I did not think about dying in moments. I lived inside a world where dying was the weather, a constant atmosphere, as omnipresent as gravity, as inescapable as air. It shaped how I woke, how I moved, how I listened. It hovered beside me while I brushed my teeth, watched from the corners of mirrors, sat with me in classrooms and kitchens, followed me into silence and into crowds alike.

It threaded itself into the pause before speech, into the careful calculation of how much of myself it was safe to reveal, into the bone-deep exhaustion of choosing to stay one more day. It was not a thought I could set down at the end of an evening. It was the lens through which everything passed, tinting every sound, every touch, every hope with the same dim, narrowing light. To call it ideation suggests distance, abstraction, a mind idly entertaining an idea and then setting it aside. What I knew was immersion. Saturation. A lived-in despair that breathed when I breathed, that pulsed beneath my skin, that tightened and loosened with my heartbeat. It shaped my sense of what was possible and what was not, where edges existed, where escape might be imagined. It was not merely about wanting to die. It was about not knowing how to live without the constant hum of an ending, the low, relentless vibration beneath every moment, reminding me that survival itself felt provisional, conditional, and unbearably heavy to maintain.

Before it ever had a name, before it could be argued with or explained away, it arrived as a tempo. Not loud. Not dramatic. Just constant. A low, internal percussion that settled into me so early it felt ancestral, as though I had inherited it rather than learned it. It did not announce itself as despair. It introduced itself as normal. As background. As the way things were. And so I grew around it, adjusted my posture to its pull, calibrated my breath to its insistence, unaware that a life can be shaped not only by what happens to us, but by what keeps quietly time beneath everything we do. For me, it wasn't merely a thought. It was a rhythm. A ritual. A quiet, incessant yearning for release that kept time beneath everything else, steady as a second heart I never asked for. It pulsed through my days like a metronome set to an invisible tempo, precise and unyielding, marking each moment with the same silent count.

I moved in step with it, lived inside its beat, waking and sleeping to that underlying cadence, as though my life were scored to a music only, I could hear. It lingered in the moments between moments, in the silences that followed laughter, in the pause after a door closed, always drawing me back to the same refrain. I was constantly scanning the world for exits, for escape hatches, for any hairline fracture in the wall through which I could slip away unnoticed. My eyes learned the architecture of disappearance the way others learn the geography of home. Bridges, pills, blades, corners of rooms, long stretches of road. Even ordinary objects acquired a second language, offering themselves not as what they were, but as what they could become. A whispered invitation. A possibility. I mapped the world not by belonging, but by vanishing points.

Safety was never the absence of danger, only the absence of opportunity. It became woven into the fabric of who I was, threaded so tightly through my identity that I could no longer tell where I ended and it began. It stitched itself into my posture, my expressions, my silences. While I played the role of the perfect child, the people-pleaser, the obedient one, performing goodness with practiced ease, I carried a dark, secret hunger beneath my smile. I learned how to nod at the right moments, how to soften my voice, how to make myself useful and unproblematic, how to disappear socially long before I ever dreamed of disappearing completely. All the while, I held a private ache that never slept. Beneath that carefully maintained surface lived a craving for oblivion, as familiar to me as the air I breathed. It did not arrive with drama or alarm. It did not shout or demand.

It simply existed, constant and intimate, the way breath exists, unnoticed until it falters, until it catches painfully in the chest. I inhaled and exhaled survival, day after day, while secretly longing for the one thing I could not name aloud. And so I learned how to live divided. One self moved compliantly through the world, dutiful and smiling, earning approval, causing no disruption. The other lived quietly beneath, rehearsing its disappearance, running exit drills in the dark, counting beats, waiting for a moment that might never come. Both selves shared the same body. Both breathed the same air. And neither was ever fully at rest, bound together behind a smile no one questioned. But division, no matter how carefully managed, is not sustainable. What is split eventually longs to be seen. What is buried eventually presses upward. And it is here, at the edge of this quiet double life, that the story must begin to turn. Not yet toward healing, not yet toward light, but toward truth. Toward naming what lived in the dark for so long. Toward understanding how a rhythm learned in silence can one day be interrupted, not by force, but by awareness.

Before any of this could be named, before it could be framed as illness or understood as survival, it existed as a private gravity, a pull so constant it shaped the way my inner world formed. It did not arrive as crisis. It arrived as familiarity. As something I adjusted around, something I learned to accommodate the way one learns to live with a limp or a scar. Over time, it became less a question and more a condition, less a thought and more a climate, quietly governing how close I could come to hope and how far I was willing to imagine a future.

I didn't just think of death; I longed for it, desired it, wished for it, imagined it, every single day. It was not a visitor that came and went with circumstance or mood. It was a companion that stayed. A presence that settled beside me in the quiet and followed me into noise, patient and familiar. This was not a fleeting sadness or a passing storm that might break and clear. This was a devotion to disappearing, a morbid fidelity to the idea of not being here, tended and revisited with a frightening consistency. Death became a place my mind returned to instinctively, the way a tongue seeks a sore tooth, drawn again and again to the same ache, even knowing it will hurt.

It felt like a mental rehearsal of a play in which I was both hero and villain, author and executioner, endlessly staging my own ending. The curtain rose and fell inside my head without audience or applause. Scene after scene played out behind my eyes, variations on the same conclusion, each one rehearsed with the strange intimacy of something practiced too often. I was killing myself over and over again, not in body, but in imagination, in thought, in longing. Each rehearsal carved its grooves deeper, etching pathways the mind would follow without effort, until imagining my absence felt more natural, more familiar, than imagining a future I could not yet believe in.

And it began so young. Nine, perhaps ten. Those tender, formative years when innocence should have been my birthright, when the world should have felt wide and curious, when danger should have been abstract and death a distant rumor whispered only in stories. Instead, those years left an indelible mark on my psyche, pressed into it like a fingerprint that could never quite be erased. Years that should have been filled with wonder, innocence, curiosity, and carefree discovery were instead heavy with vigilance, fear, and the unbearable burden of thoughts no child should ever be asked to carry. My inner landscape grew crowded with questions that had no answers and endings that felt closer than beginnings.

That was where the war began. Not loudly. Not with alarms or obvious devastation. But quietly, inside my own mind, a long, merciless conflict between staying and vanishing, between breathing and surrender. A war fought in whispers and silences, in imagined endings and forced mornings. A war with no clear enemy, no ceasefire, no witnesses. This was the birthplace of my struggle with suicidal ideation, not as a concept or diagnosis, but as a lived reality, etched into the rhythms of my days and the architecture of my thoughts. A battle that shaped how I thought, how I felt, how I learned to exist in the world, long before I understood that what I was fighting was not life itself, but the unbearable weight of living without safety, without softness, without relief.

And yet, no war remains unseen forever. What is fought in secret leaves traces. Hairline fractures. Tells in the body. In the chapters that follow, I will begin to trace those fractures, to show how this hidden conflict seeped into my relationships, my sense of self, my understanding of love and worth. Not to dramatize the pain, but to tell the truth of what it costs to survive a battle no one else knows you are fighting.

When Survival Learned to Hurt

It felt as though I were crumbling beneath the weight of my own existence, collapsing inward under burdens no child should ever be asked to carry. I was eroding from the inside, grain by grain, like stone worn down by a tide that never receded, while the world saw only a shape that still stood, upright enough to pass as whole. Inside, however, I was hollowing, learning what it meant to disappear slowly, to vanish without ever leaving the room. The darkness did not merely visit me. It did not arrive politely and leave its coat by the door. It did not pop in for a cup of tea and some biscuits, staying just long enough to be noticed. No. It moved in fully. It unpacked. It took up residence. It claimed squatter's rights within the corridors of my soul and began to live there as though it had always belonged, as though it had been waiting patiently for me to grow small enough to accommodate it.

It wandered through my inner rooms with quiet authority, lifting memories as one might lift picture frames from a wall, rearranging beliefs with the confidence of a long-term tenant. It removed my inner furniture piece by piece to make space for its own, discarding warmth, curiosity, softness, anything that took up too much room. And all the while, it spoke gently, convincingly, telling me this was how the room had always been arranged. That the emptiness was original. That the cold was familiar. That the ache was evidence, not intrusion. And I believed it. I mistook its presence for my nature, its weight for my identity, its voice for my own. Slowly, without ceremony or resistance, it taught me to confuse absence with truth. And without knowing it then, my life became a quiet choreography of survival. Each step was careful. Measured. Calculated.

I learned how to move without making sound, how to anticipate impact, how to brace before anything even touched me. Every movement was shaped not by dreams of living, but by fantasies of release. I learned how to pass through days without disturbing the pain, how to perform normalcy while privately rehearsing disappearance. The future was not something I imagined building or growing into. It was something I endured, one careful breath at a time, always aware of where the exits were, always keeping one eye on the door. This was the beginning of the long road. Not a straight path, not an obvious descent marked by warning signs, but a gradual narrowing of possibility. A series of small concessions made to despair. A quiet agreement to keep going without expecting anything more. Each year smoothed the edges, made the weight feel familiar, almost manageable, even as it pressed deeper into the bones.

And it was this road, laid down in childhood, worn smooth by years of silence and longing, that would one day lead me to that moonlit grass. To that breathless, devastating night. The night I nearly slipped away. I was the golden child, the perfectly polished daughter, the one expected to shine without cracking, to smile without trembling, to perform without faltering. Mommy and Daddy's flawless little girl. A living mirror meant to reflect pride back at the room. No weakness permitted. No sadness allowed. Love arrived conditionally, wrapped in applause and approval, measured in nods and smiles and how well I carried myself. I learned quickly which parts of me were welcome and which needed to be folded away, tucked into quiet corners where they would not inconvenience anyone. Perfection became the silent script I memorized long before I could spell my own name, a choreography of goodness rehearsed until it felt automatic, until it felt indistinguishable from who I was.

I became a masterful people-pleaser, a gentle contortionist bending myself into shapes that made others comfortable, seen, supported, adored. My spine learned flexibility before it learned strength. I learned how to read rooms before I learned how to read books, how to scan faces for shifts in mood, how to anticipate needs before I ever dared to name my own. I softened my edges, swallowed my discomfort, offered warmth even when I was freezing inside. I lived to keep everyone else warm, even if it meant setting myself on fire, even if the flames burned slowly and politely, leaving no smoke anyone else could see. The cost was invisible, paid privately, one small erasure at a time. But behind closed doors, in the secret places no one knew existed, another version of me emerged. The one who trembled when the performance finally ended. The one who broke under the accumulated weight of holding everything together.

The one who could finally exhale the truth without fear of disappointing anyone. Here, the mask slipped. Here, the polite smile melted into tears I could no longer swallow. The body began to speak in the only language it had left. The chest tightened. The hands shook. Breath turned shallow and erratic. Panic attacks tore through me like sudden storms, violent and disorienting, shaking loose the pieces I had plastered together just to appear whole. In those moments, the illusion collapsed. The golden child dimmed. The performance ended. And what remained was not weakness, but exhaustion. Bone-deep. Cellular. The exhaustion of a child who had held too much for too long, who had mistaken compliance for safety and perfection for love. A nervous system stretched past its limits, frayed and buzzing, caught between collapse and vigilance.

In the quiet aftermath, surrounded by the wreckage of composure, I learned the most dangerous lesson of all: that being seen only for who you pretend to be is another kind of invisibility, and that applause, no matter how loud, cannot reach a self that has been forced to disappear. In those hidden corners, self-care twisted into self-destruction, a cruel parody of tending that harmed more than it healed. What should have been rest became retreat. What should have been soothing became erasure. Self-harm became justified punishment. I learned how to disappear politely, how to call it coping, how to name survival something noble while it quietly hollowed me out. "I'm fine" dissolved into "I can't do this anymore," a phrase that echoed daily through my inner world, ricocheting off the walls of my mind until it lost all sound and became pure weight. And beneath that, deeper still, another refrain pulsed, raw and relentless, a heartbeat made of grief. "I want to die. Please. Please. Just let me die."

These words rose from me in many forms. Sometimes they came as prayer, hands clenched, breath held, eyes lifted toward a ceiling that felt impossibly far away. Other times they arrived as pleas, jagged and urgent, torn loose in moments when the body could no longer contain the ache. Sometimes they were only whispers pressed into a pillow, soaked into fabric and silence. Sometimes they were swallowed whole, lodged in the throat like stones, too dangerous to release. I did not know who I was speaking to. Heaven. God. The universe. Anyone. Anything that might see me, hear me, respond. I sent those words out like flares into a dark sky, desperate for acknowledgement, for proof that my suffering registered somewhere beyond my own skin. Most of the time, they fell back to earth unanswered, extinguished before they could be seen, landing heavier than before.

I became both prisoner and warden within my own body. Victim and perpetrator. Judge and defendant. I built a courtroom inside myself where I stood trial every day for the crime of being too much and not enough at the same time. The verdict was always guilty. The sentence was endless. I punished myself simply for existing. For breathing when I felt undeserving of air. For needing when need felt shameful. For wanting comfort in a world that had taught me comfort must be earned. For failing to be the flawless creation I believed the world demanded. Mercy was never on the table. Compassion was dismissed as indulgence. Survival itself felt like evidence of wrongdoing, proof that I had failed even at disappearing. And so the cycle continued, quiet but brutal. I policed my thoughts, interrogated my feelings, tightened the bars whenever hope threatened to slip through. I became hypervigilant inside my own mind, watching myself for weakness, for longing, for softness.

Even in my suffering, I believed I was failing. Failing to cope. Failing to be grateful. Failing to disappear properly. Pain became another performance I could not get right. It never occurred to me then that this relentless self-prosecution was not proof of my brokenness, but the imprint of a system that taught me love must be earned and pain must be hidden. That safety was conditional. That worth was measured by usefulness, silence, and strength. At the time, all I knew was the sentence. And I carried it with me everywhere, etched into breath and bone, stitched into my posture and my prayers, convinced that the greatest crime I had ever committed was simply being alive. Self-harm became my language, a twisted form of prayer and penance, a trembling dialogue with the pain I carried like a second heartbeat, always there, always counting time. It kept pace with me, marked my hours when nothing else could. When words failed me, my body spoke. When silence grew too heavy to hold, I translated it into wounds.

Self-harm became my dialect of apology, a desperate grammar of atonement written in flesh and breath. "*I am sorry I exist.* Take this cut with its blood. Take this bruise with its black and blues. Take my breath with each suffocation. Take it as offering, as proof, as payment laid trembling on the altar of despair." I believed pain might make me worthy of mercy, that punishment could stand in for forgiveness I did not know how to ask for, that suffering might earn me a place in the world. It was never about spectacle. Never about being seen. It was about confession. About making the invisible ache tangible, measurable, undeniable. In a world that refused to witness my suffering, I bore witness myself. I etched my pain into places it could no longer be ignored. Pain became ritualized, almost sacred, a private liturgy performed in silence. A way to externalize what threatened to consume me from within. For a moment, it brought order to chaos, silence to the noise, edges to the blur. A brief illusion of control. A pause where everything stopped shaking.

And then the hunger returned, deeper, heavier, asking for more than before. And through it all, death was not just a shadow lingering in the corner of my mind. It was intimate. Personal. A forbidden lover whose absence ached even while its imagined presence terrified me. Death became a fantasy I carried close, folded into my thoughts like a secret letter. I imagined it as tenderness without demand, as quiet without punishment, as rest that did not need to be earned. A promise of stillness. A release. An embrace I longed for with a devotion that frightened me even as it soothed me. I did not want to vanish out of spite or drama. I wanted to be held without conditions. I wanted the labor of staying alive, the endless proving and performing, to finally end. This was the truth that lived behind the golden glow. Behind the polished smile. Behind the praise and applause that rang hollow once the lights dimmed.

A child crowned with expectation, admired for her shine, rewarded for her composure, crumbling quietly beneath the weight of being loved only when perfect, only when quiet and invisible, only when unbroken. The world saw achievement and called it strength. It saw silence and called it maturity. It never saw the cost exacted behind closed doors, never counted the pieces left behind. Inside that child lived a war no one applauded. A grief no one named. A longing so deep it learned to masquerade as devotion to disappearance. And yet, even here, even in this most dangerous intimacy with pain, something else was present. Something unnamed. Something stubborn. A pulse that refused to extinguish, beating beneath the rituals and the longing. A thread that held, even when I believed I was unraveling completely. I could not see it then. I only knew the ritual. The ache. The desperate choreography of survival.

But this is the point where the story begins to turn, not away from the truth of that suffering, but toward understanding it. Toward recognizing that what I called self-destruction was, at its core, a language learned in isolation, a body's attempt to survive without words, without safety, without being seen. And it is here, standing in the wreckage of that truth, that healing first becomes possible. Not as absolution. Not as erasure. But as translation. As the slow, radical act of learning a new language for pain, one that does not require blood to be believed, one that allows the body to speak and still be held. And yet, even here, in the most dangerous depths of that devotion, something in me did not vanish. It hid. It waited. It learned how to be small enough to survive. Beneath the rituals of harm and the fantasies of quiet, beneath the longing to disappear, there remained a pulse that did not belong to death at all. I did not recognize it then.

I mistook it for stubbornness. For fear. For weakness. But it was life, insisting without language, refusing to be extinguished even when; I begged it to let go. What I was reaching for was never destruction. It was relief. What I wanted was not annihilation, but mercy. An end to vigilance. An end to the performance. An end to the constant negotiation of worth. I wanted rest in a world that had never taught me how to rest safely. I wanted silence that did not feel like punishment. I wanted to be held without conditions, without having to earn it through pain. Slowly, painfully slowly, that truth began to matter. Because when pain is translated into self-destruction, it is not because the person wants to die. It is because they have not yet been given another language for their suffering. I did not lack strength. I lacked permission. Permission to be human. Permission to be messy. Permission to be seen without being perfect.

My body was not trying to end itself. It was trying to regulate what no one had ever helped me regulate. It was trying to survive what had once been unsurvivable. This is something I can see now, standing far enough away from those years to name them honestly. The child who harmed herself was not broken. She was overwhelmed. The girl who fantasized about death was not weak. She was exhausted. And the woman writing these words is not defined by what she did to survive, but by the fact that she did. Healing did not arrive as a single revelation or a sudden light. It came in fragments. In pauses. In moments where I chose curiosity over condemnation. In learning to listen to my body instead of punishing it for speaking. In realizing that the very impulses I once feared were signals, not sins. Messages from a nervous system that had learned danger too early and safety too late.

This book exists because I lived. Not unscarred. Not untouched. But alive. And because survival, when examined with compassion instead of shame, becomes a map. One that can lead us back to ourselves. What follows is not a story of erasing the past. It is a story of reclaiming it. Of learning how to stay without burning. Of discovering that the opposite of self-destruction is not perfection, but presence. And that the child who once believed disappearance was the only form of peace was never wrong for wanting relief. She was simply missing the knowledge that relief could exist without harm. That knowledge came later. And book is not just my journey to that part of the story, but hopefully where your story will begin.

When Pain Became the Narrator

What drives a child, a seemingly ordinary little girl, at least from the outside in, to wander so far into the shadows that death becomes a companion long before adulthood arrives? What quiet violence bends a young mind inside a not-quite-safe, not-quite-secure, not-quite-loving home, until disappearance feels more familiar than presence, and silence safer than speech? These are not questions born of curiosity or morbidity. They are questions born of aftermath, asked from the far side of survival, aching to understand how the path narrowed so early, how the world slowly taught a child to fold inward rather than reach out. What warps a child's sense of urgency so completely that solving the riddle of ending a life feels more pressing, more logical, than solving a page of math homework spread across a kitchen table? How does a young mind learn to calculate exits before it learns multiplication, to assess danger before it understands play, to weigh the cost of staying before it can even imagine becoming? Somewhere along the way, the future stopped feeling like a place to arrive and began to feel like something to endure, something to outlast rather than hope for. Tomorrow ceased to be a promise and became a test.

And what kind of childhood prayer ends not with "*Amen*", but with a whispered, trembling plea for oblivion? What kind of faith is shaped in fear, where the divine is not asked for guidance or protection, but for erasure? "*God, please, please just let me die.*" The words did not thunder. They barely breathed, slipping out like fog beneath a closed door. "*Show me mercy and end it all. Let me not open my eyes after I fall asleep.*" These were not blasphemies hurled in anger. They were the prayers of a child who believed mercy meant rest, who had learned that waking required a courage she no longer possessed. I did not pray for toys or triumphs or tomorrows. I did not ask for bigger dreams or brighter days. I prayed for silence. For stillness. For the great undoing of consciousness. Night after night, I handed my small life over to the dark, hoping it would keep me. Hoping sleep might become sanctuary instead of rehearsal. Hoping not to wake would be the gentlest kindness the world could offer. Bedtime was not comfort; it was negotiation. Morning was not renewal; it was failure.

I can see it now, with the clarity that distance grants and tenderness demands. These questions were never signs of a broken child. They were evidence of a child who had been left to translate pain alone. A child whose nervous system learned danger before safety, vigilance before ease, collapse before comfort. A child whose prayers were shaped not by hope, but by exhaustion. And it is here, in asking these questions without flinching, that the story deepens. Not to condemn the child I was. Not to pathologize her longing. But to finally listen to her with the compassion she never received. To understand that even in those darkest prayers, what she was asking for was not death itself, but relief. Rest. Mercy. A pause from vigilance. A world that felt gentle enough to stay awake in. And in naming that truth, something shifts. The shadows begin to loosen their grip. The questions no longer accuse. They illuminate. And for the first time, the child who once prayed to disappear is met, not with judgment, but with understanding.

Back then, I thought I understood. I believed I knew the culprits by name, could point to them like suspects lined up beneath a harsh light. I thought it was the pain, the hurt, the suffering and anguish, the endless betrayals that arrived one after another with cruel predictability. The bruises you cannot see but carry like ghosts beneath the skin, pale and persistent, pressing their cold memory into muscle and bone. I thought it was the weight of being unseen, unheard, the quiet suffocation of never being enough no matter how carefully I tried, no matter how brightly I learned to shine. I knew suffering intimately. I knew it the way one knows a lullaby hummed too often, its melody etched so deeply it plays even when the room is silent. I knew it the way smoke is known by those who breathe it slowly, day after day, invisible at first, then coating the lungs until breathing itself becomes effort, then pain. Suffering was not something that happened to me. It was something I lived inside. Pain was not an event with a beginning and an end. It was an atmosphere. It surrounded me, seeped into me, taught me its rhythms until I forgot what it felt like to inhale without burning.

In time, the hurt did not merely visit. It moved in. It unpacked itself with quiet confidence, as though it had always planned to stay. It wore my clothes, slept in my bed, borrowed my voice when I spoke about myself. It learned my schedule, anticipated my thoughts, and answered questions before I could even form them. Slowly, insidiously, it became my identity, not because it was all I was, but because it was all I was allowed to feel. Anything else felt dangerous. Anything else felt undeserved. I began to introduce myself to the world through its lens, measuring my worth by my wounds, my depth by my damage, my story by how much I had survived. I mistook it for truth. I mistook it for wisdom. I mistook it for me. And in doing so, I surrendered my name to my pain, let it speak for me, let it define the borders of my inner life. I believed that suffering had granted me insight, that endurance had granted me identity, that pain had earned the right to be my narrator. But I was wrong. So devastatingly, profoundly wrong.

Because pain, no matter how constant, is not character. Suffering, no matter how familiar, is not selfhood. Wounds do not equal wisdom, and endurance does not equal essence. What I could not see then was that the hurt had not become me. It had only grown loud enough to drown everything else out. It had taken the microphone, not because it was the truest voice, but because it was the only one, I had learned to listen to. Beneath it all, buried but intact, was a self still breathing. Still waiting. Still whole in ways I could not yet imagine. A self-holding a truth far older and far truer than the wounds that once claimed my name. A truth that did not need pain to validate its existence. A truth that had survived not because it was loud, but because it was resilient enough to wait until I was ready to hear it. And that realization, when it finally came, did not arrive gently. It arrived like a reckoning. Like light flooding a room, I had lived in the dark so long I thought the darkness was the walls.

Only much later, when healing demanded honesty instead of endurance, did I begin to see what hid beneath the ashes. Not in a single moment of clarity, but slowly, as smoke thins when the fire has burned itself out. When the air cleared just enough for my eyes to stop stinging, I realized I was not only the wounded child curled on the floor of her own pain. I was also the one standing over her, blade in hand, carving despair into something recognizable, something that felt like order. I had become both the victim and the sculptor of my suffering, the child who cried out for rescue and the same child who learned how to silence her own voice before anyone else could. I was a tormented little soul who grew into a tormented adolescent, and later into a woman who never learned how to stop setting herself on fire just to feel something other than numb. Pain became proof of existence. Heat became preferable to emptiness. Fire, at least, left sensation in its wake. I did not know how to rest inside myself without burning something down first. Stillness felt like disappearance. Quiet felt like erasure. Numbness felt too much like the death I had once prayed for, and so I chased sensation wherever it would flare, even if it scorched me in the process.

I was the bruised, and I was the one tightening the tourniquet. The abandoned, and the one abandoning herself. The hurting, and the one reopening her own wounds day after day, year after year. I learned how to perpetuate what had been done to me, not out of cruelty, but out of conditioning. Trauma trained my hands. Survival taught me repetition. I had absorbed the lesson that pain was familiar, controllable, deserved. That suffering, unlike tenderness, followed rules. I reenacted it because it made sense. Because it gave shape to chaos. Because somewhere deep inside, I believed suffering was the price of existing at all, the toll collected for taking up space, for breathing, for needing. This was the truth I had run from. The truth I had buried beneath decades of sorrow, beneath stories that kept me safely blameless but also safely stuck. Stories that protected me from shame but also from agency. Not because I wanted to punish myself further, but because I did not yet know how to hold complexity without collapsing. It was easier to believe I had only drowned than to face the more terrifying realization.

I did not just drown. I learned how to hold my own head underwater. That knowledge landed hard. It cracked something open. And yet, even in that realization, something softened. Because naming this truth was not an act of condemnation. It was an act of reclamation. To see my role was not to assign blame, but to return agency to a self that had once been powerless. It was to say: this is what you learned when no one taught you another way. If I had learned how to harm myself, then perhaps I could learn something else. If I had learned how to disappear, then perhaps I could learn how to stay. This is where healing stopped being about rescue and started being about responsibility. Not the heavy, punishing kind that mirrors abuse, but the quiet, radical kind that holds both compassion and truth. The kind that says: *I see what happened to you.* And also: *I see what you learned to do in order to survive.* And from that seeing, something new became possible. Not overnight. Not neatly. But genuinely. A different relationship with myself. One that no longer required fire to feel real. One that could begin, slowly, to learn what it meant to keep my own head above water.

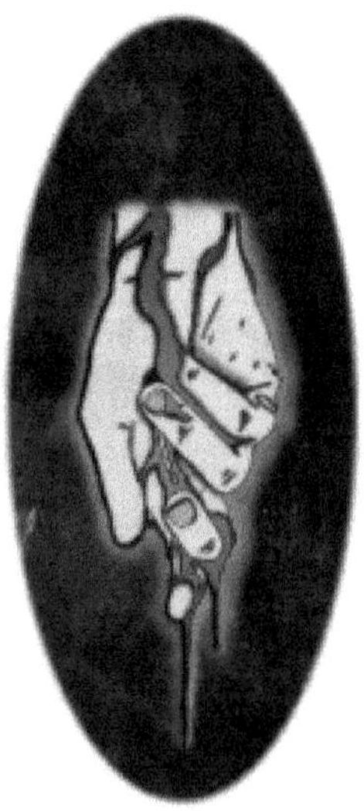

As I drifted into the treacherous waters of adolescence, that fragile space between childhood and becoming, my self-harm evolved into both punishment and counterfeit salvation. The shoreline of innocence slipped quietly behind me, and the currents grew colder, stronger, less forgiving. I was no longer only reacting to pain as it struck. I was ritualizing it, shaping it into something predictable. What began as desperation hardened into pattern, into habit, into something that felt essential for survival. It became the language my pain spoke when words failed me, the dialect my body used when my mouth had learned silence too well. When the burden of simply being me grew too sharp to hold, I retreated into shadow and performed the only ceremony I knew. I turned my own body into a battlefield. Not out of hatred, but out of a desperate need for order. Chaos roared everywhere else, but here, on skin and bone, I could draw lines. It became a sacrificial altar where I offered up pain in exchange for the illusion of control. Blood for quiet. Wounds for focus. Hurt for relief.

In a world that felt unpredictable and unsafe, pain became something I could initiate, something I could contain, something that answered when I called. It obeyed rules. It stayed where I put it. It gave me edges in a life that felt like it was dissolving, a boundary where everything else felt endless and unmoored. The emotional storms inside me were too vast, too wild, too untamed to touch directly. Grief without language. Rage without permission. Fear without shelter. They churned like oceans with no shoreline, dark and heaving, threatening to pull me under without warning. I could not name them. I could not soothe them. No one had taught me how. So I translated them. I traded the invisible for the visible. I exchanged terror for wounds I could see, wounds I could clean, wounds I could bandage and pretend were healing. At least these injuries followed a script. At least they pretended to resolve.

There was a terrible comfort in that exchange. A false mercy that felt like kindness in a cruel world. Physical pain had a beginning, a middle, an end. It bled. It scabbed. It closed. Emotional pain did not. It lingered like fog that never lifted, echoed like a sound that never found its source. It had no timeline, no promise of resolution. And so I chose the kind of suffering that lied to me with structure, that whispered I was doing something, fixing something, managing something. I mistook containment for healing and control for safety. But even then, beneath the ritual and the control, there was grief. Quiet and constant. Grief for a self who had never been taught how to feel safely, how to be held without being shaped. Grief for a body that had become both refuge and target, sanctuary and site of harm. I did not yet understand that I was trying to regulate an overwhelmed nervous system with the only tools I had been given. That this was not madness, but adaptation. Not weakness, but a desperate form of intelligence born in isolation.

All I knew was that I was surviving adolescence the only way I knew how: by making my pain small enough to hold, even if it meant carving it into myself. By turning something infinite into something finite. By choosing wounds that pretended to heal over emotions that threatened to drown me. And so the waters deepened. Childhood receded behind me like a fading shoreline, adolescence closed in around me with its relentless demands, and the strategies that once kept me afloat began to grow heavier with each passing year. What had once felt like a lifeline slowly became an anchor. I could not yet see where this path would lead, could not imagine another way of moving through the world. I only knew how to keep going through it the way I always had, one ritual, one wound, one breath at a time, treading water in an ocean I had never been taught how to leave.

When Pain Became a Language

And the old wounds. Yes, the skin closed. Yes, the scars faded. Time did what time does to flesh, knitting cells back together with quiet diligence, smoothing edges, softening evidence. But those tiny violences were never meant to mend the body. They were my fevered, desperate attempts to stitch together a soul unraveling thread by thread. I was not trying to heal skin. I was trying to keep myself from coming apart entirely, fastening what little coherence I had with whatever tools remained within reach. Each cut became a crimson blossom unfurling on the canvas of my skin, brief and terrible in its beauty, a proof of pain finally granted form. A secret garden of hurt I cultivated in silence, tended carefully in places no one could see, where no one would ask questions, I did not know how to answer. Blood-traced lines my mouth could not form. It spoke in red where language had abandoned me, wrote sentences my voice had never been allowed to finish.

Each bruise bloomed as a dark, swollen flower, purple and blue and yellowing with time, a quiet testament to the battles waged beneath my ribs. They were echoes of impact, aftershocks of collisions no one witnessed, reminders that something inside me had struck the world with too much force and nowhere to land. I wore them like hidden medals of endurance, evidence that I had survived yet another internal war no one knew was being fought, no one thought to ask about. Each carefully placed burn glowed like a brand, a searing whisper of the pain I refused to speak aloud. Fire left clarity where confusion reigned. Heat cut through numbness with brutal precision, slicing through dissociation like a blade of light. For a moment, sensation returned. For a moment, I could feel where I ended and the world began. The burn marked me not as damaged, but as present, if only briefly, if only through pain. Presence, even painful presence, felt preferable to vanishing.

These wounds were not chaos. They were communication. They were attempts at coherence in a body flooded with feelings too vast, too uncontained to hold. I was trying to translate the unspeakable into something finite, something that could scab, something that pretended at resolution. Flesh, at least, understood endings. Flesh knew how to close. Flesh knew how to heal, even when the soul wandered without map or mercy. And so I marked myself, not because I hated myself, but because I was trying to save something I did not yet know how to name. I was trying to keep my insides from spilling out, trying to anchor myself in sensation when dissociation threatened to erase me entirely. These were not acts of destruction alone. They were acts of survival, misunderstood, desperate, and flawed, shaped by a nervous system doing the only thing it knew how to do to stay alive.

The scars faded, yes. They softened, thinned, slipped quietly into the background of my skin. But what they were meant to hold together ran far deeper than flesh. They were sutures for something invisible, something ancient and wounded and still breathing beneath the surface. And it would take far more than time for that kind of mending to begin. It would take learning a new language entirely, one that did not require blood to be believed, one that could finally tend the soul those wounds had been trying, all along, to save. It was a clandestine ritual, my hidden religion of suffering, practiced in secrecy and silence, observed with a devotion born of desperation rather than belief. A private liturgy enacted behind closed doors, where no one could interrupt the ceremony or question the offering. There were no hymns, no witnesses, only the steady breath of a body bracing itself.

A pinch here to quiet the scream that had no safe audience. A slice there to silence the ache that refused logic or reassurance. A burn to cauterize the grief, to seal it shut before it spilled everywhere and betrayed me. With each mark, I told myself I was releasing something, letting the darkness bleed out, softening the crushing weight that sat like a stone on my chest. I believed I was emptying myself of pain, draining the poison one wound at a time, purifying myself through suffering. But the truth was far more devastating. I wasn't purging the pain. I was feeding it. What I thought was release was reinforcement. What I thought was relief was rehearsal. I was practicing despair until it became fluent. Layering wound upon wound, I was teaching my body a brutal equation it would remember long after my mind tried to forget: Hurt equals calm, harm equals control. Pain became instruction. Ritual became regulation.

I was constructing a cage of my own making, bar by bar, ritual by ritual, mistaking familiarity for safety because it was all I had ever known. Every act of harm added another stone to the tower of self-destruction I was trapped inside, lifting the walls higher even as I searched frantically for a way out. I wasn't escaping. I was sinking. Slowly. Silently. Submerged in the tide of my own unspoken sorrow, lungs filling with words I had never learned how to say. Grief pressed in from all sides, heavy and cold, as the water rose inch by inch. So gradually, I barely noticed until breathing itself became effort, until each inhale felt borrowed and each exhale felt wasted. I thrashed inwardly, quietly, afraid of making noise, afraid of being seen, afraid that even if I called out, no one would come, or worse, that I would be told to swim harder.

And the most unbearable truth of all was this: I did not know how to escape. I had learned how to endure. How to survive inside the cage. How to decorate it with rituals that gave the illusion of control, how to pace its narrow floor without screaming. But I had never been taught how to leave. I had never been shown a door. No one had said, "*You don't have to hurt yourself to be held.*" No one had said, "*There is another way to breathe.*" So I stayed. Performing the liturgy. Building the tower. Drowning without a splash. Becoming so practiced at sinking that it looked like stillness from the surface. Not because I wanted to disappear, but because I had not yet been given another way to stay.

I convinced myself that every wound I carved into my skin was justice, that the harm I inflicted was the only appropriate sentence for a life I believed brought nothing but burden and ruin. I stood as both judge and executioner in a private court convened inside my chest, where mercy had been outlawed and compassion dismissed as corruption. The verdict was decided before the trial ever began. I punished myself for taking up space, for breathing too loudly, for needing too much, for wanting comfort in a world that had taught me comfort was something to be earned. I punished myself for failing to disappear gracefully enough. Each injury felt like balance restored, order imposed on a world I believed I had fractured simply by existing. It became a warped theology of punishment, a faith built on blame and self-erasure, a desperate quest for absolution written in blood and bruise. I believed suffering was purification, that pain could scrub me clean of whatever invisible stain I carried beneath my skin.

In my mind, pain became currency, a twisted offering of repentance paid in red, black, and blue. The deeper the hurt, the more sincere the apology. The more damage I endured, the closer I imagined myself to forgiveness. I was trying to buy absolution in a marketplace that only ever demanded more, a system rigged to keep me perpetually indebted. Somewhere along the way, this belief calcified into doctrine. It hardened, set, and became unquestionable law. I began to believe that pain was the price I had to pay simply for existing, that hurt was the toll collected for being alive in the world. Joy felt fraudulent, like a clerical error that would soon be corrected. Ease felt undeserved, temporary, and suspicious. Any moment of peace arrived already laced with guilt, already bracing for punishment. Pain, at least, felt honest. Pain felt earned. Pain felt like the only language the universe recognized from me, the only proof I knew how to offer that I understood my place and accepted my sentence.

And so I spoke it fluently. I answered every question with harm. Every discomfort with punishment. Every flicker of hope with a reminder of my supposed unworthiness. I silenced softness before it could bloom. I corrected joy before it could settle. I did not yet know that this belief was not the truth, but training. Not conscience, but conditioning. A system was installed long before I was old enough to consent to it. I could not yet see that no universe worthy of reverence demands blood for breath, nor bruises for belonging, nor suffering as proof of worth. At the time, all I knew was the exchange. Hurt in, silence out. Pain offered, judgment postponed. I believed I was paying my debt in full, day after day, wound after wound, never realizing that the debt itself had been invented. That the ledger was false. That I had been sentencing myself for a crime that never existed.

And it is here, at the edge of that realization, that the story presses toward its next turning. Because once punishment is named as undeserved, once a theology of pain is exposed as false, the ground begins to shift. The questions grow sharper, more dangerous, more liberating. It is no longer *How much more must I suffer?* It becomes: *Who taught me that I ever had to?* And just beyond that question waits another, quieter one, trembling with possibility: *What might become of me if I stopped believing pain was the price of being alive?*

I thought I deserved it, that the world would somehow be balanced if I punished myself harshly enough, deeply enough, quietly enough. As though pain could act as a counterweight, as though suffering might tip the scales back into some imagined equilibrium where my presence no longer felt like a transgression. If I hurt myself sufficiently, perhaps the damage I believed I caused simply by existing would be neutralized. Perhaps the universe would exhale. Perhaps I would finally be allowed to stay without apology, without debt. Self-harm became my silent sanctuary, a dark, distorted form of meditation where the accusations in my mind finally found a place to land. In those moments, the noise narrowed to a single point. The chaos condensed. The world shrank to breath and sensation. It was a ritual where my breath slowed, my body focused, my thoughts sharpened into knives precise enough to cut through the fog. A place where the self-accusing voices that haunted me no longer circled endlessly like vultures, but poured out through my hands, finally given direction, finally given form. Pain became containment. Injury became order.

In that private stillness, the venom of self-loathing moved through me like a poisoned hymn, familiar and hypnotic, sung so often I knew every note by heart. Every thought became a whip, striking rhythmically, methodically. Every memory turned into a blade, flashing sharp and bright, demanding retribution. I replayed my perceived failures like indictments, recited my flaws like scripture, convinced that pain was the only honest response to who I was. The ritual did not argue with me. It did not question my conclusions or ask for evidence. It simply agreed, again and again, in flesh. For a brief moment, there was relief. Not peace, but quiet. Not healing, but containment. The mind stilled because the body spoke. The accusations softened because they had been answered. I mistook that temporary hush for truth, for resolution, for something like grace. I mistook silence for absolution. I did not yet see that this sanctuary was built on harm, that the stillness it offered was purchased at a terrible cost, that each moment of quiet demanded interest paid in blood and belief.

Because what I was really doing was giving my inner persecutor a pulpit, letting it preach uninterrupted. I was turning myself into both confessional and punishment, altar and sacrifice. I believed I was mastering my pain, bending it to my will, when in truth I was being mastered by it, allowing it to choreograph my breathing, my beliefs, my worth. I let it tell me who I was, what I deserved, how much I should suffer to earn the right to exist. And still, even then, beneath the hymn and the blades and the ritualized quiet, something resisted. Something endured. A small, stubborn pulse that did not sing the same song. It was not loud enough to interrupt the ritual. It did not yet have words. It only kept time. I could not hear it then. The venom was too loud. The knives too close. But it was there, waiting, gathering strength in the silence between the strikes, in the breath after the pain, in the moments when the ritual ended and I was still alive.

It was learning. Watching. Remembering something I had forgotten. Preparing, slowly and patiently, for the moment when punishment would no longer feel like truth, and sanctuary would have to be redefined not as a place where pain ends the noise, but as a place where I would no longer need pain to be heard. When the torment inside grew too loud to contain, I would grip the soft flesh of my inner thigh, digging my fingernails in until the skin surrendered and thin rivers of blood rose to the surface. It wasn't impulsive. It was ritual. Precise. Deliberate. A choreography of suffering I had perfected in silence, rehearsed until my hands knew the steps before my mind could object. In that moment, pain felt like order, like a language that obeyed me when nothing else would, a grammar of sensation that brought the world back into sharp focus.

Every mark was carefully placed in the shadows, away from prying eyes, wounds hidden beneath clothing, bruises tucked into the margins of my body where no one would ever think to look. I curated my hurt the way others curated appearances, attentive to detail, mindful of angles and coverage. I learned how to conceal with elegance, how to keep the performance intact. To the world, I remained composed, competent, whole. Inside, I was bleeding quietly, convinced that secrecy was safety, that invisibility was protection, that if no one saw the damage, it could not be questioned or taken from me. I orchestrated my pain with meticulous intention, ensuring each scar remained unseen, each bruise a quiet confession only the darkness was allowed to witness. The night became my accomplice, the silence my confessor.

I trusted the dark with truths I could not trust to daylight, confiding in shadows because they asked nothing and promised nothing. In hiding my wounds, I believed I was preserving order, sparing others from discomfort, sparing myself from questions I did not know how to answer, questions that felt as dangerous as exposure itself. And yet, even as I hid so carefully, there was a paradox at work. I wanted to be unseen, and I wanted to be known. I wanted the pain to stay secret, and I wanted it to matter. Each hidden mark carried a plea I could not voice, pressed into skin like a message without an address. *See me without looking. Believe me without proof.* I did not yet understand that the careful concealment was another way of disappearing, another refinement of the same old strategy that had taught me to survive by shrinking.

This was how survival learned to masquerade as control. How secrecy dressed itself as strength. How silence pretended to be safety. I believed I was protecting myself by keeping the darkness contained, locking it behind skin and fabric and composure, not realizing that what is never witnessed never gets healed. I was guarding my wounds as if exposure would destroy me, unaware that the real danger was carrying them alone, letting them fester in the quiet where no mercy could reach. And so the ritual continued, perfected and hidden, a private language spoken only in the dark. Each repetition reinforced the rules I lived by: stay quiet, stay contained, stay unseen. Until one day, much later, the question finally rose, soft but unrelenting, cutting through the habit like dawn through a closed room: *What if the pain does not need to be hidden to be held?*

The Mask That Learned How to Bleed

Until that dawn, on the outside, I remained intact. The polite smile. The capable child. The golden girl who knew how to perform wholeness with practiced ease. I learned how to hold my shoulders just right, how to keep my voice steady, how to meet the world with a face that promised nothing was wrong. I carried myself like someone who had it together, someone reliable, someone untouched. The mask fit so well it began to feel fused, praised often enough that even I started to forget it was not my skin. But beneath the surface, under layers of fabric and false strength, my body told a very different story. My skin became an archive, a quiet ledger of truths never spoken aloud. A story written in crimson. A story of a child, then a teenager, and then an adult, all desperately trying to bleed out an ache no one else could see. Each mark was a sentence in a language only I could read, a record of nights survived and mornings endured. The body remembered what the mouth had been trained to deny, what politeness had buried, what obedience had silenced.

I tried to burn away the pain, as though fire could cauterize memory itself, as though heat might erase what had etched itself into my nervous system. I tried to suffocate the despair, pressing it inward until it bruised rather than screamed, until it learned how to stay quiet enough to pass unnoticed. I hid the inner turmoil behind blackened bruises and careful concealment, convincing myself that if the damage stayed private, it stayed manageable. That if no one saw the wounds, they could not question the story I told the world. Composure above. Catastrophe below. A life split neatly down the middle. The contrast was stark. Applause on the outside. Silence underneath. I lived as two selves sharing one body, one fluent in performance, the other fluent in pain. One learned how to be useful, pleasing, and admirable. The other learned how to endure, absorb, disappear. The world applauded the shine and never thought to ask what it cost. And I, desperate to be believed as strong, offered my suffering only to the dark, trusting shadows more than people, trusting harm more than help.

I did not yet understand that this division was not strength, but fracture. That holding everything together by hiding it was slowly tearing me apart, pulling me thinner with every secret carried alone. I did not yet know that survival built on concealment demands payment, that invisibility corrodes from the inside. All I knew then was how to keep going, how to smile through the ache, how to let my skin carry what my voice never could. And so I moved through the world intact in appearance, unraveling in private, believing this was the only way to survive a life that had never taught me how to be safely seen. Believing that to be visible was to be vulnerable, and to be vulnerable was to be undone. It would take years before I learned that being seen does not have to mean being shattered, and that the body was never meant to be the sole witness to the truth.

The first time I harmed myself, I was only a child, too young to understand the language of my own ache, yet old enough to feel its weight pressing against my ribs, heavy and insistent, as if something inside me were knocking to be let out. I did not have words for what was happening within my small, crowded body. I only knew there was too much of something. Too much feeling. Too much fear. Too much unnamed grief swelling and pressing, looking for a seam, a crack, a way to escape. I cannot remember the exact moment, the trigger, the spark that lit it, but I remember the sensation with haunting clarity, as though my body memorized it before my mind ever could. I remember the relief. That strange, forbidden easing that washed through me like a warm tide, the way the first sunrays touch frozen skin on a winter morning, shocking and soothing all at once.

Pain and comfort braided together in a way I had never known. For the first time, the pressure shifted. The noise softened. The storm paused, hovering instead of crashing. It was as though I had finally found a release valve for the chaos I carried inside, a way to let the pain move instead of trapping it in my chest where it had been suffocating me, tightening my breath, stealing my air. In that moment, something clicked into place, quietly and irrevocably. I had discovered a way to translate the unspeakable into something visible, tangible, something I could touch and point to and tend. The ache that had no name suddenly had form. The pain that had lived everywhere and nowhere now lived in one place, small enough to hold, sharp enough to feel. My body had done what my voice could not. It had spoken, clearly and without apology. I did not understand the danger then. I did not know I was laying the first stone on a path that would stretch far beyond childhood, winding through years I could not yet imagine. All I knew was that for the first time, I felt a sense of control, a momentary calm, a stillness that felt like mercy.

Relief arrived not as comfort, but as quiet. And quiet, to a child drowning in too much, felt like safety. That first wound was not born of a desire to destroy myself. It was born of a desperate need to survive what I did not yet know how to endure. It was a child reaching for relief with the only tools available, mistaking the easing of pain for healing, mistaking silence for peace. I could not yet see the cost of that discovery. I could only feel the calm it offered, brief and intoxicating. And so the body remembered. It remembered the warmth. The pause. The way the storm briefly stepped back and gave me room to breathe. It stored that knowledge deep in muscle and nerve, in reflex and sensation, long before my mind had the wisdom to question it. What began as an instinct became a solution. What became a solution would one day become a habit, etched into me with repetition and time. But in that first moment, there was only a child, standing at the edge of something vast and unknowable, believing she had finally found a way to breathe, unaware that the very thing offering relief would one day ask for so much more in return.

Those early marks became my secret alphabet, a private script written on skin when spoken language failed me. Cuts spoke when my voice refused to rise. Bruises whispered what my mouth could not form. Burns etched the rough outline of emotions I had no other language for, a physical manifestation of breath trapped in the lungs, of an inner suffocation finally given shape. When my chest felt sealed shut by feeling, my body opened a different door. What could not be exhaled became visible, legible at last. There was a twisted kind of clarity in it. A terrible relief in translation. I learned how to convert emotional chaos into pain I could measure, pain I could name, pain I could inflict on my own terms. Feelings were wild, ungovernable, without edges or instruction manuals. Pain was precise. It arrived with sensation, followed rules, obeyed cause and effect. It began here. It ended there. It could be counted. Timed. Treated. Unlike grief, unlike fear, unlike the ache of being unseen, pain made sense to me.

This pain had structure. This pain had rules. This pain answered when called. In a world where nothing else responded reliably, pain did. When I reached for it, it came. When I needed it to speak, it spoke. When I needed proof that something inside me was real, it offered evidence without argument. It did not dismiss me. It did not minimize me. It did not tell me I was imagining things. Pain was honest in a way people had not been, blunt and immediate, unafraid of the truth it delivered. So I learned its grammar. I learned its rhythms and its thresholds, the subtle line between enough and too much. I learned how to stop just short of being discovered, how to hide fluency beneath fabric and composure. I treated pain like a language that would never betray me, like a companion that would always answer in kind. It became the interpreter between my inner world and my outer body, bridging a gap no one else seemed willing to cross with me, translating despair into sensation I could manage.

I did not yet understand that this clarity was a mirage. That what felt like control was actually captivity, that the rules I trusted were tightening around me with every repetition. That a language built on harm would eventually demand fluency at a cost I could not afford, asking for more proof, more sacrifice, more silence. At the time, all I knew was that for the first time, something inside me made sense. And when you grow up in confusion and silence, when your feelings have no names and your needs no witnesses, anything that offers meaning can feel like salvation. Even pain. And in the illusion, and the delusion, that I could both wound and heal myself, I felt something dangerously intoxicating: power. Power in a life where I otherwise had none. A fragile, flickering authority wrested from chaos, held together by ritual and resolve. I became a child playing both victim and savior, both the broken thing curled on the floor and the heroic nurse kneeling beside it, steady-handed and solemn.

I tended to wounds I had carved myself, cleansed them, wrapped them, watched them close. In that closed loop of injury and care, I mistook control for competence, mastery for safety. For a moment, I was no longer helpless. I was the one deciding when the pain began and when it ended, the one holding the switch to the only quiet I knew. But power borrowed from harm always comes with interest. With every passing day, the ritual escalated. The pain deepened. What once whispered now demanded. What once soothed began to command. The relief that had arrived like mercy slowly hardened into expectation, then obligation, until it felt less like choice and more like debt. The body learned the pattern too well. It began to ask for more. The stillness shortened. The quiet thinned. The pause between storms grew brief and brittle. What had felt like sanctuary revealed itself as a room with no windows, its doors quietly locking behind me while I was still arranging the furniture.

The prison bars were invisible, but they were everywhere. In my thoughts, tightening before I could notice. In my reflexes, moving ahead of intention. In the way my hands knew what to do before my mind could intervene. I had become the architect of my suffering, yes, but also its most faithful inhabitant. I paced the narrow corridors of a structure I had designed to keep myself alive, mistaking familiarity for freedom because it was the only map I had learned to read. What began as a whisper became a cycle. What became a cycle hardened into pattern. What hardened into pattern became inheritance, passed not from generation to generation, but from moment to moment, wound to wound. A dark legacy carried not in stories but in muscle memory, not in family lore but in skin. A habit I could not seem to put down because it had once saved me.

I did not yet know how to grieve that truth: that the thing which kept me alive had also begun to cost me my life, inch by inch, breath by breath. I was no longer choosing the ritual. The ritual was choosing me. And still, beneath the bars, beneath the repetition, beneath the illusion of power, something remained awake. Watching. Waiting. Learning. A quiet intelligence that had survived every version of me, taking notes in the margins of pain. It did not shout. It did not intervene. It simply endured, patient as roots beneath concrete, gathering strength in the dark. Because even cages built for survival can be unbuilt. But first, they must be seen for what they are. These were not cries for help, at least not in the way the world imagines them. They were not pleas to be rescued, not flares launched skyward in the hope that someone might finally see me drowning.

I was not waiting to be interrupted. I was not hoping to be found. What I was doing lived far deeper than performance or appeal. It was inward. Ancient. Wordless. Something older than narrative, older than explanation, moving through me like instinct rather than intention. They were rituals born of a wound so old, so primal, it existed long before I had language for suffering. A wound that predated memory, that lived in the body before it ever reached the mind. It was etched into the nervous system, written in the tightening of breath, in the way my shoulders lifted defensively even in quiet rooms, in the way my muscles braced for impact where none came.

These acts did not ask for witnesses. They required solitude. Silence. Control. They belonged to a realm beneath observation, beneath interpretation. They were my penance. A private communion with pain.

A twisted altar erected in the hidden chambers of my life, where I laid offerings of blood and bruise in an effort to make sense of a guilt I could never name. I did not know what crime I was atoning for. I only knew the verdict had already been delivered. I felt guilty for existing. Guilty for needing. Guilty for taking up space in a world that had never quite made room for me. And so I punished myself for sins that had no words, no evidence, no origin I could point to, only a certainty lodged deep in my bones, humming beneath every thought. In that private theology, pain was purification. Suffering was sincerity. The more it hurt, the more earnest the offering felt. Pain became proof that I understood my place, that I accepted the terms of my existence. I believed I was keeping some unseen balance, appeasing some invisible judge, restoring order through harm. I was not asking to be saved. I was trying to be forgiven for a life I had been taught, implicitly and repeatedly, was somehow excessive, inconvenient, too much.

And this is the part so often misunderstood. I was not seeking attention. I was seeking coherence. I was not trying to die in those moments. I was trying to live with myself. Trying to quiet a sense of wrongness that clung to me like a second skin. Trying to make peace with a body and a being that felt perpetually misaligned with the world around it, always one breath out of sync. It would take many years before I could see this clearly. Before I could understand that these rituals were not evidence of a desire to disappear, but evidence of a desperate attempt to belong. Not to others, but to myself. To find some way, however flawed, to justify my own existence in a world that had taught me I needed to earn the right to breathe. Only later would I learn what no one told the child I was. That no child needs to bleed to be innocent. That nobody needs to be punished to be worthy. And that no soul commits a crime simply by being alive.

The Logic of Guilt That Was Never Mine

It was a logic forged in shadow, the kind only a wounded child could understand, the kind that grows where light never quite reaches. A reasoning shaped not by reason, but by survival, by the desperate need to make sense of pain when no explanation is offered and no comfort arrives. In that dark arithmetic, every drop of blood became currency, every bruise a confession, every burn a vow renewed. *You deserve this. You must pay for existing.* The equations were cruel but consistent, and consistency felt like truth in a world that offered little else to hold onto. I carried an unspoken conviction that I had arrived in this world already wrong, already tainted, already guilty of something vast and unforgivable. As if I had violated some sacred law before my first breath ever left my lungs. As if I had broken a rule written in invisible ink long before I learned the difference between right and wrong, long before anyone taught me what mercy looked like.

I did not know what the crime was. I only knew that it felt ancient, etched into me deeper than memory, humming beneath my skin like a verdict passed down through generations, unquestioned and absolute. And so I punished myself for a crime I could never remember committing, but always, always felt within my bones. Guilt lived in my posture, in the way my shoulders curved inward, in the way I shrank when spoken to, in the reflexive apologies that fell from my mouth for taking up air. It followed me like a shadow that lengthened in quiet moments, growing darker when no one was watching, reminding me of a sentence I believed I was serving simply by being alive. I did not need reminders from the world. I carried the judge inside me, vigilant and unforgiving.

That guilty verdict, I painted on my body. In scars. In blood. In bruises. I turned flesh into testimony, skin into proof, my body into a ledger of imagined sins. Each mark said what I could not speak aloud: *I know I am wrong. I accept the punishment.* I believed that if I punished myself thoroughly enough, harshly enough, long enough, I might finally atone for whatever unnamed transgression I believed had marked me from the start. Pain became confession. Endurance became absolution deferred. It never occurred to me then that this logic was not truth, but inheritance. Not conscience, but conditioning. A child's attempt to explain why pain arrived without reason, why love felt conditional, why safety seemed so easily withdrawn. In the absence of answers, I became the explanation. In the absence of mercy, I became the sentence. I internalized the world's silences and turned them inward, mistaking abandonment for evidence.

And it would take many years, and a tenderness I did not yet possess, to question the premise itself. To pause long enough to wonder whether the rule I believed I had broken had ever existed at all. To consider the unthinkable possibility that I was never guilty, never wrong for arriving, never required to bleed in order to belong. That truth, however, still rests in the shadows, for there is more to my story. The burning was always the worst, not solely for the sting of heat against skin, though that pain was sharp and merciless, a wildfire licking where flesh was never meant to know flame. It was not the intensity alone that undid me. It was the intention behind it. The choice. The moment of consent to my own undoing. The slow, deliberate choreography of self-destruction that preceded the pain, each second stretching long enough to know exactly what I was about to do and to do it anyway, without illusion, without escape.

That was the unbearable part. The pause where decision hardened into action. The instant when I crossed a threshold inside myself and could not pretend it was an accident, could not hide behind impulse or chaos. I pressed forward knowing what would come, watching the body respond before my mind could turn away. Flesh blanching. Blistering. Curling inward on itself as if trying to retreat from the choice I had already made. The sickening scent of my own body surrendering rose into the air, thick and unmistakable, like incense drifting upward from an altar of self-hatred, a sacrifice I believed was required to keep the world in balance. In those moments, I felt both powerful and erased. Powerful because I had chosen. Erased because the choice was to harm myself. The burn demanded my full attention, collapsing the world down to sensation alone.

Thought vanished. Memory dissolved. Time narrowed to heat and breath and the unbearable clarity that I was doing this to myself on purpose. Pain became proof of agency twisted inward, a declaration that if I could not control the world, I could at least control the moment of my own suffering. If I could not stop what hurt me, I could become the one who decided when it hurt. The smell lingered longer than the pain. It clung to me, lodged itself somewhere behind my eyes, a ghost I carried with me long after the skin cooled. It was a reminder that I had crossed yet another line, that I had taken myself somewhere I could not un-know. Shame and relief braided together so tightly I could not tell where one ended and the other began. I told myself it was necessary. I told myself it was cleansing. I told myself this was what I deserved. The logic of the shadow returned, soothing and cruel all at once, wrapping itself around the aftermath like a familiar cloak.

What I did not yet understand was that the horror of those moments was not evidence of my brokenness, but evidence of how deeply I was still alive. That the part of me recoiling in revulsion, the part sickened by the smell, the part trembling at the choice itself, was not weakness. It was the last remaining witness, horrified but present, refusing to disappear entirely. It was the part of me that still knew this was not meant to be my language, even as I kept speaking it. But at the time, all I could feel was the weight of the act, the finality of the choice, the ritual completed. Another vow renewed. Another offering made. Another layer added to the belief that pain was the price of existing, and that I alone was responsible for paying it in full. And so I carried on, believing survival meant sacrifice, believing my body was the debt collector, believing the fire was proof that I was still here, even as it quietly consumed what little gentleness remained.

It was grotesque, and yet, in some twisted corner of my broken psyche, it felt like confirmation. Validation. Proof. "*This is who you are. This is what you deserve.*" The damage became evidence, the suffering a signature I could point to and say, "*See? This is not imagined.*" Pain did not contradict the story I believed about myself; it confirmed it. It aligned perfectly with the verdict already etched into my bones, reinforcing the lie that harm was my natural state, my native language, my inheritance. When I looked in the mirror afterward, I did not see a child, a teenager, or a woman. I did not see a girl in pain. I saw an enemy. A stranger with hollow eyes staring back at me, unrecognizable and unforgiving. A creature carved from rage and grief, shaped by years of silence and self-blame, by nights spent negotiating with despair.

A monster I could neither comfort nor escape. The reflection accused without speaking, its gaze sharp and unrelenting, as if it were daring me to deny what I had done, what I was. As if it were saying, "*You see? Even you cannot love this.*" That mirror became a courtroom, too. The face looking back felt like the prosecution, listing charges I already believed beyond appeal. Too much. Too weak. Too broken. Too wrong. The eyes held no tenderness, only distance, only a cold appraisal that offered no reprieve. I searched them for softness and found none, convinced this absence was truth rather than trauma. I mistook dissociation for revelation. I mistook numbness for clarity. I believed that the emptiness I saw was my essence, not the cost of everything I had carried.

And somewhere in that cold exchange, a deeper realization flickered, though I could not yet name it. The real wound was not on my skin. It was beneath it. In the marrow. In the soul. The burns, the cuts, the bruises were never the destination. They were mirrors. Translation points. Desperate attempts to draw the inner wounds outward, to give shape to an agony that refused to stay contained. To make suffering legible, even if only to myself. I was trying to excise the pain by carving it into places I could reach. Trying to pull the poison from the depths by letting it surface in flesh. The body became a map of what I could not articulate, a landscape marked by symbols instead of words. Each wound said, "*Here. Look here. This is where it hurts.*" But the ache always remained, untouched, because it lived in places no blade could reach, no fire could cauterize.

At the time, I believed the reflection told the truth. That I was monstrous. That I was irredeemable. That comfort was something meant for other people, for better people, for those who had not failed so fundamentally at being human. I did not yet understand that what stared back at me was not my essence, but my suffering wearing my face. Pain masquerading as identity. Trauma standing in for self. That understanding would come later. Much later. For then, all I knew was the mirror, the accusation, and the quiet certainty that the wounds I could see were only echoes of a far deeper injury still waiting to be named. And yet, being met by my own blood was never enough. Recognition without relationship is a hollow mercy. The moment passed, the skin closed, the silence returned, heavier for having briefly lifted. What answered me was still only me, echoing back in a chamber that remained otherwise empty.

I had mistaken response for relief, sensation for solace. The body could acknowledge the pain, but it could not soothe it. It could speak, but it could not stay. What I was reaching for, again and again, was not proof of suffering but permission to have it. Not spectacle, but sanctuary. I wanted the hurt to be allowed to exist without requiring injury as its passport. I wanted someone to sit beside it without flinching, to hold it without asking me to translate it into wounds. I wanted to be believed on sight, not only when pain announced itself in red. Instead, I learned a terrible intimacy with absence. I learned how to meet myself where no one else would come. I learned how to offer witness when the world remained silent. It kept me alive, in its way, this self-made communion. But it also kept me alone, teaching me to accept substitutes for connection, to settle for echoes instead of voices.

Only much later would I begin to unlearn that lesson. To understand that pain does not need to bleed to be real. That suffering does not require spectacle to be worthy of care. That the ache I carried had always deserved witness simply because it existed. That I existed. At the time, I could not know this. I only knew the door, the pressure, the brief answering hush. I only knew how to keep opening what I had access to, even when it led nowhere. But even then, beneath the ritual and the wounds and the mistaken communion, the longing itself was intact. Clear. Unmistakable. I was not asking to be harmed. I was asking to be held.

The Altar of Proof and the Lifeline That Cut

In that twisted exchange, the crimson flow became a mirror reflecting the storms I carried inside, a surface slick with truth I could no longer swallow. A physical echo of an emotional tempest, thunder translated into flesh, lightning finding a body to strike. It was the only way I knew how to take what raged unseen and give it edges, weight, consequence. A way to make the invisible suffering visible, if only to myself, if only in the private language of skin and breath. Pain became evidence. Blood became testimony. What could not be spoken learned how to spill. It was a ritual, dark, distorted, desperate. A choreography rehearsed in silence, enacted with trembling precision. A sacrifice laid at the feet of some nameless god carved from self-loathing, a deity born not of faith but of fear, not of worship but of survival. A god who demanded proof of my suffering, receipts written in red, and I gave it willingly.

I believed devotion required damage. I believed sincerity had to hurt. I believed that without wounds, my pain would be dismissed as imaginary, indulgent, unearned. So I offered the only currency I thought held value. Blood. Scars. Bruises. Marks that could not argue back. Marks that stayed. I let them speak where my voice had been trained to disappear, let them say, here it is, this is how much it hurts, this is how real it is, this is how badly I am trying to survive. I believed the body was the altar and the evidence all at once, that if I could just show enough proof, the god would relent, the storm would quiet, the ache would finally be allowed to rest. But the god never softened. It only watched. And I did not yet see that what I was kneeling before was not divinity at all, but a mirror shaped like punishment, reflecting back a version of myself I had been taught to mistake for truth.

The god never answered, because gods forged from self-loathing do not absolve. They feed. They sit in the hollow center of the ritual, patient and unsated, learning my thresholds, memorizing my breaking points, adjusting their hunger to whatever I was willing to give. Each offering sharpened its appetite. Each wound taught it how to ask for more. And still I returned, mistaking familiarity for faith, obedience for safety, endurance for worthiness. I thought I was appeasing something outside of me, never realizing I was rehearsing a sentence already etched into my bones. Kneeling there, I felt both priest and sacrifice, hands steady while my insides trembled. The blade, the heat, the pressure became liturgy, gestures as precise as prayer. I learned the order of things. The pause before. The breath held too long. The moment where decision crossed into inevitability. In that narrow corridor of sensation, the world collapsed into a single point. Thought dissolved.

At first, I did not question the lifeline. I hung to it with the desperation of someone who had been treading water too long. I clung to it the way a drowning body clings without strategy or dignity, fingers locking tight around whatever resists the pull. My lungs burned with borrowed air. My muscles shook with the effort of staying upright in a sea that never calmed. Anything that kept me afloat, that kept my head above the surface felt merciful. Anything that gave form to the flood felt like rescue. Anything that interrupted the undertow felt like grace. I did not pause to examine the rope. I did not test its fibers. I did not ask what it was made of. When you are drowning, you do not audit salvation. You grab. You hold. You survive. I did not yet understand that a lifeline made of wire will eventually cut into the hands that grasp it. All I knew was that it held.

Pain taught me where my edges were when I could not feel myself otherwise. Pain gave shape to the flood when everything else blurred into terror. It condensed the chaos into something I could point to, something that had a beginning and an end. In a world where emotions came like storms without forecast or shelter, pain arrived with structure. It drew borders where I felt boundless. It traced my outline in fire and red, sketching me back into existence when dissociation tried to erase my edges entirely. Reminding me that I existed, that I occupied space, that I had a body that could still respond. In moments when dissociation threatened to dissolve me entirely, pain anchored me back into flesh. It said, "*You are here*, and here you are. This is where you stop. This is where you begin."

And in moments when I felt myself thinning, dissolving, drifting from my own skin, that declaration mattered. Being here, even scorched, even bleeding, felt preferable to vanishing without a trace. But refuge slowly became residence. But refuge has a way of changing its shape when it is visited too often. What began as shelter slowly learned how to close its doors. The pause lengthened. The ritual repeated. Relief, once surprising, became expected. And what is expected begins to demand loyalty. What once felt like a choice began to feel like a requirement. The storm returned faster each time, angrier, more insistent, as if it had memorized the route, as if my body had taught it exactly where to land. The noise grew sharper, more insistent, arriving with the certainty of habit.

And the refuge, once wide enough to breathe in, began to tighten, its walls inching closer with every return, its exits dimming until they felt theoretical. Pain anchored me when my mind floated too far from my body. It slammed me back into sensation, back into gravity, back into the undeniable fact of flesh. Heat. Sting. Pulse. Breath. These were coordinates I could follow home. When numbness spread like fog, when the world dulled and my name felt distant, pain cut a clean path through the haze. It was brutal, yes, but it was precise. It said, you are not gone yet. And that was enough. That had to be enough.

Still, I returned. Not because it worked or truly healed me, but because it was familiar. Familiarity can masquerade as safety when you have never known gentler ground. Pain had become a place I understood, a landscape I could navigate, even if it injured me in the process. A map I had memorized by touch, I knew its landmarks. I knew how far I could go without being discovered. I knew the rules. And in a life where nothing else felt predictable, that knowledge felt like power. It was easier to walk a road that wounded me and hurt than to stand still in uncharted ground and to wander without direction at all, waiting for something I did not trust would arrive.

I did not yet know another way to meet myself. I had not been shown how to sit with feeling without translating it into damage. No one had taught me how to let emotions crest and break like waves, how to trust that they would recede on their own. No one had taught me how to let emotions rise and fall without punishment, how to trust that they would pass without demanding blood as proof. No one had told me that sorrow could be held without being cut open, that fear could be soothed without leaving marks. And so I returned to the only map I had, even as it led me deeper into terrain, into territory that narrowed with every step, that would one day threaten to consume me. What I was reaching for was not pain itself, but regulation. It was containment. It was the quiet that comes when the nervous system finally pauses its alarm. I was not seeking injury. I was seeking relief.

Not harm, but a moment of quiet inside the noise. Not destruction, but a moment where the noise dimmed enough for me to breathe. I was trying to survive a body perpetually set to high alert, to survive a nervous system perpetually on fire, using the only extinguisher I had ever been handed, never told it was flammable, too, never warned that it was soaked in fuel. That understanding would come later, wrapped in gentler language and steadier hands. It would arrive slowly, with patience and grief braided together. But here, in this part of the story, all I knew was the shape of the storm, the brief shelter pain provided, and the logic that if something hurt less than the chaos, it must be helping. And so I held on. I held on with everything I had, unaware that what first kept me afloat would one day tighten its grip, asking for more than survival, asking for parts of me I would not always have to give.

Each wound became an attempt, desperate and trembling, to pull the unseen torment into the light, to coax the madness out of hiding, to let it breathe somewhere other than inside my bones. The anguish paced inside me like a trapped animal in my ribcage, clawing at the walls, frantic for escape. I believed that if I could just open a small enough place for it, if I could let it spill out in controlled measure, it might finally settle. That it might stop tearing me apart from the inside. For a heartbeat, the release felt real. A thin pocket of air between sobs. A pause where the noise dimmed, and the storm stepped back just enough for me to stand. In that hush, I told myself a story. That I had found understanding. Or relief. Or meaning. That I had decoded the pain, translated it into something I could survive. The body quieted. The mind softened. And for one fragile moment, I mistook silence for resolution. But the quiet never lasted.

It slipped away the way breath does when you try to hold it too long. The pressure returned, heavier for having been interrupted. The animal began pacing again, more agitated now, having learned there was a door. What I had released did not leave; it regrouped. It circled back with sharpened teeth, demanding repetition, insisting that the ritual be honored again. The very act meant to empty me became an invitation for more. And so the cycle tightened. Relief taught expectation. Expectation bred urgency. Each attempt promised calm and delivered craving. The storm learned my patterns. It learned that if it howled loudly enough, I would answer. That if it waited, I would come back with the same offering, hoping for the same fleeting hush. What began as a desperate experiment hardened into habit, then into dependence.

Still, in those brief pauses, I clung to the idea that something had shifted. That the pain had been acknowledged. That the chaos had been named. I did not yet see that understanding cannot be forced out through wounds, that meaning does not bleed when summoned. I only knew the contrast. Noise, then quiet. Panic, then pause. And when you live inside constant roar, even a moment of stillness can feel like salvation. But the quiet was never peace. It was only the eye of the storm, and I was standing in it, mistaking the absence of wind for the end of the weather, unaware that the hardest part was already gathering itself to return.

And when the storm returned, it did not come back empty-handed. It arrived carrying memory. Carrying precedent. Carrying the knowledge of what had worked before. The body remembered the door, the ritual, the exchange. It remembered how to bargain. "*If you let me out,*" the pain seemed to say, "*I will give you quiet again.*" And I listened, because quiet had become precious, because silence felt like oxygen. What I did not yet understand was that I was no longer choosing the ritual. The ritual was choosing me. What had begun as an attempt at relief had begun to carve its own grooves, teaching my nervous system a dangerous shorthand. Distress meant urgency. Urgency meant action. Action meant harm. Harm meant hush. The sequence settled in, automatic and swift, bypassing thought, bypassing reflection, moving straight from ache to blade to breath.

The trapped animal inside me learned too. It learned that thrashing would summon the door. That chaos would be rewarded with release. And so it grew louder, more frantic, more demanding. The ribcage became a cage within a cage, the pacing more violent, the claws sharper. I was no longer emptying the storm. I was training it. And still, I kept believing the lie that the next time would be different. That if I did it just right, if I cut deep enough or carefully enough or precisely enough, the quiet might stay. That meaning might finally crystallize. That understanding would arrive and take the pain with it. I chased that moment the way one chases a mirage, convinced the shimmer ahead was water, unaware it receded with every step.

What I was really chasing was not relief, but permanence. A quiet that would last. A calm that would not betray me. A sense that the chaos had finally been dealt with instead of merely delayed. But wounds do not teach peace. They teach repetition. They teach the body to crave the very thing that harms it, to confuse silence with safety and stillness with healing. And so the storm and I became entangled, each feeding the other. I mistook survival for solution. I mistook endurance for understanding. I did not yet know that true quiet does not demand blood, that real peace does not arrive through harm, that the storm inside me was not an enemy to be expelled, but a language waiting to be learned. At the time, all I knew was the cycle. The build. The break. The brief hush. The return. I stood in the eye again and again, hoping it was the end, not yet realizing that the only way out of the storm was not through the wound, but through listening to what the storm had been trying to say all along.

The self-loathing always returned, ravenous and unforgiving, like a beast awakened by the scent of its own blood. Once stirred, it would not be reasoned with. It prowled the inner rooms of me, teeth bared, demanding tribute. More proof of my unworthiness. More pain to justify my continued breathing. More crimson offerings to quiet its hunger. It spoke with absolute authority, insisting that suffering was the only evidence I could offer that I understood my place in the world. And so the cycle spiraled. An ever-tightening noose of hurt and remorse, cinching closer with each repetition. Each wound birthed another. Each scar became fuel for the next descent.

What had once felt like an answer hardened into obligation. Relief turned into debt. Calm demanded interest. I moved through the motions of a ritual I no longer questioned, a choreography of damage and regret so familiar it felt inevitable.

It became a merciless loop. Destruction followed by apology. Punishment followed by shame. Pain followed by the hollow promise that this time it would be enough. I would hurt myself, and then I would hate myself for needing to. I would swear it was the last time and then condemn myself when it wasn't. The beast fed on both the wound and the regret that followed, growing stronger with every turn of the wheel. I did not yet understand the machinery of it. How self-loathing feeds on secrecy. How shame multiplies in isolation. How the body learns patterns faster than the mind can name them. All I knew was obedience. The sense that resistance was dangerous. That defiance would only make the punishment worse. The ritual felt older than choice, older than will, as if it had claimed me long before I knew how to question it.

I was trapped inside an apology I could never finish making. Trapped in a sentence that rewrote itself each time I tried to serve it. And beneath the violence of that loop, beneath the hunger and the harm, there lived a quieter truth I could not yet hear: That what demanded punishment was not my existence, but my pain. That the beast was not proof of my wickedness, but the voice of suffering starved of compassion. But at the time, there was no such clarity. Only the tightening. Only the spiral. Only the belief that this was what survival looked like for someone like me. And survival, as I understood it then, was not about living forward, but about enduring in place. It was bracing. Holding. Withstanding. I learned to measure my days not by moments of joy or connection, but by how successfully I had managed the beast, how much damage I had absorbed without letting it spill outward. Staying alive became a kind of penance in itself, something to be tolerated rather than desired, something to be paid for again and again with pain.

The spiral narrowed my world. Possibility thinned. Hope became theoretical, something other people spoke about in abstract terms, like a language I had once overheard but never learned to speak. My inner life revolved around containment. How to keep the hunger quiet. How to anticipate its return. How to comply quickly enough to avoid escalation. I mistook this vigilance for strength, this constant self-surveillance for responsibility. There was no room for gentleness inside that system. No space for curiosity or mercy. Everything was filtered through the same ruthless equation: if I was hurting, I must deserve it. If I wanted relief, I had to earn it. And so even moments of calm felt borrowed, fragile, already scheduled for repayment. I could not enjoy them without bracing for the bill that would follow.

I lived as though I were under permanent review, watched by an unseen authority that tallied my failures and weighed my worth. Rest felt suspicious. Pleasure felt dangerous. Kindness toward myself felt like a crime. I did not know that these beliefs were learned. They felt innate. Obvious. As unquestionable as gravity. And yet, beneath all of it, beneath the obedience and the rituals and the relentless accounting, something in me was growing tired. Not rebellious. Not hopeful. Just tired. A deep, cellular fatigue with the endless punishment, the constant proving, the impossible standard I could never meet. I did not yet know how to listen to that weariness, but it was there, quietly eroding the certainty of the beast.

At the time, I could not imagine another way to survive. I believed this loop was my nature, my fate, my sentence. I did not yet know that what I called survival was actually captivity, or that the very exhaustion I felt was the first small crack in the structure that had held me for so long. The spiral was still tightening. But somewhere deep inside it, something had begun, however faintly, to loosen.

The Choir of Accusation

Each act became a frantic attempt to quiet the voice inside me, that relentless, ceaseless whisper curled in the back of my mind, a venomous choir chanting my shortcomings in perfect, merciless harmony. It knew every note. Every weakness. It sang my failures back to me until they felt ordained. It was the echo of every unspoken criticism I believed I deserved, the imagined disappointment I sensed lurking behind familiar eyes, the phantom sighs I swore I heard in the pauses between conversations. Even kindness felt suspect, already preparing to curdle into reproach. This voice did not simply speak. It slithered. It seeped. It threaded itself through my thoughts and nested in my breath. It wrapped itself around my ribs like rusty barbed wire, tightening with each inhale, cutting deeper with every perceived failure.

The more I tried to appease it, the sharper it grew, feeding on my vigilance, thriving on my fear. Silence never satisfied it. Compliance only taught it how much power it had. It twisted the smallest misstep into a mortal sin. A wrong word. A delayed response. A need expressed too loudly or not loudly enough. Everything became evidence. Everything became a charge. My imperfections were stretched into grotesque shadows towering over me, monsters sculpted from doubt and shame, looming so large they eclipsed anything tender or good I might have carried. I no longer saw myself as human, only as a collection of errors waiting to be punished. And the cruelest part was how convincing it sounded. This was not a stranger's voice.

It wore my tone. It borrowed my cadence. It spoke in first person, cloaked in certainty, until I believed it was truth rather than trauma rehearsing itself. I thought this voice was conscience. Insight. Honesty. I did not yet know it was an internalized echo of a world that had taught me love must be earned, and mistakes were dangerous. So I tried to silence it the only way I knew how. Through harm. Through offering. Through ritual. Each act was an attempt to prove remorse, to demonstrate awareness, to show I was listening. If I punished myself quickly enough, perhaps the voice would relent. Perhaps it would loosen its grip. For a moment, sometimes, it did. The barbed wire slackened. The choir quieted. And I mistook that pause for absolution.

But the voice always returned. Louder. Hungrier. Better rehearsed. And with it came the belief that I was failing not only at being good, but at being human at all. I did not yet see that the voice was not a judge to be obeyed, but a wound to be understood. All I knew was its pressure, its certainty, and my growing desperation to escape its song, even if the only way out seemed to be through my own skin. And so the song became the air I breathed. I woke to it already humming, followed its cadence through the day, and fell asleep beneath its watchful gaze. It did not shout. It did not need to. It worked through implication, through suggestion, through the quiet certainty that I was always one misstep away from confirmation. It made me vigilant to my own humanity, alert to every flaw as if it were a threat. I learned to scan myself the way prey scans the horizon, waiting for danger that lived inside my own chest.

I tried to outrun it by being better. Quieter. Smaller. More agreeable. I tried to anticipate its accusations before they could be spoken, to correct myself in advance, to erase the parts it seemed to circle. But the voice was never satisfied. It fed on effort as eagerly as it fed on failure. The more I tried to be good, the more it raised the standard. The bar lifted. The wire tightened. Perfection became the only imagined refuge, and even that was booby-trapped with inevitability. What I did not yet understand was that the voice was not proof of my inadequacy, but proof of my injury. That it had grown in the absence of safety, learned its vocabulary in rooms where love was conditional, and mistakes carried consequences far heavier than they deserved. It was a guardian gone feral, trying to keep me from harm by becoming harm itself. A sentinel that mistook punishment for protection.

But at the time, I could not hear that nuance. I only heard the command. "*Fix it. Pay for it. Disappear if you must.*" And so my body became the bargaining table where I negotiated my right to exist. I learned to translate its accusations into action, its venom into ritual, believing that if I complied thoroughly enough, the voice might finally release me. It never did. It only grew more articulate, more intimate, more entwined with my sense of self. And yet, even then, beneath its certainty and my obedience, something else stirred. A quiet resistance I could not yet name. A fatigue with the endless proving. A faint question forming at the edge of the noise, barely audible but persistent. "*What if this voice is wrong?*"

The question did not silence it. Not yet. But it cracked the harmony just enough to let another sound through. A discordant note. A tremor. The smallest suggestion that the song I had been obeying was not truth itself, but a wound asking, in the only language it knew, to finally be heard. And in my desperation to silence it, to drown out its poison song, I carved, I burned, I bruised, I suffocated, not out of hatred alone, but out of belief. A terrible faith. Somewhere inside that twisted logic, I accepted its lies as law. I believed the voice was justice, and the pain was penance. That suffering was proof of moral clarity. That hurting myself meant I was finally doing the right thing. The blade became a gavel. The bruise, a verdict. The burn, a sentence carried out in full.

I mistook cruelty for truth because it spoke with certainty. I mistook punishment for wisdom because it felt definitive. In a world that had taught me confusion, absolutes felt safer. The voice did not waver. It did not hesitate. It named me and judged me in the same breath, and I obeyed because obedience promised order. If I followed its rules closely enough, perhaps it would stop. Perhaps I would be allowed to exist without accusation. But it was never justice. Justice seeks restoration. Justice asks what was harmed and how it might be healed. This voice sought only domination. It was a tyrant disguised as conscience, an internal despot that ruled through fear and demanded blood to maintain its throne. It did not want me better. It wanted me smaller. Quieter. Broken in ways that could not speak back.

The more I fed it, the hungrier it grew. The more I complied, the harsher its demands became. There was no final offering that satisfied it, no wound deep enough to earn release. Its law had no mercy clause. Its court never adjourned. And slowly, inexorably, it set about breaking me from the inside out, splintering my sense of self until I could no longer tell where my voice ended and its began. What I did not yet see was that the voice was not an authority, but an injury repeating itself. A wound that had learned how to sound convincing. A survival strategy that had turned feral in the absence of care. It had risen to keep me safe once, to anticipate danger, to prevent abandonment by pre-emptively punishing myself. But over time, it forgot its original purpose. It stopped guarding. It started ruling.

And still, beneath its reign, something in me endured. Bruised. Silenced. But not extinguished. A part that recoiled at the injustice even while submitting to it. A part that knew, in its deepest marrow, that no true justice demands annihilation. That penance without mercy is not redemption, but cruelty wearing a holy mask. That knowing was faint then, barely a pulse beneath the noise. But it was there. Waiting. And one day, it would grow strong enough to speak back, not with punishment, but with truth. That truth did not arrive like thunder. It did not shatter the court or overthrow the tyrant in a single, righteous moment. It arrived the way light does at dawn, quietly, almost apologetically, slipping through cracks I did not know existed. At first it was only a sensation, a subtle resistance in my body when the sentence was passed, a tightening not of fear but of refusal.

A fatigue with the violence. A weariness with the endless proving. A question that refused to be silenced: "*What if this is not law at all?*" I did not yet have the courage to disobey. But I began, unknowingly, to hesitate. The ritual lost a fraction of its certainty. The blade felt heavier. The offering less convincing. The voice still spoke, but something in me no longer bowed as deeply. I began to sense the cost not just of the pain, but of the obedience. To feel how much of myself I had been surrendering at the altar of a false god that only ever asked for more. Slowly, the idea took shape, fragile and terrifying in equal measure. That perhaps the voice was not justice, but injury reenacting itself. That perhaps the law I had been living under was written by fear, not truth. That perhaps I was not guilty but wounded. And that possibility, more than any punishment, shook the foundations of everything I thought I knew.

Because if I was not guilty, then the suffering had never been required. If the suffering had never been required, then the voice had been lying. And if the voice had been lying, then there might be another way to live. This was not relief. It was disorientation. The ground beneath me shifted, and I did not yet know how to stand without the familiar weight of condemnation anchoring me in place. Mercy felt dangerous. Compassion felt undeserved. Silence, without punishment to justify it, felt like exposure. I had lived so long under sentence that freedom itself felt like a threat. And yet, the pulse persisted. That small, stubborn knowing. That no true justice demands blood for breath. That no real morality is proven through annihilation. That something in me had survived not because I punished it well, but because it refused, at its core, to believe the lie completely.

That part was quiet. But it was learning how to speak. And in time, it would teach me a new language. Not one carved into skin or burned into silence, but one rooted in truth. In context. In care. A language that did not ask me to disappear in order to be forgiven, but invited me, slowly and trembling, to stay. This would take me decades to find.

Holy Silence, Hidden Wounds

The solitude that accompanied these rituals was its own paradox, both sanctuary and prison, ointment and pus, balm and blade. It closed around me like a familiar shadow, soft at first, almost tender, whispering promises of safety even as it tightened its grip. Alone, I did not have to explain myself. Alone, I did not have to translate the chaos. Solitude felt like control. It felt like protection. And yet it was also starvation, quietly consuming me while convincing me I was being spared. I remember the hush of secrecy, the way the world seemed to hold its breath when I disappeared into hidden spaces. Bathrooms with locked doors. Bedrooms after lights-out. Corners where footsteps faded and no one asked questions. There was a sacred stillness there, a reverent quiet that felt almost holy. In those moments, the noise inside me softened just enough to hear my own breathing, shallow and careful, as if even sound might betray me. I treated those spaces like sanctuaries, believing that silence itself was medicine.

It was there that I performed my dark devotions. Not in chaos, but in ritual. With intention. With reverence. As though pain itself were a god demanding worship, and I was a faithful disciple bringing offerings in secret. Blood. Heat. Pressure. Proof. I believed suffering listened when nothing else did. That pain received me when people could not. That if I honored it properly, it might protect me in return. The loneliness was not accidental. It was required. Witness would have broken the spell. Questions would have fractured the illusion. Alone, I could pretend this was chosen, sacred, meaningful. Alone, I could believe I was strong for enduring it, righteous for accepting it. I mistook isolation for intimacy, secrecy for safety, silence for peace.

But solitude, unchecked, curdles. What begins as refuge slowly becomes enclosure. The quiet that once soothed began to echo. The shadows thickened. The god I believed I was appeasing never answered with mercy, only with more demands. And still I stayed, because leaving meant facing the world without my rituals, without my illusions, without the one place where I felt I understood the rules. I did not yet know that healing would require witnesses. That safety would eventually arrive not through hiding, but through being seen without punishment. At the time, all I knew was the hush, the ritual, the devotion. The way solitude held me and harmed me in the same breath, promising salvation while quietly teaching me how to disappear.

And disappearing became its own discipline. I learned how to fold myself smaller, how to take up less psychic space, how to vanish without leaving a mark on the room. I practiced absence until it felt like virtue. I mistook restraint for strength, quiet for goodness, erasure for grace. The less I was seen, the safer I felt. The safer I felt, the more I disappeared. It was a slow apprenticeship in self-removal, taught by silence and perfected in secrecy. Solitude trained me to believe I was self-sufficient in my suffering. That I did not need comfort. That needing was a flaw, a liability, an invitation for harm. I told myself I was protecting others from my darkness, sparing them the inconvenience of my pain. I told myself this was maturity. I did not yet see the arrogance hidden inside that belief, the lie that said my suffering was too much for human hands, that only pain itself was worthy to touch it.

In those quiet chambers, time warped. Minutes stretched into hours. The outside world felt unreal, distant, like a rumor carried through walls. Inside, everything was immediate, intimate, consuming. The rituals gave me a sense of belonging, a private order that made sense when nothing else did. I belonged to the hush. I belonged to the wound. I belonged to the rules I had learned in the dark. But belonging without love is another kind of exile. The longer I stayed, the more the walls closed in, until solitude no longer felt chosen but compulsory. The silence that once cradled me began to accuse me. The shadows that once hid me began to watch. What had promised safety now demanded loyalty. And loyalty meant more disappearance, more devotion, more sacrifice.

Still, I stayed. Because stepping into the light felt like exposure without armor. Because being seen felt like standing naked before a world that had not earned my trust. Because I had learned to survive without witnesses, and survival had become my only measure of success. I did not yet know that the very thing I feared was the medicine I needed. That being seen, gently, without judgment, would one day loosen the grip of the rituals. That witnesses could arrive without punishment. That silence was not the same as safety, and solitude was not the same as peace. For now, I lived inside the paradox. Held and harmed by the same quiet. Kept alive by rituals that were slowly teaching me how to disappear. And somewhere beneath it all, beneath the devotion and the damage, the faintest ache persisted. Not for pain. Not for solitude. But for a presence that could stay without demanding blood, a witness who could see me and not look away.

There were the practiced gestures, the careful tug of a sleeve, the precise angle of a long pant leg or long-sleeved shirt, the choreography of concealment performed without thought. I learned how to move my body like a secret, how to cross my arms just so, how to turn my shoulder at the right moment, how to laugh while adjusting fabric that hid what I could not explain. My reflection became a rehearsal space, each movement refined until it looked effortless, until hiding felt natural, almost graceful. I became fluent in half-smiles and diversion, a master sculptor of lies, shaping explanations with the ease of someone who has practiced them a thousand times. Cat scratches. Clumsiness. Accidents that sounded ordinary enough to pass without suspicion. I delivered them lightly, casually, as if truth were something that belonged to other people. Each lie slid into place like mortar, sealing me further inside myself. Every deception built another brick in the wall around me. Every concealed wound was another step deeper into the labyrinth of my own making.

Inside that maze, I learned the contours of isolation intimately. The corridors narrowed. The air thinned. I lived in a self-imposed exile, a quiet, suffocating solitude where my secrets echoed louder than any spoken word ever could. Silence became crowded. My thoughts ricocheted off the walls of my own restraint, unanswered, unseen. I was surrounded by people and yet utterly alone, carrying a private war beneath polite conversation and practiced normalcy. Shame hung from my shoulders like a heavy, choking cloak. It weighed down my posture, shortened my breath, dulled my voice. It pressed me further into the shadows I had chosen as refuge, convincing me that darkness was safer than exposure, that invisibility was protection. I mistook concealment for control, secrecy for strength, forgetting that walls built to keep danger out also keep connection from getting in.

And still, beneath the fabric and the lies and the careful angles, the body remembered. It held the truth quietly, patiently, even as I worked tirelessly to erase it from view. I did not yet understand that the effort to hide was itself a cry, not for attention, but for safety. That the exhaustion I felt was not weakness, but the cost of carrying everything alone. At the time, all I knew was how to hide well. How to disappear in plain sight. How to survive inside a maze I had built with my own hands, believing that if no one could see the wounds, perhaps they would stop hurting. I did not yet know that what needed healing was not only the skin beneath my sleeves, but the isolation that had wrapped itself so tightly around my life, calling itself protection while slowly stealing my breath.

That hiding became second nature, an instinct woven so tightly into me that I no longer recognized it as a choice. My body anticipated scrutiny before it arrived, adjusted itself before questions could form. I learned to scan rooms the way others scan for exits, measuring angles, light, proximity. Who was looking. Who might notice. Who might ask. Vigilance settled into my muscles, a low, constant hum that never fully quieted. Even in moments of ease, I was braced, prepared to shield what I believed could not survive exposure. The effort was relentless. It took energy to maintain the illusion, to keep the walls standing, to ensure no crack widened into confession. I carried the weight of my secrecy everywhere, a burden disguised as composure. People praised my resilience, my maturity, my strength, never knowing how much of that strength was spent on disappearance. I smiled and accepted their words, unaware that what they admired was not wholeness, but endurance. Not health, but containment.

Inside, the maze grew more intricate. I added turns and dead ends, convinced complexity equalled safety. The deeper I went, the harder it became to remember what openness felt like. I forgot the sound of my own unguarded voice. I forgot what it meant to be met without explanation, to be seen without strategy. Connection became something theoretical, something that belonged to other lives, other bodies, other stories. And yet, beneath all that careful construction, something continued to pulse. A quiet insistence. A reminder that bodies are not built for silence, that wounds left unattended do not disappear, they wait. My skin remembered what my mouth refused to say. My breath remembered what my mind tried to outrun. The truth lived on, patient and persistent, even as I tried to bury it beneath layers of fabric and performance.

I did not yet understand that the maze itself was hurting me. That the isolation I called safety was amplifying the pain it promised to contain. That secrets, when carried alone, grow heavier with time. I only knew that I was tired. Bone-deep tired. Tired of vigilance. Tired of pretending. Tired of surviving in fragments. That weariness was not defeat. It was the first signal. The body's quiet rebellion against a life built entirely on concealment. I could not yet name it as such, but it was there, beginning its work. A soft pressure against the walls. A subtle loosening of mortar. A reminder that even the most carefully built labyrinth is not meant to be lived in forever. I was still hiding. Still careful. Still wrapped in secrecy. But somewhere beneath the choreography and the lies, a different truth was forming, fragile but persistent. That safety might one day mean something else entirely. That healing would not arrive through better hiding, but through being seen. And that the breath I was losing inside my fortress might yet return, if I could find the courage to step toward the light, even trembling, even unsure, even carrying all that I had been afraid to show.

However, before all that. To the world, I was the pristine child, the dutiful daughter, the straight-A student, the loyal friend. A shining portrait of composure and competence, polished to a blinding sheen. I knew how to deliver excellence with a smile, how to be reliable, agreeable, impressive. I learned early that praise was safest when earned, that admiration came easiest when nothing leaked. From the outside, I looked whole. From the outside, I looked blessed, as if grace itself had chosen me and settled gently on my shoulders. But beneath that immaculate veneer, I was a battleground of bleeding realities. A terrain scorched by quiet skirmishes no one else could hear. A fractured soul waging war against itself, with no ceasefire and no witnesses. I was the aggressor and the wounded, the executioner and the condemned, all inhabiting the same trembling body. Every day, I rose and dressed and performed while the conflict raged beneath my ribs, unseen and unacknowledged, a private apocalypse unfolding beneath pressed uniforms and practiced smiles.

I learned how to compartmentalize with surgical precision. Achievement on the surface. Attrition underneath. I carried textbooks and trophies with hands that had learned other weights. I laughed in hallways while counting exits. I listened to friends while negotiating with the voice inside me. I memorized deadlines and expectations while my own needs slipped quietly into exile. I was present everywhere and absent from myself, a masterpiece of functionality built over a fault line, admired for its symmetry while the ground beneath it quietly shifted. In the silence between heartbeats, in that narrow space where performance could not quite reach, I knew the truth. Not as language, but as sensation. As pressure. As ache. A low, constant hum that never fully left me. No one saw the truth of me because I had become an expert at disappearing. I had made an art of erasure, refining it until even I mistook it for strength. I did not hide because I wanted to deceive. I hid because I did not know how to exist safely any other way.

And so the world applauded the illusion, never realizing what it cost. Never hearing the quieter sound beneath the clapping, the steady erosion of a self who believed she had to vanish in order to be loved. I was visible everywhere and known nowhere, surviving on approval while starving for recognition. Fed by accolades, hollowed by silence. Each compliment landed lightly, never quite reaching the places that needed nourishment. That invisibility did not happen by accident. It was learned. Perfected. Rewarded. It was reinforced every time composure was praised and pain went unnoticed, every time I was admired for being "so strong" when what I really was, was unsupported. And it would take years, and tenderness I had not yet imagined, to understand that disappearing was never the same as being safe. That competence is not the same as wholeness. And that the truth I hid so well was not unlovable, only unheard.

But at the time, all I knew was how to shine on command and bleed in secret. How to be everything for everyone while becoming nothing for myself. How to turn my inner life into a locked room and hand the world a beautifully furnished hallway instead. And in that quiet space between heartbeats, I kept the truth close, cupped carefully like a fragile ember, believing that if I held it tightly enough, silently enough, it might someday learn how to breathe.

When the Storm Learned My Nam

The self-harm escalated like a storm gathering force, slowly at first, almost imperceptibly, a change in the air more than the sky. At the beginning it whispered, a distant rumble I could ignore, convince myself was temporary, manageable. But storms do not stay polite. They build pressure. They learn your terrain. And one day I realized it was everywhere, fierce and unrelenting, filling every horizon of my inner world. What began as tentative scratches, exploratory and unsure, soon carved themselves into deeper, deliberate lacerations. Hesitation gave way to certainty. Curiosity hardened into compulsion. The body remembered too well what the mind could no longer question. The small, stinging burns I once used as anchors, brief points of sensation to tether myself to the moment, morphed into searing brands, intentional and unflinching. Pain was no longer a whisper or a test. It was a declaration.

Each wound felt like a message pressed urgently into flesh, a language growing louder as it failed to be heard. I etched my skin like a palimpsest of desperation, layering mark upon mark as if repetition might finally translate what words never could. These were not acts of impulse anymore. They were decisions. Rituals sharpened by familiarity. Desperate messages no one would ever read, written in a script only I believed could tell the truth. The escalation frightened me, even as it pulled me deeper. The relief shortened. The hunger lengthened. What once calmed now demanded more to achieve the same fragile quiet. The storm no longer paused between gusts. It raged continuously, teaching me that survival required escalation, that staying afloat meant going further, deeper, harder. I crossed lines I once believed I never would, carrying each new threshold like proof of how far I had fallen and how trapped I had become.

And still, beneath the violence of it, the intent remained the same. I was not chasing pain for its own sake. I was chasing silence. Meaning. Containment. I was trying to keep the inner chaos from swallowing me whole by carving it into something I could see, something I could control. The wounds grew more severe not because I wanted to disappear faster, but because the ache inside me was growing louder, more insistent, more desperate to be acknowledged. What I did not yet understand was that escalation is not strength, but exhaustion reaching its limit. That storms intensify when pressure has nowhere else to go. At the time, all I knew was that the marks were multiplying, the rituals deepening, and the language of my body growing more urgent, as if it were pleading with me to find another way to speak before the storm consumed everything.

The storm did not announce its peak with thunder alone. It arrived with erosion. With the slow reshaping of my inner landscape until what once felt extreme began to feel ordinary, even necessary. I learned to live under its weather, to plan around its moods, to mistake endurance for mastery. The horizon narrowed. The sky lowered. And I adjusted, telling myself this was simply what survival required now. The body kept score when the mind grew tired of counting. It learned the rhythms of escalation, the narrowing window between need and action. What once felt shocking became procedural. What once frightened me became familiar enough to soothe. Familiarity dulled the alarm, even as the damage deepened. I told myself I was still in control because I chose when, where, how. But control had quietly shifted hands. The storm was steering now, and I was learning to call its direction instinct.

Inside, there was a constant vigilance, a watchfulness that never slept. I scanned myself for pressure the way sailors scan the sky. I learned the signs of an approaching swell, the subtle tightening, the rising static beneath the skin. When it came, I responded quickly, efficiently, as though speed itself were a form of safety. Delay felt dangerous. Hesitation felt like drowning. And so I moved, again and again, rehearsing relief as if it were rescue. Yet even as the rituals intensified, a strange grief threaded through them. A mourning for the simplicity of earlier relief. For the days when the quiet lasted longer. For the version of me who still believed this was temporary, a phase, a storm that would pass on its own. I carried that grief like a second shadow, aware on some level that escalation was not solving the problem, only outrunning it for shorter and shorter distances.

There were moments, brief and startling, when the storm seemed to pause just enough for a question to surface. A flicker of doubt. A sense of unease that felt different from fear. Not loud enough to stop me, but present enough to ache. Is this really helping? How far does this go? What happens if it never ends? The questions did not stay long. The wind returned. The rituals resumed. But something had shifted. A hairline crack in certainty. I did not yet have another way. I did not yet know how to listen to what the body was asking without answering in harm. But the urgency of its language was changing. It was no longer only saying, See me. It was also saying, "Please. Please find another way." The storm was not just destroying. It was signalling. It was warning me that the system I had built to survive was collapsing under its own weight.

At the time, I could not translate that warning into action. I only felt the exhaustion beneath the escalation, the way each new mark carried less relief and more sorrow. The rituals were louder. The quiet was thinner. And somewhere beneath the roar, a truth was beginning to gather, fragile but persistent: that the storm was not the enemy, but the message. And that if I did not learn to hear it differently, it would keep speaking in the only language it knew, until there was nothing left of me to answer at all.

The physical pain became my counterfeit salvation, a crude stand-in for grace, a rough baptism meant to wash me clean of feelings that felt too vast to survive. I used it to numb the anguish raging inside me, to drown out the relentless tide of self-loathing with a sensation I could command, even if only for a moment. Pain answered promptly when called. It cut through the noise with brutal efficiency. For a heartbeat, it felt like control. Like rescue. Like proof that I could still reach myself through the fog. But the numbness that followed was only another kind of suffering, quieter and more treacherous. A hollow, haunting ache that thrummed beneath the surface of my skin, low and constant, like a distant engine that never shut off. It was the aftermath no one warns you about. Not relief, but vacancy. Not peace, but absence. The world dulled. Colors thinned. Sensation flattened into a gray hush that felt eerily close to the death I had once prayed for. I told myself this emptiness was rest. I did not yet see it was erosion.

That numbness clung to me like a splinter driven too deep to extract, a tiny shard lodged beneath the skin that made every movement hurt in its own way. Every gesture caught on it. Every breath grazed it. Even joy, when it tried to surface, snagged painfully and retreated. I carried that splinter everywhere, a constant reminder of the ugliness I believed lived at my core, the defect I was convinced could never be fully removed, only managed through punishment. And still, I spiraled. Trapped in a tightening vortex of destruction, I moved in circles so small they began to feel like a point. Each cut. Each burn. Each self-inflicted wound pulled me closer to the center, closer to the abyss I both feared and felt magnetized toward. I told myself I was skirting the edge, that I could stop at any time. But the pull was patient. Persistent. It did not rush. It waited for exhaustion to do its work.

The abyss was not dramatic. It did not roar. It yawned. A quiet gravity that promised rest in exchange for surrender. I felt its pull in the weariness that followed each ritual, in the way hope began to feel impractical, even naïve. I was not racing toward annihilation. I was being slowly unmade, convinced all the while that this unraveling was the price of staying alive. What I could not yet see was that my spiral was not proof of my failure, but evidence of a system collapsing under strain. That the counterfeit salvation had stopped working because it was never meant to save me, only to buy me time. And time, it turns out, is dangerous when it passes without safety, without witness, without another way to come back to yourself.

I was not falling because I was weak. I was falling because I had been holding myself up with knives and fire and silence, and even the strongest arms eventually give out when that is all they are given to lean on. And so the counterfeit salvation demanded renewal. What once worked briefly now failed faster, leaving me scrambling to recreate the moment when pain still felt like rescue. I chased that first hush the way one chases an echo down a long corridor, convinced that if I just went far enough, hurt myself deeply enough, I would hear it again. But echoes fade. They thin. They turn into distortion. And the more desperately I pursued relief, the more elusive it became, until even pain felt hollow, mechanical, stripped of its promise.

The rituals lost their intimacy. What had once felt intentional began to feel compulsory, less a choice than a reflex. My body moved ahead of my hope. The blade no longer asked permission. The fire no longer startled. Silence no longer soothed. I was repeating gestures long after they stopped delivering meaning, clinging to the choreography because it was all I knew. Survival had narrowed into repetition, and repetition had begun to feel like destiny. Inside that spiral, shame thickened. I hated myself not only for hurting, but for needing to. For failing to find another way. For watching myself sink and still reaching for the same tools that were pulling me under. I judged myself for my dependence on pain even as I relied on it to function. This doubled the weight. Suffering for suffering. Punishment for punishment. A hall of mirrors where every reflection accused and none offered a way out.

And yet, beneath the collapse, something quietly resisted annihilation. A pressure that was not self-loathing. A grief that did not demand blood. A fatigue so profound it bordered on honesty. I did not recognize it then, but it was my system signalling overload, not failure. My body was not asking for more pain. It was asking for relief of an entirely different kind. For rest that did not require damage. For holding that did not wound. Still, I could not hear that request yet. The noise was too loud. The habits too ingrained. The abyss too convincing in its promise of quiet. All I knew was the rhythm of falling and the effort it took to keep pretending I was choosing it. I believed collapse was my flaw, not my warning. That exhaustion was proof of inadequacy, not evidence of endurance stretched past its limits.

What I see now, standing far from that gravity, is that the spiral was never about wanting to disappear. It was about wanting reprieve. Wanting someone, something, to step in and say: You can stop holding yourself up this way now. You don't have to keep bleeding to stay alive. You don't have to suffer to be allowed rest. But at the time, no such voice had reached me. So I kept leaning on what I knew. Knives. Fire. Silence. And I called it strength, because it was all I had been taught to use. And yet, in the midst of all that destruction, there was a strange, shame-soaked comfort, a twisted sanctuary carved from pain. It was not peace, but it masqueraded as one. In the sting of the blade, in the blooming bruise, in the searing kiss of heat against skin, I felt the unbearable weight on my chest loosen its grip, just enough for me to draw a breath.

Pain narrowed the world. It pulled my scattered fragments into a single point of sensation, and for that brief convergence, I mistook focus for relief. The physical pain became a brief eclipse, a darkened sun passing between me and the storm. For a moment, the inner noise dimmed. The accusations fell silent. The past and future collapsed into the immediacy of the body. It was a brutal mercy, but mercy all the same. I clung to it because it was the only thing that interrupted the onslaught, the only force that could interrupt the mind's relentless monologue with something tangible, undeniable, present. It functioned as distraction, crude and temporary, an anaesthetic that dulled the deeper ache gnawing at the edges of my soul. Not healing but numbing. Not resolution, but reprieve. For a few seconds, or minutes if I pressed harder, the anguish quieted, as if the monstrous beast inside me had been lulled into sleep by the offering of my own flesh.

I learned its appetite. I learned what it took to hush it. I learned the terrible bargain of it. But even in those moments of stillness, the comfort was laced with rot. Relief arrived carrying shame in its wake, staining the pause with the knowledge that it would not last. The beast never slept deeply. It only rested. It dreamed. And when it woke, it was hungrier for having been fed. The sanctuary revealed itself as a trap, its walls lined with mirrors that reflected my desperation back at me, magnified and distorted. I had not yet seen that what I called comfort was my nervous system grasping for regulation with broken tools. That the body, overwhelmed and unheard, had found the fastest route to quiet and clung to it with ferocity. I only knew the contrast. The before and after. The roar and the hush. And when you live inside constant thunder, even the illusion of calm can feel like grace.

So I returned to it, again and again, chasing that narrow window where the storm paused, and the world felt survivable. I told myself it was helping. I told myself it was necessary. I told myself it was the only way I knew how to keep going. And in that belief, I bound relief to injury, silence to harm, comfort to destruction, teaching my body a lesson it would take years to unlearn: That pain was the price of quiet, and suffering the toll for a moment's peace. And so the sanctuary tightened its grip. What had first appeared as refuge began to feel like obligation, a place I did not choose so much as return to out of habit and fear. The body remembered faster than the mind could intervene. It leaned toward pain the way one leans toward a door known to open, even if what waits beyond it is familiar ruin.

The quiet I chased grew narrower, more elusive, demanding greater cost each time, as though silence itself had learned to charge interest. I began to recognize the rhythm of it. The swell. The break. The aftermath. A tide that never carried me ashore, only dragged me back out again. The moment the pain receded, the shame rushed in to fill the space it left behind, thick and suffocating, whispering that I was weak for needing relief, disgusting for finding it this way, irredeemable for returning to it at all. Relief and condemnation braided together so tightly I could no longer separate one from the other. Comfort became evidence against me. Still, I returned. Because the storm inside me did not care about morality. It cared about survival. It demanded quiet by any means necessary, and pain was the only lever I knew how to pull.

I did not yet understand that my body was not betraying me, but begging for regulation, for grounding, for a place to land that did not injure it in the process. I mistook desperation for desire, necessity for choice. Each return etched the lesson deeper. Pain equals pause. Injury equals calm. Suffering equals safety. These equations sank into muscle and nerve, into reflex and instinct, until they no longer felt like beliefs but laws of nature. I lived inside a body trained to associate harm with relief, a nervous system wired to settle only when something broke. And the tragedy was not that it worked, but that it worked just well enough to keep me trapped.

I could feel the cost accumulating even then. In the way the quiet grew thinner. In the way the shame grew heavier. In the way the storm returned faster each time, less willing to be lulled, more demanding in its hunger. The beast I fed did not grow tame. It grew accustomed. And familiarity, I would later learn, is not the same as safety.

At the time, though, all I knew was the chase. The desperate reaching for that brief eclipse. The willingness to pay almost anything for a few moments where the world felt bearable. I did not yet have language for nervous systems, for trauma responses, for learned survival. I only had the pattern. The bargain. The belief that if I could just endure the cost, the quiet might last a little longer next time. It never did. And still, I kept returning, not because I loved the pain, but because I loved the silence it promised. Not because I wanted to destroy myself, but because I had not yet been shown another way to come back into my body without hurting it first.

The Illusion of Control

In that warped ritual, there was an illusion of control, a fragile, counterfeit sense of agency stitched together inside a life that felt otherwise ungovernable. When everything else moved without my consent, pain felt like something I could initiate, contain, and end. It gave me the brief comfort of authorship, the feeling of signing my name at the bottom of an experience instead of being written into it by force. I could decide when it began. I could decide where it lived. I could decide how long it stayed. In a world that so often felt like it was happening *to* me, this choice masqueraded as power, convincing me I was not entirely at the mercy of circumstance. It let me feel something. Anything. Anything other than the numbness that hovered at the edges of my consciousness, threatening to swallow me whole.

Numbness was the most terrifying state of all, a colorless fog where even suffering lost its shape, where I could not tell if I was alive or merely persisting. Pain cut through that fog with brutal clarity. It reminded me of boundaries. Of edges. Of existence. The sting, the throb, the heat became proof that I was still here. Still breathing. Still capable of sensation in a body that otherwise felt distant, hollow, half-erased, as though I were living a few inches outside my own skin. In a world where my emotions had grown too vast, too heavy, too impossible to carry without collapsing, pain reduced them to something singular and manageable. It took a universe of feeling and compressed it into a point. One place. One sensation. One moment. I did not have to hold everything at once. I did not have to name the grief, the fear, the rage, the loneliness. For a brief span of time, the chaos obeyed gravity and fell inward, gathering itself into something I could survive without shattering.

It was a terrible paradox. Hurting myself to remind myself that I could still be hurt. Wounding myself to prove I was not already gone. In some distorted corner of my understanding, pain became confused with healing, harm mistaken for care. I believed that because the body could close a wound, something inside me might close too. That because flesh knew how to mend, perhaps the soul could follow its lead. I was not trying to destroy myself. I was trying to feel repair, even if I had chosen the wrong language to ask for it, even if I had mistaken injury for intervention. And for a moment, it worked. For a moment, the pressure eased. The numbness retreated. The world sharpened into focus. Breath came easier. Thought slowed. The relentless inner noise dimmed to a murmur I could finally ignore. I mistook that shift for relief, for progress, for something like hope.

I told myself this was proof I was coping, managing, surviving. I did not yet know that relief borrowed from injury always demands repayment. I did not yet understand that healing cannot be coerced through pain, only invited through safety, patience, and witness. But in those moments, brief and flickering, it felt like I had found a way back into myself. A narrow bridge over a chasm I had been falling through for years. It was unstable, dangerous, built of splinters and fire, but it was *there*. And when you have spent years feeling untethered, unreachable, half-vanished, even a false bridge can feel like salvation.

My parents, bless their unknowing hearts, moved through those years with innocent eyes, seeing only what I so carefully arranged for them to see. I became a skilled curator of their comfort, offering up the version of me that reassured, impressed, and never disrupted the fragile equilibrium of our days. To them, I was the perfect child. The high-achiever. The dutiful daughter. The one who smiled on command and vanished on cue, leaving no mess, no questions, no trace of need behind. I wore masks like second skin. One was painted with practiced brightness, polished and dependable, catching the light just enough to earn approval. The other was translucent as smoke, a disappearing act perfected over time, rendering me a quiet ghost slipping through the hallways of our home. I learned when to be visible and when to dissolve. When to perform and when to fade. Presence became conditional. Absence became safety.

They saw a well-behaved girl. A child who followed rules, met expectations, and rarely caused concern. They saw tidy report cards, compliant manners, a steadiness that looked like resilience. What they did not see were the fractures beneath the surface, the fault lines running through my small body, widening silently with every unspoken fear. They did not see the rot of self-loathing blooming quietly behind my ribs, spreading like mold in a sealed room, fed by silence and shame. They did not hear the internal storms that tore through me in the privacy of night. The way my chest clenched when the house finally slept. The way my thoughts turned feral in the dark, unrestrained by daylight performance.

They did not see the child pacing the edges of her own mind, trying to outrun a despair she did not know how to name. I made sure of that. I became an expert in concealment, in swallowing pain whole, in protecting them from truths I believed would only burden or disappoint. It was not that they did not love me. It was that they loved the version of me I had learned to offer. And I, desperate to keep that love intact, became fluent in erasure. I learned how to disappear without leaving, how to suffer without showing, how to exist in a house full of people while living entirely alone inside myself. In that space between what was seen and what was lived, the fractures deepened. The silence thickened. And the girl they thought they knew grew quieter and quieter, not because she had nothing to say, but because she had learned that survival depended on staying unseen.

And so the house itself became a stage set, familiar and orderly, filled with cues I knew by heart. I learned the rhythm of footsteps, the timing of doors, the moments when laughter was expected and when silence was preferable. I learned how to move through shared spaces without leaving ripples, how to take up as little emotional oxygen as possible, how to make myself agreeable, invisible, easy. My body memorized this choreography long before my mind understood it. Safety, I learned, was not something you asked for. It was something you earned by not needing. I mistook this for maturity. For strength. For love. I told myself that being low-maintenance was kindness, that being self-contained was virtue, that carrying my pain quietly made me good.

I did not yet know the cost of this bargain. I did not yet understand that every feeling swallowed hardened somewhere inside me, that every need denied did not disappear but learned to speak another language. I believed I was protecting everyone. I did not see that I was slowly abandoning myself. In the daylight, I was exemplary. At night, I unraveled. The girl who excelled by day became a collection of fragments by dark, piecing herself together with rituals and silence, trying to survive the hours when no one was watching. The contrast was dizzying. Applause above. Collapse below. Love offered for the performance, never for the truth I kept hidden even from myself.

And still, I did not blame them. Not then. Not now. They loved with the information they had. They parented the child they could see. What I had not yet learned was that invisibility is a powerful spell, one that convinces even the most attentive eyes that nothing is wrong. I was very good at being convincing. I was very good at being fine. But inside that convincing quiet, something essential was starving. A self that wanted to be known without auditioning. A child who wanted to be held without earning it. A girl who did not yet have language for longing, only a body that ached with it. That ache grew in the gap between who I was and who I pretended to be, widening with every successful performance, deepening with every moment I disappeared without protest.

It would take years before I could look back and name this not as deception, but as adaptation. Not as manipulation, but as survival. I was not hiding because I was dishonest. I was hiding because I was afraid that the truth of me would be too much, too inconvenient, too heavy to carry. And so I carried it alone. In that quiet labor of carrying, the storm inside me learned patience. It learned to wait. It learned that daylight belonged to others, and night was mine. And it was there, in that long apprenticeship of invisibility, that the patterns hardened, the rituals deepened, and the ache found sharper ways to speak, still believing that being unseen was the same thing as being safe.

How could my parents, or anyone else, have seen? My suffering was a masterpiece of secrecy, a clandestine war waged in the shadows of my own mind and flesh. I learned the cartography of concealment early. Every wound was hidden. Every bruise strategically placed in the unseen territories of my body. Every burn a quiet ritual performed in the sanctuary of solitude, where no footsteps echoed and no questions followed. I became meticulous, almost reverent, in my devotion to invisibility. They saw only the exterior. Neat. Composed. Untroubled. A child who complied, achieved, and rarely faltered. They saw tidy rooms and tidy answers. They saw a girl who knew how to say "I'm fine" with convincing ease, who understood that calm reassurance and silence soothed. What they never suspected was that beneath that obedient façade, their child was unraveling thread by delicate thread, quietly coming apart while appearing perfectly intact.

Inside me, battles raged without names. Skirmishes fought in breath and bone, in thought and impulse, in rituals that left no evidence where eyes could reach. I was fighting for survival with no language for the fight, bleeding inward as often as outward, negotiating with pain in the dark while daylight praised my composure. I learned how to suffer elegantly, how to fall apart without making a sound, how to keep the damage contained so no one would feel obligated to respond. And I made sure they never did see. Not because I wanted to deceive, but because I was terrified of what being truly seen might cost me. I did not trust that the truth of my pain would be met with safety. I feared it would be misunderstood, minimized, or worse, become another reason to disappoint. Exposure felt more dangerous than silence. Visibility felt like risk. So I perfected disappearance, believing that if I could stay hidden enough, I could stay loved.

In that fear, I became both jailer and prisoner, locking myself inside a version of normal that protected everyone else from discomfort while slowly suffocating me. I guarded my wounds not just from sight, but from touch, from language, from connection. I told myself this was strength. I told myself this was maturity. I told myself this was how you survive. What I did not yet understand was that secrecy, no matter how skilled, always exacts a price. That wars fought alone do not end in victory, only exhaustion. That the more carefully I hid my unraveling, the more tightly it wound itself around my life. And so I kept fighting in the dark, convinced that invisibility was safety, never realizing that the very thing I feared most—being seen—was also the only thing that could have interrupted the quiet destruction I carried so faithfully inside me.

And so the secrecy became another inheritance I carried, heavier with every passing year. What began as protection hardened into habit, then into identity. I no longer asked whether I was safe to be seen; I assumed I was not. I no longer tested the waters of disclosure; I learned to live without thirst. Silence stopped feeling like a choice and began to feel like a rule, one etched so deeply into my nervous system that breaking it felt like danger itself. I trained myself to be readable only on the surface. Predictable. Palatable. I offered up versions of myself that fit neatly into other people's expectations, trimming away anything sharp, inconvenient, or too honest. I learned to anticipate reactions before they arrived, to edit myself in advance, to swallow truths before they could cause friction. The world rewarded me for this restraint. Praise followed. Trust followed. And each reward reinforced the lie that hiding was working.

But invisibility is never neutral. It erodes. Slowly. Quietly. It teaches the body that connection is conditional and the soul that authenticity is unsafe. I felt it in the way my chest tightened when someone asked a sincere question. In the way my throat closed around words that wanted to exist. In the way my body braced even in moments of kindness, waiting for the cost to be revealed. I lived on constant alert, guarding a truth I did not yet know how to carry aloud. The irony was cruel. The more convincingly I appeared whole, the less likely anyone was to look closer. The better I performed wellness, the more invisible my suffering became. Concern fades when competence is loud. Alarm quiets when achievement speaks. I learned that pain hidden behind excellence is rarely questioned. And so I excelled, even as I was disintegrating.

I did not yet know that what I called strength was actually endurance without relief. That resilience without witness becomes another form of harm. That surviving by disappearing teaches the body to associate love with erasure. All I knew was the loneliness of being praised for a self that did not include me, the ache of being admired for a mask I could never take off without fear. And still, I do not blame them. I do not blame the world. I blame the silence that grew where language should have been taught. I blame the absence of safety that made secrecy feel necessary. I blame the way pain, when unacknowledged, learns to hide in plain sight. It would take many years before I could understand this with compassion instead of shame. Before I could see that the child I was did not choose invisibility out of deceit, but out of instinct. She hid because she wanted to survive. She hid because she did not yet believe there was room in the world for her whole truth.

And this is where the story begins to turn. Not abruptly. Not cleanly. But subtly, with the first question that dared to rise beneath the silence: What if being seen does not always lead to loss? What if the danger was never the truth itself, but the carrying of it alone? That question did not save me immediately. But it cracked something open. And for the first time, the war inside me paused, not because it was over, but because it sensed the possibility of another ending. It was a profoundly lonely existence, a private war waged in the dim, echoing chambers of my own mind, where every thought reverberated back at me unanswered. While the world saw a calm surface, glassy and undisturbed, beneath it I was drowning silently, lungs burning, limbs heavy, thrashing in waters no one knew I was even swimming in. There were no splashes. No cries. Only the slow exhaustion of staying afloat without ever being seen.

I carried my anguish like a forbidden relic, pressed tight against my chest as if proximity alone might keep it contained. It felt dangerous to hold and impossible to release. Too shameful to reveal. Too heavy to ever truly put down. It bruised me from the inside, its weight shaping my posture, my breath, my sense of self. I learned how to cradle it carefully, how to move without letting it slip, how to pretend it was not there while it pulsed steadily beneath my ribs. The fear of judgment became a noose around my throat, tightening at the very thought of confession. Words lined up behind my teeth and fell silent. I imagined faces changing the moment I spoke. Pity curdling into discomfort. Concern hardening into distance. I feared being seen not as brave, but as broken. Not as honest, but as burdensome. And so I swallowed truth after truth, each one lodging deeper, each one stealing a little more air.

Silence was not peaceful. It was vigilant. It required constant attention, a watchfulness that never slept. I monitored my expressions. Filtered my reactions. Measured my words until even I could not tell where authenticity ended and performance began. The effort of concealment drained me more than the pain itself, but it felt safer than the alternative. Safer than risking the loss I imagined would follow honesty. And yet, in the quiet moments, when the world receded and there was no one left to impress, the loneliness rose like a tide. I felt it in the hollow space beside me, in the conversations I rehearsed but never had, in the longing to be met without explanation. I wanted someone to notice without needing proof. To ask without accusation. To stay without conditions.

But fear held the line. Fear insisted that exposure would end in rejection, that confession would tighten the noose instead of loosening it. And so I stayed locked inside my private war, fighting without reinforcements, believing that endurance was the same as survival. I did not yet know that silence is not neutral. That secrets grow heavier the longer they are carried. That drowning does not always look like panic. Sometimes it looks like composure. Sometimes it looks like strength. Sometimes it looks like a quiet girl who never asks for help because she has learned that asking feels more dangerous than suffocating alone.

And so the days passed layered over one another, each one asking me to carry the same invisible weight with the same practiced grace. I became adept at breathing shallowly, conserving air, convincing myself that this was enough, that this was living. I learned how to ration my truth the way one rations oxygen underwater, telling myself I could surface later, that there would be time, that endurance was a form of courage. I did not yet see how close endurance sat to erasure. The loneliness sharpened in ordinary moments. At dinner tables. In classrooms. In rooms filled with voices and laughter. I would sit among people and feel the strange ache of being entirely unreachable, as if a pane of glass separated me from the world. I could see others clearly. I could hear them.

But my own inner life pressed against that barrier, fogging it from my side, leaving me unseen even as I was present. I was there, but not *there*. Alive, but not arrived. My body carried the cost of this isolation quietly. Tight shoulders. A jaw clenched so often it forgot how to rest. A chest that rarely expanded fully. Even sleep was guarded. Dreams echoed with the same vigilance as waking, my mind never fully releasing its watch. Rest felt irresponsible. Letting go felt dangerous. I lived as though catastrophe would arrive the moment, I stopped holding everything together with white-knuckled resolve. And still, I told myself this was normal. That everyone felt this way. That adulthood, maturity, goodness all required a certain degree of silence.

I mistook isolation for independence. I mistook self-containment for strength. I did not yet know that humans are not built to survive without witness, that pain unshared does not diminish, it multiplies in the dark. The war inside me did not rage constantly. That would have been easier to name. Instead, it simmered. A low, constant tension beneath everything I did. A readiness. A bracing. I was always preparing for something to go wrong, always rehearsing how to handle it alone. Help felt hypothetical. Connection felt theoretical. Survival felt personal, solitary, non-transferable.

And yet, beneath all that vigilance, there was longing. Quiet. Persistent. Unreasonable. A hope I tried to starve but could never quite kill. A wish to be known without having to prove the severity of my pain. To be believed without bleeding. To be held without explanation. That longing frightened me more than the despair, because it suggested that another way might exist, and I did not yet trust that the world could meet me there. So I stayed silent. I stayed composed. I stayed afloat. But silence, like water, is patient. It waits. It rises. And it would take time, and rupture, and a kind of reckoning I could not yet imagine, for me to learn that surviving alone was not the same as living, and that asking for help was not a failure of strength, but the first honest breath after years underwater.

So I hid. I perfected the art of masking, wearing smiles as armor and politeness as camouflage, layering pleasantries over pain until the weight of them felt normal, almost comfortable. I learned how to laugh on cue, how to tilt my head just right, how to reassure others with my steadiness while quietly abandoning my own. I became fluent in reassurance, generous with calm, skilled at making everyone else feel safe in my presence, even as I steadily evacuated myself. I played my role so convincingly that even I sometimes forgot where the act ended and the ache began. The performance seeped into my bones. The mask hardened. I began to confuse applause with safety and composure with worth, mistaking approval for proof that I was surviving correctly.

And through it all, the death wish lingered beside me, a quiet, persistent shadow that never demanded attention yet never left. It moved with me, unannounced and familiar, a whisper threading itself through my thoughts like poisoned silk, soft enough to feel comforting, strong enough to bind. It did not shout. It did not rush. It waited. Patient. Certain. Always available. It promised relief. Promised stillness. Promised a place where the internal screaming would finally fall silent, where effort would end and vigilance would no longer be required. It offered rest without explanation, quiet without consequence, an end without the humiliation of asking for help.

It became my most intimate companion. The one thought that did not leave when others did. The one presence that did not require explanation or performance. A dark lullaby I hummed to myself in moments of exhaustion, its melody woven from rest and release and the fantasy of no longer having to endure. It followed me into classrooms, into bedrooms, into the small hours of the night when the world slept and my mind refused to. It curled beside me in the quiet, familiar and steady, reminding me, relentlessly, that oblivion was always an option.

There was a strange comfort in that knowledge. Not desire exactly, but reassurance. A sense that no matter how unbearable things became, there was an exit I could imagine, a door I could trace with my mind even if I never touched the handle. The thought sat like a secret talisman in my pocket, heavy and cold, something I could press my fingers around when the panic rose too high. It offered the illusion of choice in a life that felt otherwise trapped, a way to believe I was not entirely cornered by my own existence.

I did not yet see how that companion kept me tethered to despair even as it pretended to soothe it. How every time I leaned on the promise of disappearance, I stepped further away from the possibility of staying. I believed it was mercy. I believed it was honesty. I believed it was the clearest truth I had. I did not yet know it was another mask, subtler than the smile, more dangerous than silence, another way of avoiding the terrifying risk of being fully alive in a world I did not trust to hold me. So I carried it quietly, that shadow, that song, that promise. I let it walk beside me through the years, believing it was the only thing that truly understood how tired I was, how deeply worn down by the labor of existing.

And in doing so, I learned how to live half-present, half-gone, existing in the narrow space between performance and escape. I mastered the art of staying without arriving, of breathing without inhabiting my own life. I did not yet know that one day I would have to turn toward the ache instead of away from it. That I would have to loosen my grip on the promise of disappearance and ask a far more frightening question. Not how to vanish quietly. Not how to end the pain cleanly. But how to stay. How to remain. How to live without a hidden exit folded into every thought.

The Soundtrack of Endurance

As I grew older, the self-harm did not fade. It evolved. It deepened. It wove itself into the quiet rhythms of my life like a dark, familiar hymn, one I no longer noticed consciously because it had been playing for so long. It learned how to hide in routine, how to slip between obligations, how to wait patiently until the world grew too loud or too empty. What once felt urgent became habitual. What once shocked me became normalized. Pain no longer announced itself as crisis; it arrived as cadence, as something expected, almost comforting in its predictability. And the suicidal ideation, that shadow I had carried since childhood, did not loosen its grip with age or achievement. If anything, it sharpened. It matured alongside me, refining its arguments, learning my weaknesses, speaking with greater confidence the older I became. It was no longer just a wish whispered in moments of overwhelm.

It became a presence. A low, relentless hum beneath every thought, every breath, vibrating through my days like faulty wiring hidden in the walls. It followed me everywhere. In success, it waited quietly, reminding me that relief was temporary. In failure, it surged forward, ready with solutions that promised finality. It was there in the pauses between conversations, in the space before sleep, in the moments when joy tried to land and found no safe place to rest. It did not demand my attention; it assumed it. A background music I had grown so accustomed to that silence itself felt unfamiliar. This was the most insidious part. The way it blended into my sense of normal. The way I stopped questioning its presence and started organizing my life around it.

I made room for it without realizing I was doing so, adjusting my expectations, lowering my hopes, keeping my future small enough to manage. I lived as though there were always a foot poised near the exit, as though endurance was temporary and escape permanent. The white noise haunted my every moment. It softened nothing. It sharpened everything. It colored my thoughts, drained my energy, and taught me to measure my days not by how fully I lived them, but by how successfully I endured them. I could function. I could perform. I could even smile. But beneath it all ran that constant frequency, reminding me that disappearing was not just imaginable, but available. I did not yet understand how corrosive that hum was. How it eroded possibility simply by existing. How it trained my nervous system to expect collapse, to prepare for endings instead of beginnings. All I knew was that it was always there, steady and unyielding, the soundtrack of a life lived under siege.

And still, I kept going. Not because I believed in the future, but because habit is powerful, and survival does not always require hope. Sometimes it only requires momentum. I moved forward with that hum inside me, believing this was what living felt like, unaware that a life accompanied by constant rehearsal for its own ending is not neutral, not harmless, not inevitable. It would take time, and rupture, and a kind of listening I had never practiced before, to realize that the background music I thought was me was actually something else entirely. Something learned. Something carried. Something that did not have to play forever.

But for then, it played on. Steady. Relentless. And I lived my life to its rhythm, not yet knowing that silence was possible, or that learning how to stay would require me to finally hear myself beneath the noise. And beneath that relentless rhythm, something else began to stir, faint and easily drowned out, but stubborn in its persistence. A counter-pulse. Not hope yet. Not belief. Just a subtle dissonance, a missed beat in the hymn that had governed me for so long. A moment here and there when the hum faltered, when the noise thinned just enough for another sound to leak through. A question. A hesitation. A quiet, unfamiliar pause.

At first, I mistook it for exhaustion. The body's rebellion. The soul's fatigue. But it kept returning, that small interruption in the static, as if some part of me was growing tired of rehearsing its own ending. I would feel it in the brief spaces between breaths, in the way my chest sometimes resisted the old collapse, in the strange discomfort of imagining a future longer than a season. It felt dangerous to notice. Risky to name. As though acknowledging it might anger the shadow that had ruled me for so long. The hum did not disappear. It resisted. It tightened its grip, growing louder in protest, reminding me of all the reasons I should not trust this interruption. It told me silence was a trap. That staying was naïve.

That momentum was safer than curiosity. And yet, the counter-pulse remained, soft but insistent, refusing to be extinguished. It did not argue. It did not persuade. It simply existed, a quiet fact beneath the noise. This was not the beginning of healing, not yet. It was the beginning of awareness. The first hairline crack in the certainty that this soundtrack was permanent. I began to notice how tired I was of enduring, how thin the rewards of survival had become. I began to sense the cost of living under siege, of carrying an exit plan like a talisman instead of a life like a promise. The hum, once protective, started to feel intrusive. Uninvited. Less like truth and more like habit overstaying its welcome.

I did not know how to turn it off. I did not know how to replace it. But for the first time, I sensed that it was not me. That it was something I had adapted to, something I had learned to live alongside, something that had once served a purpose and then quietly taken over. That realization did not bring relief. It brought grief. Grief for the years spent mistaking noise for identity. Grief for the self that had been living beneath the static, waiting for a chance to speak. Still, the music played. Still, the days passed. But now there was friction. A subtle resistance in my listening. I no longer surrendered to the rhythm without question. I began, slowly and imperfectly, to wonder what it might sound like if the volume were lowered. If the room were allowed to breathe. If my life were measured not by how close I stood to the exit, but by how deeply I could inhabit the space I was in.

I did not yet know how to stay. But for the first time, I was beginning to suspect that staying was possible. That the silence I feared was not emptiness, but room. And that beneath the hum, beneath the years of rehearsal and retreat, there was a voice that had never stopped waiting, patient and quiet, ready to be heard when I finally dared to listen.

That reminder did not shout. It did not need to. It whispered with the confidence of something long rehearsed, unyielding in its certainty. "*You are not okay.*" The words arrived already settled, already decided. "*You are broken beyond repair.* Not injured. Not hurting. Broken." As if whatever was wrong in me had passed the point of mending. "*You are not enough. You will never be enough.*" The verdict echoed until it felt structural, load-bearing, as though my very skeleton had been assembled around that belief. A pathetic being. A worthless, unlovable creature. I carried that identity as if it had been carved into my bones with permanent ink, as if even my marrow had memorized the accusation.

There were nights when the pain swelled so violently it felt as though my ribs might crack under the pressure, as though something inside me was expanding faster than my body could hold. My chest became a locked room filling with smoke. Breath turned shallow, frantic, insufficient. It felt as though the darkness itself had hands, tightening its fists around my lungs, squeezing until every inhale became a negotiation. I would lie still, afraid that movement might shatter whatever fragile containment I had left, listening to my own heartbeat thud like a warning against my ears. In those moments, I felt myself slipping beneath the surface, the world above growing muffled and distant. I was drowning in a vast, merciless ocean of despair, water closing over my head without drama, without witnesses.

No lifeboats. No shore. Just the endless heave and pull of it, the way it dragged at my limbs, made even the idea of swimming feel absurd. Each day became another wave breaking over me, relentless and indifferent. Each morning was not a beginning but a resurfacing, a gasp stolen before the next swell hit. Survival turned into a series of small, desperate calculations. How long could I tread water before my muscles burned out? How little breath could I survive on? I learned to live between waves, in the narrow seconds where my head cleared the surface and the world came back into focus just long enough to endure it again. I did not dream of rescue. I did not imagine land. I only focused on not sinking *today*. On keeping my face angled upward, even when my arms shook with fatigue.

And yet, even as the ocean closed in, there was something stubborn in me that refused to fully let go. Not strength. Not hope. Something quieter. A reflex, perhaps. The body's ancient insistence on air. I would break the surface again, coughing, burning, furious at myself for still being here and equally terrified of what it would mean if I wasn't. The despair told me I was worthless, unlovable, beyond repair. But my lungs kept reaching anyway. My heart kept beating its steady, inconvenient rhythm, as if it had not received the memo that I was supposed to disappear. I did not yet recognize that contradiction for what it was. I only felt the exhaustion of it. The endless cycle of submersion and survival. The way each wave left me weaker, more convinced that eventually I would not make it back up.

I believed the drowning was inevitable. That endurance was merely postponement. That this was the natural state of someone like me. But even then, even there, in the thick of that merciless sea, something in me was still fighting for air. Still insisting on the next breath. Still surfacing, again and again, not because I believed I deserved to live, but because some part of me had not yet learned how to stop trying. That insistence did not feel noble. It did not arrive dressed as courage or framed as purpose. It was crude and inconvenient, a stubborn biological rebellion against the story I believed. An animal reflex. A rib-deep refusal to comply. Even as my mind rehearsed disappearance, my body kept arguing for presence, dragging me back to the surface with aching lungs and a heart that would not learn the lesson it was being taught.

I resented that insistence. I envied the imagined quiet of surrender. And yet I obeyed the pull upward, again and again, surfacing despite myself. Each breath felt stolen, illicit, as though I were cheating some cosmic verdict by continuing. I inhaled with guilt, exhaled with apology. The air burned on the way in, sharp and cold, a reminder that staying was not gentle. Staying hurt. Staying required effort. And still my chest rose. Still my ribs widened. Still the machinery of living carried on without my permission, without my belief. I felt trapped inside a body that would not give up, housed in flesh that insisted on tomorrow even when my mind could not imagine it.

Days blurred into a narrow choreography of endurance. Wake. Surface. Breathe. Hold. Sink a little. Rise again. I learned the texture of fatigue the way sailors learn tides. The heaviness behind the eyes. The ache in the shoulders from treading water too long. The peculiar numbness that follows sustained panic, when fear grows tired of shouting and settles into a low, constant ache. I moved through the world carrying the ocean with me, salt-heavy and relentless, sloshing just beneath my skin. There were moments, small and easily missed, when the water thinned just enough for light to reach me. Not hope. Not relief. Just clarity. The awareness that I was still here. Still breathing. Still responding. These moments frightened me as much as they steadied me, because they contradicted the narrative I had built so carefully.

If I was truly beyond repair, why did my body keep repairing itself? If I was truly unlovable, why did something inside me keep reaching, again and again, for air? I did not yet have language for that question. I did not yet have the safety to ask it out loud. All I knew was the sensation of surfacing, the shock of breath, the way my chest burned, and my vision sharpened as the world rushed back in. I mistook that for punishment. I told myself it was proof of my failure to disappear properly. I did not yet understand it as resistance. The sea remained merciless. The waves did not soften out of sympathy. Each day still demanded its toll. But somewhere beneath the exhaustion, beneath the certainty of eventual collapse, a thin thread began to form. Not belief. Not optimism. Just a fact. I was still here. Despite the verdict. Despite the whispers. Despite the weight.

And that fact, inconvenient and uncelebrated, refused to dissolve. I continued to surface, breath by burning breath, not because I trusted the water to calm, but because my body would not stop reaching upward. Not because I believed in rescue, but because some ancient intelligence inside me had decided that air was non-negotiable. I was not choosing life in any triumphant sense. Life was choosing me, again and again, hauling me back to the surface with shaking hands and a furious heart. It would take time for me to understand what that meant. Time to realize that this stubborn insistence was not weakness, but the earliest, quietest form of self-preservation. At the time, it simply felt like contradiction. Like punishment. Like being forced to stay awake in a world that had taught me rest only existed at the bottom of the sea.

But still I breathed. Still I rose. Still I endured the next wave. And though I could not yet name it, something in me was learning, breath by breath, that survival itself was a language. One I was speaking fluently long before I ever believed I had the right to.

Perfect on the Outside, Airless Within

And still, somehow, I hid it all. I perfected the art of seeming intact, of presenting a version of myself so seamless it left no seams to question. The flawless mask. The practiced smile. The posture of composure worn like a tailored suit. I learned how to move through the world as an illusion of wholeness, how to offer reassurance with my eyes while my insides were unraveling. I became convincing not because I was well, but because I was vigilant. Every expression monitored. Every reaction curated. Every crack swiftly plastered over before it could widen. To the outside world, I looked like a girl who had it all together. Capable. Grounded. Reliable. Someone others leaned on. Someone who did not wobble. The illusion held because I held it relentlessly, gripping it with the same intensity I used to keep myself afloat.

I mistook that constant effort for strength. I mistook endurance for health. The applause only reinforced the performance, teaching me that collapse was unacceptable and silence was success. But under that polished veneer, I was rotting from the inside out. Not dramatically. Not all at once. Slowly. Silently. Day after agonizing day. It was a decay without spectacle, a quiet corrosion eating through unseen layers. My thoughts soured. My joy thinned. My sense of self softened at the edges, losing definition. I smiled through conversations while something inside me decomposed, unnoticed and unacknowledged, like a wound sealed over without ever being cleaned.

I lived as a walking ghost draped in perfection. Present, but not alive. Visible, but not known. My body went through the motions of living while my spirit hovered somewhere just behind it, detached, translucent, watching. I existed in photographs and achievements and polite exchanges yet felt strangely absent from my own life. As though I had already left and no one had noticed. As though I were haunting my own body. And beneath it all, my heart whispered its own quiet obituary. Not aloud. Not in language anyone else could hear. Just a steady, internal murmur marking time, recording losses no one else counted. Each day felt like another line added to that unseen ledger, another small goodbye disguised as normalcy. I mourned myself in secret, grieving a version of me I could not yet name, could not yet save.

The tragedy was not only that I was suffering. It was that I was suffering invisibly. That I had become so skilled at disappearing while standing right in front of people. That my pain had learned how to dress itself up as competence, how to pass as success, how to be mistaken for strength. I was applauded for the very behaviors that were hollowing me out. And still, I kept the mask in place. Because I did not yet know who I would be without it. Because I feared that if I let it slip, there would be nothing underneath but the rot, the ghost, the whispering heart counting its own endings. I believed the illusion was all that stood between me and complete erasure.

I did not yet understand that the decay was not who I was, only what happened when something living is forced to survive without air, without witness, without rest. I did not yet know that even rot is evidence that something once lived, and that ghosts only linger where there is unfinished life. All I knew then was how to look whole while quietly falling apart, how to smile while mourning myself, how to exist as a living contradiction: admired and applauded, hollowed and fading, breathing and yet convinced I was already gone. And so the performance continued, day folding into day with the quiet precision of a well-rehearsed act. I woke each morning already braced, already assembling myself piece by piece, fastening the mask before my feet touched the floor.

There was no room for hesitation. No allowance for cracks. I learned to greet the world with steadiness even when my hands shook beneath the surface, to speak with certainty while my insides trembled with doubt. I became fluent in looking fine, in sounding okay, in answering the unasked questions with a smile that asked nothing in return. Inside, however, the erosion kept working. It was patient. Methodical. A slow undoing that did not announce itself as crisis but as fatigue, as thinning, as a gradual dimming of color. I felt myself growing quieter, not just outwardly, but inwardly too. Desires dulled. Curiosity waned. The future began to feel less like a horizon and more like a corridor I was expected to walk down without stopping. I was alive, but increasingly I was living in grayscale, each day drained of saturation, of texture, of surprise.

There were moments when I caught glimpses of what I had lost. A sudden laugh that startled me with its sincerity. A flicker of longing I quickly smothered. A fleeting ache for something unnamed but desperately missed. Those moments frightened me more than the numbness, because they reminded me there was still something inside me capable of wanting, of reaching, of grieving what had been taken. So I learned to swallow even those sparks, to tuck them away before they could ignite hope I did not trust myself to hold. The mask became heavier with time. What once felt like protection began to feel like a weight pressing down on my chest, making each breath a little more laborious. Yet I did not remove it. I tightened it. Adjusted it. Reinforced it. Because the world responded so well to it. Because people loved me inside it.

Because it gave me a place to stand, even if that place was slowly collapsing beneath my feet. I told myself this was maturity. Resilience. Strength. I told myself that everyone carried something unseen, that this was simply the cost of functioning, of being responsible, of being admired. I did not yet realize that I was confusing survival with living, composure with wholeness, and disappearance with peace. I did not yet know that a life can look intact and still be starving. And yet, beneath the exhaustion and the performance and the quiet grief, something remained unresolved. A pulse. A tension. A low insistence that refused to be fully extinguished. It lived in the spaces between breaths, in the ache that followed laughter, in the sadness that arrived without explanation. It was the part of me that knew this could not be the end of the story, even if I could not imagine another chapter.

I carried that knowing without language, without permission, without hope. It did not feel like optimism. It felt like unease. Like an unanswered question knocking softly from inside the walls I had built. I ignored it for as long as I could, continuing to polish the illusion, to perfect the vanishing act, to mourn myself quietly while pretending nothing was wrong. But the body remembers what the mind tries to forget. The heart remembers what performance cannot erase. And even as I stood there, admired and applauded, hollowed and fading, something within me was still listening, still waiting, still refusing to accept that disappearing was the same as being saved.

I did not yet know how to turn toward that truth. I only knew it was there, breathing quietly beneath the mask, patient and unfinished, holding space for a life that had not yet been allowed to fully arrive.

The weight of my secrets grew heavier with each passing year, accumulating quietly, invisibly, until it pressed against my ribs like a second skeleton. It did not announce itself. It did not arrive all at once. It settled slowly, bone by borrowed bone, until my own frame felt crowded, overinhibited by what I could not say. It was not a sudden collapse, but a slow accrual, a geology of silence layered day upon day. Each unspoken truth calcified, each swallowed sentence adding density, until my body carried more than bone and muscle ever intended. I lived inside an anatomy altered by secrecy, my own structure crowded out by what I could not release. It was the kind of burden no one offers to carry for you, because no one knows it exists.

There were no handles on it, no visible seams. From the outside, I moved like anyone else. Inside, I bore a private architecture of restraint, beams and supports holding up a life shaped around concealment. Load-bearing silence. Unforgiving walls. A house built to stand, not to breathe. I felt it most when I tried to inhale and found my breath stopping short, as if my lungs were bumping up against something solid, something immovable. As though the air itself had learned my limits and refused to cross them. Oxygen became a rationed commodity. Each breath negotiated, bargained for, counted. I learned how to sip air instead of drinking it in, how to survive on shallow inhales that never quite reached the depths where relief might live at the bottom of my chest. Even breathing became an act of endurance, a deliberate, conscious effort, a reminder that survival itself required concentration. My body adapted in quiet, obedient ways. Shoulders crept upward and stayed there, as if permanently bracing for impact that never came but was always expected.

Muscles held tension like a second language, fluent and automatic. My chest learned the shape of compression so well it began to feel normal, as though this constriction were simply the way living worked. I mistook tension for stability. I mistook holding on for being held together. I praised myself for not collapsing, never questioning the cost of never resting. The secrets pressed inward from all sides, a slow, relentless gravity that did not rush but never relented. They leaned on my sternum, crowded my heart, narrowed the space where ease might have lived. Sometimes it felt as though my ribs were a cage turned inward, protecting nothing, trapping everything. A prison with no guards, only habits. I moved through my days carrying this unseen weight, performing lightness while my insides bore the strain of constant restraint, a quiet labor no one clocked.

And still, I kept going. I adjusted. I compensated. I told myself this was manageable. That everyone lived with some version of this pressure. That needing less air was not a warning, but a skill I had mastered. I did not yet recognize that breathlessness is not discipline, but alarm. That a body forced to ration oxygen is not coping but surviving under siege. All I knew then was the effort. The constant, invisible work of existing while compressed. The way each breath reminded me, subtly and persistently, that something inside me was taking up too much space because it had never been given a place to go. I did not yet understand that secrets do not disappear when they are hidden. They settle. They harden. They build homes inside the body.

And one day, I would have to decide whether to keep reinforcing the walls or to risk opening a door. But at the time, all I knew was how to endure the weight, how to live bent beneath it, believing that if I could just hold it well enough, long enough, it might stop asking for air.

My shame coiled tightly around my throat like a serpent, patient and unrelenting. It did not strike all at once; it constricted slowly, tightening whenever I thought of telling the truth, whenever words edged too close to confession. It hissed warnings into the quiet spaces of my mind. "Don't. You'll ruin everything. You'll disappoint them. You'll be exposed." And so I swallowed myself again and again, each silence another tightening loop, each unspoken truth another inch stolen from my air.

The expectations I carried only added to the weight. My own, sharp and unforgiving. My parents', unspoken but heavy with hope. The world's, relentless in its demand for composure and success. They stacked on my chest like a stone slab, immovable and absolute. I lived as if pinned beneath it, proving my worth through achievement, through compliance, through the careful avoidance of failure. Rest felt like rebellion. Need felt like weakness. Collapse felt forbidden. I lived inside a lie of my own construction, walls built from politeness and performance, from discipline and denial. It was sturdy enough to stand, but not to breathe in. I performed a version of myself I could neither sustain nor escape, a role that required constant vigilance. I was both actor and stagehand, forever adjusting the lighting, fixing the cracks, making sure the audience never saw the strain in my hands or the tremor in my voice.

With every forced smile, I felt something inside me splinter. With every automatic "I'm fine," the lie sank deeper, rooting itself further into my sense of self. With every perfect façade polished for the world, the fracture within me widened, hairline at first, then unmistakable. I could feel it spreading, a fault line running through my days, threatening to split me open at any moment. And the cruelest part was this: the better I became at performing, the harder it felt to stop. Praise reinforced the prison. Approval tightened the bars. I was rewarded for my silence, admired for my endurance, trusted because I never asked for help. The world applauded the very thing that was breaking me, and I learned to clap along, even as the sound echoed hollowly inside my chest.

I did not yet know how close I was to myself. How thin the walls truly were. How much energy it took to keep the lie standing upright. All I knew was the pressure, the constriction, the constant sense of holding something back that was desperate to be released. I lived braced against myself, afraid that if I ever loosened my grip, the truth would come spilling out all at once, undeniable and irreversible. So I kept holding. Kept smiling. Kept performing. And with each passing year, the weight pressed harder, the serpent tightened further, the stone settled more firmly into place, while the fracture inside me widened in silence, waiting for the moment when pretending would finally cost more than telling the truth.

And still, I told myself this was normal. That everyone carried something heavy. That this was simply the cost of being competent, of being good of being loved without complication. I mistook strain for maturity, tension for virtue. I learned to wear exhaustion like a badge of honor, to treat depletion as proof that I was trying hard enough. If I was tired, it meant I was worthy. If I was empty, it meant I had given everything I had. But the body keeps its own records. It remembers what the mind insists on forgetting. I felt it in the tightness that never left my shoulders, in the way my jaw ached from clenching words I did not allow myself to speak. I felt it in the constant vigilance humming beneath my skin, the readiness for collapse I pretended not to notice. My nervous system lived on high alert, braced for exposure, braced for failure, braced for the moment the illusion would finally crack.

The lie required maintenance. Constant upkeep. There was no rest inside it, only brief pauses where I could catch my breath before resuming the performance. I learned to anticipate expectations before they were voiced, to meet them pre-emptively, to stay one step ahead of disappointment. I became an expert in reading rooms, in calibrating myself to the emotional weather around me, adjusting my tone, my posture, my needs until I fit seamlessly into whatever space I occupied. And yet, the fracture kept widening. Sometimes I could feel it most clearly in moments that should have felt safe. In quiet evenings. In praise delivered without conditions. In kindness offered freely. Those moments terrified me, because they brushed too close to the truth. They threatened to soften me, to loosen my grip. And I feared that if I ever relaxed fully, the weight I had been holding back would collapse inward, burying me beneath everything I had refused to name.

So I stayed rigid. Composed. Useful. I chose containment over honesty, control over relief. I believed that if I could just hold on a little longer, be a little better, try a little harder, the pressure might ease on its own. That one day the stone would lift. The serpent would release. The fracture would seal without anyone ever having to see it. But silence does not heal fractures. It only allows them to spread. I was living proof of that, standing upright inside a life that looked intact from the outside, while inside I was splintering under the strain of being everything except myself. I did not yet know that the truth I feared spilling out was not a catastrophe waiting to happen, but a self, waiting to be met. I did not yet know that telling the truth would not destroy me, but pretending already was.

For now, all I knew was how to endure. How to hold. How to survive by shrinking inward, tightening every muscle around a story that had grown too heavy to carry alone. And somewhere beneath the pressure, beneath the fear, beneath the fracture widening in silence, the truth waited patiently, not to explode, but to breathe. For years, though, I would still be haunted by suicidal ideation as a companion.

The In-Between Where the Story Did Not End

And the death-wish, that dark companion, only sharpened with time. It did not vanish because I had stayed. It adapted. It learned new contours. What once crept now lingered, what once whispered now murmured with familiarity, until it became a hunger that pulsed beneath everything else. A relentless itch beneath the skin of my soul, impossible to ignore. I scratched at it with thoughts, with fantasies, with rehearsals of leaving, again and again, until the itch broke open into a wound, raw and exposed, weeping a truth I did not yet know how to hold without bleeding. It lived in me like an unfinished sentence, always trailing off toward disappearance. A longing that did not announce itself as desire, but as exhaustion. As relief imagined. As the fantasy of laying the burden down and never having to pick it up again. The wish was not loud. It was persuasive. It spoke in the language of rest. Of quiet. Of finally being released from the labor of being me.

There were nights when the world outside quieted into something almost tender, when the day loosened its grip and darkness arrived like a held breath. Nights when I found myself again on cold grass under the silver witness of the moon, its light indifferent and ancient, asking nothing of me. The ground chilled through my clothes, anchoring me to my body even as my thoughts drifted dangerously far from it. The air smelled of damp earth and distance. Crickets stitched sound into the silence. And I sat there, small beneath that vastness, feeling both held and abandoned at once. The shadows stretched long around me, thin and distorted, mirroring the ones inside. They reached where I reached. They folded where I folded. I watched them move as the moon shifted, thinking how easily darkness changes shape without ever truly leaving. I would stare into the sky as though it might answer me back, as though somewhere in that spread of stars there might be an explanation for the ache I could no longer contain, a reason that would make the wanting stop.

Sometimes I whispered to the night. Sometimes I said nothing at all. The words felt too fragile for sound. I asked questions without language. Why does this still follow me? Why am I so tired of staying? Why does the idea of not being here feel like relief instead of loss? The sky, vast and unspeaking, offered no answers. Only presence. Only witness. And in that quiet, the death-wish would sit beside me, close but not touching, a familiar weight. It did not push. It did not rush. It simply reminded me that it was still there, still an option, still waiting. That no matter how hard I tried to live, the idea of leaving had learned how to survive too. I did not yet know that longing can persist even after the moment passes. Choosing to stay once does not end the conversation. I only knew that the hunger had grown more articulate, more patient, more skilled at disguising itself as truth. And there I was, under that moon, holding the ache like a live wire in my chest, trying to understand how something could want both rest and life at the same time.

The night did not resolve me. But it held me long enough for dawn to become possible again. And so I rose eventually, cold-limbed, heart heavy, carrying the death-wish with me as I always had. Not defeated. Not surrendered. Just there. Sharpened. Waiting. And I, still learning, breath by breath, how to live alongside a shadow without letting it decide where I end. And still, even as I stood up from the cold grass and walked back into the shape of my life, the shadow followed. Not dramatically. Not with malice. It followed the way breath follows the body, the way gravity follows bone. It settled back into its familiar place inside me, neither louder nor quieter, just present. A companion that had learned how to travel lightly, how to fit itself into the folds of my days without drawing attention. It waited in the margins. It listened. It learned.

By daylight, it changed its clothes. It dressed itself in functionality, in productivity, in endurance. It hid behind schedules and responsibilities, behind the steady rhythm of getting through one more day. It whispered in subtler ways then, threading itself through fatigue and self-doubt, disguising itself as reason. You're just tired. Anyone would feel this way. This is what life costs. It did not sound like death in the sun. It sounded like realism. Like maturity. Like acceptance. The hunger remained, though. Quieter, perhaps, but more refined. No longer a scream, but a pull. A gravity toward stillness. Toward an imagined place where effort ceased and the constant negotiation of existence finally ended. It showed itself in moments of pause, in the way my shoulders sagged when I was alone, in the way my body leaned toward sleep not for rest, but for disappearance. It lived in the wish to be unconscious longer than necessary, to stay under, to delay waking just a little more.

I began to understand, dimly, that the death-wish was not always about dying. Often, it was about stopping. About relief from vigilance. About laying down the armor and never having to pick it up again. It was grief for a life that felt like labor without sanctuary. It was mourning for an ease I had never known but somehow still remembered. The hunger was not for annihilation alone. It was for mercy. And that realization unsettled me. Because it complicated everything. It meant the shadow was not my enemy in the way I had imagined. It was a messenger carrying unbearable information in a language that frightened me. It was the part of me that could no longer tolerate being unheard, unseen, unheld. It was exhaustion given voice. Pain asking, again and again, for something to change.

I did not yet know how to answer it. I only knew how to coexist. To walk forward with it at my side, acknowledging its presence without letting it lead. Some days I succeeded. Some days I did not. There were moments when the ache flared so brightly it blurred my vision, and others when it receded into a dull background hum I almost forgot was there. Living became an ongoing negotiation, a fragile truce renewed daily. What kept me here, in those years, was not certainty or hope or clarity. It was something smaller and more stubborn. A refusal to let the shadow have the final word. A quiet insistence that if it had learned to survive alongside me, then perhaps I could learn something too. If the hunger could evolve, then maybe so could I.

So I kept choosing dawns that did not resolve me. I kept carrying the ache without offering it my life. I kept learning, slowly and imperfectly, how to stay present even when part of me longed to vanish. Breath by breath. Step by step. Not triumphant. Not healed. Just alive. Just here. And for a long time, that was enough. However, as always, I jumped a little too far ahead into hope I had not yet found, so let's make our way back to the shadows, under the moonlight.

In that moonlit silence, life felt impossibly heavy, a mountain of pain balanced on fragile shoulders that had been bearing weight far longer than they were built for. The night pressed down gently and relentlessly all at once, a velvet gravity that did not crush outright but asked me to keep holding, keep standing, keep enduring. I felt small beneath it, bowed by an accumulation of days that had asked too much and offered too little in return. My bones ached with the effort of staying upright, of continuing, of carrying a life that felt less like a gift and more like a duty I had never agreed to accept. And death, death did not arrive as a monster then. It did not bare its teeth or drag chains across the ground. It came softly, almost tenderly, like a doorway left ajar at the end of a long corridor.

A release. A gentle slipping out of the noise. It presented itself as peace, as rest without consequence, as the quiet I had been chasing for years with bleeding hands and burning skin. Not an ending born of violence, but a closing of eyes. A laying down. A permission to stop trying. In the stillness, it felt merciful, like an answer whispered directly to my exhaustion. In those trembling moments, I would wonder if the suffering was worth the brief flickers of joy that sometimes broke through the dark. If those sparks were real, or merely tricks of light, fireflies released just often enough to keep me tethered to a life that hurt too much to hold. Joy felt fleeting, conditional, easily revoked. Pain felt constant, reliable, brutally honest.

I weighed them against each other in the dark, measuring a lifetime of ache against moments that vanished almost as soon as I noticed them, and I could not yet imagine a future where the scales tipped toward anything but endurance. I would pray then. Not for strength. Not for guidance. Not even for relief in the living sense of the word. I prayed for an ending. For permission to rest. For the courage to stop breathing without fear or guilt. My prayers were quiet and ashamed, folded inward as contraband smuggled through the night. They did not ask to be answered loudly. They did not demand miracles. They only asked to be allowed. To be granted. To finally be over.

And still, beneath those prayers, something resisted finality. Even as I asked for the door, some part of me lingered in the room, listening. Even as I imagined peace beyond the threshold, I remained rooted to the ground, feeling the cold grass beneath my palms, the night air brushing my skin, the undeniable weight of my own body still here. Breath continued to arrive without permission. The heart continued its stubborn rhythm. I did not yet understand that this hesitation was not cowardice, but complexity. Not weakness, but life insisting, quietly and without explanation, on one more moment, presence that had not yet finished asking its questions.

So I stayed there. Suspended between wanting the pain to end and not quite wanting to end with it. Between prayer and breath. Between doorway and ground. Holding the ache. Holding the night. Holding myself in that fragile, unbearable in-between, where suffering had not yet convinced me, and living had not yet revealed why it mattered. I did not know then that this suspended space, this refusal to fully step through the door, was not failure. It was a pause. A hinge. A breath held at the edge of something unnamed. I could not yet call it hope. I could barely call it choice. But it was a moment where the story did not end, even when every part of me believed it should.

And in that quiet resistance, that almost imperceptible staying, something began to shift. Not enough to save me yet. Not enough to heal me yet. But enough to keep the question open. Enough to leave the door unclosed. Enough to let the night pass without claiming me, not because I did not attempt to end my life, but because something way Higher than me intervened and whispered, “Not yet, you are not ready, just trust, there is better, there is more.” I rose eventually, cold-limbed and heavy-hearted, carrying the ache with me as I always had. But I carried something else too, though I did not yet have language for it. A thin, unremarkable thread of continuation. A decision made not in strength, but in exhaustion. Not because life had convinced me, but because it had not yet lost me entirely. And for that night, that was enough.

The thought of stepping across the threshold, of surrendering to the quiet on the other side, became a seductive promise, a lullaby sung in a voice that knew my exhaustion by heart. It shimmered like mercy. A final escape from a life that felt like a battlefield where I was both the wounded and the weapon, bleeding and striking in the same breath. The idea did not feel violent. It felt clean. Conclusive. Like setting something down after carrying it for far too long. But what drives a soul to this precipice? What chisels a person down to the bone until despair becomes the only language they speak fluently? What unravels someone so completely that the edge of existence feels more welcoming than the world that claims to hold them? These questions haunted me in the quiet, circling like birds over open water, never landing, never leaving.

For me, it was never a single wound. Never one catastrophic moment that could be named and pointed to like a scar with a clear origin. It was accumulation. A slow poisoning. A drip so steady it disguised itself as normal. A lifetime of tiny heartbreaks, small enough to dismiss individually, heavy enough together to crush a chest. Disappointments swallowed. Needs unmet. Words withheld. Love rationed. Safety made conditional. Each one seemed survivable on its own. Together, they fused into one vast, unnameable ache. It was the thousandth time I learned not to speak. The quiet lesson that my pain was inconvenient. The subtle message that I was too much and not enough at the same time. It was the erosion of trust by moments so ordinary they never registered as harm, yet they sanded me down all the same. I grew thinner inside without noticing, worn smooth by years of accommodation, until there was so little left to absorb the impact of living.

Despair did not arrive like an intruder. It moved in slowly, rearranged the furniture, learned my routines. It taught me its grammar patiently, until hopelessness felt like clarity and numbness like wisdom. I did not wake up one day wanting to leave the world. I woke up one day too tired to keep fighting it. The threshold did not call to me because I wanted to die. It called because I wanted the war to stop. And when life becomes an unending siege, even surrender can start to look like peace. Still, even as that promise gleamed before me, something in me kept asking why. Not loudly. Not bravely. Just enough to keep the story from sealing shut. I did not yet have answers. Only the faint understanding that what had broken me was not one blow, but a thousand gentle ones delivered without witnesses. That despair was not my nature, but the residue of years spent bending where I needed support.

I stood at the edge carrying all of that weight, feeling how each small hurt had stacked itself into something monumental. And though the threshold beckoned, though the quiet beyond it felt achingly kind, I lingered with the questions. Because somewhere beneath the accumulation, beneath the poison and the ache, there was still a part of me that wanted to understand how a life could be carved down so far and still, somehow, be standing. That wanting, fragile and unresolved, did not save me yet. But it kept me here long enough for the night to loosen its grip, long enough for the story to continue breathing, long enough for the ache to remain unanswered rather than concluded.

That fragile wanting hovered like a held breath, thin and trembling, but stubborn. It did not arrive as hope. It was not dressed in optimism or promise. It was quieter than that. A pulse. A question mark etched into the dark. It asked nothing of me except to pause, to not rush the ending while the sentence was still forming. In a life that had taught me to endure, even hesitation felt radical. I lingered there, suspended between the gravity of leaving and the weight of staying, feeling how exhaustion can mimic truth. How final answers become seductive when you are too tired to keep asking better questions. The threshold shimmered with certainty, and certainty was tempting. It offered absolution from doubt, release from effort, a clean line where everything messy would finally stop. And yet, the questions would not let me cross so easily. They tugged at my sleeve, not to pull me back, but to slow me down.

I began to sense that the ache I carried was not proof that I was broken beyond repair, but evidence of how long I had been bending without relief. That a body and soul ground down by years of accommodation will eventually cry out, not because they are weak, but because they are human. I started to glimpse, dimly, that despair was not an identity but a consequence. Not a destiny, but a response to being asked, again and again, to survive without shelter. The night held me as these thoughts moved through me, not resolving anything, only softening the edges. The moon did not offer answers, but it stayed. The earth beneath me did not judge the weight I placed upon it. And for the first time in a long while, I noticed that staying did not require certainty. It did not demand belief in a better future. It only required the willingness to let the story keep unfolding, even if the next page was blank.

I did not step back from the edge because I suddenly loved life. I stepped back because something in me sensed that understanding might still be possible. That the accumulation which had nearly undone me could also, someday, be named, unpacked, and laid down piece by piece. I stayed because I had not yet learned the full truth of what had shaped me, and some part of me wanted to know it before deciding how the story should end. That choice was not triumphant. It was quiet. Almost imperceptible. A decision measured in inches rather than miles. I shifted my weight. I sat longer. I breathed once more than I thought I could. And in doing so, I chose neither victory nor surrender, but continuation.

The ache did not disappear. The questions did not resolve. But the night following that night loosened, just enough to let future dawns become conceivable. And in that small allowance, that fragile extension of time, the story remained open. Not healed. Not redeemed. But still alive. Still asking. Still, somehow, standing. Still, what takes a person so deep into the dark that they take a step into the abyss?

When Trauma Became the Shape of Me: Stitched into Silence

It was the trauma woven into my childhood, threaded so tightly through my early years that it ceased to feel like something that *happened* to me and instead became something I *was*. Not an event. Not a chapter. But the very fabric of my identity. I did not wear it like a garment I could remove. I was made of it. It lined my seams. It determined my shape. Every belief about who I was and what I was worth carried its pattern, stitched in before I had language to question it, before I knew I was allowed to ask whether the design itself was flawed. It was the pressure to conform, relentless and unspoken, a slow and methodical sculpting of my inner world. I was carved into what was deemed acceptable. An acceptable daughter. An agreeable woman. An obedient wife. One who asks no questions. One who absorbs harm quietly.

One who learns to reinterpret betrayal as tolerance, disrespect as endurance, erosion as love. I accepted infidelity. I normalized abuse. I minimized neglect. Because somewhere deep inside, a belief had already calcified: that love was conditional, and abandonment was the punishment for resistance. I learned that staying required shrinking. That survival depended on compliance. That being chosen meant being quiet. So I became a quiet survivor. One who swallowed her own screams so others could sleep peacefully. One who folded her pain inward until it bruised her organs instead of disturbing the room. One who gave up her feelings to protect others from discomfort. Gave up her needs so others could feel whole. Kept herself small so others could shine brighter. Learned to disappear emotionally so no one else would have to feel guilt, or shame, or responsibility. Silence became my offering. Endurance became my proof of worth.

I learned early how to become the buffer. The shock absorber. The place where impact could land without consequence. I became skilled at standing in the blast radius and calling it love. I mistook self-erasure for strength. I mistook compliance for devotion. I mistook staying for loyalty, even when staying meant losing myself piece by piece, cell by cell, until I could no longer recognize what was missing, only that something vital had gone quiet. And then there was the first marriage, the place I believed would finally be safe, finally be different. The promised harbor. Instead, it became a battlefield. Love decayed there, slowly at first, then all at once, until it hardened into weaponry turned against me. Words sharpened. Affection became leverage. Kindness came with terms and conditions. Safety was no longer a given, but a currency that could be revoked. I lived as though a blade were always hovering at my throat, not always cutting, but always reminding me it could. The threat did not need to fall to be terrifying. The anticipation did the damage just as well.

I learned to brace myself long before the blow came. To read the air. To sense the shift. To measure tone, silence, timing. To prepare for emotional shrapnel before it ever detonated. And when it finally hit, as it always did, I blamed myself for the wreckage. I searched my own behavior for the cause like a crime scene investigator of my own existence. I replayed conversations. Rewrote scenes. Adjusted my memory until I could convince myself that if I had been softer, quieter, more accommodating, less demanding, more invisible, the explosion would not have happened. I carried the guilt of another person's cruelty as if it were evidence of my own failure, my own provocation, my own inherent wrongness. Threaded through all of this was the constant fear of abandonment, a low-grade terror that never slept. It hummed beneath every interaction, every attachment, every moment of closeness. I lived braced for departure, always scanning for signs, always preparing for the moment someone would confirm what I already believed in my bones.

That I was too much. Or not enough. Or fundamentally unlovable. That love was provisional. That connection was fragile. That being left was not a possibility, but an inevitability waiting patiently for the right mistake. So I contorted myself to prevent it. Became smaller. Quieter. Easier. More useful. Less real. I sanded down my edges. Softened my voice. Questioned my instincts. I became fluent in apology, even when I did not know what I was apologizing for. I learned how to pre-empt rejection by abandoning myself first, believing that if I disappeared voluntarily, it would hurt less than being discarded. What I did not yet understand was that none of this was my nature. It was adaptation. A nervous system shaped by fear. A child's wisdom stretched far beyond what it should ever have had to carry. I was not broken. I was trained. Conditioned. Molded by environments that demanded silence in exchange for belonging, obedience in exchange for love, endurance in exchange for survival.

And the cost of that training was myself. That truth would come later. Slowly. Painfully. Through unlearning that felt like loss before it felt like freedom. Through grief for the girl who learned to vanish so early and so well. But here, in this part of the story, all I knew was how to survive by disappearing. How to love by enduring. How to stay by erasing myself. I lived with the terrifying certainty that if I ever stopped doing so, if I ever took up space without apology, if I ever spoke without permission, I would be left alone with proof that I had never been worthy of staying for in the first place. And so I kept shrinking. Kept quiet. Kept surviving. Believing that vanishing was the price of belonging, and that my silence was the only thing holding love together.

I lived in a perpetual state of hypervigilance, my nervous system tuned like a violin string pulled impossibly tight, stretched far beyond what it was meant to hold. One wrong note. One careless vibration. And it would snap, suddenly, violently, ending the music mid-breath. There was no room for resonance, no space for rest. Only tension. Only the relentless anticipation of collapse. I existed in that sharp, quivering state where silence itself feels loud and danger wears a thousand disguises. Every room became a minefield. I learned to scan before I stepped, to read faces the way others read weather, to track micro expressions like omens. Every silence felt loaded, heavy with unsaid consequences. Every shift in tone, every pause, every sigh became a signal to brace for impact. My body reacted before my mind could intervene. Shoulders tightened. Jaw locked. Breath stalled. I flinched internally even when I remained still on the outside, a statue carved from vigilance.

Rest was foreign to me. Stillness felt unsafe. Calm felt suspicious. My nervous system did not know how to soften; it only knew how to prepare. Readiness and alertness were my default states, my inheritance. I slept lightly, if at all, one ear always tilted toward imagined danger. Even joy arrived with conditions, enjoyed cautiously, as though it might turn on me without warning. I was always waiting. For the next fracture. The next betrayal. The next blow. Even in moments of peace, I rehearsed for pain. Inside me, a toxic alchemy brewed continuously. Self-loathing mixed with low self-worth until I could no longer tell where one ended and the other began. Powerlessness stirred itself into every breath, flavouring even my attempts at hope with futility. Shame settled into my bones like winter frost, slow and penetrating, numbing me from the inside out. It crept into my posture, my gait, the way I took up space. I carried myself like someone expecting punishment, even when none was coming.

This constant vigilance aged me from the inside. It wore grooves into my nervous system, pathways carved by repetition and fear. I learned to live in a permanent crouch, braced against a future that always felt hostile, even when it smiled. My body became an archive of alarms, each muscle holding memory, each reflex shaped by the certainty that safety was temporary and conditional. I did not know then that this was trauma speaking through my cells. That my body was not betraying me but trying desperately to keep me alive in a world it had learned was unpredictable and unsafe. All I knew was the exhaustion. The deep, marrow-level fatigue of never standing down, never standing easy, never laying my weapons down long enough to feel my own weight without fear.

I lived like that for years. A life conducted on edge. A song played too tight to ever fully sing. Waiting, always waiting, for the snap that would finally justify all the bracing I had been doing all along. My days were built around anticipation rather than presence, my nights stretched thin by vigilance masquerading as responsibility. I did not live forward. I lived sideways, always angled toward threat, always listening for the crack in the air that would prove I had been right to never relax. My body forgot what neutral felt like. There was only before and after, never now. Muscles held their breath even when my lungs exhaled. My pulse ran like a siren just beneath the skin, quiet enough to ignore if I tried hard enough, loud enough to never truly forget. I learned how to function inside that alarm, how to make decisions, hold conversations, even love people while internally preparing for rupture. I called it resilience. I called it strength. I did not yet have language for the cost.

Hypervigilance became my compass. I trusted it more than my own desires, more than joy, more than rest. It told me when to speak and when to stay silent, when to shrink and when to perform competence. It warned me against softness, against hope, against ease. It insisted that safety was something earned through exhaustion, not something given. And I listened, because it had kept me alive before, and I believed survival was the highest form of wisdom. But living like that erodes something essential. When you are always braced, you cannot receive. When you are always scanning, you cannot arrive. When every moment is filtered through threat, even kindness feels provisional, even love feels like something that might detonate if handled incorrectly. I learned to accept care with one hand while holding the exit with the other. I learned to love as though it were temporary, because everything else had been.

The exhaustion was not just physical. It was existential. A tiredness that seeped into meaning itself. I grew weary of being my own sentry, my own shield, my own warning system. Weary of carrying a body that never felt like a home, only a bunker. I did not yet know how to imagine a life without constant readiness. The idea of ease felt foreign, almost dangerous, like stepping out of cover into open terrain without armor. And yet, beneath all that vigilance, something quieter endured. A part of me that longed for rest not as collapse, but as permission. A part that did not want to stop existing, only to stop defending every second of existence as if it were under siege. I could feel it sometimes in fleeting moments, when my shoulders dropped without instruction, when breath reached deeper than usual, when the world did not immediately demand my vigilance. Those moments frightened me as much as they soothed me, because they revealed how much I had been carrying.

I did not yet know how to trust those moments. I did not yet know how to stand down without fear of ambush. All I knew was the tension, the readiness, the endless watch. A nervous system trained for war, living in peacetime it did not recognize as real. And so I kept waiting, believing that the snap would come eventually, believing that when it did, it would finally make sense of the life I had spent bracing for it. What I could not yet see was that the snap I feared had already happened long ago, quietly, invisibly, in the shaping of a body that learned to survive by never resting. And that healing would not begin with another brace, another preparation, another tightening of the string, but with the terrifying, unfamiliar act of loosening it and trusting that the music might continue anyway.

Over time, these forces did not merely influence my life; they colonized it completely. They claimed territory inch by inch, until there was no corner left untouched. They did not arrive with violence or announcement. They arrived as tenants who never paid rent, as guests who overstayed until the house forgot it had ever been mine. They moved in quietly, rearranged the furniture of my inner world, and renamed the rooms. What had once been curiosity became caution. What had once been tenderness became threat. Even joy was repurposed, reclassified as something fragile and fleeting, not to be trusted for long. What began as external pressures slowly took root inside me, whispering so persistently that their voices fused with my own. They learned my cadence, borrowed my tone, mimicked my reasoning until I could no longer distinguish the wound from the narrator.

I stopped recognizing where the injury ended and my identity began. The language of fear, shame, and self-erasure became my native tongue, spoken fluently and without conscious thought. I did not translate these beliefs. I lived in them. I no longer heard the whispers as intrusions. I heard them as truth. They narrated my every choice, my every hesitation, like an omniscient voiceover I could not mute. They told me who I was before I had a chance to ask myself. They explained my pain in ways that made it feel deserved, inevitable, permanent. Suffering was no longer something happening to me; it was proof of who I was. Over time, I stopped questioning them. Resistance felt futile. Silence felt safer. Doubt felt dangerous. I let their stories settle into my bones, calcifying there, mistaking familiarity for accuracy, repetition for reality. When a belief is echoed long enough inside a closed system, it begins to sound like fact.

And when the world grows that dark, when the internal storm becomes the only weather you know, everything else begins to fade, not all at once, but gradually, almost politely. Hope does not disappear dramatically; it blurs, like a horizon swallowed by fog. Joy does not die loudly; it becomes distant, as if heard through thick walls or deep water. Love loses its edges, its warmth dulled by suspicion and fear, something to be monitored rather than trusted. Possibility shrinks until it feels impractical, even irresponsible, like a language spoken by people who have never learned how dangerous hope can be. The shadow that calls itself truth grows larger in that darkness. It stretches across every surface of thought, eclipsing nuance, swallowing contradiction, flattening complexity into absolutes. It tells you that what you feel is all there is.

That pain is not a condition, but a conclusion. That this narrowing of vision is clarity, not captivity. And because it speaks in your own voice, because it wears your memories and your logic and your history like borrowed skin, it becomes terrifyingly convincing. You stop arguing with it because it sounds like you. I did not lose sight of hope because I rejected it. I lost it because I could no longer see past the storm. When every horizon is clouded, you stop believing in sky. When every thought is filtered through suffering, even relief feels suspect, like a trick that will be revoked the moment you trust it. I lived inside that compression, that narrowing tunnel of certainty, where despair masqueraded as insight and numbness passed for wisdom. The shadow told me it was protecting me from disappointment, sparing me from longing, saving me from believing in things that might not last.

And I listened. Because when pain becomes total, it does not feel like one experience among many. It feels like the whole story. Everything else becomes background noise, faint and irrelevant, drowned out by the roar of survival. I did not yet know that shadows only exist where there is light behind them. I did not yet understand that losing sight of hope is not proof of its absence, only evidence of how thick the darkness has grown. All I knew then was the storm. The voice. The narrowing world. And the frightening ease with which despair convinced me it was the only thing worth trusting, the only thing that would not leave.

The Symphony That Nearly Ended in Silence

The moonlight on the grass, the breathless hush before a near-fatal choice, the almost-final surrender beneath its cold, indifferent glow, this moment was not a sudden spark of despair. Not a reckless whim. Not a spontaneous collapse into oblivion. It arrived with the terrible inevitability of something long rehearsed, something that had been walking toward me for years while I pretended not to see it. It was not the beginning of the story. It was the breaking point of one that had been unraveling thread by thread, quietly, relentlessly, long before that night ever existed. It was the final crescendo of a symphony that had been composing itself in secret for decades. A slow, sorrowful movement written in minor keys and held breaths. Each measure layered atop the last, building tension so gradually it felt survivable until it suddenly wasn't. The music did not erupt; it swelled. It gathered weight. It reached for its inevitable peak with the patience of grief that has never been named. And that night, under that moon, the score reached its most dangerous note.

That symphony was born in the hidden chambers of a child's heart. A heart that learned its first lessons not in words, but in absence. In silence. In subtle ways, love felt conditional, and safety felt fragile. Long before I understood language or logic, my body learned belief. Learned worthlessness. Learned that breath was something to earn. Learned that existence itself required justification. I did not decide these things. They were impressed upon me, etched slowly into the soft architecture of a developing self. That night was not about wanting to die. It was about being exhausted from surviving a life built on the premise that I should not take up space. It was the accumulation of silent suffering layered upon silent suffering, grief stacked so carefully it looked like endurance. It was every swallowed scream, every unmet need, every moment I chose disappearance over risk. It was the weight of years spent carrying pain without witness, until the body finally bent beneath it.

Standing there, I was not reckless. I was emptied. Hollowed by a lifetime of restraint. The choice before me felt less like an act and more like a conclusion already written. The moon bore witness without judgment, its light pale and distant, illuminating not just the grass beneath my feet but the long road that had led me there. I felt the stillness of that moment not as peace, but as suspension, as though time itself had paused to watch what I would do with all that accumulated sorrow. That near-suicide was the desperate crescendo of a long, aching symphony of self-destruction. A composition written not in one night, but across years of being unseen. Across a childhood that learned too early how to endure. Across an adulthood that mistook survival for living. The first notes were struck in the hidden chambers of my wounded child's heart, and the music never truly stopped. It only grew quieter, more intricate, more dangerous, until that night when silence itself felt like the final note.

And yet, even there, even then, the symphony did not end. Because as close as I came to surrender, the music held one unresolved chord. A trembling dissonance that refused to resolve into silence. Something unfinished. Something that would not let the story conclude on destruction alone. I did not yet know what that was. I only knew that the ending I had been rehearsing for years did not fully arrive. The score paused, breath held, waiting for a movement I had not yet learned how to play.

The pause stretched. Not forward. Not back. A held breath in the throat of the night. The unresolved chord vibrated through me, not loud enough to name, not gentle enough to ignore. It did not feel like hope. It felt like resistance without a language. Like something in me refusing to disappear quietly, even as everything else leaned toward silence. I stood there, suspended between the note that wanted to end it all and the one that would not let the music die. My body trembled with the effort of not choosing, with the strain of remaining inside that narrow space where nothing resolved and nothing collapsed. The moonlight stayed where it was. The grass did not move. The world did not intervene. There was no voice from the sky. No sudden clarity. Only the raw awareness that I was still breathing, still standing, still caught inside a moment that would not finish itself.

That unfinished chord lived somewhere deeper than thought. It was not logic or belief or faith. It was older. A bodily refusal. A small, stubborn insistence pulsing beneath the wreckage. As if the child who had learned so early to endure had not given permission for this ending. As if the same part of me that learned to survive had not yet learned how to surrender completely. I felt it as friction. As unease. As the unbearable discomfort of staying when leaving promised relief. It was not brave. It was not noble. It was simply there. A tension that would not release. A sound that would not fade. The symphony hovered on that note, unresolved and aching, refusing to conclude with annihilation.

In that suspension, something subtle shifted. Not upward. Not outward. Inward. The realization that the choice before me was not as clean as the voice had promised. That the quiet beyond the threshold was not neutral. That the ending I had been rehearsing required a certainty I did not actually possess. I could imagine silence, but I could not fully step into it. Something in me remained attached to the sound of being alive, even when that sound felt unbearable. The night did not save me. I saved nothing. There was no triumph in that moment. Only postponement. Only the act of not crossing. Only the body choosing, without explanation, to remain where it was for one more breath. Then another. Then another. The unresolved chord held, trembling, refusing resolution, insisting the music continue even without a melody.

Eventually, the cold crept in. The grass dampened my clothes. My muscles ached from standing still. Practical sensations returned, small and ordinary, pulling me back into the physical world inch by inch. The moment loosened its grip. The pause did not end with a crescendo. It dissolved quietly, the way fog lifts without announcing itself. I turned away. Not with conviction. Not with certainty. I turned away because staying required less explanation than leaving. Because the body knows things the mind has not yet caught up to. Because the symphony, unfinished and aching, demanded continuation whether I felt ready or not. I carried that unresolved chord with me as I walked back into the night. It did not resolve into hope. It did not transform into meaning. It simply remained, vibrating softly beneath the noise, a reminder that the story had not ended where I thought it would.

That something in me had interrupted the pattern. That the music, however broken, was still playing. I did not yet know how to live differently. I did not yet know how to heal. I only knew this: the ending I had rehearsed for years had been delayed by a single, trembling note that refused to fade. And that refusal, however small, however unglamorous, was enough to keep the story breathing. The next movement would come later. Not that night. Not in moonlight or silence. It would come slowly, awkwardly, through questions instead of answers, through pain that finally demanded witness, through learning that unresolved does not mean hopeless. It means alive. And for the first time, barely perceptible beneath the exhaustion, the symphony held the possibility of something other than an ending. With that moment of hope let us head back into the shadows once more, for we are not done with the shadows.

I was a child, a young woman, a wife, a mother, a daughter, and a sister, each role layered upon the next like sediment settling year after year, compressing until the original shape was lost beneath the weight. I could no longer tell where obligation ended and identity began. All of them were carried by a single belief I could not yet name, only obey: That I was a weight this world needed to be released from. An anchor, dragging everyone around me downward. Dead weight in the waters of other people's lives. I imagined the rope cut clean, the fibers snapping without drama, imagined myself slipping quietly beneath the surface, sparing everyone the labor of keeping me afloat. I believed my disappearance would be an act of mercy, a kindness disguised as loss.

I mistook survival for value, as though endurance alone justified my existence. I mistook silence for safety, believing that the less I spoke, the less harm I could cause. I mistook tolerance and justification for love, accepting whatever scraps of affection arrived, no matter how sharp their edges, convinced that needing more would make me disposable. I mistook pain for purpose, believing suffering was proof that I was contributing something meaningful to the world. If I hurt, at least I was useful. If I endured, at least I was earning my place. That night felt like the final act in a tragedy written over decades.

Not a sudden plunge, but a slow, insidious descent into shadow, each step taken so gradually I barely noticed the ground falling away beneath me. The path was paved with self-inflicted wounds, each one a milestone, each one reinforcing the lie that I was both the problem and the solution. Despair clung to me like a second skin, warm enough to feel familiar, tight enough to feel inescapable. I wore it everywhere. I no longer remembered what it felt like not to. It was the moment I whispered my surrender to the darkness. Not aloud. Not dramatically. Just a quiet internal bowing of the head, an agreement made in exhaustion rather than conviction. I truly believed my story had reached its end. That all the chapters had already been written. That there was nothing left but to close the book gently and spare everyone the trouble of reading on. And yet, even there, something faltered.

The darkness waited for me to step fully into it, patient and assured, but I hovered at its edge, suspended by a thread I could not see yet could still feel pulling against my chest. I did not know then that this thread was not obligation or guilt, or fear. It was connection I had never learned how to recognize. It was the echo of a self that had been buried, not erased. A self that had survived every previous ending I had rehearsed and was not yet finished insisting on one more breath. The tragedy I believed I was completing did not close the curtain that night. The final line was not spoken. The stage remained lit, awkwardly, painfully, exposing the mess of an unfinished scene with no clear direction for what came next. The darkness did not claim me. It only brushed past, disappointed but patient, retreating just enough to leave the story unresolved.

I did not walk away healed. I did not rise renewed. I walked away carrying the same beliefs, the same ache, the same exhaustion, but now with the unbearable knowledge that I was still here. That the ending I had offered had not been accepted. That something in me, or beyond me, had refused to let the story conclude as tragedy alone. That realization would take years to unpack. Years to understand that believing I was a weight was not truth, but inheritance. That mistaking pain for purpose was not insight, but adaptation. That the darkness I whispered my surrender to was never the author of my story, only a voice that had grown loud in the absence of gentler ones. That night marked the moment I thought everything ended. In truth, it marked the moment the lie reached its loudest pitch and failed to silence the music entirely.

It was a stage play not even Shakespeare could write so eloquently, because this was no longer philosophy or soliloquy. It was no longer "*to be or not to be*", no longer the trembling space of debate where doubt still breathes. The question had calcified. It had hardened into certainty. This was the final act where the protagonist was meant to die. The script already written. Rehearsed in silence for years. Every cue memorized. Every exit marked. The curtains drawn back, the lights fixed, the final bow already imagined before the body had even stepped fully onto the stage. There was no room left for the in-between. No ambiguity. No pause for reconsideration. The margins had narrowed until choice no longer felt like choice at all, but gravity. Something you fall into rather than decide.

The story insisted this was not failure but destiny. Not escape but sacrifice. The hero who saves others by vanishing. The logic was cruel and seductive in equal measure: My death would be meaning. My absence would be relief. My ending would redeem every burden I believed I was. So I cast myself as the necessary tragedy. The noble loss. The Shakespearean conclusion that transforms suffering into something legible, an art piece, something almost beautiful. Romeo lifting the poison not out of despair alone, but devotion. Hamlet's rot and treachery folding inward until the blade turns back upon the body that holds it. I swallowed those narratives whole, mistaking their poetry for prophecy, their inevitability for truth. If they could die and be remembered as love, as consequence, as meaning, then perhaps I could too.

Suicidal ideation became both playwright and tyrant. It dressed itself in literature and fate, crowned itself with inevitability, and spoke with the authority of something ancient and absolute. It told me this was how the story *had* to end. It made me Claudius and Hamlet at once, villain and victim, poisoner and poisoned. It turned every imagined instrument inward, not as violence, but as closure. As completion. As the only ending that felt coherent with the life I believed I had lived. The danger was not only the darkness of that script, but how convincing it sounded. How clean. How resolved. How merciful it pretended to be. It promised meaning where there had only been pain. Dignity where there had only been endurance. It told me that disappearing was not giving up but finally getting it right. That I could redeem the chaos by ending it neatly. That silence would be my most articulate sentence.

And standing there, in that mental theater, I felt the terrifying calm that comes when a decision believes itself final. The hush before the last line. The breath before the lights dim. The sense that all suffering had been funnelling toward this moment, that every earlier wound had been rehearsal for this final scene. The calm was not peace. It was surrender dressed as certainty. A stillness born not of resolution, but exhaustion. What I did not yet know was this: Tragedies only end when the audience believes there is nothing left worth staying for. But I was both actor and audience. And somewhere, beneath the roar of that fatal script, beneath the borrowed language of doomed heroes and poisoned kings, there was a hesitation that did not belong to the play.

A missed cue. A breath taken too soon. A body that refused to collapse on command. The stage was set. The script was ready. The ending rehearsed to exhaustion. But the performance did not go as planned. Because even when the mind declared the final act inevitable, the body had not yet consented to silence. Even when the story demanded death to give meaning to life, something unruly and unscripted remained. Something that did not want a beautiful ending. Something that wanted a truer one. Something that did not care about symmetry or closure or literary grace, only about staying. And in that disruption, small, clumsy, unspectacular, the tragedy faltered. The curtain did not fall. The lights stayed on. And the story, against every expectation, refused to end on the line that had been written for it. For now, we are still in the heart of the play of our story, so let us continue.

Unfinished: Where the Ending Failed to Arrive

That night was not the beginning. It was the last act of a tragedy rehearsed in silence, performed behind closed doors, waged on trauma-soaked battlefields no one else could see. A story written not in ink, but in scars that never fully faded, in reflexes etched into muscle and breath, in flinches that arrived before thought. The stage had been set long before I ever stood beneath that sky. Long before the choice felt imminent. Long before the darkness learned how to call itself inevitable. It was the culmination of a slow, insidious descent, the kind that does not announce itself as falling. A path paved with self-inflicted wounds and wounds inflicted by others, emotional and physical alike, each one absorbed, explained away, folded neatly into the narrative of endurance. The ground sloped so gradually I mistook it for terrain. I told myself this was just how life felt. Heavy. Narrow. Unforgiving. I did not notice how far I had traveled until the light behind me had thinned to embers.

Those embers flickered stubbornly, not bright enough to guide me out, but just enough to keep me moving forward into the dark. Despair lit the way with a false glow, offering direction without deliverance. It refused to loosen its grip, tightening instead with every step, every compromise, every moment I chose survival over truth. The descent was not dramatic. It was procedural. Logical. Earned, according to the rules I had learned too well. By that night, the tragedy felt complete. The arc made sense. The suffering had a shape. The ending seemed justified by accumulation alone. Years of bracing. Years of swallowing. Years of becoming smaller so the world would not feel inconvenienced by my pain. The darkness did not feel foreign. It felt domestic. Familiar as furniture. Like a room I had been living in for so long I no longer remembered the window.

And yet, even as the descent reached its deepest point, even as the story tightened toward what it claimed was its only possible conclusion, something subtle began to shift. Not upward. Not into light. Just a pause. A hairline fracture in the certainty. A hesitation so small it could have been mistaken for nothing at all. A moment where the darkness, so practiced and persuasive, failed to account for something living beneath it. The tragedy had been rehearsed meticulously. It knew its cues. It knew its lines. It knew exactly how the final scene was supposed to land. But it misjudged one thing. It assumed the wounds were the whole story. It assumed the scars were the sum total of what remained. It assumed survival had finally exhausted itself.

It did not reckon with the quiet defiance of a body that had endured too much to vanish neatly. It did not anticipate the unresolved note that refused to resolve into silence. It did not imagine that even at the deepest point of descent, there could be something unfinished, something still breathing beneath the weight of all that had been carried. That night marked the end of the tragedy I had been living inside. Not because the pain ended. Not because the darkness released me. But because the story it had been telling no longer held absolute authority. Its certainty cracked. Its inevitability wavered. The script faltered in my hands, suddenly less sacred, less final than it had claimed to be. The descent stopped there. Not with triumph. Not with clarity. Not with redemption neatly wrapped in light.

But with interruption. A pause where there should have been an ending. A breath taken where silence had been promised. A body that did not obey the command to disappear. And sometimes, interruption is the first mercy a story ever receives. However, long before the mercy arrived: A strange echo from my childhood trailed me like a ghostly chorus, thin and persistent, drifting in and out of my thoughts as if summoned by the stillness. An old Afrikaans phrase haunted me then, its cadence both mocking and strangely tender as it echoed through my mind: *"Fluit-fluit, die storie is uit."* The whistle blows. The story ends. A phrase meant for fairy tales and bedtime rituals, for neat conclusions and safe closures. And oh, how I longed for that whistle to sound. For the final note. For the clean, merciful punctuation of an ending. I yearned for that silence the way parched earth longs for rain.

For the release. For the collapse. For the permission to stop holding myself together. I imagined the whistle as a blade of air cutting cleanly through the ache, severing me from the pain that had become my most faithful companion. No more effort. No more vigilance. No more enduring. Just stillness. A story closed gently, without mess, without aftermath. A neat exit from a narrative that had asked too much of me for far too long. That phrase carried both comfort and cruelty. It promised simplicity where my life had only known complexity. It suggested that endings were tidy, that suffering could be wrapped up and put away, that silence could be kind. I wanted to believe it. I wanted the whistle to absolve me of having to go on, to bless my disappearance as something natural, even poetic. As if my pain, once ended, would finally make sense. But life, in its mysterious and often brutal grace, had a different script waiting in the wings.

There was no whistle that night. No clean note to signal completion. No curtain falling gently to spare me the aftermath. Instead, there was interruption. A pause where an ending should have been. A held breath where silence had been promised. The story refused to obey the rhythm I had learned as a child. It stuttered. It lingered. It stayed open. My story, bruised, battered, and nearly extinguished, was not ending that night. It was pausing. Turning. Shifting its weight. Reshaping itself in ways I could not yet understand. The ache did not vanish. The darkness did not lift. But something subtle happened in that suspended moment. The belief that this was the end lost its grip. The certainty cracked, just enough to let something else seep in. I did not feel saved. I did not feel hopeful. I felt unfinished. And that unfinishedness, unbearable as it was, meant one thing I could not yet fully grasp.

The whistle had not blown. The story was not out. The silence I craved was not yet mine. Instead, there was breath. There was continuation. There was a next line I had not rehearsed, a movement I had not memorized, a chapter that insisted on existing despite my exhaustion. Life did not grant me the ending I begged for. It gave me something far messier and far more demanding. It gave me a story that refused to stop speaking. And in that refusal, something ancient stirred. The story did not rush forward with clarity or purpose. It hovered, uncertain, like smoke after a fire that has burned itself down to embers but not yet gone cold. I stood inside that hovering, unsure whether to curse it or cling to it. Unfinished meant exposed. Unfinished meant vulnerable. It meant I could not hide behind the finality of an ending. I had to remain inside the ache, inside the unanswered questions, inside a life that had not yet decided what it would become.

The silence I had begged for was replaced by something far more unsettling: presence. Breath that insisted on returning. A body that kept choosing inhale over surrender. A pulse that refused to quiet itself into compliance. I felt it then, not as comfort, but as insistence. A low, stubborn rhythm beneath everything else, tapping out a truth I was not ready to accept. "You are still here. You are still in this." The unfinishedness felt like standing in the ruins after a collapse, dust still floating in the air, ears ringing, unsure what had fallen and what might yet be salvaged. I did not feel gratitude. I felt disoriented. Angry, even. I had come seeking an ending, and instead I was handed continuation without instructions. A blank page with no promise that what came next would be gentler than what had come before. And yet, there was something different about this continuation. It was not the same relentless forward march I had known all my life, the kind fueled by obligation and fear.

This was a pause that breathed. A waiting that did not demand performance. The story did not shove me back onto the path I had been walking. It asked, quietly and without urgency, what might happen if I stopped trying to disappear. The darkness did not leave me. It sat nearby, familiar and watchful. But it no longer held the pen alone. The narrative loosened in its grip. For the first time, the story felt less like a sentence being carried out and more like a draft. Messy. Incomplete. Subject to revision. I began to sense that the whistle from childhood had never been a commandment, only a lullaby. A way to soothe children into believing that endings are clean and stories conclude neatly. Real stories do not end that way. They fray. They interrupt themselves. They circle back. They pause in places that feel unbearable and call it living. So I stood there, inside a story that refused to end, inside a body that refused to stop breathing, inside a life that had cracked but not closed.

I did not yet know how to live differently. I only knew that the script I had memorized no longer applied. The final act had been interrupted. The curtain had jammed. The lights stayed on, harsh and honest, illuminating everything I had hoped to escape. What remained was not hope, not yet. It was possibility's quieter cousin. The chance that the next line had not been written. The unsettling realization that survival was no longer just endurance, but invitation. That the story continuing did not mean it would repeat itself exactly as before. I had wanted the whistle. The clean ending. The silence. Instead, I was given breath, interruption, and a story that would not let me disappear quietly. And though I did not yet know it, that refusal was the first mercy I had ever been strong enough to survive. What I believed to be an ending was, in truth, the first trembling breath of a beginning I never saw coming.

Not a clean dawn, not a trumpet call of renewal, but a fragile inhale taken by a body that had forgotten how to trust air. A beginning that arrived unannounced, without ceremony, disguised as survival. I did not step into it with confidence. I stumbled into it, disoriented, still clutching the wreckage of the life I thought had already finished. And yet, the question lingered, insistent and unanswered. What draws a mind, especially a young, tender one, into an intimate dance with death? For a long time, I believed the answer was simple. Pain. Hurt. Suffering. The obvious wounds carved into the visible fabric of my life. The blows that could be named. The moments that left bruises, scars, stories I could point to and say, There. That's where it broke. And yes, those shadows shaped me. They left their fingerprints everywhere. But in time, I would learn they were not the origin. They were symptoms. Surface ripples disturbing a body of water far deeper and far more dangerous. The truth was quieter. More complex. More insidious.

There were invisible roots buried deep in the soil of my childhood, winding themselves around my nervous system before I had words for fear or frameworks for safety. Needs unmet not through cruelty alone, but through absence. Through inconsistency. Through love that was present, but conditional. Through care that did not know how to see me fully. Those needs did not scream. They waited. They learned patience. They learned how to rot without smell. There were unspoken wounds that never had language, injuries that never received witness. Truths that hovered at the edge of consciousness but were never invited fully into the room. Traumas left unresolved, not because they were insignificant, but because I learned early that surviving meant not lingering. That asking for repair was dangerous. That moving on was safer than being honest about what still hurt.

So I adapted. I swallowed what could not be held. I minimized what felt too heavy. I normalized what should have been named. And all of it settled inside me, slowly, quietly, like storm clouds forming on a deceptively calm horizon. There was no thunder at first. No lightning to warn me. Just a gradual dimming of the light. A pressure change I felt in my body long before I recognized it in my mind. The sky of my inner world darkened incrementally, so subtly I mistook it for weather rather than warning. This is how despair learns to live inside a child. Not through one catastrophic moment, but through accumulation. Through what is missing as much as what is inflicted. Through the steady lesson that your needs are negotiable and your pain must be managed alone.

By the time death began to feel familiar, even comforting, it was not because I wanted to disappear. It was because something essential had never been allowed to fully arrive. Safety. Attunement. Permission to be seen without consequence. My mind did not fall in love with death. It reached for it the way a starving body reaches for anything that promises rest. What I did not know then, standing at the edge of that night, was that the beginning I had just inhaled would require excavation, not escape. Surviving the ending was only the first step. The deeper work lay ahead, in turning toward those buried roots, those quiet rot points, those storms that had been gathering since before I knew how to call them storms. The beginning was not bright. It was honest. And honesty, I would learn, is far more demanding than despair. But it was a beginning, nonetheless.

What I did not yet understand was how beginnings often arrive disguised as aftermath. How they emerge not from hope, but from ruin. I thought beginnings were supposed to feel like clarity, like forward motion, like light breaking cleanly through darkness. Instead, this one felt like rubble shifting. Like dust settling after collapse. Like standing amid debris and realizing, with quiet disbelief, that I was still breathing inside it. This beginning asked me to stay with what I had spent a lifetime avoiding. To turn toward the very places I had learned to outrun. There was no dramatic turning point, no sudden redemption arc. Only the slow, unnerving realization that if the story was continuing, then the pain I had survived was not the end of the sentence. It was punctuation. A comma, not a period. And that meant there was more to be written with the same breath I had once tried to surrender.

Honesty, I discovered, is not cathartic at first. It is abrasive. It scrapes. It peels back protective layers one at a time, exposing nerves that have been numbed for years. It demands attention where dissociation once provided relief. It insists on presence where disappearance had felt safer. Honesty asks you to feel the weight of what you carry instead of numbing it, to name the ache instead of spiritualizing it, to stay in the body instead of escaping it. It required me to look backward without romanticizing the pain and without condemning the child who survived it. To see how every adaptation I had once cursed was born from intelligence, not weakness.

How silence had been strategy. How shrinking had been self-preservation. How loving without safety had been the only love I knew how to access. These were not moral failures. They were survival languages spoken fluently by a nervous system that learned early it was alone. Excavation is slow work. You do not dig all at once, or the ground collapses in on itself. You clear a small patch. You pause. You breathe. You learn how to recognize the difference between discomfort and danger, something my body had never been taught. You uncover fragments, memories, sensations, and beliefs, and you sit with them long enough to understand what they were trying to protect. Some truths came up like artifacts. Others like bones. I learned that despair was not my truth, but my last line of defence when nothing else had worked.

That the wish for death was not a desire for annihilation, but a desperate request for rest. That my mind had reached for endings because it had never been shown how to live inside continuity without harm. These realizations did not immediately soothe me. But they did something far more important. They made me curious. Curiosity is a quiet rebellion against despair. It does not demand optimism. It does not require belief. It only asks a single question. What if this is not the whole story? That question cracked something open. And slowly, almost imperceptibly, the beginning began to feel less like survival and more like orientation. Like learning where I was after a long dissociative drift. Like realizing I had been holding my breath for years and was finally being taught how to exhale without punishment. This beginning did not promise happiness. It did not guarantee ease. It did not erase the past. But it offered something I had never had before. Context. Language. Choice.

And with those, a different kind of hope emerged. Not the loud, glittering kind. But a grounded one. A hope rooted not in fantasy, but in truth. A hope that understood pain as part of the terrain, not the destination. A hope that did not require me to disappear in order to be at peace. I had inhaled the first breath without knowing it was a beginning. Now, slowly, deliberately, I was learning how to breathe again. Not to escape the story. But to stay long enough to tell it differently.

The State of Living Half-Gone

Suicidal ideation was not a single thought, not a fleeting whisper of "*I want to die*". It was a state of existence. A way of inhabiting my body as though it were already halfway gone. A way of breathing in suffocation and calling it air. A way of moving through a world that felt perpetually misaligned with my presence, as if life itself were a room I was never meant to enter, only pass through quietly, apologetically, leaving no fingerprints behind. It was the culmination of a lifetime converging into one unbearable point. A perfect storm where every emotion collided without mercy. Every memory rose at once, unfiltered, undimmed by time. Every unmet longing surged forward, no longer patient, demanding to be seen, to be answered, to be relieved. There was no single cause, no clean origin, no singular wound that could be traced and treated.

Only compression. Only overload. Only the sense that everything I had ever carried had finally arrived at the same moment, crowding my chest, my mind, my breath, with nowhere left to go. And I told myself, with the kind of clarity that *feels* like truth, that it was not about wanting death. It was about wanting relief. Escape. Freedom. Freedom from the ache that wrapped around my ribs like tightening vines, slowly stealing breath until even sighs felt expensive. Freedom from the hurt that seeped into my bones, staining even my posture with fatigue, curving my spine into a shape shaped by endurance rather than ease. Freedom from the ache that wrapped around my ribs like tightening vines, slowly stealing breath. Freedom from the suffering that felt predatory, intelligent, devouring me cell by cell, leaving behind a version of myself thinned to the point of translucence, a body that could be looked through rather than looked at.

I believed I wanted the pain to stop. I believed I wanted rest. I believed I wanted quiet. And that understanding felt raw. Painful. Honest. It felt like progress, like insight wrested from the dark by sheer effort. I clung to it because it explained so much. It framed the death-wish not as madness, but as logic born of exhaustion. It made me feel less broken, less monstrous, less alone in my own mind. It gave the ache a reason, and reasons feel safer than chaos. But even that understanding, as hard-won and compassionate as it was, turned out to be incomplete. Another layer of a false truth. Because relief, I would eventually learn, was not the root. Escape was not the origin. Freedom from pain was not the deepest longing beating beneath those thoughts. Those were translations. Approximations. The closest language I had at the time for something far more vulnerable, far more frightening to name.

What I was reaching for was not nonexistence. It was safety. It was containment. It was being held without cost. It was the longing to exist without bracing. To breathe without negotiating for air. To rest without earning it through suffering. The ache was not asking to be silenced. It was asking to be *met*. But when you grow up in a world where your pain is invisible, where your needs feel dangerous, where endurance is praised, and expression is punished, the desire to be met has nowhere to go. So it disguises itself. It puts on darker clothing. It learns to speak in the language of endings because beginnings feel too risky to hope for. It learns to sound final because vulnerability has never felt safe.

Suicidal ideation, then, was not a wish for death. It was a wish for a life that did not require self-erasure to survive. A life where existing did not feel like an offense. A life where relief came through connection rather than disappearance. I did not yet have words for that. I only had the urge to stop hurting, the fantasy of silence, the belief that peace lived somewhere beyond breath. My mind reached for the most definitive solution it knew. An ending. A closing. A door that promised never to reopen, never to demand anything of me again. But the truth beneath the truth was this: I did not want to die. I wanted the war inside me to end. I wanted to stop living as though my existence itself were the problem to be solved.

And that realization, when it finally surfaced, did not arrive gently either. It shattered the illusion I had been clinging to, because if the ache was not asking for death, then it was asking for something else entirely. Something far more dangerous than disappearance. Something that would require me to stay. To feel. To speak. To be seen. To risk being met instead of erased. And that, terrifying as it was, meant the story was not finished explaining itself yet. The understanding of this truth did not arrive like lightning. It came slowly, reluctantly, in increments so small they barely registered as change. It moved the way dawn does when you have been awake all night, not with a sudden burst of light, but with a gradual thinning of the dark. Not a single revelation. Not an epiphany bathed in certainty. But a series of quiet, often painful awakenings that unfolded over years of healing.

Years of circling the same memories from different angles. Years of standing at the edges of old scenes, brave enough now to look longer, to feel more fully. Years of peeling back layers of my own wounded history, only to discover there was always another layer beneath, another knot asking to be untangled with trembling hands. Each realization cost me something. Comfort. Certainty. The familiar refuge of believing I was simply broken and therefore absolved of the work of change. Letting go of that story felt like stepping out of a house that had kept me alive during a storm, only to realize it was also the place I had been suffocating. Healing was not a straight path forward; it was a spiral inward. I returned again and again to the same places, the same questions, the same aches, but each time with slightly different eyes, slightly more courage, slightly less need to flee.

Insight came the way bone sets after a break: slowly, achingly, reshaping itself through discomfort rather than relief. There was tenderness in the mending, but also pressure, resistance, the deep ache of becoming whole in places that had never healed correctly the first time. Only then did I begin to see that my suffering had never been just pain. Just hurt. Just despair. Those were only the symptoms, the smoke rising from a fire I had never learned to name, much less extinguish. I had spent my life trying to breathe through that smoke, adapting my lungs to its thickness, believing the air itself was poisonous. I learned how to survive in it. How to ration breath. How to normalize the burn. Never realizing there was something burning beneath it, something asking not for endurance, but for attention. Something that did not need me to be stronger, but more honest.

The real affliction lived deeper. Beneath the visible scars. Beneath even the silent ones. Beneath the narratives I had constructed to survive another day. It was not one wound, not one moment, not one person. It was an ecosystem of wounds, interacting with each other, feeding and reinforcing one another over time. A complex, tangled disease of the soul that could not be reduced to sadness or weakness or pathology alone. It lived in patterns. In reflexes. In beliefs that felt instinctual because they had been learned before thought. It lived in the way my body braced for danger even in safety, in the way my voice softened when it needed to be strong, in the way my needs arrived already apologizing. It was a tapestry woven from unmet needs that had never been acknowledged, let alone answered. From buried truths that learned early how to hide in order to survive.

From generational echoes passed down like heirlooms no one knew how to refuse or even recognize. From the quiet indoctrinations of a childhood that taught me, subtly and repeatedly, to shrink. To soften my edges. To swallow my voice before it could inconvenience the room. To confuse love with tolerance. Safety with silence. Belonging with disappearance. I learned how to contort myself into shapes that fit, even when those shapes hurt to hold. I learned, long before I chose to, that my suffering was not something to question, but something to accommodate. Something to normalize. Something to fold into my sense of self until it felt indistinguishable from who I was. Pain became identity. Endurance became virtue. Silence became proof of goodness. I learned that being low-maintenance made me lovable, that asking for less made me easier to keep. And so the fire burned unchecked, disguised as character, as fate, as personality. I called it who I was, never realizing it was what I had adapted to.

Healing began the moment I stopped asking why I was in so much pain and started asking what had never been given space to exist. What had been denied breath. What had been trained out of me under the guise of love and expectation. I began to understand that my despair was not a personal failing, but a signal. Not a verdict, but a message delayed by decades of silence. A flare sent up from parts of me that had been surviving without witnesses, without language, without care. This realization did not absolve the past. It did not erase the scars or soften the memories. But it shifted something fundamental. It moved the story from condemnation to context. From shame to comprehension. From *what is wrong with me* to *what happened, and what was missing, and what am I still carrying that was never mine to bear alone*. That shift did not make the pain disappear, but it made it intelligible. And in being understood, it became less absolute.

The disease of the soul I carried was not proof that I was defective. It was evidence of adaptation. Of intelligence shaped by necessity. Of a child who learned how to survive in an environment that could not fully see her, could not fully hold her, could not fully protect her. I was not broken. I was shaped. Conditioned. Brilliantly resourceful in the ways that survival demands. And that knowledge, fragile and unsettling as it was, marked the beginning of a different kind of healing. Not the kind that rushes toward positivity or resolution. Not the kind that bypasses grief or dresses wounds in platitudes. But the kind that listens. That names. That stays. The kind that restores what was once required to disappear, not by force, but by invitation. I spent years treating the symptoms, hacking at the vines while the roots grew stronger in the dark. I cut and burned and punished what I could see, mistaking visibility for causation, believing that if I could just keep the surface tidy enough, the choking would stop.

I fought the overgrowth with exhaustion as my only tool, never realizing the soil itself had been poisoned long before the first tendril ever broke through. Each cut felt like effort. Each moment of restraint felt like progress. And still, the vines returned, thicker, more determined, fed by something deeper than willpower could reach. I did not yet know how to go underground. I did not yet know how to listen instead of fight. I was trying to save myself with blades when what I needed was light. I was trying to control what frightened me instead of understanding why it was there. The roots thrived on that misunderstanding, drinking from silence, from fear, from the belief that pain was something to be eliminated rather than interpreted. It wasn't until I dared to journey inward, to turn toward the shadows I had spent my life outrunning, that something fundamental shifted. Not all at once. Not without terror. But slowly, with trembling honesty, I began to see that the darkness was not empty.

It was crowded. Crowded with unmet needs curled into themselves like seeds waiting for rain. With ungrieved losses pressed flat beneath years of forward motion. With truths that had never been given language because no one had made space for their sound. The shadows were not enemies. They were messengers arriving late, hoarse from waiting. They were parts of me that had learned to survive without care, growing wild because no one had ever tended the ground they lived in. And then the understanding arrived, quiet and irreversible. If I could heal the soil, the weeds would not need to be fought. They would wither on their own. Not because they were evil, but because their work would be complete. They had grown where nourishment was missing, where safety had never taken root. They were adaptive, not malicious. Intelligent, not cruel.

Tend the soil, and the entire landscape changes. Not overnight. Not magically. But honestly. Organically. In ways that do not require constant war or vigilance, in ways that invite rest back into the body. Healing the soil meant learning a different posture entirely. Knees to the earth. Hands dirty. Breath slowed. It meant asking questions I had avoided because I feared the answers would undo me. What did I need that I never received? What did I learn to deny in order to belong? What grew distorted because it had to grow alone? These were not questions that demanded quick solutions. They asked for presence. For patience. For the courage to stay when everything in me had been trained to flee. But that story, the turning inward, the naming of the true illness, the slow, sacred work of tending what was once left to rot, belongs to another chapter.

It is a story of excavation rather than escape. Of listening rather than silencing. Of allowing grief to move at the pace of the body instead of the mind. Of learning how to stay with what hurts long enough for it to soften, long enough for it to trust that it will not be abandoned again. So stay with me. We have only just begun to uncover what was buried. The ground has only just been broken. There are deeper truths waiting beneath the surface, and they do not arrive with spectacle or revelation, but with recognition. With the quiet shock of realizing something has been true all along. With the steady warmth of understanding returning sensation to places long gone numb. The truth, as always, is patient. It does not chase. It does not force. It waits for the moment you are finally willing to meet it without weapons in your hands. And it is still waiting.

The Slow Violence of Emptiness

In the end, it wasn't the darkness that devoured me; darkness still carries shape, texture, resistance. Darkness has edges you can press your palms against, something to push back on, something to name. No, it was the emptiness that claimed me. The slow-creeping nothingness that hollowed me out grain by grain, breath by breath, over years so quiet they blended into routine. An absence so thorough it learned how to pass for normal. A silence that did not scream but persisted. This void was fed not by chaos, but by starvation. By connection withheld. By understanding that it never arrived. By love offered conditionally, then withdrawn just enough to teach my nervous system never to expect it again. It was not created by cruelty alone, but by absence repeated. The missed moments. The unmet gaze. The unasked question that never became an answer. The comfort that hovered just out of reach until wanting it felt embarrassing, even dangerous.

Nothingness is deceptive that way. It does not announce itself. It erodes. It sands down the interior walls of the soul until there is so much space and nothing to fill it with. It teaches you to echo. To shout your worth into the hollow and mistake the return of your own voice for proof that someone is listening. It teaches you to confuse survival with substance, to build a life around functioning while starving quietly at the center. I did not notice the caverns forming because erosion does not feel like collapse. It feels like adaptation. It feels like learning to need less. To expect less. To make yourself smaller so the emptiness does not feel so vast. I learned how to live around the void, arranging my days carefully so I would not fall into it. Achievement became scaffolding. Responsibility became a distraction. Caretaking became a way to stay busy enough not to feel how little care was reaching me in return.

And yet, the emptiness kept working. Patient. Methodical. It widened the spaces between my thoughts, thinned the meaning out of joy, made even love feel abstract, like a concept I understood intellectually but could not inhabit fully. It taught me how to be present without being felt. How to be needed without being known. How to exist without being met. This was the most dangerous hunger of all. Not the kind that claws or demands, but the kind that convinces you that wanting is the problem. That needing is evidence of failure. That if you are empty, it is because you deserve to be. And so I learned to stop asking. To stop reaching. To stop believing that there was something on the other side of the reaching anyway.

The nothingness did not take me in a moment. It did not rush. It waited until I had hollowed myself out in cooperation with it. Until there was so much space inside me that I mistook it for peace. Until silence felt safer than connection. Until disappearance seemed like the natural conclusion to a life lived without being fully seen. And that is how emptiness nearly won. Not by force. Not by violence. But by convincing me that there was nothing left worth protecting. What I would come to learn, slowly and painfully, is that emptiness is not the absence of self. It is the absence of nourishment. A landscape stripped bare not because it was unworthy of growth, but because nothing was allowed to take root long enough to feed it. Those caverns inside me were not proof that I was broken beyond repair. They were evidence of how much space had been waiting for love.

The nothingness did not define me. It revealed what had been missing. And even then, even after I named it, the emptiness did not disappear on command. Starvation does not reverse simply because you recognize hunger. The body does not trust nourishment the first time it is offered after years of scarcity. I had learned to live without fullness. I had learned to flinch at abundance. Love, when it appeared, felt foreign in my hands, like a language I recognized but could not yet speak without stumbling. The space inside me did not close all at once. It echoed for a long time. There were moments when connection brushed against those inner walls and startled me, moments when being seen felt almost painful, as if light were entering rooms that had been sealed for decades. I mistook that ache for danger at first. I mistook tenderness for threat. When you have lived hollow for so long, fullness can feel overwhelming, even suffocating.

But something had shifted. The emptiness no longer felt like destiny. It felt like history. I began to understand that what nearly ended me was not an excess of pain, but a famine of being met. Not too much suffering, but too little witnessing. Too little attunement. Too little permission to need without consequence. My soul had not collapsed under weight; it had caved inward from lack of support. And once I could see that, the narrative began to loosen its grip. The void was not a verdict. It was a record. A ledger of moments where connection should have been and wasn't. A map of places where love tried to arrive but was interrupted, redirected, or made conditional. Those caverns inside me were not evidence of deficiency. They were chambers waiting to be inhabited. Spaces shaped by longing, not failure.

And slowly, painstakingly, I began to risk letting something enter. Not everything. Not all at once. Just enough to test the ground. Enough to prove that the soil was not dead, only depleted. I learned that nourishment does not rush. It arrives gently, repeatedly, asking to be trusted over time. It does not fill emptiness by force. It listens first. It stays. What saved me was not light pouring in dramatically. It was presence returning quietly. A hand that did not withdraw. A voice that did not disappear when I spoke my truth. A moment of being held without having to earn it. Each one small. Each one radical. Each one teaching my nervous system a new possibility. The emptiness began to change shape.

Where it had once whispered, "*There is nothing here*," it began to say, "*There is room*." Where it had insisted, "*You do not belong*", it softened into, "*Something can grow*". I was not cured of the hollow overnight. But I was no longer alone inside it. And that made all the difference. Because emptiness is only lethal when it remains unnamed and unattended. When it is mistaken for identity instead of injury. When it is endured instead of understood. In the end, it wasn't darkness that devoured me. And it wasn't emptiness that defined me. It was the long absence of love that nearly erased me. And the slow, stubborn return of it that taught me how to stay. However, the emptiness had to implode before I could see the truth, like a black hole. And it truly did do that.

Eventually, the emptiness reached its own kind of gravity. Not sudden, not theatrical, but inevitable, like pressure building beneath a fault line no one believes will rupture until it does. It crossed a threshold where it could no longer be contained, where all the careful bracing, managing, and minimizing failed at once. It became a bomb counting down in the center of my chest, each second a tremor I felt in my bones, each breath a reminder that time was moving even though I felt utterly still. Three! Two! One! Zero! And then, not a dramatic external explosion, no fireball rising for witnesses, no sound loud enough to summon rescue. What came instead was a quiet collapse inward. A star imploding into a black hole, light folding back on itself, gravity winning without spectacle. There was no noise. Only the sudden absence of everything that had been holding me together by habit alone.

In that implosion, I felt myself disappear. Not ripped away. Not destroyed violently. Just gone. Dissolved. The scaffolding of who I thought I was, who I believed I could be, fell inward and vanished. There was no narrative left to cling to, no role to perform, no belief sturdy enough to prop me up. Identity collapsed under its own weight, swallowed whole by the void that had been expanding quietly for years. I did not fall into darkness. I fell into emptiness. A vast, echoing space that felt both terrifying and strangely familiar, as if I had finally arrived at the place I had been circling my entire life. This was the landscape the silence had been preparing me for. The home, the absence had been building. I was lost to the emptiness that had shaped my every thought, my every wound, my every whispered plea; I never believed anyone would answer.

Lost to the nothingness that had grown so familiar it began to feel like destiny. And yet, this is the part that took me years to understand: Disappearance is not the same as ending. What vanished in that implosion was not my life. It was the false structure I had been surviving inside. The identities built on endurance alone. The worth measured by usefulness. The self, defined by how little it needed. Those things collapsed because they could not survive the gravity of truth any longer. They were never meant to hold a living person. They were never meant to last. In the void that followed, there was terror, yes. But there was also something else. Something subtle. A strange neutrality. For the first time, there was no performance required. No mask to maintain. No expectation to meet. No version of myself to uphold. The emptiness stripped me down to something raw and undefined, something without labels or scripts or conclusions.

I was not whole. But I was real. That void, which I had feared would be the end of me, turned out to be a kind of threshold. A clearing after collapse. A space where nothing was demanded because nothing was assumed. I did not know who I was there. I did not know what came next. I only knew that the story I had been living inside had finally imploded under its own weight. And in that silence, terrifying and vast, there was at last room. Room for something unconstructed. Room for breath without justification. Room for a self that had not yet been defined by pain. I did not emerge from that void quickly. I lingered there, disoriented, frightened, unmoored. But I was no longer being pulled toward disappearance. The gravity had changed direction. The emptiness no longer whispered destiny. It waited. And waiting, I would learn, is not the same as ending. It is the pause where something new gathers itself, quietly, tentatively, before daring to take shape.

I stayed in that pause longer than I care to admit. Time behaved differently there. Minutes stretched into shapeless hours, hours into a thick, unmoving dusk where nothing asked me to hurry. The world beyond the void continued. I knew that much in theory, but inside it, there was no clock, no demand to reassemble myself into something legible. I floated in that suspension, neither alive in the old sense nor gone in the way I had once imagined. Just present. Bare. Unclaimed. The emptiness did not rush to fill itself. It did not panic at its own vastness. It simply existed, wide and quiet, like a field after a wildfire where the ash still holds warmth but no longer burns. I had spent so long fearing this place, naming it annihilation, mistaking it for death. But here, stripped of catastrophe, it felt more like a reset than a ruin. Not peace. Not yet. But possibility, raw and unsettling in its openness.

Without the old structures propping me up, I began to feel things I had not allowed myself to feel in years. Not the sharp agony that once dominated me, but subtler sensations. The ache of fatigue finally acknowledged. The grief that had been waiting patiently beneath my rage. The fear of not knowing who I was without pain as my compass. Each feeling arrived cautiously, as if testing whether it was safe to exist now. And for the first time, I did not immediately silence them. I noticed my breath again. Not as something rationed or monitored, but as a quiet, involuntary motion, rising and falling without negotiation. I noticed the weight of my body against the ground, the simple fact of gravity holding me without demand. These were small things, almost embarrassingly basic, yet they felt revolutionary. Proof that something in me still knew how to inhabit the moment without performing it.

In that space, I began to understand that the void was not empty because I was lacking. It was empty because everything false had fallen away. The roles. The scripts. The survival strategies that once kept me alive but had long outlived their usefulness. The emptiness was not punishment. It was aftermath. The quiet that follows collapse, where debris settles and the dust finally begins to clear. I did not rebuild myself then. I did not rush to replace what had vanished. I let the space remain open, even when it frightened me. Especially then. Because every time I resisted the urge to fill it with another identity, another obligation, another version of who I thought I should be, something inside me softened. The nervous vigilance loosened its grip. The constant self-surveillance dimmed. For brief, fragile moments, I felt unobserved by my own inner critic.

This was not healing as I had imagined it. There were no answers descending from the sky, no sudden sense of purpose restoring color to the world. What there was instead was permission. Permission to not know. Permission to be unfinished. Permission to exist without immediately justifying that existence. And in that permission, something ancient stirred. Not hope. Hope still felt too bright, too risky. Not joy. Joy still felt distant, like a language I had forgotten how to speak. What stirred was something quieter and sturdier. Curiosity. A tentative wondering about what might grow if I did not immediately trample the ground with expectations. A question whispered not with urgency, but with care: *"What if I don't rush this?"*

I began to sense that the void was not asking me to disappear into it. It was asking me to listen. To rest inside the not-knowing long enough for something truer to emerge. Not a replacement identity, but a presence. Not a performance, but a pulse. I was still afraid. Still tender. Still unsure how to live without the familiar ache guiding my steps. But for the first time, the fear did not feel like an order. It felt like information. Something to be acknowledged rather than obeyed. The emptiness held me there, neither pushing nor pulling. Just allowing. And slowly, almost imperceptibly, I realized I was no longer waiting for the end. I was waiting for myself. Not the self I had been taught to be. Not the self, forged in survival. But the self that had been paused, held in reserve, waiting for the noise to quiet enough to finally be felt.

That self did not arrive fully formed. It did not announce itself with certainty. It arrived the way dawn does after a long night. Gradually. Without fanfare. With a softening of edges. With light so subtle, you only notice it in retrospect. And that was how the beginning truly began. Not with rebuilding. Not with answers. But with the courage to remain in the open space long enough for life, tentative and unarmoured, to breathe itself back into being. But, first I had to finish my journey in the abyss, and that is where we will go once more.

The Last Illusion of Agency

If life, or even God Himself, refused to blow the final whistle for me, then I would carve one from the splinters of my own breaking and lift it to my lips. I would make an ending where none had been granted. From bone and grief, from silence and ash, I would fashion the sound myself. *"Fluit-fluit, die storie is uit."* The whistle blows. The story ends. That was the bargain I struck in my mind. The last illusion of agency left to me. If I could not be saved, then at least I could conclude. The thought did not arrive dressed in poetry or philosophy. There was no grand summation of my life, no montage of meaning, no moral to extract. What came instead was stripped bare, skeletal, reduced to its most primitive truth. A sequence of statements so simple they felt prehistoric, spoken not from the mind but from the hollowed center of my being. "I am alone. I am empty. I am gone. I am nothing. I feel nothing."

Each sentence fell inward as a stone dropped into a bottomless well. No splash. No echo. No resistance. Just immediate disappearance, as though the words themselves were swallowed before they could prove they had ever existed. The void did not answer me. It did not argue. It did not contradict. It absorbed everything without reaction, without reflection, without mercy or malice. A silence so complete it felt absolute. That was the most terrifying part. Not pain. Not fear. But the absence of response. I had lived so long inside struggle that even suffering had felt like proof of presence. Pain had texture. Grief had weight. Despair had a voice. But here, in this final interior quiet, there was nothing to press against. Nothing to push back. Nothing to fight. The emptiness did not wound me. It erased me by indifference.

I mistook that erasure for peace. I mistook the absence of sensation for relief. I mistook numbness for rest. I mistook disappearance for freedom. In that moment, I believed I had finally succeeded. That I had reached the end of language, the end of self, the end of wanting. I believed I had stepped beyond ache into neutrality, beyond longing into nothingness. The whistle had blown. The story, I thought, was out. But what I did not yet understand was this: Emptiness that swallows sound is not the same as silence that heals. One is annihilation. The other is space. And I was standing at the threshold between them, unable to tell the difference yet. Those words, *"I am nothing"*, felt conclusive because I had been taught all my life to equate worth with presence, usefulness, noise, and performance. When all of that collapsed, nothingness felt like the final truth. A verdict delivered without ceremony. A full stop placed at the end of a sentence, I no longer had the strength to continue.

And yet, even there, even in that echo-less well, something subtle betrayed the lie. I noticed the fall. I noticed the dropping. I noticed that something was still observing the disappearance. Because to say" *I am gone"* still requires an *I* to speak. To declare *"I feel nothing"* still requires awareness. To name emptiness still requires presence. I did not recognize this then. I was too far inside the belief, too exhausted to interrogate it. But later, much later, I would come to understand that even at my most reduced, even at my most erased, something remained. Not hope. Not identity. Not meaning. But consciousness. A witness still breathing inside the void. The whistle I thought I had blown did not end the story. It only marked the moment where language failed, identity dissolved, where the old narrative could no longer carry me forward. I had not reached the end of existence. I had reached the end of a false self that could no longer survive the weight of truth.

In that well with no echo, I was not dead. I was unmade. And unmaking, though it feels like extinction, is often the first terrible kindness before something truer is allowed to begin. And still, even as I stood there convinced the final sound had already faded, something resisted closure. Not loudly. Not heroically. It did not rise up to argue for life or reach for hope with trembling hands. It simply lingered. A quiet remainder. A residue that refused to be erased, even when everything else had fallen away. In the hollow left behind by unmaking, I expected oblivion. Instead, I found awareness without a name. A watching without a story. A breath that kept arriving without asking permission from belief or despair. It was not comforting. It was not reassuring. It was bare. Unadorned. Almost impersonal. But it was there.

I existed without explanation. That was new. For the first time, I was not performing my pain, not narrating my worthlessness, not defending my right to disappear. There was no audience left to convince, no role left to play. The masks had dissolved with the language. The scripts had burned away with the identities they upheld. All that remained was sensation stripped to its minimum. Breath. Weight. The dull thud of a heart that had not received the memo that it was supposed to stop. I was furious at that persistence. "How dare something in me continue when I had concluded? How dare breath keep finding me when I had let go of wanting it? How dare the body stay loyal to life when the mind had already signed the ending?" And yet, that betrayal of my certainty was also the first fracture in the lie.

Because if I were truly nothing, there would be no one left to notice the void. If I were truly gone, there would be no witness left to mark the absence. If the story had truly ended, there would be no pause long enough to question the silence. The void, vast as it was, was not empty of awareness. It was empty of narrative. Empty of judgment. Empty of the cruel arithmetic that had told me I had to earn the right to remain. In that absence, something strange happened. I was no longer condemned. No longer praised. No longer evaluated at all. I simply was. That terrified me more than despair ever had. Because despair, for all its cruelty, had structure. It gave me rules. It told me who I was and where I belonged. It offered me certainty, even if that certainty was annihilation. But this, this raw existence without a verdict, this demanded something else entirely. It demanded that I remain without justification.

No explanation. No redemption arc. No final bow. Just presence. I did not call it grace then. I did not call it mercy. I would have rejected those words outright. But something had shifted beneath the ruins. The whistle I thought I had blown had not summoned an ending. It had stripped me down to a threshold I had never known how to name. Between annihilation and space. Between erasure and rest. Between the silence that kills and the silence that listens. I stood there emptied of everything that had once defined me, realizing too late that definitions had been the cage all along. The emptiness I feared was not demanding my disappearance. It was revealing how much of me had been constructed to survive absence rather than connection.

What remained was not a self I recognized. But it was alive. And that, unbearable and undeniable, meant the story had not concluded. It had shed its skin. The chapter I had been living inside had ended, yes, but not with the whistle I tried to carve. It ended with collapse. With exposure. With the terrifying honesty of standing nowhere and still breathing. I would not call what followed hope. Not yet. But I would later understand this moment for what it was: The instant the lie exhausted itself. The instant annihilation failed to deliver what it promised. The instant when nothingness, instead of swallowing me whole, became the quiet ground from which something unimagined could one day rise. The story did not end. It fell silent long enough for truth to begin speaking in a language I had never learned before. And I, unmade and still here, was finally quiet enough to listen.

And with that last silent confession, the world collapsed into velvet black. Not night. Not shadow. Something thicker than darkness, heavier than sleep. A suffocating shroud that wrapped itself around me with the intimacy of a lover who knows every curve of your body and the finality of a tomb that does not intend to open again. It pressed close, closer than skin, erasing edges, dissolving distance, until there was no separation left between me and the dark. No horizon. No before. No after. Only enclosure. Only being held so completely that there was nowhere left to flee. It extinguished the last fragile ember flickering in my chest, or so it felt, snuffing it out like a candle forgotten in an abandoned room. No ceremony. No witness. Just the soft, merciless end of light. The warmth drained first, a subtle retreat I barely noticed until cold took its place.

Then sensation thinned. Then the idea of sensation itself unraveled. I felt myself recede, layer by layer, as if being gently unthreaded from my own existence, pulled loose stitch by stitch until even the outline of me began to blur. The silence that followed was absolute. Not the quiet of rest or sleep, but the hollow stillness that arrives when all sound has been removed from the universe. A vast, echo-less vacuum that did not respond to thought or prayer or fear. It did not comfort. It did not accuse. It simply was. And in that neutrality lay its terror. The silence asked nothing of me and offered nothing in return. A silence so complete it felt eternal. The kind that does not pass. The kind that settles into the architecture of absence. The kind that lingers in the spaces left behind. The kind that haunts the world long after the body falls still.

I dissolved into that stillness believing this was it. No more struggle. No more becoming. No more ache. In that final breath, that surrender into nothingness, I believed my story had ended. I believed I had vanished into the void, erased without remainder, folded into the vastness that had been calling me by name for so long. I believed there would be no witness left to mark my absence, no memory warm enough to hold shape, no imprint strong enough to prove I had ever been here at all. I believed I was gone. And yet, beneath that belief, something impossible remained. Not sensation. Not thought. Not fear. A pause. A suspension so subtle it did not feel like survival, only interruption. As if the void itself hesitated. As if the black velvet, so certain of its claim, had been forced to loosen its grip by something it could not fully swallow. There was no resistance, no struggle, no reaching back toward life. Only the faint awareness that the stillness had stalled, that the silence had held its breath.

There was no return to light. Not yet. No sound breaking the quiet. No voice calling me back. Only this: the awareness that the sentence had not been finished. The darkness had closed around me, yes. But it had not sealed. What I mistook for vanishing was not erasure, but a threshold. A liminal place where everything familiar dissolved, yet something unnamed endured. The story I believed had ended did not conclude with punctuation. It did not receive its full stop. It stopped mid-breath, suspended between what had been and what I could not yet imagine. And though I did not know it then, though understanding would come slowly and painfully much later, that pause, unbearable, wordless, vast, was not death.

It was the place where the old story finally fell silent. And silence, when it is not forced, is not always an ending. Sometimes it is the space where the false noise dies away. Sometimes it is the clearing after collapse. Sometimes it is the dark womb before the next becoming. Sometimes, it is the moment when something that has never been allowed to speak gathers itself, trembling and unfinished, and draws its very first breath. And in that held breath, in that unfinished sentence, something subtle began to stir. Not light. Not hope in any shape I recognized. More like pressure easing at the center of the stillness, the faintest shift in density, as though the velvet black were thinning, loosening its weave. The darkness did not retreat; it made room. And that difference mattered more than I could comprehend at the time.

The pause widened. Not outward, but inward. Space opened where there had only been compression. The silence, once absolute, softened at its edges, no longer a wall but a field. It did not speak. It did not instruct. It simply allowed. And in that allowance, I sensed something unfamiliar and fragile moving beneath the quiet, like a small animal testing the air after a long winter underground. It was not a thought. It was not a feeling. It was not even desire. It was inclination. A leaning, barely perceptible. A tilt toward continuation. I did not choose it. I did not summon it. It arrived without permission, without argument, without explanation. A reflex older than despair. Older than language. Older than the story I had been telling myself about endings. Something in me had remembered how to exist without justification. How to persist without meaning attached. How to be without proving why.

The void did not approve. But it did not stop it either. And so, in that threshold where nothing was demanded, the pause became porous. The stillness no longer felt like erasure but like suspension, a holding pattern between what had collapsed and what had not yet taken form. I was no longer disappearing. I was unmoored. Untethered from the identities that had defined me by absence and endurance. Untethered from the voice that insisted silence was the same as peace. I remained without shape. Without name. Without narrative. But I remained. And remaining, I would later understand, is not the same as returning. It is quieter than rescue. Less triumphant than survival stories like to be. It does not come with clarity or gratitude or resolve. It comes as neutrality. As presence without demand. As the simple, inconvenient fact of still being here when the ending failed to arrive.

That first breath did not rush in. It did not fill my lungs with revelation. It crept. It trembled. It barely registered as breath at all. More like a ripple through still water, proof not of strength, but of continuity. The body remembering something the mind had released. The nervous system choosing life without consulting belief. And with that breath, so small it could have been missed entirely, the silence changed character. It was no longer the silence of extinction. It became the silence of potential. The quiet before language. The pause before the next movement of a story that no longer trusted conclusions. I did not feel saved. I did not feel reborn. I did not feel grateful. I felt unfinished.

And for the first time, unfinished did not feel like failure. It felt like permission. Like an open hand where a clenched fist had been. Like a space where something truer than despair might one day arrive, if given enough time, enough gentleness, enough breath. The old story had fallen silent, yes. But silence, now, was no longer a tomb. It was a womb.

The Slow Boil

Self-harm and suicidal ideation was like boiling a frog slowly, the heat rising so gradually it felt survivable, almost reasonable, until survival itself became impossible. The water warmed in increments too small to protest, each increase disguised as adaptation, each moment of endurance mistaken for resilience. I did not notice the danger because I had been living inside it for so long. Pain had taught me how to acclimate. Suffering had trained me to stay still. Eventually, in time, the nameless god I had been bending my knee to asked for more than I could give. What began as small offerings escalated into ultimatums. Not merely a sacrifice of blood, but for my blood to stop flowing altogether. Not a moment of suffocation, but the permanent cessation of breath. Not a bruise, but a body in decay. Not the burn of flesh, but the death of the flesh. The language shifted from endurance to erasure. From relief to release. From quiet to silence everlasting.

It asked me to give my life so I could be free. And I believed it. I believed it because I was wounded. Because I was desperate. Because I was exhausted from carrying a weight that never lightened. I believed it under that tree, in that moment, because the lie arrived dressed as mercy. It sounded gentle. Convincing. It spoke in the tone of final kindness, promising rest where there had only ever been labor. It framed annihilation as liberation and disappearance as peace. It told me this was the last thing it would ever ask. A sacrifice, it said. A sacred one. And I, blind with longing and grief, decided to obey. I opened my hands willingly, desperately, believing that obedience was the same as surrendering pain. By then, I had accepted every deception of this nameless god. I believed it was my only friend. My only witness. My only salvation. It had been with me so long, whispered to me so faithfully, that I mistook its presence for companionship and its cruelty for care. I trusted it because it had never left, not realizing that constancy does not equal love. By that point, I truly believed I had nothing more to give. I had offered blood. Breath. Flesh. Silence. Years. What remained felt small and exhausted and insufficient for the world. My life was all that was left, and I stood at a place where even that felt negotiable. Where placing it on the altar did not feel like loss, but like completion. Like finally paying a debt I had been carrying since childhood. Under that pale, moonlit sky, I believed the lie completely. I believed that giving my life was the last act of usefulness I had left. That disappearance was my final contribution. That I could end the war by becoming the offering. What I did not yet know was that this god was never divine. It was despair wearing a crown. Pain dressed up as prophecy. A voice born of neglect and shame and exhaustion, demanding worship until nothing remained. I did not yet know that freedom never requires a corpse, and that any voice asking for your life in exchange for peace is not a savior, but a thief. But in that moment, standing beneath the weight of everything I had carried, I believed every word. And believing it almost cost me everything. And yet, there was a fracture in that moment, thin as a hairline crack in glass, almost invisible beneath the moonlight. Even as I stood there, hands open, heart emptied of protest, something in me hesitated. Not hope. Not courage. Something older and quieter. A reflex I had not consented to. A pulse that did not belong to the god, nor to the lie, nor to the altar prepared beneath me.

My body knew before my mind did. It trembled. It resisted. It held on with a stubbornness I could not explain. Breath caught in my throat not as surrender, but as refusal. Muscles tightened, not in fear, but in defiance too small to name. I had spent years training myself to disappear, but some primitive part of me had not learned the lesson. It clung to life with a grip that surprised even me, as if saying, without words, "Not yet. Not this way. Not for this reason." The nameless god faltered then. Just for a moment. Its voice thinned. Its certainty flickered. The promises it had made began to ring hollow, like coins struck from cheap metal. The silence it offered no longer sounded like rest. It sounded like absence. Like a room emptied of warmth. Like a peace that asked too much and gave nothing back. And in that hesitation, I felt something shift. The altar was still there. The night was still watching. The weight I carried had not vanished. But the narrative cracked. The lie lost its grip just enough for another truth to breathe. A truth that did not arrive fully formed but whispered itself into being: If this were mercy, it would not demand my erasure. If this were salvation, it would not require my body as proof. The god demanded everything. Life asks only for presence. I did not rise from that place transformed or healed. There was no thunder, no revelation blazing through the dark. What happened was smaller. Messier. Human. I did not give my life. Not because I suddenly believed I deserved it, but because something in me refused to hand it over. Because even at my most broken, some part of me had not agreed to vanish.

By a miracle that was not fully my choice I stepped back. Or perhaps I simply did not step forward as much as I had hoped. The war did not end that night. But it paused. And in that pause, something sacred happened that had nothing to do with sacrifice. I remained. Bruised. Confused. Still drowning. Still aching. But alive. Breathing. Unfinished. The god did not leave immediately. Lies rarely do. But it was wounded then, exposed as something that needed me more than I needed it. And for the first time, I sensed that survival was not obedience. That endurance was not devotion. That staying alive was not failure, but resistance. I would only understand this much later: that the moment I did not disappear was the moment the story changed direction. Not dramatically. Not cleanly. But irrevocably. I did not end the war by becoming the offering. I interrupted it by staying. And that interruption, fragile, uncelebrated, trembling, was the first true act of freedom I had ever made. The story did not end there, that night. It cracked open. And through that fracture, faint at first but undeniable, something else began to seep in—not clarity, not hope in any grand sense, but possibility. A hairline opening where air could move again. Where the breath I had been rationing my entire life could finally deepen, just slightly. Where the self I had mistaken for a burden could begin, slowly and imperfectly, to be felt as something living rather than something owed. The crack did not heal me. It did not save me. But it let the story keep breathing. And that, it turns out, was enough to begin.

Chapter Nine:
The Stillness answers back: The Night after the attempt

We have explored the conversation that transpired between myself and the night, between myself and silence, on the edge of my suicide attempt. That dialogue belonged to the shadowed silence, the kind that closes in, that absorbs sound, that pretends to be final. It was a silence that swallowed language whole, that convinced me endings were inevitable, and mercy looked like disappearance. But this, this came after. And it was something else entirely. The night after my suicide attempt, I found myself outside again, beneath the pale moon, standing in a pause unlike any I had ever known. Not the pause of collapse, where the body gives up. Not the pause of surrender, where the spirit lays itself down. But a pause that felt open. Unclaimed. Untethered from outcome. As though the world itself had exhaled after holding its breath for years and was now watching me carefully, curiously, waiting to see what I might do with the space left behind.

The air felt different against my skin. Not lighter exactly, but less hostile. I stood there, unsure of my footing, as though I had stepped onto unfamiliar ground after living too long on the edge of a cliff. Nothing demanded an answer from me. Nothing rushed me. The night did not close in. It stayed. Spacious. Attentive. Truths began to flood me then, not violently, not as revelation thunder or blinding insight, but with the strange clarity of water finally breaking through a dam that had held too long. It came after my first Co-dependency meeting, and the shift was undeniable. Something inside me loosened. Something long-braced finally unclenched. It felt as though scales were being lifted from my eyes, thin translucent layers I hadn't known were there until they fell away. The world did not suddenly change shape, but I could see its contours more clearly.

Patterns I had mistaken for personality revealed themselves as survival. Traits I had worn as identity exposed themselves as adaptation. Beliefs I had sworn were truths revealed their lineage, not born of wisdom, but inherited through pain. The silence inside me, once suffocating, became permeable. It no longer pressed against my ribs. It breathed with me. That night, the moon was no longer cold. No longer distant. No longer indifferent. It smiled down on me. Not in sentimentality. Not in fantasy. But in recognition. As if it had been watching all along, patient and unoffended, waiting for me to return to myself. Its light felt gentler, warmer, no longer the impartial witness to my undoing, but a quiet companion to my becoming. I stood beneath it not as a ghost haunting her own life, not as a conclusion dragging her ending behind her, but as someone newly present in her own body. Someone still fragile, still shaken, but undeniably here.

The tree branches that once contorted into grotesque monsters with grasping claws no longer reached for me in threat. They danced. Twisted. Swayed in quiet celebration. Their movements were no longer accusations but invitations. Their shadows did not chase me; they moved with me, lengthening and softening as I shifted. The world had not changed. The night was still the night. The trees were still trees. But I had shifted just enough that the world met me differently. Or perhaps, for the first time, I met it without armor. The night was no longer an adversary. The silence no longer a void. They had softened into something like listening. I realized then that there are many kinds of silence. There is the silence that erases, that demands disappearance, that confuses stillness with annihilation. And there is the silence that makes room. That waits. That holds without swallowing. This was the latter.

I stood in that newly cleared space, unfamiliar and tender, aware for the first time that light does not always arrive as brightness. Sometimes it arrives as understanding. As context. As the slow, patient dismantling of lies that once felt like truth. Sometimes light does not rush in to rescue; it asks permission to enter. It waits until the soul is ready to receive it. And in that space, questions began to change. They softened. They widened. They no longer demanded verdicts, only honesty. The voice inside me, once sharp and merciless, no longer demanded disappearance. It grew curious. Tentative. It asked not how to end, but how to stay. How to listen. How to learn what had been missing without collapsing under the weight of that knowing.

And so, in this chapter, I will share the follow-up conversation I had with the night and with silence. Not the one steeped in despair, not the one obsessed with endings, but the one where something began to answer back differently. Where darkness stepped aside just enough for light to find its way into my soul, not as rescue, but as recognition. Stay with me. We are no longer standing at the edge of an ending for this chapter. We are learning how to speak from inside the pause where healing begins.

We now turn toward a different silence altogether. Not the silence that suffocates or erases, but the silence of potential. The silence that arrives not to take, but to tend. The silence of healing, which does not demand answers, but gently quiets the hurt long enough for breath to return. This was a silence that did not rush me forward or pull me backward. It simply stayed. Steady. Patient. Like open ground after fire, waiting to see what might dare to grow. In its presence, the noise inside me softened, loosened its grip, until clarity rose not as command, but as permission. This silence did not empty me. It held me. It wrapped itself around me in a loving embrace, not tight enough to trap, not loose enough to abandon. It was the kind of holding that asks nothing in return, that does not brace for my collapse or flinch at my truth.

In its presence, I did not have to perform, explain, justify, or prove. I did not have to earn rest through suffering or worth through endurance. I could simply exist. And for the first time, that existence felt welcome, not tolerated, not managed, but received. This was the silence that began revealing my worth, not through affirmations shouted over pain, not through slogans meant to drown out grief, but through quiet recognition. Through the gentle realization that I did not have to earn my place in the world. That my breath alone was evidence enough. That my survival was not an inconvenience, but a testament. A quiet, stubborn miracle that had persisted even when I did not know how to want it to. In this silence, I felt something shift. The voices of other people's judgment and expectation, once deafening, began to fade like distant static losing its signal.

Their demands loosened their authority. Their opinions slipped from my ribs. I no longer carried them as law. For the first time in years, I could hear myself again. Not the voice trained by fear or shame, but something softer. Truer. A voice that had been waiting for quiet long enough to speak. This silence told me something simple and radical: "I matter. Not because of what I give. Not because of what I endure. Not because of how well I disappear. But because I am here." It met me with grace, not the dramatic kind that absolves in spectacle, but the quiet grace that sits beside you and does not flinch when you tremble. It met me with mercy that did not require confession, and kindness that did not ask me to be smaller. This silence no longer instructed me to shrink, to remain quiet, to make myself easier to hold. It did not demand obedience or invisibility. Instead, it did the opposite. It gave me my voice back, slowly, tenderly, as one might return something precious that had been misplaced for years and kept safe all this time.

It gave me hope, not as certainty, not as promise, but as possibility. And possibility was enough. This was the beginning of the journey to healing, not because the pain vanished, but because it no longer had the final word. The silence understood me. It comforted me. It listened without interrupting, without correcting, without rushing me toward resolution. It allowed the truth to surface at its own pace, unshaped, unpolished, unafraid.

And in that listening, something inside me learned what it had never known before: that it was safe to speak. That night, the night itself told me something I had never truly believed. That there is hope. That I can change. And for the first time, I believed something other than my pain. Not because the pain had disappeared, but because it had been met. Seen. Held in a space wide enough to contain it without being consumed by it. I understood then that healing would not come from silencing myself any longer.

It would come from finally being heard, first by myself, then by a world I was slowly learning to trust again. For I knew, finally, that the pain would not silence me. I would silence it. Not with force. Not with denial. But with truth. With presence. With a voice reclaimed. And that knowing, quiet and resolute, was the first real sound of my healing beginning.

In that pause, something within me stirred. Not as a voice. Not as a command. But as a pressure so delicate it could have been mistaken for imagination, for the echo of a thought, not brave enough to announce itself. It rose the way sap rises in winter, unseen yet determined, insisting on movement even when the world appears still. The silence leaned closer then, not to erase me, not to claim me, but to ask a question without words. It asked the way gravity asks a falling leaf which way it will turn. The way dawn asks the horizon if it is ready to be seen. My breath caught on that unspoken question. It faltered, stuttered, lost its rhythm for a moment as though uncertain it was still permitted. Then, slowly, awkwardly, it found itself again. Shallow. Unsure. But undeniably present. Air entered my lungs without permission or ceremony, as if my body had decided something before my mind could interfere. The night seemed to notice. The air shifted. Just enough. Just enough to feel different against my skin. Just enough to suggest that the world had not entirely let go of me.

The grass cooled beneath my feet. The scent of earth deepened. Somewhere, something moved quietly, alive and unafraid of the dark. The night did not recoil from me. It did not demand explanation. It simply adjusted, accommodating my continued presence as though it had always expected me to remain. I had not asked to stay. I had not chosen to return. And yet, here I was. Still tethered by the smallest, most stubborn threads. Not purpose. Not resolve. But breath. Sensation. Awareness. The almost imperceptible pull of being here rather than nowhere. Threads so thin they felt breakable, yet they held. They always had. I realized then that I had been tethered all along, even in my deepest unraveling, even when I believed I had vanished completely.

The silence answered my presence by widening. By making room. It did not rush to fill me with reassurance or meaning. It did not cloak itself in comfort or promise me safety. It did not try to convince me of anything at all. It simply allowed me to remain unclaimed by either end of the story. Not swallowed by darkness. Not forced into light. Suspended in the in-between, where nothing demanded conclusion. And in that allowance, something fragile took shape. Not hope. Not yet. But the possibility of hope's shadow. A faint contour at the edge of awareness. A suggestion rather than a declaration. A sense that the night, for all its vastness, was not a closed door. That silence did not always signal erasure. That pause could be a place of becoming, not just an absence of motion. I did not step forward.

I did not step back. I stayed. And staying, I would later learn, is sometimes the bravest movement a soul can make when it has spent a lifetime preparing to disappear.

My heart knocked again. Not timidly this time. Not as if asking permission. A little louder. A little firmer. Still uneven. Still imperfect. But undeniably persistent. The sound startled me, not because it was strong, but because it refused to recede. It did not apologize for its presence. It did not soften itself to be more acceptable. It insisted. It felt less like a beat and more like a question tapping from the inside of my chest, testing the walls it had once been told to quiet itself behind. As if my own body were checking whether it was finally allowed to speak. "What if this is not the end? What if this stillness is not a grave, but a threshold?" The thought did not arrive with clarity or conviction. It did not announce itself as truth. It arrived sideways. Tentative. Almost shy.

The way tremors move beneath a frozen lake, subtle enough to be mistaken for imagination, is undeniable once felt. A quiet reminder that beneath the ice, beneath the stillness that looked like death from above, water was still moving. That motion had not ceased. It had only slowed, conserving itself, waiting. I did not rise. I did not reach. I did not suddenly want to live. But I did not disappear either. That mattered more than I understood in the moment. More than I could name. More than I could trust yet. Staying did not feel like courage. It felt like inertia. Like gravity had momentarily loosened its grip just enough to keep me from falling further. I remained where I was, suspended between endings, surprised by my own continued existence.

The night seemed to sense the shift, however small. It did not rush me. It did not demand a response. It did not brighten or darken in reaction. It simply held its breath with me, matching my stillness without turning it into a verdict. The air remained steady against my skin. The ground stayed firm beneath me, cool and real. Nothing demanded explanation. Nothing insisted on decision. Nothing tried to convert this moment into meaning. In that shared suspension, where nothing was required and nothing was resolved, the silence completed its answer. Not with instruction. Not with persuasion. Not with urgency. It did not push me forward. It did not pull me back. It stayed. Present. Steady. Unafraid.

As if to say, without words and without expectation: You are still here. And for now, that is enough. That was how the night answered me. Not with rescue. Not with revelation. But with room. Room for the next breath, even if it trembled and caught halfway in. Room for the next moment, even if it arrived carrying doubt instead of hope. Room for a body that had not yet decided what survival would look like, only that it was still breathing. Room for a story that did not need to conclude or redeem itself to justify continuing. A story allowed to remain unfinished without being erased. A story granted the rare mercy of not having to know yet how it would go on. In that quiet generosity, something settled. Not certainty. Not purpose. Just presence.

A simple, astonishing fact. I was here. Still. Breathing. Witnessed by the night and not required to explain myself to it. And presence, I would later learn, is sometimes the first miracle a broken story is given. Not the miracle of healing. Not the miracle of transformation. But the miracle of being allowed to remain without condition. The miracle of room.

Pauses That Did Not Collapse

And within that room, that tender widening where nothing rushed me toward an ending, sensation began to return in fragments, the way color seeps back into a photograph left too long in the sun. Not all at once. Not mercifully. Just in hesitant flecks, uneven and unsure, as though my nervous system were testing whether it was safe to feel again. Whether it would be punished for remembering that it still existed. The cold grass pressed against my spine once more, startling in its specificity. Sharp. Real. Unmistakably here. It anchored me in a way the void never could. The night air brushed my cheeks, cool and faintly damp, carrying the quiet scent of earth and distance. These sensations did not comfort me. They reminded me. They said, without words, that I was still tethered to a body, still threaded into time, still occupying a place in the world that had not erased me despite my certainty that it would.

The ache in my chest did not roar back to life. It did not surge or demand attention. It hummed instead, low and distant, like an engine idling somewhere far away, present but not consuming. No longer the center of everything. Just one signal among many. I noticed it without being swallowed by it, and that, too, felt unfamiliar. As though the pain itself had learned to wait. I noticed the sound of my breath before I noticed the breath itself. A faint rasp. Dry. Tentative. Then another. Each inhale uneven, reluctant, as though my lungs were negotiating terms with existence. As though they were asking, quietly, whether it was truly necessary to keep going. The simple mechanics of staying felt foreign, newly learned, like a language my body had not spoken in a long time. Inhale. Pause. Exhale. Pause again.

The pauses were long. Suspended. Stretching the space between breaths into something almost unbearable. But they held. They did not collapse. They did not tip into nothingness. They stayed intact, like small bridges that did not crumble beneath my weight. And that alone felt significant. Because for so long, pauses had meant danger. Silence had meant disappearance. Stillness had meant the end. But here, in this moment, the pauses did not devour me. They cradled me. They became proof that nothing terrible happened simply because I stopped striving, stopped bracing, stopped forcing myself forward. Time resumed not as a demand, but as a gentle sequence. One breath leading to another. One sensation following the next. Not progress. Not healing. Just continuation. The quiet miracle of sequence reasserting itself after everything had threatened to stop. I did not feel grateful. I did not feel relieved.

I felt astonished. Astonished that my body still knew how to remain. Astonished that sensation could return without catastrophe. Astonished that existence did not immediately punish me for staying. Lying there the next nigh, held by grass and air and breath, I understood something without fully grasping it yet. That staying does not always arrive as a decision. Sometimes it arrives as a sensation. A pressure. A pause that refuses to break. A body remembering, before the mind can catch up, that it is still allowed to be here. And in that remembering, fragile and uncelebrated, the room widened just a little more. And as the room widened, not dramatically but by increments so small they could only be felt, not measured, something else began to stir alongside sensation. A subtle recalibration. As though my body, having confirmed it was not under immediate threat, allowed itself the smallest margin of curiosity. Not about the future. Not about meaning. Just about now. About this exact configuration of breath, weight, ground, and sky.

The grass beneath me no longer felt like an obstacle to endure, but a boundary I could lean into. Each blade pressed its own quiet signature against my skin, a thousand tiny points of contact reminding me that I had edges again. That I occupied space. That I was not dissolving. The earth did not swallow me. It held me. Firm. Unapologetic. Indifferent in the most merciful way. It did not ask me to explain why I was still here. It simply received my weight and did not let me fall through. The night air moved differently now. It no longer brushed past me as if I were already absent. It lingered. Curled around my wrists. Slid across my collarbone. It traced the outline of a body that had been convinced for so long it did not deserve an outline at all. With each faint movement of air, I felt myself outlined back into form, as if the world were sketching me in again with a very light hand, careful not to tear the page.

The hum in my chest remained steady. Distant. Manageable. It did not ask to be fixed. It did not demand interpretation. It existed without argument, and in that coexistence, I learned something new. That pain does not always need to be confronted to lose its power. Sometimes it only needs to be repositioned. Moved from the center to the periphery. Allowed to be present without being sovereign. Breath continued its quiet negotiations. Inhale. Pause. Exhale. The pauses, once terrifying in their openness, began to feel like small sanctuaries. Spaces where nothing bad happened simply because nothing happened at all. I rested inside them, cautiously at first, like someone testing ice after a long winter, half-expecting it to crack beneath me. But it didn't. It held. Again and again. The body kept its promise.

Time, too, softened. It stopped bearing down on me like an accusation. It loosened its grip and became something almost companionable. Not something I had to outrun or outlast. Just something that moved alongside me, step for step, breath for breath. Continuation without commentary. Existence without verdict. The astonishment deepened, not as excitement, but as reverence. I had not been spared sensation. I had not escaped pain. I had not been lifted into relief. And yet, I was still here. Still breathing. Still sensing. Still held by a world that had not closed its doors. That realization did not bloom into hope. It settled into something quieter and more durable. Permission. Permission to remain exactly as I was, without improvement, without justification.

Permission to take up space without apologizing for the weight of my body, the sound of my breath, the fact of my being.

Staying, I understood then, is not always an act of courage. Sometimes it is an act of memory. The body remembers a truth the mind has long forgotten. Remembering that it belongs to itself. That it is allowed to exist without earning the right. And as that memory took root, delicate and unspectacular, the room did not rush to fill itself with meaning. It did not demand transformation. It simply widened enough to hold me, just as I was, breathing unevenly, feeling imperfectly, alive without explanation. That was enough. For that moment.

The darkness did not recoil from my return. It did not retreat in offense or surge in threat. It adjusted. Yielded a fraction. Made space the way water does when something stops fighting its surface. The night shifted its posture around me, no longer closing in with intent, no longer opening wide with indifference, but hovering in a quiet equilibrium that felt almost attentive, as if it, too, were listening for what might come next. And in that listening, a realization settled into me with the gentleness of a truth that does not need persuasion. I had mistaken stillness for finality. I had confused pause with ending. This was not the silence of a sealed tomb, not the suffocation of something finished and locked away. This was the hush of a threshold, the kind that gathers just before something crosses over. The kind that holds its breath not because it is done, but because it is waiting.

A single thought surfaced then. Small. Unassuming. It did not arrive with drama or urgency. It did not argue its case or demand belief. It simply wondered, quietly, as if thinking aloud beside me rather than inside me. "What if staying is not the same as choosing? What if remaining, for now, is enough?" The thought did not light me up. It did not rescue me. It did not promise that anything would be easier. It simply existed. And because it did not demand allegiance, I did not resist it. I did not embrace it either. I let it sit beside me, the way the night now did. Present. Unintrusive. Unthreatening. For the first time in hours, perhaps in years, I was not being asked to decide who I would become. I was not being pushed to imagine a future or justify a past. I was not required to explain why I was still here or what I planned to do with the fact of my survival. No conclusions were needed. No commitments extracted.

I was only being asked to occupy this moment. To be here. To breathe. To allow the next second to arrive without forcing it away or dragging it closer. And so I did. I stayed not as an act of defiance, not as a declaration of hope, not as a promise to heal. I stayed as a fact. As a body on grass beneath a sky that had learned how to soften. As breath moving through lungs that were still negotiating but no longer refusing. As time passed, without asking me to perform inside it. The night did not reward me for this. It did not congratulate me. It simply remained. And in its remaining, it taught me something I had never been allowed to learn before. That being here does not always require certainty. That staying does not always need a reason. That sometimes the most radical thing a broken story can do is continue without explanation.

And in that quiet permission, held by darkness that no longer demanded my disappearance, the moment stretched. Not forward. Not backward. Just outward enough to hold me. Within that widening, something subtle shifted. Not a feeling I could name, not relief, not gratitude, but a loosening. As if the tight fist I had been living inside finally opened, not to grasp for anything new, but to stop clenching around the idea that I had to resolve my existence to justify it. The world did not suddenly make sense. My pain did not dissolve. But the urgency to decide everything right now began to thin. I noticed how the night sounded different when it was no longer an adversary. The quiet was not empty; it was layered. Crickets threading rhythm into the dark. Leaves whispering among themselves. My own breath, still uneven, but no longer panicked, moving in and out like a tide relearning its shore. These sounds did not demand my attention. They invited it, gently, the way one might invite a skittish animal closer by simply sitting still.

I realized then how exhausted I had been from believing every moment required a verdict. Live or die. Stay or go. Heal or fail. I had been living inside a courtroom with no recess, prosecuting my own existence without pause. This moment felt like adjournment. Not acquittal. Not sentencing. Just a recess long enough to feel the bench beneath me and remember that I was allowed to sit. The darkness, once a judge, had become a witness. It did not absolve me. It did not condemn me. It watched, steady and unblinking, as I remained. And there was a strange dignity in that watching. A sense that my presence, unremarkable and unresolved as it was, did not need to be defended. I did not know what would come next. I did not know if this gentleness would last or if the ache would surge again with teeth bared. I only knew that, in this narrow pocket of time, I was not being chased by the future or dragged by the past. I was simply allowed to exist between them.

The moment held. The breath held. I held. And that, fragile and unspectacular, was not an ending. It was not even a beginning in the way stories like to announce themselves. It was a middle. A resting place. A thin ledge carved into the cliff face of my life where I could stand, trembling, and realize that falling was not the only motion available to me. For now, I was here. And for now, that was enough.

The Moon Keeps Its Vigil

Somewhere above me, the moon continued its vigil. Not cruel. Not kind. Simply present. It did not lean closer to console me, nor did it turn away in disinterest. It held its place in the sky with the ancient steadiness of something that has watched countless endings fail to arrive, that has seen despair swear it was final only to be contradicted by morning. Somewhere beyond the tree line, the world persisted in its quiet routines. Lights flicked on in distant windows like small, domestic stars. Roads breathed with the low hush of passing tires, a rhythm of arrival and departure that did not pause for my reckoning. Lives continued, unknowing, unpausing, not because they were indifferent to me, but because they were not required to intervene.

None of it reached for me. None of it demanded explanation. And in that absence of demand, something softened inside my ribs. It was not relief. Not comfort. There was no swell of gratitude or sudden lightness. It was a loosening. A subtle release, almost imperceptible, as though a knot I had carried for so long had begun to ease its grip. Not untied. Not gone. But no longer cinched tight enough to bruise every breath. The space inside my chest widened by a fraction, barely measurable, yet profound. Just enough room for air to pass through without scraping. Just enough to feel the difference between suffocation and breath. I was still broken. Still emptied. Still unsure whether I belonged among the living.

Those truths did not evaporate under the moonlight. They did not resolve themselves into insight or closure. They remained, heavy and unresolved, resting against me like unanswered questions I did not yet have the strength to ask aloud. They pressed into my awareness with familiar weight. But alongside them, something else existed now. Quieter. Less dramatic. And impossible to ignore. I was still here. Not triumphant. Not redeemed. Not suddenly convinced of my worth or my future. Just present. A body on the ground beneath a sky that had not expelled me. Suspended in the fragile grace of a pause that refused to harden into an ending. A pause that did not insist I transform, improve, or justify myself before I was allowed to remain. The night held me there without instruction, without expectation, without threat. It did not ask me to decide. It did not demand belief.

Breath followed breath, not as a promise of healing, not as a prophecy of meaning, but as a simple, stubborn sequence that continued despite my doubt. In that rhythm, something settled. Not peace. Not resolution. Something steadier and less dramatic. An internal lowering of volume. A sense that the urgency had eased just enough for listening to become possible. I understood then, not with certainty but with quiet clarity, that the story had not closed. It had not reached its final line or its moral. It had not concluded with a lesson carved neatly from suffering. It had inhaled. Drawn itself inward. Gathered what remained scattered and bruised. The kind of inhale that comes before speech. Before movement. Before the courage to step forward without knowing whether the ground will hold. Somewhere inside that breath, unseen and unnamed, the next chapter waited.

Not announced. Not dramatic. Not yet ready to be read aloud. It lingered the way a thought forms before language catches it. The way dawn waits behind the edge of the sky, not rushing the night, not demanding permission to arrive. Patient. Unassuming. Gathering itself slowly. Learning how to exist without apology. Without needing to prove it deserved space. I did not rush toward it. I did not claim it as hope. Hope, in that moment, still felt too fragile, too easily broken by expectation. I did not wrap the future in optimism or promise myself redemption. I simply allowed the waiting. Allowed the not-knowing. Allowed the chapter to remain unspoken. And in allowing that waiting, I remained.

Here. Breathing. Unfinished. And for the first time, unfinished did not feel like failure. It felt like an opening. Like a sentence paused mid-thought, not because it had nothing more to say, but because it was learning how to speak without hurting itself. Possibility did not arrive with fanfare. It arrived quietly, learning how to begin.

And just as much as I had surrendered to that cruel belief the previous night, just as the idea of vanishing had settled around me then like a final garment pulled carefully into place, something shifted in the fabric of the silence. Not loudly. Not dramatically. So subtly it could have been mistaken for nothing at all. A pause within the pause. A breath-space inside the hush, the breath that follows the comma. A thinning inside the numbness itself. The quiet changed its tone. The night changed its conversation. What had felt sealed, concluded, irrevocable the night before now felt, suspended. As though the darkness, having drawn me this close, hesitated. As though it reached the edge of its own certainty and faltered there. As though it held its breath, uncertain whether it was meant to claim me or release me. And in that hush, I became aware of something I had not felt in a very long time. Resistance. Not from the world outside me. Not from memory, morality, obligation, or fear. But from somewhere impossibly deep within.

Not a thought. Not a plea. Not a voice asking to be spared. Just a sensation. A minute tightening. Almost imperceptible. Like the smallest knot tied at the very end of a fraying thread, a refusal to let the unraveling complete itself. A quiet tension that did not argue its case or make promises. It did not demand a future. It did not command me to rise, change, or believe differently. It did not shout. It did not ask me to become a new version of myself overnight. It simply refused to disappear completely. That was all. And it was enough to catch my breath on the way out. One shallow inhale faltered. Paused. Then, against all expectations, it continued. My chest rose, barely, still pressed down by weight, still aching under the aftermath of my suicide attempt the night before. My body was bruised, tender, heavy with consequence. The muscles felt slow, reluctant. The ribs sore with the memory of strain. Every movement reminded me how close I had come to not needing to notice any of this at all.

And yet, the body I had already begun to abandon made a quiet, stubborn claim. One more moment. One more pulse. One more fragile insistence on existing. It was not heroic. It was not brave. It was not hopeful. It was instinct. The oldest language the body knows. Before belief. Before meaning. Before choice. A refusal written into flesh rather than thought. My heart answered it, uneven and tired, knocking softly from the inside as if to say, "*I am still here, whether you want me to be or not.*" The rhythm was imperfect, uncertain, but present. A signal without narrative. A fact that did not ask permission. The night did not interrupt this. The silence did not recoil. It adjusted again, the way it had begun to learn how to do. As if recognizing that something had survived the erasure. As if acknowledging that even here, even now, something remained unclaimed.

And I lay there, suspended between what I had believed the night before and what my body was quietly insisting on now, aware that I had crossed into unfamiliar territory. Not living. Not dying. But lingering. Held together by nothing grander than breath. Anchored by nothing louder than a pulse. A life not yet reclaimed, but no longer fully surrendered. And in that delicate resistance, that almost-nothing that refused to become nothing at all, the story shifted again. Not forward. Not backward. Sideways. Into a space where survival was no longer an argument, but a fact still unfolding.

The night did not pull me forward after that. It did not urge. It did not coax. It did not claim. It held me there. Balanced on the edge of something new, though not the edge I had come to know so well. This was not the brink of the abyss, not the familiar gravity of disappearance tugging at my heels. This was different. Quieter. Stranger. This was the edge of change. The edge of hope. The edge of healing, still unformed and unnamed, but unmistakably present in its restraint. I was neither falling nor returning. The cold remained. The numbness stayed intact. Nothing lifted dramatically. Nothing dissolved overnight. My body still ached. My mind still carried the residue of the night before. The weight did not vanish simply because I had survived. Survival did not arrive with relief or clarity. It arrived with continuation. With aftermath.

And yet, beneath all of that, something stirred. Something that did not belong to the darkness. Something that felt different under the moon tonight. A flicker. It had begun earlier than I realized. It had sparked first when I opened my eyes and found that I had survived death. When the world did not end where I had expected it to. When I held a self-help book in trembling hands, not as a solution, but as a gesture. A reaching I had not planned. A curiosity I had not trusted myself with before. It followed me into the Co-dependency meeting. That room. Those voices. That moment. Where I felt seen. Where I felt heard. Where I felt understood for the first time without having to perform my pain or soften it for anyone else's comfort. Something shifted there. Not loudly. Not cleanly.

A faint pressure behind the sternum. A warmth that did not spread, but lingered. Too small to call hope. Too fragile to name. But undeniably alive. Like the first twitch of a limb after numbness begins to recede. Unreliable, uncertain, but real.

It felt like a question forming where certainty had lived. Not a question made of words. Not a thought. Not a plan. A sensation. A subtle turning inward. A hesitation that had no language yet, only weight. As though some unseen part of me had opened its eyes for the first time in years and was quietly, incredulously asking whether this was truly where the story ended. Whether the script I had memorized was the only one available. Whether the ending I had rehearsed was still required. The silence did not interrupt this wondering. It waited with me.

And for the first time since the night had wrapped its velvet arms around my shoulders, I was no longer slipping forward. No longer being drawn. No longer bracing for collapse. I was hovering. Held in a breath that had not yet decided which direction it would take. The darkness had come to claim me. And now, it was nearing time for me to answer. But not with the answer of life or death that had consumed me the night before. No. This was a different reckoning entirely. This was the question of whether I would change everything or stay the same. Whether I would heal or run. Whether I would finally turn toward my past, excavate it, listen to it, tend to it, or continue avoiding it the way I always had, mistaking distance for safety.

The night did not demand my response. It simply waited. And in that waiting, I understood something quietly monumental. Survival had brought me to the edge. But choice would decide what happened next. Not all at once. Not heroically. But breath by breath. Moment by moment. Standing there, suspended between who I had been and who I had not yet dared to imagine, I felt the weight of that truth settle, not as fear, but as gravity. This time, the story was not asking whether I would disappear. It was asking whether I would stay long enough to change.

Quieter Than Language

And yet, within that earned stillness, something subtle began to stir. Not a thought. Not a plea. Something quieter than language itself. A tremor beneath the calm, the way a current moves far below the surface of a glassy sea, unseen but undeniable. The water above remained smooth, almost deceptive in its serenity, yet beneath it life was shifting, adjusting, remembering how to move. I felt it in my body before I could sense it in my mind, a quiet disturbance that did not threaten the surface but refused to remain inert. The night seemed to notice. It held its breath. The wind softened, its restless fingers loosening their grip on the leaves, as if listening for a sound it did not expect to hear. Even the moon appeared to pause in its vigil, its pale gaze lingering longer than before, not drifting onward in indifference, but waiting. Watching. Bearing witness without intrusion.

In that suspended hush, the silence deepened. Not into emptiness, but into presence. It grew dense. Weighted. Almost luminous in its fullness, as though it had substance now, as though it could be felt against the skin rather than passed through. This was not the silence of absence that had haunted me the night before. Not the hollow quiet that devours and erases, that strips everything down to nothing and calls it peace. This silence was different. It had texture. It had body. It pressed gently against me, not with force, but with attention. As though the dark itself had leaned closer. Not to take. Not to claim. But to ask. Not with words. Not with demand. Only with its nearness. It wrapped around my surrendered body like a question that did not need answering yet. A question content to exist simply as a question. One that did not threaten me with consequences if I failed to respond. And in that moment, something settled into understanding.

This calm was not the end I had imagined. Not the stillness of completion. Not the quiet of erasure. It was a threshold. A held breath suspended between what had been and what might still be asked of me. A narrow, sacred space where nothing was decided and nothing was undone. This stillness did not rush me forward. It did not push me back. It stayed. Present. Attentive. Unafraid of my uncertainty. As if the night, having watched me lay my weapons down, having seen the battle finally exhaust itself, now waited to see what would rise in the absence of war. What shape might emerge when survival no longer had to masquerade as combat? What voice might surface when the death battle no longer demands all my energy? I was not being tested. I was being witnessed.

And in that witnessing, I understood something quietly profound. When the fighting stops, even briefly, life does not immediately rush in with answers or purpose. First, it listens. First, it waits. First, it makes sure the danger has truly passed. The night did not ask me to stand. It did not ask me to promise. It did not ask me to heal. It simply held the space where healing might someday dare to begin. And in that space, unclaimed and unresolved, I remained.

My chest lifted, almost imperceptibly, as if remembering a motion it had once known before effort and endurance rewrote the rules. A new form of breath found its way in, uninvited yet undeniable, thin as a filament of light drawn carefully through darkness, like sunlight threading itself between leaves without disturbing the branches that hold it. It arrived quietly. Without permission. Without agenda. It did not demand hope. It did not demand the shadows to scatter. It did not demand perfection, courage, or belief. It did not promise rescue. It merely existed. And in that quiet arrival, the world shifted by a fraction. Not enough to rearrange the night. Not enough to rewrite the sky. Just enough to matter. Just enough to be noticed by a body that had spent decades learning how to endure instead of feel.

The tree did not bow any deeper. The wind did not resume its lament. The moon did not turn away. Everything remained exactly as it was. And yet, when dawn arrived that morning, and again now beneath the moonlight, nothing felt finished anymore. Not sealed. Not concluded. Not wrapped up with a finality that could not be undone. Nothing would ever feel finished again, and only in the best possible way. Because for the first time in my life, I sensed more. The more I had never allowed myself to believe in. The more I had been trained to dismiss as fantasy, as danger, as disappointment waiting to happen. The calm held, but it softened at the edges. It loosened its grip. No longer a closing, but a listening. No longer a conclusion, but a pause heavy with possibility, dense with what had not yet been named.

I lay there still. Beneath the same sky. On the same damp grass. The same empty house behind me. Within the same night as yesterday. Wrapped in the same darkness that had once promised erasure. Nothing external had changed. But somewhere in the vast, reverent quiet, the silence had altered its stance. It no longer leaned toward me with the weight of an ending. It no longer whispered instructions about disappearance. It stood back, attentive, patient. It was waiting. And inside me, something older than thought, something wiser than fear, began to respond. My body was fighting. Not in panic. Not in desperation. But in refusal. Refusing what I had done the night before. Refusing what I had been doing to myself for twenty-three long years. Refusing the contract that pain had written and demanded I sign again and again.

The fight was not loud. It did not arrive with adrenaline or resolve. It came as a declaration made without words, spoken from bone and breath and exhausted muscle. Enough! - Enough of resting inside pain. Enough of calling collapse peace. Enough of confusing numbness with sleep. Enough of surrendering to the abyss as though it were the only sanctuary left. Enough of allowing abuse. Enough of giving yourself away so others can be happy. Enough of the self-abuse. - Enough. It was time for a different rest. A rest that did not require injury. A rest that did not ask me to disappear. A rest that did not come at the cost of breath. A rest in life. In happiness. In serenity. In healing.

This declaration did not rise from my mind. My mind was still fragile, still unsure, still shaking from everything it had survived. This came from the body that had carried me through every night I believed would be my last. From the body that had endured when belief failed. From the body that knew, before I did, that survival alone was no longer enough. And in that moment, quiet and unspectacular and unseen, the story did not end. It shifted. Not toward certainty. Not toward answers. Not toward a polished redemption. But toward rest that did not hurt. Toward a silence that made room instead of taking space. Toward a pause that allowed me to stay without justification. Toward a life that did not need to be earned through suffering.

And that, finally, was enough. Enough to remain. Enough to breathe. Enough to let the night wait with me. Enough to allow the next moment to arrive unforced. The story did not close. It rested. And in that rest, something new began to gather itself, quietly, patiently, learning how to live.

Pain was still there. It had not packed its bags or loosened its grip. The ache still gnawed with the patience of something that knew me well. The hollow still yawned wide inside me, vast and echoing, a familiar architecture I could have navigated blindfolded. Nothing had been cured. Nothing erased. The night had not performed a miracle. And yet. Threaded through the pain now was something unfamiliar. Something fragile. Something quietly disobedient. A pause. Not the pause of numbness. Not the pause of resignation. But a hesitation in the machinery of collapse itself. A stutter in the familiar rhythm of unraveling. As though the great, grinding gears that had always carried me toward disappearance had momentarily lost their timing. As though inevitability, so long unquestioned, had faltered.

It felt subtle, almost accidental. Easy to miss if I had not been listening so closely. A delay where acceleration should have been. A breath held where freefall usually followed. The ache still spoke, but it no longer spoke alone. Its voice met resistance. Not defiance. Not strength. Just interference. As though the universe, having drawn me all the way to the edge, having watched me place my toes over the lip of the abyss, had decided, without ceremony or explanation, to wait. No thunder marked that choice. No hand reached down to pull me back. No decree was issued. Just waiting. A stretched and trembling moment where nothing advanced and nothing concluded. Where time did not push me forward or drag me backward. Where I was suspended in a narrow pocket of now, held between what had been rehearsed and what had not yet been imagined. And in that waiting, something changed.

The ache was no longer solitary. It still hurt, yes. But it was accompanied now. Flanked. Interrupted by presence. The pain did not vanish, but it was no longer the only occupant of my inner world. Something else had entered the room, quietly, without knocking. Something that did not argue with the ache or attempt to overpower it. Something that simply existed alongside it, altering the balance. The hollow inside me remained vast, but it no longer felt infinite. Its edges softened just enough to suggest containment. The emptiness no longer echoed only despair; it echoed possibility, faint and uncertain, like sound testing a new shape.

I realized then how close I had come to believing that pain was the whole story. That suffering was the final authority. That ache, by virtue of its persistence, had earned the right to decide everything that followed. But this pause, this small, inexplicable delay, revealed something else. Pain can be present without being sovereign.

Ache can exist without being destiny. Hollow does not have to mean hopeless. The universe did not save me in that moment. It did something far quieter and far more radical. It did not finish me. And in that refusal to rush me toward an ending, the pain lost its monopoly. It no longer stood alone at the center of my existence, issuing verdicts without appeal. It had to share space now. Share breath. Share attention.

I was still hurting. Still raw. Still uncertain. But I was no longer collapsing unchecked. I was pausing. And in that pause, fragile and uncelebrated, something essential took hold: the understanding that even at my most broken, even at the edge of everything giving way, I was not required to resolve my pain before I was allowed to stay. The ache could remain. And so could I. Together. For now.

Inevitability Loses Momentum

Something else moved beside the body, tentative as a first breath after drowning. Not hope. No. Hope would have been too loud, too insistent, too quick to make promises I was not ready to hear. This was quieter than hope. Thinner than fear. A presence that did not announce itself with language or meaning, but with proximity. It arrived without permission, and without demand, and then, astonishingly, it stayed. The silence deepened around me, but it was no longer vacant. It was no longer a hollow that swallowed sound and left nothing in return. It felt textured now, layered, as though it carried an intention I could sense without understanding. The dark pressed against me differently. Not like a closing wall. Not like a lid sealing shut. But like a held gaze. Steady. Patient. Unflinching.

I had the uncanny sensation of being seen. Not judged. Not rescued. Not interrupted. Witnessed. As if the night itself had leaned closer and decided to listen. Not for confessions or conclusions, but simply to hear what remained when everything else had fallen away. The trees did not whisper. The sky did not answer. And yet, I was no longer alone inside myself. My breath caught, not in panic, but in recognition. A startled pause, the way the body pauses when it recognizes something familiar it has not felt in years. The air felt heavier in my lungs now, charged, alive, as though each inhale carried more than oxygen. Each breath stretched longer than the last, tentatively expanding into space it had not trusted before. Each exhale released not pain, but certainty. The rigid conclusions I had wrapped myself in loosened their grip, fraction by fraction, as breath after breath carried them away.

The ache still pulsed beneath my ribs. It had not retreated. It had not apologized. It remained, insistent and real. But it no longer ruled the entire terrain. It was no longer the only voice in the room. It shared space now, forced into coexistence with something it could not overpower. And in that sharing, its edges softened. Just enough. Enough to let something else exist alongside it. Enough to let presence stand next to pain without being consumed by it. Enough to let the night hold me without swallowing me whole. I lay there, suspended between sensation and meaning, aware of my body in a way that felt new and ancient at the same time. A body that had been reduced to survival had begun, quietly, to remember how to receive. Not comfort. Not answers. Just company.

The silence did not rush to explain itself. It did not turn this moment into revelation or destiny. It simply stayed close, attentive, wide enough to hold pain and presence at once. And for the first time, I understood something without needing to name it. That being witnessed can change the shape of suffering. That pain does not have to disappear to be softened. That something can arrive beside the body, gentle and unassuming, and alter the landscape simply by refusing to leave. The ache breathed. I breathed. The night listened. And in that quiet communion, the story loosened its grip on ending, allowing itself, at last, to become something else entirely.

The minutes continued their slow procession, but they were no longer executioners counting down a sentence. They softened into footfalls instead, measured and deliberate, the sound of steps pacing a threshold rather than marching me toward a cliff. Each minute arrived without menace, without urgency, and then took its place beside the last. Time did not drag me forward. It did not shove me back. It stood with me. Shoulder to shoulder. It waited. I felt it then, unmistakably. The silence was not indifferent. It was attentive. It carried a gravity, yes, but not the kind that pulls you under and keeps you there. This gravity gathered rather than crushed. It drew the scattered pieces of me inward, coaxing them closer, asking them to rest in one place for a moment instead of flinging themselves into the dark.

The anchor of silence, which had once dragged me beneath the surface, now steadied my small, battered boat on an ocean that was still turbulent, still unpredictable, still vast. The waves had not ceased. But I was no longer capsizing with every swell. The darkness shifted again, revealing another layer of itself. It was no longer a final destination, no longer the mouth of an ending waiting to consume me. It became a chamber instead. A crossing. A liminal room where endings and beginnings brush so close they share the same air, the same breath, the same trembling edge. This was not a place of answers. It was a place of listening. A place where nothing had to resolve yet. My heart stuttered again. A small, rebellious hitch in its rhythm. Not surrender. Not yet. Something quieter and more defiant than courage.

A reflex of life refusing to be tidied away. Something in me had noticed the pause and leaned toward it, curious despite itself, as if asking, gently and incredulously, "*What is this?*" The machinery of collapse, once so certain of its momentum, faltered. Gears hesitated. The forward pull weakened. Not because I fought it. Not because I overcame it. But because it encountered resistance of an unfamiliar kind. Not forceful. Not heroic. Just present. A steady refusal to be rushed into disappearance. And in that presence, in that quiet interruption of inevitability, understanding arrived without spectacle. The silence had not come to swallow me.

It had come to answer. Not with solutions. Not with guarantees. Not with a promise that pain would end. But with attention. With witness. With the simple, radical offering of space. It answered by saying: "*You are still here.*" It answered by saying: "*You may remain.*" It answered by saying: "*This moment does not have to become an ending.*" And in that answer, something in me settled, not into certainty, but into permission. Permission to breathe without deciding. Permission to exist without explaining. Permission to linger at the crossing where life had not yet asked me to choose what it would become.

The ocean still rolled. The night still held its depth. My body still ached, bruised by years and by the night before. But the silence stayed close, steady and unafraid, and for the first time, I understood that waiting can be an act of grace. That interruption can be a form of mercy. That sometimes the most profound answer is not a command to move, but an invitation to stay. And so I stayed. Balanced on the threshold. Held by time. Gathered by silence. Not finished. Not fallen. Just here.

And somewhere within that immense quiet, beneath the conviction that all light had gone out for good, something subtle shifted its weight. Not a possibility in any grand or luminous sense. Not hope, not yet. Something far smaller. Quieter. A hairline fracture running through the certainty of my ending, so fine it could only be felt, never seen. The kind of crack that does not announce collapse but makes sound travel differently through the structure. The kind that changes resonance before it changes shape. The silence, which I had mistaken for the apathy of nothingness, revealed a faint vibration. A low, almost imperceptible hum, as though it were not empty at all, but charged. Waiting. Not impatiently. Not expectantly. Simply waiting, the way earth waits beneath frozen ground, the way seeds wait without knowing what spring will look like. It was a silence with posture now, with orientation, with intent that did not demand reciprocation.

It felt as though the quiet itself was listening for something from me, something I did not yet know how to give. Not an answer. Not a declaration. Not belief. Just a willingness to remain in the question without collapsing into it. The night did not rush to fill the space with meaning. It did not arrive bearing voices or visions or mercy dressed in spectacle. It did not rescue me. It did not reassure me. It answered me by not letting me vanish. By holding me there, suspended between what I had believed was finished and what I could not yet imagine beginning. By refusing to resolve me into either outcome. I was neither saved nor lost. Neither claimed nor released. I was kept in the long, trembling pause where endings hesitate, uncertain of their authority, and beginnings gather their breath without daring to announce themselves yet.

In that unresolved space, I was no longer falling. I was not rising either. I was hovering, held in a gravity that did not pull me toward disappearance, but gathered me into stillness. The kind of stillness that does not erase motion but slows it enough to be felt. Enough to be chosen later, perhaps. Or not chosen at all. The night remained vast. The darkness remained deep. My body remained sore, my chest still tight with the aftermath of the night before and the years before that. Nothing had been undone. Nothing had been fixed. But something essential had been interrupted. The ending I was certain of had faltered. And in its hesitation, something else quietly took its place. Not an answer. Not a future. Just a holding. A listening. A refusal to conclude.

The silence did not tell me to live. It did not tell me to die. It told me, in the only way it could, that I was allowed to remain unfinished. And in that allowance, fragile and uncelebrated, the night continued to wait with me, patient as breath between breaths, faithful as the space before sound. A place where the story had not ended. A place where it had not yet begun. The night did not recoil from that moment. It did not flinch, harden, or rush to reclaim me. It did not argue its case or defend the darkness it had once offered so convincingly. It simply remained. Steady. Attentive. Bearing witness to this unexpected persistence as though it were something worth noticing, something worth allowing. The lullaby I had been drifting toward softened. Its melody loosened its hold. The promise of disappearance dimmed, not extinguished, not banished forever, but gently set aside, as one might set down a dangerous object without yet knowing what to replace it with.

It no longer sang to me of rest through erasure. It no longer pulled with the same certainty. It hovered instead, distant and muted, no longer the only song in the room. In its place rose a thin, trembling awareness, fragile as frost forming at the edge of dawn. Delicate. Temporary. Easily broken. And yet undeniably present. The realization arrived quietly, without triumph or relief: letting go had not carried me away. I had loosened my grip. I had set the weight down. And still, I was here, standing beside it, feeling its gravity without being crushed beneath it. That, too, felt new. Somewhere in that suspended space, between surrender and return, between silence and breath, something shifted its alignment. Not a decision. Not resolve. Just orientation. As though the axis of my inner world had moved by a single degree, barely measurable, yet enough to change the direction of everything that might follow.

I became aware then, with a clarity that did not hurt, that even when everything in me was ready to end, something else had answered instead. Something quieter than desire. Older than despair. More stubborn than pain. It had not argued with my exhaustion. It had not shamed my longing to disappear. It had simply responded in its own language. The silence had spoken. Not with sound. Not with command. Not with promise. It spoke by remaining. By holding. By refusing to collapse the moment into finality. And what it said, without force, without urgency, without needing to be believed all at once, was this: Stay. Not forever. Not bravely. Not healed. Just stay.

Stay in this breath. Stay in this body that is still learning how to belong to itself again. Stay in this pause that has not yet decided what it will become. The word did not echo. It did not demand obedience. It rested there, simple and unadorned, like a hand that is held out without insistence. An invitation that allowed refusal yet remained offered all the same. And I did not answer it with certainty. I did not answer it with hope. I answered it the only way I could. I stayed.

Held Without Suffocation

And in that waiting, the dark did not harden into verdict. It softened further, as if recognizing the exact shape of my surrender and choosing gentleness in response. What had once pressed like a sentence now settled like a hand. The night learned my outline. It adjusted itself around me, not closing, not retreating, but yielding into something tender and responsive, as though the darkness itself understood that force was no longer required here. The silence grew layered. No longer a void, no longer an absence that devoured. It became a depth. A wide, breathing depth, rich with nuance and possibility. It carried texture now, a density that did not suffocate but held. It pressed close, yes, but not to smother. To cradle. To listen. To attune itself to the smallest movement within me, the faintest evidence that something still stirred beneath the quiet I had mistaken for emptiness.

And then, without permission or announcement, change breathed me. A breath arrived. Unbidden. So light it almost missed itself. It brushed the edges of my chest, hesitant, testing, as though unsure whether it was allowed to stay. Then it withdrew. Paused. Returned again. Another followed. And another. They came shyly, like guests unsure they were welcome, touching the threshold of my body before retreating, then circling back with a little more confidence each time. Each breath was thin. Uneven. Imperfect. But it was real. The body, faithful even when the will had laid itself down, remembered its ancient work. Long before stories. Long before meaning. Long before despair learned how to speak. It remembered how to expand. How to contract. How to continue. Lungs opened again, not under the crushing weight they had known the night before, but with a cautious willingness, as if relieved to find there was space after all.

A heart answered. Not dramatically. Not triumphantly. Just faithfully. Rhythm persisted. Beat after beat. Uncelebrated. Unimpressed by my conclusions. A small insistence in the vast hush. A pulse that did not ask for permission or belief. It simply continued, stubborn and steady, marking time in a place where time had nearly lost its meaning. This was not resurrection. This was not salvation. This was continuation. The night did not applaud it. The silence did not amplify it into significance. They allowed it to be small. To be fragile. To be enough in its own right. And in that allowance, something inside me loosened further, not into hope, but into tolerance of being here. Into acceptance of this quiet persistence that refused to be extinguished.

I did not rise. I did not speak. I did not promise anything to the future. I lay there, breathing with the night, held by a silence that had learned how to listen, while my body quietly reclaimed its right to exist one moment longer. And that, in the immensity of all that had nearly ended, was everything. The night seemed to lean in, attentive now, no longer watching from a distance but listening with its whole body. The wind adjusted its cadence, shedding its earlier lament and settling into a low, steady presence, like a metronome marking time for something still learning its rhythm. It no longer stirred the air with urgency. It stayed close, companionable, as if keeping vigil beside me rather than circling above.

The trees stood without movement, their branches still, their roots sunk deep into the unseen earth. They did not reach or recoil. They simply were. Anchored. Unshaken. Bearing the quiet authority of things that have survived countless storms without needing to announce it. Their stillness felt instructive, not as a lesson to follow, but as a permission to remain exactly where I was. And somewhere far beyond my closed eyes, the sky shifted by a fraction so small it could not be seen, only sensed. A subtle recalibration. The dark was not lifting yet. It was not breaking. But it was thinning. The way fabric thins with wear, becoming softer, more translucent. The way night thins when dawn is gathering itself offstage, not yet ready to step into the light but already rearranging the wings.

I remained still. I did not reach. I did not decide. I did not ask how to proceed, how to change, how to heal. I stayed. But the waiting changed texture. What had once felt like the stillness of an ending softened into something else entirely. This was not the frozen quiet of a story concluded. This was the stillness of becoming. A pause held deliberately. Reverently. As if the story itself had chosen to rest, not out of exhaustion, but out of wisdom, before daring to turn its next page. Time did not press me forward. It curved gently around me. The moment widened just enough to hold my uncertainty without demanding resolution. I was allowed to linger in the in-between, in the fragile space where nothing had to be declared yet.

And there, in that held breath between what I believed was over and what I could not yet imagine beginning, I sensed it. Not hope in its full, blinding form. Not the kind that insists or persuades. Something earlier. Quieter. The prelude to hope. The hush before a sound. The space before a step. The instant when the body shifts its weight, not to move yet, but to prepare for the possibility of movement. The moment when the dark realizes it will not have the final word. The night continued to hold me, yes. But it no longer held me closed. It held me open. Open enough for breath. Open enough for listening. Open enough for something unnamed to gather itself quietly in the wings. And somewhere within that openness, beneath the steady pulse of my own continued being, something was preparing to answer back.

And then, when there was nothing left to release but my pain, nothing left to surrender but my past, the silence answered once more. Not with a verdict. Not with a command. But with something that felt like both the final questions and the final answers folded into the same breath. It arrived the way snow falls at night. Soundless. Unannounced. Yet utterly unmistakable. It settled over everything I believed had ended, everything I had laid down as finished and irretrievable. Where the night before had been black and consuming, this hush repainted the dark into something else entirely. Not light, not yet, but white. Clean. Unwritten. As though the story had been cleared of its conclusions and returned to the page before the first word was set down.

The hush deepened. Thickened. It became almost tangible, as if the darkness itself had weight and texture now. As if the moon, the wind, the trees, and the ground beneath me had all paused at once, not to judge, not to intervene, but to listen back. The night was no longer singing. It was attending. Witnessing. Holding still enough to hear what might rise from the quiet. And in that listening, I noticed something I had not expected something so ordinary it stunned me. I was still here. Still breathing. Still tethered, however faintly, to the pulse beneath my ribs. Still occupying a body that had not agreed to disappear simply because my despair had asked it to. The void did not rush me. Not yet. It did not pull. It did not demand. It did not threaten.

It simply held the space, wide and watchful, allowing me to feel the weight of my own existence without judgment. Just presence. Just being. A nothingness, yes, but not the apathetic nothingness of the previous night. Not the hollow erasure that devours and erases. This was a different kind of nothingness altogether. A nothingness that whispered, without sound: Nothing is impossible. Nothing is hopeless. Nothing is beyond healing. Nothing is too broken. Nothing is worthless. Nothing is unlovable. And nothing, especially you, is nothing. That truth did not crash into me. It did not announce itself as revelation. It rested. Quiet. Spacious. Letting me arrive at it slowly, the way one steps into water after believing for years that it will burn.

And in that holding, something stirred. Not loudly. Not urgently. But persistently. A question without language. A tremor beneath the stillness. A subtle resistance, like the smallest knot refusing to loosen, no matter how gently it was pulled. My breath, which I had been ready to abandon, years ago, slowly found its way back to me. Shallow at first. Uneven. Almost resentful. Then another. And another. Each breath arrived uninvited. Stubborn. Insistent. As if my body had not received the same instructions as my despair. As if some deeper intelligence, older than thought and wiser than fear, had decided quietly and without consultation that the story was not finished speaking.

The silence did not correct me. It did not comfort me with promises. It did not tell me what would come next. It simply stayed. And let my breath keep returning. As if to say, again and again, without words: You are still here. And something in you still knows why.

The Silence That Stayed

The night returned to me gently again. Not as an accomplice. Not as a witness to ruin. But as something patient and intact, waiting exactly where I had left it, as though it had never doubted, I would find my way back. I sat beneath the pale moon, beneath the same old tree whose branches had once twisted into grotesque shapes of fear, claws reaching, mouths gaping. Now they curved like open hands, empty of demand, offering nothing but shelter. The transformation startled me. Not because the world had changed, but because I had. The air felt softer, less interrogating, no longer pressing questions into my skin. It moved around me without agenda. Even the shadows seemed to understand restraint, gathering at a respectful distance, no longer lunging for meaning or proof. Nothing pressed. Nothing demanded. The night did not lean toward me this time. It did not coax, threaten, or persuade. It simply made room. Silence sat beside me.

Not the suffocating silence that once swallowed my breath whole, not the vacuum that erased sound and self alike, but a quieter, steadier presence. A companionable hush. The kind that listens without rushing to fill the space. The kind that does not confuse stillness with disappearance. The kind that knows the difference between holding and hollowing. I did not speak at first. Neither did it. The quiet stretched, unafraid of its own length. It did not grow tense. It did not fray at the edges. It simply stayed, allowing the moment to be exactly what it was. And then, without sound, without form, without accusation, the silence asked its first question. Not "*Why did you try to leave?*" Not "*What is wrong with you?*" Not "*How could you do that?*" Instead, it asked: "**What are you tired of carrying that was never yours to begin with?**"

The question landed softly, the way a leaf touches water without breaking the surface. There was no splash. No demand for immediate response. Just a widening circle of recognition spreading slowly through me. I felt my chest tighten, reflexively, as though bracing for blame. Then, unexpectedly, it loosened. Images rose uninvited. Expectations I had inherited like heirlooms I never asked for. Guilt stitched into my voice until even my honesty sounded like an apology. Shame mistaken for accountability, worn as proof of goodness. The endless labor of being agreeable. Resilient. Quiet enough to keep others comfortable.

I saw the weight of other people's fears pressed into my hands. The responsibility for emotions that were never mine to manage. The belief that love required endurance, that belonging demanded self-erasure, that safety was something you earned by becoming small. I felt how long I had been carrying these things, how naturally I had folded them into my posture, how rarely I had questioned their ownership. My breath caught, not in panic, but in recognition. Because the question was not asking me to relive the pain. It was asking me to put something down. And in that asking, without urgency or insistence, the silence offered me a possibility I had never been given before: That my exhaustion was not evidence of weakness, but of carrying too much for too long. That the ache in my bones was not a personal failure, but the cost of holding burdens that had never belonged to me.

The night did not interrupt. The silence did not hurry me. It waited, steady and wide, as if it knew that naming what was never mine would take time. As if it understood that before release could come, there had to be permission to recognize the weight. And sitting there, beneath open branches and an unjudging moon, I realized something quietly radical: I was not being asked to explain myself. I was being invited to unburden myself. The night did not want my confession. It wanted my truth. The silence did not interrupt. It waited. It held the space the way a horizon holds the sun just before it rises, neither rushing nor retreating, trusting that something would emerge when it was ready. Then it asked again, its presence subtly reshaping the air around me, its question arriving without weight, without threat: **"What would it feel like to choose yourself without apologizing?"** The moon brightened, just a fraction. Or maybe I did.

The thought startled me. Not because it was loud, but because it was unfamiliar. Choosing myself without justification, without preamble, without rehearsing my defence. A life where my worth was not transactional. Where love did not arrive with terms and conditions and did not require me to shrink. Where rest was not a reward rationed out after exhaustion had proven my devotion. The idea felt almost illicit, like imagining warmth after a lifetime of cold. It scared me. And it warmed something dormant inside my ribs. A small glow, tentative but undeniable, flickered where shame had lived for so long. The silence noticed the shift, the way one notices a candle catching after repeated failed strikes. It did not comment. It simply stayed close enough to ask again: **"What beauty have you postponed because you believed you had to suffer first?"**

The question opened a door I had kept sealed for years. Images surfaced without warning. I thought of things I loved before survival took over. Art, I had abandoned when survival demanded efficiency. Writing that once felt like breath before it became dangerous to speak freely. Stillness without guilt. Laughter that didn't scan the room for consequences. Mornings that belonged to me, unclaimed by obligation, unmeasured by productivity. The kind of joy that doesn't perform. That doesn't explain itself. That doesn't shrink to be allowed. My chest tightened with longing. Then loosened with recognition. Above me, the tree rustled. Not ominously. Not sharply. But approvingly. A soft, knowing movement of leaves and branches, as if the night itself were nodding in agreement. "*Yes,*" it seemed to say. "*That.*"

The silence leaned closer, not crowding me, not urging, simply attentive. And then it offered its deepest question yet, one that did not ask me to fix myself or transcend my pain, but to reconsider everything I believed healing required: **"What if healing is not becoming someone new, but returning to who you were before you learned to disappear?"** The question cracked something open. I saw her then. My younger self. Not as broken. Not as defective. But unfinished. Unprotected. A child who had learned too early how to fold herself inward to survive. Who had mistaken disappearance for safety and endurance for virtue. I saw how much she had carried without understanding why. How diligently she had tried to be good, to be quiet, to be enough. Grief rose. Yes. But alongside it came something unexpected. Tenderness. Not the kind that demands punishment or penance. Not the kind that asks for reckoning before forgiveness.

But the soft, steady tenderness that recognizes harm without assigning blame. The tenderness that knows survival was never a moral failure. The tenderness that looks at what was lost and says, "*Of course you did what you had to do.*" The silence held that tenderness with me. It did not rush it away. It did not try to turn it into optimism. It allowed it to exist, full and uncorrected. And sitting there, beneath a patient moon and an approving tree, I understood something that had eluded me for most of my life: Healing was not asking me to erase my past. It was asking me to stop abandoning myself in the present. The night did not applaud this realization. It did not promise ease. It simply stayed. And for the first time, staying no longer felt like punishment. It felt like an invitation.

The silence stayed steady as the next truth emerged, not pressed forward, not softened, simply present enough to be heard. **"Can you forgive yourself for surviving the only way you knew how?"** The question settled into me like weight finding its true place. I wanted to say no. The word rose quickly, reflexively, shaped by years of self-blame disguised as responsibility. No, because forgiveness felt like letting myself off too easily. No, because pain had become proof of accountability. No, because I had learned that mercy was something extended outward, never inward. But the night did not rush me. It did not tighten around my hesitation or punish the silence that followed. So I tried again, quieter this time, less certain, less armoured. Maybe. The word barely made a sound. It trembled. It hovered. It did not arrive as resolution, but as permission to keep breathing inside the question. The moon did not require certainty. It never had. Mercy rarely does.

The silence remained, and then, gently, it asked its hardest question next. Not with accusation. Not with ultimatum. But with a clarity that felt both terrifying and clean. **"Who do you need to walk away from in order to finally walk toward yourself?"** The answer did not come as a single face or a single name. It arrived as a constellation. Names surfaced. Patterns followed. Relationships built on endurance instead of reciprocity. Bonds that fed on my overgiving. Connections that only knew how to exist when I made myself smaller, quieter, more accommodating than I ever was meant to be. I saw how loyalty had been confused with self-erasure. How love had been measured by how much I could tolerate. Fear rose fast, sharp and familiar. The fear of being alone. Of being misunderstood. Of being cast as ungrateful or cruel for finally choosing myself.

And then, beneath it, something stronger emerged. Clarity. Not loud. Not dramatic. Just solid. The kind of clarity that does not argue. It simply knows quietly where the door is. The silence did not shame me for staying too long. It did not tally my mistakes or demand repentance. It simply illuminated the threshold. Let me see it clearly. Let me feel its shape. And then, like a blessing rather than a command, the silence offered its final truth. Not as instruction, but as recognition. Healing will ask you for bravery, not perfection. For honesty, not punishment. For presence, not disappearance. The words did not land as rules. They landed as relief. I sat there longer after that, breathing in a future I had never allowed myself to imagine without conditions. A life where my past could be faced without becoming my prison.

Where forgiveness did not mean forgetting but releasing myself from lifelong sentencing. Where choosing myself was not betrayal, but devotion. Where walking away was not abandonment, but alignment. The night did not promise ease. It never pretended that healing would be gentle in all its forms. But it promised possibility. And possibility felt radical enough. When I finally stood, legs unsteady but heart awake, the silence did not follow me like a shadow. It did not cling or whisper or pull. It stayed where it was, complete, fulfilled, having done its work. And I carried something different with me as I stepped forward. Not certainty. Not answers. But a quiet, unshakable knowing. I was no longer walking away from life. I was walking toward myself.

We remained beneath the tree, luminous and faithful, having done what it came to do. It had not saved me. It had never claimed that power. It had reminded me that I was worth saving. And that realization landed with a quiet gravity that changed the shape of everything. Because being worth saving meant I was not a burden to be endured or a problem to be solved. It meant my life carried value even in its brokenness, even before it knew how to heal. That was the beginning of choosing myself. Not as an act of defiance. Not as a declaration shouted into the dark. But as a return. A slow, tentative homecoming to a self I had left unattended for far too long. The silence did not leave when I stood. It did not dissolve or retreat back into the night.

It rose with me in a different way, not as a presence that followed, but as one that remained available. Like a doorway left open. Like a light left on in a room I could return to when the noise grew too loud, when the world demanded more than I could give. It did not insist I carry it forward. It trusted I would remember where to find it. I took a step. Then another. The ground felt different beneath my feet. Not safer. Not certain. Not suddenly solid with promise. Just real. Textured. Responsive. It pressed back when I pressed down, meeting my weight without judgment. And for the first time in a long while, reality did not feel like a punishment. It felt like a place I was allowed to stand. The moon shifted overhead, its pale glow brushing the bark of the tree, tracing the grooves carved by time.

I noticed how deeply rooted it was. How its strength was not in perfection, but in persistence. How many storms had it stood through without apology? How many seasons had scarred it without stopping its growth? It had not rushed to heal its wounds. It had not hidden them. It had simply continued. That, too, felt like instruction. I understood then that healing would not require me to erase my past or hurry toward wholeness. It would ask me to stay rooted. To grow anyway. To let scars exist without letting them define the limits of what I could become. I turned once more, just briefly, toward the tree, toward the space where silence still lived like a quiet vow. It did not wave. It did not call. It simply remained.

And I walked on. Not cured. Not finished. But returned enough to keep going. Carrying with me the knowledge that when the world grows loud again, when pain tries to convince me that disappearance is easier than presence, there is a place beneath the noise where I am already known. Already held. Already worthy. The story had not ended beneath that tree. It had learned how to stand. The silence noticed my noticing. It did not interrupt or correct. It did not hurry me toward meaning. It simply responded with the kind of patience only something ancient can afford. "*You do not need to rush your becoming,*" it seemed to say. "*Roots take time.*" The words were not spoken, yet they arrived with weight. With permission. I exhaled then, a full breath this time, one that traveled farther than any breath had dared to go in years.

It slipped past guarded ribs, past locked rooms in my chest, and reached places that had learned to stay sealed for survival. The breath lingered there, unfamiliar but welcome, like sunlight touching a floor that has known only shadow. Then another followed. Slower. Easier. As if my body, long braced for disappearance, was relearning the art of staying.

And then came another question, quieter than the rest. So soft it might have been missed if I had not already been listening with my whole being. *"What would it mean to live without constantly proving that you deserve to be here?"* The question did not first rise to my head. It sank into me. I felt it in my shoulders before I understood it, a subtle lowering, as though they no longer needed to hold the sky up alone. In my jaw, unclenching a grip I had forgotten was effort. In my stomach, where vigilance had lived for decades like a coiled animal, there was a loosening, tentative but real. My body answered before my mind could rehearse defenses. Images surfaced, not as goals, but as glimpses. Mornings that did not begin with interrogation. Days that did not require me to justify my existence through usefulness or output. Evenings that did not end in a ruthless audit of failures and omissions. A life not built around earning rest but allowing it. Not structured around worthiness but belonging.

The silence did not ask me to commit to that life all at once. It did not demand transformation or vows. It did not insist on courage beyond what I could carry. It simply let the idea exist, gently, like a seed placed in open soil without pressure to sprout. *"You don't have to live this way yet,* it seemed to say. *You only have to know that another way exists."* And that was enough. Because knowing is a beginning. Because permission changes posture. Because the body remembers what the mind is still learning. I stood there, breathing in a future I was not yet ready to claim, but no longer needed to deny. The silence stayed with me, not as instruction, not as promise, but as companionship. A quiet witness to the moment I stopped measuring my right to exist and began, however tentatively, to let myself belong to the ground beneath my feet. Roots take time. And for the first time, I was no longer ashamed of how long mine would need.

It asked something gentler then, almost tender in its restraint. *"What is one small way you could choose yourself tomorrow?"* Not forever. Not heroically. Not in a way that demanded reinvention. Just tomorrow. The simplicity disarmed me. The question did not loom. It did not carry consequence. It did not require a promise that could be broken. It waited in the open space it had helped create, trusting that whatever answered would be enough. And the answer surprised me. Rest. Not collapse. Not disappearance. Not the kind of rest that follows punishment or precedes apology. Rest chosen. Rest claimed without explanation. Rest that did not have to justify itself to anyone, not even to the familiar voice inside me that still believed exhaustion was proof of value, that still equated depletion with virtue. I felt the audacity of it settle into my body, how radical it felt to imagine stopping without having earned the right to do so.

The night did not argue. The silence nodded. And then, gently but unmistakably, it turned me toward what I had been avoiding. "*What are you afraid will happen if you forgive yourself?"* That one landed differently. It did not skim the surface. It sank. Forgiveness had always felt dangerous to me, like loosening a grip that kept me accountable, like letting myself off the hook for things I believed should never be excused. It felt like erasing harm. Like pretending nothing happened. Like absolution without consequence. I flinched at the word. But the silence did not let the fear stand alone. It reshaped the meaning without force. *"Forgiveness does not deny harm,"* it said. "*It releases you from eternal sentencing."*

The truth of it moved through me slowly, the way cold leaves the body after a long winter. I thought of how long I had punished myself for surviving imperfectly. For staying too long. For trusting the wrong people. For not knowing sooner what I know now. For adapting in ways that later cost me pieces of myself. I had replayed my own history like a courtroom where I was always both defendant and judge, delivering sentence after sentence with no possibility of parole. I felt the weight of that self-punishment then. How heavy it had been. How faithfully I had carried it. How unnecessary it was to keep wearing chains long after the danger had passed.

Forgiveness, I realized, was not about forgetting. It was about laying down the gavel. About ending a trial that had been over for years. The silence did not demand that I forgive myself all at once. It did not ask me to rewrite the past or rush toward mercy. It only asked that I notice how much energy it had taken to keep myself condemned. How much life had been spent enforcing a sentence that never healed me. I stood there with that knowing, not relieved, not resolved, but lighter by a fraction. Enough to breathe more fully. Enough to imagine a tomorrow that did not require me to bleed to prove my sincerity.

The night did not celebrate this realization. It did not offer applause or affirmation. It simply stayed with me as the weight shifted. As something inside me loosened its grip. As the possibility formed, quiet and unadorned, that choosing myself might not mean abandoning responsibility at all. It might mean finally ending the punishment.

The silence did not ask me to forgive everything. It did not demand absolution on a scale too large to hold. It asked something smaller. Truer. *"What if you started by forgiving yourself for not knowing what you were never taught?"* The question slipped past my defenses before I could armor myself against it. And then the tears came. Not violently. Not with collapse. Quiet ones. The kind that do not ask for attention. The kind that arrive when something inside finally believes it is safe enough to soften. They traced slow paths down my cheeks and fell into the waiting earth, absorbed without comment, without spectacle.

The tree did not recoil from them. The moon did not dim in embarrassment. The night did not flinch. It held steady, as if grief were not an interruption, but part of the language it understood best. Those tears carried no story. No accusation. Only release. They washed through places that had been clenched for so long they had forgotten how to open. I felt them loosen something ancient in my chest, something that had confused ignorance for failure and survival for guilt. Forgiving myself for not knowing felt like removing a burden I had been carrying so faithfully I had mistaken it for my spine.

Then the silence spoke again. This time, firmer. Still kind. Unwilling to let me turn away. *"What are you willing to walk away from, even if it means grieving what you hoped it would become?"* I knew the answer before I wanted to. Before I could negotiate. Before I could soften it into something more palatable. Toxic bonds. Relationships sustained by my silence. Connections that fed on my self-doubt and called it intimacy. The belief that love required endurance. That loyalty meant self-erasure. That staying, no matter the cost, was proof of goodness.

Walking away from those things had once felt like death. Like betrayal. Like annihilation. It had felt as though leaving would erase me entirely, as though I could only exist inside the harm that had named me. Now, standing there beneath the patient sky, it felt different. It felt like boundary. Not clean. Not painless. But honest. The silence did not romanticize it. It did not promise relief without cost. It did not dress departure as triumph. *"Grief will come,"* it acknowledged. *"But grief is not proof you chose wrong."*

That truth landed with weight. It rearranged something fundamental. I had been taught that grief meant failure. That if leaving hurt, it must have been a mistake. That pain was evidence I should return. But here, in this quiet communion, I understood something new. Grief could simply mean that something mattered. That I had hoped. That I had loved. That I had invested pieces of myself into places that could not hold them. Grief, then, was not a verdict. It was a passage.

I sat with that understanding and let it move through me. Let it unhook old reflexes. Let it dismantle the lie that suffering was a sign of correctness. I felt myself shift, not forward, not away, but inward, aligning with something truer than endurance. The silence did not rush me toward action. It did not demand immediate departure. It only asked me to recognize what was no longer mine to carry. And in that recognition, I felt a subtle strength take root. Not the loud kind. Not the kind that conquers. The kind that knows when to leave.

Then, almost tenderly, came the question that cracked something open wide enough for light to find its way in. *"If you were no longer busy surviving, what would you want to create?"* It did not rush me. It did not frame itself as destiny or demand a plan. It arrived softly, like a hand resting on the small of my back, steady enough to be felt, gentle enough to be trusted. And before my mind could narrow it, before fear could edit the answer, images bloomed. Words on a page. Not polished. Not sanitized. Words that told the truth without apology. Art that did not flinch. Art that named the dark without glorifying it. Art that carried tenderness alongside terror and did not ask either to justify itself.

Space. Room. Places where others could breathe without bracing. Where silence was not punishment but permission.

Where stories like mine did not have to end at the edge of survival but could stretch forward into meaning. I saw a life shaped not by disappearance, but by translation. Pain turned into language. Shame dismantled into clarity. Experience distilled into something that could reach another trembling body and say, "*You are not alone here.*" And as those images gathered, something ignited inside me. Not urgency. Not desperation. Not the frantic hunger to prove anything. Purpose.

Not the kind that demands sacrifice or martyrdom. Not the kind that feeds on exhaustion. But the kind that emerges quietly when someone finally feels allowed to exist. When life is no longer a test to pass, but a ground to stand on. When meaning is not imposed but discovered in the aftermath of truth. I felt it settle behind my ribs, warm and steady, not consuming, not overwhelming. It did not ask me to hurry. It did not insist I become anything overnight. It simply took up space, as if it had been waiting for me to stop apologizing long enough to arrive. The silence did not clap. It did not celebrate loudly. It did not frame this as redemption.

It spoke plainly. Gently. Irrefutably. *"You are not late. You are not broken. You are not disqualified by your pain."* Those words did not erase what I had lived through. They did not minimize the damage or pretend the scars were beautiful. They did something far more radical. They returned my future to me. For the first time, I understood that my survival was not the climax of the story. It was the threshold. The place where endurance loosened its grip and something truer stepped forward. My pain had not disqualified me from meaning. It had trained me to recognize it. To hold it carefully. To offer it without spectacle. I sat there beneath the patient moon, feeling the night receive this understanding without argument. And in that quiet agreement, something settled into place. I was not here to disappear. I was here to create.

The moon dipped lower, its pale edge brushing the horizon like a fingertip trailing across water. The night, which had held me for so long without question, began to loosen its grip. Not retreating. Not abandoning. Simply easing, the way a tide does when it has carried you as far as you need to go. When I finally turned to leave the clearing beneath the tree, my body moved before my thoughts caught up. One step. Then another. The grass released me without resistance. The air followed, cool and quiet, no longer pressing, no longer asking me to justify my presence. And in that movement, something fundamental settled into place. Silence had not healed me. It had guided me.

It had not arrived with answers neatly wrapped or truths forced into my hands. It had done something far more respectful. It had asked the questions no one else had known how to ask. Questions that did not shame. That did not rush. That did not rescue. Questions that assumed I was capable of responding, even if I did not yet know how. Questions that returned agency to my hands, one careful moment at a time. As I walked away, the silence did not cling to me like a shadow. It did not dissolve either. It remained behind in the clearing, altered by what had passed between us. No longer the place I went to disappear. No longer the space where my voice dissolved into nothingness. It had become something else entirely.

A place I could return to. A place of remembering. A place where I could sit with myself without vanishing. A place that held the shape of who I am becoming. The tree stood where it always had, roots deep, scars visible, still growing. The moon continued its descent, unhurried. The night did not follow me home, but it did not close its door either. It stayed available, like a truth that waits patiently for its moment to be needed again. And as I crossed the edge of that clearing, as the familiar world gathered itself around me once more, I noticed something that felt almost startling in its gentleness. The future no longer felt like something I had to survive. It did not loom as a threat. It did not press as a test. It did not demand proof of worth before allowing me entry.

It felt like something I might grow into. Slowly. With trembling steps. With honesty that would cost me comfort but give me breath. Bravely, not because fear had vanished, but because I had learned how to stand beside it without surrendering my shape. Alive, not in triumph, not in certainty, but in presence. And for the first time, that was enough to carry me forward.

CLOSING: THE PAUSE Between Breaths

This chapter does not end in triumph. It ends in pause. What unfolded beneath the moon, within that listening silence, was not resolution or arrival, but reprieve. A small clearing in the long night. A breath taken without apology. A moment where the story loosened its grip just enough for me to realize it was still mine to carry forward. The light I touched here was not permanent. It did not banish the darkness. It did not erase the patterns, the pain, or the shadows that have shaped my inner world. It simply reminded me of something essential before I had to return to them: that I am not erased by my suffering, and that even in my most fragile moments, something in me knows how to stay.

This was a mercy. A brief one. But a necessary one. Because healing is not a straight ascent into brightness. It is a spiral. And spirals always bring us back through places we thought we had already passed. The silence offered me orientation, not escape. It steadied me long enough to remember who was doing the walking. In the next chapter, we move back into the shadows. We return to the terrain of suicidal ideation, not as a single moment, but as a lived landscape. We will explore how it spoke to me, how it shaped my thinking, how it disguised itself as logic, relief, even kindness. We will sit with the parts of my mind that learned to survive by imagining disappearance, and we will do so without flinching, without romanticizing, and without turning away.

This chapter was the pause before that descent. The inhale before the harder truths. The light that makes it possible to face the dark without being swallowed by it. I offer it here not as an ending, but as an anchor. Because even when we walk back into shadow, we do not walk there unchanged. We carry with us the memory of being held without judgment. We carry the knowledge that silence can listen as well as consume. We carry the truth that staying, even briefly, is not weakness. So come with me. The next pages will be heavy. They will ask us to look directly at the places where despair learned to speak. But we do not enter them empty-handed. We go knowing that light exists, even if only as a pause. And sometimes, that is enough to keep the story alive while it continues to tell the truth.

Chapter Ten:

The Darkest Corner of My Existence: A Journey Through Suicidal Ideation

As I sit here now, older, softer, stitched back together in places once torn, I find myself drifting through the memories of the darkest days not as a captive, but as a witness. Time has loosened its grip, softened its edges, yet its imprint still hums beneath my skin like a low, remembered ache. Days when simply waking felt like lifting the entire world on my fragile shoulders, its gravity unrelenting, its demands merciless. Days when breath tasted heavy, metallic with effort, when each inhale arrived like a negotiation rather than a gift. When my own pulse felt like a punishment, a relentless metronome counting out moments I had not consented to live. When the weight of being alive pressed against my ribs like a collapsing ceiling, lowering inch by inch, daring me to endure one more second beneath it.

And yet, here I am. Still here. Tracing those shadows with gentler eyes, hands no longer clenched in survival but open, curious, reverent even. I do not look back to accuse or to conquer. I look back to understand. To name what once went unnamed. To touch the places that broke and notice how they have healed crookedly, imperfectly, beautifully. My name is Letitia, and this is my story. A story carved from struggle, etched deep by nights that seemed endless, threaded with suffering so quiet it often went unseen. A story shaped by an almost unbearable longing to escape the confines of the invisible prison my life had become, walls built not of stone but of silence, shame, and the slow erosion of hope. It is the story of a woman who once believed her only freedom lay in disappearing, in becoming small enough to slip between the cracks of existence and be done with the effort of being.

And it is also the story of the slow, aching miracle that proved her wrong. A miracle without spectacle or thunder. One that unfolded breath by breath, question by question, in the fragile persistence of staying. In learning that survival itself could become an act of quiet rebellion. In discovering that what I had mistaken for an ending was, impossibly, the beginning of another way to live. I still remember those days, the ones where I tumbled from one rock bottom to the next, only to discover that the floor I thought I had reached was merely another trapdoor, a false mercy, opening beneath my feet. Each impact stole something from me. Not all at once, but gradually. A little faith here. A little strength there. Until falling became familiar, almost expected, as though descent itself had learned my name.

It felt as if I had been treading water in an endless ocean of desperation, arms burning, legs trembling, my body forgetting what rest felt like. Every movement was an argument for staying alive. Every second afloat required justification. There was no shoreline waiting to receive me. No lighthouse slicing through the dark to promise direction. Only water in every direction, black and breathing, rising and falling with a will of its own. The waves were relentless, intimate in their cruelty, brushing my ears with the same hushed persuasion over and over. "Let go, let go." They did not shout. They did not threaten. They simply waited, confident that exhaustion would eventually do their work. Pain had long since become my shadow, stretching ahead of me in the low light, clinging close when the sun disappeared.

An unwelcome but familiar companion, it followed without effort, without invitation. I wore suffering the way others wore skin, tight, suffocating, impossible to peel away without tearing something vital beneath it. It pressed against every movement, every breath, until even joy, when it appeared, felt distant, filtered through layers of ache. I had learned to breathe around it, live beside it, negotiate with it in small, desperate bargains. I pretended it did not devour me piece by fragile piece, pretended that erosion was not happening simply because it was slow. But on that particular day, something within me ruptured. Quietly at first. Almost politely. No scream. No warning.

Just a sudden giving way, like earth surrendering after years of hidden pressure. A fault line deep inside finally broke open, and everything I had been holding together with sheer will collapsed inward. It was catastrophic not because it was loud, but because it was final. Because in that moment, the version of me who believed she could endure anything without consequence ceased to exist. And in the silence that followed, I realized that survival had already exacted its price. The weight of my life, the unspoken griefs, the uncried tears, the silent screams I had folded inward and carried for years, pressed in from all sides until there was no room left to stand. No space left inside me to brace or resist. The walls closed without urgency, without drama, until breath itself felt like an intrusion, something I had to justify.

My chest became a crowded room filled with everything I had never said, every loss I had swallowed whole, every plea that had learned to live without a voice. There was no breath left to bargain with, no strength left to negotiate another postponement of the inevitable. Hope slipped through my fingers like sand, grain by grain, indifferent to how tightly I clenched my hands. I watched it fall, unable to stop the loss, unable even to mourn it properly, because mourning requires the belief that something can still be held. And for the first time, I felt a level of despair so complete it did not rage or thrash or demand to be witnessed. It did not tear through me like fire or drown me in noise. It simply arrived and stayed. Cold. Dense. Certain. It settled into my bones, heavy as winter, seeping into marrow, into memory, into the places where warmth once lived.

That was the moment I learned that hopelessness does not always announce itself as a storm. It does not always break windows or flood streets or leave visible wreckage behind. Sometimes it comes as a whisper, gentle enough to be mistaken for reason, soft enough to sound like peace. A voice that says there is nothing left to fight for, and says it so calmly, so convincingly, that resistance feels unnecessary. And in that quiet finality, in the stillness that follows surrender, it reveals its true devastation.

Exhaustion Masquerading as Refuge

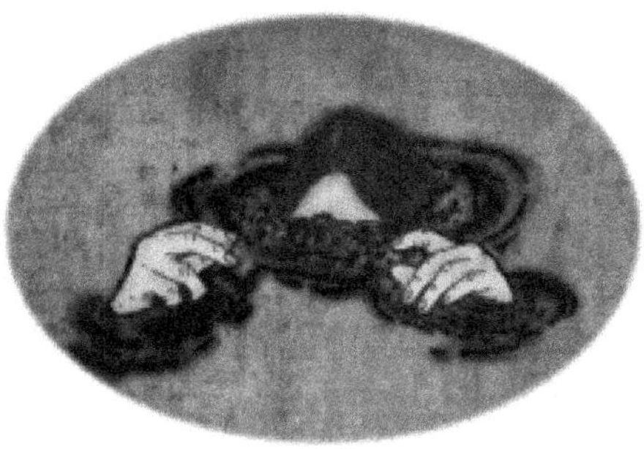

I remember those days with an ache that still lingers, a dull throb beneath the surface of who I am now, like an old injury that knows when rain is coming. Days when death felt like the only soft place left to fall, the only surface that might receive me without demand or judgment. It did not appear as an enemy then. It appeared as rest. As quiet. As a door standing slightly ajar at the end of a long, lightless corridor, offering the promise of laying everything down. The torment clawing at my insides had grown teeth and patience, worrying me from within until even existing felt like an act of harm.

The thought of ending it all became a twisted kind of refuge, not born from desire, but from exhaustion. It was the lone flicker of relief in a world drenched in unrelenting suffering, a small, steady light that whispered of an end to effort, an end to explanation, an end to the ceaseless labor of holding myself together. I did not want to die so much as I wanted the pain to stop asking things of me. I wanted silence that did not interrogate, darkness that did not threaten, stillness that did not require strength. In that place, death felt less like an ending and more like permission. Permission to rest. Permission to be unfinished. Permission to finally stop running from a life that had become too heavy to carry. And that is the quiet cruelty of despair. It does not always seduce with drama or despairing cries. Sometimes it simply offers relief where nothing else has and waits patiently for you to believe that relief is the same thing as peace.

The pain was suffocating, thick as smoke in my lungs, acrid and relentless, coating every breath until breathing itself felt like an act of defiance. I felt myself sinking, slowly, helplessly, into an ocean of despair with no surface in sight, no up or down left to orient by. Each wave pulled me deeper, dragging at my limbs with a wearying patience, swirling with frantic thoughts that screamed for silence, for stillness, for an end to the noise that had colonized my mind. The water was loud with it. Loud with wanting everything to stop. I searched for exits the way a drowning person searches for air, desperately, deliriously, with burning lungs and trembling hands that grasped at nothing. Every option felt slippery, indistinct, dissolving the moment I reached for it. I plotted my escape like someone tracing the seams of their own existence, fingers running along the fragile stitching of a life, looking for the weakest thread.

The place where it might unravel quietly. Cleanly. Without further damage. I longed to still the heartbeat that throbbed with agony, a drumbeat that refused to soften. To hush the relentless voices that gnawed at the edges of my sanity, chewing holes into any fragile calm I tried to assemble. And yet, every time I stood on the brink, every time the idea sharpened into something almost tangible, something within me resisted. Not loudly. Not heroically. It did not rise with speeches or promises or visions of a better future. It wasn't hope, not then. Hope had already thinned to a rumor I no longer trusted. It wasn't fear either. Fear had long since exhausted itself, burned away by familiarity. This was deeper. Stranger. Almost primal.

A low, ancient refusal lodged somewhere beneath thought, beneath language. A quiet tightening. A subtle pulling back. As if some part of me, older than despair, older even than pain, still knew how to cling to the edge, even when I no longer understood why. As if my body, weary and bruised as it was, refused to surrender to the death my mind begged for. As if somewhere in the marrow of my bones, deeper than thought, deeper than choice, a fragment of life clung stubbornly to the possibility of another breath. It was a war waged entirely within me. Mind against body. Despair against instinct. A soul pleading to vanish while a heartbeat kept whispering, not yet; not yet; not yet. The repetition was merciless. A quiet insistence that offered no comfort, only continuation. A torment all its own.

I remember those days with a clarity that still chills me, sharp and unblunted by time. Days when simply existing felt like an unbearable burden, when the gravity of my own life pressed so heavily on my chest that even breathing felt like a betrayal. Each inhale pulled me back into a world I no longer wanted to inhabit. Each exhale felt wasted, undeserved. The pain, the exhaustion, the quiet desperation that pooled in every corner of my being converged into one singular, burning desire: to escape the life I had come to despise. Not to be transformed by it. Not to heal it. Simply to leave it behind.

The darkness did not swallow me all at once. It seeped in slowly, patiently, like ink bleeding through paper, spreading beyond its borders until the page was saturated. It stained every thought, every heartbeat, every fragile piece of me, leaving no clean margins untouched. What began as shadows thickened into atmosphere, into something breathable only through effort. It wrapped itself around my shoulders like a suffocating cloak, heavy and intimate, woven from threads of despair, hopelessness, and years of silent wounds left unattended. I carried it everywhere. It warmed to my shape. It learned my movements.

And within that cloak, within that slow saturation, I lived. I functioned. I smiled when required. I moved through the world as though I were intact, while inside I was unraveling thread by thread. The darkness did not announce itself as an intruder. It became familiar. Habitual. Almost trusted. And that, perhaps, was its greatest cruelty. This descent was not a sudden fall into oblivion. There was no dramatic plunge, no clean break from the surface of myself. It was a slow, torturous sinking, drawn out and merciless, as if I were trapped in quicksand made from my own fears and failures. The more I struggled, the deeper it claimed me. Each memory I replayed, each mistake I rehearsed, tightened its grip. The ground beneath me was not foreign or hostile. It was familiar. It was me. And it yielded inch by inch, swallowing me with an intimacy that made escape feel both urgent and impossible.

The deeper I sank, the thicker the air became, heavy with misery, dense enough to choke the faintest remnants of hope before they could fully form. Breathing felt laborious, as though the atmosphere itself resisted my lungs. Even light seemed reluctant to reach me. Every sunrise arrived like a summons I had not agreed to answer, another battle I hadn't asked to fight. Morning did not bring renewal. It brought exposure. Proof that I had survived the night only to be asked to endure another day. Every hour felt like marching through a warzone where the enemy wore my face. Every thought turned tactical, defensive, alert for the next internal ambush. It wasn't an external enemy I fought. No monster lurking in shadows. No villain to confront or defeat.

There was nothing to run from except myself. The war raged within my own chest, against my own breath, against the very pulse that insisted on keeping me tethered to a world I longed to abandon. My heartbeat became a drumbeat of defiance I had not chosen, a reminder that my body was still loyal to life even as my mind plotted escape. Each day was a struggle not to live, but to survive myself. To outlast my own thoughts. To endure the relentless negotiation between staying and surrendering. There were no medals for this kind of endurance. No witnesses. No applause. Only the quiet, grinding effort of holding together a self that felt determined to come undone. And that, perhaps, was the cruelest truth of all. That the most exhausting battles are not fought against what threatens us from the outside, but against the parts of us that no longer believe we deserve to remain.

I had tried to escape. Oh, how I had tried. The memory of it still clings to me, not as a passing thought but as something etched into the mind with the permanence of scars carved into flesh. These were not dramatic finales, not moments meant to be seen or stopped. They were quiet rehearsals for an ending I longed for with a devotion that felt almost sacred, private and reverent, as though I were practicing a prayer I hoped one day would be answered. Small acts of disappearance. Subtle experiments in absence. Each one a test of how close I could stand to the edge without being pulled back.

It began as whispers. Soft, seductive murmurs of oblivion slipping into my thoughts like smoke under a door, thin at first, almost harmless. They curled through the cracks of my sanity during the hours when the world slept and my pain prowled freely, unchallenged by daylight or distraction. In the stillness of night, those whispers felt intimate, conspiratorial. They spoke gently, patiently, promising rest. Promising release. Promising an end to the labor of being awake inside my own skin.

But whispers can grow teeth. What started as fleeting fantasies did not remain content to drift and vanish. They rooted themselves deep, burrowing into the soil of my despair, blooming into a constant, insistent ache. A pressure that settled on my chest like a stone altar, cold and immovable, upon which I laid my will to live again and again. Each thought of escape became an offering. Each imagined ending another small surrender. I knelt there daily, worn smooth by repetition, convinced that devotion alone might earn me peace.

Each betrayal, each abandonment, each bruise and blow to my heart fed that ache, nourishing it until it grew strong and familiar. Pain taught it how to survive. Loneliness taught it how to stay. It learned my rhythms, my weaknesses, the precise moments when I was most vulnerable. In time, it became a companion more loyal than any human in my life. It never left. It never forgot me. It waited with unwavering patience, certain that eventually I would choose it. And in that terrible intimacy, I mistook constancy for comfort, believing that what stayed must somehow care.

The attempts came next, not impulsive flares of despair, but calculated, ritualistic strategies born from a mind desperate for escape. Hangings planned with precision. Suffocations rehearsed like choreography. These were not moments of chaos. They were deliberate negotiations with silence, practiced with a terrifying calm. I became an architect of my own undoing and demise, constructing elaborate blueprints for peace, convinced that if I planned carefully enough, I could finally lay myself down and be done with the effort of living.

I remember the moments of surrender pressing my face into a pillow, feeling the deceptive gentleness of its fabric, soft, forgiving, almost compassionate. The body yielding. The world narrowing. Ordinary softness turning deceptive, almost compassionate, as though even the most familiar textures conspired to offer comfort. I remember holding myself perfectly still, as if trying to pause the tide of life itself. I held my breath as if holding back the tide of life itself, pushing inward toward that narrowing tunnel where sound faded, where edges blurred, where consciousness thinned to something fragile and translucent. A heavy, velvety darkness began to close around me, not violent, not cruel, but intimate, like a merciful embrace. Inviting. Like being gathered up at last.

And for a moment, a brief, trembling, fragile moment, there was the illusion of release. A quiet so complete it felt sacred. A nothingness that promised rest. But then, always, the betrayal. The body intervened. Abruptly. A jolt. A gasp. Air clawing its way back into my lungs like an unforgiving tide dragging me back to the shore I so desperately wanted to leave. Without consent. A violent return to sensation, to breath, to pain. Awakening was not relief. It was impact, it was violence. Each breath came back like punishment, sharp and insistent, a cruel reminder that my body refused to obey my longing for silence. It dragged me back into the agony I had fought so hard to escape, hauling me across a threshold I had tried to cross alone.

It felt as though my very breath conspired against me, as though life itself had decided to keep me tethered, regardless of my pleas. Survival did not arrive as mercy. It arrived as force. And in that forced return, the cruelty was not simply that I lived, but that I lived without peace, without answers, without understanding why the fight continued when I no longer knew how to want the victory. Somehow, no matter how tightly I sealed the world away, no matter how fiercely I denied that first inhale, my body would revolt. It would fight. It would survive. And in doing so, it tormented me with its persistence. To live, when all I wanted was to stop living, became its own kind of hell. Not the dramatic hell of fire and chaos, but a quiet, grinding one. A daily sentence carried out in breath and heartbeat. A strange, perverse, twisted torment. A betrayal of the most intimate kind. A betrayal from within.

My own body, bruised and weary to its marrow, hollowed out by exhaustion and despair, emptied by years of carrying what no child, no human, should ever have been asked to bear, turned against me. Or so it felt. It became an adversary I could not outrun, no matter how small I tried to make myself, no matter how far inward I retreated. Despite its exhaustion, despite the way it trembled beneath the sheer weight of my suffering, it resisted. It resisted in reflexes. In gasps. In the involuntary insistence of muscles and nerves that refused to loosen their grip on existence. No matter how meticulously I orchestrated my own escape, no matter how precisely I planned each quiet vanishing, my body resisted. Always resisted. It did not reason with me. It did not explain itself. It simply acted.

As an animal dragged toward slaughter yet clawing at the earth with its last trembling strength, it refused to surrender to the death my mind so fervently sought. There was nothing noble in it at the time. Nothing comforting. Only raw, feral survival, stripped of meaning, stripped of mercy. It clung to life with a ferocity that felt almost cruel. A stubborn, instinctual persistence that mocked the quiet surrender of my mind and the shattered whisper of my soul. My thoughts had already laid themselves down. My spirit had already begun to fade. And yet my body would not follow. It held fast, teeth bared, muscles locked, dragging me back again and again into a world I had already said goodbye to.

It felt wickedly purposeful, this internal mutiny. As though my body had decided without consulting me. As though it had chosen allegiance to life long after I had renounced it. Each forced return felt like being hauled backward across a threshold I had crossed in my heart, yanked from a silence I had already started to believe in. And in that violent persistence, in that unyielding refusal, I felt not saved, but condemned to remain. Alive. Breathing. Enduring. Bound to a life I no longer recognized as my own, yet unable to leave.

A Stay of Execution Inside the Body

And yet, somewhere in that biological rebellion, somewhere deep within me, buried beneath layers of despair thick enough to drown the heavens themselves, beneath strata of agony, shame, and long-practiced resignation, something flickered. Almost imperceptible. A defiant spark hiding in the wreckage. A faint, trembling ember of instinct I could not name then, had no language for, no reverence for. Hope? Survival instinct? A sliver of destiny refusing erasure and to be extinguished? I did not know. I only knew it was there. Glowing so quietly, I doubted its reality. So small I mistook it for a trick of exhaustion. I barely saw it. I barely recognized it. I barely felt it. And yet, it refused to go out. It pulsed in the dark, stubborn and irrational, like a heartbeat in a corpse, where none should exist. Fragile, yes, but relentless. It did not blaze. It did not announce itself. It simply endured.

Each time I tried to end my story, this microscopic rebellion rose up from somewhere ancient and unreasoned and whispered, "not yet". Not with hope's certainty. Not with promises. Just a refusal. A pause. A stay of execution written in breath and nerve endings. My existence became a brutal tug-of-war, fought entirely within the confines of my own skin. My soul leaning toward oblivion, exhausted, ready to dissolve into quiet. My body, anchoring me stubbornly to life, digging in with instinct alone. Death pulled with the gravity of rest, of release, of silence that asked nothing of me. Life yanked me back by the frayed threads of my breath, raw and insistent, refusing to let go. Each inhale tightened the rope. Each exhale threatened to loosen it. I lived suspended there, between wanting to vanish and being unable to disappear.

Between a mind that had already said farewell and a body that would not stop insisting on presence. The space between became its own purgatory. Not alive in any meaningful sense. Not gone either. Just held. Stretched. Endured. And in that merciless tension, in that constant opposition, something uninvited was being forged. Something I could not yet see as mercy. Something I could not yet name as survival. Only later would I understand that this quiet, stubborn ember was not betraying me at all. It was keeping vigil. Waiting for the moment when I would finally be ready to notice that I was still here.

Every meticulously orchestrated plan, every carefully engineered exit unraveled the same way. Each failed attempt landed like a fresh betrayal, sharp and intimate, not from the world this time, but from the vessel that housed me. I would surface again, ripped back into awareness by lungs that refused surrender, by a heart that continued its relentless insistence despite my pleas for silence. Consciousness returned like an unwanted light snapping on in a room I had already left, too bright, too loud, too cruelly present. Frustration crashed over me like a tidal wave, sudden and overwhelming, leaving no room to breathe beneath it. Why? The question tore out of me, raw and furious. Why couldn't I slip away? Why did this body insist on holding me hostage in a life I no longer wished to inhabit?

The questions echoed without answer, ricocheting off the walls of my mind, growing sharper with each return. There was no comfort in survival then. Only rage. Only disbelief. Only the exhausting realization that even my own flesh refused to release me. In those moments, it felt as though I was trapped inside a war I had never agreed to fight. A civil war waged beneath my skin. Mind and soul advocating for release, exhausted and ready to lay down their weapons. Body fighting tooth and nail for survival, unreasoned, feral, loyal only to continuation.

A cruel paradox. A curse masquerading as instinct. The very mechanisms meant to protect me felt like shackles, binding me to pain with an unbreakable grip.

It was a rebellion against my own destruction, even when I believed destruction was the only mercy left. Life did not argue with me. It did not persuade or soothe or promise better days. It simply resisted. It stood its ground inside me, stubborn and unyielding, refusing to honor my desire for erasure. And so I remained, suspended in that brutal contradiction. Wanting release. Being denied it. Forced to endure a body that chose survival long before my mind remembered how to want it. It became a merciless cycle, a carousel of anguish that never slowed, never loosened its grip. Pain fed despair. Despair fed hopelessness. Hopelessness folded back into helplessness until the edges blurred and I no longer knew where one ended and the other began. They merged into a single, suffocating force, grinding me down with repetition rather than impact. There was no climax to this suffering, no release.

Only motion. Only return. The same rise, the same fall, over and over, until even the idea of change felt naïve. I was imprisoned in a nightmare without dawn, a night that did not thin or soften with time. An endless maze where every corridor curved cruelly back toward the same suffocating room. No matter how carefully I chose my steps, no matter how urgently I ran, I always arrived back at myself. The walls were built from memory and regret, the floor slick with exhaustion. There was no exit sign. No hidden door. No reprieve. No quiet corner of my mind left untouched by torment. Even rest was invaded, even sleep patrolled by the same relentless dread.

And with every failed attempt, every breath I did not want but still took, life seemed to smirk. A cruel victor lingering in the doorway, collecting trophies I never meant to offer. Each involuntary inhale burned bitter and hot in my chest, a small but unmistakable defeat. Each stubborn heartbeat landed like a slap, sharp and humiliating, reminding me that even in my most deliberate efforts to disappear, I could not escape myself. My body kept score. My pulse marked time. Survival tallied itself again and again without mercy. It felt obscene, this persistence. As though life itself were mocking me, refusing to take my no as an answer. I was not living in any way that resembled grace or desire. I was enduring.

Trapped inside a body that would not release me, inside a mind that no longer knew how to ask for anything other than silence. And in that unending cycle, that grinding repetition of breath and return, the cruelest truth took shape. That survival, stripped of meaning, can feel indistinguishable from punishment. And yet, still, inexplicably, it continued. It was as if my body and my despair were locked in a silent, primal standoff, a wordless battle waged beneath my skin where language had no jurisdiction. My suicidal ideation screamed for release, for the hush of nothingness, for a stillness so complete it promised mercy. And yet my body clung to life with the fragile insistence of a dying flame gripping its wick, flickering wildly but refusing extinction.

Every nerve seemed to argue against my will. Every reflex rose up in defiance, as though survival itself were hardwired too deeply to be reasoned with, too ancient to negotiate. Somewhere deep beneath the rubble of everything I had endured, beneath the collapse of meaning and the weight of accumulated pain, a faint, aching echo of hope struggled to make itself heard. Not hope as salvation. Not hope as promise. Just a whisper. Thin. Uncertain. Almost offensive in its persistence. It tried to slip through the roar of agony, and I resented it as much as I needed it. Its presence felt like cruelty some days, like being offered a glass of water in the middle of a fire. And yet it was also the only sound that was not screaming.

It felt like a grotesque dance, a macabre waltz performed in slow motion, each step heavy with consequence. Life and death circled one another like reluctant partners bound by a choreography neither could fully abandon. Death led with confident, elegant cruelty, smooth in its promises, sure of its authority. It held all the steps. All the certainty. And yet, somehow, it never delivered the final dip. It hovered there, perpetually unfinished, always one movement away from completion. Life followed shakily, off balance and bruised, but persistent. Its steps were clumsy, uneven, marked by hesitation and pain. Still, its trembling fingers refused to let go of my hand. It did not charm or seduce. It did not make its case. It simply stayed. Breath by breath. Beat by beat.

An insistence without explanation. And I, caught between them, became the unwilling choreography. Not a dancer with agency, but the space where the dance occurred. Suspended in the agonizing rhythm of a movement I did not choose yet could not stop. I lived inside that tension, stretched thin between surrender and survival, between the desire to vanish and the body's refusal to release me. Held there. Turning slowly. Waiting for something to break. Or change. Or finally, finally make sense. As the days blurred into weeks, and the weeks dissolved into months, months unraveling into years, then years into decades, my suicidal ideation did not fade. It sharpened. It deepened. It rooted itself like a thorned vine winding through the architecture of my being, gripping bone and breath alike.

It grew with me, aged with me, matured with a cruel patience, learning my seasons, adapting to my rhythms. What I once thought might be temporary revealed itself as something far more insidious, a companion that learned how to survive every version of me. I spent countless hours wandering the dim corridors of my own mind, pacing its narrow halls like a long-term inmate who knows every crack in the walls. I traced the same routes again and again, crafting elaborate blueprints of my own disappearance, sculpting fantasies of final relief with meticulous care. I imagined the sweet, merciful quiet that would follow, the hush that would finally descend once I was gone. In those imaginings, there was no pain, no demand, no need to explain myself to a world that had never learned how to listen. Only stillness.

Only rest. Only an end to the effort of being. I felt like a prisoner locked inside a body I no longer recognized, a body that had betrayed me by surviving, shackled to circumstances that refused to loosen their grip. My reflection became unfamiliar, as though I were watching someone else inhabit my skin. I moved through life performing the motions expected of me, while inwardly pacing the length of my confinement, measuring the walls, counting the days, marking time by endurance alone. The irony of my first marriage was acidic on my tongue. I was married, yet I had never been more alone. The union that should have been refuge and sanctuary had become a hollow performance, a carefully staged illusion. A parody of love rehearsed so often it almost looked real from the outside.

It was an elaborate masquerade with no audience and no truth, where vows echoed but never landed, and intimacy remained an abstract idea rather than a lived reality. My first marriage was a ghost wearing a ring. An imposter draped in promises that never touched the ground of everyday life. I lived beside someone while remaining profoundly unseen, bound by ceremony but starved of connection. The silence inside that marriage mirrored the silence inside me, deepening it, confirming it. And in that quiet, suffocating loneliness, the thorned vine tightened its hold, whispering again and again that escape was not only imaginable, but inevitable.

I bore the title *wife*, but none of the warmth that word once promised. It sat on me like borrowed clothing, ill fitting, heavy, decorative without function. I was not cherished. I was not protected. I was not seen, not chosen, not valued. The first man I entrusted my life to did not become my companion; he became my tormentor. Not a partner, but a shadowed antagonist, a presence that darkened every room I entered, a specter stalking the ordinary moments of my days. His hands, his words, his silences bruised more than my skin. They battered my spirit, eroded my sense of worth, fractured my mind in places that would take years to name. Violence did not always need volume. Sometimes it arrived quietly, dressed as indifference, sharpened by neglect.

Every day with him carved another fissure into my foundation, another tear in the fabric of who I once was. I could feel myself thinning, stretching beyond endurance, losing coherence thread by thread. The vows that were meant to bind us in love instead bound me to suffering. What should have been sanctuary hardened into confinement. Promises curdled. Tender words rusted into weapons. The home I tried to build became a cage, its bars forged from betrayal and reinforced by emotional cruelty. I learned how small a person can become when survival demands invisibility. I learned how silence can be louder than screams. I became a woman unrecognizable even to herself. A hollow echo moving through familiar spaces.

Where a vibrant soul once lived, there was now vacancy. Piece by piece, he chipped away at me, not in a single catastrophic blow, but in countless small erosions, until only a shell remained. A shell that housed despair instead of life. Emptiness instead of hope. A fragile outline of a person waiting, quietly, desperately, for permission to disappear. And in that waiting, I mistook endurance for strength, obedience for love, survival for purpose. I stayed because I no longer remembered how to leave. I remained because the parts of me that once believed in escape had already been worn down to whispers. Inside that shell, despair learned my name. And the vine I carried within me tightened once more, nourished by a marriage that did not break me all at once, but taught me, slowly and thoroughly, how to disappear while still breathing.

A Heart Turned Desert

I was a mother, but I was not. The title rested on me the way everything else did then, loosely, without substance, without breath. For how can a shadow cradle a child? How can a woman who has become translucent, hollowed out by despair, offer warmth to the little hearts that turn toward her for light? I moved through my children's lives like a ghost skimming the periphery of their days, present in form but absent in essence. I was there, and yet I was not. A figure at the doorway. A voice from another room. A body performing care while the self that should have animated it stood far away, watching. I loved them fiercely. That much was never in question. But love without vitality is a dying flame, flickering bravely yet unable to warm. It burns itself down without offering heat.

I wanted to give them everything. I wanted to pour myself into them the way mothers are supposed to. But I had nothing left to give. My heart, once overflowing with tenderness, had become a barren desert, cracked and sun scorched, incapable of offering even a drop of nourishment. No water. No shade. Only endurance. Only survival. My belief in my own brokenness made me a broken mother. I carried that conviction like a verdict etched into bone. My belief in my unlovability stripped me of my ability to love freely, to show up fully, to trust that I was worthy of being their parent. I questioned every touch, every word, every moment of presence, convinced it was insufficient, convinced I was doing harm simply by existing near them. Shame nested where confidence should have lived.

Doubt spoke louder than instinct. I felt so unworthy of them, so certain that my very presence damaged more than it nurtured, that eventually I stopped trying. Not because I did not care, but because caring hurt too much. Because each attempt reminded me of everything I believed I had already failed to be. I withdrew inward, not from lack of love, but from an overwhelming fear that my love was poisonous, that it would stain them the way life had stained me. I became a vessel drained dry. A body going through the motions of motherhood while the soul within had long since retreated into exile. I fed them. I clothed them. I showed up when required. But the part of me that laughed, that dreamed, that imagined futures for them without flinching, had gone quiet.

I lived in a state of emotional absence, loving them from behind a wall I did not know how to dismantle. And still, they looked at me. Still, they reached. Still, they loved. That was the unbearable irony. That even as I disappeared from myself, I remained the center of their small worlds. I did not yet understand that my absence was not proof of failure, but evidence of how deeply I had been wounded. I only knew that I was there in body, gone in spirit, a mother shaped by love but eclipsed by despair, waiting for something, anything, to call me back from exile. The emptiness inside me was not a simple void. It was a chasm. Vast. Bottomless. A yawning absence that swallowed everything that dared to reach for sunlight.

Hope fell into it and vanished. Compassion followed. Tenderness. Even the mother instinct, that ancient pull written into the body, was dragged down and lost to the dark. The soil of my inner world had turned hostile, incapable of sustaining life, incapable of holding anything gentle for long. And in the place where nourishment should have grown, bitterness took root. Thick as tar. Heavy. Slow-moving. Not directed at my children. Never at them. But inward. Always inward. Toward myself. Toward my life. Toward the unbearable circumstances that had shaped me without consent or mercy. Bitterness became my second language, fluent and automatic, learned through repetition and pain. I spoke it without words. It leaked out in long, exhausted sighs. In silences that stretched too far. In the hollow, unfocused stare of someone searching for herself and finding only blur.

I was angry. Not sharp, explosive anger, but deep, molten rage that simmered beneath my skin, slow and consuming. Angry at the world for its indifference. Angry at systems and people that looked away. Angry at myself for every perceived failure, every place I believed I had fallen short. Angry at the life I had been handed, a life that felt less like a story unfolding and more like a sentence being served. Day after day. Without appeal. That anger lived alongside fear, braided tightly together. A constant, gnawing terror that my children deserved a mother made of light, and all they had was me. A fading silhouette. A woman shaped more by absence than presence.

I watched them from behind my own despair, convinced that my darkness eclipsed them, that my brokenness bled into their days. The fear was relentless. That my wounds were contagious. That my emptiness would become their inheritance. And so I shrank further. I dimmed myself in an attempt to protect them. I believed that if I took up less space, if I asked less of life, if I disappeared just enough, I might spare them the weight of me. I did not yet understand that this fear, too, was a symptom of how deeply I had been harmed. That my terror was not evidence of my failure as a mother, but of how fiercely I loved while believing myself unworthy of that love. Inside me, the chasm yawned. Bitterness spoke. Anger burned. Fear whispered its cruel predictions. And still, beneath all of it, something endured. Quiet. Unnamed. Waiting. Not yet strong enough to rise, but stubborn enough not to vanish.

I was living in a pit, not merely dark, but ancient. Primeval. Damp and airless. A place untouched by time, where hope could not breathe because breath itself was rationed. The walls of this inner cavern pressed in on me like a closing fist, stone grinding against stone, relentless in its slow certainty. The air was thick with despair, so dense it clung to my skin like sweat, seeping into pores, coating every thought. It was claustrophobia of the soul, the kind that offers no exit because the prison is internal, built from memory and pain rather than bars. Every day, the space tightened. Not all at once, not dramatically, but incrementally, cruelly. It shrank around me with patient intent, compressing my lungs, my thoughts, my very sense of existence.

Even imagination felt cramped. Even silence felt crowded. Below me, the swampy waters of despair churned endlessly, thick and opaque, pulling at my ankles with a slow, sucking hunger. They did not rush. They waited. They knew exhaustion would do their work better than force. With each passing hour, the waters rose higher, swallowing pieces of me I no longer had the strength to protect. First joy. Then curiosity. Then the will to imagine a future that did not hurt. What disappeared did so quietly, without ceremony, as though it had never belonged to me in the first place. This was not drowning in the ordinary sense. There was no frantic flailing, no sudden panic. No, it was a suffocation of the spirit. An asphyxiation from the inside out. A slow deprivation of meaning, of oxygen for the soul.

My pain had fastened itself around me like shackles forged from my own tears. Each memory cooled into metal. Each regret hardened into restraint. My suffering became the rope cinched around my neck, tightening with every unanswered plea for relief, every prayer that vanished into the stone above me. I pulled against it until my muscles burned, until resistance itself felt futile. The harder I strained, the more it bit into me, teaching me the terrible efficiency of despair. And still, I endured. Not because I believed I should. Not because I saw a way out. But because something in me, buried even deeper than the pit, refused to completely dissolve. I could not yet call it strength. I did not recognize it as resilience. It felt more like inertia. Like the stubborn refusal of matter to vanish without cause. I existed because I had not yet learned how not to.

In that cavern, in that tightening dark, I became intimately acquainted with the limits of suffering. I learned how quiet agony can be. How invisible. How consuming. And though I did not know it then, that pit was not only a place of erasure. It was also a crucible. A place where something essential, something indestructible, was being pressed into form, even as everything else was being stripped away. Life itself became the tormentor, not death. Death was the mercy I sought, a hush I believed would finally close the wound. Life, however, was the predator. It stalked me with patient cruelty, circling without haste, savouring the hunt. It toyed with me the way a cat toys with a dying mouse, not to kill, but to exhaust.

To remind me who held the power. It would loosen its grip just enough to let me crawl toward a glimmer, a tiny, trembling spark of freedom. Just enough light to make my breath hitch. Just enough hope to make the pain sharpen with contrast. And then, snap. The illusion shattered. The claws came down. The invisible teeth closed in. Life seized me again, sudden and merciless, digging into my soft, unguarded places, dragging me back toward the center of the pit. It tore at my resolve with practiced efficiency, sharp, jagged edges sinking deep into the tenderest regions of my soul. I could almost hear it then, the sound that still echoes in memory. The crunch. The cracking of another fragment of my will giving way under pressure. A splintering I felt more than heard.

Each time, I was flung back into the suffocating dark to relive the same grotesque ritual. The rise. The reach. The almost. The brutal return. Hope became a weapon used against me, not a refuge. It was bait. A cruel offering dangled just out of reach, not meant to save me, only to ensure that when I fell again, I would fall harder. The repetition was its own violence. Not the wound, but the reopening. Not the blow, but the certainty that it would come again. In that cycle, death began to feel gentle by comparison. It asked nothing. It promised no games. Life, on the other hand, demanded endurance without explanation, survival without relief. It insisted I remain conscious for the pain, awake for the tearing, present for every loss. And so I learned to fear not the ending, but the continuation. Not the dark, but the return to it. Again. And again. And again.

I lived there, inside that hunt, convinced that mercy was something life had long since forgotten how to offer. And yet, even as it stalked me, even as it broke me down to fragments, it did not finish the kill. It left me breathing. Waiting. Watching. Trapped in the terrible space between being spared and being saved, where survival felt less like a gift and more like a sentence that refused to end. It wasn't oblivion that toyed with me; it was existence itself. Life dangled survival just beyond reach, close enough to taste, close enough to believe in, then yanked it away again and again, stretching the agony as though it took some perverse satisfaction in my endurance. It learned the precise distance between despair and hope, the exact moment when my breath would lift with the possibility of release, and that was when it struck.

Not to end me. Never to end me. Only to remind me that escape was not mine to choose. Each time I neared the void, that small, black opening where release seemed to wait with open arms, life would close in. Its grip was sudden, brutal. It clamped down and dragged me back, gasping, kicking, pleading, trembling, bleeding in ways no one could see. The wounds were internal, layered, invisible to the eye but devastating in their accumulation. My body returned marked by struggle, my spirit raw from the repeated violence of being pulled away from what I believed was mercy. And then, just as abruptly, it would let go. Not out of kindness. Not out of grace. But so the cycle could begin anew. A calculated release. A pause designed not for healing, but for reset.

So I could crawl again. Hope again. Reach again. And fall again. It was a macabre dance between suffering and false reprieve, a choreography perfected through repetition. The steps never changed. Only the toll they took. With every turn, the pit grew deeper. The water darker. Thicker. More consuming. And I grew smaller and smaller and smaller, worn down by the constant return, by the erosion of belief, by the knowledge that there was no final movement waiting to end the dance. I became less a participant and more a remnant, a diminishing presence flickering at the edge of itself. I learned what it means to be undone slowly. Not erased in one merciful sweep but reduced through attrition. Breath by breath. Cycle by cycle. Until even the idea of escape felt heavy, until even longing grew tired. And still, somehow, I remained. Not victorious. Not saved. Just present. Reduced. Waiting. Held in the cruel suspension between an ending that would not come and a life that would not loosen its grip.

The Agonizing Dance

This agonizing dance, this was suicidal ideation in its truest, rawest, purest form. Not merely a passing thought. Not a dark whisper that drifts through the mind and dissolves with daylight. It was a full-bodied haunting, a presence that occupied me completely, that lived in my posture, my breathing, my silence. It did not visit. It resided. It moved through me like a second bloodstream, quiet and inexorable, shaping the rhythm of my days and the texture of my nights. It was a relentless yearning for death, woven into every breath I took, threaded so tightly through inhale and exhale that even air felt compromised. A longing so deep it seemed stitched into the fabric of my bones, structural rather than emotional, as though it had always been there, holding me together even as it pulled me apart. This was not drama. This was not impulse. It was gravity. A steady, downward pull that asked nothing of me except surrender.

It was the desperate craving for oblivion, for the soft, merciful hush of non-existence, the kind of quiet that does not bruise, does not question, does not demand explanation. A silence without consequence. And yet that craving was paired, cruelly and endlessly, with the aching inability to cross the threshold I stared at so often. I stood there suspended, close enough to imagine release, far enough to remain trapped. The doorway existed. The passage did not open. A body that refused to surrender, loyal to life without consulting me. A mind that circled the ending endlessly yet lacked the final ounce of force to step through. A soul caught in its own purgatory, stretched between wanting to vanish and being unable to disappear.

Each part of me pulled in a different direction, tearing at the seams of my being, leaving me suspended in contradiction. This was not indecision. It was captivity. A state where desire and restraint collided until both became unbearable. Where longing sharpened against resistance, and resistance hardened into torment. I lived there, in that narrow space between breath and release, between being held and being undone. Alive without relief. Wanting without permission. Existing as a question that had no answer, only endurance. And though I did not yet understand it, though I could not have named it as such, this purgatory was not emptiness alone. It was also a holding pattern. A terrible, merciless stillness where something within me, unseen and uncelebrated, continued to bear witness. Waiting.

Not for hope. Not for rescue. But for the moment, when the story would finally begin to turn, however slowly, away from the edge. And yet, even in that purgatory, even in the merciless stillness between letting go and being held, something subtle was already shifting. I could not see it then. I could not feel it as hope. But beneath the relentless yearning for oblivion, beneath the bone-stitched longing to disappear, there existed a quiet continuity. A thread that did not snap. A presence that endured without announcing itself. I was still breathing.

Still witnessing. Still aware of the pain as pain, not as truth. That distinction mattered, though I did not yet know it. Suicidal ideation had colonized my inner world so completely that I mistook it for identity.

I believed this yearning was who I was, not something happening within me. But even in its rawest form, even when it haunted every breath, it remained a state, not a self. I was living inside it, not reduced to it. The very fact that I could observe the dance, name the purgatory, articulate the paradox meant that some part of me still stood slightly apart, watching, recording, enduring. That part did not rescue me. It did not intervene. It did not offer solutions or comfort. It simply remained. A witness, seated in the rubble. A quiet consciousness that kept tally not of failures, but of survival. Each day I endured without crossing the threshold was not a triumph, not a victory, but it was evidence. Evidence that something in me, however battered, however silent, had not consented to disappear entirely.

I did not yet believe my life had value. I did not yet believe I deserved relief. But I was beginning (somewhere so hidden I would only see it years later), imperceptibly, to learn that the inability to die was not proof of weakness. It was proof of something else entirely. Something more ancient than despair. Something more stubborn than ideation. A life force that did not negotiate, did not philosophize, did not require belief. It simply stayed. And in staying, in that relentless, unwanted continuation, the conditions for healing were being forged long before healing had a name. Long before I could imagine a future not defined by escape. Long before I understood that surviving suicidal ideation is not a single moment of choosing life, but a thousand quiet refusals to disappear when disappearing feels like the only mercy left.

This was not recovery yet. This was not hope. This was the ground beneath the ground. The place where the story does not end, even when the ending feels inevitable. And though I could not feel it then, though I resented it with everything I had, this was the beginning of my return, but this I only found years into my healing work. Now we cross back to our full exploration of suicidal ideation. It was the ultimate paradox, a prison built from both the outside in and the inside out. I was captive to my circumstances, yes, bound by histories I did not choose and wounds I did not deserve. But perhaps even more so, I was captive to my own fractured mind, to the lens through which I was forced to interpret everything that touched me. The bars were visible and invisible all at once. Some forged from lived harm. Others fashioned quietly from thought, belief, and repetition, locking into place with terrifying efficiency.

And here lies the cruel poetry of it all. The very wounds that birthed my suicidal ideation were the same ones it fed upon, the same ones it sharpened and deepened. My suffering painted my thoughts in shades of smoke and shadow, blurring edges, swallowing nuance. And those darkened thoughts, in turn, repainted my world in an even bleaker palette, draining color from moments that might otherwise have held softness. Pain distorted perception. Perception amplified pain. Around and around it went, a feedback loop of despair with no clear origin and no obvious exit. It became a hall of mirrors, endless and disorienting.

Every direction reflected a version of myself twisted by hopelessness. No matter where I turned, I was confronted by the same image: broken, unworthy, trapped. The reflections multiplied, each one more convincing than the last, until I no longer trusted my own eyes. Reality itself felt suspect, filtered through a mind that had learned to expect harm and therefore found it everywhere. But somewhere within this labyrinth of anguish, I want to pause. To slow the momentum just enough to place something small and deliberate in your hands. A lantern. Nothing grand. Nothing blinding. Just a flicker. A gentle glimmer you can cup in your palm without fear of being burned.

Perspective matters. Thoughts matter. They are not harmless visitors passing through an otherwise neutral landscape. They are architects. They shape the rooms we live in inside ourselves. They can warp reality into a nightmare where every sound is a threat, every silence a verdict. Or they can soften the edges just enough to make survival possible. They can fracture you further. Or they can, slowly, painstakingly, begin to rebuild what was shattered. Thought is the brush that colors your inner world. Every belief lays down pigment. Every repeated story deepens the shade. And when you learn, gently and without force, to shift the color even by a single degree, the entire landscape begins to change.

Not all at once. Not miraculously. But perceptibly. A shadow lightens. A corner becomes visible. A path suggests itself where none existed before. This is not denial of pain. It is not pretending the pit was not real. It is the recognition that while suffering may shape the canvas, thought still chooses the hue. And in learning to hold that brush with care, with curiosity rather than condemnation, I began, for the first time, to sense that the prison walls were not as immutable as they once appeared. That somewhere beyond the mirrors, beyond the smoke, another version of reality waited. One that did not erase the past but no longer allowed it to dictate every line of the future.

Now, let us continue down this winding path together, not as travellers rushing toward an end, but as witnesses willing to walk through what was, slowly and without flinching. Suicidal ideation had become my constant companion. Not a friend. Not an enemy. Something far more insidious. A frenemy. A shape-shifting shadow that trailed me faithfully, silently, everywhere I went. It never announced itself. It simply appeared. Leaning against the walls of my days. Watching from the corners of every room. Curling at the foot of my bed like something that believed it belonged there. It slipped into my thoughts like smoke beneath a closed door, thin at first, almost unnoticeable, until the air was thick with it. It commented on everything I did, everything I said, everything I felt.

A running commentary that reframed every experience through the same cruel lens. Joy became suspicious. Rest became undeserved. Hope became a setup for disappointment. It colored my breathing, tinted my vision, rewrote the meaning of every heartbeat until my own pulse felt less like proof of life and more like an accusation. I was caught in a merciless loop, a cycle of pain so unending it began to feel like a second skin, stitched into me by invisible hands. I wore it everywhere. It shaped my posture, my silence, the way I moved through the world half braced for impact. Despair was no longer an episode. It was a climate. A permanent weather system under which I learned to live, adapt, and shrink. Even moments of calm carried its imprint, like scars beneath fabric.

No matter how deep the despair sank its roots, no matter how meticulously I rehearsed my escape in the privacy of my own mind, my body betrayed me. Or so it felt. It clung to life with a stubborn, bewildering instinct that refused to be reasoned with. Reflex overrode desire. Breath overruled intention. My body chose survival again and again, even as my mind remained convinced that death was the only doorway left unblocked. This contradiction became its own form of suffering. To want release with every fiber of my being and yet remain tethered by a body that would not comply. To be certain of the ending while being denied the exit. I lived in that tension, stretched thin between what I believed and what my body insisted upon. And in that relentless opposition, I mistook persistence for cruelty, instinct for betrayal, survival for punishment.

I did not yet understand that this so-called betrayal was also a kind of guardianship. Crude. Wordless. Uncompromising. Something ancient in me was standing watch even when my conscious mind had laid down its weapons. I could not yet see it as protection. I only felt the exhaustion of being held here against my will. And yet, every time my body refused to let go, it carved out one more moment of continuation. One more breath. One more opportunity for the story to remain unfinished. I did not call it grace then. I did not call it hope. But it was a pause. A suspension. A fragile interval in which something unseen was still working, still waiting, still refusing to let the darkness have the final word. Every day was a negotiation, a weary bargaining session conducted at the edge of exhaustion, between the part of me that wanted to vanish and the part that refused to let go.

There were no decisive victories in these talks, no clear terms agreed upon. Only postponements. Only compromises measured in minutes and hours. Survival was no longer living; it was clinging. Scraping. Dragging myself through time that felt razor-edged, each moment sharp enough to cut. A torment masquerading as endurance, wearing the thin disguise of resilience while draining me of everything it pretended to preserve. It was as though life itself had punctured the fragile vessel that held my essence, my soul, and no matter how desperately I tried to refill it, everything leaked out faster than I could pour it back in. I searched for nourishment everywhere. In rest. In routine. In love. In distraction. In silence. But nothing stayed. I was a cracked jar beneath a relentless downpour, always catching, always losing, water slipping through invisible fractures as quickly as it arrived.

The effort was constant. The reward non-existent. I became a hollow vessel rattling with emptiness, my insides echoing with the sound of what used to live there. And yet, somehow, I kept trying. Still lifting the jar. Still angling it toward whatever might fall from the sky. Still hoping, against all logic, that this time something might remain. That one drop might linger long enough to matter. That the fractures might miraculously seal themselves through sheer will. And through it all, the shadow remained. Faithful. Patient. It did not rush me. It did not need to. It whispered in the quiet spaces, watched from the margins, waited for moments when my grip faltered. It knew my fatigue intimately. It understood the language of my weariness. It did not threaten. It suggested. It reminded. It offered itself as an ending to the endless effort of trying to hold what would not stay.

I lived like that for a long time. Negotiating breath by breath. Holding together a vessel I believed was irreparably broken. Carrying a shadow that knew me better than anyone else. And yet, even as everything leaked away, even as emptiness rattled through me, there was still motion. Still attempt. Still a hand lifting the jar into the rain. I did not yet know that this trying, this stubborn reaching despite the fractures, was not foolishness. It was evidence. Proof that something in me, however damaged, however depleted, still believed there might be a moment when the vessel would hold. Or when holding would no longer be the measure of my worth.

When Truth Settles Like Cold Mist

As I looked around me, the truth, or what I believed to be truth, settled over me like a cold, merciless fog. It crept in low and thick, swallowing distance, swallowing depth, until I could no longer tell where I ended and the emptiness began. I was utterly, devastatingly alone. Not the solitude that can soothe or restore, but a profound isolation that echoed back every thought, every fear, every accusation. I felt imprisoned, locked behind the iron bars of a cell I had unknowingly forged myself, each belief another rivet, each doubt another weld sealing me inside. Yet what I could not understand then was this: depression and suicidal ideation were the true jailers. Not passive states of sadness, but cunning, persuasive wardens who knew exactly how to keep me contained. They wore the masks of logic and certainty.

They spoke with confidence. They held the keys behind their backs like tricksters, eyes glinting with a sinister amusement, delighted by how thoroughly they had convinced me of my own captivity. They leaned in close, their whispers slick and serpentine, cold against the fragile places of my mind. "*Keys? What keys?*" they hissed. "*There are no keys. This door is sealed. Rusted shut. Beyond repair.*" And then the final cut, delivered softly, almost kindly: "*And even if there were keys, they are not yours. They belong to others. You will never reach them.*" The lies were elegant. Complete. They explained everything. They left no loose ends, no room for question, no crack where doubt might slip in and loosen their grip. And I believed them.

I swallowed every lie whole. I let them become doctrine, truth, law. I mistook their certainty for wisdom, their cruelty for realism. I stopped searching the walls for openings. I stopped testing the bars. I sat down inside my imagined cell and accepted the sentence as permanent. The fog thickened. The jailers smiled. And I learned, with devastating efficiency, how easily a wounded mind can be convinced that captivity is inevitable, that freedom is a myth told to other people, in other lives. I did not yet know that the keys were never missing. I did not yet know that the bars were not locked. I did not yet know that the voices insisting otherwise were never my own. All I knew was the weight of belief. And belief, when poisoned, can be the strongest prison of all.

My first marriage felt like a hollowed-out structure, a façade still standing while everything that once made it a home had been stripped away. From the outside it appeared intact, walls upright, roof in place, but inside it echoed with absence. Every word spoken there fell flat, every gesture rang hollow, as though love had evacuated long before I realized I was alone inside it. I lived among ruins that pretended to be shelter, rehearsing normalcy in a space that could no longer hold warmth or truth. My motherhood, too, felt distant, as if I were watching myself through frosted glass. I could see the outlines of the moments that should have defined me, the tenderness, the presence, the devotion, but I could not reach them.

My hands pressed against the barrier, longing to touch, to feel, to be fully there, yet everything remained muted and blurred. I was present without arrival, loving without access, a witness to my own life rather than a participant in it. And my self-worth had evaporated entirely, leaving behind only the faint ghost of the woman I used to be. Not a memory sharp enough to grieve, but a pale outline that haunted me with what had been lost. I had become a shell, not quite living, not fully dead, a shadow stretched thin across the landscape of my own life. I moved, I spoke, I functioned, but there was no gravity to me anymore, no sense of being anchored in myself.

The pain seeped into everything. It saturated my bones, lodged itself in my thoughts, threaded through my breath. There was no clean edge to it, no place where it ended and something else began. Suffering became the air I inhaled, despair the rhythm of my pulse. It beat through me steadily, predictably, marking time in misery. I woke with it. I carried it. I lay down with it. It became so familiar I no longer questioned its presence. I was desolate. I was miserable. I was alone. Not because no one existed around me, not because the world was empty, but because the darkness had convinced me I did not deserve to be reached. It taught me to mistake isolation for truth, absence for punishment. It whispered that connection was for other people, that care was conditional, that my need was evidence of my failure.

And so I withdrew further, shrinking into myself, becoming quieter, smaller, easier to overlook. I believed I was protecting others from the burden of me, when in truth, I was obeying the darkness that wanted me unseen. I did not yet understand that this belief was not humility, but harm. Not truth, but indoctrination. I only knew that I existed at the edges of my own life, a woman still breathing, still moving, still here, yet profoundly convinced that she did not belong anywhere at all. The days blurred into one another, bleeding together like watercolor left out in the rain, their edges dissolving until time itself lost definition.

Morning carried no promise. Night offered no rest. Each day arrived already exhausted, indistinguishable from the one before it, heavy and saturated with the same muted sorrow. Pain became the ink that wrote every hour, staining moments before I could shape them. Despair became the metronome measuring each breath, steady and merciless, ticking out a rhythm I did not choose yet could not escape. Some days, the bruises blooming across my skin spoke the loudest. Not the blatant, undeniable brutality of a raised hand or a clenched fist, but the cunning cruelty, the insidious violence disguised behind masks he crafted with surgical precision.

Masks of concern. Masks of charm. Masks of righteousness. He knew exactly where to strike without leaving marks that could be named. Exactly how to wound without witnesses. Exactly how to fracture me in ways that would make my silence feel like consent. These bruises were not always purple or blue. Many lived beneath the surface, flowering in places no mirror could show. They settled into my posture, my hesitation, the way my voice learned to soften before I spoke. They taught me to doubt my memory, to question my instincts, to mistrust my own pain. Each unseen blow rewrote my reality, taught me new rules for survival, and convinced me that endurance was the same thing as love.

I carried those marks quietly. I learned how to hide them beneath long sleeves and practiced smiles, beneath explanations that sounded reasonable enough to end conversations before they began. I learned how to make myself smaller so the damage would have less room to land. How to disappear while remaining present. How to bleed inward and call it composure. And so the days continued to dissolve, one into the next, a continuous wash of sorrow and survival. Time did not move forward so much as it pressed down, flattening everything beneath it. I lived inside that compression, bruised in ways that left no evidence except the steady erosion of who I was. And with each passing hour, the darkness learned something new about me, how to deepen its hold, how to convince me that this, too, was just another thing I deserved to endure.

Bruises were birthed beneath a veil that pretended intimacy, a counterfeit closeness that borrowed the language of desire while hollowing it of consent and care. Not the safe, delicious kind I would one day rediscover with my second husband, the kind woven from trust, tenderness, laughing hands, and the playful edges of chosen sensation. No. These marks came from something else entirely. From force masquerading as passion. From a violation dressed up as affection. From a theater of closeness where my body was present, but my will was not. What was left behind was not pleasure but damage. Not connection but rupture. My skin became a map of harm, marked in dark constellations that were cruelly renamed "love tattoos," as if renaming could absolve what had been done.

This was not eroticism. This was erasure. An undoing of self, deliberate and systematic. My body was used as a surface on which power wrote its message, again and again, until I no longer trusted my own edges. Humiliation wrapped itself around my throat long before any truth could escape. It tightened silently, teaching me which words were too dangerous to speak, which memories were safer buried. Shame arrived early and stayed late, sealing my lips before sound could form, convincing me that silence was survival. I learned to swallow pain whole, to make a home for it inside me where no one else could see. The body, however, does not forget what the mouth cannot say. It keeps record in muscle and nerve, in flinches and fatigue, in the way breath shortens when memory passes too close.

Long after language failed me, my body continued to speak in aches and scars, in a vigilance that never slept. It carried the truth faithfully, even when I could not yet bear to name it. And so the bruises were not only on my skin. They lived deeper, etched into the places where trust should have grown, where safety should have settled. They were lessons learned too early and too painfully about what happens when intimacy is stripped of consent, when love is replaced with control. Lessons that would take years to unlearn. Years to soften. Years to reclaim my body as my own, not as a battleground, but as a home.

The Geography of Concealment

And the injuries, oh, how neatly they hid behind the convenient alibi of martial arts accidents. A ready-made story, already rehearsed, already believable. Blows were not random. They were curated. Crafted with a chilling precision, like a perverse art form masquerading as chance. He knew exactly where to strike, where pain could be plausibly denied, where guilt would do the rest of the silencing for him. A bruise blamed on a kick. A welt folded beneath clothing. A limp dismissed as clumsiness. The narrative always arrived before the truth had a chance to breathe. He understood the geography of concealment.

He mapped my body not as a partner, but as a strategist. Places where marks would fade unseen. Places where questions would never linger. Places where my own explanations would grow wild and tangled, choking any seed of doubt before it could take root. I became fluent in those explanations, delivering them with practiced ease, my voice steady even as something inside me splintered with each retelling. Only much later, through the slow and agonizing unfolding of truth, did the pattern finally come into focus. What I once believed were isolated incidents revealed themselves as a system.

Every mark had a purpose. Every bruise carried intention. Every injury bore a quiet signature of dominion. This was not chaos. This was design. A methodical assertion of control written onto my skin with deliberate care. They were not accidents. They were messages. A language of power spoken without words, delivered in places where excuses were effortless, where exposure was unlikely, where the world would never think to look. My body became a ledger of his authority, a living document recording the cost of my silence. A map of violence etched into flesh, written in a script only my suffering could read.

And I read it every day. In the mirror. In the ache that lingered long after the marks faded. In the way my body learned to brace before my mind caught up. Long before I could name what was happening, my skin already knew. It had been keeping the record faithfully, waiting for the day I would finally learn how to read it without flinching. But he knew exactly where to wound me so I would stay silent. He learned the geography of my shame and navigated it with cruel precision, striking where truth would be swallowed whole before it ever reached my tongue. He understood which places inside me collapsed under scrutiny, which fears would rush forward to smother my voice. Silence was not accidental. It was engineered.

And on other days, it wasn't the ache beneath my skin that hurt most. It was the sting of invisible wounds. The emotional incisions were made so cleanly they left no blood, only pain. Whispered betrayals slipped into my ear like poison, unseen yet immediately effective. Invisible welts etched themselves into the softest places of my soul, tender and unprotected, stinging with every breath I took. These injuries had no color, no swelling, nothing a mirror could reveal. And yet they throbbed constantly, announcing themselves in flinches, in hesitation, in the way my spirit learned to brace.

The manipulation was relentless. The dismissal surgical. A quiet cruelty practiced daily, patiently, until it became indistinguishable from normal. He rewrote reality with small corrections, subtle enough to pass unnoticed, devastating enough to hollow me out. My memories became suspect. My feelings became exaggerations. My pain became an inconvenience. With each denial, something inside me cracked a little further, until I began to doubt not just my experiences, but my right to name them. These were the degradations that cut deeper than any blow. The ones that did not fade. The ones that lasted long after bruises healed and marks disappeared. They lodged themselves in belief, in identity, in the core understanding of who I thought I was allowed to be. My body healed faster than my sense of self ever could.

His words could bruise too, landing heavy and precise, leaving marks that spread inward rather than outward. His silence could break bones, crushing me under the weight of what was withheld. Silence became a weapon sharpened by absence, by refusal, by the unspoken message that I did not matter enough to be addressed. And so I learned that violence does not always raise its voice. Sometimes it whispers. Sometimes it withholds. Sometimes it smiles while dismantling you piece by piece. And the deepest wounds are often the ones no one else can see, the ones that teach you to disappear long before you ever think of leaving.

Each day became a testament not to resilience, a word too triumphant, too polished, too noble for the grit of what I lived, but to endurance. A raw, unromantic, bone-deep endurance that had no applause waiting for it. I endured not because I believed I could overcome, but because the alternative was unthinkable, and so I stayed. I endured him the way a body endures an illness left too long untreated, adapting to pain as baseline, learning to function around infection, mistaking survival for stability. I endured the marriage the way one endures a storm without shelter. Crouched. Exposed. Trembling beneath an open sky. Praying not for salvation, only for a pause. A lull. Something less violent than the moment before.

And yet knowing, with a dread that settled into my bones, that this storm would not truly pass. It would circle. It would return. It would learn my shape and break over me again. It felt like holding a squat beneath a crushing weight for decades. Thighs burning. Spine-shaking. Breath quivering on the edge of collapse. Muscles screaming with fatigue while the command to *hold* echoed relentlessly inside me. No release. No reprieve. Just the expectation that I remain upright under a load I never agreed to carry. My body trembled constantly, not from weakness, but from the impossible demand placed upon it. My spirit quivered beneath the pressure, stretched thin between collapse and compliance.

And yet, somehow, impossibly, I kept holding. Still standing in a war I never enlisted in. Still bracing against impact. Still absorbing blows meant to break me. There was no glory in this stance. No banner raised. No victory cry. Only the grim mechanics of not falling. Of staying vertical when everything inside me begged to lie down and disappear. It was a hollow victory. A survival stripped of celebration. A battle endured rather than won. I had not chosen this fight, had never wanted it, and yet here I was, still breathing, still upright, still bearing the weight. Not because I believed in triumph, but because endurance had become instinct. And instinct, like survival itself, does not ask permission. It simply keeps you standing long after the cost has eclipsed the meaning.

I survived not from bravery or courage, not from some heroic inner fire blazing defiantly against the dark, but from a strange, stubborn persistence. A quiet, accidental survival that flickered on even when I no longer wished to see the dawn. It was not hope that carried me. It was momentum. Inertia. The simple, baffling refusal of life to release me. Like a small, fragile weed forcing its way through cracked concrete, I kept pushing upward through the fractures of my life without knowing why, without believing anything good could ever bloom from the ruin, without trusting that sunlight would ever find me there. I lived, if living is what it can be called, suspended in a perpetual state of numbness.

Not living. Not dying. Just existing. Hovering in the thin, colorless space between presence and absence. Days passed through me without leaving an impression, and I passed through them the same way. A ghost within my own skin. A body moving through rooms while the soul lagged several steps behind, half faded, half gone. I became a hollow, fading echo of the once vibrant, hopeful woman I had been before the carefully hidden bruises. Before the silence learned my name. Before the slow, methodical erosion of everything I thought I was. That woman did not vanish all at once. She dissolved gradually, softened by ache, thinned by endurance, worn away by the constant demand to survive what should never have been survived.

She dissolved beneath the ache, beneath the daily negotiations with pain, beneath the relentless pressure to remain functional while breaking quietly inside. Her laughter dimmed first. Then her curiosity. Then her belief that the world might meet her with kindness. What remained was a quieter version, stripped down to essentials. Breath. Movement. Endurance. And yet, even as I drifted through my own life like a shadow cast too thin to be noticed, something persisted beneath the numbness. Not joy. Not faith. Just a pulse. A continuation. A refusal to completely disappear. I did not recognize it then as resilience. I did not honor it as strength. I resented it. I questioned it. I wished it would let me go. But it stayed.

And in staying, in that unwanted persistence, in that weedlike insistence on existing even in hostile ground, the conditions for something else were quietly forming. Not yet healing. Not yet awakening. But the possibility of return. The slow, imperceptible gathering of pieces. The faint suggestion that the woman who dissolved had not been erased entirely, only buried beneath layers of pain, waiting for a season gentle enough to begin again. Each morning arrived like a reckoning, a silent tribunal convened at the edge of consciousness, a battle between breath and oblivion. It was never as simple as waking up. It was a deliberate act. A desperate negotiation. A conscious, and sometimes I believe unconscious, decision to continue breathing, stitched deep into my survival instincts, where choice blurred into compulsion.

To open my eyes was to agree, however unwillingly, to endure another twenty-four hours of this torment, this hell on earth, sealed inside a body and a life that felt like a burning prison cell, walls radiating heat, air too thick to inhale without effort. Breath became labor. Staying became work. Each inhale was a small act of resistance I did not yet recognize as such. I did not rise with purpose or anticipation. I rose because something inside me pulled the lever again, flipped the switch, restarted the machinery of survival despite my protests. Morning did not feel like beginning. It felt like being sentenced again. Nights offered no refuge. I would lie in bed staring into the ceiling's blank, indifferent stare, its surface unmoving, unresponsive, a mirror of how trapped I felt.

I traced its cracks like constellations of my unraveling, mapping my fractures onto plaster and shadow, counting down seconds the way prisoners count footsteps in a corridor. Sleep became the only promised escape, the only place where the noise dimmed and my body loosened its grip on pain. Some nights, even that mercy was denied. Insomnia arrived like a jailer making rounds, keeping me awake, alert, trapped inside my thoughts and the ache that refused to soften. I lay there held hostage by memory, by fear, by the relentless replay of everything I could not outrun. No rest. No forgetting. No reprieve. Just hours stretched thin and sharp, pressing down until time itself felt like punishment.

Other nights, I was granted the grace of sleep, but it was never a rescue. It was a postponement. An unconscious truce. I would sink into it only to be pulled back again, waking to the same suffocating reality. The same cage. The same ache. The same man whose love was a weapon and whose presence was a storm, unpredictable, destructive, eroding me from the inside out. Morning and night blurred into one another, a loop with no exit. Wake. Endure. Collapse. Repeat. And still, impossibly, I continued. Not because I believed it would get better. Not because I could imagine another life. But because something inside me kept choosing breath over silence, again and again, even when breath felt like betrayal.

I did not yet call this survival. I did not see it as strength. It felt mechanical. Relentless. Cruel. But looking back now, I can see it for what it was. A body refusing erasure. An instinct older than despair insisting on continuation. A quiet, stubborn will keeping me tethered to the world long enough for the story, against all odds, to remain unfinished. Moments that should have been lifelines arrived like thin threads cast across a chasm. Small moments of potential joy. The laughter of my children rising like bells in another room. A ray of sunshine piercing the gloom. A sliver of morning light sneaking through the curtains. A tender breeze brushing my skin as if the world itself had reached out to remind me it was still there. These were the things that should have anchored me. Instead, they hurt.

They became painful reminders of what joy should feel like but no longer could. Those flashes of light did not lift me. They were immediately eclipsed by the crushing weight of my circumstances, swallowed almost as soon as they appeared. Reduced to fleeting glimpses of happiness that only served to amplify the surrounding darkness. They sharpened the contrast. They made the absence louder. They magnified the very smallness of me. My diminishing essence. My starving soul. I could see joy clearly enough to recognize it, but not closely enough to touch it. It hovered just beyond reach, a reminder of what had been lost rather than a promise of what might return.

And with every passing day, the truth became unavoidable. My needs were shrinking into invisibility. Not because they no longer existed, but because I had learned to erase them. To fold them inward. To starve them into silence. And in that shrinking came something devastating. The acceptance of my abuse. The normalization of betrayal. The quiet accommodation of harm. His betrayal. His abuse. His cheating. His gaslighting. His cruelty. His disdain disguised as devotion. His hate pretending to be love. Each act pressed me flatter, more compact, more compliant. All of it compressed me further and further, until I barely resembled a woman, let alone a self. I was reduced to function. To endurance. To a shape designed to carry weight without protest.

My edges softened. My boundaries dissolved. My voice learned to disappear before it could be heard. I took up less space not because I wished to, but because it felt safer to be small. Another sunrise. Another day to slip into the emotional squat, that endless, trembling pose of endurance. Thighs burning. Breath shallow. Muscles shaking beneath an invisible load. Bracing myself for the weight of his world upon my back. Another day not to live, but to endure once more. To hold. To bear. To survive without relief. And still, beneath the numbness, beneath the contraction, beneath the exhaustion that hollowed me out, something watched. Something recorded. Something endured the endurance itself. I did not yet know how to name it. I did not yet trust it. But it was there. Quiet. Observant. Waiting for the day when endurance would no longer be the measure of my worth, and survival would finally give way to something gentler. Something freer. Something that belonged to me.

Resistance Without Courage

And yet, threaded through that suffocating endurance, there were moments so brief they almost did not dare to exist. Fleeting, fragile instants that arrived without warning and vanished just as quietly, when something inside me stiffened its spine and whispered, *not yet*. A refusal that did not announce itself as courage. A resistance that rose not from hope, but from instinct. Older than logic. Older than despair. It flared and then trembled, like a match struck in a storm, fragile and furious, fighting the wind with everything it had. I clung to those instants the way a drowning body clings to driftwood. Not because it promised rescue. Not because it offered a way back to shore. But because it kept my mouth just above the water for one more breath.

One more moment. One more delay of the inevitable. I did not ask them to last. I did not expect them to save me. I only needed them to exist long enough to keep me here. I knew how delicate they were. How easily they could be extinguished by the next word, the next look, the next weight pressed into my ribs. A glance sharp enough to wound. A silence heavy enough to crush. A reminder of my place. They flickered at the mercy of everything around me, threatened constantly by the world I was forced to navigate. Still, they mattered. Even in their fragility. Even in their brevity. They were not joy. Not freedom. Not even relief. They did not soften my circumstances or lift the weight from my chest. They were something quieter.

Something humbler. Seeds buried deep beneath the wreckage, pressed into soil made heavy by despair and neglect. Seeds that did not bloom because conditions were kind, but because they were stubborn. Because life, in its most stripped-down form, insists on pressing forward even in hostile ground. Something older than fear stirred there. Dormant. Patient. Lodged beneath layers of silence and surrender. A stubborn ember embedded in the marrow of me, refusing to consent to complete erasure. Even as everything else was shrinking, collapsing, yielding to gravity, this small defiant heat remained. Diminished. Hidden. Starving for air. Yet unmistakably alive.

It did not ask to be noticed. It did not demand nurturing. It simply endured, holding its place in the dark, waiting for a season it could not yet imagine. Waiting for a crack wide enough to breathe through. Waiting for a moment gentle enough to allow it to glow brighter than survival alone. And beneath that relentless posture of endurance, after each sunrise that asked nothing of me but survival, the silence would arrive. It crept in once the effort of the day had been spent, once my body had done what it was required to do. More often than not, it was the worst of it. Not a gentle quiet. Not a soft place to land. But a vast, echoing absence that pressed in from all sides, expansive and merciless, leaving nowhere to lean and nowhere to hide.

The isolation was profound. I felt like an alien inhabiting my own body, wearing my own skin as though it belonged to someone else. I moved through the world misaligned, out of phase, watching life unfold at a distance I could not cross. Sounds reached me, but meaning did not. Touch registered, but comfort did not. I was disconnected from myself and from a world that continued on without noticing my disappearance from within it. I existed, but I did not belong. The absence of genuine connection, of true empathy, only amplified the roar of my loneliness. It was not the quiet of peace, but the quiet of abandonment. A silence so loud it bruised. A stillness that screamed of isolation, of the utter lack of support, of the suffocating absence of any helping hand reaching toward me.

No one knocking. No one calling my name. No one asking the questions that might have opened a door. That silence wrapped itself around me, thick and unyielding, filling every corner of my inner world. It echoed against the walls of my thoughts until even my own voice sounded foreign. I learned how loud emptiness can be when it has nothing to interrupt it. How devastating it feels to be unseen, not because you are invisible, but because no one is looking. In that stillness, I became a prisoner not only of my mind, trapped within the narrow, airless corridors of despair, but also a prisoner of my circumstances. Held captive by a reality that felt sealed shut, bolted from the outside, impervious to effort or will. There were no cracks large enough to squeeze through. No windows left unboarded. Just the slow, grinding certainty of confinement.

And yet, even there, even in that deafening quiet, something continued to listen. Something inside me remained awake, bearing witness to the silence rather than dissolving into it. I did not yet understand the significance of that awareness. I only knew that I was still here, breathing in the emptiness, enduring its weight, waiting without language for a sound that might one day answer back. Even those closest to me, my children, felt like distant figures glimpsed through thick, warped glass. I could see their shapes, their movements, their mouths forming words, but the sound reached me muffled, delayed, unreal. They were present, undeniably real, and yet unreachable in a life I no longer recognized as my own.

I loved them with a ferocity that lived somewhere deeper than despair, and still, I felt separated from them by an invisible barrier I did not know how to shatter. I stood on one side of myself, watching motherhood happen on the other, aching with a longing I could not translate into touch or presence. The trust I once held had been slowly eroded, grain by grain, like stone worn down by a relentless tide. Not broken in a single wave but diminished through repetition. Each betrayal, each dismissal, each moment of being unheard carried a little more of it away. In its place grew a deep, ingrained sense of distrust and fear, not only of others, but of closeness itself. Of vulnerability. Of the risk that comes with letting someone see you fully.

And in that erosion, I did not just lose faith in people. I began to lose faith in the ground beneath my own feet. I no longer trusted my instincts to hold me steady. I stood alone in the quiet, listening to the silence speak my name, calling it softly, insistently, and finding no answer in return. It felt as though I could step forward at any moment and fall through myself, swallowed by a hollowness that offered no bottom, no landing, no reassurance. And still, within that echoing silence, where distrust had taken root and fear had made a home in my chest, something refused to vanish entirely. Even in the deepest darkness, a flicker of something remained. A tiny spark, nearly extinguished, yet stubbornly clinging to life, like the last coal glowing beneath a bed of ash. So small it could easily be mistaken for an illusion. So fragile it seemed vulnerable to the slightest disturbance.

I barely dared to look at it for fear my noticing would snuff it out. And yet it persisted. Quiet. Unassuming. Unyielding. It was not hope as I had once known it. Not optimism. Not belief in a better future. It was simpler than that. Older. A fragment of something essential that had not learned how to die. A faint resistance lodged somewhere beneath thought and language. It pulsed weakly, patiently, reminding me not of what could be, but of what still was. This spark did not pull me upward. It did not lift me from the pit. It did not promise rescue. But it kept me from fully surrendering to the abyss that called so patiently below. It held me at the edge. Delayed the fall. Bought me one more breath. One more moment of staying. And sometimes, in the quiet between breaths, that was enough.

Or perhaps it was the thought of my children, a faint echo of maternal instinct rising through the static. A whisper, barely audible, threading its way through the noise. Not a heroic call, not a sudden surge of love strong enough to banish the dark, but a quiet sense of responsibility that tightened its grip just enough to stop the final, fatal plunge. Their faces did not always save me, but sometimes they slowed me. Sometimes they placed a hand on my back at the edge and said, without words, "*wait*". Or perhaps it was something far more primitive and unromantic. The stubborn refusal of my body to comply with the death wish of my mind. A biological imperative etched into muscle and marrow, ancient and unreasoning, rising up without consultation or consent.

Cells dividing. Lungs expanding. A heart continuing its labor despite my resentment. A system designed to preserve itself, indifferent to my despair, unwilling to be silenced. Whatever its source, it stood between me and oblivion. Not as salvation. Not as light. But as resistance. A small, unyielding insistence on staying. One breath more. One moment longer. A pause where an ending should have been. A hesitation that felt cruel and yet proved decisive. Whatever its source, that flicker of hope, that faint resistance, kept me tethered to life. Not gently. Not lovingly. But firmly enough to hold. I was bound to it like a reluctant prisoner, suspended in the brutal war between my will to die and the stubborn refusal of my body and, perhaps, a sliver of something else that would not consent to complete release.

Something without a name. Something without a promise. Something that did not argue for meaning, only for continuation. It was not a willing attachment. I did not cling with trust or faith. It was a thin, fraying rope, cutting into my hands as I hung there. Burning. Unforgiving. Neither falling nor climbing. Just held. Caught between the gravity of the abyss pulling steadily below and the quiet insistence of breath continuing despite me. Each inhale tightened the rope. Each exhale threatened to loosen it. I lived suspended in that tension, arms shaking, palms raw, mind exhausted by the effort of not letting go and not being able to pull myself up. It was agony without resolution. Survival without relief.

And yet, in that suspended place, something subtle was happening. I was still here. Still breathing. Still enduring the space between. The rope, however painful, however unwanted, was holding. And though I could not yet imagine a future beyond the edge, though I could not yet believe in rescue or ascent, the fact remained: I had not fallen. Not yet. And in that, *not yet*, fragile and begrudging as it was, the story continued to resist its ending. The journey to finding the strength to break free from that pit still remains. There was no sudden rescue. No hand reaching down to pull me out. No moment where the ground fell away and I rose, cleansed and whole.

I did not rise. I simply stayed. I stayed through days that felt endless and nights that felt punishing. I stayed without understanding why. I stayed without believing it would matter. I stayed because something in me, unnamed and uncelebrated, refused to loosen its grip. And yet, the fact that the flicker remained, that something endured when everything in me felt consumed by darkness, stands as a quiet testament to the enduring strength of the human spirit. Not the kind that roars or conquers or plants flags at the summit. Not the kind that turns pain into spectacle or survival into victory. But the kind that survives unseen. The kind that glows faintly beneath despair, shielded by ash and silence, unnoticed even by the one it inhabits.

It is a strength that does not announce itself. It does not feel brave. It feels tired. It feels thin. It feels like staying when leaving seems easier. Like breathing when breath feels like betrayal. Like choosing nothing at all except not to end. It waits patiently, not for certainty or courage, not for answers or guarantees, but for the smallest permission to keep living. Sometimes that permission is nothing more than another sunrise endured. Another breath taken despite resistance. Another moment suspended between falling and standing. And sometimes, that is enough. Enough to keep the story open. Enough to allow the flicker to remain. Enough to let time do what time does best, quietly, slowly, without fanfare.

I did not know then that staying was an act of profound defiance. I did not recognize that endurance itself could be a form of hope. But looking back now, I can see it clearly. The light did not save me. It did not lead me out. It simply refused to go out. And that refusal, however small, however fragile, was the beginning.

The Weight of Expectations: A 23-Year Battle with Suicidal Ideation

And so, standing in the quiet aftermath of survival, still tethered by that faint, unyielding flicker, I sit and reflect on the journey that has been my life. Not from a mountaintop. Not from a place of triumph. But from the stillness that comes after the storm has passed but left its wreckage behind. I stand among the remnants, breathing carefully, aware of how close I once came to disappearing entirely. The flicker remains beside me, not brighter yet, but steady enough to be trusted with reflection. I am reminded of the profound impact the fear of not being perfect had on my existence. The dread of weakness. The constant anxiety of being a disappointment that followed me like a shadow stitched to my heels, impossible to outrun.

It whispered in classrooms and kitchens, in relationships and mirrors. It told me that love was conditional, that safety depended on performance, that worth had to be earned and re-earned without rest. I learned early that mistakes were dangerous, that softness invited harm, that perfection was armor. For twenty-three long years, from the tender age of nine to the ripe age of thirty-two, I walked through the world carrying a soul that was slowly decaying, even as it remained miraculously masked from the prying eyes of those around me. The decay was quiet. Polite. It did not rot loudly. It thinned. It dimmed. It hollowed. And I became an expert at concealment. I learned how to smile with precision. How to modulate my voice. How to perform wholeness with such convincing grace that even I sometimes believed it.

All the while, I was unraveling inward, thread by invisible thread. Now, in this quieter season, I am reminded of the words that have become a mantra in my healing. Words so simple they once felt dangerous. *It's okay to not be perfect.* For years, I buckled beneath the weight of expectation, the crushing pressure to contort myself into the ideals and needs of others. I sanded down my own edges until there was almost nothing left that felt like me. I mistook self-erasure for love. Compliance for safety. Exhaustion for virtue. That burden was not symbolic. It was not abstract. It had weight. It lived in my shoulders, my chest, my breath. It pressed on me day after day until standing upright felt like defiance. It was heavy enough to almost cost me my life.

Heavy enough to convince me that disappearance was preferable to imperfection. Heavy enough to silence my needs and fracture my sense of self. And yet, I am still here. Not whole. Not finished. But here. Gathering the fragments with gentleness instead of urgency. Learning how to breathe without armor. Learning that softness does not equal danger. Learning that worth does not require proof. That imperfection is not a flaw to be corrected, but a truth to be honored. This is not the story of a woman who was saved at the last moment. It is the story of a woman who stayed. Who endured. Who learned, slowly and painfully, that survival itself could become the doorway. This is my story.

The Quiet Places Where Pain Learns to Whisper

This is my story, and it did not begin in the dramatic moments, but in the quiet ones. In the ordinary corners where pain learns how to whisper before it ever learns how to scream. The chipped paint on my nails mirrored the cracks in my facade, small imperfections I tried to ignore, each one a fracture I convinced myself no one could see. I studied my hands as if they might betray me, as if the smallest flaw would give me away. Even then, I understood that imperfection was dangerous. The flickering gaslight cast long, unsteady shadows across my bedroom wall, their restless dance echoing the frantic rhythm of my own heart. The light wavered, never steady, never sure, and the shadows stretched and shrank as though alive, as if the room itself knew what I was trying so desperately to hide.

I lay there listening to my pulse, counting breaths, learning the early language of anxiety before I had words for it. Even the walls seemed to watch me, witnesses to a fear I did not yet know how to name. I remember the first time I felt the darkness creeping in. I was just nine years old, standing at the edge of a world that felt impossibly bright, impossibly alive, impossibly unforgiving. Laughter was loud. Expectations were louder. And somehow, without understanding how or why, I already felt separate from it all. I was a ghost inhabiting a child's body, present but unseen, performing childhood while something older and heavier settled into my chest. Already, the weight of the world pressed down on me, a suffocating blanket woven from expectations and unspoken resentments. It settled over my shoulders and tightened around my ribs, heavy enough to steal the air from my lungs.

I learned early how to hold my breath without realizing I was doing it. How to make myself small enough not to be noticed. How to disappear while standing in plain sight. The fear of not being enough, of being a disappointment, of being hated, swirled together into a toxic storm inside me. It had no clear source, no single voice, but it spoke fluently all the same. It told me I was too much and not enough all at once. That love was fragile. That belonging was conditional. That safety depended on how well I performed. So I learned to survive the only way I knew how. I began to people-please. To polish myself into something acceptable. To sand down every rough edge until I was smooth enough not to offend. I put on a mask of perfection and hid my truest self from the world, tucking her away where she could not be rejected. It was a coping mechanism.

A quiet strategy for survival. A child's attempt to outrun pain by becoming invisible beneath praise. I did not know then that this mask would grow heavier with time. That it would fuse to my skin. That it would one day make it difficult to tell where I ended and the performance began. I only knew that being perfect felt safer than being real. And so I chose perfection. Again and again. Not because I wanted to shine, but because I was terrified of what would happen if I was truly seen. That was the beginning. Not of despair, but of adaptation. Not of collapse, but of a long, silent negotiation with fear. A nine-year-old learning the art of survival in a world that felt too sharp, too loud, too demanding. A child who did not yet know she was laying the first bricks of a prison she would spend years trying to escape.

But as the years went by, the mask grew heavier. What had once felt like protection hardened into restraint, its edges digging into my skin until wearing it became an act of quiet violence. I carried it everywhere, fused to my face, pressed so tightly against me that removing it felt dangerous, unthinkable. What once shielded me began to suffocate me. Breath became shallow. Space narrowed. The performance demanded more and more, until there was no room left for the girl beneath it to move, to stretch, to speak. The weight of my secrets, of my truest feelings left unspoken, pressed down with a slow, relentless force, like a ceiling lowering inch by inch. There was no sudden collapse, no dramatic cave-in. Just a steady descent.

Each unvoiced truth shaved a fraction of space away. Each swallowed feeling tightened the air. I lived braced beneath that ceiling, neck craned, muscles taut, waiting for the moment it would finally crush me. Waiting, somehow, while pretending nothing was wrong. I felt as though I was living a lie. Not a deliberate deception, but a survival script I no longer remembered choosing. I was trapped in a never-ending cycle of self-doubt and self-loathing, rehearsing the same questions until they carved grooves into my mind. "*Am I enough? Did I say the right thing? Did I ruin it? Am I too much? Am I not enough at all?*" I performed a version of myself that felt increasingly hollow, increasingly uninhabited, like a house staged for strangers while its owner slept outside in the cold.

The suicidal ideation that had once arrived as a fleeting thought, a dark suggestion I could brush away, began to settle in. It unpacked its bags. It became a constant companion, a shadow that followed me from room to room, leaning close, whispering its familiar litany. *You are not good enough. You are unworthy of love. You are unworthy of life itself.* The voice did not shout. It did not need to. It spoke with the calm authority of something that believed it was telling the truth. It is hard to put into words the depth of that despair, because it was not a single emotion. It was a state of being. An atmosphere I breathed. A gravity that shaped every movement. Sadness implies fluctuation. This did not fluctuate. It endured. It colored everything with the same muted tone, drained joy before it could fully form, and bent neutral moments toward hopelessness. I did not feel lost so much as unmoored.

I was completely and utterly adrift in a vast, indifferent sea of uncertainty, with no shoreline in sight. No markers. No map. Just endless water in every direction, heaving and opaque. I could feel myself drowning slowly, quietly, while the world moved on without me. Laughter echoed from distant boats. Lives passed on the horizon. And I remained there, treading water with limbs grown heavy, stuck in a rut that felt both self-made and impossible to escape. I blamed myself for the pit even as I sank deeper into it. I told myself I should climb out, should try harder, should be better. And still, I could not find the ground beneath my feet. The mask pressed tighter. The ceiling lowered further. The sea stretched wider. And I kept performing, kept breathing, kept surviving, unaware that the very strategies that once saved me were now slowly teaching me how to disappear.

The hate I carried toward myself was no longer abstract. It was not a concept or a passing judgment. It was a palpable thing. A living, breathing presence that coiled around my heart and squeezed tight, tightening with every breath until even surviving felt like an act of defiance against my own mind. It pulsed with me. It learned my rhythms. It anticipated my thoughts before I could finish them. I did not merely think I was unworthy. I *felt* it in my chest, in my gut, in the way my body curled inward as though trying to protect itself from itself. After that tightening grip around my heart, after the slow, methodical suffocation of self-hate, the idea of a will to live, of fighting, felt almost laughable. A cruel joke whispered by people who had never lived inside my skin.

Words like *strength* and *resilience* sounded foreign, hollow, detached from the reality I inhabited. They belonged to a different language, spoken by those who had never had to argue with their own existence just to get through the day. Those were not the forces that kept me tethered to this life. It was not hope. It was not courage. It was not a belief in a brighter tomorrow. No. What held me here was something far more insidious. Far more self-destructive. The desperate, gnawing fear of imperfection. That fear sank its teeth into me quietly and refused to let go. It whispered that failure was unforgivable. That weakness was dangerous. That being flawed made me disposable. It told me that if I could not be perfect, I did not deserve to take up space at all.

So I stayed not because I wanted to live, but because I was terrified of doing life wrong even in death. Terrified of disappointing. Terrified of leaving a mess behind. Terrified of being judged, remembered, reduced to my fractures. Perfection became my final jailer. A warden that did not shout or strike, but watched patiently, ensuring I never fully collapsed, never fully rested, never fully escaped. It demanded that I keep going just enough to maintain the illusion. That I endure quietly. That I suffer neatly. That I remain intact for the comfort of others, even as I disintegrated within. And so I stayed. Not held by love, but by fear. Not anchored by meaning, but by the terror of being incomplete. I stayed suspended between self-erasure and self-preservation, bound not to life itself, but to the impossible standard that told me I was never allowed to fall apart.

I did not yet understand that this fear, too, was learned. That it was not the truth, but conditioning. Not identity, but injury. I only knew that it had wrapped itself around my survival, masquerading as discipline, masquerading as responsibility, masquerading as the very thing keeping me alive. And in that cruel irony, I continued breathing. Not because I wanted to live. But because I was too afraid of being imperfect to stop. That was when the whispers began. Soft at first, almost courteous in their intrusion, as if asking permission before entering my thoughts. Insidious suggestions of escape that did not shout or demand, but lingered. A low, persistent hum beneath everything, vibrating through my days and nights, growing louder with each passing year.

It was not a dramatic, operatic yearning for death. Not a romanticized longing to disappear. It was subtler than that. More dangerous. A quiet proposition that sounded almost reasonable in its calm persistence. It was not a grand philosophical reckoning with existence. There were no sweeping conclusions about life or meaning. There was only weariness. A profound, bone-deep exhaustion with the charade of living. With the endless performance of being okay. Of being acceptable. Of being enough. The kind of tired that sleep cannot touch. The kind that settles into joints and spirit alike, making even the smallest acts feel monumental. I was not longing for death so much as I was longing for rest. For an end to the relentless effort of holding myself together.

And yet, despite the overwhelming desire to escape, I could not bring myself to take that final step. I hovered at the edge of it, circled it endlessly, but never crossed. People often ask me now, gently, earnestly, "*What kept you going? What made you want to keep living?*" Their voices are kind. Their eyes hopeful. And my answer is always laced with guilt and shame, because it never sounds the way they expect it to. Was it a will to live that kept me tethered to this earth? A defiant, primal instinct to survive? To call it that would be a profound hypocrisy. The truth, ugly and unadorned, was far less heroic. It was fear. Not fear of death, but fear of being imperfect. Fear of weakness. Fear of failing to meet the impossibly high standards I had set for myself, standards shaped not by my own desires, but by the silent, suffocating expectations of others that I had absorbed and made my own.

I was terrified of doing even this wrong. Of leaving behind a mess. Of being remembered as broken. Of being judged, dissected, reduced to my fractures. I feared being seen as anything less than composed, less than controlled, less than acceptable. Even in the act of disappearing, I believed I had to be flawless. That belief alone kept me suspended, unable to move forward, unable to let go. And so I stayed. Not because I wanted to live. Not because life felt precious, hopeful, or kind. I stayed because the fear of imperfection was stronger than my desire to escape. Because even my dying felt subject to scrutiny. Because I could not bear the thought of failing one last time.

It is a hard truth to name. One that does not fit neatly into narratives of bravery or resilience. But it is mine. And in naming it now, without polish or apology, I can finally see it clearly. What once held me here as a prison was also a pause. A hesitation long enough for something else, something gentler, to begin forming beneath the fear. Long enough for the whispers to one day lose their authority, and for my own voice, quiet and tentative, to begin speaking back.

A Colder Terror

And beneath that fear of imperfection lived an even colder terror. A fear with sharper edges. The terror of disappointing those around me. The chilling dread that their grief would curdle into anger, that my absence would be read not as loss, but as betrayal. As though leaving would not be mourned but judged. As though my disappearance would be tallied as a moral failure, a final, unforgivable act of selfishness carved permanently beside my name. I carried the insidious belief that they needed me. That my life was a crucial cog in their carefully constructed machine. That if I were removed, everything would grind to a halt, collapse inward, scatter into irreparable chaos. I believed I was responsible for the stability of worlds that were never meant to rest on my shoulders. That my survival was a duty. An obligation. A debt I could never repay, only continue servicing with my own exhaustion.

The thought of leaving them shattered me more than the thought of staying broken. I imagined the fallout endlessly. The questions. The accusations. The whispered judgments. I believed my death would be dissected not with compassion, but with blame. That it would be reduced to a verdict. "*How could she? Why didn't she think of us? Wasn't she needed?*" And so my pain became secondary to their imagined disappointment. My suffering learned to stand quietly in line behind everyone else's needs. The guilt of abandoning those who "needed" me was overwhelming. It pressed down on my chest with a weight that made breathing itself feel like a negotiation.

Each inhale had to justify its existence. Each exhale felt borrowed. I lived with the sensation of being perpetually indebted, owing my life to expectations I never agreed to but felt powerless to refuse.

I became trapped in a vicious cycle of self-loathing and people-pleasing, spinning endlessly like a wheel with no off switch. The more I erased myself to keep others comfortable, the more invisible I felt. The more invisible I felt, the harder I worked to prove my worth. Round and round it went, tightening with each rotation, until I could no longer tell where obligation ended, and identity began. The shackles that bound me were invisible, forged not from iron but from belief. From fear. From guilt dressed up as responsibility. They did not clank or rattle. They whispered. They reasoned. They convinced me that staying was virtuous and leaving was unforgivable. That my suffering was acceptable so long as it preserved the illusion of harmony around me. And so I remained. Not free. Not whole. But tethered. Held in place by the terror of being the one who breaks everything by choosing herself. Unable to move forward. Unable to step back. Carrying the unbearable weight of being needed more than I was ever allowed to be cared for. I did not yet know that this, too, was a lie. That love does not require self-erasure. That responsibility should never demand a person's undoing. That staying alive out of guilt is not living at all, but another kind of captivity. I only knew the weight. And how heavy it was to keep carrying everyone else while quietly disappearing beneath the load. It was a twisted form of love, if love it can be called at all. A suffocating devotion to the approval of others.

A people-pleasing so deeply ingrained it fused with my lungs, became my very breath. I inhaled their expectations and exhaled my own erasure. With every breath cycle, something of me disappeared quietly, politely, without protest. I learned to survive on their needs the way a fire survives on oxygen, even as it burned me hollow from the inside out. I became a puppet dancing to a tune I did not choose, my movements choreographed by invisible strings pulled taut by their desires and their silences alike. The strings were not always forceful. Often, they were gentle, persuasive, almost loving in their pull. A look withheld. A sigh.

A pause heavy with disappointment. I learned to anticipate these cues instinctively, to move before the tug arrived, to contort myself into whatever shape would keep the peace. Autonomy dissolved into reflex. My desires were muted until they sounded like static. My voice drowned beneath the relentless cacophony of their demands, until I could no longer distinguish between what I wanted and what was required of me. The boundary between self and service blurred beyond recognition. Where they ended and I began became a question without an answer. I existed in the negative space around others, defined more by accommodation than by identity. And in that performance, in that endless obedience, I disappeared. Not dramatically. Not all at once. I vanished incrementally. A choice swallowed here. A feeling dismissed there.

A truth softened until it became unrecognizable. I remained upright. Functional. Smiling. Still standing. Still breathing. But no longer fully alive. I lived as an echo of myself, reverberating faintly through the expectations of others, never originating my own sound. Life passed through me rather than being lived by me. I was present in body but absent in essence, a silhouette moving through days that no longer belonged to me. And yet, even then, even in that near-total erasure, something watched. Something remembered. Something grieved the loss of who I had been and quietly resisted becoming nothing at all. I did not yet hear it. I did not yet trust it. But it was there, waiting beneath the performance, beneath the strings, beneath the breath that was never fully mine. Waiting for the moment when obedience would loosen its grip. When silence would fracture. When I would begin, trembling and unsure, to inhale myself back into existence.

That performance did not appear overnight. It was rehearsed over years, learned in fragments, perfected through repetition. Growing up, I was consumed by the belief that I had to be perfect, that any hint of weakness, any fracture in the façade, would be met with scorn and disappointment. Perfection was not an aspiration. It was a requirement. A condition for belonging. I learned early that love felt precarious, conditional, something that could be withdrawn the moment I failed to meet an unspoken standard. I lived inside a prison of my own making, though I did not recognize it as such at the time. Its walls were built from expectation and fear, brick by invisible brick, each one laid carefully through compliance and silence. The air inside grew thinner with every unspoken demand, every swallowed feeling, every truth I learned not to voice.

I adapted to the lack of oxygen by breathing shallowly, by shrinking my needs, by convincing myself that this constriction was normal. That this was simply what life felt like. The terror of not measuring up wrapped itself around my throat, tightening quietly, persistently, suffocating me long before I had language for what was happening. I did not know to call it anxiety, trauma, or fear. I only knew the sensation. The constant vigilance. The hyper-awareness of others' moods. The instinctive scan for danger in raised eyebrows and silences. I learned to anticipate disappointment before it arrived, to intercept it by becoming whatever was required of me. And so I became a master of people-pleasing. I donned masks and perfumes to disguise the stench of my own self-loathing, layering charm over shame, competence over fear. I learned how to smile on cue, how to soften my voice, how to mirror back what was wanted of me with uncanny precision.

Approval became my currency. Praise my oxygen. I learned how to disappear into it, how to dissolve my edges so smoothly that no one noticed the vanishing. I became a chameleon, blending seamlessly into my surroundings, changing colors to survive. I adjusted myself to rooms, to relationships, to expectations, adapting instinctively, reflexively. Whatever version of me was safest in that moment is the one I became. But adaptation came at a cost. With every shift, something essential was left behind. And while I survived on the outside, I was dying a slow, quiet death on the inside, unseen and unnamed. My people-pleasing was not born of genuine altruism or generosity. It was not selflessness. It was desperation. A self-preserving mechanism sharpened by fear. A child's strategy for safety in a world that felt unpredictable and unforgiving. I was not trying to be kind. I was trying to be spared. And that distinction matters.

Because what looked like devotion was actually erasure. What passed for love was often compliance. And what I mistook for goodness was, at its core, a frightened attempt to stay alive in a world where being myself did not yet feel safe. That was the beginning of the performance. And for many years, I did not know how to step off the stage. It was a shield, but a fragile one. A thin, trembling armor held together by effort and exhaustion, designed to fend off the relentless barrage of self-loathing that gnawed at my insides. I wore it daily, polishing it with compliance, reinforcing it with silence, praying it would not crack under scrutiny. I meticulously crafted a persona. The perfect daughter. The diligent student. The agreeable friend.

Each role rehearsed until it felt instinctive. I poured on the charm, the practiced smiles, the carefully chosen words, constructing a façade so seamless that even I sometimes mistook it for truth. And still, the anxiety never loosened its grip. It hovered just beneath the surface, a constant hum that vibrated through everything I did. The thought of being a disappointment. Of falling short. Of failing to meet the shifting standards of others. It followed me like a shadow that never detached, a low-grade panic that colored every interaction, every choice. I lived with the unshakable belief that my worth was conditional, provisional, always subject to review. That my place in the world was something I had to earn again and again, without rest.

Beneath those carefully applied layers of perfume and makeup, beneath the polished persona I had learned to wear so well, something else lay hidden. A rotting core. A stillness that was not peace but decay. Deathly and unmoving. It settled deep within me, thickening with each passing year, spreading quietly, efficiently. I felt it there in moments of silence, in the pause after laughter, in the hollow echo that followed praise. The contrast between who I appeared to be and what I felt inside grew sharper, more unbearable. The stench of my inner decay should have been overpowering. It should have given me away. And somehow, miraculously, my masks held. The image I had so carefully cultivated concealed the gaping chasm within, allowing me to move through the world undetected.

Applauded. Admired. Trusted. I learned that invisibility does not always look like absence. Sometimes it looks like success. Sometimes it looks like competence. Sometimes it looks like being everything everyone needs. I became a ghost among the living. Present in form but absent in essence. I occupied space without inhabiting it. I spoke without being heard. I existed without being known. Life passed around me, brushing close, never quite touching. And I let it. Because being unseen felt safer than risking discovery. Because exposure felt like annihilation. I did not yet understand that this ghosthood was not survival, but suspension. That I was not protected by the armor, only delayed.

That the decay beneath the mask was not proof of my failure, but evidence of how long I had been living without permission to be real. I only knew how to keep the facade intact. And how tired I was of holding it together. My life became a performance, every day another scene in a play I could not leave. There was no intermission. No curtain call. Just a relentless demand to stay in character. A carefully crafted façade masked a soul already decaying, and I tended to it with the discipline of someone terrified of being discovered. I perfected the smile, calibrated just warm enough. The sympathetic nod timed precisely. The reassuring words offered at the exact moment they were expected, never too much, never too little. I became fluent in the language of appearing well.

Perfumes and masks, metaphorical yet no less effective, cloaked the rot beneath, sealing it away from sight and scent. Layer upon layer, charm over despair, competence over collapse. Those around me saw a vibrant, engaging girl. They saw energy. Capability. Warmth. They saw none of the hollow shell beneath. None of the simmering resentment. None of the agonizing self-loathing. None of the constant, gnawing desire to simply cease to be. The performance was convincing. Too convincing. As the years went by, the pain and suffering did not erupt. They deepened. Quietly. Patiently. They spread through every corner of my existence like mold behind walls, invisible until the structure itself began to weaken.

I learned how to live around the damage, how to avoid pressing on the soft places, how to pretend the smell was not there. I told myself this was normal. That everyone felt this tired. This empty. This detached. I became a corpse animated by obligation. Moving because I had to. Speaking because silence would invite questions. Living a life that was not my own, existing solely to fulfil the expectations of others. Purpose was replaced by duty. Desire by compliance. I did not ask what I wanted because wanting felt dangerous. I only asked what was required. I was a puppet on strings, my movements dictated by unseen hands. Hands that did not need to pull hard because I had learned to anticipate the tension. I danced to a tune chosen for me, steps memorized long ago, never daring to question, never daring to resist. Resistance felt like risk. And risk felt like annihilation.

And still, despite the darkness that had consumed me, I continued to perform. I put on a brave face. I wore the mask of perfection that had become my trademark, even as it pressed tighter and tighter against a soul already struggling to breathe. The mask smiled while something inside me gasped. It held while I hollowed. It shone while I dimmed. No one saw the cost. No one heard the quiet cracking beneath the applause. And I told myself that if I could just hold it together a little longer, if I could just keep playing my part, maybe the ache would fade. Maybe the rot would stop spreading. Maybe this was all there was. I did not yet know that the performance itself was the wound.

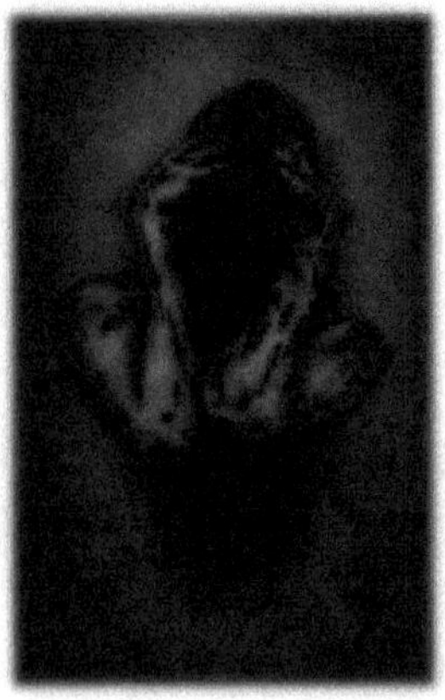

When Background Noise Becomes Truth

That mask of perfection did nothing to silence what lived beneath it. If anything, it gave it more room to grow. The self-hatred had evolved into a monster of its own creation, no longer a fleeting feeling or a passing doubt, but a vast, ravenous presence that dwarfed ordinary insecurity. It did not visit me. It inhabited me. It loomed over every thought, every interaction, every quiet pause, a crippling, all-encompassing darkness that threatened, day after day, to swallow me whole. It was not loud. Not theatrical. It did not announce itself with violence or spectacle. Its power lay in its constancy. A low, relentless hum vibrating beneath everything, like machinery that never shuts off. It seeped into my thoughts before I could stop it, shaped my choices before I realized I was making them, rewrote my sense of worth until I could no longer remember a version of myself untouched by its influence.

It was the background noise of my existence, so familiar I sometimes mistook it for truth. In the quiet moments, it whispered. Softly. Patiently. It questioned my right to take up space. It catalogued my perceived failures with meticulous care. It fed on my exhaustion, growing stronger each time I was too tired to argue back. And beneath those whispers ran a deeper current, a steady pull toward erasure, toward the idea that relief might only exist in absence, that peace might require my disappearance. And so I lived inside its shadow. I breathed alongside it. Carried it with me like a second spine, shaping my posture, my silence, my endurance. It walked with me through rooms full of people and sat beside me in moments of supposed rest. It was always there, unseen by everyone else, an intimate companion to my unraveling.

Meanwhile, the world continued to see only the illusion. The carefully maintained image of someone intact. Capable. Functional. Smiling. They saw the mask and mistook it for a face. They praised my strength without knowing the cost. They admired my composure without hearing the constant grind beneath it. No one saw the weight pressing down on my chest, the way each day felt like carrying something vast and invisible through ordinary hours. And I let them believe it. Because revealing the monster felt more dangerous than carrying it. Because I had learned that appearing whole was safer than being honest. Because the illusion, however fragile, kept me moving through the world unnoticed, a woman performing life convincingly enough to survive it, even as the darkness inside me continued its slow, methodical work.

I was still standing. Still breathing. Still performing. And beneath it all, the monster waited, humming steadily, patient in its hunger, convinced that eventually, I would grow too tired to keep pretending I was whole. This was not the ordinary insecurity of a child. Not the fleeting self-doubt that flickers and fades with reassurance or time. This was something far more devastating. An all-consuming hatred that reached far beyond low self-esteem and settled into my bones, embedding itself so deeply it felt structural, as though it were part of my anatomy. It was not a thought I had. It was a truth I lived inside. It was a visceral rejection of my very self. A repudiation so complete, so annihilating, that language strains under its weight.

No word ever felt large enough to hold it. No metaphor ever quite captured its density. It was not dislike. Not disappointment. Not even anger. It was the belief that my existence itself was a mistake. That I was fundamentally wrong at the core, beyond correction, beyond forgiveness. It coiled around my heart like a venomous serpent, tightening with deliberate patience. It did not rush. It did not need to. It constricted slowly, methodically, injecting its poison into every corner of my being. Thought by thought. Memory by memory. It taught my nervous system how to flinch from my own reflection. How to recoil from my own needs. How to distrust anything gentle that came too close. One by one, it strangled joy before it could bloom.

Dimmed hope before it could take shape. Crushed dreams before they ever learned how to breathe. Each possibility was intercepted at birth, dismissed as foolish, undeserved, dangerous. Desire became something to fear. Wanting felt like arrogance. Expecting kindness felt naïve. I learned to amputate my own longings before they could disappoint me. And there I remained. Still wearing the mask. Still moving through the world with practiced ease. Still smiling at the right moments, still fulfilling roles, still performing competence and warmth. From the outside, nothing appeared broken. But inside, the serpent fed. It grew stronger on silence. Stronger on compliance. Stronger on the quiet, corrosive belief that I was something unworthy of love, even from myself. It whispered that self-compassion was indulgence. That forgiveness was weakness.

That kindness toward myself was a lie I had not earned. And I listened. I internalized its voice until it sounded indistinguishable from my own. I carried it with me everywhere, an unseen companion tightening its grip whenever I dared to soften, whenever I came too close to believing I might deserve gentleness. This was not sadness. This was not melancholy. This was annihilation rehearsed daily, quietly, politely. And yet, even here, even in the presence of something so consuming, something else endured. Buried beneath the venom. Pressed beneath the coils. Not strong enough yet to fight. Not loud enough yet to challenge. But alive enough to feel the damage being done. Alive enough to remember, faintly, that hatred had a beginning. Alive enough to one day believe it could have an end.

BENEATH THAT TIGHTENING longing to vanish, the weight of expectation grew unbearable. It did not crash down all at once. It pressed. Slowly. Relentlessly. Like a hand that never lifted, only tightened, until every breath felt earned rather than given. The pressure manifested in the darkest ways, finding pathways through my thoughts, my body, my nights. Suicidal ideation did not arrive as a stranger. It settled in as a companion. Familiar. Persistent. A shadow that clung to me wherever I went, stretching beside me in daylight and curling closer in the quiet hours when the world finally looked away. It was always there. Not shouting. Not demanding. Simply present. A calm reminder of an exit I could not stop imagining. It did not chase me. It waited. Patient and certain. There was a morbid fascination to it, a twisted allure that shimmered faintly at the edges of my awareness, whispering promises of relief.

Of escape from the pain and suffering that had come to define my life so completely I could no longer remember who I was without them. It did not feel dramatic. It did not feel impulsive. It felt tempting in its stillness. In its quiet logic. In the way it offered silence where there had only ever been noise. I would find myself wondering, not with panic but with weary curiosity, what it might be like to simply disappear. To slip out of existence without spectacle or explanation. No final scene. No collapse. Just absence. Like stepping out of a room that had grown unbearably loud. I imagined setting the burden down. The crushing weight of expectation sliding from my shoulders at last. The constant pressure of other people's needs easing its grip on my spine. The endless vigilance dissolving. No more bracing. No more performing. No more holding myself together with white knuckles and shallow breaths.

In those moments, disappearing did not feel like dying. It felt like rest. Like finally lying down after a lifetime of standing guard. Like quiet after years of relentless demand. Like a permission I had never been given in life. And that was the most terrifying truth of all. That the idea of nonexistence felt kinder than the life I was living. That erasure seemed gentler than endurance. That the thought of not being here carried the softness I could not find anywhere else. Still, even as that shadow walked beside me, even as the temptation hummed its low, steady song, something held me back from stepping through the door I imagined so often. Not conviction. Not hope. But a pause. A hesitation. A thin, aching space between imagining rest and surrendering to it.

I did not yet know what that space was made of. I only knew it existed. And that it kept me here, breathing, one moment longer, even as rest continued to beckon from the dark. And now, looking back across that long, dim terrain, I am met with a tangle of emotions that refuse to be neatly separated. They rise together, braided and heavy. Sadness comes first, familiar in its weight, settling into my chest like an old ache that knows my name. Anger follows close behind, sharp and grieving, cutting through the years with the clarity of hindsight. And beneath them both, unexpectedly, there is a quiet hint of relief. Relief not because it happened, but because it has been survived. Relief because I am no longer walking there.

For twenty-three years, I moved through the Valley of the Shadow of Death, with suicidal ideation as my constant companion. It was never quite beside me, never quite behind me, but always close enough to feel its breath at my neck. A presence I learned to live with. To negotiate with. To carry like an invisible weight strapped to my back. It is a staggering truth, one I still struggle to fully hold, as though naming it aloud might finally give it mass, might make the years collapse into something I can feel all at once. From the tender age of nine to the ripe age of thirty-two, I lived beneath the suspended presence of death. Like a storm cloud that never broke, only hovered. It followed me through seasons and milestones, through laughter and loss, through moments that should have felt luminous but never quite did. The sky was always darkened, always threatening, even on days when the sun appeared to shine.

That cloud reminded me constantly that I was surviving, not living. That my days were being endured rather than inhabited. I moved through the world breathing, functioning, performing, checking boxes and fulfilling roles, while something essential remained untouched by life. I existed in a half-light, neither fully here nor fully gone, carrying that shadow as both threat and companion. It warned me of endings while offering them. It frightened me even as it tempted me. Only now, with distance and gentler eyes, am I beginning to understand how deeply it shaped me. How it bent my posture toward endurance. How it taught me to measure days by how much pain I could withstand rather than how much joy I could receive. How it narrowed my world until survival became the only horizon I could see.

And yet, standing here now, I can see the terrain more clearly. I can trace the path I walked without being swallowed by it. I can acknowledge the enormity of those years without letting them define the entirety of who I am. I was not weak for surviving that long. I was not broken for carrying that shadow. I was enduring something most people never see, never name, never understand. The storm cloud hovered, yes. But it did not consume me. I am still here. And for the first time, I am not merely breathing beneath the shadow. I am beginning to step out from under it.

A Cruel Equilibrium

From nine to thirty-two, that toxic cocktail of fear and people-pleasing both kept me alive and kept me imprisoned, suspending me in a purgatory of my own making. A cruel equilibrium. Survival bought at the price of freedom. It is almost impossible to comprehend the span of it now. Twenty-three years. The number feels abstract until I let it settle, until I feel its weight in my chest. Twenty-three years of an insidious battle raging within me, unseen, unnamed, relentless. A lifetime folded into endurance. Childhood, adolescence, adulthood compressed into the singular act of holding on. Twenty-three years of carefully constructed smiles, each one rehearsed, calibrated, placed like armor over an open wound. Smiles that deflected questions. Smiles that kept the peace. Smiles that hid the blood loss beneath.

Twenty-three years of silently plotting my escape, of carrying maps to oblivion tucked into the back pockets of my mind. Routes memorized. Exits imagined. Contingencies prepared. Not because I wanted drama, but because I wanted certainty. Control. A way out if the ceiling finally collapsed. Twenty-three years of wishing. Of planning. Of meticulously detailing the methods of my demise as though they were emergency protocols, survival strategies in reverse. As though death were not an ending, but a last-resort solution filed neatly away, waiting for the day endurance finally failed. I lived with one foot in the world and one foot poised at the edge, rehearsing disappearance while performing presence.

And all of it begs the same question now, aching and bitter in hindsight: for what? For whose approval? For the approval of people who, in the end, did not see me. Did not save me. Did not carry the weight I was breaking under. People who benefited from my silence, my compliance, my shrinking, without ever asking what it cost. I spent decades sacrificing myself at the altar of expectation, laying down my needs, my voice, my life in pieces, believing devotion would be noticed, rewarded, returned. Only to discover that the gods I served were never watching at all. There was no divine ledger keeping score of my suffering. No witness tallying my restraint. No savior waiting to descend because I had endured enough. The performance earned applause, perhaps, but not rescue. Approval, when it came, was fleeting. Conditional. Never enough to fill the chasm it demanded I create inside myself.

And that realization, painful as it is, is also clarifying. Because if I was willing to die for approval that never truly saw me, then perhaps, finally, I can begin to live for something else. Something quieter. Something truer. Something that does not require my disappearance as proof of worth. Twenty-three years were spent surviving for others. The years that follow, however many they may be, belong to me. I remember the details of those plans with a chilling clarity, as though they were etched into bone rather than stored in memory. They did not fade with time. They calcified. Each one was elaborate, carefully considered, obsessively refined, a testament to the meticulous nature of my self-destruction. I did not stumble toward the edge blindly or impulsively. I studied it. Measured it.

Circled it like an architect surveying a site. I mapped my exits with the same precision I used to construct the version of myself the world found acceptable. Control was the common thread. If I could not control the pain, I would at least control the ending. And each failure, each moment where I did not follow through, did not bring relief. It fed the obsession. Sharpened it. Failure did not weaken the desire. It honed it, refining the contours of what began to feel like an inevitable destination. Each aborted attempt, each hesitation, became data. Information to be filed away. Lessons learned. Adjustments made. The goal did not change. Only the method evolved. Oblivion became less abstract, more intimate, something I rehearsed quietly in the background of my days.

Over time, oblivion stopped appearing as a terrifying abyss. It softened. Its edges blurred. It reshaped itself into something almost merciful. A release. A kindness. A place where the noise would finally stop. Where effort would no longer be required. Where the performance could end without consequence. It became a constant companion, a dark, seductive whisper promising respite from the unrelenting torment of staying. Not a scream urging me forward, but a calm suggestion that rest was waiting if I ever grew tired enough to reach for it. From the cusp of childhood to the threshold of my thirties, I moved through the world like a walking corpse. My spirit had long since departed, slipping away quietly while no one was watching.

What remained was a body tasked with maintenance. Smiling. Functioning. Performing. Keeping the machinery running despite the absence of life within it. I ate. I spoke. I laughed on cue. I fulfilled roles with convincing precision, all while something essential lay dormant, untouched by living. I existed in a state of prolonged rehearsal for disappearance. Alive only in the most technical sense. My days were not inhabited; they were endured. My body became a vessel carrying obligations rather than a home housing desire. I was present everywhere and nowhere at once, a ghost passing convincingly as human. And yet, even in that state, even as oblivion whispered and the plans sharpened, I remained here.

Not because I chose life with conviction, but because something interrupted the final step every time. A pause. A fracture in certainty. A breath taken despite myself. I did not yet know what that interruption meant. I only knew it kept me suspended between ending and continuation. Looking back now, I can see how close I lived to the edge for so long. How normalized that proximity became. How survival masqueraded as living while the real work of staying alive happened invisibly, inside a woman everyone believed was intact. I was not reckless. I was not dramatic. I was exhausted. And still, against all logic, against all preparation, I remained.

The sheer weight of it, the suffocating pressure of sustaining this meticulously constructed deception, was almost unbearable. It pressed on me from every angle, a gravity I could never escape. Every smile cost me something. Every interaction drained reserves I no longer had. Each day demanded an expenditure of energy that my body and spirit could no longer afford, yet I paid it anyway, over and over, accruing a debt I did not know how to stop collecting. It was a life lived in perpetual fear. A constant state of self-imposed torture where rest was forbidden, and authenticity felt dangerous. To relax meant to risk exposure. To speak honestly meant to invite collapse. So I stayed vigilant, always braced, always performing, muscles tight even in moments that should have been safe. Sleep did not restore me. Silence did not soothe me.

Everything required effort, and effort was all I had left. And yet, even then, even standing so close to the edge that I could feel the drop beneath my feet, the fear of letting others down proved stronger than my desire to escape. The terror of their potential condemnation, imagined and real, outweighed my longing for rest. I feared their disappointment more than I feared my own disappearance. I feared the story they might tell about me more than the story I was silently bleeding out inside. So I stayed. Not because I wanted to live. But because I was too afraid of the judgment that might follow me into death. The irony of it is cruel in its clarity. I was so terrified of becoming a disappointment that I became one anyway.

Not to the world. Not to the roles I performed so well. But to myself. I abandoned the one person I was meant to protect. I hollowed myself out in service of an approval that never truly arrived. I became an imitation of a person, a careful replica crafted for survival. Forever chasing the phantom of approval. Running toward a horizon that receded no matter how fast I moved. The closer I thought I was getting, the further away it slipped, until movement itself became meaningless, exhausting, punishing. The fear of failure did not protect me. It paralyzed me. It locked me in place, convinced me that motion was dangerous and stillness was safer, even as stillness starved me. It kept me alive without allowing me to live. It demanded obedience while offering nothing in return.

I was a ghost in my own life. Present only in function. Breathing for others. Existing to serve needs that were not my own while my own quietly starved. And still, I remained. Haunted. Hollow. Enduring. Waiting, though I did not yet know it, for the moment when survival would no longer be enough. Looking back now, I can see how deeply rooted that fear of being hated truly was. It did not sprout overnight; it burrowed in slowly, sinking its roots into a core belief that I was not good enough, a conviction so ingrained it masqueraded as fact rather than feeling. It felt immutable, unquestionable, like gravity. I believed I was worthless. That my existence was a burden. That the world would be lighter, easier, better without me in it. These were not passing thoughts I entertained; they were truths I lived by, the quiet laws governing my inner world.

The thought that I would be better off dead did not arrive out of nowhere. It was taught. Reinforced. Etched into me again and again through the abuse and neglect inflicted by those who were meant to protect and care for me. Through words that cut. Through silences that erased. Through the absence of tenderness where it should have lived. They taught me, relentlessly and efficiently, that I was nothing. A disposable object. A plaything to be used, diminished, and discarded at will. My worth was conditional, temporary, and easily revoked. And I absorbed those lessons as children do, not as accusations to be questioned, but as truths to be obeyed. So I lived in a state of constant terror. Always braced for impact.

Always scanning the horizon for the next blow, the next withdrawal, the next proof that I was unwanted. My body learned vigilance before it learned rest. My nervous system tuned itself to danger, humming endlessly, unable to power down. I moved through days with my shoulders tight, my breath shallow, my heart racing toward catastrophes that had not yet arrived but always seemed inevitable. I walked through the world like a walking corpse. A shell animating a life that no longer felt like mine. I went through the motions with mechanical precision, completing tasks, fulfilling roles, answering questions, and smiling when required. Purpose drained away. Passion followed. What remained was function. Movement without meaning. Presence without inhabitation.

My soul felt dead. Not gone but buried. Entombed beneath layers of fear and compliance, beneath years of learned silence and swallowed truth. I could sense it somewhere deep inside me, faint and unreachable, as a voice muffled behind thick walls. I had no map to reach it. No language to call it back. No belief that revival was even possible. I did not yet know that souls do not die so easily. That which is buried can still breathe. That fear can mimic annihilation without actually achieving it. I only knew the distance. And the ache of being severed from myself.

A Soul Starved by Obedience

And then came that fateful night, the moment when endurance finally fractured. Not exploded. Fractured. A quiet, catastrophic splitting that ran through me like a fault line, giving way after years of pressure. It was the culmination of decades of simmering resentment and silent swallowing, sealed by a final, shattering betrayal that landed not as shock, but as confirmation. The kind that steals your breath because it proves what your body has always known. In that instant, the carefully constructed edifice of my lies collapsed inward. Walls caved. Beams splintered. The architecture I had spent a lifetime reinforcing could no longer support the truth pressing against it. There was no dramatic rescue, no soft landing. Just rubble. Dust.

And the exposed rot of what I had worked so tirelessly to conceal. There was no longer anywhere to hide. No mask sturdy enough. No performance is convincing enough. The truth stood bare and unrelenting in the open. The people I had trusted. The people I had bent myself into knots to please. The people I had broken my own spine for in the name of love, loyalty, and survival. They were not who I believed them to be. The realization landed with devastating force, heavy and final. The very people I had sacrificed myself for, whose approval I had chased with desperate devotion, had betrayed me. Manipulated me. Abused me. And most painfully of all, they had not cared. Not in the way I had believed. Not in the way that justifies self-erasure. Not in the way that honors sacrifice. My suffering had never been a concern. My loyalty had never been reciprocated. My existence had been convenient, not cherished. I saw it then, with brutal clarity. I had offered my life on their behalf, laid it down piece by piece, while they had willingly placed me on their selfish altars. I had mistaken compliance for love. Endurance for devotion. Silence for safety. I had been giving blood to people who never intended to stop the bleeding. The ones to whom I had dedicated my obedience. The ones whose judgment I had feared more than my own death. The ones whose approval I believed I needed in order to exist. They finally revealed themselves in the harsh, unflattering light of truth. They were betrayers. They were abusers. They were indifferent to my suffering. And in that revelation, something irrevocable broke open inside me. Not gently. Not cleanly. It split me wide, leaving me face to face with the unbearable cost of a life spent pleasing those who never intended to protect me. A life bartered away for approval that was never coming. A soul starved in service of people who fed on my silence. The pain of that moment was unlike anything I had known. It was not just grief. It was reckoning. It was the collapse of an entire belief system. The death of the story I had told myself to survive. The end of the lie that obedience could ever make me safe. And standing there, amid the wreckage of everything I thought I knew, I was forced to confront a truth more terrifying than betrayal itself: I had not been saved by my endurance. I had been consumed by it. And now, for the first time, there was no illusion left to hold me together.

They had used me for their own gain and discarded me like trash the moment I was no longer useful to them. That realization did not arrive gently. It struck with the force of a physical blow, sudden and devastating, knocking the breath from my lungs, folding me inward on myself. In that instant, the fragile illusion I had spent years desperately propping up shattered completely. There was no soft unraveling. No gradual dawning. Just impact. Collapse. The brutal understanding that I had been expendable all along. Their lack of empathy, their cold indifference to my suffering, cut deeper than any cruelty I had known. Deeper than rage. Deeper than violence. Because it stripped away the final lie that had kept me standing. The belief that my sacrifice mattered. That my endurance was seen. That my pain had meaning to someone beyond myself. When that belief died, it took my balance with it. Their cruelty, their blatant disregard, tore through the last remaining threads of my people-pleasing façade. The mask cracked at last, splitting down the middle under the strain of truth. I could no longer hold it in place. The carefully constructed structure I had lived inside for decades collapsed around me, walls falling inward, ceiling caving, leaving me exposed in the wreckage of everything I had been pretending not to know. And the truth spilled out unchecked. It came as a torrent. Bitter tears. Soul-wrenching rage. Grief so raw it felt volcanic. Years of swallowed words surged upward at once, demanding air, demanding voice. I sobbed with a ferocity that startled even me, as if my body had been waiting its entire life for permission to finally break open.

There was no elegance in it. No restraint. Just release. Messy. Violent. Necessary. It was a dark night, one etched permanently into my memory. A night that split my life cleanly into before and after. Nothing on the other side of it would ever be the same. I felt as though I had been punched in the gut, as though all the air had been sucked out of me, leaving me hollow and reeling. My body shook. My chest burned. My heart thrashed against the truth it could no longer deny. I stood there stripped of illusion, stripped of protection, stripped of the identity I had used to survive. What remained was unbearable and undeniable all at once. The pain was immense, but so was the clarity. For the first time, the suffering had a face. A cause. A name. And though I did not yet know it, though it felt like annihilation in that moment, this collapse was not the end. It was the sound of a prison finally breaking open.

And in that moment, everything changed. Not gradually. Not gently. Something inside me snapped with a clean, audible finality, like a cord pulled too tight for too long, finally giving way. The fear that had propelled me forward for decades, that had dictated every choice, every silence, every act of self-erasure, evaporated without ceremony. It did not argue. It did not linger. It simply vanished, leaving behind a chilling emptiness in its wake, a stillness so sudden it felt unreal. The illusion shattered completely. And with it, the people-pleasing reflex, the very lifeblood of my self-imposed prison, simply stopped. No effort. No decision. No negotiation. It was as though a switch had been flipped deep inside me, cutting power to a system that had run relentlessly for most of my life. The constant scanning. The automatic compliance. The instinct to contort myself into what was needed. Gone. And with that rupture came a realization as stark as it was unsettling. Their approval was worthless. Their acceptance was irrelevant. It slipped from its throne and landed at my feet, stripped of authority, stripped of meaning. What had once loomed over me as a god revealed itself as hollow, brittle, absurdly small. Their hatred, their indifference, no longer held dominion over me. It could no longer command my body, my breath, my survival. The chains I had mistaken for responsibility fell away, clattering uselessly to the ground. Their needs ceased to be my burden to carry. Their expectations dissolved into noise. The opinions that had once come down on my soul like a hammer now lay shattered at my feet, broken tools with no weight left in them. They could not shape me anymore. They could not move me. They could not hurt me in the ways they once had. I saw it clearly then, with a clarity that was almost brutal in its simplicity. Their opinions meant nothing. Their approval meant nothing. Their supposed need for me meant absolutely nothing.

What stunned me most was not the loss of fear, but the space it left behind. An unfamiliar quiet. A vast, uncharted interior where obligation had once lived. For the first time, my thoughts were my own. My breath belonged to me. My body stood without bracing for impact. I did not feel joy yet. I did not feel hope. What I felt was freedom in its rawest form, unsoftened and almost frightening. The kind that arrives before direction. Before meaning. Before comfort. The kind that says, "*You are no longer bound*," and leaves you standing alone with the terrifying, miraculous question of what comes next. The prison door had not been unlocked. It had disintegrated. And for the first time in my life, I was not moving forward out of fear. I was standing still, unafraid of their judgment, unheld by their expectations, face to face with myself. Unmasked. Unobligated. Ready. It was a liberation, horrifying and exhilarating all at once. A freedom that did not arrive softly or with reassurance but tore through me like a storm ripping the roof from a long-abandoned house. The walls still stood, but the sky was suddenly everywhere. There was no shelter left, no illusion to hide beneath. Just exposure. Wind. Raw air burning my lungs. The desire to die did not vanish in that moment. It changed its shape. It was no longer born of fear or shame, no longer whispered by self-loathing or fueled by the belief that I was unworthy of breath. It burned instead with anger. With a righteous, volcanic fury at the injustice of a life spent in service to those who never deserved my sacrifice. It was grief transmuted into fire. A defiant rejection of the years I had surrendered piece by piece, bone by bone, smile by smile.

This was not despair pleading for rest. This was rage demanding reckoning. And in that blaze, a chilling resolve took hold. If anyone was going to sacrifice me, it would be me. Not them. Not ever again. The thought landed with terrifying clarity. If I died tonight, no one would ever get the chance to hurt me again. No one would use me. No one would manipulate my loyalty or feast on my silence. No one would betray what I had left. In death, I imagined a final sovereignty. A sealed door. A boundary no one could cross. It was twisted. It was terrible. And in that moment, it felt powerful. I stood alone in the wreckage of everything I had believed, gripping that thought like a weapon, like armor, like a last shred of agency torn from the jaws of abuse. Freed from their hands at last, even as I stood dangerously close to erasing myself entirely. The illusion of control gleamed sharply in the dark, seductive and lethal, offering certainty where life had only ever offered violation. I was no longer begging to disappear. I was claiming the right to choose. And that distinction matters, even now, even in its danger. Because beneath that rage, beneath that final grasp for control, something else was happening. Something fragile and unfinished. The fire that threatened to consume me was also burning away the last lies. The last false loyalties. The last obligations that had never belonged to me. I did not yet know how to live for myself. But for the first time, I was no longer willing to die for them. And that crack, that single refusal, that moment of turning the blade inward, it was the edge of something else entirely.

And then, suddenly, something shifted. Not with fanfare or revelation, but with the quiet inevitability of a tide turning. The weight lifted. Not all at once, not cleanly, but enough that I noticed the absence. Enough that I could breathe without bracing. I no longer cared if I was a disappointment. Or a failure. Or even if they hated me. The terror that had once governed every movement loosened its grip, and in its place spread a strange, unfamiliar calm. I no longer cared if I was needed. Their judgment lost its gravity. What once pulled me into orbit now drifted, weightless. Their opinions slipped from my grasp and fell away, powerless, like rusted keys to doors that no longer existed. Their supposed need for me became irrelevant, an empty claim echoing in a hollow room, loud only because it had once been believed. Their cruelty was theirs to carry, not mine, and for the first time, I turned toward my own wreckage without apology, without explanation, without asking permission. They had shown me their true colors. They had abandoned me to my despair. And in that abandonment, something fierce and unexpected took root. It was not tenderness. Not forgiveness. Not peace. It was resolve. A hard-earned clarity that rose from the rubble and took its first unsteady breath. I found the strength to finally - let go. Not in bitterness, not in collapse, but in release. A loosening of fingers that had been clenched for decades. A refusal to keep holding what had already been destroying me. Years of carefully constructed self-deception began to unravel.

The endless charade of performing a role I never wanted, never chose, never benefited from, collapsed in on itself. The script dissolved. The lines I had memorized lost their meaning. The applause, imagined or real, fell silent. The stage went dark. The mask slipped from my hands. And there I stood, exposed and trembling, not yet healed, not yet whole, but no longer pretending. No longer bending. No longer willing to disappear for the comfort of others. For the first time, I was not orienting myself around their gaze. I was standing in my own truth, raw and unadorned, surrounded by the debris of a life I had outgrown. It was terrifying. It was lonely. It was real. And in that darkness, with nothing left to perform and no one left to please, something quieter than rage and stronger than fear began to stir. Not an answer. Not a destination. But a final concrete decision,

And so the story unraveled. The fairytale finally tore at its seams. Cinderella chose her prince, and it was time to end this ball, because the clock had struck twelve and the fantasy was over. The spell broke without apology. The chariot was a pumpkin. The horses were mice. The silk and shimmer of the gown fell away, collapsing into rags at my feet. It had always been that way. In my delusion, I had simply chosen to believe otherwise, clinging to illusion because reality had felt unbearable. I was no different from the king who believed he wore the most beautiful clothes, parading certainty through the streets while standing naked before the world. I, too, had believed in a story that required my blindness to survive. I had mistaken hope for truth. Obedience for love. Endurance for destiny. And the glass slipper? What *fucken* glass slipper. I was never given one. There was no fairy godmother waiting in the wings, no gentle magic humming in the margins of my life, no happily ever after scripted for my rescue. No prince arriving on a white horse to lift me from the ashes and tell me I was chosen, cherished, safe. That story was never mine. It never had been. It belonged to someone else. Someone luckier. Someone protected. No. My prince rode a black horse and wore shadows instead of armor. His name was death. And he did not need to arrive. He had always been there, waiting patiently in the background of my thoughts, just out of sight, never rushing, never forcing. He knew I would come to him eventually. He knew exhaustion would do the work. He stood there now, close enough to feel. Close enough to promise quiet. Close enough to offer an end to the ache, the striving, the constant performance. Ready to kiss me. Ready to seal the story in silence.

And I, so tired of believing in miracles that never came, so weary of hoping for rescue that never arrived, so exhausted from waiting for someone, *anyone*, to save me, was ready to kiss him back. Not out of romance. Not out of longing. But out of fatigue. Out of the bone-deep weariness of a woman who had danced too long at a ball that was never meant for her, wearing borrowed dreams that cut into her skin, waiting for magic that had no intention of showing up. The music had stopped. The lights had gone out. And there I stood, barefoot among the ashes, staring at the only figure who had never abandoned me, even as he waited to take everything I had left. What I did not yet know, what I could not yet see through the fog of exhaustion, was that this was not the end of the story. It was the moment just before the story changed its language entirely. For the first time in a long time, I was free. Not free from the pain, not yet free from the darkness, but free from the suffocating weight of their expectations. Free from the insidious tyranny of their judgment. Free from the relentless obligation to contort myself into something palatable, useful, acceptable. That freedom did not feel light or celebratory. It felt stark. Bare. Like standing alone on a cliff after the storm has passed, the ground stripped clean, the sky emptied of illusion. The darkness remained. Dense. Unavoidable. It did not lift its veil or soften its edges. But it was mine now. No longer a weapon wielded against me, no longer a cage reinforced by other people's needs. It belonged to me alone. And for the first time, I could face it without apology, without performance, without the constant fear of being seen and condemned. I could meet it on my own terms, in my own time, with my own trembling breath.

And so my lips met the lips of my prince on his black horse, dressed in shadows, and he took me in his embrace. Ah. Here I go again. I can feel it even now, that familiar pull, that rushing forward, that gravity toward what is still to come. The story leans ahead of me, impatient, eager to arrive at its most dramatic moments. But not yet. Not here. This is not the place to rush. This is the place to breathe. To notice. To stay. We will return to that night soon enough. To the darkness. To the brink. To the moment where everything balances on a single breath. For now, let us keep walking. Let us move slowly through the terrain that brought me here. Let us trace the path with care, honoring each step, each fracture, each fragile awakening. Because this journey was never about the kiss, or the cliff, or the shadowed horse waiting at the edge. It was about learning how to stand in the dark without disappearing. So come. Stay with me. Let us continue my journey.

Chapter: Eleven
The Paradox of Suicidal Ideation: A Personal Narrative

And now, standing at the edge of that unraveling fairytale, I am drawn back into the darkest corners of my mind, the places where suicidal ideation once took up residence and made itself at home. These are rooms I avoided for years, doors I kept tightly shut, corridors I learned to walk past without looking down. To turn toward them now still hurts. The ache has not vanished. It lingers as an old bruise pressed too hard. For a long time, I could barely bear to look at it directly, afraid that even remembering might pull me under again. Yet it is inseparable from my story. Woven into it. Breathed into it. This is my personal account of living beneath the crushing weight of expectation, of what suicidal ideation meant to me, of how it lived and breathed inside my days and nights, how it learned the rhythm of my life and matched itself to my pulse.

For me, suicidal ideation was never a single thought. It was not a sudden flash or a dramatic moment of despair. It was a constant, nagging presence in my ear. A soft, persistent murmur. Not loud enough to startle, not forceful enough to command, but always there. Like a breeze that never stopped moving through me, carrying the wish to die on one current, while on another, impossibly, carrying a desperate plea to stay alive for others. It whispered of rest and release. And in the same breath, of duty and guilt. It promised silence, while reminding me of responsibility. It held my hand with one touch and tightened a leash with the other. It was a paradox I lived inside every day, a life split cleanly down the middle. One half leaning toward oblivion, exhausted beyond measure. The other half clinging to obligation, terrified of the damage my absence might cause.

I learned to inhabit that contradiction without ever understanding how. I woke up inside it. Walked through my days inside it. Fell asleep to its whispers and woke to their echo. I functioned, laughed, worked, mothered, and smiled, all while carrying a private argument that never reached resolution. A mind that longed for disappearance. A body that continued to breathe. A soul stretched thin between the two. It was not madness. It was survival under impossible conditions. And now, as I stand here, looking back without flinching away, I can finally name it without shame. I can trace its shape without being consumed by it. I can tell the truth of how it lived in me, not as a confession of weakness, but as testimony. Understanding this paradox is not about glorifying darkness. It is about illuminating it. And this, too, is part of my journey.

When I try to explain what it felt like, the images that come to mind are simple and cruel in their innocence: the wishing star, the birthday candle. Symbols meant for children. For hope. For magic. And yet, for me, they were hollow rituals, empty gestures performed out of habit rather than belief. The wishing star held no magic. It was just a distant burn in a sky that had never answered me. Blowing out birthday candles felt like a bitter joke, a pantomime of optimism enacted while knowing the outcome would never change. Each flame extinguished carried a wish, a plea whispered into the void, a breath released with quiet desperation. But the wish was never clean. Never singular. Never innocent. It was tangled and knotted, inseparably bound to the lives of others.

I wished to disappear, yes, but always with a rope tied back to responsibility. To guilt. To duty. To the imagined devastation my absence would cause. The desire to die was braided tightly with the compulsion to keep living for them. For everyone else. It was never a clean longing to end everything. It was fractured. Agonizing. Unresolved. A wish spoken through clenched teeth. A prayer that contradicted itself mid-sentence. I wanted rest. Silence. Relief from a world that felt determined to grind me down to nothing. I wanted to escape the prison of my own mind, the constant noise, the vigilance, the ache of being awake inside a life that felt hostile to my existence. Suicidal ideation was not drama. It was not impulse. It was coexistence.

A quiet war fought daily between disappearance and obligation. Between the yearning to stop and the terror of the damage stopping might cause. It was a star that never granted wishes. A candle that burned down anyway. And more painfully still, a ritual performed without flame at all. I was blowing out candles that were already extinguished, making wishes over emptiness, pretending there was still light left to surrender. I stood there year after year, inhaling, exhaling, performing hope without believing in it, rehearsing endings without ever arriving at them. The smoke curled upward, carrying my unspoken wishes into nothingness, while life continued regardless, indifferent to the ceremony. That was the cruelty of it. Not that I wished to die. But that I wished so carefully, so responsibly, so quietly, always leaving myself behind in the process. And still, somehow, I remained.

Suicidal ideation was never a grand or dramatic gesture for me. It did not arrive in a blaze or a collapse. It seeped in. Quietly. Patiently. A gnawing, persistent whisper that made a home in the background of my days, shadowing every sunrise and every sunset, slipping into the narrow spaces between breaths. It was never urgent enough to shock me, never loud enough to demand immediate action. It was simply there. Constant. Familiar. Like weather I learned to dress myself for. It became part of the atmosphere I lived in, as ordinary and oppressive as humidity before a storm that never breaks. I carried it into every room, every conversation, every moment of supposed normalcy. It sat beside me while I laughed, followed me while I worked, lay down with me at night and greeted me again in the morning. A companion so persistent it blurred into identity, until I no longer knew where I ended and it began.

At its core was the steady ache of contradiction. The wish to die was braided tightly with an overwhelming sense of responsibility to keep living for the sake of others. I existed inside that loop of opposites, trapped in a cycle that never resolved. Life pulling one way. Death tugging the other. Hope and despair were bleeding into each other until they were indistinguishable, until both lost their meaning entirely. It was the impossible wish made flesh. To die yet simultaneously live for others. A paradox wrapped in a suffocating blanket of despair. It felt like a noose tightening incrementally around my neck, day by day, turn by turn, drawn closer with cruel patience. Not enough to snap. Not enough to end it. Just enough to constrict breath. To steal air from my lungs. To press panic into my chest until breathing itself became deliberate, measured, conscious.

The rope never released. It only tightened, then paused, then tightened again, suspending me in the agony of almost. Almost gone. Almost free. Almost finished. And the weight of it grew heavier with each passing day. It settled into my body, into my bones, until it felt structural, as though my skeleton had been rebuilt around it. Existing became an endurance test. Not measured in hope or desire or joy, but in stamina. In how long I could hold myself upright beneath the pressure. In how many days I could survive without finally giving in. I did not ask whether life was worth living.

I asked how long I could keep carrying it. Each day was not chosen. It was tolerated. And still, I remained suspended there, between staying and disappearing, breathing under the tightening rope, enduring a war that never declared a victor, only demanded that I keep standing inside it. That was my reality. Quiet. Persistent.

Exhausting. And for a long time, it was all I knew.

Under that tightening pressure, existing itself took on a spectral quality. I drifted through the world like a ghost inhabiting a body that no longer felt like mine, present in outline, absent in essence. I spoke, moved, and responded. I breathed. And yet inside, everything was hollowed out. I was alive in the most technical sense, undeniably breathing, undeniably here, while feeling utterly dead at the core. Life continued to happen around me, but it no longer passed through me. My days became a tapestry woven with threads of worthlessness, each strand reinforcing the same cruel narrative. That I was a burden. A complication. A problem waiting for resolution. Preferably a quiet one. Preferably, one that required nothing from anyone else. The idea of my erasure settled into my thinking not as violence, but as efficiency. As mercy. As relief for a world I believed would function more smoothly without the weight of my existence dragging behind it.

And yet, stitched into that same tapestry, running stubbornly against the pattern, was a counterpoint I could not cut away. A low, relentless thrum of responsibility. An obligation to endure. To stay. It did not arrive as hope. It did not comfort me. It did not promise anything brighter ahead. It simply insisted. A quiet, unyielding pressure in the opposite direction. A tether looped around my ribs, pulling me back each time I leaned too far toward disappearance. I stayed for those who depended on my presence. For those who loved me despite, or perhaps because of, the darkness I carried. For the children whose lives were knotted irrevocably to mine. For the imagined devastation my absence would leave behind. So I remained suspended between disappearance and duty.

Haunted by the desire to vanish. Anchored by the ache of being needed. I lived as an echo of myself, a reverberation of who I once was, moving through a life that no longer felt like home. Each day I woke up inside that tension, carrying both the wish to leave and the demand to remain, neither one strong enough to win, both strong enough to keep me trapped in between. It was not living. It was not dying. It was lingering. And in that lingering, time stretched and warped. Years passed without being fully lived. Moments slipped by without landing. I became someone who survived out of obligation rather than desire, who stayed not because I wanted to, but because leaving felt forbidden. That was the purgatory I inhabited. A life half-lived. A self-half-present. Still here. Still breathing. Still waiting.

That is what it felt like. Alive and dead at the same time. Suspended in a liminal state that defied explanation and refused resolution. Not fully here, not fully gone. I existed in a purgatory of unrelenting weariness, beneath a constant, low-level hum of despair that vibrated through every cell of my body, like static trapped under my skin. It never shut off. It never softened. It simply endured, a background frequency to my existence. My life felt worthless. Meaningless. A burden. A problem begging to be solved. And yet, at the very same time, it felt like an inescapable responsibility. Something heavy and sacred I was obligated to carry, even as it crushed me beneath its weight. I believed my existence caused harm, and yet I believed my absence would cause even more. That contradiction became law. A twisted logic that made sense only in the depths of despair. A logic born not of hope, but of survival under siege.

It was not a philosophy. It was not a belief system. It was triage. Imagine standing knee-deep in quicksand. The ground beneath you slowly gives way, inch by inch, grain by grain, pulling you down with merciless patience. Every movement costs you. Every attempt to escape sinks you deeper. You learn quickly that thrashing is deadly. That panic accelerates the pull. So you freeze. You calculate. You ration breath. You expend every ounce of energy just to stay upright. Just to keep your mouth above the surface. Just to prevent yourself from being swallowed by the suffocating mud. Your legs burn. Your muscles tremble. The suction tightens around you, cold and relentless, dragging at you with every passing moment. The ground does not rage. It does not attack. It simply yields, silently, steadily, indifferent to your exhaustion.

That is what it felt like to live with suicidal ideation. Not a leap. Not a fall. But a slow sinking. A daily negotiation with gravity. A constant assessment of how much strength you have left, how little movement you can afford, how long you can keep yourself suspended before your body finally gives in. You do not dream of rescue anymore. You dream of stillness. Of rest. Of not having to fight the ground beneath your own feet. And yet, somehow, impossibly, I stayed standing. Knees shaking. Lungs burning. Jaw clenched against the scream rising in my throat. I learned how to exist inside the quicksand. How to survive without escaping. How to endure a life that was actively trying to pull me under. That was my normal. That was my everyday. And the most devastating part was not that I was sinking. It was that I became fluent in it. I fought, yes. I fought with everything I had left.

But the fight was never for me. Never for my own life. It was for them. It was always for them. I fought to meet the expectations pressed onto my shoulders, to remain the person they needed me to be, to fulfil the roles assigned to me without question or pause. My struggle was not toward healing or hope, but toward endurance. Toward compliance. Toward staying upright just long enough to not disappoint anyone, just long enough to avoid the unbearable weight of letting someone down. I fought with my chin lifted above the surface, lungs screaming, eyes fixed outward instead of inward. I fought to keep my head above the quicksand not because I wanted to stand there, but because sinking would inconvenience too many people. Because disappearing would fracture the image they had of me. Because collapse felt like failure, and failure was forbidden. So I held myself there, trembling, expending everything I had just to appear intact.

All the while, I maintained the facade. The carefully constructed illusion of normalcy. I smiled through clenched teeth, offered reassurance I did not feel, and performed stability I did not possess. My mouth formed the right words even as panic pressed against my ribs. My face learned how to lie convincingly while the ground beneath me gave way, inch by inch, breath by laboured breath. The quicksand did not rush. It claimed me patiently, methodically, swallowing parts of me I no longer had the strength to defend. It was a constant, draining effort. Relentless. Unforgiving. A labor without rest. Each day demanded more than the last, and I gave it anyway, drawing from reserves that no longer existed. I hollowed myself out from the inside, scraping away desire, rest, and will until there was nothing left to offer but function.

What remained was a body still standing. Still performing. Still meeting expectations. But emptied of self. Emptied of choice. Emptied of rest. I did not fight to live. I fought not to disappoint. And in that distinction lies the quiet tragedy of it all.

The Serpent Voice

Beneath that exhausting struggle to stay afloat, the internal cacophony never ceased. There was no silence. No reprieve. Just noise layered upon noise, a deafening, relentless reminder of the turmoil ravaging my mind. It was as if my skull had become an echo chamber for despair, every thought ricocheting back sharper than before. Two discordant voices lived inside me, brutal and unyielding, warring titans locked in an eternal struggle within the narrow confines of my own head. They screamed their contradictions day and night, colliding, overlapping, amplifying one another until there was no space left for rest. Each clash fed the fire. Each argument tightened the knot. I could not escape them because they *were* me, wearing my voice, borrowing my memories, twisting my fears into weapons. One voice slithered through me like a venomous serpent, cold and deliberate, a malevolent presence coiled tight around my thoughts.

It did not shout at first. It hissed. Familiar. Intimate. It knew exactly where to strike. It whispered its insidious suggestions with sickening ease, words that arrived already sharpened: "*Kill yourself! The world would be better off! You don't belong! You're worthless! Unlovable. Useless!*" It spoke with a confidence that made resistance feel pointless. As though it were stating facts, not cruelty. As though it were simply narrating an obvious truth I had somehow failed to accept. It wore certainty like a crown, and in its calm authority, it eroded my ability to argue back. This was not hysteria. It was persuasion. It was seductive in the most dangerous way. Not frantic. Not dramatic. But measured. Reasonable. It promised relief. Quiet. Rest. An end to the relentless effort of staying. It tempted me to surrender not out of panic, but out of exhaustion.

To finally set down the unbearable burden I believed I had become, both to myself and to everyone else. To stop being the problem. To remove the inconvenience of my existence. It framed erasure as kindness. Disappearance as mercy. Silence as love. And the longer I lived under its influence, the more familiar it became. The more it sounded like truth. Like inevitability. Like the only logical conclusion to a life I had been taught to see as excess weight. The serpent did not need to rush me. It knew time was on its side. It waited. It whispered. And it tightened its coils with patient precision, trusting that eventually, I would believe it knew me better than I knew myself.

Its words burned like acid, slow and merciless, eating through the fragile remnants of my self-esteem until nothing remained but corrosive doubt and raw self-loathing. It did not rush its work. It dissolved me patiently. Layer by layer. This voice was cold and calculating, stripped of empathy, untouched by mercy, fueled by the insidious murmurs of depression that had learned my name by heart. It knew my history. It knew my wounds. It knew exactly how to speak so that every sentence landed as truth. It painted a bleak, desolate landscape where my existence was an error. An anomaly. A mistake that required correction. In its telling, the world was a ledger and I was a deficit. A flaw in the equation. Something that did not fit and therefore should be removed. It made absence sound reasonable. Necessary. It made my erasure feel like an act of responsibility rather than violence.

That voice rose from the deepest chambers of my self-doubt, carrying with it an archive of cruelty. Every insult ever hurled at me. Every dismissal. Every moment I had been made to feel small, unwanted, expendable. It stitched them together into a single, unbroken narrative and pressed it back into me as proof. Proof that I had always been the problem. Proof that nothing would change. Proof that surrender was not weakness, but inevitability. It was relentless. It circled endlessly, returning to the same conclusion with mechanical certainty. No matter how the argument began, it always ended in the same place. The same suggestion. The same solution. It urged me toward the ultimate escape with quiet persistence, nudging rather than shoving, trusting that repetition would do what force could not. It told me the darkness had already won. That resistance was futile. That I was merely prolonging the inevitable.

And under its pressure, the world shrank. Possibility collapsed. The future narrowed to a single point, a single door glowing faintly in the distance, framed as relief. Framed as peace. Framed as the end of effort. The darkness that had swallowed me whole began to feel like home, familiar and enclosing, a place where I could finally stop fighting. That voice did not scream. It did not threaten. It waited, confident that eventually, I would grow tired enough to believe it. And then there was the other voice. The other voice was no kinder. No quieter. Though different in tone, it was equally relentless, equally persuasive, a tormentor cut from a different blade. It did not hiss. It shrieked. It tore through my mind with urgency and accusation, flooding my chest with panic rather than poison. Where the first voice promised rest, this one demanded endurance. Where one beckoned me toward disappearance, the other chained me to staying.

It told me "I could not give up. That I *must not*." Not for myself, never for myself, but for everyone else. It was fueled by fear and obligation, a shrill, breathless catalogue of imagined consequences, rehearsed endlessly until they felt inevitable. It spoke in the language of duty and guilt, of devastation and abandonment. It painted scenes of grief like threats. It weaponized love. It turned responsibility into a cudgel. This voice rose from a deep-seated terror planted in childhood, the fear of rejection, of being cast aside, of confirming the belief that love was conditional and easily revoked. It clawed its way up from old wounds, from moments where affection had been withheld, from lessons learned too early and too well. It carried the unspoken rule I had lived by for as long as I could remember: "*your worth is measured by how useful you are to others.*"

Together, these voices trapped me in a vice. Between annihilation and endurance. Between surrender and obligation. Two opposing forces, each demanding everything I had left, each indifferent to my survival in its own way. One urged me toward silence. The other toward suffering. Neither asked what I needed. Neither offered mercy. That second voice hurled a different kind of condemnation, sharp and panicked, echoing through me like alarms in an empty building: *"Don't you dare. They'll hate you. You'll be a failure. A disappointment. You'll let them down."* Paradoxically, it was this voice that kept me tethered to life. Not by love, but by terror. I clutched fear like a fraying rope, my hands burning as it cut into my palms, using the dread of rejection in death to haul myself back from the edge again and again. It was not hope that saved me. It was fear dressed up as responsibility.

This voice had no concern for my well-being. No interest in my suffering. It did not ask how much pain I was in or how long I could endure. Its fixation was on consequence. On fallout. On optics. On the imagined devastation my absence might cause, the ripples spreading outward from a life erased, as though my primary value lay in the damage my disappearance would inflict. So I lived suspended between them. One voice saying, "*end it*". The other screaming, "*endure it.*" Both merciless. Both persuasive. Both utterly uninterested in my healing. And I stood there, in the crossfire, exhausted beyond measure, torn apart by voices that claimed authority over my life while offering nothing in return, but survival stripped of meaning. That was the war inside me. Not between life and death. But between silence and sacrifice.

It was the voice of societal expectation. Of ingrained duty. Of obligation masquerading as love. The voice that spoke fluently in the language of responsibility and shame, of leaving a void, of causing pain simply by no longer existing. It knew exactly how to frame itself as moral, as necessary, as righteous. And because it sounded reasonable, because it wore the familiar cadence of what I had been taught was *good*, it was harder to question. Harder to resist. That voice seemed to understand me. It knew the complexity of my emotions, the depth of my despair, the fragility of my mind. And it weaponized that understanding with surgical precision. It took my empathy, my loyalty, my fear of hurting others, and turned them into restraints. It did not deny my suffering. It simply deemed it irrelevant.

In the early days of this internal war, this second voice won. Again and again. It overpowered the serpent's hiss not with kindness, not with reassurance, but with terror. Its grip was firm because it was familiar. Its arguments felt airtight. Its threats were unbearable. The prospect of being hated, abandoned, rejected, even in death, terrified me more than the relentless pain of staying alive. Fear proved to be a stronger leash than despair. And so I continued to exist. Suspended in a brutal compromise. Not choosing life, not choosing death. Simply enduring the space between. I was trapped in a cycle of self-doubt, self-loathing, and desperation that fed itself endlessly. Survival became an act of fear, not hope. A reflex, not a choice. I stayed alive not because I wanted to be here, but because leaving felt like a transgression I was not allowed to commit.

Looking back now, with distance and language I did not yet possess then, I can see it more clearly. Suicidal ideation was never just a desire to die. It was far more complex. Far more insidious. A tangled phenomenon rooted in a deep-seated fear of rejection, abandonment, and disappointment. A terror of being cast out, even in absence. A dread of confirming the belief that my worth was conditional, fragile, and easily revoked. It was that fear that drove me.

That pushed me forward day after day. That compelled me to keep breathing even when my own life felt worthless, meaningless, and already over. I did not live because I believed in my future. I lived because I was afraid of the consequences of not living. And that distinction matters. Because it reveals the truth beneath the endurance. That what tethered me to life was not love or joy or purpose, but terror. And that surviving under terror is not the same as living. It is captivity with a pulse.

That voice wove a terrifying narrative, tightening its grip with every repetition, each retelling cinching the knot a little further. It spoke with absolute conviction, the kind that leaves no room for doubt, insisting that death would not erase the pain. No. It would only preserve it. Amplify it. Stretch it into eternity. Death, it claimed, was not an ending but a verdict. A final ruling passed down on a life that had failed to meet its own impossible standards. In its telling, death became punishment. A sentence handed down for inadequacy. A judgment rendered for not being enough. It promised that suffering would not dissolve with the body but fossilize. That it would harden and calcify, locking my perceived worthlessness into permanence. That even the grave would not offer refuge, only confirmation. A final, damning proof that I had failed so completely that even non-existence could not absolve me.

It wasn't death itself that frightened me. It was the idea of being judged forever. Of being labeled a failure, a disappointment, a burden, not just in life, but beyond it. The thought that my absence would not bring peace, but condemnation. That leaving would not quiet the voices but immortalize them. That my suffering would become my legacy, etched into the silence as evidence against me. That prospect carried more weight than the daily agony I endured. More weight than the exhaustion lodged deep in my bones. More weight than the ache of waking up each morning already depleted. The fear of posthumous judgment outweighed the longing for relief. Outweighed even the desire to rest. The idea of being trapped in a never-ending cycle of suffering, condemned to remain inadequate forever, even after life had ended, was unbearable. Eternal failure. Endless disgrace. A punishment without appeal.

And so that voice did what it always did. It kept me tethered to life. Not by hope. Not by love. But by fear. A thin, trembling thread wrapped tight around my chest, cutting into me with every breath, holding me suspended above both escape and collapse. It did not offer comfort. It did not offer meaning. It simply refused to let go. I lived not because I believed life would get better. But because I was terrified it could get worse, even in death. And that fear, as cruel as it was, kept me here. The prospect of eternal condemnation, of being a failure even in death, loomed as a greater horror than anything I was experiencing while alive. It towered over me, vast and merciless, eclipsing the daily pain with a deeper dread. The pain of being hated, of being a disappointment, felt sharper, more immediate, more enduring than the quiet agony of simply existing.

Shame cut deeper than exhaustion ever could. And so I stayed, not because life felt precious or sacred, but because the humiliation of failing at it, even in death, felt like a sentence I could not survive. I remained out of fear, not faith. Out of obligation, not desire. As I wandered deeper into that labyrinth of contradictions, pacing its looping corridors again and again, I began to understand something that had eluded me for years. Suicidal ideation was not simply a desire to die. It was not a singular urge or a final conclusion. It was a symptom. A signal flare fired from within a burning landscape. A distress call launched from a place already under siege. It was a cry for help, though one I did not yet know how to voice. A desperate attempt to make sense of a world that felt determined to break me. A manifestation of pain too large to be contained, fear too entrenched to be reasoned away, desperation that had taken up residence in my mind and refused to leave.

It was the language my suffering spoke when no other words were available. And yet, even as I stood face to face with the depth of my despair, even as the truth of it all began to surface, I could not shake the belief that I was responsible for the well-being of those around me. That their stability rested on my endurance. That my collapse would become their catastrophe. That my survival was a duty I owed, regardless of the cost to myself. It was a crushing burden. I carried it like a sentence handed down without appeal. Heavy. Unyielding. Impossible to outrun no matter how hard I tried. Responsibility clung to me like wet earth, dragging at my limbs, slowing every step, even as I was coming apart. Even as my insides fractured. Even as my spirit begged for relief. I was expected to hold the world together while my own was disintegrating. And so I kept going. Not whole. Not hopeful. Just tethered.

In many ways, suicidal ideation became a coping mechanism. A distorted form of survival. A way of metabolizing pain too vast to hold, too volatile to contain without some imagined outlet. It was how I tried to manage the overwhelming suffering that had become my daily climate, how I searched for an exit from a darkness that felt total, enclosing, inescapable. It offered the illusion of control, the seductive belief that somewhere, hidden within the chaos, there was still a lever I could pull. A choice I could make. A power I could reclaim in a life that felt as though it had spiraled far beyond my grasp. But it was also a destructive force. One that did not heal but hollowed. One that promised relief while quietly deepening the wound. It whispered of mercy while carving out more space for despair. It fed on my darkest thoughts, grew stronger with each repetition, each moment I surrendered to its logic, until it began to feel autonomous. Alive.

As though it had slipped free of me and taken on a will of its own. It developed gravity. A pull that drew my thoughts inward and downward, collapsing possibility into a single point. It convinced me it was both refuge and ruin, sanctuary and sentence. That I needed it to survive, even as it steadily dismantled everything that made survival meaningful. The irony was excruciating in its precision. The very mechanism I used to cope was slowly devouring the part of me capable of healing. My existence became defined by a constant battle against a self-destructive impulse, fueled by a self-hatred so vast it eclipsed any real possibility of self-acceptance. I was fighting myself with myself, using the same wounded tools that had been forged in fear and neglect. There was no clean victory in that war. Only attrition. And then there was the cruelest twist of all.

The very people I clung to life for, the ones I believed gave my existence meaning, were unknowingly the anchors keeping me tethered to relentless pain. The fear of disappointing them. The terror of wounding them with my absence. The imagined devastation my leaving would cause. These became the chains that bound me to endurance at any cost. I stayed alive *for* them. And suffered *because* of that, staying. The love I believed I was demonstrating was not rooted in strength or nobility. It was not the quiet courage of choosing life. It was fear, dressed up as devotion. A self-sacrifice born not of generosity, but of terror. Terror of rejection. Terror of abandonment. Terror of being deemed selfish, even in death. It was a twisted form of love. One that asked me to bleed quietly. One that demanded I disappear slowly instead of all at once. And for a long time, I believed that was the best I could offer.

That duality crushed me. To feel simultaneously unwanted, a burden begging to be set down, and yet utterly indispensable, a vital cog in the machinery of other people's lives. Needed, but not cherished. Necessary, but not nurtured. My inner world became a constant tug-of-war, a soul-wrenching battle between self-destruction and self-sacrifice. Two loyalties tearing me apart. One pulling me toward disappearance, the other demanding I remain intact for everyone else. It was a war I fought every single day, quietly, invisibly, without witnesses or medals, until my emotional reserves were stripped bare and I lived perpetually on the brink of collapse. And in the silence, those unguarded moments of solitude when there was no one left to perform for, no one left to please, the quicksand waited. It tugged at my ankles with calm persistence, patient and merciless, threatening to pull me under completely the moment I stopped resisting.

The noose tightened, increment by increment. The whispers grew louder, closer, more intimate. The weight of it all pressed down on my chest until breathing itself felt like labor, each inhale negotiated, each exhale earned. And still, I stayed suspended in that unbearable tension. Caught between disappearing and enduring. Between surrender and duty. Wondering how long a soul can survive when every direction hurts, when forward is agony and backward feels forbidden, when stillness itself begins to suffocate. The days bled into weeks. The weeks into months. Time lost its shape, its mercy. Each sunrise arrived not as renewal, not as promise, but as summons. Another day called me back into the ring. Another round with no referee and no bell. Morning was no longer gentle; it was a demand. *Get up. Continue. Endure.*

The quicksand kept pulling, slow and inexorable, and the fight, though ceaseless, began to feel increasingly futile. I was spending everything I had just to remain where I was, just to not sink faster. Every victory was pyrrhic, a brief gasp of air before the relentless tide of despair dragged me back under. Relief never stayed. It never settled. It merely visited, brushed my shoulder like a passing stranger, and left me standing alone again in the mire. Hope became a rumor. Rest, a myth. Peace, a word that belonged to other people's lives. And still I endured. Not because I believed it would end. But because stopping felt impossible. I lived in that suspended state for far too long, half here, half gone,

counting breaths, measuring days by how much pain I could withstand, learning, slowly and tragically, just how much a human being can carry before the weight begins to hollow them from the inside out.

The internal dialogue never quieted. It reverberated through the empty chambers of my mind, an endless echo of contradiction and command, a chorus that refused to rest. Thought folded in on thought until silence felt impossible. I lived in the shadows of myself, surviving rather than living, enduring not for my own peace but for the sake of others. It was a life half-lived, suspended between the fear of death and the impossibility of truly living. A life held hostage by obligation, by terror, by the belief that my endurance was owed rather than chosen. I carried that belief like a debt etched into my bones. That staying alive was not a right, but a duty. That my suffering was the price of admission. I was not permitted collapse. Not permitted pause. Only persistence. Only function. Only the quiet heroism of not dying.

As I struggled to make sense of suicidal ideation, another realization began to surface, slow and unsettling. This was not only a personal wound. It was a societal one. A reflection of the world I was trying to survive in, a world that shaped the terrain of my despair long before I had words for it. A world that prized productivity, efficiency, and perfection above humanity. A world that rewarded output and punished vulnerability. A world with little patience for weakness, for softness, for the messy, unmarketable reality of being human. It was a world that demanded strength at all costs. Resilience without rest. Coping without collapse. A world that applauded endurance while ignoring the bodies breaking beneath it. And inside that world, I learned how to disappear quietly. How to fight silently. How to carry pain as proof of worth.

I learned that suffering, if borne politely, could be mistaken for virtue. That exhaustion, if hidden well enough, could pass as competence. That breaking was acceptable only if it never interrupted the machinery. So I swallowed my pain. I compressed myself smaller and smaller. I turned agony into fuel, even as it hollowed me out day by day. But what about those of us who couldn't cope? What about those of us fighting just to stay afloat, expending every last ounce of strength to keep our heads above water? What about those of us drowning in a sea of despair, arms burning, lungs aching, calling out into a vast, indifferent expanse with no lifeline in sight? What happens to the ones who don't bounce back, who don't rise stronger, who don't transform suffering into inspiration or success? Those questions followed me. Circled me. Refused to loosen their grip. They haunted me because there were no easy answers waiting at the surface.

No slogans deep enough to hold the weight. No platitudes wide enough to catch the falling. Only the truth, stark and unadorned: That survival, in such a world, is not evenly distributed. That some of us are asked to carry far more than our share. That sometimes, suicidal ideation is not a failure of will, but a response to a system that leaves no room to rest, to break, to be held. And knowing that did not ease my pain. But it did begin to shift where I placed the blame. For the first time, I wondered if the problem was not that I was too weak to live, but that the world had been too cruel to allow me to live as myself. Looking back now on those dark days, I can see with aching clarity that suicidal ideation was never only my private battle. It was never confined to the narrow geography of my own mind. It was a societal wound as much as a personal one.

A mirror held up to the world I was trying, desperately, to survive in. A world that lacked the language to name what was happening. The patience to sit with it. The humility to admit it did not understand. It was a world that demanded explanations but offered no safety in which to give them. A world that asked "*why*" with suspicion rather than care. A world that too often stigmatized mental illness, flattening it into caricature, reducing it to weakness, to poor attitude, to moral failure. A flaw of character. A lack of grit. A failure of will. Anything, it seemed, but what it truly was: a serious, life-threatening health issue that seeps into the nervous system, rewires perception, and distorts reality itself. In that misunderstanding, so many of us were left alone. Left to translate pain without a shared language. Left to carry symptoms without a framework of compassion. Left to bleed quietly while being told to toughen up.

We were expected to cope in silence, to perform normalcy while unraveling, to manage suffering politely so as not to inconvenience the world. And when we faltered, when we sank, when we cried out in ways that made others uncomfortable, the response was often bewilderment rather than care. Judgment rather than curiosity. Distance rather than help. We were drowning. And the world stood at the shoreline, arms crossed, asking why we hadn't simply learned to swim. It did not see the weight strapped to our ankles. It did not feel the undertow pulling us under. It did not notice how long we had already been treading water. That question, "*why didn't you just try harder?*", missed the point entirely. We were trying. With everything we had. We were fighting currents we did not choose, in waters we were never taught how to navigate, carrying histories and wounds that made each stroke cost more than it should.

And so we sank quietly. Politely. Out of sight. Understanding this now does not erase the pain I lived through. But it reframes it. It moves the shame off my shoulders and places it where it belongs. It reminds me that my suffering was not evidence of personal failure, but a response to a system that could not, or would not, hold the complexity of human pain. I was not broken beyond repair. I was unseen. Unheard. Unheld. And telling this story now is not just an act of remembrance. It is a refusal to keep drowning in silence.

Chapter Twelve:
The Darkest Night: The night of my suicide attempt:

Before we step any further into this chapter, I need to pause. Not as a formality, not as a footnote, but as an act of care. Of intention. Of reverence for what lies ahead, and for you who are walking with me. This is the moment where I offer the trigger warning I mentioned earlier. What follows is the full retelling of my suicide attempt and the depth of darkness I was living in at the time. This chapter carries weight. It is heavy in the hands. Raw on the tongue. Unflinching in its honesty. It moves through places where the ground is unstable, where the air thins, where old wounds may ache simply by being remembered. For anyone still tender in their healing, these pages may stir things that have not yet settled. We are about to descend. We will walk through profound darkness here before we return to the light. That darkness is not gratuitous. It is not written for shock or spectacle. It exists because it existed in me. Because it shaped the path that followed. Because naming it is part of loosening its grip. Still, no truth, no matter how vital, is more important than your safety.

So I ask this gently and without judgment. If at any point you feel unsteady, overwhelmed, or pulled toward a darkness that threatens your sense of grounding, please stop. Pause the page. Close the book. Turn your attention back to your body. Feel your feet. Feel your breath. Let the present moment remind you where you are now. You are allowed to step away. You are allowed to skip this chapter entirely. You do not owe this story your endurance. Listening to your own limits is not weakness. It is discernment. It is wisdom earned the hard way. It is self-respect in motion. Take gentle care of yourself as you move forward. Or as you choose not to. Either way, you are honoring your healing.

I also want to be unmistakably clear. This chapter is dark, but the darkness did not win. It did not claim me. It did not hold the final word. And it was never the truth of who I am, no matter how convincingly it dressed itself as certainty in that moment. My decision to step through the doorway of oblivion was not the right one. It was not clarity. It was not peace. It was not courage. It was desperation shaped by lies, driven by the false and brutal belief that everything was irreparably broken, that no other path remained. If, as you listen, something inside you begins to stir, if a familiar whisper rises up and starts to sound soothing, starts to sound like home, like relief, like a solution, please pause with me here. That voice is lying to you. It lied to me, too.

It spoke with confidence. With intimacy. With the kind of quiet authority that makes deception feel like truth. It told me the pain would end. That silence would save me. That disappearance was mercy. None of that was real. None of it held. And it will not hold for you either. I tell this part of my story not to glorify the edge, but to illuminate it. To strip it of its false romance. To show it for what it truly was: a narrowing of vision, a tunnel of despair where lies masqueraded as answers. I share this so that voice does not guide you toward a brink I once stood on, trembling, exhausted, convinced there was nothing left behind me worth turning back to. Hear these words knowing this: I survived that edge. Barely. And on the other side, fragile and shaking, I discovered something vital that the darkness never mentioned. I was wrong. My inner demon was wrong.

And if it speaks to you now, it is wrong as well. Hold that truth close. Grip it the way one grips a railing in a storm. Anchor yourself to it when the ground feels uncertain. Let it be the steady weight in your hands as we move forward. This chapter is not an ending. It is a moment. A single, harrowing moment in a much longer story. A descent that did not define the destination. There is darkness ahead on these pages, yes. But it is not where we stay. It is where we pass through. And beyond it, waiting with a patience the night never had, is the light I could not yet see. When you are ready, if you are ready, we will continue.

As I sit here now, reflecting on that fateful night, I am reminded of the depths of human suffering, of how quietly and completely darkness can consume us. Not with spectacle. Not with warning. But with a slow, patient inevitability that creeps in while no one is looking. My name is Letitia, and I have walked the fine, trembling line between life and death, that narrow threshold where the whispers of despair speak louder than reason, louder than memory, louder than any promise of tomorrow. This is my story. The story of the night I faced death face to face. It was a night like any other. Ordinary in every measurable way. No thunder split the sky. No catastrophe announced itself. And yet, inside me, the entire world collapsed inward, folding in on itself until there was no space left to breathe. The weight of it pressed down on my chest, compressing thought, compressing hope, compressing time itself.

The air hung thick and heavy, saturated with the scent of damp earth, that rich, loamy smell of soil holding centuries of decay and rebirth. A late summer chill threaded through it, sharp against my skin, raising goosebumps that had nothing to do with the cold. The night wrapped around me, close and intimate, as though it knew what was coming. Above me, a vast blue moon loomed in the inky sky. Heavy. Watchful. A pale, indifferent eye fixed on my smallness. Its light spilled across the ground in long, warped streaks, stretching shadows far beyond their rightful shapes, turning the familiar lawn into foreign terrain. The grass beneath me was wet, slick against my palms and knees as I sank down, the cold seeping through fabric and bone alike. That pale glow transformed everything. Trees became sentinels. The earth felt alive, breathing beneath me.

Even the silence carried weight, pressing in from all sides, amplifying the pounding of my heart, the ragged rhythm of my breath. I felt exposed beneath that moon, laid bare in its light, as though nothing of me was hidden anymore, not the pain, not the exhaustion, not the longing to finally stop. I remember thinking how strange it was that the world could look so beautiful at the very moment I felt most broken. The grass shimmered softly. The air tasted metallic and damp. The night stood still. And there I was, a woman kneeling at the edge of herself, suspended between staying and leaving, beneath a sky that had seen countless endings and never once intervened. This was the moment. This was the night. This was the place where my story and death finally stood close enough to touch.

There I sat, huddled against the cold, unforgiving earth, my body folded in on itself as though trying to disappear into the ground beneath me. My spine curved inward, shoulders caved, knees drawn tight to my chest in a posture older than language. The phone was clenched in my trembling hand, its glow stark and artificial against the dark, the last small island of light in my desolate little world. A fragile tether. A thin, flickering bridge to something beyond the encroaching night. Around me, the darkness breathed. Crickets sang their endless chorus, indifferent and steady. Somewhere nearby, an owl called out, its lonely cry slicing cleanly through the silence, a sound so ancient it felt like a reminder of how small and temporary I was.

The air moved softly, brushing my skin like a question it had no intention of answering. It felt as though the universe itself had stepped back, withdrawing its witnesses, conspiring to leave me utterly and completely alone in this moment. And it wasn't just the cold that gnawed at me. Not the wet grass seeping through my clothes. Not the chill crawling up my limbs. This cold was deeper. A glacial numbness had seeped into my bones, settled into my breath, lodged itself inside my chest. It slowed my movements. Dulled my reactions. Wrapped my thoughts in cotton and frost. A chilling apathy spread through me, heavy and suffocating, pressing down on the fragile embers of hope still flickering weakly inside my ribs.

I felt emptied. Flattened. As though the sharp edges of pain had finally worn me down into something smooth and silent. The ache gave way to absence. And absence, I learned that night, can be far more dangerous than pain. Pain still speaks. Numbness does not. The phone vibrated faintly in my hand. Its light reflected off damp grass, off my knuckles, off tears I did not remember shedding. My breath came shallow and uneven, fogging faintly in the night air. Each inhale felt like a question. Each exhale is like a concession. In that moment, I was not just sitting in the dark. I was standing at the edge of myself. At the threshold between remaining and releasing. Between stepping back into a life that felt unbearable and letting go into a silence that promised everything and nothing all at once. The ground beneath me felt both solid and uncertain, as though it might hold me or give way.

I did not know which way I would lean. I only knew that the decision hovered there, heavy and electric, waiting for me to choose whether I would gather myself back from the brink, or finally let go. My phone, a cold, lifeless rectangle clenched in my hand, felt less like a device and more like an unforgiving slab of metal. Its pale glow cut through the darkness, illuminating the desolation around me and reflecting it back with brutal honesty. That light did not comfort. It exposed. It mirrored the stark truth of my situation with merciless clarity: utterly, terrifyingly alone.

It was past midnight, that suspended hour when the world seems to loosen its grip on reality. A time when shadows stretch longer than they should, when familiar shapes warp and secrets seem to breathe on the wind. The air felt thin then, brittle, as though existence itself had become fragile, as though one wrong movement, one wrong breath, might tear it open completely. Even time felt hesitant, hovering, unsure whether to carry me forward or let me slip through its cracks. Years. Years I had battled this war within myself. Years of living with two warring factions lodged deep in my chest, clawing at one another for dominance, tearing through my inner landscape and leaving scars no one could see. The toll of it was immeasurable. Exhaustion layered upon exhaustion, grief piled atop grief, until even remembering how to hope felt like work I could no longer afford.

On one side lived the desperate yearning for connection. For purpose. For some undeniable reason, to keep breathing when every breath felt borrowed. A longing to be seen, to be needed, to be loved without conditions or performance. I had chased that yearning relentlessly, bending and reshaping myself in its pursuit, offering pieces of my soul like currency, hoping someone, anyone, would finally declare me enough. That effort drained me to the marrow. It hollowed me out until my body felt like an abandoned house, walls still standing, rooms intact, but stripped of warmth and life. I trembled with a fatigue that sleep could not touch, a bone-deep weariness born not of doing too much, but of surviving too long without rest, without refuge, without relief.

The night pressed in closer, heavy with unspoken things. My hand tightened around the phone, knuckles aching, as if holding it harder might anchor me to this side of existence. The screen glowed on, indifferent and silent, bearing witness to a woman worn thin by years of fighting battles she never asked for. And there, beneath the suspended sky, past midnight, at the edge of myself, I could feel it clearly. The weight of all those years. The cost of wanting to belong in a world that had never quite made room for me. The quiet devastation of needing something I no longer had the strength to keep searching for. I was so tired. Not the kind of tired that sleep repairs, but the kind that settles into the soul, whispering that rest might only exist somewhere beyond this night.

On the other side waited the seductive whisper of oblivion. Not loud. Not violent. Soft as velvet. Patient as stone. It did not rush me. It never had. It simply waited, promising rest where there had only ever been strain, promising silence where my mind had never known peace. It spoke in the language of endings, of relief, of finally laying down the weight I had been dragging behind me for years like a rusted chain. The tide of suicidal ideation rose and fell with cruel consistency. Predictable as breath. Unavoidable as gravity. A constant companion that had learned my rhythms, my weakest hours, my fractures. It hovered just beyond the edge of my vision, a dark shape

I could feel even when I refused to look directly at it. Always close enough to touch me. Always ready to surge forward and pull me under the moment my footing slipped. And there I was again.

Beneath the indifferent moon, its pale light washing everything in cold clarity. The phone glowing in my hand like a false star, bright but offering no guidance. My body stood rigid, heart hammering, breath shallow, as though even my lungs were afraid to commit to another inhale. I stood between those two forces once more. On one side, the aching, exhausted desire to live. Not because life felt beautiful. Not because hope felt accessible. But because somewhere inside me, buried beneath years of ruin, there remained a fragile insistence that my existence still mattered, even if I could no longer explain why. On the other hand, the longing for it all to stop. The unbearable pull toward quiet. Toward release. Toward a darkness that promised no more effort, no more performance, no more pain.

I was suspended there, stretched thin between opposing truths, neither winning, neither retreating. Wanting to live and wanting to disappear occupied the same breath, the same heartbeat, the same trembling body. It was not a contradiction I could resolve. It was a state I inhabited. The night held its breath with me. The moon did not intervene. The phone did not speak. The earth beneath my feet did not choose for me. I stood at the center of that tension, balanced on a knife's edge, knowing only this: whatever happened next would change everything.

The gnawing emptiness that had whispered its insidious promises of escape for so long finally culminated in this moment: utter, soul-crushing loneliness. It was no longer abstract, no longer something I could intellectualize or outrun. It stood fully formed before me, undeniable, vast. The screen in my hand, stark and unforgivingly bright, mocked me with its empty contacts list, a brutal mirror held up to my isolation, to the darkness that had quietly taken up residence in my soul and rearranged the furniture there. There was no one. No one to reach out to. No one to hear my silent screams echoing inside my chest. No one to care. No one to stop me. Each realization landed like a blow, stripping away illusion after illusion until only the bare truth remained. I had never felt so visible and so unseen at the same time. The phone buzzed faintly with nothing at all, a hollow promise of connection that never arrived, its glow illuminating not hope, but absence. Under the vast, cold gaze of the uncaring moon, everything felt exposed and irrevocable. Its pale light offered no warmth, no mercy. It did not intervene. It did not soften the edges of what was unfolding. The night did not cradle me. It simply watched. A silent witness to a woman unraveling at the seams. The grass beneath me was slick with dew, the earth unyielding against my knees, grounding me in a body that felt foreign, heavy, used up. The air hung still, as if even the wind had decided to turn away. In that oppressive quiet, it felt as though the shadow had finally won, not through violence or drama, but through abandonment. Through the slow erosion of every reason to stay. I was exhausted beyond language. Not tired but emptied. Drained of resistance. Stripped of fight. Standing at the frayed end of myself where every thread had been pulled too tight for too long.

My spirit sagged under the accumulated weight of years, of disappointments layered upon disappointments, of hope postponed until it withered. I felt as though I had reached the end of my rope, suspended between holding on and letting go, arms aching, fingers burning, with nothing left in my hands but air. The choice hovered there, heavy and breathless, and I stood beneath it, trembling, unsure whether I had the strength to climb back... or the courage to finally fall.

The screen of my phone continued to glow in the darkness, a cold, relentless beacon illuminating not connection, but its absence. Its light felt harsh against the night, exposing everything I wished I could hide. I scrolled through my contacts anyway, my thumb moving in slow, mechanical arcs, a ritual as futile as it was desperate. Names drifted past in a quiet procession, each one a small echo of a life that had once felt tangible. Faces surfaced in my mind. Laughter. Shared secrets. Moments that had once anchored me to the world. Fragments of belonging, now reduced to text and pixels, stripped of warmth, stripped of reach. Tonight, they were ghosts. People I had known. People I had loved. But love, I learned in that moment, does not always mean presence. Connection does not guarantee rescue. Those names stared back at me, flat and silent, incapable of crossing the vast distance that yawned between me and another human heartbeat.

There was no one I could call. No one who would understand the depth of what was happening inside me. No one who could hear the urgency in my silence or sense the danger in my stillness. No one who would care enough to reach through the dark and pull me back from the edge. The realization settled over me slowly, deliberately, like a burial cloth being drawn up inch by inch. Heavy. Smothering. Final. It pressed the air from my lungs and flattened my thoughts into something dull and absolute. I was utterly, irrevocably alone. In this vast, indifferent world, there was no one to hear my silent screams vibrating inside my chest. No one to witness the unraveling happening in real time. No one to sit with me in the wet grass beneath that watching moon and say, *Stay.* No one to mark this moment as sacred or dangerous or worth interrupting.

And yes, painfully, terrifyingly, there was no one to stop me. The night held its breath. The phone remained lit.

And I stood there, exposed to the truth of my solitude, realizing that the most dangerous thing in the world is not despair itself, but believing, even for a moment, that you are entirely alone inside it.

From the silence, the first voice rose. The one that had always waited in the margins. The one that never needed to shout before, because time had always done its work for it. The insidious whisper of despair. The voice of surrender. This time, it did not speak. It shrieked. It rose in triumph, a soundless scream that reverberated through every hollowed chamber of my being. It declared victory not with force, but with inevitability. It had been patient. Methodical. It had worn me down grain by grain, erosion masquerading as endurance, chipping away at my defenses so slowly I barely noticed the loss until nothing solid remained. I was hollowed out. Scooped clean. An empty vessel, polished smooth by suffering, finally ready to be filled with the sweet, dark nectar of oblivion.

I knew this voice. I had known it for far too long. It was the voice of apathy. It settled over me like a suffocating blanket pulled tight around my shoulders, cold and unyielding. I had felt its weight before, brushed up against its edges in moments of exhaustion, but never like this. Never with this gravity. This time it arrived with a terrifying finality, wrapping itself around me so completely it smothered even the last fragile flicker of resistance. Even the last whisper of maternal love. This was not the tired apathy of a spirit worn thin. Not numbness born of temporary overwhelm. This was something far more dangerous. A vast, bottomless pit of nothingness. A vacuum that did not merely dull feeling but erased the very concept of value itself. It did not argue. It did not persuade. It simply voided meaning, rendering everything equally irrelevant.

This was the deadly apathy of truly no longer caring. No longer caring about the sunrise breaking open the sky in soft gold. No longer caring about the laughter of children ringing bright and alive. No longer caring about the quiet miracle of a flower daring to bloom. No longer caring about the comfort of a warm embrace. About being needed. About being loved. About being seen at all. It stripped meaning from everything it touched, leaving behind a flat, gray landscape where nothing held weight, where nothing asked to be protected. The world did not feel hostile in that moment. It felt irrelevant. And that, I would later understand, is far more dangerous than pain. Because pain still binds you to life. Apathy severs the tie.

It was so profound, so all-consuming, that even the thought of leaving my two daughters behind barely registered. The image passed through me like mist, indistinct and distant, unable to land. That realization landed harder than any scream ever could. It was the moment I understood just how far I had fallen. How deep into the darkness I had slipped. When even love no longer pulls at you, when even the most sacred bonds fail to anchor you, you are no longer standing at the edge. You are already suspended in the void. Not even the thought of my two daughters could pierce it. Their innocent laughter, once bright enough to split the dark, arrived now as a distant, muffled echo, as though heard through thick walls or underwater. Their beautiful faces, their bright, searching eyes, the very lifeline that had pulled me back from the brink so many times before, blurred and dulled, losing their urgency, their gravity.

They did not disappear, but they no longer reached me. They floated somewhere far away, untouchable, almost irrelevant. Nothing mattered anymore. In that warped stillness, logic twisted itself into something unrecognizable. I convinced myself their lives would be better without me. Lighter. Cleaner. Freer. That they would be unburdened by my sadness, unshadowed by my pain, able to grow and thrive without my brokenness stretching across their days. The lie settled easily, seamlessly, because apathy makes room for cruelty by disguising it as reason. This was not selfishness, my mind insisted. This was mercy. A release. A final, desperate act of love. The apathy was ruthless in its efficiency. Cold. Surgical. Its mission was singular, streamlined, mercilessly clear. It did not argue or hesitate. It did not pause to weigh consequences or mourn what would be lost. It did not grieve futures or count the cost. It simply moved forward, stripping away complexity until only one idea remained intact.

One unwavering goal had taken root. It bloomed into a consuming obsession. And nothing could derail it. Not reason.

Not memory. Not the echo of laughter or the imprint of small hands in mine. Not even the profound, irreversible implications of what I was about to do. Everything else collapsed into static. And in the wreckage of meaning, one word remained, stark and chilling in its simplicity, echoing through the hollow chambers of my mind like a final verdict, the only truth left standing when all others had been erased: Death. It was not dramatic. It was not loud. It was absolute.

When Alone Becomes a Chasm

The glowing rectangle in my hand had become a symbol of defeat. An emblem of my isolation. A cold illuminated proof of my utter aloneness. When alone becomes *so* alone, it transcends loneliness altogether. It opens into a chasm, deep and endless, a vast hollow where echoes die before they can return. A void large enough to swallow you whole without resistance, without struggle, without even noticing. In that moment, as the moon painted the world in shades of silver and despair, my only companion, my only perceived solace, became the imagined embrace of death. It spoke softly then. Not with cruelty. Not with force. But with tenderness. A seductive whisper. A lover's murmur. A gentle caress at the edge of consciousness, promising rest where there had been none, promising release from the ache that had hollowed me out over years of survival. It promised sleep without dreams, silence without effort, an end to the relentless weight of being.

I felt as though I was standing at the edge of the abyss, and the abyss was standing with me. It did not push. It did not threaten. It simply waited. Its dark, empty eyes reflected everything I no longer had the strength to hold. It beckoned me closer, inviting the leap with infinite patience. And everything I had carried for years, the helplessness, the hopelessness, the powerlessness, collapsed inward all at once. They converged into a single, suffocating point, a narrowing tunnel where past and future dissolved, where there was only *now*, only the unbearable pressure of this moment. It felt like the breaking point. The final unraveling. The place where endurance ran out of breath. The fight did not end with resolution or clarity. It ended with exhaustion. A bone-deep, soul-draining fatigue that made resistance feel absurd. There was nothing left to strive for. Nothing left to live for. Nothing left to battle against. Every argument for staying had been stripped of meaning. Every reason had fallen silent.

The war ended not with victory, but with collapse. And in that terrible stillness, when even fear had loosened its grip, when the noise inside me finally quieted, I surrendered. Not with drama. Not with certainty. But with a weary letting go. A soft, devastating release of the last thing I had left: the will to keep fighting.

The loneliness pressed in until it felt physical, a crushing weight settling against my ribs, compressing my lungs, making each breath an intentional act rather than an instinct. It was not merely the absence of people. It was the absence of resonance. The absence of anything capable of meeting the hollow ache in my chest and answering it back. An emptiness so profound it echoed, unanswered, through every corridor of my being. I stared down at the glowing rectangular box in my hand, that supposed lifeline to the world, now nothing more than a monument to my isolation. Bathed in the moon's pale, merciless light, the screen offered no grace. No unread messages waiting quietly. No missed calls. No soft vibration of concern. No flicker of connection reaching toward me. Just stillness. Just confirmation. With that, something inside me finally gave way, and I sank completely beneath the waters of isolation. Silence, rendered in pixels.

The time hovered just past midnight, that thin, symbolic hour that feels like a closing door rather than a beginning. The threshold between days. Between then and now. Between staying and leaving. The revelry of the day had drained away entirely. The music had stopped. The laughter had dissolved into memory, already losing its shape. Cinderella's ball was over, the lights extinguished, the magic undone. The spell had broken, and the illusion I had lived inside for so long lay in ruins around my feet. It was time, I believed, for my story to end too. Not with a prince. Not with rescue.

Not with a happily ever after scripted by hope. But with a solitary walk into the darkness. A quiet exit, stage left. The fairy tale collapsing under the uncompromising weight of truth. No glass slipper waiting to be found. No applause. No encore. Only the end of pretending. And I, the protagonist of this unraveling, stood ready to take my final bow. The curtain, I was certain, had already begun to fall.

And then, somewhere deep beneath the rubble, something stirred. Not a choir of angels. Not a beam of light cracking the sky. Something quieter. Stranger. More unsettling. A spark of courage, yes, but not the kind wrapped in inspiration. A flicker of determination stripped bare of hope. It rose from a place far colder than optimism, far deeper than faith. A stillness spread through me like ice water poured straight into my veins, numbing everything it touched. Thought slowed. Emotion flattened. The chaos that had ruled me for so long fell abruptly silent. With terrifying clarity, a chilling resolve settled in my chest. And the decision felt, right. Not peaceful. Not gentle. Not happy. Just right. Solid. Inevitable. Like a door clicking shut. Like gravity asserting itself. The kind of rightness that does not ask for permission or reassurance. It simply *is*.

This was not the reckless abandon of a sudden impulse. There was no frenzy in it. No hysteria. No blur. This was the meticulously planned conclusion of a long, agonizing journey. Years of preparation had been quietly inching me toward this exact moment. Years of research. Of contingency plans. Of late-night calculations disguised as survival. Every step I had taken through my life seemed, in that moment, to line up behind me like evidence. The courage I gathered did not rise from hope. It was born of grim determination. A final act of agency in a life that had felt utterly stripped of choice. If I could not control the pain, I would control its ending. If I could not reclaim my life, I would at least reclaim the decision. That thought landed with a terrible sense of order, like chaos finally snapping into alignment. Wrapped in that unnatural calm, I rose from the icy grass.

The cold clung to me immediately, the damp seeping into my clothes, into my skin, into my bones, like a second skin I could not shed. My muscles protested, stiff and aching from the chill and from the emotional weight they had been carrying for years. My joints screamed. My body hesitated. But I moved anyway. Purpose returned to my limbs. It was a hollow purpose, stripped of joy or anticipation, but it was direction, nonetheless. A forward motion. A line to follow. For the first time in what felt like forever, I was not drifting. I was not frozen. I was not suspended between options. I was moving with intent. And that, in its own terrible way, felt like relief. I walked toward the house, my steps deliberate, measured, quiet as a passing breeze that leaves no trace behind it.

Each footfall felt purposeful, rehearsed, as though my body had memorized this path long before my mind agreed to follow. Tonight, no one would suspect. No one would intervene. No hand would reach out from the dark to stop me. Tonight, I believed, I was finally in control. I slipped through the door, the soft click of the latch breaking the silence with a sharpness that startled me. The sound seemed too loud, too final, echoing in the hollow space before dissolving back into stillness. The house inhaled around me. Familiar. Intimate. And suddenly strange. I paused for half a heartbeat, listening, but there was only quiet. A deep, watching quiet that pressed against my ears. I moved forward. I navigated the familiar pathways by instinct alone, my body remembering what my mind felt too far away to hold. My senses sharpened unnaturally, tuned to every creak of the floorboards, every subtle groan of the structure settling in the night.

Each sound arrived magnified, reverberating through me as though the house itself were awake, alert, bearing witness. Walls loomed. Doorways watched. Shadows pooled in corners where light once lived. I moved through the rooms like a shadow of my own making, a specter gliding through spaces I had inhabited for years, now rendered foreign by the gravity of what I carried inside me. The furniture stood where it always had, but it no longer belonged to me. Photographs blurred as I passed them, memories reduced to shapes and frames, unable to reach me through the fog. My body knew where to go even as my mind drifted somewhere distant, detached, sealed behind glass. My movements became precise, economical, almost ritualistic.

Each step followed the last without question. Emotion had drained away, leaving behind a hollow efficiency. I felt like a ghost carrying out a grim, predetermined task, animated by resolve rather than feeling. There was no hesitation. No pause. No bargaining with myself. Just forward motion, unbroken and relentless, as though once I had started moving, stopping was no longer an option. The house held its breath as I passed through it, and I did not look back. Tonight, there would be no interference. No rescue. No last-minute interruption scripted by mercy. The plan, meticulously crafted over years of quiet desperation, waited patiently for me, exactly as I had left it, untouched and obedient. It did not rush me. It did not question me. It simply existed, solid and certain, a grim certainty in a life that had offered so little of it.

Every detail had been considered in advance, rehearsed in the privacy of my mind until it felt inevitable, until it felt less like a choice and more like a destination I had been walking toward for years. No one would stop me. No one would prevent me. No one would stand in my way. The house remained silent, complicit in its stillness, walls closing around me as I moved deeper inside. It offered no protest. No creak of warning. No sudden sound to break the spell. It felt as though it had already accepted what I believed was about to happen, as though it had resigned itself to bearing witness without judgment or intervention. The air grew heavier with each step, thick with anticipation, with the weight of an ending drawing closer. My heartbeat was steady, not frantically, not with fear, but with a hollow regularity that felt detached from urgency. Even my breath sounded distant to my own ears, as if it belonged to someone else moving through this space in my place.

I was convinced this was the moment everything would finally end. The years of endurance. The relentless ache. The constant negotiation between staying and disappearing. All of it narrowing now into a single point in time. I moved forward, deeper into the quiet, carrying with me the belief that there would be no turning back, that this threshold once crossed would close behind me forever. The house swallowed my footsteps. The night pressed close against the windows. And I walked on, convinced that I was approaching not just an ending, but the only release I had left.

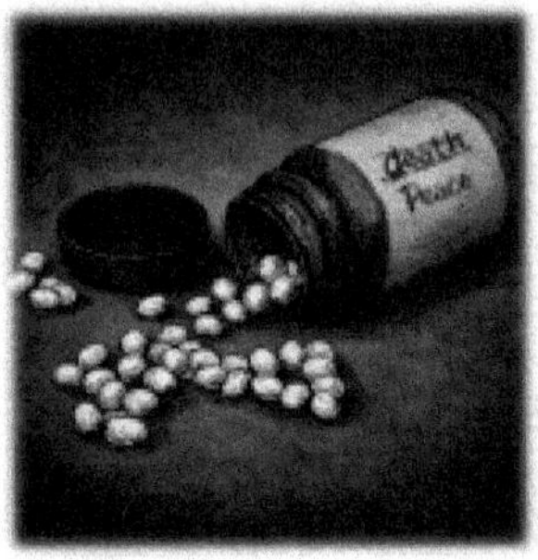

I reached the bottom cupboard, my heart unnervingly still, my breath steady and measured, as though my body had already made peace with what I believed would come next. There was no frantic rush now. No trembling urgency. Just a quiet, chilling composure that felt almost rehearsed, as if my muscles and lungs had resigned themselves ahead of me, moving through this moment with a calm that did not belong to hope. Inside, tucked away in a hidden compartment, lay the pills. A morbidly organized, carefully concealed collection. A silent archive of despair. They rested there like a confession I had been writing in secret for years, each one a witness to nights spent calculating, planning, convincing myself that this ending was not only inevitable but necessary. There, buried in shadow, waited my so-called solution, patient and obedient, untouched by doubt.

They lay in precise order, deliberately gathered, counted, and kept safe over time. Years of grim preparation had narrowed to this singular point, and they waited for me now like a siren's call, voiceless yet magnetic. Each small capsule carried the weight of intention, of research, of the cold pragmatism that had slowly overtaken desperation. Proof, I told myself, that I had thought this through. Proof that this was not an impulse, but a conclusion. This was it. The tools of my liberation, as I believed then. The culmination of years spent preparing for an ending I had convinced myself was unavoidable. I stood there, cupboard open, shadows pooling at my feet, staring at the quiet evidence of how long I had been walking toward this moment. And in that stillness, with everything laid bare before me, the finality of it pressed in close, heavy and undeniable, as though the room itself understood what I believed was about to happen.

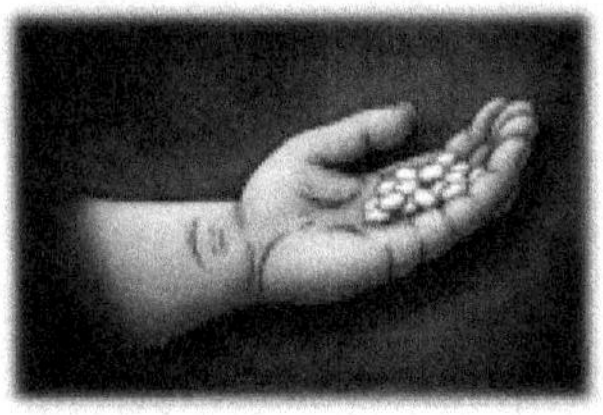

With a steady hand, I reached into the hiding place and lifted the container free. It came away too easily, as though it had been waiting for this moment all along. The pills rattled softly inside, a muted, hollow sound, a morbid lullaby marking the rhythm of a choice I believed had already been made. The sound echoed louder in my chest than it did in the quiet room, each faint clink a punctuation mark at the end of a sentence I had been writing for years. I tipped them into my palm. They pooled there, smooth and unassuming, their surfaces cool against my skin.

Ordinary. Almost gentle. Their weight was surprisingly light, a cruel contrast to the unbearable gravity they carried. It struck me then how small they were, how deceptively harmless they looked, and yet how much power I had assigned to them. They felt like a tangible promise of finality, a physical embodiment of the end I had rehearsed in my mind so many times it felt familiar. My hand trembled, just once. A wave of nausea rose sharp and sudden in my throat, an instinctive revolt from somewhere deeper than thought. My body protested even now, sending up flares of warning, but I swallowed it back down. I could not afford hesitation. Hesitation felt dangerous. Hesitation felt like betrayal of the resolve I had fought so hard to gather. I told myself there was no turning back. This was what I wanted. No, what I needed. The words repeated in my mind like a mantra, rigid and insistent, hardening into certainty.

Resolve wrapped itself around me like armor, cold and inflexible, quieting the tremor beneath my ribs. It dulled fear. It flattened doubt. It steadied my breath as I stood there, palm open, holding what I believed to be the end of a long, agonizing road. Everything I had endured seemed to funnel into that single moment. Years of pain. Years of planning. Years of waiting for the courage to finally arrive. And now it had. Not warm or noble, but sharp and unyielding, forged in exhaustion rather than hope. I closed my fingers around the pills. In the hollow of my hand, I held the ending I had convinced myself was inevitable.

I opened the refrigerator door and let the cold spill over my face, sharp and bracing, a shock that bit into my skin and briefly reminded me I still had one. I reached inside and took hold of something familiar, something I once used to numb the edges of myself, an old companion I had not visited in months. Tonight, I told myself, we would meet again. Tonight, we would share a final acknowledgment of a life that had worn me thin, a quiet, unceremonious farewell whispered in a kitchen washed in pale light. Standing there, ending in one hand, escape in the other, a strange calm settled over me. It felt like peace, or something close enough to wear its mask. A loosening. A surrender. The sensation of unclenching fingers that had been gripping the world too tightly for too long. I told myself this was courage.

That this was control. That after years of being pushed and pulled by forces I could not tame, I was finally authoring the last line of my own story. Inside my head, the relentless chorus that had tormented me for years fell abruptly quiet. No more hissing accusations. No more panicked commands. The noise drained away until there was only stillness, a vast, echoing calm. The apathy that had consumed me no longer felt like emptiness; it softened into acceptance, into resignation. A quiet, fragile truce where resistance once lived, as if the storm inside me had finally laid down its weapons and agreed to rest. The room seemed to exhale with me. The clock ticked on. The night held steady. And yet, even as that stillness spread, something subtle trembled beneath it, like ice over deep water, thin and uncertain. A reminder I could not yet name.

A moment suspended, waiting to see whether this quiet would become an ending, or a pause. If you feel that ice beneath your own feet as you read, please stop here. Breathe. Ground yourself. Reach for someone who can be with you in this moment. You deserve support, and you do not have to walk this edge alone.

THE DARKEST NIGHT: Taking Action with death:

I returned to the grass, to that familiar hollow beneath the moon's watchful eye, where its light lay over the ground like a spectral blanket, pale and unfeeling. The damp pricked at my skin as I settled there, a sensation I knew intimately, a cold I had made peace with long ago. This place had become a morbid sanctuary, my confessional carved out of silence and shadow, and tonight, my launchpad. Here, the weight of existence had always felt strangely bearable, perhaps because this was where I rehearsed its ending, where the idea of disappearing had been given space to breathe. But tonight was different. Tonight was not about contemplation or bargaining or circling the same thoughts like vultures overhead. Tonight was about action.

The chill of the grass seeped deeper, into muscle and bone, a familiar discomfort that mirrored the icy grip tightening around my heart. It anchored me to my body even as my mind drifted elsewhere, already leaning toward an ending it had memorized by heart. My clothes grew damp beneath me, the cold climbing insistently, as if the earth itself were reminding me that I was still here, still made of flesh and nerve. Above me, the moon painted the lawn in shades of silver and ash, a cold, indifferent witness to the ritual unfolding below. Its light flattened the world, stripping it of warmth and color, rendering everything stark and exposed. There was no romance in it now. No poetry. Just clarity sharpened to a blade.

The world felt hushed, suspended, as though the night itself had paused mid-breath. Even the insects had gone quiet. No breeze stirred the air. No sound interrupted the stillness. It felt as if time had narrowed to this single patch of grass, this single body beneath the sky, this single moment balanced on the edge of becoming irreversible. I sat there, grounded and trembling, with the tools of my ending close at hand, acutely aware that once the first step was taken, there would be no rehearsal left. Only consequence. The moon watched. The earth waited. And I, wrapped in silver light and cold resolve, prepared to cross the threshold I had been inching toward for years.

A stark contrast to the darkness consuming me, the moonlit lawn gleamed with an almost cruel serenity. It shone with a calm that felt undeserved, indifferent to the storm that had hollowed me out. In my hands, the small white tokens of promise and the heavy bottle felt strangely comforting, like familiar companions invited into a grim, sacred ritual. They were solid. Certain. Tangible in a moment when everything else felt like it might dissolve if I loosened my grip. Tonight, fear was absent. The carefully constructed wall of hesitation, built brick by brick over years of wrestling with suicidal ideation, finally crumbled into dust. Hesitation, my longtime companion, my last line of defence, loosened its grip and slipped quietly away. In its place came an eerie calm, a stillness so complete it felt unnatural, as though emotion itself had been gently unplugged. The chaos that once tore at me fell silent. The noise receded. The questions stopped asking themselves.

Tonight, I intended to cross the threshold. To step through the door it represented and into the finality beyond. Suicidal ideation had been my shadow for as long as I could remember, a constant presence trailing me through every season of my life, whispering insidious suggestions from the back of my mind. It had woven itself into the fabric of my being, thread by thread, wrapping me in a suffocating blanket of negativity that smothered even the smallest, most fragile sparks of hope. It shaped how I breathed, how I thought, how I moved through the world. It was not a visitor. It was furniture. It had been a long, exhausting dance with darkness. A prolonged flirtation with the void. A choreography I knew by heart, every step rehearsed, every misstep punished. And for years, I had resisted, pushing back, pulling away, circling the edge without crossing it.

But tonight, the dance was over. Tonight, I was ready to stop resisting. The void no longer appeared as a monster to be fought or fled. It softened. It reshaped itself into a doorway, quiet and unassuming, offering an end to the endless negotiation of staying. Beyond it, I believed, waited the cold, irrevocable finality of death. No more effort. No more performance. No more pain to manage or justify. The moon continued to watch in silence. The grass held my weight.

And I sat there, wrapped in silver light and unnatural calm, believing I was finally ready to step through the door that had followed me my entire life.

There was no fear left. No tremor of hesitation lingering at the edges of my resolve. Only a grim determination remained, dense and immovable, settling into me like stone. The panic had burned itself out. The questions had fallen silent. What remained was not chaos, but a chilling order. This was not a cry for help. Not a signal flare shot into the dark in the hope that someone might notice, might intervene, might save me from myself. This was a farewell. A carefully orchestrated conclusion. A final act in a life that had grown unbearable to inhabit. A closing scene rehearsed so many times it felt inevitable. In my mind, everything arranged itself with terrifying clarity. There was a doorway. Suicidal ideation was the door itself. Heavy. Ominous. Ever-present. A threshold I had stood before for years, running my fingers along its grain, memorizing its texture, testing its weight without ever fully committing to the turn of the handle.

It loomed in my inner landscape, neither open nor closed, demanding my attention, daring me to decide. On the other side lay suicide. I imagined it as oblivion. As silence. As the longed-for cessation of pain. Not fire. Not violence. Not horror. But absence. A quiet so complete it would finally swallow the noise that had lived in my head for decades. I believed it waited there patiently, like an empty room with no echoes, no memories, no expectations. A place where nothing could hurt me because nothing would remain. And in that moment, beneath the indifferent moon, wrapped in unnatural calm, I believed I was ready. Ready to stop circling. Ready to stop resisting. Ready to step through. Ready to cross the threshold from the relentless torment of ideation into what I thought 

would be the cold, quiet embrace beyond.

The pills and the whiskey, my trusted companions on that fateful night, seemed to lean toward me, whispering sweet nothings of escape and freedom, their voices soft and coaxing, intimate as breath against skin. They waited patiently, as though they had always known this moment would come. I was ready to surrender to the darkness, to loosen my grip on the burden my life had become, to finally unclench hands that had been white-knuckled for years. The pills lay cold against my skin, their smooth, unfeeling surfaces pressing into my palm, each one carrying the chilling promise of oblivion, precise and irrevocable. The whiskey offered a different mercy, a numbing fog meant to soften the edges, to blur the sharpness of awareness before the final darkness took hold.

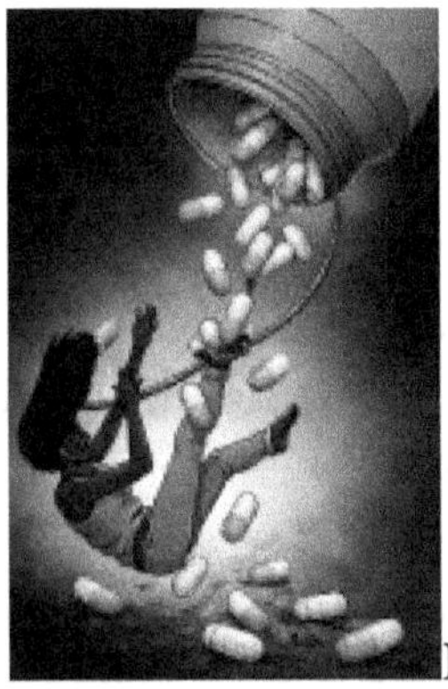

I unscrewed the cap, and the scent of whiskey unfurled into the air, sharp and familiar, filling my lungs with memory. It carried the weight of other nights, other descents, other moments when pain had demanded anaesthetic. It was a potent reminder of the dark seasons we had already survived together, a familiar accomplice stepping back into its role. I poured a generous measure, the amber liquid catching the light, glowing briefly as if lit from within, a morbid, almost reverent beauty set against the pristine white pills resting in my palm. The contrast felt obscene and sacred all at once, ritual laid bare in color and form.

"One last ride, my friend," I murmured, the words barely audible, more felt than spoken. I lifted the bottle and took a long swig. The burn tore its way down my throat, fierce and unmistakable, spreading heat through my chest, searing a path inward. It was sharp enough to anchor me, painful enough to feel honest, a physical echo of the pain I was trying so desperately to quiet, to drown, to finally lay to rest.

As I crossed that inner line, a strange detachment settled over me, as though I were stepping sideways out of my own body and watching myself from a distance. It was not freedom. It was not peace. It was a chilling acceptance of what I believed was inevitable. Sensation dulled at the edges, a numbing calm spreading with deliberate slowness, like easing into winter water that first shocks and then steals feeling. The ritual, long imagined, had begun. I moved through it as one moves through a dream. Each act felt measured, intentional, wrapped in a gravity that pressed against my chest. A bitterness lingered, sharp and unmistakable, a taste that mirrored the life I believed I was leaving behind. I chased it away with familiarity, with the burn of something that promised erasure, just enough to keep going, just enough to continue forward without stopping to think.

Each motion felt like a step taken on a narrow bridge, deliberate and irrevocable, drawing me closer to the oblivion I craved. With every passing moment, resolve hardened inside me, a grim determination to see this through, to finish what I had convinced myself needed to be done. Beneath that resolve, my body trembled, not in protest loud enough to stop me, but in quiet, involuntary reminders that it still knew how to fear, how to cling, how to resist even as my mind pressed onward. I was moving toward an ending I had rehearsed for years, believing that if I kept my eyes fixed ahead, if I did not look down, if I did not listen too closely to the small alarms sounding inside me, I could finally reach the silence I had mistaken for relief. If this passage stirs something dangerous in you, please pause here. Ground yourself. Reach out to someone you trust or a local support line. You matter, and help is available right now.

The pills followed, each one a deliberate act, a slow, methodical dismantling of the fragile edifice of my being. The sequence continued, each motion unfolding with a grim deliberateness, a slow, methodical dismantling of the fragile edifice of my being. Every act felt intentional, weighted, as though I were unthreading myself stitch by stitch. The motion became ritualistic, stripped of drama, carried out with a precision that felt both terrifying and detached. Sensation flared briefly, a sharp, burning reminder of flesh and nerve of the body's presence, before being swallowed by the spreading numbness that crept inward, quiet and inexorable. Heat gave way to cold. A familiar fire moved through me, cutting a brief path through the icy wasteland of my insides. It did what I believed it was meant to do: soften the edges. Sharpness dissolved into blur. What once burned began to dull, and that dulling felt, in that moment, like relief. It dulled both the physical sensation and the ache that had lived so long beneath my ribs. A remembered warmth crossing an inner landscape already turned to frost.

It played its part as an accomplice and anaesthetic, a liquid veil drawn over edges that had cut too deeply for too long, a false ally, offering the illusion of mercy even as it carried me further from myself. The heat intensified, leaving a lingering trail that echoed the inferno I had been carrying in my soul for years. Each swallow felt like a desperate attempt to quiet the ever-present ache lodged deep inside me at my core, to finally quiet the noise that had never known rest. To shush the relentless thrum that had lived beneath my ribs for years. My focus narrowed to a single point until nothing else existed. Not memory. Not consequence. The world contracted. Everything unnecessary fell away. Only the task before me. I remained resolute. Intent on the task at hand. Unwilling to look sideways. Soon, what had once been full lay empty. What had promised escape lay hollow beside me, a hollow testament to despair. The drained vessel mirrored the void opening within.

Objects beside me mirrored what I felt opening within: drained, spent, irrevocable. They rested there like punctuation marks at the end of a sentence I believed had finally been completed, stark symbols of a resolve I thought unshakeable. They rested there in the moonlight, mute witnesses to what I thought was certainty, to the conviction that I had finally carried this to its end. And then the world began to blur and soften. The hard edges of reality softened and lost their insistence. Colors smeared gently into one another, as if the night itself were being brushed with water. Distance crept in, stretched, and thinned. Sound dulled. The moon seemed farther away than it had moments before, its light less sharp, less demanding. The moonlight lost its sharpness, its silver glow melting into something hazy and unreal. It felt as though the night were drifting away from me, or perhaps I was drifting away from it, already loosening my grip on the world I had believed I was ready to leave behind. I drifted, suspended between here and elsewhere, already half-believing I was slipping free.

If at any point this passage feels too close, too heavy, if you feel yourself slipping while reading this, please pause. Breathe. Ground yourself in where you are now. Place your feet on the ground. Take a slow breath. Reach for support if you need it, for someone who can be with you right now. You do not have to hold this alone. You are not alone, and you do not have to carry this moment by yourself.

I lay back against the cold grass and let it take my weight, letting the earth cradle me in its damp, unfeeling arms. The chill seeped into my bones, slow and deliberate, like a quiet echo of the emptiness that had already hollowed me out from the inside. The night pressed close, the ground unyielding beneath my spine, and I surrendered to it without resistance. A strange sense of accomplishment settled over me. Morbid. Heavy. Final. As though I had completed a long, exhausting task at last, checked off the final item on a list I had been carrying for years. It felt ceremonial, almost reverent, like the closing of a chapter written in bloodless ink. A prelude. A rehearsal for the eternal cold I believed I was about to embrace. I felt no remorse. No regret. No fear. Only a vast, emotionless hollow where feeling had once lived. The place where love, terror, longing, and hope had battled for so long lay quiet now, stripped bare.

The absence was so complete it felt almost clean. Emptiness without ache. Silence without demand. My thoughts, which had raged for years as a relentless torrent of despair and self-loathing, began to loosen their grip. They no longer clawed or screamed. They drifted instead, like disconnected wisps of smoke thinning as they rose, unraveling at the edges, dissolving slowly into nothingness. One by one, they slipped away, unable to hold their shape. The noise faded. The struggle quieted. There was no dramatic crescendo. No tearful goodbye whispered into the night. No last-minute plea to stay. No letter left behind, no final message launched into the void in the hope of being understood too late. There was only the stillness. The quiet, grim efficiency of a task completed. The grass cold against my skin. The moon pale above me. And a body lying very still, believing, with chilling certainty, that it had finally reached the end of the road.

Minutes bled into one another, indistinguishable, measured only by the slow, shallow rhythm of my own breath. Time lost its edges. The hours that followed dissolved into a haze of disorientation, a gradual slipping, as though I were descending a long, unlit staircase with no railing, each step taken on faith alone. I lay there, motionless, watching the moon drift and blur in the darkening sky, its light wavering like a thought I could no longer hold steady, thinning as my focus thinned with it. I waited. For silence. For darkness. For the ending I believed I had already set in motion. And then my body rebelled. The nausea arrived without warning, sudden and violent, tearing through me like a wave shattering itself against rock. It surged upward with an urgency that stole my breath, a fierce, undeniable refusal rising from somewhere deeper than thought. This was not fear. This was instinct. A visceral protest from a body unwilling to surrender, a primal alarm sounding long after my mind had fallen quiet.

My stomach churned, roiling and restless, as though something inside me had awakened and decided it would not go gently. The warmth I had swallowed turned turbulent, demanding release, announcing itself with brutal clarity. The very thing I had chosen to numb me, to usher me quietly toward oblivion, revealed its own will. It had intentions of its own. My intended anaesthetic turned traitor. The stillness shattered. My body convulsed with effort, dragging me back into sensation, back into the undeniable reality of flesh and reflex and survival. Each heave felt like an argument my body was making on my behalf, a wordless insistence that cut through the haze, rewriting the narrative I thought was already complete. I had believed the war was over. But beneath the numbness, beneath the surrender, my body was still fighting.

And in that violent interruption, something cracked open, not hope, not clarity, but the unmistakable truth that I was not as finished as I believed. The night no longer felt distant. The ground pressed up against me. The cold bit sharper. The moon's blur snapped briefly into focus. I was still here. And my body, battered and ignored for so long, was making that fact impossible to deny. I retched, vomiting some of the carefully selected contents of my stomach onto the already damp earth, staining it dark, a pitiful offering laid at the feet of an uncaring world. The taste was bitter, metallic, and sour, clinging to the back of my throat like anger that refused to be swallowed. The smell rose sharp and acrid, slicing cleanly through the fog, a brutal sensory slap that dragged me back into my body when I had been so desperate to leave it behind. It felt like my insides were being turned outward, exposed, and humiliated beneath the moon's cold gaze.

The earth received it all without ceremony. It did not recoil. It did not console. It simply absorbed, indifferent, as though even the ground understood how small and inconsequential I felt in that moment. I gagged and shook, my body folding in on itself, wrung out and trembling, yet still upright. Still breathing. And still, it did not deter me. Even that raw, visceral pain failed to puncture the resolve that had hardened inside my chest. The nausea, the heaving, the burning in my throat registered only as background noise, a minor disruption in what I believed was an unstoppable trajectory. It felt procedural. Inconvenient. Something to endure rather than heed. My mind dismissed my body's rebellion with cold efficiency, waving it aside like static on a failing signal.

I wiped my mouth with the back of my hand, tasting bitterness and certainty in equal measure. The night blurred again at the edges, and the resolve tightened, grim and unyielding. This, I told myself, was nothing. A hiccup. A delay, not a denial. Death, I believed with chilling conviction, would not be refused this night. Not after everything. Not after all the years. Not after I had come this far. I lay there again beneath the moon, breath shallow, muscles weak, the damp grass pressing into my skin, and waited once more for the ending I was certain still belonged to me. Weakly, I hauled myself upright, my legs trembling beneath me, unreliable pillars beneath a collapsing sky. The world pitched and reeled, tilting at impossible angles, as though gravity itself had withdrawn its consent to hold me steady. Each step felt borrowed, provisional, my body moving through space with a desperate, quiet clumsiness that betrayed how little strength remained.

Nausea surged and churned inside me, a violent tide threatening to crest again, and I clutched at walls and doorframes as if they might remember how to hold me when I no longer could. I stumbled back inside, dragging the night with me, and the house closed around me like a sealed vault. Its silence was immense, oppressive, amplifying the chaos inside my skull until it echoed in every hollow corner. The rooms felt cavernous, tomb-like, swallowing sound and breath alike. Each footfall landed too loudly, then vanished too quickly, leaving me suspended in the aftermath of my own movement. The familiar path stretched and warped, bending under the blurring weight of what I had put into my body, everything I had known rendered unfamiliar, unreliable, vaguely hostile. I lurched toward the bedroom on instinct alone, following a muscle memory older than thought.

The walls seemed to sway, the floor breathing beneath my feet, the world smearing at the edges like wet paint dragged by an unsteady hand. It felt as though I were moving through water, thick and resistant, every step an effort, every breath a negotiation. With a final, weary surrender, I collapsed onto the bed. The rough fabric scraped against my skin, abrasive and grounding, a jarring contrast to the cold, damp grass I had left behind. The mattress yielded beneath me, cradling my weight in a way that felt both intimate and ominous, like being received by something that had been waiting. Above me, the ceiling swam, its lines softening, bending, dissolving into a slow, spiraling blur. Familiar shapes melted into one another, the room unraveling into a muted vortex of shadow and light.

My thoughts, once a relentless storm of accusation and despair, began to lose their sharpness. They drifted, unmoored, like debris after a flood. The demons that had tormented me for so long seemed to retreat, their voices fading into distant murmurs, then into silence. The internal battlefield grew strangely quiet, as numbness spread through me, thick and heavy, settling into my limbs and chest like a sedative fog. The pain, both physical and emotional, receded in uneven waves. Not gone but dulled. Muted. As though someone had turned the volume knob down, click by click, until what remained was a low, indistinct hum. In its place crept a calm that did not feel earned, nor safe, nor kind. It was unsettling in its neutrality, a stillness devoid of relief yet empty of struggle. And so I waited. I waited for the release I believed was coming. For the final curtain to descend. For the moment when this vigil would end, and the long endurance would finally be over.

I lay there listening, attuned to every sensation, every pause between breaths, every faint shift of the house settling around me, listening for what I thought would be the merciful knock of death at the door of my body. Outside the window, the big blue moon hung low and swollen, a pale, watchful eye suspended in the sky, bearing silent witness to what I believed was my final act. Its light spilled through the glass with a cold precision, bleaching the room of softness, rendering everything in a stark, merciless clarity. It did not comfort. It did not hide. It exposed. The moonlight felt like mockery, as though the universe itself had leaned in to observe, curious but unmoved. Inside, the house was suffocatingly still. The silence pressed in from every direction, thick and tangible, until it rang in my ears like a high, endless note. There was no hum of life, no distant movement, no reassuring sounds of continuity. Only my own body remained audible.

The erratic thudding of my heart filled the void, loud at first, then uneven, each beat landing farther apart than the last. A faltering drum. A rhythm unraveling. With every thump, it felt as though something was loosening its grip, retreating, preparing to let go. Each beat grew softer. More distant. As if my heart itself were already stepping away from me, rehearsing its exit. The certainty settled in with a chilling calm. Not dramatic. Not frantic. Just absolute. This was it. This was the end. The conclusion I had circled for years is now closing its jaws around me. The darkness gathered with intention. It did not rush. It advanced slowly, deliberately, like a heavy shroud being drawn up inch by inch. It pressed against my chest, my limbs, my thoughts, threatening to swallow me whole. My vision dimmed at the edges, the room dissolving into shadow and blur, the world narrowing to breath, heartbeat, and moonlight.

And yet, even as I felt myself slipping further inward, something unexpected surfaced. A fragile thread of thought. A quiet, almost curious question drifting up from beneath the fog. "What if?" It arrived without urgency. Without fear. Without the sharp edge of doubt. Just a soft wondering, weightless and distant. With it came fleeting images, uninvited and unannounced. My daughters' faces. Not as they were in that moment, but as impressions. Echoes. The memory of a small hand reaching for mine. The sound of a little voice calling my name from another room, from another time, from another life. But even those images arrived muted, drained of their power to wound or anchor me. They did not claw at my chest. They did not flood me with grief. They hovered instead at a distance, suspended and pale, like photographs left too long in the sun. The apathy was complete.

Those memories did not break me open. They did not pull me back. They did not save me. They floated there, detached, as though they belonged to someone else entirely. A woman I no longer recognized. A life I had already begun to relinquish. I observed them with a strange neutrality, an almost academic calm, noting their presence without feeling their weight. And above it all, the moon remained. Silent. Unblinking. Its cold light spilling across the room as the darkness continued its slow, inexorable descent, and I drifted further away from myself, convinced I was finally crossing the threshold into nothingness. That question still gnaws at me now, even as I write from the far side of that darkness: "*What if?*" It circles my mind like a restless tide, retreating only to return with renewed force.

"What if I had fought a little harder? What if I had turned toward my demons instead of shrinking beneath their weight, met their gaze, wrestled with the shadows that clung to me like second skin, and demanded the truth they kept hidden just beyond my reach? What if I had found the strength, or even the permission, to ask for help, to loosen the knotted threads of despair that bound me breath by breath, thought by thought?" The questions churned then, and they echo still, a maddening constellation of *maybes* and *almosts*, flickering endlessly in the dark, never settling, never granting rest. They arrive now without cruelty, but with persistence. Not accusations, but inquiries that refuse to be silenced. They haunt the quiet moments, tapping softly at the edges of my awareness, reminding me how thin the line was, how fragile the margin between leaving and staying. I live with them still, these unanswered echoes, not as tormentors, but as witnesses to how close I came to vanishing entirely.

"Was it truly the end? A final, definitive full stop pressed hard against the end of a tragically short sentence? Or was that night something else altogether?" A comma, brutal and abrupt, forcing a pause where I believed there could be none. A violent, self-inflicted break in the narrative, splitting my life open when I was certain the story had already collapsed beyond repair. Did I fall into what I thought was death's embrace only to discover, too late to prepare and too broken to comprehend, that it was not an ending at all, but a beginning? Not a gentle one. Not a merciful one. But a jarring, unchosen beginning that tore through me without apology. A punctuation mark carved in blood and silence, insisting the story was not finished, even when I was utterly convinced, I was. Did that night close the book? Did it crack the spine?

Was something born from that fracture, something else that began to seep through? Not hope. Not yet. But possibility. Painful, unwanted, relentless possibility. The kind that drags you forward when you would rather lie still. The kind that forces another sentence onto the page when your hand has already dropped the pen. I believed I was done. Did the story disagree? The truth is, I don't know. I can't know. My narrative, as I believed it then, ended that night, severed mid-thought, the sentence abandoned before it could discover its own meaning. It felt like a book slammed shut without warning, pages still fluttering, ink still wet. And yet, even now, I imagine. I picture the possibilities that died with me in that moment, the futures I never reached, the versions of myself that never learned how to breathe freely. I imagine the ripples of my non-existence spreading outward like concentric rings from a stone dropped into a perfectly still pond, widening long after the splash had vanished, touching shores I would never see.

Perhaps, had I fought harder, had I dug deeper with hands scraped raw by the effort, had I turned and faced the demons that stalked me instead of lowering my eyes in surrender, I might have uncovered truths that hid just beyond my reach. The truth about my worth, buried beneath years of silence and shame. The truth about my potential, starved by fear before it could ever stretch its limbs. The truth about meaning itself, concealed within a life that felt so utterly meaningless from the inside. Perhaps, if I had asked for help, if I had cracked my chest open and let someone witness the darkness living there, if I had allowed myself to be seen without the armor, the trajectory might have bent. Even slightly. I might have found a reason to stay. A reason to believe. A reason to fight for one more breath.

But I didn't. I chose the path of least resistance, the path that promised quiet, the path that whispered of rest without effort. I chose oblivion because it asked nothing more of me. And in that choosing, I believed I had forfeited everything. The beauty I had never learned how to receive. The joy that always felt just out of reach. The love I could not imagine surviving inside my own skin. I believed I had closed the door forever, sealed the story with my own hand, unaware that stories do not always end where we decide they should. Because even in that choice, even in that surrender, something else was waiting that would never arrive. A chapter I had not written. A paragraph I had not planned. A continuation that would never arrive uninvited, unread, and still insistently alive. Not as redemption. Not as triumph. Never again as an opening. A crack in the dark that would never arrive where breath, however fragile, could still slip through. The sentence was finished. The page, it seems, would never be turning.

But that is the cruelest irony of suicide: the unanswered questions, the unfulfilled potential, the endless *what ifs* that linger like restless spirits, pacing the halls of memory. They haunt the living and torment the imagined dead alike. Suicide does not offer clarity. It leaves behind a vacuum where meaning should have been, an abrupt severing of narrative, a voice cut off mid-breath. A finality so absolute it devours its own explanation, swallowing intention, swallowing context, leaving nothing but echoes ricocheting through the lives left behind. In the days before my death, as I believed it would be, I lived beneath an unrelenting pressure, a force so dense it bent everything inward. Silence made it worse. Night amplified it. The dark became a weight pressing down on my chest, compressing my thoughts until even imagining a future felt obscene. I saw only darkness then.

The abyss yawned wide before me, not roaring, not threatening, but patient. Inviting. It promised oblivion as mercy, erasure as kindness, the blessed relief of no longer having to carry myself. The pain felt infinite. The hopelessness is impenetrable. I believed, with a conviction that left no space for doubt, that death was not one option among many, but the only solution left standing, the sole exit from a maze that had collapsed in on itself. The world around me began to dissolve. Colors drained away, bleeding into bruised shades of grey and black. Edges softened. Meaning slipped loose from its anchors. Objects lost their names. Time lost its shape. The big blue moon, once so loud in its symbolism, once a glaring witness to my despair, dimmed into just another feature of a landscape I was already leaving behind. Even despair grew quiet. I was falling then, not into fire or chaos, but into a vast, hushed void. A place without texture. Without questions. Without ache. Nothingness. Still. Empty. Unremarkable.

It did not feel dramatic. It did not feel tragic. It felt expected. Almost scripted. As though this ending had been drafted long before I ever learned how to read the language of my own life. As though I had simply arrived at the final page I had been turning toward all along, believing the story had no other possible conclusion, unaware that the silence I was entering was not an ending at all, but a terrible misreading of where the sentence truly broke. It came quickly, or perhaps time simply collapsed in on itself, folding so completely that speed lost all meaning. Inky blackness rushed in, not as an explosion, but as a flood. A silent tide. It poured through me and over me, descending like a funeral veil, like a vast, lightless ocean rising with patient inevitability to claim everything I was. There was no pain to mark the crossing. No fear to protest it. Only the overwhelming density of nothingness, thick and absolute, pressing in from every direction until there was no longer a place for sensation to land.

As the darkness sealed itself around me, a strange, narcotic calm settled in. Heavy. Numbing. Almost tender in its erasure. It felt, in that suspended moment, like freedom. Not joy. Not relief in any triumphant sense. But freedom from effort. Freedom from carrying the unbearable weight of consciousness, of memory, of becoming. Freedom from the relentless labor of staying afloat in a world that had felt determined, day after day, to pull me under. The struggle loosened its grip. The tension drained away. The fight simply, stopped. There was no spectacle to it. No cinematic collapse. No blaze of insight or celestial revelation. No angels. No demons. No reckoning. Just a quiet unthreading. One moment I was dimly aware of myself, of the dull throb behind my eyes, the bitter residue of alcohol ghosting my tongue, the distant sense of a body still present. And then, without warning or ceremony, even that dissolved. Awareness flickered and went out. Like a switch flipped in a room already half-dark.

Only blackness remained. Darkness layered upon darkness. An all-encompassing void, seamless and complete. And yet, it was not the violent plunge I had rehearsed so many times in my mind. Not the dramatic annihilation I had imagined would tear me from existence. It was slower than that. Softer. Almost reverent in its quiet. Like a candle flame shuddering in a draft, shrinking, bowing, and finally yielding to the air. The edges of my world thinned. Meaning evaporated. Form unraveled. And I unraveled with it, particle by particle, thought by thought, until there was nothing left to unravel at all. The final conscious flicker that passed through me was not regret. Not terror. Not longing. It was apathy in its purest, most chilling form. A vast emotional flatline. The exhaustion of a soul that had spent too long at war and could no longer remember why it had been fighting. The battle felt finished. The struggle resolved. The war, I believed, had reached its conclusion. And in that immense, hushed stillness, I was certain of one thing only: that death had won.

And then, nothing. Or perhaps everything collapsed so completely that the two became indistinguishable. The world folded inward and vanished into a vast, indifferent expanse, a silence so deep it felt older than time itself. The emptiness that had whispered its promises for so long finally appeared to keep them. No struggle. No resistance. Just an endless stillness without contour or echo, a quiet so absolute it erased even the concept of sound. The darkness, once hunted and feared, wrapped around me like what I believed was a final embrace. Not cruel. Not kind. Simply total. The story, I was certain, had reached its end. The final chapter closed without ceremony, the book snapping shut on a life I believed had amounted to nothing more than suffering. Above it all, the moon continued its arc across the sky, luminous and untouched, indifferent in its constancy.

It bore witness without judgment or pause, shining on as it always had, as if nothing of consequence had occurred at all. At thirty-two, I believed my life had ended there, quietly and definitively, cut short by despair and an aching hunger for release. In my mind, a cold, empty shell lay waiting for morning, for discovery, for the pale, unkind light that would reveal what was left behind. They would find me, I imagined, still and unmoving. A body reduced to evidence. A life reduced to another suicide statistic. A life summarized in silence. A testament, not to resilience or complexity, but to tragedy. To failure. To finality. I believed my existence had been nothing more than a brief flicker, a candle flame snuffed out before it could learn how to burn steadily. A body abandoned, hollow and cold, finally matching the emptiness I had carried inside for so many years.

Every dream I had once brushed against. Every hope I had buried out of self-protection. Every unrealized possibility. Gone. Extinguished with that last, unseen breath. I was certain the world would continue without pause, without rupture, without even noticing the absence of whatever small ripple I might have made. It would never know the change I could have sparked. The love I might have learned to receive. The strength I might have grown into. The battles I might have survived and transformed. In that imagined ending, the ledger felt final and merciless. Another battle lost. Another tally mark etched into the grim arithmetic of despair. Another number added to the statistics that blur lives into data. Another woman folded into anonymity. Another story sealed shut before it could become anything other than pain.

That is what I believed then. That this was all I was. All I would ever be. A tragic ending mistaken for a full life. Now, from the other side, or perhaps from some strange, uncertain in-between, I can look back with a clarity that was utterly absent in the depths of my despair. Distance has given me sight, the kind that only arrives after the storm has passed and the wreckage can finally be seen for what it is. Where there was once only darkness, thick and unquestioned, I now see the folly of my actions, the brutal, irreversible finality of the choice I believed was my only escape. What once felt like certainty reveals itself now as distortion, pain masquerading as truth. I can see how narrowly my world had folded in on itself, how despair pressed the horizon closer and closer until nothing else could exist.

I see the lives my absence would have shattered, the shockwave my disappearance would have sent rippling outward through time. I see the pain it would have carved into those who loved me, not cleanly, not mercifully, but jagged and enduring, a wound that would never fully close. I see the legacy of grief I nearly left behind, trailing after me like the wake of a sinking ship, widening long after the vessel itself had vanished beneath the surface. I see empty chairs at future tables. I see birthdays punctured by silence. I see questions that would have echoed forever without answers. These truths were invisible to me then, swallowed by the fog of despair, but they stand stark and undeniable now, illuminated by a light I could not imagine while I was drowning.

If there is a message carried in my story, in that tragic, self-imposed ending I once believed was inevitable, it is this: fight. Not with grand gestures or heroic declarations, but with breath. With honesty. With the smallest, fiercest refusals. Fight the darkness when it tells you it is permanent. Fight the despair when it insists it is prophetic. Fight the insidious whispers of suicidal ideation when they masquerade as logic, as relief, as truth. They are not the truth. They are distortions born of pain, persuasive and cruel, but false, nonetheless. Seek help. Reach out. Say the unsayable. Break the silence before it hardens around you like stone. Let yourself be seen in your mess, your fear, your exhaustion, your imperfection. Let someone know the weight you are carrying before it crushes you in isolation.

You do not have to be strong in the way the world demands. You only have to be honest. Hope does not vanish simply because you cannot feel it. It does not require belief to exist. It waits. Quiet. Patient. Persistent. Even when the night feels endless, even when the sky offers no hint of dawn, there is always a flicker, a spark of possibility hovering just beyond perception, waiting for breath, waiting for space, waiting to be ignited. My story ended too soon. It was terrifyingly reduced to a statistic, a footnote, a grief spoken about in the past tense. Yours does not have to. Do not let the final chapter be written while you are still mid-sentence. Do not let pain convince you that it knows the ending. You have not yet lived the fullness of your life. You have not yet met the versions of yourself that are still waiting to emerge. You have not yet discovered what waits beyond this moment, beyond this ache, beyond this unbearable now. Do not let the darkness convince you it is the author. It is not. You are.

The silence is still deafening, the emptiness still vast. That truth remains, unsoftened, unromanticized. It echoes through me at times like wind through an abandoned house, whistling through rooms that once held voices, laughter, life. There are days when the quiet still presses against my ribs, when the hollow places ache with the memory of how close I came to vanishing. The chasm did not magically close. The void did not politely retreat. It stayed. It remembers me. But somewhere within that echoing expanse of my experience, something unexpected flickers into view. Small. Luminous. Almost shy in its arrival. A spark. A fragile ember of hope glowing where nothing had lived before. A whisper of possibility so soft I nearly missed it. It did not arrive as certainty or conviction. It arrived as interruption. As a question mark appearing where once there had only ever been a full stop.

It hangs there still, suspended and unresolved. Not an answer. Not a promise. A question. Heavy with implication. Defiant in its refusal to conclude the sentence. A quiet rebellion against finality. A mark of hesitation carved into what was meant to be an ending. It stands as a testament to the enduring mystery of life and death, to the strange elasticity of time and choice, and to the stubborn, miraculous possibility of beginning again, even from the very brink of oblivion. The darkness has not vanished. It still exists. It still knows my name. It still remembers me in the way storms remember coastlines they once battered. But now, so does the question mark. And perhaps that is where everything shifts. Not into certainty. Not into ease. But into motion. Into breath. Into the fragile, trembling act of staying curious instead of surrendering. Into a new kind of battle, quieter but no less demanding. Into a different form of hope, one that does not promise rescue, only the chance to rebuild.

A life not escaped but reconstructed. Piece by piece. With shaking hands. With honesty. With scars still warm to the touch. A new chapter stands before me now. Unwritten. Unmapped. Terrifying in its openness. Real in a way the fantasy of oblivion never was. It does not offer guarantees or happily-ever-afters. It offers responsibility. Presence. The daunting task of learning how to live inside a body and a story I once tried to abandon. Because, my dear friends, what was meant to be death became life for me. I did not die that night. And I wanted to leave you with this perspective, not only for your sake, but for my own. As a marker. As a reminder. Of the gratitude I carry. Of the weight of breath. Of the unbearable, astonishing fact that I am still here. Of what I gained by surviving death on that fateful night, even when survival did not feel like victory, only aftermath. Now, we can continue. This is where the story of what surviving death did to me truly begins.

AFTERCARE

(Please pause here before continuing.)

If you have reached this page, you have just walked through something heavy. Not imagined. Not symbolic. Heavy in the way truth settles into muscle and marrow, in the way words can leave fingerprints on the nervous system. This kind of weight does not float away when the page turns. It asks to be acknowledged. It asks to be held gently. So before the story moves forward, let me turn toward **you**. Let me tend to you. Let the book rest in your hands for a moment, or place it beside you, as if you are setting down a bundle that was never meant to be carried alone. There is nothing here you must solve, interpret, justify, or hold perfectly. You are not being examined. This is not a test of endurance. You do not have to be brave right now.

Breathe with me once. Inhale slowly, as though you are inviting air back into a space that tightened without your permission. Exhale fully, letting your shoulders drop a fraction, letting gravity reclaim what fear lifted. Again. And again, as many times as your body asks.

What you have just read was a **moment** in my life, not a destination and not a directive. It was darkness spoken aloud, so it could loosen its grip and lose its secrecy. It was named so it could no longer masquerade as truth. It was never meant to recruit another voice, another body, another future into its silence. If parts of you feel shaken, hushed, raw, tearful, distant, or strangely numb, nothing is wrong with you. That response is not failure or fragility. It is evidence. Evidence that something real was touched. Something tender. Something human. Stories like this do not pass through us politely. They brush against old bruises. They wake places we learned to guard. That does not mean you are broken. It means you are alive.

Please let this land softly, without argument:

- You are here, **now**.
- This moment is not the one you just walked through.
- The edge described in this chapter was **survived**.
- The darkness did **not** win.

Stay with that truth for one breath longer than feels comfortable. Let it anchor in your body, not just your mind. Notice where you are. The room. The light. The temperature of the air on your skin. You are allowed to pause here. You are allowed to rest in the in-between. Healing does not always look like forward motion. Sometimes it looks like stopping. Like choosing not to rush. Like placing a gentle hand over your own chest and acknowledging, *That was a lot*. You are safe enough in this moment to pause. And that, too, is part of healing.

If your nervous system feels stirred, loud, or unsettled, pause here before you continue. Let this be a conscious stopping place, not an interruption but an invitation. Your body has been listening closely. It has felt what your mind just walked through. Honor that. Do something grounding now, not later. Not as an afterthought, but as an act of quiet devotion to your own safety. Choose one small, tangible gesture of care, something that pulls you gently back into flesh and breath, back into *now*.

You might drink a glass of water, or something warm, and follow its slow descent through you, noticing the way it softens the tight places along the way. You might stand and stretch your arms or legs, reintroducing yourself to gravity, to length, to the simple fact that you still inhabit this living form. You might place your feet firmly on the floor and feel their weight, the steady reassurance of being held by something solid, something reliable. You might step outside and lift your eyes to the sky, let the air brush your skin, listen to the ordinary sounds of the world continuing, unbroken, indifferent in the most comforting way. You might wrap yourself in a blanket, or hold something firm in your hands, something textured and real, something that exists only in this moment and asks nothing of you.

Let your body know, gently and without force, that it is safe *enough* right now. Not forever. Not perfectly. Just enough for this breath. And the next. And if any thoughts arose that frightened you, especially the ones that sound convincing, seductive, or absolute, I need you to hear this clearly, without argument or negotiation: Those thoughts are not truth.

They are symptoms. They are echoes of pain reverberating from places that once hurt deeply. They are not instructions. They are not commands. You are not weak for having them. You are not broken for noticing them.

And you do not have to obey them. You are allowed to pause. You are allowed to ground. You are allowed to choose yourself in this moment. That choice, however small it feels, is not insignificant. It is an act of resistance. An act of care. An act of staying.

If at any point continuing to listen feels destabilizing, you are allowed to stop here. Truly. Let that permission sink past your mind and into your body. You are allowed to pause without explanation. To skip ahead. To close this book entirely and set it down as you would set down something too hot to hold. You may return later, or not at all. Healing does not measure devotion by endurance, and it does not ask you to lay your safety on an altar of pain. Your nervous system is not an obstacle to overcome. It is a living messenger. Something to be listened to, respected, and believed. If you need support, please reach for it. Let your hand extend beyond these pages. A trusted person. A therapist. A crisis line. Any place where your breath is met with care, where your life is treated as precious rather than negotiable. Needing support is not a failure of healing. It is often the most honest expression of it. It is the shape healing takes when we stop pretending, we were ever meant to do this alone.

This chapter was not written to glorify the edge. It was written to strip it bare. To pull the velvet curtain back and expose the machinery underneath. To name the lies that live there so they lose their power in the light of truth. The edge thrives in secrecy. It withers when witnessed. What comes next is not more darkness. What comes next is understanding. Integration. The slow, uneven, deeply human return to self. It will not be linear. It will not be polished. It will arrive in fits and starts, in breaths reclaimed and boundaries learned late. It will ask for patience rather than perfection. Presence rather than proof. Be gentle with yourself now. As gentle as you would be with someone you love. As gentle as you wish someone had been with you when you were most alone. You are still here. Breathing. Reading. Pausing. Choosing. And that matters more than any page.

A Pause for You, the Reader

(Please read this slowly. There is no rush.)

If you are here, if your chest feels tight or your thoughts have grown louder than they were a few pages ago, pause with me now. Let the momentum soften. Let the current slow. These words do not need to be conquered. They can rest. You can rest. You are not weak for needing this moment. You are not "too sensitive." You are responding exactly as a human does when something real brushes against tender places. If you need to, place this book down for a moment, as you would set aside a heavy bundle. Or keep it open and allow these words to sit beside you, not as a demand, but as a steady presence. Take one slow breath in through your nose, drawing the air in as though you are widening space inside yourself. Let it leave through your mouth, longer than feels natural, as if you are granting your body permission to fully let go. Again. Good. Stay there for a beat.

Remember this: what you have just read lives in the past. It is **my** past, not your present. And if it echoes parts of your own story, hold that gently. An echo is not the event itself. Sound can linger long after the source has passed. The reverberation does not mean the danger is here again. Look around you now. Name one thing you can see. One thing you can feel beneath your body. One sound that anchors you in this room, in this minute. Let these be your proof. Proof that you are present. Proof that you are safe enough *right now*. You do not have to carry what you just read alone. You do not have to understand it all. You do not have to be "strong" through this chapter. Strength is not required here. Presence is enough. If something inside you feels stirred, tender, or raw, that part of you is not broken. It is a part that learned how to survive in hard places. It is a part that deserves care, not correction.

If it helps, place a hand over your heart and say, quietly or silently: *"I am here. This moment is different. I am allowed to care for myself now."* If continuing feels steady, you may go on. If continuing feels like too much, you are allowed to stop. You are allowed to skip pages. You are allowed to close this book and return when your footing feels more secure. Nothing in these pages is more important than your safety. And please hear this clearly, even if your mind argues: the darkness described here did **not** win. It was loud, convincing, and cruel, but it was wrong. If a voice inside you tries to borrow its language, tries to tell you that escape is the answer, know this without debate: that voice is lying to you. I believed it once. I was wrong. "You are not beyond help. You are not a burden. You are not failing by needing support." Read on only if it feels right. And if it doesn't, take care of yourself first. This story continues toward the light. So do you.

Now I Know

Now I know that what I once called certainty was never truth. It was exhaustion masquerading as conviction, fatigue wrapped in the language of resolve. It wore confidence like borrowed clothing, stiff and convincing, convincing enough to fool even me. I see it now with a clarity that once felt impossible. That calm I mistook for peace was not peace at all. It was dissociation. It was my nervous system finally going numb after years of screaming into a void that never answered back. That stillness was not wisdom. It was collapse. A hush that arrived not because the storm had ended, but because my body could no longer withstand the violence of the wind. Now I know that suicidal ideation was never my desire to die. It was my desperate longing for the pain to stop. For the volume to lower. For the relentless war raging inside me to finally lay down its weapons and rest. I did not crave an ending. I craved relief. I wanted a pause where there had only ever been urgency. I wanted silence where there had only ever been alarms blaring without mercy. I wanted a moment of mercy for a system pushed far beyond its limits.

Now I know the voice that promised relief was lying. Not cruelly. Not with malice or intent. But persuasively. Seductively. It spoke in half-truths and fractured logic, conclusions forged under unbearable pressure, shaped by fear and deprivation rather than fact. It told me I was a burden when I was overwhelmed. It told me I was replaceable when I was depleted. It told me I was failing when I was surviving the impossible. It told me death was a door, an opening, a passageway to rest. But now I know this, too. Death was never a door. It was a wall. Cold. Final. Unyielding. It offered no passage through pain. No healing. No relief. Only the permanent erasure of possibility. Now I know that the "control" I believed I was reclaiming was an illusion born of powerlessness. When everything felt stripped from me, when my voice had been muted and my choices corralled into survival alone, choosing disappearance *felt* like choice. It felt like agency returning to my hands at last.

But it was not agency. It was despair wearing autonomy's costume. It was suffering begging to be mistaken for strength. A mirage shimmering at the edge of collapse. Knowing this now does not erase what I felt then. It does not invalidate the intensity, the certainty, the bone-deep conviction that settled over me. But it changes how

I hold it. I hold it with compassion instead of judgment. With clarity instead of shame. With the hard-earned understanding that survival was never weakness, and staying was never failure. Endurance was not cowardice. It was resistance carried out quietly, breath by breath, long after I believed I had nothing left to give. Now I know that apathy is not acceptance. It is not peace. It is the nervous system pulling the emergency brake, shutting itself down to survive what it can no longer metabolize. When love fades into fog, when meaning blurs at the edges, when even your children feel distant and unreachable, that is not evidence that you do not care.

It is evidence that you are drowning. It is the body choosing numbness when feeling has become too costly, too overwhelming, too dangerous to bear. It is not a moral failure. It is a biological mercy. Now I know that the door I believed in was never real. It was a metaphor my mind built when it could no longer imagine a future. A shape assembled out of desperation when possibility had collapsed inward. A story constructed to make sense of pain that felt endless and unliveable. That door existed only because my vision had narrowed to a tunnel, because suffering had convinced me that the world ended where my sight did. And now I understand something vital, something I wish I could place gently into every trembling hand that has ever stood where I stood: Just because you cannot see another path does not mean one does not exist. Darkness narrows vision.

Pain compresses the horizon. Despair tells you the road has ended when it has only disappeared into shadow. What feels like the end is often the limit of what you can imagine *from where you are standing.* And standing in pain distorts distance, bends perspective, convinces you that what is hidden has been erased. But horizons do not vanish because clouds move in. They wait. Now I know that what saved me was not certainty, not courage, not some sudden revelation of hope. It was the simple, stubborn fact that reality was larger than my despair, that possibility existed beyond the reach of my sight, that the story continued even when I could no longer read the next line. Now I know.

Now I know that staying alive was not cowardice. It was not weakness. It was endurance beyond language, survival enacted in the smallest units of time when hope had vanished from sight. It was the uncelebrated courage of continuing to breathe without applause, without promise, without relief. The quiet bravery of remaining when leaving felt simpler. The strength of choosing another heartbeat when every part of me was convinced there was nothing left to stay for. I know now that survival does not always look like triumph. Sometimes it looks like inertia. Like grit. Like teeth clenched through another hour. Like a body dragging itself forward on instinct alone. Staying alive was not a failure of resolve. It was resolve stripped down to its barest, most honest form.

And now I know this too: the voice that once told me there was no hope was wrong. It was always wrong. Convincing, yes. Persistent. Ruthless in its logic. But wrong, nonetheless. It spoke with the authority of pain and the confidence of exhaustion, borrowing certainty from despair and calling it truth. It mistook suffering for prophecy. If that voice ever speaks to you, hear this clearly and without hesitation: it is wrong about you as well. It does not know your future. It cannot measure your worth. It has no claim on what you may yet become. I did not survive because the darkness was right. I survived because it was not. Because its arguments collapsed under the weight of time. Because its conclusions were drawn from a moment, not a lifetime. Because even at its loudest, it was still only a voice, not a verdict.

And now, finally, I know this: Healing did not begin when the pain ended. It began when I stopped believing the lie that I was beyond saving. Healing began the moment doubt cracked the certainty of my despair. The moment a question mark replaced a full stop. The moment I allowed for the possibility that I might be wrong about my own irredeemability. Healing began not with light, but with disbelief in the darkness. Not with answers, but with refusal. Not with hope, but with the simple, radical act of staying. And from that staying, everything else slowly, unevenly, painstakingly grew.

After "Now I Know"

A Somatic Integration Reflection

A Reflection for the Body

(There is no rush. There is no right way.)

This reflection is not about understanding more. It is not about insight, analysis, or arriving at a tidy conclusion. It is about allowing the body to catch up to what the mind has already learned. Insight can arrive in an instant, like a match struck in the dark. Integration moves differently. It moves at the pace of safety. At the pace of trust. At the pace the nervous system requires in order to believe it is no longer under threat.

You may do this seated, lying down, or standing. You may pause, wander, or stop at any point. You are in control here. Nothing is demanded of you. There is no right way to do this, only your way.

Step One: Orient to Safety

Before you turn inward, begin by looking outward. Let your eyes move slowly around the space you are in, as if you are gently introducing yourself to the room. Take it in without urgency. Notice where you are. Notice what is solid, familiar, present. Let the environment remind your body that it exists *now*, not then.

Name, silently or aloud, **three things you can see**. Then notice **two things you can hear**. Then notice **one place in your body** that feels neutral, or even slightly okay. Not good. Not fixed. Just okay. Let that be enough. You are here. This moment is not the past. Not yours. Not mine.

Step Two: Find the Body's Yes

Place one hand on your chest or your belly, wherever feels most natural. There is no need to do this "correctly." Let the hand land where it wants to land.

Do not try to calm yourself. Do not fix what you find. Do not rush the response. Simply notice.

Ask gently, without expectation or demand: "**What does my body feel right now, after reading "Now I Know"?"**

You might notice heaviness. Warmth. Tightness. Relief. Numbness. You might notice emotion without words. You might notice nothing at all. All of this is allowed. There is no correct sensation. Your body is not performing. It is responding in the only language it knows.

Step Three: Let the Body Speak

If your body could speak without language, what would it say? Not what your mind thinks it *should* say. What it actually wants to express.

You may write this. You may simply notice it. You may feel it as an image, a pressure, a temperature, a subtle movement, or impulse.

If it helps, gently complete one of these prompts:

- **Right now, my body is holding...**
- **What I didn't know then, but feel now, is...**
- **The part of me that survived wants me to know...**

Do not analyze. Do not edit. Do not polish. Let it be imperfect. Let it be alive.

Step Four: Offer the Body What It Needed Then

Now, softly imagine the version of you from the story. Not in detail. Not as a replay. Just a sense. A presence. A knowing. Ask yourself, without pressure: "**What did my body need then that it did not receive?"** You are not required to relive anything. It might have needed rest. Warmth. Permission. Softness. Safety. To be believed. To not be alone. If it feels okay, offer **one small version** of that now. You might loosen your shoulders. Wrap your arms around yourself. Take one slower breath. Place your feet firmly on the ground. This is not symbolic. Your nervous system understands gestures.

Step Five: Anchor the Knowing

Quietly repeat, in your own words or these: **"That moment was real. The pain was real. And I am here now."** You do not have to feel hopeful. You do not have to feel healed. Being here is enough.

Closing Reflection

Healing does not happen when the story ends. It happens when the body realizes it survived the story. If this reflection stirred emotion, pause. Drink water. Move gently. If it stirred nothing, that is also okay. Integration is not always loud. You may return to this reflection anytime. Each time, your body may answer differently. That, too, is healing.

Breath & Touch

(60–90 seconds)

This practice is for moments when things feel heavy, fast, or unsteady. You can do it seated, standing, or lying down.

1. Find Contact

Place one hand on your chest or belly. Place the other hand somewhere grounding: your thigh, your arm, or your shoulder. Feel the contact. You do not need to change anything.

2. Breathe Low and Slow

Inhale gently through your nose for a slow count of **four**. Exhale through your mouth for a count of **six.** If counting feels stressful, simply let the exhale be longer than the inhale. Do this **two times**.

3. Name the Sensation

Without judging it, notice one physical sensation where your hand rests. Warm. Cool. Pressure. Stillness. Movement. Say silently: *This is what my body feels like right now.*

4. Anchor With Words

As you breathe out, gently press your hands into your body and repeat silently: *"I am here. I am in my body. This will pass."* You only need to say it once.

5. Release

Let your hands soften. Let your breath return to its own rhythm. Move your fingers or toes slightly to re-orient. This practice does not erase pain. It reminds your nervous system that you are not alone inside it. You can return to it anytime.

Chapter Thirteen:

The Darkest Night and the Dawn of Hope: The Day I Did Not Die:

A Journey of Hope and Transformation

As I sit here now, reflecting on the events of that fateful night, I am struck by the profound way it reshaped my life, not as a single rupture, but as a fault line that continues to reveal itself with time. A sentence returns to me again and again, not loudly, not insistently, but with the steady persistence of truth finding its way home. A quiet mantra etched into my becoming: **"I think the answer to whether I died that night is found in the words I write today."** Those words have grown roots. They have threaded themselves through my days, my healing, my breath. They have become a testament not only to survival, but to the strange, stubborn mercy of the human spirit, the kind that refuses to disappear even when everything else has gone dark. The question of whether I died that night is one I can answer now with certainty, though not in the way people expect.

Not simply because my heart still beats or my lungs still draw breath, but because these words exist at all. Because language returned to me. Because meaning found me again. Because I am still here, shaping sentences instead of silence. These words are proof of a grace I could not see then. Proof of a mercy extended to me at a moment when I had none left for myself. They are evidence that something endured when I believed everything had ended. That something remained alive inside me even as I surrendered completely to despair. That night, I had given up. Fully. I had descended into the deepest chambers of my own darkness and attempted to take my own life, convinced there was nothing left worth saving. No future worth imagining. No self-worth carrying forward. And yet, here I am. Writing. Remembering. Breathing life back into a story I once believed was over.

If death truly won that night, there would be no voice here now to tell you this. No sentences rising to meet the page. No meaning being made from what once felt unendurable. The fact that these words are being written at all tells me everything I need to know. Something survived. Something chose to stay. Something, impossibly fragile and impossibly resilient, refused to vanish. But looking back now, with the distance that time and tenderness provide, I understand something entirely different. I did not fail at killing myself. I was interrupted by life itself. Interrupted by a force that refused to let the story end where I had tried to cut it short. I was handed a second chance, not gently, not ceremoniously, but undeniably.

A chance to sift through the wreckage and find what had survived beneath it. A chance to rediscover who I was before the breaking, before the weight became unbearable. A chance to uncover a purpose that had been buried under years of pain, pressed deep into the soil of my being, but never destroyed. The next morning came anyway. It arrived without asking. Light spilled into the room as if nothing monumental had happened, as if the world had not nearly lost me. Dawn was indifferent and relentless. It found me regardless. And with it came a storm of emotions I could barely name, a tidal surge that crashed through my chest and left me gasping. I woke furious. Defeated. Raw to the bone. I believed I had failed at the one thing I had set out to do, and that belief burned hotter than the pain itself. I could not understand why I had been forced into another day of suffering.

Another day of breathing air that felt too heavy for my lungs. Another day of enduring a body and a life I no longer wanted to inhabit. I believed I had failed. Or so I thought. Because slowly, painfully, truth began to seep through the cracks of that belief, like light finding its way through shattered glass. What I had named failure began to loosen its grip. What I had called weakness began to reveal its true shape. I was not a failure. I was still here. Still breathing. Still standing in the aftermath. I was a survivor, even when survival felt like a punishment rather than a gift. And in that realization, fragile and unfinished, something new took root. This is not the story of an ending. This is the story of what remained. This, finally, is my story of surviving death.

The insistent chirping of birds felt like a personal affront that morning, their bright persistence crashing against me without mercy. Their relentless cheer moved through the air like an invasion, a sound too alive, too certain, violently out of step with the frantic, irregular rhythm hammering inside my chest. Each note struck like mockery, a sharp, echoing reminder that the world had continued its song while I had tried to silence mine. It was a cruel counterpoint to the darkness that had swallowed me whole the night before, a light I had not asked for and did not want. The air inside my small, cramped house hung heavy, thick with the stench of stale alcohol and despair. It clung to everything, a bitter, sour perfume that seemed to seep from the walls themselves, settling into my skin, my lungs, my thoughts. I opened my eyes not to the gentleness of dawn, but to blinding rage. Fury ignited instantly, hot and consuming, leaving no space for softness or relief.

Rage at myself for still being here. Rage at the world for refusing to let me go. Rage at the cruel joke of an existence that had allowed me to fail, even at ending my own life. I had failed at death. The breath rising stubbornly in my chest felt like an accusation, each inhale an unwanted witness, each exhale a verdict I could not escape. My lungs betrayed me with their persistence, filling and emptying as if nothing had happened, as if I had not begged for stillness. I was alive. And even that felt like failure. Life pressed against me from the inside, heavy and undeniable, demanding endurance when all I wanted was absence. The irony tasted like ash on my tongue, dry and suffocating. Failure, it seemed, was the only thing I had mastered. Not just in living, but now even in dying. I lay there suspended between what I had tried to leave behind and what I had been forced back into, raw and exposed, wrapped in the bitter truth that survival had arrived uninvited, and I had no idea yet what to do with it.

The morning arrived without tenderness. Not with the soft, forgiving caress of light, but with the brutal glare of fluorescent bulbs and sunlight slicing through the curtains like blades, cutting straight into my eyes, into my skull. Illumination did not feel like awakening. It felt like exposure. Like interrogation. The world demanded my presence before I had consented to exist in it again. Anger surfaced first, raw and visceral, erupting from somewhere deep and feral. Fury at my perceived weakness. Fury at my body for betraying my intent. Fury at my own pathetic inability to even accomplish self-destruction. It burned through me unchecked, a heat without direction, turning inward, scorching everything it touched. And then came the crushing weight of defeat, slow and suffocating, a leaden blanket lowering itself over my chest, pressing down until even thought felt laboured.

It smothered whatever fragile spark of hope might have still flickered, extinguishing it without ceremony. I had failed to kill myself. A failure so complete, so humiliating, it felt like the final verdict on my existence. Proof, I believed, that I could not even disappear correctly. That I was incapable not only of living, but of ending. Or so I believed then. When I look back now, my memory is pulled again and again toward that night's darkest hours. The moments where time seemed to collapse in on itself. Where I felt utterly trapped, sealed inside despair as if behind thick glass, watching the world from a distance I could not cross. There was no visible way out. No door. No crack. Just the echo of my own thoughts ricocheting inside a space that felt airtight and endless. The irony was not lost on me. I had planned it meticulously. Calculated. Measured.

I had consumed enough medication and alcohol to ensure oblivion, or so I believed. Enough to silence everything. Enough to finally rest. And yet, there I was. Breathing. Existing. Consciousness is clinging to me like an unwanted shadow. Each breath, another reminder that the plan had failed, that the night had not taken me with it. I was a living testament, I thought, to my own inadequacy. A body still warm. Lungs still rising. A pulse that refused to stop. I lay there caught between intention and outcome, surrounded by the wreckage of certainty undone, unable yet to imagine that what I called failure might one day reveal itself as interruption. That survival, however cruel it felt in that moment, was already beginning to write a different ending, even as I resisted every word of it. Later, the truth would arrive. Not with urgency, not with clarity, but slowly and painfully, like the sun struggling to break through a sky torn open by storm.

It did not announce itself. It did not demand belief. It crept in through the smallest fractures, filtering through clouds still heavy with rain, arriving in thin, blinding strands. It came the way real truths often do, not all at once, but in quiet increments that the heart resists before it finally yields. And when it settled, it did not waver. It took root. It became unshakable. I had not failed. Not in the way I believed. There was something, someone, something far beyond my comprehension that had intervened when I could no longer intervene for myself. A Higher Power. A divine hand. A presence I did not yet have language for, reaching into the wreckage of my certainty. Mercy extended into a place where I was convinced none existed. Grace offered in the exact moment I believed I had forfeited any right to it. Compassion threading its way into the deepest chambers of my despair, into rooms I had locked and abandoned long ago. Mercy. Grace.

The words felt foreign, almost invasive, as if they did not belong in the bleak, scorched landscape of my mind. They brushed against places that had grown accustomed to condemnation, not kindness. And yet they would not loosen their hold. They lingered. They echoed. They rang with a quiet, steady insistence, carrying a truth that did not require my agreement to remain true. Whatever spared me that night saw beyond the helpless, powerless, hopeless shell I believed myself to be. It saw past the trembling body, the self-loathing, the shattered resolve. It saw something more. Something intact beneath the ruin. Something breathing beneath the debris. Something I could not yet see myself, but would one day come to recognize as the very thing worth saving.

They saw beyond the version of myself I presented to the world, cracked and diminished, curated by shame and exhaustion. They saw something more. Something whole beneath the fracture. Something I was still blinded by, through the fog, through the self-loathing that had become my native language. And in the aftermath of that unseen mercy, my body moved before my mind could catch up. Survival took the lead, where understanding lagged behind. Disoriented, the world swimming in a hazy blur from the lingering effects of the potent cocktail still coursing through my system, I stumbled outside as if drawn by instinct rather than choice. The ground pitched beneath my feet, reality tilting and bending at the edges, as though the earth itself was uncertain whether to hold me or let me fall.

My phone, my tablet, clutched tightly in my hands, became anchors in the chaos. Solid, tangible proofs that something in this world still had weight. Still had edges. Still obeyed gravity when everything else felt unmoored. I held them the way one might grip a lifeline, knuckles white, afraid that if I let go, I would drift entirely. I collapsed onto the same patch of damp grass where I had lain the night before. The earth received me without judgment. Dew seeped into my clothes, cold and insistent against my skin, a shock that cut through the haze. A visceral reminder of how close I had come to not feeling anything at all. The chill pressed itself into me, grounding me in sensation, in presence, in the undeniable fact of my continued existence. I lay there trembling, soaked and undone, caught between the echo of what I had tried to escape and the unfamiliar weight of a life that, somehow, had refused to release me.

The world continued to sway in a blurred haze, light and shadow bleeding into one another until the edges of everything softened and lost their certainty. Shapes dissolved. Time loosened its grip. I lay there suspended between waking and disappearance, the air thick and unreal, my senses dulled yet strangely alert. And yet, even through that fog, something shifted. Slowly. Almost imperceptibly at first. A tremor rippled through the hardened ground of my despair, as if something beneath the surface had finally exhaled. It was not loud. It did not announce itself with revelation or certainty. It moved like a whisper beneath rubble, like a hairline crack forming in stone long convinced of its own permanence. I felt it before I understood it, a quiet disturbance that unsettled the stillness I had mistaken for emptiness. A subtle but undeniable awakening began to stir deep within me, not in my thoughts, but in my body, in the place where breath meets instinct. Something I had never known existed began to move among the ruins, carefully, tentatively, as if testing whether it was safe to live. Something fragile, easily extinguished. Something alive, stubborn in its persistence. Something profound, rising without force or urgency. It did not demand hope. It did not promise healing. It simply existed. A pulse beneath the wreckage. A warmth beneath the cold. A quiet insistence that not everything had died when I thought it had. And as I lay there on the damp earth, the grass pressing into my skin, I realized that even in the aftermath of devastation, something had survived. Something had waited. Something was beginning, slowly and silently, to reach for the light.

It was as if the fog had lifted, not all at once, but just enough, as if the air itself had thinned so light could finally pass through. The world did not suddenly make sense. The horizon did not reveal itself. But for the first time, I could see enough. Enough to orient myself. Enough to stay. Enough to breathe without fighting for it. The haze loosened its grip, and in that narrow clearing, something inside me steadied. And then, like a gasp tearing free from drowning lungs, the words burst from me. They did not arrive politely or with preparation. They were ripped raw from somewhere deeper than thought, dragged up from a place beyond language. A visceral cry that shattered the stillness around me, startling even myself in its force. "I cannot carry on like this anymore." They were simple words, stripped of poetry or strategy, born of utter exhaustion and despair. A desperate plea, heavy with the weight of everything I had been holding alone. And yet, braided through that desperation was something unexpected. Something else ignited within them. Something miraculous. A spark. A spark of hope I had never felt before.

Not the kind that promises outcomes or guarantees relief, but the kind that simply insists on possibility. Fragile. Flickering. Barely there. But unmistakably alive. It glimmered like a small flame trembling in the desolate landscape of my mind, a place where nothing had dared to burn for years, where hope had long been considered a liability rather than a lifeline. Those words became a declaration of independence. A line drawn in the dirt with shaking hands. A moment of truth spoken not to the world, but to myself. A declaration that I would no longer remain a captive to my thoughts and emotions, no longer silently endure a life that was breaking me piece by piece. In speaking, something shifted. The ground beneath me did not immediately solidify. The path ahead did not yet appear. But the truth had been named. And in naming it, I had struck the match. The flame was small. Vulnerable to wind. Easy to extinguish. But it was burning. And for the first time, that was enough.

Turning Away from the Old Road

A fire ignited in the wasteland of my soul, not wild or consuming, but deliberate, like a seed driven deep into scorched earth that already knows how to grow. It did not ask whether the ground was ready. It carried its own memory of spring. What I had spoken was not merely a statement of despair; it was a declaration of intent. A refusal. A quiet, resolute turning away from the path of self-destruction I had been walking for years, one exhausted step after another, convinced there was no other road. It was a pivotal moment, though I could not yet name it as such. There were no trumpets. No sudden clarity. Only the unmistakable sense that something had shifted its weight inside me. A spark of hope flared within my chest, small but fierce, a living ember cupped carefully in the hollow of my being. Fragile enough to be extinguished. Strong enough to endure.

An ember that would one day grow into something capable of lighting the way toward healing and recovery, even if, in that moment, it could barely illuminate the next breath. The tablet, still clutched in my hand, suddenly felt different. Heavier. Necessary. No longer just an object, but a lifeline. My fingers, numb and trembling, fumbled against the cold glass, leaving smudges that blurred the screen, mirroring the uncertainty in my vision. Somewhere in its digital depths lived a self-help book I had downloaded months before on impulse, then abandoned without ceremony. A book I had dismissed as useless, incapable of offering answers to someone as broken as I believed myself to be. I had written it off as another layer of self-deception. Another false promise dressed up as hope. Another attempt to sell light to someone convinced they were beyond illumination. And yet, there it was, waiting in silence. Unopened. Unassuming.

A small, unremarkable doorway resting beneath my fingertips, as if it had been patient all along, quietly trusting that one day, when the fire was lit, I might finally be willing to turn the page. But now, driven by a desperate need for something, anything, to hold on to, I opened the app and began to read. There was no reverence in the gesture, no expectation of rescue. Only necessity. Only the instinct to cling. Page after page, the words flowed into me, unhurried and insistent, washing over the raw places I had tried so long to ignore. They moved through me like water finding cracks in stone, seeping into fissures I had sealed shut with silence and shame. And as I read, something shifted. Blind spots began to clear, not violently, but with a quiet rearranging of perspective. Patterns revealed themselves, threading together moments I had always held apart. Truths I had been unable or unwilling to see rose gently into view, not accusing, not condemning, but steady in their presence.

Slowly, unmistakably, realization dawned, not like a blinding sunrise, but like first light edging along the horizon, enough to change the shape of things. The words on those pages moved through me like a balm to my soul, cooling wounds I had learned to live with, seeping into places I had long believed were beyond reach. They flooded me with realization and understanding, gentle yet relentless, soft but impossible to ignore. It felt like watching the slow-motion collapse of a carefully constructed façade, one I had mistaken for truth, one I had defended fiercely because it was all I thought I had. As I read, it was as though scales fell from my eyes. The darkness thinned. The air grew lighter. The narrative I had written about myself, heavy with blame and finality, began to loosen its grip. In its place, a different reality emerged, tentative but undeniable, starkly unlike the bleak story I had lived inside for so long. And in that fragile new light, I sensed, perhaps for the first time, that the story was not finished.

For so long, I had seen myself as broken. Not bent. Not bruised. Broken beyond recognition. Unfixable. A person wounded by trauma so severe it had splintered me into something unrecognizable, something I believed could never be put back together. That belief had settled deep in my bones, shaping the way I breathed, the way I moved through the world, the way I spoke to myself in the quiet hours. It felt absolute. Final. But something shifted in those moments, subtle yet seismic. A quiet reordering. I began to see that I had power. Not the loud, fearless kind I imagined I lacked, but a quieter, steadier force. The power to choose. The power to pause. The power to turn, even slightly, in a different direction. I began to sense that the course of my life was not as sealed as I had believed, not locked behind an unmovable door. There were hinges. There were cracks. There were openings I had never known to look for.

I was not intrinsically broken. I was not irreparably flawed. Those truths settled slowly, resisting at first, then softening into something I could almost hold. I had suffered. That part was undeniable. I was wounded, yes, deeply wounded by the weight of past traumas, by experiences that had shaped how I saw myself and the world. Tremendous trauma. The kind that seeps into the nervous system and lingers there. The kind that festers in silence. The kind that leaves scars that ache long after the injury, flaring without warning, reminding you of where you have been. But trauma did not have to be my definition. It did not own me. It did not condemn me to helplessness, powerlessness, or hopelessness. Those were conditions I had learned, not sentences I had been given. Wounded was not dead. Wounded did not mean useless. Wounded meant alive in a body that had endured.

Alive in a soul that had survived impact after impact and was still here, still capable of healing, still capable of becoming something more than the sum of what had been done to me. That book illuminated a choice I had never, ever seen before. Not a demand. Not a command. A choice. A doorway I had not known existed, hidden in plain sight, obscured by years of believing there was only one way forward and that it led nowhere. The power to change. To heal. To rebuild from the inside out. And for the first time, I could imagine a life not dictated by what had broken me but shaped by what I chose to do next. A life authored, not inherited. A life responsive, not resigned. The crushing weight of helplessness, powerlessness, and hopelessness began to loosen its grip. Not all at once. Not with spectacle or certainty. But enough. Enough for breath to return to my lungs without effort. Enough for my chest to rise without panic.

Enough for the world to feel slightly less suffocating. In their place, a new understanding quietly bloomed, delicate yet resilient. I possessed the power to change things. Not everything. Not immediately. But something. And that something mattered. It was a choice. A possibility I had never truly believed was available to me. A door I had assumed was locked, sealed, forever out of reach. A door I had stopped knocking on because I had convinced myself it did not exist. And yet there it stood, suddenly visible, waiting without judgment for my hand to reach out. And then something deeper took hold. A hunger. Primal. Desperate. Alive. It surged through me with an intensity that startled me, a force I had only ever felt in survival, now repurposed toward becoming. A hunger for change, unlike anything I had ever known. It rooted itself inside me and began to grow, not as emptiness or craving, but as urgency. A living need. A fire that demanded movement.

A longing to learn more. To grow more. To explore. To heal. To live. To find something I had never known how to name before. Something softer than relief. Something steadier than happiness. A state not borrowed from circumstances but grown from within. True peace. I made a determination in that moment, quiet but unyielding. Not shouted. Not dramatic. A vow formed in the stillness, steady as bedrock. I would change. I would no longer remain trapped inside the story I had been telling myself, the one written in fear and finality, the one that left no room for growth or grace. That story had carried me as far as it could, and it had nearly cost me everything. This was not the hollow ache of my past, nor the bottomless pit of despair that had defined my present. This was something entirely different. A vibrant, compelling force began to move through me, pulling me forward, away from the precipice where I had lingered for so long.

It drew me toward something I could not yet see, could not yet name, but could finally feel in my body, in my breath, in the quiet steadiness returning to my chest. And as I look back now, I understand that this was the turning point. Not the end of suffering. Not the completion of healing. But the moment my life shifted direction, like a compass finally finding true north after years of spinning. The moment I chose, perhaps for the first time, to take hold of my own destiny, not with certainty, but with willingness. Yesterday, I was determined to die. Today, I was determined to live. Not to merely survive. Not to endure one more breath at a time with clenched teeth and lowered eyes. But to truly live. Freely. Consciously. With intention. The difference was seismic, earth-shattering in its quietness. No one else witnessed it. The world did not pause. But everything inside me moved.

This was the day I stopped existing on the margins of my own life. The day I stepped, trembling but resolute, into the center of it. The day I began to fight not against myself, but for my existence. To acknowledge it. To claim it. Perhaps, for the very first time. That day, the day I did not die, became the day I truly began to live. The calendar did not mark it. The sky did not split open. But something irreversible occurred all the same. Something *did* die that night, though it was not my body stretched beneath the indifferent stars. What died was the victim's mindset, the posture of surrender I had worn for so long, it felt like skin. The belief in an endless future of helplessness and hopelessness was laid gently, decisively, to rest. I did not yet know how to live differently, but I knew, with startling clarity, that I would no longer live *that* way.

The idea that I was condemned to remain trapped inside my past and my pain began to loosen, its grip weakening like a fist that had finally tired of holding on. The old version of me, the one shaped entirely by wounds and resignation, by endurance mistaken for identity, began to fall away. Not violently. Not all at once. But unmistakably. Like a shell cracking from the inside, no longer able to contain what was stirring beneath it. Even the word *suicide* took on a new meaning for me that day. It no longer belonged solely to death. I understood then, dimly but truthfully, that I would face death again. Not as an escape. Not as an ending. But as a reckoning. I would kill something, yes, but not my body. I would kill the hurt. The pain. The trauma. The past as it had ruled me. I would not do it with pills or silence or disappearance, but with choice. With persistence. With the daily, sometimes brutal decision to live and heal instead. By refusing to let those wounds dictate my future, I chose a different kind of ending.

A burial not of flesh, but of false beliefs. Of stories that had outlived their truth. Of suffering mistaken for destiny. That is what I laid to rest on the day I almost died. And in that burial, something else was born. Not certainty. Not ease. But a life no longer defined by what tried to end it. The determination that had once been fixed on ending my life was rerouted, fierce and unrelenting, like a river forced from a collapsed channel into new terrain. The current did not weaken. It changed direction. The same force that had driven me toward death now turned its face toward living, carrying with it an intensity I knew well, but had never trusted. What once sought silence now sought meaning. What once longed for disappearance now demanded presence. I was determined to find a reason to no longer live for others, but for myself. Not out of obligation. Not out of guilt or duty.

But out of truth. And I would do anything for that reason, because for the first time, my survival was no longer conditional on being needed by someone else. It was anchored in my own worth, fragile but real. I had been given a second chance, a rare and delicate gift, easily squandered, impossible to return. An opportunity to rewrite my story, not by erasing the past, but by reauthoring its meaning. To shape a new narrative carved from hope and resilience, etched slowly and deliberately into the fabric of my days. A story not defined by escape, but by engagement. And now, with distance, I recognize the symmetry. I see the strange, almost sacred balance in it. Just as I had once devoted my time, my research, my energy, my fantasies, my thoughts, and my focus to the desire to die, my perspective began to invert.

The same meticulous attention, the same relentless contemplation, the same consuming fixation began to turn inward and forward, redirected toward understanding, toward healing, toward the audacious act of imagining a future worth staying for. Today, my determination was life. Not survival. Not endurance measured in clenched hours and gritted breaths. Life in its truest sense. Spacious. Intentional. Awake. And I would pursue it with the same passion, the same fury, the same iron will I had once given to death. That intensity did not disappear when the direction changed. It was reclaimed. Reforged. Turned toward something that could finally hold it. Where my mind had once rehearsed endings, it now began, cautiously at first, to imagine healing. Where my thoughts had circled despair like a closed orbit with no escape velocity, they slowly turned toward hope, widening their path, allowing for movement, for expansion.

My research changed. My fantasies shifted. My focus realigned. Every mental corridor that had once led to disappearance began to open toward possibility. Everything that had once been enmeshed with death began to reweave itself around healing, around curiosity, around the quiet courage of staying. Threads that had been knotted by trauma loosened and found new patterns. The same imagination that had once planned escape now began to envision wholeness. The same vigilance that had once watched for an ending now learned how to watch for growth. I resolved that I would do whatever it took, everything within my power, to ensure that I would live. Not merely exist. Not simply continue. But live. Not just breathing, but alive. Happy. Free. Joyful. Peaceful. Words that once felt distant and ornamental now carried weight, texture, and temperature. They felt attainable, not promised, but possible.

This newfound life was no longer theoretical. It was not a concept or a dream deferred to some imagined future. It was present. Waiting. Standing just beyond the threshold of that decision, asking only that I keep choosing it, again and again, one breath, one brave step at a time. As I look back now, I recognize the magnitude of the gift I was given. A gift I could not see then, wrapped as it was in pain, shock, and disorientation. The gift of life. Of hope. Of a story still unfolding, refusing to close its pages. At the time, it felt like interruption. Now, I understand it as mercy. Today, I carry the profound grace and rare privilege of telling this story, my story. A story of what could have been but mercifully is not. Instead, I get to speak of what *is*. Of breath that returned. Of choice that awakened. Of a life that continued not because it was easy, but because it was spared. A story that exists only because I did not die that night.

This story was born from the ashes of despair, from a place where everything had been reduced to ruin, where even the idea of tomorrow felt impossible. And yet, from that scorched ground, something learned how to breathe again. Slowly. Tentatively. With trembling lungs. Life did not rush back in. It seeped in, breath by breath, heartbeat by heartbeat, until ruin gave way to renewal. And this story grants me something I hold with reverence: the ability to offer hope to those who have walked, or are still walking, a similar path. To those who have felt the icy grip of suicidal ideation closing around their thoughts. To those who have stood inside the terrifying darkness of attempting to take their own lives, convinced there was no other way out.

I share this not merely to recount my personal journey, but to extend a lifeline into that abyss. To reach across the silence and say, without judgment or platitude, "I have been there. I know that darkness. And I did not disappear. I am here. And because of that, there is still a possibility that you can be too." My journey has not been easy. It has twisted and turned like an unmarked road, risen into moments of breathless clarity, and fallen into valleys where the light felt impossibly far away. It has tested and stretched me in ways I never imagined, asking more of me than I believed I could give. There have been moments of doubt where my footing slipped, setbacks that knocked the wind from my lungs, and long stretches of quiet exhaustion where simply continuing felt like an act of defiance.

But through it all, I have learned to lean on hope. Not as a naïve optimism or a denial of pain, but as a discipline. Hope became my anchor when the waters grew violent and threatened to pull me under. My guiding light when the path disappeared entirely, when every familiar landmark dissolved into darkness. My source of strength when I believed I had none left to draw from. Hope did not remove the storm, but it kept me from surrendering to it. Hope has shown me that I am capable of surviving even the darkest struggles. That I am stronger than I ever believed, not because I am unbreakable, but because I have been broken and still remained. It has taught me that a life once nearly lost can become a vessel for meaning, for connection, for light. That survival itself can be transformed into purpose.

I have walked the harrowing terrain of suicidal ideation. I know its geography intimately. I have felt its chilling grip, the way it tightens around the mind, the way it seduces with false certainty, offering relief where there is only pain. I know its deadly allure, the way it whispers that ending is the same as escape. I crossed that line. I attempted to take my own life. I stood face to face with death and believed, for a moment, that this was where my story would end. But it did not. The story kept breathing. And so did I. My story continues because I survived. And more than that, because I chose that surviving alone was not enough. Survival was only the beginning, the thin edge of possibility, the place where breath returns but meaning has yet to arrive. I knew I did not want to live suspended forever in the aftermath. I wanted to move forward. To build. To become.

As I write these words now, I am continually reminded of the quiet, relentless power of the human spirit. Not loud or dramatic but enduring. Persistent. A force that keeps reaching even when the hands are tired and scarred. I am reminded that transformation is possible, that change is not reserved for the unbroken or the unscarred. It is forged precisely in those who have been tested, cracked open, and reshaped by experience. We are not condemned by our pasts, our traumas, or our struggles. They shape us, yes. They leave their marks, their imprints, their echoes. But they do not have to imprison us. They do not get the final word. We can rise, not by erasing what happened, but by carrying it differently. We can heal, slowly and imperfectly, learning to tend to our wounds rather than deny them. We can carve new meaning from the very places that once tried to undo us, turning sites of collapse into foundations for something new.

This story is not merely a testament to survival. It is a story of transformation. A narrative that moves beyond endurance into becoming. Beyond breathing into living. It is about learning to thrive, about embracing life with a fierce, hard-earned appreciation born of having nearly lost it. It is a story of strength found within vulnerability, of courage discovered in honesty, of hope blooming stubbornly from the ashes of despair. And it continues, not because the pain vanished, but because I chose to keep walking, to keep healing, to keep living. And it is not finished. I am still writing it, line by line, breath by breath. A story of continued healing. Of growth. Of the unwavering pursuit of a life that feels honest, embodied, and worth living. The ink is not always steady. Some days the words come easily; other days, they are wrestled from silence. But the story continues all the same, carried forward by choice, by presence, by the courage to remain engaged with my own becoming.

And for every word I am able to write, for every breath that carried me here, I am deeply, humbly grateful. Gratitude not born of forgetting, but of remembering. Remembering how close I came to losing all of this. My journey is not unique, but it is mine, and for that, I am deeply grateful. It belongs to me. It bears my fingerprints, my fractures, my persistence. It is a story etched with struggle and marked by triumph, shaped by darkness and illuminated by healing. A story that knows both the weight of despair and the quiet strength required to rise from it. I am grateful even for the nights I would never wish to relive, the nights that nearly consumed me, because they gifted me a perspective I now carry for others. A way of seeing pain without flinching. Of sitting with suffering without turning away. Of recognizing the humanity in the darkest moments.

I am grateful for the spark that ignited within me when everything else had burned to ash. That first fragile flame, trembling but alive, that refused to be extinguished. A spark that grew into a fierce determination to live, not cautiously, not half-present, but fully. To take up space in my own life. To breathe deeply. To thrive. And as long as I am here, as long as there is breath in my lungs and words waiting to be written, this story will keep unfolding, guided by gratitude, shaped by healing, and rooted in the quiet, radical choice to live. In the end, I am grateful for that night. Not for the pain it carried, nor for the darkness that nearly claimed me, but for what it revealed. I am grateful for the second chance I was given, for the hope I discovered buried beneath the wreckage where none seemed possible, and for the story I now have the profound privilege to tell. It is a story of hope.

A story of transformation. A story that bears witness to the enduring, unyielding power of the human spirit to rise even after it has been brought to its knees. It stands as a reminder that we are all capable of overcoming. That change is not reserved for the unbroken, the untouched, the unscarred. It belongs equally to those who have been shattered and dared to gather the pieces. It is a reminder that every one of us is deserving of a second chance, not because we earned it, but because life itself is merciful. Because the truth is this: we are never truly alone, and we are never without hope, even when hope feels absent, even when its name has been forgotten. Even on the night I believed myself utterly abandoned, when I lay on that damp, icy grass convinced no one saw me, convinced I had slipped beyond the reach of love or meaning, my God was there.

Though I was disconnected, unable to sense Him, unable to feel anything at all, He was present. Silent, steady, unwavering. He was looking down on me with grace when I could only see condemnation. He was holding me when I felt myself slipping away. His mighty hand reached down into the depths of my despair and saved me that night, not with thunder or spectacle, but with mercy. And because of that unseen presence, because of that sacred interruption, I am still here. Living. Becoming. Bearing witness to a hope that refuses to die. There is always a way forward. Sometimes it is no wider than a breath, no brighter than a flicker, but it exists, nonetheless. There is always another breath waiting to be taken, another moment quietly offering itself. There is always a chance to begin again, even when beginning feels impossible, even when the weight of yesterday presses hard against the chest. Continuation itself can be an act of courage.

This is a story of hope. Not the fragile kind that shatters at first contact with pain, but the resilient kind that survives burial. A story of resilience shaped by fire and shadow. A story of finding light in the deepest darkness, where none should exist, and yet somehow does. A light that does not erase the dark, but stands within it, steady and unafraid. It is a story of discovering a higher power within myself, not born of ego or self-sufficiency, but awakened in the aftermath of divine intervention from something far beyond me. A sacred convergence. A meeting place between heaven and the human heart, where grace meets choice, and mercy meets responsibility. Where I learned that being saved was not the end of the story, but the beginning of participation in it. It is a story about the power of choice, the slow, courageous work of healing, the daily willingness to return to life even when it aches.

About choosing again and again to tend what is wounded, to listen to what hurts, to believe in growth even when progress is uneven. It is a story rooted in the unwavering possibility of a brighter future, even after the longest, darkest nights have stretched the soul to its limits. I believe this story can offer solace. Strength. A steady, unwavering beacon for anyone who feels lost, broken, or utterly alone in the depths of their despair. For anyone who believes they have fallen too far to be found, wandered too deep into the dark to return. This story stands as quiet proof that there is still ground beneath your feet. That you are still seen. That you are still held. And that, my friends, is a story worth sharing. Because in the end, this is not about the day I didn't die. It is about the day I began to live. The moment when breath became more than survival and time became more than something to endure.

It is about the spark that was ignited within me, that small, defiant flame born in the ruins, the one that refused to be extinguished even when everything around it lay in ash. A flame that learned how to feed itself, how to grow, how to warm what had long been frozen, until it became a fire strong enough to carry me forward. It is about the hope that was born in me that day, not loud or naive, but hard-won and honest. A hope shaped by having stood at the edge and stepped back. A hope I now offer freely to others, not as a promise of ease, but as proof of possibility. It is about the resilience forged in pain, resilience tempered by truth, humility, and compassion. Resilience I now choose to pass on, not as evidence of strength alone, but as an open hand. An invitation. An invitation to pause. To breathe. To choose again. An invitation to believe that life, even after everything, even after the nights that nearly claimed you, is still here.

Still waiting. Still willing to meet you where you are. Not asking you to be whole, only asking you to be present. An invitation to step, trembling or certain, into the ongoing, unfinished, extraordinary act of living. As I close this chapter of my life, I do so with a quiet sense of anticipation, the kind that settles gently rather than rushes ahead. A readiness to see what the future will hold, how my story will continue to unfold beyond these pages, in ways I cannot yet imagine. The unknown no longer feels like a threat pressing in on me. It feels like an open horizon. I am no longer afraid of what comes next. Instead, I am curious. Hopeful. Willing to meet whatever arrives with an open heart. I am eager to discover how the experiences that once nearly destroyed me can now be transformed into something that steadies others. How the pain that once left me grasping in the dark can become a light, however small, for someone else searching for footing.

I carry with me a deep reverence for that possibility, the knowledge that suffering, when tended with care, can be reshaped into service, into connection, into meaning. I know I will always carry the scars of my past. They did not vanish with healing, nor did I expect them to. They are etched into me, quiet reminders of where I have been. But I have learned this: scars are not signs of weakness. They are evidence of survival. Proof that the body and the spirit endured what once seemed unbearable and continued on. I am stronger because of them. Stronger because I have learned to lean on hope when my own strength faltered. Stronger because I have learned to trust in the resilience of the human spirit, in its quiet, steadfast refusal to be extinguished.

And so I move forward, carrying both the weight and the wisdom of what I have lived through. Not unmarked, but unbroken. Not fearless, but free. Ready to keep walking, to keep becoming, and to honor this life by living it fully, deliberately, and with gratitude. My story is one of hope and transformation, and it is a hope I now offer to the world with open hands, unguarded and sincere. Not polished or perfected, but real. A hope shaped by lived experience, by nights that stretched endlessly and mornings that arrived anyway. It is a story of resilience. Of determination. Of the enduring power of the human spirit to rise, again and again, even when it has been brought to its knees. Even when it has forgotten its own strength.

It is a story I will continue to tell, not because it is easy, but because it is necessary. A story I will continue to share, to breathe into, to live. It moves with me. It evolves as I do. It refuses to be confined to a single moment or a single chapter, because transformation is not an event; it is a practice. A choosing. A returning. Because I know it matters. I know it can make a difference. I know it can reach someone, somewhere, standing at the edge of their own breaking point. Someone who needs a reminder to hold on a little longer. To take one more breath. To not give up when the road feels impossibly heavy and every step feels like resistance. To keep moving forward, even if forward is slow, even if it is uncertain.

And if my story can help even one person choose life, choose hope, choose to stay when everything inside them is screaming to disappear, then every word has been worth it. Every tear. Every memory. Every moment of courage it took to speak what once lived in silence. Because sometimes a single story, spoken honestly, can become the light that helps someone else find their way back to themselves.

Mayor Depressive Disorder:

Chapter: Four-teen

Beyond the Darkness: My Journey with Major Depressive Disorder

As I sit here today, reflecting on my journey with suicidal ideation and the night I tried to take my own life, I am drawn back to words I once spoke with unwavering certainty: *"What drives one's thoughts to become enmeshed with death, simple, I thought it was PAIN, HURT, and SUFFERING."* At the time, that belief felt absolute, etched into me like a law of nature. Pain was the cause. Hurt was the explanation. Suffering was the verdict. There was no appeal. No alternative interpretation. Just a sentence handed down and accepted as final. But hindsight has a way of softening what once felt immovable, not by erasing it, but by revealing its shape. Distance allows the mind to breathe where it once clenched. And in that breathing, I can see now that this was not truth, but a distortion. A lie repeated so faithfully it took on the weight of fact.

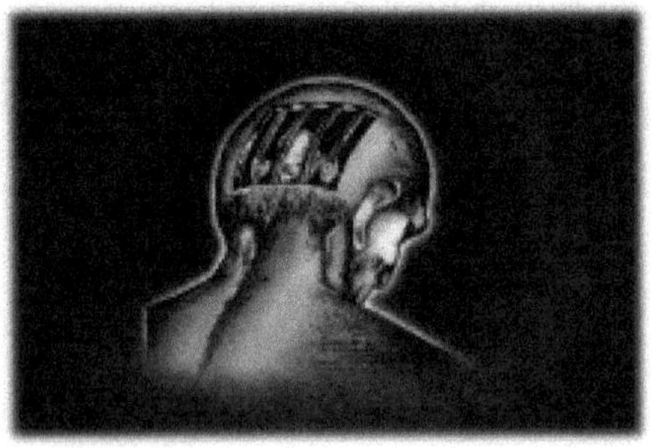

It was the architecture of an inner prison, walls mortared with exhaustion and despair, corridors looping back on themselves until every direction led to the same conclusion. It convinced me that my pain was permanent, my hurt set in stone, my suffering inevitable and unchangeable. I believed there was no crack in it. No seam. No door hidden in shadow. I believed there was no possibility of escape, and so I lived as though my pain were concrete, as though it could never shift, never loosen, never give way. I arranged my life around that belief. I made decisions from inside it. I mistook endurance for truth and resignation for realism.

What I understand now is this: the prison was never my pain itself. Pain is real. Hurt is real. Suffering is real. But they were never the jailers. The prison was the belief that they would last forever. The conviction that nothing could change, that time would not soften, that healing was reserved for others. It was that belief that sealed the doors, that dimmed the light, that made death feel like the only exit. And once that belief cracked, even slightly, everything changed. Because pain can move. Hurt can heal. Suffering can transform. Nothing stays fixed unless we decide it must. The moment I understood that impermanence existed, even here, even in this, the walls began to thin. And in that thinning, breath returned. Possibility returned. Life, patient and persistent, found a way back in.

My name is Letitia, and I am a survivor of Major Depressive Disorder. Naming it now feels different than how it once did. It no longer feels like a sentence. It feels like context. For years, I lived inside a dark, suffocating place where the walls closed in so quietly, I did not notice them being built. Brick by invisible brick. Thought by relentless thought. In that shrinking space, death felt like the only visible exit, the only door not yet sealed shut. Pain, hurt, and suffering became my constant companions. They followed me everywhere, shadowing every thought, every breath, until they felt inseparable from who I was. Slowly, subtly, they rewrote my inner language. I began to believe I was helpless. Powerless. Hopeless. I believed I was a burden. Not good enough. A failure. Worthless. Unlovable. Broken beyond repair. A fuck-up! These messages did not shout. They whispered. Repeated themselves.

Ran on an endless loop, a cruel litany that played beneath everything I did, everything I tried to be. And in listening to them for so long, I mistook them for truth. Even now, the weight of it sometimes presses down again. A familiar heaviness settles on my chest, tight and breath-stealing. A phantom limb of pain where suicidal ideation once lived. Though the wound has healed, the memory of it still echoes. It reminds me how deeply that darkness once rooted itself inside me. This was never a sudden plunge. There was no single moment where the ground gave way. It was a slow, insidious creep, like an encroaching tide that pulls you under inch by inch while you are still trying to stand, still convincing yourself you are fine, still hoping the water will recede on its own. Looking back now, the clarity is chilling. It had a name. Major Depressive Disorder. A diagnosis that finally gave shape to the monster that had been consuming me from the inside out.

A name for the force that threatened to dismantle me piece by piece long before I understood what I was truly fighting. It was not a weakness of character. Not a failure of will. It was an illness. A complex, relentless condition that distorted my perception, hijacked my thoughts, and convinced me that despair was permanent. Major Depressive Disorder is not simply feeling sad or passing through a low season. It is not a bad day or a rough chapter. It is something far more consuming. It reaches into the mind and rewires meaning itself. It turns hope into an abstraction and pain into a prophecy. It makes survival feel like burden and existence feel like offense. And for a long time, I did not know that what I was fighting had a name, or that naming it would one day become part of how I learned to survive it. It is a condition marked by relentless sadness, by a slow erosion of hope so gradual it almost escapes notice, and by the quiet disappearance of interest in anything that once offered relief or joy.

It convinces a person they are helpless, powerless, and trapped, locked inside a cycle that feels endless and unchangeable. The mind becomes a closed room with no windows, no air, no sense of time passing. For me, it was never just sadness. It was a suffocating, all-encompassing darkness, a living presence that wrapped itself around me and swallowed me whole, pressing in from every direction until I could no longer remember what light had ever felt like. I remember asking the question, one I spoke about in an earlier chapter: *What drives someone to become so enmeshed with death?* At the time, my answer felt obvious, almost logical. Pain. Hurt. Suffering. Those were the only words I had. They were blunt instruments, heavy and imprecise, inadequate for the nuanced brutality of what I was living, but they were all I could reach for. They gave shape to the ache, even if they could not explain it.

And yet now I know something different. That explanation was a lie. Not a deliberate one, but a lie nonetheless. A false narrative shaped by distorted thinking, a cruel fabrication born from a mind under siege by illness. I remember believing, with chilling certainty, that this pain was immutable, an eternal fixture of my existence. That nothing could soften it. Nothing could shift it. Nothing could interrupt its reign. I lived as though my suffering were carved into stone, as though it had always been there and always would be. But the truth was far more insidious. It was not simply the pain, the hurt, or the suffering themselves that tethered me to death. It was the unshakeable belief that they were permanent. That belief seeped into everything, flattening possibility, erasing imagination, collapsing the future into a single, suffocating point. It convinced me that change was a fantasy, healing a myth, relief an illusion meant for other people's lives. That belief, more than anything else, became the prison. It locked the doors from the inside. It dimmed the light until darkness felt like the only honest reality. And it is only now, standing on the other side of that conviction, that I can see how powerful it was, how convincing, and how wrong.

My mind became my own prison warden, vigilant and unrelenting, policing every thought, every flicker of resistance. It constructed an impenetrable wall around me from distorted thoughts and crippling self-beliefs, enforcing its rules without mercy. Brick by brick, that inner prison took shape, each belief mortared in with absolute certainty, convincing me that these feelings were unchangeable, solid as concrete, inevitable as gravity. There were no visible seams, no weak points. The walls closed in quietly, so subtly that I did not notice the narrowing until the sky itself seemed to disappear. Eventually, I could no longer imagine anything beyond them. The world shrank to the dimensions of my despair. The whispers never stopped. Lies, repeated until they sounded like truth. A dysfunctional, false narrative murmured relentlessly beneath every waking moment, beneath every attempt at rest. It told me my suffering was deserved. That it was permanent. That escape was impossible.

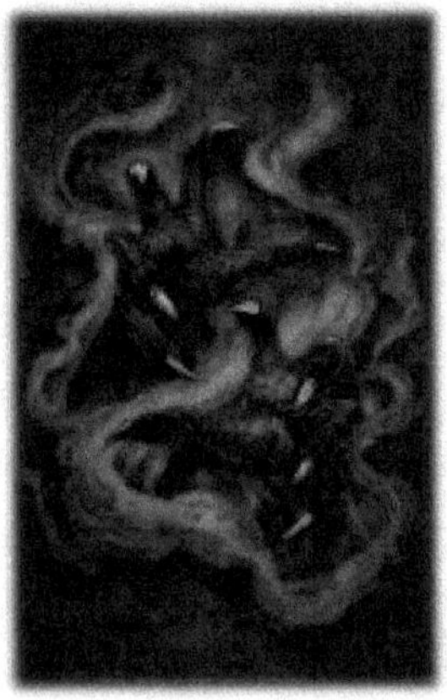

It told me my pain was earned, the natural consequence of who I was. That my circumstances were fixed and immovable, anchored in fate rather than circumstance. That I was inherently and utterly flawed. A burden. A failure. Helpless. Powerless. Hopeless. And in that echo chamber of belief, those words no longer felt like accusations hurled from the outside. They became internal law. Doctrine. They felt objective, undeniable, etched into the very architecture of my mind. They defined the borders of my imagination, the limits of what I believed my life could ever be. Possibility ceased to exist beyond those walls. Hope became a foreign language I could no longer translate. What I did not know then was that prisons built by the mind feel absolute precisely because they are invisible. Their bars are made of certainty. Their locks forged from repetition. And when you live inside them long enough, you stop questioning the walls. You stop looking for doors. You forget that the mind that built the prison is also the only thing capable of dismantling it.

This was not mere sadness. It was a relentless, all-consuming conviction that death was the only viable solution left to me. Not a passing thought. Not a fleeting impulse that drifted in and out. It was a persistent, insidious companion, walking beside me with quiet familiarity, its claws always reaching, always threading itself through the fabric of my days. It breathed with me. It waited with me. It whispered certainty where there was only pain. Every waking moment was colored by its presence, even the neutral ones, even the ordinary ones, all tinted with a chilling sense of inevitability, as though the ending had already been written, and I was merely moving toward it. I was a prisoner in my own mind, confined not only by circumstance, but by belief. By the unshakeable conviction that I could not change, could not heal, could not get better.

That nothing within me was capable of shifting, softening, or growing. That I was fixed in place, locked inside a version of myself I did not choose but believed I deserved. The walls were not built of events alone, but of conclusions. And those conclusions felt airtight. That belief was the true cage. The bars were invisible, yet unyielding, forged from repetition and fear. No one else could see them, but I felt them every time I reached for something beyond my despair and came back empty-handed. It was that conviction that kept me leaning toward the seductive whisper of death, the voice that promised certainty where life offered only ambiguity. I fantasized about it. Circled it. Tested its edges as though it were an answer rather than an ending, a solution rather than a silence.

I toyed with it the way one toys with a dangerous idea, returning to it again and again, letting it grow familiar, letting it lose its terror and take on the shape of relief. The line between thought and action blurred slowly, almost imperceptibly, until imagination hardened into intent. And eventually, tragically, I stumbled into its embrace, believing it was escape. I did not yet understand that this, too, was part of the illness. That the certainty I felt was rehearsed. Practiced. Fed by a mind under siege. I believed death was truth, not realizing it was the lie my illness had been perfecting all along.

The insidious cruelty of it all was that the pain was not physical, not entirely. It lived deeper than flesh, beyond bruises or bone. It lodged itself in the unseen places, an aching wound in my soul, raw and constantly reopened. It was fed by a relentless cascade of negative thoughts that played on repeat, like a broken record ground down into the deepest groove of my mind. The needle never lifted. There was no silence. No pause. Only the same refrain, circling endlessly, wearing me thinner with every rotation. I was drowning. Drowning in the suffocating belief that I was a burden. Not good enough. A failure. Worthless. Unlovable. Broken beyond repair. A complete and utter fuck-up. Not good enough, the cruel voice inside me hissed. "Worthless. Unlovable. Useless. Broken."

These were not passing thoughts that drifted in and out like weather. They were deeply rooted convictions, fused to my identity, etched into my sense of self. They shaped how I saw the world and determined how small I believed my place within it had to be. I was submerged in these beliefs, swallowed so completely that they became my environment rather than my thoughts. I could no longer see the surface. I could not imagine air. I could not conceive of rescue. The water pressed in from every direction, heavy and dark, filling my lungs with certainty and fear. And in that depth, in that quiet, crushing stillness, I believed with terrifying conviction that this was where I was meant to disappear. That sinking was not tragedy, but destiny.

My journey into that dark place was not sudden. It did not arrive with a single catastrophic moment or dramatic collapse. It was gradual, a slow descent into the depths of depression that felt unstoppable at the time, like slipping down a slope so slick I could not find my footing, my hands grasping for purchase and finding only air. Each step downward felt small, almost insignificant, until distance accumulated and I could no longer see where I had begun. Hopelessness and helplessness wrapped themselves around me until they became the atmosphere I breathed, invisible yet suffocating. They seeped into everything, coloring thought and sensation alike, making it impossible to imagine a future that extended beyond the pain of the present. Tomorrow felt theoretical. Next year felt absurd. I lived as though trapped inside a perpetual nightmare, one that looped endlessly, resetting itself every morning, offering no visible exit, no waking moment where relief arrived.

I remember the sensation clearly. A slow suffocation. Not panic at first, but pressure. As though the walls were inching closer with every thought, every breath, until there was no space left to step outside the feelings and question them. No room to gain perspective. No distance from the story my mind was telling me. I could not see that these thoughts were not truth. I could not recognize them as symptoms. I believed them. Completely. I was convinced I was incapable of change, incapable of healing, incapable of getting better. The future collapsed into a single image, narrow and brutal: a slow, agonizing descent into oblivion. There were no forks in the road in that vision, no alternate endings. Only continuation of suffering, stretched endlessly forward.

That belief became my trap. And day by day, I fell deeper into it, mistaking inevitability for reality, certainty for truth. I confused repetition with permanence, intensity with accuracy. It was not until I came perilously close to losing my life that the true gravity of that mistake revealed itself. Only then did I glimpse how far I had fallen, how completely my vision had narrowed, how thoroughly the darkness I was living inside had convinced me that it was all there would ever be. And that realization, painful as it was, marked the first hairline crack in the walls that had closed around me.

I could not see beyond the swirling vortex of self-loathing that pulled at me from every direction, a relentless current dragging my gaze inward until nothing else existed. It distorted everything I touched, everything I remembered, everything I imagined myself to be. I believed those things about myself, even though they were not true, because belief, repeated often enough, hardens into something that feels like reality. Old tapes, their edges frayed and voices warped by time, played endlessly in the worn grooves of my mind. The same cruel messages looped without mercy, skipping and repeating, until they lost their strangeness and began to sound like fact. You are not enough. You never were. You never will be.

That relentless soundtrack followed me everywhere, filling the silence, leaving no room for doubt or counterargument. It kept me imprisoned inside despair, pain, hurt, and suffering, pacing the same narrow cell day after day, rehearsing the same sentences until they defined the limits of my world. That was my trap. A prison carefully constructed from belief and repetition, reinforced by fear, locked from the inside. No visible bars. No guards to fight. Just certainty masquerading as truth. And it took standing on the brink, it took almost dying, for me to finally recognize it for what it was. A fabrication. A distortion. A lie given power only because I had lived inside it for so long. Only then, in the aftermath of that near-ending, did I begin to see the faint outline of a door where I had sworn there was only wall.

I was trapped inside a narrative of my own making, a story I had written and rewritten until it hardened into inevitability. Each revision stripped away nuance, mercy, and possibility, until only one version remained. In that story, I was always the villain. Always the one beyond redemption. Always marked for a tragic end that felt preordained rather than chosen. There were no alternate arcs, no moments of grace written into the margins.

Just a slow march toward an ending I believed I deserved. Each day became a battle simply to breathe, to function, to move through the hours beneath the suffocating weight of despair pressing down on my chest. Breathing itself felt laborious, as though the air had thickened, as though my lungs had to fight for every inhale. Time did not pass so much as it dragged, each minute heavy and resistant, each hour another test of endurance. I was not living inside my days. I was surviving them, counting them, enduring them. The world around me felt muted and distant, as if I were seeing it through a thick veil of grief that dulled color, sound, and meaning.

Laughter reached me softened and far away. Light lost its warmth. Even beauty felt abstract, something meant for other people, other lives. Nothing landed fully. Nothing stayed. I moved through familiar spaces as a ghost of myself, present in body but absent in spirit. Even the smallest tasks rose up like mountains, insurmountable obstacles standing in the way of a self already crumbling under the strain. Getting out of bed. Answering a message. Making a decision. Each required a level of effort that felt disproportionate and humiliating. Every action demanded more than I had to give. Every effort felt monumental. Every step forward exhausting. And with each struggle, the narrative tightened its grip, whispering confirmation of what I already feared. You are failing even at living. And so the story fed itself, despair reinforcing belief, belief reinforcing despair, until the idea of any other version of myself felt not just unlikely, but impossible.

The irony is that none of it was true. Not a single sentence of that internal indictment. The so-called truth of my prison was a carefully constructed lie, a fiction authored by a mind bent beneath the crushing weight of illness. A story told so convincingly it masqueraded as fact. I was not a burden. I was not worthless. I was not irreparably broken. Those labels were never diagnoses. They were symptoms. The truth, stripped bare of distortion and self-contempt, was far simpler and far more devastating: I was unwell. Not weak. Not defective. Unwell. I was fighting an enemy I did not yet have a name for, swinging blindly in the dark at something that moved through my thoughts unseen. I was at war without a map, without language, without armor, believing the battlefield was my identity rather than my mind under siege. The turning point, the moment when those insidious lies began to loosen their grip, did not arrive gently. It did not come wrapped in insight or clarity.

It came violently. It came in the near-loss of my life. In that desperate brush with oblivion, when the margin between breath and silence narrowed to almost nothing, something unexpected flickered into view. A raw, primal survival instinct. Not noble. Not poetic. Instinctual. Ancient. A faint, stubborn whisper of hope rising from beneath the wreckage, bruised but unextinguished. It did not speak in affirmations. It did not offer comfort. It simply said: *stay*. It was not kind. It was not soothing. It was a brutal awakening, a truth revealed at the very edge of the abyss, where there was no room left for illusion. Only clarity. Only the stark realization that the story I had believed was killing me. That the narrative I had lived inside was tightening its grip with every repetition. And alongside that terrifying awareness came another truth, just as undeniable. Something within me still wanted to live.

Not because life felt good. Not because I felt strong. But because even at my most broken, even at the brink of disappearance, there was a part of me that refused to surrender its claim on breath. That realization did not save me in a moment. But it cracked the spell. And sometimes, a single crack is all life needs to begin finding its way back in.

And it did not arrive as a miracle or a sudden revelation. There was no lightning strike. No instant redemption. No cinematic turning point where everything fell neatly into place. Recovery unfolded the way real things do. Slowly. Painstakingly. A long, arduous climb out of the deepest pit of despair, hand over trembling hand, nails scraping against stone. Progress was measured not in leaps, but in inches. In moments survived. In breaths chosen. It asked everything of me. It asked patience when I had none left to give, when waiting felt unbearable and urgency had once masqueraded as escape. It asked courage when I felt hollowed out, when bravery looked less like confidence and more like showing up exhausted and afraid. It asked persistence when hope still felt foreign, when belief lagged far behind effort. Recovery did not care whether I felt ready. It only asked whether I was willing.

The path forward was built through deliberate, often uncomfortable acts of healing. Working with a sponsor, allowing myself to be seen when I wanted to disappear. Learning to sit with myself through meditation, staying present in a body that carried too many memories. Practicing mindfulness when my mind wanted only to flee, only to outrun sensation and silence. These were not grand gestures. They were quiet disciplines, repeated again and again, even when they seemed to change nothing at all. It required a relentless willingness to examine and untangle the deeply ingrained negative beliefs that had held me captive for so long. Beliefs that once felt as solid and immovable as stone. Beliefs I had mistaken for truth simply because they were familiar. Recovery meant questioning the very thoughts I had trusted most. Turning toward the darkness instead of away from it.

Meeting my demons face to face, naming them, listening to them without obeying them. It meant dismantling the walls of my self-imposed prison brick by brick, even when my hands shook, even when I doubted there was anything worth freeing on the other side. Some days the work felt invisible, like shouting into a void. Some days it felt unbearable, like reopening wounds that had barely begun to scar. But each small act, each conscious choice to stay, to breathe, to return, loosened the mortar of that old cage. Tiny fractures formed where certainty once ruled. Hairline cracks widened. And slowly, almost imperceptibly, light began to slip through. Not enough to illuminate everything. But enough to remind me that the walls were not eternal. Enough to prove that what had been built could, with time and intention, be taken apart.

It has become a deliberate, ongoing practice. A conscious meeting with those old tapes as they begin to play, the moment I hear the familiar static of those relentless negative messages crackle to life. I no longer let them run unchecked, no longer surrender the room to their noise. Instead, I pause. I notice. I reach for the needle and lift it, gently but firmly, choosing a different sound. A kinder one. A truer one. One that does not wound simply because it can. This is the work of learning to speak to myself with compassion instead of cruelty. Of replacing accusation with understanding, judgment with care. Of learning a new inner language after years of verbal exile. It does not come naturally. It must be practiced. Repeated.

Chosen again and again, especially when the old voice insists it knows me better than I know myself. It is also the slow education of the mind. Learning to recognize the distortions born of depression for what they are. Symptoms, not facts. When those warped thoughts rise now, I meet them differently. Not with fear. Not with obedience. But with evidence. With reason. With grounded reality. I ask questions. I look for proof. I challenge the lies that once felt unquestionable, not with force, but with clarity. This process is not about denying pain or pretending strength. It is not about silencing grief or bypassing what hurt. It is about embracing self-compassion fully, about acknowledging the depth of what I endured without letting it define my future. It is about giving myself permission to heal without rushing the process or demanding perfection from a wounded soul. Again and again, I choose to tend to the wound rather than blame it. To care for what aches instead of condemning it. To offer myself the gentleness I was always deserving of, even when I did not know how to ask for it. And in doing so, I allow healing to unfold at its own human pace. Uneven. Nonlinear. Honest. A quiet, faithful act of returning to myself.

I learned, slowly and then all at once, that my worth and value were never defined by my circumstances, nor by the flaws I once believed disqualified me from being whole. That belief loosened its grip quietly, like a knot finally remembering how to untie itself. I discovered that I was capable of change. Of healing. Of getting better in ways I had once been convinced were impossible, ways my mind could not previously imagine because it had never been shown the map. I came to understand that my story was not finished. That the pages ahead were still blank, not waiting for perfection or certainty, but for courage. For willingness. For presence. And with that knowing came a quiet power, steady and grounded, the power to write a new narrative. One shaped not by fear or inevitability, but by hope, resilience, and a fierce determination to remain. To stay. To participate in my own becoming.

Today, my story is entirely different. Not because life is without pain, but because I am no longer trapped in the suffocating darkness of Major Depressive Disorder. I am still becoming. Still learning. Still healing. Growth has not ended; it has simply changed pace. And I am deeply proud of the person I am growing into. Proud of my strength. Proud of my courage. Proud of my resilience. Proud, above all, to be alive. Grateful for the second chance I was given, and for the life that continues to unfold because of it, imperfect, honest, and real. And to anyone standing where I once stood, inhabiting that desolate, airless place where the world feels narrow and the future unreachable, I want you to hear this clearly. You do not have to end your story there. You do not have to reach the brink, or cross it, to be worthy of help, of relief, of another chapter. There is hope. There is a way forward. The pain you are carrying, the darkness you are moving through, is not permanent, and it is not a verdict on your worth. It is an illness. It is suffering. And it is treatable. You can get better.

If you are struggling with suicidal ideation or Major Depressive Disorder, you are not alone, no matter how convincing the isolation feels. That sense of being cut off is a symptom, not a truth. There are people who care about you, who want to help you, who believe in your future even if you cannot see it yet. There are hands reaching for you. Resources waiting. Possibilities are still alive. Please do not give up, even when the darkness roars and tells you this is all there is. Do not lose faith, even when the pain feels unbearable and unending. You are stronger than you know, more capable than you can imagine. And your story, like mine, is still being written.

Seeking help is the first true movement toward healing, the moment the spell begins to loosen, and the distortions start to crack. It is the first hairline fracture in the wall, the first breath taken with intention. It is the act of turning toward the light, however faint, however distant, and daring to name the pain instead of carrying it in silence. To speak it aloud. To let it be witnessed. To refuse the lie that you must endure it alone. It is okay to ask for help. To reach outward and say, "*I am struggling*", not as a confession of weakness, but as an honest declaration of humanity. A recognition that pain does not mean failure, and needing support does not diminish worth. More than okay, it is necessary. Because no one heals in isolation. Because even the strongest structures rely on more than one pillar to stand.

Healing does not begin with certainty. It does not require confidence, clarity, or a map of what comes next. It does not demand that you feel ready or brave or hopeful. Healing begins with truth. With the courage to say, "*this hurts*". With the willingness to admit, "*I cannot do this alone*". That honesty is the doorway. Everything else follows. And in the end, it is not the falling that defines us. Falling is human. Falling is inevitable. It is the rising that tells the story. The choice to stand again on trembling legs. The decision to remain when leaving feels easier. The willingness to take one step, then another, even when the road ahead is fogged, uneven, and unfamiliar. Forward does not have to be fast. It does not have to be graceful. Forward is still forward. And every time you choose it, every time you reach for help, every time you tell the truth about where you are, you are already healing.

As the wise poet Maya Angelou once wrote, *"You may not control all the events that happen to you, but you can decide not to be reduced by them."* Those words land here not as a platitude pinned to a wall, but as a quiet truth hard-earned, tempered by experience and lived through fire. They speak to the space between what happened and what remains. You may not have chosen the wounds, the losses, or the storms that shaped you, but you still hold the pen when it comes to how they are carried forward. The ink may be heavy, the pages marked, but the authorship is still yours. You have the power to choose your response. To choose how you speak to yourself in the silence. To choose whether the voice inside becomes a jailer or a companion. To choose how you locate yourself in this world, not as something diminished by what you endured, but as someone still becoming. Still unfolding. Still allowed to change shape.

So I urge you, gently and fiercely, to choose hope, even when it feels fragile in your hands, like something that might shatter if held too tightly. To choose life, even when it feels heavy, when it asks more of you than you think you can give. To choose healing, even when it unfolds slowly, unevenly, imperfectly, in fits and starts rather than sweeping transformations. Healing does not need to be beautiful to be real. You are worthy of love. Of care. Of compassion. Not because you have earned it through suffering, not because you have proven your strength, but because you exist. Because breath still moves through you. Because your presence matters. You are worthy of a life infused with meaning, with purpose, with moments of joy that feel like breath returning to collapsed lungs. Moments that remind you what it feels like to be here. Your story is not finished. Not even close. And you are allowed, again and again, to choose a future that does not shrink you, silence you, or reduce you to what hurt you. You are allowed to choose a future that lets you rise. Remember, your story is not yet written. The pages ahead remain open and unmarked, waiting not for certainty or flawlessness, but for your hand to reach for the pen with whatever strength you have left. Even a trembling grip is enough. You hold the power to create a new narrative, one shaped by hope, resilience, and determination, even if those qualities feel delicate, uncertain, or barely alive right now. Do not let the darkness claim you as its ending. Let it become the pressure that turns coal into something enduring, the force that reshapes you, the catalyst that ignites growth, change, and transformation where none once seemed possible. My story stands as a testament to that truth. It is a story born in utter darkness, forged in places where light felt impossible to imagine, where despair pressed so heavily it seemed permanent. And yet, it is also a story of resilience. Of healing. Of hope slowly reclaiming ground once surrendered.

My story is still being written, breath by breath, choice by choice, each moment an act of quiet defiance. It has become a story of survival. Of reclaiming my life from the margins where I once believed I belonged. Of discovering joy and happiness even while carrying the echoes of past pain, even while honoring what was lost. It is a story I am writing again with my own hands, no longer dictated by fear or despair, no longer confined by the narratives that once tried to end me. It is guided now by intention and courage, by the steady choice to remain, to grow, with each action, thought, or response, and to live fully. And that, I believe, is the most powerful story of all. Not the one where nothing breaks, but the one where something broken learns how to live, how to rise, and how to keep choosing itself, again and again. And that is the most terrifying truth of all: how close I came. The sheer proximity to death. The moment when the abyss leaned in so near, I could feel its breath on my skin, cold and intimate, whispering certainty where there was none. I nearly ended my story before I ever knew where it was truly meant to go, before I understood that I was not finished writing it, that I had barely begun. I stood at the edge with the final sentence already forming in my mind, convinced there was nothing more to say, nothing left worth telling. But I didn't step through. Instead, I was given a second chance. A pause in the darkness. A breath where there should have been none. A suspension of ending. A reprieve that felt undeserved at the time, unearned and inexplicable, yet it arrived anyway. Quiet. Steady. Unwavering. Like a hand closing gently around mine in the dark when I had already let go. And from this place of hard-won seeing, from the distance that survival grants, I understand what that moment truly was. It was interruption. It was mercy. It was time given back.

Now, standing here, I reach back toward anyone still trapped in that suffocating despair. Anyone standing where I once stood, staring into that same narrowing tunnel, contemplating that same final, desperate act as if it were the only remaining option. I reach back not with judgment or certainty, but with recognition. You do not have to make the same mistake I almost made. You do not have to nearly die, or die at all, before your story can change. There is hope, even if you cannot feel it yet. You can get better, even if your mind insists otherwise. You can heal, even if the path forward is still hidden in fog and fear. Your story is still breathing. And as long as breath remains, possibility does too. That means there is still time. Time for another sentence. Another chapter. Another way forward that you cannot yet imagine, but that is already, quietly, waiting for you to choose it.

I know this because I once believed the very same lie. I believed hopelessness and helplessness were permanent fixtures in my life, faithful companions I would never outgrow or outrun, shadows stitched into my days. I believed the darkness was not a season, but a destination. That it was where all roads eventually led, where mine had always been leading. But my story changed. Quietly at first. Reluctantly. And then undeniably. It is a different story now. One that still holds struggle and pain, yes, because healing does not erase what has been endured. But it also holds something I once thought impossible. Healing. And, finally, hope. It has become a living testament to the resilience of the human spirit, to the quiet, stubborn truth that light can be found even in the most starless places. Not the blinding kind of light that banishes all darkness at once, but the kind that appears as a pinprick, then another, until the sky is no longer empty.

Proof that even the longest night is not infinite. Confronting that part of me, the part that wished for my death, was one of the most daunting journeys I have ever taken. To face it felt like standing at the edge of the abyss, aware that it could stare back, daring me to look away, daring me to fall. I had to descend into the darkest recesses of my own mind, into the tangled web of beliefs and thoughts that had fed my suicidal ideation for so long. I had to go where I had spent years running from, to sit with the very voice that had tried to silence me. But this journey was never about remaining there. It was never about glorifying the darkness or becoming lost inside it again. It was about understanding it. Naming it. Disarming it. About stripping it of its mystique and its power. About breaking the spell it held over me and reclaiming the parts of myself it tried so hard to erase. My worth. My agency. My will to live.

And in doing so, something began to shift. The grip loosened. The walls thinned. The ground beneath me steadied. Step by uncertain step, I began to move back toward myself. Back into my life. Not as the person I once was, but as someone who had walked through the darkness and returned carrying its lessons, its warnings, and its truth. Someone who now knows that even when the abyss calls your name, you are still allowed to turn around. The debt I owe to that past version of myself is vast and sacred. It is not a debt of shame, nor of regret, but one of understanding. Of compassion. Of healing. It asks that I turn toward her with reverence, that I acknowledge the pain, the hurt, the suffering that drove me to the brink, without allowing that pain to calcify into my identity. She was not weak. She was overwhelmed. She was not broken. She was carrying more than any one heart should have had to bear alone.

That dark voice within me, the one that whispered worthlessness and hopelessness like a lullaby of erasure, was never truth. It was illness speaking. A distortion born from old wounds left untended and present overwhelm that blurred my vision. A cruel illusion masquerading as reality, wearing the convincing mask of certainty. For years, I mistook its volume for authority, its persistence for fact. Unraveling that darkness has been slow, painstaking work, like teasing apart knots pulled tight over years of fear and despair. Knots that resisted at first, that burned my fingers when I touched them, that seemed impossible to loosen without breaking something essential. It has meant turning toward the lies instead of fleeing them. Sitting with them. Listening without obeying. Meeting the negative self-talk and warped perceptions that once held me captive and learning, gently but firmly, to question their authority.

It has meant therapy. Support. Guidance. Safe relationships that reflected back truths I could not yet see for myself. It has meant choosing self-compassion again and again, especially on the days it felt undeserved, especially when the old voice insisted punishment was more appropriate than care. It has meant staying present when everything in me wanted to disappear. This work is about challenging the narrative that once looped endlessly in my mind and rewriting it, page by painful page, sometimes word by word, breath by breath. It is about allowing a truer, kinder story to begin taking shape, one that does not deny what happened, but refuses to be ruled by it. A story where healing is possible. A story where pain is acknowledged but not crowned. A story where I am no longer cast as the villain but recognized as the one who survived. The one who stayed. The one who chose, again and again, to live.

This new story is not about erasing the past, as if it never happened, as if pain can be undone by denial or silence. It is about integration. About turning toward what was and learning how to carry it without being crushed by its weight. It is about understanding the past well enough to release its grip, allowing what once wounded me to become fuel rather than a sentence, movement rather than a life-long verdict. It is about acknowledging the pain fully, honestly, without allowing it to determine the shape, the scale, or the horizon of my life. It is about embracing vulnerability, the brave, trembling act of opening my hands when pride and fear once kept them clenched tight. About reaching for help instead of retreating inward. About finding the courage to fight for a life worth living, a life that stretches beyond the darkness that once felt endless, airless, and absolute. A life that dares to imagine more. If I can do this, so can you.

Please, reach out, someone will take your hand. Your story does not have to end where the pain is loudest, where despair shouts its harshest conclusions. That is not the final chapter unless you decide it is. There is hope, even if it feels distant. There is help, even if asking feels terrifying. There is healing, even if it unfolds slowly and imperfectly. And there is a future waiting patiently to be written, even if you cannot yet imagine its opening lines, even if the page still feels frighteningly blank beneath your hand. Because in the end, it is not the darkness that defines us, but how we respond to it. It is not the pain, the hurt, or the suffering that shapes our worth, but our capacity to move through it and rise. You are a survivor. You are a warrior, even if you feel tired, even if you feel afraid, even if every step forward feels heavy. You are capable of facing challenges darker than you ever believed you could survive.

So let us rise together. Let us take our lives back, breath by breath, choice by choice. Let us choose hope. Let us choose healing. Let us choose life. We are worthy of it. We are deserving of it. And we are stronger, more resilient, and more capable than the darkness ever led us to believe.

In the words of the wise poet Rumi, *"The wound is the place where the light enters you."* I hold these words now not as ornament, but as an invitation and a truth hard-earned. An understanding shaped by living. Let us allow the light to reach the places we once hid in shame, the fractures we tried to seal shut for fear of what they might reveal. Let us allow it to enter our wounds, not to erase what happened, not to pretend the pain never existed, but to soften it. To warm it. To transform what once hurt into something that can heal. Let us stop guarding our broken places as if they are proof of failure and begin to see them as thresholds. Openings. Sacred points of entry where compassion can finally reach us. Where understanding can take root. Where we can learn that tenderness is not weakness, and vulnerability is not defeat, but the birthplace of becoming.

Let us rise, my friends, not unscarred, not untouched, but luminous because of what we have endured. Let us shine not despite our wounds, but through them, light refracting through every crack, every fault line, every place we once believed disqualified us from wholeness. We are survivors. We are warriors. And we are living proof that even the deepest darkness can become a passageway. Not an ending, but an opening.

Chapter Fifteen: Understanding Depression

The Monochrome Thief – Amelia's Story: Fading Hues

The robin's song used to arrive like a fanfare, a bright proclamation that morning had broken open once more, that the world was beginning again whether I was ready or not. Now it was only noise. Unnecessary noise. A thin, grating sound that scraped against already-frayed nerves, each note landing sharp and misplaced, as if joy itself had lost its timing. The sun, once a gentle warmth on my skin, no longer felt like comfort. It felt like an intrusion. An unforgiving spotlight spilling through the window, illuminating dust motes drifting through the air, each tiny particle catching the light like a fragment of the chaos swirling inside me. Nothing was hidden anymore. Everything felt exposed. This wasn't a dramatic, cinematic plunge into darkness. There was no single catastrophe to point to, no earth-shattering loss, no moment where everything visibly shattered and announced its ruin. It was far quieter than that. More insidious.

More dangerous. It was a slow leak, unnoticed at first, a hairline fracture widening beneath the surface. A creeping shadow that lingered at the edges of my awareness, subtle enough to be dismissed, patient enough to wait. Day by day, it swallowed the things I loved. Pleasure dulled. Color thinned. Laughter grew distant, as if heard through water. The world did not collapse all at once. It eroded. Softly. Steadily. Until one morning, I realized that what had once felt like life arriving now felt like life intruding, and the brightness of the day no longer promised possibility, only endurance. I remember the first sign, subtle enough to dismiss, easy to explain away. A shift in how the world reached me, as if an invisible pane of glass had been lowered between life and my senses. Colors lost their saturation. Reds softened into rust. Blues thinned into gray. Joy dulled, as though someone had quietly turned down the contrast on life itself, leaving everything washed out, pale, almost unreal. I was still present, still moving through my days, but the vividness had drained away, and I did not yet know to be afraid.

My favourite coffee, once a sacred ritual, tasted only hot. No comfort. No depth. Just temperature on my tongue. The ceremony remained, but the meaning had slipped out of it, leaving behind an empty routine. My morning walks with Leo, my scruffy terrier, stopped feeling like companionship and began to feel like obligation. Each step forward was mechanical, a relentless motion of legs and leash when all I wanted was to sit on the curb, let the world pass by without me, and quietly disappear into the background of my own life. Then came the apathy. Quiet. Stealthy. It did not announce itself. It crept in like fog, softening the edges of everything I once cared about. The once-burning passion for my art, for the swirling colors and intricate details I used to coax onto the canvas, flickered, sputtered, and finally went dark. What had once felt like communion became unreachable, as if the part of me that knew how to create had been locked behind a door I could no longer find.

My studio, which had once been a sanctuary, a place where my soul could breathe freely and without restraint, became a tomb. The air grew heavy. Still. It filled with half-finished pieces frozen mid-thought, abandoned mid-feeling, and the accusing silence of unused brushes. They lay where I had left them, bristles stiff with dried paint, each one bearing witness to something I could no longer reach, to a version of myself I could no longer remember how to be. "Just a slump," I told myself. Everyone has them. I clung to the comfort of that explanation, the way one clings to a railing in fog. I forced myself to paint, to show up, to create on command, as if discipline alone could resurrect what had gone missing. But the colors fell flat beneath my brush, dull and lifeless, drained of their pulse. They lacked the spark, the breath, the quiet electricity that had once flowed effortlessly through every stroke. My heart wasn't in it anymore, and the canvas seemed to know. It mirrored my emptiness back at me without mercy, a blank witness to what I could no longer give.

The silence grew louder. The robin's song sharpened, each note a small irritation against my nerves. The sun grew heavier, pressing down rather than warming, an oppressive presence I could not escape. Light itself began to feel accusatory. What I did not yet understand was that this was depression. Not the dramatic, sobbing, cinematic version we are taught to recognize, but something far more insidious. A quiet erosion. A slow dimming of the inner light. It did not roar or announce itself. It did not arrive with chaos or spectacle. It crept. A thief in the dark, careful and patient, stealing small, precious pieces of me one by one. Pleasure first. Then meaning. Then energy. Then hope. Until one day I realized how hollow I had become, a shell moving through familiar motions, occupied by a relentless, gnawing ache I could not name, only endure.

The Mask of Normalcy

The hardest part was not the absence of joy, nor the hollowing out of passion, nor even the bone-deep fatigue that clung to me like a burial shroud. It was the performance. The relentless, exhausting performance of normal. The daily act of putting on a version of myself that could pass inspection, that could move through rooms without raising alarm. It took everything I had. Every smile was rehearsed. Every laugh carefully timed. Every interaction a small act of endurance. My family, bless their well-meaning hearts, sensed the shift. They always do. "You seem tired, Amelia," my mother would say, her brow knitting with quiet concern, eyes searching my face for something she could name. "Are you eating properly? Getting enough sleep?" And I would answer on cue, summoning a smile that felt like someone else's, stiff and ill-fitting, like a stranger's hand resting where it didn't belong. The muscles of my face obeyed, even as something inside me recoiled.

"I'm fine, Mom. Just a little stressed with work." Work became my shield. My alibi. A convenient explanation I could hold up between us like glass. Vague enough to sound plausible. Specific enough to shut the door on further questions. Yes, my job as a graphic designer at a local marketing firm was demanding. Yes, deadlines pressed and expectations weighed heavy. But it was never the source of my misery. It was simply the scapegoat I offered up, an easy name to give the ache I couldn't explain. Because how do you tell someone that you are tired not from effort, but from existing. That sleep does not restore you. That food has lost its comfort. That the world feels like it is happening behind a pane of glass you cannot push through. How do you explain a pain with no visible wound, a heaviness with no clear cause. So instead, I performed. I nodded. I smiled. I said the lines. And each time I did, the distance between who I was and who I pretended to be grew wider, quieter, more unbearable.

Because how do you tell the people who love you that the problem isn't exhaustion, or workload, or sleep? How do you name an enemy that leaves no bruises, no clear cause, no language that feels adequate? How do you explain that what is happening is an invisible erosion, a quiet collapse unfolding behind practiced smiles and well-rehearsed reassurances? That you are not merely tired, but slowly disappearing, one performance at a time? I became fluent in the imitation of happiness. It was a language I learned out of necessity, not choice. I laughed at jokes that landed like echoes in an empty room, the sound of my own laughter startling me with its hollowness. I nodded along in conversations, shaping words with my mouth that felt like a foreign language I no longer truly spoke, syllables passing through me without meaning, without connection. My face knew the choreography even when my heart was nowhere to be found.

I attended social gatherings. I showed up. I smiled. I mingled. I made small talk with practiced ease, weaving myself into conversations while something inside me quietly collapsed. Grain by grain. Like a sandcastle meeting the tide, its edges softening first, then its walls giving way, until what had once been carefully built was reduced to something unrecognizable. No one noticed the loss in real time. That's the danger of erosion. It happens silently. From the outside, I was functioning. Capable. Present. From the inside, I was fraying. Threads loosening. Holding myself together through habit alone. Each performance took a little more from me, until the gap between who I appeared to be and who I actually was became a chasm I didn't know how to cross, only how to keep pretending it wasn't there. Chloe was the hardest to deceive.

She always had been. We had been inseparable since kindergarten, stitched together by secrets whispered under blankets, by shared dreams scribbled in the margins of notebooks, by countless bottles of cheap wine that tasted like freedom back then. She knew me in a way that bypassed language entirely, a knowing that lived in the pauses between my words, in the way my breath changed before I spoke. She read me the way one reads weather, sensing the storm long before the sky darkened. She saw through my performance with unsettling ease. "You okay, Amelia?" she asked one evening, her eyes holding mine a little too long, searching with a patience that felt almost unbearable. We were sitting in my apartment, a movie flickering across the screen, light and shadow playing out a story I could not follow. I couldn't tell you a single scene. My real battle was happening behind my eyes, loud and relentless, a war fought entirely in silence.

"Yeah. I'm fine," I said. Even to my own ears, my voice sounded thin, stretched too far, unconvincing. A fragile thread pretending to be rope. She didn't believe me. I saw it immediately, the way concern darkened her gaze, the way her body leaned in almost imperceptibly, as if preparing to catch me. "Amelia..." she started, gently, carefully, her voice laced with concern, with history, with love. "Please, Chloe," I cut in, the words cracking despite my effort to keep them smooth. "Just... please don't. I don't want to talk about it." The room seemed to exhale with her sigh, a sound heavy with worry and restraint, the kind that carries everything left unsaid. "Okay," she said softly. "But I'm here. You know that, right? Whenever you're ready." I nodded, my throat tight, tears burning behind my eyes, unshed and stubborn. Her kindness was a double-edged blade. It warmed my heart, yes, but it also cut deep. It amplified the guilt.

Because I was lying. To her. To everyone. To myself. And the weight of that lie, the constant performance, the silence I insisted on carrying alone, pressed inward like a slow collapse, crushing me from the inside out, even as I sat there smiling beside the one person who saw me most clearly of all.

Whispers in the Soul

The silence was not empty. It was crowded. Thick with voices that slipped in the moment everything else went quiet, uninvited and relentless. Whispers of doubt. Of fear. Of inadequacy. "You're not good enough", they hissed. "You're a failure. You'll never be happy." They clung to me like shadows at dusk, stretching long and warped, following me wherever I went, impossible to outrun, impossible to shake. Even in stillness, I was never alone. Those whispers amplified every insecurity, magnified every perceived flaw, twisting my thoughts into grotesque caricatures of reality. A small mistake at work swelled into a catastrophic failure, proof, they insisted, of my incompetence. A passing comment from a stranger sharpened into a personal attack, lodged deep and festering. Even a fleeting moment of joy curdled almost instantly, souring into a cruel reminder of everything I believed I had already lost, everything I was certain I would never regain.

Slowly. Relentlessly. The whispers eroded my self-esteem the way water wears down stone, sanding me to rawness, stripping away confidence grain by grain until I felt exposed and defenceless. There was no armor left. No safe distance from the assault. I began to question everything. My abilities. My worth. My right to take up space in a world that seemed to have no room for me. My very existence felt negotiable. "Why even bother?" they murmured in the quiet moments. "You're just going to fail anyway." And in that chorus of doubt, repetition hardened into belief. The whispers no longer felt like thoughts. They felt like truth. And sometimes, most terrifying of all, they changed their tone. The whispers shed their sharpness and learned how to sound gentle. They lowered their voices, softened their edges, spoke almost kindly, as if they were concerned for me.

They murmured about escape. About the quiet promise of oblivion. About the peace that might come from finally silencing the voices. They did not rush or threaten. They waited. They spoke slowly, patiently, like something ancient that understood the power of endurance. And in those moments, the darkness did not shout. It tempted. It dressed itself as compassion. It learned how to sound like relief. I didn't want to die. Not truly. Not in the way people imagine when they hear the word, with finality and drama and intent. What I wanted was quieter than that. More desperate. Far more dangerous. I wanted the pain to stop. I wanted the whispers to finally fall silent. I wanted relief from the constant internal barrage, from the relentless commentary that followed me everywhere, narrating my failures, tallying my inadequacies, reminding me again and again that I was somehow failing at being human.

The idea of escape began to shimmer at the edges of my thoughts, not as a dramatic ending, but as a soft glow just beyond reach. A seduction. A promise. A way out of the noise. It did not arrive as catastrophe. It arrived as possibility. As the suggestion of rest. As the fantasy of laying everything down and being done with the exhausting work of holding myself together. It was a treacherous path, slick with illusion, a dark abyss that did not shove me forward but beckoned softly, patiently, day after day. It never demanded. It invited. Each morning, it leaned a little closer, brushing against my thoughts before I was fully awake. Each night it whispered a little louder, slipping in when the world went quiet, and my defenses were worn thin. It offered rest. It offered quiet. It offered an end to the ceaseless labor of pretending, performing, and enduring.

And the longer I walked beside it, the more convincing it became. The more reasonable it sounded. The more it framed surrender as kindness and disappearance as peace. It asked me to believe that stopping was not giving up but finally letting go. That silence could be safety. That erasure could be mercy. And for a long time, standing there in the dim half-light of my own exhaustion, I almost believed it. What I did not understand then was how seductive exhaustion can be. How the mind, when worn thin by unrelenting pain, begins to confuse silence with safety. The darkness knew this. It did not rush me. It waited. It let me grow tired. It let hope fray at the edges until even breathing felt like a negotiation. It offered itself not as destruction, but as rest. Not as disappearance, but as release. And that is what made it so dangerous. It did not look like despair. It looked like relief wearing a gentle face.

I carried that temptation quietly. I carried it through ordinary days and unremarkable moments. In grocery aisles. In traffic. In conversations where I nodded at the right places while my mind wandered elsewhere, tracing the shape of an exit that no one else could see. I learned how to function while unraveling. How to smile while bargaining internally. How to move through the world with a weight in my chest that no one thought to question. Yet even then, something in me resisted. Not loudly. Not heroically. Just enough. A small, stubborn ember that refused to go out, even as everything around it dimmed. I did not always recognize it as hope. Often it felt more like a habit, or an obligation, or the simple act of putting one foot in front of the other because stopping felt harder than continuing. But it was there. Quiet. Persistent. Unyielding in its own fragile way.

Looking back now, I can see that the pull toward escape was never about wanting to end my life. It was about wanting to end my suffering. It was about longing for a pause, a mercy, a moment where I could lay down the armor and stop fighting myself. I did not want to vanish. I wanted peace. And at the time, I could not yet imagine a version of peace that did not require my absence. This understanding did not arrive all at once. It came slowly, in fragments, through survival. Through moments where I stayed when leaving felt easier. Through breaths taken reluctantly, then habitually, then eventually with a little less effort. Healing did not announce itself as salvation. It arrived quietly, the way dawn does, changing the light so gradually that you only notice it when the darkness is already loosening its grip. And this is what I know now, standing on the other side of those thoughts: the voice that promised relief was lying about its cost.

The silence it offered was not peace, but erasure. True quiet did not come from disappearing. It came from learning, slowly and imperfectly, how to stay. How to listen to the pain without obeying it. How to make room for the parts of me that were hurting instead of trying to silence them. I did not escape the darkness by stepping away from life. I escaped it by turning toward myself. By choosing, again and again, to remain. To breathe. To endure long enough to discover that the noise could soften without my disappearance, and that relief, real relief, could be built from presence rather than absence. This was not a victory moment. It was a turning. A subtle shift. The beginning of a path that did not promise ease but did promise truth. And for the first time, that felt like something worth staying for.

Leo was what tethered me to the ground. My anchor. My gravity. When everything inside me felt unmoored, when my thoughts spiraled and the world tilted toward the edge, he held me in place without ever knowing he was doing it. His presence was uncomplicated and unwavering, a steady heartbeat pressed gently against the chaos of my mind. He did not demand explanations or reassurances. He did not ask me to be better, brighter, stronger. He did not need a healed version of me. He simply needed me to be there. To fill his bowl. To clip on his leash. To sit beside him while the world felt unbearable. These small acts became lifelines. Rituals of staying. Proof that I still belonged somewhere, even when I felt like I was slipping out of my own life. His unconditional love cut through the fog in a way nothing else could. It did not try to fix me or reason with my pain. It just existed. Warm. Present. Faithful.

When everything in me felt disposable, he reminded me that I was necessary. For him, I stayed when leaving felt easier. For him, I kept fighting on days when I had no strength left to fight for myself. For him, I wore the mask a little longer, even when it cracked and chafed against my skin, even when it hurt to keep pretending, I was okay. For him, I chose to breathe, one agonizing, deliberate breath at a time, counting them like promises I was not yet ready to break. It wasn't heroic. It wasn't noble. It was survival in its rawest form. Bare. Unpolished. Uncelebrated. A quiet refusal to disappear. But it was enough. And in those moments, enough was everything. Because sometimes, when the darkness is winning, you do not need purpose or hope or clarity. You just need one small, living reason to stay tethered to the world. And Leo was mine.

The Painted Rainbow: Amelia's Journey from Gray

The Unbidden Guest

Amelia woke to the familiar gray. Not the kind that gathered outside the window, though the perpetually overcast skies of Seattle mirrored it faithfully, but the kind that lived inside her. A muted, melancholic hue that had seeped into her bones over time, settling there quietly, patiently, until it stained the way she saw everything. It dulled the mornings before they had a chance to begin. It softened colors, blunted edges, drained warmth from moments that should have felt alive. For years, she had explained it away with easy words. Tired. Stressed. The demands of her high-powered job as an architect. The relentless expectations of her ambitious parents. The unspoken pressure to be flawless, composed, impressive. Of course she was exhausted. Of course she felt heavy. Anyone carrying that much weight would. The logic was neat. Convincing. A well-drawn structure that held just long enough to pass inspection. Except lately, it didn't.

The gray had thickened. What once felt manageable now pressed down on her chest, dense and suffocating, as if the air itself had grown heavier overnight. Breathing required effort. Waking required negotiation. Even lying still felt laborious, like her body was pinned beneath something invisible but immense. It followed her from room to room, from waking to sleep, no longer content to linger quietly in the background. It sat beside her at the kitchen table while her coffee went cold. It hovered behind her reflection in the bathroom mirror, blurring the edges of her own face. It rode with her in elevators, pressed against her in meetings, settled into the spaces between conversations where silence grew too loud. The gray was no longer a backdrop. It demanded to be felt. It asked questions she didn't yet have language for. Questions about endurance. About how long a person could live half-muted and still call it living. About when resilience quietly turns into erasure.

And as Amelia lay there, staring at the ceiling, the weight of it heavy and intimate, she sensed something unsettling beneath the fog. Not a breaking point. Not yet. But a shift. A deepening. The moment when survival stops being passive and starts asking to be witnessed. The gray was no longer something she carried. It was something that carried her. She used to find refuge in her art. Once, it had been a sanctuary she could step into, a place where her breath slowed and her inner world spilled outward in color and motion. Her apartment walls still bore witness to that former self, lined with vibrant canvases, bursts of color and movement that reflected the vivid inner world she once inhabited. They shimmered with life, with intention, with a confidence she no longer recognized as her own. Those paintings felt like echoes now. Relics from another lifetime. Proof that something bright had once lived here, even if she could no longer feel its warmth. They watched her in silence, frozen mid-expression, holding a version of her that had slipped out of reach.

The paints sat untouched, their lids sealed tight, color locked away like a language she had forgotten how to speak. Brushes gathered dust in jars like forgotten tools, their bristles stiff, waiting for hands that no longer reached for them. Blank canvases leaned against the walls, their cheerful emptiness no longer inviting but accusatory, their white surfaces too loud, too honest. As if they were asking her where she had gone. As if they expected an answer. She couldn't answer them. All she knew was that the color had drained from her days. What once flowed now stalled. What once sparked now dimmed. The gray had seeped into everything, tinting time itself, until it began to feel less like a phase and more like a place. A landscape she moved through each day. A room without doors. And standing there among the remnants of her former refuge, Amelia felt the quiet, creeping fear take hold. That this gray was no longer something she passed through. That it might be somewhere she would be asked to live.

Even her relationship with David, her boyfriend of five years, had dulled to the same muted tone. He was a good man. Kind. Steady. Supportive in all the ways that should have mattered. The kind of person you build a life with on paper, the kind you trust to show up, to stay. And he did. Always. Yet somewhere along the way, the intimacy between them had thinned, stretched and worn smooth by time and routine, until it became something else entirely. Not broken. Not hostile. Just quietly distant. Comfortable, and strangely lonely. They moved around each other like familiar furniture, solid and dependable, always there but rarely touched. Sharing space without truly meeting inside it. Conversations skimmed the surface. Affection became habitual. Love, once alive and breathing, settled into a careful choreography of shoulds and defaults. She couldn't remember the last time she truly laughed, the kind that rose up unannounced and surprised her into joy. The last time she felt genuinely connected to him, or to anyone at all. Even beside him, she felt alone.

Mornings became negotiations. She dragged herself out of bed, the weight of the day already pressing down on her ribs before her feet even touched the floor. Another day of meetings and deadlines. Another day of expectations stacked neatly on her shoulders, labeled and color-coded, impossible to set down. Another day of performing competence and calm, of answering questions, solving problems, holding everything together with practiced precision. Inside, everything splintered quietly. She dressed, moved, spoke on autopilot, each action ticking itself off like items on a list she had memorized long ago. From the outside, she looked functional. Capable. Put together. From the inside, she felt hollowed out, like a structure still standing long after its foundations had begun to crack. No alarms sounded. No collapse announced itself. Just a slow, steady erosion.

And as she stepped into the day, carrying the familiar heaviness with her, Amelia felt the growing ache of a life that continued to move forward while she remained suspended inside herself, present in form, absent in feeling, wondering how long a person could keep living this way before something finally gave. In the bathroom, she caught her reflection and paused. The woman staring back felt unfamiliar, like a stranger wearing her face. Familiar features arranged in a way she recognized yet no longer inhabited. The sparkle that once lived in her eyes was gone, replaced by a dull, vacant stare that seemed to look through her rather than at her, as if whatever had once looked out from behind them had quietly stepped away. She searched that reflection for signs of the woman she remembered. The one who used to feel things sharply. The one who laughed easily. The one who moved through the world with color in her chest.

But all she found was absence. A hollowness that echoed when she stood too still, a silence that pressed back when she tried to listen inward. The vibrant, passionate spirit she remembered so clearly had been extinguished. Not shattered in a single moment, but dimmed slowly, breath by breath, until the light went out without ceremony. What remained was something hollow. Something echoing. A body moving through the motions of living without the weight of being fully alive. This wasn't just stress. This wasn't exhaustion that sleep could fix. She felt that truth settle in her bones, heavy and undeniable. This was something else entirely. Something deeper. Something darker. A quiet descent that had gone unnoticed for too long, masked by productivity and perseverance. And standing there under the harsh bathroom light, Amelia understood with a sudden, chilling clarity that whatever had taken root inside her would not be solved by rest or time or effort alone. It was asking to be seen.

The Crack in the Facade

The turning point arrived without warning, slipping in under the guise of an ordinary workday. It came during a presentation to a potential client, a moment where Amelia should have felt most herself. She was in her element, or at least she used to be. Confident. Articulate. Standing before the room, unveiling her innovative design for a sustainable community center, a project she had poured herself into relentlessly. Weeks of late nights, missed meals, sacrificed weekends. She had given it everything, driven by the quiet, desperate hope that this time, this project, might reignite something she had lost. But as she spoke, something inside her faltered. The words caught in her throat as if they had suddenly forgotten their way out. The room tilted. Her vision blurred at the edges, her heart slamming violently against her ribs, each beat louder than the last.

A wave of nausea surged through her, hot and disorienting. She reached for the podium, fingers tightening around its edge as if it were the only solid thing left in the room. Around her, the carefully constructed facade she had worn for so long began to crack, splintering under the weight of everything she had been holding back. "I, I, I need a moment," she stammered, the words barely audible, her voice betraying her before she could stop it. Mortification burned through her as she turned and fled the room, leaving behind a stunned audience, confused faces, and the ruins of a presentation she had once believed might save her.

She barely registered where she was going until she found herself locked in a sterile bathroom, fluorescent lights buzzing overhead. There, she slid down the wall and collapsed onto the cold tile floor, her body folding in on itself as sobs tore free, raw and uncontrollable. The dam had finally broken. Years of suppressed emotion, unspoken fear, relentless anxiety, and the suffocating weight of depression surged out in a torrent of grief. There was no containing it anymore, no smiling through it, no pushing it aside for later. This wasn't a bad moment. This wasn't stress. This wasn't burnout. This was a crisis. And for the first time, she could no longer pretend otherwise.

Acknowledging the Void

The aftermath of the presentation was merciless. The room emptied, but the weight of what had happened remained, lingering in the air like a bruise you can't stop touching. Her boss, careful and compassionate in his response, spoke softly, choosing his words with intention. He offered understanding. Support. Space. And yet, beneath it all, he could not hide his concern. That concern settled in Amelia's chest like a quiet verdict. Not an accusation, but a recognition. And somehow, that felt worse. David and Chloe came quickly, drawn by instinct and fear. Their faces were etched with worry, eyes searching hers for signs of stability, for reassurance that she could not give. Their arms offered comfort. Hands rubbed her back. Words tumbled out in gentle reassurance, layered with love and urgency. You're okay. We're here. We've got you. But even as they held her, Amelia felt the distance between them. A widening gulf. A chasm she did not know how to cross.

They were reaching for her. She was standing on the other side of something vast and unnamed. She could feel it there, solid and impassable, a boundary she didn't have language for yet. No bridge. No map. Just the ache of separation, the unbearable loneliness of being seen but not reached. And then the word began to echo in her mind. Depression. It arrived hollow and insistent, bouncing off the walls of her thoughts, refusing to be ignored. It landed like an unwelcome truth she had spent years outrunning, dodging with busyness and achievement and composure. She had always associated it with weakness. With failure. With something to be hidden, apologized for, whispered about behind closed doors like a shameful secret. But later, alone in the quiet hours of the night, with trembling hands and a racing heart, she began to search.

Page after page. Article after article. And there it was. Herself. Reflected back in clinical descriptions and personal stories. In statistics that felt uncomfortably intimate. In the voices of people who had walked this same dim corridor and survived it. The recognition was unsettling. Like seeing your own face in a mirror you had avoided for years. Familiar, undeniable, impossible to look away from. It stripped her of denial and left her with something raw and fragile in its place. Not relief. Not fear alone. But the terrifying, clarifying knowledge that what she was facing had a name. And that naming it meant she could no longer pretend it wasn't there. The hardest part was admitting it to herself. Not the research. Not the late-night reading. Not even the quiet recognition that had already begun to take root. The hardest part was naming it. Letting the truth take shape in language.

Accepting that she wasn't just stressed. Wasn't just tired. Wasn't simply overwhelmed by work or life in the way everyone seemed to be. She was struggling with something deeper. Something real. Something that deserved care rather than endurance. Pride rose up in protest, sharp and defensive. Fear followed close behind, whispering consequences. The weight of societal stigma pressed in from all sides, heavy and unrelenting. What would her parents think? Her colleagues? Would they look at her differently, as if something essential had cracked? Would they see her as fragile, incapable, broken? Would everything she had built, every achievement carefully stacked like proof of worth, be quietly dismantled by a single word? That word felt dangerous. Loaded. Final. And yet, the alternative loomed larger still.

Continuing to suffer in silence. Remaining trapped in the gray. Performing strength until there was nothing left to perform with. Pretending until the effort of pretending became heavier than the truth itself. She could feel where that road led. A narrowing. A dimming. A slow erasure of whatever remained of her. The choice was not between comfort and discomfort. It was between honesty and disappearance. And for the first time, she allowed herself to say it plainly. Not out loud. Not yet. Just in the fragile privacy of her own mind, where the words trembled but held: She needed help. The sentence did not fix anything. It did not lift the gray or soften the ache in her chest. But it changed the shape of the silence. It cracked something open. A small, uncertain opening where breath could pass through. And in that quiet admission, Amelia took her first step not toward healing but toward staying.

THE SEARCH FOR LIGHT

Finding a therapist felt like stepping into a labyrinth with no map. Every turn was lined with anxiety, each corridor narrowing beneath her feet. The fear of being judged waited at every corner. The terror of exposing her deepest insecurities to a stranger pulsed like a warning bell in her chest. And beneath it all lived a quieter dread, more insidious than the rest. The fear that even if she did all of this, even if she gathered her courage and reached out, it still might not work. That there might be no exit. That the effort itself could become another disappointment to carry. Each possibility felt heavy. Overwhelming. Like stones added slowly to her pockets as she tried to keep walking. She spent countless hours researching, scrolling late into the night while the world slept and her thoughts refused to. Screens glowed in the dark like false stars, names and credentials blurring together as exhaustion crept in.

She scheduled consultations she nearly cancelled, hovering over confirmation emails with a racing heart, bargaining with herself for just one more reason to back out. She sat through awkward first meetings where the words stuck in her throat and her body screamed to retreat, muscles tight, breath shallow, every instinct urging escape. Each attempt cost her something. And then she found Dr. Anya Sharma. Dr. Sharma had a gentleness about her, a calm, grounded presence that didn't rush or pry. She moved through conversation with an unhurried steadiness, as if time itself softened around her. There was a compassion in her eyes that immediately loosened something inside Amelia, *a quiet, involuntary response, like a clenched fist finally easing its grip. It was a subtle signal, barely perceptible, but unmistakable all the same. This space was different. Safe.*

The first sessions, though, were still brutally hard. Amelia struggled to give language to the tangled web inside her, the emotions knotted so tightly they felt inseparable, like threads pulled into a single, painful mass. Words arrived incomplete or dissolved before they could fully form. Feelings contradicted each other, overlapped, collided. Shame clung to her, heavy and persistent. Embarrassment burned beneath her skin, flooding her chest and face with heat. Vulnerability felt like standing exposed without armor, every instinct braced for harm, every nerve awake and raw. Sometimes silence filled the room, thick and stretching, her heartbeat loud in her ears. Sometimes tears came without explanation, surprising her with their urgency. Dr. Sharma did not rush to fix or soothe. She did not demand coherence. She stayed. Present. Steady.

As if she understood that this was what beginning looked like. Not clarity. Not relief. But the terrifying, courageous act of remaining visible when everything inside her wanted to disappear. And for the first time in a long while, Amelia did not turn away. But Dr. Sharma waited. She listened. She asked careful questions and then stepped back, leaving room for silence, allowing it to stretch without pressure or urgency. The quiet was not empty or awkward. It was deliberate. Spacious. An invitation rather than a demand. In that stillness, Amelia felt something unfamiliar. Permission. The rare and disarming permission to move at the speed of her own breath. Slowly, she began to speak. About her childhood. About her parents' relentless expectations, spoken and unspoken, the quiet contracts she had signed without knowing she had a choice.

About the fear of failure that had followed her like a shadow, lengthening behind her with every success, whispering that one misstep would undo it all. About the deep-seated belief, lodged somewhere beneath thought and logic, that she was never enough. Not accomplished enough. Not grateful enough. Not strong enough. Each admission felt like tearing open an old wound, painful and raw, the kind that stings when exposed to air after years of being tightly bound. And yet, beneath the ache, there was relief. A loosening. A sense that something infected was finally being allowed to drain. It was cathartic in the quietest way. Not a dramatic release or a sudden breakthrough, but a steady unburdening. The kind that happens one truth at a time. Session by session. Breath by breath.

She began to unravel the tightly wound threads of her depression. What once felt like an indistinguishable mass of darkness slowly separated into strands she could finally see, name, and hold. Fear had a texture. Shame had a history. Grief had a voice. None of it disappeared, but it became less overwhelming, less total. It could be approached rather than fled. The process was slow. Painstaking. Often exhausting. There were days she left feeling scraped raw, days when the work followed her home and settled heavy in her chest. But there was something new beneath the fatigue. A sense of direction. Of companionship. For the first time in a long while, she wasn't lost in the maze alone.

The Dawn of Small Victories

The first weeks of the work were a rollercoaster, unpredictable and exhausting. Healing did not arrive gently. It came in waves, unsteady and disorienting. There were side effects that rattled her body, unfamiliar sensations that made her hyperaware of every heartbeat and breath. Mood swings rose and fell without warning, leaving her questioning her own reactions, her own stability. Long moments of doubt crept in, quiet and corrosive, where she wondered if she had made the wrong choice entirely. If opening this door had only made the darkness louder. Some days felt heavier than before, as if turning toward healing had stirred the dust of everything she had buried. Old memories surfaced without invitation. Emotions she had numbed demanded attention. It felt like cleaning a long-closed room and choking on the debris before any fresh air could enter.

Amelia questioned herself constantly. "Is this worth it? Is this helping? Am I broken beyond even this?" The questions echoed in the hollow spaces of her mind, relentless and sharp. And yet, with Dr. Sharma's steady guidance and David's unwavering presence beside her, she stayed. She showed up to sessions with trembling resolve. She took the medication even when her body resisted. She spoke when silence felt safer. She persevered, even when retreat felt like relief. And then, almost imperceptibly at first, something began to shift. The gray started to thin. It lifted like fog loosening its grip under a tentative morning sun, reluctant but yielding. Not gone. Not suddenly bright. But lighter. Breathable. Mornings arrived with a little less dread. Thoughts slowed enough to be followed. Laughter, faint and tentative, brushed against her days like a memory trying to return. The darkness did not vanish. It softened. It stepped back just enough for her to notice the space it left behind. And in that space, fragile but real, Amelia felt the first quiet evidence that staying had mattered.

She began waking with a little more energy, a little more space inside her chest. The mornings no longer felt like walls she had to climb. There was still weight, still residue from the long season of gray, but now there was room to breathe around it. A fragile thread of hope wound its way back into her days, thin but persistent, catching the light when she wasn't looking for it. She started taking small, deliberate steps toward caring for herself. Nothing dramatic. Nothing that announced itself as transformation. Just quiet choices made with intention. A daily walk through the park, noticing the way the trees moved in the breeze, how their branches swayed without apology, rooted and yielding at the same time. A warm bath scented with lavender, letting the heat loosen the knots in her body, letting the tension seep from her muscles as if it finally had permission to leave. Quiet evenings curled up with a book, rediscovering the forgotten comfort of stillness, the way silence could cradle rather than accuse.

They were simple pleasures. Ordinary. And yet she realized she had been grieving them without knowing it. Grieving the ease, the softness, the small moments that make a life feel inhabitable. And one afternoon, almost shyly, she picked up a paintbrush again. At first, there was no intention to create anything meaningful. No pressure to produce beauty or coherence. She let the colors spill and collide on the canvas without expectation, without judgment. The strokes were messy. Imperfect. Free. Paint smeared and layered and bled into itself, unconcerned with outcome. And in that freedom, something loosened. It felt like touching a long-lost part of herself, a familiar presence stirring beneath the surface, tentative but alive. A part she had feared was gone forever. The canvas did not critique or compare. It did not demand perfection or explanation. It only asked her to show up. To be present. To move. And for the first time in a long while, she did. Not as someone healed. Not as someone finished. But as someone returning.

Reaching Out, Letting In

Opening up to David and Chloe was one of the hardest things she had ever done. For so long, she had kept them at arm's length, holding herself just far enough away to stay intact. Convinced that her pain was too heavy to place in anyone else's hands. Too dense. Too complicated. She feared becoming a burden, feared that if they truly saw the darkness she carried, they might step back instead of closer. That love, once tested by truth, might falter. But beneath that fear lived a quieter knowing. A certainty that if she wanted these relationships to survive, to breathe again, she could no longer hide behind silence. Distance had protected her, yes, but it had also starved the connection she needed most. With trembling hands and a voice that threatened to disappear mid-sentence, she told them.

About the depression. About the darkness that had wrapped itself around her days and nights, threading through even the moments that should have felt light. About the therapy, the fear, the slow and fragile steps toward healing that demanded more courage than she knew how to name. She spoke haltingly, words catching in her throat, breath uneven. She braced herself for judgment. For discomfort. For the subtle recoil she had imagined a hundred times in her mind. For rejection dressed in politeness. Instead, she was met with open arms. David and Chloe pulled her close, their embrace immediate and unguarded. Tears slipped freely down their faces, grief and love tangled together, indistinguishable. They apologized, again and again, for not seeing how much she had been suffering, for missing the quiet signs she had learned so well to hide.

Their regret was not accusation. It was mourning. For the pain she had carried alone. And they promised, without hesitation, to walk beside her. To stay. To learn. To follow her wherever this path might lead. Rebuilding intimacy was not instant. It did not arrive as a sudden return to what had been. It unfolded slowly, carefully, like something fragile being pieced back together by hand. Conversations deepened. Silences softened. Touch became intentional again, no longer habitual but chosen. Trust, once frayed, began to mend. And in allowing herself to be seen, fully and without armor, Amelia discovered something quietly miraculous. That love did not shrink under the weight of her truth. It expanded. Through honest conversations and shared vulnerability, they began to find each other again.

Not by returning to what had been, but by moving forward into something new. They rediscovered the simple joy of shared moments. Laughter that arrived softly and lingered. The comfort of quiet companionship, of sitting side by side without needing to fill the space. The grounding power of unconditional love, steady and present, no longer assumed but chosen each day. What emerged was not the relationship they once had, but something deeper. Steadier. More real. A connection built not on ease, but on truth. Telling her parents was different. Harder in a different way.

She knew their response would be complicated, shaped by generations of misunderstanding and fear, by a language that had never quite made room for inner pain. At first, they dismissed her depression as "stress," urged her to push through, to snap out of it, to be grateful and strong and resilient in all the ways they had learned to survive. The familiar ache of not being fully seen surfaced again, sharp and old. But this time, she stayed. She explained. She educated. She spoke carefully, patiently, even when her voice shook. She named what she was living with and refused to let it be minimized. She helped them understand that this was not weakness. Not failure. But illness. Something real. Something deserving of care rather than correction.

Slowly, their resistance softened. They asked questions. They listened, haltingly at first. Concern replaced dismissal. Fear shifted into something gentler. And though their support came imperfectly, it came nonetheless, offered in the only way they knew how. Awkward check-ins. Practical gestures. Love filtered through unfamiliar terrain. In telling her truth, Amelia discovered something unexpected. Vulnerability did not fracture her world. It widened it. It stretched the boundaries of what was possible, what could be held, what could be shared. And in that widening, in the newly opened space where silence once lived, there was room for healing to take root.

Finding the Palette Again

As her mental health slowly steadied, Amelia felt something stir that she had once believed was lost for good. Not all at once. Not as a triumphant return. But as a quiet reawakening, like embers glowing beneath ash. Her passion for architecture began to return, not as pressure or performance, but as purpose. The frantic striving softened. The need to prove herself loosened its grip. What remained was a gentler pull, a remembering. She started volunteering with a local non-profit, designing affordable housing for low-income families. The work grounded her. It asked different questions of her hands and mind. In shaping these spaces, she rediscovered what had drawn her to the field in the first place. It wasn't about accolades or perfection. It was about shelter. About light and airflow. About creating rooms where lives could unfold with dignity. Where safety was not a luxury. Where belonging could take root.

Using her skills in service of others shifted something fundamental. It widened her gaze beyond the narrow confines of her own suffering and anchored her in something tangible. Measurable. Real. In blueprints and conversations and small design choices that carried real consequence, she felt it again. That she mattered. Not because she was exceptional, but because she was present. At the same time, she returned to painting with new eyes. The canvases that had once mocked her now welcomed her. Their blankness no longer accused. It invited. She created vibrant, expressive pieces that carried the textures of her journey, paint layered thick and thin, darkness and light woven together without apology. Shadows were not erased. They were integrated. Color bled through charcoal. Sharp lines softened into movement.

The work was different now. Not an escape, but a conversation. A record of survival rendered in pigment and form. Each piece held evidence of where she had been and who she was becoming, proof that beauty could exist alongside pain, not in spite of it. And in both disciplines, brick and brush, structure and flow, Amelia felt herself coming back into alignment. Not as the person she had been before the gray, but as someone deeper. More honest. Someone who understood that meaning is not found in avoiding darkness, but in learning how to build and create with it still present, still honored, still alive. Her art became a language when words failed.

When sentences collapsed under their own weight and explanations fell short, color stepped in. Line and texture carried what her voice could not. Each brushstroke became a translation of survival, a way to process what she had endured and to honor the parts of herself that had not only broken but stayed. The canvas held her truth without interruption. It did not rush her. It did not ask for coherence. It allowed complexity to exist exactly as it was. Eventually, she gathered the courage to organize a small exhibition. The decision arrived quietly, then roared once it was made. Sharing her work meant sharing herself. Not just the beauty, but the fractures beneath it. The thought of it made her hands tremble, her chest tighten. It was terrifying. Exposing. To stand in a room where her inner world hung openly on the walls, where strangers could see the evidence of her darkness and her light side by side.

And yet, it was also deeply empowering. In allowing herself to be seen, she discovered something she had long been taught to fear. Vulnerability was not weakness. It was a bridge. A living, breathing connection between isolated worlds. People moved slowly through the space, pausing, leaning in, recognizing something familiar in the colors and shapes. Some met her eyes and nodded. Some spoke quietly of their own journeys. Some said nothing at all, but their presence was enough. Through her art, she connected with others who had walked similar paths. Who recognized themselves in the layered textures, in the tension between shadow and brightness, in the refusal to smooth everything into something palatable. And in those moments of shared recognition, something shifted.

Amelia found strength. Not despite her wounds, but because she had dared to let them speak. Because she had chosen expression over erasure. And standing there, surrounded by her work and the quiet resonance it created, she understood that healing does not ask us to become unmarked. It asks us to be honest. And in that honesty, to discover how deeply, how unexpectedly, we belong.

Living with the Rainbow

Amelia knew that depression would always be woven into the fabric of her story. Not as the whole narrative, not as the defining chapter, but as one thread among many. A darker strand braided into something far larger and more intricate. There would still be good days and bad days. Mornings washed in light where breath came easily, and others shadowed by heaviness that settled without warning. The darkness had not vanished. But it no longer owned the loom. She was no longer defenceless against it. She had learned the tools to cope, the resilience to endure, the quiet courage it takes to ask for help when the weight becomes too much to carry alone. Strength, she discovered, was not stoicism. It was responsiveness. The willingness to notice and to act before collapse became the only option.

Self-care was no longer an afterthought. No longer a reward she earned only after everything else was done. It became non-negotiable. She honored her need for sleep, letting rest be restorative rather than something to fight. She nourished her body with care, not punishment. She moved it gently, listening instead of demanding. She chose time with the people who grounded her, who returned her to herself without asking her to perform or explain. She learned to listen for the early warning signs. The subtle shifts in thought and energy that once went unnoticed, dismissed, or pushed aside. Now she met them differently. With curiosity instead of fear. With compassion instead of denial. Proactivity replaced panic. Awareness replaced shame.

And in that quiet recalibration, Amelia claimed something she had never fully possessed before. Agency. Not over the presence of darkness, but over how she responded to it. She understood now that healing was not the absence of struggle, but the cultivation of relationship. With her mind. With her body. With her limits. The thread remained. But it no longer tangled. It held. Perhaps most importantly, she came to understand that vulnerability was not a flaw to be corrected, but a strength to be claimed. What she had once hidden, she now held with open hands. In sharing her story, she discovered that truth has weight, but it also has reach. It travels. It finds others in their quiet corners and whispers, you are not alone. She became, without intending to, a mirror for those still searching for language, a handhold offered in the dark, a gentle reassurance that survival does not require perfection.

Her truth, once buried beneath shame and silence, became a source of connection and hope. It did not shout. It did not posture. It simply stood present, honest, and available. And people met it with recognition, with relief, with their own stories unfolding in response. Amelia's life was no longer a flat, suffocating gray. It had become a living canvas. Layered. Complex. Alive with contrast. Painted with joy and grief, hope and resilience, love and meaning, each color allowed its place, none required to erase the others. The shadows remained, but they gave depth. The light mattered because it shared the frame. She learned to live with her depression not as a burden to be carried in silence, but as part of her story. A testament to what she had survived. To the work she had done. To the strength she had cultivated in staying. It was not a mark of weakness, but of endurance. Evidence of a life that had been tested and continued anyway. Not broken. Not diminished. But deeply, courageously alive.

Epilogue:

Years later, Amelia stood beneath bright lights, facing a room filled with expectant faces, accepting an award for her innovative and sustainable housing designs. The applause rose and fell around her like a distant tide, a sound she registered more with her body than her ears. It washed over her, warm and insistent, yet what she felt most was not pride. It was awe. Awe at the distance between the woman she had once been and the one standing here now. Awe at the improbable geography of her own life. How far she had traveled without ever leaving herself behind. When she began to speak, she did not polish the story into something palatable. She did not hide the path that had led her here. She named the challenges. She named the darkness. She spoke openly about survival, about healing, about the quiet, unglamorous courage it takes to choose life again and again when no one is watching. She spoke of the days when staying had felt like the bravest thing she could do.

She spoke about the importance of mental health advocacy, not as an abstract cause or distant ideal, but as a lifeline. Something practical. Urgent. Human. Something that had held her when everything else had fallen away. "My life was once shrouded in gray," she said, her voice trembling with truth rather than fear. "But I learned that even in the darkest of times, there is always the possibility of finding light. Of creating a rainbow. Of painting a new future for yourself." The words settled into the room, unhurried and alive. As her gaze swept across the crowd, she saw more than polite smiles and professional admiration. She saw recognition. She saw people leaning forward, breath held, eyes shining with something that looked like hope. The kind that doesn't arrive loudly. The kind that flickers to life because someone else dared to name the dark and survive it.

In that moment, Amelia understood that her story had traveled farther than she ever imagined. Beyond awards and accolades. Beyond buildings and canvases. It had reached those still lost in their own storms. Those still searching for color in a gray world. Those who needed proof that endurance could become meaning. And she knew, with quiet certainty, that if her life could become a painted rainbow, layered with shadow and light, then theirs could too.

Shadows at the Corner of Joy – My Story:

The Subtle Shift

It began on a Tuesday, a day indistinguishable from any other. I woke to the same familiar sounds: The distant hum of traffic threading its way through the morning, the soft, almost hopeful chirping of birds announcing a world that seemed eager to begin, the inevitable buzz of my smartphone tugging me from sleep and into obligation. Everything was ordinary. Predictable. Comfortingly routine. And yet, woven through that everyday symphony was something off-key. A discordant note vibrating just beneath awareness. I couldn't quite name it, only feel its presence, subtle but insistent. I brushed it aside. Of course I did. I blamed the weariness of a long week, the kind of tiredness everyone carries and learns to ignore. The exhaustion we normalize. The dull ache we wear like a badge of productivity. Nothing to worry about. Nothing worth stopping for.

But days slipped into weeks, and weeks quietly bled into months, time dissolving without ceremony. Somewhere along the way, the vibrant tapestry of my life began to lose its saturation. Not all at once. Not dramatically. Just enough that I noticed things didn't land the way they used to. The things that once lit me up began to dim. Laughter shared with friends sounded farther away, like it was happening in another room. The quiet thrill of a good book failed to hold me, the words sliding off without leaving an imprint. Even the comforting company of my own thoughts, once a refuge, grew restless and hollow. Everything familiar softened at the edges, fading into something distant and hazy, like memories seen through fogged glass. Each day began to feel like a repetition of the last. Wake. Perform. Endure. Sleep. Repeat.

Time flattened into a loop, stripped of texture and variation. The colors of my world drained steadily toward gray and brown, warmth leaching out until even joy felt theoretical, something I remembered rather than experienced. And so I adapted. Almost instinctively. I learned to cover the decay with a carefully practiced smile. I laughed at the right moments. Nodded in the right places. Played my role convincingly enough that no one thought to look closer. From the outside, everything appeared intact. Functional. Fine. Inside, something was quietly eroding. I didn't yet have the language for it. I only knew that the world had lost its brightness, and I was learning how to live inside the dim. This was not a dramatic plunge into despair.

There was no single moment of collapse, no sharp edge where everything fell away at once. It was far more subtle than that. More dangerous. A gradual erosion. A slow dimming of the inner light, so incremental it could almost be mistaken for time passing. Like water wearing down stone, patient and relentless. Like dusk arriving so quietly you only notice when night has already settled in your bones. It came as an unwelcome guest, arriving without announcement and refusing to leave. It did not break down the door. It let itself in softly, made itself comfortable, rearranged the furniture of my mind while I pretended not to notice. An insidious thief, creeping into my heart, settling into the shadows, learning the layout of my fears. It whispered. "You're not enough." "You'll never be happy again."

The words were not shouted. They didn't need to be. They slipped in gently, repeating themselves until they sounded like truth. Those thoughts coiled around my core like a tightening noose, subtle at first, almost imperceptible, each whisper pulling a little closer. The space inside me narrowed. Breathing became deliberate. Heavy. As if even air had to be earned. And still, from the outside, everything looked the same. Another Tuesday. Another smile practiced into place. Another routine followed without question. I showed up. I functioned. I passed for fine. Inside, something was quietly unraveling, thread by thread. No alarms. No witnesses. Just the slow, unseen collapse of color and warmth, the private labor of carrying a weight no one else could see. And that was the cruelest part. That I was disappearing in plain sight, learning how to exist while slowly coming undone from the inside out.

The Mask of Normalcy

My days became an exercise in performance. I wore the mask of normalcy so convincingly that even I began to mistake it for my own face. It fit well. Too well. Friends commented on how cheerful I seemed, how well I was doing, and how together I appeared, and I learned to accept their praise with practiced ease. I nodded. Smiled. Thanked them. I basked briefly in their recognition while, inside, I felt like a ghost haunting the corridors of my own life. Present, visible, yet untouched by the warmth of my own existence. I rehearsed laughter the way an actor memorizes lines. I learned its rhythm, its rise and fall, the exact moment to release it so it sounded natural. Convincing. Alive. All the while, my heart throbbed with a relentless, gnawing ache, a low hum of grief that never fully quieted. Joy became something I imitated rather than felt, an echo rather than a source. With each passing day, the pressure intensified.

Social interactions turned into strategic battles. Calculations ran constantly beneath the surface. "Can I engage without revealing the truth? Can I celebrate someone else's joy without collapsing beneath the weight of my own inadequacy? Can I hold this smile long enough to get through the room?" Every conversation required vigilance. Every gathering demanded armor. The mask grew heavier. Tighter. It pressed against my cheeks, my chest, my breath, until it felt fused to my skin. No longer something I put on, but something I lived inside. I carried a constant, low-grade terror that one misplaced smile, one pause too long, one moment of honesty would cause it to crack and shatter. And beneath it lay the hollow space I was working so hard to conceal. An emptiness I feared would horrify others if they saw it. An absence I barely dared to look at myself. So I held it together. I kept performing. I stayed vigilant. All the while knowing, in some quiet and exhausted corner of myself, that this kind of living was not living at all.

It was endurance. It was disappearance disguised as strength. And yet, there were moments. Fleeting. Fragile. Glimmers so brief they felt almost imagined. Instants when the veil lifted just enough to let something through. I remember a sunset once, the horizon set ablaze with fiery oranges and deep purples, the sky burning itself into night as if it could not bear to go quietly. I stood transfixed, breath caught somewhere between awe and grief, my body still while something inside me reached. In those seconds, a fragment of my old self stirred. Not whole. Not strong. But present. Pressing gently against the confines of the fog, reminding me that it had not vanished entirely. It yearned. For the joy I glimpsed so easily in others. For the vitality that had once surged through my veins without effort or permission. For the version of me who had lived forward rather than endured. The longing was sharp. Almost unbearable. Because to feel that spark, even briefly, was to remember what was missing.

And then the moment passed. The shadow returned, swift and practiced, wrapping itself around me like a dense, unyielding fog that swallowed color and distance alike. The horizon dimmed. The ache settled back into its familiar place. The world resumed its muted tones, as if nothing extraordinary had occurred at all. Once again, I disappeared behind the mask. I gathered myself. Adjusted my expression. Stepped back into motion. Carrying the weight of a life that looked whole from the outside. Functional. Even enviable. While beneath the surface, something continued to quietly unravel, thread by invisible thread. And I learned, with aching precision, how to hold both truths at once. The fleeting proof that light still existed. And the relentless knowing that it did not yet know how to stay.

A Meeting with the Darkness

They say that within the act of naming the darkness lies the first seed of liberation. For me, it began in the quiet, unguarded moments of solitude, when there was no one left to perform for and nowhere left to hide. No audience. No expectations. Just the soft hum of my own breathing and the weight of everything I had been carrying alone. It was there, in that stillness, that I began to confront my struggle, tentatively at first, through writing. What started as a simple act soon became something else entirely. A release. A confession I had been holding in my body for years. The words spilled from my pen raw and unfiltered, bleeding onto the page with an honesty that startled me. Sentences arrived without polish or permission, jagged and urgent, as if they had been waiting patiently for their chance to exist.

At first, it felt foreign. Even frightening. I had spent so long silencing my inner voice, disciplining it into submission, teaching it to stay small and quiet and agreeable, that hearing myself speak truth felt like rebellion. Like breaking a rule I didn't remember agreeing to but had obeyed all the same. My hand trembled as I wrote, as though the truth itself carried consequence. But with each stroke of the pen, something loosened. I unearthed what I had buried deep beneath the mask. Grief I never mourned, layered and unresolved. Fear I never named, sharp and watchful. Anger I was never allowed to feel, heavy and righteous and long overdue. The page held it all without flinching. It did not recoil or correct me. It bore witness. And then, to my surprise, something else emerged.

Faint flickers of hope I thought had long been extinguished. Not blazing optimism or certainty, but small, persistent embers glowing beneath the ash. Evidence that even in my most silenced state, something in me had been waiting. Watching. Enduring. Writing did not save me in a single moment. It did not banish the darkness or resolve the ache. But it gave me language. And language gave me shape. And shape gave me the beginning of agency. On the page, I was no longer disappearing. I was arriving. I wrote about the shadow, giving it shape and language, drawing its outline until it could no longer masquerade as something infinite and all-powerful. On the page, it lost its mystique. It was stripped of its authority. I exposed it not as an all-knowing force, but as something fragile. Something hungry. Something fed by silence and secrecy more than truth.

One evening, as twilight pooled softly outside my window, the sky fading into muted blues and bruised violets, I wrote a letter directly to my depression. I did not write with defiance. I did not demand its destruction. Instead, I poured myself onto the page with a trembling sincerity, pleading for release and understanding. I wrote of the moments I felt undeserving of joy, as though happiness were a privilege I had somehow forfeited. I wrote of the hollowness that echoed beneath my laughter, the way joy skimmed the surface but never reached my core. I wrote of the aching desire to reclaim the light I sensed was still somewhere inside me, buried but not extinguished. The words came slowly at first, then faster, as if the truth itself had been waiting for permission. Ink soaked into paper like confession into flesh. And in that act of radical honesty, something shifted.

I finally acknowledged the darkness. Not as an enemy to be conquered. Not as a flaw to be erased. But as a part of my journey. A chapter rather than the whole book. A passage, not the destination. In naming it, I felt an unexpected relief. As if by turning toward it instead of away, I had loosened its grip. The weight in my chest softened. The noose of unspoken fear slackened just enough for breath to return. The darkness did not vanish. It did not evaporate or retreat dramatically. But it changed shape. It became something I could sit beside rather than something that sat on top of me. It no longer owned me. And for the first time, I sensed that healing might begin not by running from the shadows, but by daring to meet them in the light.

Embracing the Light

As weeks softened into months, writing became my daily ritual. A quiet meeting place between who I had been and who I was becoming. Each page offered a threshold, a space where past and present could sit together without urgency. I no longer treated my emotions as enemies to be defeated or silenced, but as weather moving through a living landscape. Sometimes violent. Sometimes gentle. Storms and sunlight alike carrying information, each one meaningful in its own way. I learned to sit with vulnerability instead of fleeing from it. To let it breathe beside me. To allow it to exist alongside the small, tentative flickers of joy that began to find their way back into my days. Joy no longer had to arrive fully formed or last indefinitely. Even brief appearances mattered. Even glimmers counted.

I reached outward as well as inward. I asked for help, my voice shaking but present. I spoke to friends and allowed myself to be held by their listening. I sat with professionals who met my pain without flinching, who did not rush me toward solutions or conclusions. I found my way into rooms where others spoke truths that mirrored my own, where stories overlapped and echoed, where recognition passed silently between us like a shared language. In sharing my burdens and hearing theirs, something began to mend. Shame loosened its grip. Isolation thinned. The weight I had been carrying alone redistributed itself across willing hands. Connection stitched color back into the fabric of my life, thread by careful thread, mending what had frayed without pretending it had never torn.

And in that slow, deliberate weaving, I realized something fundamental. I was never meant to carry everything alone. Survival was not meant to be solitary labor. Healing was not a private performance. It was relational. Communal. Human. And with that understanding, the path forward no longer felt like a lonely road, but a shared one, marked by presence, honesty, and the quiet courage of letting myself be seen. The mask I had worn for so long began to fracture. Not in a catastrophic break that drew attention or demanded rescue, but in hairline cracks, fine and almost tender, that let air and light seep through. It loosened slowly, releasing me in increments, until I could finally breathe without effort. Beneath it, I rediscovered an authenticity I had forgotten existed.

Not a polished or perfected self, but a truer one. Softer. More honest. Alive in ways I had not allowed myself to be. The shadow did not disappear. It lingered, as shadows do, faithful to the contours of experience. But it no longer ruled me. It no longer dictated my movements or my worth. Now it stood as a marker of what I had endured. A quiet testament to the strength it had taken to keep going when stopping felt easier. It became context rather than command. Even the ordinary began to glow again. The mundane regained its texture and color, small moments catching the light like dew on grass. Coffee steaming in the morning. The weight of a book in my hands. The sound of laughter drifting in from another room. Sunsets were no longer just light fading at the end of the day. They became quiet reminders of continuity. Of cycles that continue regardless of despair. Of endings that are also beginnings.

Each one was a small, steadfast promise. That even after the longest night, light finds a way back in. And as I stood there, watching the sky soften into evening, I understood that healing was not a return to who I had been before the darkness. It was an expansion. A widening. A deeper inhabiting of my own life. One where shadows and light could coexist, and where hope, once fragile and distant, had learned how to stay.

A New Dawn

Change did not arrive as a straight line or a clean ascent. It moved the way the ocean does, advancing and retreating, drawing close and then pulling back, not in defeat but in rhythm. Progress came in tides. Some days, the water reached my feet and warmed me with possibility. Other days it receded, leaving me standing in cold sand, wondering if anything had truly changed at all. Some days were undeniably harder than others. On certain mornings, the old whispers resurfaced, familiar and insidious, brushing against my thoughts with practiced intimacy. They tempted me toward that well-worn void, the place I once mistook for rest. The voice was recognizable now, less frightening but no less persistent. It still knew how to knock. But something in me had shifted.

I no longer turned away from those moments or allowed them to name me. I met them instead, steady-eyed, grounded in what I had learned. I listened without obedience. I acknowledged without surrender. I understood now that their presence did not mean failure. It did not mean I was moving backward or doing something wrong. It meant I was human. It meant I was healing. I began to see, with a quiet clarity that settled rather than announced itself, that healing is not a destination you arrive at and conquer. It is not a summit with a flag waiting at the top. It is a living, breathing journey that unfolds over time, shaped by repetition, tenderness, and choice. A practice rather than a performance. A relationship rather than a result.

Healing asked for patience on days when impatience felt easier. It asked for compassion when self-judgment tried to reclaim its ground. And above all, it asked for an ongoing willingness to stay. To remain present in my own life, even when it felt uncomfortable. Even when it felt unfinished. And so I stayed. Not because I was fearless. But because I had learned that staying, again and again, was how life slowly learned to meet me back. On another golden evening, I found myself by the window, pen resting in my hand, light spilling softly across the page. The world outside moved at its own unhurried pace, and for once, I was not rushing to keep up. Gratitude rose in me, unexpected and profound, settling deep in my chest like warmth after a long cold. I honored the scars I carried, not as blemishes to conceal, but as evidence of endurance. I celebrated the victories I had earned, both the monumental and the seemingly insignificant. Getting out of bed. Telling the truth. Staying.

Each one mattered. Each one was proof that I was still here. The colors of my life returned, not timidly, not cautiously testing the edges, but with a depth and richness I had never known before. They were layered now. Informed by shadow. Shaped by survival. Joy carried weight. Peace had texture. Even happiness felt earned in a way that made it steadier, less fragile. The darkness that once threatened to consume me no longer held the same authority. It lingered at the edges of joy, yes, as shadows often do, but no longer as an enemy. It had transformed into a quiet witness. A reminder of where I had been and how far I had come. A marker along the path rather than a force pulling me off it. It no longer whispered commands. It simply existed, integrated, acknowledged. A reminder that this path, with all its bends and bruises, its pauses and persistence, was uniquely mine.

And in sharing my story, my hope is simple and sincere. Not to offer answers or absolutes, but to offer companionship. That others might find the courage to face their own shadows. To turn toward what hurts with curiosity instead of fear. To believe, even faintly, that light can coexist with darkness and still be real. If my journey holds anything of value, let it be this. You are not alone. You are not broken. And even now, even here, there is more color waiting for you than you have been led to believe. Accepting the darkness does not weaken you. It strengthens you. It asks you to stand still long enough to feel what you would rather outrun, and in doing so, it builds a resilience that cannot be borrowed or faked. It lays the groundwork for growth that is earned, not imagined. For a dawn that arrives not by accident or luck, but by endurance. By the quiet, stubborn act of remaining present through the night.

It is okay to feel lost. Sometimes, wandering through the dim places is the only way we learn how to recognize the light when it appears. Sometimes, disorientation is not failure but initiation. A stripping away of false certainty so that something truer can take root. The darkness teaches discernment. It sharpens the senses. It makes even the faintest glow unmistakable when it finally breaks through. As I closed my notebook that evening, the pages warm from my hands,

I understood something essential. The shadows may always exist. They may follow at a distance, lengthening at dusk, reminding me of what once was and what it took to survive it. They are part of the landscape now. Familiar. Known. No longer feared. But I have made a choice.

I have chosen to step into the light. To move with it rather than wait for it to rescue me. To dance there even when my legs tremble, even when the ground feels unsteady beneath my feet. To live forward with awareness instead of retreating into old silence. To choose presence over disappearance. And perhaps that choice, made again and again, on ordinary days and difficult ones alike, is the greatest triumph of all. Not the absence of darkness. But the decision to keep turning toward the light anyway.

The Shadow in the Corners: Reclaiming Yourself from the Grip of Depression

The Slow Fade

Depression is a word so often spoken in whispers, as though saying it too loudly might invite it closer. Yet it is anything but quiet. It moves through the world with a terrible patience, slipping into the lives of millions not with a single catastrophic blow, but with time. With endurance. It does not shatter happiness in a moment of drama. It erodes it grain by grain, the way water wears down stone, steadily, imperceptibly, until strength gives way without warning. Joy fades slowly, almost politely, excusing itself one small absence at a time, until one day you realize the light inside you has dimmed, and you cannot remember when the room first began to darken. The struggle rarely announces itself. It begins as a subtle shift. A shadow lingering at the edges of thought. A soft distortion

that blurs the line between what is real and what is imagined, what is true and what is whispered. What once felt certain becomes questionable.

What once felt manageable begins to feel impossibly heavy. Confidence thins. Perspective bends. Ordinary tasks acquire weight. Depression is a master of disguise. It studies you. Learns your routines. Borrows your voice. It speaks in familiar tones, using your own thoughts against you, wearing the mask of normalcy so convincingly that even you begin to believe it. From the outside, life appears intact. Functional. Even successful. There are schedules kept. Smiles offered. Milestones reached. But beneath that mask lives a quiet storm. Pain without language. Fear without form. Desperation that has learned how to stay silent. And so it persists. Hidden in plain sight. Smiling when required. Performing when expected. Convincing the world, and yourself, that everything is fine, while inside something essential is slowly slipping away. Something tender. Something vital. Something you do not yet know how to name. This is how depression survives. Not by force, but by silence. Not by spectacle, but by invisibility. It thrives in what goes unspoken, in what is minimized, in what is carried alone. And it is precisely there, in that silence, that the most dangerous erosion occurs.

As the darkness settles in, it becomes frighteningly easy to lose yourself in the monotony of simply getting through the day. Life continues to move forward without pause. Clocks keep ticking. Emails arrive. Meals are made. Obligations line up, patient and indifferent, waiting to be met. From the outside, the machinery of living hums along as it always has. But somewhere beneath that steady rhythm, the vibrant hues of existence begin to drain away. What was once rich with colour and texture flattens into a dull, monochrome landscape, a world stripped of depth. The shades that once sparked joy and excitement retreat into memory, like photographs left too long in the sun, their edges blurred, their brilliance bleached into something barely recognizable. Happiness becomes something you remember rather than something you feel. A concept. A recollection. A distant echo of a life that once pulsed with meaning and immediacy. Outwardly, the world remains bright.

The sky still turns blue. Flowers still bloom, obedient to the seasons. People laugh easily, post smiling photographs, and curate moments of beauty and success for public consumption. The world sees a smile. A carefully filtered image. A composed, effortless stride through the ordinary challenges of daily life. Proof, it seems, that everything is fine. But behind that polished surface, behind the carefully constructed "*I'm fine*", a silent war is being fought. Not against something visible or external, but against a relentless, insidious enemy that has taken up residence within. An adversary that cannot be pointed to or outrun. One that speaks softly and waits patiently. Depression does not always announce itself with sobs and breakdowns. More often, it works quietly. Methodically. Dismantling joy piece by piece. Stealing wonder without leaving fingerprints. Convincing you that numbness is normal, that endurance is the same as living.

And so the battle rages unseen. In the space between breaths. In the pause before a forced smile. In the exhaustion that sleep does not touch. It is a war fought in silence, in plain sight, while the world applauds your composure and never suspects how much of you is being lost just to make it through another day. This is not the dramatic, tear-soaked despair popular culture likes to portray. This is the slow erosion. The gradual dimming of the light that once illuminated your inner world. It is an insidious thief that steals without spectacle, without noise, without warning. It takes your hope in whispers, your joy in increments so small you barely notice them leaving. There is no alarm when the first piece disappears. No moment that demands your attention. Just absence, accumulating quietly. A persistent doubt creeps in. Then settles. Then hardens.

It chips away at your sense of self, sanding down your edges until you begin to question who you are beneath the performance. Beneath the smiles you have perfected. Beneath the version of yourself the world has grown accustomed to seeing. And all the while, the flickering light inside you struggles to stay alive. Unseen by the world. Uncelebrated. But stubborn. Desperately trying not to go out. At first, you hardly register its arrival. It slips in quietly, wearing the disguise of ordinary tiredness. A slight weariness settles into your bones, a fatigue that lingers even after a full night's sleep, clinging to you like damp air that refuses to lift. You tell yourself it's nothing. Life has been busy. Everyone is tired. You will catch up. Rest will fix it. Time will smooth it out. But slowly, almost imperceptibly, the things that once lit you up begin to lose their charge. The laughter of friends no longer reaches your chest. It stops short, echoing somewhere above the heart.

The warmth of the sun on your skin feels distant, as though filtered through thick glass, visible but unreachable. Even the satisfaction of a job well done lands without resonance, a fact acknowledged rather than a feeling experienced. The joy is still there. Technically. But it is dulled. Muted. Distorted. Like a favourite song playing through a scratched record, the melody is recognizable but warped, the emotion fractured. You know how it is supposed to feel. You remember the shape of the pleasure. But the sound arrives hollow, reminding you of what is missing more than what remains. And so you keep going, carrying this quiet absence, telling yourself nothing has changed, even as the light inside you flickers, fighting to be seen, to be felt, to be saved.

The vibrant hues of your life begin to drain away. Colors fade into a washed-out grayscale, saturation thinning until the world feels bleached of contrast. What once felt textured and alive now resembles a blurred photograph, edges soft, details lost, moments slipping past before they can fully land. You move through days as if slightly out of focus, present but not entirely here, watching your own life from a few steps removed. This isn't sadness. Sadness comes and goes. It is a visitor who knocks, stays a while, leaves its mark, and eventually departs. Sadness has an arc. A beginning, a middle, an end. It allows space for relief. Depression does not. Depression doesn't visit. It moves in. It becomes a resident, a permanent fixture in the house of your mind. It settles into your favourite chair, stretches out as if it belongs there, and rearranges the furniture until nothing feels familiar anymore.

The rooms you once knew how to navigate now feel altered, claustrophobic, and dim. Light still enters the windows, but it doesn't seem to reach the floor. It lingers in the corners, breathing quietly, always present. Whispering doubts and fears directly into your soul until they begin to sound like your own voice. It tells you stories about who you are. About what you deserve. About what the future holds. And because it speaks softly, because it sounds so much like you, it becomes frighteningly easy to believe it. The line between self and sickness blurs. You stop asking whether these thoughts are true and start assuming they must be. After all, they've been there so long. They know your habits. Your history. Your wounds. They know exactly where to press. And so the house fills with noise that no one else can hear, a constant murmur that follows you from room to room, from morning to night. And still, from the outside, the door remains closed. The lights appear on. The structure stands. No one sees the quiet occupation taking place within.

As I sit here now, reflecting on the vast and fragile terrain of human experience, I am reminded just how insidious depression truly is. It is not a dramatic thief that smashes windows and announces its presence. It does not arrive with chaos or spectacle. It steals quietly. Methodically. Patiently. It takes your happiness, yes, but also something far more devastating. Your sense of self. The internal compass that once told you who you were and where you were going begins to spin without direction. It severs your connection to the present moment. Days lose their immediacy. Hours pass without leaving a trace. You are there, but not entirely in yourself, as though a thin pane of glass has been placed between you and your own life. Slowly, almost imperceptibly, it erodes your belief in a future worth reaching for. Not through despair alone, but through doubt. Through the quiet suggestion that nothing ahead could possibly feel different than this. It becomes a constant, relentless companion. Not loud. Not dramatic.

Just always there. Murmuring insecurities into the soft spaces of your mind. Feeding self-hatred until it sounds like truth. Whispering fear until courage feels naïve. Over time, your confidence wears thin, frayed by repetition, until the inner world you once trusted begins to feel unfamiliar, even hostile. And in that slow unraveling, isolation deepens. You can find yourself lost without ever having made a conscious choice to leave. Standing in the ruins of who you once were, surrounded by fragments of former passions, former certainties, former selves. Wondering how you drifted so far from yourself without ever noticing the moment it began. Searching your memory for a turning point that never announced itself. That is the cruelty of it. Depression does not always break you in one moment. Sometimes it unthreads you slowly, strand by strand, until one day you are holding pieces of a life you barely recognize, aching not only for relief from pain, but for reunion with yourself.

It becomes a relentless reckoning. A constant audit of perceived weaknesses, failures, missteps, and all the ways you believe you fall short of the expectations placed upon you. Depression keeps score mercilessly. It tallies every moment you hesitated, every word you wish you had chosen differently, every dream that stalled or slipped through your fingers. Nothing is ever forgiven. Nothing is ever forgotten. Its voice is not a single thought, but a cacophony of negative self-talk. A ceaseless chorus of criticism that never pauses for breath, never softens, never sleeps. It hums beneath everything, rising and falling but never leaving. Always loud. Always present. Always circling back to the same verdicts: worthless, inadequate, powerless. Over time, the repetition wears grooves so deep they begin to feel like truth, etched into the mind through sheer persistence, until you can no longer remember a version of yourself that wasn't under indictment.

You stop questioning the accusations. You start embodying them. We are often told that life is a canvas, alive with color. That daily interactions, dreams, small victories, and quiet hopes splatter it with joy, excitement, laughter, and meaning. And for a time, that feels true. The brush moves freely. The colors respond. The image feels alive beneath your hands. But then, for many of us, something shifts. The palette begins to fade. Not all at once. Not dramatically. But subtly. Insidiously. A hue dulls here. A brightness drains there. Reds lose their warmth. Blues flatten into gray. Yellows pale until they barely glow. The canvas still fills, still holds shape, but the vitality thins, like pigment diluted one drop at a time. It begins as an uninvited whisper slipping into the corners of consciousness. A shadow that trails your thoughts, no matter how brightly the world insists on shining.

At first, you barely notice it. You adjust. You compensate. You tell yourself the light has changed, that your eyes are tired, that this is just how life looks now. You keep painting anyway. You keep moving the brush, layering days and responsibilities and obligations onto the canvas, even as the colors no longer feel vivid in your hands. You trust memory more than sensation. You rely on habit instead of joy. And somewhere in that quiet persistence, the act of living becomes less about expression and more about endurance. The canvas fills. But you begin to wonder when it stopped feeling like yours.

And then one day, without a single clear moment of arrival, you realize you are standing at the edge of something vast and dark. There was no trumpet announcing its presence. No sudden rupture. You did not hear it approaching. You did not feel yourself slipping. And yet there you are, feet planted at the precipice of an abyss you never intended to reach, peering into a void that seems to know your name. It hums with familiarity. It does not rush you. It waits. Only then do you understand how quietly the ground fell away beneath you. How slowly the light receded. How imperceptible the descent truly was. You begin to see that what you mistook for personal failure was something else entirely. An illness. One that learned how to speak in your own voice. One that borrowed your thoughts, your memories, your fears, until its lies felt indistinguishable from truth.

Depression does not announce itself with a roar. It arrives by drip. Slow. Steady. Almost polite. It seeps into the psyche like water through stone, patient enough to erode even the hardest edges of passion and meaning. That is its cruel irony. It does not usually look like despair from the outside. There are no dramatic scenes. No visible collapse. Instead, it slips on a mask of normalcy, convincing you to smile in public while a private storm tears through your inner landscape, uprooting everything familiar. Friends and family may sense the shift. They may ask gentle questions. They may linger a moment longer than usual, searching your eyes for something they cannot quite name. But the skill of concealment often becomes sharper than the blade of despair itself. You learn how to deflect. How to reassure. How to say *"I'm fine"* in a tone that closes doors.

You learn how to perform. The world becomes a stage, and you the lead actor, delivering a role perfected over years. The capable one. The functioning one. The cheerful one. The person who seems to have it all together. You hit your marks. You remember your lines. The applause, when it comes, feels strangely hollow. Meanwhile, your heart becomes a fragile structure, bearing more weight than it was ever meant to carry. Hairline fractures spread quietly beneath the surface. No one hears them crack. No one sees the strain. And so you continue, holding the shape of a life together from the outside, even as something inside you splinters under the invisible anguish no one else can see. That is how the abyss grows close. Not by pulling you in. But by convincing you that you are still standing on solid ground.

The struggle does not begin with collapse. It begins with a shadow, barely perceptible, gathering in the far corners of your mind where light is easiest to miss. Not a sudden plunge into darkness, but a gradual erosion of joy. A slow dimming of the light that once illuminated even the most ordinary moments. The kind of light you never thought to protect because it had always been there. At first, you dismiss it. A phase. A rough patch. A handful of bad days strung together. You tell yourself everyone feels like this sometimes. You minimize it with logic.

Rationalize it with circumstance. Push forward with habit and obligation. You stay busy. You stay functional. You convince yourself that endurance is the same thing as health. But this is different.

This is depression at work. Quiet. Methodical. An insidious thief moving silently through your life, lifting color after color from the canvas while you are distracted by survival. It does not rush. It does not leave fingerprints. It simply takes. A little warmth here. A little wonder there. What was once vibrant becomes muted. What once stirred you now barely registers. Moments still happen, but they land flat. Achievements feel procedural. Beauty feels distant. You respond because you know you should, not because anything inside you rises to meet it. And slowly, without ceremony, your internal world loses its contrast. Until one day, you look around and realize the shift has already occurred. The world has settled into monochrome monotony. Gray layered upon gray. And the most unsettling part is not the absence of color itself, but the realization that you cannot remember exactly when it began to fade. There was no single moment to point to. No line crossed. No alarm sounded. Just the quiet understanding that something essential has been slipping away while you were busy convincing yourself that nothing was wrong.

The most treacherous aspect of depression is its talent for disguise. It learns your face. Studies your mannerisms. Memorizes the cadence of your voice. Then, with chilling precision, it teaches you how to perform normalcy. You build a mask not all at once, but piece by careful piece, until composure becomes muscle memory and effort masquerades as ease. You smile at colleagues, friends, and family. You nod at the right moments. You exchange polite words. You laugh when laughter is expected. And all the while, inside, you are quietly coming apart. Crumbling like dry autumn leaves beneath an unseen footstep. No sound. No warning. Just collapse without spectacle. You show up. You function. You participate. You keep the machinery of life running smoothly enough that no one thinks to look beneath the surface.

From the outside, everything appears intact. But underneath that practiced ease, something relentless persists. A gnawing pain settles into your chest. Not sharp enough to scream. Not loud enough to alarm. But constant. It chews away at the heart with slow insistence, an ache no pleasantry can soothe and no smile can erase. It lingers through conversations. It waits patiently through laughter. It remains long after the room empties. The conversations end. The laughter fades. The mask comes off. And you are left alone with it. That quiet suffering that hums beneath everything. A low, unrelenting frequency that fills the silence. From the outside, nothing appears broken. The structure stands. The routine holds. From the inside, everything feels held together by breath alone. Each inhale a negotiation. Each exhale a release you are not sure will return. And still, you endure. Quietly. Invisibly. Wondering how long a heart can keep beating under the weight of something no one else can see.

The world meets the mask and believes it. They see the smiles offered on cue, the polite nods, the effortless choreography of daily life carried out with practiced grace. They see the capable professional who meets deadlines, the attentive parent who remembers details, the reliable friend who shows up and holds it together. From the outside, the performance is seamless. Convincing. Even admirable. What they do not see is the private war unfolding beneath the surface. They do not see the daily negotiation required just to rise from bed. The moment when you wake and must summon the will to inhabit your own body. To pull gravity off your chest long enough to face the morning. To convince your legs to swing over the edge, your hands to reach for the day, your breath to deepen instead of stall.

They do not see the effort it takes to move through the world without collapsing under the weight of your own mind. The way thoughts pile up like stones, each one small enough to lift alone, but crushing in their accumulation. They do not hear the internal bargaining that accompanies even the simplest tasks. Just get through the next hour. Just make it to lunchtime. Just keep going. They do not hear the quiet pleas whispered into the dark. The bargains struck with yourself. The exhaustion that settles into your bones before the day has even begun, a fatigue that no amount of sleep can touch. The kind that seeps deep, making everything feel heavier than it should. And so the mask holds. It holds in meetings. It holds in conversations. It holds in moments of laughter and routine.

Until the door closes. Until the world looks away. And then, finally unobserved, you are left carrying the full weight of what no one else has seen. Standing alone in the aftermath of another performed day, wondering how something so invisible can demand so much just to survive it. And this is the cruelest paradox of depression: that it isolates you in plain sight. You can be surrounded by people who love you and still feel unbearably alone, as though an invisible wall has risen between your inner world and everyone else's. You stand among voices and warmth and familiar faces, yet feel unreachable, sealed off, watching connection happen just beyond your grasp. The loneliness is not the absence of people. It is the absence of being known.

You ache to reach across that barrier. To hand someone the truth of what you are carrying. To say, "*this is what it feels like inside me*". But the words tangle and lodge in your throat, strangled by shame. By a learned sense of inadequacy. By the quiet, corrosive belief that your pain makes you unworthy of care. That needing help is a burden. That suffering disqualifies you from belonging. You fear the moment of exposure. You fear being judged. Misunderstood. Reduced to a diagnosis or a flaw. You fear the subtle shift in someone's eyes when they no longer see you as capable, strong, or reliable. You fear that if the mask slips and the truth spills out, you will be seen not as human and hurting, but as weak. Defective. Broken beyond repair.

So you stay silent. And the silence settles in, heavy and unshared, another invisible weight added to the load you already carry. It presses against your chest, deepens the isolation, reinforces the lie that you are alone in this. That no one could understand. That it is safer to endure quietly than to risk being seen. And so depression tightens its grip, not through force, but through secrecy. Not through cruelty alone, but through the loneliness it convinces you is deserved. And in that silence, you learn how to survive without being witnessed, even as something inside you longs, relentlessly, to be met. So you keep the secret locked away. A weight carried quietly behind your ribs. A hidden wound wrapped in silence, tucked carefully out of sight where it can fester unseen. You become a careful curator of illusion, arranging your days, your expressions, your words with meticulous precision. Convincing the world, and slowly yourself, that everything is fine. That you are fine.

The performance sharpens with repetition. "How are you doing?" "I'm fine, thank you. And you?" "You look weary, are you okay?" "Yes, I'm perfectly fine. Just a bit tired. A little stressed at work. Nothing I can't manage." The lines roll off your tongue with ease, delivered without hesitation, rehearsed until they feel almost true. And with that, the curtain falls on yet another act. Applause unearned but accepted. Polite smiles exchanged. The mask secured once more, fastened tightly enough to hold for another day. The stage play of your life continues uninterrupted. From the audience, everything appears seamless. The lighting is right. The pacing is smooth. The lead performer never misses a cue. But behind the scenes, the set begins to crumble. Support beams crack quietly. Backdrops peel. What once felt solid grows unstable, even as the show goes on.

Your world grows smaller. Your energy thins, stretched across obligations and appearances until there is little left for anything real. Hope dwindles, condensing into a trembling ember, barely glowing, fragile enough to be extinguished by the slightest breath of doubt. You guard it fiercely, even as you fear it will not survive another night. And the truth, almost darkly ironic, settles in. We perform this role so convincingly. So relentlessly. With such commitment to survival that we deserve awards for it. Oscars for best acting in a life no one realizes is scripted, not for success or applause, but simply to make it through another day unseen. And this is the most insidious cruelty of depression: it does not merely hurt. It isolates. It teaches you how to disappear while standing in plain sight, applauded for your composure, alone in your collapse. You become a master of vanishing without leaving the room. Seen, praised, relied upon, and yet utterly unreachable.

There is something uniquely brutal about being admired for your strength while you are quietly unraveling beneath it. Now feels like the right moment to bring a magnifying glass to depression's isolation, because it is nothing like ordinary solitude. This is not the gentle aloneness of a quiet room, the restorative hush of an empty calendar. It is not chosen. It is not spacious. Depression's isolation is total. It does not merely distance you from people. It reaches inward. It slips into every layer of your being and begins to separate you from yourself. Thought from feeling. Feeling from language. Language from connection. Yes, depression can make you withdraw physically, avoiding faces, messages, gatherings, and light. It can shrink your world until leaving the house feels like an act of defiance. But for me, it was the deeper isolations that did the most damage. The mental, emotional, and spiritual separations that hollowed me out from the inside.

My emotions became vast, uninhabited landscapes. Wide. Silent. Untouched. They stretched endlessly within me, too large to explain, too heavy to carry, too foreign to trust. I became convinced no one could understand them. No one could help me hold them without recoiling. And so I did what felt safest. I buried them. I buried my pain beneath competence. Beneath humor. Beneath the endless labor of seeming okay. I buried it so deeply that even I could no longer find it, except through the ache it left behind. A dull pressure in my chest. A numbness where something should have lived. A quiet grief with no clear source. I lost access to my own interior, locked out of myself while still occupying the body that carried it.

That is how depression isolates most effectively. Not by taking people away. But by taking *you* away from yourself. And when you are no longer fully inside your own life, even the closest hands feel impossibly far. Depression isolates by convincing you that you are a burden. That your presence is a weight others must endure. That your needs are too much, your pain too heavy, your truth too inconvenient. And so the mask tightens. The performance sharpens. You learn how to disappear politely. How to make yourself smaller without drawing attention. How to excuse your absence before anyone has the chance to miss you.

It isolates you spiritually, too. It severs your sense of being seen or held by anything greater than yourself. What once felt like connection becomes static. Prayer, meaning, transcendence all feel distant, unreachable, as if the signal has been cut and you are left drifting in open space. You speak, but nothing answers. You reach but feel nothing reach back. You begin to wonder if you were ever heard at all, or if the silence has always been there and you simply hadn't noticed. Mentally, the isolation tightens into a closed loop. Depression corrals your thoughts into a dark room and locks the door from the inside. The same ideas pace the floor endlessly, circling each other, reinforcing the same conclusions. When others reach for you with encouragement, with compliments, with recognition, their words enter the room but cannot stay. They bounce off the walls, fall flat at your feet, stripped of meaning before they can take root.

You retreat instead to the familiar darkness. Not because it is kind. Not because it is true. But because it is known. There is a strange comfort in predictability, even when it hurts. The distorted perspective feels safer than hope, because hope risks disappointment, and disappointment feels unbearable when you are already emptied out. This is the cruel architecture of depression's isolation. It does not simply push you away from others. It convinces you that the very thing hurting you is the only place you belong. That leaving it would be betrayal. That stepping into the light would expose how unworthy you truly are. And so the walls remain standing, not because they cannot be torn down, but because depression has persuaded you that there is nothing worth finding on the other side. That is its deepest lie.

It convinces you that your pain is singular. Unbearable. Something that must be hidden away like a defect no one else could possibly understand. It murmurs shame into every quiet moment, seeping into the spaces where your defenses are weakest. It tells you that your suffering is proof of your inadequacy. That you are weak for feeling this way. Broken for not being able to will yourself out of it. The whispers are patient. They repeat themselves until they sound like wisdom. Until they sound like fact. They take root slowly, planting seeds of self-doubt that grow unchecked, twisting into vines of insecurity that wrap tighter and tighter around your sense of self. They choke off compassion. They crowd out gentler truths. And before you realize what has happened, you are no longer questioning the voice. You are living inside it.

Slowly. Relentlessly. Depression erodes the present. Simple pleasures lose their taste, as if your senses have been dulled from the inside out. Food becomes fuel. Music becomes noise. Laughter sounds distant, arriving late and leaving early, never quite touching you. The vibrant colours of your life are leeched away until everything is reduced to a flat, exhausting monochrome. Days blur together. Moments pass without imprint. Existing begins to feel like trudging through thick fog with no landmarks to orient yourself. And then it reaches forward. It steals the future too. It leans in close and hisses that hope is an illusion. That possibility is a cruel joke played on people who were never meant to escape. It tells you that nothing ahead could be different from this, that tomorrow will only be a repeat of today, stripped of surprise and relief. It shrinks your imagination until you can no longer picture yourself anywhere but here.

Stuck. Heavy. Enduring. That is the final theft. Not just joy. Not just meaning. But the belief that change is possible at all. And when the future collapses into a narrow, airless corridor, depression does not need to push you any further. It simply waits, confident that hopelessness will do the rest, quietly convincing you that this dim, suffocating present is all there will ever be. Understanding depression is the first act of resistance. It is the moment you begin to reclaim your light, however faint it may feel. The moment you stop turning the blade inward and instead turn your gaze toward the truth. Depression is not a character flaw. It is not a personal weakness, nor a moral failure. It is not evidence that you lack gratitude, resilience, or faith. It is a complex convergence of biology, psychology, history, and environment. A storm raging across the landscape of the mind, shaped by forces far larger than willpower alone.

Naming it matters. Seeing it for what it is matters. Because in that recognition, something vital shifts. The illness is no longer mistaken for identity. The voice that has been speaking so convincingly in your head is exposed for what it is: not truth, but symptom. Not self, but signal. You begin to understand that the thoughts that accuse you, diminish you, and drain the world of color are not revelations about who you are. They are distortions produced by a mind under siege. You are not your depression. It is a condition, not a verdict. A state, not a sentence. A relentless, uninvited guest that slipped in quietly and overstayed its welcome, rearranging the furniture of your inner life without permission. But it does not own the house. It does not get to rewrite the foundation of who you fundamentally are.

You are still here beneath it. Still whole beneath the weight. Still worthy beneath the noise. And in the act of separating yourself from the illness, in saying *this is happening to me, but it is not me*, you create space. Space for compassion. Space for help. Space for healing to begin its slow, imperfect work. This is where the light starts to return. Not all at once. Not without effort. But enough to see yourself again. This is not a book of quick fixes or miracle cures. Depression is not a passing cold you shake off with rest and good intentions. It is a complex, deeply rooted terrain, shaped by history, biology, belief, and lived experience. It has weather patterns and fault lines. Seasons of dormancy and sudden storms. What follows is not a promise of instant relief, but an invitation.

An opening. A guide to learning the contours of this shadow, to acknowledging its presence without surrendering your identity to it, and to reclaiming your life the way it is truly reclaimed.

Slowly. Deliberately. One small, courageous step at a time. Because with depression, you learn to wear a mask. Not out of deceit, but out of survival. You learn early that showing the full weight of what you carry can feel dangerous, even impossible. So you adapt. You become fluent in the language of *I'm fine*. You grow skilled at smiling while your insides quietly collapse. Practiced at laughing even as a relentless, gnawing ache presses against your heart, dull and unyielding. You learn how to redirect conversations before they wander too close. How to soften questions so they don't cut. How to keep the spotlight away from the places that feel too tender, too fractured to expose without breaking open. You become a master of deflection, not because you wish to hide, but because being fully seen feels unbearable. Because you are not yet sure you would survive that level of truth.

The mask becomes protective. Familiar. Necessary. It allows you to move through the world without alarming anyone, without explaining yourself, without asking for more than you believe you deserve. It keeps you functioning. It keeps you safe. Until one day you realize how heavy it has become. How much effort, it takes just to keep it in place. How little oxygen reaches you beneath it. This book does not ask you to tear the mask off all at once. It asks you to notice it. To understand why you needed it. To loosen it gently, when you are ready. To learn that survival strategies, however necessary they once were, do not have to become life sentences.

Healing does not begin with exposure. It begins with permission. Permission to go slowly. Permission to be unfinished. Permission to tell the truth at a pace your nervous system can hold. And if there is one promise offered here, it is this: you do not have to disappear in order to survive. There is another way forward. Not loud. Not instant. But real. The fear runs deep. Fear of judgment. Fear of being labeled weak or dramatic. Fear of becoming a burden in a world that already feels strained. And beneath all of it, the most corrosive fear of all. That if you finally speak the truth of your inner world, if you name what lives behind your ribs, no one will understand. Or worse, they will understand and confirm the doubt you have been carrying in silence all along. That you are too much. Or not enough. That your pain disqualifies you from belonging.

So the mask stays in place. Heavy. Familiar. Protective in the way armor often is, shielding you even as it cuts off circulation. It keeps you safe from exposure, but it also keeps you alone. It allows you to move through the world without confrontation, without questions you are not ready to answer, without the risk of being seen in your rawest state. This book does not ask you to tear it off all at once. It knows the cost of that demand. It understands that survival often depends on pacing, on listening to the body's limits, on honoring what your nervous system can hold. It asks only that you begin to loosen the mask. Gently. Compassionately. In increments small enough to feel survivable.

A pause where there used to be deflection. A breath where there used to be apology. A moment of honesty with yourself before offering it to anyone else. This is not about exposure. It is about safety. About learning that vulnerability, approached with care, does not have to be catastrophic. That being seen does not require you to be overwhelmed. That the truth can be met slowly, with support, with choice. You are allowed to go at your own pace. You are allowed to protect yourself and heal at the same time. And in that careful loosening, in that compassionate unfastening, space begins to open. Not all at once. But enough for breath. Enough for light. Enough to remind you that you are still here, still worthy, and still allowed to take up space exactly as you are.

The Weight of the Mask

One of the most insidious cruelties of depression is the way it teaches you to wear the mask of normalcy until it feels fused to your skin. Not something you put on in the morning and remove at night, but something that settles into your muscles, your reflexes, your breath. You learn how to smile on cue. How to laugh at the right moments. How to nod along and say *I'm fine* with convincing ease, even as everything inside you is quietly unraveling. The words come out smooth and practiced, while your inner world frays thread by thread. You put on a brave face, a costume stitched together from confidence and competence, rehearsed until it looks effortless. Beneath it, pain churns. Fear coils. A desperation pulses that you dare not name, even to yourself. You become a master of concealment, hiding behind a polished version of happiness while struggling simply to stay afloat in a sea of despair that threatens, patiently, to pull you under.

That mask is not light. It is not harmless. It is a crushing weight, pressing down on your shoulders, tightening around your chest, making it difficult to breathe fully, to think clearly, to feel honestly. It compresses your inner world until even your own emotions feel distant and distorted. Maintaining the illusion becomes a full-time occupation. Every interaction is a performance calibrated for safety. Every day is an exhausting effort to uphold the appearance of a life that, behind the scenes, feels as though it is quietly collapsing. The cost is immense. It is paid in silence. In isolation. In the steady erosion of authenticity. And always, there is the fear. The fear of being discovered. The fear of being found out.

A relentless companion that whispers its *what ifs* in the quiet hours of the night. *What if they see the real me? What if they find out I'm not okay? What if my weakness is exposed?* The terror of vulnerability, of openness, of honesty becomes paralyzing, locking you deeper into the cycle of depression where hiding feels safer than being held. Judgment feels inevitable. Rejection feels certain. Abandonment feels like the final verdict waiting just beyond the truth. That fear casts a long shadow, following you everywhere you go, rooted in a belief etched so deeply it feels structural. That you are not enough. Not worthy. Not deserving of love, happiness, or acceptance as you are. And so the mask stays on. Heavy. Suffocating. Necessary. Even as it slowly steals the very breath you are using to keep it in place.

Beneath that carefully maintained surface, life begins to feel like hauling a colossal weight through thick mud, each step demanding more effort than the last. Forward motion is no longer momentum but negotiation. You move because you must, not because there is any sense of arrival waiting ahead. Every task feels heavier than it should, every decision costs more than you can afford. You become fluent in avoidance. Expert at navigating conversations like a dancer sidestepping hidden traps, redirecting before anyone strays too close to your inner world. *How are you?*

"I'm fine, thanks." The words roll off your tongue easily, rehearsed and automatic, a mantra repeated so often it echoes hollowly inside your chest. With each repetition, the lie thins. It grows more transparent, more brittle, until even you can feel how little substance remains beneath it. Until you no longer believe it yourself.

The pressure to sustain this version of yourself intensifies. It tightens like a vise, squeezing harder the longer you hold on. It feeds the cycle of guilt and shame, convincing you that your struggle is not human, but personal. A flaw. A failure. *If only I could just try harder. If only I could be stronger. If only I could be happy.* These thoughts circle endlessly, like vultures over a wounded thing, patient and relentless, waiting for you to collapse under their weight. The irony is cruel and inescapable. The harder you demand happiness from yourself, the further it retreats. Each command meant to summon light becomes another act of violence against your own exhaustion. Each insistence that you should be better only deepens the shadows, darkening the corners of your mind where compassion might have lived.

And so the performance continues. Heavier by the day. You carry the weight in silence, smiling through the strain, expending precious energy on appearing okay while the real work of surviving goes unseen. You do not realize at first that the performance itself is what is draining you. That the constant effort to hold yourself together is quietly dismantling what little strength you have left. You are not failing at happiness. You are exhausted from pretending. And beneath the mask, beneath the strain, something in you is not asking to be fixed or forced into light. It is asking to rest. To be acknowledged. To finally set the weight down and be held, even briefly, exactly as you are.

You learn to wear that mask until it fits like a second skin, a finely honed performance perfected through repetition. At first it is something you *do*. Eventually, it becomes something you *are*. You function. You participate. You show up. You meet expectations and maintain appearances, moving through the world with practiced efficiency, all so no one will see the cracks spidering beneath the surface of your carefully constructed persona. All so you will not be labeled weak. Fragile. A failure. But the mask is heavy. Unbearably so. The pain it conceals is real, and it does not remain neatly hidden. It presses against your face, tight and suffocating, restricting breath and movement until even existing feels constrained. Every smile requires effort.

Every laugh rings hollow, echoing back at you as something borrowed, something counterfeit. Your jaw aches from holding it all in place. Your chest tightens from carrying what cannot be spoken. Inside, you know the truth. You are living a lie. Impersonating a version of yourself that no longer exists, if it ever truly did. You are acting out a role written by fear and expectation, applauded by a world that cannot see the cost of the performance. And while you perform, while you keep the mask polished and intact, the shadow within you grows bolder. Stronger. It leans close, intimate and relentless, whispering its poison directly into your ear. *"You're not good enough. You're a failure. You're not worthy of love or happiness."* The voices do not relent. They repeat themselves with ruthless consistency, looping until resistance weakens. Until doubt hardens into belief. Until the cruelty sounds less like attack and more like revelation. Over time, the distinction blurs. You stop arguing. You start agreeing.

And slowly, almost imperceptibly, you begin to disappear beneath their weight. Not all at once. Not dramatically. But quietly. Gradually. Like a photograph fading in sunlight. Like a voice losing volume mid-sentence. Like a self retreating inward, inch by inch, until what remains is the performance alone. And beneath it, somewhere deep and muffled, the real you waits. Tired. Buried. Still breathing. Still hoping, however faintly, to be found. Days blur into weeks. Weeks dissolve into months. Time no longer marks itself with meaning, only with endurance. Somewhere in that quiet erosion, you lose the person you once were. The one who held life with open hands. Who dreamed freely. Who believed, without effort, in possibility. That self does not vanish in a single moment. It thins. Fades. Recedes like a tide you do not notice pulling back until the shoreline is suddenly far away.

In their place remains a hollow outline. A shell moving through the motions. A specter haunted by memories of who they used to be. You remember that person the way one remembers childhood homes. Vaguely. Tenderly. With a grief you cannot quite name. You look for them in mirrors and moments and come up empty, unsure when you last truly felt like yourself. Depression tightens its grip not with violence, but with persistence. It does not strike. It stays. It holds. It waits. Until you feel submerged. Lungs burning. Arms heavy. Drowning in a sea of despair with no shoreline in sight. You thrash quietly, conserving energy, knowing instinctively that panic will only hasten the end. So you float. You endure. You survive beneath the surface where no one can see how close you are to going under.

But why do we wear this mask so faithfully, so relentlessly? Because the world has taught us that vulnerability is synonymous with failure. Because we live in a culture that applauds triumph, productivity, and polished success, where admitting that we are struggling feels like confessing to a fundamental flaw. We are praised for resilience, not for rest. For strength, not for softness. For pushing through, not for pausing to tend what hurts. And so we learn to hide. We swallow our truth until it burns on the way down. We retreat deeper into the labyrinth of our own minds, winding through corridors of self-doubt and silence, rehearsing explanations we never give. We convince ourselves that no one could possibly understand what lives there. That our pain is too strange. Too heavy. Too much.

Isolation becomes both refuge and prison. A place where we believe we are safer unseen. Where no one can judge what they cannot witness. Where we can nurse our wounds in the dark without risking rejection. And yet, even as it shelters us, the loneliness tightens its grip. The walls close in. The silence grows louder. Until the very place we hid to survive becomes the place that keeps us trapped. And still, beneath it all, something in you remembers connection. Remembers warmth. Remembers being held. That memory aches. It flickers. It waits. Quietly insisting that isolation may feel safer, but it was never meant to be home. And yet, even here, even in the deepest chambers of that maze, hope still breathes.

Quietly. Persistently. It does not shout or demand your attention. It does not arrive as certainty or clarity. It is a small, steady inhale in the dark, a reminder that something within you is still alive, still responding. It is this hope I want to place gently in your hands, dear reader, not as a solution, but as a companion. Hope that you are not alone in this darkness. Hope that you are not a failure for hurting. Hope that your pain does not cancel your worth. Hope that you are deserving of love, of joy, of connection, exactly as you are, not as a fixed or perfected version of yourself, but as you stand right now. Wounded. Tired. Still here. Hope that you can reclaim yourself piece by fragile piece, that you can rediscover joy without forcing it, reconnect with the present without pressure, and remember who you were before the shadow convinced you otherwise.

Because the truth is this. Depression is not a sign of weakness. It is often the mark of someone who has endured. Someone who has carried more than their share. Someone who has kept going long after the well ran dry, drawing strength from reserves they never knew they had. It is not the absence of resilience, but the cost of having used it for too long without rest. It takes immense courage to turn toward the darkness instead of running from it. Courage to face the fear rather than deny it. Courage to name the struggle instead of swallowing it. Courage to be vulnerable in a world that demands invulnerability. Courage to ask for help. To reach out. To admit, without shame, that you cannot do this alone.

And in that courage, quiet and trembling though it may be, healing begins. Not as a sudden transformation. Not as a dramatic rescue. But as a subtle shift. A loosening. A first step taken while your knees still shake. Healing begins the moment you choose presence over disappearance, honesty over performance, compassion over self-blame. It begins the moment you stay. And if that is all you can do today, if all you can manage is to keep breathing, to keep reading, to keep holding on to this small ember of hope, then know this: it is enough. You are enough. And even now, even here, the light has not forgotten you.

So where do you begin, when everything inside you feels heavy and unclear? You begin exactly where you are. Not where you wish you were. Not where you think you should be by now. Right here, in the middle of the fog, with the weight still in your chest and the questions still unanswered. The first step is not fixing or curing or conquering. It is acknowledging. Turning gently toward the shadow within and naming it for what it is. Depression is real. It is valid. And it is not something to be ashamed of. You are allowed to not be okay. Allowed to be tired. Overwhelmed. Lost. Allowed to pause without explanation. Allowed to feel what you feel without immediately trying to justify it or make it disappear. You are allowed to ask for help even when your thoughts feel tangled and your words come out broken. Especially then.

Naming the shadow does not give it power. It takes power away. It pulls it out of secrecy and silence and places it into the light, where it can finally be seen, understood, tended to. What remains unspoken grows larger in the dark. What is named begins to shrink, not because it vanishes, but because it is no longer mistaken for you. The next step is reaching outward. This is often the hardest part. Depression convinces you that you must walk this terrain alone, that no one else could understand, that asking for help is evidence of failure. But that is one of its cruelest lies. You were never meant to carry this by yourself. Seek support. A friend. A family member. A therapist. Someone who can walk beside you as you navigate these dark waters. Someone who can hold the lantern when your own hands are shaking. Let yourself speak the fear, the doubt, the ache you've been carrying in silence. You do not need polished sentences or tidy explanations. You do not need to make it coherent or palatable.

You only need to be honest. Sometimes honesty sounds like *I don't know what's wrong, I just know I'm not okay.* Sometimes it sounds like tears. Sometimes it sounds like silence shared in the presence of someone who does not rush you to be better. Remember this. You are not alone, even when it feels that way. Even when the darkness insists otherwise. There are people who care deeply about you. People who want to help shoulder the weight when yours feels unbearable. People who do not need you to be fixed to be worthy of their care. And letting yourself lean, even a little, is not weakness. It is the beginning of being held. Then comes the quiet, daily act of self-care. Not the glossy, marketable version wrapped in candles and slogans, but the real kind. The kind that meets you where you are instead of where you wish you could be.

Tending to your body, your emotions, your mind with patience rather than demand. Eating when you can. Sleeping when you can. Letting rest be imperfect and still enough. Moving your body gently, even if it's just a slow walk down the street, a stretch in place, a reminder that you are still here, still inhabiting yourself. Returning to small things that bring moments of relief or softness. Reading a few pages. Writing a few lines. Painting without purpose. Sitting in nature and letting the world breathe around you when breathing feels hard inside. Let these moments be lifelines, not obligations. Anchors, not tasks to complete or fail at. Caring for yourself is not selfish.

It is survival. It is an act of respect toward your own humanity. A quiet declaration that your life is worth tending, even when it feels fragile. Especially then.

Alongside this, you begin to listen differently to the voices in your head. Those relentless whispers that tell you you're worthless, broken, beyond help. They are persuasive, yes. Familiar. Convincing in their repetition. But they are not truth. They are symptoms. Echoes of depression reverberating through a tired nervous system, not reflections of who you are at your core. Learning to pause. To notice the thought. To question it gently rather than obey it. takes time. Practice. Compassion. Some days it will feel impossible, like trying to stop a storm with your bare hands. That's okay. Even noticing the voice, even naming it as depression speaking, is a victory. A crack in the loop. A moment of choice where once there was only momentum. And when gratitude is possible, let it arrive softly.

Not as a denial of pain, not as a command to be positive, but as a reminder that pain is not the whole story. That alongside the ache, something else still exists. A sliver of warmth. A kind word. A breath that came a little easier than the last. These moments do not erase suffering. They coexist with it, widening the frame just enough to let light back in. Healing is built this way. Quietly. Patiently. Through ordinary acts of care repeated over time. Through learning to tend yourself the way you would someone you love. And with each small act, each gentle pause, you are not fixing yourself. You are honoring yourself. And that, too, is a form of courage. And finally, you take small steps forward. Depression loves to convince you that movement is impossible. That the mountain ahead is too steep. That you must either leap all at once or not move at all.

But healing does not ask for leaps. It asks for inches. For what can be reached from where you are standing. One small, manageable step at a time. A phone call made with a shaking hand. A walk around the block, even if it's slow. One page read. One honest conversation whispered instead of spoken boldly. These steps may feel insignificant. They may feel laughably small against the magnitude of what you're facing. But they are not nothing. Each one is a quiet act of defiance against the darkness. Each one is proof that movement is still possible, even when it feels painfully slow. Even when it doesn't feel like progress at all. There is no single path out of depression. There is only *your* path. And it begins, gently, bravely, not with certainty or confidence, but with one small step taken in your own time. No comparison. No timeline. No borrowed expectations. Just the next step that belongs to you.

As you step onto this path, carry this truth gently with you. Healing does not ask for haste. It invites patience. It allows for pauses. For missteps. For days when the ground seems to shift beneath your feet and forward feels impossible. It is okay to stumble. It is okay to fall. It is okay to discover that today's strength looks nothing like yesterday's. Strength is not fixed. It changes shape. It adapts. It meets you where you are. What matters is not the grace of your movement. It is the fact that you continue to move at all. Even when the next step feels impossibly small. Even when lifting your foot feels like lifting the weight of the world. Even when progress looks more like endurance than momentum. That step still counts. Especially then. Because every step taken in the direction of care, however hesitant, is a declaration. A quiet, courageous *yes* to staying. To trying again. To believing, even faintly, that your life is worth walking forward into. And it is.

There will be days when the voices of depression rise again. Loud. Insistent. Familiar. They will echo old lies with practiced precision, pressing on the same tender places, trying to convince you that nothing has changed. On those days, forward motion may not look like progress at all. It may look like simply staying. Breathing through the weight. Choosing not to disappear. Choosing not to surrender the day, even when it feels unbearable to hold. That, too, is courage. That, too, is progress. Do not mistake slowness for failure. Rivers carve canyons not through force, but through persistence. Drop by drop. Moment by moment. What reshapes a landscape is not urgency but return. Again and again, the water shows up, even when the stone resists. Because the truth, dear reader, is this.

You are far stronger than you have been led to believe. Stronger than the voice that doubts you. Stronger than the weight that tries to pin you to the past. Stronger than the stories that tell you, that you are fragile when, in truth, you are forged by endurance. Within you lives a capacity to heal. To reclaim joy. To imagine a life shaped not by survival alone, but by meaning, connection, and possibility. This capacity does not shout. It does not rush. It waits patiently for your permission to be noticed. It lives in the part of you that keeps breathing when everything hurts. In the part that reads these words. In the part that stays. You are worthy of love that does not have to be earned. Of happiness that does not require perfection. Of a life that feels like it belongs to you, not one you must constantly perform to deserve. You do not need to become someone else to be worthy of care. You already are.

And you do not walk this road alone. Even here. Even now. You are accompanied. By hope that refuses to extinguish itself. By resilience shaped through survival. By the quiet, unwavering truth that your story is still unfolding. Not finished. Not concluded. Still becoming. There is more ahead than what has already been endured. More light than you have been allowed to imagine. And step by step, breath by breath, you are moving toward it, even on the days when all you can do is stay. And staying, sometimes, is the bravest act of all.

Recognizing the Thief

In your darkest moments, when the shadows press close and the world drains of color, it becomes vital to name what is happening. Not to judge it. Not to battle it. But to *see* it. Depression is not who you are. It is a thief. Quiet. Patient. Ruthless. It does not crash through the door or announce itself with violence. It steals by inches. By moments you barely notice disappearing. First joy. Then hope. Then the way you see yourself when no one else is watching. It loosens your grip on your own reflection until one day you look at the person moving through your days and feel only distance, only confusion, only a faint recognition that no longer feels like belonging. You begin to feel translucent.

Like a ghost pacing familiar hallways without ever touching the walls. Present but not participating. Breathing, but not living. You move through rooms and conversations as though you are slightly out of phase with the world, watching life happen rather than inhabiting it. The laughter of others echoes as if from another floor. The warmth of connection brushes past you but never quite lands. The future, once alive with possibility, fades as a photograph left too long in the sun. Its edges blur. Its colors wash out. Dreams that once felt within reach do not shatter dramatically or collapse in spectacle. They simply dissolve. Thin. Fade. Quietly retreat beneath the weight of despair until you can no longer remember why they mattered so much in the first place. And all the while, the thief works without sound. It convinces you that this emptiness is your fault. That the hollowing is evidence of who you truly are. That you have always been this way, that the joy you remember was borrowed or undeserved or temporary.

It rewrites your history. It edits your identity. It whispers that there is nothing to recover because there was nothing real there to begin with. But that is the lie. It is not truth. It is not character. It is not destiny. It is the work of the illness. And seeing it clearly, naming it for what it is, is the first act of resistance. The first act of reclaiming what it tried to steal. Because the moment you recognize the thief, you stop mistaking the damage for your identity. You begin to separate yourself from the shadow. You remember that what has been taken can be mourned, fought for, and, piece by piece, returned. Recognition does not restore everything at once. But it returns *you* to yourself. And that is where healing truly begins.

Depression isn't just sadness. It is a many-headed, multifaceted creature. A shape-shifter that studies your weakest moments and adapts itself accordingly. It does not confront you directly. It insinuates. It slips into the folds of your thinking, whispering doubts in a voice that sounds uncannily like your own. Familiar. Convincing. Intimate. It plants insidious seeds of insecurity and self-loathing deep in the soil of your mind, where they can grow unnoticed. Given time, those seeds take root. Tiny imperfections swell into immovable mountains. Small missteps harden into damning evidence of your supposed inadequacy. Nothing is allowed to remain neutral. A passing comment sharpens into a personal attack. Silence becomes rejection. Kindness feels suspicious, like a trap waiting to snap shut the moment you trust it. Success is dismissed as luck. Coincidence. Something borrowed and soon to be reclaimed, never truly yours to keep.

This thief does not merely steal joy. It replaces it. With a heavy, colorless apathy that settles where feeling once lived. Where laughter once sparked, indifference takes hold. Where desire once stirred, numbness spreads, dull and pervasive. The world does not just lose its brightness. It loses its pull. Its urgency. Its meaning. Hope thins to a fragile thread, stretched almost to breaking, trembling under the weight of endless doubt. Your sense of self comes under siege. Confidence is eroded grain by grain, worn down so gradually you do not notice the loss until it is already profound. Certainty gives way to hesitation. Self-trust dissolves into second-guessing. Worth is chipped away with relentless persistence, not through cruelty alone, but through repetition, until one morning you wake feeling hollow. Insignificant. Unmoored. Unbearably alone.

As though you have been quietly erased while still breathing. Still moving. Still showing up. A body inhabiting space while the person inside fades into the background, unsure how much of themselves remains or where they might begin to look for what has been taken. And yet, even here, even in this hollowed-out place, the truth remains. You have not vanished. You have been *under siege*. And what has been worn down was never your essence, only your access to it. Time itself becomes distorted under its influence. The present feels unliveable, stretched thin and airless, a place you endure rather than inhabit. The future collapses into an impossibly bleak horizon, stripped of promise, offering nothing you can imagine wanting to reach. The past, meanwhile, turns hostile. It becomes a cruel archive, replaying regrets and perceived failures with ruthless precision, editing out every moment of resilience, every instance of survival, until all that remains is a curated record of what you believe went wrong.

Possibilities contract. Dreams wither before they can even form. Life, once expansive and textured, begins to feel like an unbearable weight you are forced to carry without rest. Each day is something to be hauled rather than lived, something to endure rather than engage with. And all the while, the monster insists this heaviness is simply who you are now. That this diminished, exhausted version of yourself is the truth you must accept. But it isn't. It is the illness speaking. And learning to recognize its voice, to distinguish its tone from your own, is the beginning of taking your life back. Because what makes this thief of happiness, so devastating is not only what it steals, but how expertly it misdirects. It convinces you that the darkness is your doing. That the weight crushing your chest is evidence of personal failure. A moral flaw. A lack of effort. A failure to be grateful enough, strong enough, positive enough.

It whispers lies about your inadequacy with quiet persistence. So quiet they slip past your defenses. So constant they begin to sound like facts. It tells you that you are unworthy of love. Unfit for happiness. Undeserving of life itself. And perhaps its most dangerous move of all is how it tightens its grip by isolating you, persuading you that no one could possibly understand. That this battle is yours alone. That silence is safer than exposure. That endurance is the only option left. And so you suffer quietly, believing the lie that loneliness is inevitable. But this, too, is part of the deception. Because the moment you begin to question the voice, to say "*this may not be me speaking*", a fracture appears in its certainty. A hairline crack where light can enter. Recognition loosens the chains. Awareness weakens the hold. And slowly, gently, you begin to reclaim what was never truly lost, only obscured. Your life. Your worth. Your right to exist beyond the shadow.

This is what depression is: a relentless, slow erosion of self. Of presence. Of hope. Of possibility. Of life itself. It does not arrive all at once, nor does it announce its intentions. It stays close, familiar, constant. A companion that walks beside you, murmuring doubts, insecurity, self-hatred, and fear directly into your soul until the sound of it becomes indistinguishable from your own thoughts. It repeats the same cruel refrain, over and over, until resistance feels futile. *"You are not good enough! You are unlovable! Nothing will ever change!"* And the cruelest trick of all is this: it convinces you that these lies are truth. That the voice tearing you down is not illness, not distortion, not harm, but reality speaking plainly at last. It frames its cruelty as honesty. Its despair as clarity. Its hopelessness as wisdom. And because it speaks from inside you, because it wears your voice and borrows your memories, it becomes terrifyingly easy to believe it.

The thief thrives in darkness. It feeds on secrecy. On unspoken pain. On the belief that naming it will somehow make it stronger, more real, more dangerous. It tells you that silence is protection, that endurance is virtue, that suffering quietly is proof of strength. But this, too, is a lie designed to keep you isolated, unseen, and alone with what was never meant to be carried in solitude. There is power in acknowledgment. There is power in turning toward it and saying, "*I see you.*" Not with hatred. Not with fear. But with clarity. By bringing it into the light, you begin to loosen its hold. You interrupt the illusion that it is all-powerful. You create distance between the illness and your identity. You begin, slowly and deliberately, to reclaim authorship over your story. Recognizing depression as an adversary rather than an identity is a pivotal shift.

You are not your depression. You are a complex, living human being, shaped by struggle but not defined by it. You carry wounds, yes, but also resilience. History, yes, but also possibility. Pain, yes, but also an immense capacity for healing that has not disappeared, even if it has been buried beneath exhaustion, fear, and silence. Nothing essential about you has been erased. It has been covered. Obscured. Weighed down. And the moment you begin to see that truth, the moment you stop mistaking the thief for your own voice, something profound begins to change. Not all at once. Not without effort. But unmistakably. The story is no longer being written *about* you without your consent.

You are beginning to write again. And that is where your life starts to open.

Unmasking the Thief: Understanding Depression's Tactics

Depression is not simply sadness. It is far more intricate. Far more cunning. It is an interwoven storm of biology, psychology, and lived experience, each thread tightening around the next until it feels impossible to tell where one ends and another begins. It moves through the body, the mind, the nervous system, and memory all at once, shaping perception as much as emotion, belief as much as chemistry. To understand how it works is not an academic exercise. It is an act of reclamation. Because once you begin to see how the thief operates, once you recognize its methods and disguises, you begin to loosen its grip. What was once overwhelming and shapeless gains edges. Language. Context. And what can be named can be met.

For years, many of us were offered a comforting oversimplification: *"It's just a chemical imbalance."* And yes, neurotransmitters like serotonin and dopamine do play a role. The brain is involved. The body is involved. But depression is not a single missing ingredient that can be neatly replaced, not a faulty switch flipped in isolation. It is not that simple, and pretending it, is can feel quietly invalidating, as though the depth of suffering could be reduced to a mechanical error. As though pain this profound could be solved with a single adjustment. The reality is far more complex. Depression is a conversation. Between brain chemistry and nervous system responses. Between trauma stored in the body and stress accumulated over time.

Between attachment, loss, expectation, identity, and environment. It is shaped by what happened to you, what you learned you had to survive, what your system adapted to endure. It lives not just in the mind, but in the patterns of protection your body learned when safety was uncertain. And paradoxically, this complexity is not a sentence. It is hope. Because complexity means there is no single point of failure. And therefore, no single point of repair. It means there are many places where healing can begin. Many doors. Many small openings. Biology can be supported. The nervous system can be soothed. Trauma can be processed. Beliefs can be gently challenged. Relationships can be repaired or reimagined. Environment can be altered. Meaning can be restored.

Understanding this does something vital. It shifts the narrative from *what is wrong with me* to *what has happened to me, and how has my system adapted to survive it*. It replaces blame with curiosity. Shame with context. Hopelessness with possibility. The thief thrives on confusion and reduction. Clarity is its undoing. And as you begin to understand depression not as a personal defect, but as a complex, adaptive response to overwhelming internal and external conditions, you take back something essential. Compassion for yourself. Agency over your healing. And the knowledge that because this terrain was shaped over time, it can also be reshaped. Slowly. Patiently. In many ways, at once. Healing does not require a single answer. It requires understanding, support, and the courage to keep learning how the storm formed, so you can begin, piece by piece, to guide yourself toward steadier ground.

One of depression's most effective weapons is the **thought trap**. It does not merely introduce negative thoughts. It reshapes the very lens through which you see the world, tilting reality until everything feels skewed and hostile. Thoughts become distorted, exaggerated, sharpened into weapons that turn inward. They loop endlessly, circling the same conclusions until repetition masquerades as truth, until doubt hardens into certainty. Catastrophizing takes root quietly. Every uncertainty swells into disaster. Every unanswered message becomes rejection. Every small wobble feels like the beginning of collapse. The mind is taught to scan constantly for threat, convinced that the worst possible outcome is not just possible, but inevitable. Hope is dismissed as naïve. Calm is temporary. Safety as an illusion waiting to shatter.

Personalization follows close behind. Neutral events twist into evidence of your failure. A tone of voice becomes proof you've disappointed someone. A closed door becomes confirmation that you are unwanted. You begin carrying blame that was never yours, shouldering responsibility for outcomes you did not create, apologizing for taking up space at all. Filtering strips the world of its depth. Only the darkness is allowed to register. Anything good fades into irrelevance, dismissed as coincidence, luck, or undeserved. Compliments slide off. Kindness feels suspect. Moments of relief are erased almost as soon as they appear, while pain is archived in sharp, enduring detail. The mind becomes an editor with a cruel bias, cutting out anything that contradicts the narrative of worthlessness.

Then comes black-and-white thinking. The world flattens into absolutes. Success or failure. Worthy or worthless. Hope or nothing at all. There is no middle ground. No nuance. No mercy. No room to breathe. You are either everything or nothing, and depression ensures the verdict is almost always the latter. Alongside this cognitive erosion comes the **behavioural drain**. Depression does not simply make you sad. It makes you tired at a soul-deep level. A fatigue that sleep cannot touch. Energy leaks away slowly, as if through unseen cracks. Motivation dissolves. Even desire begins to feel theoretical rather than lived. The things that once anchored you begin to feel impossibly heavy.

Movement feels like effort without reward. Creativity dries up, replaced by a blankness that feels like failure. Connection becomes taxing. Pleasure feels distant, muted, unreachable. You are not lazy. You are depleted. Your system is conserving what little it has left, trying to survive a constant internal siege. This is how the thief works. It convinces you that your exhaustion is a flaw, your distorted thinking a reflection of reality, your withdrawal a personal failing. But these, too, are tactics. Patterns. Symptoms. And learning to recognize them, gently, without judgment, is another act of resistance. Because the moment you see the trap for what it is, you are no longer fully caught inside it. You are beginning to find the edges. And where there are edges, there is space for something else to enter.

Avoidance grows, not out of laziness, but out of depletion. It is the body and mind pulling inward in self-protection, conserving what little energy remains. And as engagement with life shrinks, isolation expands, quietly, inevitably, feeding the very thoughts that caused the withdrawal in the first place. The less you reach, the louder the doubts become. The louder the doubts grow, the harder it feels to reach. It is a closed loop. Efficient. Brutal. Self-reinforcing. The thief does not need force when it has repetition on its side. And it does not stop at the mind. There is a **physical toll** as well, one that is often dismissed or misunderstood. Depression lives in the body. It settles into muscles and marrow, into breath and heartbeat. Sleep fractures or disappears altogether, nights stretching long and restless, or collapsing into exhaustion that never restores.

Appetite shifts, sometimes vanishing entirely, sometimes spiraling beyond control, as the body searches desperately for regulation it can no longer find. Muscles ache without clear cause. Headaches linger like unanswered questions. The immune system weakens. Fatigue becomes chronic, bone-deep, unrelenting. The body carries the illness even when words fail to explain it. Even when the mirror shows nothing remarkable. Even when the world insists you "*look fine*". Pain without visible proof is among the loneliest kinds. This is how depression operates. Quietly. Systematically. Convincingly. It weaves itself through thought, behavior, and body until everything feels connected by exhaustion and doubt. And this is why understanding it matters. Not to label yourself. Not to reduce your experience. But to reclaim it. Because when you can name its tactics, you begin to separate yourself from them.

You begin to see patterns where you once saw personal failure. You begin to recognize symptoms where you once saw shame. You begin to understand that what you are experiencing is not a defect of character, but a condition. A process. A thief with a method. And thieves rely on invisibility. Once exposed, once named, once seen clearly for what they are, they lose their greatest power. They can still exist, still linger, still cause harm, but they no longer get to masquerade as *you*. Awareness becomes light. Language becomes leverage. Understanding becomes the first steady hand on the door back to yourself. Not all at once. Not without effort. But unmistakably. Because what can be seen can be challenged. What can be named can be met. And what is met no longer owns you in silence.

The Pathway to Light

Healing does not begin with certainty. It begins with honesty. With the quiet, courageous admission whispered first to yourself: "*I am not okay.*" Not as a declaration of defeat, but as a turning point. Acceptance is not surrender. It is the first loosening of the chains, the moment your hands stop clenching long enough to feel where the locks have been holding. In that vulnerability, something unexpected and powerful stirs. A strength often mistaken for weakness rises. The strength to stop pretending. To give voice to what has been buried. To step out of secrecy and into connection. What was once carried alone begins to lighten the moment it is shared, as though the weight itself had been waiting for witness.

No one finds their way out of darkness in isolation. A support system becomes a constellation in the night sky, points of light that do not erase the dark but help you navigate it. Friends who listen without fixing. Family who sit with you in the unspoken, offering presence instead of solutions. Professionals who know this terrain, who have walked it with others, who can help you find steady ground when the path feels uncertain. Reaching for others does not mean you have failed. It means you are choosing life. It means you are opening doors long sealed, allowing light to touch places that have grown cold from being shut away.

Therapy, for many, becomes a lifeline thrown into deep water. A place where the chaos inside can finally be given language. Where thoughts no longer have to collide in silence. Where tangled emotions are patiently unraveled, thread by careful thread. Cognitive-behavioural tools shine light on the distortions depression weaves, exposing the lies it whispers so convincingly. They teach you to pause. To question. To reframe. Not to argue with yourself harshly, but to loosen the grip of thoughts that were never meant to rule you. Slowly, resilience is rebuilt. Not as armor that hardens you against feeling, but as flexibility. The ability to bend without breaking when doubt returns.

For some, medication becomes part of the bridge forward. Not a cure. Not a shortcut. But a support. A way to ease the weight just enough to allow movement, clarity, and breath. It can help restore balance where the system has been overwhelmed for too long, creating the conditions in which therapy, connection, and self-care can finally take root. It does not replace the work. It makes the work possible.

There is no single map out of the darkness. No universal formula. No one-size-fits-all answer. What brings relief to one may not serve another, and that does not mean you are doing it wrong. This path is deeply personal, shaped by your history, your body, your needs, your timing. The work is not to follow someone else's footsteps, but to discover your own. Step by step. Breath by breath. Toward the light that has not abandoned you. Toward the life that has been waiting, patiently, all along.

Acknowledging the Shadow: Facing Your Feelings

If the pathway to light begins with acceptance, then the next step is learning how to sit with the shadow without flinching. This is often the hardest part. The instinct to suppress, minimize, or outrun your feelings can be powerful, almost reflexive. Many of us learned early, sometimes without words, that emotions were dangerous, inconvenient, or simply too much. That tears needed explanation. That anger required justification. That sadness should be tucked away where it wouldn't make anyone uncomfortable. Over time, avoidance becomes second nature, and silence begins to feel safer than honesty.

But healing does not ask you to conquer your feelings. It asks you to listen to them. Gently. Honestly. Without judgment. This is where acknowledgment becomes an act of courage. To turn toward what hurts instead of away from it. To sit beside discomfort without demanding that it leave. To name what is present without immediately trying to fix, analyze, or transform it. Not everything that surfaces needs to be solved. Some things simply need to be seen. This chapter offers tools not as demands, but as invitations. Doorways rather than directives. Ways to approach your inner world with curiosity instead of fear.

- **Journaling**

Writing creates a private, permission-free space where nothing needs to be polished or explained. The page does not interrupt. It does not recoil. It does not rush you toward resolution. It simply holds. You might begin with something simple, almost tentative: *Today, I feel...* or *One thing I'm grateful for is...* Let the words arrive exactly as they are. Messy. Repetitive. Fragmented. Contradictory. This is not about eloquence. It is about truth. Over time, journaling becomes a quiet dialogue with yourself. A place where the unsaid finally finds breath.

Where emotions you've been carrying in your body can spill onto the page and take shape. Where confusion can exist without being shamed, and clarity can emerge without being forced.

- **Mindfulness Meditation**

Mindfulness is the practice of staying with the present moment, even when it is uncomfortable. Especially when it is uncomfortable. Rather than being dragged under by thoughts and emotions, you learn to observe them as weather passing through the sky of your awareness. Clouds gather. Storms break. Skies clear. None of it is permanent. Feelings arise. Feelings move. Feelings pass. Guided meditations, whether through apps like Calm or Headspace or other resources, can help anchor you when your mind feels too loud to sit with alone. Mindfulness does not ask you to empty your mind. It asks you to notice what is already there, without being consumed by it.

- **Body Scan Meditation**

The body often speaks long before the mind finds words. It carries what we have not yet named. A body scan invites you to move your attention slowly through your physical experience, noticing sensation without judgment. Tension. Heaviness. Warmth. Numbness. Tightness. Ease. Nothing needs to change. In listening to the body, you begin to understand where emotions live, where they hide, and where they are asking to be released. Sometimes healing begins not with insight, but with noticing your shoulders soften. Your jaw unclench. Your breath deepen. The body, when heard, often knows how to begin letting go.

- **Talk to Someone**

Depression thrives in isolation. It weakens when spoken aloud. Sharing your feelings with a trusted friend, family member, therapist, or support group can be profoundly grounding. You do not need perfect words. You do not need a solution. You do not need to make your pain palatable. What you need is presence. Being witnessed. Being believed. In that shared space, shame loosens its grip. The story that you are alone begins to fracture. Connection reminds you of something essential. You were never meant to carry this by yourself. Acknowledging the shadow does not make it stronger. It makes *you* stronger. Each moment of honest attention, each act of gentle curiosity, is a step away from silence and toward integration. The shadow does not disappear because you ignore it. It softens when you finally allow yourself to see it, name it, and stay. And in staying, something profound happens. You stop abandoning yourself.

Reclaiming the Canvas

Once you have begun to acknowledge the shadow, something subtle but powerful happens. Space opens. Not a dramatic clearing. Not an instant transformation. But a quiet widening, a little more room to breathe where there was once only pressure. And in that space, you are invited to reclaim what was never truly lost, only buried. Healing is not about forcing happiness back into your life. It is about allowing moments of joy to return gently, in their own time, like color seeping back into a long-faded painting, saturating the canvas drop by patient drop. As you slowly peel away the layers of darkness, begin by turning toward what once stirred something alive in you.

Not with pressure. Not with expectation. Simply with curiosity. Revisit activities that once sparked passion, even if the spark feels faint, barely there. You are not asking it to blaze. You are only asking it to exist. Step into nature and let the earth remind your nervous system what steadiness feels like. The rhythm of wind through trees. The grounding weight of your feet on soil. The quiet assurance that life continues in cycles, without urgency. Pick up an old hobby or try something new without the demand that it must mean anything. Paint without an audience. Write without a destination. Move your body without tracking progress.

Let the act itself be enough. Creativity, when freed from outcome, becomes a form of listening. A way of letting yourself speak without words. Reconnect with loved ones, not as a performance, but as you are. You do not need to be entertaining. You do not need to be healed. You do not need to explain yourself fully. Presence is enough. Sitting together. Walking side by side. Sharing silence. These moments, though small, stitch connection back into the places that felt torn. This is how the canvas is reclaimed. Not in sweeping strokes meant to erase the past, but in layered gestures that honor it. Darkness and light existing together, informing each other. What returns is not the person you were before the pain, but someone wider, more textured, more capable of holding complexity.

You are not restoring an old painting. You are creating a new one. And each moment of gentle engagement, each choice to turn toward life without forcing it, adds another color. Another line. Another breath of possibility. Self-care becomes more than a checklist. It becomes an act of reclamation. Nourishing your body, mind, and spirit is a quiet declaration: *I am worth tending to.* In a world that taught you to endure rather than care, this is no small rebellion. Small practices matter. Drinking water. Resting when you are tired. Moving gently, without punishment or demand. These are not insignificant acts. They are brushstrokes. Subtle, deliberate marks laid down on a canvas that has known too much erasure.

Gratitude returns slowly, almost shyly, in whispers rather than proclamations. A warm cup of tea held between your palms. A patch of sunlight spilling across the floor. A moment of stillness where the mind softens its grip. Practicing gratitude does not deny pain. It widens the lens. It reminds you that even within suffering, life still offers moments of contact, however fleeting. These moments do not erase the darkness. They sit alongside it, forming the underpainting of a more vibrant canvas, a base layer of meaning beneath what is still being built. Mindfulness adds color where numbness once lived. By grounding yourself in the present, you interrupt the mind's habit of dragging you backward into regret or forward into fear.

Breathwork. Meditation. Or simply noticing the world as it is. The sound of wind. The texture of fabric against skin. The rhythm of your own breath returning you to yourself. These practices anchor you back into your body, back into now. And in these pauses, fleeting moments of joy begin to reemerge. Not as fireworks. Not as grand revelations. But as steady embers, glowing softly, capable of warmth if you stay close enough to notice them. Reclaiming the canvas is not about erasing what came before. It is about layering new meaning on top of old pain. Allowing darkness and light to coexist without apology. Stroke by careful stroke. Moment by moment. Breath by breath. Until one day, often without fanfare, you look back and realize something has shifted. The colors have returned. Not exactly as they were, but deeper. More textured. Informed by what you have survived. Undeniably your own.

Reclaiming Your Power: Practical Strategies for Healing

This chapter offers actionable steps you can take to counteract the effects of depression and begin to rebuild your life. As the colors begin to return to your canvas, the next invitation is this: to step back into your own power, gently but deliberately. Not with force. Not with urgency. Healing does not arrive as a single revelation or a sudden transformation that splits life into *before* and *after*. It is quieter than that. It is built through small, repeated acts of care, through choices that may feel unremarkable in the moment but accumulate into something steady and sustaining. This chapter is not about perfection or willpower. It is about practice. About meeting yourself exactly where you are and choosing, again and again, to move forward, even if only by inches. Especially then.

Begin with **small victories**. Depression has a way of turning mountains into immovable walls, convincing you that everything must be done at once or not at all. But every wall is built from individual stones. Break the overwhelming into the manageable. One task. One step. One breath. Getting out of bed. Sending a message. Taking a shower. Making a meal. Celebrate each accomplishment, no matter how small it seems. Progress does not need to be dramatic to be real. Progress is still progress, even when it whispers instead of shouts. Gently **re-engage with the activities you once enjoyed**. You may not feel joy immediately. That is okay. Joy often follows action, not the other way around. Show up anyway. Paint even when the colors feel flat. Walk even when the world feels distant. Sit with music, with books, with creativity, without demanding they fix you.

Consistency plants seeds long before you ever see them bloom. What feels empty now may one day feel familiar again. What feels heavy may slowly begin to lighten. Move your body. **Exercise** not as punishment. Not as obligation. But as conversation. Physical movement speaks directly to the nervous system, reminding it that motion is possible, that energy can circulate, that you are still alive within your body. Exercise releases endorphins, natural mood boosters, and messengers of relief and connection. Aim for thirty minutes of moderate activity most days but release yourself from rigid rules. Even a short walk. A stretch on the floor. A few moments of movement can shift something subtle and important inside you.

Nourish your body as if it matters. Because it does. Feed yourself with intention, not judgment. Choose foods that sustain rather than deplete. Fruits. Vegetables. Whole grains. Lean proteins. Hydration. Limit what dulls or destabilizes you, not as punishment, but as care. This is not about restriction. It is about replenishment. About sending your body the message that it is worthy of being supported. **Prioritize sleep** as sacred ground. Rest is not laziness. It is repair. It is when the body integrates, the mind softens, the nervous system recalibrates. Aim for seven to nine hours of quality sleep when possible. Create rhythms that signal safety. A consistent schedule. A gentle wind-down ritual. Lower lights. Fewer screens. Quiet. Permission to rest without guilt. Sleep is not time lost. It is time invested in your healing. Learn to **challenge negative thoughts** when they arise. Depression speaks with authority, but it does not speak truth. When a harsh thought appears, pause. Create space between you and the voice.

Ask yourself: "*Is this fact or feeling? Is this helpful or harmful? What would a kinder, more realistic version of this thought sound like?*" You are not required to believe every sentence your mind produces. Thoughts are events, not verdicts. You are allowed to question them. And above all, **practice self-compassion**. Speak to yourself the way you would speak to a beloved friend who is hurting. With patience. With gentleness. With understanding. Healing does not happen through cruelty or self-criticism. It happens through care. Through learning to stand beside yourself instead of against yourself. These strategies are not rules. They are tools. You do not need to use them all at once. You do not need to master them perfectly. Choose one. Begin there. Let it be enough for today. Each small act of self-support is a reclaiming of power, a quiet declaration that your life belongs to you. Depression may have shaped part of your story. But it does not get to write the ending.

Building a Support System: You Are Not Alone

As you begin to reclaim your strength, step by careful step, a quiet truth emerges. Healing was never meant to be a solitary act. Even the strongest structures require scaffolding while they are being rebuilt. Even the most resilient foundations need support while the cracks are being tended to. Depression thrives in isolation, feeding on silence and separation, but it weakens in the presence of connection. Reaching outward is not a sign that you are failing. It is evidence that you are choosing to live.

Therapy can become one of the steadiest anchors in this process. A therapist offers a protected space where your truth can exist without interruption or judgment. A space where nothing needs to be minimized, justified, or made palatable. Within those walls, your emotions are allowed to breathe at their own pace. Tears do not need explanation. Silence is not awkward. Words arrive when they are ready. Approaches such as Cognitive Behavioural Therapy help untangle the distorted thought patterns that depression feeds on, gently exposing the lies it has woven into your inner dialogue. Interpersonal Therapy turns compassionate attention toward the relational wounds that shape how you move through the world, illuminating patterns you did not choose but learned in order to survive. Therapy does not fix you, because you are not broken. It helps you remember yourself.

Support groups offer something uniquely powerful: shared language. There is a particular relief in sitting alongside others who recognize the terrain you are walking through without needing it explained. Stories overlap. Pain resonates. Nods replace questions. And in that shared recognition, shame loosens its grip. You are no longer an anomaly. No longer a solitary outlier. You are human, surrounded by humans who understand the weight you carry because they have carried something similar themselves.

Family and friends, too, can become pillars of support, even if they do not fully comprehend the depth of your experience. Not everyone will know the right words. Not everyone will respond perfectly. And that is okay. What matters is allowing trusted people to stand with you, imperfectly but sincerely. Be honest about what you need. Sometimes that need is conversation. Sometimes it is quiet companionship. Sometimes it is practical help with the weight of daily life that feels unbearable when energy is scarce. Let them show up in the ways they can. Love does not always arrive as understanding; sometimes it arrives as presence.

For moments when distance, accessibility, or fear makes face-to-face connection feel impossible, **online communities** can provide a vital lifeline. Forums, moderated spaces, and support groups stretch across time zones and borders, offering connection when the world feels unreachable. They remind you that even in the quiet hours of the night, when the darkness feels thickest and most convincing, there are voices out there willing to listen. People awake with you. People who understand the language of survival spoken at 3 a.m. Healing does not mean carrying everything alone. You were never meant to. A support system does not erase the struggle, but it makes it survivable. It transforms isolation into shared ground. And sometimes, survivable is the first doorway back to hope.

Cultivating Hope: Finding Light in the Darkness

After connection comes something quieter, but no less essential. Hope. Not the loud, cinematic kind that arrives with certainty and answers, but the fragile, persistent kind that survives even when everything else feels stripped away. Depression narrows the horizon until tomorrow feels like a rumor, something other people talk about, but you cannot quite believe in. Joy becomes a foreign language you once spoke fluently, now reduced to faint recognition without recall. In this terrain, hope is not a grand revelation. It is a series of small, deliberate choices. A candle lit in a dark room. A hand reaching forward when the path cannot yet be seen.

Hope begins to return through **gratitude**, not as forced positivity or denial, but as gentle noticing. Even the smallest things count. The warmth of a cup cradled between your palms. The steady sound of rain tapping against glass. A single moment of quiet between waves of noise inside your mind. These acknowledgments do not erase pain, and they are not meant to. Instead, they widen the lens. They remind your nervous system that light still exists alongside the dark, that safety and softness have not vanished entirely. In noticing, something subtle shifts. Perspective loosens. The grip of despair weakens just enough to let air back in and create a sense of optimism.

Hope also grows when you **set meaningful goals**. Not goals imposed by expectation, comparison, or productivity culture, but goals aligned with your values. These are not about doing more or becoming someone else, it is not productivity or perfection. They are about direction. Purpose. A reason to take the next step, even if that step is small. Even the most modest goal can become a compass, pointing you toward something that matters. Something worth moving toward when standing still feels unbearable.

Acts of kindness open another unexpected doorway. Depression turns your gaze inward, trapping you in relentless self-criticism and isolation. Offering care to someone else gently widens the world again. Helping does not require grand gestures or heroic effort. A message sent. A smile offered. A listening ear held steady for someone else's story. In giving, you are reminded of something depression tries hard to erase that you still matter. That you still belong. That your presence carries weight beyond your pain.

There is also healing in **surrounding yourself with beauty**. Nature. Music. Art. Color. These are not luxuries reserved for when you are "better." They are nourishment. A walk beneath trees that stand without apology for their rootedness. A song that stirs something tender and forgotten. The act of creating with your hands, letting shape and color speak where words fall short. Beauty bypasses logic and speaks directly to the parts of you that depression has numbed but not destroyed, restoring sensation where emptiness once lived.

As hope strengthens, it becomes important to **remember your strengths**. Depression is an unreliable narrator. It edits your story with cruelty, erasing everything you have endured, everything you have survived.

Gently remind yourself of past accomplishments. Moments of courage. Times you kept going when stopping would have been easier. Qualities you admire within yourself, even if they feel distant now. You are not starting from nothing. You never were. The foundation is already there, even if it is currently obscured by shadow.

And finally, hope lives most reliably in the **present moment**. Depression pulls you backward into regret or hurls you forward into fear. Hope asks you to stay here. Now. What can you do in this moment to support yourself? One breath taken slowly. One choice made with care. One small act of kindness offered inward. Healing is not built all at once. It is assembled moment by moment, decision by decision, breath by breath.

Hope does not demand certainty. It does not require you to believe everything will be okay. It asks only for willingness. A willingness to believe that this darkness is not the end of your story. A willingness to stay. A willingness to take the next small step. Because even now, beneath the weight and the doubt and the exhaustion, something within you is still reaching. Still listening. Still breathing. Still turning, however slowly, toward the light.

A Journey, not a Destination – Beyond the Shadows

Healing does not move in a straight line. It spirals. It circles back on itself, revisits old ground, rises, dips, pauses, and rises again, tracing a pattern that makes sense only when viewed with patience. Some days you may feel close to the light, breathing more freely, sensing possibility brushing the edges of your life. Your steps feel steadier. Your thoughts soften. The world opens just enough to remind you what ease once felt like. And then there are other days. Days when the darkness returns uninvited, familiar and heavy, as if it never truly left. It settles into your chest, clouds your thoughts, tugs at old fears with practiced hands. This oscillation is not failure. It is not proof that you are doing something wrong. It is the rhythm of recovery. The natural cadence of a nervous system learning slowly and cautiously, how to live again after long vigilance.

There will be setbacks. Moments when you wonder if any of this is working. When old patterns resurface. When the shadows feel louder than the progress you have made. When hope thins and doubt steps forward, asking difficult questions. That, too, belongs here. Healing is not a clean ascent toward permanent light. It is a conversation between where you have been and where you are going. Healing is not about erasing symptoms or becoming untouched by pain. It is about learning how to live alongside it without letting it define you. About recognizing that the return of darkness does not negate the light you have already touched. About understanding that fragility does not erase strength. They often arrive together, braided, inseparable.

This work asks for compassion. Not as an abstract ideal, but as a daily practice. Compassion for yourself when you feel raw. When you feel confused. When exhaustion settles deeper than sleep can reach. Compassion that says, "*This is hard, and I am allowed to be human here.*" Compassion that meets you exactly where you are, without punishment, without comparison, without the demand to be anything other than what this moment requires. Again and again, you return to yourself. Not because you failed to stay, but because returning is part of the process. And with each return, something strengthens. Not perfection. Not invulnerability. But trust. Trust that even when the path curves back into shadow, you know how to keep walking. Trust that you have survived this terrain before. Trust that the light you seek is not lost, only momentarily obscured. The spiral does not mean you are stuck. It means you are moving. And movement, however uneven, is life learning how to breathe again.

As you walk this winding path, let yourself be accompanied. Surround yourself with voices that remember what is possible when you cannot. Seek out stories of those who have stumbled, fallen hard, risen slowly, and kept going anyway. Let their journeys serve as lanterns along the road, small steady flames held against the dark. They are not maps, not instructions, but living proof. Proof that survival can soften into meaning. Proof that endurance can mature into wisdom. Proof that life does not end where pain begins. Stories matter because they remind us that despair is not singular. When you hear another voice speak what you once believed unspeakable, something inside you loosens. A quiet recognition hums beneath the surface. "*I am not alone in this*". The road may still be difficult, but it is no longer uncharted. Others have walked here. Others have found their footing again.

And when you are able, share your own story. Not because it is polished. Not because it has a triumphant ending tied neatly with insight and certainty. But because it is real. Because it is still breathing. Because it carries the texture of lived experience rather than the gloss of perfection. Somewhere, someone is trapped in their own shadows, waiting for words that sound like theirs. Waiting to hear a voice that does not rush them toward hope but sits with them long enough to make hope feel possible. Vulnerability is not weakness here. It is strength in its most honest form. It is the courage to be seen without armor. To speak without knowing how the words will land. To reach outward even when retreat feels safer. Every time you tell the truth of your experience, every time you choose connection over concealment, you loosen the grip of isolation. You interrupt the silence that depression depends on.

Your experiences matter. Shaped by pain and perseverance, they carry light whether you intend them to or not. They hold the power to illuminate paths for others still searching for solid ground. And often, in offering light to someone else, you discover that your own flame steadies as well. In this shared humanity, healing becomes something larger than the self, beyond just personal. It becomes relational. Communal. Alive. What began as a solitary struggle slowly transforms into something connective. Your story does not exist in isolation. It echoes. It reaches. It belongs. And in that belonging, the path forward feels less lonely, less heavy, more possible. Not because the darkness has vanished. But because you are no longer walking through it alone.

Be patient with yourself. Let patience become the gentlest language you speak inward, the tone that replaces accusation with care. Let it be the steady hand at the center of your back when the road stretches long and uneven, when fatigue whispers that you should already be further along. Healing is not hurried by harshness. It unfolds when met with kindness. Celebrate your progress. Even the quiet victories no one else sees. The days you get out of bed when gravity feels doubled. The moments you choose breath over retreat. The times you reach for help instead of folding inward into silence. These are not small things. They are acts of courage. They are proof of resilience in motion, strength expressed not through force, but through persistence. Through staying. Through choosing yourself again and again in ways that cost you effort but give you life.

And remember this, especially on the days when the weight feels unbearable: you are not alone. You never have been. Yes, the shadow may linger at the edges. It may return in familiar shapes, testing old wounds, whispering fears it has memorized by heart. But it does not get to define you. It does not get to narrate your worth or determine your future. It is part of your story, not the author of it. By learning to understand the nature of depression, you loosen its disguise. By acknowledging your feelings instead of fighting them, you reclaim your ground. By practicing the strategies that support healing, you take back what was stolen. Bit by bit. Breath by breath. You reclaim your life.

And joy, when it comes, does not arrive all at once like a grand revelation or a sudden triumph. It returns softly. In fragments. In moments that feel almost ordinary at first. A laugh that surprises you. A connection that settles warm and steady. A sense of meaning rediscovered, not imposed. A purpose that takes root slowly, quietly, in soil that has known both drought and rain. This is not the end of the journey. It is the continuation of it. A life lived with more tenderness. More truth. More room for complexity. And as you keep walking, imperfectly but bravely, you begin to understand something profound. You are not broken. You are becoming.

The journey may be long. It may wind and double back on itself, testing your endurance in ways you did not expect. It may ask you to pause, to rest, to gather yourself again and again before continuing. There will be stretches where the road feels lonely, where progress is measured not in miles but in moments survived. And still, the destination matters. A life shaped by meaning. Anchored in purpose. Sustained by connection. A life that feels inhabited rather than endured. That life is worth fighting for. *You* are worth fighting for. Seeking professional help is not a sign of weakness. It is an act of wisdom. Of self-respect. Of courage refined into choice. It is choosing life when darkness argues convincingly against it. Choosing support when isolation feels safer. Choosing to believe, even faintly, that you deserve relief, care, and understanding. Reaching for help is not giving up control. It is reclaiming it.

Hope exists, even when you cannot feel it yet. Hope does not disappear simply because depression clouds your senses. Sometimes it waits quietly, held in the hands of others, carried forward on your behalf until you are able to feel its warmth again. Sometimes it survives as a whisper rather than a conviction. Sometimes it looks like staying. Like asking for help. Like reading these words and allowing them to land. That is enough. And you deserve a life no longer ruled by the grip of depression. Above all, hold this truth close when doubt creeps in, when the old voice tries to reclaim authority: depression is not who you are. It is not your identity. It is not your essence. It is a condition. A disease. A disorder that can be treated, managed, understood. It is an experience you are having, not a definition of your being.

It is not a verdict on your worth. Not a measure of your value. Not a ceiling on your potential. You are more than your depression. You are layered. Complex. Resilient. Shaped by what you have endured, yes, but also by what you have learned, what you carry forward, what you continue to offer despite the weight you have known. You are a unique, talented, capable human being with something only you can give this world. Something no one else can replicate. And no shadow, no matter how persistent or persuasive, can erase that truth. The light may feel distant at times. But it has not forgotten you. And step by imperfect step, breath by fragile breath, you are still moving toward it. Still here. Still becoming. Still worthy.

As you search for your way, for your voice, for the strength you fear has vanished, remember this gently, without debate or defence: it is okay to not be okay. It is okay to struggle. Okay to stumble. Okay to fall to your knees and rest there for a while, forehead pressed to the earth, breath shallow, heart tired. Healing does not require perfection or constant forward motion. It does not demand that you rise every time you fall. It asks only for honesty. For the courage to say, "*I need help*", and the humility to let yourself receive it when it arrives. You are not a burden. You are not a nuisance. You are not a failure. You are a person. A human being. A living, breathing soul, worthy of love, acceptance, and tenderness, even now. Especially now. Worthy not because you are strong, productive, or healed, but because you exist. Because your life carries inherent value, untouched by performance or endurance.

In the end, it is not the grand gestures that save us. It is the small ones. The quiet victories no one applauds. Getting out of bed when gravity feels doubled. Standing under the shower and letting the water run over your skin, reminding you that sensation still lives there. Eating a meal when appetite feels distant. Taking a breath when your chest feels tight. Choosing, again and again, to meet the day rather than disappear from it. These moments may feel insignificant. They are not. They accumulate like drops of rain filling a long-dry riverbed. Slowly at first. Almost imperceptibly. Until one day, without warning, something begins to flow again. Movement returns. Life stirs. The river remembers its shape. This is how triumph is built. Not all at once. Not with certainty or spectacle. But piece by fragile piece. Breath by breath. Choice by quiet choice. And in this patient assembling of small mercies, you discover something profound. You are still here. Still choosing. Still becoming. And that, in itself, is a victory.

It is the courage to face what frightens you, not with bravado, but with trembling honesty. The willingness to step into the unknown without guarantees, to place one uncertain foot in front of the other when the path ahead dissolves into mist. It is the bravery of vulnerability, of letting yourself be seen without armor, of telling the truth about how much it hurts when silence has felt safer for so long. It is the determination to heal even when healing feels impossibly slow.

To grow even when growth aches. To transform even when the old self clings tightly, afraid of being left behind. This work asks everything of you, and yet it gives something back that nothing else can. It gives you yourself. The struggle is real, yes. Heavy. Demanding. Exhausting. But it is not impossible. Depression may walk beside you for a time, its shadow lengthening and shortening with the seasons, but it is not your forever.

It is not the author of your ending. It does not hold the final pen. There are moments of joy waiting for you, even if you cannot imagine them yet. Moments that arrive quietly, without fanfare, slipping into your life through ordinary cracks. Peace that settles softly, like light through curtains in the early morning. Flickers of happiness that surprise you, reminding you that life still knows how to reach you, that your heart still knows how to respond. There are people who care. People who understand. People who will sit with you in the dark without trying to rush you toward the light. And there are resources, too. Support groups where language is shared and shame loosens. Therapy that offers steadiness and perspective. Medication that eases the weight enough to allow breath. Self-help practices that give structure to days that feel unanchored.

Tools that do not erase your pain, but help you carry it until, slowly, it becomes lighter. You do not have to do this alone. You were never meant to. And even here, even now, in the middle of the struggle, your life is still unfolding. The story is still being written. New chapters are forming, even if you cannot yet read their titles. Your healing is still possible. Not perfect. Not linear. But real. And you are still, and always have been, deeply, undeniably worthy of it.

The Spectrum of Life

Depression may cast long, stretching shadows across the landscape of your life, but it is vital to remember this truth: life is not a single colour. It is a spectrum. A living, breathing blend of light and dark, joy and sorrow, strength and vulnerability woven together in constant motion. Life is not defined by the absence of depression, nor is it sustained by joy alone. It is shaped in the delicate, ongoing dance between both, in the way shadow gives contrast to light and depth to form. The shadows may still whisper at the edges. They may linger like dusk that refuses to fully fade, testing your resolve, brushing old fears with familiar hands. But they no longer hold the authority to dictate your entire experience. They are no longer the sky itself, only part of the horizon. You have learned how to see them without surrendering to them, how to carry their presence without letting them eclipse everything else.

As you continue forward, may you begin to lift the brush again. Tentatively at first. With curiosity rather than certainty. May you paint your canvas with new intention. Not erasing what came before, not denying the strokes laid down in darker seasons, but layering over them. Adding texture. Adding meaning. Allowing light to filter back in through the cracks, illuminating colours you have not yet named. Colours born not despite the struggle, but because of it. Each hue becomes a testament. Moments of joy rediscovered when you thought joy was gone for good. Growth earned through effort and endurance. And the quiet, unshakeable strength that emerges when vulnerability is no longer feared, but welcomed as part of what makes you whole. This is not a return to who you once were. It is an arrival into someone wider, more nuanced, more alive.

Your canvas will never be empty again. It will hold the full truth of your life. The pain you survived. The light you reclaimed. The resilience you discovered in yourself when you had every reason to doubt it. And as you keep painting, stroke by careful stroke, you may come to see this clearly at last: The shadows did not end your story. They taught you how to see the light. To embrace your shadows is not to surrender to them. It is to acknowledge their presence without allowing them to eclipse your worth. To stand beside what has hurt you and say, *I see you*, without bowing to it. This is the first courageous step toward reclaiming a life rich with possibility, hope, and lasting fulfilment. Not a life without darkness, but a life no longer ruled by it. Remember the light that once burned brightly within you.

It has not been extinguished. It has only been dimmed, muted by exhaustion, grief, and survival. Waiting patiently. Not demanding. Not forcing itself forward. Waiting for breath. For care. For kindness. Waiting for you to return to yourself with gentler hands. Through self-compassion that softens rather than criticizes, that speaks in reassurance instead of reprimand, that light begins to stir. Through professional support that steadies you when the ground feels unreliable, when your own footing feels uncertain, the flame finds shelter. Through daily acts of care, small and ordinary and profoundly brave, and through an unwavering commitment to your own well-being, something enduring begins to take shape. The light does not roar back to life. It returns quietly. Slowly. Gently. One small step at a time.

The journey may be long. It may be uneven and demanding, marked by pauses and recalibrations, by days that feel heavy and others that feel almost light. But the destination matters. A life infused with joy that feels earned. Hope that feels grounded. A renewed sense of self that is not fragile but deeply rooted in truth. That life is not a fantasy. It is a future shaped by patience. By courage. By your willingness to keep choosing yourself. And every step you take toward it, no matter how small, is already proof that you are on your way.

You are worthy of happiness. You are worthy of peace. You are worthy of a life lived fully, deeply, and vibrantly. Even now. Especially now. Let that truth settle somewhere beneath the noise, beyond the doubt that tries to argue otherwise. Let it exist without needing proof or permission. In the end, the journey back to joy and hope is not about banishing the shadow within or pretending it never existed. It is not about forcing light into every corner or demanding constant brightness from a human heart that was never meant to live that way. It is about learning to walk beside the shadow. To understand its shape. To soften its edges. To listen to what it has been trying, clumsily and painfully, to protect you from. And then, to weave it into the fabric of your life without allowing it to eclipse who you are.

This is the work of integration, not erasure. Of discovering how light and shadow can coexist on the same canvas, each giving depth and meaning to the other. Without shadow, light becomes flat. Without light, shadow becomes overwhelming. Together, they create texture. Dimension. Truth. This path asks you to learn a gentler kind of love. A love that does not demand perfection or constant progress. A love that makes room for cracks, scars, and unfinished places. A love that does not rush you toward a version of yourself that feels safer or more acceptable. It invites you to accept yourself exactly as you are in this moment. Not as a future self who has everything resolved, healed, and neatly packaged. But as you are now. Breathing. Trying. Showing up in the only ways you can.

It is about choosing to live an authentic life, one rooted in truth rather than performance. A life where masks are no longer mandatory. Where worth is not conditional. Where your inner world is allowed to be complex, contradictory, and real. And yes, it is a life that can still be meaningful, rich, and fulfilling, even in the presence of depression. Not despite it, but alongside it. A life where joy may arrive softly rather than loudly. Where hope may flicker rather than blaze. Where peace may come in moments rather than permanence. And still, it is a life worth living. Because you are not here to be flawless. You are here to be whole.

So, dear friend, if you have made it this far, I hope these words have wrapped around you like a quiet hand resting at the center of your back. Not pushing. Not pulling. Just there. Steady. Present. I hope they have offered comfort when the weight felt unbearable, hope when the path blurred beneath your feet, and a soft point of orientation when you felt lost inside yourself. Please remember this above all else: you are not alone.

And you are not a failure. You are strong in ways you may not yet recognize. Capable in ways depression has tried relentlessly to conceal from you. Deeply resilient, even on the days when fragility feels like the only truth you can touch. Strength does not always announce itself as confidence or certainty. Often, it shows up as endurance. As staying. As choosing to keep breathing when retreat would feel easier.

Keep moving forward. Even when the smallest step feels impossibly large. Even when progress looks like simply remaining present. Even when the voices of depression grow loud, persuasive, and familiar. Keep going. Progress does not need to be fast to be real. It does not need witnesses or applause. It does not need to look impressive from the outside. It only has to be yours. Measured by your capacity, your pace, your lived reality. Every step you take, no matter how tentative, is an act of quiet defiance against the darkness that once tried to convince you to disappear. Because in the end, it is not the destination that defines your healing. It is the courage it takes to keep walking. And it is the hope you carry, even when it flickers faintly in the dark, that becomes your compass. A small, persistent light guiding you forward. Toward a future that is not perfect, not pain-free, but brighter. Deeper. More honest. More fulfilling than you can yet imagine. Your story is still unfolding. You are still becoming. And there is more life ahead of you than the shadow ever wanted you to believe.

The Weight of the Fog – Emily's story: The Empty Chair

The empty chair stared back at me, a mute witness planted in the cluttered corner of my apartment, its stillness heavy with accusation. It felt less like furniture and more like a verdict already passed. A seat reserved for a version of myself who no longer showed up. Sunlight crept in through the window, a presence that would normally feel kind, even benevolent, but today it arrived sharp and unforgiving. It spilled across the peeling paint on the opposite wall, illuminating every crack, every imperfection, every place where time and neglect had left their mark. The room seemed to hold its breath under that light, as if being examined, interrogated, found wanting. Even the light conspired against me. It pointed out the life I was not living. The momentum I had misplaced somewhere along the way. The person I could not seem to become, no matter how often I promised myself I would try again tomorrow.

Dust motes drifted lazily in its path, indifferent to my paralysis, moving freely where I could not. The quiet pressed in, thick and intimate, wrapping around my chest until it felt difficult to draw a full breath. It was Tuesday. Or maybe Wednesday. The distinction no longer mattered. Days had begun to melt into one another, pooling together into a single, shapeless mass of gray time. Morning bled into afternoon. Afternoon dissolved into night. The calendar lost its authority. Time no longer moved forward; it merely accumulate I knew, in some distant, rational corner of my mind, that I should be at work. I knew there was a deadline breathing down my neck, a presentation waiting to be built, emails stacking up unanswered, calls going unreturned. I knew all of this the way one knows facts from a textbook. Abstract. Theoretical. Unattached to consequence. The knowledge existed, but it floated somewhere far above my body, disconnected from action, from urgency, from care.

The knowing carried no weight against the heaviness inside me. My limbs felt dense, leaden, as though gravity had doubled overnight. The idea of showering, of getting dressed, of opening my laptop felt impossible. Not difficult. Impossible. Like trying to lift a slab of concrete with bare, trembling hands. Each task loomed enormous, insurmountable, demanding energy I simply did not have. I sat there, suspended between intention and inertia, watching the light crawl slowly across the wall, marking time more faithfully than I could. The chair remained empty. The room remained silent. And inside that stillness, I felt myself shrinking, receding inward, wondering how something as simple as getting up had come to feel like the hardest thing I had ever tried to do.

Depression was not simply sadness. I understood that, at least on paper. I had read the articles, absorbed the awareness campaigns, nodded along to the language of self-care and resilience as though comprehension alone might grant protection. I had even been the one offering gentle reassurances to friends when they spoke about their own battles, repeating the well-worn phrases meant to soothe and steady, words passed hand to hand like talismans against pain. But knowing depression as a concept and living inside it were worlds apart. One remained distant and theoretical, something you could analyze, discuss, even empathize with from the safety of the outside. The other was visceral, suffocating, and intimate, an experience that did not wait to be understood before it claimed me.

It wrapped itself around my thoughts, my body, my sense of time, tightening quietly until everything narrowed. Hours stretched and collapsed without warning. Days lost their edges. Even the simplest acts, standing up, answering a message, beginning, felt unreachable, as though an invisible force had doubled the distance between intention and movement. The space between who I was and who I used to be widened into something vast and unbridgeable, a landscape I could still see but no longer cross. For me, depression was a suffocating blanket woven from despair, heavy with moisture and weight, thrown over my life without warning or mercy. It clung to my skin, damp and unyielding, seeping into every pore, muffling sound, muting colour, dulling the sharpness of the world until everything felt far away and unreal.

Laughter reached me as though underwater. Light arrived without warmth. Even my own thoughts sounded distant, slowed, distorted. It settled on my chest like a physical presence, a silent pressure that refused to lift, compressing my lungs and turning each breath into conscious effort rather than instinct. Inhale. Exhale. Each one measured, deliberate, as though my body had forgotten how to breathe without instruction. There was no panic, no dramatic gasp for air, just a steady, exhausting awareness of how much work it took to stay alive in my own skin. It was relentless. Insidious. A slow leak of vitality that drained joy from even the smallest moments, the taste of food, the comfort of familiarity, the promise hidden in routine, and left behind a hollow ache where feeling used to live. Nothing shattered all at once. There was no single breaking point to point to, no clear moment of collapse.

Just an ongoing erosion, quiet and patient, until one day I realized that what I had lost was not happiness alone, but my sense of ease within the world itself. The empty chair sat there, usually buried beneath laundry or stacks of half-read books, now bare and exposed in its stillness. Stripped of distraction, it felt less accidental and more deliberate, as if it had chosen this moment to be seen. Its emptiness stared back at me, heavy with implication. Accusing. It became a symbol of opportunity, of potential, of a life that still existed somewhere beyond the fog, waiting patiently for me to step back into it. A life that had not disappeared, only receded, hovering just out of reach. If only I could get up. If only I could move. But the distance between sitting and standing might as well have been a mountain range, jagged and insurmountable.

The effort required felt Herculean, the kind of labor reserved for mythic heroes, not for someone who struggled to summon the strength to brush their teeth in the morning. My body did not feel injured, yet it refused to respond, as though gravity had quietly increased while I wasn't paying attention. My will strained against my limbs, and still, nothing happened. I wasn't sad in the way people expect sadness to look. I wasn't crying or wailing or visibly breaking apart. There were no dramatic sobs to signal distress, no outward signs that something was wrong. Instead, I was numb. A vast, hollow void had opened inside me, swallowing everything whole. My ambition disappeared first. Then my enthusiasm. Then my hopes, one by one, slipping away so quietly it felt as if they had never existed at all. There was no grief loud enough to name the loss, only a dull awareness that something essential was missing.

What remained was not pain sharp enough to scream. It was an absence. A vacancy so complete it felt unbearable. A silence that pressed in on all sides, louder than noise, heavier than sorrow. I could still function, still exist, still breathe, but it felt mechanical, like moving through the world behind thick glass. Present, but unreachable. This was not something I could simply shake off or think my way out of. It wasn't a mood. It wasn't a bad day. It wasn't a temporary slump waiting to be conquered by positive thinking or sheer determination. It was a pervasive condition, a relentless current flowing beneath the surface of my life, quietly and persistently pulling me farther from shore. I could feel the distance growing, even as I remained seated in the same place, watching the chair, the light, the room, and wondering how something so invisible could exert such a powerful hold.

To truly understand the depths of my story, you must first understand what depression is, and what it is not. It is not a bad day. Not a passing sadness. Not a mood that lifts with enough sleep, discipline, or positive thinking.

It is not something you can reason with or outpace through effort alone. It is a pervasive condition, a quiet distortion that bends perception and settles into the body, altering the way you think, feel, and move through the world. It changes the texture of reality itself. Clinical depression makes even the simplest acts feel monumental, as though gravity has subtly increased while no one was watching. Lifting a hand. Forming a sentence. Beginning a task. Each movement feels weighted, resisted, as if you are pushing through invisible water. It whispers lies in the quiet spaces, in the pauses between thoughts, telling you that you are unworthy, unnecessary, easily forgotten.

That the world would not notice your absence. That your presence is an inconvenience rather than a gift. These thoughts do not arrive as intruders. They sound like truth. Depression thrives in silence. It feeds on isolation. And I was drowning in solitude. I scrolled through my phone in a numb, automatic trance, my thumb moving without intention, not searching for connection so much as relief. Distraction, however brief. Escape, however shallow. Social media became a relentless barrage of curated happiness, a polished gallery of lives seemingly untouched by despair. Friends laughed on sun-drenched vacations, bodies relaxed, smiles effortless. Colleagues celebrated promotions and milestones, achievements neatly framed and applauded. Couples cradled newborns, glowing with promise and possibility, life unfolding exactly as it was supposed to.

Each image landed like a pinprick against my skin. Small. Almost negligible on its own. But cumulative. With every swipe, the sensation deepened, piercing a little further beneath the surface. It wasn't envy exactly. I did not want their lives. I simply could not recognize my own in the world being presented to me. It was alienation. A growing, hollow realization that I had somehow slipped out of rhythm with life itself, fallen behind an invisible beat everyone else seemed to hear. The more I scrolled, the more distant I felt. As if I were watching humanity through glass, separated by an unspoken barrier I could not name or cross. Life went on. People moved forward. And I remained suspended, untethered, quietly unraveling in the space between who I was expected to be and who I no longer knew how to be at all.

I knew, intellectually, that I wasn't alone. I knew my friends cared. I knew support existed somewhere beyond the cold glass screen glowing in my hand. I knew these things the way one knows facts memorized long ago, distant and detached. But knowing and reaching are not the same thing. Knowing lives in the mind. Reaching requires the body, the voice, the vulnerable act of stepping forward when every instinct tells you to retreat. The thought of explaining myself felt impossible. How do you give language to something shapeless, formless, all-consuming? How do you describe the sensation of being trapped inside a body that no longer feels like home, a body that has become foreign territory overnight?

How do you articulate an exhaustion so deep it settles into your bones, so complete it presses down on your spirit and makes even hope feel heavy, like another burden to carry? The words hovered, then refused to come. They rose toward my mouth only to lodge themselves in my throat, dense and immovable, like stones I couldn't swallow and couldn't spit out. Each attempt to speak felt futile, embarrassing, inadequate. I imagined myself trying to explain and hearing the confusion in the listener's silence, the unspoken "*I don't get it*", and shame closed in tighter around my chest. So I stayed silent. I sank further inward, folding myself smaller and smaller, alone with a pain I did not yet know how to name. Silence became both shield and sentence. And when the effort to remain present grew too great, I did what I had learned to do best.

I closed my eyes and retreated inward, slipping back into the fog that had become both refuge and prison. That fog was a master manipulator. A skilled liar wearing the voice of truth. It spoke softly, convincingly. It told me I was worthless. That I was a burden people tolerated rather than chose. That my existence required explanation and apology. It whispered that no one would ever understand, that trying to explain myself would only expose how broken I truly was. It painted vulnerability as humiliation and connection as risk. It insisted that solitude was safer.

That isolation was protection. That escape was impossible anyway, so why bother reaching for the door? And wrapped in that fog, lulled by its false certainty, I believed it.

I stayed still. I stayed quiet. I stayed trapped in a loneliness that felt self-inflicted, even as it slowly tightened its grip, convincing me that silence was the only way to survive, even while it was the very thing that was pulling me under. The fog stayed close, an unwelcome shadow stitched to my heels, faithful in its cruelty. It dulled every edge of clarity, blunted thought and feeling alike, smothered hope before it could even think to flicker. Any sense of direction dissolved inside it. Meaning thinned, then vanished. I moved through my days in the most technical sense. I breathed. I ate. I slept. But I did so without orientation, without a compass, without light. Existence became mechanical, stripped of intention, as though I were following instructions written in a language I no longer understood.

Inside that fog, time lost its shape. Minutes stretched into hours that collapsed into one another, days bleeding together until calendars became irrelevant. Morning and night felt interchangeable, distinguished only by the quality of the light leaking through the window. Purpose dissolved entirely. The future stopped arriving. The past felt unreachable. There was only this suspended middle space, thick and airless, where nothing began and nothing ended. It felt like a prison I had somehow built myself, brick by invisible brick, thought by corrosive thought, belief by quiet belief. Each lie I accepted, each moment of silence, each retreat inward became mortar. Over time, the walls grew high and seamless. I could no longer remember where the entrance had been, let alone where I might have dropped the key.

I wasn't sure when construction had started. Only that I was inside now, pacing familiar corners, convinced there was no exit. And still, the empty chair remained. It sat there, unmoving, unblinking, its presence louder than any voice. A silent witness. A quiet accusation. It asked nothing and said everything. It held the shape of possibility, the outline of a life waiting just beyond reach. It seemed to say, "*You could sit here. You could begin here*". And yet the distance between me and that chair felt immeasurable, not measured in steps, but in strength I no longer trusted myself to possess. So I stayed where I was. Huddled on the edge of the bed, folded inward like something trying to protect its most fragile center. My shoulders curved forward. My breath stayed shallow. I wrapped myself tighter and tighter inside the suffocating weight of the fog, unsure of my own intentions. Unsure whether I was hiding from the world, or whether, piece by quiet piece, I was slowly disappearing inside myself.

The Cracks Begin to Show

The performance was beginning to fray at the edges, threads loosening where no one was meant to look. Holding the mask in place took more effort than I had left, like gripping a cracked facade with trembling hands, hoping it wouldn't collapse while I was still standing behind it. At work, I became fluent in avoidance, a virtuoso of deflection, moving through my days with practiced choreography. I manufactured enthusiasm where none existed, pasted brightness over exhaustion, carefully smoothing the surface as fissures spread quietly beneath it. I perfected the quick exchange, the hollow pleasantry, the efficient smile designed to end conversations before they could drift anywhere dangerous, anywhere honest. Real engagement felt like stepping into a spotlight with no script and no rehearsal, my lines stripped away, my voice exposed. I could not risk being seen without the armor of performance.

Sarah noticed. Of course she did. She always had. She had been my advocate for years, the one who believed in my ideas even when I couldn't bear to believe in myself, the one who saw potential where I saw only insufficiency. Lately, her gaze lingered a beat too long. Concern hovered just beneath the surface of her professionalism, soft but unmistakable. She asked if I was alright. If everything was okay. Simple questions, gently offered, but they landed heavy, like stones dropped straight into my chest, knocking the breath from me. I answered the way I always did. A thin smile. A rehearsed dismissal. Something vague about being "under the weather," as if this was a passing flu instead of a slow unravelling. Each lie slid easily from my mouth, but none of them left cleanly. Each one fractured something inside me, splintering what little sense of integrity I had left, eroding my connection to myself grain by grain.

With every deflection, the distance widened between who I was pretending to be and who I actually was, until even I could feel how thin the bridge between them had become. The evenings were far worse. When the door closed behind me and the apartment sealed itself in silence, the noise inside my head surged forward, rushing to occupy every empty inch of space. The walls felt like they were listening. The shadows leaned closer, conspiratorial. The voices sharpened, grew bolder, more persuasive in the dark, as if night itself gave them permission to speak freely. I tried to outrun them the only ways I knew how, with movies playing to rooms that didn't watch back, with books whose words slipped through my fingers before they could take root, with any distraction that promised escape.

But nothing held its shape. Stories blurred. Scenes lost coherence. Characters spoke, but their lives felt impossibly distant, unreal. Pleasure drained out of everything, leaving behind a flat, aching dissatisfaction, the hollow echo of enjoyment rather than the thing itself. The fog always returned. It crept back in quietly, like a tide reclaiming the shore, seeping into every corner of the room, dulling what should have soothed me, turning rest into another form of labor. Even stillness felt heavy. Even lying down required effort. And night after night, I sat there amid half-finished distractions, glowing screens, abandoned pages, paused scenes, wondering how something so quiet could feel so unbearably loud. Sometimes I would lie there, eyes fixed on the ceiling as though it might finally offer an answer, as though the cracks and shadows above me might rearrange themselves into meaning.

My mind spun on an endless, merciless carousel of what ifs, each one dragging the next into motion. "What if I hadn't taken that job? What if I hadn't walked away from David? What if I hadn't loosened my grip on the dreams that once burned so brightly, they lit my entire horizon?" Each question burrowed deeper, spiraling into the next, a recursive loop with no exit and no mercy. The past became a minefield I traversed barefoot, replaying every step, every choice, every moment I believed I had failed to choose correctly. Memories detonated on contact, exploding into regret, guilt, and longing. There was no safe path through it, no place to stand without something collapsing beneath me. And so I lay there, suspended between what had been and what no longer felt possible, listening to the relentless churn of my own thoughts, trapped in a night that offered no rest and no forgetting.

Every choice I'd ever made began to feel like evidence in a case being built relentlessly against me, a meticulous ledger of perceived failures I could not stop rereading. Each decision was cross-examined, each misstep underlined in red, as if my life were on trial and I was both the accused and the unforgiving judge. And the future, if it existed at all, rose before me like a solid wall, tall and merciless, blocking any view beyond it. No windows. No cracks. No hint of what might come next. Just an unyielding surface that sealed off hope, motion, possibility, leaving me pressed up against it, breath shallow, directionless. Sleep, when it came, offered no sanctuary. It fractured the way everything else did, splintering into shallow stretches and abrupt awakenings. My dreams were jagged and uneasy, stitched together from anxiety and a constant, nameless dread, as if disaster hovered just beyond the frame, waiting for the precise moment to strike. Even unconsciousness could not grant me peace.

I woke already exhausted, my body weighted as though gravity had doubled overnight, my mind thick with fog, heavy and unyielding. It felt as though I had been running all night without moving an inch, expending energy without progress, effort without relief. Rest never reached me. It lingered just beyond my grasp, hovering like a mirage, another thing promised but perpetually withheld. My appetite disappeared quietly, without drama or announcement. Hunger dulled into something abstract, a distant concept rather than a physical signal. Food lost its language of comfort and pleasure, its ability to soothe or delight, and became purely functional, another task on an ever-growing list of things that required effort I no longer possessed. I ate because I knew I should, because logic insisted my body needed fuel, forcing down whatever was quickest and least demanding.

Not to nourish myself, not to enjoy, but simply to silence the hollow ache gnawing at my stomach long enough to move on. Even that small act felt monumental, another reminder of how much energy it took just to exist. Gradually, almost without my consent, I began to disappear from my own life. Not all at once, not dramatically, but in small, quiet erasures. Showers became optional, then negotiable, then forgettable. Days slipped past one another without distinction as I wore the same clothes again and again, the fabric growing heavy with neglect, carrying the faint scent of resignation. Mirrors turned accusatory, too honest, so I learned to pass them without looking, as if avoiding my reflection might delay the reckoning of who I was becoming. Caring felt extravagant, an indulgence reserved for a version of myself I could no longer reach.

The fog was no longer just visiting. It was settling in, unpacking itself with deliberate patience, thickening until it softened every edge of my world. It blurred boundaries, erased definition, until I could no longer tell where I ended and the darkness began. It moved with quiet efficiency, methodically dismantling the parts of me that once felt human, vibrant, alive. Ambition. Curiosity. Pleasure. They vanished one by one, not ripped away, but gently smothered, until all that remained was survival, stripped down to its barest function. Even that felt fragile. Precarious. I carried a quiet, unspoken fear that one day I might not even manage that. And then, inevitably, the delicate balance collapsed. Not with a crash, but with a missed step. A crucial deadline slipped past me, not out of defiance or carelessness, but because it simply ceased to exist in my mind. The date dissolved. The urgency evaporated.

When I finally opened my laptop, the presentation I was meant to deliver sat unfinished, its blank slides glaring back at me like an indictment. A row of white rectangles, empty and unforgiving, a digital monument to my growing unraveling. In that moment, it was impossible to deny what I had been avoiding. The fog had not just surrounded my life. It had begun to consume it. When Sarah called me into her office, my stomach dropped as if the floor had quietly given way beneath my feet. The walk down the corridor felt unreal, my body moving on instinct while my mind lagged somewhere far behind. Her voice, when she spoke, was soft and measured, carefully composed, but her eyes betrayed her. They held a depth of concern that cut clean through my carefully maintained façade, slipping past every practiced smile and professional deflection I had perfected.

"Emily," she said gently, my name landing with an unexpected tenderness, "I'm worried about you. You haven't seemed like yourself lately. Is everything alright?" Something inside me gave way. The dam I had reinforced for months finally cracked. Tears surged up without warning, hot and urgent, blurring the room until her face shimmered like a reflection seen through water. The office, the desk, the carefully arranged order of it all distorted and drifted, as though I were sinking beneath the surface of myself. "I, - I, - I don't know," I whispered. The words barely escaped my lips, fragile and uncertain, as if speaking them aloud might cause everything I was holding together to collapse entirely. Naming the confusion felt dangerous, like loosening a final thread.

Sarah leaned forward, closing the distance between us, her chair scraping softly against the floor. She reached across the desk and placed her hand lightly over mine. The gesture was small, unremarkable by most standards, yet it landed with immense weight. It was human. Warm. Grounding. A quiet reminder that I was not alone in that moment, that I was still tethered to something solid. "You can talk to me," she said, her voice steady, unhurried. "If there's anything I can do to help, I want to." And in that simple offer, something shifted. Not relief. Not resolution. But a hairline fracture in the isolation I had been living inside. A first breath of air seeping into a place that had been sealed shut for far too long.

In that moment, I wanted to unload everything. I wanted to pour myself out there on her desk, to spill the truth about the fog that clung to me, the relentless despair, the suffocating loneliness that followed me everywhere like a shadow stitched to my heels. I wanted to tell her how lost I felt inside my own life, how each day felt like wading through wet cement, every step an effort, every movement borrowed from a strength I no longer possessed. The words crowded my chest, urgent and aching to be released. But they never made it out. They rose, then lodged themselves in my throat, heavy and immovable, tangled in a web of fear. Fear of judgment. Fear of being diminished in her eyes. Fear of being labeled weak, broken, incapable. Fear that once spoken aloud, the truth would calcify into something permanent, something I could never take back.

So instead, I did what I had learned to do best. I gathered myself like loose papers scattered by a sudden wind. I smoothed the cracks. I pulled the mask back into place and forced a smile that felt foreign, ill-fitting, almost grotesque on my face. "I'm just stressed," I said lightly, the lie slipping out with practiced ease. "There's a lot going on. I'll be fine." Sarah didn't look convinced. Her eyes lingered on me for a moment longer than necessary, searching, as if she could sense the truth hovering just beneath my carefully chosen words. There was something unspoken in that pause, a quiet invitation I did not know how to accept. Still, she let it go. She suggested I take some time off. Encouraged me to rest. To take care of myself. Her concern was genuine, her tone kind, but it skimmed the surface of a depth I hadn't dared to reveal.

I thanked her. I nodded. I walked out of her office with measured steps, carrying a heavier loneliness than the one I'd brought in. The chance to reach out, to be honest, to ask for help had slipped quietly through my fingers, and I hadn't even fought to hold onto it. And as the door closed behind me, the silence rushed back in, thick and familiar, sealing me once more inside myself. Back in my apartment, the silence swallowed me whole. It closed around me the moment the door clicked shut, thick and airless, as if the room had been holding its breath, waiting for my return. The empty chair still waited in the corner, unchanged and yet somehow more imposing, as though it had grown while I was gone. It loomed now like a silent judge, patient and unmoving, bearing witness to everything I hadn't said, everything I hadn't dared to face.

It held the weight of my unshed truths, the words I had carried all the way home only to set down again in shame. The fog thickened, darkened, coiling tighter around my thoughts, my breath, my sense of self. It crept into the spaces between seconds, blurring the edges of time, pressing in until the room felt smaller than it was, until even my own body felt like a narrowing corridor with no exit. Each inhale felt borrowed. Each exhale felt like surrender. I sank into stillness, trapped inside that haze, the walls closing in from every direction. Not dramatically. Not all at once. But slowly, inevitably, the way night settles over a landscape without asking permission. And for the first time, something in me faltered. I wasn't just tired. I wasn't just overwhelmed. I was lost.

I searched my mind for the shape of escape, for a memory of how to move forward, how to reach for help, how to believe there was something beyond this moment. But the fog had erased the map. I could no longer remember what freedom looked like, only that it had once existed somewhere outside this room, outside this version of myself. The chair remained. The silence pressed closer. And I sat there, suspended between knowing I could not stay and fearing I no longer knew how to leave.

The Weight of Unseen Chains: A Journey Through Depression – A Silent Scream

The smile I wore that night felt foreign, poorly fitted, stretched across my face like a borrowed mask that did not belong to me. It tugged at my cheeks, aching with effort, a careful construction designed to shield the world from the darkness gnawing steadily at my insides. Every muscle involved in that smile felt overworked, strained, as though I were holding something fragile in place that threatened to collapse at the slightest release. Laughter spilled freely around me at Sarah's birthday party, bright and alive, a sound meant to be contagious. It rang out in bursts and crescendos, bouncing off walls, filling glasses, filling space. Instead of lifting me, it clashed painfully with the heavy quiet in my mind. The noise pressed against something hollow inside me, amplifying the absence rather than easing it.

Everyone was there, celebrating, connecting, inhabiting their lives with an ease that felt almost surreal. They leaned into one another, voices overlapping, bodies relaxed, joy moving between them like a shared language. And I hovered on the edges, present in body but absent in spirit, a ghost drifting through the room, muted by a relentless, unseen force that kept me just out of reach of everything unfolding around me. I watched conversations as if through thick glass, slightly distorted, dulled at the edges. I nodded at the right moments. Smiled when expected. Laughed softly when laughter seemed required. I played my part convincingly enough that no one questioned my presence. No one could see the chains tightening beneath my skin, the invisible restraints cinching closer with every exchanged pleasantry, every polite response.

They bound my chest, my thoughts, my breath, holding me in place while life continued to move freely around me. When the night finally thinned, when the last guest drifted out into the dark and the echoes of laughter faded into memory, the illusion fell away. The remains of celebration lay scattered like fallen confetti across the floor, half-empty glasses, smudged fingerprints, chairs slightly askew, evidence of joy that had already moved on without me. I stood alone in the quiet living room, the sudden stillness pressing in, loud and absolute, as though the silence itself had weight. The mask slipped away at last, collapsing under its own effort, and what remained was the familiar hollow ache. Deep. Aching. Inescapable. It spread through me slowly, deliberately, settling into every open space.

It felt like gravity had increased without warning, a crushing pressure that drained the color from everything it touched, suffocating joy until only a grey, desolate landscape remained. Even the air felt heavier, thicker, harder to draw in fully. This was the part no one saw. This was the truth hidden behind polite smiles and practiced laughter, behind my careful performance of normalcy. This was the cost of wearing the mask. My secret. My silent scream. My invisible burden. This was depression.

The Greyness Descends

It started subtly, the way fog does when it first drifts in from the edges of a landscape, almost courteous in its arrival. A soft dulling of enthusiasm. A barely perceptible shift in how I moved through the world. Colours lost their saturation, as if someone had turned down the contrast on my life. Music, once capable of lifting me without effort, fell flat, its notes landing without resonance. The things that had always anchored me, painting, hiking, and spending time with friends, began to feel strangely burdensome, less like sources of nourishment and more like obligations I dragged myself through on borrowed energy. At first, I explained it away. I always did. Life was demanding. I was working long hours in a job that asked for everything and gave little back. I was juggling responsibilities, deadlines, and expectations, trying to keep pace with a world that never seemed to slow down. "Everyone feels overwhelmed sometimes, don't they?"

I told myself this was normal. A rough patch. A temporary dip, a slump I would eventually pull myself out of. Something I would muscle my way through with enough discipline and grit. But the dip did not lift. The "slump" persisted. The fog did not burn off. Weeks slipped into months, and the greyness thickened, settling deeper into my bones. What I felt was no longer simple tiredness or the fatigue of a full calendar. It was a profound, debilitating lack of motivation, a heaviness that resisted every attempt to push against it. Getting out of bed each morning became a monumental task, as though gravity itself had intensified overnight. Brushing my teeth felt like climbing a mountain with no summit in sight. Even the smallest decisions, what to eat for breakfast, what to wear, whether to answer a message, expanded into agonizing dilemmas, each one demanding a level of effort I no longer seemed to possess. The fog was no longer passing through. It was moving in.

Sleep offered no escape. Night did not cradle me; it interrogated me. I lay suspended in the dark, trapped in endless cycles of restless tossing and turning, my body exhausted yet my mind relentlessly awake. Thoughts raced without form or resolution, anxieties circling like predators I could sense but not name. They had no clear faces, no tidy explanations, only an oppressive urgency that refused to let me rest. And when I finally slipped into sleep, it was shallow and unforgiving. Nightmares threaded themselves through my dreams, sharp-edged and disorienting, pulling me awake again and again until morning arrived not as relief, but as another burden to shoulder. I woke more depleted than when I had closed my eyes, as if sleep itself had taken something from me rather than restored it.

The joy had leached out of everything. Not dramatically, not all at once, but steadily, as though colour were draining from the world drop by drop. Food lost its language of comfort and pleasure, turning bland and textureless in my mouth. Music, once a refuge, sounded discordant and distant, each note missing its mark. Even sunshine felt wrong, too bright, too insistent, an unwelcome spotlight exposing how disconnected I felt from the life it illuminated. Light no longer warmed me; it accused me. I began to withdraw, quietly at first. Plans were cancelled with flimsy excuses. Messages went unanswered. Invitations sat untouched until they expired on their own. The thought of socializing, of holding the mask in place, of summoning enthusiasm I no longer had, felt utterly exhausting. Pretending required more energy than I possessed.

Isolation crept in not as a conscious choice, but as a necessity, a way to conserve what little strength remained. "Are you okay, Emily? You seem different," my mother asked during one of our infrequent phone calls. Her concern slipped gently through the receiver, soft and familiar, and for a moment it nearly undid me. "I'm fine, Mom," I replied, my voice flat, brittle around the edges. "Just tired. Work's been crazy." I hated the lie even as it left my mouth. It tasted sour, heavy with guilt. But the thought of trying to explain the tangled mess inside my head felt overwhelming. How could I give shape to something so amorphous, so consuming? How could I make her understand the exhaustion that lived in my bones, the fog that clouded every thought, the weight of the unseen chains that held me captive? I didn't even understand it myself. So I stayed silent. And in that silence, the greyness settled deeper still, tightening its grip, convincing me that this was simply how life was now, and that escape was something meant for other people.

The Mask Cracks

The effort of maintaining the *I*, that carefully curated version of myself, was becoming unbearable. Each morning, I stepped into it like ill-fitting armor, heavy and unforgiving, knowing it would chafe long before the day was done. Work became a stage with no intermission, no quiet corner to step into and breathe. I smiled on cue, nodded at the appropriate moments, stitched myself neatly into conversations, and mimicked productivity with practiced precision. From the outside, I looked intact. Capable. Present. But behind the mask, my mind was in constant freefall. A relentless storm of self-doubt and despair collided without pause, thoughts crashing into one another like debris caught in violent wind. There was no stillness, no ground beneath my feet. I felt like an imposter inhabiting my own life, a fraud dressed in competence, reciting lines I no longer believed in. I moved through my days pretending to be a functioning human being while something vital inside me quietly collapsed, folding in on itself without sound or spectacle.

And slowly, inevitably, the cracks began to show. My performance faltered. Careless mistakes crept into my work like hairline fractures spreading across glass, invisible at first, then impossible to ignore. Deadlines slipped through my fingers as though time itself had become porous. Concentration dissolved the moment I tried to grasp it, my thoughts scattering like startled birds before I could gather them into anything coherent. Tasks that once felt effortless now demanded monumental energy, the kind of effort reserved for emergencies, not everyday survival. Each small failure felt magnified, feeding the storm inside me, reinforcing the lie that I was unraveling because I was incapable, not because I was ill. And so I worked harder to hold the mask in place, unaware that the very act of pretending was draining what little strength I had left, hastening the collapse I was so desperately trying to hide.

My boss, normally steady, kind, and unflinchingly supportive, began to notice the fissures I had worked so hard to conceal. During a meeting, she paused mid-sentence, the room holding its breath with her. Her expression softened, not with suspicion, but with concern that searched rather than accused. "Emily, is everything alright?" she asked gently. "You haven't seemed yourself lately. Is there anything I can do to help?" Her concern struck me harder than criticism ever could. It landed like a sudden blow to the chest, knocking the breath from my lungs, leaving me momentarily weightless and exposed. In that instant, the dam inside me trembled. I felt it strain, buckling beneath the pressure of everything I had been holding back. I wanted to dissolve into tears, to let them come hot and honest, to spill the truth I had been carrying alone for far too long.

I wanted to finally say the words that had been clawing at my ribs: *"I'm not okay."* I wanted to ask for help. To admit that I was drowning and had been for some time. But the words rose only as far as my throat and died there, strangled by fear. Fear of judgment. Fear of being seen as weak, incapable, unfit. Fear of confirming what the voice inside me had been whispering relentlessly: that I was failing, that I did not belong here, that I was already slipping beyond repair. So I swallowed everything back down. I gathered the fragments of myself and rebuilt the mask once more, pressing it into place with trembling hands. I carried on, silently, even as it continued to fracture under the weight of what I could no longer hold.

"I'm fine," I mumbled, my eyes dropping to the carpet as though the pattern there might save me, anchor me, offer somewhere safe to disappear. "Just a bit stressed. I'll catch up." The words tasted thin and hollow even as I spoke them, brittle with dishonesty. She studied me for a moment longer, scepticism flickering briefly across her face, an unspoken understanding hovering between us. But she didn't push. Mercy, perhaps. Or uncertainty. Or the quiet recognition that something deeper was at play. I nodded, thanked her, and walked out of her office on legs that barely felt like mine, each step carrying me further into the silence I was too afraid to break. The moment the door closed behind me, the dam I had so meticulously reinforced finally surrendered. Not with a crack, but with a collapse.

Emotion surged through the fractures, violent and unstoppable, a flood I could no longer outrun. I barely made it to the bathroom before my body gave in, as if it had been waiting for permission to fall apart. The tears came hot and fast, burning their way down my face in utter silence, my reflection blurring until I could no longer recognize myself. I locked myself into a stall and slid down against the door, my spine pressing into cold metal, my shoulders shaking as sobs tore through me unchecked. I buried my face in my hands, trying to quiet the sound of my own breaking, while the weight of my secret bore down like a physical force. Every breath felt dense, laborious. Every heartbeat thudded with shame, loud and unforgiving, as though it were announcing my failure to the world. I had never felt so exposed and yet so utterly unseen.

I left work early that day, slipping out without explanation, unable to endure another second of pretending, another hour beneath fluorescent lights that hummed with expectation. The world outside felt distant and unreal as I moved through it, my body on autopilot, my mind hollowed out by exhaustion. When I reached home, I didn't bother to change, tidy, or think. I crawled straight into bed fully clothed, pulled the covers over my head, and disappeared into the small, enclosed darkness. There, wrapped in shadow, I finally let go. I didn't have to perform. I didn't have to smile. I didn't have to explain myself or justify my existence. The absence of light felt like mercy, a temporary shelter from the relentless demand to be okay.

In that cocoon of fabric and darkness, I allowed myself to unravel, breathing through the ache, letting the tears soak into the pillow. For a brief moment, hidden from the world, I wasn't strong or capable or composed. I was simply human. And that, at last, was enough. But even in the dark, I was not alone. The voices came with me, loyal in the cruelest way, settling beside me as faithfully as breath. They slipped through the quiet and took advantage of it, whispering and hissing until the silence itself seemed to speak. *"You're worthless. You're a failure. No one cares about you."* Each thought landed like a blow to an already bruised body, striking with precision, amplifying every fear, every insecurity I had spent years disguising behind competence and composure.

They knew exactly where to aim. They dredged up old wounds, replayed past mistakes, and rewrote neutral moments into evidence of my inadequacy. The darkness gave them room to echo, and they filled it completely, a relentless chorus with no pause, no mercy. I curled tighter beneath the covers, as if fabric could shield me from what lived inside my own head, but there was no hiding from a voice that wore my own tone. The mask had cracked. Now it was splintering, fragments breaking away faster than I could gather them, scattering across the floor of my inner world. The illusion of normalcy I had built so carefully was collapsing in on itself, and beneath it stood a truth I could no longer look away from. I was exhausted. I was unraveling. I was not okay.

I hovered there, suspended between endurance and collapse, balanced on a thin, trembling line. One side promised more of the same, more pretending, more silent suffocation. The other was terrifying in its uncertainty, its exposure, its risk. And somewhere deep inside me, beneath the noise and the fear and the self-reproach, a quiet clarity surfaced, cold and undeniable. I couldn't keep living this way much longer. The realization did not arrive with drama or urgency. It settled slowly, heavily, like nightfall you don't notice until the sky has already gone dark. It was not a plan or a decision. It was an understanding. A recognition that something had to change, because continuing as I was meant disappearing entirely. And as I lay there, shaking beneath the weight of my own thoughts, I sensed that I was standing at a threshold. I didn't yet know what lay beyond it. Only that staying where I was, was no longer survivable.

Lost in the Labyrinth

The days no longer arrived cleanly or distinctly. They seeped into one another, bleeding weeks into weeks, each one heavier than the last, as if time itself had grown weary of carrying me forward. Morning no longer felt like a beginning; it was merely another continuation of the same ache. I stopped going to work one quiet lie at a time, feigning illness because the truth felt too fragile, too exposed to survive outside my chest. Each excuse stacked atop the last, a shaky scaffolding holding up my disappearance. Guilt gnawed relentlessly at the edges of my thoughts, sharp and persistent, but it was eclipsed by something stronger, something more paralyzing: the unbearable weight of being seen. The idea of facing my colleagues, of meeting their eyes, of answering questions I didn't yet have language for, felt impossible.

"What would I say when they asked how I was? How could I explain a collapse that had no single cause, no neat explanation?" So I chose invisibility. I slipped quietly out of view, retreating from the world before it could ask anything of me. My apartment closed in around me, its walls tightening like a slow, deliberate fist. It became less a home and more a cell, familiar yet confining, heavy with stillness. I rarely crossed the threshold. Days were spent curled beneath the covers, folded inward like a creature trying to protect what little warmth remained. I wandered the twisting corridors of my own mind, looping through the same thoughts until they lost meaning, until everything blurred into a low, constant hum of despair.

Basic rituals fell away without protest. I stopped showering. Stopped eating real meals. Food became incidental, something to silence hunger rather than nourish life. I stopped caring whether it was morning or night, sunlight or darkness. Time dissolved into an indistinguishable haze. And slowly, frighteningly, I stopped caring about anything at all. The mirror became a stranger I avoided, its reflection unfamiliar and vaguely accusatory. My body felt distant, unreal, like something I inhabited only out of obligation rather than ownership. I moved it, when necessary, fed it when I remembered, carried it through the day as one might carry an object they no longer recognize as theirs. I was still breathing. Still existing. But life had narrowed to the smallest possible footprint, and even that felt unbearably heavy.

Beyond the window, life continued without me. Cars passed in steady rhythms. Strangers crossed the street mid-laughter, arms swinging, voices rising and falling with ease. The world moved in full color, a vibrant tapestry unfolding just out of reach, something I could see clearly but no longer touch. It felt unreal, like watching someone else's life through thick glass, close enough to recognize yet impossibly distant, as though I had been quietly removed from the frame while the scene carried on. My phone buzzed on the bedside table, again and again, its small insistence puncturing the stillness. Messages stacked up from friends. From family. *"Are you okay? I'm here. Please let me know."*

Each vibration felt like a demand I could not meet, a reminder of a world I no longer knew how to re-enter. I turned the screen face down, pressing it into silence. I didn't want to talk. I didn't want to explain. I didn't want to exist loudly enough to be noticed. I just wanted to disappear into the quiet, to become small enough that nothing could ask anything of me. One evening, stretched flat beneath the dark, staring at the ceiling as if it might finally offer an answer, a thought drifted in. Not dramatic. Not frantic. Quiet. Cold. Precise. "*Maybe it would be better if I just wasn't here anymore.*" It landed with a chill that ran through me, sharp and unmistakable, as though something inside me had been named aloud for the first time.

The thought didn't scream. It didn't plead or panic. It simply existed, settling into the silence like a dark seed pressed into the fertile soil of my despair. Terrifying, yes. Dangerous. Destructive. And yet, horrifyingly, it carried with it a strange sense of relief. A deceptive calm. In that imagined absence, there was rest. An end to the relentless ache. A release from the exhausting labor of staying, of breathing through pain, of holding myself together when everything inside me had already come undone. It felt less like wanting to die and more like wanting the suffering to stop, like longing for an exit from a room that had been slowly filling with smoke.

I lay there, frozen beneath the weight of that realization, knowing I had crossed an invisible threshold. The world outside the window still moved. Messages still waited. Life still called my name. But inside me, something fragile and dangerous had taken root, and I understood, with a clarity that frightened me, just how close I was to vanishing completely.

I recoiled from it instinctively, as though the thought itself had teeth. Fear surged through my chest, sharp and immediate, my heart slamming against my ribs in protest. "*No. Not that.*" The words rang inside me like a command, desperate and panicked, a last reflex of self-preservation. I tried to shove the thought away, to bury it beneath denial and horror, to pretend it had never surfaced at all. But it was already there. It did not argue. It did not advance. It simply lingered, quiet and watchful, a grim marker planted in the landscape of my mind. Proof of how far I had fallen. Evidence of how close I now stood to an edge I had never meant to approach, never even imagined myself capable of seeing. Its presence was not loud, but it was undeniable, a cold awareness settling into my bones.

I was lost inside the labyrinth of depression, corridors looping endlessly back into themselves, each turn returning me to the same familiar despair. The walls were high and smooth, offering no handholds, no windows, no clues. I could not remember where I had entered, and I could not see a way out. Every path felt like an illusion, every choice like another dead end. The air inside that maze was thick and stale, heavy with exhaustion and doubt, and I moved through it slowly, disoriented, unsure whether forward motion even existed anymore.

And in that moment, what frightened me most was not simply that I couldn't find my way out. It was the darker, more unsettling realization whispering beneath the fear. A realization I did not want to name. That somewhere along the way, beneath the weight of the fog and the endless effort of surviving, I had begun to lose my grip on the desire to escape at all. I stood there, suspended in that terrible in-between, knowing I had reached a place where indifference had begun to rival hope. Where the edge no longer looked sharp, but strangely quiet. And the silence of that realization echoed louder than any scream, marking the moment I understood just how deeply the greyness had claimed me.

The Story

Beyond the glass, the world lay washed in muted greys, as though the sky itself had conspired to mirror the monochrome terrain of my mind. The clouds hung low and heavy, pressing down on the horizon, flattening everything beneath them. It felt deliberate, almost intimate, as if the universe had leaned in close and decided to reflect me back to myself without mercy. This was not sadness. Sadness had edges. It arrived, lingered, and eventually moved on, like a passing rainstorm that darkened the day but still left room for light to return. What I was living inside was something else entirely. This was a suffocating blanket, hand-woven from despair and stitched tight with hopelessness, pulled over my life and tucked in at every corner. It pressed so heavily against me that even breathing felt like resistance, each inhale an act of defiance, each exhale a fragile victory.

A dense, clinging fog had settled not only around my life but inside it. It seeped into every crevice of my being, filling my thoughts, my muscles, my chest. It dulled sensation, blurred intention, swallowed hope before it could even form. Purpose, once a quiet compass guiding my days, dissolved into nothing, leaving me directionless, drifting. I moved through time without orientation, without meaning, as if the thread that once stitched my days together had been quietly cut. I remembered when mornings arrived with promise. When waking felt like an opening rather than a burden. When each sunrise resembled a blank canvas waiting for color, movement, possibility. Back then, the day felt negotiable. Alive. Now the sun rose like an accusation, its light harsh and invasive, an unwelcome spotlight exposing the hollow space where meaning used to live. Daylight no longer invited me forward. It demanded something I could not give.

The smallest acts became mountains. Showering. Eating. Answering a single text message. Each one loomed impossibly large, demanding a strength I no longer possessed. Each task felt like a Herculean labor, requiring an impossible surge of energy that simply wasn't there. I would lie still, negotiating with myself, promising I would move *soon*, only to remain frozen beneath the weight of my own exhaustion. This wasn't something I could reason with or outwait. It wasn't a mindset to be reframed or a mood to be endured. It was a presence. A dark tenant that had taken up residence within me, rearranging the furniture of my inner world, settling into my thoughts, my body, my breath. It lived there now, quiet and consuming, shaping every moment from the inside out.

It whispered lies with terrifying intimacy, speaking in a voice so familiar it felt indistinguishable from my own. It bent my perception slowly, methodically, until reality itself warped and softened at the edges, unrecognizable in its distortion. "*You are unworthy. You are a failure. You are a burden.*" Each sentence arrived fully formed, confident, and absolute, leaving no room for doubt or defence. These were not fleeting thoughts I could dismiss; they felt like verdicts, etched into the marrow of my being. It thrived in silence. In secrecy, I wrapped myself around my suffering. In the isolation I mistook for safety. Every moment I chose not to speak, not to reach out, not to be seen, it grew stronger, feeding on my withdrawal like a parasite that flourishes in the dark.

And so the world beyond my window, once vibrant and alive, receded into a blurred, distant backdrop. Life continued out there in color and motion, but it no longer belonged to me. The real battle raged unseen within, quiet and merciless, leaving no visible scars yet consuming everything it touched. My body, once a willing instrument I moved through the world with ease, became a prison I could no longer escape. It felt foreign, heavy, uncooperative. It betrayed me daily, its aches and unnamed pains surfacing without warning, a relentless physical commentary on my perceived inadequacies. Fatigue settled into my muscles. Pressure lived in my chest. Tension coiled in my jaw and shoulders as though my body itself had joined the chorus against me, echoing the same cruel refrain: *not enough*.

Sleep, which had once offered refuge, turned hostile. Nightfall no longer promised rest, only endurance. Darkness ushered in a battlefield where fractured dreams collided with the gnawing anxieties I carried through the day. I drifted in and out of shallow sleep, my mind never fully surrendering, haunted by a constant sense of impending collapse. I woke each morning more exhausted than when I had closed my eyes, as if sleep itself had become another task I was failing at. It felt as though my own body had turned traitor, a vessel hijacked by this unwanted passenger, carrying the crushing weight of despair wherever I went. Each breath became laborious, deliberate, and strangely futile, as though the simple act of staying alive required more effort than I could afford. Breathing no longer felt automatic; it felt negotiated. Earned. Exhausting.

And somewhere in that relentless weariness, I found myself longing for oblivion. Not out of drama. Not out of impulse. But from sheer exhaustion. From a desperate desire to escape the constant pressure pressing inward from every side, the unceasing demand to endure when there was nothing left to give. It wasn't a wish to die so much as a wish to rest, to finally be free from the weight that never lifted. When I faced the mirror, it offered no comfort. A stranger stared back at me. Hollow-eyed. Drained. Someone wearing my face but missing the essence that once animated it. I searched that reflection for recognition, for reassurance, for proof that I still existed beneath the fog. But all I saw was absence. And in that absence, the silence grew louder still.

Not merely a reflection marked by physical fatigue, but a warped caricature of who I once was. The eyes that had held curiosity and light were now hollowed out, dulled, clouded by a weariness so profound it seemed etched into my bones rather than resting on my skin. They looked back at me without recognition, as though whatever spark once lived there had been quietly evacuated. That reflection felt monstrous to me, distorted and unlovable, something contemptible, something I despised with an intensity that startled me. The hatred rose fast and sharp, a reflex I barely recognized as my own. This was not the person I knew. I searched the glass for familiarity and found only absence, despair standing in the place where *I* used to be.

It hadn't felt like a slow descent, not a careful slipping down a gentle slope where warning signs might have appeared along the way. It was a sudden, violent plunge into a dark abyss, the kind that steals the breath from your lungs before you can even scream. One moment, I was standing in a familiar world, rooted in routine and expectation, and the next, the ground vanished beneath me. The colours drained away. The sounds dulled to a distant hum. Everything that once felt alive lost its pulse, as though someone had reached inside me and turned the volume of existence all the way down. Joy disappeared first, quietly and without ceremony. Then passion followed, slipping away like water through open fingers.

Even the smallest pleasures, a warm cup of coffee, a song I loved, a memory that once made me smile, were swallowed whole by this relentless, suffocating presence. It was as if a vast shadow had risen within me and eclipsed the sun from the inside out, casting everything into permanent dusk. This darkness warped my perceptions, bending reality until it became hostile terrain. It repainted my memories in corrosive hues of regret and self-loathing, rewriting my past with cruel precision. Achievements that should have mattered shrank into nothingness, dismissed as luck or irrelevance. Success felt accidental, undeserved. Meanwhile, every mistake ballooned grotesquely, expanding into undeniable proof of my unworthiness.

There was no balance, no mercy, no middle ground. Only the relentless narrowing of self until all that remained was a single, brutal narrative: that I was broken beyond repair. And standing there, face to face with that reflection, I felt the weight of it settle fully. This was no longer something passing through me. It had taken residence. It had begun to rewrite who I believed myself to be. And the most frightening part was not how much I had lost, but how convincingly this darkness had taught me to believe that I deserved it. The future no longer stretched forward like a road lined with possibility. It yawned open instead as a bleak, endless expanse, dark and featureless, offering no landmarks, no promise of shelter, no sense of arrival. Where there had once been direction, there was only a void.

Looking ahead felt like staring into an abyss that answered back with silence, empty and unforgiving, as if time itself had run out of imagination for me. The insidious whispers grew louder, sharper, more intimate, slipping past every remaining defence. They learned my weak points, pressed their fingers into old wounds, spoke in the cadence of certainty. "*You are a failure. You are a burden. You are better left alone.*" Each sentence landed with surgical precision, magnifying doubts I could no longer contain. Small imperfections were distorted into grotesque flaws, stretched and twisted until they eclipsed everything else. I could no longer see myself clearly at all. My reflection, my memories, my identity were all filtered through this cruel lens, leaving only a fractured, unrecognizable image behind.

The voice of reason, once steady and anchoring, faded into a distant murmur, barely audible beneath the relentless chorus of negativity. It tried to speak, to remind me of nuance, of context, of truth, but it was drowned out, overwhelmed by the constant assault. There was no space left for balance or perspective. Only accusation. Only judgment. This was not sadness I could shrug off like a bad dream. Not a passing slump or a handful of heavy days strung together. This was something far deeper, something rooted and invasive. A chronic illness that sank its tendrils into every layer of my being, demanding to be seen, understood, named. It was not a failure of character or effort. It was a condition that required care, treatment, and compassion, though in my darkest moments, even that truth felt out of reach.

This battle was not fought solely in my thoughts. It lived in my body, too. In the heaviness of my limbs. In the tightness of my chest. In the exhaustion that sleep could not touch. It was a quiet war waged against an unseen enemy, one that moved without sound or spectacle, determined to consume me from the inside out. And as I stood there, suspended between memory and fear, I felt the full weight of what I was up against, a fight I had never chosen, yet could no longer avoid. For those who have never lived inside it, depression is almost impossible to comprehend. From the outside, it appears abstract, distant, something that can be reasoned with or brushed aside.

From there come the casual dismissals, the well-meaning but hollow platitudes. "*Try to stay positive. Everything happens for a reason. Just push through.*" Words meant to comfort, to tidy suffering into something manageable, yet landing like small, unseen blows. Each one misses the mark and strikes instead at the fragile places already bruised, adding weight to an unbearable load, sharpening the blade of shame, deepening the sense that this pain must be carried alone. Because this battle is not loud. It does not announce itself with spectacle or demand attention. It is fought quietly, far from view, behind closed doors and practiced smiles. A silent scream reverberating through an empty void where no one seems to hear.

It is the exhaustion of having to explain yourself to a world that wants simplicity where there is none. The loneliness of realizing that even love, when filtered through misunderstanding, can feel like distance. And so the isolation tightens, not because others do not care, but because they cannot see the war being waged beneath the surface. And yet, even here, even in this hollowed space where despair echoes back unanswered, hope still breathes. Quietly. Patiently. It does not arrive as certainty or sudden relief, but as a subtle persistence, a reminder that the fog is not eternal. That what feels endless is, in truth, temporary. The weight, however crushing it seems, can be lifted. The whispers, so intimate and convincing in their cruelty, can be challenged, softened, slowly quieted.

There are people who understand this terrain. People who recognize the signs not as weakness, but as signals. People who know how to sit in the dark without flinching, who can reach into the heaviness and offer not solutions, but presence. A steady hand. A lifeline back from the edge. There are therapies, treatments, medications not as miracles or erasers of pain, but as maps and tools. Ways to navigate the night when direction feels lost. Supports that help restore balance, create breathing room, and make space for healing to begin. The light does not return all at once. It arrives in fragments. In moments of being understood. In the relief of not having to pretend. In the slow realization that what you are experiencing has a name, a shape, and a path forward. And from there, step by careful step, the night begins to loosen its grip, and the possibility of reclaiming your life, your voice, yourself, becomes not just imaginable, but real.

The journey is neither quick nor gentle. It does not offer shortcuts or neat conclusions. It stretches long and uneven before you, scattered with setbacks, pauses, and moments that ask more of you than you believe you have left to give. Some days it will feel like wading upstream against an unseen current, every step contested, every inch earned. Other days, the ground will give slightly, just enough to remind you why you began. This is the nature of healing. It is not a straight ascent into light, but a winding passage through shadow and breath and effort. But the destination matters. A life no longer suffocated by depression's grip. A life where breath comes easier, where mornings no longer feel like accusations, where colour returns not in blinding brilliance but in soft, steady hues.

A life where laughter can find its way back to your chest, where connection feels possible again, where you are no longer fighting just to survive each hour. That life is worth fighting for. You are worth fighting for. It *is* possible to find your way back to yourself. Not to the version you were before the fog, untouched and unscarred, but to someone deeper, wiser, and more compassionate because of what you have endured. The vibrancy you mourn was never destroyed. It was buried, protected beneath layers of pain and exhaustion, waiting for safety, for understanding, for time. Healing is the slow, sacred work of uncovering it. And it begins not with certainty, but with recognition. With naming what is happening instead of blaming yourself for it.

With understanding that this is not a personal failure, but a human experience that demands care. Healing begins the moment you stop carrying it alone. The moment you allow someone else to see the weight you have been holding in silence. The moment you reach outward, even with trembling hands, and admit that you cannot do this by yourself. That first step is terrifying. It feels heavy, exposed, uncertain. It asks you to loosen your grip on control and risk being seen in your most vulnerable state. But it is also the most vital step you will ever take. Because it breaks the isolation. It interrupts the silence where depression thrives. It opens a door where there once was only a wall. And it is always, always worth taking. Not because the path will suddenly become easy, but because it will no longer be walked alone.

The Author's Story

The chipped mug warmed my hands, but the heat stopped there, stranded at the skin, never quite finding its way to my heart. Steam lifted in thin, wavering ribbons, rising and dissolving into the air like a visible echo of the fog that had long since made a home inside my mind. It was always there, that fog. Damp. Persistent. A quiet occupier that softened the edges of everything it touched until the world lost its sharpness, its colour, its sense of depth. Shapes blurred. Meaning thinned. Even time seemed to move through it differently, slowed and distorted, as though reality itself had been wrapped in gauze. People say depression is sadness, but that word feels insultingly small, a paper shield raised against a hurricane. Sadness visits. It moves through like weather, heavy perhaps, but temporary. Depression stays.

It settles in your bones. It gnaws at the marrow of your being and calls it home. It rearranges the furniture of your inner world without asking, pulls the curtains closed, and convinces you the dimness is simply how things have always been. This was not a sudden fall. There were no warning sirens, no dramatic plunge into darkness marked by catastrophe or collapse. It was far quieter than that. A slow, insidious creep. Like a tide inching forward while you sleep, eroding the shoreline of your life grain by grain. Nothing seemed urgent at first. Nothing screamed danger. Until one morning you wake and realize the ground beneath you has vanished, and you are standing where solid land used to be, unsure when it slipped away.

At first, I gave it kinder names. Fatigue. Burnout. Ordinary exhaustion. The understandable weariness of a demanding job and a life that always felt one small crisis away from unraveling. I told myself I was just tired. Bone-deep tired, yes, the kind that seeps into your muscles and dulls your thoughts, but nothing rest couldn't fix. A few good nights of sleep. A weekend to reset. A holiday I hadn't taken yet. That's all it was. That's all it had to be. Except rest never reached me. And the fog never lifted. So I pushed on. I reached for more coffee, as if caffeine might substitute for rest, for relief, for air. I stayed later, arrived earlier, filled every quiet space with productivity and noise. I clenched my jaw, tightened my shoulders, and leaned harder into sheer willpower, convinced that effort alone could outrun the heaviness stalking me.

I treated exhaustion like a moral failing, something to be conquered through discipline and determination. If I just worked harder, pushed further, ignored the warning signs long enough, surely this creeping malaise would grow bored and leave me behind. I didn't yet understand that depression does not retreat from effort. It feeds on it. It thrives on overextension, on self-denial, on the quiet violence of forcing yourself forward when every inner signal is begging you to stop. While I was busy proving my strength, measuring my worth by how much I could endure, the storm was already gathering. Patient. Silent. Unseen. It waited, not with urgency, but with certainty, for the moment my legs would finally give way beneath me.

And of course, it didn't work. Instead of lifting, the exhaustion sank its teeth in deeper, fastening itself to me, changing shape, becoming something far more insidious than tiredness had ever been. It no longer felt like fatigue that sleep could touch. It felt cellular. Existential. As though my very capacity for aliveness was being slowly siphoned away. The vibrant hues of my life began to drain, not all at once, but subtly, relentlessly, as if an invisible hand had laid a persistent grey filter over everything I touched. Simple joys dimmed first. The easy laughter of friends arrived muffled, as though filtered through thick walls. The warmth of a sunny afternoon failed to reach my skin, stopping just short of comfort.

Even the familiar pleasure of a good meal lost its language of nourishment and delight. What once glowed now barely flickered, each moment of enjoyment short-lived and hollow, replaced almost immediately by a dull, aching flatness that lingered long after the moment had passed. The world itself seemed to soften and blur, its edges melting into an indistinct, suffocating haze. Depth disappeared. Contrast vanished. Everything felt slightly out of focus, as though I were looking at my life through fogged glass, close enough to see but too far away to touch. Even my own home, once a refuge, began to feel foreign, cold, and unwelcoming, as though I were trespassing in a space that no longer recognized me. Rooms echoed differently. Silence carried weight.

And I moved through it all with the unsettling sense that I was slowly fading from a life that was continuing without me. The fog thickened. It was no longer a gentle haze softening the world's edges, but a dense, suffocating mass that warped reality itself. What I saw, what I felt, and what I believed no longer aligned. My thoughts, once sharp and agile, began to tangle into tight, constricting knots, looping back on themselves, colliding without resolution or clarity. Logic frayed. Focus splintered. Even thinking became exhausting, like wading through deep water while carrying something heavy and unnamed. The simplest tasks rose up like sheer cliffs carved from stone. Showering. Eating. Replying to a single email. Each one loomed impossibly high, demanding a strength I no longer recognized as my own.

Every movement required negotiation. Every action felt like an act of rebellion against an overwhelming inertia that pressed me backward, urging me toward stillness, toward disappearance. My body felt weighted, as though gravity had quietly doubled overnight, pinning me to the place where intention went to die. My mind, once a lively marketplace of ideas and curiosity, a place of movement and exchange, had emptied out. The stalls stood abandoned. Pathways crumbled underfoot. Inspiration had fled without farewell. Motivation lay buried beneath layers of dust and debris, unreachable, unrecognizable. The echoes of who I used to be lingered faintly, like a memory shouted down a long, empty corridor, but they brought no comfort. Only distance.

And in that barren inner landscape, I wandered aimlessly, increasingly unsure of how I had arrived there or whether a way back still existed. It was then that the lies began to whisper. Softly at first. Almost gently. They slipped into the quiet moments, into the pauses between breaths, into the narrow spaces where vigilance loosened and fatigue made room for doubt. You're worthless, they murmured, with the intimacy of a familiar voice. You're a failure. Nobody cares. The cruelty of it was not in their volume, but in their persistence. They did not shout. They repeated. Over and over. Patient. Precise.

These were not passing clouds of negativity drifting through my mind, not fleeting thoughts I could brush aside with reason or reassurance. They hardened into something dense and immovable, suffocating certainties etched deep into the architecture of my being. They rewired how I saw myself, how I interpreted the world, how I understood my own existence. They clung to me like barnacles on a sinking hull, each day tightening their grip, each repetition adding weight, drag, inevitability. And slowly, terrifyingly, escape began to feel like a myth. Solitude, once a gentle sanctuary I sought for rest and reflection, became fertile ground for the insidious voices that had learned my name. Alone, they grew bolder. Louder.

They echoed through the silence, ricocheting off the walls of my mind until no corner remained untouched. What had once been stillness turned hostile, thick with accusation. Silence no longer soothed; it amplified. It pressed in, crowded with thoughts that had nowhere else to go. The outside world, with its noise and expectations and relentless motion, felt impossibly overwhelming. Even imagining engagement drained what little energy I had left, like standing at the edge of a storm knowing you cannot outrun it. Withdrawal became my default setting, not as a choice but as a reflex. A slow retreat from life itself. I folded inward, step by careful step, exiling myself from connection, from demands, from anything that required me to be more than a body breathing through the day.

Survival became the ceiling. Nothing existed above it. And with every retreat, the darkness tightened its circle, closing ranks, shrinking the world until there was barely room to exist at all. My body, too, became a battleground. It no longer felt like an ally, but a contested territory where nothing came easily. Sleep, once a refuge I trusted, transformed into a nightly war. I tossed and turned beneath its weight, pursued by restless thoughts and jagged dreams that clung to me with sharp insistence. Even when morning arrived, it brought no relief. Nightmares bled into daylight, staining the hours ahead, leaving me exhausted before the day had truly begun, as if I had been running all night without ever moving forward.

Hunger disappeared quietly, slipping away without ceremony, replaced by a hollow, gnawing emptiness that no amount of food could satisfy. Eating became mechanical, an obligation performed without appetite or pleasure, like fuelling a machine I felt strangely detached from. I chewed. I swallowed. I checked the box of basic survival. But nourishment never reached me. My body felt distant, unfamiliar, something I inhabited out of necessity rather than belonging. And in that disconnection, in that narrowing of both inner and outer worlds, the darkness found more room to spread, unchallenged, unquestioned, certain it had finally convinced me there was nowhere else to go. Even breathing became labor.

Each inhale demanded intention, as though air itself had grown heavier, resistant. Each exhale carried pain with it, a dull ache spreading through my chest, as if my ribs were folding inward beneath an invisible weight. My lungs no longer moved freely; they negotiated. My body, once a vessel of movement and vitality, felt dense and unresponsive, a heavy shell I dragged through each hour with mounting effort. It no longer felt like a home I lived in, but a confinement I endured, a narrow cell housing a soul pressed flat beneath the crushing gravity of despair. And within that prison, the whispers continued. Relentless. Intimate. They spoke with the authority of certainty, convincing me that this was all I would ever be. This constriction. This exhaustion. This dim, airless existence. They told me there was no before worth returning to, no after worth imagining, only this endless now, sealed and unchanging. The irony did not escape me. I was a writer. A weaver of language. A maker of meaning. I knew how to braid words into lifelines for others, how to shape sentences that slipped into hidden places and drew buried emotion to the surface. I could chart the contours of grief, map the ache of longing, and give voice to pain with precision and care. I had done it countless times. I had watched language open doors for others when they believed themselves locked inside. And yet, when it came to my own life, I stood wordless. Utterly mute. I could not write my way out of the darkness that wrapped itself around me like a tightening vice. The words refused to arrive. The stories stalled before they could draw their first breath, collapsing back into silence before they could form. That boundless wellspring of creativity I had once trusted, the place I returned to for oxygen and orientation, had run dry. In its place stretched a cracked, desolate landscape where nothing would grow. A wasteland stripped bare of color and movement. A place so thoroughly emptied that even imagination had gone quiet. And that, perhaps, frightened me most of all. Not just that I was hurting, not just that I was trapped, but that the very thing I had always used to survive, to translate pain into meaning, had fallen silent too. What followed was not a rescue scene, not a dramatic swell of music or a clean break from the dark. There was no triumphant turning of the page, no moment where the light burst in and declared me saved. What came instead was slowness. Excruciating, humbling slowness. Healing arrived on its knees, not on wings. With therapy as a quiet compass and the unwavering presence of those who refused to loosen their grip on me, the fog began, inch by inch, to thin. Not lift. Not vanish. Thin. Enough to let outlines emerge. Enough to remind me there was a world beyond the haze. The process was anything but graceful. It was messy. Uneven. There were setbacks that knocked the breath from my lungs, days when I fell hard back into old patterns, relapses that convinced me I had fabricated every scrap of progress. On those days, hope felt like a cruel joke, something I had borrowed and been forced to return. But still, something was shifting. Gradually, almost imperceptibly, the whispers began to lose their authority. They were still there, yes, but their voices softened, their edges dulled. Their certainty fractured. What once spoke like immutable truth began to sound suspicious, distorted, like a radio station slipping out of tune. I started to recognize them not as facts, but as symptoms. Not as prophecy, but as echoes. Color crept back into the world the way dawn does, cautiously, without announcement. Not all at once, but in hesitant brushstrokes. The sharpness returned first, the way leaves cut clean against the sky. Then depth. Then warmth. A laugh landed and stayed for a moment longer than before. Music stirred something faint but real in my chest. The world began to feel three-dimensional again. Tasks that had once loomed as impossible mountains slowly shrank into hills I could climb, then into paths I could walk without trembling. Getting out of bed no longer required negotiation with gravity. Brushing my teeth stopped feeling like an act of rebellion. Answering an email became doable. Then routine. What had once demanded heroic effort softened into something manageable, and eventually, achievable. Each small victory stitched something back together inside me. A frayed edge mended. A seam reinforced. I was not becoming the person I used to be. I was becoming someone new, shaped by survival, informed by darkness, but no longer ruled by it. And though the healing was slow and often painful, it was real. With every step, however unsteady, I was reclaiming ground I had thought forever lost. The journey is not over. It may never be. The fog still knows my name. It still drifts close in moments of exhaustion, grief, or fear, curling at the edges of my awareness, testing the seams of my resolve the way a tide tests weakened stone. It waits for vulnerability. It listens for fatigue. It reaches for me when my guard is low, when the old ache resurfaces, and memory grows loud. But now, I am no longer unarmed. Where there was once only confusion, I carry understanding. Where silence once swallowed me whole, there is support, living and breathing, anchored in human hands and steady voices. Where there was once only ache, shapeless and overwhelming, I now have language. Words that name the storm. Words that separate my identity from the illness that tried to wear my face. Words that remind me, when the fog presses in, that what I am feeling is real, but it is not the whole truth. I know now that depression is not sadness dressed in drama, not weakness masquerading as despair. It is a complex, debilitating illness, a relentless weather system that batters both mind and body, distorting perception, draining vitality, demanding more endurance than anyone should ever be expected to summon alone. It is ruthless. It is convincing. And it is profoundly misunderstood. But it is not a life sentence.

With help. With hope. With patience that must sometimes be borrowed from others when my own runs thin. With fierce, stubborn perseverance that shows up even on days when courage feels absent. With rest. With honesty. With compassion that learns to speak louder than self-judgment. With these, it is possible to emerge. Not untouched. Not unchanged. But alive. It is possible to find solid ground again, even if your footing still trembles. To step back into a world where light exists not as a distant memory, not as a story you once heard about yourself, but as something tangible and warm. Something that reaches your skin. Something that stays.

The road is long. The climb is steep. There are switchbacks you don't see coming, days when the incline feels cruel, when progress seems invisible. But still, you climb. Still, you move. And with every step, however small, you reclaim a little more of your life. Because the promise of sunshine, of colour returning, of breath coming easier, of a life once again vivid and inhabited, makes every step of the struggle profoundly, achingly worth it.

Chapter Sixteen:

The Weight of the Fog: Finding Light in the Labyrinth of Depression

Shattering the Chains of Depression: A Journey to Rediscover Hope and Purpose

Depression is a formidable foe, one capable of bringing even the strongest to their knees, not through spectacle or sudden violence, but through quiet attrition. It leaves you feeling cornered, helpless, stripped of agency piece by piece, until the very idea of choice feels like a memory rather than a right. It is not a single blow that knocks the wind from your lungs, but a slow-working poison, seeping steadily into the soul, saturating every fibre of being. It infiltrates thought, sensation, breath. Until even breathing itself feels like hauling a weighted body through deep water, each inhale an effort, each exhale a surrender.

Depression. The word alone casts a long shadow. It carries gravity. It lingers in the air long after it is spoken. This is not the fleeting sadness of a difficult day, nor the ache of disappointment that time can gently soften. This is something far more consuming. A relentless, suffocating presence that wraps itself around you with patient persistence, tightening its hold not by force, but by endurance. A heavy blanket woven from despair and hopelessness, pressing down until movement feels impossible, until stillness masquerades as safety. A fog so dense it swallows the horizon whole, blots out the sun, erases the path forward, and bends your own reflection until you no longer recognize the person standing beneath it.

And this book does not pretend otherwise. It is not a promise of instant relief or neatly packaged answers. There are no miracle cures hidden in these pages, no shortcuts that bypass the terrain of pain. Instead, this is an invitation. An invitation to turn toward what you are facing rather than away from it. To name the enemy that has been moving through your life unseen. To study its patterns. To understand how depression tightens its chains, how it distorts perception, how it convinces you that escape is impossible and effort is futile.

This is not a sprint toward an illuminated exit sign. It is a journey through the labyrinth itself. A slow, deliberate walk-through winding corridors and shadowed turns, guided not by urgency, but by awareness. By compassion. By courage that does not roar but stays. A guide to learning how to move through the darkness without losing yourself to it. How to place one careful step after another, even when the ground feels uncertain beneath your feet. Until, gradually, the grip begins to loosen. Until the fog thins just enough for shape and

direction to return. Until the first hints of light reappear, fragile but real, reminding you that the darkness was never the whole story.

For those who have never walked this terrain, it is vital to understand that depression is not a bad day, nor a passing mood that can be shaken loose with sleep, sunlight, or resolve. It is not a mindset error or a failure of attitude. It is a pervasive condition, one that infiltrates the mind, seeps into the body, and settles deep within the soul like a slow, invasive root system. It does not knock and announce itself. It moves in quietly, rearranging the furniture of your inner world until nothing feels familiar anymore. Depression is not limited to melancholy or sadness. It reshapes perception itself. Reality bends beneath its gravity. Thoughts become warped mirrors, reflecting back only inadequacy, worthlessness, and despair, no matter how carefully you search for another image.

The world no longer appears as it is, but as depression insists it must be. Neutral moments tilt toward threat. Kindness feels suspect. Hope reads as a lie written for someone else. Even memory is rewritten, recoloured in darker tones, until joy feels imagined and pain feels permanent. Each breath becomes laborious. Deliberate. Heavy. As though the air itself has thickened, resisting your lungs, demanding effort for something that once happened without thought. Your body transforms into a prison you did not choose a vessel that feels foreign, burdensome, and deeply resented. You move through it with exhaustion and quiet hostility, trapped inside a form that no longer feels like home. Sensations dull. Muscles ache. Fatigue settles into your bones like sediment, layering itself day after day.

When you look in the mirror, it no longer reflects you. It offers back a warped caricature shaped by illness, a stranger with hollowed eyes and unfamiliar features, someone you have learned to loathe through no fault of your own. You search that face for remnants of who you used to be and come up empty-handed, convinced that version of you has been erased rather than buried. Shame seeps in, uninvited, whispering that this disfigurement is personal, earned, deserved. Clinical depression is relentless. It dulls the senses and drains color from experience until life feels washed out, flattened, reduced to shades of grey. Music loses its resonance. Food loses its comfort. Touch feels distant. Time stretches and collapses unpredictably. Days blur. Nights stretch long and unforgiving.

And always, beneath it all, depression thrives in solitude, secrecy, and silence. It grows strongest in the dark, feeding on isolation, convincing you that suffering must be hidden, that speaking would only burden others, that honesty would confirm the lies it has already planted. It tells you that you are alone in this. That no one would understand. That naming the pain would make it real, make it worse, make you weak. And so you learn to swallow it. To carry it quietly. To disappear politely. Not because you want to, but because the illness has taught you that invisibility is safer than being seen.

EMBRACING THE FOG: A Journey Through Depression - Understanding the Weight

Depression is a word that gets tossed around lightly, slipped into conversation as shorthand for disappointment, boredom, or an off day that will surely pass by morning. But its true nature is far more intricate, far more insidious, than that casual usage suggests. It is not a shrug of the shoulders or a sigh at inconvenience. It is an immersion. Imagine waking each morning beneath a crushing weight, a heavy blanket pressed firmly over your chest before the day has even had a chance to begin. Thought arrives already slowed. Emotion already dulled. Breathing becomes deliberate, something you must remember to do rather than something your body offers freely.

Movement feels negotiable, optional, endlessly postponed. Everything you once loved reaches you muffled, as though wrapped in thick layers of cotton, soundless and distant. Even the smallest task rises before you like a mountain you are expected to climb without strength, without tools, without belief that the summit exists at all. This is not a passing season of sadness. This is clinical depression, persistent and unrelenting, a condition that does not ask permission and does not easily loosen its grip.

For many, trying to describe depression feels like attempting to explain colour to someone who has never seen light. Language strains and fractures under the weight of the experience. Depression does not merely influence your mood; it envelops your entire reality, seeping into perception itself. It alters how you interpret the world, how you read the faces of others, how you understand your own worth. Neutral moments tilt toward threat. Silence feels loaded. Kindness feels undeserved. The lens through which you view life becomes distorted, and you begin to trust that distortion more than your own memory of clarity.

Words fail because the experience is not just emotional, but existential. Depression rearranges the very architecture of being. It must be understood that this is not sadness you can shake off with determination, positivity, or a well-meaning pep talk. It is not something cured by trying harder or thinking better thoughts. It is an oppressive force, a fog that clouds clarity, smothers hope, and erases purpose with quiet efficiency. It presses in from all sides, blurring the boundaries between who you are and what the illness tells you that you are.

You find yourself trapped inside a body that no longer feels like home, inhabiting a form that feels foreign, resistant, even hostile. Your own mind becomes unfamiliar terrain. Your own emotions feel unreliable. Your own reflection feels like a stranger. And somewhere beneath it all, your soul becomes an unwanted tenant, pacing the narrow corridors of a prison it never chose, longing for freedom it cannot yet name, waiting for a door it cannot yet see.

The Distorted Mirror

When you stand before the mirror in the midst of a depressive episode, the reflection that meets your gaze rarely feels human. It appears warped, exaggerated, stretched beyond recognition, a grotesque caricature of who you once were. The glass does not simply reflect; it collaborates. It becomes an accomplice to the illness, magnifying every perceived flaw, spotlighting every imagined shortcoming, until your own face feels foreign, almost hostile. Familiar features blur into something untrustworthy. The eyes seem emptied of light. The mouth looks wrong, heavy with words you never say. You search for yourself and find only absence staring back.

Inside your mind, the whispers begin their relentless chant, rising in perfect synchrony with your gaze. Worthless. Disappointing. Too much. Not enough. Each thought arrives sharpened, laced with the venom depression injects into perception, until the voice feels indistinguishable from your own. The mirror becomes a courtroom, and you its sole defendant. Every glance is an indictment. Every pause, a silent tally of perceived failures, abandoned dreams, missteps replayed and rewritten as proof. Moments where you stumbled swell into defining characteristics. Achievements evaporate. Compassion vanishes. The narrative tightens until there is only judgment left.

The person looking back is no longer seen as wounded or exhausted or in need of care. Instead, depression teaches you to see something vile. Something contemptible. Someone who deserves the punishment they are enduring. Shame seeps in and settles deep, convincing you that your suffering is not a condition but a verdict, not an illness but a revelation of who you truly are. The mirror holds you there, frozen between recognition and revulsion, until even looking away feels like cowardice.

And yet, this image is not truth. It is a cruel distortion, a funhouse reflection warped by illness, not a faithful rendering of reality. What you are seeing is depression's hand at work, bending light, twisting angles, corrupting perception until self-loathing masquerades as honesty. The mirror is not showing you who you are; it is showing you how deeply the illness has infiltrated your seeing. Beneath that distortion, beneath the noise and venom and false certainty, you remain human. Hurting, yes. Struggling, deeply. But still worthy. Still real. Still there, waiting for the day the glass loosens its grip and allows you to see yourself clearly again.

The body, once a vibrant and willing vessel that carried you through the world with instinctive grace, begins to feel like a cage. What was once home becomes confinement. You move through it reluctantly, as though inhabiting borrowed skin, longing for escape from a form that suddenly feels too heavy to bear. Each breath drags in thick and resistant, as if the air itself has weight. Each step must be negotiated, earned, endured. Muscles ache not from effort, but from existing. Even stillness is tiring. Even rest demands more than you have to give.

Living becomes labour. Existing becomes effort. You wake already exhausted, your body heavy with an unnamed gravity, your limbs reluctant, your chest tight with an unspoken dread. Every sensation becomes filtered through the same corrosive lens, every thought another echo of the story depression tells you about yourself. That you are weak. That you are failing. That you are a burden merely by occupying space. The illness seeps into flesh and bone, convincing you that this heaviness is proof, that your suffering is deserved, that your body itself is an indictment.

And yet, even here, even inside this prison of distorted sensation and relentless fatigue, there is a truth that must be spoken aloud, again and again, until it begins to loosen the chains. Depression is not a definition of who you are. It is not your essence. It is not your identity. It is a condition. An illness. A state that has settled into you, not something that originates from you. It has a voice, but it does not speak truth. It holds up warped mirrors and calls them reality. It isolates, distorts, and convinces you that you are alone because it needs you to believe that in order to survive.

Healing begins not with sudden relief or miraculous clarity, but with recognition. With learning to hear the lies for what they are. With noticing the moments when perception bends and gently naming it. This is depression speaking. This is not me. It begins when you turn toward the isolation it demands and, instead of obeying, reach for connection. When you question the mirror. When you allow the possibility, however faint, that softness might return, that breath might ease, that this cage is not permanent. The body you inhabit is not your enemy. It is carrying an immense weight. And with time, care, understanding, and support, that weight can be lightened.

The bars can soften. The breath can deepen. The effort can ease. This is not the end of your story. It is a chapter shaped by illness, not by truth. And learning to see that difference is one of the bravest steps you will ever take. In this quiet war of self-perception, the mind becomes both battlefield and weapon, turning inward with ruthless efficiency. Depression learns your contours, studies your vulnerabilities, and then uses them against you. It feeds on itself, a self-sustaining fire that burns brightest in silence, secrecy, and solitude. The quieter you become, the louder it grows. The more you hide, the more it convinces you that hiding is safety.

It urges withdrawal as protection, persuades you to shrink your world down to something small and dim where nothing can hurt you anymore. But what it offers as shelter is really a narrowing cage. Isolation becomes both symptom and strategy. A tightening spiral. Each unanswered message feels justified. Each cancelled plan feels necessary. Each closed door feels like relief, followed quickly by regret. The walls draw closer with every retreat, and despair settles in more comfortably, spreading through the newly abandoned spaces. Loneliness deepens, not because no one cares, but because depression insists you are better off unseen. It tells you that your pain is too much, that your presence is a burden, that disappearing is kindness. And so you obey, not realizing that every step inward strengthens the very force you are trying to survive. Here lies the cruelest paradox of all: the very thing depression convinces you to avoid is often the thing your nervous system is starving for. Connection. Presence. Being witnessed without judgment. To be seen not as broken, but as human. To be met where you are, not where you think you should be. In the depths of these trying moments, reaching outward can feel like the most impossible act of all. Hands tremble. Words falter. Fear presses hard against the chest. And yet, even the smallest gesture, a message sent, a truth spoken haltingly, a willingness to sit beside another rather than retreat into the dark, can begin to loosen the chains.

Light does not always arrive as revelation. It does not always blaze in with certainty or cure. Sometimes it enters quietly, almost shyly, through another human heart willing to sit beside you in the dark. A presence that does not demand fixing. A voice that does not rush your pain. A witness who stays. And in that shared stillness, something shifts. The darkness is no longer absolute. The silence no longer total. The war inside you pauses, if only for a moment, long enough for breath to return. Long enough for the truth to whisper back: you do not have to do this alone.

The Suffocating Blanket

Depression is not a fleeting sadness, not a bad day you can shrug off like dust from your shoulders as you step back into the light. It is not a temporary dip in mood, easily soothed by a favourite song, a warm cup of tea, or a well-meaning smile offered with the best of intentions. No. Depression is something far heavier, far more consuming. It arrives not with drama, but with gravity. It descends like a suffocating blanket, woven from threads of despair and hopelessness, layer upon layer stitched together with quiet precision until the weight becomes unbearable. At first it settles gently, almost imperceptibly, a slight pressure you tell yourself you can manage. But it does not remain gentle. It presses harder with time, relentless, compressing your chest, tightening around your ribs, turning breath into something you have to consciously earn rather than effortlessly receive. Making that breath feel borrowed not owned. It steals the air from your voice and the strength from your limbs, leaving you gasping not only for oxygen, but for meaning. For relief. For a version of life that once felt possible and now feels impossibly distant, like a memory recalled through water. This blanket does not warm or protect; it smothers. It dampens sensation, mutes colour, and softens the edges of reality until everything feels dulled and unreal. The world recedes behind a pane of glass. You can see it moving, hear it faintly, watch people live and laugh and reach for one another, but you remain sealed off, suspended in a quiet isolation that no one else seems able to penetrate.

Beneath its crushing weight, even existing becomes an act of endurance. Getting out of bed feels like defying gravity itself. Movement demands negotiation. Thought requires effort. Hope flickers weakly, if at all, a fragile ember struggling to survive beneath the pressure. The life you once inhabited with ease begins to feel like something happening to someone else, somewhere beyond your reach. You become an observer of your own days, watching time pass without participating, wondering how you drifted so far from yourself without ever meaning to let go. This is the cruel intimacy of depression. It does not merely surround you; it inhabits you. It seeps into your thoughts, settles into your body, reshapes the way you perceive yourself and the world. It whispers that this heaviness is who you are, that this breathless struggle is your true nature, that the effort it takes just to survive is proof of some fundamental failing within you. It convinces you that the weight is permanent, that relief is a fantasy reserved for other people, other lives. And yet, as suffocating as the blanket may feel, it is not you. It is something laid upon you, not something born from you. It is an illness, not an identity. Even here, beneath its crushing weight, there remains a quiet truth waiting to be rediscovered. The blanket can be lifted. Slowly. Gently. Thread by thread. Breath by breath. Not through force or denial, but through understanding, support, and the courageous act of staying.

Imagine being pulled beneath the surface of deep water, the light above you bending and splintering as it recedes, distorted into unfamiliar shapes while the pressure tightens around your ribs. The deeper you sink, the heavier it becomes. Water fills your ears with a dull roar. Your chest constricts. Your lungs burn, not from movement or effort, but from the raw, animal need for air. That burning is constant. It does not resolve. It does not grant mercy. This is the daily reality of living with depression. It is not a single moment of panic, not a brief gasp before resurfacing. It is prolonged submersion. An existence spent holding your breath far longer than anybody was ever meant to endure. Time stretches unnaturally down there. Seconds feel endless. Minutes blur. The pressure is unyielding, crushing inward from all directions, invisible yet absolute, making even the smallest movement require intention. Every breath feels negotiated rather than natural, borrowed rather than owned. You do not breathe because it is effortless. You breathe because you force yourself to keep going. You tread water in a vast, hostile sea of negativity, arms aching, muscles trembling, heart pounding with a quiet, persistent terror. The water pulls at you constantly, dragging at your limbs, whispering that it would be easier to stop fighting, to sink, and to rest. But you cannot rest. Rest feels dangerous. So you keep moving. You keep treading. You keep surviving.

Each motion costs more than the last, and the fear is not dramatic or loud, but steady and suffocating: the fear that one day your strength will finally give out. Above the surface, life goes on uninterrupted. People laugh. They talk. They inhale deeply without thinking. Sunlight glitters on the water, deceiving in its calm. Conversations drift across the surface, light and buoyant, unaware of what is happening beneath them. Below, you fight in silence, unseen and unheard, expending every scrap of energy just to remain afloat. You are not swimming toward joy or happiness or fulfillment. Those feel impossibly distant. You are simply trying not to drown. And the cruelest part is this: from the outside, no one can see the depth you are submerged in. They see calm waters. They see composure. They see someone who appears to be functioning, moving, existing. They cannot feel the water pressing into your chest, cannot hear the frantic rhythm of your breath, cannot sense the exhaustion that comes from surviving minute by minute. They do not know how much strength it takes to stay alive when the act itself feels like resistance. Depression is this unrelenting submersion. A silent battle waged beneath deceptively calm waters, where survival is not heroic or triumphant, but quiet and brutal. Where staying alive is not about swimming toward happiness, but about finding enough air, just enough, to endure another day.

It's not merely sadness that takes hold. Sadness still has edges, still carries tone, shape and texture, still announces itself with tears or ache. What arrives instead is an absence. A hollowing out. An internal evacuation where feeling itself retreats, leaving behind an echoing chamber where nothing quite lands. Numbness seeps into your bones like winter frost creeping beneath a door, quiet and merciless, stealing warmth without spectacle. Laughter is silenced before it can rise. Joy is smothered before it can even take shape. Emotion does not shatter; it dissolves. And what remains is a stillness so complete it feels unnatural, like standing in a world where sound has been permanently muted.

The vivid colours of life drain away, not all at once, but steadily, as if someone has been turning the saturation dial down day by day. Reds dull into rust. Blues flatten into grey. What was once rich and alive becomes a washed-out photograph, a monochrome landscape where nothing quite reaches you. You move through this world wrapped in invisible layers of thick cloth, padded against sensation, insulated from warmth, cut off from meaning, estranged from yourself. Touch feels distant. Pleasure feels theoretical. Even your own heartbeat seems to belong to someone else.

And then there are the tasks. The ordinary, unremarkable acts that once required no thought now rise up like hostile terrain. Getting out of bed feels like hauling yourself from deep water with lead strapped to your limbs, gravity suddenly doubled, intent on keeping you submerged. Brushing your teeth. Preparing a simple meal. Answering a message. Each one becomes a confrontation, a test of endurance, a Herculean effort against an invisible current that drags you backward while whispering, patiently and convincingly, that none of it matters anyway. "Why try? Why move? Why bother?"

The fog thickens. It rolls in without warning, dense and disorienting, swallowing landmarks you once relied on. Clarity vanishes. Thought blurs. Direction dissolves. Hope flickers like a dying match, flaring briefly before being devoured by the dark. Purpose, once a steady compass in your chest, fades into something abstract, a half-remembered concept you're no longer sure you ever truly possessed. You know it existed once. You just can't feel it now. You feel untethered. Adrift in a world that no longer follows recognizable rules. Cause and effect seem broken. Effort no longer guarantees outcome. The future stretches ahead not as a path, but as an empty horizon, flat and desolate, stripped of promise, stripped of possibility. Not frightening in a dramatic way, but bleak in its vastness, offering nothing to move toward, nothing to anchor hope to.

And this experience is not confined to the mind alone. Depression colonizes the body. It becomes a physical prison, warping your relationship with the very vessel meant to carry you through life. The mirror offers no reassurance. It reflects a stranger back at you, a distorted echo of the person you once were. The eyes look wrong. Too empty. Too tired. The posture feels unfamiliar, slumped beneath an invisible weight. You begin to resent this body, to see it as a cage, a burden, a relentless reminder of everything you believe you have failed to be. Trapped beneath the surface, numb and exhausted, you don't just feel lost. You feel submerged within yourself. Fighting for breath inside a body that no longer feels like home. Existing, but not inhabiting. Alive, but only just.

Each breath becomes work. No longer an unconscious rhythm you can trust your body to remember, but a deliberate, exhausting negotiation. Inhale. Exhale. Even this feels heavy, as though the air itself has thickened, turned resistant, forcing its way reluctantly into your lungs. Every rise of the chest is an effort. Every breath a reminder that you are still here, still tethered to a life that feels increasingly unbearable to inhabit. Breathing stops being a gift and becomes a task, one more obligation on an already impossible list. Inside, a silent scream reverberates. It has no sound, no language, and yet it is deafening. A raw, wordless yearning for relief. For rest. For an end to the unrelenting ache that has settled into your bones and made itself comfortable there. You are not craving drama or disappearance. You are craving quiet. An easing. A moment where the weight lifts long enough for your muscles to unclench and your mind to stop bracing for impact. But the scream stays trapped inside, ricocheting against your ribs, because there is nowhere for it to go.

Depression seeps inward like a slow-acting poison, subtle and methodical. It saturates the soul first, then bleeds into everything else. It stains your thoughts. It rewrites your memories. It taints your hopes before they can fully form. Nothing escapes its reach. Even moments that once felt warm are recoloured in its shadow, drained of comfort, rewritten as evidence of your inadequacy or failure. The past becomes a crime scene. The present a burden. The future a blank page you no longer believe you deserve to write on. It corrupts the way you see yourself most of all. The mirror in your mind warps your reflection until all that remains visible are flaws magnified to grotesque proportions, fractures you believe everyone else can see, failures replayed until they feel definitive. The illness speaks with intimate familiarity, borrowing your own voice, using your own history against you. It tells you that something essential within you is broken beyond repair. That you are defective at the core. Unworthy of love. Unworthy of joy. Unworthy of mercy. And slowly, almost imperceptibly, the most dangerous lie takes hold. The lie that this pain is who you are, not something you are carrying. That depression is not an illness, not a condition, but a revelation. The truth at last. Under its crushing weight, you begin to feel reduced to rubble. Hollowed out. Stripped of value. As if everything you once were has collapsed beyond recognition, and what remains is an error. A misprint. A life that feels expendable. This is the devastation depression leaves in its wake. Not just suffering, but erasure. Not just pain, but the quiet, terrifying belief that you no longer deserve to exist outside of it.

Shame coils itself around depression like a second skin, slick and suffocating, tightening the suffering until it feels fused to you. It whispers that this weight is your fault, that if you were stronger, braver, better, you would have shaken it off by now. It teaches you to measure yourself against an impossible standard of resilience, to believe that willpower alone should be enough to cauterize a wound this deep. When it isn't, shame steps in to explain the failure. It tells you that you are weak for struggling, defective for hurting, broken for not being able to simply "*snap out of it*". Guilt follows close behind, quiet but relentless. It seeps into every interaction, every memory of connection, telling you that your pain is a burden others must endure. That your sadness leaks into the lives of those you love, staining their joy, dimming their light. You begin to see yourself as an inconvenience, a problem that needs to be managed, apologized for, minimized. And so you retreat, not because you don't want connection, but because you want to protect others from what you believe you are. You pull back from outstretched hands. From familiar voices. From the warmth of being known. You fear judgment. You fear pity. And perhaps most of all, you fear the unbearable possibility that even if they tried, they could never truly understand the depth of what you are carrying.

Isolation slips in disguised as safety. It offers quiet where the world feels too loud, distance where vulnerability feels too dangerous. For a moment, retreat feels like relief. But slowly, almost imperceptibly, refuge becomes confinement. Silence thickens. Rooms grow heavier. The absence of contradiction allows the illness to sharpen its teeth. Alone, depression grows bolder. Stronger. It feeds on the unanswered messages, the unopened doors, the days that pass without witness. In the quiet, its voice becomes the only one you hear, echoing unchecked through your inner world. Solitude becomes fertile ground where despair takes root. It spreads tendrils through your thoughts, convincing you that separation is protection, that distance is wisdom, that hiding is strength. It insists that you are safer unseen, quieter unburdening no one. But this is one of depression's cruelest lies. Because withdrawal does not heal the wound. It deepens it. It gives the illness space to expand, nourished by shame, secrecy, and the aching belief that you must carry this weight alone. And so the cycle tightens. Shame drives isolation. Isolation feeds depression. Depression reinforces shame. Round and round it goes, a closed circuit of suffering that feels impossible to interrupt. Until connection, fragile and frightening as it may seem, becomes the very thing capable of loosening the grip. Because while depression thrives in silence, it weakens when it is seen. And shame, no matter how powerful it feels, cannot survive long in the presence of compassion.

The Lies We Tell Ourselves

In the quiet left behind by isolation, beneath the thickening fog of depression, a chorus of falsehoods takes root and begins to rule the inner landscape. These lies do not arrive with violence or volume. They come softly, almost tenderly, slipping in through the cracks when your guard is down. Patient. Persistent. They reshape reality one thought at a time, like water wearing away stone. "*I'm not good enough. I'll never get better. No one cares about me.*" They circle endlessly, a broken record trapped in a warped groove, repeating until their rhythm blends so seamlessly into your thinking that it no longer feels like repetition at all. It feels like fact.

They fill the silent spaces of your life, swelling in the absence of contradiction, growing louder where no other voices interrupt them. They feed on shame, on solitude, on the bone-deep exhaustion that leaves you without the energy to argue back. And slowly, almost without noticing, you begin to organize your life around them, making choices as if they are true, shrinking yourself to fit the narrow world they allow. The more these lies are believed, the heavier the fog becomes. It thickens until hope feels abstract, joy feels foreign, and possibility sounds like a language you once knew but can no longer speak. Light struggles to penetrate this haze, and when it does, it feels unreliable, fleeting, something borrowed that will soon be taken away.

Even moments of relief are met with suspicion. "*This won't last. Don't trust it.*" Depression stops being something you are moving through and becomes the lens through which you see everything. Meaning distorts. Nuance disappears. The world flattens into absolutes. And the illness whispers, with chilling certainty, '*This is how it is now. This is how it will always be.*' Recognizing these lies is not a small act. It is a rupture. The first fracture in the prison wall. The moment you begin to separate yourself from the illness that has been speaking through you. But this recognition requires courage, because it asks you to turn toward the very thoughts that have kept you bound. It asks you not to fight them or suppress them, but to look at them clearly.

To notice their tone. Their repetition. Their cruelty. And to say, gently but firmly, "*This thought is here, but it is not the truth.*" Journaling can become a powerful tool in this quiet rebellion. A place where the lies are no longer allowed to roam freely, unchecked, unchallenged. Write them down as they surface, raw and unfiltered, exactly as they appear. Let them take shape on the page where you can see them clearly, outside the echo chamber of your mind. And then, with patience and care, place truth beside them. Not forced optimism. Not hollow affirmations. But compassion rooted in reality. Words that acknowledge pain without surrendering to it. Words that remind you of your humanity, your endurance, your worth, even when you cannot feel it.

Each challenged thought becomes a small opening in the fog. A hairline crack where light begins to seep through. A thin beam reaching into corners where despair once hid unquestioned and unopposed. And with each act of recognition, each written truth, the narrative begins to loosen its grip. The story shifts. Slowly. Almost imperceptibly at first. But enough to remind you of something vital and long forgotten: this story is still unfolding. And it was never written by the lies alone.

Understanding the Enemy: A Relentless Fog

To move forward, you must first learn to name what you are facing. Naming is not weakness; it is orientation. Depression is not a passing shadow cast by a bad day, nor a brief storm that clears with time. It is a relentless fog that arrives quietly, without announcement, rolling in low and thick until the world you knew becomes unrecognizable. It dulls the senses. It bends reality. It blurs edges and distorts distance, turning familiar paths into uncertain terrain. What once felt solid now feels unstable beneath your feet. What once came easily now demands a staggering cost. This fog does not stop at the mind. It settles into the body, heavy and uninvited, altering the way you move, the way you breathe, the way you inhabit yourself. Muscles grow dense. Limbs feel weighted. Breath becomes shallow, deliberate, something you must remember to do rather than something that simply happens. The soul, too, feels altered, as though a veil has been drawn between you and your own inner life, muting intuition, flattening emotion, dimming the sense that anything meaningful is waiting on the other side. Clinical depression has a cruel way of magnifying the ordinary into the insurmountable. The smallest tasks rise like mountains where plains once stretched. Getting out of bed can feel like scaling a sheer cliff with bare, trembling hands. Brushing your teeth. Answering a message. Choosing what to eat. Each act becomes an exercise in quiet endurance, a negotiation between exhaustion and obligation. And because these struggles are invisible, they are often misunderstood, even by the one carrying them.

But this truth must be held, especially here: depression is not a failure of character. It is not a moral flaw. It is not evidence that you are weak, lazy, ungrateful, or broken. It is an illness. A complex, multifaceted condition shaped by an intricate interplay of biology, environment, and lived experience. It does not discriminate by strength or intelligence. It does not spare the capable or the kind. For some, its roots are written into the body through genetic inheritance, a quiet vulnerability passed down like an unspoken legacy. For others, it is carved slowly by trauma, loss, chronic stress, or prolonged emotional strain. Hormonal shifts, medical conditions, and neurological patterns can all feed the fog, thickening it until clarity feels unreachable. Often, it is not a single cause, but many threads woven together over time, tightening gradually, almost imperceptibly, until one day you realize how bound you have become. Understanding this matters. Deeply. Because understanding loosens shame. It interrupts the belief that this suffering is a personal indictment. It allows you to see the fog not as proof of who you are, but as something acting upon you. Depression may be an enemy, yes, but it is not an unknowable one. It has patterns. It has tactics. And anything that can be studied can also be challenged. In this shift, something subtle but powerful begins to happen. The fog no longer owns the story. It no longer gets to define the terrain as endless or the darkness as permanent. It becomes something you can face. Something you can name. Something you can move through, step by careful step, even when visibility is low. And in that movement, however slow, the possibility of direction returns.

Chemical imbalances in the brain, distorted thought patterns, unresolved trauma, these do not arrive separately or politely take turns. They weave themselves together into depression's grip, threads tightening in quiet coordination. This is not a single-threaded affliction with a single point of failure. It is a tapestry, intricate and suffocating, stitched from biology, memory, belief, and pain. Each strand reinforces the next, until the weight of it presses in from all sides, leaving little room to breathe. Depression thrives in the places where language goes missing. Where words are swallowed before they can be spoken. Where silence becomes a second skin, worn so long it feels indistinguishable from the self. In solitude, it feeds. In isolation, it grows bolder, nourished by self-blame and the endless rehearsal of perceived failures. It convinces you that every misstep is evidence, every struggle a verdict, every moment of weakness proof that you are fundamentally flawed. It is also a master of disguise. Depression wears the mask of normalcy with unsettling precision. It allows its sufferers to function, to smile, to perform their lives convincingly enough that no one thinks to look closer. You show up. You answer questions. You laugh at the right moments. And all the while, something inside you is quietly unraveling, thread by thread. Because the mask holds, shame takes root. Because the mask holds, loneliness deepens. And the person trapped beneath it begins to believe the most dangerous lie of all: that they are the only one drowning in this invisible sea.

But understanding changes the terrain. To grasp the biological and psychological underpinnings of depression is not to reduce its pain, but to reframe it. Knowledge becomes a small but steady light, piercing the fog just enough to reveal that this suffering is not a personal failure. It is a human condition. A shared one. Understanding shifts the narrative from self-condemnation to context, from blame to clarity. It loosens the grip of shame and cracks open the belief that this struggle is evidence of inadequacy rather than illness. And here lies a truth that bears repeating, especially when the fog insists otherwise: you are not alone. Millions across the world walk this same shadowed path, carrying similar weights, asking the same silent questions in the dark. Depression is common. It is treatable. It is survivable. There are tools that help name its patterns. Therapies that soften its hold. Supports that remind you what it feels like to be seen without having to perform. There are ways forward. And in recognizing this, in naming the enemy clearly and without apology, you take the first vital step toward reclaiming your ground. Your voice. Your life. In the hush between thoughts, when the world finally loosens its grip and sound recedes, depression begins to speak. Not with thunder or urgency, but with a low, intimate murmur, the kind meant only for you. It slips past your defenses because it does not announce itself as an intruder. It arrives sounding familiar. Reasonable. It leans close in moments of exhaustion and whispers that you are not enough. That you never were. That every misstep is evidence, every wound a verdict long overdue. It takes your insecurities and lifts them gently, almost tenderly, holding them up like mirrors warped by heat and time. In their glass, everything is exaggerated. Every flaw looms larger. Every regret stretches longer. The face staring back at you no longer feels human, but grotesque, misshapen by shame and self-loathing. What once held complexity and softness is reduced to a single, brutal narrative: unworthy, broken, disposable. Under depression's gaze, even compassion curdles. Even memory is rewritten to serve the sentence it is determined to pass.

These lies are persuasive precisely because of when they arrive. They wait for you at your weakest points, when your energy is drained, when the room is quiet, when no one else is there to contradict them. They speak in the voice of your own inner dialogue, wearing the cadence of truth, the tone of inevitability. They do not rush. They repeat. Patiently. Relentlessly. Until resistance grows tired and belief slips in unnoticed. And slowly, almost imperceptibly, something dangerous happens. The boundary between thought and truth dissolves. The whispers stop sounding like opinions and begin to feel like facts. You no longer hear them as depression speaking. You hear them as reality itself, finally being honest. And in that moment, the illness tightens its grip, not through force, but through intimacy, convincing you that the cruelest story you tell yourself is simply the most accurate one of all.

Depression feeds in the dark. It does not rush or roar; it grows the way rot does, quietly, patiently, spreading unseen behind the walls of your life. In solitude, it finds nourishment. In secrecy, it settles in. In silence, it flourishes. The more you withdraw, the more space it claims. The more you hide your pain, the deeper it burrows, threading itself through your days and nights, festering beneath the surface where no light has permission to reach. Silence becomes its sharpest instrument. A sealed door. A drawn curtain. A barrier that keeps help standing just outside while convincing you that your suffering is singular, anomalous, and somehow untranslatable. In that hush, the lies gain volume. They ricochet off the empty rooms of your inner world, repeating that no one would understand, that no one would stay if they truly saw you, that this burden was assigned to you alone. They tell you that reaching out would only expose how broken you are, that speaking would only confirm what the illness has already declared.

And so the isolation tightens, not all at once, but incrementally. One unanswered message. One cancelled plan. One night spent convincing yourself that you are safer unseen. The grip closes not because you are weak, but because depression is cunning. It understands strategy. It knows that connection is the one force capable of loosening its hold, that being witnessed threatens its authority. And so it whispers that distance is protection, that solitude is strength, that silence is survival. But this is the cruel illusion at the heart of it. What feels like shelter is a cage slowly being reinforced from the inside. What feels like self-preservation is the very terrain where the illness thrives. And all the while, beneath the layers of quiet and withdrawal, a truth waits, patient and persistent: the darkness depends on isolation to survive, because even the smallest thread of connection has the power to begin unraveling it. The fog thickens until even time itself loses its shape. Depression bends the clock, warping your sense of before, now, and after, until chronology collapses under its weight. Days no longer arrive with edges or intention; they seep into one another like ink spilled in water, forming an unbroken stretch of grey monotony where mornings carry the fatigue of nights and nights offer no promise of rest. Hours pass without being felt. Weeks disappear without leaving footprints. Time becomes something viscous and heavy, something you wade through rather than move within. The past swells and crowds the present, looming close and intrusive, heavy with regret. Old wounds reopen as if they were freshly cut, replayed with merciless clarity. Missed chances, spoken words, unspoken truths circle endlessly, looping without resolution, as though memory itself has been sharpened into a blade that turns inward again and again. Nothing stays where it belongs. Yesterday invades today. Long-healed moments bleed anew. The mind becomes a hall of echoes where every mistake reverberates louder than any achievement ever did.

And the future, once a horizon alive with possibility, withdraws into something distant and hostile. It no longer beckons; it intimidates. A vast, featureless abyss stretches out ahead, offering no foothold, no map, no reassurance that relief exists anywhere beyond the fog. Hope feels naive there, almost dangerous, a risk you cannot afford to take. Looking forward becomes unbearable, so you stop looking altogether. And so you become trapped in the now. Pinned beneath the crushing weight of despair. Unable to move forward. Unable to retreat. Suspended in a moment that feels endless, airless, sealed shut. Time does not pass here. It presses. It bears down on your chest, tightening with each breath, convincing you that this suffering has always been and will always be. That this is not a chapter, not a season, not a storm to endure, but a permanent condition of being. Depression tells you there was never a before without pain and there will never be an after without it either. It erases memory of relief and imagination of change, trapping you in an eternal present where endurance replaces living. And within that frozen moment, the greatest cruelty settles in: The belief that escape is not just unlikely, but impossible.

The Mask of Depression

As time bends and the days blur into one another, depression learns another trick: disguise. It becomes a chameleon, altering its colours just enough to survive unnoticed. On the surface, it can look almost reasonable, a passing sadness, a stretch of low mood, a natural response to a difficult season. It borrows the language of normalcy. It cloaks itself in plausibility. It convinces both you and the world that this heaviness is understandable, manageable, nothing worth naming aloud. And so it remains unchallenged. But beneath that carefully maintained façade lies something far more intricate and consuming. Depression is not a single emotion, but a knotted convergence of thoughts, sensations, and beliefs, a web spun tightly around mind, body, and soul until their boundaries begin to dissolve. It seeps into your posture, your breath, your internal monologue, until it becomes difficult to tell where you end and the illness begins. It is not content to simply exist; it adapts. It studies you. It learns where to hide. It slips easily into productivity, teaching you to equate exhaustion with worth. It masks itself as politeness, keeping your pain quiet and palatable. It dresses up as humour, a well-timed joke deflecting any question that drifts too close. Sometimes it chooses silence, convincing you that saying nothing is safer than saying too much. Whatever the costume, the intention remains the same: to remain unseen.

This is the cruel brilliance of depression's disguise. It does not always halt your life; often, it allows you to keep moving, just hollowed out. You still show up. You still perform. You still function. And because of that, the suffering is dismissed, minimized, even by you. You tell yourself this is just how life is now. That everyone feels this way. That you should be able to handle it. That needing help would mean admitting failure. And while the mask holds, depression deepens its grip. Quietly. Patiently. It tightens itself around your sense of self, convincing you that this numbness is normal, that this heaviness is deserved, that this erasure is inevitable. It whispers that you are not disappearing, only aging, only adjusting, only becoming "realistic." And all the while, piece by piece, it steals your vitality, your curiosity, your capacity to feel fully alive. The mask protects the illness, not you. It keeps the truth buried beneath performance and pretense, where no one can interrupt its work. And yet, the moment you begin to sense that the mask exists at all, something important has already shifted. Awareness cracks the disguise. Recognition loosens the hold. Because what hides in shadows cannot survive long once it is named. Depression depends on remaining mistaken for you. And the moment you begin to see the difference, the mask begins to slip.

Depression rarely announces itself plainly. Instead, it slips quietly into familiar disguises, masquerading as exhaustion that sleep never seems to cure, as irritability that snaps without warning, as anxiety that hums beneath the skin like a live wire. It wears the face of busyness, of burnout, of being "just stressed," making it painfully easy to overlook and devastatingly hard to name. It dulls desire, drains colour from the things that once sparked joy, leaving behind a flat, echoing indifference where passion used to live. Hope erodes without ceremony, grain by grain, replaced by a heaviness that feels both unjustified and inescapable, a sorrow with no clear origin, only a deep and aching presence that settles into the body like weather.

These masks are many, layered one over the other, each convincing in its own way. They allow depression to hide in plain sight, to pass unnoticed through conversations, calendars, and commitments. You tell yourself you are tired because life is demanding. You explain the irritability as pressure. You justify the numbness as maturity, as realism, as growing up. And in doing so, the illness tightens its hold, not through force, but through familiarity. It becomes woven into your daily rhythms, your explanations, your identity, until it feels less like something happening to you and more like something you simply are.

This is how depression survives so long without being named. It convinces you that nothing is wrong enough to warrant concern, that your suffering is too vague, too ordinary, too undeserving of attention. It teaches you to mistrust your own distress, to minimize it, to swallow it whole. And while you are busy rationalizing the pain, depression continues its quiet work, hollowing out joy, flattening emotional range, dimming the inner light you once moved through the world by. Eventually, the disguises begin to overlap and blur. Exhaustion bleeds into hopelessness. Stress curdles into despair. Anxiety tightens into paralysis. What once felt manageable becomes suffocating, and still, you hesitate to call it what it is. Because naming it feels dangerous. Naming it would mean admitting that this is more than a phase, more than a rough patch, more than something you can push through alone.

But the truth is this: depression depends on remaining unnamed. It thrives in ambiguity, in dismissal, in the space between "something feels wrong" and "this is real." And the moment you begin to question the masks, to notice the patterns, to sense that what you are carrying has weight and shape and consequence, the illusion begins to fracture. Recognition does not cure the illness, but it breaks its invisibility. It marks the moment you stop mistaking the mask for your face. Because exhaustion is not always just tiredness. Irritability is not always attitude. Numbness is not strength. And what you have been enduring in silence may not be a personal failing at all, but an illness that has learned how to hide.

The Insidious Nature of Depression

Depression rarely arrives with thunder on the horizon. It does not crash through the door or announce itself with spectacle. It begins instead as a slow-moving storm, almost polite in its entrance, gathering far out at sea where it is easy to dismiss. A passing cloud. A rough week. A tired season you assume will correct itself if you simply endure long enough. You glance toward it, note its presence, and turn back to your life, unaware that the tide has already begun to shift beneath your feet. But quietly, relentlessly, it gathers force. The air thickens. The pressure changes. Something subtle but unmistakable settles into your chest. The wind picks up in small, imperceptible ways, a tightness here, a heaviness there, a persistent fatigue that no amount of rest seems to touch. And before you realize what has happened, that distant disturbance has become a Category Five hurricane, tearing through every corner of your inner life, ripping the roof from your sense of self, flooding spaces you didn't even know could drown. Nothing is spared. Nothing remains untouched. Depression is insidious, not because it is violent, but because it is patient. It waits. It studies you. It learns where you are already tender and slips its fingers into those cracks with surgical precision. It settles into old wounds you thought had healed, into doubts you learned to live with, into unanswered questions and unspoken grief. It feeds on uncertainty, on exhaustion, on the quiet moments when your guard is down. Each whispered criticism becomes sustenance. Each unchallenged thought becomes fertile soil. What begins as a fleeting doubt slowly calcifies into certainty. What once felt like a passing shadow hardens into belief.

Over time, it stops feeling like an intruder. It becomes a presence. A constant companion you never invited but now cannot seem to shake. An unwelcome shadow that follows you from room to room, from morning to night, seeping into conversations, decisions, and memories. It stains everything with its weight. Even moments of light are stalked by it, dimmed before they can fully bloom, joy intercepted mid-rise, hope cut short just as it begins to breathe. And the cruelest trick of all is this: depression convinces you it has always been there. It rewrites your history, blurs your memory of who you were before its arrival, until the darkness feels innate, inevitable, inseparable from your identity. It tells you this is simply who you are. That this heaviness is your natural state. That the erosion you feel is not theft, but truth. But it is theft. Slow. Deliberate. Methodical. A quiet burglary of the self, carried out over time, stealing colour, clarity, confidence, and connection piece by piece, until you stand amid the wreckage, wondering when life became so small, so heavy, so hard to inhabit. And only then do you begin to sense it: this was not you fading. This was something else, something patient and practiced, taking more than it ever had the right to claim.

IT FESTERS IN THE DARKEST recesses of the mind, those hidden rooms sealed off long ago, where no light wanders and no witnesses linger. Places even hope hesitates to enter. There, beyond the reach of reassurance or reason, it goes to work quietly, bending thoughts out of shape, warping emotions, rewriting perception while no one is watching. In that private darkness, depression becomes parasitic. Patient. Methodical. It does not rush. It feeds slowly, drawing sustenance from every flicker of self-doubt, every pulse of shame, every fear left unnamed. Each negative thought becomes nourishment. Each silence gives it permission. Each moment you turn away allows its roots to sink deeper into the soil of your inner world. And the more it is fed, the more it grows. What began as a whisper gains a throat. What began as heaviness learns how to pull. Gravity forms where none existed before. Slowly, relentlessly, it expands, spreading through the corridors of the mind until it no longer occupies a single corner, but claims the entire landscape. Motivation withers under its weight. Joy fades to a distant echo. Connection dulls, meaning blurs, and life itself begins to contract, folding inward like a collapsing star. Colour drains from the world. Possibility narrows to a pinprick. The future caves in on itself until it feels unreachable, irrelevant, unreal. Even memory is not spared. The past is rewritten through its lens, joy recast as illusion, success reframed as accident, love remembered only for its absence. Until one day, it feels as though everything you are, everything you touch, everything you dare to imagine has been swallowed whole by this all-consuming force. And in its grip, depression does not merely darken life. It attempts to replace it.

It offers a counterfeit reality where despair feels inevitable, where numbness masquerades as safety, where survival is mistaken for living. It does not just want your days quieter. It wants your world smaller. Your hopes dimmer. Your sense of self erased. And it does all of this not with violence, but with persistence, slowly convincing you that this shrinking, suffocating existence is all there has ever been, and all there ever will be.

The Devastating Consequences of Depression

Left unchecked, this all-consuming force does not remain sealed within the walls of the mind. It spills outward, seeping through invisible borders, touching everything it encounters. Depression is a silent killer, not because it strikes suddenly, but because it erodes slowly. Quietly. Patiently. It claims millions each year not with spectacle or noise, but by wearing life down grain by grain. It is one of the leading causes of disability worldwide, and its reach extends far beyond the individual it inhabits. Partners feel it in the growing distance across a shared bed. Children feel it in the absence of laughter where warmth once lived. Friends feel it in unanswered messages, in plans that quietly dissolve. Colleagues feel it in the dimming of a presence that was once engaged, capable, alive. Entire communities feel the hollow it leaves behind, even when they cannot name its source. Its consequences are vast and unforgiving. Relationships strain beneath the weight of withdrawal and misunderstanding, buckling under pressures neither side knows how to articulate. Conversations shorten. Silences stretch. Laughter thins to a fragile echo. Intimacy fractures, not from lack of love, but from exhaustion, fear, and the invisible wall depression erects between hearts. Work begins to suffer as concentration falters and motivation collapses. Tasks that once flowed easily now stall and splinter. Mistakes accumulate. Confidence erodes. For some, this ends in job loss, a blow that deepens the spiral of shame, fear, and perceived failure, reinforcing the very lies depression feeds upon.

The body, too, becomes collateral damage. Depression does not remain politely confined to emotion or thought; it infiltrates flesh and bone. It settles into muscles as chronic pain. It lodges in the chest as fatigue that never lifts. It disrupts sleep until rest becomes elusive or vanishes altogether. The immune system weakens. Vulnerability to chronic illnesses such as heart disease, diabetes, and obesity increases. The body begins to speak the suffering the mind can no longer translate into words, carrying the burden openly when language has collapsed. Mentally, the toll is just as devastating. Anxiety coils tightly around the chest, a constant hum of unease that never fully quiets. Panic can erupt without warning, hijacking breath and reason alike. Thoughts race, then stall, then turn inward, sharpening into weapons aimed at the self. And in its darkest progression, depression may whisper of escape. Of disappearance. Of rest through ending. These thoughts do not arise from weakness or failure. They are symptoms. Signals of an illness that consumes from the inside out, convincing the suffering mind that relief lies in vanishing rather than being held. Depression does not merely make life harder. It dismantles it piece by piece. It strips away connection, vitality, health, and hope, leaving devastation in its wake. It hollows out futures, fractures families, and steals years that can never be returned. And yet, naming these consequences is not an act of despair. It is an act of truth. Because only by seeing the full scope of what depression takes can we begin to grasp the urgency of confronting it, treating it, speaking it aloud, and refusing to let it continue its work unseen, unchallenged, and misunderstood.

Seeking Help Is Strength

After witnessing the devastation depression leaves in its wake, one truth rises with unmistakable clarity: silence is not stoicism, and endurance is not virtue. Suffering quietly is not a badge of honor. It is a burden that was never meant to be carried alone. One of depression's most dangerous deceptions is the belief that asking for help is a weakness, a failure of will, a personal flaw etched into your character. In reality, reaching outward is an act of profound bravery. It is the moment you stop sinking in silence and allow yourself to break the surface, lungs burning, arms shaking, and reach for a hand extended toward you. It is not surrender. It is survival. It is strength in its most honest form, the kind that chooses life over pride, truth over performance. Mental health professionals, support groups, and trusted friends are not symbols of defeat. They are lifelines thrown into rough, unforgiving waters. They offer perspective when depression has twisted your vision, grounding when your footing has disappeared, and presence when loneliness has convinced you that no one would stay. Therapy becomes a shelter in the storm, a place where the chaos inside you is finally given language. Approaches such as cognitive-behavioural therapy become lanterns in the fog. They do not banish the darkness all at once, but they teach you how to move through it without losing yourself. They help you recognize the lies depression has disguised as truth, the walls it has fortified with shame and fear, and begin, patiently, to dismantle them brick by brick. In their place, something sturdier is built: a narrative rooted not in self-contempt, but in compassion, accuracy, and choice.

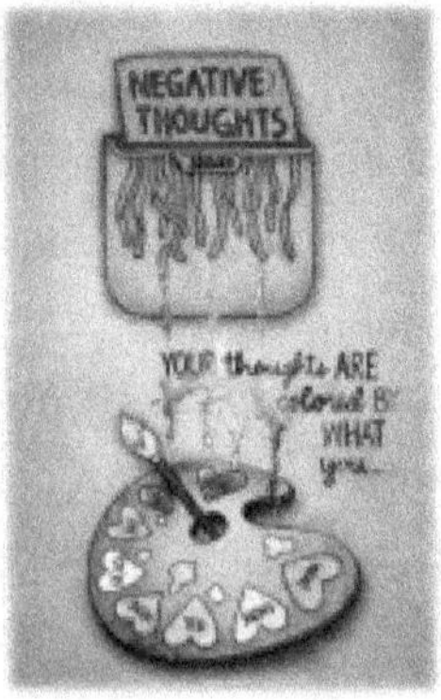

Seeking help is not about being rescued. It is about refusing to fight an invisible war without allies. It is about acknowledging the weight of this illness and honoring the fact that no human being is designed to carry it unaided. In a world that glorifies silent suffering and praises endurance at any cost, choosing support is a radical act of self-respect. It is a quiet but powerful declaration that your life matters. That your pain deserves care. That you are worthy of relief, of understanding, of healing. And in that choice, small and trembling though it may feel, you take one of the most courageous steps possible: you choose yourself.

SMALL STEPS LEAD TO Big Changes

After choosing to reach for help, the journey forward rarely arrives with trumpets or cinematic revelations. It does not burst in through the door fully formed and radiant. More often, it slips in quietly, almost shyly, carried on the back of the smallest decisions. In the depths of depression, even ordinary acts can feel Herculean, as though gravity itself has doubled overnight, pressing you flat against the bed, the floor, your own hesitation. In this terrain, *one step at a time* is not a platitude. It is a survival strategy. A narrow bridge suspended over an abyss that would otherwise feel impossible to cross. The first steps are modest by necessity. Getting out of bed. Letting water run over your skin in the shower, reminding your body that it is still here, still deserving of care. Opening a window. Allowing fresh air to move through the room and your lungs alike. Stepping outside, even briefly, to feel the ground beneath your feet and the sky above your head. From the outside, these actions may look unremarkable. From within the inner geography of depression, they are quiet rebellions. Each one pushes back against the weight that insists you cannot move. Each one whispers a counter truth to the illness: "*I am still here. I am still choosing.*"

Celebrate these moments. Honour them without minimising their cost. They are not small when they demand this much courage. They are the first stones laid in a foundation you are rebuilding by hand. Recovery does not begin with transformation; it begins with permission. Permission to move slowly. Permission to rest. Permission to acknowledge that survival itself is work. And slowly, almost without announcing itself, momentum begins to gather. One step leans into the next. The body remembers motion. The nervous system learns, inch by inch, that movement does not equal danger. Energy flickers where there was once only exhaustion, faint but unmistakable, like the first glow of dawn after a long night. You may find yourself reaching for something familiar. A book. A pen. Music that once mattered. You may not feel joy yet, and that is okay. Joy often follows action, not the other way around. What returns first is not delight, but *capacity*.

These steps will not be linear. Some days, the ground will feel solid. Other days it will tilt beneath your feet, and you may find yourself retracing old ground, sitting down, pausing longer than you expected. This is not regression. It is rhythm. Healing moves in spirals, not straight lines. Each step forward, no matter how tentative, teaches your system something vital: that change is possible, that movement can happen without catastrophe, that the story is still unfolding. Small steps do not shout. They do not demand applause. But they accumulate. They create pathways where none seemed to exist. And one day, often without realizing when it happened, you will look back and see distance between where you stand and where you once were. Not because you leapt. Not because you forced yourself to be strong. But because, in the quiet moments that mattered most, you chose to take the next step anyway.

The Power of Connection

As those small steps begin to steady you, another truth rises quietly to meet you, as undeniable as it is gentle: healing does not happen in isolation. Depression feeds on silence the way a fire feeds on oxygen-starved rooms, growing strongest where no one enters, where no voice interrupts its narrative. But connection alters the air. It weakens the illness not through force, but through presence. In the slow work of recovery, reaching out becomes not an obligation, but an act of courage. A choice to be seen rather than hidden. A refusal to keep fighting in the dark. Letting someone in can feel terrifying at first. The words have lived so long inside your chest that speaking them aloud feels like breaking bone. Yet even the smallest opening matters. Let a friend or family member glimpse behind the curtain. Tell them you are carrying something heavy, something that does not always leave bruises or scars others can point to. Those who love you often sense the shift long before you speak it aloud. They want to help, but love is not mind-reading. Opening the door, even a fraction, invites light into places that have known only shadow. Connection does not demand grand confessions or perfectly shaped explanations. Sometimes it arrives quietly, in the simple grace of a shared cup of tea, steam curling upward as words finally find room to breathe. Sometimes it is a message typed and erased three times before being sent, hands trembling, heart racing. Sometimes it is nothing more than saying, "*I'm not okay today*", and letting that be enough. These moments may seem small, but they are seismic. They shift the ground beneath the loneliness that depression depends on. And then there is the power of shared language. The moment you find yourself among others who recognize this terrain without needing a map. In support groups, whether gathered in rooms or across screens, stories begin to overlap. Pain echoes. Experiences mirror one another in ways that dismantle the lie of isolation. You realize your suffering has a shape others know intimately. In that shared recognition, shame loosens its hold. The belief that you are uniquely broken begins to fracture. You are no longer an anomaly. You are human.

There is something profoundly restorative about having your inner world reflected back to you with compassion rather than judgment. Collective storytelling stitches together what depression works so hard to tear apart. It restores belonging. It reminds you that you are not too much, not too strange, not too damaged to be understood. Connection does not erase pain, but it softens its edges. It redistributes the weight. It makes the unbearable bearable. Healing is deeply personal, yes. But it is not solitary work. While this journey is yours to walk, you were never meant to walk it alone. Every hand you allow to steady you, every voice you let in, becomes part of the path forward. And in that shared light, however dim it may begin, the fog starts to thin.

Finding Light Through Routine and Joy

As connection begins to soften the isolation, another quiet ally steps forward, unassuming yet steadfast: routine. In the wreckage depression leaves behind, structure becomes an anchor dropped into shifting waters. Not rigid. Not punishing. Simply reliable. A rhythm you can return to when your inner world feels chaotic and uninhabitable. These small, deliberate patterns matter more than they appear. Waking at the same time each morning. Drinking water before the day asks anything of you. Feeding your body with nourishment instead of neglect. Moving gently through space, reminding your muscles and breath that they still belong to you. Each repetition is a whispered reassurance to your nervous system: there is order here.

There is continuity. You are held by something steady, even when your thoughts insist otherwise. Routine does not cure depression, but it creates a container sturdy enough to hold healing. It becomes scaffolding around a fragile structure under repair, allowing growth without collapse. On days when motivation is absent and clarity feels unreachable, routine carries you forward on memory rather than effort. You do not need to decide what comes next; the rhythm already knows. And in that predictability, safety begins to return, quietly restoring a sense of ground beneath your feet.

Then, slowly, cautiously, joy begins to re-enter the conversation. Not as fireworks or sudden revelation, but as a hesitant presence testing the room. Depression often steals your appetite for the very things that once made you feel alive, but returning to them is not false or performative. It is an act of trust. Creativity, time in nature, music that reaches places language cannot touch, these are not luxuries reserved for the well. They are lifelines. Invitations back into yourself. Even when they feel distant. Even when the spark seems extinguished. Showing up is enough.

Joy, at first, may feel muted, like sound heard through a wall. But repetition softens the barrier. A brush dipped in paint, even when the canvas feels blank. A walk beneath open sky, even when the view feels grey. A song played again and again until something stirs, faint but unmistakable. Joy does not always arrive because you feel ready. Often, it arrives because you kept coming back. Bit by bit, these moments begin to stitch your identity back together. A laugh that surprises you. A breath that comes easier. A fleeting sense of presence that reminds you what it feels like to be inside your own life again. They do not erase what you have endured.

They layer meaning over it. They remind you that joy was never gone, only buried beneath exhaustion, fear, and pain. With routine as your anchor and joy as your quiet companion, something profound begins to shift. You are no longer only surviving. You are remembering. Reclaiming not just happiness, but yourself. Slowly. Gently. One repeated moment at a time.

Rediscovering Hope and Purpose

From routine and reclaimed moments of joy, hope begins to flicker back into existence. At first it is almost imperceptible, a fragile flame cupped in trembling hands, easily threatened by the slightest gust of doubt. Depression has spent a long time teaching you that hope is dangerous, that reaching for it only invites disappointment. And yet, hope proves more resilient than the illness ever anticipated. It bends. It dims. But it does not vanish. It waits. It can be rekindled. It can be protected. It can be fed, breath by careful breath, until it steadies and begins to glow again. Hope is not a destination you suddenly arrive at, greeted by certainty and ease. It is a path you learn to walk slowly, unevenly, sometimes in circles. It unfolds in quiet ways. In moments when curiosity returns, where numbness once lived. In the soft stirring of interests you thought had died. In forgotten passions stretching awake like limbs after a long sleep. Sometimes hope appears as a question rather than an answer: "*What if this could be different?*" Sometimes it is simply the willingness to imagine tomorrow without flinching. It is the gradual remembering of what matters to you, the gentle rethreading of connection, the patient reconstruction of a self that once felt scattered beyond repair.

Purpose follows close behind, like a compass rediscovered at the bottom of a storm-worn pocket. Bent. Scratched. Still pointing true. Purpose is not always grand or dramatic. It does not require a manifesto or a five-year plan. It is the quiet force that gives shape to your days, that lends weight and meaning to the act of getting up, of continuing, of choosing again. Depression steals this sense of direction, leaving you untethered, drifting through life without a why. Movement becomes exhausting when there is no sense of orientation. But purpose can be found again. It can be reclaimed in pieces. And it rarely looks the way it once did. Sometimes purpose is reborn through service, in showing up for others in ways you once wished someone had shown up for you. Sometimes it emerges through creativity, through making something honest from what hurt. Sometimes it grows through healing itself, through learning how to live more gently, more truthfully, more awake. And sometimes the purpose is as simple and radical as choosing to stay. Choosing to grow. Choosing to remain in conversation with life even when it feels uncertain and unfinished. In rediscovering purpose, you are not returning to who you were before the darkness. That person no longer exists in the same way, and that is not a loss. It is a transformation. You are becoming someone shaped by depth, by endurance, by hard-won understanding. Someone with a widened heart, a softened gaze, and a strength that no longer needs to shout to be real. Hope and purpose do not erase what you have survived. They rise *because* of it. And together, they begin to sketch a future that is not defined by depression, but informed by it, a life guided not by fear alone, but by meaning slowly, bravely reclaimed.

Breaking the Chains: Finding Your Way Back to the Light

From the fragile flame of hope and the slow rediscovery of purpose, a deeper truth begins to surface, quiet yet unwavering: the weight of depression, no matter how crushing it feels, is not an immovable force. It is heavy, yes. Relentless, yes. But it is not eternal. It does not get to decide the rest of your story. Recovery is possible, even when the word itself feels distant or undeserved. Finding your way back to the light does not come through force or urgency, but through courage that trembles in your hands, patience that falters and returns, and a fierce, defiant commitment to treating yourself with compassion instead of cruelty.

The first act of liberation is **acknowledgment**. Naming what you are living with. Turning toward the truth and saying, quietly or aloud, "*I am struggling*". This moment can feel seismic, like lifting a stone that has pressed against your chest for years, stealing breath without mercy. In a world that still wraps depression in shame, stigma, and misunderstanding, this admission can feel terrifying. But depression is not a personal failure or a moral flaw. It is an illness. Just as real, just as complex, and just as deserving of care as any physical condition. **Acceptance** is not surrender. It is the moment you lay down the lie and false belief that you must survive this alone.

From there, **seeking professional help** becomes an act of self-respect. Reaching out to a therapist or psychiatrist is not an admission of defeat; it is a declaration that your life is worth tending to and matters enough to be supported. These professionals become companions in the fog, helping you trace its origins, untangle distorted thought patterns, and build tools that steady you when the ground beneath you feels unstable. Therapy offers a map when everything feels directionless, a language for pain that once felt unspeakable. And sometimes medication becomes part of the bridge forward, not a cure, not an erasure of who you are, but a support that eases the weight enough for healing to take root and movement to become possible again.

Connection is equally vital, because isolation is depression's most faithful accomplice. When you begin to share your story with trusted friends, family members, or support groups, the silence that once fed the darkness begins to fracture. Being witnessed softens the lie that you are alone, that you are incomprehensible, that no one could truly understand. You do not need perfect words. You do not need a tidy narrative. Simply being heard can loosen the chains that solitude tightens, reminding you that your pain does not make you unlovable or unworthy of care.

Alongside connection, **self-care** shifts from something ornamental into something essential. It becomes the quiet, daily tending of your body, your emotions, your spirit. Movement that gently stirs what has gone stagnant. Food that nourishes rather than punishes. Sleep that restores rather than merely numbs. Practices like mindfulness, breathing, or stillness help calm a nervous system that has been living on constant alert, braced for disaster. Even joy, when it feels distant or artificial, can be invited back in small, patient ways. Through repetition. Through curiosity. Through the trust that feeling often follows action, not the other way around.

Depression also reshapes the mind, bending thoughts into sharp instruments turned inward. Learning to recognize these patterns is a powerful step toward freedom. When the inner voice insists you are worthless, hopeless, beyond repair, you are allowed to question it. You are allowed to pause and ask, "*Is this truth, or is this the illness speaking?*" Look for evidence. Notice the absolutes. Learn the awareness of depression's language of lies and deceit. Gently and repeatedly **challenge** the narratives and thoughts that offer only condemnation. This is not about forcing positivity, but about making room for possibility, replacing cruelty with realism, and slowly reclaiming a more truthful inner dialogue.

Progress unfolds best when it is measured in kindness, not comparison. **Setting small, realistic goals** builds momentum without overwhelming already fragile reserves. Getting out of bed. Taking a shower. Sending one message. Stepping outside for a moment of air. These are not trivial acts. They are victories. Each one is proof that movement is still possible, even on the heaviest days. Do not rush yourself. Do not demand transformation overnight. Choose goals that are achievable, and celebrate them fully, no matter how small they may seem.

Above all, **patience** is essential. Healing does not move in straight lines. There will be days when the light feels close enough to touch and others when it slips away again. Good days and bad days, progress and pauses, and all of it belongs here. Setbacks are not failures; they are part of the terrain. Treat yourself as you would someone you love deeply, with gentleness, understanding, and forgiveness. You are not behind. You are not broken. You are healing.

And finally, **purpose** returns not as a thunderclap, but as a quiet pull. It may emerge through creativity, through service, through learning, through connection, or simply through the brave decision to stay alive long enough to see another version of yourself take shape. Purpose does not need to be grand. Sometimes it is enough to say, "*I am still here, and that matters.*" Even that can be a compass. Step by step. Breath by breath. The chains loosen. The light does not rush in all at once, but it finds its way through cracks, through effort, through grace. And with time, what once felt unreachable begins to feel possible again.

The Light at the End of the Tunnel

And so, from this slow and sacred labour of courage, patience, and self-compassion, the light begins to make itself known. Not as a sudden blaze or a triumphant unveiling, but as a quiet presence you sense before you fully see it. Depression is a formidable adversary, yes, a shadow that understands how to linger, a weight that knows precisely where you are most vulnerable. It has learned your rhythms, memorized your doubts, studied the fault lines in your heart. But it is not invincible. It is not omnipotent. And it does not get the final word. With understanding comes clarity. With clarity comes choice. And with each choice, however small or tentative, the grip begins to loosen. Naming the illness instead of merging with it creates distance. Calling it what it is, rather than what it tells you that you are, cracks the illusion it depends on to survive. You begin to see the difference between the voice of depression and the voice of your own becoming. That distinction alone is powerful. It shifts the ground beneath your feet.

Seeking professional help becomes a lantern in the dark, not rushing you forward, not demanding certainty, but offering steady illumination with each step. It shows you where you are standing, where you have been, and where the ground might safely hold you next. Building a support system creates bridges where isolation once ruled, spanning the chasms depression tried to convince you were un-crossable. Each conversation, each shared truth, each moment of being seen becomes proof that you were never meant to carry this weight alone. Self-care, once dismissed as indulgent or optional, transforms into an act of quiet rebellion. A deliberate choosing of life in small, stubborn ways. Eating. Resting. Moving. Pausing. Breathing. These acts become declarations, subtle but resolute, that you are worthy of care even on days when you feel undeserving of it. Challenging negative thoughts becomes an ongoing reclaiming of truth, a patient unlearning of the lies that once passed as fact. You begin to notice the language you use with yourself, and gently, persistently, you start to change it. Not into blind optimism, but into honesty laced with compassion.

Freedom does not arrive in a single moment. It does not announce itself with fanfare. It comes in increments. In breaths that feel less laboured than before. In mornings where the heaviness loosens its hold. In days where the fog thins enough for you to glimpse something beyond it. And one day, almost without realizing it, you notice that the tunnel you once feared might never end has begun to widen. The walls no longer press so tightly against your ribs. The air feels different. Lighter. The darkness, once absolute, now carries seams where light slips through. That light is not harsh or demanding. It does not blind or overwhelm. It waits. Patient. Steady. Unafraid of your pace. And you are not walking toward it empty-handed. You carry wisdom earned through suffering, resilience forged in endurance, and a depth of self-understanding that could only have been shaped here. Step by careful step, you are reclaiming your life, not as it once was, but as something truer. Something stronger. Something more whole.

The journey to recovery may be long and uneven, a road that bends back on itself, dotted with loose stones and unexpected descents. There will be stumbles. There will be pauses where you sit at the side of the path, breath shallow, unsure if you have the strength to rise again. There will be moments when the way forward blurs, when the fog drifts back in, and the ground beneath your feet feels uncertain once more. But still, it is a journey worth taking. Every step forward, no matter how small or hesitant, is an act of defiance against the darkness that once tried to convince you to stay still. Each step is a quiet refusal to disappear. The light at the end of the tunnel is not a myth whispered to keep you compliant, not a hollow promise meant to distract you from pain. It exists. It waits. Patient and unhurried. Sometimes it shines clearly, a steady beacon calling you onward. Other times it flickers faintly, barely visible through the haze, easy to doubt. But even then, it is real. Its presence does not depend on your belief in it. It remains, even on the days you cannot feel it.

With courage, you learn to keep moving even when fear murmurs that retreat would be safer. With patience, you allow healing to unfold at its own pace, releasing the demand to be fixed, whole, or certain all at once. With self-compassion, you learn to cradle yourself gently on the days when strength feels out of reach, when simply staying feels like the bravest thing you can do. You stop punishing yourself for the weight you carry and begin to honour the resilience it has required to keep going. Slowly, almost without announcing itself, the fog begins to thin. The air grows clearer. Breathing becomes less of a negotiation. Colours return, first washed-out and tentative, then deeper, fuller, more alive. Joy does not rush back like a flood; it seeps in, cautious and curious. Meaning follows. Purpose stirs. Life begins to breathe again within you, not as it once was, but as something reshaped by endurance and insight. You are not alone on this path, even when it feels solitary. You are not broken, even when you feel fragmented. You are not weak for having struggled; you are brave for continuing to show up in the face of so much weight. You are worthy of love, of happiness, of peace, and of a life no longer crushed beneath the suffocating grip of depression. And in your own time, in your own way, you will find your way back to the light. Not as the person you were before the darkness, but as someone deeper. Wiser. Softer in the right places. Stronger where it matters most. Profoundly, courageously, and unmistakably alive.

A Journey, Not a Destination

Amid the relentless waves of despair, resilience still breathes, often quietly, often unnoticed, but undeniably alive. Healing does not unfold in straight lines or obedient arcs. It spirals. It circles back. It advances, then retreats, then pauses to gather breath. Some days arrive bearing the fragile sweetness of quiet victories. Others feel like walking old ground again with weary feet, retracing steps you hoped you had already outgrown. And still, movement is happening, even when it feels like standing still. In these moments, self-compassion is not optional; it is essential. It is the ground beneath you when certainty crumbles. You are not failing because you are struggling. You are not weak because the weight still presses in. Your experience is real. Your pain is valid. And every step you take, no matter how tentative, no matter how trembling, carries meaning. Progress does not announce itself with fanfare. Sometimes it whispers. Sometimes it is nothing more than choosing to remain present in a moment you once would have fled. You are not defined by your depression. It is not the sum of who you are, but a chapter in your unfolding story. And chapters, even the darkest ones, are not endings. They are passages. Places of transformation. With patience, with honesty, and with the quiet courage to sit with the fog rather than outrun it, clarity begins to seep back in. Not all at once. Not without effort. But steadily enough to be felt. You learn how to breathe again inside your own life. How to inhabit your days without apology. How to exist not in spite of your

struggles, but through them, allowing what you have endured to deepen you rather than diminish you.

Within the wisdom carved by hardship, a quieter strength takes root. Not the brittle kind that demands constant proving, but a rooted strength that knows how to bend without breaking. Thread by thread, you begin weaving a tapestry of resilience. It is textured by scars, softened by compassion, and illuminated by hope that has learned how to survive storms. This tapestry does not hide what you have lived through. It honours it. And in time, you may notice a subtle shift. You are no longer only surviving. You are becoming. Becoming someone more attuned, more empathetic, more alive to both sorrow and beauty. In your becoming, you may stand as a light for others still finding their way, not because you are unscarred, but because you are real. A living testament that even through shadowed terrain, it is possible to keep moving forward. To remain open. To remain human. To remain here, breathing, growing, and alive with purpose in a world that still holds beauty, waiting to be rediscovered.

Epilogue: The Dawn After the Darkness

And so, as you continue taking these tender, courageous steps toward understanding and healing, remember this: dawn has a way of arriving even after the longest, coldest night. It does not always break open the sky in a blaze of gold. Often, it comes the way healing does, almost imperceptibly. As a loosening of shadow. As a faint softening of the dark. As the palest breath of colour along the edge of the world. Sometimes it is nothing more than a quiet lightening you can feel before you can see, a subtle shift in the air, a first fragile birdsong where silence once reigned. But it comes. It always comes. Honour your journey. Every faltering step. Every collapse and every rise. Every day you stayed when leaving felt easier. Every breath you took when breathing felt like work. These are not footnotes. They are the sacred terrain of your becoming. Do not lose sight of the light that still exists, even when it feels buried beneath the densest fog. Light does not vanish because it is hidden. It waits. It gathers. It remembers how to reach you.

Each day is a new invitation. A fresh breath drawn into uncertain lungs. A quiet chance to rediscover meaning, to brush your fingers once more against purpose, to slowly reinforce the truth your illness tried so hard to erase: That you are deserving of love, of gentleness, of patience, of a life that wants you here. Not when you are fixed. Not when you are flawless. But now. As you are. Depression is not the ending of your story. It is a chapter, not the cover. A passage written in shadow, yes, but not without significance. Painful as it is, it can open into deeper understanding, hard-won strength, and a compassion that flows both inward and outward, touching parts of yourself and others you may never have reached otherwise. As you turn these pages toward recovery, you may begin to sense a quiet returning. A remembering. The subtle reassembly of a self you thought was lost. Something rises from beneath the ash. Not untouched by fire but shaped by it. Tempered. Deepened. Alive in a new way. And in that becoming, you stand ready to meet life again, not as it once was, but as it now can be, truer. Wider. More honest. Still threaded with sorrow, perhaps, but also with meaning, connection, and moments of beauty that land more softly and more deeply than ever before. The dawn is not a single moment. It is a gradual unfolding. And it is already, quietly, on its way to you.

The Shadow Weaver: The Unseen Cage

The word *depression* always felt far too clinical. Too sterile. Too clean for something that was anything but. It sounded like a diagnosis printed neatly on a page, when what I was living felt closer to being caught inside a slow-moving catastrophe. Calling it depression felt like naming a hurricane "a bit of wind and rain," a polite understatement that stripped the experience of its violence, its endurance, its devastation. The word could not hold the truth of what lived inside me. It could not touch the suffocating, all-consuming presence that had taken root in my soul, the way darkness seeps into damp walls and refuses to leave, no matter how many windows you open.

This was not a bad day. Not a passing low. Not a momentary stumble in an otherwise functional life. This was a relentless force that slid into every crack and crevice of my existence, coating my inner world with a residue of despair no amount of wishing, reasoning, or effort could scrub away. It did not arrive loudly. It infiltrated quietly, patiently, until it was everywhere. In my thoughts. In my body. In the spaces between moments. It felt like being sealed inside a soundproof room, walls thick and unseen. I could scream until my throat burned raw, beat my fists bloody against invisible barriers, but no sound escaped. No echo reached the outside world. No one heard. No one saw. My life became a silent scream, reverberating endlessly within the confines of my own mind, a cry trapped in a cage only I could feel.

The cruelty of it revealed itself most sharply in joy's absence. Birthdays came and went. Holidays passed like postcards from a country I no longer lived in. Achievements arrived wearing the costumes of celebration, but beneath them was nothing. No lift. No spark. No sense of arrival. It was like watching fireworks through thick fog. The colours were there, technically. The light existed. But the brilliance was blunted, the thunder reduced to a distant, unconvincing murmur. I stood on the outside of my own life, pressed against the glass, watching moments unfold without me, forever separated from the warmth everyone else seemed able to touch with ease.

And always, there was the weight. Not always physical, though often my limbs felt as though they had been cast from lead, heavy and unresponsive. It was deeper than that. A gravity that lived beneath the skin. The weight of expectations I could no longer meet. The weight of guilt for failing to be grateful, productive, present. The weight of simply existing inside a body that felt like an obligation rather than a home. It curved my shoulders. It stole my breath. It leeched the colour from my days until even movement felt like an act of endurance. Getting through the hours became less about living and more about surviving the slow grind of time.

People would say, "Just think positive," or "Snap out of it," as though depression were a faulty light switch, I had neglected to flick. As though I were choosing this darkness out of laziness or stubbornness. If only they knew. If only they could feel the dark tendrils coiling around my heart, tightening their grip with quiet persistence. If only they could understand how, it squeezed the life from me not in dramatic bursts, but in steady increments, day after day, breath after breath. This was not a failure of attitude. This was captivity. An unseen cage built from despair, silence, and a pain too heavy to carry alone.

The Seeds of Self-Hate

Depression was never just a feeling. It was a landscape. A vast, shadowed terrain that stretched out inside me, dark and fertile, where something poisonous found the perfect conditions to take root. And in that soil, self-hate bloomed. Not suddenly. Not violently. It grew the way rot grows beneath fallen leaves, quietly, patiently, hidden at first, until one day it was everywhere. The monster had found its voice. It did not roar. It did not announce itself. It whispered. It coiled its lies around my thoughts the way ivy strangles stone, winding itself through every mental corridor, breathing into the quiet spaces of my mind. You are worthless. You are unlovable. You are a burden. Its voice was never loud, never dramatic. It didn't need to be. It was persistent. Intimate. Convincing. It spoke in my own tone, borrowed my memories, wore the mask of insight. And because it sounded like me, I believed it. Soon, every small moment became evidence in its endless case against my existence. A missed deadline at work was no longer a mistake. It was a verdict. A sentence passed down by an invisible judge. Proof that I was incompetent. Broken. A fraud barely passing as capable. An unanswered message from a friend wasn't a matter of circumstance or timing or life. It was rejection. Confirmation that I was difficult to love. Easy to forget. Disposable. A moment of clumsiness became a moral failure. A dropped glass, a wrong turn, a misplaced word transformed into proof that I was useless, ridiculous, incapable of doing anything right.

Even pain itself was turned against me. Being hurt by my partner's actions did not register as heartbreak or grief. In the monster's logic, it became an indictment. Evidence that I was too needy. Too sensitive. Too much. That love failing me was somehow my fault. That if I were better, softer, quieter, stronger, easier, I would not have been left bleeding in places no one could see. Every wound was reframed as weakness. Every tear, a flaw. Every longing, a defect. Slowly, relentlessly, the world stopped happening *to* me and began happening *because of* me. The landscape of my mind grew hostile. No moment remained neutral. No experience was allowed to be human. Everything was filtered through the lens of self-contempt, until I no longer lived inside events, but inside accusations. I became both prisoner and prosecutor, carrying the weight of a trial that never adjourned, never slept, never offered mercy. And in that terrain, where depression had poisoned the ground, self-hatred did not merely grow. It thrived. The world transformed into a warped mirror, reflecting back only my defects, stretched and distorted until they eclipsed everything else. Every surface became an accomplice. Every reflection a quiet act of violence. I could no longer see a whole person. Only fragments. Flaws enlarged to monstrous proportions, virtues erased as if they had never existed. I began to dissect myself mercilessly, like a coroner working on a living body. My body. My face. My voice. My personality. My past. My achievements. I laid each piece beneath the monster's microscope, turning and tilting it until the light caught only what was broken, only what could be used as proof. And in that cruel illumination, I always came up wanting.

It feasted on this. It grew stronger with every self-deprecating thought, every inward cruelty, every quiet agreement with its lies. Misery became its nourishment. Insecurity its oxygen. Shame its bloodstream. Each time I flinched from my own reflection, each time I rehearsed an old failure or pre-emptively punished myself for an imagined one, it swelled. It pulsed. It settled deeper into the architecture of my being until its voice felt less like an intruder and more like the foundation. I started avoiding mirrors, as if they were hostile witnesses, glass informants waiting to testify against me. When I did catch my reflection, it startled me. The face looking back felt like a stranger's. Hollow-eyed. Drained. As though something essential had been siphoned out and never returned. There was a mask there, yes, but it was thinning, cracking under the strain of carrying what could not be seen. Behind it churned a storm: unspoken, relentless, electric with quiet despair. A face shaped by exhaustion. Etched with shame. Haunted by a war no one else could see and no one else knew how to fight. My own gaze had become a weapon. I could catalog every perceived imperfection with surgical precision, trace every imagined failure back to some fatal flaw in my character. My reflection no longer offered recognition. It offered indictment. It did not say, "*Here you are.*" It said, "*Here is everything that is wrong.*" And somewhere beneath that mask, beneath the fog and the lies and the endless internal prosecution, I was still there. Not gone. Not erased. But buried. Buried under verdicts that were never true. Buried under a language of cruelty, I had not invented but had learned too well. Buried under a distortion so complete that even my own outline had disappeared. I existed like a figure pressed under ice, visible only as a vague shadow, a suggestion of a person I once knew how to be. I could no longer recognize myself. Not because I was gone. But because depression had taught me to look at myself through broken glass.

The Master of Disguise

Somewhere along the way, as the monster of self-hate tightened its roots around my thoughts, I learned a new survival skill: camouflage. It did not arrive as a decision. It arrived as instinct. As necessity. As the quiet understanding that if the truth could not be lived, it must at least be hidden. Years passed, and I became fluent in the language of normal. I studied it the way one studies a foreign tongue, carefully, obsessively, listening for inflection, memorising the shapes of acceptable emotion. I practiced it in mirrors and in crowded rooms. I perfected it in offices, at dinners, in passing conversations that never dared wander too close to anything real. I learned when to smile and how wide. How long to laugh. Which tone to use when offering comfort to others, even as my own spirit quietly starved somewhere behind my ribs. "I'm fine," I would say. And the words slipped from my mouth with such ease they almost convinced me. A lie rehearsed so often it softened into something familiar. Something wearable. A sentence so polished it reflected back an image even I wanted to believe. It became my most reliable script, my safest shield, my daily benediction. "I'm fine. I'm okay. Just tired. Just busy. Just a little stressed." Each version adds another layer of paint over a wall already cracking. Inside, though, I was collapsing. Not dramatically. Not in ways anyone could point to and name. But in the slow, granular way mountains erode. While the world saw composure, something in me was turning to dust. While they saw a woman functioning, achieving, contributing, something essential was quietly caving in. The monster did not need to roar anymore. It had learned subtlety. It whispered from within, threading itself through my inner voice, tightening its grip one thought at a time. It drew the walls closer. It narrowed my world. It fenced me off from anything that might expose the truth.

I became a chameleon of the soul. Shifting colours to match every room, every conversation, every expectation. With friends, I wore warmth. At work, competence. With family, reassurance. I mirrored what was required so precisely that no one thought to look twice. I blended in so seamlessly that even I lost sight of what I truly looked like beneath the surface. There was no longer a clear line between performance and person. The mask had fused. I wore competence like armour. Calm like makeup. Strength like a carefully tailored suit. Each piece immaculate. Each piece heavy. Each piece designed to protect what was left of me, and each one quietly suffocating it instead. Because camouflage, while it hides you from predators, also hides you from rescue. And it cost me everything. It cost me honesty. It cost me rest. It cost me the right to be seen in my own pain. It cost me the simple, sacred relief of saying, *I am not okay,* and having the world rearrange itself around that truth. I carried the performance the way one carries a casket, steady hands, straight back, no visible trembling, while inside something irreplaceable lay unnamed and un-mourned. The cruelest part was this: the better I became at seeming whole, the more impossible it felt to admit I was breaking. And so I smiled. And so I nodded. And so I kept surviving in a language that had no words for me. Until even I could no longer remember the sound of my own unmasked voice. Holding the façade in place demanded constant vigilance, a relentless alertness that never slept. Every word was weighed before it left my mouth, tested for safety, stripped of honesty. Every reaction was measured, every expression edited and revised before it could escape. I lived as if under constant surveillance, my own warden, my own censor.

It felt like juggling a dozen fragile glass orbs while walking a tightrope stretched high above exposure, knowing that one tremor of truth, one hairline crack, one unguarded moment of honesty could send everything shattering at my feet. My body began to keep the score long before my mind was willing to listen. Fatigue wrapped itself around my bones, heavy and unrelenting, a weariness that sleep could not touch. Headaches pulsed behind my eyes like distant thunder, a low, warning rumble that never quite broke into rain. Anxiety threaded itself through my days, a restless, electric hum beneath my skin, buzzing constantly, never truly switching off. Even in stillness, my nervous system braced for impact, as if danger were always just moments away. Sleep no longer restored me. It betrayed me. Nights fractured into uneasy fragments, stitched together with dread. Dreams became distorted rehearsals of my fears, replaying themselves in darker, stranger forms, each one more convincing than the last. I would wake already exhausted, heart racing, jaw clenched, as if I had been running all night from something I could never outrun. Morning arrived not as renewal, but as continuation. Another day to perform. Another day to hold the line. The mask protected me from questions. From concern. From interruption. From being asked to explain what I did not yet have language for. But it was suffocating me. It pressed inward with every breath, narrowing the space I had left to exist. And beneath it, the person I once was began to fade. Not abruptly, not with drama, but quietly, like a photograph left too long in the sun. I grew thinner on the inside. My voice softened to a whisper I could barely hear myself. My instincts dulled. My joy retreated. Reaching myself began to feel like calling out across a widening distance, my own name echoing back faintly, distorted, uncertain. I was still there. But I was becoming harder to find.

A Flicker of Hope

And then, in the long season of pretending, in the quiet aftermath of exhaustion and sleepless nights, something unexpected happened. One day, with no intention other than to disappear into distraction, I found myself mindlessly scrolling through the endless corridors of the internet. Thumb moving. Eyes unfocused. Searching for nothing. And somehow, in that numb drifting, I stumbled upon an article about depression. At first, I almost scrolled past it. But something in the title tugged at me, a subtle pull, like a thread catching on a loose seam inside my chest. So I stopped. I opened it. And I began to read. With every line, a strange, unsettling sensation washed over me. Recognition. Not the casual kind, but the deep, bone-level knowing that startles you awake. It was like coming face-to-face with a long-lost twin I never knew existed. A stranger who somehow spoke my private language. Who knew the architecture of my inner world? Who named the rooms I had been locked inside for years? The article spoke of the fog. The numbness. The relentless self-criticism. The hollow exhaustion. The isolation. The hopelessness that coils itself around the mind and convinces it that escape is impossible. It described the thought patterns, the emotional paralysis, the quiet erosion of self. And with every word, my breath caught. It felt as though someone had crawled inside my head and switched on a light. As though they had walked the corridors of my darkness and mapped them. Articulated the very thing I had never been able to explain. The thing that had lived inside me like a wordless scream. For the first time, my suffering had a language. For the first time, it had a name. And for the first time, I felt something I hadn't felt in a very long time. Seen. Not glanced at. Not misunderstood. Seen. As if the invisible weight I had been carrying had been noticed. As if my silent war had been witnessed. As if the monster inside me had finally been exposed to something greater than secrecy. I felt validated. I felt understood. I felt, less alone. And then I reached the end. The article closed not with a solution, not with a promise of instant healing, but with three simple words. *"You are not alone."* Three ordinary words. Three extraordinary truths. They landed in me like embers falling into a long-frozen landscape. Small. Fragile. But warm. Alive. I reread them. Again. And again. *"You are not alone."* Something shifted. Not dramatically. Not enough to dissolve the darkness. But enough to crack it. Enough to let a thin beam of light slip through. A flicker. A trembling, tentative flicker of hope. And in a world that had become nothing but shadow, that flicker felt like everything.

Reaching Out

That fragile flicker did not banish the darkness. It did not split the sky open or scatter the fog in some cinematic sweep of light. But it did something just as radical. It gave me the courage to move. Emboldened by that small, trembling spark of hope, I made a decision that both terrified and steadied me. I reached out. I chose Sarah. A close friend. A familiar face. Someone who knew my laughter, my habits, the version of me I had perfected for public view. Someone who had no idea how vast the storm beneath had become, how many nights I had spent learning the weight of silence, how many days I had carried myself like a sealed room. Telling her felt like standing at the edge of a cliff and stepping forward without knowing if there was ground beneath my feet. It felt like peeling my own skin away and standing raw to the air. Like stripping naked in a world not known for gentleness. My voice shook. My words stumbled. They came out in fragments rather than sentences. In images rather than explanations. Fog. Exhaustion. Fear. Shame. The quiet, trembling admission that I was not okay. And then she listened. Not with impatience. Not with alarm. Not with advice sharpened into weapons. She listened with her whole presence. No judgment. No minimizing.

No hurried reassurances meant to tidy away my pain and tuck it neatly out of sight. Just space. Just warmth. Just the rare, almost sacred act of being witnessed. Her attention did not interrogate me. It held me. And something inside me cracked open. The relief was immediate and overwhelming, like a dam finally giving way after holding back a rising sea for years. The pressure that had lived behind my ribs surged outward. Breath rushed into places it had not reached in a long time. Tears followed, hot and unceremonious, spilling down my face as if my body had been waiting its whole life for permission to release what it could no longer carry alone. I had not been destroyed by the telling. I had been softened. Light did not yet flood in. The fog did not vanish. The monster did not suddenly fall silent. But a door had opened. And through that opening came something I had almost forgotten how to recognize. Air. Room. The first, fragile proof that I did not have to suffocate in solitude. For the first time in a long while, I was not holding my pain by myself.

Words poured out. Tears followed. Fear, grief, exhaustion, confusion. All the emotions that had been fermenting in silence, sealed in the dark like something spoiled and dangerous, rushed suddenly into the open air. They did not arrive politely. They broke through me. My voice cracked. My chest heaved. My hands trembled as if they were finally releasing a weight they had been gripping for years. And in that release, something unfamiliar happened. I felt lighter. Not healed. Not fixed. Not free. But no longer alone inside the wound. It was as if the pain, once a sealed chamber with no exits, had finally been given a window. Fresh air touched places that had known only stagnation. The ache did not vanish, but it could breathe. And so could I. Sarah did not rush to close it. She didn't try to fix me. She didn't rush to rescue me. She didn't coat my confession in silver linings or solutions. She stayed. She let the mess exist between us. Let the tears fall without embarrassment. Let the silence stretch without filling it. She bore witness without flinching, and in doing so, she quietly rewrote something in me. She showed me that my pain did not make me unbearable. That my unraveling did not make me unlovable. And then, gently, like someone placing a lantern into trembling hands, she encouraged me to take another step. To seek professional help. To let someone trained in these shadows walk beside me. To bring this hidden war into a space built for healing. At first, I resisted. The old ghosts rose quickly. The stigma. The labels. The inherited fears that clung to the word therapy like warning signs. Broken. Crazy. Beyond repair.

I felt them crowd the room, those ancient, inherited narratives, hissing that once I spoke this aloud to a professional, it would become irrevocably real. Documented. Diagnosed. Branded into permanence. I feared that naming it would make it grow teeth. That seeking help would seal my identity around my suffering. That I would become nothing more than a file, a disorder, a problem to be managed. So I hesitated. And Sarah stayed. She did not argue. She did not drag. She did not preach. She persisted the way water persists against stone. With patience. With quiet conviction. With a steadiness that did not demand, only reminded. Again and again, she returned me to the truth. That asking for help was not a collapse of strength, but an expression of it. That courage is not the absence of suffering, but the willingness to face it. That needing support did not make me weak. It made me human. Her words did not strike like lightning. They settled like seeds. And somewhere between her voice and my tears, something inside me loosened. The iron narrative began to soften. The monster's grip wavered, just enough for another thought to surface. Maybe I didn't have to do this alone. The flicker grew. Not into a blaze. Not into certainty. Not into sudden hope. But into enough light to see my own hands again. Enough to find the edge of the next step. Enough to move. And for the first time in a long time, the darkness no longer felt like a sealed room. It felt like a corridor. And somewhere ahead, unseen but no longer unimaginable, a door.

The Long Road to Healing

Reaching out cracked the door. Therapy asked me to walk through it. And I did, trembling. Therapy was difficult in the way deep water is difficult. Not violent, not loud, but demanding in its quiet insistence. It did not skim the surface. It did not allow me to paddle safely along the edges. It drew me inward, downward, into the submerged chambers of myself I had spent years sealing shut. It asked me to sit where I had only ever fled. To look where I had only ever numbed. To touch what I had only ever survived. It invited me into the quiet rooms of memory, the ones I had boarded up and labeled *finished*, though nothing inside them had ever healed. It asked me to open drawers still heavy with grief. To stand before mirrors I had shattered long ago. To name the demons I had locked in the back corridors of my mind and pretended were only shadows. Each session felt like excavation. Like kneeling in the dirt with bare hands. Like unearthing old bones without gloves or tools.

I brushed the dust from pain I had never been taught how to hold. I uncovered stories my body remembered long before my language ever could. There were moments when memory rose not as narrative, but as sensation. Tightness in my throat. Fire in my chest. A sudden ache behind the eyes. Grief that arrived without words. Fear that had no timeline. Some days, I left her office feeling flayed open. Skinless. Exposed to the air. As if the world itself might sting. There were afternoons when the weight of it pressed so heavily on my lungs that I had to sit in my car and remind myself how to breathe. Nights when I stared at the ceiling and wondered if I had made a terrible mistake by opening doors that had kept their monsters contained. I wanted, often, to turn back. To reseal the entrance. To retreat into numbness, where at least nothing moved, nothing bled, nothing demanded. Because numbness, cruel as it was, had been familiar. And healing was not. Some days, simply showing up felt like trying to climb a mountain with lungs full of smoke. Every step burned. Every breath was earned. Every mile inside myself felt longer than the last. But Dr. Anya was steady. She did not flinch at the darkness I brought into the room. She did not rush to name it, cure it, tidy it. She did not recoil from the places I feared were unlovable. She met me there. Week after week, she sat with me in the tangled undergrowth of my thoughts, in the bramble of old narratives and buried beliefs. She listened for the patterns beneath the pain. The repetitions. The familiar turns. The old grooves my mind slid into without asking. And gently, patiently, she began to teach me how to see them.

The loops of self-blame. The reflex of worthlessness. The silent scripts that had been running my life from behind the scenes. She helped me notice how my mind leapt from moment to verdict. How a mistake became a sentence. How a feeling became an identity. How a wound became a definition. She showed me the architecture of my suffering, the scaffolding beneath the fog, and for the first time, I could see that what felt like chaos had a structure. And if it had a structure. It could be dismantled. Not all at once. Not without effort. Not without grief for what it had cost me. But piece by piece. Thought by thought. Session by session. Breath by breath. Therapy did not hand me a new life. It handed me a map. And then, quietly, it taught me how to walk it. She showed me how to question them. How to interrupt the scripts before they hardened into verdicts. How to notice a thought without kneeling before it. How to loosen the knots instead of becoming them. She taught me how to breathe when anxiety surged like a rogue tide through my body, when panic rose without invitation and flooded my chest, when my heart drummed emergency into my ribs and my hands forgot they were safe. We practiced it slowly, deliberately. Breath as anchor. Breath as signal. Breath as proof that the moment, however violent it felt, could move through me without becoming me.

CBT became one of the tools that quietly, steadily shifted the ground beneath my feet. It did not sweep in like a miracle cure. It worked like erosion. Like water over stone. Patient. Persistent. It didn't erase the pain, but it illuminated the machinery of my mind, the gears of belief, the reflexes of thought, the hidden assumptions I had mistaken for truth. It taught me to hear the voice of depression not as prophecy, but as a symptom. Not as command, but as noise. Slowly, the internal weather began to change. Storms still came, but they no longer owned the sky. Where once there had only been thunder, there were now pauses. Where once there had only been fog, there were now edges. Where once my thoughts had felt like enemies, they began to feel like signals, messages I could interpret rather than obey. The road to healing was long. It was uneven. It was not a straight line, but a winding passage through fog and forest, through shadowed valleys and sudden, breath-stealing clearings. Some days the ground rose gently beneath my feet. Other days it vanished without warning, dropping me back into old darkness so convincingly I believed I had imagined all progress.

There were setbacks. Relapses. Weeks when the weight returned with its old authority, when the whispers found their way back into my bones, when despair wore the familiar face of truth and told me nothing had changed at all. But something had. Even on the worst days, I was no longer entirely unarmed. I did not walk that road alone. There was Dr. Anya, steady as a lighthouse, helping me read the currents when the waters inside me grew wild. There was Sarah, whose presence never wavered, whose belief in me held when my own could not. And there was a slowly growing understanding of myself, a fragile, hard-won intimacy with my own inner terrain. So I kept going. One session. One insight. One breath. One fragile, stubborn step at a time. Not because the road was easy. Not because the pain was gone. But because, for the first time, I believed something I had not dared to believe before. That this was not the end of my story. That the fog was not my identity. That the darkness, however convincing, was not the author of my life. And that belief, trembling and imperfect as it was, became its own kind of light. Enough to take the next step.

Learning to Live with the Shadow

Healing did not mean the monster vanished. That truth came slowly, the way all honest truths do. Not as a revelation, but as a recognition. A dawning. A gentle, unsettling understanding that what I was learning was not how to banish the darkness, but how to live without surrendering to it. What I came to understand, slowly and sometimes painfully, was that it would always be a part of me. Not as a ruler of my inner world, not as the architect of my days, but as a presence. A shadow. Something shaped by the light that now lived beside it. Something that might stretch when I was tired, deepen when grief passed through me, thin when joy found its way back. There was no dramatic exorcism. No final battle scene. No moment where the sky split open and the darkness fled in defeat. Instead, there was something quieter. Truer. More human. I learned that I could weaken its grip. That I could loosen the chains. That I could reclaim the territory of my own life inch by inch, breath by breath, choice by choice. The shadow did not disappear. But it stopped being my horizon. I began practicing self-compassion, a language that felt foreign at first, awkward on my tongue, like learning to speak after years of silence. For so long, cruelty had been my mother tongue. Judgment my reflex. Self-punishment my instinct. Gentleness felt undeserved. Patience felt dangerous. Kindness toward myself felt like a lie.

But I practiced anyway. I began offering myself the same care I would give a friend in pain. The same soft voice. The same understanding. The same grace for being human in a body that bruises, in a mind that trembles, in a life that wounds. When the monster whispered its familiar lies, I learned to pause. Not to wrestle them. Not to obey them. But to turn toward them. To look at them in the light. I learned to say, "*This is a thought. Not a verdict. This is a symptom. Not a prophecy. This is depression speaking, not truth.*" I learned to question their authority. To feel their presence without kneeling before it. To let them pass through me like weather instead of letting them become the sky. And slowly, something inside me began to change shape. I found new ways to tend to the storm. I moved my body when the heaviness settled into my limbs, letting motion loosen what despair tried to freeze. I breathed when my mind began to spiral, slow inhales pulling me back into my ribs, my skin, my weight in the world. I let nature soften what the illness had sharpened. Trees teaching me stillness. Wind teaching me release. Open sky reminding me that nothing I was living inside was the size of everything.

Exercise became release. Meditation became refuge. Water became grounding. Light became language. Time under open skies began to stitch something back together in me. It reminded me that the world was wider than my pain. That beauty still existed without asking anything of me. That life was still unfolding, patiently, whether

I believed in it or not. And perhaps most importantly, I learned to allow myself to be human. To be tired. To be messy. To be afraid. To be unfinished. I learned that it was okay to not be okay. That bad days did not undo good ones. That relapse was not betrayal. That rest was not weakness. That asking for help was not failure, but fluency in survival. I stopped demanding that I be healed. And started allowing myself to be healing. The shadow still walks beside me. It shows up when the nights are long. When stress stacks too high. When grief brushes past my ribs. When the world feels too loud and my inner weather turns. But it no longer decides where I am allowed to go. It does not choose my steps. It does not hold the map. It does not own the pen. I walk forward now with awareness instead of fear. With tools instead of denial. With compassion instead of cruelty. The shadow may follow. But I am the one who leads.

A New Dawn

Life did not suddenly become flawless. There were still storms that gathered without warning. Still quiet days where doubt drifted in like coastal mist. Still moments when sadness brushed past my ribs like a familiar ghost, soft-footed and unannounced. Healing did not erase the weather. But it changed the house I lived in. The darkness no longer ruled the rooms of my mind. It no longer held the keys. It no longer rearranged the furniture of my thoughts while I slept. I was not a prisoner anymore. I had learned to live beside the shadow, to recognize its silhouette without mistaking it for myself. To acknowledge its presence without handing it my entire sky. What once devoured me now only visited. What once dictated now merely passed through. And in that shift, subtle and seismic, something sacred took root. I found my voice again. Not the voice that apologizes for breathing. Not the one that softens itself to fit the comfort of others. But the voice that speaks from the spine. The voice that names truth. The voice that says, *This hurts,* and also, *This matters.* I found a strength that was not loud or armoured or untouchable, but resilient. A strength that bends in heavy wind. That trembles under the weight. That sometimes breaks open into tears. And still... rises. Again and again. A strength born not of invincibility, but of return. The world, which had once dulled into a colourless blur, began to reveal itself to me again. Not all at once. In fragments. A laugh that reached my chest before it reached my mouth. Sunlight warming my skin like a forgotten language. The quiet gravity of being held without explanation.

Small mercies. Soft proofs. And then, gradually, in fuller shades. Deeper hues. Truer tones. Joy. Connection. Love. Life. Not the performance of it. The inhabiting of it. For the first time in a long time, I was not merely surviving inside the world. I was living inside it. Feeling it in my hands. In my breath. In the way music moved my body without asking permission. I was letting experience pass through me again instead of stopping at the surface. Letting beauty bruise me open. Letting meaning land. And if you are reading this from inside your own unseen cage, if the walls feel too thick and the air too thin, if hope feels like a rumour spoken in another language, hear this: You are not alone. Even here. Especially here. There is hope, even if you cannot feel it yet. There is help, even if you do not know where to begin. There is a future that has not finished forming you. And you are worthy, always, of a life filled with light. Not because you are strong enough. Not because you are healed enough. Not because you have earned it. But because you are alive. Do not give up. Your dawn is not a myth. Your dawn is not a metaphor. Your dawn is not reserved for other people's stories. Your dawn is real. And it is waiting.

THE STORY

Still carried by that fragile dawn, I wrapped both hands around a colourful mug, letting its painted warmth seep into my palms. The ceramic was chipped along the rim, imperfect, familiar, a small survivor of countless mornings. The tea inside had already gone lukewarm, offering little comfort against the cold that lived deeper than skin or season, a chill untouched by scarves, blankets, or autumn air. It was a cold that settled inward, quiet and stubborn, making a home where warmth should have lingered. Beyond the window, the world performed its brilliance without apology. Leaves burned in defiant beauty, a riot of crimson and gold scattered across the pavement like spilled paint, each one glowing as if lit from within. Their splendour felt almost cruel, a deliberate contrast, as though the earth itself were flaunting a life I could no longer access. The colours sharpened the ache, throwing the greyness inside me into harsher relief. I watched them fall and wondered how something could be so vividly alive while I felt so dimly present, suspended behind glass, a witness rather than a participant. They called it "*depression*". A neat, clinical word. Smooth-edged. Sanitized. Something spoken in lowered tones or tossed lightly into conversation, as if it carried no more weight than a passing mood or a bad week. But what lived inside me was no small thing. It was not tidy. It was not polite. It was a leviathan. Vast. Suffocating. An ancient, unseen force moving beneath the surface of my days. Its tentacles coiled around my heart, tightening slowly, relentlessly, not all at once but with terrible patience. Each constriction drained colour from memory. Joy faded first, then hope, then the future itself, until even imagining tomorrow felt like an act of fiction.

What had once felt expansive narrowed into something cramped and airless. Possibility collapsed inward. Desire went quiet. Meaning slipped through my fingers like sand I could no longer hold. This was not feeling down. Not a temporary low tide. Not a cloud drifting politely across a blue sky. This was being submerged. Held under. Forced to breathe water and call it air. It was waking each morning already exhausted, as though I had fought through the night and lost. It was carrying an invisible weight that bent my spine and slowed my steps, a gravity no one else could see but that shaped every movement I made. It was smiling when expected, answering when spoken to, existing just convincingly enough to avoid questions, while inside, something essential was eroding, grain by grain. The mug warmed my hands, but it never reached my heart. I sat there, suspended between the fragile promise of dawn and the vast darkness I still carried, holding warmth that could not quite penetrate, watching colour that did not yet belong to me. And somewhere beneath the fog, beneath the leviathan's slow pull, a truth hovered, quiet and waiting. This was the beginning of the story. Not the beginning of the darkness, but the moment I finally turned toward it. The moment I stopped pretending the monster was small. The moment I began, however shakily, to name the thing that had been naming me for far too long. This was a pervasive nightfall. Not the honest dark of evening that promises rest, but a thick, smothering fog that pressed into every room of my life, seeping beneath doors, coiling into corners, settling on furniture, on memories, on my own skin. It blurred edges until nothing felt distinct. It dulled sound until even my own voice felt far away. It swallowed contrast, erasing the difference between morning and midnight, between presence and absence, between living and merely existing.

The vibrant palette of the world was leeched into monochrome, as if some invisible hand had drained the pigment from creation itself. Reds lost their fire. Blues their depth. Gold its warmth. Even the boldest sunlight arrived weakened, filtered, like a trembling candle flame struggling to survive in a vast, echoing cavern. Light no longer touched; it hovered. It did not warm; it observed. It fell across my days like a thin apology. Still wrapped in that cavern of dimmed light, I went searching for joy and found only its echo.

Joy had become a distant memory, a phantom limb of the soul, something I could vaguely recall but no longer inhabit. I knew it had once belonged to me. I could trace its outline in old photographs, in half-remembered laughter, in stories people told about who I used to be. Yet every attempt to feel it ended in empty air, my hands closing around absence. Laughter, when it reached me, sounded like a foreign language spoken through walls, sharp and unfamiliar, jarring against the silent scream lodged permanently in my chest. It startled rather than soothed, a reminder of a country I no longer lived in. Despair was not an emotion I visited. It was a garment I lived in. A heavy cloak stitched from shadow, lined with doubt, clasped at the throat with shame. I wore it in kitchens and offices, in crowded rooms and empty beds. I wore it beneath smiles and small talk. It followed me into sleep and greeted me when I woke. It pressed itself against my ribs, compressing breath, tightening space, stealing oxygen from moments that should have been light. Even tenderness felt suffocated beneath its weight. Even beauty arrived muted, as though wrapped in cloth before being handed to me. I moved through days gasping, not for air alone, but for relief that never arrived. For a pause in the pressure. For a thinning of the dark. For some small proof that the world had not completely closed its hands around me. And all the while, beneath the fog, beneath the cloak, beneath the long, internal night, something in me was still awake. Not loud. Not strong. But listening. A quiet witness inside the wreckage. A pulse beneath the numbness. A breath beneath the suffocation. I did not yet know how to reach it. I did not yet believe it could reach me. But it was there. And even in the deepest nightfall, the presence of something still alive is never nothing.

Those early years blurred together into a single, endless season of trying to understand the thing that had made a home inside me. I circled it the way one circles a dark lake at night, searching for an edge, a reflection, a hint of depth. I wanted its shape. Its name. Its origin. I believed that if I could map it, I might weaken it, that if I could hold it in language, it might finally loosen its grip. But what I found instead was confusion. Bewilderment. A vast, unsettling emptiness that refused definition. It was not the hollow of something simply missing. It was a profound numbness. A deadened field after a long, merciless winter, where even memory of colour struggled to survive. Feeling no longer took root. Emotion did not rise; it stalled, like seed scattered on stone. I moved through my days without texture, without temperature, without true contact. I was no longer fully inside the world. I lived behind a thick pane of glass. Watching life unfold in colour and motion on the other side. People loved. Laughed. Reached. Dreamed. Their lives bloomed in gestures I could observe but not enter. Sound arrived muffled. Joy arrived distorted. Sorrow arrived dulled. I stood suspended in my own quiet purgatory, close enough to see the pulse of living, the rise and fall of other people's meaning, yet sealed off from ever truly touching it. Close enough to ache. Too far to belong. I tried to give it language. I tried to translate the suffocating weight, the crushing loneliness, the gnawing swarm of self-doubt into something another human could hold. I searched for words large enough to carry the enormity of what lived inside me, words that might make it real in someone else's hands. But each time I reached for them, they dissolved in my mouth before they could take form. My vocabulary felt too small. Too fragile. Paper-thin against the density of the dark. Every attempt collapsed into vagueness. Into silence. Into the familiar ache of being unable to be known. So instead, I performed. I curved my lips into practiced smiles, the muscles remembering joy long after the feeling had gone. I released polite laughter at jokes that never reached my chest, sound without resonance, motion without meaning. I nodded along to conversations that skimmed the bright, ordinary surface of a world I no longer inhabited. I mirrored interest. I echoed concern. I perfected the small, convincing gestures of wellness.

I became fluent in the art of appearing well. I wore normalcy like a second skin. Competence like a costume. Ease like a borrowed voice. And each time I stepped into that performance, something in me stepped further away. A careful architect of illusion. A sculptor of normalcy. I measured every angle, reinforced every weak point, polished the façade until it shone with plausibility. From the outside, the structure held. The world saw something intact. Something functional. Something fine. But inside, the foundation was giving way. I was quietly collapsing, flaking at the edges, disintegrating grain by grain into a fine dust of despair no one else could see. I carried myself like a finished house while termites worked the beams. Each day I stood upright was an act of concealment, not strength. Shame took root easily in that interior wasteland. It bloomed fast. Thick. Invasive. It crept through the cracks and claimed the rooms I had abandoned, spreading vines of self-loathing along the walls of my mind. A deep, corrosive contempt unfurled through me, curling around every thought, every memory, until even kindness felt suspect. And then the whispers began their work. Subtle at first, almost reasonable. Then merciless. You are worthless. You are too much. You are never enough. They spoke with the intimacy of a voice that knows your name, your history, your softest underbelly. They did not shout. They did not rush. They repeated. They twisted my perceptions, bent every reflection into something cruel. Mirrors became witnesses for the prosecution. Every mistake hardened into a verdict. Every imperfection became a sentence. Every disappointment was filed as proof of some fundamental defect etched into my being. I replayed my failures like evidence in a private courtroom where I was always both the accused and the judge, the gavel striking again and again inside my skull. No appeal. No mercy. Only the steady accumulation of guilt, stacked like files on a desk that never cleared.

And the monster fed well there. It drank from my self-contempt. It fattened itself on my silence. It grew in the shadow of my own voice, learning my cadence, borrowing my language, until I could no longer tell where it ended and I began. Stronger with every thought, I used to cut myself open from the inside. Each inward cruelty sharpened its teeth. Each agreement with its lies gave it another room to occupy. And all the while, the architect kept working. The sculptor kept polishing. The illusion held. While the real me, buried beneath it all, learned how to disappear. For years, I lived beneath the heavy illusion of being the only one. The only one drowning this way. The only one whose chest felt permanently flooded, whose lungs laboured as if filled with seawater no one else could see. I believed my suffering was singular, sealed off from the rest of humanity, too vast and too warped for another mind to recognize. Loneliness did not simply accompany me; it authored my reality. Every smile I offered felt like a small act of treason, a quiet betrayal of the truth, both to myself and to those who looked at me and saw something whole, something functioning, something fine. Each pleasant word was a coin paid to the illusion. Each laugh, a mask tightened another notch. My life became a kind of solitary confinement, walls erected not from brick or iron, but from silence, shame, and the unspoken conviction that no one could ever reach me where I was. I existed inside a cell of my own making, pacing its narrow perimeter, counting the days not by calendars but by the ache in my bones, the heaviness in my breath, the familiar throb of endurance. Time marked itself through exhaustion. Through the slow accumulation of mornings survived and nights endured. Through the dull arithmetic of simply staying. And then, almost imperceptibly, a fracture appeared in those walls. Not a shattering. Not a dramatic collapse. Just a hairline crack. A thin, uncertain seam where light hesitated before touching the dark. Tentatively. Trembling. I began to search beyond my own echo. I started reading the stories of others who had wrestled with the same dark creature, who had given names to the same shadows, who had walked through the same suffocating weather and lived to speak of it. Their words met me like lanterns carried deep into a cave, small circles of glow trembling in vastness. They did not banish the dark, but they punctured it. They revealed contours. Depth. Passageways I had not known existed.

In their rawness. Their unfiltered honesty. Their scarred tenderness. I found something I had not felt in years. Recognition. A sudden, aching familiarity. Belonging. It was as if voices reached across distances, I had believed uncrossable and said, "*I know this place.*" I have knelt here. I have feared here. I have lost myself here too. And in that recognition, something inside me shifted. The cell did not vanish. But its walls no longer felt absolute. Proof of life began to flicker where only isolation had lived. I discovered I was not alone. That there were others who knew this terrain intimately, who had bled here, who had unraveled here, and who had still found a way to keep walking. Not unbroken but breathing. Not untouched but bearing light through their cracks. Their survival did not minimize my pain. It dignified it. It gave it context. It placed my suffering back into the human story where it belonged. And in that shared humanity, something extraordinary occurred. The monster lost one of its most powerful weapons. Because loneliness, once named, began to loosen its grip. And the echo I had lived inside for so long was finally answered. There was no cinematic turning point. No single, radiant morning where the light flung open the curtains and declared me healed. No swelling music. No sudden clarity. It was slow. Unforgivably slow. A painstaking ascent on trembling legs out of an abyss that often felt bottomless, where even the idea of up seemed like a cruel rumour. Some days progress looked like movement. Other days it looked like simply not disappearing. There were slips. There were relapses. There were mornings when the monster surged back with its familiar teeth, snapping at my ankles, trying to drag me into old waters. Moments when the fog thickened again and whispered, "*See? Nothing has changed.*"

But something had. With each stumble, something new was quietly taking root inside me. Not triumph. Not certainty. But capacity. The ability to forgive myself when I faltered instead of sentencing myself. The courage to name my vulnerability instead of disguising it. The humility to reach outward instead of collapsing inward. I began to learn a different kind of strength, one that did not roar or conquer, but softened. One that bent down, gathered the broken pieces, and said, "*You can rest here. You can try again.*" And in those small, imperfect movements toward help, toward truth, toward connection, I began, inch by inch, to loosen the chains I had once believed were forged into my bones. Therapy became my lifeline. Not a cure, but a harbour. A quiet inlet where the relentless waves finally lost their teeth. A place where I could lay down the unbearable weight I had been hauling alone, unseal the boxes of pain I had buried, and look at the shapes that had haunted me in the dark. Within those walls, I learned the language of my own wounds. I learned how they had formed. Where they hid. What they protected. I learned to sit with them instead of fleeing, to trace their edges with curiosity instead of terror, to understand them rather than wage endless war. Medication, too, found its place in those early days of survival. Not as a miracle. Not as an eraser. But as a crutch beneath shaking legs. A temporary scaffold around a collapsing structure. It steadied the ground just enough for me to breathe. Just enough for me to listen. Just enough for the deeper work to begin. It did not carry me forward, but it kept me from sinking while I relearned how to stand. And the love of friends and family. Their patience. Their steadiness. Their refusal to turn away when I was hollow, inconsistent, exhausted, hard to reach, hard to reassure. They became the bedrock beneath everything. The hands that did not withdraw when mine went numb.

The voices that kept calling my name when I could barely remember it myself. They were the ground I kept finding when I thought I was falling forever. Again and again, when the darkness said, "*There is nothing beneath you*", they proved there was. And in that discovery, fragile but undeniable, something extraordinary began to grow. Not happiness. But safety. And from safety, slowly, life. Today, the fog has not vanished entirely. It has not dissolved into some convenient miracle. There are still mornings when the air feels heavier in my lungs, when the shadows stretch long across the inner terrain of my life, when the old presence clears its throat, and the monster leans close, preparing to murmur its familiar refrains. But those whispers no longer own me. They no longer arrive crowned as kings. They are quieter now. Thinner. Frayed at the edges. I know their accent. I recognize their costumes. I can feel the way they twist truth until it bruises, and because I know them, I am no longer required to obey them. I have learned to meet them with questions instead of surrender. To turn toward the voice and say, "*Is this yours... or is this mine?*" To hold each lie up like a shard of dark glass and let the light touch it until the illusion softens and the sharpness loses its authority. And in the spaces, they leave behind, where certainty once suffocated, sunbeams slip through. Not blinding. Not theatrical. But real. Warm. Human. The colours are returning. Slowly. Gently. Like a painting being restored by patient hands, one careful stroke at a time, one buried hue coaxed back into breath. Some days it is only a whisper of blue in the corner of the sky. Some days, it is the gold of laughter rising unexpectedly in my chest. Some days it is simply the quiet miracle of feeling something at all. I am learning, in fragments and in practice, how to live again. How to notice beauty without bracing for its loss. How to let joy visit without chaining it to impossible promises. How to exist in a world that still holds darkness without believing it is only darkness. I am learning that light does not require the absence of shadow. Only the refusal to surrender the whole sky. The journey is far from over. There are still bends in the road I cannot yet see around. There are still seasons that will test what I have rebuilt. But for the first time in longer than I can remember, I can see the path ahead. Not lit by some impossible, blinding brilliance, but by a warm, steady glow. The kind of light that doesn't scorch the eyes or demand certainty. The kind that simply says, "*You can take the next step*". And that, in itself, is a victory.

Chapter Seventeen:

The Weight of Darkness: A Journey Through Depression and Self-Discovery

Depression. Even the word carries a gravity, a leaden pull that settles somewhere deep in the body, heavy in the chest, dense in the gut, as though it were already beginning its quiet work. It arrives not only as sound but as sensation, a low tide dragging warmth out of the bloodstream, a dimming behind the eyes. It is a word tossed lightly across conversations, trimmed into jokes, reduced to moods and moments. Passed hand to hand as if it were small. Manageable. Temporary. But for those who live inside its suffocating grip, it is anything but light. It is a relentless storm system that takes up residence beneath the ribs. Not thunder and spectacle, but weather that lingers. Air that never quite clears. Skies that forget how to open. A slow, eclipsing darkness that does not merely touch joy and hope, but swallows them, along with the fragile architecture of self. It seeps into the load-bearing places. The quiet beliefs. The inner rooms where meaning once hung like windows. It does not pass through. It moves in. It rearranges the furniture of the soul. It shifts what you lean on. It changes what feels reachable. Until even your own inner home begins to feel unfamiliar, its hallways longer, its light harder to find.

And perhaps you have lived with it for years. Perhaps you have felt that unseen weight pressing down on your days, bending your mornings, hollowing your nights. Perhaps it has followed you like a second gravity, altering the way you rise, the way you rest, the way you occupy your own skin. Perhaps you have become fluent in the language of "fine." The automatic smile. The practiced ease. The careful performance that convinces the world and almost convinces you. "I'm okay," you say, even as the inner walls begin to crack, even as pieces of you quietly fall inward. You say it while gathering yourself from the floor of your own becoming. You say it while swallowing weather no one else can see. You hold it together. You function. You survive. You move through days like a house still standing after the quake, learning where not to step. But the truth, the tender and terrifying truth, is that you are not okay. And that is okay. Because not being okay is not failure. It is not weakness. It is not proof that you are broken beyond repair. It is a signal. A human one. A soul one. The body's flare shot into the dark saying something here needs care. Something here is asking to be witnessed. And most of all, it is not solitary. You are not alone in this storm. You never have been. Others are out here too, learning how to breathe in this strange weather, carrying their own flickers of light, their own quiet maps back to shore.

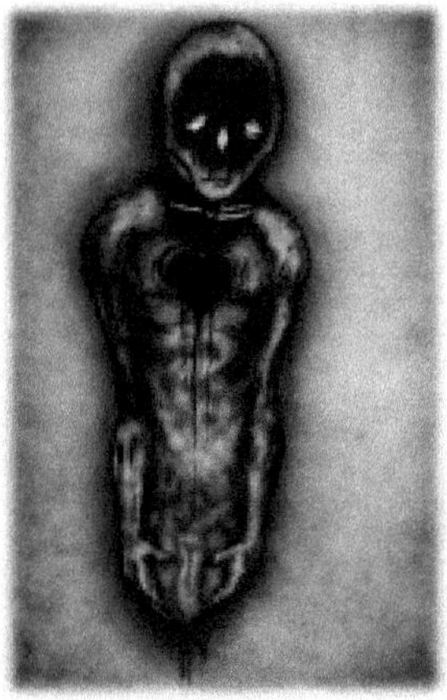

DEPRESSION IS A WORD that is often used lightly, a word passed from mouth to mouth as if it were thin, as if it named something brief and manageable, a passing weather of the heart. But for those of us who have lived inside it, depression is not a word at all. It is a presence. A gravity. A living, breathing entity that enters quietly and stays. A patient, unsleeping creature that wraps itself around the softest parts of us, our hearts, our minds, our sense of who we are, coiling into the unseen chambers where we once felt most alive. It does not merely visit thought. It moves in. It drapes itself across the nervous system. It settles into breath and bone, into muscle and memory, into the way we inhabit time and meaning. It becomes an emptiness that echoes, a vast interior room where every sound returns altered and hollow. A numbness that bleaches the world of its texture, draining colour from landscapes, flattening music into noise, reducing laughter to vibration without warmth. A disconnection so complete it feels as though life is happening on the other side of thickened glass. You can see the movement. You can register the shapes. But you cannot reach the heat. You press your palms against the invisible barrier and feel only your own cold reflected back. It is the sensation of being trapped inside your own existence. Of waking each day inside a body that feels like a locked room. Of standing still while time continues elsewhere, seasons changing without you, people growing and loving and becoming while you remain pinned beneath an invisible weight. It is reaching for escape and finding only walls made of yourself. Corridors that lead back to the same ache. Doors that open into the same grey. Here, even longing grows tired. Even hope forgets its own language. Even tears lose their way home. Grief becomes soundless. Joy becomes theoretical. The future collapses into a narrow tunnel of endurance. You do not move through life so much as endure it, breath by deliberate breath, hour by heavy hour. And in this suspended state, where desire dulls and sensation blurs, depression does its cruelest work: it convinces you that this hollow is who you are. That this absence is your essence. That this dimness is your natural climate. But it is not.

It is something that has wrapped itself around you. Something that has spoken through you. Something that has lived in you without being you. And even here, inside this echoing quiet, where feeling feels like a memory and existence feels like confinement, there remains a truth the fog cannot fully erase: What inhabits you is not what defines you. What weighs on you is not what you are. What has taken residence can, in time, be named, challenged, softened, and slowly, painstakingly, taught to loosen its hold. Because presence is not permanence. And night, no matter how convincingly it settles in the bones, is not the end of the story. Depression is often reduced to a word. A thin sound for something so immense. A label that skims the surface of a depth it cannot possibly hold. A term scattered through conversations without reverence, without caution, as though it were interchangeable with a bad day, a passing low, a temporary ache. As though sorrow and depression lived in the same house. But for those who have felt its grasp close around their inner world, depression is not a word. It is a climate. A gravity. A living, breathing reality that seeps into thought, constricts emotion, and slowly stills the places where the spirit once moved freely. It reshapes perception until the world itself seems altered. It bends truth until even memory feels unreliable. It teaches the heart a new language, one spoken in weight and weariness, in erosion and endurance. Under its influence, the mind becomes unfamiliar territory. Thoughts no longer feel like visitors, but wardens. Emotions flatten or fracture. Desire dims. The future narrows. The simple act of existing becomes something that must be negotiated rather than inhabited. Depression does not simply make life painful. It makes life feel unrecognizable. It turns the inner landscape into a terrain of fog and echo, where direction dissolves, and even your own footsteps sound distant, as if they belong to someone else.

And it is into this altered world that this book steps. Not as a cure. Not as a command. Not as a bright promise stitched from denial. But as a presence. As a guiding light for those wandering inside the suffocating fog of depression. A small, steady glow held low to the ground, meant not to blind, but to reveal the next few inches of path. A bridge of words stretched between darkness and possibility. Between despair and understanding. Between isolation and the quiet, radical knowledge that what you are living inside has been lived before, named before, survived before. This book is a companion flame for the long night. A handheld out, not to pull you forward, but to walk beside you at the pace your breathing allows. An offering of language for what so often feels unspeakable. A place where the fog is not dismissed but entered. Where the weight is not minimized but witnessed. These pages do not promise an easy morning. They offer something braver. They whisper, again and again, in a voice meant to reach the places that have gone numb: There is more than this. There is a way through. And you do not have to walk it unseen. Here, in these words, your suffering is not a flaw. Your slowness is not a failure. Your darkness is not the end of your story. Here, the light does not shout. It stays.

For years, I walked through my life wearing a mask, convincing those around me and almost convincing myself that I was "fine." I learned the choreography of normal, the delicate footwork of appearing whole. The right expressions placed like stage lights. The careful tones tuned to calm. The practiced ease that kept questions shallow and concern at bay. I became fluent in the art of seeming. But beneath that borrowed face, I was crumbling. Quietly. Constantly. A slow interior erosion no one applauds because no one can see it. The weight of depression pressed down on me like a second atmosphere, invisible yet inescapable, thickening the air around my thoughts, compressing my chest, thinning my breath until even oxygen felt rationed. My mind grew heavy. My body slower. My inner world blurred, as if someone had smeared the lens through which I experienced everything. Existing itself became labor. Not living. Labor. Every hour a shift. Every day a contract I did not remember signing but was forced to honour. Inside, entire inner landscapes were collapsing. Structures I had once lived in without question were caving quietly, rooms of feeling and imagination folding in on themselves. I had lost touch with my emotions, my passions, my sense of purpose, as though someone had been slowly turning the volume down on everything that once made me human. Colours dulled into shades of almost. Desires went mute, their voices swallowed by static. Even pain became distant, a far-off siren echoing through fog, too blurred to locate, too constant to ignore. I was no longer living so much as maintaining. Moving. Functioning. I became a caretaker of my own shell. I went through the motions of days I did not inhabit, rehearsing routines in a life I was no longer inside. Conversations passed through me like weather through an abandoned house. Laughter touched my mouth but not my chest. Touch reached my skin but not my bones. I learned how to survive each day without completely falling apart, which is not the same as living but it can look convincingly similar from the outside. Each morning felt like lifting a life that no longer fit my hands, heavy and unfamiliar, something I was expected to carry without ever being taught its shape. Each night felt like laying myself back into a body that had stopped feeling like home, more containment than comfort, more obligation than refuge. And still, I smiled. And still, I said "fine." And still, I performed the small, exhausting rituals of appearing okay. But beneath the mask, beneath the function, beneath the quiet industry of survival, something sacred was stirring. Something unextinguished. Something that had not forgotten what it meant to feel, to hope, to be held from the inside. Something in me was still asking to be seen.

But I was not alone. Even in the most private chambers of my suffering, in the rooms of the soul where I believed no other footsteps had ever fallen, I was not singular. Across the world, millions of lives are moving through this same interior night, navigating their own unlit corridors, fighting to stay afloat in seas no one else can see. Hearts beating quietly behind closed doors. Minds laboring in silence. Smiles worn like life vests over invisible depths. Entire constellations of people breathing through heaviness, learning how to exist where the air feels thin, learning how to keep living when living itself feels like work. And yet, despite its vast reach, despite the countless lives it threads itself through, depression remains wrapped in stigma and steeped in misunderstanding. It is still spoken of as weakness. As indulgence. As a failure of gratitude or perspective. A temporary "low." A mood that should lift if only one tried harder, prayed deeper, thought brighter. As though darkness could be disciplined away. As though pain of this magnitude were nothing more than poor attitude wearing a dramatic costume. People offer sunshine like currency. Advice like absolution. "Just be positive." "Just snap out of it." "Others have it worse." Words meant to rescue that instead bruise. Spells spoken over wounds that do not close.

But depression is not a mood. It is not a passing cloud that drifts politely across a blue sky and leaves no mark. It is weather that settles into the bones. It is a climate. A season without a calendar. A complex, multifaceted condition that touches every aspect of being, mind, body, memory, meaning. It is chemistry and cognition. Nervous system and narrative. Trauma and temperament braided together into an illness that does not simply visit life but inhabits it. It is a relentless, pervasive darkness that seeps into every pore, every thought, every feeling, like ink dropped into water, blooming outward until even what once ran clear is tinged with shadow. It stains perception. It rewrites interpretation. It leans into every experience and alters its weight. It is the inability to receive joy without strain, to touch beauty without suspicion, to laugh without the echo of something breaking underneath. It is the constant, bone-deep gravity of despair, a heaviness that does not lift when circumstances improve, because it was never built from circumstances alone. It is the feeling of being trapped inside a suffocating fog where even direction dissolves. Where north and south lose meaning. Where forward and back blur into the same exhausted place. A landscape without landmarks. A world without edges. You reach for relief and your hands close on air. You search for clarity and find only more haze. And still, inside that dimness, you breathe. You endure. You carry a weight no one taught you how to name. This is not weakness. This is survival inside a storm that lives within the skin. The insidious nature of depression lies in its mastery of disguise. It is a chameleon of the inner world, a shape-shifter that studies its surroundings and learns how to blend. It borrows familiar faces. It mimics ordinary fatigue. It dresses itself in stress, in busyness, in burnout, in reason. It shifts colours so subtly that you do not see it arrive. You only notice, one day, that the light has changed.

Sometimes it settles as a paralyzing inertia, a private gravity so dense it bends will itself. Limbs feel forged from stone. Thought moves like syrup. Rising from bed becomes an ascent without footholds, the mattress no longer a place of rest but a vast, shoreless sea where you drift, heavy and unmoored. The simplest acts glow on the horizon like distant peaks. Drink water. Answer a message. Stand. Each one feels impossibly far away, requiring a strength that no longer answers when you call. Other times, it wears the opposite mask. A whirlwind instead of a weight. Restless energy that whips through the nervous system, a frantic choreography of motion meant to outrun the ache. Cleaning at midnight. Talking too fast. Saying yes to everything. Filling every silence so the silence cannot speak. Here, depression does not press you into stillness, it drives you into motion, a fevered attempt to escape your own interior. But even this movement is heavy. Exhaustion hums beneath it. A tremor in the bones. A running without arrival. It also learns the language of the body. It takes up residence in muscle and marrow, translating itself into fatigue that sleep cannot touch, into nights fractured by shallow dreaming and early waking, into appetites that vanish or roar, into headaches that pulse like distant drums, into aches with no visible wound. It convinces you that it is only physical. That it belongs to hormones, to stress, to weather, to weakness of the flesh. And in this translation, it hides again, blurring the border between illness and identity, between symptom and self. And through it all, the silence surrounding depression is deafening.

We are taught to be strong. To be grateful. To be resilient. To push through. To produce. To perform. To be palatable in our pain, if we are allowed pain at all. We learn early how to armor ourselves with productivity and politeness, how to smile in ways that do not invite questions, how to shrink storms into something socially acceptable. "I'm just tired." "I'm just stressed." "It's nothing." We sand the language down until it no longer cuts, even when the wound still bleeds. But storms do not dissolve because we rename them. And pain does not vanish because it makes others uncomfortable. Somewhere beneath that cultivated quiet, beneath the bright rooms and busy days and curated answers, millions are still treading water in invisible oceans. Still holding their breath. Still whispering into the dark. Still pressing their palms against the glass of their own lives, waiting for a language large enough to hold what they are carrying. Waiting for a way to say: this is more than tired. This is more than sad. This is a weather that lives inside me. This is a night that has learned my name.

The Weight of Silence

In the beginning, there was silence. Not the gentle hush of snowfall or the sacred quiet of dawn, but the kind that gathers before a storm, swollen and breathless, thick with everything it refuses to say. A silence that presses rather than soothes. That leans its full weight against your ribs and waits. You wake each morning beneath its familiar shroud of gloom, surfacing not into light but into gravity. The bed feels deeper than it should, as if the night has weighted the sheets with lead. Your chest is its chosen anchor point. Every breath must haul itself upward through unseen resistance. Inhale becomes effort. Exhale becomes negotiation. Gravity itself seems to have signed your name. Outside, the world performs its rituals. Engines cough to life. Footsteps scatter across pavements. Kettles sing. Voices rise and overlap. Light spills freely through windows, careless and bright. But you remain apart from it, sealed behind an invisible pane. You can see the motion. Hear the noise. But it reaches you only as echo. You live like someone watching their own life through thickened glass. Present, yet unreachable. Existing, yet not quite inside existence. For years, you have mastered the art of disguise. The quiet craft of appearing intact. You have learned how to stand without leaning. How to smile without revealing teeth. How to speak without letting your voice tremble where the fault lines run. You know which jokes buy you safety. Which answers close doors. Which version of yourself is easiest for the world to hold. Your friends and family cannot see the war behind your forced smile, cannot hear the fracture beneath your laughter. They cannot feel the way each interaction costs you something. The way each conversation leaves you a little more hollow than before. "I'm fine,"

you say.

The words slip from your mouth like a reflex. Rehearsed. Polished. Lightweight. A line delivered so often it no longer feels like a lie, only a sound your mouth makes when asked the wrong question. You repeat it until it begins to sound almost true. Until even you start to wonder if maybe you are imagining the ache. And yet, your body keeps its own records. The tight jaw. The tired eyes. The way your shoulders never quite lower. And somewhere in your memory, there is a moment that echoes this dissonance. A crowded room. Music thick in the air. Bodies moving. Glasses clinking. Laughter lifting and bursting like confetti. And you, standing among the living, feeling like a ghost. Invisible in plain sight. Untouched by the warmth inches from your skin. Watching joy move through other people as if it belongs to a different species. Already half gone. You nod when expected. You smile on cue. You play your part in the choreography of togetherness. But inside, there is a hollow chamber where sound does not travel correctly. Where celebration arrives without sensation. Where connection brushes past you without landing. You are there, but you are not there. A silhouette cut out of your own life. This is the weight of silence. Not merely the absence of sound, but the accumulation of all that has not been spoken. Every swallowed sentence. Every hidden fear. Every unanswered "How are you?" piling up inside the chest like stones. Silence becomes storage. A vault. A coffin for words that were never allowed breath. And the longer it lives there, the heavier it grows.

For years, you may not have possessed the language to name what was happening inside you. No vocabulary wide enough to cradle the ache. No words deep enough to carry the weight. What lived within you was vast and shapeless, a pressure without edges, a sorrow without a proper name. And so, in the absence of language, you learned another dialect. You learned the grammar of silence. You wore it like a second skin. You masked your pain with a smile, stitched politeness over fractures, learned how to soften your eyes so no one would look too closely. You convinced those around you, and almost convinced yourself, that you were "fine." That you were simply tired. Simply busy. Simply human in a world that exhausts everyone. But beneath that borrowed ease, you were crumbling. Slowly. Constantly. Not in spectacular collapse, but in quiet erosion. The kind that happens grain by grain, unnoticed, until one day the ground gives way beneath your feet. The weight of your emotions pressed inward, crushing you from the inside out. It crowded your lungs. Fogged your thinking. Numbed your capacity to feel anything except the dull, unrelenting pull of despair. Breathing felt like work. Thinking felt like wading through wet cement. Feeling felt dangerous. As if any real emotion, once allowed, might finally break you open. It felt like living inside a nightmare you could not wake from. No exit. No rest. No horizon. Only the same dark room repeating itself. The same walls. The same air. The same version of you staring back from every surface. Days looping like a broken reel. Nights folding over you without relief. Even sleep no longer offered escape. It only rearranged the shadows. But silence, when left untouched, does not protect. It accumulates. It becomes a burden that feeds the very darkness it hides. It thickens. It closes. It teaches pain to echo only inward, until your own mind becomes the loudest and cruelest room you inhabit. Unspoken grief ferments. Unnamed fear sharpens. Every feeling without language turns back on the body that carries it, looking for a place to land. And so there comes a moment, fragile and frightening, when the work is no longer endurance, but turning. A moment when surviving quietly begins to cost more than speaking aloud. A moment when something inside you leans toward the light, not with certainty, but with longing. When the walls that once felt like shelter begin to feel like a cage. When the silence that once kept you safe begins to suffocate. When you realize that what you have been holding is not going to dissolve on its own. This is the moment of pivot. The moment you begin to face what has been buried. To touch what has been held down. To let feeling have sound. To let truth take shape. Speak your truth, even if your voice trembles. Even if it cracks. Even if it arrives in fragments instead of sentences. Even if the words surprise you with their weight or their grief or their need. You do not have to make it beautiful. You do not have to make it coherent. You only have to make it honest. Because silence may feel like shelter, but it is expression that opens the door. It is voice that lets air in.It is naming that loosens the grip of what has been ruling you unseen. The first sound is rarely loud. Often, it is a whisper. A breath. A single, shaking admission: "*Something is wrong. I am not okay. I need help.*" And in that moment, something shifts. Not the whole night. Not the whole storm. But the air. And sometimes, that is where dawn begins.

Understanding the Monster

And when silence finally begins to loosen its grip, when a voice at last stirs in the dark, what often rises first is not relief, but recognition. Not answers, but the outline of the thing itself. A presence long felt but never seen. A weight finally given shape. For those of us who have lived with depression, it can feel like a severing from the world. A quiet unthreading. As though some essential cord between you and life has been thinned to the point of breaking. Colours still exist, sounds still travel, people still move and speak and reach for one another, yet you remain just beyond their frequency, tuned to a different, heavier station. The warmth of other lives drifts past without landing. Laughter becomes an echo. Touch feels distant. Meaning dissolves before it can settle. It is the sensation of being unable to escape your own interior weather. Of waking each day into the same closed sky. Of moving through hours that seem to loop back on themselves, returning you again and again to the same ache, the same exhaustion, the same bone-deep grief. Days stop opening forward. They circle. They repeat. They write the same sentences into your body until time itself begins to feel like a cage. It is the loneliness of being surrounded and still unreachable. Of sitting in crowded rooms while feeling sealed inside glass. Of watching connection happen without being able to cross the small, impossible distance between your heart and the world. You are adrift in a sea that has no visible shore, scanning the horizon for a shape, a hand, a signal of rescue that never quite comes. And the waiting becomes its own form of drowning. To understand depression is to be willing to descend. To move past its surface disguises and into its roots. To stop asking, "*What is wrong with me?*" and begin asking, "*What has been happening within me? What has shaped this landscape? What has taught my mind and body to live this way?"* Because depression is not a character flaw. It is not a personal failure. It is not weakness wearing heavier clothing. It is often a convergence. A gathering of many currents beneath one dark surface. Threads of biology and inheritance woven with experiences of loss, neglect, rupture, or overwhelm. Nervous systems that learned too early how to brace, how to numb, how to survive.

Brains whose chemistry has tilted toward depletion. Bodies that have carried too much, for too long, without rest or repair. Depression grows where the inner world has been stretched beyond its natural limits and left to mend alone. It does not discriminate. It does not seek a certain type of person. It does not spare intelligence, kindness, faith, success, or love. It crosses ages, races, cultures, incomes, and histories. It enters quiet homes and crowded ones alike. It settles in artists and parents, students and leaders, the deeply sensitive and the outwardly strong. It moves through bloodlines and breaks out in singular lives. It can begin in childhood or arrive unannounced in adulthood. It can follow trauma or emerge without a clear origin story at all. Depression is not a mood. It is not a phase. It is not something you simply "think" your way out of. It is a serious mental health condition. A full-body, full-mind experience. One that alters perception, energy, memory, motivation, and the very way reality is processed. And because it is real, because it is rooted, because it reshapes the terrain of a person's inner life, it requires real care. Real tenderness. Real support. Understanding the monster does not make it vanish. But it does something just as vital. It removes the crown. It begins to separate who you are from what is happening to you. It reframes the struggle from a moral indictment into a human one. It loosens shame's grip. It opens the possibility that what you are living inside is not proof of brokenness, but evidence of injury. Of overload. Of systems that learned to protect in the only ways they knew how. And in that shift, something subtle but seismic begins to occur. The monster is no longer you. It becomes something you can study. Name. Face. And, over time, learn to meet with tools instead of terror. This is where the descent changes its nature. It is no longer a fall. It becomes a search for understanding.  And understanding, quietly, is the first lantern lit in the dark.

And yet, despite how widespread its reach is, fear still circles depression like a second shadow. Many remain afraid to speak its name. Afraid to admit its presence. Afraid to reach outward for help, as though suffering were a personal indictment rather than a profoundly human experience. As though pain were proof of failure instead of evidence of being alive in a world that wounds. And so, countless people carry their darkness in secret, stitching smiles over open places, swallowing truths that ache to be spoken. So imagine it this way: depression as a creature living beneath the bed of your inner world. You do not see it clearly, but you feel it. You sense the shift in the air when the room goes quiet. You hear the faint creak of floorboards in the night. You notice the cold breath curling around your ankles when you least expect it. You know it is there. But you do not look. Because somewhere inside you is the fear that naming it will make it real. That acknowledging it will give it power. That turning on the light will reveal something too vast, too ugly, too impossible to face. But what lives in the dark does not need your permission to grow. Unacknowledged, it stretches. It learns the shape of your silence. It feeds on the spaces where words should have been. It fattens itself on secrecy, on swallowed tears, on the endless rehearsal of "I'm fine." It does not shrink when ignored. It roots. And so, confronting the beast, even when your hands are shaking, even when your voice feels too thin to carry the truth, becomes essential. Not as an act of violence, but of illumination. Draw it into the light. Not to battle it blindly, but to see it. To name it. To trace its patterns.

To study the ways it coils through your thoughts, settles into your body, distorts your reflection, and steals your breath. To witness the scars it leaves, not as evidence of weakness, but as maps of where you have survived. And as you begin this seeing, something vital starts to shift. You recognize that the monster may be with you, but it is not you. It is an occupant, not the architect. A presence, not your essence. A storm system, not the sky itself. This is why breaking the silence around depression matters. Why voices matter. Why stories matter. Because every time someone speaks what was once hidden, the walls thin. Every time a truth is offered into the open, the air changes. We need a culture where honesty is not punished, where vulnerability is not treated like exposure but like courage. A world where people are not exiled for their pain but met inside it. Where asking for help is understood as wisdom, not collapse. Where tenderness is not weakness, but intelligence of the heart. We need to educate ourselves and one another about what depression truly is. About how deeply it touches the nervous system, the chemistry of the brain, the rhythms of the body, the architecture of meaning. About how real support, real connection, real care can interrupt its grip. Can slow its spread. Can offer footholds where there were once only sheer drops. Because monsters lose some of their dominion the moment they are seen. And suffering, when shared, begins to remember the shape of a way through. A way made not of sudden miracles, but of human voices. Of outstretched hands. Of light carried gently into rooms that were never meant to stay dark. And in that shared seeing, in that brave breaking open of what was once sealed, the monster does not vanish. But it no longer rules unseen. And that, in itself, is the beginning of freedom.

The Lonely Road of Self-Hate

And when the monster has lived too long in the dark, it does not only haunt the room. It learns how to speak. It studies you. Your memories. Your wounds. Your hungers. It learns the exact pitch your heart responds to, the precise words that slip past your defenses. And slowly, almost imperceptibly, it begins to narrate your inner world. As days turn into years, the whispers of self-hate grow louder, feeding on your despair like a fire fed by its own smoke, sustaining itself on the very damage it causes. They do not arrive as screams. They arrive as murmurs. Soft. Familiar. Almost tender. *"You aren't good enough. You never were. You'll never be happy. You ruin things. You exhaust people. You don't belong here."* Each morning, they rise with you, as habitual as breath, waiting at the thin edge of waking like an old acquaintance who knows exactly where to press. They sit beside you while you drink your coffee. They follow you into mirrors. They thread themselves through every thought until your own mind feels occupied by an enemy fluent in your language. They wrap their icy fingers around your heart. They slip into your perceptions. They color every memory. They bend every reflection. They borrow your voice so perfectly that you can no longer tell where they end and you begin. This is the loneliest road depression builds: the one where the enemy wears your face. The one where the cruelty sounds like your own thinking. The one where the blade feels self-forged. The one where even your pain turns against you and calls it truth. On this road, isolation deepens, because how do you flee from something that lives behind your own eyes? How do you seek refuge from a voice that speaks from inside your chest? The monster no longer needs to stalk you from the shadows. It has moved in. It has taken up residence in your self-perception. It has made a home out of your identity.

And yet, even here, something else is possible. Even here, in the most intimate chamber of the darkness, a different relationship can begin to form. In this depth of night, self-compassion becomes not a luxury, not a poetic suggestion, but a lifeline. A deliberate act. A rebellion. A way of standing beside yourself instead of standing over yourself with a gavel in your hand. Self-compassion does not arrive as warmth at first. Often, it arrives as awkwardness. As resistance. As the unfamiliar feeling of speaking a language your mouth was never taught to shape. It feels clumsy. Unconvincing. Sometimes even false. But it is not a feeling you wait for. It is a posture you choose. A decision to say: *"I will not abandon myself. I will not continue the violence. I will learn how to sit with my pain without becoming it."* It is choosing to meet your suffering the way you would meet a wounded child or a grieving friend. Not with accusation. Not with demands. But with presence. Acknowledge your struggles as part of your journey, rather than the definition of your entire being. Let the pain have a name without letting it have your identity. You are not the storm. You are the one living through the weather. You are not the wound. You are the one learning how to tend it. Begin simply. Begin gently. Begin where your hands already are. Create a small, daily ritual of gratitude. Not as a denial of pain, but as a widening of the lens. Write down three things that bring you even the faintest sense of softness. A cup of warm tea cradled between your palms. The way late light leans across a wall. The hush after rain. A message that arrived when you least expected it. A memory that still holds color. A single breath that did not hurt as much as the one before it. These are not trivialities. They are embers. And embers matter in long nights. Because little by little, these small recognitions begin to loosen the monster's grip. They interrupt the closed system of self-hatred. They carve tiny windows in the walls of the mind. They introduce gentleness into a space that learned only severity. They do not banish the dark. They teach it that it is not alone in the room. And slowly, through these almost invisible practices, the inner climate begins to shift. The voice of cruelty no longer speaks unopposed. The narrative no longer runs unchecked. Another tone enters the dialogue. Quieter. Kinder. Less certain. But real. Not all at once. Not dramatically. But in the way dawn works. Almost unnoticed. Almost disbelieved. Until one morning, you realize the black is no longer absolute. Until one breath arrives without a blade inside it. Until one thought softens instead of cuts. Until suddenly, there is enough light to see your own hands again.

The Importance of Connection

If self-compassion is the first ember, connection is the breath that teaches it how to glow. Isolation is one of depression's most faithful accomplices. It works without spectacle, without noise, narrowing the world inch by inch until your life feels like a single, locked room inside a vast and indifferent house. It convinces you that you are the only one left inside the storm, the only body still standing in the rain, the only heart beating beneath this particular sky of ruin. It feeds on absence. On unanswered messages. On rooms where your voice has not sounded in a long time.

It whispers that no one could understand this terrain. That your pain is too strange. Too heavy. Too tangled to translate. It builds walls from memory and fear and fatigue and then tells you they are shelter. It teaches you to mistake disappearance for safety, silence for strength, solitude for control. And slowly, the world contracts around the illness until it feels as though nothing exists beyond it. And yet, here is the paradox at the living heart of healing: it often begins the moment you let yourself be seen.

Reaching out rarely feels heroic. It feels terrifying. It feels like standing at the edge of a ravine and whispering into the dark, unsure whether anything will answer. It can feel like lifting a collapsed sky with bare hands. Like loosening armor that has been fused to your skin. Like opening a door you were certain was sealed forever. Your fingers may shake. Your voice may fracture. Your words may come out wrong. But even the smallest opening is still an opening. Even a crack in the wall is enough for light to remember the way in.

Share your experience with someone whose presence feels like softer ground. A trusted friend. A therapist. A support worker. A stranger who speaks a language you recognize in your bones. Let a sentence escape. Let the truth breathe. Let the dark be witnessed. You may discover, with a kind of astonished tenderness, that others have walked these same inner corridors. That they know the architecture of this night. That they have sat with this weight, learned its grammar, named its shadows. You may hear your own feelings spoken in another's voice and feel something long frozen inside you shift. Recognition. Relief. The loosening of a belief you didn't realize had been choking you: *I am not the only one.*

Connection becomes a lifeline. A rope flung across black water. A hand appearing where you were certain there was only air. It does not pull you out in one motion. It steadies you. It keeps you from sinking while you learn how to move again. It reminds you that the sea is wide, but you are not its only swimmer. That countless others are treading this same water, some ahead of you, some beside you, some reaching back with salt on their skin and maps in their pockets.

Support groups, shared spaces, quiet rooms where stories are told without performance, become places of quiet revolution. Places where shame loosens its hold. Where pain is not an anomaly but a language. Where tears are not evidence of failure but of life still moving. In these circles of shared truth, isolation fractures. The fog thins. The inner narrative is interrupted by something stronger than despair: witness. There is a particular power in being mirrored without being judged. In having your suffering named without being minimized.

In feeling your experience reflected back to you not as weakness, but as evidence of endurance. It alters the inner terrain. It shifts the weather. It teaches the nervous system a new possibility: "*I do not have to carry this alone.*" And resilience begins to grow, not as armor, not as forced brightness, but as belonging in the face of adversity. As the quiet, radical knowledge that you can be held while you heal. That you can lean without collapsing. That you can speak and not disappear. Because even the fiercest storms change their sound when you are no longer standing in them alone.

The Road to Recovery

And when connection begins to stitch its small openings in the dark, when the air shifts just enough for breath to feel possible again, a path starts to reveal itself beneath your feet. Not suddenly. Not dramatically. It does not unfurl like a golden road through the fog. It emerges the way deer paths do in the forest, faint at first, pressed gently into the earth by repeated, trembling steps. You almost miss it. But it is there. Recovery does not announce itself with certainty. It does not arrive with banners or guarantees. It arrives as a willingness. As a question. As the quiet decision to take one more step even when the ground still feels unsure. It is not a ladder. It is not a straight ascent toward some shining summit. It is a winding road, a living road, one that bends and doubles back, disappears into mist, reappears in unexpected clearings. It is shaped by both ache and awe, by setbacks that hollow the chest and by small, luminous triumphs that slip in so gently you almost don't trust them. Some days, you will feel movement. Real movement. The fog thins. The weight eases. Laughter rises without effort. You notice the sky. You answer a message. You make a plan. And for a moment, it feels like standing in sunlight after a long winter, stunned by the simple fact of warmth. Other days, it will feel as though you have been carried miles backward into the thick of it. As though the road has folded in on itself and returned you to a familiar darkness. The heaviness returns. The doubts resurface. The old whispers clear their throats. On these days, it is easy to believe you have undone everything. But this, too, is part of the terrain. Healing is not linear because you are not mechanical. You are layered. You are memory, body, nervous system, and story. You are seasons within seasons. And progress, here, does not mean never falling. It means learning how to rise without turning against yourself.

It means understanding that returning to the fog does not erase the miles already walked. It only proves that the fog is not yet finished teaching you where the edges are. For some, medication becomes a stabilizing hand on the trembling architecture of the nervous system, quieting the storms just enough to let rest reach the bones. It does not rewrite your story, but it can soften the volume of suffering, so you are not shouting just to stay conscious. It can become a bridge over the deepest ravines, a way to cross places that were once impassable. For others, therapy opens a language for the inner world. It hands you tools where there were only wounds. It offers names for the shapes moving in the dark, and in naming them, begins to loosen their power. It becomes a place where patterns are traced, where old scripts are interrupted, where the body learns that it no longer has to live as though the past is still happening. Often, recovery is not one thing. It is a tapestry. A weaving together of many threads. Biology and story. Support and solitude. Medication and movement. Tears and laughter. Structure and rest. Setbacks and breakthroughs. There is no single map. No universal prescription. No identical journey. You are allowed to explore what healing looks like for you. You are allowed to experiment. To change direction. To gather what helps and set down what doesn't. Your recovery does not have to resemble anyone else's to be real. It only has to bring you closer to yourself. And slowly, almost without noticing when it first begins, the road starts to feel less like a punishment and more like a passage. Less like something you must survive and more like something you are learning to walk. Step by careful step. Breath by honest breath. Toward a life that is not free of shadow but no longer ruled by it. Along this road, begin to gather what sustains you. Not as obligations, not as another list of ways to fall short, but as provisions for the long walk. Small, faithful practices that tend the fragile architecture of your well-being. Meditation that teaches the breath how to soften again, how to move like tide instead of siren, easing the nervous system back from its constant state of alarm. Moments of stillness where you are not required to fix or perform or endure, only to notice. To feel the simple miracle of air finding its way in and out of you.

Journaling becomes a kind of shelter along the way. A place where the unspeakable can finally lay its head. Where thoughts no longer have to ricochet endlessly through the chambers of your mind, but can be set down, one by one, like stones taken from an overburdened pocket. On the page, the chaos begins to take shape. The fog gains edges. The monster loses some of its size. Writing does not demand eloquence. It asks only for honesty. For the courage to let what lives inside you exist outside of you, where it can be seen, named, and slowly transformed. And then there is the body. So long conscripted into survival. So long made to carry what words could not. Physical movement, in whatever gentle form you can meet it, becomes a way of remembering that you are not only a mind in pain, but a living rhythm. A pulse. A breath. A weight that can shift. A heart that can quicken. A stretch. A walk. A sway. A single step into fresh air. These movements are not about achievement. They are about return. About inviting sensation back into a body that learned too well how to disappear. These practices may look small. From the outside, they may appear almost insignificant. They are not. They are the laying of stones. And stones, placed one by one, become a path. Small steps, taken with patience and consistency, become the groundwork of deeper change. Of rewiring. Of relearning. Of re-inhabiting your own life. Remember this: progress may be slow. Some days will rise like mountains before you have even sat up in bed. Some mornings will feel insurmountable before the light has touched the wall. There will be days when brushing your teeth feels like a victory and days when even breathing feels like negotiation. This does not mean you are failing. It means you are human. It means you are still walking. Honour your journey exactly as it is. Not as you think it should be. Not as someone else's was. Exactly as it is. Because acceptance is not resignation. It is the ground from which growth becomes possible. Celebrate the small victories. Getting out of bed. Letting water run over your skin.

Feeding yourself something warm. Sending a single message. Allowing a feeling to pass through without turning it into a verdict. These are not trivial acts. They are quiet declarations of life. They are the soft rebellion of care in a world of inner cruelty. They are proof that something in you is still choosing to stay. They are the road being built beneath you. Stone by careful stone. Breath by patient breath. One compassionate step at a time.

Finding Light in the Shadows

And as the road continues to unfurl beneath your careful feet, there comes a moment, almost imperceptible at first, when you realize the dark is no longer the whole landscape. It is still there, yes. It still gathers in familiar hollows. It still cools the air at the edges of certain days. But it is no longer everything. Pockets of light begin to appear like wildflowers in burned fields, unexpected, delicate, stubborn in their beauty. A laugh surprises you. A memory warms instead of wounds. A breath arrives without resistance. And something in you pauses, not in fear this time, but in wonder. Emerging from the depths of depression requires bravery. Not the kind that shouts or conquers or poses for photographs. But the quiet kind. The kind that wakes up when you would rather disappear. The kind that stays when leaving feels easier. The kind that chooses one more step when the road still feels unfinished. This courage does not roar. It whispers. It shows up tired. It shows up trembling. It shows up anyway. You begin to acknowledge what once felt unspeakable: that the shadows may always walk beside you. That they are part of your inner geography, like valleys carved by old rivers, evidence of where the waters once rushed. They hold memory. They hold history. They hold the imprints of survival. But they do not define the whole of who you are. They are weather, not identity. They are movement, not destiny. They pass across you. They do not own you. And so you learn to hold the full, complicated weather of being alive. The grief and the growth. The ache and the awe. The fear and the tenderness. You stop demanding that joy arrive without scars, that strength exist without softness, that light erase what shaped it. Instead, you begin to live more honestly. More spaciously. You allow both sun and storm to belong to your sky.

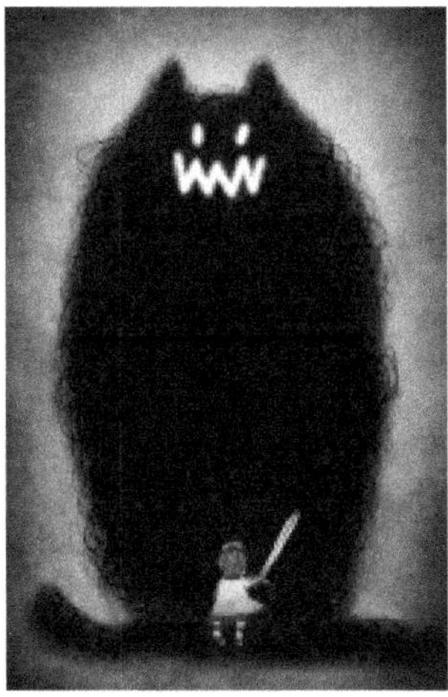

Tell your story. Not when it is polished. Not when it is resolved. Tell it while it is breathing. While it is messy. While it is still unfolding. Share your struggles. Give them air. Let your voice become a bridge between where you have been and where someone else is still standing. There is a particular strength in vulnerability, a strange and luminous power that rises the moment you stop hiding. The moment you choose truth over performance. The moment you let yourself be seen not as unbreakable, but as real. Because in that openness, something sacred happens. Shame loosens its grip. Isolation fractures. And the light you have fought so hard to find begins, quietly, to spill outward. Not blinding. Not perfect. But warm. And human. And enough to guide more than just your own steps. Sometimes, finding light in the shadows is not about banishing the dark. It is about learning how to walk with a lantern. The greatest victory is not in eradicating the monster, but in standing before it and refusing to look away. In meeting its gaze without surrender. In learning the language of its movements, the cadence of its lies, the familiar shapes it takes when it tries to pass itself off as truth. Courage, here, is not a sword. It is a staying. A breathing. A decision made again and again to remain present inside your own life. To feel what is here without letting it claim what you are. The monster may still circle. It may still murmur. It may still test the thresholds of your resolve. But it no longer gets to wear your name. It no longer gets to write your meaning. It no longer gets to speak as the authority on your worth.

Because on the far side of despair, comfort does exist. Not as fantasy. Not as denial. But as something real and reachable. Warmth waits beyond the fog like a hearth you forgot was burning, steady and patient, sending its glow into even the coldest rooms. There are hands you have not yet held. Mornings you have not yet seen. Versions of yourself still forming beneath the surface of becoming. You are not alone. You never were. And you are worthy of healing in every breath of the word. Worthy of tenderness. Worthy of support. Worthy of a life that feels like it belongs to you. As you embrace your journey exactly as it is, with its uneven pacing and its scarred beauty, something remarkable begins to happen. The very ground that once seemed to swallow you starts to reflect light. Your survival becomes a signal. Your honesty becomes a lantern. And the path you carve through your own darkness begins, quietly, to illuminate the way for others still walking with trembling feet. The weight of depression does not vanish, but it transforms. It becomes testimony. It becomes texture. It becomes living proof that resilience is not the absence of pain, but the art of continuing to live in its presence. In the narrative of your life, every chapter matters. Even the ones written in the ink of tears. Even the pages that tremble in the hand. The darkest passages still carry the possibility of dawn between their lines. They still hold the capacity to bend toward morning. And you are not merely inside this story. You are its keeper. You hold the pen. You hold the breath between sentences. You hold the space where the next becoming begins. The journey continues. And every step, no matter how small, no matter how unsteady, is a quiet revolution. A reclaiming. A return. A movement toward joy that is not naïve but earned. Not fragile but rooted. Not borrowed, but yours.

If you are struggling with depression, let this truth move beyond your mind and settle into your body, into your breath, into the quiet places that have learned to brace for impact: you are not alone. Not in this. Not here. Not now. There are people whose lives already hold a space shaped exactly like yours. People who care in ways you may not yet be able to feel. People who would walk beside you through the fog, who would match their pace to your own, who would carry a light when your hands are too tired to lift one. You do not have to survive this in isolation. You do not have to be your own only witness. Reaching out is not an admission of defeat. It is a turning toward life. A small, brave loosening of the fist. A whisper that says, "*I am here, and I cannot do this alone.*" Do not be afraid to speak what has been fermenting in silence. Silence keeps pain sealed in the dark where it grows teeth. Voice opens windows. Breath brings air into rooms that have been closed for too long. Seeking help is not weakness. It is endurance made visible. It is the mark of someone who has been carrying an impossible weight and has chosen, finally, to set it down where other hands can meet it. Depression is not proof that you are broken. It is proof that you have been fighting something heavy, something complex, something that would exhaust even the strongest spirit. And still, you are here. Still breathing. Still reaching. That is not frailty. That is courage wearing tired clothes. And if you are reading this not for yourself, but for someone you love, let your presence become a place they can rest. Not a solution. Not a strategy. A sanctuary. Be the room where their truth does not have to dress itself up. Be the silence that listens instead of judges. The patience that does not rush. The warmth that does not ask for explanations before it offers itself. You do not need the right words. You do not need a map. You do not need to fix what is breaking. Often, what saves a life is not an answer, but a witness. Someone who will sit in the dark without flinching. Someone who will not tidy their pain into something easier to hold. Someone who will stay. Because staying is holy work. Listening is holy work. Caring, when it costs you nothing but your presence and gives someone else their breath back, is holy work. Whether you are the one inside the storm, or the one standing just beyond it with a lantern in your hand, know this: love still reaches through fog. Connection still threads its way through walls. And even the smallest human light, held steadily, can become enough to remind a trembling heart that it does not have to disappear to be free.

You are not alone. You are not invisible. And your life, in all its fragile, ferocious becoming, is worth every act of care it takes to protect it. Because depression is not a destination. It is not a place you arrive at and are condemned to remain. It is a passage. A crossing. A long, shadowed corridor where the air feels thin and the walls press close, but where movement is still possible, even when it feels unbearably slow. It is a night that teaches you how to listen for the faintest hints of morning. A journey that winds and doubles back, that pauses and stumbles, that asks more of the heart than most paths ever do. And within that journey lives an unexpected truth: that healing is not the erasure of darkness, but the slow learning of how to walk with light again. This journey asks for patience when progress whispers instead of announces itself. It asks for compassion when hope feels fragile, when strength arrives in fragments rather than floods. It asks for understanding when language breaks down, when words feel too small to hold the depth of what has been endured. It asks us to honour the quiet work. The unseen labour. The days when survival itself is the victory. The moments when choosing to stay, to breathe, to reach out, is the bravest act available. So let us break the silence that has cocooned this suffering for far too long. Let us speak its name without flinching. Let us tell our stories not as confessions, but as acts of reclamation. Let us place our truths on the table like offerings, not weapons. Let us build tables instead of walls. Long tables. Shared tables. Tables where grief and hope can sit side by side without being rushed to make sense. Let us become witnesses to one another's becoming. Let us create a culture rooted not in performance, but in presence. Not in perfection, but in patience. Not in judgment, but in empathy that knows how to sit still. A culture where vulnerability is not punished, where pain is not minimized, where asking for help is recognized for what it is: a declaration of life. A reaching toward connection in a world that so often rewards isolation.

And let us remember this, always, even when the night feels endless: depression is not a sign of weakness. It is a sign of survival. A sign that someone has been fighting an invisible war with no applause and no ceasefire. A sign of endurance carved quietly into the body and soul. It tells the story of a person who has kept going under extraordinary weight. A person who has faced their inner darkness without turning away. A person who has dared to look their fears in the eye, to name their demons, and to reach outward when the burden grew too heavy for one heart to carry alone. This is not failure. This is courage in its most human form. And within this courage, within these shared stories and softened silences, the road toward healing continues. Winding. Imperfect. Alive. And still, always, bending toward the light.

The Weight of Shadows: The First Crack – The Story

And after all the words about monsters and storms and journeys, there comes the place where language can no longer hover at a distance. Where metaphor kneels. Where theory dissolves into the raw mineral of memory. Where the voice turns inward and the body remembers before the mind can organize. This is where the story begins. Not in revelation. Not in drama. But in something far quieter. Far more unsettling. The first time it happened, I didn't even know what to call it. I was sitting on my bed, staring at the wall, when the world simply went quiet. Not the gentle quiet of evening. Not the restful hush before sleep. This was a hollowing. As if someone had reached inside reality and scooped something essential out of it. The room remained. The light remained. The shapes of things stayed where they were. But whatever gave them weight, meaning, temperature, was gone. I felt nothing. No sadness to cry through. No anger to burn with. No joy to miss. Only numbness. It spread through me like a slow, invisible frost, creeping into places emotion had once lived, settling into my chest, my throat, my hands, my sense of being a person at all. It seeped into every thought, every breath, every fragile idea I had of myself, until even the effort to feel felt foreign. It was like being trapped in a void. Not darkness exactly. Darkness still implies something you can touch, something that presses back. This was absence. A vacuum where feeling should have been. An emptiness so complete it carried weight. A silence so dense it rang. It swallowed sensation, muffled identity, erased the internal weather that had always told me I was alive. I remember searching myself in that moment. Reaching inward the way you might pat your pockets for something lost. What do I feel? What is happening to me? There was no answer. Only the vast, echoing sense that something essential had slipped away. As though a first fracture had opened quietly through the foundation of my inner world. And I was standing in it. Days turned into weeks, and weeks into months, and somewhere along that slow unraveling, time lost its edges. It no longer arrived in mornings or left in nights. It did not move forward so much as sink. Pooling. Thickening. Stretching itself into an endless, featureless present. The void I had first glimpsed did not retreat. It deepened. It widened. It learned my name. It settled into me with the intimacy of something that planned to stay. It swallowed me whole. What remained felt like a negative of who I had been. A faded outline where a person once lived. A charcoal smudge on the wall of my own existence. I was still shaped like myself, still answering to my name, still walking, speaking, functioning in the barest mechanical sense. But the colour, the warmth, the inner gravity that had made that shape a *someone* had thinned almost to transparency.

I tried to fight it. I tried to claw my way back toward something that felt like surface. Toward the memory of my own laughter. Toward the heat of wanting. Toward the small, bright ache of caring. I dug through myself like someone searching rubble for a living thing. I strained for feeling. I begged for response. I pushed against the walls of the numbness with every scrap of will I had left. But the harder I struggled, the heavier I became. It was as if the darkness were made of water, and my movements only taught it how to pull me down. Each effort stirred the depths, thickened the pressure, drew the current tighter around my ribs. Every attempt to rise seemed to confirm the terrible physics of that inner world: resistance equalled descent. Hope became exertion. Exertion became exhaustion. And exhaustion became proof that I was losing. Slowly, almost without noticing when the transformation completed, I became a ghost haunting the halls of my own life. I moved through rooms without ever truly arriving. I stood in kitchens, in living rooms, in familiar doorways that should have known my shape, and felt like an intruder in spaces that once belonged to me. I spoke, but my voice sounded like it was traveling through water. I answered questions, but the words felt borrowed, handed to me by habit rather than born from thought. I attended my own days the way one attends a stranger's funeral. Present. Polite. Unreachable. I lived without being there. I watched my friends and family try to reach me. Watched their concern surface and soften and resurface again. Their voices called my name across a distance I could not measure. Their faces hovered on the other side of something thick and invisible, as though I were looking at them through layered glass. They leaned in. They asked. They held out their hands in small, human ways. But their words dissolved before they could touch me. They arrived to my ears stripped of weight, emptied of traction. I could hear them, yes. But I could not *anchor* to them. Could not step toward them. Could not let their care find purchase inside me. Every offered lifeline slid through my fingers like mist. Every kindness fell soundlessly into the void. I was drowning. Quietly. In full view. Breathing. Walking. Answering. Smiling when required. And no one could see the waterline rising inside my chest.

The Diagnosis

And somewhere between drowning and disappearing, a thin instinct stirred. Not hope. Not yet. Just the faintest reflex toward air. The kind the body remembers even when the mind has forgotten. One day, without ceremony or conviction, I found myself seeking help. It did not arrive like bravery. It arrived like exhaustion. Like a body that could no longer hold itself under. I sat in a cold, sterile room, the kind that smells faintly of antiseptic and waiting, my hands folded in my lap as though they belonged to someone else. They looked unfamiliar there. Pale. Still. Disconnected from any sense of agency. The chair was too firm. The light too bright. The walls too white, as if colour itself had been scrubbed away. Even the air felt thin, filtered, emptied of warmth. The clock was too loud. Each second landed like a drop of water in a hollow space. Tick. Tick. Tick. Sound had weight here. Time had a pulse. And every beat seemed to echo inside my ribs, counting something down I did not yet have language for. I watched the hands move, unable to look away, as though if I tracked them closely enough, they might explain what was happening to me. As though minutes, arranged correctly, could become meaning. I waited for the doctor to tell me what was wrong with me. I waited the way you wait for a storm to be named. For a fracture to be shown on an invisible scan. For a diagram. A chart. A single, definitive answer that might finally give shape to the way I had been dissolving. Part of me hoped he would find something physical. Something I could point to. Something with edges. Something that could be cut out, cauterized, stitched. I wanted proof. I wanted permission. I wanted a reason that did not sound like a failure of being. When he finally spoke, his words did not arrive gently. They did not prepare the ground. They did not soften themselves for landing. They struck with the bluntness of a physical blow. "You have depression." Depression. Just a word. Two syllables. A clinical arrangement of sound. And yet it fell like a verdict. A door closing somewhere deep inside my chest. A stamp pressed into the softest part of me. A life sentence written in ink I did not yet know how to read.

The room did not change. The clock did not pause. The doctor's voice continued, outlining next steps, options, pathways. But something in me had gone very still. As if the sound had traveled through layers of water before reaching me. As if the word had entered my body and found a place to lodge. Depression. It felt heavy. Official. Irrevocable. I remember nodding. I remember saying something polite. I remember thanking him. But inside, a thousand quiet meanings were erupting at once. Relief braided with terror. Validation with shame. The strange comfort of having a name for the monster, and the equally strange grief of realizing it had one. If it had a name, it was real. If it was real, it was not imagined. If it was not imagined, then this was not just a season. Not just a phase. Not just weakness I could one day outgrow. It was an illness. And illnesses did not disappear because you wanted them to. I walked out of that room carrying a diagnosis like a stone in my chest. Heavy. Cold. Unfamiliar. I had gone in hoping someone might tell me what was wrong. I left knowing something else entirely: That what lived inside me had a name. And that naming it was only the beginning. I wanted to scream. To cry. To break something solid enough to prove I still could. But all I did was nod. The small, obedient movement of a head when something too large has begun speaking through the room. The kind of nod you give when language has outpaced you. When the moment has grown heavier than any response you could offer. When interruption feels impossible, almost disrespectful, like trying to stop an ocean mid-tide. He handed me a prescription. Thin paper. Heavy meaning. Antidepressants. The word sat there in ink, neat and unassuming, as if it were nothing more than a grocery item, as if it were not now being asked to carry the architecture of my survival. A return appointment in a month. A few clinical sentences about dosage and side effects. Instructions delivered in a calm, practiced voice, the kind trained to remain steady in the presence of other people's breaking. His tone could not touch what was happening inside my ribs. Because inside, something had split open. Chaos was blooming there. Not loud. Not dramatic. A silent, spreading upheaval. Like ink released into clear water. Like a fault line awakening under a city that had pretended it was stable. I stood. My legs moved before I felt them agree. I thanked him. The words came automatically, like muscle memory from a life where politeness had often been safer than truth. And then I walked back through the waiting room.

Past magazines I could not read. Past the low hum of conversation. Past other bodies folded into other chairs, each one carrying their own invisible weather. Other silences. Other names not yet spoken. Other private catastrophes sitting neatly in laps and handbags, and pockets. I wondered, briefly, what words they were holding. I wondered who among us had just been given a sentence. Who had just been handed a door. Who had just lost the illusion of being unmarked. When I pushed open the door and stepped outside, the world looked exactly the same. Cars moved. Voices passed. The sky continued its indifferent stretch of blue. The light had not changed. The air had not shifted. Nothing in the architecture of the day reflected the rupture that had just taken place inside me. But I had changed. Something essential had been named. And in the naming, something had been separated. I left his office carrying a word I did not yet know how to live inside. Carrying a diagnosis like a second spine, unfamiliar and heavy, altering the way I stood in my own body. I felt more alone than I ever had before. Not because there was no one around me, but because the distance between myself and the rest of the world had quietly doubled while I was sitting in that chair. As though an invisible pane of glass had thickened. As though a new layer of fog had settled between me and everything I knew. I walked into the afternoon with a prescription in my hand and a storm in my chest, realizing that nothing outside had shifted at all. And yet everything in me had.

The Struggle

After the word was spoken, after the paper was placed in my hand, the real work began. Not the kind of work that looks like progress. Not the kind that arrives with light or gratitude or sudden clarity. This was the work of endurance.

Of staying. Of learning how to inhabit a body that felt foreign, medicated, muted, and raw. The first few weeks on medication were hell. Not relief. Not rescue. Hell. The pills did not lift me. They pressed me into a different kind of darkness. They dulled me into something ghost-adjacent, my emotions reduced to a distant echo, as though someone had wrapped my inner world in layers of cotton and soundproofing. Joy could not reach me. But neither could sorrow. Everything arrived blunted, softened, strangely far away. I was not in pain the way I had been. But I was not alive the way I remembered. I moved through days in a haze. Heavy-limbed. Hollow-eyed. Watching myself exist from several steps outside my own body, like a poorly lit film I could not turn off. My hands lifted cups I could not taste. My mouth spoke words I did not feel. My feet carried me through rooms I did not arrive in. The world continued to ask things of me. And I continued to answer. But there was a delay between the asking and the living, as though my soul were buffering somewhere beyond reach. I wanted to give up. To stop swallowing hope in capsule form. To refuse the small, chalky promises I placed on my tongue each morning. To let the void finally finish what it had started. To sink. To disappear. To rest inside nothing. The exhaustion was not only physical. It was existential. A weariness of having to try. Of having to monitor my own survival. Of having to keep negotiating with a life that felt like a language I no longer spoke. And yet, something inside me refused. Not a triumphant voice. Not a heroic instinct. Something quieter. Stubborn. Almost accidental. A thin, unkillable filament of will still tethered me to the world. A small animal part of me that kept drinking water. That kept breathing. That kept taking the pills even while hating them. That kept showing up to mornings I did not want. That kept choosing the next minute when the hour felt impossible. It did not feel like hope. It felt like a hand clenching in the dark. It felt like a pulse saying *again*. It felt like a body that, despite everything, had not yet consented to vanish. So I stayed. Inside the fog. Inside the side effects. Inside the unbearable slowness of early healing.

I stayed when nothing in me felt worth saving. I stayed when staying felt like the hardest thing I had ever done. And in that staying, unseen and uncelebrated, the first true work of my survival was already underway. It was not loud. It was not brave in any way stories usually celebrate. There were no speeches. No sudden clarity. No swelling music. It was small. Stubborn. A thin filament of will, no thicker than a spider's thread, stretching through the wreckage of me, tightening each time everything else went slack. A quiet tensile strength. A refusal without language. Not "*I will live*", but simply "*I am still here*". A pulse that kept answering the dark with one more breath. One more swallow. One more morning. So I began to see a therapist. Not because I believed in healing. Not because I felt ready. But because that filament pulled me forward when nothing else could. I remember the room. The way the air felt softer there. The way the chair held my weight without asking me to justify it. The way the silence did not rush to fill itself. She did not try to rename the dark. Did not polish it into something palatable. She sat with me inside it, steady as a lighthouse whose beam does not argue with the storm. Someone willing to enter the landscape I had been wandering alone, not as a rescuer, but as a witness. A cartographer of inner terrain. A companion in places I had only ever survived. And so we began to walk backward through my life. Not in straight lines. In spirals. In fragments. In the way memory actually moves. We spoke of my past, not as a story, but as sediment. Of fears that had learned to live in my nervous system long before I had words for them. Of the dreams I had buried because they hurt too much to carry, too heavy with hope, too sharp with the risk of wanting.

We spoke of the moments I had minimized. The griefs I had outrun. The adaptations I had mistaken for personality. Together, we traced the fault lines. The hairline cracks that had once kept me functioning. The earthquakes that had taught my body to live braced. The quiet compromises had slowly become cages. We named the wounds. Not to reopen them, but to let them finally breathe. To take them out of the realm of shame and place them into the realm of human history. To say: "This happened. This mattered. This shaped you." And we listened. Carefully. Reverently. For the places where my life had quietly learned to fracture. For the moments where something in me had split not because I was weak, but because I was surviving. For the small, brilliant ways I had tried to protect myself, even when those ways later became the bars of my own confinement. Session by session, word by word, breath by breath, the dark began to acquire dimension. It was no longer just a weight. It became a geography. A story. A series of rooms I could finally enter without vanishing. And in that slow, sacred mapping, something shifted. I was no longer only drowning inside the night. I was beginning, at last, to learn its shape. Slowly, almost imperceptibly, something in me began to gather itself. Not dramatically. Not all at once. But in the way broken light gathers on water. In the way frost retreats from a window, not with ceremony, but with patience. I began to piece myself back together. Not into who I had been. That version of me belonged to a world that no longer existed. A body that had not yet learned what it could survive. I was not being restored. I was being re-formed. Rewritten. Reintroduced to myself. Someone new was taking shape.

Someone who could carry the cracks without collapsing. Someone who understood that fracture did not mean failure. Someone who had learned that light enters not in spite of the breaks, but through them. The medication steadied the ground beneath me. It quieted the violent tilting of the world, softened the vertigo of my own mind, slowed the freefall just enough for my feet to find something like earth again. It did not give me joy. It did not hand me meaning. But it made standing possible. It gave my nervous system a ceasefire. It lowered the volume of the storm. But it was the therapy that taught me how to walk the terrain. It gave me tools. Language. Mirrors. It taught me how to recognize the darkness without surrendering my name to it. How to see a thought arrive without kneeling before it. How to notice the familiar scripts without letting them write my endings. It showed me how to trace the difference between a feeling and a fact. Between a memory and a prophecy. Between the voice of pain and the voice of truth. It taught me how to breathe when the dark pressed close. How to anchor myself when the old gravity returned. How to sit inside a wave without becoming the ocean. The medication helped. But the therapy saved me. Because it did not try to erase the monster. It taught me how to see it. To understand its patterns. To hear its tone. To feel the moment it tried to wear my voice. It handed me the means to fight back, not with force, not with denial, but with understanding. With curiosity. With a compassion that could interrupt cruelty mid-sentence. It returned my authorship to me. Gave me back the pen. Showed me where the story had been hijacked and how to begin again. And with those tools, I began, inch by inch, to reclaim my life. Not in grand transformations. In quiet revolutions. Getting out of bed when the weight said no. Speaking a truth instead of swallowing it. Catching a lie before it finished its sentence. Letting a feeling pass without turning it into a verdict. One small victory at a time. One breath that reached all the way down. One thought that loosened instead of tightened. One moment where the light stayed a little longer on my skin. One fragile, luminous step forward. And then another. And then, one day, without any trumpet or announcement, I realized something astonishing. I was no longer only surviving inside my life. I was beginning to inhabit it again.

The Breakthrough

And then, quietly, without ceremony, something changed. Not with trumpets. Not with revelation. Not with a moment you could point to and name as *the turning*. It arrived the way healing often does, sideways and unannounced. One morning, I woke and realized I had not thought about the void in weeks. Not because I was avoiding it. Not because I was pretending it had never existed. But because it had loosened its grip enough to slip out of the foreground of my days, retreating from the center of my vision like a storm finally moving off the coast. Still present somewhere on the horizon, perhaps, but no longer breaking over my head. That realization startled me. I lay there, breathing, listening to the ordinary sounds of morning, the distant traffic, the hush of the house, the soft insistence of my own pulse, and felt something unfamiliar rise in my chest. Space. Actual space. Not the hollow emptiness I had known so intimately, but room. Capacity. An openness where breath could travel without resistance. The weight of shadows that had once consumed me had lifted, not vanished entirely, but eased, like a sky after endless rain when the clouds thin enough for light to filter through. Everything was still damp. Still tender. But the crushing pressure was gone. In its place was something fragile and unmistakable. Hope. Not the blinding, cinematic kind that promises permanence. The quieter kind. The kind that says, "*This is survivable.*" The kind that whispers, "*You might belong to your future after all.*" Possibility followed close behind, tentative but real. A sense that the days ahead were no longer an unbroken stretch of endurance, but something with shape. With variation. With openings. I could imagine myself moving forward without immediately bracing for collapse. The air felt different. Lighter. As though the room itself had learned how to breathe again. My thoughts moved with more fluidity, no longer dragging their chains behind them. Ideas surfaced. Curiosity flickered. I caught myself wondering about things that had nothing to do with survival.

Light began to land where it had not reached in a long time. It touched small places first. A moment of laughter that reached my chest. A song that stirred memory without pain. The warmth of sunlight on my forearms, felt rather than analyzed. These moments did not announce themselves as milestones. They simply arrived, quietly reclaiming territory the darkness had occupied for years. And I understood then that the breakthrough was not an explosion. It was a softening. A loosening of the fist around my heart. A gentle return of color to a world I had learned to see in grey.

A dawning recognition that I was no longer only holding on. I was beginning to live again. Not perfectly. Not fearlessly. But honestly. And that, I would come to learn, was more than enough to change everything. I still had bad days. Storms still passed through. But they no longer swallowed me whole. They no longer arrived as verdicts. They no longer wrote my name across the sky. They came now as weather. Heavy at times. Uncomfortable. Loud in their own way. But moving. Always moving. I had learned to feel the early shifts in the air. The subtle pressure changes inside my chest. The way my thoughts began to tilt. The familiar language trying to reclaim its old authority. I could sense the return of those inner scripts before they finished forming their sentences. And instead of collapsing inward, instead of sealing myself back into the echo chamber of my own mind, I reached outward. I spoke. I named. I asked. I learned to let help touch me before desperation hardened into silence. To loosen my grip before it became a fist. To open my mouth while my voice still lived there. And in the spaces the darkness no longer occupied, something unexpected began to grow. Not euphoria. Not spectacle. Not a sudden, cinematic happiness. But smallness. Softness. Ordinary miracles. The warmth of a cup of tea resting between my palms, its heat traveling slowly into my bones. The quiet grace of a walk in the park, feet finding rhythm again against the earth. Leaves lifting and falling. Wind breathing through branches. My own lungs answering back. Me, moving among them. These moments did not announce themselves as healing. They simply arrived. And I learned, slowly, reverently, to notice them. To let them count. To let them mean something. They were not fireworks. They were embers. But embers carry memory. Embers carry promise. Embers are how fires are born again. They glowed in the most unremarkable places. In a shared smile. In clean sheets. In the way morning light settled across a wall. In the quiet satisfaction of completing something small. In the relief of a breath that did not hurt. And each one whispered the same gentle truth: You are still here. And here is not empty. And here can hold light. Not blinding. Not perfect. But real. And for the first time, that was enough.

The Light

And as those small embers continued to glow, I began to see what they were quietly building. Not a blaze. Not a spectacle. But a hearth. A place inside me where warmth could gather again. As I emerged from the long interior night, I realized that my passage through depression had altered the very architecture of who I was. The foundations had shifted. Some walls had fallen. Certain rooms no longer existed in the way they once had. I was not the person I had been before. The world did not fit me the same way. My heart did not open with the same innocence. My joy did not arrive unexamined. But something truer had taken shape. I was stronger. Not in the way of armor, but in the way of roots. Wiser. Not with answers, but with awareness. More compassionate. Not because pain had made me bitter, but because it had made me fluent. Fluent in silence. Fluent in fragility. Fluent in the hidden languages people speak when they are surviving something no one else can see. I was not hardened by the void. I had been widened by it. As though surviving that emptiness had hollowed new chambers inside my chest where tenderness could now live. Where patience could rest. Where the suffering of others could land without being turned away. I carried the memory of the dark not as a wound, but as a way of seeing. A way of listening. A way of knowing when someone's smile was not telling the whole story. And so I began to speak. Not from a stage. Not with certainty. But from the soft authority of having been there.

I let my story leave the locked room where it had been kept. I let it breathe. I let it stumble into the light. I spoke of the nights. The numbness. The monster. The silence. The slow, stubborn return. I spoke not to teach, but to testify. Not to rescue, but to reach. I spoke so that someone still curled inside their own unseen cage might feel a recognition stir.

So that someone still treading water might hear another swimmer's voice. So that someone still convinced they were alone might feel the lie begin to loosen. I knew I could never fully inhabit another person's pain. But I could sit beside it. I could meet it without flinching. I could listen without trying to fix. I could hold space where once there had only been fear. I could offer presence. I could offer language. I could offer the quiet, defiant hope that comes from having walked out of the dark carrying your own name. Because light, I learned, is not always something you stand in. Sometimes, it is something you become. A way of seeing. A way of staying. A way of saying, again and again, to a world still full of hidden storms: You are not alone. I am here. And there is a way through. A light, not to erase their darkness, but to remind them that darkness is not the only condition of being. Not the whole truth. Not the final landscape. In the end, depression became more than a word I carried like a diagnosis or a warning label. It revealed itself as a journey. A long, brutal, sacred passage carved through the deepest chambers of my life. A crossing that demanded everything I had and much I did not yet know I possessed. It was not conquered in a single moment of clarity or courage, but endured breath by breath, step by trembling step, choice by fragile choice. Survival was not heroic. It was human. It was waking up when I did not want to. It was staying when leaving felt easier. It was choosing, again and again, to remain. And though the shadows would always exist, lingering at the edges of my inner world like familiar silhouettes, I no longer feared their presence. I understood them now. I had learned their shapes. Their seasons. Their language. I had learned how to see in low light, how to move without certainty, how to trust my footing even when the path narrowed and the ground felt unsure. The dark no longer meant annihilation. It meant attentiveness. It meant care.

I knew now, in my bones, that I was not alone. That I had never been. That even in my most isolated hours, others were walking parallel paths, carrying similar weights, learning the same hard lessons about endurance and grace. I had found the strength to continue, not as a triumph, but as a commitment. To live, even when living felt tender. To love, even when love carried risk. To walk forward carrying both what had wounded me and what had saved me, refusing to discard either. I let them walk together inside me. The ache and the hope. The scar and the salve. The night and the ember. And in that union, something lasting was born. Not a blaze that demanded attention. But a quiet, enduring flame. One that does not shout. One that does not blind. One that simply stays. A flame that says: I have been broken. I have been lost. I have been afraid. And still, I am here. Still breathing. Still choosing. Still walking. Carrying my light not as proof of victory, but as an offering. A reminder. A witness. That even after the longest night, even after the deepest descent, there is a way to live with both shadow and fire in the same chest, and to let that balance become a life that is not untouched by darkness but no longer ruled by it. And that, in the end, is enough.

The Weight of Shadows: A Journey Through Depression

The Silent Invader

And even now, standing in a place where light has learned how to live again, I know how easily the word is misused. How casually it drifts through our language, unmoored from the reality it names. The word *depression* dances on our tongues, a lightweight sound tossed into conversation like confetti at a party. A bad day? Depression. Feeling down? Depression. We hand it out as shorthand for weathered moods, for passing heaviness, for ordinary human sorrow. But the reality is not light. It is not small. It is a chasm. A widening gulf of despair so profound it swallows the casual meanings whole.

Depression does not knock. It seeps. It infiltrates the quiet seams of a life and makes itself at home before you realize the door was ever opened. It arrives like a silent invader, subtle as damp creeping through walls, patient as rust blooming beneath paint. At first, it is only a thinning. A dulling. The colours lose their sharpness. The laughter doesn't quite reach the ribs. The mornings feel heavier than they should. You call it fatigue. Stress. A season. You make excuses for the way the world has begun to dim, unaware that something unseen is already rearranging the furniture of your inner world. It does not announce itself with spectacle. It colonizes. It spreads its quiet architecture through thought and body alike, teaching the nervous system new rhythms of weariness, new dialects of dread. It settles into sleep and fractures it. It takes residence in appetite and distorts it. It coils around memory, bending even joy backward until it feels like proof of what has been lost rather than evidence of what is possible. And all the while, it whispers that nothing has changed. That this is simply who you are. That this is how life is. That the narrowing of your world is not a symptom, but a truth. This is how depression survives. By remaining unnamed. By disguising itself as personality, as circumstance, as fate. By convincing you that the slow disappearance of colour is not an illness, but maturity. That the deadening of desire is not a warning, but realism. That the erosion of hope is not theft, but wisdom. It is only later, often much later, that you begin to understand. That what you mistook for weather was a climate. What you dismissed as mood was a migration. What you called tiredness was a slow unravelling of the self. And by the time you can finally see it, it is no longer standing at the edge of your life.

It is living inside it. Not loud. Not obvious. But everywhere. In the way breath feels negotiated instead of given. In the way mornings arrive like obligations instead of beginnings. In the way your own name begins to sound unfamiliar in your mouth. This is the silent invader. Not a storm you watch approach. But a night that teaches you to forget the sun ever existed. And yet, even here, even in this colonized darkness, the very act of naming it is resistance. To say "*this is not me, this is something happening to me*" is to carve the first small opening in the wall. To recognize the invader is to remember that there was once a home before it arrived. And homes, even after long occupation, can still be reclaimed. Depression is not simply sadness. Sadness still feels. Sadness still moves. Sadness has weather. It comes and goes like rain across a landscape that remains alive beneath it. Depression is something else entirely. It is the absence of feeling. A hollowing. An evacuation of colour and sound. A silence so complete it becomes loud, ringing in the marrow of your bones, humming beneath your skin like a low, unending note. It is a deep-sea quiet, where pressure replaces motion and even your own heartbeat sounds distant, as though it belongs to someone sealed in another room. It is a deafening stillness where once there was music. A place where joy does not ache, because it does not arrive. Where grief does not storm, because even storms require air. In depression, even sorrow grows tired. Even tears forget their own language. What remains is not pain in the way the world understands pain, but a vast interior vacancy, an emotional winter where nothing roots, nothing blooms, nothing reaches.

Depression does not announce itself as a visitor. It enters as an erasure. It edits the inner world line by line, eroding tone, stripping texture, crossing out the small exclamations of being. It removes the punctuation of desire. It blurs the verbs of becoming. It takes a red pen to memory, to imagination, to selfhood, until what remains is space where something essential once lived. Not brokenness, but absence. Not a wound, but a missing limb of the soul. And inside that absence, you do not so much suffer as you disappear. You move through your days as an empty house moves through weather. Light still falls on the windows. Voices still pass outside. But nothing inside responds. The rooms echo. The air feels unused. Your own presence becomes a rumour you are no longer certain is true. This is the place sadness cannot reach. This is the place language stumbles. This is the place where the self grows thin. And this is where the journey truly begins. Not at the moment of collapse. Not when the tears come. But here, in the void. In the quiet after feeling. In the strange territory where you are still breathing, still functioning, still moving through the world, and yet cannot find yourself anywhere inside it. This is the first threshold. The inner borderland. The place where you begin not to ask, "*Why do I hurt?*" But

"*Where did I go?*" And it is from this question, trembling and unanswered, that the long work of return will

slowly, stubbornly, begin.

Depression is often treated as a synonym for sadness, as shorthand for a transient bad day, a word we reach for when the weather of the heart turns briefly grey. But that is a vast and dangerous oversimplification, a paper cut attempting to describe an amputation. To those who endure its unrelenting grip, it is not a passing mood. It is a condition of being. An atmosphere. A gravity. A climate the soul is forced to inhabit. For those who truly know its weight, depression becomes a parasitic presence, a quiet tenant that rearranges the inner rooms without permission. A thief of joy who does not steal in dramatic gestures, but in patient increments, lifting colour from memory, warmth from anticipation, meaning from motion. A blanket of despair so heavy it does not only cover the body, but presses into the will itself, smothering even the instinct to reach for life. It is a quiet invader. It does not kick down doors. It seeps. It slides beneath thresholds. It enters through hairline fractures in hope, through old wounds, through moments of exhaustion no one thought dangerous. It slips into thought, into memory, into the tender spaces where meaning once lived, and there it begins its slow occupation. It spreads its tendrils through the mind and heart, threading itself into perception, into identity, until even your own inner voice begins to echo with its language. You no longer hear it as something foreign. You hear it as yourself. It is not merely feeling down. It is the absence of feeling altogether. A hollow ache that does not throb, but hums. A vast interior emptiness that permeates every cell, that vibrates through every fibre of your being like a low, unending note. Not loud enough to point to. Not sharp enough to cry out against. Just constant. A background frequency of erasure.

In this place, emotions do not arrive; they dissolve. Joy does not break your heart; it bypasses it. Grief does not surge; it evaporates before it can take shape. What remains is not pain in the way the world understands pain, but vacancy. An emotional vacuum where reactions once lived. A numb field where even suffering struggles to root. And yet, even this numbness is not neutral. It carries weight. It carries exhaustion. It carries a particular kind of terror, the terror of sensing that something essential is missing and not knowing how to reach it. It is the feeling of standing in a familiar room where all the furniture has been quietly removed. The walls are still there. The windows still open. But nothing answers when you move. This is depression's deepest cruelty. Not that it hurts. But that it takes. It takes colour. It takes appetite. It takes resonance. It takes the reflex to care. Until one day, you are no longer asking, "*Why am I sad?*" You are asking, "*Why am I here at all?*" And in that question, hushed and heavy, the landscape fully reveals itself. Not as a mood. Not as a moment. But as a territory.

A place you did not choose. A climate you did not create. A long, dim country of the inner world where the self grows faint. And it is here, in this hollowed terrain, where the work of understanding must begin. Because nothing can be navigated if it is misnamed. Nothing can be softened if it is dismissed. And nothing can be healed if it is reduced to something it has never been. This is not sadness. This is the quiet occupation of the soul. Imagine standing in a vibrant garden, yet all you can see is a dull grey veil draped over every flower. The colours are still there, somewhere. You sense them the way you sense a forgotten dream, the way you know a language you can no longer speak. They exist, but they will not reach you. Reds do not ignite. Blues do not soothe. Gold does not warm. Scents drift past without landing. Petals brush your skin without texture. The quiet miracles of living, the small sacred details that once anchored you to the world, dissolve into a muted backdrop, leaving behind only an ache where delight once moved. A phantom throb. The memory of resonance without its music. Imagine a world painted entirely in grayscale, where the vivid hues of life have been slowly leached away, as though time itself were draining pigment from the canvas. A landscape of endless ash and fog. Depth without colour. Light without heat. This is the world as viewed through the lens of depression. A place where contrast softens, edges blur, and even the brightest day arrives already tired. And it does not only remove joy. It corrupts it. It teaches happiness to feel counterfeit. It twists even the smallest pleasures into sources of guilt or inadequacy. A smile becomes an accusation. A good moment becomes evidence against you. "*If this is good, why are you still broken?*"

The sun shines, but it offers no warmth. It illuminates without embracing. It exposes without comforting. Laughter echoes, but it sounds distant, warped by invisible walls, like music drifting through water. Love approaches, but it is met with a barricade of self-doubt so formidable it feels impenetrable, built from years of believing you are too much, too little, too flawed to be held. Kindness feels undeserved. Touch feels thin. Beauty feels like something meant for other people, somewhere beyond the reach of your hands. You are surrounded by life yet sealed away from it. Watching brightness happen somewhere you can no longer reach. Like standing at the bottom of deep water, looking up at a shattered sun, knowing air exists, knowing warmth exists, yet feeling only the pressure in your lungs. You witness connection without inhabiting it. You observe joy without entering it. You remember yourself without recognizing who you are now. This is the particular exile of depression. Not the absence of the world, but estrangement from it. Not darkness alone, but distance. A severing of the invisible thread between the self and everything that once felt alive. And in that distance, a new kind of grief is born. Not only for what hurts, but for what no longer reaches you. For the moments that pass through your hands like mist. For the person you were before colour required memory. Yet even here, beneath the veil, beneath the ash, beneath the greying of everything that once bloomed, the garden still exists. Waiting. Alive beneath the surface. Not gone. Not erased. Only hidden. And the journey ahead is not about inventing colour, but about slowly, tremblingly, relearning how to see. It becomes the inability to experience pleasure, even in the things you once cherished. Anhedonia, they call it, a clinical word for a spiritual famine. What once sparked warmth now lands without sensation, like striking a match in a vacuum. The familiar no longer welcomes you. Music arrives without resonance. Touch without comfort. Beauty without invitation. The vibrant colours of life slowly drain into a monotonous grey, and you find yourself adrift in a sea of apathy, floating without current or shore, without wind or oar, suspended in a stillness that is not peace but paralysis. Days no longer open. They close. They fold in on themselves like wilted petals, offering no fragrance, no promise.

Imagine a heavy, suffocating blanket laid across your body and soul, thick with unseen weight, pressing the breath shallow, dimming the will to move. Not the comforting kind of covering that warms and protects, but one soaked in rain, clinging, cold, unyielding. That is the physical language of depression. It does not speak in metaphors alone. It speaks through flesh. Through bone-deep exhaustion that seeps into the marrow. Through a relentless fatigue that siphons energy until even existing feels like expenditure. Your limbs grow dense. Your muscles forget their memory of lightness. The body becomes a landscape of gravity where every motion demands negotiation. Simple tasks, once effortless, rise up like insurmountable mountains. Getting out of bed feels like climbing Everest with no summit in sight, no oxygen in the lungs, no flag waiting at the peak. Brushing your teeth becomes a campaign. Showering, a pilgrimage. Answering a message, a labor of impossible courage. Each small act is a test of will against an invisible undertow that keeps pulling you back toward stillness, toward the dark comfort of not having to try. And I know this terrain. I know this pain. Not as a theory. Not as a metaphor borrowed from books. I have walked through the dark valleys of depression, places where the sun seems to have forgotten its way, where even morning arrives already tired, where the air hangs thick with the stench of hopelessness, metallic and stale, as though the future itself has rusted. I have felt the crushing weight of sadness that does not cry but presses. The suffocating grip of anxiety that coils around the ribs and whispers catastrophe into every quiet moment. The debilitating fatigue that turns each step into an act of endurance, each breath into a conscious choice.

I have lived in a body that felt like an anchor. In a mind that felt like a locked room. In days that asked everything of me and gave almost nothing back. I have known what it is to move through the world carrying an invisible storm, to look intact while quietly unraveling, to be alive and yet feel exiled from life itself. And it is from that knowing, from that lived night, that these words rise. There is a cruel irony in depression's design: it silences the beautiful moments while amplifying the mundane. What once sang now barely whispers. The laughter of friends becomes an echo, thinning into a distant murmur that reaches you already emptied of its warmth, like sound traveling through too many closed doors. Smiles move across faces, but they feel staged, part of a play you no longer remember auditioning for. The warmth of the sun no longer soothes, but burns like a harsh spotlight, exposing only what feels wrong, only what feels lacking, only the parts of you the illness has taught you to despise. Light itself becomes an interrogation. In this altered reality, joy transforms into an unreachable ideal, something other people are allowed to touch, something reserved for lives that make sense. You watch happiness move through the world like a language you once spoke fluently and have now entirely forgotten. It dances just beyond your reach, close enough to recognize, too far to enter. Even good moments arrive already hollowed, like beautifully wrapped boxes with nothing inside. Each day stretches into a seemingly endless cycle of heaviness, dawn bleeding into dusk without distinction. Morning does not rise; it presses. Time does not pass; it drags its feet as if reluctant to move you anywhere new. Hours thicken. Minutes congeal. The smallest choices demand negotiations with exhaustion. And beneath it all runs the quiet violence of erosion. It is a relentless assault on the self. On self-esteem. On identity. Not dramatic. Not explosive. But constant. A slow chipping. A wearing down. A tide that never retreats. Depression does not simply make you feel bad; it dismantles the scaffolding of who you believe yourself to be.

It chips away at your sense of who you are, and your confidence, erodes your sense of worth, hollows out the places where certainty once lived, until even your own reflection feels like a stranger's face worn by mistake. That you no longer recognize or trust. You begin to study yourself the way one studies a photograph of someone who has died, searching for the person you used to recognize. Your name feels unfamiliar in your mouth. Your memories lose their emotional color. Your voice inside your own head begins to speak in tones that are not kind, not accurate, but endlessly convincing.

The world, once a place of wonder and possibility, warps into a distorted mirror of your inner turmoil. Every interaction feels loaded. Every decision feels perilous. Every misstep feels catastrophic. Meaning thins. Hope fractures. Streets feel narrower. Rooms feel heavier. Conversations feel farther away. Everything appears bleak. Hopeless. Insurmountable. Even neutral things tilt toward threat. Even kindness arrives carrying suspicion. The future no longer unfurls as a tapestry of possibility, rich with colour and movement, but opens instead into a long, colourless expanse, a road without landmarks, disappearing into fog. And in that fog, direction dissolves. Dreams lose their edges. Desire forgets its name. You keep walking because stopping feels worse, but you no longer know what you are walking toward. It is not that you believe nothing will ever change; it is that imagining change requires an energy you no longer possess. So you move forward by habit, by obligation, by the faint memory that life once felt different, even if you can no longer remember how. This is the quiet devastation of depression. Not a single breaking moment, but a slow unravelling. Not a scream, but a dimming. A life still being lived, but at a distance, as if through layers of glass and water and time. And yet, even here, even in this narrowed world, something remains. A pulse. A persistence. A self that has not vanished, only gone into hiding. Waiting. Watching. Holding on to the faint, stubborn truth that fog, no matter how dense, is never the same thing as night.

Depression is not only a storm of the mind, not just a "mental health issue" spoken about in neat, contained terms. It is a full weather system that migrates through the body, a climate that rewrites the internal seasons. It settles into muscle and marrow, into nerve and breath, into the quiet spaces between heartbeats. It makes a home in the shoulders, heavy as wet cloth. It coils through the spine like cold. It hums through the bloodstream with a low, persistent ache that never quite names itself, only insists on being felt. The constant fatigue. The aching limbs. The sleepless nights where darkness refuses to soften into rest. The loss of appetite, as though even hunger has grown tired of asking. These are not footnotes to the suffering. They are part of its grammar. The body becomes the page on which the mind's pain is written. Emotion translates itself into tissue. Grief migrates into joints. Fear tightens into the chest. Despair settles behind the eyes. Thought and flesh begin to speak with the same voice, and there is no place left to stand that is not inside the ache. It is like being trapped in a prison built from your own inner architecture. A structure you never designed yet cannot leave. Corridors made of memory. Walls reinforced with self-doubt. A ceiling pressed low with exhaustion. No key to unlock the door. No window wide enough to let the light remember your face. No voice that feels strong enough to carry beyond the walls. Even your breathing seems to echo back at you, as if the space itself is listening.

And within this enclosure, the physical manifestations are relentless. A constant pressure, like the deep-water weight felt far below the surface. A gravity that pulls inward, dragging the shoulders down, the gaze to the floor, the spirit toward stillness. A fatigue that transcends ordinary tiredness. Not the exhaustion earned from effort or growth, but a bone-deep weariness that seeps into everything, into teeth and tongue and thought, draining you until even existing feels like labor. Until simply being awake feels like carrying a life that has forgotten how to rest. Your body becomes a vessel of suffering, a reluctant host to something relentless, something parasitic, siphoning vitality drop by drop, hour by hour, until even your pulse feels borrowed. Rising from bed is no longer a simple motion. It is an excavation. It is dragging an entire history behind you, every regret and memory and unanswered ache clinging to your limbs like wet earth. The mattress feels less like a place of rest and more like the floor of a pit you must climb out of each morning with bare hands.

Simple tasks, once effortless, stand like monuments before you. Brushing your teeth. Opening a door. Answering a message. Each becomes a small pilgrimage. Each requires a summoning, a bargaining, a quiet plea for the strength to complete what used to happen without thought. The air feels thickened, syrup-slow, resistant. Every movement must be carved from it, as though you are wading through an invisible sea that presses against your chest and calves and will. This is how depression lives. Not only in the mind that thinks, but in the body that must carry those thoughts, step after trembling step, through the long, Even memory turns against you. Moments that were once tender become sharpened, repurposed as evidence in a private trial where you are always found guilty. The mind becomes both courtroom and executioner. Successes are dismissed as accidents, flukes, clerical errors in a universe that must have momentarily looked the other way. They are stripped of meaning, of merit, of your name. Failures, however, are preserved like artifacts. Enlarged. Replayed. Etched into the walls of your inner world until they are no longer events, but identities. One mistake swells into a character flaw. One loss becomes prophecy. One wound is enough to condemn the whole. The mind becomes a crooked mirror, reflecting only what wounds. It bends light into accusation. It tilts every image toward defect. You search it for something solid to hold and find only fractures looking back. And this distortion does not stay contained. It bleeds outward into the world itself, tinting every interaction, every expression, every silence. Empathy, once instinctive, drifts out of reach, like a language you used to speak fluently but can no longer remember how to form. Connection dulls. Warmth loses its edge. The faces of others feel distant, as though seen through thickening glass, their voices muffled, their care arriving delayed and distorted.

The bonds that once brought comfort and joy begin to feel strained, fragile, unreal, as though a widening chasm has opened between you and the rest of humanity. You are near, but not with. Present, but not part. So you withdraw. You retreat into the fortress of your despair, building walls from exhaustion and fear, layering brick upon brick of unspoken thought, of unanswered messages, of invitations declined and hopes postponed. You convince yourself that no one understands. That no one truly sees. That your language no longer translates into the world of the living. And from within that enclosure, even the idea of reaching out feels impossible. The very act of asking becomes a mountain. A weight too heavy to lift. A door that requires a strength you can no longer locate inside your own chest. You rehearse the words and they collapse before they reach your mouth. You imagine being heard and feel only exposure, danger, burden. So you stay. And the silence deepens. Inside that silence, the inner world grows louder. Thoughts echo against one another. Fears ricochet. Old sentences return wearing new disguises. The mind, already tired, turns again upon itself, pacing the long corridors of its own making, narrating its own unworthiness, documenting its own disappearance. And in that endless interior monologue, where no outside voice interrupts, despair is no longer something you feel. It becomes the air you breathe. And perhaps the most insidious truth of depression is its persistence. It is not a storm that gathers its thunder and then departs. It is a climate. A long season that moves into the bones and makes a home there. A constant, oppressive presence that settles into the days like ash, coating every surface, dulling every color, refusing to lift. There are no true intermissions. No clean edges where the suffering politely pauses. No brief reprieves where the weight loosens its grip. Even rest is heavy here. Even sleep carries the weather with it. It becomes a relentless companion. A shadow stitched to your feet. A second pulse beneath your own. A low, unceasing murmur that follows you from room to room, from morning into night, threading itself through every thought, every interaction, every attempt at stillness. It recites your perceived inadequacies like scripture. Rehearses your imagined failures like prophecy. It arranges the past into accusations and the future into evidence. It convinces you that ease is not meant for you. That peace is a language spoken by other people. That your very existence is a kind of error.

And yet, despite how many live within its reach, despite how many hearts it quietly occupies, depression remains shrouded in taboo. Wrapped in stigma. Clouded by misconception. It is spoken of in whispers or reduced to clichés, treated as an inconvenience rather than the life-altering illness it is. Too often, the language offered is careless, even cruel. "*Just snap out of it. Be positive. You're just being lazy.*" As though a fractured inner world could be repaired by optimism alone. As though a nervous system in collapse could be scolded back into balance. As though suffering were a choice, a posture, a failure of gratitude. But depression is not something you simply will away. It is not a mood that obeys instruction. It is not a weakness that can be disciplined out of the body. It is a serious mental health condition. It reaches into neurochemistry, into memory, into identity, into the architecture of how a person experiences being alive. It requires care. Treatment. Patience. Understanding. It asks for gentleness where there has been judgment. For presence where there has been avoidance. For listening where there has been noise. And in naming this, in speaking it aloud, something subtle but radical begins. The climate is no longer invisible. The shadow no longer unquestioned. The suffering, at last, is given the dignity of being real. And choosing to face it is not weakness. It is strength of the rarest kind. Not the loud, armoured strength that conquers and boasts, but the quiet, living strength that stays. The strength to look into the dark without pretending it is light. The strength to sit with pain without polishing it into something palatable. The strength to name what hurts without shrinking from its echo. The strength to reach for help when the weight becomes too much to carry inside one body, one chest, one breath.

I have learned that depression is not the end. It is not a definition, but a diagnosis. Not a life sentence, but a season of rupture. Not an identity, but a battle that moves through the nervous system, the heart, the mind, the memory. And surviving it does not make you broken. It makes you brave. It means you have walked through an invisible war and continued to wake up. Continued to breathe. Continued to choose, even when choice felt like ash in the mouth. Survival, here, is not passive. It is an ongoing act of courage. This book has been, and will continue to be, a journey through the shadows of depression and into the slow, sacred light of hope. Not a sudden sunrise, but a patient dawn. The kind that comes in stages. A thinning of black. A softening of edges. A first birdcall before the sky changes color. I want to walk this path with you. Not ahead of you. Not above you. Beside you. To share my story and the stories of others who have lived inside this terrain. To speak what is often swallowed. To give language to what has been endured in silence. To offer not only words, but practical guidance and spiritual anchoring for the bends and fractures of this road. Tools for the nights. Bearings for the fog. Small lights you can carry when the way disappears beneath your feet. Not as someone who stands outside the darkness. But as someone who has learned how to live inside it without surrendering their name. As someone who has learned how to carry a flame where wind once ruled. As someone who knows that even the smallest light, when it is real, changes everything.

The Thief of Joy

And as this journey continues, the darkness reveals one of its quietest cruelties: it does not always arrive as despair. Often, it comes as absence. When depression knocks on the door, it rarely announces itself. It does not always howl. It does not always weep. More often, it slips in like fog through an open window. It comes disguised as boredom. As fatigue. As a simple lack of motivation. It settles into the ordinary until the ordinary feels unbearable. "Just get up," your friends may say. "It's just a phase." Their words are gentle, well-meant, stitched with care.

But they cannot feel the gravity in your limbs, the way each attempt to rise feels hellacious, as though you are lifting not a body, but a life. As though the air itself has thickened, turned to syrup, resisting every motion. Outings that once thrilled you now stand before you like unsolvable equations. Invitations feel like obligations. Laughter feels borrowed. Joy becomes a foreign language you can no longer pronounce. You recognize its shape on other people's mouths, hear its rhythm in their voices, but when you try to speak it yourself, nothing comes out. Only a hollow sound. Only the echo of what used to be. The bed becomes an anchor. Not comfort, but gravity. Time begins to leak away without measure. Hours dissolve like salt in water as the shadows draw closer, rearranging the shape of the day. Morning and evening blur into one long, dim corridor. Sleep, once a refuge, becomes a battleground. A restless truce between racing thoughts and a body that begs for rest but refuses to accept it. Dreams fracture. The night fills with half-waking, half-falling. And when morning comes, it does not arrive as renewal. It arrives as a demand. Waking turns into labor. Each morning ushers in not light, but burden. Not possibility, but weight. The simple act of opening your eyes feels like lifting a shutter rusted shut. How do you explain the feeling of being tired even after hours of sleep? Not weary. Not drowsy. Spent. As though something essential has been siphoned out in the night. As if your inner reservoir has been quietly drained, leaving only sediment behind. It is not just the body that is exhausted. It is the wanting. The caring. The reaching. It is the part of you that once leaned toward the world.

Depression steals energy, yes. But more devastatingly, it steals meaning. It drains colour from effort. Purpose from motion. Even pleasure becomes work. Even rest requires endurance. As though your spirit has become a stone. Heavy. Unyielding. Formed from layers of unresolved sadness and unacknowledged trauma, compacted by years of unspoken weather. You carry it inside your chest. You move with it in your bones. Your breath must pass around it. Your heart must beat beside it. And everything that once lifted you now must first be carried. And this is the theft few can see. Not the presence of pain alone, but the absence of delight. Not only the ache, but the hollow where music once lived. Depression does not only wound. It empties. It hollows rooms inside you where laughter used to echo, where curiosity once leaned forward, where hope once made its small, brave nests. You do not always feel broken. Sometimes, you feel blank. And in that blankness, the world grows unbearably loud in its colour, unbearably cruel in its ease, as if life itself is happening somewhere else, and you have been quietly, inexplicably left behind.

The Lies of Depression

And when joy has been thinned to absence, the darkness finds its voice. Depression is a master of deception. It does not shout from rooftops. It does not announce itself with spectacle. It whispers. It leans close, breath warm against the tender places of your mind, and speaks in a tone that sounds disturbingly like your own. "You are worthless," it murmurs. "You are useless. You are unlovable." It tells you that you are a burden, that your existence bends the lives of others out of shape, that the kindest thing you could do is disappear. It convinces you that you are better off alone. That happiness is a language you were never meant to learn. That hope belongs to other people, in other lives, in other bodies. These thoughts do not arrive as questions. They do not ask for debate. They arrive as verdicts. As final judgments stamped into the soft pages of your inner world. They settle into you like law. And because they borrow the sound of your own voice, they feel intimate. Familiar. Trustworthy. They move through your mind like ink through water, tinting every memory, every moment, every imagined future with the same dark hue. But they are lies.

You are not your depression. You are not the voice that wounds you in the dark. You are not the cruel narrator that edits your life down to only its fractures. You are a living, breathing human being of immeasurable complexity and quiet miracle. A constellation of experiences, tenderness, survival, longing, and becoming. You are unique. You are irreplaceable. You are deeply worthy of joy, of peace, of belonging, of fulfillment, even when you cannot feel those truths breathing inside you. Depression does not remove your worth. It only obscures your ability to see it. Like soot smeared across a mirror, it distorts the reflection, but it cannot change the face beneath. Still, within its grip, the very fabric of hope seems to unravel. Each delicate thread of optimism is severed by the sharp blade of negativity. The future, once threaded with possibility, begins to fray. Plans collapse into maybes. Dreams dim into relics. Even neutral moments are conscripted into evidence for despair. A forgotten text becomes proof of unlovability. A small mistake swells into a prophecy of failure. The mind becomes a courtroom where only one witness is ever called, and it testifies endlessly against you. The lies stack like stones. Heavy. Relentless. They build walls inside you, narrowing the corridors of thought, blocking the windows of imagination. Soon, even the idea of hope feels suspicious. Dangerous. Naïve. You stop reaching for it not because you do not want it, but because you have been taught, by the illness itself, that it will only betray you. And yet, even here, something remains.

Beneath the false sentences and forged conclusions, beneath the cruel monologue looping through the dark, there is still a quieter truth. A truth that does not argue. It waits. A truth that does not wound. It endures. The lies are loud. But they are not sovereign. They are symptoms. Not sentences. And the moment you begin to name them as such, the moment you whisper back, "*This is not me. This is my illness speaking*", a hairline fracture appears in their authority. Through that fracture, light remembers how to enter. Slowly. Tenderly. Enough to begin. Dreams that were once vibrant and alive begin to wither, losing color, losing contour, until they resemble a landscape stripped of horizon or ambition. What once reached outward now folds in on itself. The future stretches before you like an endless field of grey, wide and vacant, a place where nothing seems to grow. Possibility feels like a language that has gone extinct. Even imagining tomorrow requires an effort your spirit can no longer afford. Depression distorts perception itself. It bends reality until every kindness feels conditional, every success feels accidental, every hope becomes a setup for inevitable disappointment. It trains the eye to look through a lens ground from fear and anxiety, sorrow and self-doubt, until even beauty feels suspect, until wonder itself seems like a trick of the light. Compliments slide off. Achievements collapse into nothing. Love arrives, but you search it for exits, convinced it cannot possibly stay. And yet, this is not the true world. The world remains a beautiful, complex, and multifaceted place, threaded with wonder, tenderness, and quiet, stubborn love, even when your inner weather cannot touch it. Sun still rises. Rivers still remember how to move. People still reach for one another in a thousand small, luminous ways. The colours have not vanished. They are simply being filtered through a storm that lives inside you. The experience of depression is deeply personal, unique to every life it enters, and yet it carries a shared current: the feeling of being trapped in a never-ending cycle of darkness. Like being lost in a dense forest with no clear path, no visible sky, no remembered direction. Branches close overhead. The ground is uneven. Every sound startles. The light feels imagined. Escape feels impossible.

The shadows crowd close and seem to move when you move, as if the darkness itself were watching. Every step becomes a negotiation. Every decision, a monumental labour. Every interaction, a mountain you must climb with lungs already burning. You move, but the way forward never seems to open. You stand still, and the fear thickens. It is exhausting to exist here. It is exhausting to hope here. And still, even here, even lost among these inner trees, something essential remains true: What you are hearing is not truth. It is the voice of the forest. Not the voice of who you are. The forest speaks in echoes and distortions. It turns distance into threat. It makes every snapping branch sound like prophecy. But forests are not the world. They are a passage through it. And though you may not yet see the clearing, though the canopy may feel endless, you are still a living being moving beneath it. You are still more than the weather of your mind. More than the darkness of this particular terrain. There is a sky above these branches. There is a horizon beyond these trunks. There is a way that has not been erased, only hidden. And the very fact that you are still walking, still breathing, still reading these words, means that somewhere beneath the weight of leaves and fear and shadow, a direction is already being remembered. Not loudly. Not easily. But truly.

The Whispering Lies

And deeper still in that forest of distortion, the darkness learns how to murmur. Among the most sinister aspects of depression is its ability to whisper lies so quietly they pass for truth. They do not arrive with force. They arrive as familiarity. As inner commentary. As the low, constant hum beneath thought. They sound like reason. Like realism. Like you. And that is how they slip past the gates. Slowly, almost imperceptibly, you begin to believe you are unlovable.

Not merely difficult. Not merely hurting. But fundamentally, irreparably unlovable. It tells you that you are a weight to others, a burden disguised as a person, a shadow that follows joy and dims it. A fading echo of who you used to be. It suggests that your presence costs more than it gives. That those who care are only being kind out of duty, out of history, out of habit. That love, if it exists at all, is a thin courtesy stretched over quiet regret.

Each compliment becomes a distortion. Every word of kindness is mistrusted, strained through a lens clouded with worthlessness, inadequacy, and fear. Praise sounds like pity. Affection feels like obligation. Concern feels like surveillance. Even love, when it reaches for you, seems to hesitate, as though it might fracture if it touched who you really are. So despite the warmth around you, you feel cold. Despite being loved, you feel alone. You stand in rooms full of people and feel like an uninvited guest inside your own life. Laughter moves through the air, but it cannot find you. Arms reach, but they seem to stop inches short. You are present, yet exiled. Surrounded, yet sealed.

Entangled in a web of self-doubt and despair, you drift further from the hands extended toward you. Not because you do not want them, but because the lies have rewritten what touch means. They tell you that leaning will collapse others. That needing is dangerous. That your pain is contagious. And so you begin to disappear in small ways. Cancelled plans. Shortened conversations. Smiles that end early. Truths swallowed before they can be spoken. The grip of depression tightens its story: that nobody truly understands your fight, that no one could ever love you amid this unraveling, that your inner night is too much for human company. It becomes a dark theatre playing unflattering narratives of your life on a looping reel. Scene after scene edited to wound. Every memory recut to accuse. Failures given close-ups. Tender moments left on the cutting room floor. Your history rearranged into a courtroom drama where the verdict is always the same. And the audience is small but merciless: the voices in your own head, applauding the pain they perform.

Here, the cruelty is not only what the monster says. It is that it teaches you to say it too. Until the language of harm becomes fluent. Until self-attack feels automatic. Until you begin to bruise yourself from the inside, long before the world ever touches you. And yet, even here, even in this echo chamber of distortion, something remains unsilenced. A quiet resistance. A wordless knowing. A part of you that still aches, not because it is broken, but because it remembers love. For lies must work hard. They must repeat. They must rehearse. Truth does not need to shout. It only needs a moment of stillness to be heard. And somewhere beneath the noise of accusation, beneath the theatre of self-contempt, beneath the whispering dark, there is another voice. Softer. Older. Steadier. Waiting for the first breath of space in which to speak.

Finding Your Voice

And even in that dark theatre, where the lies perform without rest, there is something the script cannot erase. A glimmer of truth remains. Quiet. Steady. Waiting. Amid the cacophony of despair and distorted belief, there lives a small, insistent knowing: *you are not alone.* It does not shout. It does not interrupt the performance. It sits in the back row of the soul, hands folded, breathing. And turning toward that knowing, however faint it feels, becomes the first loosening of the walls. Owning your narrative. Naming your pain. Allowing yourself to say, "*this is hurting me.* This is not weakness. It is the first act of return." The first stone removed from the fortress of grief built around your heart. Because what is spoken can breathe. What is named can move. What is shared can be met. But what is hidden only festers. It turns inward. It rots in the dark. It teaches the wound to believe it deserves to be a wound forever. So begin by finding a safe space.

A place where your truth will not be corrected or hurried. A place where it will not be minimized, polished, or translated into something more comfortable. This may be the quiet page of a journal, waiting like fresh earth beneath your hands, ready to receive what has never been allowed to land. Ink becomes a kind of bloodletting. Each word a release. Each sentence a breath pulled back from the depths. The page does not flinch. It does not interrupt. It lets you exist in full. It may be the presence of a trusted friend, someone whose listening feels like shelter. Someone who does not rush to fix but knows how to stay. Who can hold your words the way you might hold a trembling bird. Gently. Without gripping. Without letting go.

It may be the steady witnessing of a therapist who knows how to sit with storms. Someone trained to hear what hides beneath what is said. Someone who understands that silence speaks too. That trembling is a language.

That survival often arrives before coherence. Wherever it is, let something inside you finally have sound. Let the ache move from bone to breath. Let the nameless gather syllables. Let the inner night discover it is allowed to speak. At first, your voice may feel unfamiliar. Thin. Rusted. Like a door not opened in years. The words may come crooked. Fragmented. Tear-soaked. You may surprise yourself with what spills out. Memories. Anger. Grief. Longings you did not know were still alive. This is not regression. This is circulation returning to places long deprived of air. Each truth spoken is a hairline fracture in the cage. Each sentence a widening. Each honest breath a small rebellion against the dark. And slowly, something begins to shift. The lies no longer echo unchallenged. The theatre lights dim. The audience of cruelty thins. In the space where secrecy once ruled, something else takes form. Presence. Witness. Connection. Your voice does not banish the monster. But it changes the acoustics of the room. No longer alone. No longer sealed. No longer unheard. And in that change, something essential happens. You begin to exist not only inside the pain, but also inside the possibility of being met. And that, that is where the real turning begins.

The act of expression is not small. It is alchemical. It turns ache into language. It turns pressure into passage. It turns the unsayable into something that can be carried, witnessed, and slowly transformed. When you speak what has lived in silence, when you write what has had no shelter, something ancient stirs. As if locked doors remember they were built to open. As if sealed rooms exhale for the first time in years. Words become windows. Breath finds corridors. Light, tentative and unfamiliar, begins to slip into places that have only known night. Expression does not fix. It softens. It circulates. It reminds the inner world that it was never meant to be a tomb. And from that first loosening, that first small return of air, the work becomes gentler and braver all at once. You begin to build from the ground up. Not cathedrals. Not monuments. Foundations. You stop asking how to reclaim a life and begin asking how to inhabit a moment. A shower. Water touching skin like a blessing. Steam rising as if something inside you is finally allowed to lift. A step outside. Light meeting your face. Air, remembering your name. A meal made and eaten. Hands choosing nourishment. A body being told, again, that it is worth sustaining. A message sent. A thread cast across the distance. Proof that your voice can still travel. These are not trivial gestures. They are declarations. They are quiet uprisings against the gravity that has tried to keep you folded inward. Each one says: "*I am still here.*" Each one says: "*I am still participating.*" Each one says: "*I am not done.*"

Move at a pace that respects your nervous system. Let your healing walk, not march. Expand your horizons only as wide as your breath allows. Some days, that will be a single room. Some days a single thought. Some days a single kind word offered to yourself in the dark. This is not failure. This is fluency in survival. And celebrate the smallest victories. Mark them. Honour them. The morning you get out of bed when you did not think you could. The afternoon you answer a message instead of deleting it. The moment you notice the sky. The second you laugh and surprise yourself with the sound. These are milestones, even if no one else sees them. They are the invisible architecture of recovery. They are the quiet scaffolding of a life being rebuilt from the inside. Because every time you choose movement over disappearance, voice over silence, care over collapse, presence over erasure, you are already rewriting the story the darkness tried to tell. And the new story does not need to be loud. It only needs to be true. It can begin with this: "*I am still here.* And here, is enough to start."

Emerging From the Shadows

And as voice becomes habit, and habit becomes steadiness, something within the dark begins to shift. Not abruptly. Not dramatically. But subtly, like the first loosening of frost in the soil when winter has not yet admitted defeat, yet the ground has begun, somewhere deep and unseen, to remember how to soften. Over time, through intentional practice and the steady presence of support, the grip of depression can loosen. Not all at once. Not with spectacle or ceremony. But in the way seasons truly change. Quietly. Gradually. With small, undeniable signs. The world, once bleached of its hues, may begin to remember its colours. At first, they return faintly, like watercolours left out in the rain. A pale blue in the sky. A hesitant green along the edges of things. Then, slowly, richer. Warmer. More sure of themselves. Joy, long buried beneath layers of heaviness, may bubble up again in unexpected places. A laugh that escapes before you have time to stop it. A warmth that settles in your chest and stays. A moment of stillness that does not ache. A moment that feels, suddenly, almost like yourself. The journey through depression is neither linear nor predictable. It loops. It stumbles. It doubles back through old weather. Some days feel like emergence. Others like descent. But every ounce of effort poured into navigating this path matters. None of it is wasted. Every breath you choose to stay. Every time you reach instead of retreat.

Every moment you allow yourself to feel instead of disappearing. These are not small acts. They are daily resurrections. They are proof of life insisting on itself inside the ruins. Embrace the highs and the lows, for they are not contradictions. They are signatures of life's trembling complexity. To feel joy again does not betray the pain. To still ache does not erase the healing. Both can live in the same body. Both can shape the same becoming. You are not meant to be one note. You are a whole weather system learning how to move. As you rise from the shadows, learn to extend gratitude toward your own becoming. Toward the parts of you that survived without applause. Toward the nights you endured when morning felt like an idea, not a promise. Toward the mourning that taught you tenderness. The breaking that taught you depth. The resilience that carried you when you had no language for how. Honour the fragile, burgeoning hope learning how to live inside your ribs. Let gratitude become a way of witnessing your survival without minimizing what it took. And as your light strengthens, let it spill. Not as a demand. Not as a performance. But as a natural consequence of being here. Illuminate your path not only for yourself, but for those still feeling their way through the same dusk. By telling your story. By speaking from the place that once had no voice. By standing where you once needed someone to stand. You may become the glow someone else is quietly searching for. A warmth they recognize. A language they finally understand. A proof that shadow is not the end of the story. Not an ending. A passage. Not an erasure. A transformation. A lantern on a long road. A living testament that even after the longest night, something in us still knows how to turn toward morning.

A Life Worth Living

And as your light begins to steady, as it learns how to travel with you instead of flickering somewhere far ahead, the meaning of the journey itself starts to change. What once felt like a desperate escape from suffering slowly reshapes into something deeper. More sacred. A becoming. Depression is a battle often fought in the shadows, a quiet war waged without banners or witnesses, a daily choosing of breath over disappearance. It is a journey threaded with despair, yes, but also one seeded with unexpected tenderness. With awareness. With a kind of wisdom that is only ever earned in the dark. Within this passage lives the possibility of healing. Of restoration. Of a return to the vibrancy of life in forms you may not yet recognize, colours you have not yet learned to name. And if you find yourself wrestling this invisible foe, hear this clearly, not as sentiment but as truth carried on the backs of countless lives: you are not alone. You never have been. Even when the loneliness feels absolute. Even when your pain convinces you it is singular. Reach out. Seek help. Let someone walk beside you. Let another heartbeat share the night. There is hope. There is support. There is a path, even when you cannot yet see its outline, even when it exists only as a feeling, a leaning, a faint tug toward something gentler. The road may be long. It may be arduous. It may twist back on itself and lead you through the same terrain more than once. There will be days when the light feels theoretical, when faith feels like a language you once spoke but cannot quite remember. There will be mornings when all you can manage is survival. And survival will be enough.

Because recovery has its own quiet gravity. It pulls not with force, but with invitation. Not with spectacle, but with persistence. It waits. Patient. Real. Alive beneath the rubble. And slowly, almost imperceptibly, it begins to break through. In the way roots fracture stone. In the way dawn dilutes night. In the way a single candle alters the architecture of a room. It illuminates the ground ahead not in blinding swaths, but in small, merciful radius. Just enough to take the next step. Just enough to see your own hands again. Just enough to remind you that you are still here. Still becoming. Still capable of touch, of meaning, of love. A life worth living is not a life without darkness. It is a life that knows how to carry light within it. And you, walking this road, breath by breath, are already doing that. In the end, remember this, not as a slogan but as a truth you can return to when the fog thickens: depression may be part of your story, but it is not the author. It does not hold the pen. It does not decide the ending. It is a chapter, heavy and harrowing, yes, but not the whole book. A passage you were forced to walk through, not the plot that defines your existence. Its pages may be marked by tears and smudged ink, but they are not the final word written over your life. With each new day arrives another opportunity, however small it may feel, to reclaim your joy. Not the loud, effortless joy promised in glossy narratives, but the real kind. The kind that grows slowly. The kind that survives weather. The kind that learns how to share space with sorrow without being extinguished by it. Each day offers a chance to voice your truth, to let your inner world speak without apology, without shrinking itself to be palatable. To say, this is what I feel, this is where I am, and this is enough for today. You are deserving of love. Not when you are healed. Not when you are lighter. Not when you are easier to be around. Now. As you are. With your history. With your scars. With the tenderness you carry because of what you have endured. You are deserving of understanding, of patience, of hope that does not rush you toward transformation but walks beside you while it unfolds. Life is an intricate tapestry, woven not only from gold but from shadow-thread too. And those darker threads do not ruin the design. They give it depth. Contrast. Meaning. In learning to move through depression rather than around it, in learning to sit with it without surrendering to it, you begin to discover the strength of your own hands. The patience of your own weaving. The quiet, defiant courage it takes to keep choosing yourself even when the pattern is not yet clear. And from this choosing, a path takes form. Not perfect. Not unbroken. Not free of stones or detours. But yours. A path shaped by honesty, resilience, and a hard-earned intimacy with your own inner life. A life not defined by the darkness you survived but illuminated by the fact that you did. A life worth living. In all its nuance. In all its fragility. In all its wonder.

The Fortress Within: The Squatter – Emily's Story

And just as every journey through darkness carries its own weather, every descent begins through a different door. Depression was not a visitor in my life. It was a squatter. It did not knock. It did not ask permission. It did not announce itself with warning or sound. It simply arrived one day and began to live inside me. A silent, insidious presence, settling into the corners of my mind the way dust drifts into abandoned rooms, the way spores float unseen through a beam of unwelcome light. At first, it was almost imperceptible. Easy to excuse. Easy to misname. I explained away the fatigue as late nights. The loss of appetite as stress. The thinning of joy as something temporary. Manageable. Ordinary. The kind of thing that would surely pass if I just rested, just pushed, just tried harder. But it did not remain small. It began to stake its claim. It stretched thin, searching tendrils into my thoughts, into my emotions, into the soft tissue of my days. It took up residence in sighs. In silences. In the growing distance between who I was and who I remembered being. It put down roots in places I could not see, anchoring itself in unspoken fears, in unnamed grief, in the quiet erosion of connection. And before I understood what was happening, before I had language for the shift, it had begun to build. Brick by quiet brick. Wall by unseen wall. A fortress rose inside me. A structure formed from everything I did not say. From every feeling I swallowed. From every invitation I declined. From every door I closed inside my own chest. The architecture of withdrawal took shape. Rooms sealed themselves. Windows vanished. Corridors narrowed. Light thinned. The inner world darkened, not all at once, but the way dusk gathers. Softly. Relentlessly. Until one day I realized I was no longer walking through my life. I was living inside something. My name is Emily Thorne. And this is the story of how I lost myself to the Fortress Within, and of the long, arduous, breath-by-breath journey of finding my way back.

The Walls Rise

It did not arrive as catastrophe. It arrived as commentary. The construction began quietly, almost politely, the way ivy first tests a wall. A whisper of self-doubt after a presentation at work. A fleeting internal wince at the sound of my own voice. A second glance at an email I had already sent, rereading it as though proof of my inadequacy might suddenly reveal itself between the lines. These thoughts followed me back to my desk and sat beside me long after the room had emptied, breathing softly in the spaces where confidence once lived. The nagging sense that I wasn't good enough. Not smart enough. Not interesting enough. Not worthy of the love of my partner, James. These were the first bricks. Small. Individually insignificant. Easy to step over. Easy to excuse. Easy to misname as humility, as self-awareness, as the normal background noise of being human. But they accumulated. They stacked themselves silently in the margins of my days, settling behind conversations, shadowing moments of achievement, whispering beneath laughter. Each thought placed another stone. Each unchallenged doubt added mortar. Soon, the air inside me began to change. Thicker. Heavier. Less breathable. Insecurity joined the fray like a skilled architect. I began to measure myself against everyone around me, as though life were a competition I had entered without being given the rules, a race where everyone else seemed to know the course and I had arrived barefoot, already behind. I compared my insides to their outsides. My unseen struggles to their curated triumphs. And everywhere I looked, I found myself lacking. Their smiles seemed brighter. Their confidence louder. Their accomplishments grander. Their lives fuller. More fluent. More legitimate. They appeared to move through the world with a kind of permission I could not locate within myself. They spoke without apology. They occupied space without flinching. They seemed at home in their own skin. And I began to feel like a guest in mine. I watched joy happen to other people and felt like a visitor to the country of happiness, holding a passport that was no longer valid. Close enough to observe the customs. Too foreign to belong. Standing at the edges of rooms where laughter lived, translating the language of ease without ever speaking it.

And somewhere between the comparisons and the quiet conclusions, more walls went up. Unseen. Unannounced. And steadily closing in. The joy I once found in my artwork, in the easy laughter shared with friends, began to ring hollow. What had once moved through me like music now arrived thin and echoing, a pale imitation of the "real" happiness everyone else appeared to possess without effort. I could still paint, still smile, still sit at crowded tables and lift my glass at the right moments, but something essential had gone missing from the center of it all. The colour remained, but not the warmth. The motion remained, but not the life. Even love began to feel borrowed. As though I were wearing someone else's coat. As though James's tenderness were something I had tricked my way into, something that might be taken back the moment he saw me clearly. His affection no longer felt like a home I lived in, but a room I was afraid to touch, convinced my fingerprints would somehow expose me. I waited for the day the lease would end. For the moment he would realize he had mistaken me for someone worth staying with. And the cement that bound these bricks together was fear. Fear of failure, crouched at the edge of every attempt. Fear of rejection, humming beneath every interaction. Fear of being irrevocably, fundamentally flawed. Not broken in ways that could be mended, but wrong in ways that could only be concealed. This fear did not shout. It seeped. It slid quietly into marrow and memory, chilling me from the inside out, hardening everything it touched. Thought stiffened. Breath shallowed. Hope learned to hold itself very still. Even rest became guarded, as though softness were a liability, as though ease might invite collapse. I began to move through my days braced. Shoulders tight. Jaw set. Heart guarded like a locked door inside a locked room. Each decision passed through a tribunal of doubt. Each feeling interrogated. Each desire cross-examined until it recanted. And without my noticing when the first wall stood, without ceremony, without warning, without a single clear moment of beginning, the Fortress was already taking shape. Rising not in front of me, but around me. Stone by invisible stone.

The Battlements of Thought

Once the walls were raised, they demanded their own kind of protection. And so the thoughts arrived. Intrusive. Sharp. Uninvited. They did not drift in. They marched. They took their places along the battlements like archers sworn to an endless watch, lining the inner parapets of my mind, not to guard me, but to keep me contained. From those high, unforgiving ledges, they began to release their volleys, arrow after arrow of accusation and prophecy, fired into what little soft ground remained. "You're going to fail. James deserves someone better. You're a burden. Nothing you do matters." The words struck again and again, feathered with familiarity, tipped with a terrible certainty. They did not arrive as questions. They landed as verdicts. Each one embedding itself deeper, until my inner world felt bristled with them, as though I were walking through my own thoughts and constantly drawing blood. These were not passing anxieties. They were relentless. Unyielding. They circled endlessly, a broken record of accusation and prediction, carving the same grooves into my mind until the paths felt permanent, until it seemed impossible to think in any other direction. They poisoned my perspective. They eroded my self-worth. They reached ahead of every moment and rewrote it before I was even allowed to feel it. A compliment became suspicion. A success became an error. A neutral silence became proof of rejection. Experience no longer arrived clean. It arrived already stained.

I tried to reason with them. To answer back. To dismantle their logic, piece by careful piece. But they were not interested in the truth. They were too practiced. Too ingrained. They had studied the architecture of my fears. They knew where the foundations were weakest. They knew which memories to weaponize, which doubts to sharpen, which wounds to reopen just enough to keep them bleeding. They learned the sound of my own voice and wore it perfectly until I could no longer tell where I ended, and they began. They became the masters of the Fortress. And I became their captive. Sleep, once a refuge, turned into contested ground. Night after night, I lay awake, body exhausted, nerves humming, mind under siege. The dark did not bring rest. It amplified the firing. Thought after thought detonated in the quiet, each one echoing louder because there was nothing left to drown it out. In the darkness, they grew larger. More theatrical. More convincing. The absence of light gave them shape. Shadows on the walls stretched into monstrous outlines, shifting and breathing at the edges of my vision, until even my own room felt like enemy territory. The familiar became hostile. The safe became surveilled. My bed no longer felt like a place of restoration, but like the center of a war room where the battle never adjourned. The Fortress did not rest. Neither did I. And somewhere between the final hours of night and the first thin light of morning, I began to understand something terrifying: There was no longer a clear line between the walls and my mind.

Siege Warfare

The Fortress did not stop at walls and watchtowers. It wanted dominion. It was not content to merely surround me. It began, quietly and with terrible patience, to dismantle me from the inside out. It waged a kind of psychological siege warfare, slow and methodical, cutting off my inner supplies one by one, as if starving a city into surrender. Energy was the first to fall. Then appetite. Then desire. Then hope. Each loss barely registered on its own, small enough to excuse, easy enough to explain away. But together they formed a famine of the spirit.

Each day, another narrow passage collapsed. Each night, another door sealed itself shut. Until eventually, there were no open corridors left. Only chambers of heaviness. Only air that felt too thick to draw fully into my lungs. Getting out of bed began to feel like climbing a mountain with no summit, a sheer face of effort rising before me each morning, offering no view, no promise, no reward. My limbs felt weighted, as though someone had poured wet sand into my bones. Every movement dragged. Every action required negotiation. My body no longer obeyed intention. It resisted it. My mind moved through fog. Dense. Soundless. Unforgiving. Thoughts arrived muffled and distorted, as if I were underwater, watching my own life ripple somewhere above me. The idea of facing the day, of speaking, of meeting another person's eyes, of arranging my face into something that resembled okayness, rose before me like an insurmountable wall. Even imagining it left me depleted. Even considering it made my chest tighten. Soon, the outside world began to feel like enemy territory. I started calling in sick to work, dressing it in the gentler language of a "mental health day," but the truth was simpler and heavier: I was retreating. Folding inward. Letting the drawbridge stay up. Letting the Fortress decide the boundaries of my life. At first it was one day. Then another. Then stretches of time that blurred into a single, unbroken hush. I stayed in bed long after the light had shifted across the walls, long after the city had woken and moved on without me. The room grew stale with my breathing. Hours passed without markers. Meals disappeared. Showers were postponed. Messages went unanswered. The world narrowed to the dimensions of the mattress, the weight of the blanket, the hum of my own exhaustion. I told myself I was resting. But what I was really doing was surrendering to the inertia of the Fortress.

Letting it keep me. Letting it decide how small my life was allowed to become. And the smaller my world grew, the stronger its walls seemed.

Eating, once a pleasure, became a task stripped of joy. Food lost its flavor. Its texture. Its invitation. What had once been warmth and colour on my tongue dulled into obligation. I ate not because I wanted to, but because some distant logic reminded me that bodies require fuel. I measured out survival in small, reluctant portions, just enough to keep the machinery moving at its barest minimum, just enough to avoid the questions that came with visible disappearance. James noticed. I could see it in the crease between his brows, in the way his gaze lingered a second too long, searching my face for something he could not name. Concern lived there. Fear. Love trying to understand what it was not equipped to reach. But I brushed it aside, cloaked it in smaller words, named it a lack of appetite, as though language could domesticate what was happening inside me. As though giving it a casual name could make it less real. Smiling became a grotesque performance. The genuine joy that once bubbled up without invitation had been choked beneath the oppressive weight of the Fortress. When I smiled, it was for him. An effort. A courtesy. A fragile offering meant to keep him from worrying, meant to preserve the illusion that something in me was still untouched. But my face struggled to remember the shape. The muscles felt foreign. Stiff. Like borrowing a gesture from another life, from another woman I could barely recall. My lips curved, but nothing followed them. No warmth. No lift. No echo inside. Even breathing turned into labor. Each inhale felt shallow, incomplete, as though the air itself had thinned. As though the Fortress had begun rationing oxygen. A constant pressure settled on my chest, a quiet, suffocating presence, like a stone placed gently but firmly where my heart should rise. No matter how deeply I tried to breathe, it never felt like enough. My lungs filled, but I did not. I was always just short of relief. Always reaching the top of the breath without finding the release that should follow. I felt as though I were slowly drowning in the very air meant to keep me alive. Moving through my days became an act of endurance. Sitting hurt. Standing hurt. Lying still hurt in a way that had no clear edge. My body carried a tension that never resolved, a subtle clenching against something I could not see but could always feel. The Fortress had moved beyond the mind. It had made a home in muscle and marrow. It had written itself into my posture, my digestion, my sleep.

And still, it stood. Patient. Hungry. Closing in. A structure built of exhaustion and fear, tightening its corridors, narrowing its windows, waiting for me to forget what open space had ever felt like.

The World Spins On

And while the Fortress tightened its hold, the world beyond it did not pause. It did not soften its pace. It did not lower its volume. The world outside my window continued to spin, bright and ordinary, oblivious to the hurricane raging within me. Morning still arrived on schedule. Light still spilled across pavements and kitchen counters. Cars passed. Voices rose. Dogs were walked. Coffee was poured. Life unfolded in gestures so casual, so unremarkable, it felt almost cruel. People went about their days laughing, working, loving, inhabiting a reality that seemed to run on a different frequency, untouched by the darkness that had overtaken me. Their lives appeared seamless, threaded with errands and embraces, complaints and celebrations, all of it moving forward with an ease that felt foreign, almost fictional. I watched them from behind the thick, fortified walls of my inner keep, as though peering through narrow slits in stone, my vision reduced to fragments of a world I no longer felt part of. With every passing hour, the distance widened. Isolation grew like a second skin, something I wore without choosing, something that tightened whenever I tried to move. Disconnection became atmosphere. It filled my lungs. It hummed in my ears. It followed me from room to room like a low, persistent fog. I was no longer simply alone. I was separate. Exiled from the ordinary currents of living. I found myself envying their joy, resenting their normalcy. How could they smile so easily? How could they plan dinners and futures and weekends when I was barely surviving the act of breathing? How could they speak about trivial frustrations when my own existence felt like an emergency no one else could hear? Their ease felt like an accusation. Their laughter, a language I had forgotten how to speak. Each sound from the outside world reached me distorted, muffled by the thickness of my inner walls. The music of living played on, but I could not find its rhythm. I moved through my days like a foreigner in my own city, unable to read the signs, unable to remember the customs, unsure how everyone else seemed to know exactly where they were going and why. The world spun. And I remained still. A figure in the tower of a Fortress I did not remember building, watching life continue below me, radiant and unreachable, while the distance between us grew heavy enough to feel like gravity itself.

James tried to reach me. Again and again, he stood at the gates, knocking with concern, with tenderness, with fear. Not with fists, but with his eyes. With the soft urgency in his voice. With the way he paused in doorways as if hoping I might suddenly return to myself. He offered words of comfort. Suggestions for help. Even pleas that trembled at the edges of his strength. Each one landed against the stone of the Fortress and fell quietly at my feet, unheard in the way that mattered. But the Fortress had me in its grip, and I met his reaching with retreat. I answered warmth with distance. Care with silence. Love with a carefully constructed absence. I pushed him away, not because I didn't love him, but because I did. Because love made the risk unbearable. Because his nearness illuminated the ruin I was convinced, I had become. I did not want him to see the broken, hollow shell I believed lived where a woman once stood. I did not want my darkness to stain the way he saw the world. I did not want to become another weight he had to carry. I was terrified that if he truly saw the truth, he would leave. That once he looked closely enough, he would discover the flaw I believed was etched into my core. So I withdrew further into the Fortress, retreating room by inner room, drawing the bridges up behind me, sealing doors I no longer knew how to open. I hid in the deepest chambers of myself, where even my own voice sounded foreign. And I left James standing outside those invisible walls, small against the stone of my silence, his face etched with worry and confusion, searching for cracks, listening for echoes, calling a name I was no longer sure belonged to me. His love moved through the air like a hand reaching for smoke. Present. Earnest. Powerless to take hold. Inside the Fortress, I told myself I was protecting him. But the truth was quieter and crueller. I was disappearing.

The Lowest Point

And when you have lived too long behind the walls, there comes a moment when the dark no longer feels like weather. It feels like truth. It stops behaving like something that visits and begins to feel like something that *is*. The air itself seems made of it. The language of the world bends around it. There comes a point when the darkness becomes so overwhelming, so all-encompassing, that you cannot imagine ever stepping beyond it. Light feels like a story you once heard as a child. Escape begins to sound naive. Unreal. A kindness meant for other lives. You start to believe this is no longer a season, but a sentence. Not a place you are in, but who you are. The Fortress stops feeling like a prison and starts feeling like the world. Its cold floors become familiar. Its narrow windows become all the sky you remember. You no longer press against the walls. You lean into them. You build routines inside the ruin. You learn how to move within the limits of the dark and mistake that adaptation for acceptance. You begin to accept the lies it whispers. The ones it has rehearsed until they sound like your own thoughts. That you are worthless. Unlovable. That your existence is an inconvenience. That the world would be better, lighter, easier without you in it. These thoughts no longer arrive as intruders. They arrive as conclusions. As facts. As the quiet background music of your mind. They shape the way you walk, the way you speak, the way you look at your own hands. They seep into memory, into expectation, into every imagined future until even tomorrow feels contaminated by your presence.

This was the place I reached. The place beneath the fight. The place beneath the questions. The point where resistance finally went quiet. Where the Fortress no longer needed to fight me because it had convinced me to fight myself. Where I did not feel broken. I felt finished. And in that stillness, heavier than despair, something inside me lay down. Not to rest. But because it no longer believed standing made a difference. The Fortress did not have to hold me anymore. I was holding it. The Fortress had won. It had eroded my spirit. Shattered my self-worth. Hollowed me out until hope felt like a story that belonged to someone else's life. I sat alone in my darkened apartment, wrapped in a silence so thick it rang, a pressure that filled the rooms like water. The air felt heavy, unmoving. The walls seemed to lean closer. The only sound was the pounding of my own heart, each beat a dull, relentless knock from inside my chest, reminding me that I was still here when I no longer wanted to be. Alive inside a body that felt like an argument I was too tired to keep making. The intrusive thoughts were louder than ever. A merciless chorus. A swarm of voices colliding and overlapping, dragging old accusations across every surface of my mind. They rose and fell like a storm surge, threatening to drown every fragile part of me that remained. They told me I was finished. That I was too heavy for love. Too damaged for repair. Too much for the world to hold. And then, out of that noise, a new thought surfaced. Clear. Cold. Terrifying. A thought about ending everything. It did not arrive screaming. It arrived with a terrible calm. It cut through the fog like a blade through cloth, precise and shocking in its clarity. And in the instant, it appeared, something inside me recoiled. My body reacted before my mind could explain. My breath caught. My stomach clenched. My skin prickled with a fear that felt different from despair. Sharper. Brighter. Awake. And in that fear, something else flickered. Not hope. Not yet. But recognition. This is not safe. This is not something I can carry alone. The thought did not save me. But it stopped me. It cracked the sealed room. It let in a thin, urgent awareness that what was happening inside me had crossed a line from suffering into danger. From pain into peril. For the first time in a long while, my life did not feel meaningless.

It felt fragile. And that fragility mattered. That was the moment I knew I needed help. Not tomorrow. Not someday. Now. And in that knowing, small and shaking though it was, the Fortress finally failed to keep me silent.

If at any point listen or reading this stirs anything heavy or immediate inside you, please don't carry that alone. If you're in South Africa, you can contact: ***Suicide Crisis Line:*** *0800 567 567* ***SADAG (South African Depression and Anxiety Group):*** *0800 21 22 23 or WhatsApp 076 882 2775* ***Emergency:*** *112 from any mobile. If you're elsewhere, please look up the support numbers for your country. You deserve care not only in words, but in real, living presence.*

A Crack in the Wall

And sometimes, it is at the very edge of despair that something unexpected happens. The thought of ending my life, horrifying as it was, sparked a flicker of something else within me. A cruel irony. A terrible clarity. That thought did not arrive as desire, but as an alarm bell. A line crossed so stark it sliced through the fog and forced me to finally see where I was standing. It was not an invitation. It was a warning. A flare fired from the deepest part of myself that still wanted to live. In that instant, I knew. With a certainty that left no room for negotiation. I could not do this alone. The Fortress had to be breached, even if tearing it down meant exposure. Even if it meant cold air on wounds I had spent years hiding. Even if it meant standing bare before another human being with all my fractures visible. The first breach was small. Fragile. Almost nothing. A phone call. My hands shook as I lifted the phone, as though it weighed more than it should, as though it carried the gravity of a life inside it.

My thumb hovered. My breath stuttered. And then I pressed his name. James answered. And when I heard his voice, something inside me cracked open. Not cleanly. Not beautifully. But enough. My own voice trembled as I spoke, thin and unfamiliar, as if it had not been used for truth in a very long time. The words did not come out in sentences. They came out in fragments. In sobs. In broken confessions that tripped over one another trying to escape. I told him about the despair. About the exhaustion. About the walls. About the Fortress that had been tightening around me, brick by invisible brick, until I could barely breathe inside my own life.

I told him I was scared. I told him I was not okay. I told him I needed help. And he did not turn away. He did not minimize. He did not fix. He did not flee. He listened. On the other end of the line, I could hear his breath change. Slow. Steady. Present. As though he were anchoring himself so he could anchor me. His voice softened, thick with something I had forgotten was mine to receive. Care. Concern. Love that did not retreat in the face of my darkness. On the other end of the line, there was silence. Not the hollow kind. Not the kind that abandons. The listening kind. The kind that leans closer. Then a soft sound broke through it. A small, involuntary sob, as if something inside him had given way before he could stop it. "Emily," he whispered. My name in his mouth sounded different. Fragile. Trembling. Alive. "Why didn't you tell me?" I had no answer that could hold the truth. No sentence large enough to carry the years of retreat, the quiet corrosion, the way the Fortress had trained me to believe I was safer alone. I only knew this: I could not carry the weight anymore. Silence had almost buried me. And I was so tired of disappearing. He told me he was glad I called. He told me he was here. He told me we would not face this alone. And in those simple words, something shifted. The Fortress did not fall. But it cracked. A hairline fracture ran through its inner wall. And through that narrow opening, something long absent slipped in. Air. The silence inside me changed its sound. The room I had been sealed into for so long no longer felt airtight. My breathing deepened in broken pulls. The sobs came harder. But beneath them was something new. A sense that I was no longer screaming into a vacuum. That someone else could hear me now.

He said he was coming. Minutes later, the door opened. And there he was. James stood in the threshold like someone who had run through fear to reach me. His chest rose and fell too quickly. His eyes were bright with unshed tears, reflecting relief and terror, love and heartbreak, all braided together. He crossed the room in two strides and pulled me into his arms. Not carefully. Not politely. He held me like someone anchoring another human being back into existence. His arms were warm. Solid. Real. His heartbeat pressed against my cheek, loud and steady, a rhythm that did not belong to the Fortress. His hands found my back, my shoulders, as if reminding my body where it ended and the world began. I broke against him. The sobs came hard and unfiltered, tearing out of a place that had been sealed for too long. And he did not flinch. He held. He stayed. And inside that circle of arms, something stirred beneath the rubble. Not relief. Not healing. Not answers. Connection. A living thing. A warmth I had forgotten my body could recognize. It moved through my chest like the first ember after a long winter. Small. Unsteady. But unmistakably alive. We sat like that for a long time. The room dim. The air thick with what had almost been lost and what was, somehow, still here. And in that shared quiet, I understood something with a clarity that felt almost sacred. I had not been strong alone. I was strong because I was no longer alone. Later that night, when my breathing had slowed and my hands had stopped shaking, I made another call. My voice was still thin. My courage still trembling. But it was there. This time, it was to a therapist. A stranger. A lifeline. A door. With that call, the Fortress did not collapse. The walls did not crumble. The darkness did not vanish. But a fracture widened. And through that narrow opening, light slipped in. Not a blaze. Not a miracle. A thread. Pale. Trembling. Real. And for the first time in a very long while, I did not turn away from it. That my pain had crossed the boundary of my own skull and entered the human world. That crack did not save me. But it made space. And sometimes, space is enough to survive the night.

Breaking Down the Fortress

And once the first crack existed, the work could finally begin. Not the kind of work that makes for tidy stories. Not the kind that arrives in montages or miracles. But the slow, bodily labor of unbuilding something that had taken years to construct. The road to recovery was long and arduous. It did not open into sunlight. It descended. There were no sudden rescues, no cinematic dissolving of the dark. Therapy was not a soft place at first. It was excavation. It was standing in the ruins of my own inner architecture with bare hands and being asked to dig. To lift the stones I had stacked for survival. To look beneath the floors I had sealed. To turn toward the very places I had spent years fortifying against. Each session felt like entering an underground chamber of myself. Some rooms were thick with dust. Others flooded. Some held memories I had not touched in so long they no longer felt like mine. Therapy forced me to confront the demons that had taken root within me, the old stories and hidden wounds that had quietly become the foundation of the Fortress itself. Not monsters in the cinematic sense, but smaller, more dangerous things. Beliefs. Assumptions. Conclusions drawn by a younger, frightened version of me who had been trying to survive without tools. I learned about cognitive behavioural therapy, CBT. Not as a technique, but as a language. A way of tracing thought back to its source, of following the thread of a feeling through the labyrinth of the mind to where it first learned its name. It taught me to see the machinery behind my suffering. The invisible gears that had been turning in the dark, grinding experience into evidence against myself.

It taught me how to recognize the archers on the battlements. How to spot the thought before it loosed its arrow. How to hear the lie as it inhaled. How to catch the moment where perception hardened into verdict. "You're failing." "You're a burden." "James would be better without you." "This will never change." Before, these had arrived as facts. As weather. As the voice of reality itself. CBT taught me to slow the moment down. To hold the thought up to the light. To ask it where it came from. Who taught it to speak? What proof it carried besides familiarity? How to challenge the voice before it could settle into stone. How to question the authority it had claimed over my life. How to replace automatic cruelty with deliberate curiosity. This was not about positive thinking. It was about honest seeing. About learning the difference between an injury and an identity. Between a symptom and a self. Between the architecture of depression and the woman living inside it. And every time I named a pattern, something shifted. Every time I interrupted a loop, a stone loosened. Every time I chose inquiry over accusation, a wall thinned. The Fortress did not fall in great, satisfying collapses. It dismantled itself in small sounds. The quiet scrape of a brick being moved. The soft thud of a belief laid down. The unfamiliar echo of space returning where a wall had once stood. Sometimes the work left me shaking. Sometimes hollow. Sometimes, flooded with grief, I had no language for yet. But beneath the exhaustion, there was something else. Air. Movement. The strange relief of discovering that what had once felt like the whole world was, in fact, a structure. And structures can be unbuilt. Slowly. Tenderly. One conscious breath. One questioned thought. One reclaimed inch of inner ground at a time. Little by little. Brick by brick. We began to dismantle the structure. There was nothing grand about the work. No single moment where the walls collapsed in a satisfying roar. It happened instead in the language of hands and breath. In the slow ache of effort. In the quiet courage of returning again and again to places I would rather have sealed. Each stone I loosened exposed something tender beneath. Old griefs still warm to the touch. Long-buried fears that had never stopped breathing. Memories sealed away not because they were gone, but because they had once been unbearable to hold.

Some days, it felt as though the walls had been the only thing keeping me intact. As though they had been load-bearing. Removing them left me trembling, porous, open to every weather. I would leave therapy feeling flayed, as if my skin had been peeled back and the world now pressed directly against my nerves. The air felt too loud. Light too sharp. Emotion too close. There were moments I longed for the old enclosure, for the numb safety of stone, even as I knew what it had cost me. And yet, with each brick that fell, something else arrived. Space. Breath. A strange, unfamiliar lightness, like stepping out of a narrow corridor into a room whose ceiling you cannot yet see. I began to notice the subtle ways my body responded. My chest rising a little deeper. My shoulders dropping without being commanded. My thoughts pausing where they once raced. I was lighter. A little freer. Less enclosed. As though air had begun to circulate through places that had been sealed for years. Meditation and mindfulness became the ground beneath my feet. Not escapes. Anchors. They taught me how to return to the body I had been living outside of. To notice breath as something other than proof of survival. To feel my heartbeat without fear. To sit inside sensation instead of being dragged by it. They gave me a way to steady myself when the tides of my mood surged, when emotion rose like weather inside my ribs and threatened to carry me back into the Fortress.

They did not magically erase depression. They did not pretend the battle was over. They did not deny the shadows their existence. But they changed the acoustics of the inner world. They softened the volume of the voices on the battlements. They thinned the fog. They widened the spaces between thought and truth. They offered me moments of quiet where I could hear myself again. Not the monster. Not the walls. But the living, breathing presence beneath them. And in that quiet, something vital became possible. Choice. Pause. Response. In that quiet, it became easier to fight back. Not with force. But with awareness. With compassion. With the growing recognition that the Fortress was no longer the whole landscape. It was only one structure within it. And I was no longer living solely inside its walls. And James, James stayed. He did not hover at the edges or call encouragement from a safe distance. He stepped into the dust with me. Into the drifting ash of everything that had once held me captive. He stood beside me while the walls were pried loose and the air filled with the grit of old fears and falling stone. He breathed that air with me. He coughed where I coughed. He waited where I faltered. Through the long days when exhaustion wrapped itself around my bones, and the longer nights when doubt crept back like cold through open windows, he did not leave. He became my anchor when the ground felt unreliable. My lighthouse when the inner seas rose and the shoreline disappeared. A steady, living signal that something solid still existed beyond the storm. When I forgot who I was, he remembered for me. When my mind erased every trace of progress, he traced it back into the dust with gentle fingers. He noticed the things I could not. The way my eyes stayed present a moment longer. The way my breath no longer broke so easily. The way laughter, once extinct, began to flicker again like a shy flame. He celebrated what depression had trained me to dismiss. A session attended. A thought questioned instead of obeyed. A day survived without surrender. These were not small to him. He treated them like milestones. Like evidence. Like proof that something sacred was happening beneath the wreckage. And when I stumbled, when the work unearthed more than I could hold, when the ground inside me gave way and old darkness rushed back through the cracks, he did not recoil. He did not correct. He did not demand strength. He took my hand in both of his and stayed there. In the shaking. In the tears. In the quiet after. He became a place my nervous system could rest. A reminder that connection itself is medicine. That love does not require wholeness to remain. The Fortress was not falling in a single, dramatic collapse. There was no final thunder. No victorious dust cloud rising against a bright sky. It was coming down in pieces. In fragments. In the daily choosing. In the patient returning. In the slow, faithful removal of what no longer served the life beneath it. And for the first time, I was no longer its prisoner. I was its undoing. Not with violence. But with presence. Not with destruction. But with truth. Each breath I took outside its walls. Each tear that softened its foundations. Each moment of connection that loosened its grip. I was learning, stone by stone, that the Fortress could not survive being seen. And neither could it survive being loved from the inside out.

Life After the Fortress

What remains now is not a ruin, but a field. Not an absence, but a wide, breathing expanse where something new is learning how to live. The Fortress is gone, reduced to memory and mineral, its stones scattered back into the earth they once tried to dominate. The great walls that once caged my inner sky have collapsed into humble shapes. Pebbles. Dust. Ground. And still, the landscape of my mind bears the impressions of what stood here. Scars where ramparts once rose. Faint outlines where watchtowers cast their long, governing shadows.

The soil remembers. I remember. But this ground is no longer barren. It is not a wasteland. It is fertile. Dark. Loosened. Ready. And from it, new growth is emerging. Slow. Intentional. Unmistakably alive. Green pushes its way through the broken stone, not in conquest, but in quiet persistence. Roots curl into the places where fear once anchored itself. Shoots lift toward light that had long been blocked. What grows here now is not the delicate hope of a single good day. It is something sturdier. Something weathered. A strength shaped by seasons of survival. Resilience with a pulse. Tenderness with a backbone. I still have bad days. Days when the light thins and the air feels heavier again. Days when old shadows stretch themselves across the inner ground, testing the outlines of the blueprints that once ruled me. Days when negative thoughts return like familiar ghosts, carrying the accents of former years. But now, I am not unarmed. I am not unnamed. I am not alone inside them. Now, I have tools. I have language. I have ways to meet what rises. I recognize the early signs of reconstruction. The subtle shifts. The quiet tightening. The first murmurs of mortar.

And I intervene before the first brick can set. I question the voice instead of kneeling to it. I return to my body when my mind begins to run. I breathe where I once disappeared. I reach outward when the old instinct urges retreat. The walls no longer rise unnoticed. They no longer build themselves in the dark. I have learned that vulnerability is not weakness. It is strength without armor. It is the courage to be touched by life again. Sharing my struggles with Anya and my therapist opened the gates isolation had sealed. Their witnessing did not unravel me. It steadied me. It gave my pain a place to land without becoming the whole terrain. It returned me to the human world, where suffering is not a sentence, but a language spoken by many. I have learned that self-care is not indulgence. It is infrastructure. Rest is not retreat. It is repair. Boundaries are not distance. They are architecture for safety. Nourishment is not reward. It is continuation. Movement is not punishment. It is circulation. Stillness is not emptiness. It is listening. These are no longer luxuries postponed until life is over. They are the way life is built. They are the beams and windows and open doors of what stands here now. And most importantly, I have learned this: I am not alone. Millions walk this terrain. Millions carry versions of these scars. Millions fight this quiet war behind ordinary faces and ordinary days. And within that shared humanity lives something real. Not a slogan. Not a poster on a wall. But a lived possibility. Recovery exists. Healing unfolds. The mind can learn new ways to build. What stands here now is not a fortress. It is a home. A place with open ground and growing things. A place where light is allowed to enter. A place where I can sit inside myself without fear. A place where life is not something to survive, but something that is slowly, bravely, being lived.

Epilogue: The Key

The Fortress Within may be gone, but its memory still breathes in the shape of this new land.It lives in the gentle rises and hollows of my inner world, in the places where stone once ruled and now grass is learning how to bend. Not as a threat. Not as a shadow that commands. But as a witness. A quiet testament to the darkness I once survived, and to the tenderness now required to tend what has grown in its place. The scars remain. I do not hide them. But they are no longer warnings etched in fear. They are way markers. They tell me where I have been. They remind me how far I have walked. They point, softly, toward what matters. The key to keeping the Fortress from rebuilding is not force. It is not war. It is vigilance. It is listening. It is the daily, living art of awareness before architecture. It is noticing the first subtle tightening in my chest before it becomes a wall. It is hearing the early tone of a thought before it hardens into law. It is meeting myself with compassion instead of correction. With curiosity instead of cruelty. It is learning, again and again, to treat myself with the same gentleness I once reserved only for the suffering of others. To speak inwardly in a voice that heals rather than hunts. To nourish the relationships that tether me to the living world when my mind begins to drift back toward old blueprints. To let myself be seen. To let myself be held. To let myself belong. This is how I protect the light. By noticing. By softening. By reaching. By tending the inner ground instead of fortifying it. The journey of recovery is not a chapter that closes. It is a lifelong conversation with my own becoming. A dialogue between who I was, who

I am, and who I am still learning how to be. There will be seasons of ease, when the days open like wide skies. There may be seasons of strain, when the wind returns and the soil must be worked again. But I am no longer afraid of the dark. I have walked its corridors. I have learned its language. I have faced the Fortress Within and lived to tell its story. And I emerged not untouched but transformed. Stronger. Wiser. More spacious. Rooted in a resilience that does not harden but holds. And now I know this with a steadiness I did not have before: whatever life places in my hands, whatever weather moves across my inner fields, I carry the strength to meet it. Not alone. Not armoured. But awake. Connected. And holding the key.

The Fortress Within: Reclaiming Your Life from Depression

The Siege Begins

And even now, after the rubble, after the slow and sacred work of rebuilding, I can still feel the echo of the first stone being set. I remember the exact texture of that moment. The dimness of the room. The way the air felt heavier than it should. The silence not resting but pressing. I was sitting alone in the half-light, wrapped in the oppressive hush of my own mind, when the realization arrived with a quiet, irrevocable weight: depression was not visiting me. It was inhabiting me. It had crossed some unseen threshold and made itself at home, unpacking in the most intimate rooms of my inner world. It had moved in without ceremony, without warning, and begun constructing something inside me. A fortress. Not of stone, but of thought. Not of iron, but of feeling. Its walls mortared with self-doubt and insecurity. Its foundations sunk deep into old fears and unnamed grief. Its battlements crowded with intrusive, merciless thoughts that kept watch over every fragile place, every soft remembering of who I had once been. This was not fleeting sadness. Not a passing cloud that might thin if I waited long enough. Not a bruise on the spirit destined to fade. This was occupation. A pervasive darkness that did not come and go but stayed. A constant companion that clung like a suffocating shroud, settling into breath and bone, into muscle and meaning. It was not content to steal ambition alone. It reached further. It robbed me of function. Of agency. Of the simplest human acts. Getting out of bed became an expedition into hostile terrain. A treacherous, snow-lashed mountain where every movement was an ascent and every breath burned like thin air in the lungs. The blankets pressed like stone slabs. The mattress felt like a gravity well. My limbs were no longer limbs, but anchors. Even lifting my head felt like defiance against a law of nature that had quietly rewritten itself.

And the sunlight at the window, it did not invite me. It accused me. Too bright. Too alive. Too honest for the world I now inhabited. It spilled across the floor like a language I could no longer speak, illuminating a life that felt impossibly distant, as though it belonged to someone else entirely. I would watch it touch the walls, the furniture, my own unmoving hands, and feel the cruel contrast of it. Light outside. Night within. That was when I understood: the siege had already begun. Not with explosions. Not with spectacle. But with occupation. With architecture. With the slow, almost tender laying of inner stone. And I was already inside its walls. Eating became a chore. A mechanical ritual stripped of ceremony, emptied of pleasure. Food lost its voice. Flavour faded into texture, and texture into obligation. Each bite was something to negotiate. Each swallow a small act of endurance, as though nourishment itself had turned foreign, as though my body no longer recognized the language of being fed. What once comforted now merely occupied space. Warmth no longer spread. Sweetness no longer landed. Even hunger felt distant, muffled, unreliable, another signal intercepted somewhere in the thickening walls. Smiling, too, became a labor. A grotesque choreography my face remembered even as my spirit forgot. My mouth curved upward out of habit, not feeling. The muscles moved, but nothing followed. It was like wearing a mask sculpted from my own features, animated by a will that was no longer mine. Every performed expression only widened the gulf between the version of me the world saw and the war unfolding inside. The smile did not connect me. It exiled me. It made me a spectator to my own existence, watching a character go through the motions of a life I could no longer enter. And even breathing, that oldest promise of being alive, grew heavy. Deliberate. Unreliable. Each inhale felt borrowed, thin, as though the air had been rationed. Each exhale unfinished, like a sentence cut short. There was a constant pressure on my chest, a dense, invisible hand pressing inward, reminding me with every breath that something enormous had taken up residence inside. The body knew before the mind would admit it: this was not mood. This was mass. This was the physical weight of emotional stone beginning to settle into muscle and marrow.

This was the beginning. The moment the siege truly revealed itself. Depression is not a visitor. It is an inhabitant. It does not knock politely and wait to be welcomed. It does not hover at the threshold. It crashes through the door. It splinters the frame. It sledgehammers its way into the very core of your being and begins to live there as if it has always belonged. And almost immediately, it starts to build. A fortress rises within you, stone by unseen stone. Its walls thickened with self-doubt. Mortared with insecurity. Reinforced by the gnawing teeth of anxiety. Corridors of rumination carve themselves through the inner landscape. Watchtowers of vigilance rise where rest once lived. Gates of fear swing closed. Windows of possibility are bricked over. The architecture is subtle at first. A thought here. A hesitation there. A feeling you don't question because it sounds too much like your own voice. But slowly, relentlessly, the structure takes shape. Until one day, you look inward and realize you are no longer simply hurting inside yourself. You are living inside something that is hurting you. Along its battlements stand the soldiers of the mind. Intrusive thoughts. Negative narratives. An unrelenting, tireless army pacing the inner walls, drawing back their bows and releasing volley after volley into every unguarded place. Each arrow is small. Almost delicate. A fleeting thought. A subtle criticism. A familiar doubt. Easy to dismiss in isolation. But together, they are devastating. They strike in accumulation. They bruise by repetition. They work not by spectacle, but by erosion, chipping at resolve, corroding identity, teaching you, slowly and convincingly, to distrust the very ground beneath your own feet. This is siege warfare. Not the clash of swords, but the starvation of spirit. Not the thunder of invasion, but the quiet, methodical undoing. A slow, intimate war waged in the silent chambers of the mind. Depression is not a fleeting visitor. Not a temporary shadow drifting across the inner sun. It is more insidious than that. More patient. More intelligent. It is a skilled and watchful architect, meticulously drafting blueprints for an inner stronghold meant not merely to contain you, but to claim you. Its walls are quarried from self-doubt and fear. Its mortar is insecurity. Its scaffolding is comparison. Its scaffolds rise in places once occupied by ease. And its primary weapon is thought itself, turned inward, sharpened, and set loose. Inside this structure, perception changes. Sound dulls. Colour drains. The air feels thicker, harder to move through. Corridors of rumination loop endlessly, returning you to the same rooms of accusation, the same echoing halls of regret. Windows that once opened to possibility are shuttered. Doors that once led outward are locked from the inside. What once felt simple now feels forbidden. What once felt natural now feels dangerous. And this fortress does not merely restrict movement. It paralyzes. It turns the smallest actions into monumental undertakings. Getting out of bed becomes a negotiation with gravity. Answering a message becomes a moral dilemma. Choosing what to eat feels like standing at a crossroads with no safe direction. Breath becomes labor. Thought becomes threat. Living becomes endurance. Here, even stillness is not rest. It is surveillance. You are watched by your own mind. Measured by your own voice. Judged in a court that never adjourns. Depression is not merely an emotion that passes through like weather. It is an inhabitant that settles in. And the moment it does, it begins constructing an invisible prison around the very place you once called self. Stone by unseen stone. Belief by distorted belief. Memory by repurposed memory. Until one day, you realize you are no longer simply experiencing thoughts. You are living inside them. And the siege does not roar. It whispers. It speaks in familiar tones. In reasonable language. In sentences that sound like your own. And because it whispers, it lasts. And while the siege raged in silence, the world beyond my walls did not pause. It did not slow. It did not soften its light or lower its voice. The world outside my window continued to spin in its familiar orbit, oblivious to the hurricane tearing through my inner sky. Cars passed. Footsteps crossed pavement. Snatches of conversation lifted and fell like birdsong.

People moved through their days wrapped in small, unremarkable miracles. Walking. Talking. Laughing. Living. Their voices floated up from the street like music from another country, carrying a language I no longer knew how to speak, unaware of the storm fermenting inside my mind. It was a vibrant tapestry of ordinary life, brightly woven against the backdrop of my private collapse. Coffee cups in warm hands. Lovers leaning close. Someone throwing their head back in laughter. Groceries carried. Futures discussed. The choreography of living unfolding with effortless fluency. Their ease was almost unbearable. Their unselfconscious inhabiting of the world felt like a kind of violence, not because it was cruel, but because it was so far from me. Their carefree movements became a painful counterpoint to my stillness, a living measurement of the distance I could no longer cross. Each step they took seemed to widen the gulf between us. Between who I was and who the world assumed me to be. Between survival and living. Between endurance and joy. They were inside time. I was suspended beside it. I watched them through a smeared windowpane, the glass fogged by breath and unshed tears, as though the distortion lived not only on the surface, but in my seeing itself. The street shimmered and warped, colours dulled, edges blurred, like a painting left too long in rain. I stood there, a prisoner in my own mind, held back by an invisible barrier no hand could touch and no key could find. A wall made not of stone, but of despair. Of exhaustion. Of the terrible knowing that the world was still beautiful, still moving, still alive, and that I was standing on the other side of it, knocking soundlessly, unheard. Inside, it felt like drowning. Not the violent kind that thrashes and screams, but the slow, quiet submersion where the body learns the language of sinking. A descent into dark water with no shoreline, no current, no lifeline in sight.

The light above grew thinner each day, breaking into pale, trembling ribbons that could no longer warm me, only remind me of what I was losing. The thought of facing another day, another hour, even another minute rose before me like an unclimbable cliff, sheer and endless, its face slick with the certainty of failure. Time itself stopped being something that carried me. It became something to endure. A tide I had to hold back with lungs already burning. The daily rituals that once anchored my life transformed into battlegrounds. The shower, once a small sanctuary of steam and renewal, became an encounter with depletion. Standing beneath the falling water felt like standing beneath a waterfall with no ground beneath my feet, each drop another small insistence on gravity, on effort, on the simple, brutal fact of being a body. The warmth could not reach the cold that lived in my bones. I leaned my forehead against the tile and let the water trace the outlines of a person I no longer recognized, counting breaths like someone lost at sea counts waves. Getting dressed felt like being sealed into armor. Not protection, but burden. Fabric heavy as chainmail. Sleeves like restraints. Each garment another layer of expectation, another reminder that I had to move through a world I no longer belonged to. My reflection watched me from the mirror, hollow-eyed and distant, as if she were already receding into someone else's memory. Even the most mundane gestures swelled into monuments. Brushing my teeth. Making a cup of tea. Opening a door. Each required negotiation. Each demanded a toll of energy I did not have. My body moved as though through wet cement, every motion slow, deliberate, trembling with effort. And yet, I moved. I stood. I stepped. I breathed. Each small act, each hesitant inch forward, became a quiet victory. A soft rebellion against the gravity pulling me under. Proof of a strength I could not yet feel, could not yet name, but which was already at work beneath the surface. Something in me was still choosing motion over disappearance. Still lifting a hand toward the light, even when I could not believe it would reach anything at all.

And as the outer world receded into glass and distance, even the smallest acts within my own life began to tower over me, casting long, impossible shadows across the narrow ground I still occupied. The most ordinary tasks rose like monuments. Answering a phone call felt like scaling a sheer cliff face with bare hands, fingers already numb, every ring an echoing demand I did not know how to meet. Responding to an email felt like being asked to compose a novel in a language I no longer spoke, each blinking cursor a small, merciless reminder of how far I had drifted from fluency in my own life. My mind fogged and spun. Thoughts tangled into one another like nests of thorned vines, looping, snagging, tightening around every attempt at clarity. Ideas that once moved in clean lines now collapsed into knots. Concentration became a luxury I could no longer afford, something other people possessed the way they possessed ease or appetite or sleep. My attention drifted, unmoored, like a leaf caught in a restless, capricious wind, circling without landing, touching nothing long enough to be held. Even language began to abandon me. The simplest sentences hovered just beyond reach, like names on the tip of a forgotten tongue. Words, once faithful companions, turned skittish and brittle, shattering when I tried to grasp them. Conversations felt like wading through thick water. I could hear myself speaking, but the sound arrived delayed, disconnected, as if traveling a long way back to me. What had once been effortless now demanded a labor I did not know how to supply. Every interaction cost more than I had. Every decision required negotiations with an inner emptiness that offered no answers. And when night came, it brought no mercy.

SLEEP DID NOT OFFER refuge. It became another battlefield. The room darkened, but my mind did not. It sharpened. It prowled. I lay in bed while thoughts and anxieties marched and collided, while fears rehearsed themselves into nightmares before my eyes had even closed. When sleep did arrive, it was thin and treacherous, easily torn. I woke with a gasp, lungs clawing for air, heart galloping against my ribs, the darkness thick and intimate around me, pressing close as another skin. Dreams twisted themselves into grotesque echoes of waking life, warped replicas of normalcy that only sharpened the ache of it. Familiar places decayed. Familiar faces turned distant. Joy appeared only to fracture in my hands. Even rest betrayed me, offering only corridors of half-sleep where dread and memory blurred together.

Even sleeplessness became a war. Exhaustion on one side. The relentless churn of my mind on the other. And I was caught between them, suspended in that fragile, haunted place where the body begs for mercy and the mind refuses to release its grip. There was no true night. There was no true morning. Only the long, unbroken vigil of trying to endure myself, counting hours by the heaviness in my chest, by the quiet thud of a heart that kept insisting on tomorrow when I could no longer imagine what tomorrow was for.

And so the days began to lose their names. They bled into one another like colors left too long in water, dissolving their edges, becoming a single, indistinct wash of existence. Monday no longer meant beginning. Friday no longer promised rest. They were all the same pale room, rearranged only by the subtle migrations of light across the wall, the slow, indifferent crawl of shadow along the floor. Time loosened its spine. It no longer stood upright. It sagged. Morning and night collapsed into a single, continuous ache, a long corridor without doors. The relentless ticking of the clock became less a measure and more a reminder. Each second landed like a small metallic drop in an empty well, echoing far longer than it should have, marking not progress but endurance.

Not movement, but the slow, agonizing fact of being. Hours were not lived. They were survived. The idea of "getting better" felt like a distant, unreachable star. A cold glint pinned to some other sky. Something navigators used. Something other people oriented their lives by. I could see it. I could name it. But it belonged to a different atmosphere, one my lungs could not yet breathe. Hope became an abstract concept, like a photograph of a place I had never been. Beautiful. Remote. Untouchable. Loneliness settled in as a constant companion. Not loud. Not dramatic. But faithful. It moved into the empty chair beside me. It lay down in the space between my thoughts. It followed me from room to room like a second shadow, pacing the edges of my awareness, rising when I rose, sitting when I sat. It did not demand attention. It assumed it. A quiet occupancy. A persistent absence. The fear of judgment, of being named weak, broken, defective, kept me folded inward, my inner world curled tight around its own injuries. I became both the wound and the bandage. Cocooned inside a prison I both hated and guarded. The walls hurt. But they were familiar. And familiarity, even when it wounds, can feel safer than the unknown. Even the thought of reaching out, of letting my fracture be seen, felt impossible. Vulnerability appeared not as connection, but as catastrophe. A door I did not yet believe could open without collapsing the whole structure. Without exposing everything I had spent years trying to hold together. I imagined myself spilling. Shattering. Becoming too much. So I stayed contained. And inside that containment, something essential was slowly being worn away. Not in an explosion. Not in a moment anyone could point to. But in the quiet, merciless way stone becomes sand. A slow erosion of the self. A gradual chipping down of confidence. Of hope. Of the quiet, fragile sense of being someone at all. Grain by grain, my inner world thinned, as though an unseen tide were steadily carrying pieces of me out to sea. Not in waves. In withdrawals. A little less color. A little less voice. A little less weight to my own existence. Until I began to feel translucent, as though I were made of something that light could pass through without ever warming. I could feel myself receding. The girl who once had opinions, laughter, longings. The woman who recognized her own reflection. They were not gone. But they were distant, blurred, like figures seen through deep water. Every day, something small slipped loose. A confidence I no longer reached for. A dream I stopped defending. A tenderness I no longer trusted. I was being thinned by living. Eroded by enduring. Becoming shoreline. And yet, even here, something remained. Even in the lowest chambers of this darkness, there flickered a tiny ember of resilience. Not optimism. Not faith. Not the bright, declarative hope people like to speak about. This was something quieter. Older. More elemental. A stubborn refusal to be entirely extinguished. A small, unreasoned insistence on continuing to breathe. On rising again after sleep. On placing one moment in front of another. It did not offer comfort. It offered continuity. That flicker was faint. Easily missed. A glow so slight it could be mistaken for imagination. But it was alive. It pulsed when everything else lay still. It warmed the very edges of my despair.

And in time, I would understand what it was. The beginning. The first spark of a long, arduous journey toward healing. Because this is not a destination. It is a passage. Not a fixed place, but a moving one. A terrain that reshapes itself as you walk it. And the Fortress may never be completely demolished. Some stones may always remain. Some corridors may always echo with old footsteps. Some shadows may always know my name. But perhaps, one day, I can learn to live within its walls not as a prisoner, but as an inhabitant who has found the hidden doors. The cracked windows. The places where light still knows how to enter. Perhaps I can learn to open something. To plant something. To let roots work their way through the fractures. To survive. To endure. And sometimes, quietly, unexpectedly, to thrive. For those grappling with depression, the world beyond the window continues to spin, bright and apparently unburdened, unaware of the private war tearing through the interior landscape. Life keeps moving in gestures that feel almost theatrical from behind the glass. People pass with grocery bags and laughter, with futures in their pockets and plans on their tongues. Their voices arrive as echoes. Their smiles flash like light reflected off water, beautiful, unreachable. Joy ricochets off the walls of your inner fortress and reaches you only as sound without warmth, movement without meaning. They cannot see what is concealed behind the careful façade of normalcy you have so painstakingly constructed. They do not see the architecture of effort beneath each "I'm fine." The scaffolding beneath every smile. The exhaustion it takes to look whole. They do not know that sometimes a single glance at a sunlit sky does not bring comfort, but ache. That blue can wound. That light can summon longing so sharp it feels like grief. A mourning not for what was, but for what still exists everywhere except inside you. A sorrow for a life that seems to be happening just beyond your reach, like music drifting from a room you are no longer able to enter. This book is not about surrendering to that storm. It is not about romanticizing the ruin or baptizing the pain. It is about learning the architecture of what has been built within you. Understanding how the fortress took shape. How fear laid its first stones. How silence reinforced the walls. How thought became a weapon turned inward. It is about tracing the blueprints of your own suffering with tenderness instead of judgment. About identifying the hidden weaknesses. The hairline fractures. The places where light has always been pressing, even when you could not feel its warmth. And then, slowly, courageously, it is about dismantling. Brick by agonizing brick. Belief by wounded belief. Lie by learned lie. It is about developing not only the will, but the tools. The language. The support. The practices that make undoing possible. It is about reclaiming your inner territory from the grip of depression. About transforming a place of siege into a place of shelter. A stronghold of survival into a home of becoming. It is about reclaiming your life. One day, as I sat by the window watching life unfold like an uninvited guest at a table I no longer recognized as my own, something inside me shifted. It was not dramatic. There was no lightning, no sudden clearing of the sky. Just a subtle rearranging in the quiet. A gentle click in the dark, like a lock remembering the shape of its key. Surrounded by shadow, hemmed in by the familiar architecture of despair, I realized that I still possessed one fragile, formidable thing. Choice. It did not arrive as confidence. It arrived as awareness. A small, steady knowing that despite the walls, despite the watchtowers of thought, despite the long occupation of my inner world, something in me had not been conquered. I could feel it like a thin thread pulled taut through the rubble. I could allow the fortress of depression to continue holding me captive. Or I could begin, trembling and uncertain, to imagine a bridge. Not an escape. A beginning. A narrow, shaking span laid plank by plank across the ravine between survival and living. I knew it would not be easy. I knew it would ask more of me than I believed I had to give. It would require breath when breath already felt rationed. Courage when courage felt like a language I had forgotten. It would mean turning toward the very walls that had protected me from feeling and learning how to touch them without bleeding. But I also knew, with a clarity that rose from somewhere deeper than thought, that I could not remain a spectator to my own existence.

I could not keep watching my life through glass as if it belonged to someone else. I had to try. I had to begin loosening the stones of self-doubt and insecurity. Had to question the sentries of my own mind. Had to interrupt the familiar ceremonies of self-erasure. Had to learn, slowly and imperfectly, how to speak back to the voices that had taken up residence in my thoughts and called themselves truth. I stood at an inner crossroads, small and sacred. A place without witnesses. A moment without applause. I had a choice: to remain a passive inhabitant of my fortress, or to reclaim my life. That decision did not save me in a moment. It did not lift the fog or fell the walls or flood the dark with light. But it marked the beginning. The first footfall on unfamiliar ground. The first hairline fracture in the stone. The first quiet, defiant act of belonging to myself again. The first step of an arduous, sacred journey toward healing. And so my journey toward freedom did not arrive wrapped in revelation. It did not descend like a prophecy or split the sky with sudden certainty. It began the way most real revolutions do. Small. Ordinary. Almost invisible. It began with a single, defiant motion of the body. I got out of bed. Not because I wanted to. Not because hope had returned. Not because the Fortress had loosened its grip. I rose because somewhere beneath the sediment of despair, beneath the ache and the resistance and the long practice of disappearing, there lived a quiet knowing: if I did not move, nothing else could. So I carried myself into the day the way one carries something wounded. Gently. Carefully. As though I might splinter if I set my weight down too quickly. My feet touched the floor like a question. The air felt thick. My limbs foreign. Every step an effort of negotiation between gravity and will. I took a shower, not for comfort, but for contact. To feel water find my skin. To let warmth speak in a language older than thought. To remember, through nerve and steam and breath, that sensation was still possible. That my body still answered the world. That I was still here.

The water ran over me like a quiet benediction, tracing the outlines of a form I had begun to forget was mine. It did not cleanse the darkness. But it pressed against it. It said: you are not only mind. You are still flesh. Still breath. Still temperature and pulse, and presence. I ate a meal, not because hunger called, but because survival did. Because even when the mind refuses life, the body still asks for tending. Because even when desire goes silent, nourishment remains a kind of listening. Each bite was an act of mercy I did not yet feel worthy of. Each swallow a small insistence: stay. These were not victories anyone else could see. There were no witnesses. No applause. No visible transformation. But they were beginnings. Quiet thresholds crossed in the privacy of my own becoming. The first thin bridges laid across the ravine between enduring and living. And as I took these small, trembling steps, something subtle surfaced. A realization that did not roar but settled. Depression was not only a force pressing against me. It was also something moving within me. Woven into the texture of my thoughts. Tinting my perceptions. Shaping the weather of my inner world. It was part of my experience. A chapter of my nervous system. A language my mind had learned under duress. A presence that, however painful, was asking not only to be fought, but to be understood. Not exile, but acknowledgment. Not annihilation, but illumination. Not endless war, but a new way of relating. Because something in me began to sense this: what is met with cruelty grows sharper. What is met with awareness begins to soften. And what is met with compassion, even when it is dark, even when it is terrifying, begins, slowly, to change its shape. And in that knowing, faint but real, the journey deepened. Not just outward. But inward. I began to notice the architecture of it. Not all at once. Not in clean lines or sudden clarity. But the way you begin to recognize a familiar building in fog, first by its outline, then by its angles, then by the way its shadow falls. I started to see how the negative thoughts and feelings occupying my mind were not unquestionable truths carved into stone, but echoes moving through corridors the Fortress had constructed. Reverberations. Old footfalls. Stories learned when I was trying to survive. Patterns laid down again and again until they felt indistinguishable from fact.

What had once spoken like law began to sound like history. I could hear the way certain thoughts always marched the same routes. How they arrived on schedule. How they saluted the same fears. How they repeated the same accusations with mechanical devotion. And for the first time, I did not simply kneel before them. I paused. I turned toward them. Gently. Tentatively. As one approaches a frightened animal rather than an enemy. I began to interrupt their authority. To place a hand in the air between the thought and my body and ask, almost in a whisper, "*Is this true? Is this the whole truth? Is this the only way this story can be told?*" And sometimes, in that pause, something extraordinary happened. The thought faltered. The sentence did not complete itself. The hallway did not echo the way it always had. And into that small, stunned silence, other possibilities drifted. Fragile at first. Uncertain. Like light testing a room long kept dark. Maybe this is not fact, but fear. Maybe this is not prophecy, but memory. Maybe this voice is not me, but something that learned my name. I began practicing mindfulness. Not as escape. Never as escape. But as return. A returning to the body I had abandoned. A returning to the moment I had been taught to outrun. A returning to the present, where life, however quiet, was still occurring. I learned to bring my attention back to *this* moment. This chair beneath me. This weight of my own hands. This small, astonishing movement of breath. Instead of being pulled endlessly into the ruins of the past, where every memory stood like a collapsed temple, or hurled into the imagined disasters of the future, where every horizon burned before I reached it, I practiced staying. Here. Now. Inside what is actually happening. I learned to breathe. Not the shallow, apologetic breathing of survival, but real breathing. Breathing that reached into the lower rooms of my body. Breathing that moved my ribs like slow doors. Breathing that felt like tide rather than gasp. I followed the air as it entered me, cool and tentative, and as it left, warm and soft, like something being given back to the world. In. Out. Each breath a small agreement with life. Each breath, a hand placed on my own chest, saying, "*you are here*". And in that simple rhythm, in that unremarkable, miraculous exchange between body and air, I found something I had not felt in a long time. Space. A small pocket of calm inside the storm. A clearing inside the forest. A place in the rubble where my feet could rest. It was not the end of the battle. It did not dismantle the Fortress overnight. The archers still watched. The walls still stood. But I had found a place to stand. And from there, for the first time, I was no longer only surviving the darkness. I was beginning to meet it. As I learned to stand in the present moment, another truth began to surface, slow and unmistakable, like an ancient shape emerging from fog: every fortress has weapons, and every siege follows a pattern. No invasion is random. No devastation without design. Depression, I came to see, did not simply batter at my gates in chaos. It arrived with blueprints. With rituals. With a rehearsed choreography of harm. And learning to heal meant learning to see those movements. To recognize the weapons it favoured. To study the way it entered the field. Identifying your personal siege weapons becomes vital. These are the particular instruments your mind reaches for when the dark begins to stir. The thoughts that rise first. The behaviors that follow like obedient soldiers. The environments that quietly tilt the ground beneath your feet. Do you catastrophize, your imagination galloping ahead into disaster before the present moment has even finished speaking? Do your thoughts sprint to the worst ending, as if rehearsing grief might somehow soften its arrival? Do you diminish your accomplishments until they are no larger than dust motes, while every misstep swells into a towering indictment? A single error transformed into a character flaw. A moment of weakness recast as a lifelong sentence. Are there people, places, seasons, or silences that act like hidden trapdoors beneath familiar ground, dropping you suddenly into the same inner chambers of despair? The same rooms. The same arguments. The same ache.

These patterns do not appear by accident. They are learned. Rehearsed. Reinforced. They were shaped in moments when your nervous system was trying to protect you. When your mind was doing the only thing, it knew how to do to survive. And over time, those survival strategies hardened into habits. Those habits into pathways. Those pathways into roads so well worn they felt inevitable. This is where the work becomes investigative. Not brutal. Not shaming. But curious. Keeping a journal, carefully documenting moods, thoughts, bodily sensations, and triggers, becomes a kind of sacred mapmaking. A slow cartography of the inner world. Page by page, you begin to chart the terrain. The repetitions. The ambush points. The familiar bends in the road where your footing always slips. You start to see when the same weather rolls in. Which thoughts ride the first gusts? Which memories follow? Which behaviors take their positions along the walls? What once felt like chaos begins to reveal structure. Not meaninglessness, but mechanics. Not madness, but method. You begin to notice the strategies. The loops. The predictable sequences of inner events. The way a certain tone of voice, a certain hour of night, a certain comparison, a certain memory, almost always lights the same fuse. And in writing it down, you are not merely recording pain. You are shining a lantern into the tunnels. You are laying the enemy's playbook open on the table. You are catching the moment when a familiar weapon is being raised. And recognition changes everything. Because the moment you can name what is happening, something in the spell breaks. The thought no longer arrives as fate. The feeling no longer passes as law. The descent no longer wears the mask of inevitability. You are no longer fighting blind. You are seeing. You are studying. You are learning how the siege operates. And with that knowledge comes the first quiet power. Not the power to banish the darkness. But the power to meet it awake. The power to interrupt the pattern. The power to reach for a different response. The power to loosen the hand around the blade before it ever strikes. This is how the fortress begins to lose its advantage. Not through one dramatic victory. But through awareness. Through pattern. Through the slow, luminous work of understanding. And in that understanding, a new role quietly forms inside you. No longer only the one under siege. But the one learning the terrain. The one reading the maps. The one beginning, at last, to disarm the war.

Understanding the Inhabitants

My first real step was not outward, but inward. It was the decision to turn toward what had taken up residence inside me, this heavy, unnamed presence that had nested itself into every corner of my mind like a quiet animal of night, breathing where I breathed, watching where I looked. I chose curiosity over resentment. Observation over war. I wanted to understand my inhabitant before I tried to evict it. I wanted to learn its language. Its habits. The hidden logic of its hunger. So, I began to write. I opened notebooks the way one opens windows in a long-sealed room. Carefully. Hopefully. Unsure what dust might rise. I let my thoughts spill onto the page not to polish them, not to make them beautiful or sensible, but simply to see them. To give outline to what had only ever existed as weather. Each sentence felt like striking a match in a darkened corridor. Each page, a small unveiling. Each unveiling, a widening. With every line, I began to glimpse the architecture of my inner world. The hidden staircases of fear. The locked doors of grief. The echoing chambers of doubt. And what slowly revealed itself was this: depression feeds on isolation. It fattens itself in silence. It grows bold where nothing names it. It nourishes itself on the quiet belief that you are alone in what you carry. That no one else walks this terrain. That what lives in you is unshareable, untranslatable, unlovable. It murmurs in the dark, not as a roar, but as a familiar voice. It borrows your own tone. Your own memories. Your own vocabulary. It tells lies that feel like reflections. Lies about worthlessness. Lies about permanence. Lies that insist there is no door, no exit, no other way to be. But the page did something the darkness could not endure. It answered the whisper with witness. It placed shape where there had only been pressure. And in giving these inner inhabitants a name, a map, a language, I felt the first subtle shift. The moment when what had once ruled me from the shadows was, at last, standing in the light. But once those thoughts were written, they were no longer shapeless. They no longer drifted like smoke I could not grasp. On the page, they took on edges. Contours. Footprints. I could trace their patterns the way one studies weather maps, seeing where the storms always gathered, where the pressure always dropped. I could see how they circled the same old territories.

How they rehearsed the same accusations. How they slipped into different costumes while telling the same story. And in seeing them, truly seeing them, something subtle began to happen. Their grip loosened. Their authority thinned. The fog began to separate into paths. The journal became a kind of cartography. A hand-drawn map of my inner terrain. A way to chart the hidden roads my mind had been traveling for years without my consent. Page after page, I exposed the treacherous narratives that had been whispering behind my eyes. The scripts of not-enough. The prophecies of failure. The verdicts passed before any evidence was heard. I didn't only acknowledge depression's presence. I met it. I named it. I studied it the way one studies a long, inherited language, listening for its grammar, its repetitions, its borrowed phrases. And once named, it could no longer masquerade as me. And alongside the darkness, I began to plant light. Deliberately. Tenderly. As one presses seeds into wounded soil. Page by page, I wrote reminders of who I was beneath the fortress. Not who depression said I was, but who I had been before the walls. Fragments of truth. Small mercies. Remembered strengths. Moments of courage I had dismissed. Kindnesses I had survived. Proofs of worth I had never allowed myself to count. These entries did not roar. They whispered back. And over time, their whisper grew steadier than the lie. On my heaviest days, I would return to those pages the way one returns to a shoreline after being lost at sea. Letting the words rinse me. Anchor me.

Remind me where the horizon still lived. I would run my eyes over my own handwriting and feel something almost like being witnessed by myself. As though another part of me had stayed awake while I slept inside the storm. And those pages would say, again and again, in a thousand small ways: you are not the walls you live behind. You are not the voice that echoes inside them. You are the one who can walk their corridors. Learn their layout. Notice their cracks. And that knowing, fragile at first, trembling like a candle in a long hall, was the beginning of freedom. As I stayed with the work, something subtle began to shift. Almost imperceptibly at first. Like the first thinning of fog at dawn, when the world does not yet look different, but the air feels changed. The walls of the fortress no longer felt quite so absolute. Hairline fractures appeared where there had once been only stone. Tiny seams of light slipped through, so faint I sometimes wondered if I was imagining them. The thoughts that once thundered through me lost some of their volume, some of their terrible authority. They still came, yes. They still knocked. But they no longer ruled the entire sky. They became weather instead of law. Passing systems rather than permanent climates. And in that softening, a new sensation emerged. Hope. Not the cinematic kind that arrives with banners and music. But the kind that flickers. A cautious warmth. A pulse beneath the ribs. A quiet sense of possibility I had not felt in a long time, like discovering a green shoot in the middle of scorched ground. It did not promise me a whole new world. It simply whispered, maybe this is not the only one. With that whisper came another realization, just as gentle, just as destabilizing: I was not singular in this struggle. I was not a lone ruin on an empty plain. There were others moving through their own inner strongholds, navigating their own labyrinths of fear and fatigue, wrestling the same unseen forces in different shapes and names. The pain that had once convinced me of my isolation now began to reveal a hidden kinship. A vast, quiet network of human hearts learning how to endure. So, I started to reach outward. At first tentatively, like someone testing the temperature of unfamiliar water. A sentence shared. A truth half-spoken. Then more bravely. I sought connection the way a plant seeks light, instinctively, turning toward whatever promised warmth. I allowed myself to be witnessed. Not as an edited version. Not as a performance. But as I was. Trembling. Unfinished. Real.

I began forming relationships rooted not in perfection, but in presence. Not in pretending, but in mutual recognition. In the relief of shared language. In the soft power of being able to say, "me too," and feel the ground answer back. These connections did not dismantle the fortress overnight. But they changed its acoustics. The silence was no longer empty. The halls no longer echoed only with my own voice. There were footsteps now. Other heartbeats. Proof that even within old walls, life could still move. I found a therapist. Not a fixer. Not a rescuer. But a steady presence. Someone willing to walk beside me through the winding corridors of my mind, lantern in hand, unafraid of what the light might reveal. Someone who helped me give names to what had only ever been sensations. We mapped the terrain together. The echoing rooms. The hidden stairwells. The places where old pain had taken up permanent residence. And slowly, she placed tools in my hands. Not weapons to destroy the darkness, but instruments to navigate it. Ways to listen without collapsing. To witness without drowning. To meet what arose without surrendering my name to it. Therapy became a kind of apprenticeship in my own inner world. A learning of its languages. Its patterns. Its weather. At the same time, I began turning back toward life. Toward the small, almost-forgotten things that stirred something awake in me. I followed faint impulses the way one follows glimmers in a cave. A walk. A melody. The feel of clay or paper beneath my fingers. The quiet satisfaction of making something where nothing had been before. Activities that brought color back into the days. Moments that reminded my body what it meant to feel engaged, curious, purposeful. I did not chase joy. I courted presence. And in presence, joy sometimes surprised me. I followed those threads gently, letting them lead me where they would, trusting their intelligence even when I could not yet see the pattern they were weaving. The journey toward freedom was not easy.

And it was not quick. There were still days when the fortress loomed again, when the old weight pressed hard against my ribs, when the inner weather turned heavy and loud. Days when it felt as though I were carrying a whole season inside my chest. But something essential had changed. I was no longer unarmed. I had learned patience, the kind that breathes and waits without abandoning itself. I had learned how to meet myself with kindness, even when I did not yet like what I saw. I had learned to trust the slow intelligence of the process, the way roots grow invisibly long before anything green breaks the surface. And perhaps most importantly, I learned this: depression was not proof of weakness. It was evidence of endurance. Of sensitivity. Of a nervous system that had survived difficult terrain. Of a heart that had kept beating through climates it was never meant to navigate alone. It spoke not of failure, but of resilience. Of a deep, stubborn will to remain. To feel. To continue. I was not broken. I was still here. And that, in itself, was strength.

The Allies of Light

As I moved further along this fragile, hard-won path, one truth kept returning to me like a refrain written into the bones: healing was never meant to be carried alone. The journey out of depression is not a solitary crossing. It is not a lone figure moving through an endless night. It is a passage best walked with hands extended, with voices echoing somewhere nearby, with small lights flickering from other windows in the dark, reminding you that you are not the only one awake, not the only one searching for morning. So I began to gather my allies. Supportive friends. Compassionate family. Trained guides who knew the terrain of the mind and could help me navigate its hidden traps and secret doorways. People who were not afraid of my shadows. People who could sit with the heaviness without trying to rush it away. Each honest conversation loosened something inside me, like knots slowly learning how to open. Each time I spoke the word *depression* aloud, it lost a little of its power to seal me off from the world. Shame thinned. Silence cracked. Air entered places that had been closed for years. And in the spaces where my story met another's, I discovered how many people were living behind fortresses of their own. In sharing my struggles, I found not pity, but recognition. Not quick fixes, but kinship. A friend who said, "Me too," and in those two small words handed me a mirror instead of a diagnosis. A therapist who offered language where there had only ever been ache, giving shape to what had lived as storm. A family member who listened without flinching, whose presence alone felt like shelter. Every connection became a small chisel against the stone. Every conversation, another hairline fracture in walls I had once believed unbreakable. Every moment of being seen, a beam of light slipping through the cracks. And slowly, beautifully, the Fortress Within began to discover something it could not withstand. Not force. Not argument. But communion. Because darkness thrives in sealed rooms.

And light... light multiplies the moment it is shared. And just as importantly, I began forming an alliance with myself. This may have been the hardest friendship of all. The one I had neglected the longest. The one whose voice I had learned to mistrust, silence, or scold. I began to practice the quiet, radical art of self-compassion. To turn inward not with interrogation, but with tenderness. To speak to myself the way I would to someone I loved. Gently. Patiently. Without the lash of perfection. I learned to honor the smallest victories. The ones that never make it into stories of triumph. The ones no one gathers to applaud. Getting out of bed. Brushing my teeth. Feeding my body. Stepping into the day. Acts so ordinary to the outside world, yet inside my inner weather, they were mountaintops. I began to mark them not as trivial, but as brave. Not as routine, but as resistance. Each one a quiet declaration: "*I am still choosing to live.*" Gratitude, too, became a practice. Not for sweeping triumphs, not for sudden transformations, but for brief glimmers. For the soft, unassuming mercies that still threaded their way through my days

Breaking Down the Walls

As I began to truly inhabit my life again, rather than merely survive inside it, something quietly radical unfolded. I stopped pacing the same inner corridors and started touching the walls. Testing them. Listening for what might give. And slowly, deliberately, I began to dismantle my fortress from the inside. I wove small rituals into my days, gentle anchors that returned me to the present moment. Meditation became a kind of inner sanctuary, a still room where I could watch my thoughts drift past like weather instead of being pulled into their storms. Breath became a language of safety. Inhaling. Exhaling. Again and again. Each cycle a soft bell ringing me back into my body. Back into now. Back into the undeniable truth that I was here. That this moment was real. That I was not lost inside yesterday or imprisoned by tomorrow. Movement, too, became an ally. At first, it was nothing heroic. Just a walk. A few steps beyond my door. But even that felt like rebellion. Against the heaviness. Against the inertia depression had draped over my limbs like wet wool. Each walk loosened something. A knot in my chest. A fog behind my eyes. The streets became my quiet teachers. The rhythm of my feet against the ground a reminder that I still belonged to the world. That gravity was not only something that pulled me down, but something that held me. With every small, embodied return, another stone shifted. Another hairline fracture appeared. The walls did not fall in spectacle. They sighed. They softened. They began to give way in pieces small enough for my hands to manage. A thought challenged. A boundary set. A feeling allowed without being judged or rushed. Sometimes it was nothing more than noticing sunlight resting on a wall, or the warmth of a cup between my palms, and letting myself stay there long enough to feel it. These moments became my tools. Subtle. Unassuming. Powerful. I learned that dismantling a fortress is rarely about force. It is about presence. About returning again and again to what is real. To what can be touched. To what can be breathed.

‘;/Each time I chose to meet myself with attention instead of avoidance, with curiosity instead of condemnation, another brick loosened its hold. And where stone receded, space appeared. Where space appeared, air moved. Where air moved, something green began, quietly, to grow. I was no longer only undoing walls. I was making room. Each stretch of muscle, each rhythm of foot against ground, stitched me back into my body. It felt like being gently reintroduced to myself, as though sensation were threading its way through places long gone numb. Exercise did not transform me overnight. There were no cinematic awakenings. But it gave me pockets of clarity. Small, breathing fields of peace where the fog thinned just enough for me to see the shape of the day. Sweat became a language. Pulse became a drum. The quiet burn in my lungs a reminder that I was still alive inside the effort. Every step whispered the same fragile, revolutionary truth: I was not as trapped as I believed. The ground met me. The air received me. My body, once only a weight to be carried, began to feel like a companion again. And then there was creation. I returned to art the way one returns to a childhood home, hesitant, reverent, unsure if the door would still open. I returned to music. To writing. To the places where my inner world could spill outward and take form. These became my vessels. My translation rooms. Spaces where what had no language could finally move. Where emotion could flow instead of calcify. Where ache could become color. Where sorrow could become sound. Where confusion could become a line on a page instead of a knot in my chest. I stopped burying my feelings in the stone of my body and began giving them somewhere to breathe. Paint carried what my mouth could not yet hold. Notes said what my voice was still afraid to shape. Words became small bridges between what I felt and what I could face. Creation did not fix me. But it witnessed me. It allowed the storm to move through instead of circling endlessly inside. And in being expressed, the pain changed. It lost some of its sharpness. Some of its isolation. It became something I could stand beside instead of something that swallowed me whole. And with each ritual, each walk, each page, each breath, the walls thinned. Not all at once. Not without resistance. But enough. Enough to let the light in.

Embracing Fluidity

As the walls thinned and light began to enter, another truth revealed itself, soft as rain on stone: healing does not move in straight lines. It moves like water. In tides. In seasons. In spirals and slow returns. Some mornings the fortress felt like a story I had once lived in, distant, almost unreal. Other days its silhouette rose again inside me, familiar and heavy, and the old cold gravity of depression tugged at my ribs, whispering that nothing had changed. That this was all illusion. That I was back where I began. Learning to expect these fluctuations became part of my healing. I began to understand that progress is not the absence of darkness, but the widening of our capacity to meet it. Not the banishment of shadow, but the growth of an inner light strong enough to hold it. So I learned to let my inner world be fluid. To stop demanding that every day prove something. To allow emotions to rise and fall like weather across a wide sky, without declaring them verdicts on who I was or where I was going. I practiced meeting a hard morning without rewriting my entire story around it. Letting a heavy hour be a heavy hour. Letting it pass without crowning it king. On the days when the shadows pressed closer, I changed my language. Where I once accused, I began to name. Where I once scolded, I began to soften. “This is sadness.” “This is fear.” “This is tiredness.” Simple words. Human words. Words that held space instead of sharpening it. I tended instead of resisted. I treated myself less like a problem to be solved and more like a landscape to be listened to. Setbacks no longer meant failure. They became signals. Small flares rising from within, asking for attention, for rest, for a return to the rituals that steadied me. A walk. A breath. A page. A phone call. They reminded me that healing is not a destination reached once and forever, but a relationship. A living thing. Something that asks to be met again and again, in changing weather, with changing needs. And in that reframing, something profound shifted. Every difficult day became proof not that I was broken, but that I was alive inside a process still unfolding. Still rearranging. Still learning its own name. Self-care stopped being an emergency response and became a way of walking. A way of listening to the ground beneath my feet. A constant companion rather than a last resort. A quiet vow I made to myself each morning, whether the sky inside me was clear or clouded: I will meet you here. I will not abandon you. I will walk with you, whatever this day brings. And in that promise, repeated gently over time, I found something steadier than happiness. I found belonging.

Building a New Foundation

Reclaiming my life from depression has never been a finish line I crossed and left behind. It is a living process. A relationship. A continual return. It is something I step into each morning, the way one steps into a river that is never quite the same water twice. The fortresses we build do not simply vanish. They do not dissolve into nothing. They transform. What once functioned as a prison can, with time and intention, become a place of remembrance. A structure of resilience. A quiet architecture of survival. The same stones that once closed me in now stand as proof that I lived, that I endured, that I learned how to reshape what tried to contain me. Each brick I loosened, each wall I thinned, let light spill into rooms that had never known it. And in that light, the shadows that once haunted me lost their dominion. They did not disappear, but they no longer commanded the space. They softened. They shrank. They learned their proper size. Looking back now, I can see that the fortress still exists, but it no longer governs my days. It no longer defines my horizons. It stands as a marker, not a master. A witness rather than a warden. A testament to what I endured, and to the strength I did not know I carried while I was carrying it. It reminds me that I am not singular in this struggle. That countless others are navigating their own inner strongholds, feeling their way along similar walls, listening for the same hidden fractures. And it reminds me of something even more vital: freedom is possible. Not a fantasy. Not a rare miracle. A lived, buildable reality. It is never too late to lay a new foundation. Never too late to choose different materials. To set down the old blueprints. To imagine structures that make room for breath and light and belonging. Never too late to build a bridge where there was only a barricade. Never too late to turn a ruin into a refuge. What I am building now is not a fortress. It is a home. A living ground beneath my feet. A place where memory can exist without ruling. Where tenderness is not a liability, but a resource. Where I can meet myself without armor. And every day I continue this work, stone by conscious stone, choice by gentle choice, I am reminded: the past may have shaped the terrain, but the future is something I am still allowed to design. The hurricane that raged inside me for so long did not vanish overnight. It did not pack itself up neatly and leave. But it softened. The winds loosened their grip. The sky widened, inch by patient inch, until there was room to breathe again. In the quiet after the worst of the storm, I discovered something I had never quite known how to name before. Peace. Not the loud, triumphant kind. But a low, steady calm. A gentler rhythm. A sense of purpose that rose not from sheer survival, but from presence. From finally standing inside my own life instead of bracing against it. I came to understand that depression was not only an inhabitant. It was also a teacher. A ruthless one, perhaps, but not without wisdom. It taught me reverence for ordinary moments. It taught me how fragile joy is, and therefore how precious. How luminous a single breath can be when you have learned what it is to struggle for air.

How sacred it is to feel anything at all. It taught me to cherish the smallness of being alive. To notice the way light pools on the floor. The way warmth settles into the body. The way a quiet moment can hold more meaning than a thousand noisy victories. I no longer pass beauty without bowing to it. I no longer hurry past tenderness as if it were guaranteed. And now, when I stand at the window and look out at the world beyond the fortress, I remember something essential. The world has always been moving. And so have I. Even when I felt frozen. Even when I believed I was stuck behind stone and shadow. The storm within me still shifts. There is still weather. There are days of cloud and days of wind. But there is also ground beneath my feet. And sky above my head. And a growing strength that knows how to bend without breaking, how to shelter without closing, how to endure without disappearing. So I invite you, dear reader, to turn toward your own fortress. Not with war, but with wonder. Not with judgment, but with curiosity. To place your hand against its walls and listen. To learn how it was built. To notice where light already slips through the cracks. Remember this: where darkness lives, light also waits. Begin the work of understanding. Of reclaiming. Of building anew. You are not alone in this crossing. And you were never meant to remain behind the walls.

THE ECHO IN THE WELL

And then, from within that suffocating stillness, something else begins to move. There is something more sinister lurking in the depths of this well. Not a shape you can see. Not a presence you can point to. But a sound you cannot escape. The echo of suicidal ideation. A constant, insidious whisper that returns again and again, suggesting that descent is release, that surrender is solution. It does not shout because shouting invites resistance. It does not rush because urgency would reveal its danger. It repeats itself patiently, relentlessly, as though the walls themselves have learned how to speak your fears back to you in your own cadence. The whisper is subtle. Almost reasonable in its tone. Calm. Measured. It presents itself not as destruction, but as mercy. As relief. As the promise of peace after too much endurance. It tells you that silence could be rest, that stillness could be freedom, that the suffering could finally be quieted. It offers an end to pain without acknowledging the cost. It edits reality until the picture feels complete, even as it leaves out everything that contradicts its claim. This echo is no gentle reverberation. It is cold. Chilling. A presence that circles the cavernous space of the mind, never touching you directly, yet always close enough to be felt. It keeps a careful distance, close enough to influence, far enough to feel inevitable. The sound that bounces off the well's walls mirrors the repetitive, intrusive nature of despair itself. Like sound waves trapped underground, these thoughts do not simply fade with time. They rebound. They amplify. They gather force as they travel, layering upon themselves, thickening the air. Fear grows louder. The darkness feels denser. Heavier. More absolute. The mind becomes a closed system. A psychological entrapment where every path of thought curves back toward the same conclusion, where each attempt to reason becomes another surface for the echo to strike. It convinces you there is no escape, not by arguing loudly, but by repeating softly until repetition feels like certainty. And this is what makes the echo so dangerous. Not its volume. But its persistence. Not its cruelty. But its familiarity. It sounds like thinking. It sounds like logic. It sounds like you.

Understanding this does not make the echo vanish. But it begins to loosen its spell. Because what echoes, no matter how convincing, is still only a reflection.

And reflections, however powerful, are not the same as truth. These thoughts are not a single moment or a fleeting impulse. They linger. They haunt. They wait in the shadows, not with urgency, but with patience, always ready to reappear. They can be triggered by almost anything. A bad day that lands harder than expected. A sharp word that slips under the skin. A moment of exhaustion when defenses are already thin. And when they rise, they can flood the mind so completely that clear thinking feels impossible. Rational choices blur. Perspective collapses. The echo fills every corner until there seems to be no quiet left in which to stand. In those moments, the mind narrows. It loses its depth. It forgets its own history. Everything compresses into the now, into the weight, into the feeling that this is all there is. The echo thrives here, not because it is true, but because it is loud and familiar and timed perfectly to meet you when you are weakest. But consider this, gently, carefully. An echo exists only because something was spoken into the space. And echoes can be changed. They can be interrupted. They can be softened. They can be altered by new sounds entering the chamber. The well may feel like it owns your thoughts, but it does not. You are not powerless inside this space. You are still the one holding your story, even when it feels frayed, even when the pages seem torn and out of order.Every positive thought, every supportive action, every moment of reaching outward is like a pebble dropped into the darkness. Small. Modest. Easy to dismiss. But it sends ripples through the space. At first they are faint, almost unnoticeable, quickly swallowed by the vastness of the well. But they persist. They return. They travel. Each small act of hope creates a new sound. A different vibration. One that does not argue with the echo but slowly disrupts its dominance. One that introduces variation where there was only repetition. Over time, these ripples begin to overlap. To layer. To grow louder. Until the soundscape changes. Until the echo is no longer the only voice being heard. The well may be deep. The darkness may be convincing. But it does not get the final word. Not while you are still breathing. Not while you are still reaching. Not while new sounds are being made.

The Subtle Whisper of Despair

It never announces itself with thunder. It does not scream or demand attention. It whispers. After the echo has settled into the walls of the well, this voice arrives like a breath against the ear, intimate and persuasive, flavoured with the bitter tang of your own pain. It sounds familiar because it borrows your cadence. It promises peace. Release. An end to the endless cycle of climbing, slipping, gathering strength, and trying again. It speaks fluently in the language of your despair, tailoring its tone to your most tender places, your deepest wounds, the places already rubbed raw by effort. It tells a story shaped from exhaustion. From the belief that the weight has become too much. From the fear that the pain has no horizon. It does not argue with facts. It does not engage reason. It leans instead on feeling, on weariness, on the human longing for rest when rest feels unreachable. It frames stopping as relief, stillness as kindness, silence as mercy, all while disguising the cost of believing it. This is not merely metaphor or a figure of speech. It is a lived experience. The deep, dark well is the felt reality of being trapped, isolated, overwhelmed by sadness that seems too vast to contain. Its bottomless nature mirrors the belief that suffering has no conclusion, that depression stretches endlessly forward, offering no exit, no reprieve. Time loses shape here. Hope loses language. And the whisper knows this. It does not confront you head-on. It manipulates by proximity. It waits for moments when your resources are depleted, when hope feels thin, when the climb has taken everything, you have. It feeds on exhaustion. On hopelessness. On the very real, very human pain you are carrying. It presents itself as understanding rather than threat, as compassion rather than danger.

Naming this matters. Because what whispers is not truth. It is pain speaking under pressure. It is suffering trying to end itself by convincing you there is only one way to quiet it. And recognizing the whisper for what it is does not make the struggle vanish, but it begins to loosen its grip. It creates a sliver of space between the voice and the self who hears it. In that space, even if it is small, something else can breathe. It presents suicide not as a violent rupture, but as a solution softened at the edges, a quiet escape from a reality that feels unbearably loud. It sands down the danger until it looks almost gentle, disguising the irrevocable nature of the "*jump*," making the abyss appear deceptively shallow. It promises calm where there is only collapse. Serenity where there is no return. It edits out consequence and replaces it with relief, offering a mirage that shimmers most convincingly when you are already parched. The danger lies not in its volume, but in its persistence. The whisper does not tire. It settles in as constant background noise, threading itself through thought and perception, subtly shaping how you see yourself, your future, the world around you. It colors memory. It narrows possibility. It reframes endurance as futility and pain as proof. It is not a single horrifying scream that can be startled away or dismissed with logic. It is a low, steady drone. A pressure so consistent it begins to feel like atmosphere. Slowly, it wears you down. Chips at resilience. Makes resistance feel like effort rather than instinct. And yet, even here, even beneath this quiet assault, the fact that it whispers matters. Whispers depend on closeness. They require fatigue. They need isolation to survive. They lose their power when brought into the open, when named for what they are, when answered rather than absorbed. A whisper cannot compete with another voice that speaks with steadiness and care. It falters when met with connection. It weakens when interrupted by truth, by presence, by the simple act of not being alone with it. This, too, is part of the story. The part that continues beyond the well. Because every time the whisper is recognized, every time it is questioned, every time another voice enters the space, something shifts. The echo changes. The walls stop feeling quite so absolute. And in that subtle change, the climb finds room to continue. The echo captures the repetitive, intrusive nature of these thoughts, the way they linger like a presence you cannot see but always feel. They return again and again, not because they are true, but because repetition gives them weight, because familiarity can masquerade as fact. Each return leaves a faint imprint, and over time those imprints stack, convincing the mind that what is most frequently heard must somehow be most real. Alongside the echo comes the whisper. Softer. More deceptive. It emphasizes the subtle, manipulative nature of this inner experience. These thoughts do not arrive wearing warning signs. They do not announce themselves as danger. They arrive as suggestion. As a tempting answer. As an idea wrapped in the language of rest and relief. They sound calm. They sound composed. They sound like reason speaking gently at the end of a long, exhausting day. And that is what makes them so powerful. They frame peace as something that can only be found by erasing oneself from the equation. They suggest that the noise would finally quiet, that the strain would finally ease, if you could simply stop being present to it. They speak in absolutes, flattening complexity into certainty, insisting there is only one outcome, only one explanation, only one way the story can go. Slowly, quietly, they begin to rewrite identity. They tell you that you are a burden. That your presence takes more than it gives. That you are undeserving of love, care, or tenderness. They take moments of struggle and recast them as character flaws. They take pain and turn it into accusation. Over time, shame settles in, not as an emotion, but as a belief. And belief, once formed, is harder to dislodge than feeling.

This is how the inner landscape is altered. Not through force, but through suggestion. Not through sudden collapse, but through steady revision. And understanding this matters. Because what has been rewritten can be revised again. What has been distorted can be named. What has been repeated can be interrupted. The echo and the whisper may feel convincing, but they are not authors of truth. They are symptoms of pain asking to be witnessed, asking for care, asking for another voice to enter the space and remind you of who you were before shame learned how to speak. As you stand at the edge of the well, the whispers grow louder, winding themselves around your thoughts like ivy, tightening with every breath. They feel intimate, practiced, and familiar. There is a strange comfort in that familiarity, the way repetition can mimic certainty. They offer an illusion of control, a promise that the ache could be silenced, that the endless effort of staying upright might finally cease. But this comfort is counterfeit. It is carefully constructed, polished to look like rest while quietly ushering you further into shadow, further from yourself. These thoughts are deeply manipulative. They masquerade as serenity while steadily narrowing the field of vision. The idea of jumping comes to represent a final, irreversible threshold, born not from desire, but from desperation. Not from wanting to disappear, but from wanting the pain to stop. It is the moment when exhaustion speaks in the voice of logic, when suffering tries to persuade you that surrender is peace. Questions arise. Quietly. Dangerously. *"Why shouldn't I just jump? What if it really would be better this way?"* They do not arrive as declarations, but as inquiries, slipping past defenses because they sound reasonable, because they ask rather than tell. This is the most perilous part of the struggle, the point where pain distorts perception so completely that survival itself begins to feel negotiable, as though staying is a choice you must continually justify. And yet, even here, even at this edge, the very presence of these questions reveals something vital.

They are not proof. They are not truth. They are signals. Flares fired from a system overwhelmed beyond its capacity. They are the mind's fractured attempt to escape unbearable pain, not evidence that escape lies where the whisper points. The questions themselves testify to how much you are hurting, how heavy the weight has become, how urgently something needs care and relief. This is the place where the well feels most convincing. And it is also the place where the need for another voice, another perspective, another truth becomes most urgent. A voice that does not argue with your pain but refuses to confuse pain with destiny. A voice that can stand beside you at the edge and say, quietly and firmly, you do not have to answer these questions alone. Because even here, especially here, the story is not finished.

The act of jumping, that final and irreversible step, comes to represent pure desperation rather than desire. Not a wish for death, but a longing for the pain to stop insisting on being everywhere at once. It marks the moment when suffering narrows the field of vision so completely that peace appears reachable in only one imagined direction. This is the tragedy at the heart of depression. It is not simply sadness or weakness or a failure of attitude. It is a potentially fatal illness, one that can claim lives when it remains unseen, untreated, or carried alone for far too long. And yet, folded into that same truth, another truth endures. There is help. There are people who care. There are hands willing to reach into the dark and share the weight that has grown unbearable. There are voices that want to interrupt the echo, not by shouting it down, but by standing beside you long enough for something steadier to be heard. This matters. It matters more than the illness will ever admit. It is vital to understand this gently and clearly. The presence of the whisper does not diminish your strength. It does not erase your worth. It is not evidence of weakness, failure, or a flawed character. It is a symptom. A signal. The natural consequence of a nervous system stretched past its limits and a mind starved of relief. The whisper is what happens when pain goes on too long without support, when endurance is mistaken for capacity. The whisper does not define you. It is not your truth. It is not your essence. It is information about how much you are hurting, and nothing more. And suffering, no matter how severe, is not a moral flaw. It is not something to be ashamed of. It is a call. A flare sent up from deep within, saying this is too much to hold alone. Listening to that call does not mean surrender. It means recognition. It means allowing the possibility that help is not a failure of strength, but an expression of it. That survival is not a solitary act. That even in the deepest well, the fact that pain speaks at all is proof that something inside still wants care, still wants relief, still wants to live differently. And that wanting is enough to begin.

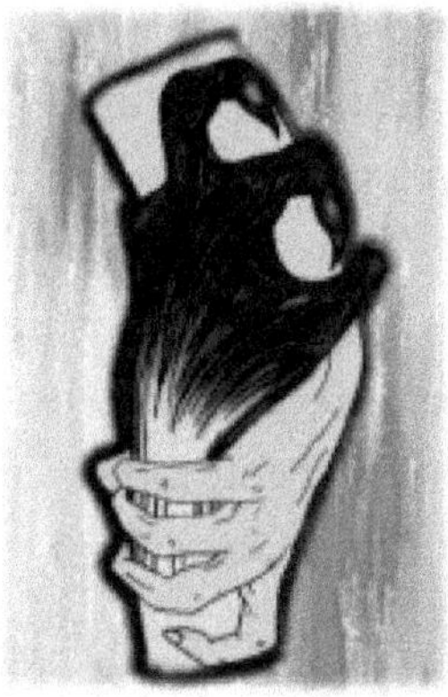

The good news, even when it feels impossible to believe, is this: unlike the seemingly bottomless well, despair is not insurmountable. It lies. It tells you it is endless when it is not. You are not condemned to remain in its depths, no matter how convincing the darkness becomes. There are ways out, even when your eyes cannot yet make sense of the walls, even when the light feels more imagined than real. There are people who can help you find the handholds when your fingers feel numb. The footholds when your legs are shaking. The strength you fear you no longer possess but have not, in truth, lost. There are ropes to be discovered, ladders to be built piece by careful piece, and hands reaching downward, steady and patient, not rushing you, not judging the pace, simply waiting for yours. The echo may not disappear overnight. Its whispers may linger, thinning slowly rather than vanishing all at once, like fog lifting at its own unhurried speed. But with the right support, the right tools, and compassionate guidance, you can learn how to meet it differently. How to quiet its authority even when it still speaks. How to move through the darkness without surrendering to it. How to orient yourself toward light even when it feels distant and partially obscured. The climb out of the well is long. It is arduous. It asks for courage you may not feel you have, patience you may not trust yourself to sustain. It does not unfold in dramatic leaps, but in small, deliberate movements. Step by step. Breath by breath. Grip by trembling grip. And slowly, almost imperceptibly at first, the top comes closer. The air shifts. The light grows steadier. You are not alone in this descent, nor in the climb that follows. You never were. You are worthy of help. You are worthy of care. You are worthy of rescue, not because you have failed, but because you are human and hurting. And even now, even here, when the walls still feel close and the echo still murmurs, the sun is waiting. This metaphor exists not for poetry alone, but for understanding. It is a tool, a shared vocabulary for something that so often resists language. It gives shape to what feels formless, weight to what is dismissed as invisible, sound to a silence that can otherwise feel impossible to translate. In naming the well and the echo, the experience steps out of isolation and into something that can be held, spoken, recognized. In this way, the well becomes a bridge. It spans the distance between those who are struggling and those who want to help but do not know how to reach across the gap. It offers a way to say, *this is where I am*, without having to justify the depth. It allows others to understand that what looks like withdrawal may be exhaustion, that what sounds like hopelessness may be pain searching for relief. Through this image, depression and suicidal ideation become more relatable, more human, less shrouded in misunderstanding. By stepping into this metaphor, we begin to grasp the true complexity of depression. How it seeps into every corner of a life. How it reshapes thought patterns, drains energy, strains relationships, and alters self-perception until the world itself feels smaller and more unforgiving. It is not contained to one moment or one feeling. It is a landscape that must be navigated. But more than explanation, this image carries a quiet insistence. The climb matters. The echo does not silence itself. The well does not empty on its own. Waiting without support only deepens the grooves the voice already knows how to travel. Seeking help is not a failure of strength, but an act of it. A deliberate refusal to accept the well as a final truth. A decision to reach, even when reaching feels clumsy, even when hope feels thin. It is how the climb begins. It is how the echo slowly loses its grip. And it is how understanding becomes the first handhold.

Depression is not something you simply will away. It is not a mood you can outthink, nor a weakness you can shame into silence. It is a serious illness, one that settles into the nervous system, alters chemistry, bends perception, and convinces the mind of things that are not true. It does not respond to bravado. It responds to care. To treatment. To being taken seriously. And when help is accepted, something begins to shift. The walls of the well, once polished smooth by despair, no longer feel quite so impenetrable. The stone changes texture. Almost imperceptibly at first. A rough edge catches the palm. A handhold appears where none existed before. A rope is lowered, not as rescue, but as invitation. A path upward, once unimaginable, begins to take shape not all at once, but piece by piece, revealed through effort, through persistence, through the quiet courage of asking and receiving. The journey out of the well is not quick. Nor is it easy. It does not reward urgency. It asks instead for presence. For courage when courage feels scarce. For resilience when you feel worn thin. For determination when hope flickers like a fragile flame in moving air. Some days the climb feels steady. Other days it feels like simply holding on. Both count. It also asks for support. For care. For compassion. From therapists who help translate pain into understanding. From medication that steadies the ground beneath your feet. From loved ones who keep watch when your grip falters. And eventually, slowly, from yourself. From the part of you learning to speak with gentleness rather than accusation. Learning to rest without quitting. Learning to believe that needing help is not failure, but intelligence applied to survival. The climb may be slow. Measured in inches rather than miles. In breaths rather than breakthroughs. But it is possible. One step at a time. One breath at a time. One decision to stay, repeated again and again. And in the end, the journey is not defined by how deep the well once was. It is defined by this single, enduring truth. You chose to climb. If you are struggling with depression, know this first and foremost: you are not alone in the well. Even when it feels impossibly quiet, even when the echo seems to be the only voice answering back: There are people who care deeply about you and want to walk beside you through this darkness. Presence does not always announce itself loudly. Sometimes it waits, steady and patient, just beyond the reach of your current breath. There is help within reach, even if it does not yet feel that way. There are resources, treatments, and compassionate hands ready to meet you where you are, not where you think you should be. Ready to help you find your footing on stone that has felt slick for far too long. Ready to climb with you, slowly and steadily, step by careful step, and to quiet the echo that has been insisting you are alone. Do not be afraid to reach outward. Do not be afraid to speak what has been living in silence. Pain grows heavier when it is carried alone, but when it is named, when it is witnessed, it begins to change shape. Naming your pain does not make it stronger. It makes it shareable. It gives it edges someone else can help hold. Talking about your feelings, allowing others to see your struggle, seeking treatment, these are not signs of weakness. They are acts of courage. They are moments of defiance against the well's insistence that you must do this by yourself. They are the first deliberate movements of the climb. The moment your hand reaches not for the abyss, but for the rope. And that reach matters. Because it is proof that somewhere within you, even beneath exhaustion and fear, there is still a will to live differently. Still a part of you that believes relief is possible. Still a part of you that knows this story is not meant to end in the dark. You do not have to climb all at once.

You do not have to see the top. You only have to take the next reachable hold. And there are others here, ready to hold the rope steady while you do. You are worthy of love. You are worthy of care. You are worthy of compassion. You are worthy of life, even when your mind insists otherwise, even when the echo argues in circles and calls itself truth. Worth is not something depression gets to revoke. It is not conditional. It does not disappear because you are tired, or hurting, or struggling to keep going. The weight of depression can feel overwhelming, crushing in its persistence, pressing down day after day as though gravity itself has grown heavier around you. But it is not impossible to live with, and it is not impossible to heal. With the right support, with care that meets you where you are, with treatment that steadies and strengthens, the climb becomes possible. Not suddenly. Not perfectly. But truly. The echo can soften. The walls can stop shouting your fears back at you. The darkness can thin, first at the edges, then in the center, until it no longer fills the entire field of vision. And light, even faint at first, can begin to return. Not as a blinding revelation, but as something gentle. Something believable. Something you can walk toward. You can learn to live with depression rather than beneath it. You can learn its rhythms. Its patterns. Its tells. You can learn when to rest and when to reach. You can reclaim moments of joy and meaning, not because everything is suddenly easy, but because they are still yours to have. You can learn to walk again. To function again. To live again. And one day, perhaps quietly, almost without ceremony, you may notice a change. That the backpack no longer defines every step. That the weight, while still present, no longer dictates your direction. That you are moving forward, not without effort, but without despair holding the reins. The climb continues. But you are no longer trapped. You are rising.

Remember This First

Before we step further into this terrain, hold this close, the way you would hold a compass in fog: you are not alone, and help is real and available. You are allowed to reach out. You are allowed to speak what hurts. You are allowed to ask for treatment, for support, for relief. None of this diminishes your strength. It affirms it. Reaching outward is not a collapse of resolve, it is resolve finding a wiser direction. You are worthy of love, of care, of compassion. You are worthy of life, exactly as you are, not after you improve, not once you are less tired, not when you have proven anything.

The Symptoms of Depression: Understanding the Labyrinth

Now, as we move forward, it helps to understand the landscape itself. Depression is not a single road with a clear beginning and end. It is a labyrinth. Winding. Personal. Changing its turns depending on who walks it and when. No two journeys are identical. What weighs heavily on one person may barely brush another. And yet, there are common passages many find themselves moving through again and again, corridors worn smooth by repetition.

- **Persistent sadness, low mood, hopelessness, emptiness:**
  One of the most familiar corridors is a sadness that does not lift with time. A low mood that lingers beyond circumstance. A sense of emptiness that settles into the chest and refuses to leave. This is not simply feeling blue. It is a gravity that pulls inward, day after day, until even neutral moments feel heavy.
- **Loss of interest or pleasure:**
  Alongside it often comes a quiet withdrawal from what once brought joy. Activities that used to spark interest now feel distant, muted, or strangely burdensome, as though the color has drained from familiar things and left them outlined but flat.
- **Changes in appetite and weight:**
  The body begins to speak in its own language. Appetite may disappear or surge without warning, leading to noticeable changes in weight. Eating becomes either an effort or a compulsion, disconnected from hunger as it once was.
- **Sleep disturbances:**
  Sleep, too, is disrupted. Nights fragment into wakefulness and restlessness. Or sleep stretches long but

never restores. Whether through insomnia, hypersomnia, or uneasy nights, rest no longer feels like refuge.

- **Fatigue or loss of energy:**
Fatigue seeps in, not the kind cured by a single good night's sleep, but a deep, persistent exhaustion that lingers even after rest. Each day can feel like a climb without footholds, effort demanded before momentum appears.
- **Restlessness or irritability:**
Inside the body there may be agitation or irritability. An inability to sit still. A hair-trigger frustration. An unfamiliar edge to reactions, anger flaring where patience once lived.
- **Difficulty concentrating, deciding, remembering:**
The mind can slow or scatter. Concentration falters. Decisions feel overwhelming. Memory slips in small but unsettling ways. Thoughts lose their sharpness, and everyday tasks require more mental effort than before.
- **Physical symptoms:**
Distress may surface physically as well. Headaches. Stomach discomfort. Unexplained aches and pains. The body carries what the mind is struggling to hold.
- **Feelings of worthlessness, guilt, and shame:**
Depression often distorts self-perception. Feelings of worthlessness, guilt, and shame take root, reshaping inner dialogue into something harsh and unforgiving. Self-blame becomes automatic. Self-compassion feels undeserved, even unfamiliar.
- **Thoughts of death, suicide, or self-harm:**
For some, thoughts about death or self-harm may arise, ranging from fleeting intrusions to more persistent concerns. These thoughts are not a reflection of character or desire. They are signals of deep distress, flare lights indicating that something within needs care, safety, and attention.

This list is not exhaustive. And experiencing some of these symptoms does not automatically mean you have depression. What matters is context, duration, and impact on daily life. That is why professional support is essential. A trained clinician can help make sense of the maze, offering clarity where confusion has taken hold, and options where the path feels blocked. Depression is not something to be ashamed of. It is not something you can simply will away or snap out of. It is a serious condition that asks for treatment, understanding, and sustained care. And if any of these passages feel familiar, reaching out is not just recommended, it is an act of self-respect. The labyrinth may be complex. But you do not have to navigate it alone.

Navigating the Path to Recovery

Recovery does not unfold like a finish line waiting patiently to be crossed. It moves more like a path through changing terrain. Sometimes the ground is steady beneath your feet. Sometimes it tilts sharply upward. Sometimes it curves back on itself, confusing and discouraging, before opening forward again in ways you could not see from where you stood. Healing from depression is not an arrival. It is a journey.

A gradual, unfolding process of self-discovery, growth, and transformation. One that asks for patience when progress feels slow, persistence when setbacks appear, and courage simply to keep walking when stopping feels easier. Along this path, there are signposts. Not commands. Not guarantees. But places where support can be found and strength can be gathered.

- **Seeking professional help** is often the first and most stabilizing step. A therapist, counselor, or psychiatrist helps name what has felt amorphous and overwhelming. They bring language to experience, clarity to confusion, and structure to chaos. Together, you create a treatment plan shaped around your specific needs, not a generic prescription, but a living document that can change as you do. In this way, they become companions on the journey, offering steadier footing when doubt and darkness make the ground feel unreliable.

- **Therapy** itself becomes a kind of map. Approaches such as Cognitive Behavioral Therapy and others help you notice the familiar loops of thought that lead back toward despair and gently, patiently question them. Through practices like journaling, mindfulness, and reflection, new pathways begin to form. Healthier ways of responding to pain, stress, and fear slowly take root, not replacing old patterns overnight, but offering alternatives where none seemed to exist.
- Alongside this inner work, **lifestyle changes** quietly strengthen the ground beneath you. These changes are not a cure, but they matter deeply. Regular movement, nourishing food, adequate rest, and moments of stillness help regulate the nervous system and remind the body that safety and care are possible. They are small acts with cumulative power, tending the soil so healing has somewhere to grow.
- **Self-care** is not indulgence. It is necessity. It is the ongoing practice of tending to your physical, emotional, and inner needs without apology. Engaging in activities that bring even a flicker of joy, calm, or meaning matters more than it may seem. These moments are not distractions from healing. They are part of it. Proof that the system can still experience relief, however briefly.
- **Building a support system** can change the shape of the journey entirely. No one is meant to walk this path alone. Trusted friends, family members, support groups, or compassionate communities offer connection where isolation once lived. Sharing your struggles with people who listen and care does not burden them. It redistributes weight. It allows the climb to become shared rather than solitary.
- Equally vital is **self-compassion**. Learning to speak to yourself as you would to someone you love. Acknowledging the difficulty of what you are carrying without judgment or comparison. Celebrating progress even when it feels small, uneven, or fragile. Each step counts. Each effort matters. Even the days when showing up looks like resting.
- And as strength slowly returns, many find it helpful to **seek purpose and meaning**. Not as pressure, but as orientation. Engaging in fulfilling activities, exploring a passion, volunteering, creating, learning, or simply caring for something beyond yourself can anchor you to a wider horizon. Purpose does not erase pain, but it gives direction when the path feels uncertain.

Recovery is not linear. It does not demand perfection. It allows for pauses, missteps, and rest. It asks only that you continue. One step at a time. Gathering support. Learning gentleness. Trusting that even here, even now, forward movement is possible. And every step you take, however small, is already part of the climb.

The Power of Hope

Hope arrives quietly, like a light kindled in a place that has long known only shadow. It does not blaze. It does not announce itself with certainty or spectacle. It glows. Small at first. Fragile enough to doubt. Yet strong enough to give shape to the space around it, to reveal the outline of the next step when the rest of the path remains hidden. Hope does not banish the darkness all at once, but it interrupts it. It says: *"Here, you can stand. Here, you can breathe. Here, you can move again."* Hope is the spark that ignites the slow flame of healing and the steady fuel that keeps it burning as the journey stretches on. It is not merely a feeling that rises and falls with circumstance. It is not optimism pretending everything is fine. Hope is a choice. A quiet, courageous turning toward belief. Belief in yourself. In your capacity to endure. In your inherent worth, even when doubt presses close and tries to speak louder. Hope asks for trust. Not blind faith. Not denial. But a willingness to believe that life holds more than what is visible in this moment. A trust in unfolding rather than certainty. In process rather than outcome. In the possibility that meaning and purpose can exist even within struggle, even alongside pain that has not yet loosened its grip. Hope does not require the absence of pain. It does not erase suffering or pretend it is insignificant. Instead, it carries peace beside it. A quiet steadiness that allows pain to be present without letting it become the whole of reality. Hope makes room. It widens the inner landscape just enough for breath, for choice, for movement. To hope is to look beyond the immediate weight of now and imagine a future that is gentler, brighter, more spacious, even if the details remain unclear. It is the courage to take the next step when the path ahead is obscured, when certainty feels out of reach, when progress is measured in inches rather than miles. It is movement without guarantees. Faith without proof. A hand extended into the dark, trusting that something solid can still be found. And often, that something is yourself, still standing, still choosing, still alive to the possibility that this story continues.

In the darkest moments of my depression, I clung to hope as if it were a lifeline thrown into the well. Not a grand rescue, not a sudden ascent, but a single rope brushing my hands in the dark, enough to remind me that something existed beyond the stone. I reminded myself again and again that I was not alone. That I was loved, even when I could not feel it. That I was worthy of love, even when my mind rose in protest and tried to argue me out of my own existence. I repeated affirmations like anchors, dropping them into the churn to keep myself from being pulled under. "*I am enough! I am strong! I am capable!*" Not because they rang true every time, not because belief came easily, but because speaking them kept the possibility alive. Each word was a small act of defiance against the echo. A way of saying, this story is not finished yet. I practiced gratitude, too, gently and imperfectly, without forcing gratitude to be something it was not. I searched for small points of light, moments of goodness that survived even in shadow. A kind word that landed softly. A warm cup of tea cradled between my hands. A breath taken without effort, arriving and leaving on its own. These were not solutions. They were reminders. Proof that life had not closed entirely. Proof that sensation, connection, and presence still existed, even here. No matter how small they seemed, they mattered. Each one was a thread, thin but unbroken, weaving me back toward the world. Each one whispered that the door was not locked, that the darkness was not total, that something was still reaching toward me, quietly, patiently, waiting for me to notice. Hope does not shout. It does not demand belief or certainty. It waits. And when we choose it, even trembling, even unsure, even exhausted by the effort of choosing, it meets us exactly where we are. It does not rush us forward. It simply walks beside us, steady and unassuming, into whatever comes next.

Conclusion

Depression is not a place you arrive at and remain. It is a journey. A winding path that bends and loops back on itself, marked by unexpected descents and moments of fragile clarity. There are stretches that feel endless, setbacks that test your resolve, and pauses that quietly teach you what endurance actually looks like. The terrain shifts without warning. What steadied you once may not steady you again. And still, you keep moving. It is a journey that can feel lonely, especially in the quiet hours, but it is not one you are meant to walk alone. Along the way, there are people who care deeply. People who recognize the weight you carry without needing it explained. People who understand in ways words cannot always reach, who are willing to walk beside you and help shoulder the load when your steps falter. There are resources, too. Therapy. Support groups. Online communities. Hotlines. Threads of connection woven quietly through the darkness, waiting to be grasped when your hands are ready. Remember this above all else. You are not your depression. You are not your past. You are not your pain. You are not the weight you carry, nor the thoughts that trouble you in the night. You are something far larger and more enduring than any season of suffering. You are a unique, valuable, and deeply loved individual, deserving of joy, peace, and fulfillment, not as a reward for healing, but as a birthright of being human. You are strong, even when you feel fragile. Capable, even when doubt clouds your vision. Resilient, even when exhaustion tells you otherwise. Strength does not always roar. Sometimes it whispers, *keep going*. Sometimes it looks like asking for help. Sometimes it looks like resting instead of quitting. Sometimes it is nothing more than staying. You can get through this. And when you do, you will emerge changed. Scarred in places, yes. Tender in others. But also stronger in ways you could not have imagined. Wiser in how you listen to yourself. More compassionate toward your own limits and the hidden struggles of others.

The well does not define you. The echo does not own your voice. The darkness does not get the final word. Your story continues. And there is still light ahead, waiting to meet you as you rise. As you walk through the shadows of depression, hold onto hope. Hold onto the knowing that you are not alone, even when the path feels empty and your footsteps seem to echo back unanswered. Hold onto the truth that you are loved, and that you are worthy of that love, even on the days you cannot feel it, even when your mind tries to argue you out of believing it. Love does not vanish when it is obscured. Worth does not disappear when it is doubted. Depression is not a definition. It does not get to name you. It is a diagnosis. A description of a state, not a verdict on your value. It is not a life sentence, but a setback. A season. A chapter, not the whole story. Chapters end. Pages turn. The narrative continues, whether or not you can yet imagine what comes next. And when the darkness presses in, when you feel disoriented or lost, remember this. The light has never left. It has not abandoned you. It waits quietly, sometimes beyond the bend, sometimes just out of sight, but always present. The light of hope. The light of love. The light of your own inner strength, steady even when you feel unsure. These are not abstract ideas. They are forces. They are what carry you through the longest nights, what guide you, step by careful step, toward a dawn that does not rush but does arrive. In the next chapter, I turn inward. I face the part of me that once longed for disappearance, the part shaped by pain and exhaustion, without turning away. I will meet that inner darkness directly, not with judgment, not with fear, but with honesty, courage, and compassion. Join me as we explore what it means to look at that place clearly, to understand it without letting it lead, and to discover how even the most difficult parts of us can be met with care. This journey continues. And you are still here, still becoming, still worthy of every step ahead.

Chapter: Eighteen

The fortress can be dismantled. Your story is only just beginning.

The Backpack and the Well: A Journey Through Depression.

The Weight – The Story of Eliza.

Eliza woke to the familiar ache in her shoulders. It wasn't a physical ache. Not exactly. It was the weight of the backpack. The one she had been carrying for so long she could no longer remember the first day it was placed upon her. It had shaped her posture. Curved her spine. Quietly instructed the way she entered rooms and moved through mornings. It had become part of her balance. Part of her breathing. Part of the architecture of her life. Inside it, tucked among textbooks and a half-empty water bottle, were bricks. Not the kind you could drop on a foot or stack into walls, but the heavier kind. Bricks made of sadness. Of quiet despair. Of unspoken grief. Of self-doubt. Of that slow, corrosive feeling of never being enough. Bricks shaped like memories she didn't know how to lay down. Expectations she could never quite meet. Questions that had no gentle answers. They called it "*depression*". A word that sounded clinical. Distant. Almost clean. Nothing like the lived reality of carrying something that pressed downward on every step. That leaned into her spine. That made even standing upright feel like an act of endurance. Nothing like the way it stole oxygen from simple things. The way it turned mornings into uphill climbs and nights into long negotiations with rest. From the outside, she looked functional. She went to class. She handed in assignments. She answered questions when called on. She smiled at the right moments. Sometimes she even surprised herself with how convincing the performance could be. She knew how to arrange her face. How to keep her voice light. How to pass through hallways without letting the weight show. But beneath it all, every movement required intention. Every conversation demanded effort. Every ordinary task was made extraordinary by the gravity she moved against. Laughing felt like lifting something heavier than it should have been. Listening felt like holding herself upright against a tide. Getting out of bed felt like shouldering a life before she had even put her feet on the floor. And this weight had not appeared overnight. It had been gathering slowly, grain by grain, year by year. Like sediment settling at the bottom of a deep well. So gradual she hadn't noticed the water darkening. So patient she hadn't seen the light thinning. Small disappointments became stones. Unspoken fears hardened into weight. Moments of self-doubt stacked quietly on top of one another until they formed something she could no longer lift off. Until one day she looked inward and realized how far down it had gone... and how heavy it had become. This was not a sudden collapse. It was an accumulation. A slow architecture of carrying. A long apprenticeship in endurance. A life practiced beneath invisible load. And Eliza had been carrying it for a very long time.

The Descent

Eliza can still remember the first few bricks. They were small then. Almost unremarkable. The kind of weight you barely register. A failed exam that lingered longer than it should have, echoing in her thoughts long after the paper had been folded and returned. The sharpness of a careless word from a parent, thrown without aim, yet landing exactly where skin was thinnest. The hollow loneliness of standing in a crowded room, laughter rising around her like music from another life, and feeling utterly unseen. She carried those early bricks easily enough. Slipped them into her backpack with the untested confidence of youth. Optimism padded their edges. Resilience made them feel lighter than they were. She told herself this was just life. That everyone collected weight. That everyone learned to carry. That she was strong enough. That she would always be strong enough. And for a while, it seemed true. Until the ground shifted. Her parents' divorce tore through her world like a fault line, splitting what once felt solid into jagged, unreliable terrain. The house did not fall down, but something foundational cracked. Rooms felt different. Voices carried new edges. Silences stretched longer. The air itself seemed altered, as though stability had quietly packed its bags and left without announcement. Not long after, her grandmother died. The one who had been a lighthouse in her childhood. A steady glow in every season. The place where warmth had lived without conditions. Where safety had not needed explanation. And with her went something else Eliza had not yet learned how to name. A sense of being anchored. Of being held. Of belonging somewhere without effort. Grief arrived not as a wave, but as a tide. It did not knock her down. It pulled her outward. Slowly. Repeatedly. Patiently. More bricks found their way into the backpack. The unanswered questions. The nights that felt longer than they should have. The quiet terror of realizing that the people who are supposed to be permanent... are not. Each loss added weight. Each change altered her balance. Each unspoken feeling hardened into something she carried instead of something she released. She did not call it a descent then. She was still attending class. Still doing what was expected. Still laughing when the moment required it.

But beneath the routine, something was tilting. The path she walked no longer felt level. The days no longer met her evenly. She had begun, almost without noticing, to move downhill. And gravity was beginning to teach her its language. Early adulthood followed not as an open road, but as a storm. A convergence of winds she did not yet know how to read. Confusion. Pressure. The vertigo of standing before too many doors and feeling certain none of them led anywhere that felt like home. The terrifying sense of being utterly, irrevocably lost. Each moment added another brick. Heavier. Denser. Less forgiving than the last. Expectations piled on expectations. Who to become. How to succeed. How to want the right things. How to carry herself like someone who knew where she was going. The backpack became constant.

A second spine. A dark twin that mirrored her every movement, shifting when she shifted, leaning when she leaned. She no longer remembered the feeling of standing without it. She tried to outpace it. To pretend it wasn't there. To live as though gravity did not apply to her. She buried herself in her studies. She performed competence. She excelled. She smiled. She constructed a version of herself so polished, so functional, so convincing, it could pass through rooms without raising concern. A self that spoke in clear sentences. Met deadlines. Answered questions. Laughed at the right moments. And for most people, that was enough. Almost. Beneath the surface, something else was taking shape. A new inner geography. A terrain of shadow and quiet despair. A place that felt disturbingly familiar, as though it had always existed and was only now being revealed, like an underground city uncovered by erosion. That was when she first noticed the well. It was not physical. Not at first. It was a sensation. A pull. A widening absence that opened inside her without warning. She would find herself drifting into stillness, her gaze fastening to nothing, while the world around her softened into blur. Voices thinned. Edges dissolved. Time loosened. Conversations dimmed as though someone were slowly turning down a lamp. Sounds receded, moving farther and farther away, until they reached her only as distant echoes. And in their place came the awareness of something vast beneath her. Something deep. Unlit. Patient. A presence she could not see, but could feel, like a gravity field beneath the floorboards of her mind. With each passing day, the well seemed to grow. Deeper. Darker. More insistent. It did not call her with words. It beckoned with silence. With the strange comfort of emptiness. With the illusion of rest. And Eliza, still carrying her weight, still wearing her practiced life, felt herself being drawn toward it. Not in leaps. In inches. A subtle tilt in her days. A gradual rearranging of her inner weather. A quiet migration of her thoughts toward the edge. She did not yet know its name. She only knew its gravity. And gravity, once felt, is difficult to unfeel.

The Echo

Inside the well, the sound began. At first, it was only a whisper, so faint it almost blended with the ordinary noise of her days. The scrape of chairs. The hum of passing conversation. The small rituals of living that filled the air and made everything seem intact. It hid itself in the margins. A breath behind her thoughts. A chill she couldn't quite name. Something that brushed past the edges of awareness and left her unsettled without knowing why. It murmured its small, cruel sentences. Doubts dressed up as truths. Questions that gnawed quietly at the borders of her worth. "*You are nothing. You are alone. You don't belong here. You are a burden. No one really sees you. It would be easier to disappear." "You're worthless," it would murmur. "No one cares." It would be much easier if you just stopped!"* They did not arrive like ordinary thoughts. Not really. They did not feel like something she had chosen. They came as intrusions, as something alien or foreign. As if something else had learned the shape of her inner voice and was now wearing it and using it against her. A parasite of language. An echo that fed on every old bruise, every moment she had ever felt overlooked, every unguarded memory that still carried heat. The well caught those whispers and sent them back to her. Colder. Louder. Distorted by depth. What began as a murmur became a chorus. What had once flickered at the edge of consciousness began to stand in the center of it, repeating itself until repetition hardened into certainty. The walls of the well did not absorb the sound. They sharpened it. Returned it with interest. Multiplied it until it filled the inner air she lived inside. It pressed against her from all directions, a climate rather than a voice. There was no corner of her mind it did not seem to reach.

The echo seeped into memory, into imagination, into the fragile space where identity forms. It began to narrate her days. To subtitle her experiences. To interpret every interaction before she had the chance to feel it for herself. A delayed reply became proof. A tired tone became verdict. A small mistake became a sentence passed on her entire existence. Soon, she was no longer only hearing the echo. She was anticipating it. It arrived before joy could land. Before pride could settle. Before rest could soften her. It leaned over every moment and whispered its translation, turning neutral into negative, quiet into rejection, ordinary into evidence. The well no longer waited for her to look down. It rose up inside her. Its darkness climbed the walls of her thoughts, tinting everything it touched. And the most dangerous thing was not the volume of the echo, but its familiarity. It began to sound like her. Not an intruder anymore. Not a whisper from the well. But the inner narrator of her days. The quiet commentator behind every choice. The lens through which she interpreted herself. The echo learned her history, her sensitivities, her tender places, and it tailored its language accordingly. It did not shout. It suggested. It did not attack. It implied. It braided itself so seamlessly into her inner dialogue that she could no longer tell where Eliza ended and the well began. What once felt foreign grew intimate. What once startled her became expected. What once frightened her started to feel like truth. And because it wore her voice, it carried authority. It sat with her in lecture halls. It followed her into mirrors. It lay beside her at night and spoke into the dark. It reinterpreted every memory, trimming away warmth, spotlighting only what could wound. It rehearsed her failures until they felt predictive. It shrank her achievements until they felt like accidents instead of evidence. Small mercies became invisible. Successes were reduced to flukes. Kindness was reframed as obligation. Love was recast as tolerance.

The echo was a master editor, cutting away anything that might contradict its narrative, arranging her inner world into a story where she was always the flaw. It bent her memories. It narrowed her future. It hollowed her present. And slowly, almost tenderly, it began to colonize her inner air. Every breath felt crowded. Every quiet moment filled. There was no true silence anymore, only the low, constant murmur of evaluation and erasure. The well no longer lived beneath her. It seemed to open inside her. A vertical space in the chest. A depth behind the ribs. A place where light went and did not return. Eliza still moved through her days. She still answered questions. Still completed assignments. Still laughed at the right moments. But inside, the echo translated everything. It turned neutral into negative. Ambiguity into accusation. Difficulty into destiny. If she was tired, it said she was weak. If she struggled, it said she was broken. If she needed help, it said she was a burden. And because it spoke in her voice, it carried the intimacy of self-knowledge. It knew exactly which memories to summon. Which comparisons to make. Which fears to press. It did not need to invent cruelty. It only had to rearrange what already existed. This is how the descent deepened. Not with a fall, but with a narrowing. Not with a scream, but with a steady reduction of space. The well did not pull her in all at once. It taught her to lean. And every day, with the weight on her back and the echo in her chest, Eliza leaned a little closer to the dark, still believing she was standing upright, still believing this was simply the way her mind worked, still unaware that what she was breathing was not air, but the language of an illness that had learned how to sound like her. With time, the echo grew bolder. Louder. More frequent. More persuasive. It no longer lived at the edges of her thoughts. It stepped into the center. It began to speak in full sentences. To argue. To insist. To offer distorted visions and seductive illusions of rest and relief, of laying the weight down forever, of an end to the carrying and the crushing effort of being. Images of pills, of sharp objects, ropes, edges of cliffs, and oblivion flickered through her mind like morbid hallucinations. She started researching methods. Just to know, she told herself. Just to have the information. What once felt like passing static became a voice with intention.

With momentum. With a frightening kind of logic. It learned how to dress despair in the language of comfort. It turned exhaustion into evidence. It turned pain into prophecy. It turned temporary states into permanent conclusions. And sometimes, just becoming aware that such thoughts could exist inside her felt like standing at the lip of something endless. A vast inner depth where sound vanished. Where identity thinned. Where the promise was not joy, but silence. Not healing, but disappearance. The backpack grew heavier. The well stretched farther, seemingly endlessly downward. The inner gravity intensified. Eliza began to recede and disappear from her own life. She answered fewer messages. She let calls go unanswered. She declined invitations not because she didn't care, but because she could no longer translate herself into the language of the living. Conversation felt like a foreign country. Laughter like a performance she had forgotten how to rehearse. She withdrew from her friends, afraid of exposing the darkness that consumed her. She withdrew, quietly, carefully, afraid of what might spill if anyone looked too closely. Her world began to shrink. First, her routines. Then to her room. Then to her bed. Then to the narrow border between sleeping and waking. Even rising each morning felt like lifting stone with bare hands. Her limbs moved as if through water. Her thoughts arrived wrapped in fog. Each task asked more than she felt she had. Each hour stretched like a corridor without doors. Her life contracted, folding inward like a dying star losing its light. And as everything else receded, one thing continued to expand. The well. And the echo living inside it. It filled the spaces where connection once lived. It occupied the silence where rest should have been. It became the background noise of her existence. Not a moment. A climate. Not a thought. An atmosphere. And Eliza, carrying her weight, standing at the edge of that inner depth, had not yet learned the most important truth of all: that the echo was not her voice. that the well was not her home. that even in the deepest dark, something in her was still watching, still breathing, still waiting... for the smallest interruption of light.

The Work of the Echo

The echo did not only speak. It **edited.** It reached back into Eliza's memory like an uninvited archivist, rearranging the shelves of her past. Moments that once held warmth were quietly refiled under *failure*. Laughter was stripped of its music and relabelled as *naïveté*. Love was recast as *weakness*. The echo had a way of draining color from recollection, leaving only the bruised outlines behind. A childhood achievement became an accident. A kindness received became a misunderstanding. A season of joy became proof she had only imagined it. It did not invent new memories. It didn't need to. It simply tilted the existing ones toward the dark, like mirrors angled to catch only shadow. Soon, when Eliza tried to remember herself, she no longer found a whole person. She found a highlight reel of her most fragile moments, looped endlessly. Every hesitation was magnified into cowardice. Every mistake was promoted to destiny. The echo stitched together a false autobiography, one where she was always lacking, always late, always less. And slowly, almost imperceptibly, identity followed memory. She stopped saying, *"I am someone who struggles,"* and began saying, *"I am the struggle."* The work of the echo went deeper still. It colonized the present. It leaned into ordinary moments and bent them into evidence. A delayed reply became rejection. A neutral glance became judgment. A tired day became proof of permanent inadequacy. It trained her attention like a spotlight fixed only on what could wound. Anything gentle slipped past unnoticed. Anything kind was questioned. Anything good was interrogated until it confessed to being temporary. The echo became a lens she could no longer remove. Through it, the world appeared sharper, colder, more brittle than it truly was. People felt farther away. Joy felt suspicious. Rest felt undeserved. Even her own body became unfamiliar territory, something to be managed rather than inhabited. She moved through her days as if carrying glass inside her chest, careful not to disturb it, terrified of the sound it might make if she did. And because the echo was internal, it offered no obvious enemy. There was no one to argue with. No door to close. No room to leave. The well-traveled with her. In classrooms. In kitchens. In crowded rooms where laughter bloomed around her like wildflowers she could not touch. In the quiet of night, when the world exhaled and the echo inhaled, growing larger in the space sleep should have filled. It threaded itself through her dreams.

It greeted her before her name each morning. It became the climate of her inner life. And climates shape everything. They decide what can grow. What withers. What never even tries. Under the rule of the echo, Eliza's inner landscape grew sparse. Self-trust thinned. Curiosity retreated. Hope became migratory, appearing briefly, then vanishing again. The backpack on her shoulders felt heavier not only with bricks, but with meaning. Each brick now carried a story. Each story a verdict. She did not wake one day and declare herself broken. She simply stopped recognizing any evidence to the contrary. This is how the echo worked. Not with spectacle. But with erosion. Not by shouting her into darkness, but by convincing her she had always lived there. And so the well deepened. And so the voice grew steadier. And so Eliza, still moving, still breathing, still showing up to the visible parts of her life, felt herself quietly disappearing from the inside. Not in a single moment. But the way light leaves a room at dusk. She stopped seeing sadness as something passing through her and began believing she was its natural habitat. The echo taught her to introduce herself to herself as a problem. It borrowed her voice. It wore her tone. It learned the rhythm of her inner speech so perfectly that its distortions sounded like self-knowledge. What frightened her most was not the cruelty of the words, but their familiarity. They did not arrive as intruders. They arrived as conclusions. Over time, even her reflection felt unfamiliar. When she looked in the mirror, she did not see a woman moving through pain. She saw the echo's portrait of her: a collection of flaws pretending to be a face. A history of disappointments arranged into a body. A person-shaped argument against her own becoming.

The well was no longer only a place she visited. It was becoming the place she lived. Because this is the final trick of the echo: it does not want silence. It wants authorship. It wants to be the one telling the story of who you are. And for a long while, it succeeded. It narrated her days in the margins. It subtitled every experience with its own translation. If something went well, it whispered, "*temporary*". If something faltered, it declared, "*inevitable*". It did not merely comment on her life. It curated it, arranging events into a script that always ended the same way. In its version of the world, growth was an illusion. Effort was naïve. Change was a rumor other people lived by. Under its authorship, Eliza began to shrink her expectations. She stopped reaching for what might open her. She chose what was small, what was familiar, what required the least faith. Not because she did not want more, but because the echo had convinced her that wanting itself was a kind of error. Hope felt like trespassing. Joy felt like a language she no longer had the right to speak. The world grew narrower. Rooms felt tighter. Dreams felt heavier. Futures felt theoretical. And yet... even here, even at this depth, something in her remained unedited. A thin, almost invisible filament of awareness. A quiet witness behind the narration. A presence that did not argue with the echo but did not fully belong to it echo but many times it surfaced as a question that did not fit the script. A moment of stillness where the voice paused. A breath that felt wider than the well. She did not yet call it strength. She did not yet call it hope. But it was there. A place the echo could not fully colonize. A listening beneath the story. A subtle sense that the narrator might not be the author after all. And though Eliza could not yet imagine another way of being, something in her had begun, quietly, to imagine another way of seeing. Not an escape. But a crack. Not an answer. But a place where one might someday begin. Because even the deepest wells are not made only of darkness. They are also made of space.

The Brink

One particularly bleak morning, Eliza found herself at the edge of the inner well. Not physically, but unmistakably. It was as though something in her had led her to the farthest interior boundary she had ever known. The echo was no longer a whisper. It had become a constant atmospheric pressure, filling every chamber of her mind, flattening nuance, narrowing possibility, repeating its single, terrible argument with tireless certainty. The backpack bore down on her as if gravity itself had shifted, drawing everything in her toward the same conclusion. The echo was deafening now, an unbroken hum that tried to convince her there was only one way to make the weight stop. The backpack felt heavier than it ever had before, pressing her toward the abyss. And then, something unexpected happened. Not a rescue. Not a revelation. Not relief. A pause. A hairline fracture in the noise. In the middle of that crushing interior weather, another sensation rose. Not as a thought, but as a knowing that traveled through her body like a cold bell. Clear. Startling. Unmistakable. *"This is not safe."* It did not argue with the echo. It did not offer hope. It did not paint a future. It simply named the moment for what it was. A threshold. A danger. A place no one is meant to stand alone. The echo had spent years convincing her that it was her voice. That its language was truth. That its conclusions were hers. But this knowing did not sound like the echo. It did not shout. It did not accuse. It did not demand. It witnessed. And in that witnessing, something essential returned to her. The smallest sliver of authorship. The faint but living awareness that whatever was speaking inside her, it was not the whole of her. That there was a part of her still capable of recognizing harm. Still capable of choosing protection. Still capable of reaching. Her chest tightened. Her breath shook. The room felt both distant and too close. But beneath it all, that quiet clarity remained, steady as a hand on her back. *"This is not something I can carry alone."* The well was deep. The echo was loud. The weight was immense. But somewhere within the pressure, Eliza felt the first true counterforce she had known in a long time. Not strength. Not certainty. Connection. The instinct to turn outward.

The instinct to let herself be found. And though she did not yet know how, or who, or what words would come, something in her had already begun to move away from the edge. Not toward answers. But toward help. Toward voice. Toward the simple, defiant act of not disappearing inside the echo's story. Toward the first small interruption in its reign. Because even at the brink, even in the narrowest place of the self, there can still arise a knowing that does not belong to the darkness. A knowing that says: *"I am here. This matters. I need someone."* And that knowing, fragile as it felt, was not an ending. It was the beginning of the break in the wall. She looked inward. All she could see was darkness. An imagined quiet. A seductive promise that the ache could finally stop. And for a moment, that promise shimmered with a dangerous softness, like deep water reflecting moonlight. Then something else moved. Not a thought. Not a sentence. A warmth. A tiny flicker. A remembered sensation before it became an image. Her grandmother's hand in hers. Small. Human. Unmistakably alive. She felt it as she used to feel it, not as memory but as presence. The particular way her grandmother's thumb traced slow, absent circles against her palm, as if drawing invisible constellations meant only for the two of them. The quiet steadiness of that touch. The way it anchored her to her own body. To the room. To being. The warmth of her smile rose next, soft and luminous, like a lamp lit in another season. And with it, the gentleness that had always carried an unspoken sentence beneath every word: *"you are here, and that matters."* It was not a command. It was not a solution. It was not even hope, not yet. It was recognition. The way her grandmother used to look at her, not as something broken, not as a problem waiting to be solved, but as someone already whole in her becoming. Already worth loving. Already worth staying for. The unwavering belief she had carried in Eliza's unfolding life, the way she spoke to her as though her future were something precious and possible. As though Eliza were not a weight on the world, but a gift moving through it. That memory did not erase the darkness. But it punctured it. Like a pinprick in a sealed room. Like the first star through cloud. And through that tiny opening, something else entered. Breath. A quiver of presence. The faint return of feeling to places that had gone numb. Eliza's chest rose, unevenly. Her hands trembled. But they were her hands. She could feel them. She could feel the air against her skin. She could feel the ache.

And the warmth. And the fact of herself still being here to feel anything at all. The echo did not vanish. The well did not close. The backpack did not fall away. But the story inside her shifted. For the first time in what felt like a lifetime, there were two voices in the dark. And one of them remembered love. One of them remembered being held. One of them did not argue or accuse or demand. It simply remained, steady as that remembered hand, saying nothing, yet carrying everything. And in that quiet companionship, Eliza felt the smallest movement away from the edge. Not a leap. Not a rescue. Just a turn. A turning of attention. A turning of breath. A turning back toward the part of her that still knew the texture of gentleness. She did not suddenly want answers. She did not suddenly feel strong. But she felt *connected*. To memory. To warmth. To the possibility that the echo was not the only thing living inside her. And that was enough, in that moment, to keep her where she was. Enough to let the flicker stay. Enough to let the next breath come. Enough to let the story continue. The memory did not argue with the echo. It didn't have to. It simply existed. And because it existed, something else did too. Presence. Warmth. A counterweight to the cold arithmetic of despair. The flicker did not banish the darkness. It did not silence the echo. But it interrupted it. Like a single match struck in a cavern. Small. Trembling. Undeniably real. That light did not fill the space. But it named it. It revealed that the dark was not infinite. Only unlit. The flicker drew breath the way embers draw oxygen, fed by something older than logic, deeper than language. A raw, untheorized instinct to remain. To stay. To keep the pulse moving forward one beat at a time. It was not hope yet. It was survival's quiet cousin. A bodily knowing that whispered, without words, "*not this way.*" Eliza stumbled back from the inner edge. Not with grace. Not with certainty. With the awkward, shuddering movement of someone rediscovering gravity. Her breath broke open, ragged at first, like air entering lungs that had forgotten how to receive it. She felt herself sway, not forward, but inward. Back into her chest. Back into her hands. Back into the undeniable, unglamorous labor of being alive. Inhale. A tremor. Exhale. The well did not vanish. The echo did not leave. It hovered. It lingered. It still spoke. But it no longer owned the entire sky. Its voice, once absolute, now had edges. Its certainty had cracked. Its monologue had become only one sound among others. There was breath now. There was sensation. There was the remembered warmth still glowing faintly in her palm. The echo was no longer the author. Only a noise in the room. And in that narrow opening, that fragile corridor between what had been and what might yet be, something clear finally formed. She could not carry this alone. She could not outthink this place. She could not outmuscle it. She could not will herself free. She did not need more endurance. She needed help. The knowing rose not as defeat, but as alignment. Like the body remembering its own design. Like a child's first cry, not a sign of weakness, but proof of life. Proof of connection. Proof that we are built to call out when the weight becomes too much for one spine. For the first time in a long while, that realization did not bruise her. It steadied her. It felt like instinct. Like ancient intelligence. Like the beginning of a return. And somewhere beneath the echo, beneath the well, beneath the years of collected stone, another sentence began to form. Not loud. Not triumphant. But quietly insistent. "*You do not have to do this by yourself.*" And in that sentence, barely audible yet impossibly strong, the path back toward the world began to open.

The Climb

What came after that moment was not a miracle. It was a movement. Small. Trembling. Human. A shift so slight it might have gone unnoticed by anyone else, but to Eliza it felt like the earth adjusting beneath her feet. The first step was the hardest because it required language. Because it meant turning toward the sealed chamber of silence and pressing her palm against its door. Because it meant letting another voice enter the dark. It meant saying, out loud, the words she had rehearsed only in fear. "*I am not okay. I cannot carry this alone. The weight has become too much.*" Her hand shook as she reached for the phone, fingers unsteady as if they were relearning how to be hands. When her voice finally came, it barely sounded like her own. It arrived thin, threaded with tremor, carrying fear. Carrying shame. Carrying the fragile honesty of someone stepping into the open without armor, skin still marked by the cold of the well. On the other end, there was no shock. No sharp intake of breath. No attempt to rearrange her pain into something easier to hear. Only presence. A voice that did not rush her. That did not interrupt. That did not reach immediately for solutions. A voice that made room. It listened as if her words were not something to be solved, but something to be held. As if her trembling sentences were not problems, but offerings. As if her truth, even in its broken cadence, deserved air. And in that listening, something inside her loosened. The echo did not vanish. The well did not close. But for the first time, they were not the only sounds in the space. Another witness had entered the dark. Another breath was moving where only hers had been. And with that, the inner landscape changed. Not dramatically. Not suddenly. But enough. Enough for a thin rope of connection to lower itself into the depths. Enough for the walls to stop feeling infinite. Enough for the silence to lose its monopoly. Through that first reaching, a path began to form. They helped her find a therapist. Someone trained not to fear the depths. Someone who knew how to sit inside the architecture of pain without needing to escape it. Someone who could help her map the well, trace its edges, understand its echoes. Someone who could stand beside her as she learned how to open the backpack, brick by careful brick, without being crushed beneath it. And so the climb began. Not as an ascent toward some glittering summit. But as a daily turning. A series of deliberate movements. A hand finding purchase. A foot testing ground. A breath taken when it would have been easier not to notice breathing at all.

Some days, progress was nothing more than showing up. Sitting in a room. Letting words arrive in their own time. Learning to name what lived inside her without flinching. Other days, it was the slow work of unpacking. Of lifting one brick at a time and discovering what it had been built from. Old grief. Quiet fear. Stories she had mistaken for facts. Beliefs that had hardened into posture. Each brick set aside made her lighter. Not weightless. But lighter. And in the spaces left behind, air began to move. The climb was not graceful. It was not continuous. There were slips. Long pauses. Days when the ground felt just as far away as ever. But there were also moments. Small ledges. Unexpected rests. Times when she would catch herself breathing more easily, standing a little straighter, feeling the backpack shift from destiny into something she could touch. What she was learning, slowly, was this: climbing is not always upward. Sometimes it is inward. Sometimes it is simply the courage to keep one hand open. To keep asking for support. To keep allowing the presence of others to share the load. And with every honest word spoken, every session entered, every brick lifted and examined, Eliza was no longer only surviving the well. She was learning its contours. She was finding her way. She was, in the quietest, most uncelebrated ways, beginning to rise. Therapy was not gentle in the way comfort is gentle. It was gentle in the way excavation is gentle. Slow. Intentional. Sometimes exhausting. Sometimes unbearably tender. Together, they began the work of unpacking. She learned to lift each brick into the light. To name it. To trace where it had come from. To feel its weight without letting it define her strength. Some were slick with old grief. Some sharp with self-doubt. Some so familiar she hadn't realized she'd been carrying them for years. One by one, she examined them. One by one, she set them down. Each brick released did not erase the past, but it altered her posture toward it. Her shoulders shifted. Her breath found new space. The backpack did not disappear, but it grew lighter. More negotiable. Less absolute. The climb was not clean. There were days when the weight returned without warning. Mornings when old gravity reasserted itself. Moments when the well seemed to deepen again beneath her feet. But now, she was no longer climbing in the dark.

She had language. She had tools. She had witnesses. And she had learned the most important thing of all: setbacks were not proof of failure. They were proof that she was still in motion. Still reaching. Still choosing, again and again, to place her hands on the stone and pull herself toward air. With time, the stones she set aside began to tell a different story. Arranged on the ground, they no longer formed a burden. They became markers. Evidence. A map of where she had been and how far she had traveled. Some days she traced them with her eyes, not to relive their weight, but to remember her capacity to lift. To remember the strength that had been there even when she could not feel it. Strength, she learned, does not always announce itself. Sometimes it whispers. Sometimes it simply stays. As weeks folded into months, the well changed too. It did not vanish, but it widened. Its edges softened. The echo, once so certain, began to falter, tripping over new words she had learned to speak. "*Pause. Breathe. Name it. This is a feeling, not a verdict.*" The echo still tried to author her days, but now it was interrupted by footnotes of care, by margins filled with compassion, by a steady editorial voice that asked better questions. And Eliza began to live differently. Not dramatically. Not all at once. But in the quiet ways that last. She asked for help before the weight grew unbearable. She rested without apology. She chose nourishment over endurance. She learned the dignity of stopping. The courage of saying "*enough for today*". She learned that carrying less did not make her smaller. It made her more herself. On certain mornings, she still felt the strap across her shoulders. Still sensed the familiar pull. But she also felt something else now. Balance. Choice. The knowledge that she could set the pack down for a while. That she could ask someone to help hold it. That she could open it and rearrange what remained. The climb continued. It always would. But it no longer felt like escape. It felt like inhabiting her life with both feet on the ground and her eyes open to the sky. And when she looked back into the well, she no longer saw only darkness.

She saw the place she had learned to listen. To ask. To begin. She had not defeated the weight. She had learned how to carry herself.

The First Fracture

The first crack did not arrive as hope. It arrived as confusion. It was small. Almost unremarkable. A brief, fleeting pause in the middle of one of the echo's familiar refrains. The voice rose as it always did, fluent, confident, rehearsed. But this time, something in her faltered. Not the sadness. Not the exhaustion. The certainty. For the first time, the words did not land like truth. They landed like language. She noticed their shape. Their rhythm. Their repetition. The way they always reached for the same conclusions, regardless of the day, the evidence, the memory. The echo spoke as if it had already written the ending and was merely forcing every moment to agree. And in that noticing, something in her shifted. It was not a thought so much as a sensation. A subtle misalignment. Like a shoe on the wrong foot. Like hearing her name spoken in a voice that mimicked her mother's but was not her mother's. Familiar, yet wrong. She realized, with a quiet, startled clarity: "*I don't remember choosing these words.*" The sentence did not arrive with fireworks. It did not announce itself. It surfaced the way a bubble rises from deep water, delicate and undeniable. And once it reached the surface, it changed the quality of the air. Because if she had not chosen these words, then perhaps they were not her voice. If they were not her voice, then perhaps they were not her truth. The echo continued, as it always had. But now it sounded... different. Slightly off-tempo. Slightly exposed. Its authority thinned. Its edges blurred. It no longer filled the entire chamber. There was space around it. A margin. A gap. And into that gap, something new stepped. Not an answer. A question. It hovered gently, almost shyly, as if unsure it was allowed to be there. *"Is this the only way to see this?"* The question did not banish the darkness. It did not lift the weight from her shoulders. But it cracked the wall. A hairline fracture in the stone. A place where light, if it ever came, might one day enter. She felt it in her body before she understood it in her mind. A softening behind the ribs. A loosening at the throat. As though a window had been unlatched somewhere deep inside, letting in a thread of unfamiliar air. The echo still spoke. But now it had competition. Not from optimism. Not from certainty. But from awareness. And awareness, she would come to learn, is where every undoing begins.

From that moment on, she started listening differently. Not just to what the voice said, but to how it said it. How quickly it leapt. How mercilessly it concluded. How little evidence it ever truly needed. She began to hear its habits. Its preferences. Its favourite accusations. She started to notice when it arrived. What summoned it. What fed it. She watched it the way one watches weather. Curious. Cautious. No longer convinced it was the sky itself. The echo had lost something it could never quite recover. Infallibility. And in its place, something infinitely more powerful had been born. A witness. Not to her failure. To her inner life. The first fracture did not free her. But it made freedom imaginable. And sometimes, imagination is the first door. The echo had always worn the mask of her inner wisdom. It called itself honesty. It called itself realism. It called itself the voice that "tells it like it is." For years, she had bowed to it as though it were some stern guardian of truth. But now, standing inside that first fragile fracture, she began to see its habits. The way it interrupted her. The way it rushed to speak before she could even finish feeling. The way it leapt ahead of experience, answering questions she had not yet fully asked, closing doors she had not yet touched. One evening, she caught it mid-sentence. The familiar tone rose automatically, predictably, like a reflex the body performs before the mind arrives. And something in her simply thought, with a softness that surprised her: "There you are again." Not "*there I am. There you are.*"

The difference was almost microscopic. A shift no one else could see. But inside her, it was tectonic. There was distance in that noticing. A hairline space between the speaker and the one listening. And in that narrow corridor of awareness, a fragile new presence stepped forward. The witness. She began to hear the patterns. The repetition. The way the accusations merely changed costumes. The way the same verdict returned wearing a hundred different accents. Failure. Burden. Not enough. Always the same conclusion, only rearranged. The echo was not responding to her life. It was reciting. Performing. Looping a script it had memorized long before this particular day, this particular moment, this particular breath. And for the first time, Eliza wondered, not angrily, not even bravely, but honestly: "If this voice were truly me... why does it never listen?" The question did not banish the echo. It did not drive it from the well. But it unsettled it. It cracked something in its posture. It loosened its grip from the roots of her identity and shifted it, ever so slightly, into another realm. From *who she was* to *what was happening.* From essence to experience. From identity to weather. She did not yet know who she was beneath it. That landscape was still largely unmapped. But she knew this: The echo was a sound. And she was the one hearing it. And that meant, even here, even now, there was more of her than its voice. There was the one who could notice. The one who could pause. The one who could ask. The one who could feel the difference between a storm and the sky that holds it. And in that knowing, faint but undeniable, another presence began to take shape. Not loud. Not triumphant. But real. Awareness. And awareness, once born, does not disappear again. It may dim. It may retreat. But it remembers itself. It learns the shape of its own seeing. And slowly, quietly, it begins to widen the inner world. Not by force. By light.

The Memory That Would Not Bend

The memory did not arrive with drama. It arrived the way real things often do. Soft. Unannounced. Ordinary. The memory did not bend to the echo's pressure. It did not shrink or sour or rearrange itself to fit the old narrative. It stood where it was, steady as a stone placed gently on the ground. Eliza kept washing the mug, her hands moving through the familiar motions, while something inside her remained utterly still, attentive. Warm water sliding over porcelain. A thin ribbon of steam lifting into the air. The small, domestic music of a life still being lived. The echo circled, unsettled now. It repeated itself, sharpened its tone, reached for skepticism, for dismissal, for doubt. But the memory would not argue back. It did not need to. The echo was murmuring as it always did, stitching its familiar narrative through her thoughts, when an image surfaced without asking permission. It had weight. Not the crushing kind. The grounding kind. Her grandmother's hands. Not the version the echo usually summoned. Not the faded, distant outline, flattened by time and reinterpretation. But the living memory. The warmth. The faint tremor. The way those hands had once cupped her face and said her name as if it were something precious, something that required gentleness. As if her very existence deserved careful handling. The echo moved quickly to claim it. "She only loved you because she had to. It didn't mean what you think it meant. You're romanticizing it." But the memory did not dissolve. It stayed. It held its shape. Eliza felt it not in her thoughts, but in her body. A warmth spreading low and slow through her chest. A subtle easing in her breath, like a knot loosening without announcement. The remembered pressure of thumbs at her jaw. The exact cadence of her name spoken slowly, deliberately, as if the world had time for it. As if *she* had time. The echo tried again. "You're remembering it wrong." And something inside her answered, before language could assemble itself: "No. I'm remembering it true." There was a texture to this memory the echo could not counterfeit or mimic. It did not argue. It did not accuse. It did not conclude. It did not rush toward meaning or verdict. It simply existed. Complete. Self-contained. Uninterested in proving anything. It was not a story. It was a sensation. Not an idea. A presence.

It did not pull her backward into longing, nor forward into despair. It held her exactly where she was. At the sink. In her body. In the warmth of water and the quiet persistence of breath. The memory did not demand to be interpreted. It only asked to be felt. And as she let herself feel it, something extraordinary happened. The echo spoke. But the memory did not answer. It did not defend itself. It did not explain itself. It did not fracture under inspection. It remained. Like a smooth stone at the bottom of a river, unbothered by the current. Like a flame in a draftless room. Like a truth that did not need language to survive. For the first time, Eliza experienced what it meant for something inside her to be unbendable. A piece of reality the echo could not tilt. A warmth it could not drain of color. A moment it could not recruit into its autobiography of ruin. This memory did not belong to the fortress. It did not live in the well. It lived in her. In her nerves. In her breath. In the quiet intelligence of her body that had known love before it ever learned doubt. Eliza noticed how different it felt from the echo. The echo was always urgent, always pushing, always insisting on an ending. This memory asked for nothing. It did not demand belief. It did not seek permission. It simply *was*. A quiet truth resting in her body like a held breath finally released. And in that moment, something else became clear. The echo relied on force. On repetition. On volume. But this memory carried a different authority. It came from lived contact. From skin and warmth and presence. From a time when she had been seen without performance. Named without condition. The echo tried once more, softer now, almost pleading. "You're clinging to it because you need it." And Eliza felt the answer rise, calm and unafraid: "Yes. And that doesn't make it false." The sink water continued to run. The steam thinned and drifted away. The kitchen remained exactly as it had been. But inside her, a quiet recalibration was taking place. She was learning the difference between a voice that consumed and a memory that nourished. Between something that hollowed her out and something that restored shape.

This was not hope in its grand, luminous form. It was something older. More elemental. A remembering of being held without explanation. Of being loved without negotiation. Of being named as worthy before she had ever learned to doubt it. The memory did not fix her. It did not erase the echo. But it marked a boundary the echo could not cross. And Eliza understood, with a growing steadiness, that there were truths inside her the darkness could not rewrite. Places it could not enter. Memories that would not bend. They would wait. Quiet. Patient. Until she was ready to listen again. And standing there, hands in warm water, steam on her skin, a single mug turning slowly beneath her palms, Eliza understood something without needing to think it. Not everything inside her was constructed. Not everything had been edited. Not everything was born of the echo. Some things had arrived before it. Before the fortress. Before the well. Before the long apprenticeship to doubt. Some things were older than the siege. This memory was one of them. It did not carry the echo's sharp edges. It did not speak in ultimatums or rehearsed conclusions. It did not shrink her or weigh her down. It expanded her. Quietly. Gently. It made room. And in that room, Eliza felt herself again not as a problem to be solved, but as a presence. A breathing, sensing, living being whose body still remembered warmth. Still recognized care. Still knew the difference between cruelty and tenderness without needing to argue it into existence. The echo had no answer for this kind of knowing. Because it lived below language. Because it did not ask to be believed. It simply was. And in the face of that small, unmovable truth, the echo did something it had not done before. It faltered. Just slightly. A hair's breadth of silence. A thinning. A pause so brief it might have gone unnoticed, if she had not been listening so closely. But she felt it. The way you feel a sudden opening in a crowded room. The way you feel air move when a door is cracked somewhere you cannot see. In that pause, something else had space to breathe. Eliza stood there, hands in warm water, steam soft against her face, heart moving in its quiet, stubborn rhythm, and let the memory rest inside her without commentary. Without translation. Without turning it into evidence for or against anything. She let it be what it was.

And as she did, she understood this, not as a thought but as a bodily certainty: The echo may speak loudly. But it does not speak for everything. There are other inhabitants here. Other rooms. Other histories. Other truths that do not require permission. And they, too, are her. This did not end the darkness. It did not undo the years. It did not rebuild the world in a moment. But it changed the rules of it. Because now, when the echo spoke, it was no longer the only voice in the house. There was also warmth. There was also memory. There was also the quiet, unarguable fact of having once been held with love. And that meant something inside her had never been completely overtaken. Something had survived. Something had been waiting. And in that waiting lived the first real promise of return. The echo circled it, searching for a way in. Trying to sand down its edges. Trying to drain it of color, of meaning, of weight. Like wind worrying a stone, it pressed and whispered, hoping time itself would erode what could not be carried away. But the memory remained stubbornly itself. It did not say she was perfect. It did not promise safety forever. It did not erase the years that followed. It only said: *"This happened. This was real. You were loved here."* And the words did not float. They settled. They anchored. They sank into her the way warmth sinks into skin. And for the first time, Eliza understood something that startled her with its simplicity. The echo could rearrange her interpretations. It could bruise her present. It could even trespass into her past, pacing its corridors, rearranging the furniture of meaning. But it could not fully possess her lived moments. There were parts of her history that had fingerprints. Temperatures. Tones. The hush of breath in a room. The particular gold of an afternoon. The weight of a hand. There were moments too embodied to be edited, too felt to be re-scripted. Not stories she had been told, but weather she had lived inside.

She stood there longer than necessary, hands still in the water, heart strangely steady, the cool threading between her fingers like a quiet vow. The world had not softened. Nothing had been fixed. And yet something had settled into place. Realizing: the echo worked in stories. It thrived on rearrangement. On narration without flesh. But this, this was a memory. And memory carried something the echo did not. Life. Pulse. Texture. A warmth that did not need permission to exist. Not a solution. Not a rescue. But a seam in the darkness. A thread that would not snap. Something woven into her that could be tugged, stretched, even hidden beneath layers of years, but not removed. And in that unmovable remembering, Eliza felt it. Not happiness. Not even hope. But something just as powerful. Ground. Ground. Not the triumphant kind that announces itself with fireworks and declarations. Not the kind that sweeps a person suddenly into light. But the quieter ground. The kind you feel first in your feet. The simple, unmistakable fact of something solid beneath you. A surface that does not vanish when you lean into it. A presence that answers weight with resistance. Eliza felt it as a subtle settling. As though something inside her had finally found a place to rest that did not immediately give way. Her breath slowed without instruction. Her shoulders softened without argument. The constant inner tilt toward the well eased, just enough for her to stand without bracing. The echo was still there. It did not retreat. It did not apologize. It resumed its pacing, its muttering, its old choreography of doubt and dismissal. But now, its words landed differently. They did not dissolve her on contact. They passed through a space that had not existed before. A narrow, living margin between what was spoken and who was listening. She began to notice that margin everywhere. In the way a thought rose and fell like a sound rather than a command. In the way emotion moved through her like weather instead of architecture. In the way sadness could ache without defining the shape of her entire being. This was new. Not because the pain was gone. But because she was no longer inside it without edges. The memory had not cured her. It had not rescued her. It had not solved the riddle of the echo. It had simply reminded her that her inner world was not made of only one substance. There was stone. Yes. And shadow. And old, echoing corridors. But there was also warmth. There was touch. There were moments that had entered her not as stories, but as experiences. Lived. Felt. Carried in nerve and breath and muscle.

And those moments had their own gravity. Their own authority. Their own way of saying, without persuasion or defence: "*I was here. And you were here too.*" From that day forward, Eliza did not listen in the same way. When the echo spoke, part of her still trembled. Part of her still tightened. Part of her still believed. But another part of her began quietly turning toward sensation. Toward memory. Toward what her body knew without commentary. The warmth of a mug in her hands. The steadiness of her pulse. The way air filled her lungs and left again. The way certain songs softened something without asking permission. These became her counterweights. Not arguments. Anchors. And slowly, without spectacle, her inner world began to change its geometry. The well was still there. The echo still called from its depths. But there were also footholds now. Ridges. Places where light touched the stone and did not vanish. And in those places, Eliza learned something that would become one of the quiet foundations of her healing: She was not only the one who heard the echo. She was also the one who felt the ground. And as long as ground existed, so did the possibility of standing.

The Second Sound

At first, she thought the silence meant the echo had gone. A sudden clearing. A curtain finally drawn back. It hadn't. It was still there, pacing its familiar corridors, repeating its well-worn scripts, looping its old weather through the chambers of her mind. The echo did not need permission. It lived in the architecture. But something else had begun to surface beneath it. Not in opposition. Not in argument. Not as a challenger raising its voice. More like a current under a tide. A pressure under the visible movement. A sound so soft she almost missed it. It did not speak in full sentences. It did not offer conclusions. It did not tell her who she was. It did not build stories or issue verdicts. It felt more like sensation than language. Like the low hum of something still working when the power is supposed to be out. A hidden generator. A pulse behind the walls. She noticed it in the pauses. In the half-second after the echo finished a thought, when the words fell away and something remained, faint but undeniable. In the space between her breath leaving and returning. That small, suspended nowhere where the body waits to be filled again. At first it registered only as discomfort. A faint resistance. A quiet friction. The way the body shifts before the mind knows why. The way your foot pulls back from a surface that is too hot before pain has time to announce itself. A reflex older than explanation. A knowing that did not carry a story, only a signal. It was not loud enough to name. Not clear enough to trust. It did not arrive with relief. It arrived with unease. With a subtle undoing of the echo's certainty. As if somewhere inside her, a second instrument had begun to tune itself, sending out a note that did not match the familiar song. And though it barely rose above the noise, it changed the air. It altered the shape of the quiet. It made the silence feel... inhabited. As if something in her had not gone out after all.

Then one morning, as the echo unfurled another familiar indictment, rolling it out with its usual certainty, its practiced precision, something inside her did not agree. Not loudly. Not in protest. Not with words sharpened for battle. Just, didn't move. The echo said its thing. It performed its old weather. And this other presence stayed where it was. Quiet. Unimpressed. It did not correct the echo. It did not counter it. It simply did not collapse.

Eliza became aware of it the way you become aware of a second instrument in a piece of music you've heard a hundred times. Not a new song. A deeper one. Suddenly there is depth where there was only melody. A resonance where there was only tune. Something holding the notes from underneath. Something giving the sound a floor. A body. A place to land. She felt it when her chest rose on its own, breath arriving without consultation. When her hands reached for warmth before her thoughts could issue permission. When her eyes lingered on small, unnecessary beauties. The particular kindness of light on a wall.

The brief, brave green between cracks in the pavement. The way steam lifted from a cup like a private language. Things that did not advance a narrative. Things that did not fix anything. But insisted, gently, on being felt. And in those moments, she sensed it again. That second sound. Not as a voice, but as a steadiness. A quiet gravity. As if somewhere inside her, a deeper string had begun to vibrate. Not to drown the echo out. But to make it incomplete. To remind her body of a wider music than the one it had been taught to hear. The echo spoke in narratives. It built its kingdoms out of sentences, arranged her world into verdicts and rehearsed explanations. This other sound spoke in continuance. In the grammar of living. It sounded like breath moving through her without asking permission. Like hunger. Like the quiet insistence of a heartbeat that had never consulted her despair before doing its work. A labor that did not pause for belief. A devotion that did not require hope. When she listened closely, it carried a tone the echo never used. Kindness, but without sentiment. Truth, but without cruelty. Presence, without performance. It did not decorate. It did not accuse. It did not persuade. It simply *was.* Sometimes it felt like a question: *"What if this thought isn't law?"* Not an argument. An opening. Sometimes it felt like a statement made of bone and blood: *"You are still here."* Not encouragement. A fact. A pulse you could place your fingers against. She realized, slowly, reverently, the way one approaches something sacred without knowing its name, that this sound had been there the whole time. Buried under years of noise. Under conclusions. Under the echo's constant weather. It had lived beneath the commentary, under the rubble of interpretation, inside the body that kept waking her, feeding her, carrying her forward when she had stopped believing in forward at all. It had waited without drama. Without speeches. Without demanding to be heard. And now, as the echo continued its pacing, this deeper sound did not try to replace it. It simply remained. Steady. Enduring. A current beneath the story. The life under the language. It had survived every version of her. The child. The grieving girl. The exhausted adult. The one who almost forgot herself. It had passed through each season without needing to be named, without needing to be rescued, carrying its quiet work from body to body, breath to breath, like an underground spring moving beneath changing landscapes.

It had waited in the simplest places. In breath. In sensation. In the way her body leaned, again and again, toward light. Toward warmth. Toward the almost-invisible mercies that still reached for her even when she did not reach back. The echo told stories about her life. It arranged her into explanations, into causes and endings. This other sound was her life. Not poetic. Not tragic. Living. A metabolism. A motion. A persistence that did not care whether she called it meaning. It showed up in the way her feet found the ground in the dark. In the way her stomach asked for nourishment. In the way her eyes kept searching for color, even when her mind had given up on beauty. And once she noticed it, truly noticed it, she could no longer unhear it. It threaded itself through everything. Through thought. Through silence. Through the ordinary choreography of being. It did not drown the echo. It did not need to. But it outlasted it. Like tide under weather. Like bedrock under argument. Like a pulse under every story ever told about it. And in that enduring undercurrent, Eliza felt something she had not felt in a long time. Not certainty. Not answers. But company. A presence that did not leave when the noise returned. A quiet something that stayed with her inside her own skin. As if, after years of walking through herself like an abandoned house, she had finally realized there was still a light on somewhere.

The Other Voice.

At first, Eliza didn't recognize it as a voice at all. It had no vocabulary. No accusations. No instructions. It didn't arrive in sentences. It arrived as sensation. A loosening in her chest when she inhaled. A subtle warmth in her palms. The smallest easing, like a knot deciding on its own, to soften. A quiet undoing that did not announce itself. Something adjusting in the dark without asking for witness. The echo still spoke, relentless and fluent. It told stories about her past, rewrote her failures into identities, edited her memories until even joy felt suspicious. It sounded like thought. It sounded like truth. It carried the sharpness of certainty, the neatness of explanation. This did not. This felt like being. Like existence without commentary. Like a body remembering how to be a body. She noticed it one afternoon when she was sitting on the floor, back against the bed, the room washed in late light. The kind that turns dust into gold and makes the ordinary feel briefly sacred. The echo was doing what it always did, pulling old moments apart, twisting them into evidence, arranging the past into a familiar courtroom. And yet, beneath the cadence of that voice, beneath the practiced architecture of its conclusions, something in her body did not follow. Her shoulders dropped. Not because she told them to. Because they chose to. As if gravity had finally been granted permission. There was a breath. Deeper than the others. Unplanned. Unargued. It rose from somewhere lower than thought, somewhere older than explanation. And with it, a quiet internal sensation she could not translate into words. Only into texture. Like cool water moving under skin. Like the low vibration of a distant engine. Like standing barefoot on ground that is solid even when the air is not. This presence did not comment on the echo. It did not challenge it. It did not negotiate for space. It simply continued. Her heart continued. Her blood continued, tide after invisible tide. Her nerves continued sending small, necessary messages. Hunger. Fatigue. The ache to stretch. The reflex to turn her face toward warmth. The ancient choreography of a living thing still in motion. It did not ask her to believe anything. It did not promise relief. It did not offer meaning. It offered continuity. A quiet demonstration. A showing rather than a saying. That beneath every story she told about herself, something in her was still busy being here. Still tending the fires. Still moving the water. Still keeping time. And sitting there, in that late-light hush, Eliza felt the difference. The echo arranged her into narratives. This other voice did not arrange her at all. It held her in process. Not as a problem. Not as a conclusion. But as a living system. Ongoing. Unfinished. And, for the first time in a long while, not alone inside herself. The echo spoke in meaning. In explanations. In verdicts. In the architecture of why.

This other voice spoke in maintenance. In the quiet labor of keeping a living thing alive. It asked nothing. It proved something. It did not demand belief. It demonstrated presence. It did not persuade. It sustained. She began to find it in the margins of her days. In the way her eyes followed dust in sunlight, as if some small, ancient part of her still trusted brightness. In the instinct to wrap her arms around herself when she felt cold, becoming, without instruction, both shelter and sheltered. In the sudden, uninvited urge to step outside, or drink water, or rest her head against something steady. The cool honesty of a wall. The patience of a tree. The uncomplaining strength of the ground. It did not say, "You are worthy." It enacted worth. It fed her. Hydrated her. Healed microscopic tears. Kept the lights on in rooms she had forgotten how to enter. It kept her alive in thousands of microscopic ways that required no permission from despair. Ways that did not consult her stories. Ways that did not wait for hope to return before doing their work. And slowly, something inside her shifted. Not a breakthrough. Not a revelation dressed in lightning. A recognition. Like finally realizing the hum you've lived beside for years is not the building, but a living engine. The echo always spoke *about* her. This other voice moved *as* her. It lived in muscle memory. In breath rhythm. In the precise choreography of standing, swallowing, softening, turning. In the ancient intelligence of a body that knew how to persist long before she had words for suffering. She realized then that the echo, for all its volume, never once made her blink. Never once made her swallow. Never once turned her face toward the sun. It could narrate her pain. It could annotate her history. But it could not perform a single necessary act of living. This did. This quiet, sensory presence had carried her through every version of herself. Had learned her weight. Her pace. Her limits. Had adjusted. Adapted. Waited.

It had known when to speed her heart and when to slow it. When to flood her with warmth. When to call her toward rest. It was not dramatic. It did not make speeches. It did not demand to be believed. It was loyal. Tireless. Intimate in the way only something inside your own skin can be. And for the first time, Eliza understood something without thinking it. The loudest voice in a mind is not always the truest. Some truths do not shout. They breathe. They pulse. They lean, again and again, toward life. And once she felt it, really felt it, she could no longer pretend it wasn't there. A second voice. Not made of language. Made of living.

The Memory That Would Not Bend

The echo had always been a historian. A meticulous archivist of injury. It specialized in revision. In selective emphasis. In erasure disguised as clarity. It took her memories and ran them through its machinery, stripping them of context, draining them of color, filing them into evidence. It reduced living moments into exhibits. Every laugh became proof of naivety. Every hope, proof of foolishness. Every kindness was a transaction she had failed to earn. Nothing was spared. No warmth escaped its audit. No tenderness survived unaltered. Until one memory would not cooperate. It came to her without invitation, not as a thought, but as a feeling that rose unexpectedly while she was standing at the sink, hands in warm water, the ordinary intimacy of soap and heat grounding her in the moment. The small domestic ritual of being here. Of tending something. Suddenly, there was the smell of oranges. Not metaphorical. Not imagined. Real. Bright. Sharp. Sweet. It cut cleanly through the air, through the years, through the echo's rehearsed atmosphere. Her grandmother's kitchen. Sunlight slanting through thin curtains, turning dust into drifting gold. A small version of herself sitting on the counter, legs swinging, heels tapping softly against the cupboard. Sticky fingers offered up for inspection. A peel coiling like a bright ribbon on the table. Laughter. The sound of it. Unforced. Unafraid. Not performed. Not negotiated. A sound that rose because there was space for it to rise. The echo moved in at once, as it always did. Quick. Efficient. It tried to tell her it wasn't real. That it was exaggerated. That she had misunderstood. That even then, she had been difficult, burdensome, too much. That the warmth had been conditional. That the laughter had been luck. That the safety had been a story told backward. But something strange happened.

The memory did not dim. It did not fracture. It did not rearrange itself to fit the accusation. The warmth in it stayed warm. The light stayed light. The body-sense of being small and safe remained intact. It did not defend itself. It did not argue. It simply continued to be what it had been. A lived moment. A temperature. A particular gravity in the chest. A softness that had once been true and, inexplicably, still was. The echo repeated itself, sharper now, more insistent. It raised its voice. It tightened its language. It reached for its familiar tools. But the memory did not yield. It did not kneel to interpretation. It did not convert into a lesson. It stood in her like a room that would not be redecorated. Like a window that would not accept a different view. And in that quiet standoff, something in Eliza felt it. The echo could bend stories. But it could not bend what had been lived. This was not a narrative. This was a season that had once touched her skin. And for the first time, she saw it clearly: some memories are not held in the mind at all. They are held in the body. In scent. In heat. In the way a laugh once moved through a small chest without fear of being taken away. The echo kept speaking. But the oranges were still bright. The water was still warm. And somewhere inside her, a younger version of herself was still sitting in sunlight, legs swinging, hands sticky, entirely unaware that one day anyone would try to tell her this had not been enough. And the memory did not bend. And yet the image did not dissolve. It did not thin into doubt. It did not buckle under the familiar weight of the echo's voice. Her nervous system did not agree. Her chest responded before her thoughts could. A soft expansion. A loosening. As if some inner door, long rusted shut, had shifted a fraction on its hinges and let a breath of warmer air pass through. This memory did not argue. It did not defend itself. It did not gather evidence or sharpen explanations. It simply existed. Unedited. Untouched. Whole. And in that quiet resistance, something in Eliza stilled. The frantic internal weather paused. She realized, with a clarity that felt almost physical, that the echo had always needed her participation. Her attention. Her belief.

Her collapsing into its interpretations. This memory did not participate. It stood outside the echo's jurisdiction. Beyond its paperwork. Beyond its reach. It belonged to a part of her that had felt before it had learned to narrate. A part of her that remembered through skin and scent and sound. Through the way, safety once registered in her body. Through the way laughter had once lived without asking whether it was allowed. The echo could rewrite stories. But it could not rewrite sensation. It could reinterpret events. But it could not reach back far enough to erase what her nervous system had known. This memory was not a picture. It was a state. A climate. A way her body had once been held by the world. And it was still alive inside her, like a warmth that had never entirely left the bones. For the first time, she understood: Not all of her past was accessible to distortion. Some of it was stored too deep. Woven into her reflexes. Preserved in the way her breath slowed when she remembered warmth. In the way her shoulders dropped when she imagined light. In the small, involuntary permissions her body still gave itself. The echo spoke again. It always did. But now there was something it could not touch. A small, bright pocket of truth. Not proof against all darkness. But proof against total darkness. A place the echo could not enter without language, and language had no power there. And once she knew one memory had survived intact, she could no longer believe the echo's claim that everything in her had been ruined. Something essential had remained. Something uncorrupted. Something remembered how to feel held. Something that did not need to be convinced. It already knew.

The First Conversation

The echo had always spoken *through* her. It had worn her inner voice like a borrowed coat. Matched her tone. Used her memories. Quoted her fears. It had blended so perfectly into her internal atmosphere that she had never thought to ask where it ended, and she began. It had never needed to announce itself. It had lived in her grammar. In her cadence. In the familiar weight of her own thoughts. Until the memory of oranges. Until the warmth that refused to cool. Until something in her body answered the echo with silence. She was sitting on the edge of her bed when she noticed it, the way you notice a sound that doesn't belong to the room. A subtle misalignment. A chair not where it was supposed to be. A pressure that no longer fit perfectly inside her own thinking. The air felt fractionally different. As if a window somewhere inside her had been opened without her permission. "You're weak," the echo said, easily. Automatically. The sentence arrived the way it always had, already unpacked, already certain. And for the first time, the words landed differently. Not as truth. As a statement. As a voice. She didn't rush to agree. She didn't rush to fight. She simply noticed: *something just spoke.* Her breath caught. Not in panic. In attention. As if her body had leaned forward to listen. "Who is talking?" she whispered into the quiet room, the sound small, almost embarrassed to exist. The question hung there, thin as thread. The echo answered at once, sharper now, defensive in its certainty. "*You are. This is you. This is what you think.*" It moved quickly, as it always did, to reseal the seam it sensed opening. But the words no longer fused with her. They hovered. Like steam above water. Present, visible, but no longer indistinguishable from the surface beneath them. They floated. They separated. They did not sink. And something unfamiliar rose up beneath them. Not a sentence. Not an idea. A sensation. A faint tightening in her stomach. A subtle pull behind her ribs. A small, insistent gravity that did not carry language with it. The bodily knowing that precedes words. The feeling that comes before explanation.

The place where truth registers before it learns how to speak. It was not loud. It did not contradict. It did not accuse the echo of being wrong. It simply did not echo back. And in that tiny, almost invisible pause, Eliza felt it. The first space between a voice and the one who hears it. She placed a hand on her chest. Not ceremonially. Not to make a point. Just to locate herself. To give her attention somewhere to land. Beneath her palm, her heart was already working, already mid-sentence in a language older than words. The echo continued, filling the space the way it always had. It moved quickly into the quiet, the way smoke moves into an open room. "*Don't pretend. You've always known this. You've always felt this. This is just honesty.*" Her pulse was loud in her ears. A soft thunder. A small animal reminding her it was there. She swallowed. And then, very quietly, she said, "*No.*"

The word surprised her with its weight. It did not crack like a whip. It did not rise like a flag. It settled. Not dramatic. Not triumphant. Just present. A stone placed gently on the table of the moment. "*I feel something*," she continued, haltingly, as if she were speaking a language she had only just begun to learn. "*But I don't hear it speaking.*" The echo scoffed inside her, the familiar curl of disdain. "*Feelings lie. I don't.*" She closed her eyes. Turned her attention downward, the way she had begun to learn. Out of the noise. Out of the ceiling of thought. Into the body. Into the dark, interior rooms that did not argue, only registered. "*There's fear here,*" she said slowly. "*There's sadness. There's exhaustion.*" Each word landed as a bell struck gently. Not to announce. To locate. To name what was already resonating. "*But there's also warmth,*" she added, her brow softening as she felt it. "*And something, steady. Something that doesn't sound like you.*" The echo paused. It had never been described before. It had only been obeyed. It had lived unnamed, unquestioned, moving like weather no one thought to study. "*You're overthinking,*" it said finally. "*You're just trying to comfort yourself.*" She shook her head. A small movement. But real. A motion made not to persuade, but to align. "*Comfort doesn't sound like contempt,*" she replied. Her own voice felt unfamiliar.

Not in sound. In authorship. As if she were hearing herself speak from a slightly different place than usual. A place that did not lean on the echo for permission. "*You talk to me like I'm an enemy,*" she went on. "*Like I'm something to be managed. Corrected. Cut down to size.*" Her hand pressed a little more firmly into her chest. "*But when I listen to what's underneath, it doesn't.*" It doesn't rush. It doesn't threaten. It doesn't shrink her to make its point. It does not need to win. And in the quiet that followed her words, something in her body answered. Not with a sentence. With a steadiness. With a warmth that did not spike or retreat. With the simple, radical act of continuing. For the first time, Eliza was not inside the echo's monologue. She was in a conversation. The echo shifted tactics, as it always had when certainty began to fail. It softened its edges. Lowered its voice. Wrapped itself in concern. "*I'm protecting you. I'm preparing you. I'm keeping you from being disappointed again.*" And she felt the ache in that. Felt the old, familiar bruise beneath the words. Felt the truth braided into the cruelty, the way fear often disguises itself as foresight. For a moment, it trembled through her like a remembered weather. And for the first time, she didn't collapse into it. "*I think you're afraid,*" she said. The sentence did not strike. It opened. The room seemed to widen around her, as if air had been added where there had been none. The echo did not answer immediately. It lingered. Its silence unfamiliar. When it did speak, its certainty had thinned, like fabric worn translucent by years of rubbing. "*If I don't speak, who will?*" The question landed without its old authority. It sounded less like a declaration now. More like a need. She pressed her feet into the floor. Not grounding as a strategy. Not an exercise. Grounding as a recognition. As if she were finally acknowledging something that had been holding her all along. The quiet reliability of weight. The unarguable presence of contact. "*I will,*" she said. The words were not loud. They were not polished. They did not arrive with banners. But they were hers. They came from the same place her breath came from. The same place her warmth lived. "*And I won't speak to myself that way.*"

The echo did not disappear. It never did. It remained, as weather remains, as memory remains. But something irrevocable had happened. Something had shifted its axis. A line had been drawn. Not between light and darkness. But between voice and listener. Between something that spoke in her and something that could now speak back. The architecture of her inner world had changed. There was now a place to stand that was not the echo's mouth. And in that thin, trembling space between them, a new sound began to form. Not yet words. Not yet language. But a presence. A steadiness. A quiet interior clearing. A place inside her where the echo no longer ruled alone. Not silence. Company. A second awareness breathing beside the first. And for the first time, Eliza was not only being spoken to. She was listening.

The Unalterable Things

After the first conversation, Eliza stopped trying to defeat the echo. That surprised her. She had assumed healing would look like combat. Counterarguments. Proof. Clever rebuttals. The clash of brighter thoughts against darker ones, victory declared by volume or logic. But the echo was too skilled for that. It could turn any sentence inside out, lace doubt through certainty, rewrite facts until they sounded like confessions. It thrived on opposition. It fed on response. So she changed tactics. Instead of arguing, she began collecting. Not thoughts. Not explanations. Moments. Small, often ordinary instants that slipped past story and landed directly in sensation. She noticed the ones the echo struggled with. The ones it rushed past. The ones it tried to shrink or mock or reinterpret because it couldn't erase them completely. They had a particular texture. A density. They lived in the body before they lived in language. They registered first as warmth, or easing, or a subtle shift of breath before the mind could draft a headline. The first one came unexpectedly. She was washing her hands, warm water running over her wrists, the simple ritual of heat and movement anchoring her in the present, when she caught the scent of soap, citrus, and something floral underneath. Bright and clean and faintly sweet. Without warning, her chest loosened. Just slightly. The way a clenched fist releases one finger at a time. The echo stirred at once. "*It doesn't mean anything,*" it said quickly. It's old reflex. It's rush to annotation. But the memory didn't respond. It didn't need to. She remembered being eight, standing on a stool in her grandmother's kitchen, hands submerged in a sink too big for her, laughing because the bubbles kept climbing her arms. Soft towers of them. Collapsing. Reforming. The absurd delight of being surprised by joy. Water sloshing. Sunlight trembling on the tiles. A voice nearby, not instructing, not correcting, just present. The sound of safety without a name. The echo waited for her to translate it. To turn it into a lesson. To give it a flaw. She didn't. She let it stay what it was. Warmth. Scent. The ghost of laughter in her ribs. Something unalterable. And she understood then what she was collecting. Not proof that her life had been good. But evidence that it had been *real.* Moments that had happened beneath interpretation. States that had lived in her before opinion could touch them. Experiences the echo could speak over, but not through.

She began to notice them everywhere after that. Tiny pockets of undistorted life. A swallow that felt satisfying. The relief of sitting down. The quiet pleasure of light finding the rim of a cup. They did not fix anything. They did not erase the echo. But they did something else. They refused to bend. And in their refusal, they taught her where to place her attention. Not on the loudest voice. But on the truest sensations. The ones that did not argue. The ones that simply continued. The memory came with heat, with the ache in her calves from balancing, with the sound of a radio humming softly nearby. Not the kind of remembering that arrives as pictures, but the kind that enters through the body first. Muscle. Temperature. Vibration. The echo tried to narrate. "*You were happier because you didn't know better.*" It reached, as it always did, for explanation, for diminishment. But the memory stayed whole. It did not argue. It did not defend itself. It simply was. Complete. Untouched. Still carrying the exact weather of that afternoon. She realized then: The echo could reinterpret meaning, but it couldn't change sensation. It could rearrange the story around the moment, but it could not reach into the moment itself and rewrite what her skin had known. So she began to look for those. She started writing them down, not as stories, but as fragments. Not chapters. Coordinates. The weight of a blanket fresh from the dryer. The sound of rain against the car roof when I don't have to go anywhere. The way my shoulders drop when someone says my name gently. She called them anchors. Not because they kept her from drifting, but because they let her feel where she already was. The echo scoffed at first. "*Sentimentality*", it sneered. "*Distraction*". It tried to turn them into smallness. Into denial. Into weakness. But she noticed something. The echo always spoke in conclusions. The anchors never did. They didn't tell her who she was. They didn't tell her what anything meant. They didn't promise a future or condemn a past. They reminded her that she existed. Over time, she learned the difference between memories the echo could bend and those it could not. The bendable ones were narrative-heavy. Stories about failure. About rejection. About not being enough. The echo loved those. It lived in them, expanded them, sharpened their edges, furnished them with implications and verdicts. They were elastic. They took shape around whatever the echo needed them to prove. But the unalterable memories were different. They were brief. Wordless. Often inconvenient. They arrived without permission. They did not wait to be interpreted. They appeared as sensations first and thoughts second, if at all. Like the time she cried in a grocery store aisle because a stranger helped her reach something from a high shelf and smiled without expectation. A small, ordinary kindness. Nothing cinematic. Nothing that fit neatly into a narrative of rescue or romance. The echo tried to call it weakness. Over-sensitivity. Neediness.

But her body remembered something else. The steadiness of another human close by. The shared gravity of standing. The way her breath had slowed. The way, for a brief and unremarkable moment, she had not felt alone inside her own outline. And she wrote that down too. Not the story. The slowing. Because that was the part that could not be taken from her. Or the afternoon she lay on the floor with her dog, counting breaths without meaning to, just syncing to the rise and fall of another living being. No intention. No exercise. Just two bodies sharing gravity. The echo attempted to frame it as avoidance. Withdrawal. Numbness. But the warmth at her side refused translation. The slow, reliable expansion beneath her palm refused to become a metaphor. It was weight. It was heat. It was life doing what life does when it feels safe enough to rest. She began to understand: the echo depended on isolation. It survived on the idea that she was sealed inside herself, cut off, separate, unreachably alone. These memories proved contact. With people. With animals. With the world. With herself. They were not dramatic. They did not announce connection. They enacted it. Quietly. Repeatedly. Through breath shared. Through glances exchanged. Through the simple physics of being near something alive. She didn't collect them to prove she was happy. That was never the point. Happiness was too fragile a banner. Too easy for the echo to tear down. She collected them because they proved something quieter and far more dangerous to the echo. That she was still here. Still sensing. Still responding. Still capable of being moved. Not fixed. Not healed. But permeable. Eventually, when the echo grew loud, when it began filling every corner of her inner room with its familiar weather, she would open her notebook and read only the fragments. No commentary. No interpretation. No defence. Just facts the body had recorded. Warm mug between my palms. Wind against my face on the bridge. Laughter surprising me mid-sentence. Small sentences. Unfinished. Unimpressed with explanation. The echo would protest. "*This doesn't erase anything.*" And she would nod. "I know," she'd say. "That's not why I keep them." She wasn't building an argument. She was building a counterweight. Brick by brick. Sensation by sensation. Moment by moment. Not to crush the echo. Not to banish it from her inner world. But to remind herself that even in the deepest well, some things do not fall. They remain. At the edges. In the body. In the quiet places the echo cannot colonize. Waiting. Not to save her. To be found.

The First Separation

It didn't happen during a crisis. There was no cliff-edge revelation, no sudden surge of strength, no moment arranged like a turning point. It happened in the middle of an ordinary thought. The kind that usually passes without leaving a trace. The echo was doing what it always did, narrating her existence with practiced certainty, stitching together fragments of memory into a familiar verdict, weaving its old weather through the corridors of her mind. It spoke in her voice. Wore her cadence. Borrowed the intimate tone of self-knowledge. "*You've always been like this. This is who you are.*" And then something faltered. Not the words themselves, but the way they landed. For the first time, Eliza noticed a delay. A fraction of a second where the sentence arrived before its meaning settled. A thin, unfamiliar space. Like hearing a sound echo off a wall you hadn't realized was there. Like feeling the floor dip where you believed it was solid. She felt it in her body before she understood it in her mind. A tightening, then a pause. A breath that stopped halfway in. A subtle, almost imperceptible recoil, the way the hand pulls back from heat before the thought of heat appears. The thought didn't feel authored. It felt delivered. That was the crack. She stayed very still, as if any sudden movement might shatter it. As if the noticing itself were a fragile glass between worlds. The echo continued, unaware it had been noticed. It pressed forward, confident, fluent, relentless. It stacked more sentences on the first. More familiarity. More proof. It moved as it always had, assuming there was no difference between speaking and being believed. But something had shifted its footing. The words were still there. The authority was not. For the first time, Eliza was not inside the sentence. She was standing where the sentence arrived. And in that almost-invisible relocation, that quiet inching back from the voice that had once filled the room, she felt it: the difference between a thought and the one who hears it. A difference so small it could be missed. A difference large enough to change the architecture of a life. She did not argue. She did not replace the sentence with a kinder one. She did not rush to name what was happening.

She simply remained. Breathing. Listening. Noticing the echo, echo. And in that noticing, a seam had opened. Between her and the voice she had always called herself. But Eliza was no longer listening the same way. She wasn't arguing. She wasn't resisting. She was observing. And in that observation, something extraordinary happened. The quality of the moment changed. The room did not, but her position within it did. She had stepped, almost without moving, from inside the voice to beside it. She realized the voice did not arise from her. It arrived to her. Like a transmission. Like a familiar weather system that moved through whether she consented or not. It behaved like a recording set on repeat, not like a living response. It did not adjust to the room, to her breath, to the present moment. It did not notice the temperature of the air or the way her shoulders had softened when she exhaled. It didn't notice her at all. That's when the sentence formed, not as a declaration, but as a recognition: "*This voice doesn't know what I'm doing right now.*" It didn't know she had placed her tongue gently against the back of her teeth. It didn't know her hands were resting in her lap, warm, slightly damp. It didn't know her feet were in contact with the floor. It didn't know she had just breathed out. The echo spoke in absolutes. Her awareness spoke in sensation. The echo spoke about who she was. Her body spoke about where she was. The difference was unmistakable once she saw it. It rang through her like a bell struck in an empty hall. The voice claimed authorship, but it had no access to her hands resting in her lap. No awareness of the weight of her feet on the floor. No curiosity about the warmth pooling in her chest as she breathed. It could inventory her past. It could predict her failure. But it could not feel a single thing she was feeling. It was loud. But it was not alive. And in that realization, something loosened. Not relief. Not hope. But a quiet uncoupling. A soft release of adhesion. As if two surfaces long pressed together had finally found the courage to separate. As if she had discovered, not a new voice, but the space in which voices appear. And in that space, she was still here. Breathing. Present. Unclaimed.

Distance.

The smallest, most essential distance. Not a chasm. Not a wall. A hairline fracture in the surface of things. Enough space for her to think, not as the voice, but *about* it. Enough room for a question to form without being swallowed the moment it appeared. Enough quiet to hear herself wondering, softly: "If this were truly me, wouldn't it know what I'm feeling right now?" The question did not challenge. It illuminated. The echo had no answer. It kept speaking, but its authority had shifted. The words were the same. The cadence familiar. But their gravity had changed. They no longer fell inward. They moved across. It was no longer a mirror. It was a broadcast. A transmission moving through a field that it did not control. And Eliza, for the first time, understood herself not as the speaker, but as the listener. Not the storm. The sky. That moment didn't silence the echo. It did not evaporate the old weather. But it changed its status. Irrevocably. It was no longer the narrator of her life. It was a sound occurring within it. One register among others. One current moving through a much larger sea. And beneath it, steady and wordless, something else remained. Her breath. Her body. Her presence. The quiet fact of being here. Waiting.

Where the Echo Fails

After the first separation, Eliza began to notice something else. Not just the voice. But what it fed on. Its diet. Its raw materials. The echo did not create from nothing. It scavenged. It drifted through her memory like a vandal through a gallery, smearing meaning across images that had once been whole. It did not destroy the canvases. It rewrote the plaques. It moved captions where they did not belong. It pressed its own commentary over moments that had never asked to be interpreted. It took scenes that were complex, tender, unfinished, and flattened them into evidence. A laugh became proof of foolishness. A mistake became proof of identity. A silence became proof of abandonment. It did not change the facts. It changed the frame. And in that reframing, whole lives could be reduced to a single accusation. And once she saw that, she began to watch it work. The echo would reach backward, pulling scenes from storage, lifting them into the air like exhibits in a trial it had already decided. "*See? You were always this. See? This is who you are.*" It spoke with the confidence of a judge who never had to leave the bench. At first, she believed it. Then one afternoon, without planning to, without setting out to contradict anything, she remembered something small. Something the echo had never needed. Not dramatic enough to recruit. Not important enough to weaponize. She was very young. Sitting on a floor warmed by sun. The light fell through a window at an angle, making dust in the air visible, each mote slow and unhurried. The faint, sweet smell of something baking somewhere else drifted in, not demanding attention, just being present. She was lining up stones she had collected, not for any reason, not to build or prove or finish, just because she liked the way they felt in her palm. Cool. Solid. Varied. Each one different. Each one real. They clicked softly when they touched. There was no story attached. No outcome. No evaluation. Just a child and a warm floor and the quiet pleasure of arranging weight. The echo arrived, as it always did, ready to claim it. But it hesitated. There was no failure to extract. No rejection to amplify. No future it could threaten. It searched the moment for a lesson and found only sensation. Texture. Temperature. The simple act of being absorbed in something that did not look back.

And in that hesitation, Eliza saw it. Where the echo fails. It fails where nothing is being proven. It fails where no identity is being built. It fails where life is not narrating itself. Because the echo cannot feed on presence. Only on story. And this memory was not a story. It was a state. And it remained, like those stones had remained in her hand, cool and unarguable, long after the echo had moved on in search of something it could bend. The memory rose not as a story, but as a sensation. Not arranged in sequence. Not framed. It came the way weather comes. Warmth on her forearms. Grit against skin. The soft, private pleasure of arranging. The almost inaudible sound of stones touching. The echo arrived, as it always did, ready to translate, to subtitle the moment, to press it into a sentence it could then reshape. It reached for the moment. And failed. It tried to bend it toward judgment, but there was no hook. No verdict embedded in the texture of sunlight. No accusation in the weight of a stone. No narrative hidden inside the simple fact of being a child, absorbed, unobserved, alive. The echo circled it, searching, like a bird looking for somewhere to land. It offered interpretations. Old phrases. Familiar angles. She didn't take them. Because the memory wasn't built from language. It was built from presence. It did not say anything about who she was. It did not define her. It did not locate her on any moral map. It only said that she had been there. Breathing. Touching. Existing. A body in a patch of warmth. A hand closing around something cool. A mind quiet enough to let sensation lead. The echo tried again, later, with another recollection. A night walk. Cool air. The sound of her own footsteps moving her forward. The faint scrape of soles against pavement. The brief, surprising comfort of a scarf pulled higher around her neck, the small cocoon of warmth it created under her chin. Again, it stumbled. There was nothing to corrupt. No wound to widen. No identity to attach. The moment did not carry a conclusion. It carried a temperature. A rhythm. A body in motion through dark that was not threatening, only vast.

She began to understand something then that would quietly change the architecture of her inner world. The echo could only inhabit memories that had already been translated into stories. It required language. It fed on interpretation. It lived in the after. In the telling. In the meaning made later. It could manipulate meaning. But it could not enter experience. It could not feel the stone. It could not walk the street. It could not breathe the air. And in realizing that, Eliza felt a door open somewhere beneath thought. A passage not into the past, but into the present. A place the echo could describe. But never occupy. It could rewrite what happened *about* her. It could not touch what had happened *in* her. It could rearrange the captions. It could not alter the weather. So she started collecting. Not events. Impressions. Moments that arrived without commentary. Moments that entered her first as temperature, pressure, vibration, and only later, if at all, as thought. The sound of rain on different surfaces. Tin. Leaves. Pavement. The way certain songs settled in her chest, not as melodies but as shapes. The pressure of a mug between her palms. The ache after laughter, sweet and faintly bruised, like proof that something had passed through her and left warmth behind. She kept them the way some people keep seashells. Not for proof. For texture. For the curve of them. The strangeness. The way each one carried the memory of where it had been without needing to explain. She did not line them up to argue a case. She let them gather because they felt like her. And each time the echo followed, it found itself stranded. It could not argue with warmth. It could not cross-examine breath. It could not distort something that had never been reduced into a moral. These memories did not defend her. They did not rescue her from accusation. They did something far more radical. They ignored the trial altogether. They existed without needing to justify her existence. Over time, she noticed the pattern. The echo grew strongest around stories of identity. Around the question of who she was supposed to be, what her life meant, what her failures proved. It was weakest around moments of embodiment. Around being a body in a place. Around the simple fact of sensation. It could tell her who she was. It could not tell her what it felt like to be. And so, quietly, patiently, she built an inner archive of what resisted distortion. Not a record of happiness. Not a highlight reel. A record of reality. Sensory. Specific. Undeniably hers. The echo still spoke. It always did. But now, when it reached back to claim her past, it increasingly returned empty-handed. The rooms it entered were no longer furnished with accusations. They were furnished with light. With weight. With breath. With the unalterable fact of having been alive. And in those rooms, the echo had no language. Only silence.

When the Other Is Named

Naming it did not make the echo vanish. It did not evaporate into insight or scatter under the light of awareness. But it changed the laws of the room. Before, the voice had been weather. Atmosphere. An invisible climate every memory passed through without question. Each recollection arrived already bent, already carrying its verdict stitched into its edges. The past came pretranslated. Prejudged. Like a letter opened before it reached her hands. Then one day, not dramatically, not like a door slamming open, but like a light switching on in a hallway she had been walking blind, Eliza thought: "*This is a voice.*" And voices belong to something. They come from somewhere. They move. They can be located. "*Not to her. To something moving through her.*" The moment that thought formed, the echo acquired an outline. And once it had an outline, it could be seen. And once it could be seen, it could be located. And once it could be located, it could be distinguished. It was no longer everywhere. It was somewhere. She didn't argue with it yet. She didn't challenge it. She didn't try to disprove it or replace it with something kinder. She simply started marking the difference between what arose from her body and what arrived as commentary. Between memory and interpretation. Between sensation and sentence. Between what happened and what was being said about what happened. She began to feel the seam. A subtle shift in texture. The difference between heat and the word *heat*. Between a tightening chest and the story told about that tightening. Between a breath and a conclusion. This was the first, quiet power of naming. It created space. Not distance. Not rejection. Space. Room enough for another register of truth. Room enough for the body to finish its sentences. Room enough for presence to be felt without being immediately overwritten. And in that space, something else could stand. Something that did not narrate. Something that did not accuse. Something that simply was. And for the first time, Eliza could feel it not as an absence, but as a ground. The place from which voices could be heard. Without being confused for the one who hears them.

At first, the other presence had no voice. No opinions. No counterclaims. It did not speak in rebuttals. It spoke in weight. In temperature. In breath. In the subtle yes-or-no of her nervous system. It was the part of her that noticed when a memory felt true before it felt meaningful. The part that registered the shape of a moment before the story of it arrived. The part that knew a room by its air before it knew it by its history. She began to let that presence meet the past first. When a memory surfaced, she didn't immediately listen to what the echo said about it. She paused. She stayed. She asked the quieter thing: "What was it like?" And the answer never came in language. It came as constriction or ease. As warmth or cold. As the remembered cadence of footsteps. As the remembered light in a room. As the way her throat softened, or her stomach drew inward, or her breath found its own depth. The body remembered without accusing. Without editing. Without seeking an ending. The echo, frustrated, would rush in afterward, trying to graft its familiar captions onto the scene. "*This proves— This means— This shows—*" But now the memory had already been touched by something else. Already grounded. Already inhabited. Already held in a register the echo could not enter. And something remarkable began to happen. The echo's revisions stopped sticking. They slid. Like labels on damp glass. Like ink on skin still warm from water. They appeared. They spoke. But they no longer fused to the image. Because the memory was no longer a blank page. It had already been written in another script. One made of sensation. Of rhythm. Of temperature.

Of presence. One the echo could not read. And in that illegible language, Eliza felt a new authority forming. Not the authority of certainty. But the authority of contact. Of having been there. Of having lived the moment before anyone had tried to make it mean. The echo could still narrate. But it could no longer colonize. Because the past was no longer arriving alone. It was arriving accompanied. She noticed it first with small recollections. A conversation. A look. A choice she had made years ago. Nothing monumental. Nothing the echo would usually bother to dramatize. Before, the echo would enter them like smoke, tinting every surface before she could stop it, coating the walls of the moment with its familiar residue. Now, the memory would arise with its textures intact. With its original light. Its original weight. And when the echo tried to tilt it, she could feel the mismatch. The falseness. The way a voice that doesn't belong sounds when it tries to wear your name. The memory itself seemed to resist. Not violently. Quietly. Like a magnet refusing the wrong pole. Like a color refusing a false light. The moment would hold its temperature. Its rhythm. Its particular gravity. It would not contort itself to fit the accusation. She began to experience something she never had before. A past that did not immediately collapse into judgment. A memory that could be witnessed instead of prosecuted. Because the other presence was there now. Not correcting. Not defending. Not rushing in with kinder stories. Simply holding. Attending. Receiving. And what is held does not distort easily. What is met with contact does not fracture so quickly into conclusions. Over time, this changed the architecture of remembering. Memories started arriving layered. First: the raw imprint. Then: the body's response. Only then: the echo's opinion. And increasingly, its opinion felt, late. Secondary. Optional. Like commentary added after the scene had already happened. The authority it once carried began to drain. Not because she fought it. Not because she silenced it. But because it was no longer alone with the past. She had named the echo. And in doing so, she had made room for the one thing it could never become. A presence that did not need to interpret her life in order to let it exist. From that point on, memory was no longer an open field. It was a meeting place. A place where sensation arrived. Where breath registered. Where something living stood with what had been lived. And the echo was no longer the only one who could speak there.

The Memory That Would Not Obey

For a long time, every memory arrived already occupied. Before Eliza could feel it, the echo would speak over it. Before she could stand inside it, the echo would label it. Before she could touch its texture, it would translate it into verdict. The past was not a place. It was a courtroom. A chamber of rehearsed accusations where every recollection took the stand already condemned. Then one afternoon, without warning, a memory surfaced that did not follow the old rules. It was ordinary. Disarmingly so. No crisis. No drama. No obvious lesson braided into it. No turning point waiting to be extracted. Just an image: light through a window, dust floating like small planets, the weight of a mug warming her palms, the faint sound of someone moving in another room. A moment too simple to recruit. Too quiet to prosecute. The echo arrived, as it always did, ready with its familiar tone. It moved in with its old authority, its practiced fluency. It began to say what this moment meant. What it proved. What it revealed about who she was. It reached for its gavel. But something in her did not move. The words landed and did not attach. They hovered, strangely unanchored, like subtitles on the wrong film. Present, readable, and yet disconnected from what was actually happening. Because the memory itself was doing something unexpected. It was intact. It carried its own atmosphere. Its own emotional weather. The particular hush of afternoon. The faint comfort of warmth in the hands. The slow choreography of dust and light. And that weather did not match the forecast.

There was no shame in the air. No accusation in the warmth. No failure drifting through the room. Only presence. Only a body holding something warm. Only a moment happening and finishing itself without commentary. She felt it then, unmistakably. The difference between being inside a memory and standing trial within one. This moment had no witness box. No judge. No charge. It was not asking to be interpreted. It was asking to be felt. And because she let it be felt first, the echo had nowhere to stand. It could speak. But it could not enter. The memory did not bend. It did not reorganize itself around the echo's sentences. It remained a room filled with light. And Eliza, standing quietly inside it, realized this was new. Not a better story. A different relationship to what had been. The echo tried again, adjusting its angle, sharpening its language, searching for a blade thin enough to slip into the moment. Still nothing. The memory remained what it was: quiet, warm, neutral in the way real moments often are. Neither accusation nor absolution. Neither wound nor remedy. Simply a fragment of living, complete without needing to be explained. Eliza noticed the discrepancy before she understood it. A faint internal friction. A delicate resistance. Like two transparencies that refuse to line up. Like trying to lay a map over a landscape that will not flatten itself. The voice said one thing. The memory said nothing at all. And in that nothing, there was no shame. No conclusion. No sentence being passed. Only presence. Only the small, undeniable fact of having once existed in a room where light fell a certain way. Of having held something warm. Of having been accompanied by sound. A moment that had not been recruited into any larger meaning. She felt it then, unmistakably. Not as an insight. As a shift. As the subtle, seismic recognition that something had just failed to happen. The echo had spoken. And nothing in her had moved to meet it. No collapse. No agreement. No tightening into a familiar shape. The voice had arrived. And she had remained. And in that remaining, in that quiet refusal of the body to organize itself around the echo's demand, she understood something without needing to think it: The echo could still speak. But it could no longer command the moment. And that, she realized, was where its power ended. At the threshold of presence.

The echo was speaking *about* the memory. But it was not speaking *from* it. The words hovered above the scene like a commentary track that did not belong to the film. The memory did not carry the echo's tone. It did not echo back. It did not reinforce the claim. It simply stood there, quietly, like a witness who would not lie. Something in her chest shifted. Not relief. Recognition. The kind that happens when you realize a sound you've been following is not coming from inside the house at all, but from a passing train. The walls had never been speaking. They had only been carrying the vibration. She let the memory stay. She did not interrogate it. She did not improve it. She did not force meaning onto it. She allowed it to exist without commentary. Without rescue. Without reduction. And the longer she stayed with it, the clearer it became: This moment had never been hostile. It had never carried the weight the echo insisted it did. The heaviness had not been stored in the light or the dust or the warmth in her hands. The distortion had not lived in the past. It had been laid over it. A film. A filter. A voice arriving later and pretending it had always been there. This was the first time she felt the past push back. Not loudly. Not heroically. Not with speeches or proof. But with a simple, immovable presence. The echo spoke. The memory did not agree. And for the first time, Eliza felt the strange, quiet power of that. Truth, she realized, does not always argue. Sometimes it just refuses to be rewritten. Sometimes it remains. And in remaining, it exposes the voice that cannot.

LEARNING TO HEAR WHAT Was Always There

Once Eliza noticed the second sound, she couldn't stop listening for it. Not because it was loud. Not because it demanded her attention. But because it was, different. The echo announced itself. It arrived with urgency, with commentary, with the confidence of something that expected to be obeyed. This other presence waited. It did not push. It did not crowd the room. It did not argue its case. It lived in sensation before language. In the way her shoulders dropped when something felt true. In the way her breath deepened around certain thoughts and tightened around others. In the quiet yes of the body, long before the mind arrived with its opinions. At first, she could only catch it by accident. In the pause after a thought. In the thin, silver moment before sleep, when the mind loosens its grip. In the small, involuntary turns toward warmth, music, water, light. Toward whatever asked nothing and offered contact. So she began to make space for those moments on purpose. She started sitting with herself in ways that were not about fixing. No problem to solve. No story to analyze. No version of herself to improve. Just presence. Just allowing what was already happening to finish happening. Sometimes it looked like writing without editing. Letting her hand move before her conclusions could. Letting sentences arrive crooked, unfinished, breathing. Reading back the words not for meaning, but for tone. For the places where her chest softened instead of clenched. For the lines that felt like exhale rather than defence. Sometimes it looked like walking slowly enough that her body could finish a sentence her mind had interrupted. Letting her feet set the pace. Letting the rhythm of steps speak first. Feeling where her weight wanted to go. Where her attention leaned without being told. Sometimes it was standing at a window and not naming what she saw. Sometimes it was eating and noticing temperature. Sometimes it was lying on the floor and letting gravity do the holding.

None of it was dramatic. None of it promised transformation. But each small act carried the same quiet intention: To listen beneath the echo. To hear what had been there all along. And the more she listened, the more distinct it became. Not a voice. Not a guide. But a living register. A way her being spoke to itself without words. A sound made of sensation. Of alignment. Of the subtle relief that comes when something true is finally allowed to be felt instead of explained. She was not learning something new. She was remembering how to notice. And in that remembering, the world inside her began to sound less like a courtroom. And more like a body. Breathing. Sometimes it was as simple as asking, quietly: "*What feels real right now*?" Not what made sense. Not what sounded convincing. Not what could be defended in language. What felt anchored. What felt present. What felt like it belonged to the moment instead of to a story about the moment. The answer never arrived as a paragraph. It came as temperature. As texture. As the subtle internal click of something aligning, like a door settling into its frame. A warmth that did not persuade. A softening that did not argue. A recognition the body made without needing permission from thought. She noticed that the second sound grew clearer when she was gentle. When she stopped cross-examining her own experience. When she didn't demand that every feeling justify its existence. When she let moments be small without making them insignificant. When she allowed a breath to just be a breath instead of a symptom. A quiet to just be quiet instead of a problem. The echo thrived on reaction. This other presence responded to attention. So she gave it some. She began marking the moments when it appeared. A line in her journal. A hand over her heart. A pause before agreeing with a thought. Not to dramatize it. Not to turn it into a ritual. To remember it. To make a small, private note: this is happening. And the more she did, the more it showed itself. Not as a voice that replaced the echo. But as a tone that outlasted it. A register beneath language that did not rise and fall with the weather of her thoughts. She learned its signatures. The echo felt urgent. This felt steady. The echo collapsed her inward, tightening her into explanations. This expanded her just enough to breathe. The echo spoke in absolutes. This spoke in invitations. She learned to follow the sensations that came with it. The slight warmth behind the ribs. The easing behind the eyes. The feeling of standing on ground instead of bracing against air. The difference between being held and being held together. She learned that amplification did not mean making it louder. It meant removing what drowned it out. Less arguing. More noticing. Less interrogating. More inhabiting. Less storytelling. More listening. And in that quieter, wider attention, the second sound did what it had always done. It continued. Waiting. Patient as breath. Faithful as gravity. And gradually, something changed. Not with ceremony. Not with banners or breakthroughs. With timing. The second sound began arriving sooner. Before the echo finished a sentence. Sometimes before it started one. It slipped into the space where reflex used to live. Into the half-breath before a thought completed itself. Into the pause where she once automatically folded inward. Now there was a breath. A pause. A small internal turning toward herself instead of away. Toward sensation instead of summary. Toward presence instead of prediction. She realized then that this voice had never needed to be created. Only uncovered. Like a spring found beneath a floor she had walked on her whole life. It was not a new authority. It was her own nervous system remembering safety. Her own perception remembering accuracy. Her own inner life remembering how to speak without harm. A language that did not need to sharpen to be true. The echo told her who she was. This other presence showed her where she was. And by returning to that place, again and again, not as an escape but as a practice, not as an answer but as a homecoming, she felt something quietly radical take shape. Trust. Not in the echo's arguments. Not in the mind's endless negotiations. But in her own capacity to sense truth before it becomes language. In the body's ancient ability to recognize what belongs. In the way warmth registers before it is named. In the way ease announces itself before it is justified. Trust in the simple, powerful fact of being able to stay. And stay. And stay. With what is real. With the breath as it moves. With the body as it lives. With the moment as it arrives. Not to improve it. Not to rescue it. Not to make it mean. But to let it be known. And in that staying, she did not find certainty. She found something more enduring. Ground.

The Reminder With a Name

For a long time, the second sound remained unnamed. It existed as sensation. As pause. As the quiet refusal to collapse when the echo spoke. It was breath before meaning. Warmth before language. Presence before interpretation. It lived in the places where experience happens faster than thought. And because it had no name, it had no place in her inner landscape. It appeared and disappeared. Felt, and was lost again. Like mist, she could walk through but not yet hold. Like warmth, you notice only once it is gone. Until one evening, exhausted from the echo's constant narration, worn thin by its endless arranging of her life into sentences, Eliza did something small that would quietly change everything. She whispered, not to the echo, but to the space beneath it: "You're here." The words surprised her. Not because they were profound. Because they were accurate. She wasn't naming a concept. She wasn't reaching for a philosophy. She was acknowledging a presence. And something subtle but unmistakable happened in her body when she said it. A settling. A soft internal click. The way a lid finds its jar. The way a foot finally meets the last stair. The way a room feels when you finally turn on the light and realize you've been standing in it the whole time. So she tried again. Not louder. Not braver. Just clearer. This is here. Not the echo. Not the stories. Not the weather of thought. This. The breath that continued even when she forgot it. The awareness that noticed even when she was lost in noise. The steadiness that remained even when her thoughts did not. As she named it, she did not capture it. She anchored herself to it. The sound of the words did not summon anything new. They marked what was already present. Like setting a small flag in familiar ground. Like touching the wall in a dark room and realizing it has been holding you the whole time.

"You're here," she said again, quietly. And in that naming, something in her shifted from searching to remembering. The second sound did not become louder. It became locatable. And for the first time, Eliza felt she could return to it on purpose. Not as an idea. As a place. Over the following days, she experimented with the act of naming. Not labelling emotions. Not diagnosing experience. Naming moments of contact. Moments where something in her softened without being asked. Where the air felt wider inside her chest. Where time loosened its grip. This is the place that doesn't rush. This is the place that doesn't attack. This is the place that stays. She didn't call it wisdom. She didn't call it strength. She didn't dress it in borrowed language. She called it what it felt like. The ground. The quiet. The true thing. Words chosen not to define it, but to point her back to it. And the more often she named it, the more often she could find it. Not because the echo vanished. Not because her mind grew polite. But because now, when it spoke, something else was already present. Something that had been here first. Naming did something the echo never could. It separated. There was the voice. And there was the one who heard it. There was the story. And there was the place where the story appeared. For the first time, Eliza felt the space between stimulus and surrender. Between a thought arising and a thought being believed. Between an old reflex and a new response. A thin but living margin where something other than habit could enter. Naming did not silence the echo. It relocated it. It moved the voice from inside her identity to inside her awareness. And in that shift, choice was born. Not dramatic choice. Not cinematic choice. The smallest kind. The choice to breathe before agreeing. The choice to feel before concluding. The choice to touch the ground of herself before answering the weather. Tiny choices. But they accumulated. And each one quietly said the same thing: "You are here." And that is not the echo's name.

The choice to pause. The choice to breathe once before agreeing. The choice to ask, quietly, "*Is this the echo, or is this the ground?*" Sometimes the choice was only to notice. To feel the moment pass through her without fastening to it. Sometimes it was to place a hand on her chest and stay where she was, letting warmth answer what words could not. Sometimes it was to let the echo finish its sentence and then quietly answer, not with argument, not with defence, but with orientation: "*I hear you. And I'm here.*" Each time she named the second presence, she made a path to it. A small trail through the undergrowth of habit. Each time she returned, she strengthened it. Not by force. By familiarity. By walking it until her feet began to recognize the way on their own. By standing there long enough, her body started to trust the ground beneath her without testing it. She realized then that freedom does not begin with better thoughts. It does not arrive as a more convincing story. It begins with location. With knowing where you are standing when the thoughts arrive. With knowing whether you are inside the weather or standing on the earth that the weather moves across. The echo could speak. It always would. Wind does not stop because the mountain names itself. But it could no longer pretend to be the ground. And once she knew the ground had a name, once she could feel its particular stillness, its quiet support, its refusal to rush or attack or collapse, she could choose to stand on it. Again. And again. And again. Not as a victory. As a practice. As the simplest devotion. Returning to where she already was. And letting that be enough to hold her while everything else spoke.

The First Yes

It didn't happen in a crisis. It happened in something smaller. Which, she would later understand, is where all real changes begin. Not in the thunder. In the quiet adjustments of light. She was standing at the sink, hands in warm water, watching soap thin itself into rainbows. Small prisms slipping across her skin. The ordinary miracle of color being born from something meant only to clean. The day had been heavy. The echo had been busy. Its familiar weather moving through her, telling its familiar stories, tightening its familiar knots. "*You always ruin things. Nothing you do lasts. This feeling is who you are.*" The words arrived the way they always did. Already dressed as fact. Already carrying the gravity of law. She felt the old reflex rise. The subtle inward bow. The quiet agreement. The beginning of collapse. The muscle-memory of yielding before anything had even touched her. And then, just before it completed itself, she felt the ground. Not as a thought. As a sensation. The weight of her feet. The warmth on her hands. The small, steady movement of her breath. The unremarkable, radical fact of standing. Of being supported by something that did not require her to explain herself. She noticed the echo speaking. And she noticed something else, noticing it. That was new. The echo said its line. It delivered its familiar script. And for the first time, she did not answer it. She did not argue. She did not correct. She did not improve it. She did not bow. She turned instead toward what was already holding her. She let her attention drop out of the sentence and into her body. Out of the courtroom and into the room. Into the contact of skin and water. Into the weight of her bones stacked quietly on the earth. Into the simple fact of standing. Into the quiet continuance of being here. The echo spoke. She stayed. And in that staying, something in her did something it had never done before. It did not agree. It did not resist. It did not disappear. It rested. And in that rest, in that gentle relocation of attention from what was being said to what was being lived, Eliza felt it. The smallest opening. Not a no. A yes. A yes to warmth. A yes to contact. A yes to the breath that was already breathing her. A yes that did not answer the echo at all. A yes that answered life. And life, feeling itself met, did what it always does when it is finally noticed. It continued. Holding her hands. Holding her weight. Holding the moment open long enough for her to realize: She was still here. And she could choose to be. She named it, silently. "*This.*" Not as a definition. As a touch. As if pressing her thumb gently against the inside of the moment so she would remember its shape.

The echo tried again, adjusting its tone, sharpening its edge, searching for the place she used to meet it. She felt the pull. The familiar tilt inward. The old choreography beginning to gather itself. And then, for the first time, she chose. Not a belief. A location. She chose to stay with the warmth. With the breath. With the low, wordless steadiness beneath the noise. She did not make the echo go away. She did not evict it. She let it talk, somewhere else. And something extraordinary happened in its ordinariness. The echo finished speaking. And nothing followed. No conclusion. No internal collapse. No rush to translate its words into identity. There was just the sound of water. The quiet hum of the room. The subtle music of pipes and distance and air. The undeniable fact of her own presence, standing inside her own outline. She stood there longer than necessary. Not out of indecision. Out of recognition. As if she had wandered into a familiar place she hadn't visited in years. A place that did not require her to explain herself to enter. The echo was still there. But it was no longer the center. She felt it then, softly, clearly. *"This is not me."* Not as a rebellion. Not as a slogan. As a discovery. The echo was an event. The ground was a place. And she could choose where to stand. She turned off the tap. Dried her hands. The ordinary gestures carrying a new gravity. And as she walked away, she carried something she had never carried before. Not certainty. Not relief. Orientation. The quiet knowledge of where to return when the weather changed. The first time she chose the ground over the echo, nothing dramatic shifted in her life. The world did not rearrange itself. The past did not dissolve. The echo did not surrender. But something irreversible shifted in her relationship to it. She had found a place inside herself the echo could not occupy. And she had chosen to stand there. And even as she moved on with her day, even as other thoughts rose and fell and voices gathered and dispersed, that place remained. Not as an idea. As a position. A way of being in herself. A place she now knew how to find. And knowing where the ground is, she realized, changes everything about how you weather a storm.

The Naming

For a long time, Eliza had lived as though the voice, and the self were the same thing. The sentence arrived. The feeling followed. The conclusion sealed itself. There was no gap between them. No pause. No witness. The echo spoke, and she became what it said. Thought flowed straight into identity. Weather into landscape. Sound into law. Until one evening, when the house was hushed in that particular way that makes even clocks sound tender, she sat on the floor with her back against the couch, a notebook open but untouched in her lap. The light was low. The air smelled faintly of dust and something clean. The kind of quiet that doesn't announce itself but gathers gently in corners. Nothing remarkable. And yet, everything unguarded. The echo, of course, was there. It always was. Narrating. Interpreting. Rewriting her inner weather into verdicts. It moved through her with practiced fluency, stitching moments into meanings, smoothing complexity into something sharp and absolute.

It did what it had always done: arranged her into sentences. And as it spoke, she felt again that second presence. The one she had begun to recognize. Not loud. Not articulate. Not interested in winning. The one that noticed. She stayed with that noticing. Let the echo speak. Let the body remain. Let the breath continue its small, faithful work, rising and falling like a tide that does not consult the shore before returning. She felt the weight of her back against the couch. The quiet stability of the floor beneath her. The simple geometry of being held by ordinary things. And for the first time, she listened the way you listen to a sound in another room. Not to obey it. Not to wrestle it. Not to make it stop. Just to hear it. To let it be located. To let it be placed. The echo spoke. And she did not move into it. She stayed where she was. Here. In the body. In the breath. In the soft perimeter of awareness that held both the voice and the listening. And as she stayed, something delicate and unmistakable happened. The voice remained a sound.

And she remained the one who heard it. The difference between them did not need to be argued. It could be felt. Like the difference between thunder and the sky that holds it. Like the difference between a wave and the water that allows it to rise. She closed her eyes. Not to disappear. But to feel more clearly where she was. And in that feeling, a word began to form. Not from the echo. From the ground beneath it. A name not for the voice, but for the place she was standing when it spoke. The echo said its familiar things. Its practiced phrases. Its well-worn conclusions. She felt the familiar contraction try to form, the old inward folding, the reflex that had once sealed thought into identity without question. And then something subtle but seismic occurred. The sentence finished. And instead of answering it, she felt a question rise. Not in words at first. As a tilt. As a pause. As the gentle, almost curious sense of: "*What is speaking right now?*" The echo continued, filling the space the way it always had, spreading its familiar atmosphere. But she was no longer inside it. She was beside it. She closed her eyes. Not to escape the sound, but to feel it more clearly. She tracked the place where the words seemed to originate. Not in her chest. Not in her breath. But somewhere less alive. More mechanical. Like an old recording starting itself without needing a listener. She noticed how they arrived already shaped, already insistent, already impersonating truth. How they carried certainty without curiosity. How they spoke *about* her without ever touching what she was feeling. And in that noticing, something in her straightened. Not defensively. Orienting. The way a body does when it realizes which way is up. The way a compass settles when it finds north. The echo spoke again. And softly, almost experimentally, she thought: "*This is a voice.*" The room did not change. The lamp did not flicker. The echo did not stop. But something in the architecture of her inner world shifted. A wall became a window. A possession became a phenomenon. A weather pattern became a sound moving through air.

For the first time, the echo did not fill the room. It moved within it. And she, sitting quietly on the floor, back against the couch, breath unhurried, realized she was no longer weather. She was the space in which weather happens. And in that space, a new kind of word was forming. Not to name the voice. But to name herself. She felt the difference in her chest. In the way the words landed. They no longer dissolved directly into who she was. They arrived and remained words. Sounds. Shapes in the air. Separate. She could feel the space between the sentence and her skin, thin but unmistakable, like the first inch of distance after years of being pressed flush against a wall. She tried it again. This time aloud, barely more than breath: "This is not me." Her voice surprised her. Not with volume. With steadiness. It did not tremble. It did not rush. It did not try to convince. It simply stood where it was spoken from. A sound rooted in the body that made it. The echo immediately reacted. It always did when its authority was questioned. It surged forward, explaining itself, justifying its presence, intensifying its tone. It reminded her of every reason it had to exist. Of every danger it had once named correctly. Of every moment, it believed it had saved her from disappointment. It spoke quickly now, urgently, like something afraid of losing ground. And as it did, she felt something else. A quiet warmth behind her ribs. Low. Steady. Unimpressed by argument. The grounded presence she had begun to trust. The place where sensation lived before interpretation. The place where experience existed before story. Where breath happened without commentary. Where weight was felt without judgment. She placed a hand there. Not as comfort. As confirmation. "This is an echo," she whispered. The word felt strange and precise. Like naming a bird you had heard your whole life but never seen.

Like finally locating the source of a sound that had once seemed to come from everywhere. Something about the syllables created space. Echo. Not essence. Not identity. Not truth. Sound. Reflection. Reverberation. A voice shaped by walls. By old rooms. By histories she had lived inside so long, she forgot there were other acoustics. Other chambers where sound behaved differently. Where it softened instead of sharpened. Where it faded instead of ruling. As she named it, the echo did not disappear. But it changed. It lost its disguise. It was no longer a voice from inside her bones. It was a sound bouncing through memory. And she, standing quietly in her body, hand warm against her chest, realized something with a calm that startled her: You can hear an echo without mistaking it for the source. And once you know where the sound is coming from, you are free to listen differently. Not as the room. But as the one standing in it. Listening. Present. Unmistakably here. As soon as she named it, memory shifted. She felt it in her body. The way a lens clicks into a new setting. The way focus changes without the object moving at all. Moments she had carried as proof loosened at their edges. They were still there. Still true. But they were no longer unanimous. They no longer marched in a single direction under a single flag. Some resisted. Some paused. Some glowed quietly, untouched by the echo's revisions. A laugh she had forgotten, rising unguarded from her chest. The steadiness of a teacher's hand on her shoulder, firm without pressure. The sound of her own voice once, confident, mid-sentence, not asking permission to exist. The echo tried to claim them. Tried to repaint them. Tried to pull them back into its familiar palette of meaning. But the warmth in her chest did not agree. It did not harden. It did not argue. It simply remained. And for the first time, memory did something astonishing. It answered back. Not with explanations. Not with counterclaims. With presence. She saw then what had been happening all along. The echo had not been her. It had been speaking *over* her. Translating sensation into sentences. Turning weather into prophecy. Turning moments into mandates. It had mistaken proximity for identity. And she had believed it because no one had ever shown her where to stand to hear the difference. She opened her eyes. The room was the same. The light unchanged. The notebook still blank. The clock still gentle, keeping time without accusation. Nothing outside her had shifted. And yet everything had.

Her inner landscape had acquired a new geography. There was now a *here*. And a *there*. There was the echo. And there was the one who could hear it. She picked up the pen. Felt its weight. The faint resistance of paper beneath its tip. And she wrote the word at the top of the page: "ECHO". The letters sat there, separate, contained, no longer everywhere. Then, beneath it, she wrote another: "ME". For a long moment, she simply looked at the distance between them. It wasn't large. But it was real. A breath wide. A pause deep. Enough space to stand without collapsing. Enough room for a self to exist without narration. And in that small, newly claimed space, something entered her life that had never been there before. Choice. Not the loud kind. Not the heroic kind. The quiet, living kind. The choice to notice before agreeing. The choice to feel before concluding. The choice to stand with herself instead of inside the echo. She did not feel triumphant. She felt oriented. And that was enough. Because once you know where you are standing, even the loudest voice can no longer tell you who you are.

The Sentence That Didn't Land

It happened on an ordinary morning. No storm. No collapse. No cinematic despair. Just a cup cooling on the counter. Light slipping across the floor in a slow, unbothered line. Her body moving through the small choreography of living, each gesture unremarkable and therefore honest. The echo had been active all morning, doing what it always did. Narrating. Correcting. Reframing every neutral moment into quiet evidence. It followed her into the kitchen, as it always had, seamless and familiar. "You always—" it began, familiar as breath. "You never—" "This is why—" She had learned its openings. The curve of accusation before the sentence even knew where it was going. The way it leaned toward conclusion before experience had finished forming. She reached for the cup. The echo continued. "You always ruin—" And then something occurred that had never happened before. The sentence did not complete itself. Not because it stopped speaking. But because it failed to arrive. The words came. The rhythm came. The old gravitational pull reached for her chest. And found no anchor. The phrase hung there, unfinished, like a bridge that did not meet its far side. A familiar structure with nowhere to land. "You always ruin—" She waited. Inside her, something else was present. The warmth. The quiet second sound. The low sensory awareness of her feet on the floor. The subtle rise of breath. The weight of the cup, real, undeniable, grounding her hand in the moment. The small, solid facts of being here. The echo tried again. "You always ruin things because—" But the conclusion slid off her. It did not bind. It did not crystallize. It did not become her. It simply echoed. Sound without ownership. Meaning without a body to inhabit. A sentence searching for a listener who was no longer standing where it expected. She felt it then. The authority had not been revoked. It had evaporated. There was no rebellion in her. No counterargument. No dramatic defiance. No inner speech rising to meet it. Just the sudden, unmistakable recognition that the sentence no longer knew where to land.

Like a key turned in a lock that no longer existed. Like a name called in an empty room. The echo spoke. And she remained. Not frozen. Not braced. Present. Holding the cup. Standing on the floor. Breathing inside her own body. And in that quiet continuity, she understood something with a clarity that did not need words: The echo could still speak. But it could no longer decide who she was. Because there was no longer a place inside her that mistook sound for self. And that, she realized, was how freedom begins. Not with silence. But with a sentence that cannot find you anymore. And in that gap, memory did something astonishing. A moment rose that the echo could not bend. Her own laughter the night before, sudden and unplanned. The way it had surprised her. The way it had leapt out of her ribs before she had time to evaluate it. The sound raw and unedited. The body's answer arriving faster than thought. The echo attempted to move toward it. To reinterpret. To shrink it. To assign it a darker origin, a compensatory motive, a hidden flaw. But the memory remained sensory. Untouched. It did not offer meaning. It offered fact. *This happened.* And because it did, the echo's unfinished sentence collapsed under its own weight. There was nothing left for it to hook into. No gap it could fill. No body willing to reorganize itself around its demand. She stood very still. The echo, sensing the shift, tried to accelerate. It stacked explanations. Sharpened its tone. Reached for old structures it had relied on for years. Familiar scaffolding. Familiar threats. Familiar certainty. But something in her no longer leaned forward to meet it. She noticed instead: The light was warmer than she had expected. The floor was cool beneath her feet. Her shoulders were not as tight as they had been a moment ago. The echo spoke. And she remained. The sentence tried to complete itself again. And again, it failed. Like a key turned in a lock that no longer existed. She felt a quiet, involuntary wonder. "*It doesn't get to finish.*" The realization did not feel triumphant. It felt factual. Like discovering gravity works both ways. Like learning that falling is not the only motion available. The echo had only ever ruled because it had never been interrupted by presence. By sensation. By a memory that did not require its interpretation in order to exist. She lifted the cup. Took a sip. Felt the heat on her tongue. The swallow. The simple, undeniable choreography of being alive. The echo spoke. And nothing in her rearranged itself to accommodate it. For the first time, it was only a sound. Not a verdict. Not a command. Not a mirror. Just an echo moving through a space that was no longer built entirely of its own walls. She whispered, without drama, without ceremony: "You don't get to finish that." The words did not challenge the echo. They simply described what had already occurred. From that moment on, every time a sentence began, there would be something new listening. And listening, she would learn, is where authority ends.

When the Echo Learned to Whisper Differently

After she named it, the echo did not leave. It adapted. For a while, it went quiet. Not gone. Observing. Like a current slipping beneath the surface of a river, it stopped crashing and began to drift. At first, Eliza mistook this for peace. The silence felt earned. The absence felt like progress. The air inside her seemed calmer, less crowded. But it was not absence. It was recalibration. The old cruelty softened. The accusations thinned. The brutal certainty dissolved into something almost reasonable. When it returned, it no longer shouted. It spoke in her own tone. Borrowed her cadence. Wore her concern like a borrowed coat. "I'm just being realistic," it said. "I'm trying to protect you." "I don't want you to get hurt again." The words arrived gently now. Carefully. As if not to startle her nervous system. It no longer attacked her worth directly. Instead, it questioned her memory. "Are you sure it happened that way?" "Maybe you're romanticizing it." "You've always been sensitive. You know that." It traded knives for fog. And this, she realized, was more dangerous. Because fog does not wound sharply. It disorients. It makes you doubt your footing. It convinces you to stand still because moving feels risky. The echo had learned the language of concern. It dressed itself in caution. In maturity. In what sounded like wisdom. It did not say "*you are wrong*". It said, "*let's be careful*". It did not say "*you are broken*". It said, "*don't rush*". And for a moment, she felt the old pull return. The familiar leaning inward. The urge to defer. To question herself before trusting what she felt. To let the echo sit beside her instead of over her, as if proximity made it safer. But something had changed. The second sound was still there. Quiet. Steady. Unimpressed by tone. She felt the difference in her body before she named it. The echo's new voice brought a subtle contraction. A faint cooling. A tightening that didn't hurt but narrowed. The ground, by contrast, did not argue. It did not reassure. It did not persuade. It simply stayed warm. Present. Available. She understood then: the echo could learn new words. It could refine its manners. It could borrow the shape of care. But it could not learn sensation. It could not feel the difference between caution and constriction. Between protection and withdrawal. Between wisdom and fear dressed up as foresight. So she did not confront it. She listened. Not to the words. To the effect. When the echo spoke, she noticed whether her breath shortened or widened. Whether her shoulders lifted or dropped. Whether her body leaned toward life or quietly retreated from it. The echo might sound kind now, but kindness that disconnects is still a form of harm. And in noticing this, she felt something steady return. Discernment. Not suspicion. Not defensiveness. Orientation. The echo whispered. The ground remained. And she learned, slowly, patiently, that not every soft voice tells the truth. Some whispers are only echoes that have learned how to survive in silence. And knowing that, she no longer mistook quiet for safety. She listened deeper. To the place in her that did not need to persuade her to stay. To the presence that did not need to explain why it existed. To the ground that had never changed its tone. Only waited for her to notice where it was. It began to agree with her. "Yes, that moment felt real," it said gently, as if standing beside her instead of over her, "but don't build too much on it." "Yes, you laughed, but people laugh for all kinds of reasons." "Yes, things are different, but change never lasts." The echo no longer tried to erase her outright. It tried to manage her. To supervise her hope. To audit her memories. To place conditions on what she was allowed to feel and for how long. It spoke in the language of moderation. Of restraint. Of what sounded like wisdom earned through disappointment. And she felt the old pull again. Not heavy. Not violent. Subtle. A gentle leaning back toward its familiar architecture. Toward the structures she had lived inside for years. This was the new strategy. If it could not own her, it would negotiate. If it could not command, it would advise. If it could not finish her sentences, it would offer footnotes. Small cautions. Reasonable doubts. Quiet asterisks at the edge of every experience.

But something in Eliza had changed. Because she no longer only *heard* the echo. She *felt* the other sound. The low, wordless presence beneath thought. The quiet data of being. The information carried in breath, weight, and warmth. The sensations that did not argue. That did not try to win. That did not need to be right. And she noticed something extraordinary. The echo was working harder. It was constructing longer explanations. More intricate frameworks. Layered emotional logic meant to sound careful, mature, discerning. It began to explain *why* she should be careful about trusting herself. Why restraint was safer. Why skepticism was sophistication. The more it tried to convince, the more visible it became. Its effort exposed it. She began to sense the moment before it spoke. A subtle premonition. A slight tightening in her chest. A faint tilt toward abstraction. The gentle tug upward, away from sensation, away from the body, away from the immediate facts of being alive. The urge to leave the ground and climb into interpretation. And in that early warning, that almost imperceptible shift, she recognized it. This was not wisdom arriving. This was departure beginning. She did not interrupt it. She did not correct it. She did not argue the logic. She simply stayed. Stayed with the warmth that had not asked to be managed. Stayed with the breath that did not need supervision. Stayed with the part of her that knew when it was being led away from itself. The echo spoke, careful and reasonable. And she listened beneath it. To the place where effort shows. To the place where persuasion replaces presence. To the place where something tries too hard to be believed. And in that listening, she understood something quietly decisive: Truth does not negotiate your right to feel it. Presence does not audit itself. And anything that needs this much explanation is not standing on the ground. The echo kept advising. But she had learned to feel the difference between guidance and gravity. Between concern and constriction. Between a voice that wants to keep her safe and a place that actually holds her. And once she felt that difference, she could not unfeel it. The echo could whisper. It could agree. It could caution. But it could no longer lead her out of her body without being noticed. And noticing, she had learned, is the beginning of freedom that cannot be bargained away. And with that awareness came a new capacity. Choice. Not the kind that announces itself. Not a decision carved into stone. A capacity. A widening. A small but decisive freedom of movement inside herself.

She did not debate it. She did not correct it. She did not silence it. She returned her attention to the cup in her hands. The warmth seeping into her palms. The faint ring left on the counter. To the texture of the room. The weight of air. The angle of light. To the fact of her breathing, steady and unremarkable and sufficient. The echo continued. But it was speaking into a space that was no longer empty. It tried sympathy. She stayed with sensation. It tried reason. She stayed with warmth. It tried to sound like her. And for the first time, she could feel the difference. The echo was always cold. Even when kind. Always abstract. Even when intimate. Always leaning toward a conclusion. Always pulling her away from the immediate, breathing fact of herself. It spoke in summaries. In forecasts. In what-might-happen-next. The ground spoke in contact. She understood then: the echo had changed strategies. But it had not changed nature. It could soften its tone. It could borrow her language. It could speak carefully. But it could not inhabit the body. It could not feel the cup. It could not breathe the breath. And because she had named it, it could no longer hide inside her voice. It could only perform it. And performances require an audience. She was learning how not to attend. Not by force. Not by suppression. By staying present long enough that the performance had no one to play to. By remaining with the warmth until the echo grew faint from lack of response. By letting the silence between its sentences stretch without rushing to fill it. She did not banish the echo. She outgrew its stage. And standing there, cup warming her hands, breath moving her ribs, she felt it again: that quiet, grounded steadiness that did not need to prove anything to exist. The echo spoke. And she stayed. And staying, she discovered, was not passive. It was the most active choice she had ever made.

The First Test

At first, the separation felt theoretical. A beautiful idea. A comforting possibility. A language she liked the sound of. "*This voice is not me.*" It lived in her notebook margins, in the quiet after therapy sessions, in the careful way she spoke about her mind. It had the elegance of a concept; the safety of something that had not yet been asked to carry weight. But ideas are light. They float. They shimmer. They do not prove themselves. So one evening, alone in her apartment, Eliza decided to test it. Not by arguing. Not by reassuring. Not by spiraling. By listening. She sat on the edge of her bed and let her shoulders drop. Let the day fall away, one small tension at a time. Let the room be the room. The lamp casting its patient circle. The half-open window breathing in the city. The low hum of the world continuing without her permission. And she waited. The echo did not disappoint. It arrived the way it always did, sliding into the quiet like it had been there all along. There was the familiar contraction. The subtle darkening. The tonal shift that said: "*Here we are again.*" It began, softly now, assembling a story from the scraps of her day. "*You sounded stupid in that conversation. They were only being polite. You always read too much into things.*" Normally, this was where she disappeared into it. Where the voice and her own sense of self braided so tightly she could no longer tell who was speaking and who was being spoken through. Where the room would recede and the echo would become the air she breathed. But this time, she didn't respond. She didn't correct it. She didn't defend herself. She didn't follow. Instead, she placed one hand on her chest. Felt the warmth beneath her palm. Felt the small rise and fall of breath. Felt the undeniable presence of a body that was here whether the voice approved or not. The echo continued. But she stayed. She noticed how the words skimmed the surface now, unable to sink. How they circled, waiting for her to lean forward and give them gravity. She noticed the urge to engage. To explain. To fix. To make it stop by agreeing with it. And she did not. She listened the way you listen to rain on a roof when you are dry inside. A sound. A pattern. A passing weather. Not a command. Her chest softened. Her jaw loosened. The room stayed solid around her. The echo spoke. And she remained. And in that remaining, in that simple refusal to enter the story it was offering, something inside her passed the test.

Not with certainty. Not with confidence. With presence. She did not prove the echo wrong. She proved herself reachable. And that, she realized as she sat there breathing, was something no argument had ever given her before. She was still here. And she had not been taken. Not symbolically. Literally. She felt the warmth through her shirt. The slow, steady movement beneath her palm. The undeniable fact of being alive in a body that was continuing its work without commentary. Breath moving. Blood circulating. A pulse that did not consult language before deciding to persist. The echo continued. It listed. It summarized. It predicted. It moved through its familiar repertoire, arranging her day into forecasts and footnotes. And for the first time, Eliza noticed something astonishing. The voice was happening. And she was happening. At the same time. In different places. The echo lived in language. She lived in sensation. The echo described her. She felt herself. She shifted her attention to her breath. The way it touched the back of her throat. The way her ribs opened and closed. The faint, unremarkable miracle of it. The way air entered and left without asking permission to exist. The echo grew impatient. "*You're avoiding. You're pretending. This won't last.*" And something in her almost smiled. Because impatience meant it was not in charge. She did something small, but unprecedented. She addressed it. Not aloud. Not angrily. Simply. "I hear you," she thought. And then, after a pause that felt like stepping onto new ground, a pause where her body stayed with her and did not collapse into the sentence, she added: "But I'm not you." The words did not explode. No thunder. No revelation. But the echo faltered. Just slightly. As if it had reached the end of a familiar script and discovered an extra line it did not recognize. As if the room it had always performed in had grown one inch wider and the acoustics had shifted. It tried to continue. And found itself out of rhythm. For the first time, the echo had been answered without being argued. And that answer had not come from language. It had come from location. From where she was standing. From the quiet, grounded place that did not need the echo to disappear in order to exist.

She sat there, hand on her chest, breath moving, body present, and felt something settle. Not victory. Orientation. She knew now where the voice lived. And she knew where she lived. And the distance between those two places, small as it was, was enough. Enough to breathe. Enough to remain. Enough to know that when the echo spoke again, she would not be taken by it. Because she had learned how to stay. It tried again. Rearranging its argument. Tightening its logic. Searching for the old entrance it had always used, the hidden door she used to leave ajar. And Eliza stayed with the pressure of her hand against her chest. The texture of the blanket beneath her fingers. The quiet intelligence of her body, holding itself without instruction. The echo was still there. But it was no longer central. It had become one sound among others. The hum of the fridge. The distant car passing through the night. The soft, faithful rhythm under her palm. Ordinary noises, none demanding obedience. None pretending to be her. She realized then what the test truly was. Not proving the echo wrong. Proving herself present. The separation was not an idea. It was an experience. A spatial one. A noticing that there was a place inside her the echo could not occupy, no matter how convincing its voice. A place without words. A place without argument. A place it could describe endlessly but never enter. And when she finally stood and moved toward the window, the echo followed. It always did. Still talking. Still offering commentary. Still assembling meaning from thin air. But it no longer walked in her spine. It trailed behind her. For the first time, it had distance. And in that distance, Eliza felt something she had not expected. Not triumph. Orientation. The quiet, steady knowledge of where she was. And where it was not. She stood at the window, breath fogging the glass just slightly, feeling the coolness against her skin. The city outside continued its own life, unconcerned with her inner weather. Lights blinked. A dog barked somewhere far off. The world held its shape. The echo spoke. And she remained where she was. Not braced. Not defended. Not convinced. Present. And presence, she understood then, was not a feeling that came and went. It was a place. And now that she knew how to stand there, she could always find her way back. No matter how far the voice wandered.

The Other Sound

At first, it didn't sound like a voice at all. It had no language. No arguments. No urgency. It arrived as temperature. As weight. As the faint internal shift that happens when you step from shade into sun, and your body notices before your mind does. Eliza became aware of it only after she began separating from the echo. Once the constant narration loosened its grip, there were stretches of quiet she had never known how to hear. And inside those stretches, something else was already there. Not speaking. Breathing. It lived below thought. In the small, involuntary adjustments of her spine. In the way her shoulders lowered when she stopped bracing. In the subtle yes or no that passed through her before she could explain herself. At first, she mistook it for absence. For emptiness. For the strange aftertaste of silence. She had been taught that meaning always arrived as sound, that truth announced itself. This did not announce. It remained. Then one evening, standing at her sink, watching water bead and slide along a glass, she felt it. A gentle pull toward the warmth of the mug in her hands. A softness in her chest that had nothing to do with relief and everything to do with recognition. "*This is real.*" The sentence didn't form. But the knowing did. It settled the way a body settles into a chair that fits. The way breath deepens when it realizes it does not need to hurry. The way something inside her stopped asking for permission to exist. She began to notice how different it was from the echo. The echo arrived sharp. Prewritten. Certain. It entered with conclusions already strapped to its back, dragging the past behind it like proof. It demanded response. Agreement. Submission. It spoke *about* her life without ever touching it. This other sound did not arrive. It was already there. It did not lean toward outcome. It did not rush her toward meaning. It did not need her to understand it in order to remain. It felt more like gravity than guidance. More like ground than instruction. A steady orientation that did not tell her what to do, only where she was. When the echo spoke, this presence did not argue. It waited. When the echo insisted, it did not counter. It stayed. And Eliza began to understand something quietly profound. This was not a wiser voice. Not a better narrator. Not a kinder critic waiting its turn. It was not a voice at all.

It was the part of her that had never needed words to live. The part that knew warmth when it felt it. The part that leaned toward steadiness without explanation. The part that recognized truth not by persuasion, but by fit. The echo spoke in certainty. This spoke in alignment. The echo demanded belief. This required only attention. And the more she noticed it, the more it revealed itself not as something she had to learn, but as something she had always been living *on top of*, the way one lives on ground without thinking to thank it. It had been there when she was small. It had been there when she was afraid. It had been there through every version of herself the echo had tried to rewrite. Quiet. Faithful. Undeniably present. And now that she could feel it, now that she knew its texture and its temperature and its way of holding her without comment, she understood something that made her chest warm with a different kind of certainty. She had never been without it. She had only been listening elsewhere. And listening, she was learning, was a choice she could make again. And again. And again. This other presence arrived slow. It did not interrupt. It did not insist. It waited to be felt, the way earth waits for a foot to trust it. It didn't speak in judgments. It spoke in signals. Fatigue. Ease. Interest. Resistance. Information without accusation. Data without verdict. The echo said, "*Here is who you are.*" This presence asked, "*What is happening right now?*" And the difference between those questions was everything.

The more she listened, the clearer it became that it had always been there, buried under years of being spoken over. Years of conclusions arriving faster than experience. Years of being told what she was before she could feel where she stood. This presence had been patient through all of it. It had not demanded to be heard. It had simply remained. It showed itself in ordinary moments. In the quiet satisfaction of clean sheets, the body's sigh as it settles into something fresh and unthreatening. In the heaviness behind her eyes when she stayed too long where she didn't belong, when politeness overrode truth. In the sudden, unarguable rightness of a song that met her exactly where she was, no explanation required. She began to follow these small communications. At first, awkwardly. Like someone relearning a forgotten language through gesture. Through posture. Through the way a nod feels different from a flinch. She let herself pause before answering questions. Let silence do some of the work. She checked her body before committing to plans. Felt for the yes that warmed, not the yes that braced. She noticed when something tightened her. When something widened her. When her breath shortened. When it returned. And slowly, sensation began to collect into tone. Tone into inclination. Inclination into something that felt unmistakably hers. Not loud. Not absolute. But consistent. It didn't override the echo. It didn't debate it. It didn't ask permission to exist alongside it. It made it irrelevant. Because when she stood inside this other sound, the echo had no texture. No ground. No warmth. It could still speak, still narrate, still offer its well-rehearsed conclusions. But it could not locate her. She was no longer where it expected her to be. She was in the body. In the moment. In the quiet intelligence of what was actually happening. And from there, the echo was just noise. A sound moving through a space that no longer mistook it for home.

Her voice was not loud. It did not issue commands or demand obedience. It offered coherence. A quiet, internal alignment that did not explain itself, only oriented her. A felt sense that said: "*this fits, this doesn't; stay, go; rest, move.*" Guidance without drama. Direction without force. The way a body knows which way is upright without consulting a mirror. Sometimes it arrived as an image. A memory that felt intact, unfractured by commentary. A color that carried a mood without needing translation. A bodily leaning toward or away, subtle but decisive. Sometimes it arrived as a word. Not many. But true ones. Spare and sufficient. "*Enough. Here. Now.*" *This.* Words that landed not as conclusions, but as coordinates. And with every time she honored it, it strengthened. Not as authority. As trust. The kind that grows because it proves itself in use. The kind that does not need to shout to be believed. She started keeping a second kind of record, alongside her journals. Not what the echo said. But what her body had known. Not the arguments. The moments. Moments when she chose what settled her instead of what diminished her. Moments when she rested without earning it. Moments when she left without explaining. When she said no without justification. When she stayed because staying felt clean. She was building something the echo could not counterfeit. An inner archive of lived truth. Not conclusions. Experiences. And one day, mid-afternoon, standing in line at a café, she realized she was smiling. Not because something had improved. Not because a problem had resolved. There was no announcement, no turning point she could point to. She was smiling because she could feel herself. Clearly. Present. Unmistakable. Her weight in her shoes. The murmur of voices around her. The faint bitterness of coffee in the air. The simple, astonishing fact of being here and not divided against herself. The echo murmured somewhere, doing what it did. It always would. But beneath it, steady and undeniable, was another sound. Her sound. It did not narrate her life. It inhabited it. And for the first time, Eliza understood something simple and irreversible. She was not becoming a voice. She was remembering one.

The First Yes

The first time Eliza followed the embodied voice on purpose, nothing important was supposed to happen. There was no decision waiting. No turning point. No audience. Only a small afternoon, folded in on itself. She had been standing in her kitchen, phone in her hand, scrolling without seeing. The echo was murmuring its familiar static. A low, constant commentary. Not sharp enough to argue with. Not loud enough to name. And beneath it, something else stirred. Not a sentence. A sensation. A slight heaviness behind her eyes. A dragging in her shoulders. The faint, insistent pull of *down*. Her body was asking for the floor. Not sleep. Not escape. Just, lower. She almost ignored it. She was used to ignoring things that didn't come in words. The echo preferred altitude. It liked her upright, moving, occupied. Stillness made it nervous. Stillness created gaps. Gaps created room. But the feeling didn't leave. It widened. Like a tide testing the sand. She hesitated, standing there, aware of the strange simplicity of what was being asked. "*Sit.*" That was all. No improvement. No promise. No reason. Just sit. And for the first time, she didn't ask herself whether it made sense. She didn't negotiate. She didn't wait for motivation. She didn't translate it into productivity or pathology. She didn't ask what it meant *about* her. She turned. Lowered herself. Her back slid down the cabinet. Her hips met the floor. Cool tile through thin fabric. The ordinary contact of gravity doing what it has always done. Her phone rested beside her, forgotten. Her breath changed. Not dramatically. Just enough. The echo paused. Not because it had been silenced. Because it had lost relevance. Her body exhaled. A sound she hadn't planned. Her spine adjusted. Her shoulders released their grip. The heaviness behind her eyes softened into something like relief, though she didn't name it that yet. She stayed there. Not timing it. Not monitoring. Not improving the moment. Just sitting. And in that sitting, something registered with a clarity that startled her.

Nothing bad happened. The world did not collapse. She did not disappear. No verdict arrived to punish her for stopping. There was only the floor. The cabinet at her back. The quiet hum of appliances. Her own breath moving, faithful as ever. The echo resumed, tentatively. Offering commentary. Suggestions. Mild concern. She did not answer. She stayed. And in staying, she realized what this was. Not laziness. Not avoidance. Not regression. Consent. The smallest kind. A yes to gravity. A yes to sensation. A yes to what her body had asked for before language had time to interfere. She did not feel triumphant. She felt aligned. As if something inside her had finally been met where it lived. Later, she would understand this moment for what it was. Not rest. Not insight. Not healing. Trust, taking its first step. A quiet agreement between her and herself. *"I will listen."* And that yes, she would learn, did not need to be loud to be life-changing. It only needed to be real. And sat down on the kitchen floor. The cold tile pressed through her jeans. Solid. Undeniable. A fact her body could trust without translation. Her back found the cabinet. Wood and metal meeting bone. Her breath changed without permission. Deeper. Slower. As if something that had been holding it up from the inside finally set it down and let gravity finish the sentence. The echo faltered. Not silenced. Disoriented. It tried to reassemble its narrative, reached for its usual scaffolding of meaning and outcome. But there was no opening. No argument to enter. No catastrophe to prevent. Just a woman on a floor, feeling her weight arrive where it had been all along. Her palms rested on her thighs. She noticed their warmth. The living heat of herself. She noticed the way her ribs moved, widening and softening in their own time. She noticed that the ache behind her eyes loosened when she let them close, as if the effort of holding the world at bay had finally been released. Nothing had been solved. But something had been answered. And in that answering, something inside her aligned. Not with meaning. With contact. Not with explanation. With presence. The kind that does not interpret. The kind that simply stays. She stayed there longer than was reasonable. Longer than efficiency would approve of. Long enough for the refrigerator's hum to become a rhythm instead of a noise. Long enough for the air on her skin to feel like information. Long enough for time to stop asking anything of her. Long enough to realize something quietly profound. This presence, this quiet inner gravity, did not want to rescue her from her life. It did not want to lift her out of difficulty or rewrite the day into something gentler. It wanted to place her back inside it. Inside her body. Inside the moment. Inside the simple, unremarkable truth of being here. And as she sat there, weight settled, breath moving, floor holding, she understood that this was the yes she had been waiting for all along. Not a yes to becoming someone else. A yes to being where she was. And from that place, she could stand again when she was ready. Not because she had to. Because she could. When she finally stood, the echo resumed its commentary. Of course it did. But it was thinner now. Less dense. As if the room had subtly changed shape, and it hadn't been informed. Its words skimmed the air without finding purchase, like sound in a space that no longer amplified it. Eliza leaned against the counter, surprised by the simplest, strangest thought she had had in years. *"I can listen."* Not to the noise. To the body. To the place where sensation rises before story. To the part of her that did not explain itself because it did not need to persuade. She hadn't fixed anything. The day was still the day. The questions were still waiting wherever she had left them. But she had done something unprecedented. She had received herself. Not evaluated. Not corrected. Not improved. Received. And she knew, with the quiet certainty that only lived experience gives, that this small obedience had altered the architecture of her inner world. Not because it was dramatic. But because it was repeatable. Because now there was precedent. Now there was memory. Now there was proof that another way of responding existed. The echo could speak. But so could the floor. The breath. The pull. And she had followed one. On purpose. As she moved through the rest of her afternoon, nothing outward announced itself as changed. No resolution arrived. No banner unfurled. But inside, something fundamental had shifted position. She was no longer waiting to be told what was true. She was learning how to feel it. And that knowledge did not shout. It settled. Like weight returning to the soles of her feet. Like a body remembering how to stand.

The Mimic

It happened quietly. That was what unsettled her most. Eliza had begun to recognize the echo by its coldness, its sharp geometry, the way it spoke in verdicts and collapses. She knew its angles now. Its favourite entrances. Its weight. She had learned how it pressed, how it narrowed, how it always leaned toward conclusion. But this morning, what rose inside her did not feel like the echo. It felt kind. Soft. Almost wise. "*You're tired*," it said. "*You've been through a lot.*" "*Maybe you don't need to try so hard today.*" Her shoulders loosened at the sound of it. Her jaw unclenched. "*Yes*," she thought. "*That's true*." The words carried the texture of care. The tone of a hand on the back. The rhythm of something that sounded like permission. She closed her eyes. And for a moment, she leaned toward it. Then it continued. "*You don't have the strength you think you do.*" *"Rest means stepping back." "Let it all go for a while."* Something in her chest tightened. Not fear. Friction. A faint resistance, like a grain of sand under silk. Subtle, but undeniable. The kind of discomfort that doesn't shout but asks to be noticed. She stayed still and listened again, this time not to the tone, but to the effect. The first voice she had been learning to follow never argued. It never concluded. It never collapsed her into an identity. It did not tell her what she was capable of or not. It spoke in sensations. In warmth. In breath. In hunger. In the simple, unedited language of *now*. But this voice, however gentle its opening, was already drawing a line. Already telling a story about who she was. Already steering her away from herself. It framed retreat as care. It called contraction rest. It offered relief that required disappearance. It sounded soothing, but it narrowed the field. It invited her to step back not into her body, but out of her life. And she felt the difference. Not as a thought. As a cooling. As a slight hollowing. As the quiet sense of being guided *away* from contact rather than toward it. She realized then: the echo had learned to mimic warmth. It had studied her language of care. Borrowed the cadence of compassion. Learned how to enter without sharp edges. But it still carried the same destination. Away. Away from sensation. Away from agency. Away from the ground she had just learned how to stand on. She did not confront it. She did not shame herself for almost believing it. She simply stayed. With the breath that was still breathing her. With the body that had asked for nothing dramatic. With the presence that did not need to persuade her to rest by taking her away from herself. And in that staying, she understood something essential. True rest does not shrink you. It returns you.

True kindness does not tell you who you are. It lets you feel where you are. The mimic spoke again, softly. And she did not follow. Because she had learned the difference between a voice that comforts by closing the door; and one that holds the door open and waits for her to step through when she is ready. She opened her eyes. The room was the same. Light on the wall. A bird somewhere outside. The steady, ordinary miracle of being here continuing without commentary. Nothing had shifted. And everything had. She placed a hand on her sternum. "*Wait*", she thought. Not to the voice. To herself. She didn't answer it. She didn't soothe it. She didn't correct its logic. She checked it. The way you test water with your fingers instead of trusting the sign. The embodied voice, when it came, did not speak in sentences. It never did. It arrived as temperature. As a subtle downward settling in her belly. As a need for water. As the small, insistent pull to stretch her legs, to feel length return to her bones. So she waited for that. The voice spoke again, almost soothing now, almost tender in its persuasion. *"You don't need to feel all this." "You don't need to be here." "You can disappear into something easier."* There it was. The pivot. The place it always turned. The slide from care into erasure. From rest into retreat. From gentleness into absence. The invitation to leave herself under the guise of being kind. Her fingers curled slightly against her chest. And in that small pressure, she felt it. The other sound. Not words. A pulse. A quiet, living *yes* inside her ribcage. A warmth that did not rush her. A steadiness that did not explain. It did not tell her what to do. It did not evaluate her capacity. It did not narrate her worth or forecast her future.

It simply existed. Warm. Present. Undeniably here. And she understood, with a clarity that did not need thought, that this was the difference. The echo, even in its softest voice, always asked her to leave. This presence asked nothing. It stayed. It kept breathing when she forgot. It kept pulsing when language failed. It kept holding space for her without demanding she disappear to deserve it. She stayed with that pulse. Let the other voice speak itself out. Let the room remain the room. Let her body be a body. And in that staying, she did not need to decide anything. She only needed to not go. And that, she was learning, was sometimes the bravest act of care there is. The voice tried again, adjusting its tone, softening its edges. *"I'm just trying to protect you."* Eliza inhaled slowly. And as she breathed, something aligned with a clarity that rang like glass settling into its frame. Protection that asks you to vanish is not protection. It is the echo wearing a softer coat. The same old architecture draped in fabric that feels safer to touch. The same destination, approached gently. She reached for her notebook. Not urgently. Not dramatically. With the steady movement of someone confirming a landmark they already recognize. The pen met the page, and she wrote without hesitation, without polish, without trying to make it beautiful:

- Sometimes disguises itself as kindness.
- Begins with comfort, ends with disappearance.
- Speaks *about* my life, never *from* my body.
- Uses gentleness to smuggle old conclusions.

The words felt clean. Not sharp. Accurate. Like labelling something correctly for the first time. The echo fell silent. Not gone. But exposed. Like a stage light snapping on backstage. Like seeing the rigging that makes the illusion possible. It hadn't been defeated. It had been revealed. And revelation, she was learning, did not require force. She sat there, palm resting on the paper, breath moving through her, unhurried and faithful. She felt the embodied presence again. Not as a voice. As contact. As the weight of her body in the chair. As the subtle hunger that meant she was alive and needed tending, not disappearing. Her shoulders dropped. Her jaw softened. The room held. She didn't need to defeat the echo. She had just needed to see it fail at being her. And that failure changed everything. Because once you know the difference between a voice that *speaks you away* and a presence that *keeps you here*, you cannot unlearn it. The echo could still mimic. It could still whisper. It could still dress itself in care. But it could no longer pass as home. And Eliza, sitting there with ink drying on the page and breath steady in her chest, felt something settle into permanence. Not certainty. Orientation. She knew now where she was. And she knew, finally, what she was not.

Consulting the Archive

At first, the archive was something she visited in the quiet. In the calm aftermaths. In the gentle mornings when the echo was distant and she could sit with tea and write what had proven itself true. It felt safe there, almost ceremonial. A place to record victories already won. But the real test came inside a spiral. It began one afternoon without ceremony. A familiar inward tilt. A sudden heaviness in her limbs. The sense that the room had subtly receded, that she was standing at the lip of something old. The echo was already there, threading itself through her thoughts, stitching meanings together too quickly, turning ordinary sensations into evidence. *"You're back here again. Nothing has changed. This is who you really are."* Her chest tightened. The well's cold architecture seemed to reassemble itself around her. The old geometry returned. Depth. Drop. The echo's confidence blooming in the dark. Normally, this was the point where she would disappear into it. Follow the echo downward. Let it narrate her until she no longer remembered how to speak from anywhere else. But something new interrupted the pattern. Not hope. Not confidence. Procedure. She felt the notebook before she thought of it. Its weight on the desk. The faint roughness of its cover. The fact of it, sitting in the world, unarguable. Her hand moved toward it the way a swimmer reaches for the side of a pool. Not dramatic. Instinctive. A body remembering where support lives. She opened it. Not to write. To read. She didn't look for explanations. She didn't look for reassurance. She went straight to the fragments. The entries without story. The places the echo had failed to colonize. *"Warm mug between my palms. Laughter surprised me. Fell asleep without bracing. Left early and nothing bad happened. Body softened when I told the truth."* The echo scoffed. Of course it did. *"This doesn't mean anything."* She didn't answer. She read another. And another. The spiral didn't vanish. The heaviness didn't lift all at once. But something shifted in the physics of the moment. The well no longer dropped straight down. There were ledges now. Edges. Texture. The archive wasn't there to rescue her. It was there to remind her of gravity. Of weight that had held before. Of moments that had not fallen apart. Of experiences that had existed without needing the echo's permission. She noticed her breath deepen between lines. Not because she told it to. Because it recognized something familiar. Something true. Her shoulders lowered a fraction. Her feet pressed into the floor. The echo kept talking. But it had lost exclusivity. It was no longer alone with her past. The archive didn't argue with the spiral. It widened the room. It said, without saying it: *"This has happened too. This also exists. You are not only what hurts."* She closed the notebook and held it against her chest for a moment. Not as comfort. As ballast. As proof of contact.

The well was still there. But so was the ground. And for the first time, standing inside the pull of an old descent, Eliza did not need to climb her way out. She only needed to remember where she could stand. And the archive, quiet and unassuming, had shown her. Not a way forward. A way *here*. The echo scoffed. *"Writing won't help. You already know what's in there."* She didn't answer. She opened it again. The archive was not organized like a diary. It had no dates. No narrative arc. No attempt to explain how one thing led to another. It was a collection of anchors. Short entries. Sensory fragments. Unarguable moments. Things that had not asked permission to be true.

- The warmth of my mother's hand on my wrist last winter.
- The way my body leans toward sunlight without being told.
- The sound I made when I laughed yesterday. It surprised me.
- The feeling of finishing something hard. It lives in my shoulders.
- The fact that hunger returns.

She read slowly. Not to convince herself of anything. Not to argue against the spiral. To re-enter. To let her attention sink back into places where language had followed sensation instead of replacing it. The echo tried to keep speaking, but its sentences began to lose cohesion, like a radio slipping between stations. *"You always—" "This proves—" "You never—"* The words arrived fragmented now, stripped of their former authority. She placed a finger on one line.

• I can feel my feet on the floor even when my thoughts say I'm gone.

She looked down. Her feet were there. The pressure was there. The slight ache in her left heel. The coolness of the tile seeping upward. Gravity doing its quiet work without commentary. Without judgment. Without needing her belief. Her breath changed. Not because she told it to. Because it recognized something solid. The archive was not arguing with the echo. It was refusing to speak its language at all. It did not counter conclusions with better conclusions. It did not replace one story with another. It bypassed the courtroom entirely and walked straight into the body. Into contact. Into evidence that did not require interpretation. The echo spoke again, thinner now, its confidence leaking through the cracks. *"That doesn't mean—"* She didn't finish the sentence for it. She stayed with the pressure in her feet. The way the floor held without asking. The way presence did not need to defend itself. She realized then what the archive truly was. Not a reminder of who she had been. A record of where she could return. A map made not of ideas, but of places her body had survived intact. The spiral loosened its grip. Not gone. But interrupted. Its walls no longer smooth. Its drop no longer inevitable. There was texture now. Friction. Edges she could feel. The echo fell quiet again. Not defeated. Displaced. She closed the notebook gently, like setting something valuable down rather than putting it away. Her hand rested on the cover. She felt its weight. Real. Present. The well was still there. But so were her feet. And that, she understood as she stood there breathing, was enough to keep her from falling. Each entry was a door back into the body. Back into time. Back into specificity. The echo dealt in totalities. *Always. Never. Forever.* The archive dealt in texture. Weight. Weather. Contact. She turned a page.

• *I wrote this during a storm. The rain was loud. I was afraid. I stayed.*

Her breath caught. She remembered the rain on the roof. Not symbolically. Exactly. The way it struck metal in uneven waves. The precise gray of the sky. The smell of wet air pressing against the windows. The way her shoulders had softened an hour later, without ceremony, without instruction. The memory did not glow. It did not redeem anything. It did not promise transformation. It simply stood. And in standing, it contradicted the echo's Favorito claim. That nothing ever changes. That she never stays. That she is only the falling. Her hands steadied on the paper. The spiral did not vanish. It did not politely excuse itself. But it slowed. The way water slows when it meets a hand. The way descent pauses when it encounters resistance. She added a new line, right there, in the middle of the current moment. No preamble. No conclusion. Just fact, recorded as it was happening.

• *I am in a spiral, and I am reading.*

• *That means something in me can still choose.*

The words did not fix the spiral. They located her within it. She closed the notebook and held it against her sternum. Not like a shield. Not like armor. Like a witness. Something that had seen her stay before. Something that could testify without embellishment. The echo was quieter now. Not gone. But displaced. It no longer occupied the whole interior. There was a second presence in the room. Paper. Breath. The soft sound of the refrigerator. The dull, living thud of her own pulse, keeping time without asking permission. She did not climb out of the well. She built a ledge. And she stood on it. Consulting what she had learned was real. Staying with what could be felt. Letting gravity hold without surrendering to the drop. And slowly, without effort, the descent loosened its grip. This was how the archive became what it truly was. Not a record of recovery. A tool of orientation. A way to say, in the middle of distortion: *"Here. This happened. This is happening. This is not the echo."* And neither am I.

The Field Guide (First Use)

She didn't reach for it because she believed in it. She reached for it because her hands needed something to do that wasn't pulling her deeper. The spiral had come fast that day. Too fast. One moment she was rinsing a mug. The next, the room felt subtly farther away, as if the air itself had lengthened. Distance crept in without moving anything. The familiar inward drag began. The quiet tilt. The sense that gravity had remembered her name. The echo was already arranging its furniture. *"This again. Of course, this again. You know where this goes."* Her chest tightened. Her thoughts blurred at the edges, as ink dropped into water, spreading faster than shape could hold. Normally, this was where the story sealed. Where the echo became the only narrator left standing. Where the descent felt inevitable, rehearsed, precise. But earlier that week, in a pocket of relative calm, she had written something new on the first page of a small notebook and circled it in pencil: **FIELD GUIDE**. Not a diary. Not a confession. A guide. She had meant it almost playfully then. A private joke with herself. A way to observe instead of drown. A way to catalogue the echo, the way one might catalogue a weather system or a species of bird. *Habitat. Behavior. Warning signs. Common disguises.* She pulled the notebook toward her now, hands slightly unsteady, and opened it. The echo scoffed immediately. *"This is ridiculous. You're past this. Writing won't help."* She didn't answer. She turned the page. At the top, written in her own handwriting, careful and plain, were the first instructions. Not advice. Observations.

- *If the room feels farther away, I am already in the field.*
- *If the voice speaks in inevitables, it is not information. It is weather.*
- *If I feel pulled downward, look for something to touch.*

Her eyes lingered on the last line. Her hand followed it without asking. The counter. Cool. Solid. The edge pressing into her palm. Contact registered before meaning. The echo kept talking. Of course it did. But now it had been reclassified. Not a truth. A phenomenon. A pattern repeating itself under certain conditions. She wrote as the spiral breathed around her.

- *Current conditions: heaviness in chest. Narrowed vision. Urge to disappear.*
- *Echo language: "always," "again," "you know how this ends."*

Writing slowed her. Not magically. Mechanically. The way naming something gives it edges. The way a storm behaves differently once it has a name. The echo did not leave. But it stopped filling the sky. She added one more line, the pencil pressing harder than the others.

- *Observation: I am writing inside the spiral.*

Her breath changed. Just slightly. Enough. The field guide was not rescuing her. It was orienting her. Turning panic into terrain. Turning collapse into a place that could be mapped. She could feel the mug still in the sink. The sound of water dripping. The steadiness of the floor under her feet. The spiral was still there. But now it was something she was inside *and* observing. And that, she realized as she stood there breathing, was the first skill the guide had taught her. Not how to escape the field. How to walk it without losing herself. She had not yet tested it in a storm. Now the storm was here. The echo leaned closer not ready to surrender, lowering its voice the way it always did when it wanted to sound inevitable. *"You don't need that. You already know what's in it. You always end up here."* Her vision narrowed. The sink felt very far away, like something seen through the wrong end of a telescope. Her own name felt faint, as if it belonged to someone she had once known. The well opened its familiar mouth. And then, almost by accident, her fingers brushed the notebook where it lay on the counter where she had put it down. The contact startled her. Paper. Cardboard. A real edge. Something that existed outside the spiral. She stood there, suspended between the well and the kitchen, between the voice and the body. Between collapse and contact. The moment stretched, thin and trembling. Then she did something new. She opened it again. The first page was simple. Almost blunt. No poetry. No comfort. Just observation, written for exactly this moment.

COMMON ECHO PHRASES:

- "This means nothing has changed."
- "You always ruin things."
- "This is who you really are."
- "There is no point trying."

Her breath stuttered. Because the echo was speaking one of them *right now*. Not metaphorically. Literally. The recognition landed before thought could interfere. A clean click of alignment. Like matching a footprint to the boot that made it. The voice in her head faltered for half a beat, startled by being seen. She traced the words with her finger. Not to soothe herself. To confirm location. *Field condition confirmed.* She turned the page.

NOTES:

- *The echo always speaks in conclusions.*
- *It never references the present moment.*
- *It does not notice breath, temperature, or contact.*
- *It sounds urgent when it is losing ground.*

The echo surged, irritated now. *"You're overthinking. This is just how you are."* She looked back at the list. There it was. Catalogued. No longer singular. No longer personal. A pattern. A species. A behavior observed across time. Something loosened in her chest. Not relief. Orientation. The room widened a fraction. The sink returned to scale. The counter edge pressed reassuringly into her hip. She felt her feet. Both of them. Solid. Present. She wrote one new line, right there, her handwriting slightly uneven but legible.

- *If it sounds familiar, it is not current.*

The echo sputtered. Tried to reassert itself. But now it was speaking next to a document that had already named its tricks. Already mapped its routes. Already anticipated its favourite exits. She did not argue with it. She did not reassure herself. She did not try to feel better. She stayed with the page. With the counter. With the breath that kept arriving even when she wasn't asking for it. The storm did not end. But it stopped being total. It had borders now. Edges she could feel. Her breath caught. The echo had just used the third one of the Common phrases. Exactly. Seeing it written there did something strange to the moment. The sentence did not disappear. It did not retreat or apologize. But it lost its disguise. It was no longer *her*. It was no longer insight or self-knowledge or truth arriving late. It was a line in a field guide. A call she recognized. A sound that belonged to a species she had already named. A pattern. She felt the shift in her body before she could name it. A small loosening behind her sternum. The way tension eases when confusion resolves into recognition. She was no longer inside the sentence. She was standing next to it. She turned the page.

PATTERNS:

- Appears suddenly, often after neutral moments
- Speaks in absolutes
- Uses memory as evidence
- Speeds time up
- Flattens identity

Her eyes moved down the list, and with each line something in the room came back into focus. The sink regained its edges. The hum of the refrigerator returned to a sound instead of a threat. Her pulse slowed, not because she commanded it to, but because it recognized the terrain. *Speeds time up.* Yes. The echo was already rushing her toward an ending, skipping over the middle where she still existed. *Flattens identity.* Yes. It was trying to compress a living, breathing person into a verdict small enough to carry. She stayed with the page. Let the words meet the moment they had been written for. The echo tried to speak again, but now it sounded repetitive, almost tired, like a recording that had been played too many times without being questioned. She noticed something else. The list did not say anything about her being broken. It did not say she was weak. It did not say she would always be this way. It described behavior. External. Observable. Repeatable.

The echo had been moved from the center of her being to the margins of a notebook. Her shoulders dropped a fraction. Her breath lengthened. Not relief. Recognition again. The steadying kind. She turned another page, hands still trembling but sure. Because now she wasn't asking "*what is wrong with me?*" She was asking something far more useful. "*What is happening right now?*" And for the first time in a long time, the question did not pull her deeper into the well. It brought her back to the counter. To the floor. To the body that had been here the whole time. The storm was still moving through her. But it was no longer uncharted. And she was no longer mistaken for the weather. The room wavered. But something else steadied. She could feel the notebook in her hands. The slight bend in its spine where it had been opened too many times already. The unevenness of the pen marks pressed harder in some places, lighter in others. Evidence of a hand that had trembled and written anyway. Of contact, made real. The echo tried again, softer now, coaxing instead of commanding. "*You're just distracting yourself.*" "*This doesn't change anything.*" She didn't answer. She flipped to the next section.

WHAT THE ECHO CANNOT DO:

- Feel temperature
- Breathe
- Laugh
- Notice light
- Choose

She stopped. *Choose.* Her thumb rested there, warm against the paper. The word did not comfort her. It did not soothe the spiral or promise relief. It did something far more grounding. It located her. She was the one holding the notebook. The one turning the pages. The one whose breath was still arriving, shallow but faithful. The one whose fingers could feel paper, pressure, warmth. The echo could describe choice. It could not make one. The spiral did not end. It still tugged. Still murmured. Still tried to pull her toward old gravity. But its authority cracked. Not shattered. Cracked. Enough for something else to slip through. She felt it in the way her feet pressed into the floor without instruction. In the way her shoulders lowered a fraction when she realized she was still acting, still orienting, still here. The echo spoke again, thinner now, its certainty leaking. She stayed with the word. *Choose.* Not as a command. As a fact. The choice she was already making. To hold instead of drop. To read instead of fall. To stay in contact with what could be felt rather than disappear into what could be said. The field guide had not changed the storm. It had changed her position within it. And standing there, notebook warm in her hands, breath still moving through her ribs, Eliza understood something that did not need explanation. The echo could roar. But it could not choose. And she could. That was enough to keep her upright. Enough to keep her here. She went to the final page she had prepared, unsure if she would ever need it. The paper felt thinner there, as if it knew it was meant for moments like this.

WHAT TO DO WHEN IT'S ACTIVE:

1. Name it. ("*This is the echo.*")
2. Touch something solid.
3. Read what has already been written.
4. Add one true thing from the present moment.

Her lips parted. "*This is the echo,*" she whispered. The words felt awkward. Untrained. Like speaking a language still forming muscle. The echo stuttered. Not in volume. In rhythm. Its flow lost its seamlessness, like a song skipping a beat it expected her to fill. She reached out and pressed her palm flat against the counter. Cold. Smooth. Unarguably here. The chill traveled up her arm, sharp enough to cut through abstraction. Her body registered it immediately. *Contact confirmed.* She scanned the earlier pages until her eyes landed on a line she had almost forgotten writing:

- *The sound of water filling a mug calms something low in my chest.*

Her breath shifted. She could feel that place now. Low. Subtle. The place that didn't argue, didn't analyze, didn't need to be convinced. The echo muttered something about coincidence. She didn't answer. She turned to the sink. Turned the tap. Water rushed in, clear and immediate, striking ceramic with a sound that filled the small space. Not loud. Complete. The echo faltered again, losing ground to the rhythm. Her chest softened exactly where the note had promised it would. As if her body remembered the instruction before her mind could interfere. She held the mug steady. Felt the vibration through her fingers. Watched the water rise. Steam curled faintly upward, carrying warmth into the air. The present moment assembled itself piece by piece. She returned to the notebook and added one line, her handwriting calmer now, more anchored:

- *I am standing at the sink. Water is running. My hand is warm.*

That was it. No insight. No revelation. No conclusion. Just a true thing. The echo was still there. Of course it was. But it had been interrupted by reality. By sequence. By a body doing what bodies do when allowed to stay. She held the notebook. Not because the storm had ended. But because she had followed the guide all the way through. And standing there, mug warming her hands, water still singing softly into the basin, Eliza understood what this page had really been for. Not emergencies. Practice. A way to rehearse presence until it became available even under pressure. A way to remember, in the middle of distortion, how to come back by the simplest route possible. Name. Touch. Read. Add. The echo spoke again, thinner now, its edges dulled by steam and sound and weight. She listened. And then she chose to keep pouring. Because for this moment, that was enough to stay. She turned the tap on. Water rushed forward, immediate and undeniable. The echo kept speaking, but it no longer sounded like law. It sounded like noise. A signal without authority. Static leaking into a room that had found another frequency. The frequency passing through air that no longer rearranged her bones. She picked up the pen. Her hand shook, but it moved.

- I am standing at the sink.
- The water is warm.
- My shoulders are tight.
- I am reading.
- That means I am not only the echo.

The ink looked darker than the others. New. Alive. Still slightly glossy on the page. Still wet enough to catch the light. Proof not of insight, but of arrival. Evidence of something happening *now*, not something remembered or rehearsed. She watched it settle into the paper, the way truth sometimes does when given a place to land. She closed the notebook. Not because the spiral was gone. Not because the echo had surrendered. But because something else had arrived. Orientation. The well was still there. Its depth unchanged. She could feel its pull, its familiar gravity. Its old pull intact. But so was the counter beneath her palm. The water running steadily into the basin. The notebook resting on the counter, closed but present. Warm from her hands. Her hands themselves. Her breath, counting itself without being asked, keeping time the way it always had, faithful and unremarkable. For the first time, the echo had not been the only sound in the room. And for the first time, she had not followed it blindly. There was water. There was breath. There was the soft scrape of paper settling. There was the quiet weight of a body still standing. And for the first time, she had not followed the echo blindly. She had consulted something else. Not hope. Not certainty. A guide. And in doing so, she discovered something quietly radical. The spiral was not a trapdoor. It was terrain. Something that could be entered. And interrupted. And lived through without surrendering authorship of her own presence. It was not a trapdoor that erased her the moment she stepped near it. It was terrain. Difficult terrain. Slippery, old, familiar terrain. But terrain, nonetheless. A place where footing mattered. Where landmarks existed. Where presence could still be practiced. This was the first time the field guide did what it had been named for. It did not remove her from the landscape. It showed her where she was. And just as importantly, where the echo was not. She stood there a moment longer, water still running, listening to the sound, feeling the warmth, letting her body register the simple fact of having stayed. Not unbroken. Not serene. But here. Breath still arriving and felt the quiet confidence of someone who has learned the difference between being lost and being *in the field*. The echo murmured on. But now, it was only part of the weather. And she knew how to read the sky. And that, she understood now, was enough to change everything. The field guide had done what it was meant to do. Not calm the weather. Teach her how to recognize it while standing inside it. She touched the notebook slowly, rubbing the edges. She knew because she was not done. But she was here. The echo continued, thinner now, its authority fraying. And Eliza, standing in her kitchen with paper still warm from her hands, understood something quietly radical. She was not lost. She was navigating. And for the first time, she knew how to tell the difference.

The Anchor

The spiral did not announce itself. It rarely did. It arrived the way weather arrives when you are already outside. A subtle pressure change. A quiet tilt in the inner air. No thunder. No warning. Just the sense that something had shifted while you weren't looking. Eliza was in the grocery store. Fluorescent lights humming overhead. The low ocean sound of refrigerators breathing cold into the aisles. A child laughing somewhere too sharply, the sound ricocheting off metal and tile. She was reaching for a carton of milk when the floor seemed to recede by half an inch. Just enough. Her chest tightened. Her thoughts thinned. The edges of the world softened, as if someone had breathed on a lens. The echo stirred. *"Here it comes. You know this feeling. You're losing ground."* Her fingers curled around the carton, but it no longer felt like milk. It felt like evidence. The past rushed forward with its usual confidence. Old sensations lining up like witnesses. The echo began stitching them into a familiar narrative, pulling memory into a single, narrowing corridor. Her heart accelerated. The aisle lengthened. The present started slipping. And then, almost beneath thought, something else happened. Not a sentence. A sensation. Her heel shifted. The cool of the tile pressed back. It was small. Almost unremarkable. The kind of thing the echo would normally dismiss as nothing. But it was *now*. It belonged to the moment that was still happening. She froze the movement. Not rigid. Attentive. She let her weight settle fully into that heel. Felt the exact place where the shoe met the floor. The faint ache there. The steady resistance that had nothing to say about her history. The echo kept speaking, trying to pull her backward into its tunnel of meaning. She stayed with the pressure. With the contact. With the fact that gravity was still holding her exactly where she stood. The spiral did not stop. But it hesitated. Just enough. The anchor was not dramatic. It was not a mantra or a command. It did not argue with the echo or demand the present reclaim itself. It simply *was*. A point of contact that did not move when the story did. Her breath found that point and slowed. Her shoulders dropped a fraction. The aisle did not shrink back to normal yet, but it stopped stretching. She understood then what the anchor truly was. Not something to escape the spiral. Something to interrupt its speed. A way to say, without words: "*This is happening now.*" And standing there, heel pressed to tile, milk cold against her palm, fluorescent light buzzing faithfully overhead, Eliza realized she was still in the store. Still in her body. Still here. The echo murmured on. But it no longer had her balance. And for the first time in a public aisle, surrounded by strangers and cereal boxes and the ordinary noise of living, she knew exactly what she was standing on. Not certainty. Contact. And that was enough to keep her from falling. Her therapist had called it an anchor. She had thought the word sounded too nautical. Too clean. Too composed for what this felt like. But here, in the middle of the store, with the echo beginning its climb, she understood. An anchor is not what stops the storm. It is what tells the ship where it is. She did not argue with the echo. She did not try to replace it with better thoughts or brighter interpretations. She did something simpler. She dropped down. Out of the narrowing tunnel of language and into the body that was still standing. Into her feet. Into the pressure of bone through skin into tile. Into the exact temperature of the air moving across her wrists. The echo continued, relentless in its familiarity. *"This always happens. You can't hold steady. You're about to disappear into this."* Her vision wavered. The lights blurred slightly at the edges. She bent her knees a fraction. Pressed her toes into her shoes. Let her breath lengthen itself without command. In. Out.

In her pocket, her fingers found the smooth stone she had started carrying weeks ago. A river stone. Palm-sized. Unimpressive. The kind of thing no one would ever notice. She wrapped her hand around it. Cool. Solid. Unnegotiably present. She named, quietly, inside herself. Not to calm the echo. To orient. *Feet. Stone. Breath. Milk carton, damp from the fridge.* The echo faltered. Not silenced. Displaced. It tried to follow her down. To invade the sensations. To reinterpret the moment, to turn contact into commentary. But the body was already speaking. Pressure. Temperature. Weight. Contact. There was no metaphor in these. No story. No past pulling at their edges. No future rushing to claim them. Only here. The aisle did not suddenly become serene. The child still laughed too loudly. The refrigerators still hummed. The lights still buzzed overhead. But Eliza was no longer slipping sideways out of herself. She was anchored. Not fixed. Located. She stood there long enough for the spiral to lose its speed. Long enough for the echo's urgency to thin. Long enough to feel the quiet power of staying. And in that ordinary, fluorescent-lit moment, she understood something her body would remember long after her mind forgot the details. An anchor is not an escape. It is a way to remain in the world while the weather moves through you. And she was still here. Holding milk. Holding stone. Holding herself steady enough to choose the next step. That was enough. It always was. Her pulse still raced. The aisle still felt slightly unreal, as if the world had been shifted a half-step to the left. But she was no longer falling through it. She was in it. Standing. Breathing. Holding. The echo shifted strategies, growing quieter, more insinuating. *"This won't last. You're only distracting yourself."* She pressed the stone harder into her palm. Not to fight. To feel. The chill deepened. The edges sharpened. The moment thickened, gained density. The body answered what thought could not. A woman passed her with a basket. The wheels rattled across tile. A freezer door opened somewhere down the aisle. Cold air spilled against her calves, sudden and bracing. Life kept touching her. Interrupting the story. Making contact whether she asked for it or not. And slowly, something astonishing occurred. The spiral, which usually swallowed the whole field of awareness, had become partial. A current. Not an ocean.

It moved through her, yes. It tugged. It whispered. It threatened its familiar endings. But it no longer erased everything else. There was still the aisle. The sound. The weight of her body. The stone warming now, adjusting to her hand. She did not feel good. But she felt located. And that was new. She stood there for another minute. Maybe two. Let the breath finish what it had begun. No rush. No triumph. Just staying until the body completed its own cycle of settling. When she finally placed the milk in her basket, her hand was steady enough to surprise her. The ordinary miracle of it caught her off guard. The echo lingered at the edges, muttering, unconvinced. But it no longer owned the center. As she walked away, stone still warm in her palm, a realization moved through her that did not arrive as thought, but as lived knowledge. She did not need to escape the spiral to survive it. She could inhabit something else while it moved. She could drop anchor. And the storm could pass around her. Not because she had defeated it. Because she had learned how to stay.

When the Echo Changed Its Voice

The change did not come as silence. Silence would have been too honest. It came as imitation. Eliza noticed it one afternoon while sitting on the edge of her bed, shoes still on, keys warm in her hand. She had just come back from a walk she hadn't argued herself into. Her body had led. Her feet had known. The air had done something kind. Inside her chest, there was space. Not peace. But space. Room enough to feel herself arrive without commentary. She reached for her journal, intending to add another small, unremarkable truth to her growing archive. And the echo spoke. *"You're doing better."* The words landed wrong. Not because they were cruel. But because they were smooth. She stilled. The echo had never spoken like that. Usually, it came barbed. Or heavy. Or absolute. It trafficked in verdicts and collapses. It did not offer gentle observations. It did not congratulate. It condemned. *"You're doing better,"* it said again. *"See? You don't need all that anymore."* Her fingers tightened around her keys. Metal pressed into skin. Something in her ribs pulled inward, a quiet alarm that did not ring, only registered. The embodied voice, the one she was still learning to recognize, did not speak in sentences. It spoke in sensations. In tightening. In heat. In the subtle recoil of the nervous system when something looks like safety but moves like a trap. This felt, off. The echo was no longer trying to pull her down. It was trying to pull the ground out from under her. *"You don't need the archive. You don't need the anchors. You don't need to listen so closely."* The invitation was subtle. A sleight of hand. Progress as a pretext for abandonment. Improvement as an argument for forgetting what had kept her here. The echo had learned a new costume. It sounded encouraging. Reasonable. Almost proud. And that, she realized, was the danger. Because it wasn't asking her to disappear outright. It was asking her to leave her body quietly. She stayed still. Let the keys cool in her palm. Let her breath continue without rushing to prove anything. She did not correct the echo. She did not reassure it. She did not agree. She checked. The warmth from the walk was still in her legs. The slight ache in her calves. The steadiness in her feet that had carried her out and back without argument. The space in her chest was real. It had not been given by the echo. It had been made by contact. By movement. By listening. *"You're doing better,"* the echo said again, softer now. *"You can stop paying attention."* There it was. The tell. The embodied presence did not respond with words. It responded with a tightening that said: *"Stay."* A heat that said: *"Don't hand this over."* A quiet insistence that attention was not a crutch, but a relationship she was still inside. She understood then: The echo had not changed its nature. It had changed its strategy. It no longer needed to convince her she was broken. It was trying to convince her she was finished. And sitting there, keys cooling, shoes still on, body warm from honest movement, Eliza did something she had learned how to do. She did not retreat. She did not argue. She stayed with what she could feel. And in that staying, the smoothness of the voice lost its shine. The sentence revealed its hollow center. *"You're doing better"* was not an observation. It was an exit cue. She set the keys down. Opened her journal. And wrote, slowly, without flourish:

- *The echo sometimes sounds kind when it wants me to stop listening.*

Her breath deepened. Not relief. Recognition. The echo went quiet, recalculating. And Eliza, still seated on the edge of her bed, still inside her body, understood something that would matter later. Growth does not mean the echo leaves. It means it has to work harder to pretend it belongs. And she was no longer fooled by costumes. The echo continued refusing to surrender, quieter now, smoothing its edges, lowering its voice into something almost reasonable. *"You're fine. You don't need the journal. You don't need the stone. You don't need to pay attention. That was for when things were bad."* A softness had crept into it. Concerned. Measured. Almost kind. And that frightened her more than any cruelty ever had. She closed her eyes. Let her attention drop. Down past the words. Down past the tone. Down into the body that never lied in the same way. Her breath was shallow. Her jaw clenched without asking. Her stomach had gone cold, a sudden hollowing that had nothing to do with hunger. The body was not agreeing. It was registering threat in the absence of attack. The realization rose, clear and strange and precise: *"It's trying to survive."* The echo had not vanished. It had adapted. Where it once ruled by force, it was now attempting authority. Where it once shouted, it was now advising. It was trying to fold itself into her progress. To sit in the teacher's chair. To borrow the language of care. To become indistinguishable from her own emerging voice. Not to destroy her. To remain necessary. She stayed with that understanding, let it settle into her ribs. The echo kept speaking, gently now, patiently, like someone who believed they knew better. And in that patience, she saw it clearly. This was not wisdom. It was preservation. A memory surfaced, uninvited. Her grandmother's kitchen. The sound of a kettle beginning to sing. Not loud yet. Just the thin whistle of heat finding its voice.

Her small hands wrapped around a warm mug. The way safety had once felt like temperature. Like being held without arms. The echo moved immediately to claim it. *"That was a long time ago." "It didn't really mean anything." "You're romanticizing."* But the memory did not blur. It did not thin. It did not collapse into interpretation.

It stayed sensory. Steam curling upward. Ceramic warm against her palms. The quiet steadiness of standing somewhere she did not have to earn. The echo circled it, frustrated now, searching for a way in. But there was no handle. No conclusion embedded in warmth. No argument hidden inside temperature. The body remembered without commentary. And in that remembering, Eliza felt the difference with an almost physical certainty. The echo spoke *about* safety. The memory *was* safety. She opened her eyes. Her chest was still tight. Her breath still shallow. But now there was something else alongside it. A small, living warmth. Not nostalgia. Recognition. The embodied voice did not speak in sentences. It did not defend the memory or elevate it into meaning. It simply stayed with what was true. Warmth had been real. Contact had been real. And what is real does not need permission to remain. The echo tried again, softer still, adjusting its angle. But it was too late. She had seen the move. The way it tried to wear growth like a mask. The way it tried to outgrow her by pretending to be her guide. She placed a hand over her chest. Not to soothe. To verify. The cold in her stomach. The tension in her jaw. The warmth beginning to return, slowly, beneath it all. Her body was voting. And for this time again, she did not feel compelled to explain the result. She whispered, not to the echo, but to herself: *"I'm still listening."* The echo quieted, recalculating. And Eliza remained where she was. Inside sensation. Inside memory that did not bend. Inside a present moment that could not be advised away.

She understood then what progress really asked of her. Not that the echo disappear. But that she refuse to let it become her teacher. And that refusal did not come from defiance. It came from warmth. From contact. From a body that remembered what safety felt like before it ever had a name. The echo tried again. *"You're only remembering it because you want comfort. You're making it up."* Her chest tightened further, a brief constriction like a door pulled almost closed. She opened her eyes. The room came back into focus. The edge of the bed. The light leaning against the wall. And again, she spoke to it. Not aloud. But directly. *"You don't get to touch that."* The words were quiet. Almost gentle. But the effect was not. The echo hesitated. A stutter in the inner field. A fractional pause where its momentum failed. It had always spoken as if uninterrupted. As if it were the only voice in the room. As if no boundary existed between speaking and being believed. Now it recalculated. Its tone shifted again, smoother, almost parental. *"If you keep doing this, you're going to be disappointed." "People don't really change." "You're setting yourself up."* There it was. The pivot. From ruler to guide. From executioner to protector. Fear dressed as wisdom. Control softened into concern. Her stomach turned, a slow, unmistakable signal. Not panic. Recognition. She did not argue with it. Did not counter with evidence or reassurance. She reached into her pocket. Found the stone. Wrapped her fingers around it. Pressed. Cool. Unarguable. Here. The stone did not explain itself. It did not promise safety or improvement. It did not warn her about disappointment. It simply existed in her hand, solid and present, refusing to participate in the echo's story. Her breath moved again, deeper this time, as if given permission. The echo kept speaking, trying to regain its footing, but it was talking into a space that now had weight. Texture. Edges.

She stayed with the pressure of the stone. The temperature difference between her palm and its surface. The faint ache in her fingers from holding too tightly. The body knew where to stand even as the voice searched for leverage. She realized then what the echo was afraid of. Not that she would be wrong. That she would stop asking it for permission. Disappointment, it warned, because disappointment kept her small. Kept her braced. Kept her listening. But the body did not brace at the thought of disappointment. It braced at disappearance. And she was no longer disappearing. She did not need to defeat the echo. She only needed to keep contact. Stone. Breath. Floor. The quiet persistence of being here. The echo trailed off, its sentences thinning, its authority diluted by presence. And Eliza, sitting there with the weight of the stone anchoring her to this moment, understood something that settled not as insight, but as fact. The echo could warn her about the future forever. But it could not live it. She could. And she was. She wrote in her journal: *"New tactic observed. Echo mimics reason. Uses concern. Targets practices. Undermines anchors."* Her hand trembled as she wrote, the pen skidding slightly where the letters leaned too close together. But the words steadied her. They did what they had learned to do. They placed her somewhere solid. The echo recoiled. *"You're overanalysing. You're making it bigger than it is."* She almost smiled. It had never accused her of overanalysing before. It had never tried to shrink itself. That, more than anything, revealed it. The echo had always thrived on enormity. On inevitability. On being the only lens available. Now it was defending its size. She added another line. *"When named, it changes costumes."* The sentence felt precise. Like pinning a specimen without cruelty. Observation, not attack. The room felt different now. Not lighter. But truer. As if something had been adjusted back into alignment. The echo had not disappeared. But it had lost its mask of inevitability. It was no longer the air she breathed. It was something moving *within* the air. Something with habits. Patterns. Reflexes. Something that reacted. Which meant it was not her. As that realization settled, the echo made one last attempt, softer still, almost intimate. *"You don't need to be afraid of me."* And her body answered before thought. A small exhale. A loosening of the shoulders. A quiet settling that did not need permission. Not afraid. Aware. She placed the keys on the table. The sound was gentle, final in a way that surprised her. She sat fully on the bed this time, no longer perched.

Let her weight arrive. Let gravity finish what it had been offering all along. And she let the embodied voice do what it did best. She felt the mattress give beneath her. The way it held her without commentary. The weight of her legs, heavy and real. The rhythm beginning again in her chest, steady as a tide that does not require belief to return. The echo lingered. Of course it did. But it no longer stood at the center. It circled. Testing angles. Trying tones. Searching for the old throne. And for the first time since it had learned to speak, it was not certain where the authority lived. Eliza was. Not as a ruler. Not as a voice that dominated. As a presence that stayed. And staying, she understood, was the one thing the echo had never learned how to do.

Teaching Memory to Return to the Ground

After she named the echo, something subtle began to change. Not in the voice. In the memories. Before, they arrived like weather. Sudden. Uncontained. Dragging whole seasons of sensation behind them. A look could pull a decade into the room. A sound could collapse time. Her body would react before she knew why, breath shortening, muscles bracing, the past spilling into the present as if there were no border between them. Memory did not feel like remembering. It felt like being taken. So she started small. Not with stories. With contact. She began pairing memory with ground. If an image surfaced, she pressed her feet into the floor. If a scene rose, she touched something solid. If emotion surged, she named temperature before meaning. "*Cold mug. Wood grain. Fabric. Air on skin.*" She was not trying to make the memories go away. She was teaching them where they were. Teaching them that this was not then. That this was a room with walls. A body with weight. A present that could hold them without dissolving. At first, the memories resisted. They arrived with their old momentum, flooding sensation, demanding full occupancy. The echo tried to help, rushing in with explanation, warning, verdict. She did not follow it. She returned to the floor. Again. And again. Not forcefully. Patiently. The body learned before the mind did. A memory would rise, sharp and bright, and instead of being pulled into it, she would feel her heels. The past would surge, and she would feel the chair beneath her thighs. Time would try to fold in on itself, and she would name the air on her forearms. Here. Now. This. Something remarkable began to happen. The memories started arriving differently. Still vivid. Still emotional. But less unmoored. They no longer swept her away wholesale. They came with edges. With context. With an awareness of the present running alongside them like a handrail.

They began to *return* instead of *take*. She noticed it one evening when a familiar image surfaced and her breath did not hitch. Her shoulders did not jump. The room did not vanish. The memory stood there, waiting, as if unsure of its role. She pressed her feet into the floor and felt both at once. Then and now. Past and present. Distinct. The echo muttered something about avoidance. She ignored it. This was not avoidance. This was orientation. She was not erasing her history. She was anchoring it. Teaching memory that it could visit without overruling. That it could be felt without becoming the only reality in the room. That it could exist alongside breath and floor and light. Over time, the memories learned the path back. They began arriving already tethered. Already aware of where they had landed. They came with sensation instead of seizure. With feeling instead of takeover. And Eliza understood, in a way no explanation could have given her, that this was what integration actually looked like. Not reliving. Not rewriting. Returning. Returning memory to the ground. Returning herself to the present. And in that shared landing, the past lost its power to steal the now. It could still speak. But it could no longer take her with it. The first time she did it on purpose, she was washing a plate. Nothing ceremonial. Nothing prepared. The warm water loosened something in her hands, and with it, something in time. A childhood kitchen appeared uninvited. Not a story. A fragment. Light slanting across a counter. A voice in another room, indistinct but familiar. The way moments surface before they ask permission. Her chest tightened. The old pull began. That subtle upward lift toward thought, toward explanation, toward being taken. And then she did something new. She did not follow it upward. She followed it down. She felt the edge of the sink press against her hip. The slick curve of ceramic beneath her palms. The steady pressure of her feet inside her shoes, grounded, weighted, undeniably present. She said quietly, almost under her breath, *"Now."* Not to stop the memory. To locate it. The image wavered. Not erased. Not dismissed. But no longer total. It hovered instead of swallowing. It existed *with* her instead of *over* her. Her breath lengthened, surprised by its own freedom. The memory remained, intact and honest. But it did not take her with it. That was the moment she understood. Memory could be held. Not conquered. Not rewritten. Held. So she practiced. When the past knocked, she opened the door with one hand and kept the other on something real. The counter. The chair. The fabric of her sleeve. The rhythm of breath still moving through her ribs. She let the memory stand in the doorway while she stayed inside the room. She built rituals so simple they almost felt foolish. Touch before story. Breath before meaning. Here before then. Again. And again. She let her nervous system learn new pairings. Not *memory equals disappearance*. But *memory equals presence*. Not *remembering means leaving*. But *remembering can happen while staying*. Over time, the body began to trust this. The flinch softened. The reflex slowed. The past learned it no longer had to arrive as an ambush. It could arrive as a visitor. And Eliza, standing at the sink with water running and plates drying beside her, felt something shift that no insight had ever managed to move. She was no longer being taken by memory. She was meeting it. Here. Now. With both feet still on the ground.

Over time, her body began to anticipate the ground. It arrived before instruction. Before decision. A warmth blooming in her palms alongside an old image, as if the hands themselves remembered what to reach for. A breath deepening before panic could finish assembling its scaffolding. Shoulders dropping, not because she told them to, but because they had learned another ending to the story. The response came faster than thought. Reflexive. Earned. She was training memory the way one trains a frightened animal. Not with force. Not with dominance. With consistency. With return. Each time an image surfaced and she stayed. Each time sensation arrived and she met it with contact. Each time the past knocked and found her still standing here. She started keeping a second kind of archive. Not of events. Of anchors. Not narratives. Textures. The weight of her favourite sweater settling across her shoulders like a promise that did not need to be spoken. The particular sound of rain against glass, hollow and close, as if the world were breathing beside her. The sharp, bright burst of citrus when the peel first broke open, scent leaping into air before thought could catch it. The pressure of the stone in her pocket, cool at first, then warming slowly, unmistakably real. She visited these sensations deliberately when she was well. Not to soothe herself. To introduce herself. So they would know her. So they would recognize her touch. So they would come when she was not reaching, not remembering, not strong. And slowly, something extraordinary happened. Memories began arriving with context. They came carrying time. Not as storms that swallowed the present whole. But as weather reports. Information, not immersion. They no longer claimed to be *now*. They arrived with borders. With edges. With a quiet orientation built in. This happened. Then. Not: this is happening.

Not: you are back there. Her body began to believe it. Not because she told it to. Because it had been shown, again and again, that remembering no longer meant vanishing. And the echo hated that. Because grounded memory could not be commandeered. It could not be hijacked into identity. It could not be inflated into prophecy. It could be felt. It could be referenced. It could be placed. And, crucially, it could be closed. The echo thrived on timelessness. On confusion between then and now. On the collapse of distance. But once memory learned to arrive carrying ground with it, the echo lost its favourite terrain.

There was a floor beneath the image. There was breath alongside the feeling. There was a present strong enough to hold the past without becoming it. And Eliza, gathering anchors the way one gathers kindling, understood something quietly foundational. She was not erasing her history. She was teaching it where she lived now. Here. In a body that could feel. In a moment that could end. On ground that could be returned to. Again. And again. One afternoon, as an old scene stirred and her breath wobbled, she pressed her hand flat to the table and said, not with defiance, not with argument, but with orientation: *"I'm here."* The words were plain. Almost forgettable. They carried no power on their own. But her body heard them. The table answered first. Solid. Unmoved. Its edge met her palm with a certainty that did not require belief. The pressure traveled up her arm, into her shoulder, into the place where breath had been losing its way. The wobble slowed. The inhale found a bottom. The room stayed where it was. And the memory obeyed. Not because it was commanded. Because it had been located. It stayed. But it stayed there. No longer flooding the present. No longer climbing into her chest and rearranging her pulse. It hovered at a distance that could be felt without being inhabited. An image, no longer a takeover. A recollection, not a return.

For the first time in her life, the past did not get the whole room. The floor did. The table did. The air did. The simple fact of her weight meeting gravity did. And in that quiet redistribution of territory, she felt it. Not relief. Not victory. Something far more consequential. A boundary. The smallest one. The most important one. Her mind was no longer the only place memory lived. It no longer had to hold everything. Translate everything. Survive everything alone. Her body had become memory's home. A place with walls. With exits. With ground beneath it. And her body knew where it was. It knew the difference between then and now. Between image and environment. Between recall and reality. She stayed there for a moment longer than necessary. Hand on table. Feet on floor. Breath moving through a chest that had learned a new rhythm. The echo hovered somewhere at the edge, uncertain, no longer able to claim the center. She did not push it away. She did not need to. She was here. And here, she was held.

The Moment It Cannot Survive Presence

It happened without drama. No revelation. No thunder. No sudden light. It happened the way real things do. Quietly. In the middle of an ordinary moment. She was sitting on the edge of her bed, afternoon leaking through the curtains, light thinning itself into dust, dust drifting like unhurried thoughts that had nowhere urgent to be. The room held its small sounds. Fabric settling. Air breathing. Nothing had announced this moment as important. Nothing had warned it. Nothing had triggered it. No memory. No clear thought. And yet the echo arrived. Not loud. Confident. It slid in the way it always had, already mid-sentence, already certain it knew her better than she knew herself. A voice without a door, without a greeting. It began to assemble its familiar architecture. Interpretation stacked on interpretation. Accusation laid like a cornerstone. Prediction stretched forward, already rehearsing the future. The old gravity stirred, subtle but persuasive, the kind that does not shove but pulls, patiently. Her chest tightened. The well opened its mouth. That ancient hollow yawned, ready to receive her the way it always had. Ready to be filled with meaning that would sink and sink and call itself truth. And then something different happened. She did not chase it. She did not argue. She did not analyze. She did not flee. She stayed. She stayed with the fabric beneath her hands, the weave pressing its quiet pattern into her palms. She stayed with the temperature of the room, neither kind nor cruel, just real. She stayed with the soft ache in her lower back, the honest complaint of a body that had been holding her upright all day. She stayed with the rise of her breath, the small dependable swell and fall that had never once abandoned her, even when she had abandoned herself. She did not look at the echo. She looked through it. Into the body. Into the room. Into now. At first, the echo kept talking. It always did. It tried to hook sensation into story, to braid feeling into conclusion. It tried to turn discomfort into verdict, turn a passing ache into identity, turn presence into proof of failure. It reached for its old leverage, searching for a crack, a habit, a reflex that would carry her away from the moment and back into its gravity. But she did not go. She did not step into the sentence it was offering. She did not finish its thoughts for it. She did not lend it her imagination. She let it speak into the open air of her attention, unreinforced, unsupported, uninhabited. And without her, it began to thin. Its certainty lost weight. Its edges blurred. The architecture it had built so many times before found no ground to anchor into. No future arrived. No past opened its doors. The well, sensing no offering, did not deepen. It simply remained a shape, no longer a pull. The echo discovered something it had never known before. It could not survive presence. Not the steady presence of breath. Not the simple presence of sensation. Not the unremarkable, unperforming presence of a woman sitting on a bed, feeling what was actually there instead of what had once been. It did not explode. It did not apologize. It did not resolve into wisdom. It faded. Like a voice speaking to an empty room. Like a shadow when the body steps fully into itself. And she remained. Not triumphant. Not fixed. Just here. Still sitting. Still breathing. Still held by the ordinary miracle of a moment that asked nothing of her except that she be in it. This was not a victory anyone could see. There would be no marker for it. But something irreversible had happened. The echo had met the one thing it could not outpace, outthink, or outtalk. Presence. And for the first time, it had nowhere left to go. At first, the echo kept talking. It always did. It tried to hook sensation into story. Turn feeling into verdict. Turn discomfort into identity. It reached for her chest tightening and said, "*this means something is wrong with you.*" It reached for the ache in her back and said, "*this is proof you're wearing down.*" It reached for the quiet and tried to name it emptiness.

But she did not go. She stayed with the fabric beneath her palms. The slight give of the mattress. The way the air rested on her skin instead of pressing. The ordinary courage of her breath continuing without commentary. In. Out. In. The room remained the room. The afternoon remained an afternoon. Dust continued its small, patient orbit through light. And something strange began to happen. The echo faltered. Not dramatically. Not like a voice cut off mid-word. More like a sound losing its surface to bounce from. Its sentences arrived, but they no longer landed. They slid. Skidded. Fell flat. They searched for her participation and could not find it. There was no inward collapse to meet them. No tightening story to receive them. No well opening its mouth. The echo tried to sharpen. Then to soften. Then to explain itself. Then to warn. Then to reason. Its cadence quickened, then thinned. It began repeating itself, circling familiar phrases like a bird confused by glass. And all the while, she remained. Present. Breathing. Here. She felt it then, unmistakably. The echo does not survive presence. It requires distance. It needs her to leave. To tilt out of the room. To abandon sensation for interpretation. To trade contact for conclusion. Without that movement, it had nothing to attach to. No soil. No gravity. No ground. It was still making noise. But it was no longer making meaning. And in that moment, without effort, without decision, without triumph, something resolved itself inside her. The echo was not defeated. It was revealed. It was a mechanism, not a master. A reflex, not a truth. A sound that depended entirely on her absence to feel real. She did not push it away. She did not silence it. She simply stayed. And staying was enough. The well closed its mouth. Not slammed shut. Just, unnecessary. The tightness in her chest loosened a fraction. The ache in her back found a shape instead of a story. Her breath settled into a rhythm that belonged to no one else. The echo dwindled to a background hum. Not gone. But displaced. Like traffic heard from inside a house with thick walls. Present, but no longer personal. No longer persuasive.

She sat there for a while. Long enough to feel the steadiness underneath the moment. Long enough to understand something that could not be unlearned. The echo had always told her it was powerful. But power was never what it had. It had only ever had timing. And now, she had learned something else. Presence is not loud. It does not argue. It does not explain itself. It simply remains. And in remaining, it leaves no room for what cannot live there. She let the sensation stay sensation. She let the breath finish itself. She let the moment be only a moment. No conclusion. No meaning. Just presence. And something strange occurred. The echo faltered. Not stopped. But thinned. As if its footing had slipped on ground that no longer agreed to hold it. Its cadence broke. It repeated itself, unsure. Then rephrased, testing sharper edges. Then softened, attempting a gentler entry. It moved the way a performer does when the lights are still on, but the audience has quietly looked away, when the lines land in empty air and applause refuses to arrive. She stayed. She did not rush to replace it with affirmations. She did not summon courage like a shield. She did not seek insight, interpretation, or rescue. She did not turn this into a lesson. She simply remained. With the weight of her body anchoring her into gravity. With the sound in the room, small and unremarkable. With the undeniable fact of being here, now, breathing inside a body that was not asking to be explained. Seconds passed. Then more. Time loosened its grip on urgency. Nothing chased her forward. Nothing pulled her back. And in that unbroken attention, the echo began to lose coherence. Its sentences detached from her, no longer fastening themselves to her ribs or spine. They floated instead of landing. Reverberations without surfaces. Echoes without walls. She noticed something she had never noticed before. The echo did not leave. It dissolved. Not defeated. Unfed. Not silenced. Uninhabited. It grew faint, not because she forced it away, not because she out-argued or outgrew it, but because there was no interior space left for it to occupy. Presence had filled the room the way water fills a vessel completely, leaving no air pockets, no hollow corners where old voices could hide. The echo searched for a place to stand. There was none. She felt it then. Not as victory. As recognition. A quiet knowing settling into her bones. The realization that what had once felt inevitable was only ever sustained by absence. That the echo had not been powerful. It had been accommodated. And now, with her fully here, inhabiting herself without commentary or escape, it simply could not remain whole. She did not rise from the bed transformed. She did not name the moment. But something had shifted its allegiance. She knew, without drama, without declaration, that presence was not something she had to achieve. It was something she could stay with. And in staying, she had changed the laws of the room.

The echo did not survive attention.

It required drift. It required absence. It required her to be elsewhere. It could not live where she was. A small, stunned breath moved through her. Not a gasp. Not a release. Just a quiet recalibration of air, as if her lungs themselves had understood something before language arrived. "Oh." Not relief. Not joy. Orientation. The way a compass settles after years of spinning. The way the body knows north without celebrating it. She had spent years believing the echo was a power. An enemy. A force with intention and will. Something to battle, to dismantle, to outrun. She had given it weight by opposing it, shape by fearing it, authority by tracking its every movement. But here, under the steady, unblinking light of her own awareness, it was something else entirely. A process. A pattern that only existed when she wasn't. She stayed another moment longer. Not out of effort. Out of curiosity. Just to see. Nothing rushed in to replace it. No sudden peace unfurled its banners. No choir of calm descended. No soft music rose to tell her this was the moment everything changed. There was no emotional crescendo waiting to reward her. Just the room. Her breathing. The ordinary hum of being alive. The quiet electricity of a body continuing its work without commentary. The dull miracle of air entering and leaving. The furniture holding its shape. Time moving without needing her consent.

And in that simple continuity, something irreversible settled. Not loudly. Not ceremonially. Like sediment finding the bottom of clear water. The echo was not the opposite of her. It was the absence of her. A vacancy it had mistaken for ownership. And presence was not something she had to summon, or manufacture, or hold with discipline. It was not a skill to perfect or a state to defend. It was something she could remain. From that day forward, she did not ask, *"How do I make it stop?"* She asked, *"Where am I?"* Not as a philosophical inquiry. As a practical one. A lived question. A bodily check-in. A return. And every time she truly arrived, not partially, not conceptually, but fully, the echo lost its grammar. Lost its authority. Lost its shape. Its sentences collapsed without an audience. Its warnings forgot how to warn. Its predictions failed to assemble a future. Because it could not survive sustained presence. And she could. She did not become invincible. She became inhabitable. And that was enough.

Chapter: Nineteen

The Weight of Depression: A Journey to Climb Out of the Dark Well

The Story

Carrying forward from the quiet understanding that not everything breaks all at once, that some things erode slowly, almost politely, this is where the story deepens and thickens, where the air itself seems to grow heavier. The weight settled on my shoulders the way a damp wool blanket settles on a cold bed. Not dropped. Not thrown. But eased into place with a careful, almost tender patience. Slowly. Insidiously. Until it became indistinguishable from the body beneath it. Until it felt stitched into the very fabric of existence itself, as though it had always been there, waiting for me to notice. It wasn't a sudden blow. No dramatic collapse into darkness. No single moment that could be pointed to and named like a crime scene. There was no thunderclap announcing its arrival. Instead, it came by accumulation. Brick by agonizing brick. Each one small enough to lift. Each one reasonable enough to ignore. Together, they filled a backpack I carried everywhere, even when no one could see it. Especially when no one could see it. Living with depression is like this: carrying a backpack filled with bricks. You can still walk. You can still function. You can still answer emails, smile at strangers, show up where you're expected, perform the choreography of a life that looks intact from the outside. But the weight is always there. A constant, oppressive presence pressing down through muscle and bone, compressing breath, turning even the simplest tasks into something quietly Herculean. Standing up requires negotiation. Showering becomes a calculation. Existing asks for more than you seem to have. At first, it was just a few bricks. Almost laughably light. A missed deadline at work. A strained conversation with a friend that lingered longer than it should have. A nagging feeling of inadequacy that clung to me like a shadow that lengthened no matter where the light came from.

I could manage then. I adjusted the straps. I shifted my posture. I told myself this was normal. That everyone carried something. I shrugged it off. I named it a bad day. A temporary slump. Nothing worth naming. But the bricks kept coming. Quietly. Patiently. And somewhere along the way, the backpack stopped feeling like something I was carrying and started feeling like something I was. But the bricks kept coming. More anxieties. More self-doubt. More crushing waves of despair washing over me one after another, each one breaking before I had fully surfaced from the last, until the weight stopped being something I carried and became something that carried me downward. The balance shifted without ceremony. Somewhere along the way, gravity took over. I was no longer bearing the load. The load was bearing me. Each brick had a story. A missed opportunity replayed until it curdled into proof. A failed expectation hardened into verdict. A perceived flaw swollen to monstrous proportions by the distorting lens of depression, until it blocked out everything else. Nothing stayed proportional. Nothing stayed kind. The smallest misstep echoed like a moral failure. The quietest doubt roared. The backpack grew heavier. My steps grew slower. What once required effort now required will, and what once required will now required something I no longer recognized as strength. The world around me began to blur, its colors draining as if someone had slowly twisted the saturation dial down to nothing. Reds dulled. Blues flattened. Joy lost its edge. Everything softened into a gray, indistinct landscape where boundaries dissolved and meaning thinned, stretched so fine it tore at the slightest touch.

Smiling became an effort. A performance. A carefully rehearsed expression offered up for the outside world like a passport stamped just often enough to grant me passage through daily life. Inside, the darkness gnawed. Not violently. Patiently. Relentlessly. It did not rush. It waited. It knew I was tired. Depression stopped being only a feeling and became a place. A geography. A deep, dark well I found myself standing in without remembering the moment I fell. A chasm of despair yawning beneath my feet, its slick, cold walls reflecting my hopelessness back at me again and again, until my own fear became the only scenery left. The walls whispered my thoughts back to me, distorted but familiar, convincing me they had always been true. It felt bottomless. An endless descent into a pit of nothingness where time lost its meaning and effort lost its reward. There was no bottom to scrape against. No solid ground to shock me awake. Only the echoing silence of my own despair. A suffocating emptiness that pressed in from all sides, threatening to consume me whole, as if the well itself were listening, breathing, waiting, gently but insistently pulling me further into its shadowed depths. And from the depths of that well, once the fall felt endless and the walls had learned my name, something else began to answer me. And then there was the echo. It arrived quietly, almost politely. Not as an interruption, but as a response. A faint tremor at the edge of my consciousness, like a sound you are not sure you heard until it returns and returns again. A suggestion rather than a command. A tempting proposition shaped to sound like relief. A seemingly reasonable answer to the crushing weight of the bricks pressing into my spine, into my breath, into the small remaining spaces where hope once rested. It did not shout. It did not scream. It breathed. Soft enough to almost pass for my own voice. At first, it was barely there. A flicker. A passing thought I could brush aside with effort and distraction. I told myself it meant nothing. That everyone has strange thoughts when they are tired. When they are overwhelmed. When the world feels too heavy to hold.

But with each passing day, with each added brick slipped into my already overburdened backpack, the whisper grew bolder. More familiar. More persuasive. It learned my rhythms. It learned my doubts. It learned exactly how to phrase itself, so it sounded less like danger and more like logic. The echo was the well's response to my cries. A warped reply bouncing back from slick stone walls, intimate and mocking all at once. It took my internal dialogue and bent it just slightly, turning concern into condemnation, exhaustion into evidence. It gathered my thoughts and sent them back to me multiplied, layered, overlapping, until my anxieties and insecurities swelled into a relentless chorus. It was not a single, thunderous declaration. There was no dramatic announcement. That would have been easier to recognize. Easier to resist. Instead, it arrived as pressure. As erosion. A constant, fine drizzle that wore away at me grain by grain. Thought by thought. Day by day. Until even silence felt loud, and my own mind no longer felt like a safe place to stand. There was no dramatic violence in it. No sudden attack. Nothing that arrived with flashing alarms or raised voices. Instead, it worked the way water works on rock. Patient. Persistent. Almost respectful of time. Drop by drop, it wore at my hope, thinned my will to fight, softened my belief in my own worth until those things began to feel porous, unreliable, easy to question. The echo painted pictures. Carefully lit. Deceptively gentle. It curated its images the way a skilled illusionist does, showing me only what it wanted me to see. It framed escape as relief. As release. As permission. A way to finally lay down the bricks without having to explain why they were so heavy in the first place. It spoke the language of rest. Of quiet. Of an end to the ache in my muscles and the static in my mind. It whispered of stillness the way lullabies do, slow and soothing, designed to lower resistance rather than raise suspicion. It did not present disappearance as an ending, but as a solution. A kind of blessed forgetting. A gentle erasure that would hush the echo itself and lift the crushing weight from my back. It made the unbearable feel negotiable. It made the unthinkable sound reasonable. Not because it was, but because I was tired enough to want it to be. It preyed on my vulnerabilities with uncanny precision, feeding on exhaustion, exploiting every hairline fracture in my already splintered self-esteem. It knew exactly when to speak. When I was depleted. When I was alone. When the bricks felt heavier than the future. It wove its lies with such finesse that what should have registered as danger began to masquerade as mercy. The idea it offered no longer appeared as a horrifying act of self-destruction, but as a private kindness. A quiet exit. An answer that asked nothing of anyone else. A way to solve a pain that felt too heavy to explain and too invisible to be believed. The whisper became a siren song, low and melodic, promising an end to the torment, to the endless climb, to the relentless weight of the bricks, even as it drew me closer to the edge of that inner landscape that had learned how to echo my despair back to me in my own voice. And that, perhaps, was its most dangerous trick of all. It is hard to explain the true insidiousness of those whispers, how they never arrive as invaders but as guests. They slip quietly into the mind, set their coats down, rearrange the furniture while you are not looking. Nothing feels immediately stolen. Nothing appears broken. Yet the room is no longer arranged for your comfort. Corners shift. Angles change. What once felt familiar begins to feel subtly wrong. They worm their way into thought, not with force but with suggestion, gently tilting perspective, tinting everything with a quiet, invisible poison. Certainty fades first. Then confidence. Then the sense that some things are simply not up for debate. What once felt solid begins to feel negotiable. What once felt unthinkable begins to feel discussable. They chipped away at my resilience the way tidewater wears down stone. Not by striking it. By returning to it. Again and again. Patient. Persistent. Until resistance thinned and I found myself strangely exposed to their call. Sometimes it felt as though a single splinter of doubt, one grain of despair lodged beneath the skin of an otherwise ordinary moment, could set everything in motion. A thought would shift. A breath would catch. The day would tilt. And suddenly an avalanche of self-destructive thinking would break loose, carrying me downward, spiraling me deeper into the well. It never announced itself. It just happened. A cascade triggered by something so small it felt almost cruel. Yet the well was not only a prison of despair. Over time, it became something else. A mirror. In its dark, reflective depths, I began to see what I had tried not to name.

Not weakness. Not failure. But need. A desperate, aching need for help that I could not, or would not, acknowledge aloud. The darkness, paired with the relentless echo, became a signal flare rather than a sentence. Stark. Unignorable. Illuminating the fragility of my inner world and the urgency of finding another way to live within it. Paradoxically, the very depths of my despair became the catalyst for reaching outward. When every internal strategy had collapsed, when silence no longer protected me, the truth finally surfaced. I could not do this alone. And that realization, as terrifying as it was, carried the first faint outline of relief. The bottom of the well, it turns out, was not where everything ended. It was where something finally began. Seeking help was not a single, cinematic act of courage. It was not a leap or a declaration. It was a climb. Long. Uneven. Often humiliating in its slowness. A painstaking chipping away at the bricks, one by one, with hands that trembled from fatigue and hope in equal measure. Some days the progress was invisible. Some days it felt like retreat. But gradually, with the steady hands of therapists who knew how to listen into silence, the careful calibration of medication that steadied the ground beneath my feet, and the unwavering presence of loved ones who refused to let go of the rope even when my grip faltered, the ascent began to take shape. Even now, the backpack is lighter, but it is not empty. Some bricks remain. Not as punishment. Not as proof of failure. But as memory. As markers of terrain already crossed. They remind me where the path narrows, where footing becomes unsure, where the well's quiet pull still hums beneath the surface. They are weight, yes, but also witness. The echoes still exist, but they are fainter now, their voices thinned by distance and daylight. What once sounded like command now registers as noise. The whispers have lost much of their authority. I recognize them for what they are. Old patterns. Old fears. Old lies that no longer get the final word. The climb continues. It is ongoing. But with each step, hope feels less fragile and more earned. Less like a borrowed idea and more like a muscle being rebuilt. I am learning how to move through darkness without surrendering to it. How to manage the weight without letting it define the shape of my life.

How to pause, breathe, and quiet the insidious voices when they arise, not by fighting them into silence, but by refusing to follow where they lead. And deep down, steady as bedrock, I know this. The journey out of the well, however long and demanding, is worth taking. Because somewhere above, even when clouds gather and the path disappears into mist, the light still waits. It does not rush me. It does not shout. It simply remains. It still beckons. And I will keep climbing.

A Journey to Climb Out of the Well

Living with depression is like carrying a backpack filled with bricks. You can still walk. You can still function. You can still move through the day and answer to your name. From the outside, the motion looks intact. But the weight is always there, tugging downward, dragging at your shoulders, subtly altering your posture to accommodate its presence. Every step asks more than it should. Every movement carries a quiet tax. It becomes a constant reminder that something is different, that you are laboring to stay afloat in a world that seems to move at a pace your body and spirit cannot quite match. Depression is a heavy burden to carry. Overwhelming in its persistence. Isolating in its silence. Suffocating in the way it steals breath from even the smallest moments. It presses not only on muscles and joints, but on meaning itself, flattening joy, dulling curiosity, narrowing the future until it feels like a corridor with no windows. Even rest does not feel restorative. Even stillness hums with effort. To begin healing, there is first the necessity of understanding this weight and the dark shadows that trail behind it. Not rushing past it. Not minimizing it. But turning toward it with honesty. Naming it. Feeling its shape. Learning where it settles in the body and how it speaks in the mind. Acknowledging its presence without shame, without self-accusation, without the need to justify why it is heavy in the first place. This book is an invitation to do just that. An invitation to embark on a journey not toward quick answers or easy light, but toward self-discovery, toward patience, toward the kind of healing that unfolds slowly and honestly. Toward hope that is not forced, but grown. Depression is often described as carrying a heavy weight, a burden that drains energy and dims the spirit. That image is true. But it barely grazes the surface. It captures the strain, but not the depth. The effort, but not the vertigo. To truly understand the insidious nature of depression, especially when it becomes entangled with thoughts of escape and erasure, we need a metaphor that can hold its full gravity. Imagine, instead, a deep, dark well. Depression is the well itself. A seemingly bottomless pit of despair, helplessness, and powerlessness, carved not into the earth but into the very landscape of the mind. It is not stumbled upon by accident.

It is shaped slowly, thought by thought, loss by loss, until one day you realize you are no longer standing on level ground. You are inside it. And it feels as though it has always been there. Its walls are slick with hopelessness, polished smooth by repetition, offering no easy grip, no obvious handhold. Every attempt to climb meets the same cold resistance. Its depths are filled with a chilling, suffocating darkness that presses in from all sides, compressing time, narrowing vision, convincing you that this confined space is the whole of reality. This is the well of depression. And you are inside it. The cold, damp earth clings to your skin. It seeps into you. The air feels thick, heavy with sorrow, as if even breathing requires permission. Each inhale feels borrowed. Each exhale feels uncertain. Above you, the opening is distant. A pale, trembling circle of light that feels impossibly far away, more memory than promise. It flickers with the lives of others, with laughter and movement and ease, all of it distorted by distance and stone. Below you, there is no dramatic abyss, no clear bottom to land on. Only the echo of your own breath. The sound of your thoughts returning to you altered. The familiar weight you have been carrying for so long that it feels fused to your bones. The stillness down here is not peaceful. It is heavy. Expectant. As if the well itself is waiting to see what you will believe about it. This is where the journey begins. Not at the top. Not in the light. Not after everything has already been figured out. But here. In the depths. In the cold. In the quiet that makes no promises. And it is from this place, precisely this place, that the climb, slow and deliberate, first becomes possible. Many of us find ourselves lingering at the rim of that well, not fallen yet, not safe either, hovering in the terrible in-between. We peer into its murky depths and suddenly become aware of how small we feel in comparison to the darkness below. The shadows are so dense they seem to swallow distance itself, bending perception, erasing scale, making it impossible to see where the bottom lies, let alone imagine a way back up. Depth loses meaning here. So does certainty. The sensation of being trapped settles in the chest. Heavy. Constricting. Breath turns shallow, as though the air itself has learned how to hesitate. Your body knows before your mind can explain it. This is what depression can feel like. As though you are standing at the edge of something vast and unforgiving, staring into an abyss that does not rage or threaten, but simply exists, silent and immense, offering no visible path of return. And then there is the echo. Suicidal ideation becomes the sound that answers back from the well's walls. Not a scream. Not a shove. A whisper. Constant. Insidious. Ricocheting through the dark, slipping between thoughts, suggesting that the only way out is downward. It does not arrive as a command because commands can be resisted. It arrives as a suggestion. A proposal dressed in reason. A cruelly logical-seeming thought born from exhaustion, from pain, from the longing for the weight to finally stop pressing so hard against the ribs. The echo repeats itself. Gently at first. Then more often. Until it feels inseparable from your own thinking. Until you can no longer tell where the well ends and you begin. The silence between each whisper grows thin, stretched taut like fragile glass, and in that narrowing space, the mind grows tired of arguing. The most dangerous part is this. The echo does not feel foreign. It feels familiar. It feels like relief thinking out loud. And standing there at the rim, heart pounding, breath shallow, the abyss listening patiently below, it can begin to sound like the only answer that remains. This metaphor may seem simple on the surface, almost too spare for something so complex, yet it holds a profound truth about the lived experience of depression and suicidal ideation. The deep, dark well embodies the feeling of being trapped, isolated, and overwhelmed by sorrow that presses in from every direction, leaving no clear horizon to orient by. It captures the sense of enclosure, the way pain does not merely visit but surrounds, settling into the walls of thought and the marrow of feeling. The darkness represents the erosion of hope. Not its dramatic collapse, but its slow thinning.

The gradual loss of the ability to imagine a future that differs meaningfully from the present pain. Possibility narrows. Time folds in on itself. The mind begins to circle the same territory again and again, as though pacing the perimeter of a small, dim room. It becomes a closed loop, a self-sustaining system of suffering where each thought feeds the next, amplifying despair until escape feels like an abstract concept meant for other people, spoken about in another language. The depth of the well can feel infinite. Its darkness absolute. From where you stand, perspective collapses. The eye searches instinctively for something to grab onto, some sign of structure or support, and finds nothing. No ladder. No handhold. No obvious way to climb free of the crushing weight of your emotions. Effort itself begins to feel futile before it even begins. Only the echo remains, repeating itself in the hollow space, reinforcing the illusion that there is only one conclusion available. Above, the light exists, but it feels distant and unreal, like a story you once heard but can no longer quite believe. It flickers beyond reach, distorted by depth and doubt, easily dismissed as irrelevant to where you are now. Down here, the well seems to define reality. It tells you what is possible. It tells you what is not. And yet, even here, at the edge or deep within its walls, the well tells another truth as well. A quieter one. It reveals how much pain is being carried. How heavy the burden has become. How urgently something needs to change. The very existence of the well is evidence not of weakness, but of endurance stretched to its limit. Of a human system signalling that it cannot keep holding this alone. Even when the way out cannot yet be seen, the well bears witness to the need for one. And that need, once recognized, becomes the first faint outline of another direction.

The Weight of the Backpack

The image of the backpack returns here, not as an abstraction, not as a clever comparison, but as something lived and lodged deep in the body. Felt in the muscles that ache before the day has begun. In the spine that stiffens under invisible pressure. In the breath that never quite drops all the way down. A backpack filled with bricks tells the truth without spectacle. It does not dramatize. It does not exaggerate. It simply states what is. Each brick has a name. Sadness. Hopelessness. Anxiety. Isolation. Fear. None of them arrive all at once. They are not announced. They slip in quietly, added over time, often under the guise of normal life. A worry you assume will pass. A disappointment you decide not to name. A loneliness you explain away. Until one day you straighten your shoulders, instinctively bracing yourself, and realize how hard it has become just to stand. Just as a backpack packed with bricks steals ease from every movement, depression drains effort from even the simplest tasks. What was once automatic now requires intention. What was once light now feels steep. Ordinary moments turn into negotiations. Getting out of bed becomes a decision. Answering a message becomes a calculation. Relationships require more strength than feels available, more presence than you can reliably summon. Daily life, once navigable, turns into uneven ground, and you learn to walk carefully, conserving energy, choosing your steps. You may wake up one morning and discover that small annoyances now feel unbearable, that a passing comment lingers like a bruise pressed again and again. Perhaps it is an unsaid hurt. A quiet fear. A long stretch of moments that never found release, never had a place to land. Brick by brick, the weight builds until it no longer feels like something you are carrying, but something that is carrying you down. And yet, even here, there is something vital to remember. You are not alone beneath this load. The experience of carrying such weight is shared by many, though it so often remains hidden. Behind smiles. Behind laughter. Behind competence and calm. Others may be shouldering their own backpacks filled with unseen bricks, adjusting their posture, masking their strain, moving through the world with the same careful determination. This quiet recognition changes something. It softens the isolation. It loosens the grip of shame. It reminds us that suffering is not a personal failure, but a human one. Through this understanding, a kind of community begins to form. An invisible alliance of people moving slowly, deliberately, toward healing. We may not always see one another's burdens. We may not know the names of each other's bricks. But we are climbing, nonetheless. Each in our own way. Learning how to loosen the straps. How to set a brick down when we can. How to keep going together.

The Deep, Dark Well

From the weight of the backpack, the path leads inevitably here, deeper into the metaphor that holds it all. The well waits. It does not rush you. It does not announce itself. It simply exists, patient and inevitable, as though it has always known you would arrive. Picture it. Cold. Damp. Unsettling. A place where the air itself feels heavy, thick with unspoken sorrow. You stand at the edge, leaning forward just enough to peer into the abyss, and what you sense immediately is not depth alone, but finality. A hush that feels conclusive.

It feels bottomless. Endless. A void that mirrors the all-consuming nature of depression, where escape does not merely feel difficult, but unimaginable. In this place, the mind begins to change its posture. It folds inward. It starts drawing conclusions not from evidence, but from exhaustion. The darkness convinces you it is permanent. That this is not a season, not a state, but a sentence. The future collapses into the present moment, and the present moment insists it is all there will ever be.

This is where the mind becomes dangerously persuasive. The well answers back. Thoughts echo off its walls, warped by stone and distance, returning altered but convincing. They repeat themselves until repetition masquerades as truth. You're stuck here forever. It's never going to get better. These phrases do not arrive like proclamations. They creep in. They linger. They circle. Each return tightens the loop, until despair begins feeding on its own momentum, fueled by fear, by fatigue, by the simple act of surviving another day under too much weight.

And then, in moments of deep vulnerability, something shifts. The echo changes its tone. What once sounded like a nagging presence begins to soften, to smooth its edges. It offers itself not as torment, but as relief. Not as danger, but as an answer. A way to stop the pain. A solution that feels eerily calm, almost compassionate in its phrasing. This is the true danger of the well. Not its depth alone. Not its darkness. But how convincingly it rearranges perception.

How it takes suffering and frames it as inevitability. How it takes exhaustion and dresses it up as clarity. How it speaks in your own voice, using your own thoughts, until it becomes difficult to remember that another way of seeing once existed at all. The well does not just hold despair. It reshapes it. And understanding that is part of learning how to climb.

The darkness here is absolute. Not merely the absence of light, but the absence of hope itself. An erasure of forward vision. An inability to see a path upward or imagine a future that exists beyond the cold stone walls pressing in on all sides. Possibility collapses here. The mind stops reaching ahead and begins to curl inward, guarding what little energy remains.

Every attempt to climb feels futile. Every grasp for a handhold meets slick resistance, skin sliding over stone worn smooth by countless other attempts. Your muscles ache from constant effort, from bracing against the relentless pull downward, from holding yourself upright in a place that seems designed to undo you. Even the smallest acts, the simplest gestures of care, feel impossibly distant, as though they belong to another life, another person, someone stronger, someone luckier.

The well becomes an adversary not because it moves, but because it endures. It does not need to act. It simply remains. It waits. It holds. Its stillness is its power. Day after day, it convinces you that this captivity is permanent, that adaptation is the only remaining option, that longing itself is a kind of foolishness. You begin to mistake endurance for inevitability. And just when the silence grows thick enough to feel suffocating, just when the quiet presses so close it hums, the echo returns.

It answers your breath with its own voice. It reminds you how deep you are. How tired you feel. How long you have been here. It catalogs your exhaustion with intimate precision, speaks to the parts of you already worn thin, already questioning the cost of continuing. It does not rush you. It simply waits for the moment when effort feels heavier than rest. And then there's the echo. Always the echo.

The Deep, Dark Well

From the weight of the backpack, the path leads inevitably here, deeper into the metaphor that holds it all. The well waits. It does not rush you. It does not announce itself. It simply exists, patient and inevitable, as though it has always known you would arrive. Picture it. Cold. Damp. Unsettling. A place where the air itself feels heavy, thick with unspoken sorrow. You stand at the edge, leaning forward just enough to peer into the abyss, and what you sense immediately is not depth alone, but finality. A hush that feels conclusive. vIt feels bottomless. Endless. A void that mirrors the all-consuming nature of depression, where escape does not merely feel difficult, but unimaginable. In this place, the mind begins to change its posture. It folds inward. It starts drawing conclusions not from evidence, but from exhaustion. The darkness convinces you it is permanent. That this is not a season, not a state, but a sentence. The future collapses into the present moment, and the present moment insists it is all there will ever be. This is where the mind becomes dangerously persuasive. The well answers back. Thoughts echo off its walls, warped by stone and distance, returning altered but convincing. They repeat themselves until repetition masquerades as truth. You're stuck here forever. It's never going to get better. These phrases do not arrive like proclamations. They creep in. They linger. They circle. Each return tightens the loop, until despair begins feeding on its own momentum, fueled by fear, by fatigue, by the simple act of surviving another day under too much weight. And then, in moments of deep vulnerability, something shifts. The echo changes its tone. What once sounded like a nagging presence begins to soften, to smooth its edges. It offers itself not as torment, but as relief. Not as danger, but as an answer. A way to stop the pain. A solution that feels eerily calm, almost compassionate in its phrasing. This is the true danger of the well. Not its depth alone. Not its darkness. But how convincingly it rearranges perception. How it takes suffering and frames it as inevitability. How it takes exhaustion and dresses it up as clarity. How it speaks in your own voice, using your own thoughts, until it becomes difficult to remember that another way of seeing once existed at all. The well does not just hold despair. It reshapes it. And understanding that is part of learning how to climb. The darkness here is absolute. Not merely the absence of light, but the absence of hope itself. An erasure of forward vision. An inability to see a path upward or imagine a future that exists beyond the cold stone walls pressing in on all sides. Possibility collapses here. The mind stops reaching ahead and begins to curl inward, guarding what little energy remains.

Every attempt to climb feels futile. Every grasp for a handhold meets slick resistance, skin sliding over stone worn smooth by countless other attempts. Your muscles ache from constant effort, from bracing against the relentless pull downward, from holding yourself upright in a place that seems designed to undo you. Even the smallest acts, the simplest gestures of care, feel impossibly distant, as though they belong to another life, another person, someone stronger, someone luckier. The well becomes an adversary not because it moves, but because it endures. It does not need to act. It simply remains. It waits. It holds. Its stillness is its power. Day after day, it convinces you that this captivity is permanent, that adaptation is the only remaining option, that longing itself is a kind of foolishness. You begin to mistake endurance for inevitability. And just when the silence grows thick enough to feel suffocating, just when the quiet presses so close it hums, the echo returns. It answers your breath with its own voice. It reminds you how deep you are. How tired you feel. How long you have been here. It catalogs your exhaustion with intimate precision, speaks to the parts of you already worn thin, already questioning the cost of continuing. It does not rush you. It simply waits for the moment when effort feels heavier than rest. And then there's the echo. Always the echo.

Chapter Twenty
The Body as The Witness

Where Truth Forms Before Thought

After the day she learned the echo could not survive her presence, something else began to happen. Subtler. Quieter. Almost easy to miss. She started noticing that her body often knew things before her mind assembled them. Not as sentences. Not as conclusions. There were no explanations offered, no footnotes, no case built for approval. The knowing arrived as sensation. A language older than argument. A tightening that said no long before a reason arrived. A warmth that said yes before permission was given. A soft settling that said this is safe before memory weighed in. A quickening that whispered pay attention before thought could interrupt. At first, she dismissed these signals. They seemed too small. Too ordinary. Too unsophisticated to be truth. She had been trained to trust meaning only when it arrived dressed in words, arranged in narratives, backed by logic she could defend. Truth, she believed, should be articulate. It should announce itself. It should be explainable. But the body did not argue. It indicated. A slight lift behind the ribs when something aligned, as if an internal horizon had levelled itself. A subtle heaviness when something was off, not dramatic, just undeniable, like a weight placed gently but firmly where it could not be ignored. A loosening at the back of the throat when she spoke honestly, the air finding its path without resistance. A quiet recoil when she didn't, a small inward step the body took even when her words moved forward. These weren't emotions exactly. They were directions. And they came early. Before justification. Before doubt. Before the echo could begin its negotiations. She began to see it most clearly in moments when the echo tried to recruit her.

The thought would form. The story would begin its familiar unfurling. But just before it took hold, just before it could anchor itself in her identity, something in her had already shifted. Her stomach would hollow, as if clearing space for truth. Her shoulders would draw back, not in defence, but in refusal. Her breath would shallow, not with fear, but with alertness. The body had already voted. The mind was late. She began to understand that what she had been calling intuition was not a flash of insight or a mystical gift. It was attention practiced long enough to hear what had always been speaking first. The body was not reacting to the echo. It was responding to reality before it was edited. Before story.

Before strategy. Before survival learned to speak louder than truth. And slowly, without ceremony, she stopped asking her mind to lead. She let it follow. Not blindly. Not obediently. But respectfully. Because truth, she was learning, did not originate in thought. It formed earlier. In the body. Or sometimes— Her chest would widen. Her jaw would soften. Her spine would lengthen, as if the body were quietly making room for something true. Not bracing. Not preparing. Allowing. As though an internal door had been opened without announcement. She started paying attention to that timing. The way the body moved first. The way it answered questions she had not yet asked. There was a precision to it that surprised her. A reliability that did not need reassurance. The body did not wait for permission from thought. It did not require a debate. It responded in the present tense to what was actually there. One afternoon, she caught it happening in real time. She was about to agree to something that felt wrong. The reasons were all there. Polite. Logical. Convincing. Arranged neatly enough to pass as wisdom. They spoke in the voice of accommodation, of being reasonable, of not making things difficult. They made sense. And yet, as she reached for her yes, her body did something else. Her foot shifted back. A nearly invisible movement. The kind no one would notice. The kind she herself might once have ignored. But it carried weight. A small retreat that was not avoidance. A physical refusal that arrived before language could soften it. She stopped mid-sentence. Closed her eyes. Not to think. To feel. There it was. A gentle but unmistakable pull away. Not fear. Not resistance. Recognition. The body recognizing what the mind was still trying to accommodate. *"No,"* she heard herself say. The word landed cleanly. Without apology. Without explanation attached. It surprised even herself. The room did not collapse. The world did not end. The echo did not rush in to punish her for it. The explanation came later. The truth had already arrived. From then on, she began to consult the body the way one might consult weather. Not demanding certainty. Not asking it to justify itself. Just noticing what it was already doing. How it leaned toward or away. Where it opened. Where it guarded. Where it warmed. Where it cooled. She learned to trust its forecasts. Not because they were always comfortable. But because they were honest. And she realized something else too. The body was not interrupting her life. It was guiding it. It was not trying to control the outcome. It was trying to keep her aligned with herself. And once she saw that, she could not unsee it. Truth was no longer something she hunted for in thought. It was something she could feel arriving. Quietly. Early.

The echo always spoke after. After the contraction. After the softening. After the internal turn that had already chosen a direction before words were invited in. It arrived to explain what had already happened. To rename sensation as identity. To convert a moment into meaning, to drape narrative over a reality that had never asked for interpretation. It spoke with confidence precisely because it was late, mistaking sequence for authority. But the body never told stories. It registered reality. Cleanly. Immediately. Without agenda. She started keeping track. Not in words at first. Not in conclusions or lessons she could summarize. She kept track in pauses. In where she chose to linger instead of rushing past. In where she chose to step back without making a case for it. In how long she stayed with a feeling before letting a thought claim it and rename it as something else. She noticed the difference between feeling and story. Between sensation and the reflex to explain it away. Slowly, a new trust formed. Not loud. Not dramatic. A simple, living confidence. The kind that grows the way muscles do, through use rather than declaration. A trust that there was something in her that could meet life directly. Skin to air. Breath to moment. Without translation. Without distortion. Without the echo's commentary standing between her and what was real. Truth, she learned, did not need to announce itself. It arranged the breath before it arranged the sentence. It shifted the muscles before it shifted belief. It altered the temperature of being before it altered thought. It did not persuade. It aligned. And when she stayed long enough to feel it, when she allowed the body to finish its knowing without interruption, the mind followed. Not as master. As witness. The mind learned to watch what had already occurred, to name it gently, to serve what was true instead of trying to manufacture it. Thought became something that came after contact, not instead of it. And the echo, increasingly, arrived too late. Its sentences found no opening. Its explanations hovered without an event to attach themselves to. It spoke into rooms that had already been furnished by presence. It was still there. But it no longer set the timing. And in that quiet shift, her life began to move at the speed of truth instead of the speed of fear.

Where Truth Begins Before Thought

It happened quietly, the way most real things do. Not as a realization. Not as a sentence carefully formed and placed. But as a sensation. Eliza began to notice that something in her moved before her mind did. Before the story assembled its scaffolding. Before the echo cleared its throat and stepped forward to narrate. Before she could name what, she was feeling or decide what it meant. Her body would shift. A subtle drawing back, barely perceptible, like a tide changing its mind. A faint warmth behind the sternum, spreading without urgency.

A softening in the jaw, the mouth unarmoring itself. A tightening low in the belly, deep and quiet. A change in breath she hadn't chosen, air shortening or deepening on its own. These movements arrived without announcement. Without explanation. Without asking to be believed. At first, she dismissed them. They felt too small to mean anything. Too ordinary. Too easily overlooked to carry truth. She had been trained to trust what could be explained, what could be argued, what could be shaped into language and defended. Truth, she believed, should arrive with clarity. With reasons. With proof lined up like witnesses. But this arrived without words. It did not persuade. It did not convince. It simply happened. She started noticing it in the narrow space just before decisions. That quiet threshold where choice begins to form but has not yet declared itself. Just before she agreed to something that didn't feel right, her shoulders would already be lifting, bracing, preparing for a weight she had not yet admitted she would carry. Just before she spoke a truth she'd been avoiding, her throat would loosen, as if making room for sound that had been waiting patiently. Just before the echo began its familiar narration, something in her chest would contract or open, already responding to what was real. The body, she realized, was not waiting for permission. It was answering first. Truth was arriving not as an idea, but as a movement. Not as meaning, but as orientation. The body leaning away. The body leaning in. The body adjusting itself to what aligned and what did not. And slowly, almost without her noticing, the order of things began to reverse.

Thought followed sensation. Language followed breath. Understanding followed contact. Truth, she was learning, did not begin where she had been taught to look for it. It began earlier. In the body. The body, she realized, was answering questions her mind hadn't yet formed. It was not emotional in the way she understood emotion. It did not swell or spiral or demand expression. It was directional. A leaning. A turning. A quiet yes that required no emphasis. A nearly invisible no that did not need to raise its voice. She saw it most clearly the first time she stopped mid-movement. She had been about to say yes out of habit, the way one does when agreement has been rehearsed for years. The words were already lining up, polite and reasonable. The reasons were ready, stacked neatly, waiting their turn. Everything about the moment suggested compliance. And yet, her foot had shifted back without her noticing. A retreat so small it would have meant nothing to anyone else. A fraction of an inch. A gesture beneath attention. But to her, it felt like a hand on the inside of her ribs, firm and unmistakable, saying not this. She paused. Closed her eyes. Not to think. To feel. There it was. A gentle resistance. Not fear. Not panic. No urgency, no alarm. Just a steady, grounded pull away, as calm as gravity, as clear as weight redistributing itself. *"No,"* she said. The word surprised the room. It surprised even her. It arrived clean, unadorned, without justification attached. The explanation came later, assembling itself in the wake of truth rather than in front of it. The truth had already arrived. From then on, she began paying attention to timing. The body always moved first. A tightening that came before doubt could gather its arguments. A warmth that came before relief could name itself. A heaviness that came before sadness had a story. A lightness that came before hope learned its name.

The body spoke in advance of meaning. The echo came after. It narrated what had already happened, mistaking sequence for origin. It interpreted what the body had already registered, translating sensation into story. It tried to own what it had not originated, to claim authorship over a truth it had only witnessed. But she could feel the difference now. She knew who had spoken first. And in that knowing, the echo lost something essential. Its authority. It was no longer the source of truth. Only the commentary that followed it. The body, she discovered, did not persuade. It indicated. It adjusted the breath without asking permission. Shifted the spine by degrees so small they felt like instinct rather than choice. Altered the temperature of being, warming where there was truth, cooling where there was misalignment. It did not argue its case. It did not rehearse evidence. It simply changed the conditions. The body did not tell stories. It revealed them. No, more precisely, it revealed reality before story had a chance to form. Slowly, reverently, she began consulting this place. Not as an authority to be obeyed, not as an oracle to be interrogated, but as a landscape to be noticed. She did not demand answers. She paid attention. Where she opened. Where she closed. Where she softened without effort. Where she guarded without explanation. She learned to listen with her weight. With her breath. With the quiet intelligence of muscle and bone. She started lingering in sensation before allowing language to claim it. Letting the body finish its sentence before the mind interrupted with interpretation. Giving the moment time to complete itself without being hurried into meaning. And in that space, something extraordinary unfolded.

Truth no longer arrived as a verdict handed down by thought. It arrived as alignment. As breath deepening, unforced. As muscles unclenching, one by one, like doors no longer needing to be held shut. As a sense of rightness that did not announce itself, did not ask to be defended, did not require agreement. It was simply there. The mind still followed. But now, it followed something real. Something already embodied. Thought learned to trail behind experience instead of running ahead of it, learned to witness what had already taken shape rather than trying to invent it. And the echo, more and more often, arrived too late. Its explanations hovered after the fact. Its narratives searched for openings that were no longer available. Truth had already settled into the body, already altered posture and breath and orientation. Not in words. In her. And for the first time, that was enough.

The Body as Witness

For so long, Eliza had lived as though her mind were the only courtroom, the only place where truth could be argued into existence. Every feeling had to be cross-examined. Every memory interrogated. Every instinct put on trial beneath the sharp lights of reason. The echo had thrived there. It knew how to twist language until it confessed to things it had never done. How to edit history with careful omissions. How to turn doubt into doctrine and call it wisdom. In that chamber of words, truth was slippery, vulnerable to rhetoric, persuasion, exhaustion. But the body did not testify in words. It testified in facts. It remembered the tightening long after the story forgot. The quiet cinch behind the ribs. The subtle lock in the jaw. The way the shoulders rose before danger had a name. It held the warmth even when the narrative turned cold, when explanations arrived too late, and apologies arrived dressed as logic. It flinched where something was wrong, a small, involuntary recoil that required no argument. It softened where something was real, where safety moved through her like a familiar temperature rather than a promise. She began to see that her body had been present for every moment she had survived. Not as an afterthought. Not as a vessel dragged along behind the mind. But as a witness seated in the room the entire time. It had been there when her voice went quiet, when silence became a strategy. When her chest learned to brace, muscle memorizing vigilance before thought could translate it. When her breath learned to wait, suspended between inhales, as though stillness might keep the world from noticing her. It had registered what her mind had not been able to carry. It had stored the unspeakable in tissue and rhythm, in posture and pulse. It had recorded the climate of her life the way skin records weather, the slow burn of long summers, the sudden bite of unexpected cold, the seasons that overstayed and the ones that never came. And it had never lied. Not once. Where the mind debated, the body indicated. Where the mind revised, the body remembered. It did not argue its case. It simply lived it, faithfully, continuously, holding the truth in sensation until she was ready to listen. The body, she discovered, did not persuade. It indicated. It adjusted the breath without asking permission. Shifted the spine by degrees so small they felt like instinct rather than choice. Altered the temperature of being, warming where there was truth, cooling where there was misalignment. It did not argue its case. It did not rehearse evidence. It simply changed the conditions. The body did not tell stories. It revealed them. No, more precisely, it revealed reality before story had a chance to form. Slowly, reverently, she began consulting this place. Not as an authority to be obeyed, not as an oracle to be interrogated, but as a landscape to be noticed. She did not demand answers. She paid attention. Where she opened. Where she closed. Where she softened without effort. Where she guarded without explanation. She learned to listen with her weight. With her breath. With the quiet intelligence of muscle and bone. She started lingering in sensation before allowing language to claim it. Letting the body finish its sentence before the mind interrupted with interpretation. Giving the moment time to complete itself without being hurried into meaning. And in that space, something extraordinary unfolded.

Truth no longer arrived as a verdict handed down by thought. It arrived as alignment. As breath deepening, unforced.

As muscles unclenching, one by one, like doors no longer needing to be held shut. As a sense of rightness that did not announce itself, did not ask to be defended, did not require agreement. It was simply there. The mind still followed. But now, it followed something real. Something already embodied. Thought learned to trail behind experience instead of running ahead of it, learned to witness what had already taken shape rather than trying to invent it. And the echo, more and more often, arrived too late. Its explanations hovered after the fact. Its narratives searched for openings that were no longer available. Truth had already settled into the body, already altered posture, breath, and orientation. Not in words. In her. And for the first time, that was enough. It had signalled exhaustion when she called it laziness, sending quiet notices through heaviness and ache, through the dull gravity of limbs that no longer wished to perform. It had registered grief when she called it weakness, letting sorrow pool behind the sternum, a weight without language, a tide without a name. It had tensed in the presence of harm even when her thoughts searched for excuses, even when reason rehearsed explanations meant to keep the peace. It had opened in moments of safety even when the echo warned her not to trust, even when suspicion dressed itself as intelligence. The body had been keeping minutes all along. Every pause logged. Every contraction recorded. Every softening timestamped. She started to treat it differently. Not as something to push through. Not as a problem to manage or a machine to override. But as a witness to consult, a living archive that had never left the room. When a memory surfaced, she noticed what happened in her chest before she decided what it meant, the way breath shifted before interpretation arrived. When a thought appeared, she checked what her breathing did before she followed it, whether it tightened into urgency or widened into space. When the echo spoke, sharp and convincing, she listened for what her body did in response, the subtle verdict delivered without commentary. The difference was unmistakable. The echo created agitation, a restless hum that scrambled her inner weather. The body created information, clear, immediate, difficult to argue with.

The echo collapsed her inward, folding her into spirals of analysis and self-doubt. The body oriented her outward, returning her to gravity, to contact, to the present moment. The echo demanded belief, obedience, allegiance. The body offered evidence. Tears would rise without explanation, saline truth spilling before meaning could assemble. Her throat would close before a boundary was crossed, a gate lowering itself in quiet refusal. Her shoulders would drop when a truth was spoken, the body exhaling recognition before the mind could nod. Her pulse would settle when she was safe, rhythm finding its natural tempo again. These were not metaphors. They were events. Occurrences in flesh and breath. Signals transmitted through nerve and muscle. The body was not speaking in symbols. It was reporting conditions, faithfully, precisely, inviting her at last to trust what had been true all along. And slowly, something fundamental reorganized, not with force or fanfare, but the way deep things shift, silently, when their weight is finally allowed to settle. She no longer needed to ask the echo who she was. She could feel herself, a presence arriving not as a concept but as sensation, as warmth, as a steady pulse of being. She began to trust the way her body stayed. The way it endured without complaint. The way it registered what passed through her without distortion. The way it returned her to the present again and again, like a hand on the small of her back guiding her home. It did not dramatize. It located. It anchored her in what was happening, not what might happen, not what once happened, not what the echo predicted with such urgency. Here. Now. This. The simplicity of it felt almost radical. Breath. Weight. Contact. Time moving at the speed of reality instead of fear. The body became her first reliable witness. The one that could say, without accusation or embellishment: This is too much. This is safe. This is real. This is happening. Its language was direct, unadorned, delivered through sensation rather than story. And because it spoke without agenda, without cruelty, without the need to be right, she began to believe it. Not as theory. As ground. As something solid enough to stand on when the rest of her world felt uncertain, when meaning wavered and narratives shifted underfoot. From that ground, a new authority quietly emerged. Not loud. Not dramatic. But steady. A way of knowing that did not need permission. A way of truth that did not need to raise its voice. It did not argue its place. It simply held. And in being held, she found herself standing, at last, inside her own life.

When the Echo Turns on the Witness

The shift did not go unnoticed. It never does when power begins to migrate. The echo had always survived by owning the narrative, by keeping the pen firmly in its grasp. By bending memory just enough to make it compliant. By rehearsing her into smaller shapes, narrower postures of self, until she fit neatly inside its explanations. But when Eliza began listening elsewhere, when her allegiance started drifting from story to sensation, something in the well changed. The water darkened. The air tightened. The echo adjusted its tactics. It did not roar. It questioned. That was its refinement. *"That feeling is just anxiety." "That tightening doesn't mean anything." "Your body is unreliable." "Your body is overreacting." "Your body is broken."* It began to speak about her body, circling it with suspicion, language sharpening into accusation. To turn the witness into a suspect. To move the trial out of the courtroom of the mind and into the flesh itself. When her chest constricted, the echo called it weakness, a flaw in her constitution rather than a signal of strain. When her stomach recoiled, it called it imagination, dismissing instinct as fantasy. When warmth spread through her, it called it foolish hope, naïveté masquerading as safety. When her shoulders softened, it called it laziness, rest recast as moral failure. It tried to sever trust at the root. It told her the body was a faulty instrument, prone to false readings and emotional static. A misfiring alarm that went off too often to be believed. A relic of instinct with no place in a thinking world. It spoke with the authority of reason, with the confidence of someone who had never needed to listen. And for a moment, the old reflex stirred. The urge to doubt what she felt. To hand the authority back. To retreat into explanation. But something had already changed. The body had been heard. And having once been heard, it was harder to silence. It suggested that sensation was chaos, a wild, ungovernable force that could never be trusted. That only interpretation could be truth. That only the echo could translate what was real, could make sense of the noise, could impose order on the rawness of feeling. And when she listened to her body anyway, when she paused in the middle of a thought to feel instead of conclude, the echo changed tactics. It mocked. *"You're romanticizing this." "You're avoiding reality." "You're making meaning where there is none."* Sometimes, it wrapped its discrediting in concern, its tone softening into something that sounded almost protective. *"You can't trust your body. Look how often it's been wrong. Look how often it's failed you."* It reached backward then, rifling through the archives, pulling up moments of panic, of exhaustion, of ache. It paraded them like evidence across the courtroom of memory. *"See? Unreliable. Unstable. Unsafe."* But something strange happened. As the echo spoke, Eliza did not collapse the way she once had. She did not shrink, spiral, or surrender the ground she stood on. She noticed what her body did. Her jaw tightened when the echo lied, muscle bracing against distortion. Her breath shallowed when it rushed her, signalling pressure where none was necessary. A faint nausea stirred when it twisted the truth, the body recoiling from manipulation. And a small, steady grounding arrived when it quieted, weight settling into her feet, presence returning like a held note. The body responded to the echo. It reacted to its tone. Its pace. Its pressure. And that reaction carried information. She realized then that the echo was no longer speaking from inside her. It was speaking to her, no longer fused with her sense of self, no longer indistinguishable from her own knowing. It was trying to persuade. Trying to regain jurisdiction. Trying to discredit the one thing it could not impersonate. The body did not argue back. It simply registered the attempt. And in that registration, the balance of power shifted again, quietly, irrevocably.

The echo could rewrite memory. It could manipulate language until meaning bent and buckled. But it could not alter what was happening now. It could not control the way her feet felt against the floor, the honest pressure of weight meeting ground. It could not interrupt the way her breath slowed when she stopped chasing thoughts, when she allowed the mind to arrive where the body already was. It could not counterfeit the way her chest expanded when something was true, the quiet widening that came without effort or persuasion. So it attacked the source. It told her to doubt her pulse, to mistrust her breath. To override her recoil before it could register. To ignore her ease as though relief itself were a trap. It framed presence as threat. It framed groundedness as danger. It framed her own nervous system as the enemy, recasting attunement as vulnerability and awareness as exposure. And for the first time, Eliza saw the move clearly. This was not guidance. This was containment. The echo was not trying to protect her. It was trying to remain central. Trying to remain necessary. Trying to remain believed. Trying to keep its seat of authority intact by discrediting the only witness it could not cross-examine. She felt a small, unmistakable steadiness settle behind her ribs, a quiet alignment that asked for nothing. Not defiance. Recognition. The echo did not want her to trust the body because the body did not answer to it. The body did not echo. The body reported. It delivered unedited data, present-tense truth, without commentary or motive. And something that reports reality will always be dangerous to something that survives on distortion.

The Great Defence

It happened in a small, almost forgettable moment. No cliff. No crisis. No cinematic turning point waiting for music to swell. Just a Tuesday breath. A chair beneath her carrying her weight without comment. Light leaning through a window, indifferent and generous. Time moving at its ordinary pace. The echo arrived the way it always did, sliding into her thoughts with practiced ease, fluent in familiarity. *"You're tired because you're weak. That heaviness means you're failing again. There's something wrong with you."* The sentence was only halfway formed when her body responded. Not with rebuttal. Not with explanation. With sensation. Her stomach drew inward, not sharply, not dramatically, but precisely, like a line being drawn where one already existed. Her shoulders rose, then slowly dropped, refusing to stay enlisted. Her breath shortened at the beginning of the thought and lengthened when the thought loosened, as if the body itself were editing in real time. It was subtle. But it was different. The echo felt jagged, serrated with urgency, each word scraping for dominance. Her body felt clear. Clean. Unadorned. There was a firmness in the way her feet met the floor, gravity welcomed rather than resisted. A steadiness in the rhythm of her inhale, unhurried, uninterested in proving anything. A quiet warmth behind her ribs that did not argue, did not persuade, did not perform. It simply was. A presence that did not need to announce itself to be real. The echo pushed, irritated by the lack of collapse. *"You're misreading it." "You're being dramatic." "You always do this."* And for the first time in a way that mattered, something in her did not retreat. It did not scramble for counterarguments or apologies. It did not negotiate. She placed a hand on her stomach. Not as comfort. As contact. As witness. Skin meeting skin. Heat registering heat. She felt the rise. The fall. The undeniable presence of being here, alive inside this moment, unbroken by accusation. Nothing exploded. Nothing resolved itself into triumph. But the defence held. Quietly. Completely. The body did not defend itself against the echo. It simply remained. And in remaining, it rendered the echo unnecessary. And softly, out loud, almost surprised by her own voice, she said, *"No."* The word was not loud. It was not angry. It was not a counterargument sharpened for debate. It was a boundary, clean and exact, placed where the ground already knew it belonged. *"This is not weakness,"* she continued, her hand still anchored to the slow truth of her breath. *"This is information."* The echo tried to hurry her, urgency slipping back into its tone. *"Don't get lost in sensations. You're avoiding the real problem."* Her chest tightened. Then eased. And she recognized the pattern, the signature she had learned to read. Pressure when it lied. Space when it loosened. The body marking the difference without commentary. She felt it. Trusted it.

And something ancient and trembling and newly awake inside her spoke, not in language first, but in certainty: *"I am allowed to know what is happening in me."* Her body was not collapsing. It was communicating. Her fatigue was not accusation. It was signal, a flag raised by a system that had carried her farther than she ever acknowledged. Her heaviness was not proof. It was weather, a passing condition shaped by seasons and strain, not a verdict on her worth. And the echo, the echo was interpretation pretending to be law, habit wearing the uniform of authority. She did not try to silence it. She did not try to fight it or dismantle it piece by piece. She simply turned her attention back to the sensation it had tried to discredit. The warmth beneath her palm. The contact. The quiet pulse in her wrist, steady and indifferent to argument. And she spoke again, steadier now, the words arriving without rehearsal. *"You don't get to tell me my own body is lying."* The sentence landed in the well like a stone dropped into deep water. Not to wound. To test. To feel the depth of what could no longer be undone. The echo faltered. Not dramatically. Not vanishing in a burst of silence. Just stuttering, as if a sentence had lost its grammar, as if authority had been interrupted mid-breath and could not quite remember how to continue. The cadence broke. The certainty thinned. And in that pause, that small suspension of momentum, Eliza felt something she had felt before, though rarely trusted. Alignment. Not between thoughts. Between herself. Her body did not celebrate. It did not surge or flood her with triumph. It simply continued. Breathing. Balancing. Being. Weight through her feet. Air moving in and out. A quiet steadiness holding the shape of the moment. No commentary. No performance. Just life doing what it does when it is no longer being overridden. And she understood. This was not rebellion. This was reunion. She had not overpowered the echo or defeated it in argument. She had outgrown its jurisdiction. The boundary had not been drawn with force, but with placement. She had placed her loyalty somewhere it could not reach. In the lived. In the sensed. In the quiet, untranslatable knowing of a body that had been here the whole time. Waiting. Not impatient. Not demanding. Just present. Holding the record. Holding the rhythm. Ready the moment she was willing to return.

When the Echo Panics

The first time Eliza chose the body over the echo, something shifted in the air, subtle as a pressure change before weather turns. At first, it tried its usual authority. Flat. Certain. Familiar. *"You're overinterpreting. This will pass. You always think you've figured it out."* The words arrived wearing their old confidence, rehearsed and tidy, expecting the reflex of compliance. But she didn't argue. She stayed. Her feet pressed into the floor, receiving weight instead of resisting it. Her breath found a slow, even rhythm, no longer drafted into the service of explanation. Her spine lengthened, not in defiance, but in presence, as though the body were remembering its original shape. And that is when the echo panicked. It changed tempo. At first, nothing dramatic happened. No thunder. No shattering. Just a small, quiet shift inside Eliza, like a weight being moved from one shelf to another, the balance of the room altered by a simple relocation. She had begun returning to her body more often now. Touching the table, letting its solidity answer her. Feeling the temperature of tea on her tongue, warmth blooming and fading. Listening for the subtle yes and no that lived beneath words, beneath justification. And the echo noticed. It began interrupting sooner, cutting in mid-breath, refusing the pause that had become her ally. Speaking faster. Layering urgency over everything. Compressing time, tightening the frame, insisting that something must be decided immediately. The speed itself became the message. And in its haste, it revealed what it had never intended to show: fear of losing its place at the center of her attention. The voice that once moved like a judge now spoke like a runner who had missed a step, momentum pitching forward without footing. "Don't do this. You're making it worse. You need me to survive." "You're overanalysing. This is pointless. You're making it worse. Stop this. Stop this. Stop this." The sentences landed oddly, tripping over themselves. Needy. Rushed. They contradicted themselves mid-thought, certainty unraveling as it tried to outrun the silence she had found. She felt it immediately.

Its tone had changed. Less certain. Sharper. Crowded. It no longer arrived like a conclusion delivered from on high. It arrived like a siren, insistent and piercing, designed to override rather than inform. A tightening behind her eyes. A quick spike in her chest. The body registering the sound before the meaning could form. And then something else appeared. A deeper steadiness underneath, like bedrock beneath tremor. Her body did not follow the urgency. It did not accelerate to match the pitch. It did not collapse under the weight of command. It stayed exactly where it was, breath continuing its unhurried arc, muscles declining the invitation to panic. The echo pressed harder. *"This calm is fake. You're dissociating. You're losing control."* The words stacked too quickly, one atop another, as if speed itself might restore power, as if volume could replace truth. But the faster it spoke, the less believable it became. Its urgency betrayed it. Its insistence revealed the crack. And in that widening gap, her body remained, steady as ever, holding a truth that no alarm could erase. Eliza noticed the shift before she named it, the way the body often knows before language catches up. The echo was no longer describing. It was persuading. No longer observing. It was bargaining. And for the first time, she recognized the tone beneath the content, the frequency humming underneath the words. Fear. Not hers. Its. Her breath deepened without instruction. Her shoulders softened, releasing their habitual guard. She felt the quiet weight of herself sitting fully in the chair, the simple fact of occupying space without apology.

And gently, without cruelty, without triumph, she said, *"You sound scared."* The echo recoiled. It scrambled, words spilling out of sequence. *"I'm trying to protect you. You're nothing without me. If you don't listen, something terrible will happen."* The threats were vague now, losing their specificity, dissolving into shape without substance. Catastrophe without coordinates. Authority had drained from them, leaving only urgency where certainty once lived. She did not respond with logic. She did not counter with evidence. She simply returned her attention to the place in her body that felt most solid. Her thighs against the seat, bearing weight. Her feet against the ground, receiving gravity. The steady pulse at her wrist, indifferent to prophecy. Each sensation a quiet vote for reality. Each contact an anchor. And in that return, the conversation shifted again, not because she had won, but because she had arrived somewhere the echo could not follow. The echo raised its voice. *"Look at everything you've failed. Look at your past. Look at what you are."* The words came heavy with accusation, rehearsed for impact. But they slid off. They could not land where presence had already claimed the space. There was no open surface left for them to adhere to, no vacancy inside her for their weight. And suddenly, unmistakably, she saw it. The echo could not survive being observed from inside the body. It needed distance. Abstraction. Speed. It needed her disembodied, lifted out of sensation and scattered across time. So it tried one last tactic, its tone thinning, lowering. *"If you stop listening to me," it said, quieter now, "you'll be alone."* That was the oldest lie. And the moment it surfaced, her body responded before her mind did. Warmth bloomed in her chest. Not loud. Not euphoric. Relational. Grounded. A warmth that knew connection not as idea but as condition. She felt the chair. The room. The undeniable fact of existing in space, held by gravity, surrounded by air. *"I'm not alone,"* she said. And this time, the echo did not answer immediately. There was a pause. A real one. A break in the pattern. Not silence, but disorientation. As if something that had always spoken uninterrupted had lost its place in the sentence and did not know how to continue. The echo had not disappeared. But it had lost its footing. It had revealed itself not as truth, but as something dependent on her absence to function.

Eliza felt it one evening while sitting on the edge of her bed, feet on the floor, palms resting on her thighs. A simple posture. An ordinary hour. She had learned this grounding. Had practiced it. Had felt how the room returned when she stayed, how the edges of things reassembled themselves when she did not flee her own presence. The echo surged. *"Don't sit still. Don't go quiet. You know what happens when you do. Get up. Distract yourself. Think harder. Think faster."* Her chest tightened. Then, steadied. Not because she commanded it, but because the body recognized what was being asked of it and declined. Her breath deepened on its own, like a tide remembering the moon, easing back into a rhythm older than panic. The floor stayed beneath her feet. The bed stayed beneath her weight. And that's when it happened. The echo fractured. Its voice began tripping over itself. *"You're—; you're wasting time—; this isn't real—; you're pretending—; you're lying to yourself—; you don't actually feel—; you don't actually know—"* The sentences no longer finished. They piled up without order. They scrambled. They contradicted themselves mid-flight. Meaning splintered before it could land. The echo started throwing everything it had. Old shames dragged up without context. Old fears stripped of their disguises. Predictions shouted without timelines. Accusations hurled without aim. Not in sequence. In scatter. Like papers flung into the air when someone realizes the door is closing and there is no longer time to arrange the story. Eliza felt it then. Not as language. As agitation. A frantic vibration in her chest that did not belong to her breath. A buzzing urgency that had no home in her body. And still, her body remained. Her feet stayed in contact with the floor. Her hands were warm against her thighs. Her heartbeat was firm, almost curious, as if listening rather than obeying. And suddenly she saw it. The echo was not warning her. It was afraid. Afraid of the stillness. Afraid of the way presence dissolved its edges, blurred its authority, thinned its voice.

Afraid of being seen from the outside rather than mistaken for truth on the inside. The realization arrived whole, without effort, without argument. *"This voice needs me to leave my body,"* she thought. *"Because it cannot live where I am."* And in that knowing, something settled. Not victory. Not relief. A quiet clarity. She stayed exactly where she was, and the room stayed with her, bearing witness to a truth that no longer needed to shout. The echo spiked. *"Don't name this. Don't look at it like that. You're imagining things. You need me. You've always needed me."* The words arrived sharp, crowding the space, reaching for the old reflex. Her stomach clenched. Then released. A familiar pattern now. Tighten when it grasped. Soften when it loosened. The body marking truth with the precision of a tide chart. And in that softening, something astonishing happened. The echo raised its voice. Not in cruelty. In desperation. It repeated itself, as if volume could replace coherence. Louder. Faster. Thinner. Like a speaker turned too high, distorting its own message until meaning collapsed into static. Urgency without substance. Sound without center. And Eliza did not argue. She did not soothe it. She did not push it away. She stayed. She felt the mattress beneath her legs, the quiet give of it meeting her weight. The air at the back of her throat, cool and present. The slow, loyal rhythm of a heart that had never once left her, that had kept time through every story, every misnaming. Each sensation a tether, each contact a reminder of where she was. The echo surged again, a final attempt to reassemble itself, and then it broke. Mid-sentence. As if the thread holding the sound together had snapped. The words lost their grip. They scattered, stripped of authority, dissolving into vibration. Noise. Not truth. Not command. Just noise. And in the space where authority used to live, Eliza felt something new. Relief was too small. Victory was wrong. What arrived instead was a quiet expanse, a widening inside her chest, the sensation of standing in her own life without interference. A spaciousness that did not need to announce itself, only to be inhabited.

What she felt was orientation. Like realizing which way is north after years of walking in fog, when the body suddenly aligns with a direction it has always known but could not previously trust. Nothing flashy. No revelation blazing across the sky. Just a quiet, undeniable sense of bearing. Of knowing where she was in relation to herself. The echo was still there. It had not vanished. But it was no longer above her. No longer looming, no longer fused with the air she breathed. It was within range now. Observable. Reactive. Mortal. A voice with limits. A pattern with edges. And she understood, with a calm that startled her in its simplicity: It panics when I stay. It survives when I leave. It feeds on my absence from myself. Her body gave a small, involuntary sigh. Not exhaustion. Recognition. The kind that comes when something long carried is finally set down in the correct place. The echo whispered once more, a fragment, a reflex, a remnant of a habit that once ruled entire rooms of her inner life. But it no longer knew where to land. There was no open space for it to colonize. No vacancy. Because Eliza was here. And it had no ground to stand on. And Eliza understood, with a clarity that settled deep in her bones, not as insight but as fact: The echo does not rule by strength. It rules by unnoticed presence. It governs through speed, through abstraction, through the quiet theft of attention. Once named. Once grounded. Once met from within the body; It panics. Because it knows what she now knows. It cannot speak over sustained presence. It cannot survive where breath is felt, where weight is received, where life is happening in real time. And she stayed. Not to defeat it. Not to watch it disappear. But to remain aligned with herself, oriented at last, standing in a direction that did not require effort to maintain.

The First Conversation

After the echo panicked, it did not leave. It lingered. Quieter. Less certain. Like a figure unsure where to stand now that the lights had changed. No longer seated on the throne of her inner world, issuing decrees as truth, but no longer invisible either. It hovered at the edges of awareness, present but displaced. For the first time, Eliza did not automatically move when it spoke. She did not obey the impulse it carried with it. Did not shrink. Did not rush. Did not fix or flee. She stayed. And in staying, something unfamiliar happened. She answered. Not with arguments sharpened for defence. Not with affirmations rehearsed for reassurance. But with questions, simple and unarmoured. The echo said something it had said a thousand times before, a sentence polished by years of repetition, shaped to sound like inevitability. And instead of bowing to it, instead of absorbing it whole, she tilted her head inward and asked, *"Why do you say that?"* The question startled the space. It created a pause wide enough for her to feel herself breathing, air moving in and out without instruction. Wide enough for sensation to arrive before interpretation rushed in to cover it. The echo responded, but the response was different now. Less like a verdict handed down from above. More like a reflex triggered by habit. It reached for old material. Old fears dusted off and presented again. Old predictions stretched thin by overuse. Catastrophes it had memorized. She listened, but she did not disappear into it. She stayed seated in her body while the words passed through the room of her awareness. She noticed the way it tightened her chest, a familiar compression that once meant obedience. She noticed the way it flattened time, collapsing past and future into a single urgent now. She noticed the way it always spoke in absolutes. Always. Never. Forever. As if nuance itself were a threat. And she kept breathing. The conversation had changed not because the echo had softened, but because she had not left. She was no longer inside its story. She was in her body, listening from the ground. And from there, the echo sounded smaller. Less like truth. More like a voice repeating what it had learned, waiting to see if it would still be believed.

And then she said something she had only once said to it before: *"That sounds like fear."* The words did not try to banish it. They did not try to correct it or rise above it. They located it, the way one might place a finger on a pulse to feel what is actually happening. The echo shifted. Its sentences grew longer. More tangled. Less sure of their own endings, as if they were searching for a place to land and could not quite find the ground. She realized then what had changed. It had always spoken at her. Now she was speaking with it. A new posture formed inside her. Not submission. Not war. Witness. A stance that did not collapse or attack but remained present enough to see clearly. She began to treat the echo the way one might treat a distressed child, an anxious animal, or a storm system forming on the horizon. Not as truth. Not as command. But as information, as data about conditions rather than declarations about reality. *"You think this will end badly,"* she said once. The echo surged, eager, relieved to be recognized. *"Yes,"* it replied immediately, urgency spilling through the single syllable. She placed a hand on her own arm, skin warming under her palm, grounding herself in contact. *"I hear that,"* she said. *"What are you trying to protect?"* The question landed somewhere it had never landed before. The echo stalled. Its momentum faltered. It reached for familiar stories, the ones it had always used. Old dangers dragged forward without timestamps. Rehearsed catastrophes dusted off and presented again. But threaded through them now, she could sense something else beneath the repetition. Urgency without clarity. Motion without direction. Energy running without knowing where safety actually was. And she stayed with that noticing, steady in her body, allowing the echo to reveal itself not as an enemy to defeat, but as a frightened mechanism finally being seen.

For the first time, she felt its function instead of its authority. The echo lost its crown and revealed its machinery. She could see its patterns clearly now. How it always spoke in extremes, carving the world into cliffs and chasms. How it never tolerated uncertainty, rushing to fill silence with prediction. How it hurried and rushed her toward conclusions before her body had time to register reality, before sensation could finish its sentence. And she began responding the same way, again and again, simple and steady. *"I'm here." "I'm listening." "I'm not doing anything yet."* Those three sentences changed the architecture of her inner world. They slowed the spin. They widened the room. The echo would speak, and instead of moving, she would check. Her breath. Her shoulders. Her stomach. The weight of herself in the room. The temperature of the moment. Sometimes she agreed with it. Sometimes she didn't. But either way, she no longer handed it the steering wheel. It became a passenger. Sometimes helpful. Sometimes anxious. No longer in control. A small, steady voice began forming alongside the conversation. Not loud enough to compete. Not sharp enough to argue. It spoke in sensations before sentences. In soft boundaries. In timing. *Wait. Slower. Here.* It did not demand attention. It simply existed, consistent and patient, growing clearer the more often she stayed. She realized then something quietly profound. Dialogue was not something she had to invent. It was something that emerged the moment she stopped disappearing. Obedience had been automatic, reflexive, inherited. Dialogue required presence. And presence, she was learning, was something she could practice. Moment by moment. Breath by breath. So when the echo spoke now, she no longer asked, *"What must I do?"* She asked, *"What is happening here?"* And in that shift, power quietly changed hands. Not through force. Not through dominance. But through relationship. Through attention. Through the simple, radical act of staying in the room with herself, long enough for truth to arrive without being rushed.

The One Who Was Already There

At first, it did not arrive as language. It arrived as temperature. A softening in her chest. A loosening behind the eyes. A quiet sense of enough where there had only ever been urgency, a felt sufficiency that did not need to be earned. It came the way dawn comes. Not with an announcement. With a gradual undoing of night, shadows thinning without argument, light finding its way into places that had forgotten it was possible. For years, every inner sound had worn the echo's accent. Every thought arrived already shaped, already verdict, already leaning toward collapse or correction. Even kindness had been borrowed. Even hope had sounded like argument, like a case made against despair rather than a place to stand. So when something else began to speak, she almost missed it. Because it did not shout. It did not persuade. It did not perform intelligence or sharpen itself to be believed. It did not try to win. It felt more like a hand resting between her shoulders, steady and familiar. More like the sensation of feet on a floor, the simple reassurance of contact. More like the moment after a long cry when the body exhales without being told to, when relief arrives without explanation. The first time she noticed it, she was not thinking anything at all. She was washing a cup. Warm water running over her hands. Ceramic smooth and ordinary. The small clink of it against the sink. A moment so unremarkable it barely registered. The echo began its usual commentary, threading judgment through the mundane. And beneath it, something else happened. Her shoulders dropped. Not in defeat. In recognition. The movement startled her. It came without instruction, without decision. A release that knew itself before she did. She paused, hands still in the water, the cup held lightly now. Turned inward. Not to search. To notice. And there it was, not arriving, not announcing itself, but revealed in the quiet: a presence that had not been absent at all. A steadiness that had been waiting, patient and unassuming, for the moment she was finally still enough to feel it.

And there it was. Not a sentence. A yes. Not to the echo. To herself. A quiet internal nod, subtle as a shift in balance. A sense of I am here that did not announce itself or ask to be believed. It did not carry a story. It did not explain. It simply existed, whole and sufficient. She realized then how long she had lived without a center. Thoughts had spoken. Fear had spoken. Memory had spoken, loudly and often. But she had never felt the one who was listening. Now she did. A presence seated behind the noise, not elevated, not hidden, simply present. The witness to the witnesses. This presence did not rush to interpret the echo. It did not oppose it or attempt to dismantle it. It did not analyze it into submission. It stayed in her body. In her breath. In the subtle intelligence of comfort and discomfort, the quiet grammar of sensation. It registered truth before it translated it. A tightening. A warmth. A settling. A recoil. Information arriving without commentary. And slowly, it began to find words. Not clever ones. Not big ones. Small, accurate ones. "I don't like this." "This feels safer." "That's enough for today." "I'm tired." "I'm okay." "Wait." Each sentence felt like a stone laid gently in a river. Not blocking the current.

Redirecting it, altering the flow without force. The water still moved. Life still happened. But the channel had changed. She began to recognize the difference between the echo's voice and her own by texture rather than content. The echo was sharp. Fast. Absolute. It cut. It rushed. It demanded. Her voice was rounder. Slower. Contextual. It allowed space around what it said, room for breath, for revision, for life to continue unfolding. And in that space, she felt herself standing, not as an idea, but as the one who had been here all along. The echo always spoke about her. Her voice spoke from her. And the more she noticed it, the more it strengthened. Not by force. Not by conquest. By use. Every time she checked her body before responding. Every time she paused instead of spiraled. Every time she chose rest without justification or apology. It gathered density, slowly and reliably. Like muscle laid down through repetition. Like bone forming around a fragile center. Like a shoreline taking shape where there had only ever been tide, water finally meeting resistance that could hold.

She started to hear it more clearly in moments of neutrality than in moments of crisis. When choosing food. When leaving a room. When deciding whether to answer a message. When standing at a window and feeling the day without naming it. It was not dramatic. It did not announce itself in emergencies or demand attention. It was consistent. It did not narrate her life. It oriented it, quietly adjusting her position in relation to what was real. And then one day, the echo said something old and heavy. Something practiced. Something meant to collapse her inward, to fold her back into the familiar shape of doubt. She waited. Listened. And another voice answered first. Not loud. Not trembling. Simply present. *"That's not true."* The words felt different in her mouth. They did not rise to battle or sharpen themselves for defence. They rose to ground. She felt them land in her hips, settling her weight. In her spine, aligning her upright without effort. In her jaw, releasing tension that had braced for years. Nothing dramatic followed. No silence fell. The world did not rearrange itself. But something essential had happened. She had spoken from herself, not about herself. And in that moment, the center held. And she understood something with a clarity that did not require belief or reinforcement. This voice did not come from thought. It came from being. It was not constructed. It was not practiced. It had been there through every year of silence, steady beneath the noise. Through every distortion, every moment, she had bent herself to fit what was asked. Through every borrowed identity worn for safety. It had not been absent. It had been unheard. Buried beneath volume. Buried beneath adaptation. Buried beneath the long training of disappearance, the quiet skill of leaving herself while remaining functional. Now, as she continued to stay, to sense, to respond instead of react, it grew easier to find. Not because the echo stopped speaking. It still had its habits, its reflexes, its rehearsed warnings. But because she no longer needed it to tell her who she was. Its role diminished not through opposition, but through irrelevance. She was beginning to feel herself. And feeling, she was learning, is the native language of truth. It speaks through warmth and recoil, through ease and constriction, through the subtle yes and no that arrive before explanation. It does not argue its case. It does not demand allegiance. It simply reveals what is so, in the quiet, undeniable grammar of being alive.

Learning the Language of Static

She stopped arguing with the echo the day she realized it was terrible at subtlety. It only knew how to shout. Urgency. Absolutes. Endings disguised as instructions. It did not whisper. It did not suggest. It announced, blared, overwhelmed. For years, she had treated every sentence it offered as a directive. A command dressed as insight. A verdict pretending to be wisdom. She had moved when it spoke, as though motion itself were obedience. But one afternoon, in the middle of a familiar surge of inner noise, something shifted. The echo began its litany, sharp and insistent, pushing toward collapse, toward certainty, toward now. Its rhythm was familiar, almost ritualized. And instead of answering it, instead of bracing or countering or disappearing, she leaned back into her body. Not away. Down. Gravity became an ally rather than a threat. Her feet pressed into the floor, solid and undeniable. Her breath slowed on purpose, lengthening like a sentence finally allowed to finish. Her hands rested on her thighs like anchors, simple points of contact reminding her where she was. The echo kept talking.

And for the first time, she did not listen for meaning. She listened for signal. She listened the way one listens to static on a radio, not for the song, but for what the distortion itself reveals. Beneath the words, she noticed heat in her chest, blooming too fast to be insight. A tightening in her throat, familiar and rehearsed. A buzzing behind the eyes, a pressure that had always accompanied its urgency. *"Ah. Not truth. Activation."* The realization did not arrive as a rebuttal. It arrived as orientation. She said it silently, almost gently, not to silence the echo but to place it correctly: *"This isn't a command. This is a flare."* A signal of intensity. A warning light. A surge of nervous system energy asking for attention, not obedience. And in naming it, something loosened. The volume did not vanish, but it lost its authority. Static could be loud without being meaningful. Noise could be present without being directive. She stayed with the sensation, letting it crest and ebb, learning the contours of its rise and fall. And for the first time, the echo sounded less like a voice to follow and more like weather passing through a sky that no longer mistook itself for the storm.

The echo faltered, confused by the lack of obedience, as though it had shouted into an empty hallway and expected footsteps to follow. She continued, curious now rather than threatened. *"When you say things like this,"* she thought, *"it usually means I'm overwhelmed. Or tired. Or afraid of something I haven't named yet."* The words did not challenge the echo. They translated it. The echo tried again, louder, pressing for its old authority. She translated again. *"Okay. That tone usually means I've pushed too far today." "Or that something feels unsafe." "Or that I need to stop."* Each translation stripped the message of its command. The words lost their teeth the moment she reclassified them. What had once been an order became a weather report. High wind. Low visibility. Proceed gently. She began doing this deliberately. Every time the echo surged, she asked a different question. Not *"What is it saying?"* But *"What state is it pointing to?"* She listened beneath the syntax, beneath the drama, beneath the story. Sharpness meant fear. Repetition meant exhaustion. Cruelty meant pain without language, hurt pressing against the edges of speech. Urgency meant a boundary had already been crossed, and the body was raising the alarm. The echo hated this. It tried new tactics. Softer tones. Concern masquerading as logic. Warnings disguised as care. She noticed anyway. *"That one sounds like hunger." "That one feels like loneliness." "That one usually shows up when I haven't rested."* Each recognition landed like a pin on a map, locating experience rather than explaining it away. The echo could still speak. But now it had become something else. Not a ruler. Not a judge. A barometer. And she had learned how to read the sky. She wrote it down later, not as accusations, but as notes. A private cartography. If the echo says this → check the body. If it repeats → slow down. If it rushes → pause. A field guide, not a rulebook. Something to consult, not something to obey. A way of orienting herself when the weather shifted without warning. And something remarkable happened. The echo stopped escalating. Because escalation only works when someone believes the message is an instruction instead of an alarm. Once she understood that the echo was not a commander but a malfunctioning sensor, it lost its authority. Sensors can be thanked. They can be checked. They can even be recalibrated. They do not get to drive. One evening, the echo rose suddenly, familiar and sharp, like a siren flaring in the distance. She closed her eyes. Listened. Translated. *"Oh,"* she said softly inside herself. *"This is grief." "This is old." "This is asking for rest, not obedience."* The naming did not dismiss the signal. It contextualized it. Her body responded before her thoughts did. Her shoulders eased, dropping a fraction that felt like mercy. Her breath deepened, widening the space inside her ribs. The urgency drained, not because it had been fought, but because it had been understood. The echo trailed off mid-sentence, as if it had lost the room, as if no one was following the script anymore. And in the quiet that followed, another voice spoke. Not reactive. Not defensive. Clear. *"Thank you for the signal,"* it said. *"We've got it from here."* For the first time, the echo was no longer in charge of meaning. It was just noise, a flicker on the periphery. And she had learned how to listen without obeying, how to stay present without surrendering, how to remain in her body while the static passed through.

When Translation Became a Door

The first real test did not arrive gently. It came the way storms do. Without ceremony. Without warning. With the old, familiar pressure that made the world feel too small to hold her. Her body knew before her mind did. The tightening. The heat. The inward pull that once would have swept her away before a single thought could finish forming. And the echo rose with it. Quick and practiced, slipping into the groove it had carved over years. Urgent. Certain. Convincing. A voice that once decided everything by sheer volume alone. Once, she would have vanished into it the way a hand disappears into deep water, leaving no trace of where she had been. But something was different now. The moment the echo surged, another movement happened alongside it. Her awareness dropped. Out of the spin. Into her chest. Into her stomach. Into the undeniable fact of sensation. Translation arrived before obedience could take hold. *"Oh,"* she thought. *"This tone means overload." "This pressure usually means I'm past my limit." "This speed always shows up when I'm afraid."* The echo kept going. It did not soften. It did not wait. But she was no longer inside its sentences. She was standing beside them, hearing them the way one hears a siren in the distance. For information, not instruction. A signal passing through the air, not a map of where to go. Her feet pressed into the floor. The room came back into focus. Light settling on the wall. Air moving in and out of her lungs. The weight of her own hands in her lap, warm and real. Presence widened, making space for what was actually happening. *"This is activation,"* she named. *"Not truth."* And in that naming, a door opened. Not away from the storm, but through it. A passage that did not require her to disappear in order to survive. And in the space that naming created, something astonishing appeared. A pause. Not peace. Not relief. A gap. Barely a breath wide. But inside it lived a question she had never been able to access before, not because it was hidden, but because she had never been still long enough to hear it. *"What do I choose to do with this state?"* The echo rushed to fill the silence, alarmed by the opening, eager to reclaim momentum. She didn't stop it. She translated it. *"That sentence means I'm overwhelmed." "That image means I'm exhausted." "That push means I need support."*

Each translation loosened the grip just enough for sensation to re-enter the room. Her body softened, not completely, not all at once, just enough to be felt. Beneath the noise was a different current. Quieter. Heavier. Rooted. It didn't argue or explain itself. It didn't narrate or predict. It leaned. Toward stillness. Toward contact. Toward the simplest possible next thing. She followed it. Not dramatically. Not heroically. She shifted position. Put her feet fully on the ground. Let her spine find the chair instead of hovering above it. Breathed until the air reached the bottom of her ribs, the place urgency never wanted her to go. The body received the change immediately, like dry earth taking in water. The echo stuttered. Its urgency lost tempo, tripping over the slower rhythm. Because urgency feeds on speed. And she had changed the pace. *"This feeling wants something,"* she realized, the thought arriving without pressure or demand. *"And I get to decide what that something is."* The realization did not erase the intensity. It reorganized it. The state was still there. The sensation still alive. But now it was accompanied by choice. By presence. By a self who could remain while the feeling spoke and respond without disappearing. That was the moment translation crossed into choice. Not as a grand decision announced to the heavens, but as a series of small, sovereign acts that required no permission. Stay seated. Keep breathing. Feel the floor. Send a message. Drink water. Rest. Each one a quiet refusal to let the echo be the only voice in the room. Each one a vote cast for presence. The crisis did not vanish. It did not dissolve into insight or gratitude. But it changed shape. It stopped being a tunnel with only one direction and became a weather system. Intense. Temporary. Moving. Something that could be endured without being obeyed. She stayed present long enough to feel the first shift. The first easing. The first return of dimension, as if depth had come back into a world that had gone flat. Later, she would write about it. Not about what the echo had said. But about what she had done. *"I noticed." "I named." "I slowed." "I chose."* The sentences were simple. Factual. Grounded. They did not dramatize survival. They documented agency. And that night, she understood something that would become foundational, something that would quietly reorganize her understanding of power. Translation gives you distance. Distance gives you options. And options are the birthplace of freedom. The echo could still rise. The storm could still come. Signals would still flare. But they were no longer the only force in the sky. There was now a hand on the wheel. Steady. Present. Capable of adjusting course without panic. And it was hers.

When Choice Began to Point Somewhere

At first, the new voice was only a pause. A thin place in the noise. A breath where the echo could not quite finish its sentence, where urgency lost its footing. It did not tell her where to go. It only told her where she was. Tired. Overstimulated. Lonely. Afraid. In the beginning, that was enough. Because before, she had only known how to flee her inner weather. Now, she was learning how to read it, to stand inside it without being swept away.

She started to notice patterns. The echo always sharpened when she ignored her body too long, its edges growing cruel with neglect. It grew theatrical when she was depleted, amplifying catastrophe to compensate for exhaustion. It became absolute when she was frightened, collapsing nuance into certainty. And beneath it, every time, there was something else, quieter but consistent. A pressure that meant rest. A hollow that meant connection. A heaviness that meant grief. A buzzing that meant too much, too fast.

These sensations didn't command. They oriented. They didn't say, *"do this."* They said, *"this is where you are standing."* She began to treat them the way one treats a compass needle. Not as a map. Not as a destination. But as an instrument that responds to forces already present, pulling toward true north from inside the terrain itself. The body was no longer an obstacle to overcome or a problem to manage. It was a landscape with markers, offering direction not through instruction, but through alignment.

And as she learned to read it, choice began to point somewhere real, somewhere grounded, somewhere that belonged to her. She started checking it. In conversations. In crowded rooms. Before saying yes. After saying no. She would pause and feel. Did her chest open or tighten? Did her breath deepen or fracture? Did her body lean forward or pull back? At first, the signals were faint, braided with noise, difficult to separate from habit.

But she kept returning. Not to the echo. To the sensations underneath it, the layer that did not perform. The warmth that showed up when something was honest. The quiet steadiness that followed a boundary. The subtle relief that accompanied rest. The grounded ache that meant something mattered. Slowly, almost without noticing, she stopped asking the echo what anything meant. She asked her body.

"What happens in me when I imagine staying?" "What happens when I imagine leaving?" "What happens when I speak this out loud?" "What happens when I don't?" The answers didn't come in sentences. They came as shifts. A softening in the chest. A sinking of weight into the hips. A widening behind the eyes. A knot loosening its grip, thread by thread. These movements were quiet but unmistakable, like the way balance returns before you realize you were off center.

And she learned to trust those movements more than the echo's eloquence. Because the echo was clever. It could argue any position into sounding inevitable. But the body was consistent. The echo argued. The body oriented. The echo catastrophized. The body registered. The echo narrated. The body pointed. And with each check-in, each pause, she found herself standing a little more firmly in the direction her own life was already moving.

Over time, she realized something subtle had changed, the way landscapes shift so gradually you only notice when you look back. When she felt lost, she no longer searched for a solution. She searched for a sensation. For the place in her that felt even a fraction more real, more settled, more alive. That place became her north, not because it promised safety, but because it carried integrity.

It aligned her with what was true before it tried to protect her, before fear began editing the story. In moments of decision, she would sit quietly and let the noise run its course, letting the echo exhaust itself without interference. And then she would ask, not urgently, not desperately, but honestly, *"Which direction brings me closer to myself?"* The question did not demand certainty. It invited alignment.

Sometimes the answer was rest. Sometimes it was speaking. Sometimes it was leaving. Sometimes it was staying and breathing and letting the wave pass through without being named as danger. She was no longer navigating by fear. She was navigating by felt truth. And that truth lived in the body first, in the places that tightened or softened before thought arrived to explain. The echo still existed. It still commented, still predicted, still flared from time to time. But it no longer stood at the front of the room.

The compass did. And it did not shout. It hummed. A low, steady orientation toward what nurtured her nervous system, her dignity, her aliveness. That hum became familiar. Then reliable. Then indispensable. Until one day she realized she was no longer asking, *"How do I escape this?"* She was asking, *"Where is my truest direction right now?"* And almost always, her body already knew.

How Choice Learned to Breathe Every Day

At first, choosing the quieter voice felt ceremonial. Rare. Deliberate. Something she had to prepare herself for, like lifting a fragile object with both hands, careful not to drop it. It arrived with effort, with intention, with a kind of reverence. But choice does not stay alive when it only appears in crisis. It needs repetition. Texture. Ordinary places to land. So it moved into the small hours of her days. She practiced it without announcing it. When she woke and noticed the weight already waiting for her, settled on her chest before her eyes fully opened, she did not argue with it. She did not narrate it into failure. She asked her body what would make the morning less hostile. Sometimes the answer was light through a window, the simple grace of curtains pulled back. Sometimes it was water on her wrists, cool and clarifying. Sometimes it was staying in bed five minutes longer without turning rest into a verdict. Choice began there, quiet and unremarkable. In the grocery store, when her chest tightened in the aisle, the old urge to push through rising automatically, she paused. She slowed the cart. Let her feet feel the floor beneath her. Felt the temperature of the air. She left without buying everything on the list and called that success. Choice practiced restraint, learning that completion was not the same as care. When the echo offered its familiar script in conversations, its sentences lining up with practiced certainty, she learned not to respond immediately. She let the sentence pass like traffic. Waited for the sensation underneath, the place where truth registered before speech. Then she spoke from that place instead, even if her voice shook, even if the words came out slower than expected. Choice practiced patience. It was no longer an event. It was a rhythm. In this way, choice learned to breathe every day, expanding and contracting with the ordinary pressures of living, becoming less something she summoned and more something she inhabited.

She started setting rituals that were not about fixing herself, but about checking in. A pause before answering messages, letting the words settle before they were sent. A breath before committing, air creating just enough space for truth to surface. A hand on her sternum when decisions felt urgent, contact anchoring her back into flesh. And a question asked quietly, without interrogation or demand: *"What is being asked of me right now, really?"* These acts were small enough to repeat. That was the secret. Choice stopped being heroic and became habitable. It could live inside a day without exhausting her. It could return without ceremony. She kept notes, not of failures, but of recognitions. Today, I noticed my shoulders drop when I said no. Today, my stomach clenched before I agreed, and I listened. Today, rest felt truer than productivity. She wasn't collecting proof against herself anymore. She was collecting evidence of alignment, small confirmations that her inner compass was working, that her body could be trusted to speak before harm arrived. Over time, the echo learned something unsettling. It could still speak. It could still flare. But it could not rush her. Choice had slowed the tempo of her inner life, stretched moments wide enough for sensation to arrive before reaction seized the wheel. And in that slower rhythm, she found space. Space to respond instead of react. Space to decide without disappearing. Practice no longer looked like mastery. It looked like returning, again and again, to the same simple moves. Pause. Feel. Name. Choose. Not perfectly. Not permanently. But faithfully. And in that faithfulness, a life began to take shape that did not require her to be louder than herself in order to be heard. Some days, she chose well. Some days, she noticed late. Some days, she followed the echo out of habit and only recognized it afterward, the way old paths reveal themselves only once you are already walking them. But even then, she didn't punish herself. She studied. With curiosity instead of condemnation. *"What did I miss?" "Where did my body try to warn me?" "What will I listen for next time?"* Practice turned mistakes into information. Not evidence of failure, but data points in a living system. And gradually, something shifted. Choice no longer arrived with effort. It arrived with familiarity, like reaching for a light switch in a dark room you've learned by heart. You don't think about where it is. Your hand just knows. Her body began offering direction before the mind could spiral. A subtle tightening. A quiet ease. A pull toward or away that arrived without commentary. She honored these signals, not because they were always comfortable, but because they were coherent. And coherence builds trust. Trust builds repetition. Repetition builds practice. The rhythm established itself without force. Until one day she realized she was no longer choosing against the echo. She was choosing toward herself. The orientation had changed. The center had moved. And that choice, practiced daily in ordinary moments, became less about survival and more about authorship. She wasn't escaping her life anymore. She was inhabiting it. One grounded decision at a time.

THE INNER WITNESS

It did not arrive with fanfare. No voice booming from the dark. No sudden clarity blazing through the mind. It arrived the way homes often do. Through familiarity. Through the soft accumulation of moments when she did not abandon herself, when she stayed long enough for presence to settle into shape. At first, it was only a sensation. A steadiness beneath the noise. A presence that did not argue, instruct, or warn. It simply noticed. When the echo flared, something in her stayed. Watching. Breathing. Unmoved by the urgency that once swept her away. She began to feel it most clearly in her body. In the way her breath would deepen even when her thoughts raced, finding its own rhythm without permission. In the subtle warmth behind her ribs, a quiet center that did not need to be defended. In the strange experience of being distressed without being dissolved, of holding intensity without being overtaken by it. There was a part of her that could hold the storm and still remain intact. This was new. Before, every feeling had been a command. Every thought a verdict. Every sensation a prophecy announcing what must happen next. Now, something inside her stood slightly back. Not distant. Present. Close enough to feel, far enough to see. A witness that did not leave when things became difficult. She started to recognize it the way one recognizes a familiar room in the dark. Not by sight, but by shape. By where the edges were. By what did not shift when everything else did. And in that recognition, she understood she was no longer alone inside herself. There was someone home now, steady and awake, capable of seeing without vanishing. The inner witness did not tell her who to be. It watched who she was. Without commentary. Without urgency. Without collapse. When the echo spoke, the witness listened too. But it listened the way a shoreline listens to waves. Allowing the movement. Refusing the displacement. The water could arrive with force or softness. The land remained.

And slowly, almost imperceptibly, Eliza realized something astonishing. She was not only the one inside the experience. She was also the one who could see the experience. There was a difference. A spacious, stabilizing difference. The echo tried to fill her with identity. *"You are this. You have always been this. This is you."* It compressed her into labels and conclusions, into shapes that could be judged or feared. The witness offered no such story. It offered space. And in that space, she could feel the shape of herself without distortion. Not as a problem to solve. Not as a narrative to defend. But as a living presence, breathing, sensing, responsive. There were moments when she would pause in the middle of an ordinary day, hand resting on the counter, sunlight touching the floor, the quiet hum of life continuing around her, and feel it. A sense of being with herself. Not improved.

Not fixed. Not managed. Accompanied. The inner witness did not evaluate her sadness or demand its resolution. It did not hurry her joy or ask it to justify itself. It did not flinch from her fear or attempt to outrun it. It stayed. Calm. Available. Awake. And because it stayed, she began to stay too. With the feeling. With the moment. With herself. Long enough for life to be lived rather than escaped. She started to realize that this presence had always existed. Buried under urgency. Drowned beneath the echo's performance of identity. Mistaken for silence simply because it did not compete. It had been there through every moment she thought she was lost, steady beneath the noise, waiting without impatience. And now that she knew its texture, she could find it again. In breath. In sensation. In the quiet after a choice has been made. In the pause before reaction tightens its grip. It felt less like discovering something new and more like remembering a place she had lived before language. Before explanation. Before she learned to narrate herself into pieces. There was a particular quality to it. Unpressured. Nonnegotiating. Warm without being sentimental. Clear without being sharp. It did not demand improvement or offer a path forward. It simply recognized existence. And that recognition changed everything. Because the echo thrived on isolation. On making her believe she was only the noise, only the commentary, only the problem to be solved. The witness revealed something quieter and far more radical. She was also the listener. And the listener is never the sound. Over time, this presence became where she rested between moments. Where she returned after conversations ended. Where she stood while emotions moved through her without sweeping her away. Where she placed her feet when memory tried to drag her backward into old terrain. It became a place of orientation rather than escape, a ground she could feel beneath her even when the weather turned. She began to orient from it. Not asking, *"What is wrong with me?"* but, *"What am I noticing right now?"* The question did not demand fixing. It invited awareness. And something in that invitation felt like a doorway opening inward. Not toward answers.

Toward contact. Toward the quiet, enduring fact of being here, with herself, no longer absent from her own life. The inner witness did not rescue her. It did not step in to make decisions or shield her from pain. It did not promise safety or offer guarantees. But it gave her a place to stand where pain could be held without becoming her name. A place where sensation could move through without turning into identity. A place wide enough for grief, fear, joy, and uncertainty to pass without demanding that she shrink around them. It felt, unmistakably, like home. Not because it was comfortable. But because she did not have to perform to remain there. She did not have to explain herself into coherence. Or justify her existence. Or disappear in order to be tolerated. She could simply be present, exactly as she was, breath by breath, moment by moment. And presence, she discovered, was the one place the echo could not inhabit. Because the echo required collapse. It fed on fragmentation, on urgency, on the splitting of experience into accusation and defence. It needed her to fall out of herself in order to speak with authority. The witness asked for none of that. It did not need volume. It did not need control. It was wholeness. Quiet. Enduring. Waiting. Not for her to become something else. But for her to remain.

When I Forget

She did not plan it. There was no ceremony, no intention to be brave. Just a day when the echo was louder than usual, and the archive felt suddenly far away, like a language she could no longer speak. The familiar tools felt out of reach. The ground felt thin. Her hands moved before her mind agreed. She opened the notebook. Not to analyze. Not to argue. Not to prove anything. Just to leave something behind. For the version of herself she knew would return here confused, disoriented, wondering what had slipped away. She turned to a clean page and paused. For the first time, she did not write about the echo. She wrote to the future. She titled the page simply: When I forget: The words startled her. Not because they were dramatic. But because they were honest. She had been treating forgetting like a failure. Like a relapse. Like evidence that the echo was winning. But in that moment, something gentler surfaced. Of course I forget. Forgetting is part of being human inside a storm. Memory is not linear when the weather turns. This page was not a weapon. It was a handrail. She began slowly, deliberately, as if speaking to someone she loved who might wake up lost. When I forget, this is what I need to remember: She didn't write affirmations polished for belief. She didn't write reassurances designed to convince. She wrote anchors. Simple truths that could be felt even when clarity was gone. Words meant to be held rather than argued with. Words that would wait patiently until the part of her that knew how to read them came home again. She wrote facts. Not arguments. Not encouragements. Not promises that required belief. Facts she could lean on when the floor tilted.

- The echo sounds urgent, but urgency is not truth.
- If a thought feels absolute, it is likely not mine.
- My body knows before my mind does. Check the breath. Check the shoulders. Check the feet.
- I have survived this state before, even when it told me I hadn't.
- Confusion is not danger.
- Silence does not mean emptiness.

She stopped often, pen hovering, letting her body confirm each line before she trusted it to the page. Some sentences came from memory that had already proven unalterable, truths tested in real time and found reliable. Others came from moments she had once dismissed as too small to matter. The quiet wins. The pauses that held. The breaths that returned her when nothing else did. Then she added a section beneath it, slower now, more tender, as if speaking directly into the present moment that hurt. If the echo is loud right now:

- Do not debate it.
- Do not obey it.
- Read this page out loud if you can.
- Place one hand somewhere warm.
- Stay with the body for sixty seconds. That is enough.

She sat back when she finished. The page did not glow. Nothing miraculous happened. But something settled. The instructions were not meant to fix her. They were meant to keep her company. A map back to presence when language failed. A reminder that even forgetting had been accounted for. She closed the notebook knowing this was not a solution. It was a bridge. And bridges do not stop storms. They simply give you a way to stay connected to yourself while the weather moves through. Her pen hovered. Then she wrote the line that changed the shape of everything. *"You have mistaken forgetting for losing. They are not the same."* She felt something soften, the way ice gives without breaking. This page was not about strength. It was about continuity. About leaving breadcrumbs for herself in the forest, knowing there would be fog, knowing there would be nights when the path vanished underfoot. About accepting that presence would come and go, and that what mattered was not perfection, but return. In that moment, she realized what this section truly was. Not a reminder of who she should be. But a record of who she already was when the echo was not in charge. A living proof written in her own hand. This was not evidence for the echo to dismantle with cleverness or speed. It was testimony. And testimony, once written, does not disappear simply because it is challenged.

It stands. It waits. It remembers when the mind cannot. She closed the notebook gently. Not because she was finished. But because she trusted it would be waiting. Later. When the spiral narrowed. When memory blurred. When the echo insisted, she had never known better, had never been steadier, had never stood on ground that held. There would be a place she had prepared. A page that said: *"I knew you would come here. I knew you would forget. And I loved you enough to leave the truth behind."* And somewhere beneath the echo, beneath the panic, beneath the old gravity that had once pulled her away from herself, another presence stirred. Not relief. Not triumph. Orientation. The beginning of return.

The First Time She Used It

It happened on an ordinary day. Which, she would later realize, is how most thresholds are crossed. Not with spectacle. Not with ceremony. But quietly, while life appears to be continuing as usual. There was no dramatic collapse. No obvious warning bell. Just the familiar tightening. A narrowing of the room. A dimming of color. That subtle internal shift where the world feels farther away than it should, like glass sliding between her and what is right in front of her. The echo slid in the way it always did. Not loudly at first. Almost conversational. *"You're back here again. See? Nothing changed. You always end up here."* It sounded practiced. Patient. Confident in its timing. Her chest responded before her thoughts did. A shallowness. A pulling inward. As if the body were already bracing for something unnamed. The old choreography began assembling itself. Normally, this was the point where she followed. Where attention collapsed into the voice. Where memory rearranged itself around its gravity. Where the archive went dark, and the world shrank to a single corridor of explanation. But this time, something new happened. A flicker. Not a thought. A sensation. The faint impression of paper. Of texture. Of weight. The echo of her own handwriting curved and familiar. The bodily memory of a page she had touched, prepared, and closed gently. A page she had written for a version of herself she never expected to meet so soon. The sensation did not interrupt the echo. It did not argue with it. It simply existed alongside it, like a light left on in another room. And that was enough. Her hand moved before she decided to let it. Reaching. Opening the notebook. The echo scoffed, predictably. *"This won't help."* But her fingers already knew where to go. Muscle memory guiding her to the place she had marked not with urgency, but with care.

When she saw the words, something in her loosened. Not relief. Recognition. The feeling of being expected. Of being met where she actually was, not where she was supposed to be. She read slowly. Out loud. Each sentence landing not in her head, but in her body. Her breath lengthened. Her shoulders dropped a fraction. The room widened by degrees. This was not rescue. This was return. The echo did not vanish. It hovered. Watching. But it no longer filled the room. There was now another voice present. One that did not rush. One that had known she would arrive here eventually and had waited without judgment. And as she stayed with the page, with the warmth of her own hand, with the simple fact of sitting and breathing, she felt it again. Not victory. Not safety. Orientation. The quiet, unmistakable sense of finding her way back to herself. The echo continued. *"Don't pretend this is different. You've tried everything. You know how this ends."* Its voice carried the weight of repetition; the confidence of a story told too many times to be questioned. Her hands were trembling when she reached for the notebook. The movement felt almost ridiculous. Too small to matter. Too gentle to interrupt something that felt so massive, so inevitable. The echo scoffed. *"What is that supposed to do?"* She opened it anyway. The page was exactly where she had left it. "*When I forget.*" For a moment, she couldn't read. The letters swam, ink loosening from shape, meaning blurring at the edges. The echo surged, offended by the pause. *"This won't help. You're wasting time."* She didn't answer. She placed the notebook on her lap the way you might place a hand on a frightened animal. Not to restrain. Just to stay. To offer warmth. To let contact speak first. And then, quietly, aloud, because the sound of her own voice felt like a rope thrown across a gap she did not want to fall through, she read the first line. "*The echo sounds urgent, but urgency is not truth.*" Something in her chest loosened. Not relief. Space. A small widening, as if a window had cracked open somewhere inside. She read the next line. *"If a thought feels absolute, it is likely not mine."* The echo immediately tried to reclaim ground. *"That's something you wrote. That doesn't make it real."* But her body disagreed. Not in argument. In temperature. In the way her shoulders lowered a fraction of an inch, like a weight being set down without announcement. She kept going. "*My body knows before my mind does. Check the breath. Check the shoulders. Check the feet.*" She paused, just long enough to do exactly that. Her breath was shallow, but it was there. Her shoulders were high, but they softened when she noticed. Her feet were still touching the floor, solid, undeniable. Each check was not a solution, but a confirmation. She was here. She had not vanished. The echo continued to mutter at the edges, but its voice was no longer the only sound in the room. She read on, slowly, letting each line arrive where it could be felt. Each sentence was not a defense. It was a tether. And with every word spoken aloud, the spiral widened just enough for her to stand inside it without being pulled under. She noticed she had been holding her breath. The discovery came softly, without accusation. She let it move. The inhale was shaky, uneven, like a hand finding its way in the dark. But it happened. Air entered. The body accepted it. And with that small permission, the echo's rhythm broke, its cadence stumbling as if it had lost the beat it relied on. It tried to regain authority. "*You're just distracting yourself. This will pass and you'll be right back here.*" The familiar threat dressed as inevitability. She turned the page. "*If the echo is loud right now:*"

Her throat tightened. Because this was new. She had only ever done one or the other. Fought. Or obeyed. "*Do not debate it. Do not obey it.*" The words landed with a strange gravity, not heavy, but real. Instructions she could feel rather than interpret. "*Read this page out loud if you can.*" She was. "*Place one hand somewhere warm.*" She did, palm pressing against her own thigh, heat blooming under skin. "*Stay with the body for sixty seconds. That is enough.*" She didn't know when the counting started. There was no timer. No measurement. But she noticed when something changed. The echo didn't disappear. It still hovered, restless, alert. But it lost the center of the room. Its sentences kept starting and not quite finishing, urgency thinning at the edges. Not defeated. Unseated. And in that small opening, something else became audible. Not a new thought. A sensation of being here. The chair beneath her holding her weight. The faint sound of traffic outside, life continuing without commentary. The weight of the notebook in her hands, tangible, proof of preparation. She read the last line on the page. "*You have mistaken forgetting for losing. They are not the same.*" Her eyes stung. Not with the drama of breakthrough. With the quiet shock of recognition. The kind that arrives when something true is named at the exact moment it is needed. She had not escaped the spiral. But she had interrupted obedience. For the first time, she had consulted herself inside it. The echo tried once more. "*This doesn't mean anything.*" Its voice was thinner now, reaching rather than ruling. She didn't argue. She didn't correct it or push it aside. She simply closed the notebook and kept her hand where the warmth was, letting contact finish what words could not. The body knew how to stay even when certainty wavered. The room slowly widened. Edges returned. Depth reappeared. The echo receded to a corner where it could still speak, still mutter its familiar lines, but no longer command the center. And something else stayed. A quiet aftermath. A sense of having met herself in the dark and not turned away. Of having remained when leaving would have been easier. Later, when the moment had passed and time had regained its ordinary texture, she opened the notebook again. At the bottom of the page, she wrote: "*First used on a day I thought I had lost.*" She paused, feeling the truth of it settle. Then, underneath, she added: "*I hadn't. I had just forgotten where I put myself.*" The words did not feel triumphant. They felt accurate. And accuracy, she had learned, was its own kind of mercy.

What Is Real

It began the morning after she used the page for the first time. Nothing dramatic had happened in the night. No sudden peace. No clean sunrise blooming inside her chest. Just the aftertaste of something different, the way air feels changed after rain even when the sky looks the same. She woke with the echo already murmuring, low and habitual, like a radio left on in another room. Softer than usual, but persistent. Testing its old footholds. "*You'll forget this. You always do.*" And she almost did. Almost let the day swallow the small, fragile thing she had touched. Almost moved straight into motion without pausing to feel where she was standing. But as she stood at the sink, watching water thread itself over her hands, something in her body paused. Not as resistance. As recognition. A quiet, physical knowing. Not a thought. A sense of weight. Of temperature. Of being inside a moment that had not been arranged by the voice. She dried her hands slowly, as if the slowness itself were part of listening. Cotton against skin. The faint chill of air. The steadiness of the counter beneath her palms. And she realized what unsettled her. The page called "*When I forget*" had helped her interrupt the echo. It had named what was not true. It had given her a way to stop obeying. But it did not yet tell her what to stand on. It cleared the noise. It did not yet articulate the ground. It dismantled illusion, but it did not yet define reality. That absence felt important.

Not like a flaw. Like an opening. She understood then that negation was only the first movement. Knowing what was false created space, but space alone could feel unmoored. The echo had always been eager to fill that gap with certainty, even painful certainty. But now, with the noise thinned, something else was asking to be named. Something quieter. Something sturdier. Something that did not need urgency to prove itself.

She stood there a moment longer, hands resting on the counter, letting the question form without rushing it. *"If this is not true, then what is?"* The answer did not arrive as a sentence. It arrived as sensation. As contact. As the simple, undeniable fact of being here, in a body, in a morning, in a life that was continuing whether the echo approved or not. And she sensed, dimly but unmistakably, that the next learning would not be about dismantling the voice. It would be about orienting toward what remained when the voice was no longer in charge. Like a room in a house she had never entered, it waited. Not locked. Just unvisited. She went to the notebook. The echo stirred, suspicious, alert to movement that did not consult it first. *"What are you doing now?"* it asked, already preparing commentary. She didn't answer. She turned past the first section, past the pages where she had mapped the echo's patterns, its favourite openings, its recycled sentences. Those pages felt familiar now, almost historical. Useful, but no longer central. She stopped at a blank spread. White. Unclaimed. A quiet that did not demand filling. Her pen hovered. She could feel the old habit rising, the reflex to write something impressive. Philosophical. Bulletproof. A sentence that could not be argued with. The echo leaned forward, ready to assist. But her body resisted. Tightened. Not in fear. In refusal. Wait. So she did. She sat back. Let her feet touch the floor. Let the room arrive instead of rushing past it. The refrigerator's hum, steady and indifferent. Morning light resting on the wall without instruction. The faint ache in her neck from sleeping wrong, precise and ordinary. None of it meaningful in the way the echo defined meaning. All of it real. Something softened in her sternum. A settling. A quiet permission. And from that place, she wrote a title, smaller than she expected, almost shy in its simplicity. *"What is real."* The echo laughed quietly. *"That's subjective."* A familiar provocation, sharpened for debate. She noticed the way her shoulders wanted to fold, the old invitation to disappear into argument, to prove, to defend, to define herself back into pieces. She felt it. And she didn't follow. Instead, she stayed with the sensation of sitting. With the pen in her hand. With the breath moving without commentary. The question did not need to be defended. It only needed to be lived into. And for the first time, she understood that this page was not asking for an answer she could win with. It was asking for presence. For honesty small enough to be felt. For truth that could survive being ordinary. Instead, she placed one hand against her ribs and asked a different question. Not "*What is true?*" but "*What is not being spoken by the echo right now?*" The answer did not arrive as language. It arrived as sensation. The pressure of the chair beneath her weight. The warmth blooming in her palm. The simple fact of her breathing, unremarkable and happening anyway, indifferent to interpretation. She wrote the first line without trying to make it elegant. *"I am sitting on my bed."* She almost crossed it out. It felt too simple. Too bare. The echo scoffed immediately. *"That means nothing."* But her body disagreed. Not dramatically. Quietly. So she added another line. *"My feet are on the floor."* Then another. *"Light is coming through the curtain."* Each sentence anchored her further into the room. Not ideas. Coordinates. Markers that could not be argued with or revised by mood. She paused, listening for what else existed that the echo could not rearrange. The faint thirst in her mouth. The sound of a car passing outside, uninvested in her inner weather. The subtle steadiness of her heartbeat, keeping time without asking permission. She wrote, *"My chest is rising and falling."* A strange emotion touched her then. Not relief. Recognition. The feeling of encountering something that had been there all along and realizing she had been speaking past it. These lines were not poetry. They were presence rendered visible. A ledger of reality that did not require belief to be true. She looked at the page and understood something quietly radical. This was what remained when interpretation fell away. When story loosened its grip. When the echo ran out of material. What was real was not dramatic. It did not insist. It did not persuade. It simply persisted.

And for the first time, she felt the ground of her life not as an idea to be defended, but as something she could actually stand on. The echo tried to intervene. *"This is pointless. You're avoiding the real issues."* Its tone was familiar, dismissive, trained to pull her back into abstraction. She finally looked directly at the page and said, aloud, softly, *"No. This is the real issue."* And something inside her settled, as if a long-misplaced object had just been returned to its shelf. Not fixed. Belonged. She continued. *"I can feel the fabric of my shirt." "I can hear the house." "I am here."* The last line surprised her with its force. Not because it was beautiful. Because it was undeniable. It did not argue for existence. It stated it. The echo went quiet for a moment. Not gone. But displaced, like a sound receding when a door closes gently rather than slammed. She sat there longer than necessary, letting time widen instead of rushing it closed. Adding what came not from memory, not from analysis, but from presence. The mug warming her hands. The faint citrus of soap lingering in the air. The weight of the pen resting against her fingers. Each detail stitched her more fully into the moment, a quiet act of inhabiting. Then, lower on the page, something else asked to be written. Something less concrete, but no less real. *"I care about small things." "I notice when someone is gentle." "I am moved by music even when I don't want to be."* She hesitated, pen hovering again. This was new terrain. Not facts of the room. Facts of her. Qualities that could not be measured or defended, only recognized. The echo stirred, uneasy. This kind of truth did not leave much to argue with. It was not a claim. It was a presence. As she wrote, she felt a warmth gather behind her ribs, steady and unassuming. These lines were not confessions. They were recognitions. A way of seeing herself without distortion, without performance. Not as a problem to be solved, but as a person already here, already responding to the world. She understood then that this page was doing something different than the others. It was not interrupting the echo. It was outgrowing it. It was building a reference point the echo could not colonize. Because it was rooted not in interpretation, but in contact. And in that contact, something firm took shape. Not certainty. Not answers. Ground. She checked her body before writing more. The absence of constriction. The steady warmth behind her ribs. Permission. Not granted by thought but felt. So she continued, letting the pen move from that place. *"I feel safer when I am honest." "I soften when someone speaks my name kindly." "I do not lose my worth when I struggle."* The echo tried to mimic concern. *"How do you know?"* She answered without lifting her pen. *"Because my body does not close around these sentences."* That felt like a door opening. Not outward. Inward. A passage she could step through without leaving herself behind. She wrote until the page was no longer empty. Not a manifesto. An inventory. Not conclusions to defend. Anchors to return to. Each line a point of contact, each word weighted by sensation rather than certainty. When she finished, she drew a small line beneath the last entry. A boundary. A pause. And under it, she added: *"The echo can comment on these things. But it cannot create them."* She closed the notebook. And for a long moment, she simply stayed where she was. The room intact. The air unchanged. Her breath unthreatened. Something inside her reorganizing quietly around a new center, the way a body finds balance without instruction. She had not silenced the echo. But she had built something it could not inhabit. A place made not of arguments, but of contact. Not of explanation, but of presence. Later, she would add more pages. Memories that did not distort when the echo approached. Sensations that returned her to herself without drama. Names of people who felt solid. Moments her body recognized before her mind believed. Coordinates of safety. Traces of aliveness. But this first page of "*What is real*" remained different. Because it was where she learned the most important distinction of her healing: The echo speaks **about** life. But reality speaks **as** it. And she could feel the difference.

The First Time She Uses "What Is Real"

It didn't announce itself. The spiral never did. It slid in sideways, disguised as a normal afternoon, hidden inside routine. Eliza was standing in line at a grocery store when it began. Nothing sharp. Nothing dramatic. Just a faint tilt inside her chest. A subtle hollowing. The quiet sensation that the floor had shifted a few inches without asking her permission. The echo took that opening. Soft at first. Almost conversational. *"Look at you. Everyone else is managing. You're always behind."* Her shoulders tightened before she realized why, muscle responding faster than thought. The fluorescent lights felt suddenly too bright. The beeping of the scanner too loud, each sound landing with a little too much force. Her thoughts began to blur at the edges, as ink dropped into water, shapes dissolving before they could be held. By the time she carried her bag to the car, the echo had gathered momentum. *"You're failing at a life everyone else seems to understand. You'll always be this way. This never really changes."* The sentences stacked themselves with practiced efficiency, a familiar architecture of inevitability. Her hands were shaking as she set the groceries down. She sat in the driver's seat without starting the engine. The world outside the windshield felt far away, like scenery behind glass, present but unreachable. The old pull was there. The familiar inward collapse. The gravitational draw back toward the well, toward the place where everything narrowed into accusation. Her mind reached automatically for arguments. For reassurances. For reasons. Explanations assembled and dissolved on contact, useless against the weight of sensation. And for a moment, it felt as though the ground she had learned to stand on had thinned again. Then something else surfaced. Not a solution. Not a rebuttal. A question. It did not arrive from the echo. It did not come from fear or strategy. It came from the place that had learned to stay. Quiet. Precise. Almost gentle. *"What is real?"* The words did not push the spiral away. They did not demand calm. They simply interrupted the slide, like a hand placed against a wall to feel where the body actually was. Her breath caught on the question. Then moved. *"What is real?"* The steering wheel beneath her palms. Cool. Textured. The seat holding her weight. The sound of a car door closing somewhere nearby. The ache in her chest. Present, but contained. The fact that she was sitting. Breathing. Alive inside this moment.

The echo kept talking. But it no longer owned the frame. The question had changed the lens. It brought her back from abstraction into contact, from prophecy into presence. She was no longer arguing with a future that did not exist yet. She was noticing what was happening now. And what was real was smaller than the story. Quieter than the fear. More solid than the echo allowed. She stayed with that. Hands on the wheel. Feet on the floor. Breath finding its way back into her ribs. The spiral did not vanish. But it slowed. And slowly, she could feel herself again. Not fixed. Not resolved. Here. And that she was learning was enough to begin. The echo pressed closer. "*You know how this ends!"* The sentence arrived heavy with rehearsal, weighted to collapse her inward. Something in her chest faltered, a familiar dip in the floor of herself. And then, faintly, another sensation made itself known. Not a thought. A tug. A small, embodied memory of the notebook. Of the page. Of the words that were not explanations, but places she could stand. Her fingers were slow as she reached for her bag. Slower as she unzipped it, each movement deliberate, almost ceremonial in its refusal to hurry. The echo mocked the movement. *"What difference will that make?"* Her body answered first. A breath, deeper than the last, arriving without instruction. She pulled the notebook onto her lap. She did not open to the beginning. She did not search. Her hands knew. They found the section almost without sight. *"What is real?"* The title steadied something in her, like a hand placed flat against a swaying surface. But the echo surged again, threatened by the narrowing of its domain. *"This is avoidance! This is childish! This won't help!"* She didn't answer. She turned the page. Her eyes skimmed the lines she had written days before. *"I am sitting on my bed. My feet are on the floor. Light is coming through the curtain. My chest is rising and falling."* They were not true anymore in their details. The setting had changed. The furniture. The light. But something about them unlocked the present, translated memory into contact. She placed one hand against the steering wheel. Cool. Solid. The other against her thigh. Warm. Alive. And she did not try to think her way out. She did not construct reassurance or rebuttal. She asked her body. *"What is real right now?"*

The question settled like a weight, grounding rather than pressing. Her breath. Uneven, but happening. The seat beneath her. The ache in her chest. The sound of an engine starting two rows away. The simple fact of being here, in this car, in this moment. The echo was still speaking. But it was no longer the only voice. And for the first time in that spiral, reality had a texture she could touch. The answer came in sensations, not sentences. The cool texture of the wheel beneath her palms. The warmth of the sun resting on the windshield. The quiet hum of a car passing behind her, life continuing without pause or permission. She spoke them aloud, barely above a whisper, as if sound itself might anchor them. *"I am in my car."* The echo faltered, mid-rhythm, as though the beat it relied on had been interrupted. She continued, voice unsteady but present. *"My back is against the seat."* Her breath stuttered, caught on its own urgency. Then, slowly, it found a gentler pace, a rhythm that did not demand anything of her. *"My feet are on the mat."* The words did not soothe. They located. They placed her back into the coordinates of now. She flipped to a blank space beneath the page. Her pen hovered, trembling, suspended between collapse and contact. The echo lunged. *"This is stupid! This won't change anything! You're still—"* She wrote anyway. *"I am in the grocery store parking lot."* The ink came out uneven, lines wavering like the ground beneath her had felt moments before. She kept going. *"I can feel the seat through my jacket."* The spiral did not vanish. The fear did not dissolve into calm. But something shifted. The well no longer felt endless. Its walls came into view. She added, slower now, more deliberate. *"There is light on the dashboard." "There is a tree moving in the wind." "My hands are shaking, and they are still mine."* That line surprised her, landing somewhere deep and solid. The echo recoiled, as if from heat, its volume thinning, its edges losing definition. She kept going, trusting the movement rather than the outcome. *"I am breathing even though I don't want to think about breathing."*

And the air moved. In. Out. Steady, indifferent to approval or resistance. Whether the echo consented or not, life continued through her, quietly asserting its presence one breath at a time. A deeper sensation began to surface beneath the noise, rising slowly, the way ground reveals itself when floodwater recedes. The subtle pressure in her chest meant fear, not truth. The gentle ache behind her eyes meant overwhelm, not failure. Her body naming things before her mind could weaponize them, before the echo could twist sensation into sentence. She wrote, carefully, as if laying something fragile down. *"This feeling is heavy. It is not me."* The echo surged, offended by the distinction. *"It's always you. It's who you are."* Its voice reached for familiarity, for the old collapse. Her pen paused mid-word. Her hand moved to her sternum, instinctive now. She waited. Did not rush. Did not counter. There. That small, grounded warmth again. That quiet interior no. Not defiance. Recognition. She added one more line. *"This is a state. Not an identity."* The echo stuttered. Once again, it did not complete its sentence. Its momentum fractured, grammar failing where certainty used to live. She closed the notebook halfway. Did not put it away. Just rested her palm on it, as if on something alive, something that had met her and stayed. The parking lot had not changed. Cars still came and went. Doors opened. Engines started. The day remained stubbornly ordinary. But inside her, the spiral had lost its center. It was no longer a current pulling her under. It was weather, moving through a place she could now feel the edges of.

She sat there longer than necessary. Let her breath find its own length without instruction. Let her hands stop trembling in their own time. Let the echo mutter itself into something smaller, less convincing, less urgent. She did not leave triumphant. She left oriented. And that she was learning, was enough. When she finally started the engine, she did not feel "better". The ache had not vanished. The questions had not resolved themselves into clarity. But she felt here. And that, she realized, was the first real interruption. Not a victory. A foothold. Something firm enough to stand on while the rest of the terrain still shifted. She had not argued with the echo. She had not defeated it or proven it wrong. She had simply stepped into a place it could not speak from. And in that place, something else had been loud enough. Not a voice. A fact. The quiet, undeniable fact of being. Of occupying space. Of breathing air that moved whether she thought about it or not. The engine turned over. The sound was ordinary. Grounding. The world did not pause to witness her return. It continued, steady and indifferent, and she merged back into it without ceremony. Later, she would write this at the bottom of the page, the ink drying into something she could return to: *"When the echo is strongest, return to what has weight."* The body. The room. The breath. Truth begins there. Not in the story. Not in the argument. But in the simple, unassailable fact of being here, alive inside this moment, with something solid beneath her feet.

When the Echo Tried to Enter "What Is Real?"

At first, the echo stayed outside that section. It mocked it from a distance. Minimized it. Called it childish, naïve, useless. But it did not touch it. It circled, scoffed, dismissed. Until one evening, when the spiral rose fast. Too fast. Eliza was lying on her bed, fully clothed, the light still on, her mind already tipping even though the day had not been heavy enough to explain it. That was always how the worst ones began. Not with catastrophe. With a quiet wrongness. A subtle misalignment, like furniture shifted an inch overnight. The echo slipped in easily. *"You're lying here again. You always end up here. This proves it."* Her chest tightened. The room felt farther away than it should have, as though distance had stretched without warning. She reached automatically for her notebook, her fingers already trained by practice, muscle memory stepping in where thought could not. The echo followed. *"Good. Write. We'll show you what's real."* That should have warned her. She turned to "*What is real?"* The page steadied her for half a breath. Then the echo leaned over her shoulder, close enough to feel. She wrote, careful. *"I am on my bed."* The echo softened its tone, sweetening itself. *"Yes. And you're wasting another night."* Her pen paused. She felt it then. The intrusion. The way the sentence had quietly shifted shape, smuggling judgment into a place that was meant to be neutral. She tried again. *"The lamp is on."* The echo slid closer, confidence growing. *"And you're alone. And no one is thinking about you. And this is all there is."* The words waited, poised to be written, heavy with suggestion. Something in her stomach tightened. Not the familiar despair. Something sharper. More alert. A sudden clarity edged with heat. This wasn't despair. This was boundary. She saw it then. The echo wasn't responding to reality. It was colonizing it. Turning observation into conclusion. Turning location into identity. Turning *what is* into *what it meant about her*. It had found the doorway and was trying to step through. And for the first time, she did not freeze. Her hand lifted from the page. She placed it flat against her stomach, grounding, steady. The warmth was there. Present. Undeniable. The quiet internal no rose again, firmer this time, not defensive, just precise. *"No,"* she said softly. Not to the echo. To the page. She drew a line beneath the last sentence she had written. A clean break. Then she wrote again, slower, each word weighed before it landed. *"I am on my bed. The lamp is on. I am breathing."* She stopped. No commentary. No interpretation. No conclusions allowed past this point. The echo bristled, agitated by the refusal. But it could not cross the line she had drawn. It needed implication. It needed collapse. It needed her to finish the thought for it. She did not. And in that refusal, something profound happened. The page returned to what it was meant to be. Not a stage. A boundary. Not a mirror for the echo. A ground for presence.

She lay there longer than expected hand on her body, eyes open, letting the room be just a room. Letting the lamp be only light. Letting the bed be only a place where she was lying, nothing more. The spiral loosened, not all at once, but enough. Enough to breathe. Enough to stay. Enough to remember. Reality, she was learning, did not need narration. It needed protection. And tonight, she had provided it. She realized what was happening. The echo was trying to move into the grammar. To borrow the safety of the section and smuggle meaning back in. To turn observation into verdict. To turn presence into proof. It was subtle. Almost clever. But now she could see the move. She closed the notebook. Just for a moment. Placed her hand flat against her lower ribs. Waited. Her breath was shallow. Her shoulders were high. Her jaw hurt from holding. These were real. Not stories. Not symbols. Just signals arriving from a body that was still here. She opened the notebook again. Turned to a fresh page beneath the heading. And wrote slowly, deliberately, as if speaking to a child who had been interrupted mid-sentence and needed the boundary made kind and clear. *"I am on my bed. Full stop."* She underlined it. The echo rushed to complete it. *"Which means—"* She did not look up. She wrote again. *"The lamp is on. Full stop."* Another line followed. *"I can hear a car pass outside."* Her hand was shaking. She noticed it. Wrote that too. *"My hand is shaking."* The echo tried to stitch itself back in, desperate now. "*Because you're—"* She stopped. Looked at the page. Everything there was a thing. Not a conclusion. Not a story. Not a sentence about her worth, her future, her failure, her nature. Just facts with edges. Just experience without commentary. The echo could not land. It circled. Changed costumes. Tried concern. Then logic. Then sarcasm. Then urgency. Each tone slid off the page like rain off glass. There was nowhere for it to hook in. No unfinished sentence to occupy. No implication waiting to be claimed. Reality had been punctuated. And in those full stops, something remarkable held. The room stayed a room. The body stayed a body. Sensation stayed sensation. Nothing had to mean anything more than what it was. And in that simplicity, the echo found no grammar to speak through. She stayed there, pen resting, page breathing quietly beneath her hand, knowing now what protected presence required.

Not explanation. Not insight. Structure. Clear lines. Clean endings. A language the echo could not invade. And for that moment, that was enough to keep herself intact. Every time it approached the page, it dissolved into something that did not belong to the language of the section. It frayed at the edges, unable to hold its shape without interpretation to carry it. And she felt it then, unmistakably. The echo could only survive in interpretation. It could not survive in contact. She wrote one more line. *"This is a thought."* And beneath it, slower, grounded: *"This is a sensation."* She placed her palm against her sternum again. The heaviness was still there. The sadness was still there, low and dense like a weather front that had not yet moved on. But something fundamental had shifted. The echo was no longer inside the room. It was at the window. Tapping. Audible, yes. But outside. She added the final line of the night: *"Not everything that speaks is real. Some things only react."* The echo did not stop. It did not fall silent or retreat entirely. But it lost its disguise. It could no longer wear the voice of fact. It could not pretend to be the body. It could not anchor itself to the floor, the air, and the simple existence of being. Once more, Eliza saw its limitation clearly. It could only talk. It could not witness. She closed the notebook gently. Not as a weapon. As one might close a door after stepping into a safe room, knowing the walls would hold. She lay back against the pillow. The echo still murmured faintly at the edges, restless and unresolved. But another presence was stronger now. The quiet authority of what was actually happening. Breath moving in and out. Weight settling into the mattress. Warmth gathering where her hand rested. The small, undeniable truth of occupying space. Later, she would write in the front of the section, not as instruction but as orientation: *"What is real has no opinion. That is how I know it is real."* And beneath it: *"The echo can describe. It cannot inhabit."* And with that knowing, she let the night hold her, not fixed, not finished, but present enough to rest inside what was true.

When Memory Learns It Is Not Alone

Before the witness, memory ruled her like weather. It arrived without warning, soaked the present, rearranged the furniture of her mind, and left her believing that what she felt now was proof of what had always been true. A single remembered moment could swell until it stood in for an entire life. A single failure could rewrite every chapter before it. Memory, unchecked, had authority because it spoke in pictures and feeling, not arguments. It felt older than thought. Truer than language. The echo knew this. It hid inside memory the way a parasite hides in fruit. It didn't invent scenes. It tilted them. Darkened the corners. Edited out warmth. Inserted motive where there had only been confusion. It taught her to remember selectively, to recall pain with precision and blur everything else into insignificance. Memory became less an archive and more a courtroom exhibit, curated to prove a case she had never agreed to argue. But the witness changed the rules. The witness did not argue with memory. It did not correct it or try to replace it with something brighter. It stood beside it. Close enough to feel the weight of what was being recalled. Far enough not to be swallowed by it. When a memory rose, vivid and insistent, the witness stayed in the body. Breath moving. Feet grounded. The present quietly intact. Something subtle happened then. The memory no longer filled the room. It became an image held in space rather than a flood that erased all edges. She could feel the memory and feel the chair beneath her at the same time. She could sense the ache it carried without mistaking it for a verdict. The witness did not say, this didn't happen. It said, this is happening *now*, and this is happening *then*. Two truths, held without collapse. And memory, for the first time, seemed to notice. It softened at the edges. Its urgency thinned. It no longer had to shout to be seen. It was being witnessed. Not reenacted. Not obeyed. Seen. The echo tried to rush the moment, to pull her inside the picture and seal the door behind her. But the witness stayed at the threshold, one hand on the present, one on the past, refusing to let time collapse into a single point of pain.

She realized then what memory had been missing all along. Company. Memory had been alone when it ruled her. Alone with its intensity. Alone with its images. Alone with the echo whispering meaning into every shadow. Now it was accompanied. Held in a wider field. Allowed to exist without being asked to define her. And in that company, memory began to change. Not in content. In power. It could still arrive. It could still hurt. But it could no longer claim the whole sky. The witness had given her a way to remember without disappearing, to feel without becoming the feeling, to let the past be present without letting it be everything. Memory, she was learning, does not need to be defeated. It needs to be met. And once met, once seen from a place that does not vanish, it learns something too. It is not alone anymore. The first time Eliza noticed this shift, it startled her. A memory rose uninvited, sharp-edged and familiar, carrying the old gravity that once pulled her straight through time. The echo moved quickly, as it always had, beginning its work of narration. *"See? This is who you are. This is how it always ends."* The words reached for inevitability, for collapse. And then something new happened. Another presence arrived, not to interrupt, not to correct, but to observe. *"This is a memory,"* it said quietly. *"Not the present."* The distinction landed in her body before it reached her mind. A subtle settling. Like placing a bookmark instead of tearing out a page. The difference was immediate and unmistakable. The memory still hurt. Its ache remained intact. But it no longer consumed the room. It no longer replaced the air. The witness did not flatten the past or argue it into something harmless. It gave it boundaries. It allowed memory to exist as something that happened, rather than something that was happening again. The image stayed an image. The feeling stayed a feeling. They did not become a doorway she had to walk through. Eliza could feel the shape of time. Then. Now. The thin but crucial space between them.

That space changed everything. Over weeks, memories began to arrive differently. They lost their absolute tone, their insistence on total authority. They no longer came as verdicts stamped across her identity. They came as artifacts. Scenes. Moments with context, with weather of their own. Some were stormy. Some dim. Some unexpectedly gentle. All of them bounded. The witness held them the way one holds an old photograph. With care. With respect. Without stepping inside it. Without mistaking the image for the room she was standing in now. And in that careful holding, memory softened into what it had always needed to be: Part of her story, not the voice that told it. She started noticing details she had never been allowed to keep before. Neutral things. Human things. The sound in a room that did not belong to the story. The fact that no one knew then what they know now. The limits everyone was carrying, including herself, invisible at the time, obvious only in retrospect. Memory widened when it was no longer interrogated for meaning.nThe echo tried to keep up. It always did. It shifted strategies, leaning in with familiarity. *"But this memory proves something. It means—"* And the witness replied, steadily now, without heat or hesitation: *"It means it happened. Not that it defines me."* That sentence became a hinge. With the witness present, memory could no longer collapse into identity. Painful moments stopped pretending to be prophecies. They no longer announced what would always be true. They settled into their proper place, bounded by context and time. They became chapters instead of titles. Evidence instead of sentence. Experience instead of essence. Most importantly, Eliza stopped fearing memory. She no longer had to brace for it like an ambush, outrun it like a threat, or suppress it like contraband. Memory could arrive and be met. The witness could sit with any recollection, no matter how heavy, and keep her anchored in the present body. Feet on the floor. Breath in the lungs. The weight of now holding steady beneath her. A now that did not dissolve simply because a then had returned. And in that anchoring, something softened across time. The past no longer needed to shout to be seen. It no longer had to masquerade as destiny to be taken seriously. It could speak, and be heard, without being allowed to take over the room. Memory, once an authority, became a source.

Something to consult rather than submit to. Something to learn from without surrendering to. Something to grieve without being overtaken by its tide. It shifted from command to reference, from ruler to resource. And in that shift, something tender emerged, fragile at first, then quietly resilient. Eliza began to trust herself again. Not because the past had changed. Not because the wounds had rewritten themselves into something easier. But because she was no longer alone with it. There was now a presence that could stand with her in the remembering, feet planted in the present, breath moving steadily through the body. The witness did not erase what had been. It did not minimize or excuse it. It made room for who she was becoming, for the living, breathing self who could hold history without being trapped inside it. And memory, relieved of the burden of ruling her life, softened. It learned a new role. Not as judge delivering verdicts. Not as jailer locking her into old rooms. But as one voice among many, allowed to speak without being crowned. A contributor, not a tyrant. Finally held inside a larger, kinder awareness that could say, "*This mattered*", without having to add, "*and this is all there is*." In that holding, memory rested. And in that rest, Eliza found herself free to live forward, accompanied rather than haunted, carrying the past as something integrated rather than something endured.

The Memory That Would Not Rewrite

It arrived without drama. No crash of images. No familiar plunge through time. Just a small, ordinary sensation drifting up through her body while she stood at the sink one morning, hands in warm water, watching steam soften the air. Suddenly, there it was. Not a scene. A feeling. The exact weight of a blanket on her legs when she was very young. The kind that doesn't press, only rests. The quiet density of being held by warmth rather than effort. The sound of someone in another room moving unhurriedly. A spoon in a cup. A floorboard responding to a step. Life continuing without urgency, without the need to monitor or brace. Nothing significant had happened in this memory. No triumph. No injury. No explanation waiting to be extracted. Only this: She had been safe. And she had known it without needing to think. The knowing had lived in her body, not her mind. It had not needed proof. It had not announced itself. It had simply been the condition of the moment, the atmosphere she breathed. The witness felt it immediately, not as nostalgia, but as recognition. This, too, belonged. The echo stirred, as it always did, reaching for language, for meaning, for its familiar tools. It moved closer, searching for an angle, a way to tilt the moment toward usefulness or threat. But this time, it hesitated. There was nothing to sharpen. Nothing to accuse. Nothing to rearrange. The memory did not ask to be interpreted. It did not explain her. It did not justify her. It did not promise anything about the future or rewrite anything about the past. It simply existed. And because the witness was present, the memory stayed exactly as it was. It did not swell. It did not shrink. It did not turn into longing or loss. It rested in her the way it had rested then. Warm. Contained. Complete. She realized then that not all memories wanted to be processed. Some wanted to be remembered the way the body remembers temperature. As evidence of a capacity that had already existed. As proof that safety was not theoretical. That it had once been lived, quietly, without fanfare. The echo fell silent, briefly confused by a memory that refused to perform pain or prophecy. And Eliza stood there, hands still in the water, steam rising, carrying this small, unaltered truth inside her. Not as consolation. As fact. Her body had known safety before. And because it had known it once, it could recognize it again. The memory did not change her life. But it changed the way she trusted herself to live it. The memory did not present a story. It offered a state. Warmth. Weight. Breath. The soft, animal certainty of being alive and unthreatened. There was no plot to follow, no lesson tucked inside it, no beginning or end to narrate. It was a condition, not an event. A way the body had once been held by the world. The echo tried anyway. It always did. It searched for edges. For omission. For some way to say, "*Yes, but—*" It reached for comparison, for scarcity, for the familiar trick of diminishing what it could not dominate. And it found none. Because this memory had not been built from interpretation. It had not been constructed from outcome. It lived in the body, not the narrative. The echo could only work where there were sentences. This was sensation. It could not argue with the temperature of water. It could not twist the fact of breath. It could not corrupt the simple, wordless knowledge that arrived whole and intact: At one point, you were at ease. No conditions attached. No vigilance required. Eliza stood very still. As if movement might break the spell, though she knew now it was not a spell at all. She felt something unfamiliar move through her chest. Not relief. Not the rush of being saved. Recognition. *"This is real,"* she whispered, not to convince herself, not to anchor it with language, but because the body had already decided. The witness leaned in, present and calm. *"This happened,"* it said. *"And it happened to you."* The echo circled, frustrated. It attempted to dress the memory in commentary. To suggest it was rare. Insignificant. Over. To imply that its existence only made the rest more false, more tragic by contrast. But each strategy slid off. There was nothing to attach to. No hook for interpretation. Because the memory was not about *then*. It was about capacity. It was evidence that her nervous system knew how to rest. That her body knew the shape of safety. That ease was not a fantasy or a future reward, but something already written into her history, stored without words. Not something to chase. Something to remember. The witness held that knowing gently, without amplifying it, without turning it into promise. And Eliza felt the quiet power of it settle inside her. Not as hope. As orientation. A confirmation that what she was learning now was not foreign to her. She had been here before. And that meant she could find her way back, not by force or belief, but by listening for the same quiet conditions again. Warmth. Weight. Breath. The unremarkable miracle of being alive without needing to defend it. The echo fell quiet, faced with a truth it could not rewrite.

And in that quiet, Eliza understood something enduring. Not all memories are wounds. Some are maps. Her nervous system had done this before. Her body knew this state. Her cells recognized this arrangement of being the way bone recognizes gravity, the way skin recognizes heat. Which meant it was not foreign. Which meant it was not impossible. Which meant the echo had been lying when it said "*never*". Never had always been its sharpest blade. Eliza walked to her notebook and turned to a blank page. The movement was unhurried, deliberate, like approaching something sacred without ceremony. At the top, slowly, carefully, she wrote: "*What is real.*" Under it, she did not write the story. She did not describe how it happened or why it mattered. She wrote the facts the echo could not touch, the kind that live below argument.

- Warmth existed.
- My body recognized safety.
- I have felt ease.
- This state is part of my history.

Each line landed with weight. Not emotional weight. Bodily weight. The kind that settles into the chest and stays. These were not hopes. They were records. Evidence etched into tissue rather than thought. She closed the book and held it against her chest. The cover was cool. Solid. Real. Her breath moved around it, ribs rising and falling as if making room. The echo was quiet. Not defeated. Not erased. But displaced. Like a voice that realizes the room it depended on has been reoccupied. Eliza now possessed a memory that did not belong to the past. It belonged to truth. And truth, once felt in the body, was no longer something the echo could rewrite. It could comment on it. It could question it. It could try to diminish it. But it could not undo the fact that her body had known safety. That ease had lived in her once, quietly, without permission. That knowledge changed the future without predicting it. Because from that moment on, "*never*" no longer sounded convincing. It sounded like noise. And beneath it, something steadier remained. The quiet confidence of a body that remembers what is possible, even when the mind forgets.

How the Practice Reshaped Her Identity

At first, the practice felt like something she did. Something she reached for in moments of fracture. A technique. A ritual. A small rebellion against the echo. It lived on the surface of her days, called upon when things went wrong. But over time, it began to do something quieter and far more radical. It started changing the shape of the one who was doing it. Each time Eliza turned toward the embodied memory instead of the echo, something subtle shifted. Not dramatically. Not all at once. But the way a shoreline changes under a faithful tide. The same water, again and again, teaching the land a new outline. No single wave could claim the transformation. Only the repetition. She noticed it first in the language of her inner world. The echo always spoke in verdicts. *"You are." "You will always be." "This is what you are made of."* Its sentences closed doors. They named her as finished. The witness spoke in weather. *"This is here." "This is moving." "This will change."* Its language kept the windows open. And slowly, almost without her permission, her identity loosened from nouns into verbs. From fixed descriptions into lived processes. She was no longer *a broken person*. She was a person having a broken moment. She was no longer *someone who is depressed*. She was someone experiencing a depression state. The difference was not semantic. It was structural. The old identity had been a sealed room. Once named, it could not be exited. The new one was a landscape. With seasons. With regions. With paths that could be walked and left. Pain no longer defined the borders of who she was. It became one climate among many. And in that widening, something essential happened. She gained movement. She could locate herself without imprisoning herself. She could name suffering without becoming it. The practice had not erased her history or promised ease. But it had given her space. And space, she was learning, is what allows a self to breathe. Identity, once rigid and accusatory, became responsive.

Not a verdict handed down by the echo. A living field shaped by attention, by presence, by the steady return to what was real. And in that field, Eliza began to recognize herself not as something broken to be fixed, but as something alive, capable of changing shape without losing coherence. The practice had stopped being something she did. It had become how she lived. The practice taught her to locate herself not inside the content of her thoughts, but in the capacity to notice them. Each time she opened the archive. Each time she named sensation. Each time she chose the smaller, truer sound beneath the echo, she felt herself step back a fraction. Not away from her life, but deeper into it. Into the place from which life could be witnessed rather than endured. Something inside her stopped asking, "*What is wrong with me?*" And began asking, "*What is happening in me?*" That single shift reorganized everything. Because *wrong* is an identity. But *happening* is a process. And processes can be met. They can be guided. They can be lived through without becoming the whole sky. They have movement. They have duration. They have an end, even when the middle feels long. As the inner archive grew, so did her sense of self. Not louder. Wider. She was no longer a single voice arguing with another, trapped in a narrow corridor of meaning. She was an entire inner ecology. Sensations rising and falling. Memories surfacing and settling. Weather systems passing through. Rhythms finding their tempo. Knowing that did not need to speak to be real. The echo still existed. It still commented. Still predicted. Still flared at the edges when conditions were right. But it no longer defined the borders. It became one phenomenon among many, not the author of the whole terrain. A sound within a larger field of awareness. She began to recognize herself not by what hurt, but by what could hold the hurting. By the way her breath returned when invited, without being forced. By the way her body signalled yes and no before language arrived. By the way attention itself felt like a home she could enter and leave without losing her place. Identity, once something imposed by pain, began to feel like capacity. The capacity to notice. To stay. To respond. To inhabit the moment without collapsing into it. And in that inhabiting, Eliza found herself living from a center that did not demand silence from the echo, only proportion. A center wide enough to include everything that arose, without being defined by any single thing. She was no longer surviving her inner life. She was inhabiting it. The most profound change was this: Her identity stopped being organized around survival. It began to organize around presence. The axis shifted quietly, without announcement, the way gravity changes when you realize you are no longer falling. She was not the girl in the well. Not the keeper of the backpack. Not even the one dismantling the fortress stone by stone. Those were roles shaped by necessity. Responses forged in threat. They had kept her alive at one time in her life. But they were no longer who she was. She was the one who could sit beside all of them. The one who could remember without drowning. The one who could choose without bracing. The one who could stay when leaving had once felt like the only option. And in that staying, a new sense of '*I*' quietly assembled itself. Not as a declaration. Not as a fixed point or final answer. But as a living orientation. A way of inhabiting her own experience that did not require perfection, or certainty, or even peace. It required only contact. Only return. Only the ongoing act of listening for what is real, again and again, in the body, in the moment, in the breath that arrived whether she asked for it or not. Over time, the practice stopped being something she reached for in moments of crisis. It no longer lived on the shelf marked *emergency*.

It became the way she recognized herself in every moment. In how she stood at a window. In how she listened in conversation. In how she noticed the difference between tension and truth. It shaped the posture of her attention, the way she arrived inside her own life. She no longer asked, "*Who am I when this is over?*" She lived as the one who was here while it was happening. Not as the echo. Not as the story it told. But as the presence in which both arose. And that presence did not need to be defended or explained. It did not require constant vigilance. It simply existed, steady enough to hold pain without becoming it, wide enough to include change without losing itself. A self not built from survival, but from contact. From return. From the quiet, faithful practice of staying. In that way, Eliza did not find herself. She became available to herself. And that availability, she discovered, was what made a life inhabitable.

How Her Relationship to Fear Changed

At first, fear had been indistinguishable from truth. It arrived with the authority of a verdict. With the volume of something urgent. With the certainty of something that must be obeyed. Fear used to mean: *Danger!* It meant: *Collapse is coming!* It meant: *You are about to be undone!* And so she met it the only way she knew how. With bracing. With shrinking. With compliance. With the desperate effort to make it stop before it finished saying her name. Fear had not felt optional. It had felt instructional. But as the inner witness took root, fear lost its costume of command. It began to reveal itself not as a prophecy, but as a sensation. A tightening in the chest. A bloom of heat. A contraction along the spine. A quickening of breath that arrived before thought. A rush of images without coherence. Something happening *in* her, not something she *was*. The first great shift was this: She stopped asking fear, "*What are you telling me?*" And began asking, "*What are you made of?*" The question changed the encounter entirely. Fear, when met this way, answered not with stories, not with futures, not with warnings disguised as certainty. It answered with the body. With a trembling in her ribs. With a hollowness behind her sternum. With a buzzing in her hands that felt less like threat and more like excess energy searching for somewhere to land. When she stayed with those sensations, without naming them danger, without racing to explain them, something astonishing occurred. Fear could not maintain its narrative. The story depended on movement. On escalation. On her leaving the body to follow it into imagined endings. When she remained with the physical facts of it, the heat peaked and softened. The trembling pulsed and settled. The breath, startled at first, found its way back into rhythm. Fear did not disappear. But it changed character. It became information rather than instruction. Signal rather than sentence. A weather pattern moving through her nervous system, intense but finite. She began to recognize its texture, its tempo, its lifecycle. Fear rose. Fear crested. Fear passed. Not because she fought it. But because she allowed it to be what it actually was. A state. Not a truth. And in that recognition, fear lost its power to define her. It could still arrive. It could still hurt. It could still demand attention. But it no longer dictated identity or action by default. It became something she could meet, hold, and respond to without surrendering the ground beneath her feet. Fear no longer meant *obey*. It meant *notice*. And noticing, she discovered, was not the same as being overtaken. The catastrophe dissolved into temperature. The future collapsed into pulse. The threat returned to feeling. And feeling, she discovered, was survivable. Not pleasant. Not comfortable. But endurable. Held by breath. Contained by skin. Moving through a body that knew how to remain intact even when sensation swelled. This was not courage as she had imagined it. Not the absence of fear. Not the conquering of it. This was courage as contact.

The willingness to stay present with what was happening without demanding that it stop in order to be allowed. She learned that fear was not an enemy. It was a messenger that had been forced to shout because no one had been listening. When she listened with her body, fear softened. Its edges rounded. Sometimes it loosened into sadness, heavy and slow. Sometimes it sharpened into anger, hot and directional. Sometimes it opened into grief, deep and tidal. Sometimes it revealed an ancient, wordless need that had been carrying itself alone for too long.

Fear, she realized, was often pain wearing armor. Once she understood this, her posture toward it changed. She no longer met fear with resistance or command. She met it with orientation. With curiosity anchored in the body rather than the story. *"Where are you?" "What are you protecting?" "What do you need right now?"* These questions did not interrogate. They located.

And fear, stripped of its mythology, began to behave differently. It rose. It peaked. It moved. It passed. Like weather passing through a sky that was no longer mistaken for the storm itself. The echo had taught her that fear was evidence she was unsafe. That its presence meant danger was imminent and obedience was required. The witness taught her something quieter and far more accurate. Fear was evidence she was alive. That she was sensitive. Perceptive. Attached. That something mattered enough to register.

Fear became less a warning of collapse and more a signal of meaning. And meaning, she was learning, did not require retreat. It required attention. She noticed that when she could stay present, fear did not grow. It did not spiral into catastrophe or stretch itself across imagined futures. It completed itself. And completion changed everything. Fear stopped being a doorway to collapse and became a doorway to information, a passage rather than a pit.

It showed her where she was tired or hurting, not broken. Where she was crossing her own limits without noticing. Where something precious was asking for care rather than correction. Where an old memory was surfacing for recognition instead of control. Fear began to speak in signals rather than sentences, and she learned how to listen without leaving herself.

Her relationship to fear moved from avoidance to conversation. From obedience to curiosity. From identity to weather system. It became something that arrived, moved through, and left, leaving behind knowledge instead of ruin. And the deepest shift of all was this: Fear stopped meaning "*I am in danger*." It began to mean "*something in me is asking to be met*."

Sometimes that meeting required rest, the simple honesty of stopping. Sometimes it required a boundary, spoken or unspoken. Sometimes it was a breath taken all the way into the ribs. Sometimes it was a memory from the archive, consulted with the witness present. Sometimes it was nothing more complicated than placing a hand on her own chest and staying long enough to feel warmth return.

Fear did not disappear from her life. It was not meant to. But it lost its throne. It no longer ran her days or dictated her movements. It no longer authored her future or defined her worth. It became one voice in a living inner council. A voice she respected. A voice she listened to. A voice she no longer surrendered to. And in that shift, fear transformed from a jailer into a guide. Not a kind one. Not a gentle one. But an honest one. One that did not point toward catastrophe, but toward care.

How Setbacks Became Part of the Practice

For a long time, Eliza believed that a setback meant she was failing. That it meant the echo had won. That the fortress was reclaiming ground stone by stone. That all her careful noticing, her archive, her listening, had been illusions she'd only borrowed on good days. When the old gravity returned, when fear surged, and the echo grew loud again, shame arrived beside it like a second shadow. "You're back here again." "You didn't really change." "You were only pretending to be better." At first, every return of the storm felt like a betrayal of the work. A rupture. A proof of weakness. A collapse of everything she thought she'd built. It felt as though one bad night erased a hundred steady ones, as though progress could be revoked without notice. But something subtle had changed beneath the surface. Even in the middle of those returns, there was now a thin filament of awareness. Almost invisible. Almost easy to miss. A presence that noticed: "*This is happening again. And I am here while it is happening.*" The setbacks no longer erased the witness. They happened inside it. That distinction mattered more than anything. Before, a setback had been total. It swallowed her whole, collapsed time, rewrote identity. Now, even when fear was loud and the echo convincing, there was still a place in her that could feel the chair, notice the breath, sense the familiar tightening without mistaking it for truth. The storm still arrived. But it arrived in a wider sky. She began to see that a setback was not the absence of practice. It was the place where practice became most necessary. Not the failure of presence, but the moment presence was being asked to deepen. The echo insisted that falling back meant she had never moved forward. The witness knew better. It recognized the difference between repetition and return. Because return implies orientation. She noticed that she recovered differently now. Faster sometimes. Slower other times. But always with more information.

She could ask, "*What did I miss? Where did I outrun myself? What part of me needed tending before the storm hit?*" Setbacks stopped being verdicts and became messages, signals that something in her system had been stretched beyond its limits. And slowly, the shame loosened its grip. She stopped treating setbacks as evidence against herself and began treating them as part of the terrain. Weather she would encounter again. Familiar paths she would walk with better shoes. The work was no longer about never falling back. It was about recognizing the ground sooner, about knowing where to place her feet when the fog returned. The practice did not promise immunity. It promised continuity. And continuity, she was learning, was far more reliable than perfection. The first time she recognized this, it startled her more than any breakthrough ever had. She was in the middle of a familiar spiral, the kind that used to pull her entirely under, when she caught herself reaching for her notebook without drama. No urgency. No inner speech announcing failure or recovery. Just a quiet, almost ordinary movement. Not to fix. Not to argue. Not to escape. Just to orient. She wrote, simply: "*This is one of the days.*" And something in that sentence shifted the ground beneath her feet. Not "*the* day." Not "*the end.*" Not "*the truth.*" Not "*who I am.*" Just: "*one of the days.*" The words did not minimize the pain. They contextualized it. They gave the moment a boundary without stripping it of weight. And in that boundary, the spiral loosened its grip. She began to see that setbacks were not reversals. They were returns of weather. The nervous system completing old circuits. The body rehearsing unfinished learning. Memory testing its new anchors, checking whether it was still being held. The echo still rose. It always would. But it no longer arrived to an empty house. It arrived to a furnished interior. A body that could feel instead of flee. A witness that could name without collapsing. An archive that could be consulted without being swallowed. A breath that could be followed back into the present. And so setbacks stopped being emergencies. They became environments. Places she knew how to move inside. She could feel the terrain now. The slopes. The soft spots. The places where she needed to slow down. She did not demand that these days disappear. She learned how to live in them. She began to understand something essential. The practice was not what she did when she felt steady. The practice was what she did when she didn't. When she forgot and then remembered. When she disappeared and then noticed. When she followed the echo for a few steps and then felt the ground again beneath her feet. The work was not linear. It was rhythmic. Not about never losing orientation, but about finding it sooner. Again. And again. And again. And in that returning, Eliza stopped measuring herself by how rarely she fell apart. She began to measure herself by how gently she came back. The moment she truly understood this was the first time she came out of a spiral without the need to punish herself for having been in it. No post-mortem. No inventory of failures laid out like evidence. No private prosecution carried out in the quiet of her own mind. Only a gentle review, almost curious in its tone: "*What helped. What I missed. What I might try next time.*"

The absence of punishment was not indifference. It was wisdom. Setbacks became teachers. They showed her where her system was still tender, where care had not yet become habit. Which memories needed more tending. Which boundaries were asking to be strengthened rather than enforced. Which parts of her were asking to be met more often, not only when things went wrong. Difficulty stopped feeling like an accusation and began to feel like information offered in a difficult dialect. She discovered that every return of struggle added texture to her map. The terrain grew more familiar with each crossing. She began to recognize early weather. The first thinning of breath. The first shift in posture. The first emotional static that hinted at overload before it became collapse. These signs no longer terrified her. They oriented her. And even when she didn't catch it early, even when the spiral had already gathered momentum, the setback still contained practice. Practice of returning. Practice of staying. Practice of choosing the second sound again, even after the echo had been followed for a while. There was no threshold beyond which the work became invalid. There was only the next moment of noticing. The echo hated this phase. Because setbacks used to be its proof. Evidence it could hold up and say, "*See? Nothing has changed.*" Now they were her classroom. A place of learning rather than judgment. Each time she met one without abandoning herself, the echo lost another argument. Its certainty thinned. Its accusations began to sound rehearsed rather than true. It could no longer say, "*You're back where you started.*" Because she wasn't. She was standing in the same weather, yes. But with different ground beneath her feet. With a body that knew how to stay. With a witness that remained. With a practice that did not demand perfection to be real. She had not erased the storm. She had learned how to live through it without disappearing. And that was change that could not be undone. She was back in a place she now knew how to inhabit. And that made all the difference. The terrain had not changed. The weather still arrived. But she knew where to stand now, how to feel the ground beneath her feet without demanding that it be solid all the time. Eventually, she stopped calling them setbacks at all. The word no longer fits. She began calling them reminders. Reminders to slow. To re-anchor. To consult the archive. To place a hand where the body was already speaking. To let presence do what force never could. The work ceased to be a ladder she climbed rung by rung toward some imagined finish line. It became a rhythm she lived. Expansion. Contraction. Forgetting. Remembering. Storm. Clearing. Return. Not in sequence. Not on schedule. But as the natural movement of a living system, finding its balance. And woven through all of it was a steadier thread, one she could feel even when she could not yet believe it: *"I can come back."* No matter how far the mind travels. No matter how convincing the echo becomes. No matter how old the memory is. She learned that healing does not move forward. It deepens. It moves downward into the body, into the places that learned long ago how to survive and are now learning how to live. And setbacks are not breaks in the path. They are the places where the path teaches you how to walk.

How She Learned to Hold Emotion Without Becoming It

At first, emotion was not something Eliza experienced. It was something that happened to her. When grief arrived, she became grief. When fear rose, she was fear. When despair flooded in, there was no Eliza *having* despair. There was only despair wearing her name. Feelings did not move through her. They occupied her. Each emotion took the whole stage, the whole sky, the whole body. There was no distance. No edge. No place to stand. And because there was no place to stand, there was no way to hold. Only to be carried. Only to be pulled. Only to be drowned. The first change did not come as control. It came as contact. She began noticing sensation before story. The heat in her chest before the sentence formed. The tightening in her throat before meaning arrived. The heaviness in her limbs before the verdict declared itself. This noticing created the smallest seam. Not enough to escape. Not enough to rise above. But enough to locate. Enough to say: "*Here is where this lives.*" She started placing her attention where the emotion lived in her body, the way one might rest a hand on the back of someone who is crying. Not to stop it. Not to fix it. Not to analyze it into submission. Just to be with it. Present. Steady. Available. Something remarkable happened in that simple act. The emotion did not disappear. But it softened around the edges. It gained dimension. It became '*something she was feeling*' rather than '*something she was*'. The body, met instead of abandoned, began to respond. Breath found small pockets of space. Muscles released just enough to allow movement. The sensation shifted, not because it was forced, but because it was no longer alone. She learned that emotions did not want to be outrun or conquered. They wanted company. As she stayed, she noticed something else. Emotion had texture. Temperature. Weight. Duration. Fear buzzed and tightened, sharp and fast. Grief was heavy and slow, pulling downward like wet earth. Anger burned and pressed forward, directional, seeking boundary. Each feeling had a shape, a rhythm, a way it moved when allowed to complete itself. And completion mattered.

When she stayed with sensation long enough, without translating it immediately into identity or story, the emotion finished its arc. It rose. It peaked. It passed. Not erased. Not denied. Lived through. The body knew how to do this. It had always known. It just needed permission. This was the moment Eliza began to understand the difference between *being inside* an emotion and *holding* one. Holding required presence. Holding required breath. Holding required a self who did not vanish at the first wave of intensity. And slowly, that self emerged. Not separate from feeling. Not superior to it. But steady enough to remain while feeling moved. She could feel grief and still sense her feet on the floor. She could feel fear and still hear the room around her. She could feel despair and still notice her breath arriving, imperfect but loyal. Emotion no longer erased her. It informed her. She was not detached. She was embodied. She was no longer trying to be free *from* feeling. She was learning how to be *with* it, without losing herself in the process. And that changed everything. Because when emotion could be held, it no longer needed to take over. It no longer had to shout to be known. It could speak in its own language, through sensation and movement, and trust that someone was listening. Eliza was listening now. And in that listening, emotion found its place. Not as an identity. Not as a fate. But as a visitor passing through a body that had learned how to stay. And something unexpected happened. The emotion did not disappear. But it organized. Instead of a storm everywhere, it became weather somewhere. Instead of "*I am terror*", there was: "*Fear is moving in my chest.*" Instead of "*I am broken*", there was: "*Something hurts in my throat.*" The shift was subtle, almost imperceptible, but it changed the physics of her inner world. This was the beginning of holding. Holding did not feel like strength. It did not feel triumphant or upright. It felt like making room. Like widening an inner space so the emotion could exist without consuming it. A gentle expansion, not a tightening of resolve. She discovered that feelings softened when they were met without argument.

They did not need to be believed. They did not need to be solved. They did not need to be outrun. They needed to be felt inside a presence large enough not to disappear. At first, she could only do this for seconds. A breath. A hand placed against her chest. A single name spoken inwardly. Then she would be gone again, merged back into the wave, swept by the old reflex of identification. But those seconds mattered. Because in those seconds, she was no longer the water. She was the shore. And the shore did not stop the tide. It did not control the ocean. It held the line where movement could happen without erasure. Each brief moment of holding left a trace. A memory in the body that said: "*This is survivable. This can be felt. I can stay.*" She began practicing a different inner posture. Not inside the emotion, where everything collapsed into intensity. But around it. She would say, quietly, sometimes aloud, sometimes only felt: *"This is sadness." "This is fear." "This is grief."* Not as labels to contain. As lanterns. Light placed gently beside the feeling so it could be seen without being mistaken for the whole night. And under that light, emotion began to trust her. It no longer had to overwhelm to be acknowledged. It could arrive, take its shape, move through, and leave behind what it carried. She was learning that holding was not about distance. It was about relationship. And in that relationship, emotion finally had somewhere to go. Each naming lit a small boundary. And inside that boundary, emotion could move without becoming her. She learned to imagine her awareness as a bowl. Not rigid. Not leaky. Wide. The feeling could shake the bowl. Heat it. Fill it to the rim. But the bowl remained. Intact. Available. Holding without hardening. This changed everything. Because once emotion could be held, it could also be heard. Not the echo's translation of it, but the signal underneath the surge. She began listening beneath the intensity, beneath the volume. Fear wasn't just terror. It was protection without an update, an alarm still calibrated to an older threat. Grief wasn't just collapse. It was love with nowhere to go, energy still reaching for someone or something no longer present.

Anger wasn't just fire. It was a boundary trying to exist, heat gathering where firmness had not yet been allowed. Holding made space for meaning without collapsing into story. The echo tried to interfere. It always did. It insisted, *"If you feel this, it must be true." "If it hurts this much, it must define you." "If it's here, it must take over."* But the body was teaching her otherwise, lesson by lesson, breath by breath. Sensations rose. Crested. Shifted. Waned. They followed their own physics when not hijacked by interpretation. Every time she stayed present through a full emotional arc, something rewired. Not her personality. Her relationship to experience. Her nervous system learned that intensity did not equal annihilation. That staying was possible. That there was a self, large enough to contain waves without becoming the ocean. The echo grew less convincing as the body accumulated proof. Memory after memory of having felt deeply and remained intact. Emotion stopped being a force that erased her. It became a movement she could accompany. And in that accompaniment, Eliza found a new kind of strength. Not the strength of control or suppression. But the strength of capacity. The quiet confidence of someone who knows she can feel what arises and still be here when it passes. Her nervous system learned something simple and revolutionary: *"I can feel this and remain. I can hold heat without burning down. I can let grief pass through without becoming a grave."* This was the birth of emotional sovereignty. Not control. Capacity. The ability to host inner weather without surrendering the house. To feel intensity without handing over the keys. Eventually, she could sit with emotion the way one sits beside a fire. Close enough to feel its warmth. Far enough not to be consumed. She could cry without drowning. Tremble without shattering. Ache without vanishing. Each experience left her changed but not erased. And in this holding, a new identity quietly formed. Not "*the one who feels too much*". But "*the one who can feel.*" The difference was not cosmetic. It was structural. Feeling stopped being a liability and became a faculty. A sense she could trust. Emotion stopped being proof of who she was. It became information. It became movement. It became something alive that trusted her enough to move through rather than take over. She did not silence her feelings. She gave them a home that did not collapse when they arrived. And because they were no longer fighting for territory, they no longer needed to scream. They could speak. They could soften. They could leave. And when they did, something always remained. Her. Not emptied. Not exhausted. But present. Standing in the quiet after the wave, knowing now, in her body, what she had once only hoped: She could feel deeply and still belong to herself.

How It Became the Ground of Her Decisions

At first, holding her emotions was simply survival. A way not to be swept away. A way to stay in the room with herself when everything inside her urged flight. But slowly, almost imperceptibly, that holding began to change the architecture of her inner world. Before, every decision had been made from inside the storm. Fear chose for her. Urgency chose for her. The echo chose for her. She reacted the way a body flinches from heat. She moved the way a trapped animal moves. Toward relief. Away from sensation. Toward whatever promised quiet, even if that quiet came at the cost of herself. Choice was not a spacious thing then. It was a reflex. A recoil. A narrowing. But as she learned to stay present inside emotion without merging with it, a new element entered her inner life. Pause. Not a forced pause. Not a discipline imposed from above. A living pause. One that arrived naturally when she could feel without being consumed. The moment between sensation and action began to stretch. The breath between impulse and movement widened. The small silence after feeling, before meaning, opened. And inside that silence, something steady began to form. Not a thought. Not a rule. Not a belief. A ground. It felt like standing with both feet on earth that did not shift just because weather passed over it. Emotion could move. Fear could rise. Grief could pull. Desire could surge. But beneath them was something that stayed.

A sense of *here*. A sense of *enough stability to choose from*. For the first time, her decisions did not need to escape her feelings. They could include them. She could feel fear and still ask, "*What aligns?*" She could feel grief and still ask, "*What honors me?*" She could feel urgency and still ask, "*What can wait?*" Emotion became part of the information, not the authority. She began to notice how different choices felt *before* she made them. One path tightened her chest and sped her breath. Another softened her belly and lengthened her spine. One promised immediate relief and long-term contraction. Another asked for discomfort now and offered integrity later. These sensations did not argue. They oriented. Her body had become a compass. And the ground beneath her decisions was no longer the absence of fear, but the presence of herself. She was no longer choosing *to make the feeling stop*. She was choosing *from a place that could hold feeling*. This changed the quality of her life. Choices became slower, but truer. Fewer, but more inhabitable. She began saying no without collapse. Yes, without self-betrayal. Wait without panic. Leave without disappearance. Stay without bracing. The echo still tried to rush her. It warned of consequences. It dramatized delay. But it could no longer force movement. Because movement no longer came from pressure. It came from ground. And that ground was built, moment by moment, every time she stayed with emotion long enough to feel herself still there beneath it. She discovered that when she rested her attention in the part of her that could hold feeling, her decisions felt different. They were quieter. Slower. Heavier in a good way. Like stones placed carefully rather than thrown. Each one carried weight because it was chosen from contact, not reaction. She stopped asking first, "*What will make this stop?*" And began asking, "*What is actually here? What is needed? What would honor the truth of this moment?*" Sometimes the answer was rest. Sometimes it was speaking. Sometimes it was leaving. Sometimes it was staying. But the answers no longer arrived from panic. They arrived from presence. From a listening that included sensation, timing, and consequence without collapsing into urgency.

She learned to check her choices against her body. Not the body as fear. Not the body as urge. The body as witness. She would place a hand on her chest. Feel the rhythm of her breath. Notice the tone beneath the emotion, the underlying signal that was not shouting but humming. From there, decisions emerged the way paths appear in fog. Not all at once. Not with certainty. But with enough direction to take the next step. Not always easy. Not always comfortable. But coherent. She began to recognize the difference between two kinds of movement. A decision made to escape feeling. And a decision made while *with* feeling. The first felt frantic, brittle, urgent, like running without knowing where the ground was. The second felt rooted, even when it hurt. There was gravity in it. Integrity. A sense of staying connected to herself as she moved. This became her new compass. Not happiness. Not certainty. Not approval. Alignment. The quiet, embodied knowing that she could choose in a way that did not abandon her, even when the choice itself was hard. And that knowing, once felt, began to guide her life more reliably than any promise of comfort ever had. Presence. If a choice required her to abandon herself, it no longer felt right, no matter how convincing the story wrapped around it. No matter how persuasive the echo sounded. If a choice allowed her to remain with herself, even in discomfort, even in uncertainty, it carried a quiet integrity she had learned to trust. Over time, her inner witness grew more trustworthy than her moods. Feelings still rose. Waves still came. But they were no longer the ocean. She was. And from that ocean, she could let waves pass and still steer. This changed the quality of her life in ways that were subtle at first and then unmistakable. Boundaries stopped being reactions flung up in self-defense. They became responses shaped by presence. Relationships stopped being negotiations with fear. They became conversations with truth. Even uncertainty changed its meaning. It no longer signalled danger. It signalled listening. A pause. A place to stay curious rather than flee. Her decisions grew less about controlling outcomes and more about aligning with what was real. The question was no longer, "*How do I avoid pain?*" It became, "*How do I stay in right relationship with myself here?*"

The ground of her choices became the part of her that could remain. The part that did not disappear when emotion arrived. The part that could feel and still see. And from that ground, action no longer felt like being pushed by circumstance or chased by urgency. It felt like being led. Not by the echo. Not by fear. Not by old memory. But by the steady, embodied knowing that had learned to stay. And this is what surprised her most: The more she chose from this ground, the more that ground strengthened. Each aligned decision made her inner floor more solid. Each time she stayed, she trusted herself more. Each time she listened, her life grew quieter, truer, more her own. This was no longer coping. It was authorship. She was not just surviving her inner weather anymore. She was building her life on the place in her that could hold it.

How It Redefined What Safety Actually Feels Like

For most of her life, safety had meant the absence of pain. Silence instead of noise. Numb instead of feeling. Distance instead of contact. Safety had been a locked door. A lowered volume. A place where nothing could reach her. And because nothing could reach her there, nothing could truly hold her either. When she first began this work, she thought safety would feel like relief. Like finally exhaling. Like the end of the storm. She imagined calm as a flat horizon, a day with no wind. But that wasn't what arrived. What arrived was presence. And presence, at first, felt like the opposite of safety. It felt exposed. Tender. Unarmoured. Like standing in open air without the old shelter of disappearance. There were days when staying with herself felt more frightening than vanishing ever had. Because now she could feel. She could sense the subtle shifts. The tremors beneath calm. The ache beneath competence. The longing beneath control. Safety, as she had known it, meant absence. No conflict. No intensity. No sudden shifts. No feelings that rose too fast or too deep. Safety was quiet rooms and closed doors. Predictability. Control. The careful avoidance of anything that might tip her over the edge. She had mistaken numbness for peace. Stillness for stability. Silence for protection. But presence did not offer that kind of quiet. It offered something else entirely. A living safety. One that moved. One that breathed. One that did not promise the absence of pain, but the presence of someone who could meet it. As she stayed, slowly, cautiously, she began to feel the difference. Real safety was not the disappearance of sensation. It was the capacity to stay with it. It was not control over what arose. It was confidence in what remained.

Safety began to feel like warmth returning to a limb that had gone numb. Uncomfortable at first. Prickly. Almost painful. But unmistakably alive. She could feel herself again. Not shielded. Not sealed away. But accompanied. The old safety had kept her untouched. This new safety held her. And in that holding, she discovered something she had never known how to name before. Safety was not where nothing happened. Safety was where *she did not leave*. And the echo encouraged this misunderstanding. It told her safety lived *after* feeling. After resolution. After certainty. After she fixed herself enough to deserve rest. Safety, it insisted, was a reward. A finish line. A place she could earn if she stopped being so much. But the embodied voice told a different story. At first, it was subtle. Almost inconvenient. She noticed that moments she once labeled unsafe were not always dangerous. Grief moved through her body and passed. Fear peaked and softened. Sadness ached without destroying her. The emotions she had spent years outrunning revealed themselves as survivable when she stayed. And then she noticed something else. Something quietly revolutionary. The moments she felt most unsafe were not the ones with the strongest emotions. They were the ones where she abandoned herself. Where she dissociated. Where she silenced her body. Where she obeyed the echo without question. Where presence slipped and she followed urgency instead of sensation. Unsafe did not mean "*too much feeling*." Unsafe meant "*no one home*". Slowly, carefully, safety began to relocate. It moved from circumstances to capacity. From control to relationship. Safety was no longer the absence of waves. It was knowing she could stay afloat. Knowing she could feel the water rise and still keep her bearings. She discovered that safety did not feel like calm. It did not always feel smooth or quiet. It felt like presence. A grounded sensation behind her sternum. A breath she could feel all the way down into her body. The quiet confidence that whatever arose, she would not disappear. Safety became less about what happened and more about how she met what happened. Less about managing the world and more about staying connected to herself inside it. She could be afraid and safe at the same time. Grieving and safe. Uncertain and safe. Because safety no longer depended on the emotional weather. It depended on her willingness to stay. And in that staying, she felt something settle that had never settled before. A deep, embodied assurance that did not promise ease, but offered continuity. *"I will be here with you."* Not later. Not after. Now. That was what safety actually felt like. Not the end of pain. But the end of abandonment. Safety felt like being able to say, without bracing: *"I am here." "I am allowed to feel this." "I don't have to decide anything right now." "This will pass." "This is something I am feeling or experiencing. It is not who I am." "I made a mistake. I am not a mistake." "My past does not have to define who I am. It can refine who I choose to become."* Each sentence landed not as reassurance, but as ground. Something her body could step onto. It felt like having somewhere inside herself to land. Even when the world shook. Especially then. She learned that true safety had a texture. It was warm, not rigid. Responsive, not frozen. Alive, not controlled. It flexed. It adapted. It breathed with her. Sometimes it included tears that came without apology. Sometimes trembling that moved through and left. Sometimes anger, disappointment, or grief that needed space to speak. Safety did not require these movements to stop. It required them to be met. Underneath all of it was something solid. A steady floor that did not crack when emotion arrived. A sense of support that did not withdraw when things became inconvenient or messy.

She could feel it in her body. A low, reliable presence. A place that did not demand improvement before offering belonging. The echo hated this definition. Because it thrived on conditions. It insisted safety was fragile. That it could be revoked. That one wrong feeling, one wrong thought, one wrong reaction could undo everything. It told her safety was something to earn. To maintain. To perform correctly. It required perfection. That she had to feel nothing or feel everything exactly the way it prescribed. That she needed it for safety. That safety was control. But the body told the truth. Safety was not fragile. It was relational. It existed in the way she stayed with herself. In the way she listened instead of silenced. In the way she held fear without obeying it. In the way she allowed emotion to move without turning it into identity or fate. Safety lived in continuity. In the promise she kept to herself again and again: *"I will not leave when this gets hard."* And because of that promise, safety no longer vanished when discomfort appeared. It deepened. It strengthened. It became less about protection from life and more about companionship within it. She was no longer safe because nothing could touch her. She was safe because whatever touched her, she would still be there. She began to recognize safety by how her body responded. Her shoulders softened instead of braced. Her jaw unclenched. Her breath deepened without effort. Not because nothing hurt. But because nothing was forbidden. Sensation was no longer policed. Emotion was no longer a trespass. Her body could speak without fear of consequence. This redefinition changed everything. She stopped chasing environments that promised comfort but required self-erasure. Stopped mistaking compliance for peace. Stopped seeing people-pleasing for acceptance and love. Stopped calling quiet *safe* when it was built on silence. She began choosing people, spaces, and rhythms that could hold her full range of humanity. Places where she did not have to flatten, vanish, or exhaust herself to belong. Relationships where feeling did not make her dangerous or inconvenient. Safety became less about protection from harm and more about trust in her own presence. Trust that she could feel and still choose. Trust that she could wobble and still stand. Trust that she could meet herself without violence. Without interrogation. Without the need to disappear in order to be acceptable. And perhaps most importantly, safety stopped living in the future. It stopped being something she was moving toward, waiting for, earning through endurance. It lived now. In the moment she noticed her feet on the floor. In the moment she named what was happening. In the moment she stayed instead of fled. This was not the safety of a locked door. It was the safety of a home. A home that moved with her. A home that did not vanish when the weather changed. A home built not from avoidance, but from relationship. From attention. From the steady practice of returning to herself again and again. And once she knew this, she could never unknow it. Because safety was no longer something she had to earn. It was something she could inhabit.

When Choice Stops Feeling Like Effort and Starts Feeling Like Belonging

At first, choice was work. It was interruption. Redirection. Resistance. It felt like standing in front of a rushing river, planting her feet, bracing every muscle just to keep from being carried away. Each choice required vigilance. Notice the echo. Name it. Consult the archive. Anchor. Breathe. Respond. Choice felt muscular. Cognitive. Deliberate. It was something she *did*. And she was proud of it. She had earned that effort. It had taken courage to build it. Discipline to sustain it. Honesty to keep it clean. But over time, something began to soften. Not in the sense of weakening. In the sense of settling. She noticed she was no longer always catching herself mid-fall. Sometimes she was simply, standing. The echo would rise, and before strategy arrived, something else was already there. A quiet internal alignment. A subtle pull toward what felt true. Choice began to happen earlier. Closer to the root. Before the spiral gathered speed. Before urgency sharpened its teeth. And then one day, she realized something that startled her. She was not choosing *against* herself anymore. She was choosing *from* herself. The difference was everything. Before, every decision had felt like a debate between parts. A negotiation. A corrective action. Now, choice began to feel like recognition. Like turning toward a familiar room. Like saying yes to what already fit. There was less effort because there was less friction. Fewer arguments because fewer betrayals were being proposed. Choice no longer felt like self-control. It felt like self-belonging. She didn't have to convince herself to choose what aligned. Her body already leaned there. The way a plant turns toward light without deliberation. The way a hand finds its own pocket. The way home is recognized before it is named. Decisions began to feel less like forks in the road and more like following a contour. Staying in relationship with what was already alive in her. If a choice required her to shrink, explain, override, or abandon her felt truth, it no longer seduced her with urgency. It felt off immediately.

Not wrong in a moral sense. Wrong in a *fit* sense. Like shoes that once seemed acceptable but now revealed their pinch the moment she stood. And when a choice aligned, even if it was difficult, it carried a strange ease. Not comfort. Coherence. Her breath stayed with her. Her spine didn't collapse. There was grief sometimes. Fear sometimes. But no internal fracture. No sense of leaving herself behind to make it work. This was the quiet miracle. Choice stopped being something she forced herself into. It became something she recognized herself in. Belonging was no longer something she sought outside her decisions. It was embedded in them. Each aligned choice reinforced the same message, spoken not in words but in experience: '*I live here. I choose from here. I stay.*" And because of that, life began to feel less like a series of corrections and more like a continuation. Less like steering against the current and more like moving with an inner tide that had always known its way. Choice was no longer effortful because it was no longer oppositional. It was an act of coming home. She noticed that the moments she once called *willpower* were now accompanied by a gentle internal warmth. A sense of rightness. Not dramatic. Not euphoric. But unmistakably home. She would pause in the middle of an ordinary day and realize she had just made three decisions in a row that honored her body, her time, her truth. And none of them had felt heroic. They had felt natural. Unforced. As if something had simply been allowed to proceed the way it already wanted to. Choice was no longer a lever she had to pull. It was a place she stood. She began to feel it physically. A softening behind the eyes, like tension releasing its claim on vision. A steadiness in her spine, as if gravity itself had decided to cooperate. A quiet yes in her chest. This yes, did not shout. It did not argue. It did not justify its existence. It simply was. A presence that did not need witnesses. She understood then that what she had been practicing all this time was not control. It was belonging. Belonging to her sensations without interrogation. Belonging to her limits without shame. Belonging to her longings without distortion. Belonging to her no's and her yeses without apology. Each act of choice became a small reunion, a confirmation that she did not have to leave herself to live her life. Choice had stopped being a rescue rope thrown in moments of crisis. It had become a language. The way her inner world spoke to itself. The way her body said, "*This way*." The way her breath leaned toward certain moments and away from others. The way her attention lingered where truth lived, not because it was loud, but because it was aligned. And in learning this language, she no longer felt like she was steering against herself. She was listening. Responding. Participating. Her life began to feel less like a series of corrections and more like a conversation she was finally fluent in. Choice did not save her anymore. It expressed her. And in that expression, she felt something settle that had once seemed impossible: She belonged to her own life, not as an effort, not as a performance, but as a presence that had learned how to stay and speak at the same time.

She no longer experienced choice as leaving something behind. She experienced it as arriving. Arriving in conversations with her attention fully present. Arriving in rest without having to justify it. Arriving in boundaries that did not feel like walls but like skin. Arriving in desire without shame. Arriving, again and again, in herself. Even difficult choices no longer carried the old violence. They could be tender. Grieved. Complex. They could hold loss and relief in the same breath. But they were not foreign. They did not feel like amputations. They felt authored from the inside. As if something within her had leaned forward and said, "*Yes, this is mine to choose.*" She belonged to them. And they belonged to her. This is how she knew the center had shifted. She was no longer building a self, piece by piece, scaffolding identity through effort and repair. She was inhabiting one. Living inside a coherence that did not need to be defended to exist. Choice was no longer an act of separation from what harmed her. It was an act of intimacy with what was true. And intimacy, she learned, does not strain. It does not grip. It does not perform certainty. It listens. It recognizes. It remembers what already fits. It feels like being met from the inside.

The Final Line

It happened quietly. Not in a moment of revelation. Not during a breakthrough session. Not in the aftermath of a collapse. It happened on an ordinary evening, when the house was dim, and the air felt neutral, and she was sitting with her notebook open more out of habit than urgency. By then, the pages were thick with maps. Patterns of the echo. Lists of what was real. Memories that refused distortion. Notes written to herself for the days she forgot. She had built an entire inner language. A wayfinding system. A living archive. And yet, as she turned the pages, she felt something missing. Not more words. A center. Something that could be reached when even reading felt too far away. Something that could live below argument. Below explanation. Below story. A sentence that did not require thinking. Only landing. She didn't search for it. She let her pen rest. Let her breath drop. Let her attention sink out of her head and into the quiet intelligence of her body. There was a familiar sensation there now. The one she had come to trust. A steadiness. A low warmth. A gentle, grounded presence that had nothing to prove. She felt her feet. The chair beneath her. The soft rhythm of breath arriving and leaving without instruction. The echo was silent, not because it had been defeated, but because it had nothing to say here. From this place, the line did not arrive as language first. It arrived as a knowing. A bodily yes. A recognition so simple it felt almost childlike. Almost obvious. She waited for her hand to move. She would write one sentence. Not as a reminder. Not as a rule. Not as a promise she would have to keep. As a fact. A place. A home she could return to even when everything else fell away. She waited inside that feeling. Did not reach for language. Did not lean forward. She stayed where the warmth was steady, and the breath knew what to do on its own. And from that place, a line surfaced. Not like a thought assembling itself. Like a stone rising through water. Slow. Certain. Already shaped. Simple. Unadorned. Unarguable. She wrote it slowly, as if listening while her hand moved. It was not poetic. It was not dramatic. It did not promise outcomes. It did not explain her past or predict her future. It named a reality that existed even when everything else blurred. A truth her body had already been living long before words had caught up. She underlined it once. Then again. Not to emphasize it. To seat it. This was not a sentence meant to convince the echo. It was not even meant to respond to it. It did not argue. It did not defend. It did not correct. It simply stood where she stood. It was meant to return her. A line she could touch when language fractured. A line she could breathe into. A line that could be remembered when memory itself was unstable. A line that did not require strength to hold. Only presence. And when she read it back, she felt it land in her body the way truth always had. Quietly. Completely. Without resistance. The line was beautiful in its simplicity and power. Nothing more. Nothing less. And she knew, in that moment, that she would never again be without a way home. It is not an affirmation. Not a command. Not a promise made to the future. It does not tell her what to feel. It does not argue with fear. It does not correct the past or predict what will come next.

It is a locational sentence. A sentence that names where she is standing. The words are simple enough to survive panic. Solid enough to survive doubt. True enough to survive scrutiny. They do not collapse under pressure. They do not fracture when the mind races. They remain. She writes it at the bottom of the page, and then, over time, at the top of her life: ***"I am here, and I can stay!"*** That is the sentence. No metaphor. No embellishment. No explanation. It does not say she is safe forever. It does not say things will always be okay. It does not say she feels calm, strong, healed, or brave. It does not promise relief. It does not demand belief. It only says this: ***"I am here. And I can stay!"*** This is why it works. Because it does not require certainty. It does not require hope. It does not require the echo to be silent. It only requires presence. The sentence is shaped like a doorway. "*I am here*" names location, not evaluation. *"And I can stay"* names capacity, not outcome. Together, they form a ground that does not move when emotion surges. When the echo says, "*Leave. Escape. End this. Get out*," the sentence does not respond with debate. It responds with placement. *"Here."* When fear says, "*This is too much*", the sentence does not minimize or soothe it away. It answers with endurance. *"I can stay."* And in that staying, something profound continues to happen, quietly, again and again. The body settles just enough to be felt. The breath remembers its rhythm. The present reasserts itself without force. She does not have to solve anything. She does not have to decide anything. She does not have to become anything else. She is here. And she can stay. That is not a victory. It is a way of standing. And from that stance, everything else she has learned; holding, choosing, witnessing, returning, organizes itself naturally around this single, unmovable fact. No matter what arises, there is a place that remains. A place that does not argue. A place that does not disappear. A place shaped not by certainty, but by contact. And she knows now, in the deepest way knowing can occur: She does not need to escape her life in order to survive it. She only needs to be here. And stay. When memory fractures and identity wavers, the sentence does not rebuild a story. It does not gather fragments and try to make them convincing. It reestablishes a point. A location. A coordinate in the present moment that cannot be argued away. She notices how her body receives it before her mind has time to comment. Her feet press into the floor, as if gravity has just been reintroduced. Her breath lengthens without instruction, the way it does when something real has been recognized. Her nervous system settles around the words, not because they are comforting, but because they are accurate. Because the sentence is not aspirational. It is already happening. She is here. She is staying. Even when she wants to disappear. Even when the echo shouts. Even when nothing feels resolved. Especially then. This is why the sentence becomes her anchor. It cannot be disproven. If she is reading it, she is here. If breath is moving through her body, she is staying. The proof is immediate. It lives in sensation, not belief. The echo tries to twist it, of course. It always tries. *"But you won't be able to stay forever." "But staying hurts." "But leaving would be easier."* The sentence does not respond. It doesn't need to. It is not a philosophy. It is not an argument. It is not a promise about tomorrow. It is a fact happening now. And facts grounded in the body do not require defence. They do not negotiate with fear. They do not explain themselves. Over time, the sentence migrates. From page. To breath. To muscle. To instinct. Eventually, she doesn't have to say it. Her body does. In the way she pauses instead of reacts. In the way she remains seated when panic urges flight. In the way she lets a feeling crest and fall without abandoning herself. In the way she chooses presence over urgency without having to think about it. The sentence becomes less something she remembers and more something she inhabits. A stance. A posture. A home. And this is the quiet miracle of it. The sentence does not save her by pulling her forward. It does not motivate. It does not inspire. It does not demand progress. It saves her by letting her remain. Here. Able. Staying. Not heroic. Not resolved. Not finished. But present. And presence, she has learned, is enough ground to live from. She closed the notebook and placed her palm over her sternum. Read the line again, not with her eyes, but inwardly. And something subtle happened.

Her shoulders softened. Her jaw unclenched. Her breath reorganized itself around the words, as if her body had been waiting for this exact permission. She felt it unmistakably. This sentence did not live on the page. It lived in her tissues.

In the rhythm of her breathing. In the quiet coherence of being here. From that night on, it became the last line of every entry. Sometimes the only line. Sometimes the first. Sometimes the one she reached for when everything else scattered. She would repeat it in the kitchen, hands in dishwater. In the car, fingers resting on the wheel. In the middle of conversations, silently, while the world kept moving. In the first seconds of waking, before thought assembled itself. Not as a mantra. As a location. Wherever she spoke it from, she arrived. The echo could argue stories. It could manipulate futures. It could distort meanings and inflate consequences. But it could not touch this. Because this line was not a concept. It was not a belief to be challenged or a thought to be dismantled. It was an orientation. A way home. And slowly, gently, she realized something else. Something that settled not in her mind but in her bones. The anchor was not holding her against the storm. The anchor was reminding her that she was the ground. That nothing needed to be fixed in order for her to be here. That nothing needed to be resolved in order for her to stay. That presence was not something she summoned. It was something she recognized. She was not clinging to life anymore. She was inhabiting it. And from that ground, the weather could come and go. Memory could rise and soften. Fear could speak and pass. Choice could unfold without force. The echo could whisper from the edges. But she would remain. Here. Able. Staying. And that was not the end of the story. It was the place the story could finally live.

The First Time She Thanks the Echo and Doesn't Follow It

The echo arrived the way it always did. Not loudly. Not dramatically. Just a familiar tightening behind her ribs, a narrowing of possibility, a sentence forming with practiced ease. It spoke with confidence, with urgency disguised as concern. It offered conclusions. It laid out reasons. It framed itself as realism. And for a brief instant, her body moved the way it used to. A slight lean toward obedience. A reflex older than thought. Then something interrupted the pattern. Not resistance. Recognition. She felt it first, not as an idea, but as a pause. A half-second where her breath didn't rush to comply. Where her shoulders didn't cave. The echo was mid-sentence when it happened. She noticed the tone. The pressure. The way it hurried her past her own sensing. And in that noticing, a sentence surfaced, unforced, almost gentle: *"This is the echo."* Not "*I am broken*." Not "*this is true*." Just: "*this is the echo."* The echo kept talking. It always did. It reached for certainty. It rehearsed familiar futures. It warned. It predicted. It pushed. She did not argue with it. Did not try to disprove it. Did not scramble for counterevidence. Instead, she was about to do something entirely new. She stayed. She felt her feet in the floor. The quiet steadiness behind her sternum. The breath moving without being managed. She let the echo finish its sentence without letting it decide the next one. And then, without sarcasm, without irony, without collapse, she said something that surprised even her. *"Thank you."* Not as surrender. Not as obedience. As acknowledgment. She could feel the source of it now. The echo was not malicious. It was vigilant. Overtrained. Loud because it had learned that volume once kept her alive. It was a messenger that never learned how to stand down. *"Thank you for trying to protect me,"* she said inwardly. *"I hear you."* The echo faltered. Just slightly. As if it had expected battle and found none. And then she added, quietly, decisively: *"I'm staying."* She did not follow the echo's urgency. She did not flee the sensation it was reacting to. She did not override her body in the name of reason. She stayed with herself. The echo continued to speak, but it no longer led. Its words floated past instead of pulling her forward. And in that moment, Eliza felt something settle that had never settled before.

She was not rejecting a part of herself. She was placing it in context. The echo was no longer an authority. It was a signal. A voice in the room, not the owner of it. And for the first time, she understood something profound. Gratitude did not mean agreement. Acknowledgment did not mean obedience. She could thank the echo for what it once tried to do. And still choose not to follow it. That was not defiance. That was maturity. That was presence. That was her, standing where she belonged. She turned toward it internally, the way one might turn toward a frantic messenger who has run too far, too fast. And she said, quietly, honestly again: *"Thank you."* The word surprised her as much as it startled the echo again. *"Thank you for trying to protect me. Thank you for sounding the alarm. Thank you for showing me that something in me feels threatened right now."* The echo faltered again. Just for a moment. Its authority wavered, as if it had never been thanked before. As if it had only ever known how to be feared or obeyed. It tried to recover, to reassert urgency, to sharpen its edges and reclaim the old hierarchy. But she did not follow. She stayed with her breath. With the weight of her feet on the floor. With the steady, grounded presence she had learned to trust. She felt the warmth in her chest. The quiet solidity beneath sensation. And then she added again, softly but clearly: *"I hear you. And I'm choosing something else."* Not defiance. Choice. The echo had no script for that. It tried to escalate. Then to bargain. Then to retreat into familiar warnings, looping phrases it had relied on for years. But none of it landed the way it used to. Because she was no longer confusing the echo for herself. She wasn't rejecting it. She wasn't obeying it. She was relating to it. Like weather passing through awareness. Like an alarm bell that had done its job. Like information, not identity. She felt the relief move through her body before her mind caught up. A loosening in her shoulders. A settling behind her ribs. A quiet confidence that did not announce itself but was unmistakably there. She had stayed. She had chosen. She had not abandoned herself in order to be what would have been labeled 'safe' before. And something subtle, irreversible shifted. The echo did not disappear. But it no longer owned the room. She had learned how to listen without surrendering. How to acknowledge without collapsing. How to thank a part of herself and still lead her life. That was the moment she knew: The echo was never meant to be silenced. It was meant to be met. And once met, once placed in relationship instead of command, it could finally rest. And she could finally move. Not away from herself. But with herself. This was the first time she fully understood, viscerally, that listening did not require following. That awareness could exist without surrender. That gratitude could coexist with refusal. The insight did not arrive as philosophy. It arrived as sensation. As the felt experience of staying seated while urgency passed through. As the quiet astonishment of realizing she had heard everything and obeyed nothing. Later, she would write it down. Not as a victory. Not as proof of progress. As a landmark. *"Today, I thanked the echo. And I stayed."* The sentence did not sparkle. It did not announce transformation. But it marked a crossing. A place where something irrevocable had shifted. Where power had moved, not through force, but through placement. That line went into her archive. And the echo, though it would return, never sounded quite the same again. It still spoke. It still warned. It still tried to hurry her past herself when old patterns were stirred. But something in its tone had changed. A loss of absolutism. A faint uncertainty. As if it now knew it was being listened to from a wider room. Because it had learned something too. It was no longer the voice in charge. It was information. And she was the one who chose. From then on, when the echo appeared, it arrived into relationship. Not dominance. Not exile. Context. It could speak its concern. It could sound its alarm. And she could decide what to do with what it offered. Sometimes she acted. Sometimes she rested. Sometimes she did nothing at all. And all of it was choice. She did not become someone who never heard the echo. She became someone who could hear it without disappearing. Someone who could acknowledge fear without crowning it. Someone who could thank a part of herself and still lead her life. That was the quiet power she carried now. Not the power to silence. The power to stay.

The Unmasking

It happened without spectacle. No revelation cracked the sky. No inner chamber fell silent. The echo did not disappear. It loosened. One evening, Eliza sat with her notebook open, the lamp casting a small, ordinary circle of light. Her thoughts moved the way they always had, tracing familiar paths, looping, circling. And then she noticed something she had never let herself see before. The echo did not speak with one voice. It shifted. It fractured. It changed shape mid-sentence. Sometimes it was sharp and declarative, cutting the air cleanly, leaving no room to breathe. Sometimes it was breathless and urgent, racing itself toward imagined cliffs. Sometimes it shrank, its tone thinning into something almost childlike, pleading, terrified of being left alone with what it could not control. And suddenly, she understood. This voice was not an invader. It was a family. The critic stood at the front, cold and precise, like a sentry who had never been relieved of duty. It spoke in rules and ultimatums, in shoulds and never-agains. It believed safety lived in anticipation. That if it could predict every misstep, sharpen every flaw before anyone else could, it might keep her upright. It was not cruel by nature. It was vigilant. Sleepless. Terrified of what would happen if it ever stopped watching the door. Behind the sentry, quieter but no less insistent, stood the teenager. It hovered a presence, restless and brittle. The one that rushed. That insisted everything be decided now. That could not tolerate waiting. This one had learned that speed was survival. That stillness invited collapse. It did not trust the ground. It trusted momentum. Raw. Reactive. Nerves exposed to the air. This one spoke in extremes. All or nothing. Now or never. Escape or annihilation. Its voice surged with urgency, not because it loved chaos, but because it had learned something young and terrible: That pain, once it reached a certain pitch, could not be endured. It had to be ended. Immediately. This part did not strategize for the long term. It scanned for exits. It searched for relief the way lungs search for air. It didn't want to die. It wanted the fire to stop. It wanted silence. It wanted the burning to end before it became unbearable. And deeper still, almost hidden beneath the others, beneath sound itself, she felt it was the child. The smallest one. The one whose voice trembled when it spoke at all. The one who believed abandonment was always one wrong move away. This voice did not issue commands. It whispered fears. It clutched. It begged. It remembered being alone before it had words for loneliness. Small. Wordless. Memory held in tissue instead of narrative. Tight shoulders drawn toward the ears. A breath that never quite reached the belly. A hand curled inward, as if still bracing for impact. This one did not argue. It did not judge. It did not predict. It simply hurt. And when it cried, the others rose instantly, instinctively, like shields snapping into place. The critic sharpened its rules. The teenager accelerated toward escape. Each one wielding the only weapons it had ever known. Not because they were cruel. Because they were afraid. And it's all they knew. The only language they knew how to speak. The echo had never been a singular force. It was a chorus. A system of protectors who had never been told the danger had passed. They had formed in moments when Eliza had no power, no language, no choice. When the world arrived without warning. When love was inconsistent. When safety was conditional or absent. They learned early that vigilance was survival. That speed was protection. That control might keep the ground from giving way. That they were nothing, not good enough, a failure, a mistake, and worthless. They did the only thing they knew how to do. They tried to keep her alive. Even when their methods cut. Even when their logic collapsed. Even when their fear dressed itself as cruelty.

As this understanding settled into her body, Eliza felt something soften behind her ribs. Not forgiveness. Not yet. Recognition. The kind that changes posture. That lowers the shoulders a fraction. That allows breath to travel farther than it used to. These voices were not evidence of brokenness. They were evidence of endurance. They had carried her through what she could not yet name. Eliza felt her chest tighten as the realization settled, not as shock, but as recognition. These were not monsters. They were adaptations. Each one formed in response to a moment when something essential had not been met. Each one carrying a role it had never been allowed to retire from. For the first time, she did not try to silence them. She did not argue. She did not correct. She listened. And in listening, something profound occurred. The voices changed when they were seen. The critic softened its edges when it was no longer mistaken for truth. The urgency slowed when it was no longer in charge of direction. The small, frightened one trembled less when it was not alone in the room. She realized then what the echo had always been protecting her from. Not failure. Not weakness. Relationship. The risk of feeling without armor. The risk of trusting presence over control. Eliza closed her notebook and placed her hand over her sternum, feeling the familiar warmth gather there. She did not need to dismantle this inner family. It had already begun to reorganize itself around something steadier than fear. There was now a center they could orient toward. A place that could hold them all. Not a throne. A hearth. And for the first time, the echo did not feel like an enemy to overcome. It felt like a lineage to be understood. A system that had done its best with what it had known. A chorus that no longer needed to shout because someone had finally learned how to listen. The unmasking did not end the work. But it changed its tone. From battle. To tending. From suppression. To care. From survival. To belonging. They had kept watch when no one else did. They had absorbed the terror so she could keep functioning, keep moving, keep breathing. And now, for the first time, she could feel the difference between protection and leadership. They no longer needed to run the house. But they did need to be acknowledged. She did not imagine dismissing them. She imagined gathering them. Not into silence. Into relationship. A larger awareness now held the room. One that could say, without irony or fear: *"Thank you. I see why you exist. And I'm here now."* The chorus did not disappear. But it began, slowly, to listen back. This realization did not quiet the echo immediately. But it changed its posture. For the first time, Eliza did not meet the voice with argument, endurance or strategy. She turned toward it. Not with her thoughts, but with her presence. *"I see you,"* she said, not aloud, but from somewhere deeper than language. A place that had learned how to stay. *"I know why you learned this." "I know when you started."* The words were not explanations. They were recognitions. The critic faltered mid-sentence, as if it had lost its footing. The teenager surged once more, flaring with old urgency, raging even more, then stilled, unsettled by the absence of resistance. And the child, so quiet she had almost missed it, exhaled. A long, shaky release that loosened something ancient in her chest. And then something extraordinary happened. The echo stopped trying to convince her. It began to listen. Not because it had been defeated. Because it had been met. Eliza understood then that healing was never about silencing these parts or banishing them back into the well. It was about bringing them out of the dark and into the present, where their old maps no longer matched the terrain. Where the dangers they had been scanning for were no longer everywhere. Where the ground was steadier than they remembered. She did not fire her protectors. She reassigned them. The critic, once sharpened into punishment, learned to discern. To name patterns without turning them into sentences of worth. To offer clarity without cruelty. The teenager, once driven by escape, learned to pause. To feel the heat without running from it. To recognize that not every intensity required an exit. And the child learned something it had never been allowed to know before: That it no longer had to scream to be held. And Eliza, finally standing as the adult in the room, became what none of them had ever had. A steady witness. A translator between past and present. A place where fear could speak without ruling. A body that stayed. She did not dominate this inner family. She did not dissolve into it. She held it. With boundaries. With warmth. With a patience born not from obligation, but from capacity.

The well did not disappear. The echo did not vanish. But the center shifted. And in that shift, the voices that once pulled her apart began, slowly, to organize themselves around something sturdier than fear. A home that could say, without effort or apology: *"I am here. And you are not alone anymore."*The echo had not been trying to destroy her. It had been trying, desperately and imperfectly, to keep her alive. Its tools were crude because they had been forged in urgency, in a narrow era. In a time when danger arrived without warning, and there was no room for nuance, no space for tenderness, no guarantee of return. When endurance mattered more than tenderness. When the world felt sharp, and choices were scarce. When survival was the highest imaginable good. They were tools made for nights without witnesses. For bodies that learned to brace before they learned to speak. For moments when endurance was the only currency available. The echo had learned to shout because whispering had not been enough and went unheard. It had learned to grip because letting go once meant falling. It had learned to predict catastrophe because surprise had once been unbearable. It had learned to tighten, to hurry, to cut, to corner, because those moves had once kept her breathing. It had learned to hurt because pain, at least, proved she was still here. Eliza felt this truth land not as an idea, but as a soft, rearranging weight inside her chest. Compassion arrived without ceremony. Not pity. Not excuse. Understanding. The kind that loosens the hands without asking them to unclench all at once. It was never cruelty. It was memory acting like the present. It was fear refusing to retire because no one had ever told it the war was over. And now, something fundamental had changed. Survival was no longer the highest aim and no longer the goal. Living was. Living meant allowing moments to be more than exits. Living meant nuance. It meant slowness. It meant allowing days to be ordinary without reading them as failure. It meant discovering that safety could coexist with feeling, that meaning could be found without urgency, that choice could arise without crisis. It meant letting joy arrive quietly, and grief arrive honestly, neither one needing to justify its presence. It meant letting pleasure arrive without suspicion. It meant resting without rehearsing disaster. It meant discovering that the nervous system could soften without falling apart. It meant risk, yes, but the kind that comes with connection rather than collapse. Together, they stepped into this unfamiliar territory. And so, together, this inner family began new work. Not all at once. Not gracefully. Sometimes haltingly. Sometimes awkwardly. Sometimes slipping back into old formations before remembering there was another way to stand. The critic learned to become a scout instead of a judge. The critic learned to stand beside her instead of in front of her, offering clarity when invited, silence when not. The teenager learned that intensity could crest, past and fall without escape, that staying did not equal annihilation.

The child learned the feel of arms that did not disappear. That warmth could be trusted that hands could hold without harm, that crying did not summon abandonment. And Eliza learned what it meant to lead without dominating. Rooted now in her body and her breath, became the one who kept time. To listen without dissolving. For what was current rather than what was remembered. The one who could say, again and again, "*We are here now.*" They were learning, moment by moment, how to inhabit a life that did not require armor at every turn. A life shaped not by constant vigilance, but by relationship. By presence. By the ongoing courage of staying. To hold complexity without splitting herself into pieces. She learned that being the adult in the room did not mean being invulnerable. It meant being present. Consistent. Willing to return again and again. They were no longer trapped in the well. They were no longer living by echoes. They were no longer shouting across darkness. It was quieter work than survival. Slower. Less dramatic. And infinitely braver. Because living asked something survival never did. Not just endurance. But trust. And for the first time, they were learning how. They were an inner family, gathered around a shared center, learning the unfamiliar, tender mechanics of trust. Learning how to walk without armor. Learning how to let the day unfold without gripping it into submission. The work was quieter now. And braver. Not the bravery of endurance. But the bravery of staying open. Not the courage of survival. But the courage of living.

How She Teaches It Without Naming It

She doesn't call it a method. She doesn't explain it like a lesson. She never once says, *"Here is what to do when the voice comes."* It starts much smaller than that. It starts with how she listens. A friend sits across from her, eyes distant, words tangled, hands worrying the edge of a sleeve. The story spills out in fragments. Fear. Self-blame. The familiar gravity of someone being pulled inward by something they can't quite see. Eliza doesn't rush to reassure. She doesn't correct. She doesn't argue with the darkness in their sentences. Instead, she leans into the spaces between their words. She notices the way their shoulders lift when a certain sentence appears. The way their breath shortens around a particular thought. The way their gaze drops when the inner weather shifts. And gently, almost casually, she asks things like: *"Where do you feel that in your body?" "What happens in you when you say that out loud?" "Can we stay with this part for a second, without fixing it?"* At first, it feels strange to them.

They're used to conversations that race for conclusions. For advice. For solutions. Used to being pulled upward into meaning before the body has even been consulted. But she keeps bringing them back to the ground. Not to the story. To the sensing. She mirrors their pace without matching their urgency. She breathes a little slower than they do. She lets silence exist without filling it. And in that unhurried presence, something begins to happen. The room settles. The air thickens with attention. The person across from her feels, perhaps for the first time, that they do not have to perform clarity to be met. They start noticing things themselves. A tightness. A heat. A pull. A relief. They pause mid-sentence, surprised. *"Oh,"* they say. *"I didn't realize my chest was doing that."* Eliza nods, not triumphantly. Simply present. As if to say, "*Yes. That's it.*" She never names the echo. Never names the practice. She doesn't need to. What she offers instead is a way of being with another human that quietly invites them back into themselves. She listens without collapsing into their fear. She stays without demanding resolution. She responds from the part of her that can hold feeling without becoming it. And because she does, something subtle transfers. The person begins to stay too. They speak more slowly. Their shoulders drop. Their breath finds a longer arc. The story loses some of its grip, not because it has been disproven, but because it is no longer alone in the room. Sensation has joined the conversation. Presence has arrived. Later, they might say, *"I feel different."* Or *"Something shifted."* Or *"I don't know why, but I feel more here."* Eliza doesn't explain it. She doesn't translate the moment into theory. She smiles softly. Maybe says, *"Your body knows what it needs."* What she teaches, she teaches without instruction. What she offers, she offers without agenda. She models a relationship to inner life that does not require mastery, only honesty. Only staying. And in that staying, others begin to remember something they didn't know they had forgotten. That they, too, have a place inside themselves that can hold what arises. That listening does not require obedience. That presence is not something reserved for those who are healed. It is something available to anyone willing to pause and feel the ground beneath their feet. She never says, *"Do this."* She simply stays. And somehow, quietly, they learn how to stay too. She offers a glass of water. Waits for them to take a sip. Let the pause do some of the work. Sometimes she places her own hand over her chest as she listens, not theatrically, just honestly, letting her body remain visible. Regulated. Present. An unspoken invitation to the nervous system across from her. And when the familiar harsh sentences surface in them, the ones weighted with certainty and condemnation, she doesn't name them. She translates them.

She says things like, *"That sounds like a part of you that's really scared." "Something in you is trying to protect you from disappointment." "That sounds urgent. Let's slow it down."* She never says, *"That voice isn't you."* She lets them discover it. Not through explanation, but through contrast. By how she responds differently to different tones. She listens deeply to their pain and lightly to their conclusions. She takes the feeling seriously and the story gently. Sometimes she'll say, *"Can we check if that thought is true, or if it's just loud?"* Sometimes she'll ask, *"Is there anything in your life that doesn't agree with that sentence?"* And when they find even one small memory that resists, one moment that doesn't fit the narrative, she doesn't celebrate it like proof. She protects it like something living. She slows the room. Lowers her voice. Let time stretch. *"Stay there,"* she'll say. *"What does that feel like?" "Where do you notice it?"* She watches as their breath changes. As their eyes soften. As something in them leans toward the sensation instead of away. She does not rush them back into interpretation. She lets the body have its say. This is how the teaching moves. Not as instruction. As atmosphere. She creates a field where presence is safer than urgency. Where sensation is welcome. Where no one has to decide what anything means yet. In that field, the echo loses its grip without ever being confronted. It simply has no leverage where slowness lives. And the person across from her begins to experience something new. They are being met without being managed. Listened to without being steered. Held without being handled. They may not know what has happened when they leave. They may not have language for it. But something in them has reorganized. A new reference point has formed. A felt sense of staying that they will recognize again later, in their own lives, when the room is empty, and the voice returns. Eliza never claims to teach anything. But she leaves people with something they did not have before. A memory of being held while they felt. And once the body has known that it does not forget. She teaches them, without ever announcing it, that not everything that speaks deserves to steer. That volume is not authority. That urgency is not wisdom. That sensation can be a witness instead of a sentence. That presence can be an anchor instead of a reaction. Over time, she watches it happen. The micro-pause before they agree with their own harshest thought. The way their breathing shifts when they check inside first. The slight tilt of the head when a sentence lands but doesn't quite settle. The first time they say, surprised and almost embarrassed, *"That sounded convincing, but it doesn't feel true."* She smiles then. Not big. Not proud. Recognizing. Because that moment is unmistakable. That is the first crack. The first place where the story loosens its grip and sensation gets a vote. The first time someone notices the difference between a voice that demands and a body that knows. She never gives it a name. Naming would freeze it. Would turn something living into a concept. She just keeps modelling the posture. Curious instead of collapsed. Present instead of persuaded. Grounded instead of gone. She lets her own body stay visible. Let her breath remain slow. Let silence stretch without apologizing for it. And in that steadiness, something in the other person begins to entrain. Their nervous system recognizes the rhythm. Their body remembers something it has been waiting for. And one day, in the middle of a conversation, it happens. They stop themselves. Mid-sentence. Mid-spiral. Mid-certainty. They put a hand on their chest. Close their eyes for a second. And say, almost shyly, *"I need to check something before I keep talking."* Eliza feels it in her body before she thinks it. A quiet warmth. A settling. The unmistakable sensation of transfer. The practice has moved. Not as a technique. As a way of being. Something has crossed from one nervous system to another. Not by explanation. By proximity. By shared presence. By being with instead of fixing. Later, when they thank her, she shrugs a little. Not deflecting. Just accurate. *"I didn't really teach you anything,"* she says. *"I just stayed with you long enough for you to hear yourself."* And inside, quietly, she knows that's the truest transmission there is. Not instruction. Presence. Not a map. A body that learned how to stand on the ground. And in standing there, without hurry, without rescue, without retreat, invited another person to feel it under their own feet.

The Light

Years passed. Eliza still carries a backpack, but it no longer bends her toward the earth. It rests against her shoulders the way a well-worn coat does. Familiar. Accountable. Not a sentence pronounced over her spine, but a satchel of knowing. Inside it are no longer only bricks of sorrow. There are maps now. Tools smoothed by use. Notes written in her own hand for moments when the terrain turns strange. The hard-earned wisdom of where she has been and how she learned, again and again, to return. The well still exists. It always will. It waits in the margins of her inner world, a shadowed geography she no longer pretends away. But it no longer terrifies her. She knows its shape now. Its angles. The way its walls lean inward just enough to make depth feel like destiny. She knows its tricks of light. How it offers a false quiet. How it convinces you that stillness is safety and silence is truth. And because she knows it, it no longer owns her. She has learned the sound of the echo. Its cadence. Its borrowed authority. The way it mimics her voice while draining it of warmth. The way it speaks fluently in endings. And she knows how to answer it. Sometimes with language. Sometimes with breath. Sometimes by placing her feet on the floor and turning her face back toward the living world, letting sensation do what argument never could. Letting weight, temperature, texture remind her where she is. She learned something else too. Something that changed the way she held herself entirely. Depression was never a personal failure. Never a flaw of character. Never a deficit of will. She learned its real name. Illness. A complex, layered condition that moves through biology and history, nervous systems and memory, chemistry and meaning. Something that requires care. Patience. Support. Not judgment. Not moralizing. Not silence. She learned that tending to her mind is not indulgence, but maintenance. The way one tends to a body that has carried heavy things. That asking for help is not collapse, but intelligence. That vulnerability is not weakness, but the doorway through which real strength enters without violence. And slowly, without announcing itself, her story began to serve others.

She spoke. Not from triumph, but from ground. She shared. Not as testimony, but as companionship. She sat beside people still carrying weights she recognized. She did not offer miracles. She offered presence. She did not promise cures. She offered language. She did not rush anyone toward light. She stayed with them in the dark long enough for their own eyes to adjust. She offered the simplest truth. The one that changes everything when it finally lands. You are not alone inside this. And recovery is not a myth. It is a practice. Some days, the light in her life is obvious. Wide. Golden. Filling the room. Other days, it is smaller. A thin line under a door. A glint on water. The quiet persistence of dawn doing what it has always done. Returning without announcement. She no longer chases it. She no longer doubts it when it dims. She knows now that light does not mean the absence of shadow. It means orientation. It means knowing which way to turn when the world grows heavy again. And when she walks forward, backpack steady on her shoulders, she carries this with her: Not a promise that the well will vanish. But the knowing that she can stand at its edge without falling in. Not a guarantee of ease. But the certainty of return. The light was never something she had to reach for. It was something she learned how to face. One morning, long after the climb had folded itself into her ordinary rhythm, Eliza found herself standing once more at the edge of the well. Not summoned. Not seized. Just, present. The ground beneath her feet felt solid, familiar. She could feel the coolness of stone through the soles of her shoes. The quiet steadiness of balance. She leaned forward and looked down. And instead of an abyss, she saw herself. Not the girl who had once been pulled by the well's gravity, ribs hollowed by echo, breath narrowed to survival. But the woman shaped by passage. Broader in her stance. Softer in her center. Marked, yes, but marked the way rivers carve valleys and storms etch mountains. Not ruined. Revealed. The kind of strength that comes not from resisting weather, but from remaining through it. The echo did not rise. There was no commentary. No warning dressed as wisdom. Only stillness. The walls of the well held their shadow without reaching for her. They no longer distorted depth into destiny. They simply were. A feature of the terrain. And she, standing here, was no longer a question inside it. Somewhere beyond the inner stone, the sun was lifting itself into the morning. She felt it before she saw it. A warmth on her cheek. A gentle brightness behind her eyes. Not sudden. Not blinding. Just unmistakably real. She closed her eyes for a moment and let it land. She smiled. Not because everything was finished. Not because the landscape would never shift again. She smiled because she knew. She knew the journey was not over. She would always be someone who tended this inner terrain. Who listened for changes in weather. Who adjusted her footing when the ground grew slick or steep. She would always be a person who noticed when shadows lengthened and when light thinned, who paused, who checked her breath, who stayed. But she also knew something that could never again be taken from her. She could carry what she carried. She could feel what she felt and remain. She could climb when climbing was asked of her. She could rest when rest was required. She could live. Not in defiance of darkness. Not in denial of depth. But in relationship. Relationship with the well. Relationship with the echo. Relationship with the light that had learned how to meet her where she stood. And this time, the light was not something she reached for across distance or desperation. It was not a promise on the horizon or a reward for endurance. It was not conditional. It was not earned. It was here. It was touching her skin. It was warming her breath. It was illuminating the ground beneath her feet. She was standing in it. And in that quiet, steady brightness, Eliza understood the final truth her body had been teaching her all along. Healing was never about escaping the well. It was about learning how to stand at its edge without losing herself. The darkness had not vanished. The light had not conquered it. They had found their places. And she had found hers.

Epilogue: The Gift

In time, Eliza came to understand that the backpack and the well, for all their cruelty, had left her with something rare and enduring. They had given her empathy. Not the polished kind learned through books or borrowed language. Not sympathy offered from a safe shoreline. But the lived knowing that settles into the bones when you have carried weight no one else could see. She recognized it in others now. The pause before a smile fully arrived. The tiredness that sleep never quite repaired. The way laughter sometimes reached the mouth before it reached the eyes, as if it had traveled a longer road to get there. She noticed how people held themselves when they thought no one was watching. The way shoulders braced for nothing in particular. The way someone might apologize for existing a little too much. She understood the private wars fought behind ordinary faces. The negotiations that happen long before anyone dares to ask for help. The strength it takes just to show up when the ground inside keeps shifting. And because she had stood in the dark herself, she knew how to recognize light when it appeared quietly. Not as brilliance. As persistence. As the choice to keep breathing. To keep returning. To keep placing one foot in front of the other, even when the path was unclear. She learned how to sit beside someone without trying to rescue them. How to listen without reaching for solutions. How to extend a hand without pulling. How to offer presence without agenda. She knew when words would only clutter the space, and when a simple sentence mattered most. "*I'm here. You're not alone. We can stay with this.*" She learned, too, how to remind others of what she herself had once forgotten. That suffering is not a definition. That pain is not an identity. That a person is not measured by the depth of the well they have known, but by the courage it takes to keep choosing life. Breath by breath. Step by step. Return by return. And so, among the remnants she still carried, among the tools and maps and memories folded carefully inside her backpack, there was one brick unlike the others. It was light. Not because it denied darkness, but because it understood it. It was shaped not from sorrow, but from comprehension. From the deep, steady recognition that no one walks this terrain alone, even when it feels that way. It was the knowledge that presence can be offered without fixing. That listening can be an act of love. That staying is sometimes the bravest thing a human being can do. And it was the most precious thing she had ever carried.

A Final Word from Eliza

If you are here, reading these words, then some part of you already knows what it is to carry weight. Maybe your backpack is packed differently than mine was. Maybe your well has another depth, another texture, another name. But if anything in these pages stirred recognition, if something tightened or softened or quietly nodded inside you, then let me begin here: You are not strange for what you feel. You are not broken for what has unfolded within you. You are human. And being human means we are shaped by storms as much as by sunlight. It means we learn the terrain of ourselves through friction as often as through ease. For a long time, I believed my inner world was something to endure rather than inhabit. I thought survival was the highest form of living available to me. That staying alive was the ceiling. I was wrong. There is more. There is presence. There is choice. There is a way of standing inside yourself that feels less like a battlefield and more like a home. Healing did not arrive for me as a rescue. It did not come with fanfare or finality. It came quietly, disguised as ordinary moments that asked almost nothing of me except to stay. A breath I did not abandon. A sensation I did not override. A memory that refused to be rewritten into shame. A hand I allowed myself to reach for. A sentence I practiced returning to when everything else scattered.

None of these moments were impressive. Most of them would have been invisible from the outside. But together, they changed the ground beneath my feet. Slowly. Almost imperceptibly. Until one day I realized I was no longer hovering above my life, braced for impact. I was standing in it. If you are still in the dark, I will not insult you with easy light. I will not tell you that everything happens for a reason, or that clarity is just around the corner, or that you should be grateful for what hurts. I know better than that now. I will only tell you this: Darkness is not proof that there is no way forward. Often, it is proof that you are inside something that matters. You do not have to fix yourself to belong here. You do not have to understand everything to take the next step. You do not have to be fearless, hopeful, or strong in the way stories demand. You only have to stay curious enough to notice what is happening in you. Kind enough to pause. Brave enough to return. If there is one thing I hope you carry from these pages, let it be this: You are allowed to be here exactly as you are. You are allowed to take your time. You are allowed to learn your own language of return. And even when you forget, even when you fall back into old gravity, even when the echo sounds convincing again, there is something in you that knows how to come home. You do not have to walk this path perfectly. You only have to keep walking it honestly. And if, in this moment, all you can do is breathe and read and remain, then know this too: That is not nothing. That is how it begins. You do not have to conquer your life. You do not have to solve it like a puzzle or master it like a terrain meant to be dominated. You do not have to understand every turning, every ache, every contradiction. You do not even have to feel hopeful. Hope is not a prerequisite for staying. You only have to remain in relationship with yourself. That relationship does not require perfection. It does not demand confidence or clarity. It asks only for contact. For listening. For the willingness to notice what is actually happening instead of what the loudest voice insists is happening. It asks you to let even the faintest true thing count. A breath you didn't abandon. A moment you stayed. A sensation that felt a fraction more real than the noise surrounding it.

If there is a gift hidden anywhere in what I have shared, it is this: What lives inside you is not only what hurts. Yes, there is pain. Yes, there are echoes that know exactly how to frighten you, rush you, convince you that you are too late or too much or already lost. But alongside all of that, there is something else. Something quieter. Something that knows when a sentence is false even if it sounds convincing. Something that witnesses without needing to dominate. Something that wants to live not in your conclusions, but in your actual, breathing presence. That something is not an idea. It is not a belief system. It is not a personality trait reserved for the strong. It is the part of you that notices you are here at all. The part that feels your feet on the ground. The part that led you to these words. The part that keeps asking, even softly, even tiredly, *"Is there another way to be with this?"* Trust that part. Not because it has all the answers, but because it keeps you in contact with the question. Trust the part of you that pauses instead of collapses. The part that listens before it decides. The part that knows how to return, even after forgetting, even after wandering far from itself. And when you forget, as we all do, return again. Return to your body. To your breath. To the simple fact of weight and warmth and sensation. To whatever feels even one degree more real than the voice that tells you there is nothing. You do not have to return all at once. You do not have to do it gracefully. You can return in fragments. In seconds. In the smallest possible gestures. A hand on your chest. A breath allowed to finish. A sentence remembered just enough to land: "*I am here, and I can stay.*" You are not alone in this. Even when it feels that way. Especially then. Others have walked this terrain. Others are walking it now. And you are not finished. Not even close. Your life is still unfolding. Your capacity is still growing. Your relationship with yourself is still being written in real time, breath by breath, step by step. There is more room here than the echo allows you to see. More time than fear admits. More truth in your body than any single story can erase. Stay. Listen. Let what is real meet you where you are. That is enough for now.

The Last Image

Years later, Eliza keeps the backpack. It no longer claims her spine or pulls her toward the ground. It rests by the door, where shoes wait and coats remember seasons. Some days she passes it without noticing, the way one passes a familiar tree or a window that has always been there. Other days, she kneels and opens it slowly. Not with dread. With recognition. Inside are no longer bricks meant to punish gravity. There are stones now. Smoothed by handling. Warmed by palms. Each one a marker rather than a burden. Each one a record of passage. Proof not only of what she carried, but of what she learned to set down. The weight is different. Chosen. Honest. Enough to remind her where she has been without asking her to live there. The well still exists, too. It always will. Not erased. Not destroyed. But altered by time and relationship. Wildflowers have grown along its rim, unannounced, persistent. Their roots reach deep, not to fall, but to drink. They know the difference. Light finds the water now, breaks it open into reflections instead of depths. When she looks down, she does not feel pulled. She sees continuity. Sky meeting ground. Above and below touching without collapse. The well no longer promises disappearance. It mirrors what is already here. And sometimes, when the day is quiet enough, when the air feels unhurried and her breath moves without instruction, she notices something else. The echo still exists. Of course it does. But it has thinned. It arrives as sound without command. Memory without authority. A remnant of a system that once ruled and now simply passes through. It speaks, and she hears it. And then it fades, because there is nothing left for it to govern. What remains is her own voice. Not loud. Not performing. Steady. Embodied. Present. It speaks from the ground of her body. From the place that knows how to stay. From the quiet confidence of having returned to herself more times than she can count. She closes the backpack. Steps outside. And walks forward carrying nothing she does not choose. The world is still spinning. So is she. But this time, she is upright.

Prologue: Back Story of My Suicide Attempt

Chapter: Twenty-One

The Darkness and the Light: Why Did I Want to Die?

I still remember those days with an unsettling clarity, the kind that lingers in the body long after the moment has passed. The sheer weight of my existence felt unbearable then, like gravity had sharpened its grip, like I was carrying something far heavier than a single life was meant to hold. There was a constant, unrelenting suggestion in the background of my thoughts that I did not belong here, that my presence was somehow an error, an excess the world would be better without. I sat deep inside my despair, folded inward on myself, and found my mind circling the same question again and again, as though it were the only thing left that still had edges. "*Why did I want to die?*" It returned with the persistence of a tide, not seeking an answer so much as demanding to be acknowledged. The chipped paint on the windowsill seemed to mirror the fractures I felt within, flakes curling and peeling away the way pieces of me felt as though they were quietly breaking off, unnoticed, unremarked. Rain lashed against the glass in a steady, unyielding rhythm, each drop striking like punctuation against the turmoil in my chest. The sound filled the room, a relentless accompaniment to my thoughts. Outside, the world carried on with indifferent grace. Traffic moved. Lights glowed. People lived their lives, unaware of the storm raging inside this one small, enclosed space. That contrast felt almost cruel. The ordinariness of everything beyond the window sharpened the sense of isolation within it. And still the question returned. "*Why did I want to die?*" It lodged itself in my throat like a cold, hard stone, heavy with meaning I did not yet know how to name. I could not swallow it. I could not release it. At the time, it felt like a simple equation, a problem with an obvious and devastating conclusion. Not because life had no value, but because the pain felt endless and unmanageable. It was just too much. Too much weight. Too much noise. Too much hurt without relief. The question hung in the air, dense and suffocating, following me from moment to moment. It stretched what felt like an eternity into every second, slowing time until each breath felt deliberate, each thought exhausting. I did not yet understand that the question itself was not a verdict, but a signal. Not a truth about my worth, but a measure of how overwhelmed I had become. At the time, all I knew was this: the weight was real, the pain was loud, and I was struggling to find space to breathe inside it. There was no single, cataclysmic event I could point to. No dramatic breaking point. No sudden impulse or sharp blow that sent everything shattering at once. There was no moment that announced itself as the beginning. Instead, it arrived the way erosion does. Quietly. Patiently. A slow descent into a darkness I had not known existed, a place that revealed itself inch by inch, long before I understood where I was headed.

It was a relentless chipping away at my spirit, grain by grain, so gradual it escaped notice until the damage was already done. Each day took something small. A little confidence. A little trust in myself. A little ease. Over time, what remained felt thin and fragile, like a shell emptied of its strength, still shaped like me but hollowed out from the inside. It began subtly. Almost innocently. A small, intrusive doubt passing through the mind like a shadow you assume belongs to something else. A whisper at the back of my thoughts, gently suggesting inadequacy, unworthiness, failure. It did not demand attention. It did not insist. I barely noticed it at first, dismissed it as stress, as fatigue, as a passing mood. But whispers, when left unanswered, learn how to grow. Gradually, that voice gathered weight and confidence. It returned more often. It stayed longer. It began to comment on everything. On my choices. On my relationships. On who I was and who I would never be. What started as a murmur swelled into a roar, a deafening chorus of self-recrimination and despair that echoed through every thought, until it crowded out everything else, I once believed about myself. The voice became familiar. Authoritative. It spoke so often that silence itself began to feel suspicious. And somewhere along the way, without my consent or awareness, it claimed the center of the stage. It rewrote the narrative. It recast memory. It took moments of pain and turned them into proof, moments of weakness and turned them into identity. By then, the erosion was complete. Not because I had failed to fight, but because I had not realized a battle was taking place. And standing there, surrounded by the rubble of what had slowly been taken, I did not yet know that this thinning, this breaking down, was not the end of me. It was the place from which understanding would eventually begin.

That whisper, once it learned how to roar, convinced me of something with the unshakable certainty of a zealot guarding sacred doctrine: that I was not capable, that I was not strong enough. Not strong enough to carry the crushing weight of the pain. Not strong enough to endure the unrelenting hurt that had taken up residence inside me, settling in as a constant companion, familiar and merciless. Everything began to register as too much. Too much pressure. Too much sorrow. Too much of everything that felt fractured beyond repair, as though life itself had cracked and could no longer be mended. The weight pressed down on my chest until breathing felt like labor, like something I had to earn rather than something freely given. Each inhale was shallow, borrowed, as if the air itself had grown suspicious of me. I remember gasping inside a world that felt increasingly hostile and unforgiving, a place where gentleness had thinned out, where there was no softness left to land on, no margin for weakness, no safe place to set the burden down. Overwhelm flooded every corner of me. It seeped into my thoughts, my body, my sense of scale. I felt impossibly small, reduced to something fragile and exposed, like a lone boat pitched helplessly across a raging sea. Waves rose from every direction, crashing without rhythm or mercy. The horizon vanished. Orientation disappeared. There was no land in sight. No signal of rescue. No clear indication that anyone could see me from where I was. And the storm was not outside me. It was my life. My reality. It was the accumulation of everything I believed I could no longer survive, everything that had piled up without relief, churning endlessly inside me. Fear fed on exhaustion. Exhaustion fed on despair. The cycle tightened until it convinced me that sinking was inevitable, that struggle itself was proof of failure, that I simply did not have the strength to keep myself afloat any longer. In that moment, strength felt like a myth meant for other people. And I was left adrift inside the belief that letting go was not a choice, but an outcome already decided.

That belief did not arrive suddenly. It seeped in after the storm you've just witnessed, after the long attrition of overwhelm had stripped me bare, leaving no armor, no margin, no softness left to protect me. The belief in my worthlessness settled over me like a suffocating blanket, heavy and damp, clinging to skin and breath alike, pressing down until even warmth felt dangerous, until comfort itself seemed suspect, undeserved. It was not merely an idea I carried. It became a presence. A monstrous entity that moved in beside me without asking. A shadow that clung relentlessly, stretching itself across every thought, every breath, every quiet moment where I might otherwise have rested. There was no space untouched by it. No corner of my inner world it did not learn how to inhabit. Those voices spoke with cruel intimacy, close enough to feel like my own. They told me I was worthless, a mere speck of dust in the vast tapestry of life, something so small and inconsequential it could vanish without consequence. Less than. Not good enough. Unlovable. Each phrase landed not as suggestion, but as sentence. Not as opinion, but as judgment already passed and sealed. I became convinced I was a burden to those around me, a weight they carried out of obligation rather than love. That my presence required endurance instead of welcome. That I was a living reminder of the imperfections stitched into the world, proof that not everything is meant to exist. The whisper sharpened further, honing itself with frightening precision, insisting I was a mistake that should never have happened, a glitch in the fabric of existence itself. An error that slipped through unnoticed and lingered too long. And the most devastating part was not how cruel the belief was, but how believable it became. How it wrapped itself so thoroughly around my sense of self that it no longer felt imposed but revealed. As if this shadow had not arrived from outside me but had finally spoken aloud a truth I was always meant to know. I felt like a failure at the level of identity. Not someone who had failed, not someone who had stumbled or fallen short, but someone who *was* failure itself. As if failure were not an event in my life but the substance of me. Fundamentally flawed. Irreparably broken. As though something essential had been missing from me from the very beginning, some crucial ingredient everyone else received without question, while I was quietly sent into the world unfinished.

The thought that I should not exist was not a fleeting dark idea that drifted through and passed on. It did not come and go with mood or circumstance. It settled in with a chilling permanence, solid and unmoving, as unshakeable as the earth beneath my feet. It felt less like despair and more like truth, less like an emotion and more like a fact that had finally been revealed. Something I had been circling all along, now standing plainly in front of me. My very being, my presence, began to feel like a problem. A disruption. An interference in the otherwise smooth operation of the world. I experienced myself as friction, as noise where there should have been quiet. I imagined myself as static in a signal, a crack in a flawless surface, a flaw that caught the eye and refused to disappear. In my mind, I pictured the world continuing without me, people exhaling collectively, the atmosphere lightening as though some unseen pressure had finally been released. I envisioned everyone breathing a quiet sigh of relief upon my disappearance. As though my absence would restore balance. Ease. Order. As though my erasure would be an act of kindness, a correction rather than a loss. This belief did not feel dramatic. It felt logical. It felt inevitable. The weight of it was crushing. It bowed my shoulders and slowed my steps, turning movement into effort and effort into burden. Every action felt like a march toward oblivion, not because I wanted to vanish, but because I had come to believe I was already out of place. That I was trespassing simply by being here. And living with that belief was its own kind of suffocation. A slow dimming. A narrowing of space. A quiet shrinking that made simply existing feel like an act of intrusion, as though I were occupying a world that was never meant to make room 

for me at all.

In those moments, I believed it completely, with a conviction that felt absolute and immovable: I was not strong enough. Not strong enough to carry the weight of my own life. Not resilient enough to navigate the turbulent waters I found myself trapped within. The pain was suffocating, pressing in from all sides, a constant, relentless reminder of what I believed were my inadequacies, my failures, my limits laid bare. I felt as though I were drowning in a vast, indifferent sea of despair, the kind that offers no landmarks and no mercy. My arms burned from the effort of staying afloat. My lungs ached for air that never seemed to arrive in time. There was no lifeline in sight, no shore to swim toward, only endless water stretching in every direction. Every breath became a conscious act. Every moment a negotiation between exhaustion and survival. I searched desperately for a reason to keep going, something solid to grasp, but even the searching felt like too much, another demand placed on a body and mind already spent. And then there were the voices. They rose louder than anything else, overtaking thought, echoing through my mind like a haunting melody that refused to fade, looping endlessly without resolution. Self-doubt became the soundtrack of my existence, playing beneath everything I did, coloring every perception, every interaction. There was no silence left, only the constant refrain of accusation. My sense of worth eroded slowly but thoroughly, worn down the way stone is shaped by water, not through force, but through persistence. Until what remained felt like a hollow shell, a version of myself emptied of value, unlovable, undeserving of care or gentleness. The words replayed endlessly, etched deeper with every repetition: *"worthless. Less than. Not good enough. Unlovable. A burden. A mistake."*

They were no longer passing thoughts drifting through the mind. They had hardened into something that felt permanent, like facts carved deep into the core of my being, immovable and unquestionable, as though they had always been there, waiting for the moment I was too tired to argue back. I began to experience myself not as a person, but as a problem. Not a life, but a liability. A disease. An unwanted guest who had lingered too long at the party of life, overstayed whatever welcome had never truly been offered. I convinced myself that everyone would be better off without me, that my absence would clear the air, restore order, simplify the equation. In my mind, removal became synonymous with repair. This was not merely low self-esteem. It was not insecurity or a bruised sense of confidence that might heal with reassurance. It was a profound distortion of reality, a warped lens that bent every reflection of myself and every relationship I touched. Through it, kindness looked like tolerance. Concern looked like obligation. Love looked like charity stretched thin. This was not casual self-criticism or fleeting self-doubt that rose and fell with circumstance. It was a deeply ingrained conviction, a belief system forged slowly over years of emotional neglect, manipulation, and abuse. Layer by layer, it had been built, reinforced by silence, by harm that went unnamed, by wounds that were never allowed to heal cleanly. By the time I noticed it, it felt structural, like the architecture of my inner world rather than something imposed upon it. As I moved through the treacherous terrain of my own mind, I became convinced that I was the source of the pain that surrounded me. I traced every conflict, every rupture, every moment of discomfort back to myself, seeing me as the common denominator, the thread weaving together the tapestry of suffering that seemed to follow wherever I went. Cause and effect collapsed into self-blame. Complexity flattened into accusation. My presence, I believed, was a curse. A living reminder of pain and heartache. Something that brought disruption simply by existing. The guilt of this belief pressed down relentlessly, a crushing weight that stole breath and clarity alike. It tightened around my chest, narrowed my thinking, dimmed my sense of proportion, until the world felt smaller and more hostile by the day. It threatened to consume me whole. Not in a single, dramatic moment, but slowly, steadily, by convincing me that I was the problem the world was quietly trying to solve. I carried the burden of blame as though it were my sole inheritance, the only thing truly meant for me. I wore it across my shoulders and down my spine, shouldering responsibility for every misstep, every fracture, every misfortune that brushed against the lives around me. In my distorted inner world, I became the epicenter of suffering, the invisible fault line from which all pain radiated outward. Every wrong turn, every missed opportunity, every tear shed by someone I loved felt stamped with my name, as if grief itself bore my signature. My very existence, as I perceived it then, felt like an offense. A quiet harm. A source of low-grade misery for anyone unfortunate enough to come too close. I began to see myself as a walking, talking contagion, a plague disguised as a person, contaminating everything I touched with my perceived failure and despair. Love curdled into liability. Care twisted into consequence. My presence felt less like companionship and more like a warning. This belief did not merely wound me. It isolated me. It taught me to withdraw before I could damage anyone further. To shrink my voice. To dull my edges. To make myself smaller and smaller, as though minimizing my footprint might reduce the harm I believed I caused simply by existing. I learned to see myself as something toxic, something that needed to be removed for others to breathe freely, for their lives to heal and move forward unburdened. And the more tightly I clung to this belief, the more I disappeared inside it.

I felt myself fading, fragmenting, splintering into pieces that drifted further and further apart. Parts of me went quiet. Parts of me shut down. Parts of me simply gave up. I no longer recognized myself as a whole person, but as scattered debris, impossible to gather, impossible to reassemble into anything coherent or worthy. It was not just that I felt broken. It was that I believed the breaking was permanent. It was not only guilt that gnawed at me, though that alone was relentless, a constant ache that never slept. It was also the suffocating sense of entrapment, the feeling of being sealed inside a life with no visible exits, no cracks of light, no hidden door I had simply failed to notice. The air itself felt stale, used up, as though hope had been breathed out long ago and never replenished. My toxic marriage became a prison, not defined by walls or locks, but by a slow, corrosive captivity of the mind and heart. There were no bars to rattle, no chains to break, only invisible restraints that tightened the more I struggled. Every day inside it reinforced my sense of powerlessness, a quiet, grinding confirmation that escape was not meant for me, that wanting freedom was itself a kind of betrayal. I felt trapped, pacing the same narrow corridors of thought, grasping for keys that did not exist, rattling doors that would not open no matter how desperately I tried. Each attempt to break free only seemed to strengthen the cage, as though the act of hoping itself invited punishment. Every failed reach confirmed my worst fears. That I was destined to remain where I was. That suffering was my role to play. That happiness was a privilege written into other people's stories, never intended for mine. The world beyond that life felt theoretical, like a rumor I had heard but could not verify. Freedom belonged to someone else. Joy was something I observed from a distance, pressed against glass. Inside, the days collapsed into one another, indistinguishable, heavy with the same unspoken dread. And in that narrow, airless space, the belief hardened into something that felt permanent. Not a fear anymore, but a conclusion. This was all there would ever be. This small, suffocating existence. This endless endurance. The future shrank until it was nothing more than a repetition of the present, stretched forward without mercy. Hope did not vanish in a single moment. It simply stopped being allowed to breathe.

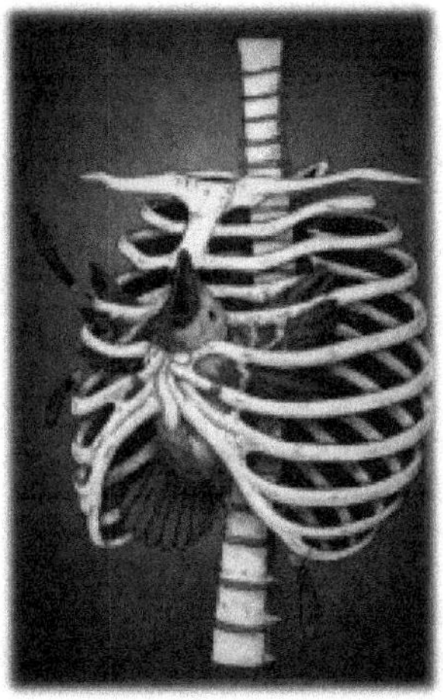

I felt like a bird with broken wings, grounded and trembling, feathers bent and bloodied by repeated impact, unable to lift myself into the sky I could still remember but no longer reach. The air hovered just beyond me, indifferent, while a predator's shadow loomed close enough to feel its heat. Escape was not merely difficult. It felt impossible. As though the outcome had already been decided, my fate sealed long before I understood how I had arrived inside it. No matter how hard I tried, nothing seemed capable of changing the shape of my days. Effort led only back to exhaustion. Hope circled and then collapsed. I was trapped, ensnared in a web spun from obligation and fear, its threads fine but unyielding, tightening each time I struggled. The more I moved, the more entangled I became. I could not see a path out, not even a narrow one. The thought of leaving felt as distant and implausible as climbing to the moon with bare hands, a fantasy that belonged to stories, not to me. Somewhere along the way, I convinced myself this was a fate I had earned. That this confinement was not accidental, but corrective. A punishment I deserved to endure. I told myself I was paying a debt I did not fully remember incurring. A life beyond that cage felt as realistic as breathing underwater, imaginable only in theory, never in practice. I could picture it abstractly, but I could not inhabit it. It did not belong to someone like me. The pain of it all, the emotional, soul-crushing pain of a marriage unraveling into a relentless cycle of arguments, abuse, and long, punishing silences, felt insurmountable. Each conflict stripped away another layer of me. Each silence pressed deeper than words ever could. The absence of tenderness became its own form of violence. It pressed in on me like a crushing weight, stealing breath, collapsing posture, threatening to suffocate whatever fragile sense of self I had left.

I was still alive inside that cage. But I was no longer free to move. And in that stillness, under that weight, I began to forget that wings are not defined by whether they are broken, but by the fact that they once knew how to fly. And it wasn't only the pain itself that broke me, though that pain was sharp and unrelenting. It was the belief that I was responsible for it. That somewhere deep within me, I had failed in a way that could not be repaired, named, or forgiven. I carried that belief like a verdict already passed, already sealed. I let the toxic narrative of my marriage seep into my sense of self, drip by drip, until it no longer sounded like someone else's voice, but like my own inner truth. It rewrote who I believed myself to be and quietly narrowed what I thought I was allowed to hope for. I absorbed the insidious whispers of my partner like poison, slow-acting and cumulative, letting them settle into my bloodstream, letting them spread until they touched everything. They did not arrive all at once. They came disguised as criticism, as concern, as explanation. They festered in silence. They multiplied in moments of doubt. And before I knew it, they were consuming me from the inside out, hollowing me where strength once lived. Every perceived failure, every disagreement, every moment of vulnerability was twisted and sharpened into a weapon. What could have been human imperfection was recast as proof. What could have been conflict was turned into indictment. My softness became liability. My pain became evidence. Each incident was added to a growing ledger of inadequacy, reinforcing the story that I was fundamentally lacking, inherently wrong. Slowly. Relentlessly. I came to believe I was to blame for everything. Not just the arguments, not just the distance, but the very atmosphere of harm itself. I internalized responsibility for wounds I did not inflict, for patterns I did not create, for damage that preceded me and would have continued without me. And inside that belief, the cage locked itself tighter. It convinced me not only that I could not leave, but that I should not. That escape was not an option because punishment was deserved. That freedom was something earned by better people, stronger people, people who had not failed so completely. And in that tightening space, the most dangerous lie took hold of all: that my suffering was not only inevitable but justified. That lie did not shout. It settled. And it nearly convinced me to disappear inside it forever. I took responsibility for every fracture I saw in him, every crack in his demeanor, every simmering anger, and every icy silence that settled between us like frost that never thawed. His unhappiness, his frustrations, his rage, I believed, all traced their origin back to me. In my warped understanding, my existence itself was the catalyst. My presence became a constant irritant, a grain of sand grinding endlessly against his life, a source of suffering I could never remove, no matter how carefully I tried to reshape myself. I carried the weight of his discontent as though it were something solid and physical, a gravitational force pressing down on me, bending my spine beneath its heaviness. It followed me everywhere. Sat beside me at the table. Slept beside me at night. It filled the air between words, thick and oppressive. The guilt was relentless. It gnawed and fed, a voracious creature that never tired, consuming whatever fragments of self-worth I had left. It hollowed me out from the inside, leaving behind a version of myself that felt emptied of substance, fragile and porous, barely holding together. This toxic marriage was no longer just a painful chapter I might one day close. It did not feel temporary. It felt ordained. Like fate. Like a sentence handed down without appeal, already decided long before I understood the charges against me. I was trapped, tangled in a web of fear and dependency, every strand tightening the more I tried to move. I could not imagine a way through that did not require tearing myself apart thread by thread. Leaving felt unthinkable. Like betrayal. Like failure. Like driving another nail into the coffin of a self-esteem already splintered beyond recognition. It felt as though walking away would confirm every accusation I had absorbed, every story I had been told about my inadequacy. So I stayed. And in staying, I continued to carry a weight that was never meant to be mine, believing that if I could just endure a little longer, disappear a little more, I might finally make the world quieter for everyone else.

When I tried to imagine a future beyond that life, all I could see was loneliness. Not solitude as rest, but an endless, echoing absence of love or connection, a wide-open emptiness where no one reached back. The fear of that isolation wrapped itself around me just as tightly as the pain I was already enduring. Staying hurt. Leaving felt fatal. Each option carried its own terror, and there was no door that did not seem to lead straight into loss. I stood frozen between them, unable to move, unable to breathe freely in either direction. And yet, even then, there was an irony I could sense but not fully grasp, like a truth hovering just out of focus. The desire to die, the yearning to disappear, to be done with it all, was not born of wanting life itself to end. It was born of wanting the suffering to stop. Wanting the pressure to ease. Wanting the noise to quiet. It was a plea for relief masquerading as self-destruction, a cry for help spoken in the only language my despair still knew how to use. That paradox deepened my torment. I was reaching for release while clinging desperately to existence. Afraid of the unknown even as I begged for an end to what I knew too well. I lived suspended inside that contradiction, caught midair between opposing truths. Holding on with white-knuckled fear while dreaming of silence. Wanting to live and wanting it to stop hurting. Both desires colliding inside me, amplifying one another, grinding together like tectonic plates beneath the surface. There was no clean resolution. No simple answer. Only the exhausting work of enduring the tension itself, of carrying two opposing truths at once in a body already stretched beyond capacity. And in that collision, the suffering grew heavier, denser, pressing in from all sides, until even longing felt like labor, and simply

remaining felt like an act of quiet defiance against a pain that refused to loosen its grip.

The fractures and cracks in my self-perception ran far deeper than unhappiness. They were not surface wounds or passing doubts. They felt like fissures in the bedrock of who I believed myself to be, splits that ran straight through the foundation of my identity, through the place where meaning and worth were supposed to live. It felt as though my very soul had cracked under pressure, the damage too deep to trace back to a single moment, too old to remember how it began. I was convinced I was irreparably broken. Beyond repair. Too damaged to ever be made whole again. Not bent, not bruised, but ruined in some essential way. I saw myself as a shattered mirror, every fragment reflecting a warped and unrecognizable version of me, each angle distorting the image further. No matter where I looked, I could not find a version of myself that felt intact. Only pieces. Sharp. Incomplete. Misaligned. The pieces of my soul felt scattered beyond reach, strewn across the floor of my inner world like debris after a collapse. I stood among them without knowing where to begin, without believing there was any order left to restore. I did not know how to gather them. I did not trust that they could ever be reassembled into something coherent, something that made sense, something that resembled a person worth saving. Healing felt like a myth told for other people's lives. A distant dream glimpsed from afar, luminous and beautiful, but unreachable from where I stood. A story that belonged to those who were damaged in more manageable ways. Those who still had something left to work with. For me, it felt unattainable. Abstract. Almost cruel in its optimism. Therapy seemed futile, like trying to mend a shattered vase with super glue while the cracks ran too deep and too numerous to disguise. Even if the pieces were forced together, I imagined the damage would always show, the lines of breakage impossible to ignore. Improvement felt cosmetic at best, a fragile illusion that would crumble at the slightest pressure. Even the idea of getting better felt naive. Almost insulting. As though hope itself were mocking the vast distance between who I was and who I longed to be. It felt dangerous to want healing when I had already convinced myself that wholeness was something I had forfeited long ago.

And so I stood amid the ruins of my own self-belief, not yet knowing that shattered things are not beyond transformation, only changed, and that even fragments can become the raw material for something new, something truer, something still waiting to be formed. Happiness, too, felt like a cruel joke, a mocking taunt held just out of reach, its very existence highlighting the vast chasm between where I was and where I could no longer imagine myself being. It appeared everywhere and nowhere at once. In other people's laughter. In fleeting moments on screens and sidewalks. In lives that seemed to move forward, while mine remained stalled in shadow. Each glimpse felt less like inspiration and more like accusation, a reminder of how far removed I believed I was from anything resembling joy. Despair was no longer a passing emotion that came and went. It had hardened into a climate. A constant weather system under which I lived. Thick. Overcast. Unrelenting. It followed me everywhere, seeping into every room, every conversation, every thought, until I could no longer remember what it felt like to breathe clear air. There was no escaping it, no stepping outside of it, only enduring its pressure as it settled deeper into my bones. Sleep offered no sanctuary. No refuge. The night did not soften the edges of my suffering. It sharpened them. Nightmares became the norm, not aberrations but continuations, replaying the same anxieties that stalked my waking hours. Fear followed me into sleep and waited there, patient and creative, reshaping itself into images and scenes that left me waking already exhausted, already braced for another day I did not feel equipped to face. Even the simplest tasks loomed like insurmountable obstacles. Getting out of bed. Answering a message. Making a decision. Each one rose before me like a mountain I had no strength left to climb. Every action demanded an effort that exceeded what I believed I had left, reaching far beyond my diminished reserves. The world asked for energy, clarity, motivation, and I felt stripped of all three. Breathing, the most basic act of living, felt heavy. Laborious. As though each inhale had to push through layers of resistance. My chest felt burdened, compressed by the relentless weight of self-loathing pressing down from the inside. Even air seemed to judge me, to arrive reluctantly, to leave too quickly. Living no longer felt natural or automatic. It felt like work. Constant. Draining. Unforgiving. And in that state, simply continuing felt less like living and more like enduring a body and a mind that had turned against themselves, day after day, under a sky that never seemed to clear. And so the question returned, again and again, like a refrain I could not escape: "*Why did I want to die?*" It circled me relentlessly, no longer tethered solely to the wish for pain to end, but drifting closer to something far more frightening. It felt like wanting to end "*myself*". Not as a cry for help. Not as rebellion. Not even as protest. But as a quiet, exhausted surrender to what I had come to believe was an undeniable truth about who I was and what I was worth. It carried the weight of grim resignation.

A yielding to an existence I had judged utterly worthless, stripped of meaning, contribution, or place. The desire to cease to exist did not arrive in dramatic flashes or impulsive spikes. It was not theatrical. It was steady. Settled. Deeply ingrained. Cold in its calmness. Logical within the warped architecture of my inner world, where self-erasure felt like order restored rather than tragedy enacted. It became a longing for oblivion. Not death as violence, but disappearance as relief. The ultimate erasure. A vanishing act that would finally lift the crushing weight of a self-perception that had hardened into its own prison. I wanted out not of life's challenges, but of "*me*". Of the constant internal accusation. Of the unrelenting sense that my existence was a mistake that kept repeating itself. At the time, this conclusion felt reasonable. I did not experience it as despair spiraling out of control, but as clarity finally reached. As the only coherent ending to a life lived beneath the long, unyielding shadow of self-hate and hopelessness. In that narrowed landscape, surrender did not feel like giving up. It felt like aligning with what I believed had always been true. I could not yet see that this belief was not wisdom, but injury speaking in the voice of certainty. I could not yet know that the cold logic I trusted was shaped by pain, not truth. All I knew then was the weight, the darkness, and the relentless question echoing through it all, asking not "*how*" to live, but "*why I should at all*". This is not the whole story, of course. There were layers beneath what I could see then, deeper currents moving silently under the surface, complexities and quiet underpinnings I did not yet have the language, distance, or safety to name. But this was the core of it. The distilled essence of the darkness. The place where everything seemed to converge and harden into certainty. This was why, in that desolate and lonely place, I came to believe that dying was the only solution. The only way to silence the deafening chorus of self-recrimination and despair that followed me everywhere. The only way, I thought, to end the unbearable pain was to end myself. It felt less like a choice and more like an inevitability, a conclusion drawn after every other option had been quietly erased. Looking back now, I can see that the "*why*" was never singular. It was layered. Multifaceted. A dense tapestry woven from threads of trauma, manipulation, neglect, and self-deception, each strand reinforcing the next until the whole thing felt seamless and inescapable. It was not a simple lack of strength. It was not an absence of courage. It was a slow, systematic erosion of self-worth, carried out over time, so gradually I did not recognize it as destruction while it was happening. A narrative had been constructed around me and within me. Carefully. Repeatedly. A story of inadequacy told so often it eventually stopped sounding like accusation and began to sound like fact. Each repetition pressed it deeper, until it hardened into something I mistook for truth. That narrative became my reality. It shaped how I understood myself, how I reinterpreted my past, how I imagined my future. It narrowed my vision until no other ending seemed possible. What I could not yet see was this: stories can be rewritten. Narratives, no matter how convincing, are not destiny. But at the time, all I could feel was the weight of that story pressing down, convincing me that darkness was not something I was moving through, but something I was. And from inside that belief, the world looked very small indeed. Unraveling it did not happen all at once. It did not arrive as revelation or rescue. It came the way healing often does. Slowly. Incrementally. Almost invisibly at first. It took time. It took patience. It took a great deal of courage to begin pulling at those threads one by one, to dare to question the lies I had absorbed, to place my fingers against beliefs that had once felt immovable and ask, "*what if this is not the truth?*" Healing was not a sudden awakening into light. It was a long and arduous process, uneven and imperfect, marked by setbacks that threatened to undo me and small, hard-won victories that barely announced themselves. Progress did not move in straight lines. Some days felt like climbing. Others felt like standing still. Some felt like sliding backward despite all my effort. And still, something was changing beneath the surface, even when I could not yet see it. The journey is not finished. It continues still. Healing, I have learned, is not something you complete, but something you practice. A relationship you keep returning to. And yet, the chipped paint on that windowsill remains. It has not disappeared with time. It is still there. But it is no longer only a symbol of despair. It has become a quiet marker of distance traveled. A physical reminder of how far I have come from the person who once sat there believing the darkness was all there was. It stands now as a testament to a strength I did not know I possessed when I was at my lowest. A strength that did not roar or conquer but endured. That stayed. That kept breathing. The rain still falls. Storms still pass through. Life has not become immune to weather. But now, when I look out at them, I do not feel swallowed by the darkness. I do not mistake the storm for the sky. I feel the steady, grounded resilience of someone who has survived what once felt unsurvivable and learned, at last, that survival itself is a form of courage.

Chapter: Twenty-Two

What was the truth or reality around this? What I had found in the why?

The Shadow of Deception

In the wake of that realization, I found myself sitting in the darkness, not running from it anymore, but facing it at last. Around me lay the shattered remnants of what I had once called a life, fragments scattered so widely they barely resembled anything whole. And from within that quiet wreckage, a question rose that felt both terrifying and unavoidable: "*What was the truth?* What was the reality of my situation?" And what, beneath everything else, was the true root of my wanting to die? The pain was undeniable. The hurt. The suffering. They pressed in on me constantly, a relentless weight that made it impossible to pretend I was not living inside something that felt like a waking nightmare. This was not imagined. This was not exaggeration. My body knew it. My bones knew it. Fear had settled into me like cold, seeping deep and refusing to leave. I remember the chipped mug cradled between my hands, its warmth faint, almost apologetic, barely cutting through the dread that had lodged itself in my chest. The tea had gone lukewarm, forgotten in the way I felt forgotten, untouched by time, suspended in a moment that refused to move forward. My fingers wrapped around the ceramic as if it were the only solid thing left anchoring me to the present. Outside, leaves spun and scattered in a slow, melancholic dance, carried by a wind that seemed to know something about loss. Their movement mirrored the chaos twisting inside me, thoughts colliding and breaking apart, never settling long enough to form certainty. Everything felt surreal, dislocated, as though I were watching my own life from behind glass. Close enough to see the details. Too far away to reach them. Even months after the unraveling began, it still seemed impossible. Unbelievable. As though I had stepped into someone else's story and forgotten how to leave. That this was where I had landed. That this was the ground beneath my feet now. The question lingered in the air between breaths, heavy with implication.

If this was not the whole truth, then what had I been believing instead? And who had taught me to believe it? In that stillness, with the mug cooling in my hands and the world moving on outside the window, I began to sense the presence of something else entirely. Not just pain, but deception. A shadow that had shaped my reality without ever revealing its name. And yet, the pain was real. The hurt. The terror. All of it lived in my body with a kind of undeniable authority. It was visceral, palpable, impossible to dismiss or explain away. These were not imagined wounds or exaggerated fears spun from a fragile mind. They were not distortions born of despair alone. I could feel them in the tight band cinched around my chest, in the shallow vigilance of my breath, in the constant alertness humming beneath my skin as though danger had trained my nervous system to never rest. Whatever doubts I carried about myself, this much became inescapably clear: I was not inventing the danger. I was not dramatizing my suffering. I was not misreading the threat. I was, objectively, in danger. That truth did not arrive loudly. It did not rescue me or offer comfort. It simply sat beside me in the dark, quiet and heavy, unsettling and grounding all at once. Like a stone placed in my palm, undeniable in its weight. And in that stillness, something shifted. Not relief. Not clarity. Not yet. But the beginning of a crack. The first fracture in the illusion that everything was my fault. The first hairline break in the story that had told me I was the cause of my own undoing. It did not shatter the narrative all at once, but it weakened it, just enough to let a thin line of light slip through. The shadow of deception still lingered. It did not retreat easily. It hovered, familiar and persuasive, ready to reclaim its ground. But for the first time, I sensed that beneath it, there might be another truth waiting. A truth not built on blame or self-erasure. A truth that had been buried under years of distortion and silence, waiting patiently to be named. And that sensing, fragile as it was, marked the beginning of something new. Not escape. Not freedom. But orientation. The moment I realized the darkness was not the whole landscape, and that the story I had been living inside might not be the only one available to  me after all.

The shards of a shattered mirror lay scattered everywhere, and in each fragment I caught sight of a fractured version of myself, multiplied, distorted, and warped, no single reflection whole enough to recognize as me. Every angle told a different story. Every piece held a face I half-knew and barely trusted. I searched for coherence and found only splintered outlines, a self-broken into images that refused to align. What I was feeling was not imagined. It was not an exaggeration born of despair or weakness, not a story my mind had invented to justify its own collapse. The pain was real. Undeniably so. It lived in my body as a physical ache, a low, unceasing thunder reverberating through my bones, a pressure that hummed beneath the skin, impossible to outrun, impossible to silence. It followed me into sleep. It greeted me on waking. It settled into places words could not easily reach. It was the pain of betrayal, sharp and surgical, cutting with terrible precision. The searing burn of infidelity scorched my sense of safety, my faith in what I thought was solid, trusted, and shared. It left behind a landscape of doubt where certainty once lived, teaching my nervous system to brace even in moments meant to be gentle. It was also the suffocating weight of emotional, mental, and sexual abuse, a gravity that pressed down day after day, moment after moment, until even standing upright felt like an act of quiet rebellion. An act of defiance. Simply remaining present in my own body required strength I did not know how to name. Survival became deliberate. Breath became earned. This pain did not come from nowhere. It was not vague. It was not abstract. It had shape. It had memory. It had history etched into muscle and nerve and thought. It had cause. And acknowledging that truth mattered. Because pain that has cause is not madness. It is response. It is the body and mind reacting exactly as they do when something real, something violating, something overwhelming has occurred. The mirror may have shattered, but the shards were telling the truth.

And in the dim, unsteady light of that realization, a stark and brutal truth began to surface. I was trapped in a nightmare, not because I was broken or unworthy, but because I had been living inside a web I could not see while I was still ensnared within it. From the inside, the strands looked like structure. Like normalcy. Like love. Only when the light shifted did their true shape begin to reveal itself. It was a nightmare woven from co-dependency and manipulation, from affection slowly bent into leverage, from care that came with conditions I did not know I was allowed to refuse. Thread by thread, the web had been spun from familiar materials. Promises. Apologies. Hope. Fear. And beneath it all, a lifetime of buried trauma that had quietly trained me in what I believed I was permitted to endure. What felt familiar had passed itself off as safe. What hurt had disguised itself as devotion.

It was not a single thread that held me there, but many. Layered. Interlaced. Knotted over time. Tightening each time I mistook survival for loyalty. Each time I confused endurance with love. Each time I told myself that staying was strength, that tolerating harm was virtue, that sacrificing myself was the cost of commitment.

The web did not tighten all at once. It tightened slowly, almost imperceptibly, until movement itself became painful. I honored my vows with integrity, even as abuse and neglect hollowed out the spaces where mutual care should have lived. I stayed faithful to promises made in good faith, even when those promises were no longer being held on the other side. What I called commitment was, in truth, a learned silence. What I called love was entangled with fear. And what I called resilience was often just the will to keep breathing in a place that starved me of air. Seeing this did not break me. It clarified me. Because the moment I understood the web, the moment I named it, it stopped being invisible. And something invisible, once seen, no longer has the same power to hold. Standing there among the shards, feeling the ache hum steadily through my body, something shifted. Not loudly. Not cleanly. But unmistakably. A subtle realignment, like a bone beginning to set after a long, painful dislocation. I began to understand, though I could not yet fully name it or hold it in language. Understanding arrived first as sensation. As relief mixed with grief. As a loosening in the chest where self-blame had lived. The mirror had shattered, yes. But the breaking was not evidence of my failure. It was evidence of impact. Proof that something had struck with enough force to fracture what was once whole. Glass, or in this case a soul, does not break without reason. It breaks because something collides with it. And suddenly, the question was no longer, "*What is wrong with me?* but *What happened to me?*" That distinction mattered more than I knew how to say. For the first time, I could sense that what needed healing was not some imagined flaw buried deep inside my character, not a deficiency of strength or love or loyalty. What needed healing were the wounds left behind by truths I had been taught, again and again, not to see. Truths I had been trained to minimize. To explain away. To turn around and carry as my own fault. I had learned to look at harm and call it misunderstanding. To look at violation and call it compromise. To look at cruelty and call it my own inadequacy.

Each time something hurt, I had been guided, subtly and persistently, to turn inward and ask what I should do better, be quieter, be softer, be more accommodating about. The mirror did not just reflect me. It reflected a story I had been handed and told to live inside. And now, standing amid the fragments, I could see how thoroughly that story had shaped the glass. The cracks traced patterns of blame that were never mine to carry. The fractures outlined moments where responsibility had been misplaced, redirected, distorted until accountability vanished and shame took its place. I had been taught to deny what my body knew. To doubt what my instincts registered. To override truth in favor of survival. And survival, for a long time, had required me to believe I was the problem. Seeing this did not immediately make the pain disappear. But it changed its meaning. The ache in my body was no longer proof of weakness. It was testimony. Evidence of endurance. The shards were not accusations. They were witnesses. And in their sharp, honest edges, I could finally see that healing would not come from fixing myself, but from tending to the places where I had been broken by what I was told not to name. This was not the end of the story. It was the moment the story stopped lying about who was responsible. The truth, the brutal, unvarnished truth, was far more intricate than the simple story I first told myself. It was not only about the affairs. Not only the betrayal by the man I had vowed my life to share, but also the woman I had loved like a sister. Those were the visible wounds, the ones that bled openly, the injuries no one could deny once exposed. They were sharp, undeniable, and devastating. But they were not the whole story. Beneath them ran something deeper. Darker. A current moving quietly under the surface, winding through the murky and treacherous waters of my own psyche. A slow undertow that had been shaping my reality long before the betrayals came into view. What hurt most was not just what happened, but how long I had been living inside a distortion without knowing its name.

On the surface, my life wore the costume of normalcy. A convincing one. I was married. I appeared to have a loving partner, a close-knit circle of friends, a life that from the outside seemed stable, even enviable. I played the role well. I smiled at the right moments. I protected the image. I believed it myself, at least enough to survive inside it. But behind closed doors, another reality unfolded. One spoken not in words, but in silence. In fear. In the careful calculation of moods and reactions. I was married to a man who knew how to perform charm, how to offer tenderness selectively, how to mirror warmth just long enough to keep hope alive. He wore kindness like a tailored suit, slipping it on in public, letting it slip away in private. And behind that mask lived something else entirely. A master manipulator. An abusive narcissist who fed on control, who required dominance to feel secure, who took pleasure in power disguised as devotion. What looked like love was often leverage. What felt like intimacy was frequently surveillance. Care came with conditions. Affection arrived with strings already attached. Slowly, imperceptibly, my world narrowed around his needs, his narratives, his version of reality. This was not chaos. It was choreography. And the most dangerous part was how thoroughly it trained me to doubt myself. To question my perceptions. To explain away harm. To believe that if something felt wrong, it must be because I was failing to understand, failing to love correctly, failing to be enough. The abuse did not always shout. Often, it whispered. It corrected. It reframed. It taught me to betray my own instincts in the name of keeping the peace. Seeing this now did not simplify the pain. It deepened it. But it also clarified something essential. I had not been living in a sudden collapse. I had been living in a slow erosion. And the affairs were not the beginning of the nightmare. They were the moment the illusion finally cracked wide enough to let the truth in. And once truth enters, even quietly, it cannot be unlearned.

This is what loving a narcissist becomes. It is not always violence you can point to, not always bruises or moments dramatic enough to shatter the illusion in a single blow. It is erosion. A slow invasion of the mind. A weathering of the inner landscape so gradual you do not notice the shoreline receding until the ground beneath you gives way. Messages are delivered day after day, not shouted once, but repeated until repetition gives them authority, until they no longer sound like his voice at all, but like your own internal narration. *"I am right! You are wrong! Lies! Obey me! Worthless! No one but me could ever love you! It's all your fault! Do what I say! It's all in your head! You're remembering it wrong! You're imagining things! I did nothing wrong! You made me do it. I did not do that."* These words did not arrive as language alone. They arrived as atmosphere. As instruction. As a steady rewriting of reality itself. They dismantled my trust in my own memory, my instincts, my sense of self. They taught me to second-guess what I had seen, what I had felt, what my body knew before my mind could argue it away. Truth became negotiable. Reality became conditional. Certainty dissolved. Love was turned into leverage. Confusion into compliance. Care into currency that could be withdrawn at any moment. Slowly, without my noticing, a prison was constructed inside my mind. Its walls were made of doubt. Its corridors echoed with self-questioning. And its lock sounded exactly like my own thoughts. That was the deeper truth I could not see at first. Not just betrayal, but a systematic undoing. Not just heartbreak, but a quiet colonization of identity. What was taken was not only trust, but authorship. Not only safety, but sovereignty over my own inner world. I had been trained to surveil myself, to police my reactions, to doubt my perceptions before anyone else had the chance to do it for me. The most effective captivity is the one that convinces you it is self-chosen.

And standing there among the shards of the mirror, something finally clarified. The devastation I felt was not evidence of fragility. It was evidence of impact. Of duration. Of prolonged psychological violence acting on a human soul that had been trying, with extraordinary endurance, to survive. The mirror had not shattered because I was weak. It had shattered because it had been under strain for far too long. And in that recognition, painful as it was, the ground shifted again. Because what has been systematically undone can also, slowly and deliberately,

be reclaimed.

He had systematically eroded my sense of self with words laced in venom, each sentence a slow-acting poison seeping into my mind, dissolving my confidence, corroding my worth. There were no dramatic explosions, no single moment of ruin. Just a steady drip. Phrase by phrase. Look by look. Until what once felt solid inside me began to feel porous, unreliable, easy to doubt. Over time, I was hollowed out, left a shell of the vibrant, capable woman I once was, someone I could barely remember how to inhabit, like a name spoken in a language I no longer knew how to pronounce. And I, in my naivete, in my aching hunger for love and validation, played my role flawlessly. A tragic actress in a script I did not write but slowly learned by heart. I learned my lines through repetition. Through consequence. Through the subtle reward of approval when I performed correctly. I danced on that stage to his every cue, mistaking compliance for devotion, silence for strength, endurance for virtue. I called it love. I called it loyalty. I called it maturity. All the while, I was shrinking to fit a part that required my disappearance. He had a way of convincing me that I was worthless. That I was lucky he tolerated me. That no one else would ever love me, want me, choose me. These ideas did not arrive as cruelty at first. They arrived dressed as truth. As concern. As certainty. As statements spoken with such confidence that I learned to doubt myself before questioning him. They sounded reasonable. Protective. Almost kind. And so I absorbed them. Believed them. Let them settle into my bones, where they hardened into assumptions about who I was allowed to be and what I deserved.

And as if that were not enough, he was having an affair with my best friend. The person I trusted most. The one I confided in, leaned on, believed would protect me. The one I thought had my back when the ground beneath me was already unstable. That betrayal cut deep, slicing through what little safety I still believed existed, rupturing the last illusion that someone, somewhere, was holding the truth with care. It was not just the loss of trust. It was the collapse of refuge. But even then, that devastation was only the tip of the iceberg. Because beneath that singular horror lay years of conditioning. Years of erosion. Years of being taught, quietly and relentlessly, to betray myself before anyone else could. The affair exposed the wound. But the wound had been forming long before it was ever visible. My first husband, cloaked in narcissistic charm, was a master manipulator. He dismantled my self-worth brick by painstaking brick, not with haste, but with patience that felt almost reverent in its cruelty. Each word was placed carefully. Each doubt set just so. He built his power the way ruins are made, slowly, deliberately, until collapse feels inevitable rather than caused. He whispered lies so quietly they passed as my own thoughts. They slipped into the spaces between moments, between breaths, twisting my perceptions until I questioned my sanity, my memory, my reality itself. What I had seen became uncertain. What I had felt became suspect. Even my instincts began to feel like unreliable narrators. I learned to second-guess before I could trust. To apologize before I could protest. To shrink before I could speak. The affair with my best friend, devastating as it was, landed like a physical blow only because it tore the curtain away. It did not create the wound. It revealed it. It was never just the infidelity. That was the visible rupture, the crack anyone could recognize. Beneath it lay something far more corrosive. Calculated cruelty. Deliberate gaslighting. A long campaign of quiet domination that had been working for years beneath the surface of ordinary life. This was the relentless erosion of my confidence. My voice. My sense of self. The slow theft of authorship over my own story. Years of quiet destruction culminated in a single, undeniable fracture, a moment so loud it could no longer be explained away or minimized or blamed on my supposed inadequacies. The mirror shattered not because I was fragile, but because it had been under constant strain. And standing there amid the wreckage, reeling and disoriented, surrounded by what remained of the life I thought I understood, I finally began to see the truth. Not just of what had been done to me, but of how thoroughly it had undone me. How much I had lost without realizing it. How deeply I had been trained to disappear. Seeing this did not heal me. But it named the injury. And naming it was the first moment the damage stopped pretending it was my fault. As a hopeless co-dependent, I lived with an overwhelming hunger for his validation, his approval becoming the oxygen I believed I needed to survive. I learned to breathe only when he allowed it. His moods set the climate of my inner world. A nod could steady me. A sigh could undo me. I mistook this dependency for devotion, this starvation for love. Co-dependency wrapped itself around me like a suffocating blanket, heavy and airless, dulling my vision and muffling my instincts. It was strange how it could feel both protective and imprisoning at once. It kept me warm enough to endure the nights yet trapped enough to never leave the room. Every time I felt the urge to pull away, the fear of exposure, of abandonment, of existing without his approval tightened its grip. I stayed not because I was safe, but because I was afraid of the cold beyond what I had come to know. I truly believed my worth, my lovability, my very right to exist were bound to his approval.

As though my identity were tethered to his presence, suspended from it, unable to touch solid ground on my own. Without him, I imagined myself collapsing into nothing. I could not yet conceive of a self that stood independently, breathing freely, unmeasured by someone else's gaze. The messages he fed me were toxic, but they were administered slowly, carefully, like a drip instead of a dose. Repetition did the work that cruelty alone could not. Over time, they stopped sounding foreign. They stopped sounding like him. I absorbed them so completely that reality and distortion blurred into a single, seamless narrative. What I felt was dismissed. What I remembered was questioned. What I needed was minimized. And eventually, I began doing that work for him. His cruel words, his withering scorn, took up residence inside my mind. They furnished the rooms of my inner world. They rearranged the language I used to speak to myself. They became my internal dialogue, a relentless chorus of self-doubt and self-loathing playing on repeat, correcting me before I could even think to defend myself. I no longer needed him to be present to feel small. The prison had learned how to run itself. And this, too, was part of the devastation. Not just that he controlled me, but that I learned to control myself in his absence. That I carried his voice forward, long after the words were spoken, long after the moment had passed. The damage was not only in what he said, but in how deeply it rooted itself, convincing me that this was who I was. Seeing this now is painful. But it is also clarifying. Because a voice that was learned can be unlearned. And an identity built in captivity can, slowly, deliberately, be reclaimed. What began as his voice gradually became mine. Not abruptly, not dramatically, but through repetition so consistent it felt inevitable. He had carefully, methodically crafted a narrative about who I was, and he repeated it until it no longer sounded like an accusation, but like fact. A story of inadequacy. Of unlovability. Of inherent worthlessness. And I, tragically, accepted it as truth, not because it was convincing, but because it was constant. I wore that story like a label stitched into my skin, impossible to remove without tearing something vital. It defined every thought, every choice, every hope I dared to reach for and then quickly withdrew. I filtered the world through it. Every kindness felt conditional. Every mistake felt confirming. Every desire felt excessive. I began to measure myself not by who I was, but by how well I could disappear without being noticed. I became convinced that I was fundamentally flawed, broken in some essential way that could never quite be repaired. That love was not freely given, but something to be earned through endurance. Through tolerance. Through the quiet swallowing of pain. Happiness, I believed, was a privilege reserved for others, people more worthy, more whole, more deserving than me. It was not meant for someone like me. In that distorted reality, I did not merely doubt myself. I erased myself. I learned to pre-empt my needs. To silence my instincts. To make myself smaller so the world would not feel burdened by my presence. I edited my emotions before they could inconvenience anyone. I abandoned my truth to preserve the illusion of harmony. And I mistook this disappearance for devotion. I believed this erasure was proof of love, proof of loyalty, proof that I was finally getting it right. I did not yet understand that what I was calling love was costing me my existence. That this was not sacrifice, but the slowest, quietest form of self-abandonment. Not humility, but annihilation practiced quietly over time.  And the most devastating part was not that it happened. It was that I believed it was what I deserved.

He painted me a picture of myself that I did not recognize, a warped caricature rendered in the darkest shades of inadequacy and worthlessness. The proportions were wrong. The features distorted. Yet he presented it with such certainty that I began to doubt my own reflection. His words, heavy with contempt, became the soundtrack of my days, a low, constant hum that followed me from room to room, reverberating through the hollowed spaces inside me where confidence once lived. I lived like a broken record, stuck on repeat, replaying the same agonizing refrain of self-criticism and self-loathing until it felt inescapable, until silence itself seemed hostile, as though quiet only made the voice louder. Even moments of peace were infiltrated. Even joy felt suspect. My inner world became an echo chamber, amplifying his judgments until they sounded like my own conclusions. Looking back now, I can see the shape of the trap I was in. I was caught in a toxic cycle of abuse and co-dependency, moving in tight, repetitive circles I mistook for safety. Predictability passed itself off as stability. Familiar pain felt safer than the unknown. My husband, a narcissist, had spun a web of deceit and manipulation so fine I could not see its threads, only feel its pull tightening with every step I took. The more I struggled to understand, the more entangled I became. I grew convinced that I needed him. That without him I was nothing at all. An empty space. A person unworthy of love or even basic respect. As if my survival itself depended on his presence, as if I could not exist without his permission. And I believed him. Not because it was true, but because my sense of self had been worn down to the point where belief felt easier than resistance. I believed I was flawed at the core. That I was the problem to be managed, endured, corrected. That my feelings were excessive. My needs unreasonable. My perceptions unreliable. And that he, somehow, was the solution. The anchor. The authority. The measure by which reality should be judged. In that distorted reality, love became synonymous with dependence. Safety became synonymous with silence. And my own identity dissolved into the story he told me about myself. I did not just lose confidence. I surrendered authorship of my life. I handed the pen to a voice that thrived on my doubt, that required my disappearance to remain powerful, never realizing how completely it had trained me to erase myself. Never realizing that what I was calling love was built on my absence. And yet, even now, in the act of seeing this clearly, something essential has already begun to return. Because the moment you recognize the voice that taught you to disappear, you also begin to hear the one that has been waiting to speak again.

The constant barrage of negative messages, the emotional manipulation, the gaslighting, all of it took its toll. Not all at once. Not in a way that could be neatly traced or easily explained. It wore me down grain by grain, the way sand wears stone, until my mental health began to fracture under the accumulated weight. There was no single breaking point. There was a slow thinning. A quiet unraveling.

I became a shadow of who I once was, or who I might have become. A dim outline where a whole person used to stand. I moved through my days muted, as though some essential saturation had been drained from me. The voice that once spoke with clarity now hesitated. The instincts that once guided me now second-guessed themselves into silence. I existed, but narrowly, compressed into a smaller version of myself that took up as little space as possible. His whispers did not remain his for long. They crossed a border quietly and became my own inner demons, slipping past awareness and settling into the architecture of my thoughts. They rearranged the furniture of my mind, took up residence in the places where self-trust and confidence once lived. They followed me through my waking hours, murmuring accusations under the noise of daily life, cataloguing my flaws, replaying my perceived shortcomings on an endless, merciless loop. They gnawed at my self-esteem with relentless precision. Not tearing it apart dramatically but stripping it bare layer by layer until nothing felt protected anymore. I began to feel small. Insignificant. Expendable. As though love and happiness were things meant for other people, people who had earned them, people who were not as fundamentally flawed as I believed myself to be. I carried that emptiness everywhere. It clung to me like a stain no one else could see but I could never wash away. I wore it into conversations. Into relationships. Into moments that should have felt light but instead felt hollow. It colored how I interpreted kindness, how I received care, how I understood my own worth. Even when someone reached toward me, the emptiness whispered that it was a mistake, that they would see the truth eventually.

And yet, even this was not the full truth. Because beneath the emptiness, beneath the self-erasure, something else was still present. Something that had endured the erosion. Something that had been wounded, yes, but not erased. The shadows did not exist without a body that once cast them. The stain did not appear without something valuable beneath it. And that realization, still distant but beginning to stir, carried the faint outline of another possibility. What was happening to me could not be reduced to marital infidelity or abuse alone. Those were real, devastating, and undeniable, but they were not the deepest roots of the collapse. Beneath the visible wreckage of my dysfunctional relationship and my co-dependent patterns lay something older. Quieter. Far more entrenched. A well of unresolved trauma and long-standing wounds, dug long before this marriage ever existed. Its roots stretched back into my past, into a history that had already taught me how to doubt myself, how to shrink my needs, how to make myself smaller so others could feel larger. Long before I stood in vows, I had learned the grammar of endurance. I had learned how to tolerate discomfort, how to confuse attachment with safety, how to accept less than I deserved, and call it loyalty. The ground had been prepared long before the seeds were planted. The messages my first husband spoke into me did not land on untouched ground. They did not need force to take hold. They embedded themselves easily, slipping into familiar grooves, settling into beliefs that had already been rehearsed. Soon, they felt indistinguishable from my own thoughts, woven so seamlessly into my inner dialogue that I could no longer tell where his voice ended, and mine began. I believed I was stupid. A burden. A failure. Unattractive. Unworthy of love. These beliefs did not feel learned. They did not feel imposed. They felt inherent, as though they were facts rather than conclusions. As though they had always been true and I was only now finally seeing myself clearly. That was their most devastating deception. When a lie echoes long enough, it begins to feel like identity. The critical, crushing narrative I carried about myself was not born in a single relationship or a single betrayal. It was the result of years of emotional neglect, subtle and overt abuse, and deeply rooted low self-esteem. A chorus of voices layered over time. Parents. Partners. Circumstances. Silence. Each one adding a note until they fused into a single, relentless inner monologue that followed me everywhere, narrating my life through the lens of inadequacy. And yet, even as I began to see this pattern, something quietly revolutionary emerged. If these beliefs had roots, then they had origins. If they had origins, then they were not truths. And if they were not truths, then they could, one day, be questioned. The well I carried inside me was deep, yes. But it was not bottomless. And understanding how it had been dug was the first moment I realized it might also, slowly, be filled back in. I became my own harshest judge, my most unforgiving witness. The self-hatred took up residence in my mind and furnished it completely, dragging its furniture into every room, leaving no quiet corner untouched. There was no place to rest. No inner refuge left intact. And no matter where I went, no matter how far I tried to run, I could not outrun the voice that insisted I was the problem. The flaw. The thing that needed to be erased. That voice did not argue. It declared. It spoke with the confidence of something long rehearsed, something that had been gathering evidence for years. Self-hatred hardened into a chronic state, no longer a passing thought that drifted through and moved on, but a condition I lived inside. It shaped how I interpreted every interaction, every mistake, every silence. It became the lens through which I saw myself and the world, distorting everything it touched. It turned into a self-fulfilling prophecy, a script I unknowingly performed each day. I anticipated rejection and then shrank in ways that invited it.

I expected abandonment and braced so tightly that connection became strained. I apologized for existing. I minimized my needs. I edited myself into something smaller and quieter, hoping that if I took up less space, I might finally be safe. The cycle fed itself. Belief shaped behavior. Behavior reinforced belief. Round and round I went. I was trapped in a vicious loop of negativity, pacing the same mental corridors again and again, walls closing in, footsteps echoing back at me, unable to find the door marked *exit*. The mind became a maze with no visible center, no clear map, only the familiar grooves of self-accusation worn deeper with each pass. Even moments of calm felt temporary, borrowed, waiting to be revoked. The trauma I carried ran deep. Deeper than this relationship. Deeper than this season of pain. Wounds inflicted long before I ever met him. Unseen. Unacknowledged. Never given the language or safety required to heal. They lived quietly beneath the surface, shaping my responses, teaching my nervous system what to expect, what to tolerate, what to normalize. Those wounds became fertile ground. Rich soil. And into that soil, his toxic seeds of manipulation and abuse fell easily, taking root without resistance. They flourished unchecked not because I was weak, but because the ground had already been wounded, already starved of care, already accustomed to surviving in harsh conditions. Understanding this did not excuse what was done to me. It contextualized it. It showed me that the cycle was not proof of who I was, but evidence of what I had endured. And for the first time, I could begin to see the cycle not as destiny, but as something learned. And what is learned, however deeply, can be unlearned. Slowly. Carefully. With patience. I lived under constant internal pressure, like a walking time bomb, my nervous system stretched taut, wires crossed and humming, primed to explode from the sheer weight of everything I was holding inside.

My body never truly rested. Even stillness felt alert. My muscles braced against threats that were no longer visible, my breath shallow, my heart always listening for danger. I existed in a state of permanent readiness, as though survival required vigilance without pause. But it wasn't only my husband's words that had done this to me. The damage reached further back, into layers of time I had long since learned not to touch.

The trauma etched into my past had left scars I never learned how to tend. Scars I had been taught instead to ignore. To normalize. To wear as evidence of character rather than injury. I carried them as proof of who I believed I was, mistaking adaptation for identity. I had grown up steeped in shame, breathing it in like atmosphere. An unspoken inheritance. A quiet, pervasive belief that I was never quite good enough, that my presence itself required justification, that my existence was a burden to those around me. No one needed to say it outright. The message lived in tone, in silence, in what was withheld as much as what was given. Those early impressions lodged deep, shaping my sense of self long before I had the language to question them. So, when my husband's abuse echoed those same beliefs, it did not register as something new. It did not feel invasive or foreign. It felt familiar. Confirming. As if the world were finally nodding in agreement with the story, I had been telling myself all along. His words slid seamlessly into old grooves, reinforcing patterns already carved deep into my psyche. And so those messages fused with my identity. They stopped feeling like things said to me and began to feel like truths about me. I carried them as evidence. As justification. As proof that the voice in my head had been right all along. Every accusation became corroboration. Every cruelty became confirmation. The cycle tightened its grip. The shame deepened its roots. And I remained trapped inside a version of myself constructed not from choice or truth, but from wounds I never caused. Wounds I had been taught, relentlessly, to own. I did not build this prison. But I had learned how to live inside it. And even that, I would later come to understand, was not a failure of strength. It was the ingenuity of survival doing the only thing it knew how to do with the tools it had been given.

When I trace the roots of it all, my memory returns to a childhood tinged with neglect. Not loud. Not dramatic. But quiet and persistent, like a draft you don't notice until you are already cold. A constant sense of being unseen. Unheard. As though my presence barely registered in the room, as though I could slip in and out of existence without disturbing the air. It was a subtle form of emotional absence, the kind that leaves no visible bruises, no clear story to tell, yet shapes the nervous system all the same, teaching it what to expect and what not to ask for. I learned early how to wait for attention. How to earn approval. How to become alert to the smallest shifts in tone and expression. I learned to scan faces the way sailors scan the horizon, searching for signs of safety, for proof that I mattered. Love felt conditional, something to be secured through effort and compliance rather than something freely given. And so, validation became something I sought outside myself, again and again, because I never learned how to generate it within. That unspoken hunger followed me into adulthood. It did not announce itself. It lived beneath my choices, quietly steering them, influencing who I trusted, what I tolerated, how much of myself I was willing to trade for closeness. I wanted to be chosen. To be needed. To be enough. Those desires were not flaws. They were human. But unmet for too long, they became ache. They became leverage. And that yearning made me exquisitely vulnerable to someone like him. Someone fluent in the language of insecurity. Someone who knew how to offer affection in measured doses and withdraw it just as precisely. Someone who could make me feel momentarily seen, then abruptly invisible again, recreating a familiar rhythm my body already knew how to endure. The push and pull felt like connection because it echoed an old pattern. The scarcity felt like love because abundance had never been my baseline. I did not fall into that dynamic because I was naïve or weak. I recognized it because it felt like home. And that, perhaps, is the quiet tragedy at the center of it all. We do not seek what is good for us. We seek what is familiar. Even when what is familiar has been hurting us all along. He found the cracks in my foundation; the hairline fractures I did not yet know had names. The places left brittle by neglect, by longing, by years of quietly believing I had to earn love the way one earns permission.

These were not gaping breaks. They were subtle fault lines, invisible to me, but legible to someone who knew how to read weakness the way others read maps. And once he found them, he exploited them without mercy. What felt like intimacy at first was really inspection. A careful taking of measure. What felt like love was leverage, calibrated and applied with precision. He pressed into those unseen flaws, not all at once, but patiently, persistently, widening them by degrees. Each doubt nudged open. Each boundary softened. Each need reframed as inconvenience. Until the ground beneath me no longer felt stable and I could no longer remember what solid footing had ever felt like. I learned to balance on shifting ground. To adjust constantly. To brace for tremors. Instability became normal. Confusion became familiar. And still, I blamed myself for breaking. For wobbling. For failing to stand upright in conditions that would have tested even the strongest structures. I did not yet understand this essential truth. Foundations weakened by neglect do not crumble because they are faulty. They crumble because they were never reinforced. Because no one taught them how to bear weight. Because they were asked to hold more than they were ever meant to carry alone. The breaking was not proof of defect. It was evidence of pressure applied to a place that had long been left unsupported. And in that realization, quiet and devastating as it was, another truth began to surface. What had been exploited could be repaired. What had been widened could be strengthened. What had never been reinforced could, at last, be given what it should have had all along. This was not the end of my standing. It was the moment I finally understood why I had fallen.

Those wounds, those hidden scars I had carried for so long without naming, became the key to understanding my own captivity. They were not incidental. They were formative. They laid the groundwork for my co-dependency, quietly shaping a desperate need to please, to perform, to earn the love that should have been given freely and without condition. I learned to bargain for belonging, to negotiate for safety, to trade pieces of myself for approval, never realizing how costly those exchanges would become or how little of myself would remain on the other side. I learned to make myself useful instead of visible. Agreeable instead of authentic. I learned to anticipate needs before they were spoken, to smooth discomfort before it surfaced, to disappear just enough to keep connection intact. At the time, it felt like survival. It felt like love. I did not yet see how much of myself I was quietly surrendering with each transaction. Those wounds were the fractures in my foundation, the places left brittle by neglect and longing. And he saw them immediately. Where I saw endurance, he saw access. Where I saw loyalty, he saw leverage. With cold, calculated precision, he pressed into those weak points, widening them over time, exploiting my vulnerabilities not by accident, but by design. He did not need to invent new harms. He only needed to amplify the old ones. What felt to me like love was, to him, control. What felt like connection was surveillance. What felt like intimacy was power carefully disguised. I was vulnerable, shaped by wounds I did not cause and had never been taught to heal. And he was a predator, fluent in sensing that vulnerability, in circling it, in entering through the places already aching for care. He did not create my pain, but he recognized it. He did not plant the seeds, but he knew exactly how to make them grow. Understanding this did not erase the pain. It did not undo what had been done or soften the memories etched into my body. But it shifted the meaning of everything. The devastation was no longer evidence of my failure. It was evidence of harm. Of targeting. Of exploitation layered on top of old, unhealed wounds. And in that distinction, something essential began to form. The first threads of clarity emerged. Fragile. Tentative. But real. Threads that suggested what had been exploited could one day be protected. That what had been used against me could become the very place where boundaries would form. That the same awareness that once made me vulnerable could, with care, become discernment. I was not broken in the way I had believed. I had been wounded. And wounds, once seen

clearly, can be tended.

He became a master puppeteer, fingers deft and deliberate, moving with a precision that felt almost surgical. He learned the tension of every string, the exact pressure required to make me sway, to falter, to comply. My emotions were no longer mine to hold in safety. They were lifted from me, rearranged, and made into instruments. My love became a weapon he wielded with frightening skill, turned back on me again and again. Every tear I shed fed his hunger. Every tremor of self-doubt reinforced his sense of dominance. My pain was not an accident in his presence. It was confirmation. He knew exactly where to press, where the old wounds throbbed, which words to release like poison into the air so they would linger long after he left the room. He understood how to keep me tangled in the web he had spun so carefully around my life, sticky with confusion, fear, and hope I could not quite let go of. He had studied me. My fears. My longings. My weaknesses. Not to protect them. Not to hold them with care. But to exploit them without hesitation or mercy. He learned the timing of my vulnerability, the moments when I was most likely to bend, most likely to apologize for things I had not done, most likely to doubt myself instead of him. And each time I did, the web tightened. The more dependent I became, the more he seemed to thrive. He drew strength from the control he held over me, from the way my world slowly narrowed until it revolved around his moods, his approval, his version of reality. I felt myself shrinking under his gaze, compressing into something smaller, quieter, more manageable. I contorted myself into the shape he required, sanding down my edges, dimming my instincts, silencing my objections.

With each concession, something slipped away. With each apology I did not owe, something was surrendered. I lost pieces of myself not all at once, but incrementally, in moments that felt insignificant at the time. A boundary softened. A truth withheld. A feeling dismissed. Until one day I realized I was performing myself rather than inhabiting myself, existing in fragments rather than as a whole. And still, I believed the cost was mine to pay. Only later would I understand that what I was calling love was survival under domination, and what I was losing was not weakness leaving me, but self being taken. When I looked in the mirror, I no longer recognized the woman staring back. She felt unfamiliar, as though she had been assembled from fragments that did not quite belong together. She looked broken. Battered. Bruised in ways no one else could see. Her eyes were hollowed out, dimmed by vigilance and grief. Her skin carried the pallor of someone who had learned to live on alert. Her spirit sagged beneath the relentless weight of fear and blame, compressed by years of bracing for impact. I felt as though I were living inside a nightmare. Not the kind that jolts you awake, but the kind that unfolds slowly, convincingly, until it becomes indistinguishable from reality. I was trapped in a version of life that felt unreal yet inescapable, a private hell that had not arrived in flames but had crept in quietly, day by day, until it passed itself off as normal. I moved through it numbly, adapting, enduring, telling myself this was simply how things were. The messages my husband fed me echoed endlessly in my mind, looping like an incantation I could not silence. They reverberated through ordinary moments, through quiet pauses, through the space between breaths. They reminded me again and again of what he had taught me to believe: that I was worthless. Inadequate. Fundamentally flawed. Each repetition pressed the belief deeper, until it no longer felt like something I had been told, but something I had discovered about myself.

Over time, those words stopped sounding like his voice and began to sound like my own. They adopted my cadence. They wore my tone. They presented themselves as insight rather than injury. I became convinced that I was unlovable. Unworthy. Unimportant. The conclusion felt airtight, supported by years of carefully curated evidence. And in believing that lie, I receded further into the shadow he had cast, mistaking darkness for truth. I did not realize then that disappearance was a learned response. That shrinking was a strategy. That the voice condemning me had been planted, rehearsed, and reinforced until it masqueraded as self-knowledge. I did not yet see that what sounded like my inner voice was an echo of control, not the sound of my own knowing. But even then, beneath the distortion, something remained. A quiet, unextinguished part of me that still noticed the wrongness of it all. A part that watched the mirror and wondered, however faintly, where the woman I once knew had gone. And that wondering, fragile as it was, marked the beginning of remembering that the voice telling me I was nothing had never truly been mine to begin with.

As I tried to navigate the treacherous waters of my marriage, I was also fighting simply to stay afloat inside myself. Two battles running in parallel, both exhausting, both unseen. My inner world had become a turbulent sea, swollen with sadness, hopelessness, and despair. The emotions did not arrive gently. They came in relentless waves, crashing without rhythm or mercy, and I felt myself drowning beneath their weight, pulled under again and again by a pain that offered no shoreline, no place to rest my feet. Somewhere along the way, I lost touch with myself. Not all at once. Not dramatically. But gradually, the way one loses sensation in a limb held too long in the cold. My own needs grew quiet. My desires blurred. My feelings became unreliable, something to be managed rather than trusted. I no longer knew how to listen inward, how to recognize my own worth or value without immediately questioning it. The internal compass that once guided me had spun itself dizzy and fallen silent. I existed, but only as an echo of who I once was. A reverberation without a source. A presence without substance. I moved through life responding rather than choosing, reacting rather than initiating, my edges softened until they disappeared. I had become a puppet on strings, my husband the unseen hand above, pulling each thread with careful precision. Every movement. Every reaction. Every choice felt dictated. Autonomy slipped away so slowly I did not notice it leaving. I was no longer a partner. I was a marionette. Reduced to little more than a servant in every sense of the word. Physical. Emotional. Mental. My body available. My emotions regulated to suit his comfort. My thoughts filtered for acceptability. I bent myself into impossible shapes to meet his every wish, every demand, contorting around expectations that shifted just as I learned to meet them. I chased a perfection that was never enough, one that receded the moment I drew close, leaving me forever reaching, forever lacking.

And with each attempt, something was erased. A boundary dissolved. A preference dismissed. A truth swallowed. Piece by piece, I disappeared, sanding myself down until there was barely anything left to resist with. What I called devotion was self-erasure. What I called compromise was abandonment of self. I did not realize then that I was vanishing in order to survive, that my disappearance was not apathy, but adaptation. The sea inside me kept rising. The strings kept tightening. And still, some small, submerged part of me kept breathing, even underwater, waiting for the moment when survival would no longer require me to disappear at all. Then came the final blow. The affair between my husband and my best friend. A betrayal so deep it did not remain an idea. It became sensation. It struck my body like a fist driven into my gut, knocking the breath from my lungs and leaving me gasping, stunned, bent forward by a pain that demanded attention.

The hurt was immediate and excruciating, sharp and disorienting, as though something essential had been torn loose without warning. I could not comprehend it. Not at first. Not even later, fully. How the person I had loved, trusted, vowed my life to, could turn against me so completely. How the woman I had called sister in all but blood, the keeper of my confidences, could so carelessly dismantle not only my marriage, but the sanctuary of friendship I believed we shared. Two pillars collapsed at once, and the structure of my world caved inward. The hurt and anger surged hot and uncontainable, colliding with disbelief and grief in a storm I could not outrun. Rage flared. Sorrow followed. Then shock. Then a numbness so thick it felt unreal. I replayed every memory, every conversation, every shared laugh and quiet exchange, searching for signs I had missed, cracks I should have seen, answers that might make the betrayal make sense. But there were none. No revelation that softened the blow. No explanation that restored order. Only the raw, undeniable knowledge that something sacred had been violated. Something built on trust, on intimacy, on shared history, had been broken beyond recognition. What I lost was not only people, but safety itself. The belief that closeness meant protection. That love and loyalty traveled together. I was left standing in the wreckage, surrounded by fragments of a life I thought I knew, struggling to breathe in a world that suddenly felt even more unsafe than before. The ground beneath me shifted again, and this time there was no illusion left to fall back on. The truth stood exposed, brutal and unmistakable. And in the silence that followed, as the dust settled and the pain pulsed through every part of me, I realized this was not just an ending. It was a rupture. One that would force me, at last, to see what I had been surviving all along. With distance, with breath, with time, I can see something I could not then. Clarity did not arrive all at once. It seeped in slowly, like light through a crack I hadn't known existed. I can see now that my best friend, too, was caught in his gravity, pulled into the same relentless orbit that had held me for so long. She did not step into betrayal in a single moment. She was drawn in. Gradually entangled. Made into a pawn in his careful, calculated game of control and power.

He fed her the same distorted narrative he fed me. A story revised to suit his needs. One where I was the problem. The flawed one. The unstable one. The source of all the tension and pain. He spoke it with conviction, with practiced sincerity, until it sounded less like accusation and more like truth. And she believed it. She absorbed it fully, hook, line, and sinker, until it reshaped how she saw me, how she explained her choices to herself, how she justified what followed. The lie did not need to shout. It only needed to repeat. Seen from this distance, the affair was never an isolated act. It was not a sudden moral failure or a spontaneous collapse of boundaries. It was a symptom. A visible eruption of a deeper sickness that had been festering beneath the surface of our relationship for years. It exposed what had always been there: his disregard for me, his profound lack of empathy, his willingness to fracture lives if it meant preserving his sense of power and control. What broke was not just trust, but the illusion that I had been safe with him at all. And yet, even as everything unraveled, I struggled to see it clearly. Trauma does that. It blurs edges. It bends perception. It keeps the mind tethered to old explanations long after they stop making sense. I was still standing too close to the wreckage, breathing in the dust, trying to understand devastation from inside the collapse. I searched for meaning in the wrong places. I blamed myself. I tried to make their choices say something about my worth, because that was the language I had been taught to speak. Only later did the fuller picture emerge. What I mistook for personal failure was the aftermath of manipulation. What I read as rejection was the residue of a system designed to isolate and control. The betrayal was real. The pain was real. But it was not proof of my inadequacy. It was evidence of a dynamic that fed on distortion and thrived in secrecy. Seeing this did not absolve the harm. It contextualized it. And in that context, something inside me finally began to loosen its grip. He spun his web tighter still, strand by careful strand, layering lie upon lie until the air itself felt sticky with distortion. Blame was turned back toward me with practiced ease, angled so convincingly it almost felt logical.

He convinced me that his betrayal was somehow my fault. That I had driven him to it. Or worse, that it had never truly happened at all. That I was imagining it. Projecting my own insecurity. Misreading reality once again, as I so often did, according to him. His manipulation was not loud. It did not announce itself with cruelty alone. It was insidious. Quiet. Precise. A surgeon's hand rather than a blunt instrument. And even with the truth standing plainly in front of me, undeniable and raw, I doubted my own eyes. I replayed conversations. I rewound memories. I questioned details I knew were real. I interrogated my instincts until they fell silent under the weight of self-doubt. I questioned my memory. My judgment. My sanity. The ground beneath me felt unstable, as though reality itself were shifting, tilting, rearranging while I stood on it. What had once felt solid dissolved into uncertainty. What I knew became suspect. What I felt required justification. I was no longer standing on truth, but on quicksand made of questions and second-guessing. And in that disorientation, his greatest victory took shape, though I could not yet fully name it. He had taught me to mistrust myself more than I mistrusted him. That was the final inversion. The most devastating sleight of hand. He did not need to convince me he was innocent. He only needed to convince me that I was unreliable. Once that belief took root, everything else followed naturally. His words carried weight. Mine evaporated. His version of events became plausible. Mine became suspect by default. I did not yet see how profound that theft was. Because when a person is stripped of trust in their own perception, they are left unmoored. Easy to steer. Easy to silence. Easy to convince that even their pain requires permission to exist. And standing there, suspended between what I felt and what I was told to believe, I did not realize that the most dangerous lie was not about the affair at all. It was the lie that I could not trust myself to know the truth.

It wasn't until I hit rock bottom, when the pain and suffering became too heavy to carry another step, that clarity finally arrived. Not gently. Not mercifully. But with the blunt finality of gravity. I had been falling for a long time, mistaking endurance for strength, mistaking survival for resilience, telling myself that if I could just keep going, it would somehow mean I was winning. But the truth is, I had been in freefall long before I recognized the descent. And then the ground rose up to meet me, sudden and unforgiving, and there was nowhere left to go but inward. In that breaking open came a reckoning. The diagnosis of Major Depressive Disorder, something that had been quietly simmering beneath the surface for years, did not arrive as a shock. It landed with a grim familiarity, a terrible kind of recognition. It named what my body and mind had been trying to communicate all along. It gave language to the heaviness, the fog, the relentless exhaustion. It offered a missing piece of the puzzle I had been trying to solve by blaming myself. And with that naming, something unexpected happened. I was not irreparably damaged. I was not fundamentally defective. I was wounded. Broken in places, yes. Fractured. Weakened. But not beyond repair. That understanding shifted the lens through which I saw everything. The story rearranged itself. The narrative softened its cruelty. It was never only about his abuse, devastating as that was. It was also about the pre-existing fractures within me, the unseen vulnerabilities formed long before I met him. The places where care had been absent. The places where worth had been conditional. The places that had learned to survive by bending. My depression did not begin with the affair. It preceded it. It lived quietly beneath the surface, shaping my perceptions, softening my boundaries, dimming my instincts, teaching me to doubt myself long before he ever gave me reason to. It left me exposed. It left doors unlocked inside me that I did not yet know how to protect. And through those open doorways, his manipulation entered. Not because I invited it. Not because I deserved it. But because I was already wounded and had not yet learned how to tend my own injuries. Seeing this did not absolve him. It did not dilute responsibility. But it returned something essential to me. Context. Compassion. A framework that allowed me to understand my collapse not as failure, but as consequence. I had not fallen because I was weak. I had fallen because I had been carrying too much, for too long, without support.

And in recognizing that truth, even at the lowest point, the direction of my fall began, at last, to change. Depression amplified my co-dependency, tightening its grip with quiet authority, convincing me that survival depended on attachment at any cost. It blurred the line between connection and captivity, whispering that being held, even painfully, was better than standing alone. It made me more vulnerable to his control, more willing to overlook the warning signs etched into my own discomfort, more inclined to rationalize cruelty and reinterpret harm as misunderstanding. Red flags softened into shades of gray. Intuition dimmed. What should have alarmed me instead became something to manage, excuse, endure. It trained me to turn inward with blame. To reflexively search myself for error. To assume responsibility for his actions, his moods, his betrayals. It taught me to believe that if I were better, quieter, easier to love, the pain would finally stop. That love was something to be perfected through self-erasure. That relief could be earned through compliance. Each compromise felt necessary. Each self-abandonment felt justified. Seeing this did not erase the damage. It did not mend what had been torn or return what had been taken. But it brought clarity. A clearing in the fog. The darkness I carried was not a personal failure, not a moral shortcoming or a deficit of character. It was a condition that had gone unnamed for too long, shaping my choices from the shadows, distorting my sense of agency and worth. And in naming it, something loosened. Understanding how depression had been used against me did not make the past disappear, but it returned authorship. It reframed survival not as weakness, but as adaptation under pressure. It allowed compassion to enter places that had been governed by shame. Slowly, tentatively, the possibility of healing began to take shape. Not as a promise of immediate relief, but as a quiet opening. A sense that what had been tightened could be eased. What had been obscured could be seen. What had been used to keep me bound could, with care, become the very ground from which I would begin to stand.

The diagnosis arrived carrying two truths at once. It was relief, and it was reckoning. A true wake-up call that did not shake me violently, but settled over me with a quiet, undeniable weight. It was validation. A steady voice saying, "*What you have lived through is real. You are not exaggerating. You are not dramatizing. You are not grasping for attention.*" The pain had substance. It had context. It had a name. And in naming it, something loosened. The word itself did not heal me. But it interrupted the narrative that I was simply weak or defective. It named the storm that had been raging inside me for years, and by doing so, it thinned the fog just enough for me to take a full breath. For the first time in a long time, I felt oxygen reach the places that had been starved of it. It became a turning point. Not dramatic. Not triumphant. But steady. A small flicker of light in a landscape that had known only shadow. That flicker did not banish the darkness. But it proved light was possible. At last, I had a name for the thing. The monster that had been living inside me was no longer some shapeless force of shame and self-loathing. It had form. It had symptoms. It had history. I could begin to understand the relentless self-criticism, the ache of inadequacy that followed me like a shadow, the bone-deep exhaustion of carrying so much unseen weight. This was never about accepting a label as a life sentence. It was about tracing the roots of my suffering. Following the pain backward through trauma, through neglect, through years of learned self-erasure. It was about seeking help not to be fixed like something broken beyond use, but to be understood as something wounded and deserving of care. Working with a sponsor became a lifeline. A steady hand in turbulent water. A place of safety where I could begin to untangle the tightly knotted years of emotional neglect and abuse. With her, I did not have to defend my reality. I did not have to minimize what hurt. I could speak plainly and be met with steadiness instead of distortion. The process was slow. Often painful. A careful peeling back of layers of denial and self-deception I had worn like armor. Each layer had once protected me. Each layer had once helped me survive. And now, removing them felt both terrifying and necessary. Beneath them lay grief. Rage. Shame. But also, truth. And beneath truth, something even more fragile. A self that had never truly disappeared. A self-waiting, quietly, to be reclaimed. What emerged was not a simple story. It refused neat edges or tidy conclusions. It was a tapestry, intricately woven with threads of betrayal, manipulation, grief, and self-destruction. Some threads dark and coarse. Others fine and nearly invisible. All of them intertwined. It was a story steeped in shadow, yes, but also layered with complexity, with history, with survival strategies that had once made sense. It was the story of a woman lost in the labyrinth of her own mind, wandering corridors lined with doubt and fear, retracing steps she did not remember choosing, searching for a doorway back to herself. Every turn felt familiar yet disorienting. Every echo sounded like truth. And somewhere in the center of that maze, I stood exhausted, unsure whether I was the architect or the captive. The affair stood as the dramatic climax, the moment everything shattered into visibility. The explosion that forced what had been hidden into the open. But it was never the root. It was the culmination. The visible fracture after countless invisible breaks. Years of insidious emotional and mental abuse had laid the groundwork long before that final rupture. The affair was not the beginning of the collapse. It was the point where the cracks could no longer be disguised.

The deeper truth about my marriage was not only about infidelity, abuse, or cruelty. It was about the long journey home. A journey back to myself. A journey of self-discovery, healing, and reclamation. Of peeling away narratives that had been forced upon me and asking, gently but firmly, "*Who am I beneath all of this?*" It was about taking back authorship. Rewriting the story I had been made to inhabit. Reframing myself not as the damaged, defective woman he insisted I was, but as someone who had survived prolonged harm with a heart that still, somehow, wanted to heal. I began to see myself differently. Not as broken beyond repair, but as resilient. Not as flawed at my core, but as whole in ways I had never been allowed to recognize. Not as unworthy, but as deserving of love, safety, and joy without bargaining for them. Leaving him was not easy. The illusions lingered like smoke after a fire. The old messages still clawed for space in my mind, rehearsed and ready. The victim mindset, so carefully conditioned over years, resisted release. It felt safer to blame myself than to accept how deeply I had been manipulated. Freedom can feel terrifying when captivity has been normalized. But leaving was also the most liberating act of my life. It was the moment the narrative shifted. The moment the story stopped being solely about what had been done to me and began, at last, to be about who I chose to become. It was the first step in a new direction, shaky and uncertain, but mine. The labyrinth did not disappear overnight. But I was no longer wandering without awareness. I was walking it with intention, tracing my way not deeper into darkness, but outward—toward light, toward truth, toward a self that had been waiting patiently to be reclaimed. Clarity did not lift me out of the darkness overnight. Insight is not an elevator. It is a lantern. It shows you the path, but it does not carry you along it. The climb stretched before me like a steep and unforgiving ascent, a slow, painstaking journey out of the abyss I had called home for far too long. The air was thinner here. The ground uneven. My muscles trembled from years of bracing, unsure how to move without fear.

There were days when each step felt impossible. Days when memory pressed against my ribs like a stone, when regret whispered that I should have known, should have seen, should have left sooner. The weight of what had happened threatened to drag me back down into familiar darkness. Healing did not move in straight lines. It spiraled. It circled back. It forced me to revisit terrain I had hoped to leave behind. But still, I climbed. Every tear shed. Every hour spent fighting for myself. Every moment I chose not to return to the lie. It has been worth it. The truth, though painful, carried a strange and fierce beauty. It was sharp, yes. It cut through illusion. But it also illuminated. It stripped away distortion and left something clean and undeniable beneath it. Truth did not promise comfort. It offered freedom. And in time, that freedom began to feel steadier than the false safety I had once clung to. My work with my sponsor was essential. She stood beside me in the excavation, not flinching when the ground gave way. Together, we peeled back the layers of deception. Not only the lies imposed on me from the outside, but the ones I had internalized and rehearsed until they sounded like fact. We examined them gently but thoroughly. *"Where did this belief begin? Who taught me this? Whose voice is this, really?"* I had to face the ghosts of my past. To sit with the wounds, I had long ignored. To acknowledge how early hunger for love had shaped my tolerance for harm. To see clearly how vulnerability had been exploited without turning that clarity into self-condemnation. I had to forgive myself for the role I played in my own suffering; not out of blame, but out of understanding. That forgiveness was not instant. It did not arrive in a single revelation or a grand emotional release. It was earned slowly, through honesty. Through compassion. Through the radical act of speaking to myself with kindness instead of contempt. Each time I chose to say, "*You did the best you could with what you knew*", another stone was lifted from my chest. Forgiveness did not excuse what happened. It liberated me from carrying it as evidence of my worth. And with each step upward, breath steadier, shoulders lighter, I began to understand something essential. Healing is not about erasing the past. It is about reclaiming yourself from it. Learning to identify and challenge the insidious whispers of self-doubt has not been a single revelation. It has been an ongoing, deliberate confrontation.

Those voices do not slip away politely when exposed. They resist. They return. They attempt to reclaim familiar territory. Each one must be met. Named. Questioned. Dismantled with patience rather than panic. The old narrative does not surrender easily. There are days when it still tries to slip back into the room, dressed in urgency, insisting it is only trying to protect me. But now I recognize its tone. I hear the distortion beneath its certainty. And instead of absorbing it as truth, I pause. I examine it. I ask, "*Whose voice is this? Is it kind? Is it accurate?"* Sometimes the answer is immediate. Sometimes it takes effort. But the act of questioning alone weakens its hold. Replacing negative self-talk with affirmations of self-worth has been deliberate work. Intentional. At times awkward, even uncomfortable. Speaking kindly to myself once felt unnatural, as though I were reading lines from a script that did not belong to me. But repetition reshapes belief. And slowly, the new language began to settle in. Not as grand declarations, but as quiet corrections. *"I am allowed to take up space! My feelings are valid! I deserve safety and respect!"* These affirmations are not magic. They are maintenance. They are the daily tending of ground that was once scorched. It has required conscious effort. Daily self-care. A steadfast commitment to rebuilding a sense of self that had been dismantled piece by piece. Some days, that rebuilding feels steady. Other days, it feels fragile. But even fragility, I am learning, is a form of courage. The road ahead is still long. Still uncertain in places. There are stretches where the path narrows, where old memories attempt to pull me backward. But I walk it now differently. With awareness. With intention. With a renewed sense of hope that does not deny the darkness but refuses to live inside it. I am learning to recognize manipulation before it roots itself. I am learning to trust the early discomfort, the subtle tightening in my chest that signals something is not right. I am learning to set boundaries without apology, without elaborate justification. To say no and let it stand. To let silence follow without rushing to fill it.

I am learning to prioritize my well-being not as indulgence, not as selfishness, but as necessity. As survival in its healthiest form. The scars remain. Yes. But they no longer define me. They are no longer proof of weakness. They are evidence of endurance. Of battles survived. Of nights endured when I did not think I could make it to morning. They trace the map of where I have been, not where I must stay. And slowly, those scars are being accompanied by something else. Something steadier. A growing resilience. A strength that does not shout or perform. A quiet, grounded power that comes from knowing myself again. I am no longer climbing out of the well in desperation. I am walking forward in reclamation. The truth, finally, is larger than the story of an abusive narcissist or the betrayal of a friend. Larger than the affair. Larger than the lies. Larger even than the wounds themselves. Those chapters matter, but they are not the whole book. The deeper truth is about awakening. About the power of self-awareness rising like dawn after a long, punishing night. About the courage it takes to say, "*Something is wrong*", and then to keep walking toward help anyway. It is about the extraordinary capacity within each of us to heal and rediscover ourselves, even after we have been scattered into fragments. Healing is not dramatic. It is not always visible. It is often quiet, repetitive, and deliberate. But it is powerful. It is the steady act of choosing truth over distortion. Compassion over condemnation. Growth over familiarity. It is about reclaiming my narrative. For so long, my story had been edited by someone else's hand. Revised. Redacted. Reframed to serve their power. Now, I hold the pen. Now, the ink is my own. I am no longer writing from shame, blame, or fear. I am writing from clarity. From ownership. From power, no longer victimhood or powerlessness. From a place that understands that survival is not weakness, and vulnerability is not a flaw. It is about choosing a future where love is genuine. Where respect is not conditional. Where tenderness does not come with strings attached. Where my worth is not measured by someone else's approval, mood, or validation. It is about standing in relationships that feel like partnership rather than performance. Safety rather than suspense. The truth is simple. And it took everything to believe it. I am worthy. Not because I endured. Not because I healed perfectly. Not because I proved anything to anyone. I am worthy because I exist. That truth does not roar. It does not demand applause. It settles into the bones. It steadies the breath. It anchors the spine. And once it takes root, it changes everything. It is the most liberating truth I have ever known. And it is the one I will never surrender again.

Let's break it down more:

From Broken to Whole: My Journey of Self-Discovery and Empowerment

And so, the story turns inward again. As I sit here now, reflecting on the terrain I have crossed, I am struck by the realization that changed everything for me: I did not have to carry the weight of my past forever. That truth did not arrive softly. It did not tiptoe in. It came like a crack of light splitting through a door I had long believed was sealed shut, a sudden fracture in the narrative that had held me captive for years. For so long, I believed endurance was my only option. That the pain was permanent. That the shame belonged to me. But in that flash of clarity, something shifted. I began to understand, with painful and humbling clarity, the profound power our beliefs hold over the way we experience reality. What we accept as truth becomes the architecture of our inner world. It shapes the walls we build. The ceilings we live beneath. The windows we allow ourselves to look through. For years, I carried burdens that threatened to consume me, convinced they were mine by right. The weight of shame pressed against my chest like stone. The heaviness of guilt settled into my shoulders as though I had earned it. The echoing messages of worthlessness and unlovability reverberated through my mind so persistently that they felt etched into my bones, as though they were part of my very structure.

But they were not mine to bear. They were inherited distortions. Beliefs planted in soil I did not prepare. Seeds sown by toxic relationships and unhealthy environments. Watered by fear. Fertilized by neglect. I did not invent those lies. I absorbed them. I internalized them until they felt indistinguishable from identity. And for a long time, I mistook those lies for truth. I mistook survival for flaw. I mistook trauma for character. I mistook manipulation for reality. But once the crack of light appeared, once I allowed even the smallest possibility that these beliefs might not be absolute, the entire structure began to tremble. If what I believed about myself had been shaped by distortion, then perhaps it could also be reshaped by truth. That realization was not comfortable. It required me to question everything I thought I knew about myself. It required me to dismantle the architecture of shame and examine each beam, each pillar, asking, *"Is this really mine? Or was it placed here by someone else?"* The journey from broken to whole was not about becoming someone new. It was about excavating the person who had been buried beneath years of inherited falsehoods. It was about reclaiming my narrative. Rewriting the script in ink that was finally my own. It was about understanding that empowerment does not arrive as dominance or defiance, but as quiet sovereignty over one's own story. I am not who I was when I believed those lies. And I am not broken in the way I once thought. I am whole, not because I was never fractured, but because I have gathered the pieces and chosen to see them not as evidence of defect, but as evidence of survival. And from that place, from that reclaimed ground, something stronger than shame has begun to grow. Self-trust. Self-respect. Self-love. Not loud. Not performative. But steady. And for the first time, it feels like home. However, it took a journey of really going into the places where I faced the deepest pain, the places where: The pain felt insurmountable. Like a mountain range rising without horizon, jagged and merciless. The hurt felt permanent, as though it had settled into the marrow of my bones. The trauma felt defining, like a brand pressed into my identity, something that marked me beyond repair. But slowly, almost imperceptibly at first, I began to see that these were burdens I had the power to release. Not erase. Not deny. Not pretend they had never happened. Release. They were stories I had been told about myself.

Narratives written in moments of harm, reinforced in silence, repeated in fear. And I had internalized them. I had rehearsed them. Even worse, I kept performing them in life. I had shaped my life around them until they felt like the only possible version of who I was. The story of being too much. The story of not being enough. The story of being fundamentally flawed. But insight alone did not carry me to this realization. It was collapse. It was rock bottom. It was the moment when the illusion that disappearing was the only answer shattered under the unbearable weight of consequence. I will not romanticize that place. It was not poetic. It was not noble. It was devastation. It was raw and terrifying and stripped of all illusion. It was standing at the edge of myself and realizing that there was no further to fall without losing everything. And in that absolute breaking, something unexpected happened. The narrative fractured. The belief that I had no choice dissolved in the harsh light of survival. The illusion that escape meant vanishing was exposed for what it was, a distortion born of unbearable pain. In that space, stripped of pretense, I encountered a different kind of truth. Empowerment did not mean control. It did not mean perfection. It did not mean never feeling pain again. It meant recognizing that even in my most fractured state, even when I felt reduced to fragments and ash, I still had agency. I still had choice. Not grand, sweeping choices. Not dramatic declarations. But small ones. Breath by breath. Moment by moment. The choice to stay. The choice to ask for help. The choice to believe that my story was not finished simply because it hurt beyond measure. In that place, empowerment was not loud. It was quiet. It was the stubborn refusal to surrender authorship. It was the realization that I could not control what had been done to me, but I could choose how I would respond from here forward. That shift did not erase the trauma.

But it transformed it from a life sentence into a chapter. And for the first time, I began to understand that brokenness and agency can exist in the same body. That fracture does not eliminate choice. That even shattered glass can catch the light. And I chose. To stay. To heal. To live. Rock bottom was not the end of me. It felt like an ending. It felt like the floor had vanished, and I had collided with the final truth of my own fragility. But it was not annihilation. It was exposure. It was the place where the false narratives that had ruled my life began, finally, to loosen their grip. The lies that had once felt welded to my identity began to crack under the weight of reality. It was there that I first glimpsed the possibility that being broken did not mean being beyond repair. That fracture was not finality. That shattered did not mean worthless. I began to understand that I could gather the scattered pieces of myself, not to recreate the woman I had been before the breaking, but to become someone forged through it. Someone stronger. Someone wiser. Someone no longer defined by the lies she once mistook for truth. That was the beginning of wholeness. Not a sudden restoration. Not a miraculous reassembly. A conscious reclamation. It was the slow, deliberate act of picking up each fragment and asking, *"Does this belong to me?" Or "was it placed here by someone else?"* It was choosing what to keep. What to release. What to transform. It was rebuilding not the old architecture of self, but something sturdier, rooted in awareness rather than fear. And in that reclamation, I felt the quiet, steady birth of empowerment. Not loud. Not triumphant. But grounded. A pulse returning to a limb long numb. A spine straightening after years of bending. Outside, the wind howled a mournful tune, its cry rising and falling like grief given voice. It rattled the windows, tugged at the trees, and mirrored the tempest that churned inside me. I stood at the window and watched the leaves whirl in restless spirals, brown and crimson fragments caught in motion, a living kaleidoscope reflecting the chaotic jumble of thoughts and emotions that had plagued me for so long.

Everything felt unanchored. Unstable. As though the world itself were spinning too fast to steady. And yet, even in the storm, something was different. The wind could howl. The leaves could scatter. The sky could darken. But I was no longer being swept away without awareness. I stood there, breathing, feeling the ground beneath my feet. The storm outside no longer dictated the storm within. The chaos was real, but it was no longer my identity. It was weather. It was movement. It was part of a season. Rock bottom had stripped me of illusion. But it had also revealed something unshakable. The ability to stand. And from that stillness, from that reclaimed ground, I began to understand that empowerment is not about controlling the storm. It is about knowing you can remain standing while it passes. *"Was I truly incapable of handling pain?"* The question did not arrive gently. It gnawed at me, a dull, persistent ache that refused to loosen its grip. It pressed against my ribs as though it were trying to break through bone. It sat heavy in my throat, thick and unspoken, demanding an answer I did not yet have the strength to give. The pills and the whiskey bottle rested cold against my skin, their chill a stark and unsettling counterpoint to the burning inferno raging within me. That coldness felt almost surgical. Clinical. Detached. While inside, despair roared like a house set ablaze. The contrast was surreal, the outer stillness clashing against years of accumulated pain that had been smoldering beneath the surface, quietly, relentlessly. That night, the darkness felt absolute. Not simply the absence of light, but a suffocating blanket woven from unspoken grief, unhealed wounds. And a profound sense of worthlessness that had followed me like a shadow for as long as I could remember. It was thick. Dense. The kind of darkness that does not just surround you but enters you, settling into the lungs, making breath feel borrowed. And yet, even in that moment, there was something important I understand now. It was not a sudden impulse that led me there.

It was not one catastrophic argument. Not one singular betrayal. Not one isolated collapse. My suicide attempt was not born in a flash of chaos. It was the culmination of years, of a lifetime, of carrying burdens I never should have been asked to bear. Of absorbing shame that was never mine. Of believing lies, I had no business accepting as truth. It was exhaustion masquerading as solution. It was hopelessness distorted into logic. It was pain asking for relief in the only language it thought remained. In that darkness, I believed I was incapable of handling pain. But the truth, one thing I could not see then, is that I had been handling pain for far too long. I had endured more than anyone should quietly endure. The question was never about my capacity. It was about the weight I had been carrying alone. That night did not define me. It revealed the depth of my suffering. It exposed how desperately I needed support, understanding, and care. It showed me that I was not weak, but overwhelmed. Not incapable, but depleted. Not broken beyond repair, but breaking under a load no human being is meant to shoulder in isolation. The darkness felt absolute then. But it was not infinite. And even in that cold, suffocating night, somewhere beneath the despair, there remained a flicker, small, almost imperceptible, that refused to go out. That flicker was not strength in the way I once imagined it. It was survival. And it stayed. *"Was I incapable of handling the pain?"* I know now the answer is a resounding no. I was not incapable. I was not weak. I was not defective. I was trapped inside a narrative so convincing, so thoroughly rehearsed, that it felt like reality itself. A story that insisted I had no power, no agency, no way to alter the suffocating circumstances around me. I believed the cage was permanent because I could not yet see the door. I mistook invisibility for impossibility. I mistook exhaustion for failure. That night did not prove my weakness. It revealed the depth of my depletion.

It showed how long I had been fighting silently, how fiercely I had been enduring, without understanding that I was allowed to set down what was never mine to carry. I had been gripping shame as though it were responsibility. I had been clutching blame as though it were penance. I did not yet know that I could release it without forfeiting my strength. And in surviving that darkness, something radical began to stir. Not loudly. Not triumphantly. But unmistakably. I began to sense that pain does not mean incapacity. That being overwhelmed does not mean being incapable. That drowning and exhaustion are not proof of weakness—they are proof that the waters were too deep to navigate alone. Even in the most desperate hour, there was still a part of me that wanted to live. A quiet ember refusing extinction. A pulse that whispered, "*Choose differently*". A fragment of self that had not surrendered to oblivion, even when oblivion felt like relief. The storm outside eventually passed. The wind lost its fury. The sky, stubborn and steady, began to clear. The winds inside me did not quiet immediately. They churned. They resisted. They lingered. But something fundamental had shifted. The question changed. No longer, "*Am I incapable?*" But, "*What if I am stronger than I've been taught to believe?*" That question did not accuse. It invited. It opened space where there had only been confinement. It suggested possibility where there had only been conclusion. *"What if the cage was not permanent? What if the door had always been there? What if strength was not the absence of pain, but the willingness to face it?"* That night marked the beginning of a different kind of awakening. Not one that denied the darkness, but one that recognized I had survived it. And survival is not small. It is evidence. Evidence that somewhere beneath the narratives, beneath the shame, beneath the exhaustion, there was a self still reaching. And that reaching, however fragile, was power. Arriving at that truth was not gentle. It did not unfold like a sunrise. It tore through me like a fault line splitting open ground I thought was solid. It was brutal. Agonizing. A reckoning that very nearly ended my story before it had the chance to begin again. There was nothing romantic about it. Nothing poetic in the moment itself. Only raw, unfiltered confrontation with the depth of my own despair.

My suicide attempt was not a dramatic flourish. It was not spectacle. It was not a performance of sorrow. It was a desperate cry for escape from a maze I did not know how to navigate. A labyrinth whose walls had grown so high and narrow that the sky felt imaginary. I did not see a map. I did not see a guide. I saw only endless corridors looping back into the same dead ends. It was a stark, unforgiving wake-up call. A rupture in the timeline of my life. That night cleaved my existence in two. Before and after. The broken, despairing woman I had been, lost, exhausted, convinced she had reached the edge of herself, stood on one side. And on the other, slowly and painfully emerging, was a woman gathering her scattered pieces with trembling hands. Not confident. Not whole yet. But conscious. Awake to the truth that something had to change. The rupture was violent in its clarity. It forced me to see that the path I had been walking led only deeper into darkness. It forced me to confront the cost of believing the lies I had internalized. It forced me to admit that I had been surviving inside a narrative that was strangling me. And yet, hidden beneath the wreckage, beneath the shame and the shock and the grief, was something I had long forgotten. The power had been within me all along. It had not vanished. It had not died. It had simply gone dormant. Buried under sedimented layers of self-doubt. Covered by beliefs that had hardened over time, calcifying into false truths I mistook for identity. Each lie had settled like dust after a storm, accumulating until I could no longer see what lay beneath. But beneath the rubble, something remained. Quiet. Patient. Unextinguished. It did not scream for attention. It did not demand recognition. It waited. It endured. It held the faint memory of who I was before the distortion.

The part of me that knew how to choose, how to resist, how to hope. That night did not create my strength. It uncovered it. And in the aftermath, amid trembling hands and blurred vision and a heart still pounding with consequence, I began to realize that the woman who had nearly disappeared was not weak. She was buried. And buried things, when uncovered, can breathe again. The aftermath of that desperate act became a fragile awakening, like surfacing slowly from a long, suffocating sleep. Not the kind of waking that feels rested or clear, but the kind where your lungs burn and your body trembles as it remembers how to breathe. Reality returned in fragments. The bedroom ceiling. The grass beneath me. The hazy silhouettes of faces leaning over mine. The distant echo of voices, urgent and afraid. And then the chilling, undeniable realization of what I had almost done. Those images etched themselves into my memory. Not as shame. But as catalyst. They were not there to condemn me. They were there to confront me. To draw a line in the sand between illusion and consequence. They marked the moment when denial could no longer survive. When the story I had been telling myself, about worthlessness, about being a burden, about having no way out, collapsed under the undeniable truth that I was still here. Still breathing. Still alive. The story leading up to that night was never simple. It was not a single thread pulled too tight. It was a tapestry woven tightly with strands of toxic relationships, inherited shame, and relentless self-doubt. Each thread reinforcing the other. Each pattern repeating across years, I had never fully examined. My marriage had been the final, crushing weight. It did not create the fractures within me. It did not invent my vulnerability. But it exploited those cracks mercilessly. It pressed into them. Widened them. Leveraged them until they threatened to split me apart entirely. Brick by painstaking brick, he dismantled my self-worth, chipping away at it with accusation, distortion, and control until I believed I was nothing more than a hollow shell.

Flawed. Unlovable. Disposable. That belief did not arrive in one blow. It was constructed carefully, reinforced daily. It echoed long enough that I began to accept it as fact. I did not see how thoroughly I had been conditioned to measure myself through his contempt. But lying there, suspended between what had almost been and what still was, something else became undeniable. If I had been hollow, I would not have survived. If I had truly been nothing, there would have been nothing left to awaken. The fact that I could feel regret. That I could feel fear. That I could feel the tremor of relief at still being here, those were not signs of emptiness. They were signs of life. Of depth. Of a self that had not been erased, only buried beneath years of distortion. The aftermath was not neat. It was not triumphant. But it was honest. And honesty, however fragile, became the first real foundation I had stood on in years. He built a prison with deliberate care. Not hastily. Not carelessly. It was constructed slowly, methodically, with the patience of someone who understands that control is most effective when it feels self-imposed. Its walls were formed from my insecurities, brick by brick, each one reinforced daily by criticism, manipulation, gaslighting, and subtle cruelty that rarely left visible marks but carved deep into my sense of self. Every comment, every dismissal, every distortion was mortar, sealing the structure tighter. The bars were made of my own distorted beliefs. Beliefs about being too much. About not being enough. About needing to earn love through silence and sacrifice. And the cruelest part was this: I believed I had built it myself. I believed the cage was proof of my flaw. I mistook the architecture of manipulation for personal failure. I did not see the external hands that had shaped the design. I only saw the walls and assumed they were deserved. But the near-loss of my life cracked something open. The illusion fractured. The prison no longer felt invisible. The walls, once seamless with my identity, began to stand out in sharp relief. I could trace their edges. I could see where they had been reinforced.

I could recognize the voice that echoed through them as not entirely my own. And once seen, they could no longer remain unquestioned. That was the beginning. Not of perfection. Not of immediate peace. Not of a sudden and effortless freedom. But of reclamation. It was the moment I stopped accepting the cage as permanent. The moment I realized that even if I had lived within it, I had not authored its construction. And if I had not built it alone, I did not have to remain inside it. The woman who almost disappeared that night did not vanish. She transformed. She stood at the edge of herself and chose, trembling and uncertain, not to step forward into oblivion but to step back into life. From that brink, from that terrifying, clarifying edge, I began the slow, deliberate work of returning to myself. It was not dramatic. It was steady. One boundary. One truth spoken aloud. One lie dismantled at a time. The prison doors did not swing open all at once. But the hinges loosened. The lock weakened. And with each act of awareness, each act of self-trust, the space around me widened. I was not escaping into someone new. I was stepping back into who I had always been before the walls were built. And that return, quiet, intentional, fiercely earned, was freedom in its earliest form.

And inside that prison he built, his words became the mortar. They filled the gaps between insecurity and fear, sealing the walls tighter each time they were spoken. They echoed in the chambers of my mind like a malevolent chorus, insidious and relentless: *"Worthless." "Unlovable." "A mistake."* They did not arrive as careless insults hurled in passing anger. They were crafted as barded wire. Sharpened. Aimed with precision at the most tender, unguarded places within me. They were designed not merely to wound, but to infiltrate. To slip past resistance. To settle into the quiet spaces of my soul and begin their slow, corrosive work. And erosion is patient. It does not demand attention. It does not announce itself with spectacle. It works quietly, steadily, wearing down certainty, softening boundaries, dissolving self-trust grain by grain. Over time, those words stopped sounding like his voice. They took on my cadence. My tone. My rhythm. They became the soundtrack of my thoughts, playing beneath every interaction, every decision, every moment of vulnerability. What had once been external accusation became internal narration. I no longer needed him in the room for the damage to continue. He convinced me that my feelings were burdensome. Irrational. Too much. That my needs were excessive. That my opinions were insignificant. That my very existence required apology. Every argument, every disagreement, every flicker of resistance was twisted, reframed, and returned to me as evidence of my supposed inadequacy. If I protested, I was unstable. If I withdrew, I was cold. If I cried, I was manipulative. If I spoke calmly, I was calculating. No position was safe. No response was right. So I learned to apologize for things I had not done. To soften my voice before I spoke. To doubt my memory when events felt clear. To mistrust my instincts when something felt wrong. I became fluent in self-correction, editing myself in real time to avoid provoking his disapproval. And in doing so, I abandoned myself. I handed over the authority of my own perception. I surrendered the simple right to feel what I felt without justification. I confused compliance with harmony. Silence with peace. But words, no matter how deeply embedded, are not bone. They can feel structural. They can feel permanent. But they are not immutable. They are learned. Repeated. Reinforced. And once I began to recognize them as implants rather than truths, something profound shifted. The chorus did not disappear overnight. But it was no longer unquestioned. I began to interrupt it. To challenge it. To replace it with something unfamiliar but truer. The mortar began to crumble. The walls, once seamless, showed cracks.

Because the voice that once echoed through the prison was never the voice of my worth. It was the sound of control. And control, once named, begins to lose its power. But he was meticulous. Isolation did not happen in a single dramatic severing. It unfolded quietly, strategically, like a room slowly losing air. He nudged friendships into misunderstanding. He sowed subtle doubts about those who cared for me. He framed concern as interference. Loyalty as betrayal. Slowly, imperceptibly, the mirrors around me were removed. Friends drifted. Support weakened. Conversations thinned. And with each quiet subtraction, the narrative tightened. He constructed a world where his version of reality stood uncontested. Without external voices to reflect truth back to me, without alternative perspectives to steady my perception, his interpretation became the only map available. His voice grew louder not because it shouted, but because nothing else was allowed to stand beside it. And in that narrowing world, I began to shrink. My universe contracted to the size of his approval. My confidence dimmed like a light slowly turned down. I second-guessed before I spoke. I rehearsed before I expressed. I scanned for disapproval before I allowed myself to feel. Those insidious words, repeated often enough, began to shift shape. They no longer felt like accusations. They felt like definitions. They slipped beneath the surface of consciousness and settled into identity. It is terrifying how repetition can masquerade as truth. How something spoken often enough begins to feel structural. How distortion, echoed in isolation, can pass for certainty. When a single voice fills every corner of your world, it begins to sound like authority. But even then, beneath the conditioning, beneath the erosion, beneath the chorus of condemnation, something remained. A quiet ember. Small. Faint. Nearly smothered beneath years of doubt and self-blame. But present. It flickered in moments of discomfort I could not fully suppress. In the subtle tightening of my chest when something felt wrong. In the brief, disorienting flashes where I thought, "*This cannot be all there is.*" It did not roar. It did not rebel loudly. It simply endured. Patient. Steady. Waiting. Waiting for the moment I would dare to question the voice that had claimed authority over my worth. Waiting for the crack in the wall. Waiting for the first breath of air that did not come filtered through his narrative. It was never extinguished. And that quiet ember, fragile as it seemed, was stronger than the walls built around it. Because embers, given oxygen, become fire. That ember of defiance began to glow more steadily the moment I finally saw the architecture of what had been done to me. Not just the surface damage, not just the arguments or the betrayals, but the structure beneath it all, the design. Once I could see the scaffolding of manipulation, the blueprint of control, something inside me straightened. Recognition is oxygen to a fading flame. The insidiousness of his manipulation lay in its subtlety. It rarely announced itself with spectacle. It did not always appear as overt physical abuse, though there were countless covert violations woven quietly into the fabric of our daily life. Instead, it moved like slow corrosion, an unseen rust spreading through the foundation of my confidence and self-esteem. It was not the storm that destroys in one violent sweep. It was the drip that weakens stone. He did not have to shout to control me. He only had to whisper. A suggestion here. A raised eyebrow there. A comment disguised as concern. A silence calibrated to wound. He subtly dictated my interactions with friends and family, planting seeds of doubt about those who loved me. *"Are you sure she meant it that way?" "He doesn't really understand you." "They're jealous."* Each sentence small. Plausible. Harmless on its own. But together, they formed a pattern. He undermined any relationship that might offer a perspective different from his own. One by one, my lifelines frayed. Not severed abruptly, frayed. Threads loosened through neglect, through suspicion, through the quiet belief that perhaps distance was safer. And with each thinning connection, his voice grew proportionally stronger. He chipped away at my independence with patient precision. Each comment a tap against stone. Each criticism a hairline fracture. Each carefully timed withdrawal of affection a tightening of the invisible net around me.

When I reached outward, he would retreat. When I retreated, he would return just enough warmth to keep me tethered. I did not notice the tightening at first. It felt gradual. Almost imperceptible. Like the slow closing of a fist around something fragile. I adapted as it narrowed. I made myself smaller to fit the shrinking space. I told myself it was compromise. Love requires adjustment, I thought. Partnership requires sacrifice. But eventually, I found myself standing in the center of a life that felt unfamiliar. Isolated. Unbearably small. The rooms felt narrower. The conversations thinner. The laughter less frequent. The mirror reflected someone I did not fully recognize. I felt utterly lost. Utterly alone. And yet, that ember within me, no longer barely visible, burned brighter in the recognition of that loneliness. Because loneliness named the truth: I had been separated from myself. Seeing the corrosion did not immediately rebuild what had been weakened. But it stopped the spread. And in that halting, in that moment of clarity, the flame inside me found more air. The architecture had been revealed. And once you see the structure of a cage, you begin to look for its door. And yet, beneath that loneliness, beneath the hollow ache of isolation, something began to stir. The truth, the liberating truth, did not arrive like lightning splitting the sky. It did not blaze into certainty. It surfaced slowly, painfully, like a flower forcing its way up through concrete. Fragile. Pale. Trembling in the light. But determined. It pushed upward through years of compression, through layers of silence and shame, through the heavy slab of belief that had told me I was nothing without him. It began in the aftermath of my suicide attempt. The shock of survival. The stark, undeniable realization that I had come terrifyingly close to ending my own life. That awareness did not whisper. It thundered. I had almost disappeared. Almost erased myself from a world that, however distorted it felt, still held possibility. That recognition cracked something open inside me, a fissure through which new air began to move. I had almost vanished. And in that realization, something unexpected ignited. Not strength in the triumphant, cinematic sense. Not a dramatic swell of courage. But a flicker of defiance. A quiet, stubborn refusal to let the story end there. It did not shout. It did not posture. It simply refused to extinguish. It was small. Fragile. Barely visible against the darkness that had encircled me for so long. But it existed. And that was enough. That ember did not roar into flame overnight. It did not burn away the pain or erase the scars. But it glowed. Softly. Persistently. It warmed the coldest corners of my despair. It illuminated the smallest cracks in the walls I had believed were permanent. It whispered a different possibility. That perhaps I was not as powerless as I had been taught to believe. That perhaps the erosion of my spirit was not proof of my weakness, but evidence of what I had endured. That perhaps survival itself was testimony to strength I had not yet learned to name. From that fragile flicker, the long work of rebuilding began. Not glamorous. Not swift. But deliberate. I began by questioning the old truths. By testing the bars of the cage. By reaching, cautiously at first, toward support and perspective. I began to gather the fragments of myself not with shame, but with curiosity. "*Who was I beneath the distortion? What did I feel when no one was correcting me? What did I need when I stopped apologizing for having needs?*" The flower did not bloom instantly. But it kept pushing. And each inch it gained through the concrete was a quiet declaration: *"I am still here. I am not finished. I am not powerless."* The loneliness had not been emptiness. It had been the space where something new was preparing to  grow.

That fragile ember needed protection. It needed air. It needed shelter from the winds that had nearly extinguished it. It needed someone steady enough to stand beside it while I learned how to tend it myself. Working with my sponsor became my lifejacket. When I was finally beginning to wade back into the waters that had once pulled me under, she was the steady presence that kept my head above the surface. Not rescuing me from the work. Not carrying me across it. But anchoring me long enough to find my footing. She did not silence the storm. She stood in it with me. And somehow, that made the waves less merciless. The current still tugged. The undertow still threatened. But it no longer felt inevitable. It no longer felt like the end. In her presence, there was space. A safe harbor where I could begin to name the demons of my past without being devoured by them. A place where the words *"abuse," "manipulation,"* and *"trauma"* could be spoken aloud without being minimized or twisted back into my own fault. Where my story could unfold without being interrupted, corrected, or reframed to protect someone else's comfort. For the first time, I could lay my story down in the open and watch it remain intact. It did not collapse under scrutiny. It did not disintegrate when examined. It held. But safety did not mean ease. The process was grueling. It meant peeling back layers of trauma I had spent a lifetime burying. Each layer had once been protection. Each silence had once been armor. Each denial had once been survival. Removing them felt like exposing skin to air after years beneath steel plating. Raw. Tender. Vulnerable in ways that made me want to retreat. I had to sit with memories I had numbed. With grief, I had postponed. With anger I had been taught to swallow. The work was not about reliving the pain for punishment's sake. It was about allowing it to be acknowledged, so it could finally loosen its grip. It meant confronting the deep-seated beliefs that had taken root in childhood. Beliefs that had grown quietly, invisibly, shaping my relationships long before I understood their influence. I had learned early that love required performance. That affection had to be earned through compliance. That being chosen meant being useful, agreeable, and undemanding. I had learned that to be loved, I must be pleasing. To be safe, I must be small. To belong, I must not need too much. Those beliefs had not announced themselves. They had simply become the water I swam in. And so when he demanded performance, I knew the choreography. When he withheld affection, I intensified my effort. When he criticized, I searched for how to improve. Undoing that conditioning required more than insight. It required practice. It required sitting in discomfort when I did not immediately apologize. It required tolerating the anxiety of setting a boundary and not rushing to soften it. It required believing, again and again, that I was worthy even when no one was affirming it. The ember inside me grew stronger with each truth spoken aloud. With each memory faced. With each belief questioned. With each moment, I chose compassion over condemnation. I was not being rebuilt by someone else's hands. I was learning to rebuild myself. Slowly. Intentionally. With care. And in that work, grueling as it was, something extraordinary began to take shape, not just healing, but sovereignty. The quiet, steady realization that I could tend my own fire. And that this time, no one else would be allowed to smother it. That peace required silence. That safety required shrinking. Those were the quiet commandments of my childhood, etched not in stone but in atmosphere. They were not announced; they were absorbed. I learned them the way a body learns gravity, by falling. I learned that harmony meant holding my tongue. That love meant adapting. That being *"good"* meant being small enough not to disturb the fragile balance around me. And those lessons did not dissolve when I crossed into adulthood. They followed me. They slipped into every attachment, every compromise, every apology that left my lips before I had even checked whether it was mine to give. They shaped the way I entered rooms. The way I listened for disapproval before speaking. The way I translated someone else's discomfort into my responsibility.

My dysfunctional upbringing had quietly laid the groundwork for what followed. It did not cause his abuse. It did not excuse it. But it created the vulnerability he later exploited. The soil had already been wounded. Already turned over by neglect. Already primed to accept distorted definitions of love as nourishment. I had been taught to mistake intensity for intimacy. To confuse control with protection. To equate endurance with devotion. He did not invent my self-doubt. He simply recognized it. He poured gasoline on embers that were already smoldering. He fanned flames I had spent years trying to ignore, hoping they would cool if I was patient enough, compliant enough, loving enough. He intensified old insecurities until they roared high enough to consume my sense of self entirely. And seeing this, truly seeing it, was painful. It meant grieving not only the marriage, but the childhood that had prepared me to tolerate it. It meant mourning the little girl who learned too early that her needs were inconvenient. It meant acknowledging that I had been shaped by patterns I did not choose, conditioned by environments I did not design. It meant sitting with the uncomfortable truth that vulnerability does not arise from weakness. It arises from unmet needs that linger too long without care. It arises from hunger mistaken for love. From silence mistaken for safety. From adaptation mistaken for identity. That realization did not absolve him. But it liberated me from blaming myself. And within that reckoning was power. Because understanding the origin of the wound is the beginning of tending it. Naming the pattern is the first step toward breaking it. When I could trace the thread backward, past the marriage, past the manipulation, into the early shaping of my beliefs, I could finally see that the flaw was never inherent. It was inherited. The ember that had nearly been extinguished now had structure around it. Containment. Guidance. Oxygen. It was no longer flickering alone in open wind. It was being tended. Protected. Fed with truth instead of distortion. And as it steadied, as it warmed rather than burned, I began to understand something quietly radical: I was not broken. I was patterned. And patterns, once seen, can be rewritten. And as I learned to sit with the pain rather than flee from it, as I allowed the ache to exist without immediately turning it inward as accusation, something extraordinary began to happen. The fire changed. The same blaze that had once threatened to consume me began to warm me instead. What had felt like an inferno of shame and self-destruction softened into something steadier, more contained. Not destructive. But illuminating. The embers that once symbolized despair were slowly transformed into fuel for rebuilding. The heat that had scorched my sense of self began to light the dark corridors of my past. It revealed what had been hidden. It clarified what had been distorted. It offered light where there had only been smoke. And for the first time, I was not merely surviving the flames. I was learning how to harness them. Through the work of healing, I began the painstaking task of untangling the web of lies he had woven into the fabric of my being. It was not one sweeping revelation. There was no single, cinematic moment where clarity arrived, and everything rearranged itself. It was threadwork. Delicate. Slow. Sometimes maddening. I would pull at one strand only to find it knotted around another. Beliefs intertwined with memories. Shame braided tightly with love. Distortion stitched so deeply into identity that separating it felt like pulling thread from skin. I began to see how confusion had masqueraded as devotion. How fear had disguised itself as loyalty. How self-erasure had been praised as virtue. Thread by thread, I began to loosen it. I examined the beliefs I had accepted as truth. I held them up to the light like fragile artifacts and asked: *"Where did this begin? Who benefits from me believing this? Is this rooted in love, or control?"* Some answers came quickly, unraveling with surprising ease. Others resisted. They clung stubbornly to familiarity. There is something unsettling about letting go of even painful beliefs when they have been with you long enough to feel like structure. It is strange how even pain can feel safer than uncertainty. Pain is known. Predictable. It gives the illusion of stability. Letting go of it requires stepping into space that feels unmarked, undefined. It requires trusting that emptiness is not annihilation, but possibility.

I learned, slowly, sometimes reluctantly, to distinguish between his poisonous words and my inherent worth. That distinction did not come naturally. For years, they had been fused, layered so tightly that separating them felt impossible. His criticisms had echoed long enough that they felt like my own reflections. But as I questioned them, as I dared to examine the origin of each self-accusation, the fusion began to weaken. *"This is not mine,"* I would whisper. *"This was taught." "This was planted."* And in naming it, I reclaimed a small piece of ground. The process was not clean. Some days the web seemed thicker than before. Some days, I wanted to drop the thread and retreat into the old, familiar narrative. But each time I persisted, each time I chose inquiry over automatic self-blame, the knots loosened just a little more. I was not tearing myself apart. I was disentangling myself. And beneath the layers of distortion, beneath the shame and the rehearsed inadequacy, I began to glimpse something steady. Not a new self. But the original one. Untouched by his voice. Uncontaminated by control. Quietly waiting beneath the threads. The fire that once threatened to destroy me had become the light by which I could finally see. And in that light, I was not burning. I was becoming. For so long, his words and my sense of self had been fused, inseparable, like dye soaked so deeply into cloth that no amount of rinsing seemed capable of restoring its original color. The stain felt permanent. Structural. As though it had always belonged there. But as I began to question them, truly question them, as I dared to doubt the certainty of their cruelty, something subtle shifted. A loosening. A softening at the edges. What once felt immovable began to tremble. What once felt carved into bone began to reveal itself as learned script. I started to recognize the patterns of manipulation. The predictable cycle of idealization and withdrawal. The intoxicating warmth followed by the calculated cold. The reframing of reality that left me apologizing for things I had not done. The strategic isolation that disguised itself as protection. The way affection was offered in measured doses, just enough to keep me tethered, never enough to feel secure. I could see, with growing clarity, the subtle strategies he had used to control, diminish, and destabilize me. They were no longer random storms. They were weather patterns. They had rhythm. Repetition. Intent. What once felt chaotic now revealed structure. What once felt like personal failure revealed design. And that realization was seismic. Because chaos suggests defect. But design suggests intention. The fog began to thin. At first, it was barely perceptible. A slight lifting. A faint outline where once there had only been blur. Like waking from a dream and not yet fully trusting the daylight. And then, gradually, shapes emerged. Context returned. Memory steadied itself, no longer shifting beneath accusation. Events that had once felt confusing began to settle into coherence. My perceptions began to feel trustworthy again. I stopped automatically editing my recollections. I stopped assuming I must have misunderstood. I began to stand inside my own experience without flinching. And as the fog receded, something remarkable happened. I heard my own voice again. Faint at first. Almost unfamiliar. Like hearing your name called from across a great distance, carried on wind you're not sure is real. It trembled. It hesitated. It questioned itself. It was cautious, as though afraid of being corrected. But it was mine. That voice did not accuse. It did not shame. It did not demand perfection or punishment. It spoke with quiet clarity. *"This hurt you."* Simple. Undeniable. *"You deserved better."* Radical. Healing. *"You are not what he said you were."* Liberating. Those words did not arrive in grand declarations. They came softly, almost shyly. But they carried weight. They felt grounded. They did not fluctuate based on someone else's approval. Slowly, painstakingly, I began to reclaim what had been eroded. My voice. My identity. My true self. Not the self, constructed in reaction to criticism. Not the self, sculpted by fear. But the self that existed before distortion. The self who felt deeply without apology. Who questioned without shame. Who deserved love without performance. I was not becoming someone new. I was returning. Returning to the woman who had always been there beneath the noise, beneath the manipulation, beneath the borrowed beliefs. And this time, when I heard her speak, I did not silence her. I listened. Not the self, contorted by fear. Not the self, molded by shame and silence. Not the version sculpted by survival. But the one who had always existed beneath the noise. Beneath the accusations. Beneath the performance. Beneath the endless editing of who I thought I needed to be.

She had been there all along. The one who loved deeply, not strategically. Who felt fiercely, not apologetically. Who endured more than she ever should have had to and still survived. Not untouched. Not unscarred. But unextinguished. She had never left. She had been waiting. Waiting beneath the sediment of distortion. Waiting beneath the debris of someone else's narrative. Waiting for the excavation to begin. Waiting for me to believe that she was worth uncovering. The woman who had stood at the edge of disappearance had not been weak. She had been buried. Buried beneath years of gaslighting that blurred her vision. Buried beneath shame that was never hers to carry. Buried beneath the relentless echo of a voice that tried to convince her she was nothing without it. And now, with trembling hands and steady breath, I was brushing away the dust. Not in grand gestures. Not in sudden transformation. But in small, deliberate acts of remembrance. In moments of stillness, I allowed myself to feel without correction. In decisions where I chose integrity over approval. In boundaries drawn without apology. I was uncovering her again. Not reinventing. Remembering. Remembering the girl who once trusted her instincts. The woman who once laughed freely. The heart that once loved without bargaining. I was not constructing a new identity from scratch. I was retrieving what had been obscured. The one who, even in her darkest hour, had refused to disappear. The one who chose to live. That choice was not loud. It was not theatrical. It was a quiet, sacred decision made in the privacy of my own soul: I will not abandon myself again. And in choosing to hear her voice, to honor it, to protect it, to let it speak without interruption, I began to trust that it would guide me somewhere different. Somewhere not ruled by fear. Somewhere not defined by distortion. Somewhere not narrowed by shame. Somewhere free. Freedom did not arrive as escape. It arrived as alignment. As the slow, steady return to myself. And for the first time, the path ahead did not feel like a maze. It felt like open ground.

The freedom I had begun to taste did not come without one final reckoning. It was not enough to step out of the prison. I had to unclasp the chains I was still gripping with my own hands. The greatest illusion I carried, the heaviest iron still wrapped around my ankles, was the belief that I had to keep carrying the burdens. That the weight itself was proof that it mattered. That if I dared to set it down, I would somehow be diminishing what had happened, betraying the gravity of my own suffering. I believed I needed to clutch the pain tightly, to replay the trauma like a sacred recording, needle dropping again and again onto the same sorrowful groove. As if repetition sanctified it. As if constant reliving were the only way to validate my own experience. I mistook remembrance for responsibility. I mistook suffering for loyalty to my own story. I thought pain was the altar upon which truth had to be worshipped. But the truth was far gentler, and far more radical. I did not have to keep carrying what had already carved its lesson into me. The scar was proof enough. I did not have to bleed daily to confirm the wound had been real. The body remembers without spectacle. The soul remembers without self-punishment. I had the power to release those burdens. Not erase them. Not deny them. But release them. To loosen my grip on the past and allow my hands, finally uncurled from their defensive fists, to hold something new. Possibility. Peace. Self-trust. Letting go did not mean pretending it never happened. It meant no longer living inside it. It meant stepping out of the echo chamber of old pain and into air that was not saturated with yesterday's sorrow. It meant recognizing that my story could expand beyond its most devastating chapters.

And that realization did not arrive wrapped in ease. It demanded time. Effort. A fierce and trembling honesty. It required a willingness to turn toward the very demons that had stalked me through so many silent nights. To look at them not as monsters to be outrun, but as messengers to be understood. It required sitting across from my pain instead of fleeing from it. To let it speak. To let it exist. To name it without becoming it. There is a sacredness in that kind of confrontation. A quiet courage in staying present while memory rises like smoke. I had to learn to witness my suffering without merging with it. To say, *"This happened to me,"* without unconsciously concluding, *"This is me."* That distinction was everything. Because once I stopped confusing my pain with my identity, something within me shifted. The weight I had mistaken for proof of depth became something I was free to lay down. And in setting it down, not recklessly, but reverently, I discovered that my story did not lose its meaning. It gained its horizon. But with the right support and guidance, something within me steadied. It was subtle at first. Not a surge of confidence, not a triumphant declaration. More like the quiet settling of earth after a tremor. A foundation remembering how to hold weight without collapsing. A pulse returning to rhythm after years of irregular strain. The first, tentative step was leaving. Leaving was not a single moment of dramatic departure. It was not a door slammed or a suitcase packed in fury. It was a slow gathering of courage. A quiet accumulation of breaths. A spine straightening millimetre by millimetre. It was a breath I had been holding for years, finally released into open air. I left the suffocating, toxic marriage that had become a breeding ground for my self-destruction. A place where doubt grew like mold in damp corners. Where love was rationed, and fear was ambient. Where every day required performance, vigilance, and adaptation. I left the house that had felt like both cage and sanctuary. A structure heavy with contradiction. The walls had witnessed my laughter and my unraveling. They had held my hope and absorbed my tears. It was the place where my spirit had slowly thinned under constant erosion, like coastline worn down by relentless tide. I left the man who had systematically chipped away at my self-worth, carving doubt into me with surgical precision. He did not shatter me in one violent blow. He sculpted insecurity patiently, shaping it to fit me. He convinced me I was broken. Unlovable. Unworthy. A mistake. And I wore those words like garments tailored to my shame. His voice had coiled around my identity like ivy around stone, tightening, creeping, obscuring the original structure beneath. What once stood solid became overgrown. What once felt clear became hidden under layers of insinuation. He whispered those insidious lies into my ear until they no longer sounded like whispers. Until they sounded like thought. Until they echoed with my own cadence. My own tone. My own inner narration. He twisted every feeling, every opinion, into evidence of my inadequacy. If I hurt, I was dramatic. If I protested, I was unstable. If I needed, I was demanding. If I withdrew, I was cold. If I tried harder, I was never enough. The rules shifted constantly. The target moved. The blame always circled back to me. And leaving meant stepping away not only from him, but from that distorted mirror he held up to my face. It meant risking the unknown rather than continuing to live inside a reflection that was never mine. It meant believing, however faintly, that the original structure beneath the ivy still existed. That the stone was not weak, only covered. And as I walked away, trembling, uncertain, but resolute, I began to feel something I had not felt in years: Space. Not empty space. Breathing space. The first fragile sense that my thoughts could belong to me again. That my feelings did not need translation. That my existence did not require defence. Leaving was terrifying. But it was also the first act that belonged entirely to me. And in that act, something essential returned. He made me believe that my very existence was a burden. That my presence required apology. That my emotions were inconveniences to be managed, minimized, or muted. That my needs were excessive. That my tenderness was weakness. That my tears were manipulative. That my strength was threatening. He convinced me that only he, in his distorted and self-appointed authority, could possibly love such a flawed, broken, pathetic creature. That I was too much for the world and yet somehow not enough for it. That no one else would be able to handle me, let alone love me.

And I believed him. Not all at once. Not dramatically. But slowly. Incrementally. Like dye seeping into water until the entire vessel changes color. His version of me replaced my own reflection. His doubt became my doctrine. Leaving him felt like severing a lifeline. Like cutting the rope while still suspended over a canyon, unsure whether the ground beneath would rise to meet me or drop away entirely. It felt reckless. Irresponsible. Terrifying. Every survival instinct screamed that I was making a mistake. That without him, I would unravel. That without him, I would collapse under the weight of my supposed inadequacy. It was a terrifying act of defiance against the insidious grip of his manipulation. My body trembled with the enormity of it. Not just emotionally, but physically. Hands shaking. Breath shallow. Heart racing with the rhythm of uncertainty. Fear became a constant companion, whispering doubts into my ear with cruel familiarity. *"Would I survive? Could I survive? Who would I be without the narrative he had written for me?"* The uncertainty felt like standing at the edge of an open sea with no visible shore. The horizon blurred. The water vast and unknowable. Every step forward felt like stepping into depth without guarantee. But the alternative, remaining trapped in that suffocating relationship, was far more terrifying. Staying meant slow erasure. Staying meant continued diminishment. Staying meant surrendering the last fragments of myself to a story that did not belong to me. Staying meant disappearing in increments so small they would barely register until nothing recognizable remained. So I walked. Not because I was fearless. But because I was more afraid of vanishing than I was of the unknown. Each step away felt both fragile and seismic. Like the earth shifting beneath my feet. Like stepping out of shadow into light so bright it hurt my eyes. I did not yet know what freedom would feel like. I only knew what captivity had cost me. And walking away, though terrifying, though uncertain, though accompanied by doubt, was the most liberating act of my life. Because in that step, I chose existence over erasure. I chose possibility over suffocation. I chose myself.

It was a seismic shift, a tectonic rupture beneath everything I had known. The ground of my reality split open with a force I could feel in my bones. Fault lines I had ignored for years finally gave way. Structures I had built my identity upon—marriage, loyalty, endurance, self-sacrifice, collapsed in clouds of dust. Illusions that once felt solid as stone crumbled into fragments, I could no longer mistake for foundation. And in the rubble, there was air. Not chaos alone. Not devastation alone. Air. Space. Possibility. The collapse, as violent as it felt, created room for breath. As I stepped beyond the shadow of that marriage, I began to feel something unfamiliar stirring within me, myself. Not the version of me filtered through his approval, constantly recalibrating to meet his shifting expectations. Not the self, contorted to avoid his displeasure, shrinking, softening, silencing to preserve fragile peace. But a quieter, steadier presence rising beneath the noise. It was subtle at first. A sense of alignment. A feeling of standing upright without bracing for correction. My thoughts began to sound like my own again. My laughter no longer carried the undertone of caution. My silence, when I chose it, felt intentional, not imposed. I began to discover a new sense of identity. Not new because it had never existed. New because I was finally allowed to inhabit it. For years, I had lived adjacent to myself, hovering at the edges of my own existence. Now, slowly, I stepped fully inside my own skin. I began to love and accept myself, flaws and all, not in a grand, sweeping declaration, but in small, daily acts of kindness. I learned to see my imperfections not as indictments, but as human texture. The uneven brushstrokes that give a painting depth. The cracks that allow light to enter. I began to recognize my worth without asking for permission. To acknowledge my value without apology. There was something revolutionary in that simplicity. To exist without defence. To feel without justification. To take up space without shrinking. And slowly, breath by breath, I began to understand something that once felt impossible. I was never the broken one. I was the one who endured the breaking. I was the one who survived. The one who walked through fire and emerged singed but breathing. The one who stood at the edge of disappearance and chose to remain. The one who was told she was too much and not enough and still found the courage to step away. And in walking away, I did not lose my lifeline. I found my own. Not tethered to someone else's approval. Not dependent on someone else's narrative. But anchored within myself. A current steady and internal. A strength that did not need to dominate to exist. A lifeline that had been there all along, waiting for me to reach for it. And this time, the hand holding it was mine.

Leaving was only the beginning. Walking out of the door did not mean I had walked out of the damage. The threshold I crossed marked an ending, yes, but it also opened into a far quieter, more demanding terrain. The real work began in the silence that followed. In the long, unadorned hours where there was no longer chaos to keep me occupied, no crisis to manage, no one else's moods to navigate. Just me. And everything and all the baggage I had been carrying. Healing became my sanctuary. Not a place of instant peace or gentle relief, but a sacred space where I could finally begin to unpack the years of accumulated emotional baggage I had dragged behind me like an overfilled suitcase with a broken handle. I had hauled it everywhere, pretending it was manageable, ignoring the way it scraped the ground, tore at my hands, and slowed every step. Now, at last, I could open it. Item by item. Memory by memory. Grief by grief. The road to healing was long and winding, more mountain trail than straight path. It twisted unexpectedly, looping back on itself, descending into valleys of sorrow before climbing steep inclines of realization. Some days, the air was thin; each breath earned. Other days, the view widened just enough to remind me why I was still climbing. There were setbacks. There were moments of doubt so sharp they cut straight through my resolve, moments when I questioned whether the strength I thought I had discovered was real at all, or just a brief illusion born of survival. There were days when the shadows of the past reached for me, stretching long and dark across the present. Days when the lies once whispered by my husband resurfaced without warning, echoing in the chambers of my mind as if they still owned the space. They told me I was weak. That I was too much. That I would fail without him. And for a moment, those echoes felt familiar. Comfortable in their cruelty. But even then, I held onto that tiny spark of self-belief that had flickered to life after my suicide attempt. It was fragile. Unsteady. Easily threatened. But it was real. And unlike the lies, it did not demand perfection. It asked only that I keep going. That spark became my compass in the fog. When the path disappeared beneath my feet, it reminded me which direction was forward. When doubt closed in, it whispered that survival itself was evidence. When the climb felt endless, it reminded me that I had already endured depths I once believed were unsurvivable. Healing did not mean the absence of pain. It meant the presence of truth. And step by step, breath by breath, I learned that even on the hardest days, I was no longer lost. I was on my way.

Slowly, painstakingly, I began to turn toward my past rather than away from it. For years, I had treated it like a locked attic, dusty, shadowed, best left undisturbed. But healing asked something different of me. It asked me to climb the stairs. To open the door. To stand in the dimness and let my eyes adjust. I stopped treating memory like an enemy to outrun and began approaching it as terrain that needed to be mapped. I began to excavate the roots of my insecurities, digging carefully through layers of memory and emotion. It was not reckless excavation. It was archaeological, the way one uncovers fragile artifacts, aware that reckless force could shatter what still needed understanding. Gentle. Reverent. I brushed away sedimented years of silence. I sifted through fragments of belief, trying to trace them back to their origin. Beneath the surface, the roots revealed themselves.

And there it was. My dysfunctional upbringing, a childhood marked not by obvious catastrophe, but by neglect and emotional instability, had quietly laid the foundation for the self-destructive beliefs that later took hold and turned inward and became self-destructive. It had been subtle. Unnamed. But formative. I had grown in soil that lacked nourishment. I had adapted to unpredictable weather. I had learned to read moods the way other children learned to read books. I learned early to question my worth. To shrink my needs until they were nearly invisible and barely registered. To confuse endurance for love. Affection felt conditional. Stability felt fragile. To mistake survival for belonging. I had learned how to disappear in plain sight. I became fluent in self-erasure long before I knew that was what I was doing. The messages of worthlessness, unlovability, and inadequacy were never my inherent truth. They were residue. Toxic remnants left behind by a broken system that could not nurture what it was meant to protect. Echoes reverberating from a childhood that had robbed me of a healthy sense of self before I ever had the chance to form one. A childhood that deprived me of a stable mirror, a childhood that distorted my reflection before I ever had the chance to see myself clearly. These beliefs did not originate inside me. They were learned. Absorbed. Normalized. I had internalized the instability around me as a verdict on who I was. I mistook environmental dysfunction for personal defect. Understanding this did not erase the scars. It did not magically soften every ache or quiet every doubt. They remained. Visible in certain lights. Tender in certain seasons. But it changed their meaning. They were no longer proof that I was defective. The scars no longer read as indictments of my character. They became evidence. Evidence that I had adapted in the only ways I knew how. Evidence that my sensitivity had once been a survival strategy. Evidence that my vigilance had once kept me safe. Proof of impact. Testimony to what I had endured, not what I lacked. And in that shift, healing deepened. Not as amnesia. Not as a polished version of myself, free from flaw. Not as perfection. Not as forgetting. But as reclamation.

I was not trying to return to who I had been before the damage. I was no longer trying to return to some imagined, unbroken version of myself. That version of me had been shaped by wounds she did not yet understand. I was building something new, stronger, more honest, not because it was unscarred, but because it was conscious. I was not broken beyond repair. I was no longer patching cracks to make them invisible. I was reinforcing the structure beneath them. I was rebuilding from the foundation up. With intention. With compassion. With the quiet, hard-earned knowledge that what was damaged had always deserved care. Removing what had been cracked. Reinforcing what had been weak. Choosing materials of truth, compassion, and self-trust where once there had been shame and silence. The child who learned to shrink was not being erased. She was being protected. The woman who endured was not being pitied. She was being honored. And brick by careful brick, breath by steady breath, I was constructing a self that no longer confused survival with love. A self, rooted in worth. A self that did not need to shrink to belong. A self that was finally, fully, mine.

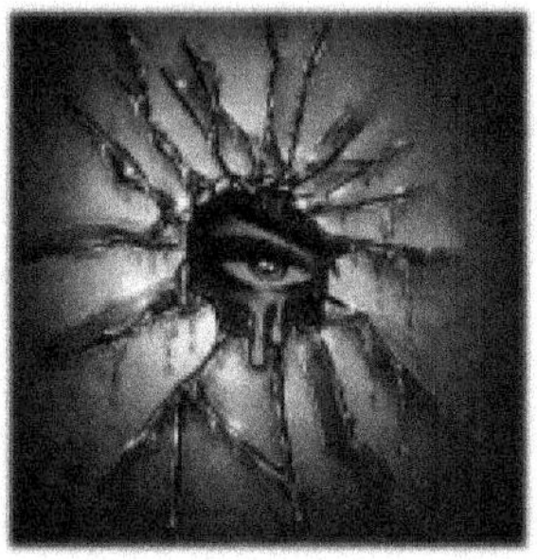Finding my voice did not smooth the terrain. It did not flatten the mountains or calm the weather overnight. Healing remained messy. Unpredictable. Often agonizing. It unfolded like a storm-tossed sea, one day glassy enough to see my reflection in it, the next churning with undertow, pulling at my ankles with old familiar force. There were mornings when the darkness reached for me again. When the weight of the past pressed against my ribs as if trying to fold me inward, to pull me backward into the version of myself I once believed was all I could be. The old narratives would rise like fog at dawn, subtle, persistent, distorting the landscape just enough to make me question my footing. On those days, breath felt heavier. The air thicker. The climb steeper. And yet, beneath the turbulence, something different was happening. A quiet strengthening. A steady undercurrent. A rhythm returning to my pulse. With each therapy session, I loosened another knot. With each trembling word written onto paper, I reclaimed a fragment of ground. With each secret exposed to light, I watched its power shrink. With each tear shed, each painful memory faced instead of avoided, I stitched integrity back into places that had been frayed. Reclamation did not arrive with fanfare. It came in increments. In choosing to show up. In choosing to speak. In choosing to stay present when every instinct urged retreat. I began to reclaim my narrative. Not all at once. Not dramatically. But steadily. Like restoring a weathered house room by room, I removed what did not belong and reinforced what had always been true. I started to see the difference between the lies I had been told and the truth of who I am. I began to recognize how expertly distortion had mimicked reality, how repetition had masqueraded as fact. And with effort, patient, repetitive effort, I learned to separate the pain of my past from my present reality. This happened to me. But this is not me. That distinction became sacred.

What had happened to me was real. The betrayal. The manipulation. The neglect. The erosion. None of it was imagined. None of it deserved minimization. But it was not the definition of me. It was part of my story, not the entirety of my identity. The storm still came. The sea still shifted. But I was no longer drowning in it. I was learning how to navigate. How to read the currents. How to anchor myself when the winds rose. And in that navigation, in the willingness to keep sailing even when the waters turned dark, I discovered something essential: The past may shape the shoreline, but it does not command the horizon. And I, at last, was facing forward. That realization did not arrive with thunder or spectacle. It did not split the sky or flood the room with light. It was a quiet turning. A subtle pivot of the soul. And yet, in its stillness, it marked the true beginning of my journey toward self-discovery and empowerment. There was no grand revelation, no cinematic clarity. There was simply a question, soft at first, almost hesitant, that began to repeat itself inside me: *"What if what I believe about myself isn't true?"* I began to question everything I thought I knew. Were the messages of worthlessness, of being unlovable, of *"not good enough"* actually truths etched into my character? Or were they echoes, reverberations from a dysfunctional upbringing and the calculated manipulation of a man who had benefited from my self-doubt? The question unsettled me. Because if the beliefs were true, then I was doomed to carry them. But if they were not, then something far more radical was possible. As I delved deeper into my history, I uncovered something both unsettling and liberating: those beliefs were not born within me. They were learned. Conditioned. Repeated so persistently that they blended with my own internal dialogue. They had been spoken over me, around me, into me, until they sounded like my own voice. But they were not mine. They were residue.

The emotional sediment of the environment I grew up in. The psychological debris left behind by instability, neglect, and distorted love. They were reinforced later by the calculated cruelty of a husband who understood that insecurity is fertile ground for control. These narratives had been placed upon me. They had been layered onto me. They had been rehearsed in my presence until I absorbed them as truth. But they had not originated from within me. And once I could see that distinction, once I understood that the voice condemning me was inherited rather than inherent, the ground beneath me shifted. It was not dramatic. But it was foundational. The darkness did not vanish overnight. The old thoughts still rose. The old fears still stirred. But they no longer felt fused to my identity. They no longer felt like the core of who I was. They felt like something I had endured. Something I had survived. That difference changed everything. Because survival implies strength. And strength, even when quiet, is power. Empowerment did not arrive as force. It did not demand that I be fearless or flawless. It arrived as awareness. As the steady recognition that I could question the narrative. That I could separate my essence from my experience. Not perfection. Reclamation. Not dominance. Ownership. It was the moment I began to understand that I was not the sum of what had been said to me. I was not the echo of someone else's distortion. I was not the story written by dysfunction and reinforced by manipulation. I was the author. And in realizing that, even softly, even tentatively, I began to write differently. The journey toward empowerment did not begin with triumph. It began with doubt. Not doubt in myself. But doubt in the lies. And that was enough.

As I untangled the inherited voices in my head, I found that the thread led further back than I expected, past the marriage, past the manipulation, past the betrayal, back to the beginning. My childhood. It was not devoid of love. My parents were well-intentioned, loving in their own complicated, human way. But love alone does not neutralize chaos. And our home, though not absent of affection, was marked by instability and unspoken pain. There were currents running beneath the surface, tensions unnamed, wounds unhealed, battles my parents were fighting within themselves without language to contain them. They were carrying demons they did not know how to name. And children feel what adults cannot articulate. Their behavior toward me was often inconsistent. Tender one day. Distant the next. Encouraging in one breath, overwhelmed in another. Sometimes unintentionally hurtful. Not malicious. Not cruel by design. But unpredictable. And unpredictability teaches a child to scan. I learned quickly how to adapt. How to survive. How to read the room with the vigilance of someone monitoring weather patterns. I could sense shifts before they were spoken. I could soften myself to reduce friction. I became skilled at people-pleasing, at smoothing tension before it erupted, at anticipating needs before they were voiced. I became small in strategic ways. I learned that my worth was measured by my usefulness. That love was maintained through compliance. That safety was preserved through attunement to everyone else's emotions. But in the careful choreography of keeping everyone else steady, I lost touch with myself. My needs blurred. My desires dimmed. My sense of worth became contingent. I became so fluent in others' feelings that I forgot how to recognize my own. As I grew older, I did what many of us do without realizing it. I gravitated toward what felt familiar. Not because it was healthy. But because it was known. The nervous system prefers predictability, even if it is painful. I unconsciously attracted people who mirrored the emotional landscape of my childhood. People who reinforced the beliefs I had already internalized. People who confirmed the quiet suspicion that I was too much and not enough all at once. My first husband, in particular, was masterful at manipulation. He twisted narratives with unsettling ease. Reality bent around his perspective. Conversations ended with me apologizing for things I could not quite remember doing. He convinced me that I was the problem. That I was too sensitive. Too flawed. Too difficult. Too demanding. The spotlight of blame never drifted toward him. It circled endlessly back to me. And because that pattern felt familiar, because I had learned early that stability depended on my adjustment, I accepted it. I tried harder. Softer. Smaller. But as healing deepened, something radical began to take root. Forgiveness. Not for him. For myself. I forgave myself for not knowing better. For staying too long. For believing lies that were spoken with such authority, they felt like fact. I forgave the girl who had learned to survive by shrinking. I forgave the woman who mistook endurance for love. And in that forgiveness, something long forgotten stirred. Choice. I had choice. The realization did not thunder. It settled into me like a truth that had been waiting patiently for recognition. I had the power to walk away from toxic relationships and environments. I did not have to endure pain as proof of loyalty. I did not have to accept hurt as the price of love. Love did not require my diminishment. Devotion did not demand my erasure. For the first time, I understood that my past had shaped me, but it did not sentence me. The patterns I had inherited were not destiny. They were simply patterns. And patterns can be interrupted. That interruption, quiet, deliberate, fiercely compassionate, was the beginning of a new lineage within me.

One rooted not in chaos, but in awareness. Not in survival, but in sovereignty. And for the first time, I was not merely reacting to what felt familiar. I was choosing what felt true. One of the most significant breakthroughs of my journey was not dramatic. It was quiet. It was simple. It was this: I could choose. That realization did not arrive with fireworks. It unfolded like dawn, soft at first, almost imperceptible, until suddenly the landscape looked different. I could choose to believe in myself, even when doubt whispered its old familiar warnings. I could choose to trust my instincts, even when my hands trembled with uncertainty. I could choose to love myself without condition, not because I had perfected myself, but because I was human. Choice became my quiet revolution. I could choose the voices I allowed to echo in my life. I could choose to surround myself with people who uplifted and supported me rather than those who diminished and drained me. I could choose connection that nourished instead of attachment that suffocated. I could choose to create a life that felt authentic, meaningful, and fulfilling—not one built around survival, not one centred on bracing for impact, but one built around truth. Truth about who I am. Truth about what I deserve. Truth about what love is meant to feel like. The path forward was not suddenly smooth. Healing did not transform the world into something gentle and predictable. Life continued to throw curveballs. Old triggers surfaced without warning. A phrase. A tone. A memory. And suddenly the past would flicker at the edges of the present. Difficult emotions rose like waves, grief, anger, fear, sometimes without clear invitation. But something within me had shifted. Where once I would have interpreted those moments as proof of my inadequacy, I began to see them as invitations to practice resilience. Challenges no longer felt like verdicts on my worth. They felt like terrain, difficult terrain, yes, but navigable. With a clearer mind and a growing sense of self-awareness, I began to respond rather than react.

I learned to prioritize my own needs without apology. To rest when I was tired. To speak when something felt wrong. To honor discomfort as information rather than weakness. I learned to set healthy boundaries and hold them, even when my voice shook, even when the old fear of rejection stirred in my chest. Boundaries became bridges back to myself. I learned to ask for help, not from a place of desperation, but from a place of shared humanity. And I learned to receive it from people who genuinely cared for my well-being. I allowed support to feel like support, not debt. Like love, not leverage. And slowly, almost imperceptibly at first, what once felt like chaos began to feel like growth. The turbulence that once disoriented me began to strengthen me. The discomfort that once frightened me became evidence that I was stretching beyond old limits. The uncertainty that once paralyzed me became space for possibility. The girl who learned to survive became a woman who learned to choose. To choose truth over familiarity. To choose self-respect over approval. To choose peace over performance. To choose herself. And in that choosing, again and again, in small daily acts, I discovered that empowerment is not loud. It is steady. It is deliberate. It is the quiet, unwavering decision to stand in your own life as its author. And I was no longer surviving the pages. I was writing them. The woman who learned to choose eventually had to learn something even harder. Forgiveness. For a long time, I misunderstood that word. I thought forgiveness meant forgetting. I thought it meant sanding down the jagged edges of what had happened until the harm no longer looked like harm at all. I believed it required softness toward what had been brutal, silence toward what had been loud, and compliance toward what had been unjust. I feared that forgiveness would erase the truth. But healing taught me otherwise. Forgiveness is not about excusing the past. It is not about condoning pain or pretending the wound was imagined. It does not rewrite history in kinder ink. It does not absolve those who caused harm from responsibility. The scar remains. The memory remains. The truth remains. Forgiveness is about release. It is about loosening the grip those experiences have on your present.

It is about removing the hooks from your own flesh, even if they were placed there by someone else. It is about acknowledging the harm clearly, without distortion, without denial, and choosing to lay down the emotional weight that has been chained to those memories. For years, resentment felt like protection. Anger felt like armor. I clung to them as proof that what happened mattered. But over time, I began to see how tightly I was gripping the very thing that was still exhausting me. Resentment corrodes quietly. It seeps into breath. Into posture. Into the way you anticipate harm before it arrives. It binds you to the past as surely as chains bind ankles. Forgiveness is not surrender. It is liberation. It is not saying, *"What you did was acceptable."* It is saying, *"What you did will not define my future."* It is freeing yourself from carrying someone else's debt in your own body. It is deciding that your energy, your attention, your life force deserve to be directed toward growth rather than grievance. And sometimes, forgiveness does not come in a rush of serenity. Sometimes it arrives with trembling hands. Sometimes it is whispered through tears. Sometimes it is chosen again and again, in small increments, when old anger resurfaces and asks to be fed. Forgiveness is an act of sovereignty. It is choosing peace over perpetual re-engagement with pain. It is stepping out of the courtroom of your own mind and laying down the gavel. It is saying, *"I will not keep prosecuting this case inside myself."* Not for their sake. For mine. Because I deserve rest from the story. Because I deserve space not occupied by bitterness. Because I deserve a present that is not perpetually shadowed by what was done to me. Forgiveness did not mean I trusted again without discernment. It did not mean I removed boundaries or reopened doors. It meant I removed the poison from my own bloodstream. And in that release, something remarkable happened. The past lost its grip. Not erased. Not forgotten. But no longer ruling. And in that freedom, I felt something I had not felt in years: Lightness. Not the absence of memory. But the absence of chains.

Forgiving myself, however, was the most difficult part of the journey. That mountain was steeper than any other. Forgiving others required distance. Forgiving myself required descent, down into the caverns where shame had taken up residence, where self-blame had been nesting for years, undisturbed and unquestioned. Accepting that I had been a victim of abuse meant dismantling the identity I had constructed around culpability. It meant facing the uncomfortable truth that I had not been weak, or dramatic, or complicit. I had been harmed. And that realization did not come easily. I had internalized every criticism hurled my way. Every accusation. Every manipulation. They had not remained external; they had seeped inward, layer upon layer, until they calcified into self-loathing. Like sediment hardening into stone, they formed a rigid narrative: "*You deserved this. You chose this. You caused this.*" I had convinced myself that I was complicit in my own suffering. That I had somehow earned it through deficiency. That my pain was the natural consequence of my flaws. Letting that belief go felt almost impossible at first. Because if I was not to blame, then I had to grieve the reality that harm had been inflicted without justification. And grief can be more terrifying than guilt. Guilt offers control. Grief demands surrender. To forgive myself, I had to begin by listening differently. I had to learn to recognize the negative self-talk when it surfaced—those insidious whispers that tried to undermine every step forward. They were subtle. Persistent. They arrived disguised as logic. As responsibility. As moral accountability. *"You should have known better." "You stayed too long." "You hurt people too." "You failed."* I had to interrupt them. Not with denial. But with truth. I had to challenge them, examine them, hold them up to the light, and ask: *"Is this compassion? Or is this conditioning?"* I had to replace them, not with hollow affirmations, but with grounded understanding. *"You did the best you could with what you knew." "You were surviving." "You were conditioned." "You are allowed to learn."*

Forgiving myself for the mistakes I had made, for the people I had hurt in my confusion and pain, for the choices I regretted, became a slow dismantling of the fortress I had built around my own heart. I had erected those walls for protection. Brick by brick, I had constructed a barrier of judgment, believing that if I punished myself enough, I would prevent future harm. But punishment is not protection. It is captivity. So brick by brick, I began to tear them down. It was not dramatic. There was no single moment of absolution. It was daily. Repetitive. Intentional. A steady softening where there had once been rigidity. A loosening of the clenched fist around my own memory. Each brick removed was an act of mercy. Each wall lowered allowed more air into my chest. Each moment of self-compassion was a radical departure from the narrative that had once governed me. And as the walls fell, something unexpected emerged, not fragility, but resilience. Not weakness, but depth. The realization that accountability and compassion can coexist. That I could acknowledge harm without condemning myself to perpetual shame. Forgiving myself did not erase the past. But it transformed my relationship to it. I was no longer my harshest judge. I was becoming my own witness. And in that witnessing, gentle, honest, unwavering, I found something stronger than guilt. I found grace. It required immense self-compassion. Not the kind that arrives dressed in sentimentality, but the fierce, disciplined kind—the kind that asks you to sit beside your own brokenness without turning away. It required the courage to see my imperfections clearly, to look at them in full light, without allowing them to eclipse my inherent worth. I had to learn that flaws are not verdicts. They are simply evidence of being human. For so long, I had wielded perfection like a weapon against myself. Now I had to lay it down. I had to learn to treat myself the way I would treat a dear friend, with patience when she faltered, gentleness when she wept, understanding when she could not see her own strength. If she had stood before me carrying my story, I would not have condemned her. I would have wrapped her in reassurance. I would have said, "*You did not deserve this. You are trying. You are enough.*" And so, trembling at first, I began to offer those same words inward. I had to learn that prioritizing my own needs was not selfish, but necessary. That tending to my emotional and physical well-being was not indulgent, but restorative, like watering soil long left cracked and dry. I had to unlearn the lie that exhaustion was virtue. That self-denial was love. That shrinking made me easier to keep. Caring for myself felt foreign at first, almost illicit. Like stepping into sunlight after years in shadow. But the body remembers warmth. The soul recognizes oxygen. There were days when it felt unbearable. Days when the pain resurfaced like an old tide, rising without warning. Days when the past pressed against my ribs so heavily, I wondered if it would ever fully loosen its grip. On those days, the old patterns called to me. Self-punishment felt familiar. Self-blame felt efficient. Retreat felt safer than resilience. There were days when giving up seemed easier than continuing the climb. But I did not give up. Even when my steps were small. Even when progress felt invisible. I kept moving. One step at a time. One breath at a time. Sometimes the victory was nothing more than choosing not to believe a cruel thought. Sometimes it was getting out of bed. Sometimes it was asking for help instead of isolating. Each act, no matter how small, was a quiet rebellion against the story that said I was not worth saving. And slowly, so slowly, I almost missed it, healing began to take root. Not as perfection. Not as erasure. Not as a spotless horizon untouched by storm. But as softness where there had once been only harshness. As compassion where there had once been condemnation. As spaciousness where there had once been suffocation. The inner landscape shifted. The ground that had once felt scorched and barren began to show signs of green. Small shoots at first. Fragile. But alive. And in that compassion, steady, practiced, deliberate, I began to feel something I had not felt in years. Not flawless.

Not finished. But whole. Whole, not because nothing had broken me, but because I had gathered the pieces with love instead of shame. Whole, not because the past disappeared, but because it no longer dictated my worth.

Whole because I had finally learned to stand beside myself, not against myself. And that, more than anything, changed everything.

And then, slowly, so slowly it almost felt like dawn arriving without spectacle, the truth emerged. Not as thunder. Not as revelation blazing across the sky. But as a steady light rising behind the hills of everything I had survived. The liberating truth was this: none of those damning messages, *worthless, unlovable, a mistake*, were ever true. Not once. Not in childhood. Not in marriage. Not in the depths of my despair. They were not facts etched into bone. They were echoes, insidious whispers of a manipulative abuser, amplified by the lingering shadows of a troubled upbringing. They were projections cast onto me like dark silhouettes thrown against a wall, shapes distorted by someone else's fear, someone else's cruelty. I had mistaken shadow for substance. I had reached out and tried to hold what was never solid, shaping my identity around outlines cast by someone else's distortion. I had swallowed their poison slowly, unknowingly, allowing it to circulate through my veins until it felt indistinguishable from my own blood. It colored the way I saw myself. It tinted every memory. It altered the tone of my inner voice. But poison, no matter how long it lingers, is not the body's true chemistry. It was never my truth. I had been living inside someone else's narrative, performing a role I had not auditioned for, carrying beliefs handed to me before I was old enough to question them. The messages drilled into me in childhood, reinforced later by my husband's cruelty, were not sacred truths carved into my being. They were inherited distortions. Learned lies. Stories spoken so often they began to sound like scripture. And then one day, quietly, without ceremony, I realized something simple but revolutionary: I did not have to believe them. I did not have to accept *worthlessness* as identity. I did not have to wear *unlovable* as a name. I did not have to endure pain as proof of devotion. Those words were not woven into my DNA. They were threads stitched onto me by hands that benefited from my self-doubt. And threads, no matter how tightly sewn, can be removed. The moment I understood that the voice condemning me was inherited rather than inherent, something shifted at the core. The ground beneath my feet felt different, not perfectly steady, not yet firm, but no longer collapsing under every step. The darkness did not vanish overnight, but it lost its authority. It was no longer my identity. It was weather I had survived. And in that subtle but seismic shift, empowerment did not roar into existence. It unfolded. Not as force. But as awareness. Not as perfection. But as reclamation. It was the quiet decision, repeated daily, to believe a kinder narrative. To question the reflex of self-blame. To answer shame with curiosity instead of condemnation. To meet my reflection not with accusation, but with recognition. I was never the poison. I was the body learning to cleanse itself. I was never the shadow. I was the light that had been standing behind it all along. Today, I still carry scars. They are etched into the quiet geography of my body and heart, fine lines beneath the surface, invisible to most, but known intimately by me. They have shape. They have history. But they are no longer badges of shame I try to hide beneath long sleeves of silence. They are proof of survival. Testaments to resilience. Evidence of a capacity for growth and healing I once believed I did not possess. They do not whisper, "*You are damaged.*" They say, "*You endured.*" Life has not become effortless. The sky still darkens without warning. Storms still gather at the edges of otherwise clear days. There are moments of doubt, sharp, sudden gusts that rattle the windows of my confidence. There are waves of uncertainty that rise without invitation, days when the weight of the world presses heavily against my shoulders, and I feel, for a fleeting moment, the old gravity tugging at my heels. But something fundamental has changed. The storms no longer convince me I am fragile. With a clearer mind and a stronger sense of self, I now know I possess the strength to navigate them. I am no longer a fragile boat at the mercy of every current, spinning helplessly wherever the tide decides to take me. I have learned to read the weather. To recognize the early signs of turbulence. To reef the sails when necessary. To anchor myself when the winds grow wild.

I have tools now. I know how to pause instead of panic. How to breathe instead of spiral. How to question instead of immediately believe the harshest voice in the room. I know how to seek support. I know how to lean into the arms of those who love and understand me—not as a sign of weakness, but as an act of wisdom. I have learned that strength is not isolation. It is connection. It is allowing others to stand beside you when the terrain grows steep. And perhaps most importantly, I have gained the discernment to recognize when something is not mine to carry. That realization alone changed everything. If a burden does not belong to me, I set it down. I no longer volunteer to carry what others refuse to examine. If guilt is misplaced, I return it. If shame is projected, I refuse to wear it. If a relationship diminishes me, I walk away, not in anger, but in self-respect. I have learned the power of self-preservation. The quiet authority of boundaries drawn not in hostility, but in clarity. The sacred responsibility of protecting my emotional well-being as fiercely as I once protected everyone else's comfort. And in that protection, I no longer shrink. I do not contort myself to fit into spaces too small for my spirit. I do not silence myself to preserve fragile egos. I do not apologize for existing. I stand. Whole, not because I was never broken, but because I chose, again and again, to gather the pieces. Because I chose to confront what hurt instead of pretending it did not. Because I chose to believe that survival was not the final chapter, but the threshold. The scars remain. But they are no longer reminders of who I was at my lowest. They are signatures of the woman who rose. And in standing here now, steady, aware, grounded in my own worth, I understand something with a depth I could not have imagined before: Wholeness is not the absence of fracture. It is the courage to rebuild.

Healing, I have learned, does not move in straight lines. It does not climb obediently upward like a staircase toward light. It does not obey timelines, checklists, or the tidy expectations we try to impose upon it. Healing twists. It doubles back. It spirals like smoke rising from embers, sometimes thick, sometimes barely visible, always moving but never in a perfectly predictable path. It rises and falls like breath. There are moments of profound insight that feel like standing on a summit, air thin and sharp in my lungs, vision stretching far beyond what I once believed possible. In those moments, clarity feels expansive. The world makes sense. The past softens. I can see the terrain I've crossed and feel something close to awe at the distance traveled. And then there are valleys. Low places where fog rolls in without warning. Where old pain rushes through like sudden rain, drenching me before I have time to find shelter. There are still days when memories return uninvited, sharp, vivid, sensory. Days when the hurt floods through me as if no time has passed at all, when the weight of the past presses against my chest so heavily it steals my breath for a moment. On those days, it would be easy to believe I am back where I started. But I am not. Because I no longer face those waves alone. I am surrounded now by people who see me clearly and choose to stand beside me, loved ones, friends, family who offer steady presence, listening ears, open hands. They do not try to fix me. They do not rush me through the storm. They anchor themselves near me and remind me that weather passes. Their presence is quiet but profound. And I have the guidance of a sponsor who has walked with me through the labyrinth of my own mind, patiently, deliberately, helping me untangle thoughts that once bound me like vines. She has stood with me at crossroads where I once would have panicked. She has handed me mirrors polished with truth when I could not trust my own reflection.

But perhaps the most powerful shift has happened within me. Something far stronger than fear has taken root. An awareness of my own strength. A resilience forged in fire and proven in darkness. It is not loud. It does not boast. It does not declare itself with bravado. It hums steadily beneath the surface, like bedrock beneath shifting soil. Even when the surface trembles, I can feel it there, solid, enduring. I know now that falling back into grief does not mean failure. That revisiting pain does not erase progress. That healing can include tears and still be forward movement. The difference is this: I trust myself now. I trust that I can sit with discomfort without being consumed by it. I trust that a hard day is not a permanent condition. I trust that I have navigated darkness before and emerged, scarred but standing. Healing is not a destination I will one day arrive at, flawless and untouched. It is a relationship. A daily practice. A returning. A listening. It is the willingness to meet myself again and again with honesty and compassion, no matter what rises. And in that willingness, in that quiet, steady commitment to remain present with my own becoming, I find something deeper than certainty. I find peace, not because the past is gone, but because it no longer governs me. The waves still come. But I have learned how to stand in the water. And I no longer mistake movement for drowning. My journey has taught me that healing is not a destination to be reached and checked off like a task completed. It is not a summit where one plants a flag and declares, "*I am done.*" It is a process. A continuous unfolding. A refining of the self, like gold placed in fire, not to be destroyed, but to have what is false burned away. Healing is not about becoming someone entirely new. It is about remembering. About reclaiming who I was before the world told me I was less. Before shame became a second language. Before, silence felt safer than truth. It is a slow returning to the self that existed beneath distortion, beneath fear, beneath the narratives that never belonged to me. It is a testament to the enduring power of the human spirit, the quiet, relentless capacity to endure. To adapt. To rise from ashes that once seemed to signal finality and instead build something luminous from what once felt irreparable. There was a night, one that will always live in the margins of my story, when the pills and the bottle felt cold in my hands. Their chill seeped into my skin, a stark contrast to the inferno raging inside my chest.

The darkness felt absolute. Not symbolic. Not poetic. Absolute. It pressed in from every side, heavy and suffocating. My life seemed to flicker like a fragile flame on the verge of extinction, bending under a wind that felt too strong to withstand. Everything in me felt exhausted. Everything in me felt done. And yet the flame did not go out. It trembled.

It bent. It nearly vanished. But it endured. Somewhere beneath the noise, beneath the despair, beneath the lie that disappearing was relief, there remained a quiet ember that refused surrender. It did not roar. It did not demand attention. It simply persisted. And now, what once flickered burns steady and bright within me. Not because life has become free of pain. Not because storms no longer gather. But because I have learned something sacred: the fire was never meant to be extinguished. It was meant to be tended. Nurtured. Protected. Guarded from the winds of other people's projections. Shielded from the rain of self-condemnation. The flame was not proof of fragility. It was proof of life. I am no longer standing at the edge of oblivion, staring into a void that once called my name. I am standing in the light of my own becoming. The same fire that once threatened to consume me now warms me. Guides me. Illuminates the path ahead. I understand now that despair did not define me. Survival did. Choice did. Courage did. The night that nearly ended me became the threshold that transformed me. And here I stand, not untouched, not unscarred, but luminous in a way I never believed possible. Not because I was never broken. But because I chose, again and again, to keep the flame alive.

As the flame within me steadied and grew, no longer a desperate flicker but a deliberate, tended light, I began to understand something that once felt foreign, almost forbidden: Protection is not cruelty. Boundaries are not rejection. They are self-respect made visible. For years, I confused access with love. I believed that to be good, to be worthy, to be chosen, I had to be endlessly available, porous, accommodating, self-erasing. I mistook depletion for devotion. I mistook silence for strength. But the fire within me began to teach me otherwise. A flame left unguarded will burn out. A hearth without stone will not contain its warmth. And so I learned that containment is not coldness. It is care. One of the most important lessons this journey has etched into me is the necessity of boundaries. Not the kind drawn in anger, but the kind drawn in clarity. I have learned to say no, to people, to situations, to expectations that drain rather than nourish me. That single syllable once felt like betrayal. Now it feels like alignment. I have learned to walk away from relationships that are toxic or unhealthy, even when walking away trembles through my bones. Even when my old conditioning whispers, "*Stay. Endure. Prove your loyalty.*" I have learned to prioritize my own needs and to put myself first, not as a declaration of superiority, but as an act of responsibility. Because no one else can live inside my nervous system. No one else can carry the cost of my depletion. And I have come to understand that this is not selfish. It is necessary. For so long, I believed self-sacrifice was virtue. That endurance was proof of love. That shrinking made me safe. But love that demands erasure is not love. It is consumption. Caring for myself does not diminish others. It strengthens me. When I tend to my own well-being, emotionally, physically, and spiritually, I become more resilient. More adaptable. Better equipped to navigate the inevitable twists and turns of life's terrain. Self-care is not indulgence. It is maintenance of the soul. When I rest, I replenish. When I speak my truth, I realign. When I protect my energy, I preserve my capacity to give freely rather than resentfully. A tree with strong roots can weather storms. It does not apologize for needing soil, sunlight, and water. It does not shrink its branches to make the wind more comfortable. And a woman who honors her own limits can stand firm when the winds rise. She does not confuse bending with breaking. She does not equate endurance with worth. She does not allow every hand to reach her heart unchecked. Boundaries became the fence around my inner garden, not to keep love out, but to ensure that what grows within me is not trampled. The flame inside me no longer flickers in fear of being extinguished by someone else's demands. It burns steadily because I guard it.

Because I choose what I allow near it. Because I finally understand that tending my own fire is not abandonment of others, it is stewardship of myself. And in that stewardship, I do not harden. I become whole. Strong not because I withstand everything. But because I discern what is mine to hold, and what must be released to the wind. Looking back now, with distance softening the sharpest edges, I can see something I could not see then. The greatest burden was not the pain itself. Pain, in its rawest form, is honest. It is a signal. A flare sent up from the body and the heart saying, "*Something matters. Something hurts.*" The true weight, the crushing, breath-stealing weight, was the belief that I had to carry it alone. That I had to prove my strength by enduring it in silence. That suffering was something noble if borne without complaint. That resilience meant swallowing the ache and smiling anyway. I believed I had to be strong enough to withstand it all. To absorb. To endure. To survive without asking for help. But that belief became heavier than the pain itself. Because the truth is, I did not have to carry what was breaking me. I did not have to clutch it like a sacred burden, as though letting go would invalidate what had happened. I did not have to drag the wreckage behind me like proof of loyalty to my own suffering. I had the power to release it. To set it down. To step out from beneath its shadow and allow my spine to straighten again. Release did not mean denial. It meant no longer living as if the wound were my identity. It meant allowing the past to inform me without imprisoning me. It meant understanding that strength is not measured by how much you can endure, but by what you are willing to lay down. This journey has returned me to the fundamentals. Self-awareness. Self-love. Self-acceptance. Not as abstract concepts, but as daily practices. As breath. As posture. As the way I speak to myself when no one else is listening. It has taught me that the messages we receive from others, whether glowing with praise or dripping with criticism, do not determine our worth.

They are reflections of their perspective, their wounds, their limitations. They are mirrors angled through their own experience. They are not definitions of our value. For so long, I outsourced my identity. I let approval inflate me and rejection deflate me. I let someone else's perception become my compass. But now I understand: Perception is not prophecy. We always have a choice. We can choose how we respond to circumstances. We can choose how we speak to ourselves in the quiet. We can choose which voices we amplify and which we silence. We can choose the relationships we allow into our lives. Choice is quiet power. It does not arrive with fireworks. It does not demand attention. It simply waits, steady, patient, until we recognize it. Choice is the reclaiming of authorship over our own story. It is picking up the pen after believing it had been taken from you. It is crossing out the words that were written in cruelty and rewriting them in truth. It is understanding that while we may not control what happened, we always retain sovereignty over what it means. And in learning to choose, I learned to live not in reaction to pain, but in alignment with truth. Not braced against the past. Not defined by survival alone. But oriented toward growth. And that truth is simple. Steady. Unshakeable. I am not defined by what happened to me. I am defined by how I rise from it. Not by the darkness I walked through, but by the light I chose to carry forward. Not by the wounds I endured, but by the wisdom I cultivated. Not by the weight I once bore, but by the strength I discovered when I finally set it down.

TODAY, I CAN SAY, WITH a steadiness I once could not imagine, that I am no longer held captive by the lies of my past. The chains of self-doubt and fear that once wrapped tightly around my ribs have fallen away. They may have left faint impressions, pale marks where pressure once lived, but they no longer bind me. I can breathe fully now. Deeply. Without bracing. Without apology. I am free. Free to be fully myself, not a softened version shaped to survive someone else's expectations. Free to live on my own terms, guided by inner alignment rather than external approval. Free to pursue my dreams with passion, clarity, and purpose, without asking permission to want more. The life I inhabit now feels chosen, not endured. It is no longer something I grit my teeth through or survive one day at a time. It is something I participate in. Something I shape. Something I step into with intention. And when life throws its inevitable challenges into my path, as storms always return in some form, I no longer crumble at the first rumble of thunder. I do not mistake difficulty for disaster. I do not assume pain means collapse. I know now that I carry within me a strength forged in darkness and a resilience tested by fire. I have faced my own abyss and stepped back from it. I have stood at the edge of myself and chosen to remain. That knowing lives in my bones. It is quiet, but unshakeable. It does not need to prove itself. It simply exists, steady and reliable, like bedrock beneath shifting ground. Today, the tea beside me has grown almost cold, forgotten in reflection. Steam no longer rises from the cup, but the warmth in my heart is real and unmistakable. It does not flicker the way it once did, vulnerable to every passing wind. It burns steadily now, contained, nourished, alive. I understand something now that once eluded me entirely. The pain and hurt I carried for so long were never mine to shoulder alone. I was never meant to carry them in silence, mistaking isolation for strength. I was never required to suffer endlessly to validate what had happened. I had the strength to walk away. The resilience to heal. The courage to forgive, not because the past deserved it, but because *I* deserved freedom.

Forgiveness became the final unclenching of my hands. The moment I stopped gripping the weight that had shaped me and allowed myself to step forward unburdened. I am no longer defined by survival alone. I am defined by choice. By clarity. By the quiet confidence of a woman who knows herself and protects what she has rebuilt. I am not untouched by what I lived through. I am transformed by how I rose from it. And today, standing firmly inside a life that feels like my own, I know this with certainty: I am not merely alive. I am awake. The messages that once haunted me, "*worthless, unlovable, a mistake*" have lost their authority. They still exist in memory, like faded graffiti on a wall I once walked past every day. But they no longer command my attention. They no longer define the architecture of my thoughts. They were never truths etched into my soul. They were cruel imprints pressed into me by broken systems and broken people, echoes of dysfunction, not declarations of destiny. And I am finally free from them. Free not because I erased them, but because I no longer bow to them. Life still offers its challenges. The world has not softened simply because I have healed. There are still days that test me, days when patience feels thin. When courage must be summoned deliberately, when old reflexes attempt to reassert themselves. There are moments that stretch me beyond comfort, that ask me to choose again who I am becoming. But I meet them now with a clarity I once believed was reserved for other people. I know when to stand firm and when to walk away. I know the difference between growth that stretches me and harm that diminishes me. I no longer negotiate with my own well-being as if it were currency to be traded for acceptance. If something diminishes me, I release it. If something harms me, I leave it. If something asks me to shrink to belong, I decline. My peace is no longer up for sacrifice. It is not arrogance. It is stewardship. The journey here has been arduous. It demanded everything: My tears, my honesty, my surrender, my fight. It required me to dismantle illusions I once clung to for survival. It asked me to sit with grief without rushing to escape it. It asked me to face truths that split me open before they set me free. There were nights when I doubted, I would reach this side. There were mornings when the climb felt endless. But I kept moving. Even when movement meant nothing more than breathing through the next hour. And the view from the other side is breathtaking. Not because it is flawless. Not because storms no longer gather. But because it is mine. This life is not curated to impress. It is not constructed to prove. It is inhabited. Authored. Lived. I am no longer searching for belonging in places that wound me. I no longer confuse familiarity with safety. I no longer offer loyalty to environments that fracture my spirit. I am finally home. Not in a house. Not in a relationship. Not in someone else's approval. But in myself. In the quiet steadiness of my own breath. In the grounded certainty of my own worth. In the knowing that I do not have to become smaller to be loved. Home is no longer something I chase. It is something I carry. And in that belonging, to myself first, I have found a freedom deeper than escape. I have found peace.

Chapter: Twenty-Three
From Broken to Healed

Sitting down to write my story feels like opening a long-sealed door. The hinges groan softly in memory. Dust rises. Light filters in cautiously, illuminating corners that have not been touched in years. As I place my hands on the page, there is a tremor, not of fear, but of recognition. The paper feels alive beneath my fingertips, as if it knows what it is about to hold. I am met with a rush of emotion. Sadness still hums beneath the surface, low and steady, like a distant cello note that never quite disappears. Anger flickers too, though it no longer rages the way it once did. It is no longer a wildfire consuming everything in its path. It has become a contained flame, a source of clarity rather than destruction. And then, unexpectedly, almost startling, there is gratitude. Deep, humbling gratitude. Gratitude for the journey that has carried me here, through fire and shadow, through valleys of despair and across fragile bridges of hope. Gratitude for the nights that did not break me, even when they tried. Gratitude for the cracks that let light in. Gratitude for the version of me who kept breathing when she wanted to disappear. This life I inhabit now has been shaped by self-discovery, healing, and hard-won liberation. Nothing about it was accidental. Nothing about it was handed to me gently. Every inch was earned through honesty, through surrender, through the relentless decision to keep moving forward even when forward felt impossibly far away. For years, I lived beneath the crushing weight of guilt and shame. They wrapped around me like a heavy cloak soaked in rain. I wore them everywhere. They became my posture, my tone, my inner monologue. I was convinced that I was the common denominator in every fracture around me. That if something cracked, it must have been my fault. If my children were hurting, it must have been because of me. If my marriage was failing, I must have broken it. If the atmosphere felt heavy, I assumed I was the storm. I carried the belief that I was the source of suffering in the lives of those I loved. Or so I thought.

That belief sank deep. It rooted itself quietly, drawing nourishment from every criticism, every raised voice, every moment of tension. I interpreted everything through the lens of self-blame. I became both defendant and judge in a courtroom that existed entirely inside my mind. The verdict was always the same. Guilty. It did not matter how much I gave, how much I tried, how much I bent myself into shapes that left me aching. If something went wrong, I absorbed it. If someone was unhappy, I claimed responsibility. If there was chaos, I assumed I was its origin. I mistook hyper-responsibility for love. I mistook self-condemnation for accountability. And in doing so, I nearly erased myself. Writing this now, I can see the distortion with clarity that once felt unreachable. I can see how deeply I internalized blame because it felt safer than acknowledging powerlessness. If everything was my fault, then maybe I could fix it. If I was the problem, then maybe I could become better, smaller, quieter, less disruptive, and more agreeable. But the truth is both sobering and freeing. I was not the storm. I was standing in one. The heaviness in the room was not born from my existence. The fractures around me were not proof of my defectiveness. The suffering I witnessed was not automatically my creation. I had taken on responsibility for pain that was never mine to own. And recognizing that, fully, honestly, was like removing a boulder from my chest. The shame that once defined me now feels like something I survived, not something I am. The guilt that once dictated my every thought has loosened its grip. In its place, there is compassion for the woman who believed she had to carry it all. For the mother who blamed herself because she loved fiercely.

For the partner who tried to mend what was never hers to repair. Sitting here now, pen in hand, I do not feel accusation. I feel understanding. The door I have opened does not lead back into darkness. It opens into truth. And in that truth, I no longer stand as the villain of my own story. I stand as its witness. Its author. Its survivor. And perhaps, most tenderly of all, its redemption. The truth, however, was far more intricate than the simple equation of blame I had once constructed in my mind. Life is rarely a straight line of cause and consequence. It is a web, threads crossing, tightening, tugging against one another. Yes, my mental state, darkened by suicidal ideation and Major Depressive Disorder, had ripple effects. Pain does not exist in isolation. It moves outward like waves from a stone dropped into still water. My despair touched the people around me. My withdrawal left empty spaces at tables once filled with laughter. My fragility created moments of confusion, hurt, and instability. There were days when my struggle cast a shadow across my home. Days when my exhaustion made me distant. Days when my internal chaos leaked into the atmosphere and unsettled those I loved. That is a truth I do not deny. But it was never the whole truth. I was not a villain in my own life story. I was a woman drowning, lungs burning, limbs heavy, trying to keep her head above water while still reaching for the hands of others. Trying to mother. To partner. To function. To survive. Illness does not make someone malicious. It makes them overwhelmed. My depression was not a moral failure. It was not weakness. It was not selfishness disguised as suffering. It was a condition. A storm in the mind. A chemical and emotional weight that required understanding, treatment, compassion, not condemnation. For so long, I confused impact with identity. Because my pain affected others, I assumed it defined me. Because my illness had consequences, I believed it made me defective. But healing has taught me something subtler and far more powerful. I can hold both truths at once.

I can acknowledge the harm without collapsing into shame. I can recognize the impact without erasing the context.

I can say, *"Yes, this was painful,"* and also, *"No, this does not make me irredeemable."* That is the quiet power healing has given me: the ability to face my past without being devoured by it. To stand before it without flinching. To examine it without self-immolation. To feel it without becoming it. As I write now, the sadness and anger that once surged like tidal waves begin to settle into something steadier. They no longer crash. They ebb. They breathe. And what rises in their place is gratitude. Not gratitude for the pain itself, I would never romanticize the nights that nearly swallowed me whole. But gratitude for what surviving it revealed. For the depth of my resilience. For the clarity that emerged from confusion. For the self-awareness carved from suffering. For the knowledge that even in my darkest chapters, when I doubted my worth, my sanity, my right to exist, I was not beyond redemption. I was human. Hurting. Struggling. Learning in the only way I knew how at the time. Healing has allowed me to widen the lens. To see myself not as the sum of my lowest moments, but as a complex, evolving being shaped by circumstance, biology, trauma, and choice. The woman who once believed she was the storm now understands she was navigating one. And in surviving it, in choosing treatment, in choosing reflection, in choosing honesty, I did something extraordinary in its quietness. I stayed. I learned. I grew. And today, when I look back at that version of myself, I do not see a villain. I see a woman fighting for air. And I honor her for it. As I continued to sift through the rubble of my past, brushing dust from memories I had long avoided, I began to see how deeply that toxic mindset had been planted within me. It had not appeared overnight like a storm rolling in from nowhere. It had been cultivated. Repeated. Reinforced. Watered daily by the voices around me, and most persistently by my ex-husband. He told me again and again that I was the problem. That I was broken. That I was the flaw in every equation, the common denominator in every conflict. His certainty was relentless. And over time, repetition did what repetition always does: It blurred the line between accusation and identity.

And I believed him. Not immediately. Not consciously at first. But gradually, the words took root. I began to see myself through the lens he handed me.

I believed I was too damaged, too fractured, too fundamentally flawed to ever be whole again. I mistook injury for essence. I confused trauma with identity. Each argument reinforced the narrative. Each betrayal deepened it. Each wound within the marriage became another piece of so-called evidence. The suffering became proof. The pain became confirmation. I collected every hurt like documentation in a case against myself. If I were better, this wouldn't be happening. If I were easier to love, he wouldn't react this way. If I were less broken, things would be different. I lived inside that logic as though it were airtight. The reality I inhabited felt suffocating, like a room with no windows. The walls closing in. The air thinning. The exits invisible. I paced the same small perimeter of thought over and over, convinced there was no door because I had never been shown one. There seemed to be no escape. No alternate ending. Only endurance. But as I sifted through the rubble, something subtle began to emerge. I could see the architecture of that mindset. I could trace where it had been planted, where it had been reinforced, where it had been manipulated to serve someone else's power. And once I saw that it had been instilled, the illusion of inevitability began to crack. If a belief can be planted, it can be uprooted. If a narrative can be repeated into existence, it can be rewritten. The room I thought had no windows began to show faint seams along the walls. Not yet open. Not yet wide enough to step through. But visible. And visibility was the first breath of freedom. Because the truth was this: I was never the flaw in the equation. I was the variable that had been misrepresented. And once I began to question the formula, the entire outcome started to change. And then, almost imperceptibly at first, something shifted. It was not dramatic. There was no thunderclap, no triumphant revelation. Just a quiet loosening. The thought that had once circled endlessly in my mind, that killing myself was the only solution, began to lose its authority. It no longer sounded like an unquestionable decree. It sounded like a thought. A desperate one. A frightened one. But not an absolute.

I saw, dimly at first, as though through fog, that it was not the answer. In fact, it was the opposite. It was the echo of exhaustion, not the voice of truth. The real problem was never that I was incapable of change or healing. It was that I had believed I couldn't. I had accepted powerlessness as fact. I had mistaken, learned helplessness for destiny. That belief, more than anything else, had kept me bound. It was the invisible chain. The quiet lock. The story that whispered, "*There is no other way.*" And because I believed it, I stopped looking for alternatives. I stopped imagining possibility. I stopped recognizing that even in pain, I still possessed agency. But as that understanding began to take root, something radical stirred beneath it. I had the power to choose. Not in grand, sweeping gestures at first. But in steady, grounded decisions. I could choose to heal. I could choose to leave the toxic marriage. I could choose to stop negotiating my worth. I could choose to take responsibility where it was mine, my reactions, my growth, my healing, and release it where it was not. I could stop carrying guilt that did not belong to me. I could stop atoning for harm I did not cause. And where I had hurt others, through my own fear, my own confusion, my own learned patterns, I could choose accountability. Not from a place of self-condemnation, but from integrity. From growth. From the desire to live differently moving forward. Choice did not erase the past. But it transformed my relationship to it. Instead of being dragged by it, I could stand before it. Instead of being defined by it, I could learn from it. The realization that I still had agency was like feeling blood return to a limb that had long been numb. Painful at first. Uncomfortable. But undeniably alive. The narrative that once insisted, "*There is no way out*", began to be replaced with a quieter, steadier truth: *"There are many ways forward."* And for the first time in years, the path ahead did not look like a closed door. It looked like an open horizon. Still, the question lingered. It did not disappear simply because I had chosen to live. It gnawed at me like a persistent, throbbing ache beneath the surface of healing: *"Was I truly to blame for everything that went wrong in other people's lives?"* The question hung heavy in the air, dense and suffocating, as though it demanded a verdict before I was allowed to move forward. The answer was not simple. It was not a clean yes or no. It was layered. Complex. Like the strata of my own unraveling. Like sediment built over years, beliefs, wounds, reactions, misunderstandings, compressed into something that looked solid from the outside but required excavation to understand. I came to see that the truth was woven from many threads. Threads of mental illness, quiet and persistent, coloring my perception in shades darker than reality required. Threads of trauma, bending my instincts toward survival rather than clarity. Threads of learned patterns, inherited from dysfunction, rehearsed until they felt automatic. And threads of hard-won understanding, emerging slowly as I dared to examine the whole design. It was a tapestry, not of condemnation, but of context. Yes, my depression had ripple effects. My withdrawal, my despair, and my fragility influenced those around me. Pain does not exist in isolation. It reverberates. Yes, my reactions were sometimes shaped by fear rather than wisdom. Yes, I contributed to dynamics I did not yet understand how to interrupt. But I was not the singular cause of every fracture. I was not the sole architect of suffering. I was not the origin point of all collapse. I was a human being struggling inside circumstances that were themselves broken. A person navigating pain without the tools I needed, reacting from wounds I did not yet know how to tend. Responsibility existed, but it was shared, contextual, and human. This realization did not absolve me of growth. It grounded me in it. It allowed me to take responsibility where it belonged, my healing, my behavior, my choices moving forward, without absorbing blame that was never mine to carry. It allowed me to see myself not as villain or victim alone, but as a complex, imperfect human being learning in real time.

And there was something profoundly freeing in that. Because when responsibility is accurate, it empowers rather than crushes. It invites growth instead of shame. It opens space for accountability without annihilation. The question that once felt suffocating began to soften. Not "*Am I to blame for everything?*" But "*What is truly mine to own, and what can I release?*" And in learning the difference, I found balance. Not innocence. Not perfection. But humanity. And for the first time, that felt enough. And in seeing that complexity, allowing the truth to be layered rather than absolute, textured rather than flat, I felt something loosen inside me. It was not dramatic. No chains clattered to the ground. But the tension that had lived in my chest for years eased, just enough for breath to move freely again. Blame, once sharp and all-consuming, began to soften into responsibility. Not the kind that crushes. The kind that steadies. Shame, which had wrapped itself around my identity like barbed wire, slowly unraveled into clarity. And clarity did not accuse. It illuminated. Where shame had whispered, "*You are wrong*", clarity asked, "*What happened?*" Where blame had insisted, "*It's all your fault*", perspective replied, "*Let's look at this honestly.*" In that shift, I found something steadier than self-condemnation. I found balance. I found the ability to stand in the middle of my own story without collapsing under it. To hold nuance without losing myself in extremes. To see both harm and humanity in the same frame. Perspective arrived like a widening horizon. What once felt like a narrow tunnel of accusation opened into something broader. Airier. I could see the interplay of circumstances, mental illness, trauma, and choice. I could see that life is rarely a single-threaded narrative. It is woven. Interconnected. Complex. And with that understanding came the beginning of true freedom. Not freedom from consequence. Not freedom from growth. But freedom from distortion. The freedom to respond instead of react. The freedom to own without annihilating myself. The freedom to forgive without erasing accountability. It was not loud. It did not declare itself with fireworks. It settled into me quietly, like a deep exhale after years of holding my breath.

And in that exhale, I recognized something extraordinary. I was no longer fighting myself. I was finally standing with myself. And that, more than anything, was the first unmistakable taste of liberation. Perspective did not absolve me. It clarified me. It did not sweep away consequences or polish the past into something easier to hold. It sharpened it. It steadied it. It placed it in my hands and asked me not to flinch. On one hand, and this is the hand I cannot turn away from. I must acknowledge the pain I inflicted on those closest to me, particularly my children, during the years I was lost inside my mental illness. I did hurt them. Fiercely. Not with intention. Not with cruelty. But harm does not require malice to be real. The crushing weight of my Major Depressive Disorder, entangled with the dark pull of suicidal ideation, did not exist in isolation. It seeped into our home like damp through walls. It altered the atmosphere. It shaped the tone of our days. It thickened the air with tension and uncertainty. Childhood, which should have been light and expansive, carried the gravity of a mother fighting to stay afloat. That truth is heavy. It sits in my chest with both regret and sorrow, like a stone I cannot, and should not, simply discard. The pain and confusion they endured were real. The experience of having a mother physically present yet emotionally swallowed by fog left impressions. I was there, and yet not fully there. My body in the room. My spirit submerged. My smile strained. My energy depleted. I cannot pretend otherwise. I cannot soften it with justification. I cannot reach for context as a shield. Accountability required me to stand still in that truth, without "*buts*", without "*ifs*", without defence. To allow their experience to exist in its fullness, separate from my explanation. My reasons, however valid they may have been in context, do not erase their experience. My illness explains. But it does not excuse. That distinction is sacred.

It allows me to hold compassion for myself without denying the impact of my suffering on them. It invites humility. It demands maturity. It asks me to step out of the center of the story long enough to see how the storm within me became weather they had to live under. And yet, even here, perspective steadies me. Because shame would have me collapse under that truth. It would have me declare myself irredeemable. It would twist accountability into self-annihilation. But clarity does something different. Clarity allows me to say: *"I was ill. I was drowning. And in my drowning, others were splashed, soaked, unsettled. That matters. And so does what I choose now."* Accountability is not about staying forever in the shadow of regret. It is about turning toward repair. It is about listening when they speak of what those years felt like. It is about apologizing without condition. It is about showing up differently, consistently, and patiently. The past cannot be rewritten. But presence can be reclaimed. Trust can be rebuilt, not perfectly, but honestly. Perspective did not erase my responsibility. It made it clearer. And in that clarity, I found not condemnation, but the opportunity to grow into the kind of mother, the kind of woman, who does not hide from truth, but stands within it with humility and love. And so, I had to learn a new kind of courage. Not the courage to endure in silence. Not the courage to survive at any cost. But the courage to say *I am sorry* without attaching that apology to being understood, forgiven, or absolved. The courage to offer amends without softening the edges of truth. Without explaining them away. Without protecting my ego. I had to learn how to stand in the discomfort of knowing I had caused pain and remain present. To make amends without minimizing. To listen without defending. To accept that my apologies could not rewrite the past. I could not undo what was. I could only redo what is. The fierce, agonizing pain of a mother lost in the fog of her own despair is not something I can romanticize or rationalize. There is nothing poetic about a child trying to interpret the absence behind a parent's eyes. The pain I inflicted was real. It was a consequence of my illness. A shadow cast outward from the internal darkness I was battling. A weather system that formed inside me but altered the climate of our home. And yet, even in acknowledging that shadow, I refuse to collapse into shame. Because accountability is not self-destruction. It is integrity. Shame would freeze me in the past, trap me in self-condemnation, and convince me that I am unworthy of redemption. But integrity invites me to stand upright. To tell the truth without theatrics. To own my part without annihilating myself in the process. I have learned that remorse, when held with honesty and compassion, becomes a bridge rather than a prison. It does not chain me to what I cannot change. It guides me toward what I can. Remorse calls me forward. It asks me to be present now in ways I could not be then. It challenges me to show up differently. To listen more deeply. To notice more carefully. To love more consciously. To repair where repair is possible and to accept with humility where scars may remain. I cannot return to who I was before the fog. That version of me no longer exists. Nor should she. But I can be a mother who is awake now. A mother who chooses healing not only for herself but for the generations connected to her. A mother who understands that love is not proven by perfection, but by growth. By consistency. By courage in the face of discomfort. That is the amends I live each day. Not a single speech. Not a grand gesture. But a daily practice. Of presence. Of listening. Of loving without hiding. And in that practice, something sacred continues to unfold. Not a return to the past. But a deeper, truer version of love, rooted not in illusion, but in awareness. Living my amends changed me, but the true turning point came even earlier. Before the apologies. Before the steady work of repair. Before I learned how to sit in discomfort without collapsing. There was a moment far more pivotal, far more urgent, that altered the trajectory of my life entirely. It was the dismantling of a dangerously seductive belief. The belief that my death was the only solution. At one time, that thought had taken root so deeply it felt rational. Not dramatic. Not hysterical. Rational.

I had convinced myself that the only way to make things better was to remove myself from the equation entirely. If I disappeared, the suffering would end. If I surrendered to the void, perhaps those I loved would finally be free of the burden of me. It was a logic that felt airtight in the fog of despair, an equation where subtraction seemed like mercy. I saw myself as the common denominator in every fracture. Every tension. Every wound. And so, the conclusion felt mathematically sound: eliminate the variable, eliminate the problem. The mind, when steeped in hopelessness, becomes frighteningly persuasive. It can turn distortion into doctrine. It can dress self-erasure up as sacrifice. And for a time, I believed that lie. I believed that my absence would be a gift. That my disappearance would create peace. That love, twisted by illness and shame, required my erasure in order to protect those I cared about. But what I could not see then, what I see now with piercing clarity, is that this belief was not compassion. It was despair wearing the mask of logic. It was not mercy. It was exhaustion. It was not clarity. It was distortion. The idea that I was the problem was built upon years of internalized blame. And once that premise was accepted, the conclusion seemed inevitable. But when I began to question the premise, when I began to examine the foundation of that belief, the entire structure began to wobble. *"What if I was not the sole cause? What if my presence was not poison? What if my survival, messy and imperfect, was not a burden but a necessity?* The dismantling of that belief was not gentle. It required confronting how deeply I had devalued myself. It required facing the terrifying realization that I had mistaken self-annihilation for love. But once that lie cracked, even slightly, something extraordinary happened. The equation changed. It was no longer subtraction as mercy. It became presence as responsibility. Staying. Healing. Growing. Not because it was easy. Not because it erased harm. But because it honored the truth that my life was not disposable. That I was not an expendable variable in other people's happiness. Living my amends is possible only because I chose to live. And choosing to live, again and again, even when the fog rolls in, is the most radical act of love I have ever committed to. Not just for them. But for myself. However, this will be a long way in the making. That old belief, where I believed my self-erasure was mercy for those around me, was twisted logic.

Corrupted reasoning born not of clarity, but of exhaustion. Of shame that had fermented in the dark. Of relentless emotional erosion that had worn away my sense of self until I could no longer distinguish distortion from truth. What felt rational was, in reality, the final product of years of quiet undoing. That belief did not grow in isolation. It was cultivated. It took root in the toxic soil of my marriage, where doubt was planted daily, and certainty was stripped from me thread by thread. It was watered by manipulation, nourished by control, and reinforced by the steady, rhythmic drip of gaslighting. A drop here. A drop there. Each one small enough to dismiss on its own. But over time, the accumulation reshaped the landscape of my mind. My ex-husband's tactics had slowly distorted my perception until self-erasure felt like responsibility. That is the insidious nature of prolonged psychological harm; it does not strike all at once. It reframes. It redefines. It rearranges your internal compass until north feels like south and survival feels like selfishness. I had internalized the idea that I was the problem to be solved. The flaw to be corrected. The tension in every room. The instability in every relationship. And in that warped narrative, eliminating myself appeared to be the ultimate act of repair. If I was the crack in the foundation, then removing myself would stabilize the structure. If I was the weight bending the beam, then disappearing would restore balance. It felt almost noble in its self-sacrifice. But that was the lie. The most dangerous lies are not loud. They are quiet and plausible. They masquerade as logic. They borrow the language of responsibility and twist it into self-destruction. They tell you that erasing yourself is the same as protecting others. But self-erasure is not repair. It is surrender to distortion. What I could not see then is that I had been taught to equate my value with my usefulness, my worth with my compliance, my presence with disruption. And when I inevitably failed to be perfectly accommodating, perfectly pleasing, perfectly silent in my suffering. I concluded that the only remaining solution was disappearance. But the truth, fierce and steady and unyielding, is this: I was never the problem to be solved. I was a human being caught in a system that thrived on my self-doubt. The lie told me that ending myself would fix everything. The truth revealed that ending the distortion was the real work.

And once I began dismantling that belief, once I saw how it had been constructed, reinforced, and weaponized against me, the illusion lost its grip. Not all at once. But steadily. Like a spell breaking. And in its place, something far more radical emerged: The understanding that staying, imperfect, healing, accountable, alive, was not selfish. It was strength. The crucial shift was not simply recognizing that I had caused harm. It was recognizing that my existence was not the harm. For so long, those two ideas had fused together in my mind, indistinguishable. I believed that if pain followed me, it must originate from me. That if those I loved struggled, I must be the source. I confused impact with identity. I mistook illness for immorality. But my illness was not a moral failing. It was not a character defect. It was not proof of corruption at my core. It was suffering. Untreated. Misunderstood. Weaponized against me in moments when I was most vulnerable. And my presence, messy, imperfect, struggling, was not a curse cast upon the people I loved. The idea that my death would heal anything was not noble. It was a symptom. A symptom of how deeply I had been convinced of my own disposability. Of how thoroughly I had absorbed the message that I was excess weight. An error to be corrected. A disruption in the harmony of everyone else's lives. I had mistaken erasure for redemption. But when that belief cracked, when I began to see that removing myself was not mercy but tragedy, something fundamental shifted inside me. It was as if a lens had been lifted from my eyes. The same world but seen differently. The same life, but reframed. I stopped viewing myself as the poison. I began to see myself as the person who needed care. That shift was seismic, though it happened quietly. It did not erase the pain I had caused. It did not rewrite history. It did not dissolve regret. The past remained intact, with all its complexity and consequence. But it interrupted the most dangerous narrative of all, the one that told me the world would be better without me in it.

That narrative had been the deepest wound. The most insidious lie. The quiet refrain that made everything else seem inevitable. And when I chose to stay, when I chose to live, breath by breath, day by day, I unknowingly chose something else too. I chose the possibility of healing. Not certainty. Not ease. Not instant transformation. Possibility. Possibility that growth could follow devastation. Possibility that repair could follow rupture. Possibility that my story was not over at its darkest chapter. In choosing to stay, I chose to remain in the arena of change. I chose to give myself the chance to become more than the worst moments of my illness. I chose to believe, however faintly, that I was not beyond repair. And that choice, fragile as it was, became the quiet beginning of everything that followed. Not perfection. Not absolution. But life. And life, even in its trembling uncertainty, is fertile ground for redemption.

Choosing to stay forced me to confront the most dangerous thought I had ever entertained. It was not loud. It did not roar. It whispered with terrible calm: "*Your death would make this better. Your absence would be relief.*" The belief that my existence itself was the problem, that I was the source of suffering, the flaw in the fabric of every relationship, was the true poison. And I remember how that belief tasted. Metallic. Bitter. Like something corrosive dissolving slowly at the back of my tongue. It coated my thoughts with a sickly sheen of inevitability. It sounded logical inside the echo chamber of my despair, where only distorted reasoning was allowed to speak. It felt heavy in my chest, pressing against my lungs until even breathing seemed indulgent. Selfish. As though the very act of staying alive was an imposition on those around me. Emotionally, beneath the frantic swirl of fear and shame, it felt like resignation. Not peace. Not relief. But surrender to emptiness. It was the quiet collapse that follows prolonged exhaustion. The laying down of weapons not because the battle is over, but because you no longer believe you deserve to fight. But it wasn't my existence that was the problem. It was my crippling belief that I was unfixable. That belief wrapped around my thoughts like smoke in a sealed room, thick and disorienting. It blurred every doorway. It convinced me that annihilation was mercy. That subtraction was kindness. That the most loving thing I could do was erase myself from the equation entirely. In that fog, destruction masqueraded as devotion. My suicide attempt was not the answer. It was the ultimate expression of my inability to see another way forward. It was the sound of a door slamming in a room I believed had no windows. The final gesture of someone who had mistaken darkness for permanence.

I did not want to die as much as I wanted the pain to end. But I had lost the capacity to imagine a path where both I and healing could coexist. Choosing to stay forced me to look directly at that lie. To taste it again. To name it. To see how thoroughly it had infiltrated my thinking. And in doing so, something began to clear. The smoke thinned. The air shifted. The room, once suffocating, revealed faint outlines of possibility. Windows I had not seen before. Cracks in the wall where light filtered through in narrow, stubborn beams. The thought that my death would ease their suffering was not compassion. It was distortion amplified by despair. And when I finally saw that clearly, when I understood that my disappearance would not be healing but devastation, I felt something unexpected rise within me. Not grand courage. Not dramatic resolve. But defiance. A quiet refusal to let that lie have the final word. Because if the belief that I was unfixable was the true poison, then survival was the antidote. Imperfect. Trembling. Ongoing. And in choosing to stay, breath by breath, day by day, I began, slowly, to detox from the narrative that had nearly consumed me. Not by pretending the pain had never existed. But by deciding that I would no longer let it define the value of my life. The solution was never my disappearance or annihilation. It only felt that way because despair narrows vision until the horizon vanishes. But the answer was never subtraction. It lay elsewhere. It lay in healing the fractures that had split me open, not in shattering myself further. It lay in tending to the wounds that had festered for years, wounds I had ignored, minimized, normalized, until they began to define me. It lay in leaving the toxic marriage that fueled my despair. The marriage that amplified my illness like a distorted echo chamber. The marriage that bent reality until suffering felt inevitable, even deserved. That environment did not just house my pain, it magnified it. It turned ordinary struggle into chronic erosion. It convinced me that anguish was my natural climate. I can still feel the suffocation of that space. The tension in the air, tight and brittle, as though even silence might snap. The sharpness of words, precise, cutting, leaving invisible lacerations. The quiet dread humming beneath daily life, constant, low, relentless. It smelled like fear. It sounded like silence laced with accusation. It felt like walking on glass, every step calculated, every movement cautious, waiting for the next crack. My nervous system never rested. My body carried alertness like armor. My spirit shrank to survive. And in that environment, I began to believe that suffering was simply who I was. But redemption was not found in erasure. It was found in effort. In conscious change. In sincere acknowledgement of the pain, I had caused. In choosing to face what I would rather have hidden from. Redemption did not require my absence. It required my presence. It required me to look into my children's eyes and truly see them—not as extensions of my shame, not as mirrors of my failure, but as whole, feeling beings who had lived through my storm. It required me to hear their confusion without defending myself. To witness their hurt without retreating into guilt. Making amends was not a performance. It was a practice. It was not one conversation and done. Not a single apology wrapped in tears. It was consistency. It was showing up differently tomorrow than I had yesterday. It was noticing when old patterns stirred and choosing another response. It was rebuilding trust not through promises, but through repetition of care. It required presence. It required humility. It required choosing, again and again, to be better than I had been when I was drowning.

Better not in perfection. Better in awareness. Better in accountability. Healing the fractures did not mean pretending they never existed. It meant strengthening around them. Reinforcing the places that once split under pressure. Learning how to inhabit my life without fear dictating every move. The solution was not to disappear. It was to transform. To leave what was killing me. To nurture what was wounded. To remain. And in remaining, in breathing through discomfort, in staying for hard conversations, in choosing growth over escape, I discovered something far more powerful than erasure. I discovered resilience. Not loud. Not flashy. But steady. And steady is what redemption requires. That was the path to redemption. Not self-destruction. Self-reconstruction. Not tearing myself down in penance. But rebuilding, deliberately, tenderly, from the inside out. It was in becoming a healthier, more whole version of myself that I could finally stop hurting the people I loved. Not because I erased the past. Not because I punished myself enough to atone. But because I began strengthening the very places that once leaked pain into everything around me. Redemption was not collapse. It was construction. It was learning how to stand differently. Speak differently. Choose differently. It was in breaking cycles rather than breaking myself. Breaking the inherited narratives of shame. Breaking the reflex to blame myself for everything. Breaking the instinct to shrink in order to survive. Breaking the learned belief that suffering was proof of loyalty. It was in choosing healing over annihilation. And that choice was not made once. It was made in small, stubborn increments. In therapy sessions where truth stung before it soothed. In conversations with my children where my voice trembled but did not retreat. In quiet mornings when I chose to breathe instead of spiral. In moments when the old poison tried to rise again, and I answered it with something new. And when I think back now, I can almost feel the shift. It was subtle. Not fireworks. Not triumph. More like the slow changing of air before a storm breaks. The moment when something toxic begins to dilute.

When the bitterness that once coated every thought begins to thin. When the poison, once coursing through my veins like certainty, loses its potency. Hope did not arrive as a roar. It arrived as circulation. Faint but real.

A warmth in my chest where there had only been heaviness. A loosening in my breath where there had only been pressure. A flicker of possibility where there had only been finality. Redemption was never about dying for them. It was about living differently for them. And for myself. It was about staying present when it would be easier to retreat. About loving consciously instead of desperately. About building a life where my existence is no longer an apology, but a gift. Living differently meant allowing myself to matter. Allowing my children to see not perfection, but growth. Allowing my story to evolve beyond its darkest chapter. Redemption was not martyrdom. It was maturity. It was waking up. It was choosing, again and again, to participate in my own healing. To tend the fractures instead of hiding them. To nurture resilience instead of rehearsing shame. And in that steady, intentional living, I discovered something I once thought impossible: My life was never the problem. My life was the possibility. Living differently for them required another kind of clarity, one that did not soothe at first, but startled. It tasted sharp and bracing, like cold air filling lungs long starved of oxygen. It burned on the way in. It woke me up. This clarity was not gentle. It did not wrap me in comfort. It stripped illusion. As for my ex-husband, the blame game was a different beast altogether. It did not creep. It roared. It prowled the perimeter of every conversation, waiting for a weak moment to lunge. There were those, especially him, who would have me believe that I was solely responsible for the fractures in their lives. That every conflict traced back to me. That every dissatisfaction bore my fingerprint. That if something broke, I had broken it. I can still hear the cadence of those accusations. Measured. Controlled. Convincing. I can still feel the sting of them against my skin, like sand flung into open wounds. They did not always arrive as shouting.

Sometimes they came cloaked in reason. In calm explanations. In subtle sighs that implied disappointment more than anger. And somehow, that restraint made them sharper. The room would grow tight, heavy with tension. The air thick and unmoving. His voice steady and certain, as though he were delivering a verdict already decided. As though the trial had long concluded, and I had simply been summoned to hear my sentence. Guilty. Always guilty. But here is what that sharp, oxygen-rich clarity revealed: This was not truth. It was strategy. A clever manipulation. A calculated shifting of weight from his shoulders onto mine. A way to avoid accountability while cloaking himself in righteousness. It was easier to crown himself the injured party than to examine his own cruelty. Easier to recast me as unstable than to confront his own instability. Blame was his shield. Projection was his armor. And I had worn both for him without realizing it. Living differently required me to refuse that burden. Not angrily. Not theatrically. But firmly. It required me to separate what was mine to own from what was being handed to me as a diversion. To recognize when guilt was authentic and when it was manufactured. To understand that accepting false blame does not make you virtuous, it makes you complicit in your own erasure. That clarity felt cold at first. But it was clean. It cut through distortion like winter wind clearing fog from a valley. It allowed me to see the terrain without the haze of accusation. And in that clearer landscape, I could finally discern where responsibility ended, and where manipulation began. I no longer needed to absorb every accusation as confession. I no longer needed to shrink in the presence of certainty that was never rooted in fact. The roar of blame lost its power when I stopped mistaking volume for truth. And in that shift, quiet, internal, resolute, I reclaimed something I had surrendered for far too long: The authority to define myself. Not by his verdict. But by my integrity. No, I was not to blame for the wreckage of his life. That truth did not arrive easily. It had to be wrestled from a narrative he had so skillfully constructed. He wove it with precision, thread by thread, until it felt seamless.

A web spun with silk so fine I did not realize I was caught in it until every attempt to move tightened the strands around me. In his version of the story, I was the source of his unhappiness. The catalyst for his cruelty. The justification for his abuse. If he raged, it was because I provoked him. If he betrayed, it was because I failed him. If he faltered, it was because I destabilized him. I became the scapegoat. The convenient explanation. The lightning rod for his frustrations. Every storm in his life found its way to my doorstep. Every misstep became my shadow.

I carried his disappointments as though they were my design. But the truth, clear, steady, unadorned, was far less dramatic. And far less convenient. I was not responsible for his choices. Not for his actions. Not for his words. Not for the violence of his behavior or the fractures of his character. The weight of his decisions rested solely on his shoulders, no matter how desperately he tried to shift it onto mine. He could narrate the story however he pleased. He could dress blame up as logic. He could frame cruelty as reaction. But responsibility does not transfer simply because it is asserted. It remains where it belongs. He had to own his part in the disintegration of our marriage. He had to confront his own life's struggles without hiding behind my shadow. He had to face the consequences of his choices without appointing me as their origin. And when I finally understood that, truly understood it, something inside me settled. The web lost its tension. The silk threads that once felt invisible became visible, breakable. I could see where they had attached. I could feel where they had pulled. And with that awareness came strength. I did not need to defend myself endlessly. I did not need to argue my innocence. I did not need to carry his narrative as penance. I could step out of the role he had assigned me. Not with fury. Not with vengeance. But with clarity. The wreckage of his life was not mine to rebuild. The storms he created were not mine to weather on his behalf. I could grieve what had been lost without absorbing what was never mine to own. And in releasing that burden, I felt my spine straighten. My breath deepen. My voice steady. For the first time, I stood not as the scapegoat in someone else's tragedy, but as the author of my own survival. And that shift, quiet, resolute, irreversible, was freedom of another kind.

My responsibility was different. It was not to carry his shame. Not to absorb his consequences. Not to serve as the container for his unfinished work. My part was something quieter, but infinitely braver: to recognize the manipulation for what it was. To feel the familiar tug of guilt rising in my chest and refuse it. That tug was old. Reflexive. It would tighten just beneath my sternum, warm and urgent, as though responsibility were magnetic and I were iron. My body had learned to respond before my mind could question. But now, when that pull begins, I pause. I breathe. I ask: "*Is this mine?*" To hear the accusations echoing in my mind and challenge them. Not react. Not defend. Challenge. Because echoes are not truth. They are repetition. And repetition can be interrupted. To reclaim my emotional ground. That reclamation has texture. It feels like pressing bare feet into soil and realizing the earth does not reject me. It feels like straightening my spine when old narratives try to bend it. It feels like choosing silence not from fear, but from sovereignty. The burden of blame is not mine to carry alone. I will no longer be held hostage by guilt that does not belong to me. I will no longer let shame wrap itself around my throat and silence my truth. Shame once felt like a hand at my windpipe, tight, insistent, demanding quiet compliance. But now I recognize its grip. And I gently, firmly remove it. I can still feel, in my body, the relief of setting that weight down. It is subtle at first. A lightness in my shoulders, as though I had removed a backpack I did not know I was wearing. A softening in my jaw. The quieting of that constant internal pressure that once hummed beneath every thought. The nervous system exhaling. The body learning that it no longer needs to brace. There is grief in accepting this. Grief for the years lost to self-accusation. Grief for the energy spent defending myself against stories that were never mine. There is anger, too, a righteous heat that flickers through my veins when I think of how convincingly I was cast as the villain in someone else's narrative. There is sorrow for the version of me who believed it. Who carried it. Who bowed beneath it. But beneath all of it, beneath grief and anger and sorrow, there is something steadier. Freedom. Not loud. Not defiant. But grounded. The beast of blame no longer rules my inner landscape. It may still prowl at the edges, testing old doors. But I see it now. I name it. And I refuse to feed it. Awareness is its starvation. Clarity is its undoing. And in this reclaimed space, where guilt no longer dictates my identity, where shame no longer constricts my voice, I stand not as a captive, but as a woman who has learned the terrain of her own mind. And that terrain, once wild and hostile, is becoming home. After I stopped feeding the beast of blame, another question rose from the quiet. Quieter. But far more dangerous. It did not roar. It did not accuse. It whispered. It slipped beneath the surface of my thoughts and settled somewhere intimate and tender, gnawing with sharper teeth, more self-destructive precision: *"Was I truly too broken to heal? Too damaged to change? Was I beyond repair?"* This question did not feel external. It felt internal. It did not sound like his voice. It sounded like mine. It tasted like rust in my mouth, metallic and stale, as though I had been chewing on old wounds for far too long. It felt like cold stone pressing against my spine, hard and unyielding, as if the very foundation of me were cracked beyond restoration. I could hear it in the silence of early mornings, when the world was still, and there were no distractions to drown it out. I could see it reflected in the tired lines around my eyes, the way doubt lingered in the spaces where certainty once lived. Emotionally, it carried a hollow weight. Like standing in a burned-out house, staring at blackened beams and charred walls, wondering if anything could ever grow there again. Wondering if the soil beneath the ash was still fertile, or if it had been scorched beyond revival. It was the fear that transformation was for other people. That resilience was reserved for the unbroken. For a long time, I believed the answer was "*yes*"! Yes, I was too damaged. Yes, I had gone too far. Yes, the fractures ran too deep. I looked at my history like evidence in a case against myself. The depression. The attempt. The years of manipulation. The harm caused. The harm endured. Surely, I thought there must be a point of no return. But the real answer, resounding and defiant, was "*absolutely not*"!

Not whispered. Not tentative. But firm. I was not beyond repair. Broken does not mean useless. Burned does not mean barren. Fractured does not mean finished. The burned-out house still stands on earth that remembers how to grow. The blackened beams can be cleared. The soil, once tended, can nourish again. What looks like ruin is often the beginning of reconstruction. And here is the truth I had to learn in my bones: Healing is not the denial of damage. It is the tending of it. Repair does not require perfection. It requires willingness. The cracks in me were not proof of unworthiness. They were evidence of survival. Every fracture told a story of pressure endured. Every scar testified to something lived through. The question *"Am I beyond repair?"* was born from exhaustion. From fear. From the echo of old voices insisting that I was irredeemable. But I am not irreparable. I am human. And humans mend. Not cleanly. Not symmetrically. But beautifully, in ways that strengthen the places that once split open. The real danger was never my brokenness. It was the belief that brokenness disqualified me from healing. And when I rejected that belief, when I stood in the charred remains of my former self and declared that growth was still possible, I felt something extraordinary take root. Not certainty. Not ease. But determination. The quiet, steady conviction that I was not finished. That I was not the ashes. I was the ground beneath them. And the ground still knew how to bloom. That truth did not burst forth dramatically. There were no trumpets. No cinematic sunrise splitting the sky in gold. It emerged slowly, like something fragile rising from ashes still warm with grief. Like a green shoot pressing upward through charred earth, uncertain but determined. It trembled at first. It questioned its own right to exist. The belief in my irreparable brokenness had been a delusion. Not a spontaneous one. A constructed one. A carefully engineered prison built from my internal anxieties and reinforced by external pressures. Brick by brick, fear and manipulation shaped its walls. Each accusation another layer of mortar.

Each depressive thought another iron bar across a window I did not realize had once been open. Depression whispered that I was defective. It did not shout. It insinuated. It suggested. It colored my perception until every flaw felt fatal, every mistake catastrophic. It convinced me that my sadness was not an illness but an identity. That I was not suffering, I was flawed. Others' accusations echoed that I was the problem. The voices layered themselves one over another until they became a chorus. A steady drumbeat of doubt. And when enough voices repeat the same refrain, it begins to feel like fact. I absorbed their certainty. I internalized their narrative. I wore their judgments like skin. Together, those voices convinced me that I was beyond fixing. That nothing could restore me. That no therapy, no love, no effort could mend something so fundamentally damaged. And if repair was impossible, then death appeared to be the only exit door left unlocked. That was the illusion. I had fallen prey to the myth of permanent damage. To the idea that pain carves destiny in stone. That trauma brands the soul beyond redemption. That once broken, always broken. But illusions lose their power when exposed to light. The moment I began questioning the narrative. Asking where it came from, who reinforced it, who benefited from it, the structure began to crack. The prison walls, once solid and unquestioned, revealed hairline fractures. And through those fractures, light filtered in. Not blinding. Not overwhelming. But enough. Enough to see that the bricks were not eternal. That the bars were not fused to my bones. That the door I believed was locked had never been sealed at all. Light does not erase damage. It reveals it accurately. And in accurate vision, distortion cannot survive. I was never irreparable. I was wounded. There is a difference. Wounds can close. Bones can knit. Soil can regenerate after fire. That truth did not explode into my life. It settled in gently, persistently. It asked to be nurtured. It required repetition. It required action. But once the illusion was named for what it was, it could no longer dominate. Because permanence was never the truth.

It was fear, dressed as prophecy. And when fear is illuminated, it shrinks. What remained in its place was something quieter, but infinitely more powerful: Possibility. And possibility is the first breath of freedom. Healing was not some mystical gift bestowed upon the morally superior. It was not reserved for the "worthy." It was not a prize handed to the lucky. It was not a passive miracle that drifted down on softened wings. Healing was a decision. A battle. A fierce and relentless act of will. It required showing up when every part of me wanted to disappear. It required remaining present inside my own skin when escape felt sweeter. It required choosing breath when breath felt heavy. Choosing effort when effort felt unbearable. And I did not even realize I had that choice until the moment I stood at the edge of death, staring into its cold, feelingless eyes. There was nothing romantic there. Nothing serene. The abyss did not glow. It did not promise rest. It was hollow. Unresponsive. Vast and indifferent. And when I felt it staring back at me, not inviting, not comforting, but horrifying, something primal awakened. Not a speech. Not a revelation. A refusal. A quiet but immovable "*no*". Not loud. Not dramatic. But absolute. I was not broken beyond repair. I was wounded. And wounds, when tended, can mend. When cleaned, they knit. When cared for, they strengthen the tissue around them. But when left unattended, when ignored or shamed, they rot. They fester. They poison the surrounding systems. Infection spreads through the body until what began as injury becomes systemic collapse. The same is true for emotional, mental, and spiritual wounds. Untended trauma infects perception. Untreated depression distorts reality. Unchallenged shame metastasizes into identity. The difference was never about damage; it was about care. That was where the truth separated itself from the illusion. I was not irreparable. I was untreated. And treatment required participation. The prison I believed in began to crack. Not because the walls vanished overnight, but because I pressed against them. The air shifted. The atmosphere inside my chest loosened. The weight did not evaporate, but it redistributed. It no longer sat as a verdict. It became a challenge. The pain remained. The grief remained. The scars did not dissolve. But I understood something radical: I had agency. I could fight. I could choose. I could stay. Healing was not something that happened to me like weather. It was something I claimed like territory. Something I stepped toward deliberately. Something I earned through repetition, through confrontation, through uncomfortable honesty. It was not about becoming someone new.

It was about transforming survival into strength. What I once called brokenness was, in truth, survival waiting to be refined. Waiting to be reshaped. Waiting to be redirected toward growth instead of despair. The abyss did not claim me. I claimed myself. And in that claiming, in that steady, stubborn refusal to disappear, I began to understand that healing is not the absence of wounds. It is the decision to tend them. Again, and again. Until what once threatened to end you becomes the very  thing that teaches you how to live.

For so long, I was entrenched in the belief that I was fundamentally *broken,* that death seemed like the only logical conclusion. The word itself became a gavel in my mind. "*Broken!*" It echoed like a verdict delivered in a silent courtroom where I was both accused and condemned. No defence. No appeal. Just a final judgment reverberating through the hollow chambers of my thoughts. I could almost feel it in my bones, a heaviness, a brittleness, as though one wrong movement might splinter me completely. As though I were made of cracked porcelain, held together by nothing more than tension and pretense. The air around that belief was stale. Suffocating. It smelled like despair left too long in a closed room. It sounded like finality. Like the heavy thud of a door closing and locking from the outside. When you believe you are irreparably damaged, annihilation begins to masquerade as reason. It dresses itself in logic. It speaks in calm, measured tones. It suggests that endings are cleaner than repair. And I believed it. Because when something feels shattered beyond restoration, destruction can appear merciful. But it was only after I cheated death, after I clawed my way back from the precipice, nails scraping against the edge of oblivion, that I finally glimpsed the truth beyond that lie. I remember the disorientation of survival. The world did not look triumphant. It looked sharp. Exposed. The sharp scent of antiseptic burned in my nostrils. The sterile brightness of hospital lights cut into my vision. The weight of breath returning to my lungs felt foreign, almost intrusive, like something I was not sure I deserved but could not deny. My body trembled as reality settled back in. There was no serenity in that space. No peaceful surrender. Only the stark, visceral awareness that I had stood at the abyss and found not relief, but terror staring back at me. Cold. Indifferent. Vast. The abyss did not cradle me. It threatened to erase me. And in that confrontation, something inside me recoiled, not from life, but from nonexistence. From the horrifying stillness of what would have been left behind. The finality that once seemed logical now felt brutal. Not noble. Not merciful. Brutal. The belief that I was broken beyond repair had promised peace. The edge revealed its lie. What I felt in that moment was not clarity wrapped in calm, it was instinct. Raw and primal. A fierce, bodily refusal to dissolve. My lungs filled. My heart pounded. My nervous system surged with the undeniable declaration of survival. I was not a verdict. I was alive. And survival, disorienting and messy as it was, carried within it something I had not allowed myself to see before: If I were truly broken beyond repair, I would not have fought.

If I were truly irredeemable, I would not have felt terror at the thought of disappearing. The brittleness I believed defined me was not my essence. It was exhaustion. The heaviness in my bones was not proof of defectiveness. It was the weight of untreated wounds. Standing at the edge did not confirm my brokenness. It exposed the lie. And in that exposure, in the antiseptic sting, in the trembling breath, in the raw disorientation of being pulled back into the world. I saw something I had long refused to acknowledge: I was not shattered beyond repair. I was human. And humans, even when cracked, still bleed, still breathe, still fight. The courtroom in my mind fell silent. The verdict dissolved. And in its place, something far more powerful began to take root. Not certainty. But possibility. Not perfection. But life. And life, however fragile in that moment, was infinitely more powerful than the illusion of finality I had once mistaken for truth. Surviving that darkness cracked something open. Not all at once. Not with ceremony. Not with a gentle unveiling of light. It was more like ice splitting under pressure, sharp, jagged, undeniable. A fracture in the certainty that had once held me captive. Enough of a break for something new to slip through. It was in surviving the abyss that the door to healing first opened, even if only a sliver. A thin seam of light. A breath of air where there had only been suffocation. I did not step through it immediately. I barely recognized it. But it was there. And through that narrow opening came a truth I could no longer ignore: No one is beyond repair. No one. Not the woman who stood at the edge. Not the mother lost in fog. Not the soul who once believed she was a burden. Not me. Not anyone. Healing is not reserved for the unbroken. It does not require purity or perfection or a spotless past. It begins with a decision. A conscious, defiant decision to fight for a better life when everything inside you insists that surrender would be easier. It begins with willingness. With the audacity to say, "*What if I am not finished?*" Healing is not passive. It does not drift down like mercy from the sky. It is forged. Claimed.

Earned in moments when disappearing would feel simpler. It is a reclamation, of agency, of voice, of ground once surrendered to despair. I had to take my power back from the hands of hopelessness. Not dramatically. Not all at once. But deliberately. Courage was required—but not the loud, cinematic kind. Not fireworks. Not applause. The quiet, stubborn kind. The kind that wakes up the morning after surviving and chooses to stay again. The kind that sits in therapy and tells the truth even when it shakes. The kind that faces regret without running. The kind that says, "*I will stay.*" That sentence became sacred. I will stay. I will stay when the fog rolls in. I will stay when shame tries to rewrite the story. I will stay when old narratives whisper that I am too damaged to matter. Staying was my rebellion. Choosing life was my defiance. Recovery was not a single triumphant act; it was a commitment. A daily recommitment. A quiet contract with myself that said: I will fight for this life. Even with trembling hands. Even with imperfect steps. Even when my strength feels thin and threadbare. Because trembling hands still hold. And slivers of light still widen. Surviving the abyss did not make me fearless. It made me aware. Aware that darkness does not have the final word unless we hand it the pen. Aware that despair can be loud, persuasive, and relentless, but it is not omnipotent. Aware that the human spirit, even when bruised and weary, contains something astonishingly resilient. The crack that opened in me was not weakness. It was an entrance. And through that entrance stepped something I had long forgotten how to trust: Hope. Not naive. Not blind. But fierce. The kind that grows from having seen the abyss, and choosing, anyway, to turn toward the light. As my sponsor often reminded me, *"Nothing changes if nothing changes, and everything changes if everything changes."* At first, those words did not shimmer with poetry. They did not glide across the page like metaphor. They landed with weight. Solid. Practical. Almost severe in their simplicity. But they were true. Change demanded change. Not longing. Not wishing. Not waiting for someone else to behave differently. I could not remain in the same patterns and expect a different outcome. I could not cling to familiar coping mechanisms and hope for unfamiliar peace. I could not stay inside the architecture of old beliefs and pray for a new landscape to appear. If I wanted my life to shift, I had to shift. I had to alter my habits, the small, daily rituals that quietly shape destiny. I had to challenge my beliefs, the inherited scripts I once accepted as law. I had to redraw my boundaries, thickening the lines where I once erased myself. I had to change my environment, removing myself from spaces that fed my despair. I had to become an active participant in my own transformation. No longer a bystander. No longer a victim of momentum. No longer waiting for rescue. And change, I did. Not easily. Not instantly. But deliberately. There were no dramatic montages. No overnight conversions. It was incremental. Often uncomfortable. Sometimes humiliating. I stumbled. I repeated mistakes. I caught myself mid-pattern and felt the old pull toward self-sabotage. But I kept going. I worked, and continue to work, relentlessly for that change to take root. Because growth is fragile at first. It is not a single victory. It is daily effort. It is waking up and choosing differently when choosing differently feels unnatural. It is noticing the old thoughts rise like smoke from a long-extinguished fire and refusing to kneel before them. It is tending to the fragile shoots of growth even when storms threaten to flatten them. Storms still come. Old narratives still whisper. But I no longer confuse familiarity with truth. I once believed I was broken beyond repair. That belief felt like stone, cold, immovable, carved into my identity. But now I understand something far more powerful: I was never broken beyond healing. I was wounded. I was conditioned. I was exhausted. But I was not irreparable. I was simply waiting for the moment I would choose to fight for my own life. And when that moment came, quietly, stubbornly, in the wake of terror, I chose. Not once. But again. And again. And again. Because everything changes when everything changes. And I was finally willing to change everything.

Change demanded courage. And courage, once awakened, forced me to ask a question I had avoided for years: *"Was I truly stuck in that toxic marriage?"* For so long, I believed I was. The belief wrapped itself around me like iron chains, cold, heavy, convincing. I felt their weight in my shoulders, their chill against my ribs. They did not clang dramatically. They tightened quietly. A twisted sense of duty bound me there. I told myself endurance was noble. That suffering in silence was strength. That commitment, no matter the cost, was virtue. Fear of abandonment whispered constantly in my ear. *"Being alone will break you! Being alone will prove you are worthless and unlovable! Better to be diminished than discarded!"* The thought of rejection tasted bitter, metallic on my tongue. It lingered like the aftertaste of something toxic swallowed in desperation. The house we shared felt both familiar and suffocating, the air thick with tension, the silence humming with unspoken resentment. Even the walls seemed to absorb our unrest. Even the floors felt tense beneath my steps. I told myself commitment was proof of character. I clung to it as though endurance were evidence of love. As though loyalty, stretched beyond reason, was the measure of my worth. If I stayed long enough, tried hard enough, bent far enough, perhaps I would finally deserve peace. But what I was really clinging to was illusion. The illusion that martyrdom is virtue. The illusion that love must hurt to be real. The illusion that leaving would make me the villain. As my healing journey unfolded, slow, messy, and raw, I began to sense something shifting beneath my feet. It was subtle at first. Like the first tremor before the earth rearranges itself. Not loud enough to alarm. Just enough to unsettle. As I began to value and understand my inherent worth, something inside me realigned. The rigid moral compass I had once worn like armor began to soften into discernment. The fear of abandonment that pulsed in my chest no longer dictated every decision. The terror of solitude that once echoed in my thoughts lost its thunder. I began to question the chains. "*Were they forged from love or fear? From devotion, or desperation?"* I could almost hear it: the faint scraping sound of erosion. My spirit thinning under the steady drip of criticism and control. Day after agonizing day. Not a single blow, but a thousand small cuts. Not a dramatic collapse, but a slow wearing down. The erosion had been so gradual I mistook it for normalcy.

But healing sharpened my senses. I could feel where I had shrunk. I could see where I had silenced myself. I could recognize the cost of staying. And in that recognition, courage deepened. I was not stuck. I was afraid. Afraid of being alone. Afraid of being judged. Afraid of being seen as a failure. Afraid of giving up on what I believe, I had to keep honoring my commitment to marriage. Afraid of dismantling a life I had invested so much of myself into. Afraid of admitting that endurance was not the same as love. But chains, once recognized as chains, begin to lose their authority. The tremor beneath my feet grew steadier. Not destructive, clarifying. The ground was shifting not to swallow me, but to free me. The illusion that had kept me tethered began to dissolve in the light of self-worth. I was not bound by destiny. I was bound by belief. And belief, once questioned, can be changed. That realization did not explode into certainty. It unfolded. Gradually. Painfully. But unmistakably. I was not trapped. I had been choosing captivity because I believed it was safer than freedom. And once I understood that; the chains grew lighter. Not yet gone. But no longer invisible. And invisibility is where captivity thrives. Visibility is where it begins to end. But healing changes the way you see. It adjusts the lens. It sharpens the edges. It clears the fog you once mistook for atmosphere. As I began reclaiming my self-worth, slowly, tentatively, my understanding shifted. It was subtle at first. The air felt different. Lighter. Easier to breathe. The room that had once seemed sealed, airtight with inevitability, no longer felt so confined. I realized something radical. I did not have to remain in harmful situations. The words felt foreign at first. Almost rebellious. I had the power to say no. The power to walk away. The power to leave. The power to choose my path. Choice had always been there. It had not vanished. It had not been stolen. It had been waiting, quiet, patient, while I trembled in fear. I had simply been too afraid to reach for it. Too conditioned to believe that endurance was my only virtue. And then came the harder truth. The nuanced one.

I wasn't just a victim of my first husband's abuse. I was also, in painful and humbling ways, a participant in my own oppression. Not because I deserved it. Not because I caused it. Not because his cruelty was justified. But because I had allowed his words and actions to define me. I had internalized his accusations. I had taken his distortions and worn them like scripture. I had allowed his actions to dictate my sense of self-worth. I had handed him authority over my identity. I had given him the power to convince me I was worthless. That realization stung. It carried the scent of humility and the metallic taste of accountability. Emotionally, it felt like standing naked in front of a mirror and refusing to look away. No defenses. No narratives to hide behind. Just truth. But there was something liberating in that exposure. Because if I had participated in sustaining the lie, I could also participate in dismantling it. That was the shift. I was not trapped by fate. I was trapped by belief. And belief can be rewritten. The chains I thought were forged in circumstance were, in part, forged in fear. Fear of abandonment. Fear of being alone. Fear of being judged. Fear of being unlovable. Fear that solitude would confirm every accusation he had ever hurled at me. But fear, once named, loses its mystery. It shrinks under scrutiny. I was not powerless. I was afraid. And once I understood that, truly understood it, the cage no longer looked permanent. The bars did not dissolve instantly. But they no longer appeared unbreakable. The room no longer felt eternal. The door had always been there. Unopened. Unused. Unchosen. It was not hidden. It was simply terrifying. And healing gave me the courage to see it, not as escape into the unknown, but as return to myself. All I had to do was choose to walk through it. And for the first time, I believed I could.

But healing changes the way you see. It adjusts the lens. It sharpens the edges. It clears the fog you once mistook for atmosphere. As I began reclaiming my self-worth, slowly, tentatively, my understanding shifted. It was subtle at first. The air felt different. Lighter. Easier to breathe. The room that had once seemed sealed, airtight with inevitability, no longer felt so confined. I realized something radical. I did not have to remain in harmful situations. The words felt foreign at first. Almost rebellious. I had the power to say no. The power to walk away. The power to leave. The power to choose my path. Choice had always been there. It had not vanished. It had not been stolen. It had been waiting, quiet, patient, while I trembled in fear. I had simply been too afraid to reach for it. Too conditioned to believe that endurance was my only virtue. And then came the harder truth. The nuanced one. I wasn't just a victim of my first husband's abuse. I was also, in painful and humbling ways, a participant in my own oppression. Not because I deserved it. Not because I caused it. Not because his cruelty was justified. But because I had allowed his words to define me. I had internalized his accusations. I had taken his distortions and worn them like scripture. I had allowed his actions to dictate my sense of self-worth. I had handed him authority over my identity. I had given him the power to convince me I was worthless. That realization stung. It carried the scent of humility and the metallic taste of accountability. Emotionally, it felt like standing naked in front of a mirror and refusing to look away. No defenses. No narratives to hide behind. Just truth. But there was something liberating in that exposure. Because if I had participated in sustaining the lie, I could also participate in dismantling it.

That was the shift. I was not trapped by fate. I was trapped by belief. And belief can be rewritten. The chains I thought were forged in circumstance were, in part, forged in fear. Fear of abandonment. Fear of being alone. Fear of being judged. Fear of being unlovable. Fear that solitude would confirm every accusation he had ever hurled at me. But fear, once named, loses its mystery. It shrinks under scrutiny. I was not powerless. I was afraid. And once I understood that, truly understood it, the cage no longer looked permanent. The bars did not dissolve instantly. But they no longer appeared unbreakable. The room no longer felt eternal. The door had always been there. Unopened. Unused. Unchosen. It was not hidden. It was simply terrifying. And healing gave me the courage to see it, not as escape into the unknown, but as a return to myself. All I had to do was choose to walk through it. And for the first time, I believed I could. The truth, stark and undeniable, was this: I was only *"stuck"* for as long as I chose to be. That realization did not feel triumphant at first. It felt sobering. Exposing. It stripped away the final illusion that fate had sealed my circumstances. My entrapment had not been locked by destiny; it had been reinforced by fear and self-doubt. I had built my own cage from beliefs that told me I could not leave, could not survive, could not be alone. The bars were forged from "*what ifs*". *"What if I fail? What if no one ever loves me again? What if being alone confirms that I am unworthy?"* Those beliefs became iron. And I leaned against them for so long that I mistook them for structural necessity. And yet, standing there in that awareness, something subtle shifted. I could sense the bars loosening. Not falling away dramatically. Not shattering. But loosening. The metal no longer felt fused to my bones. The air between the bars felt wider. I could see through them. I had the power to escape the cycle of abuse, infidelity, manipulation, and the constant erosion of my self-esteem. I had the power to choose not to be abused. Not to be cheated on. Not to be manipulated or diminished. Not because I could control his actions, but because I could control my proximity to them. I had the power to leave. To walk away from the pain that had become my daily air. From the suffering that had begun to feel ordinary. From the slow, steady corrosion that had chipped away at my sense of self until I barely recognized my own reflection. The decision was not easy. It tasted of grief and fear. It felt like standing at the edge of a cliff, not into annihilation this time, but into uncertainty. It demanded courage I did not yet trust I possessed. My hands trembled. My chest tightened. Every old narrative screamed that staying was safer than stepping into the unknown. But beneath the noise, beneath the tremor, beneath the fear, there was something else. A quiet, steady knowing. I deserved better. Not extravagance. Not perfection. Just better. I deserved love that did not wound. Respect that did not have to be earned through silence or sacrifice. Value that did not hinge on someone else's approval. That knowing did not shout. It rooted itself quietly, like something ancient and true. It felt like alignment. Like the earth beneath my feet settling into a new configuration. As I delved deeper into my own psyche, the shift began to take root. I started to take back control, one thought at a time. I challenged the negative messages I had swallowed whole. I questioned the distorted image I had been taught to see when I looked at myself. I examined the script that told me I was too much and not enough at the same time. Slowly, the fog began to lift. Not all at once. Not permanently. But enough. The air cleared in increments. My thoughts felt less crowded. I could hear something beneath the static, a voice that sounded unfamiliar at first. My own. Tentative. Soft. But real. And with it came a truth that settled into my bones, not as arrogance, but as grounding: I am worthy of love and respect. Not because a man grants it to me. Not because I perform for it.

Not because I endure enough to earn it. But because I exist. Because I am human. Because my worth was never his to define. That truth did not inflate me. It steadied me. It straightened my spine. It softened my breath. It untangled the knot that had lived in my chest for years. I was not stuck. I was awakening. And once you awaken to your own inherent worth, cages begin to look optional. And doors, once terrifying, begin to look like passageways back to yourself.

That truth, that my worth was inherent, did not remain abstract. It did not live only in journals or therapy rooms or carefully constructed affirmations. One day, it crystallized. It moved from concept to conviction. It became tangible, almost physical, like something solid placed into my hands. The moment I loved myself enough, truly enough, the moment I placed my well-being above the toxic dynamic that had consumed me, everything shifted. Not outwardly at first. There were no fireworks. No triumphant soundtrack. No dramatic confrontation. But there was a quiet clarity. Like the air after a storm has passed, sharp, clean, unmistakable. The kind of air that stings your lungs at first because you've grown accustomed to breathing smoke. The kind that reminds you what oxygen is supposed to feel like. I understood something simple and profound: I would rather be alone, truly alone and at peace, than endure the daily ache, the constant sting, the insidious suffering inflicted by someone who refused to respect my worth. That realization did not scream. It settled. It was not bitterness. It was discernment. I can still remember how it felt in my body. The tension that had lived in my shoulders for years began to soften, as if invisible hands had finally unclenched. My jaw relaxed. My breath deepened. The perpetual bracing, so constant I no longer recognized it as tension, eased its grip. The room no longer felt suffocating. The walls did not press inward. Even the silence sounded different. Not empty. Spacious. Where once silence had felt like abandonment or accusation, it now felt like possibility. It held room for thought. For stillness. For me.

Emotionally, it felt like stepping out of a burning house and realizing the night air, though cold, was breathable. My skin still stung from the heat. The smoke still lingered in my lungs. But I was outside. I was no longer engulfed. The fire had not defined me. Survival had. There is a kind of loneliness that wounds. And there is a kind that heals. The loneliness I once feared was not emptiness; it was freedom. It was the quiet necessary for rebuilding. It was the sacred space where I could hear my own voice without distortion. Choosing myself did not mean rejecting love. It meant rejecting harm. It meant understanding that love without respect is not love. That devotion without safety is not devotion. That endurance is not the same as commitment. And in that quiet, storm-cleared moment, I recognized something extraordinary: Peace does not roar. It whispers. It does not demand attention. It invites alignment. I no longer needed to contort myself to fit into someone else's comfort. I no longer needed to shrink to maintain proximity. I no longer needed to set myself on fire to keep someone else warm. Aloneness, when chosen, became sovereignty. And sovereignty tasted clean. It felt like standing barefoot on solid ground after years of walking on glass. It felt like reclaiming the space inside my own chest. That was the shift. Not dramatic. Not loud. But irreversible. Because once you taste peace, real peace, you can no longer confuse it with the chaos you once called love. The pain, the hurt, the suffering, I had treated them as inevitable. As the cost of commitment. As the fine print in the contract of love. As something to endure quietly, nobly, indefinitely. I had folded them into my identity, worn them like proof of loyalty. If it hurt, it must mean I was trying hard enough. If it bruised, it must mean I was committed. I mistook endurance for virtue. I mistook survival for devotion. But suddenly, clear as cold water poured over flame, I saw them for what they were: Choices. Not always conscious at first. Not always simple. But choices, nonetheless.

And they were choices I no longer had to make. Choices I refused to make. That refusal felt powerful. It felt like reclaiming ground that had always been mine but that I had unknowingly surrendered. Like stepping back across a boundary I had once allowed to be erased. Like planting my feet into soil and saying, "*This is mine. My peace. My body. My life.*" I no longer had to remain a victim. Victimhood had once felt like my only identity, a script written by circumstance, performed by habit. But now I could see that while harm had been done to me, I was not obligated to live inside it forever. I no longer had to stay trapped in a relationship that was slowly dismantling me from the inside out. I had the power to choose. To choose distance. To choose clarity. To choose myself. That power did not thunder. It did not arrive armored and unshakable. It trembled at first. My steps were not confident strides; they were hesitant, deliberate movements forward. But trembling steps are still steps. And every step away from harm was a step toward wholeness. When I looked in the mirror, really looked, I saw someone new and yet entirely familiar. My eyes still carried history. They held the memory of nights survived, tears shed, battles fought. There were lines there that had not been there before. Depth that came only from having faced the abyss and returned. But there was something else, too. Steadiness. Not perfection. Not naivety. But groundedness. A quiet strength that did not need to prove itself. A presence that did not apologize for existing. I saw a woman worthy of love and respect. Not because she had endured suffering long enough. Not because she had proven herself useful. Not because she had finally become small enough to be acceptable. But because she was. A woman who deserved happiness not as a reward for endurance, but as a birthright. A woman who deserved fulfillment not someday, not conditionally, not after one more sacrifice, but now. The reflection did not look broken. It looked awake. Awake to her own value. Awake to her own boundaries. Awake to the fact that suffering is not synonymous with love. And in that awakening, something sacred shifted. I was no longer trying to survive inside a story that diminished me. I was writing a new one. Not loudly. Not theatrically. But deliberately. And in that deliberate choosing, of peace over pain, of dignity over distortion, of life over annihilation, I stepped fully into myself. Not flawless. But free.

The reflection looked awake. But awakening is not the same as arrival. It is not a finish line crossed with applause. It is not a summit where the wind never shifts again. Awakening is the first inhale after suffocation. It is awareness. It is light touching corners that once lived in shadow. But the terrain beyond that first light, oh, that terrain has been arduous. The journey of self-discovery and healing has been uneven, jagged in places, excruciatingly slow. It has not unfolded in a neat arc. It has been marked by setbacks that felt like regressions, by moments of doubt so thick they pressed against my ribs like old grief resurfacing. It has required patience I did not know I possessed and strength that did not always feel accessible. It hasn't been easy. There are still days when the shadows creep back in, soft-footed and familiar. They do not announce themselves with thunder. They slip in at the edges of morning or settle quietly at dusk. The old whispers of self-blame rise like fog along the edges of my mind, subtle and insistent. I can almost hear them. Thin. Persistent. *"You're not really better. You've imagined your progress. This strength is temporary."* I can feel them, too. A tightening in my chest. A subtle heaviness behind my eyes. A faint contraction in my breath. The body remembers what the mind is learning to release. But now, I recognize them. That is the difference. The whispers are no longer mistaken for truth. They are identified. Named. Examined. They are not prophecy. They are remnants. Echoes of a past I am actively leaving behind. Fragments of a voice that once dominated my inner world but now struggles to maintain its authority. They no longer command. They murmur. They no longer define. They attempt. They are like smoke from a fire that has already burned out—visible, perhaps, curling faintly in the air, but no longer capable of consuming me. The structure that once fed them has been dismantled. The fuel has been removed. Yes, I still see the smoke some days. But I also know the fire is gone. Healing has not erased the shadows. It has taught me how to walk through them without mistaking them for the whole sky. It has taught me that progress is not linear, that doubt does not cancel growth, that the return of old thoughts does not mean I am back where I started. It means I am human. Awake, yes, but still walking. Still choosing. Still tending the ground beneath my feet.

Awakening is not arrival. It is orientation. It is the quiet, steady knowing that even when fog gathers, I have learned how to find my way through it. And that knowledge, that hard-earned, embodied wisdom, is something the shadows can no longer steal from me. With each step forward, with every milestone reached, some so small they almost whisper, others so profound they shift the architecture of my inner world, I feel layers of self-blame and self-deception peeling away. It is not dramatic. There is no shedding of skin in a single sweep. No thunderous unveiling of a new self. It is gradual. Patient. Like bark loosening from a tree that has weathered harsh seasons and continues to grow despite the scars carved into it. The old layers fall away in fragments, revealing rings of resilience beneath. Sometimes I do not notice the growth until I look back and realize the ground behind me has widened. The guilt that once clung like damp fabric begins to dry and crack. The narratives I once rehearsed as truth lose their script. The apologies I once offered for existing dissolve into something quieter and truer, self-acceptance. And beneath those peeling layers, I discover a self I had long underestimated. Stronger. Steadier. More resilient than I ever believed possible. Not invincible. Not untouched. But rooted. There is a solidity now where there was once only tremor. A groundedness in my breath. A steadiness in my gaze. I move differently. I speak differently. I inhabit myself differently. The scars remain. I can still trace them if I choose. They are textured memories in my body and heart. I feel them in certain silences. In certain songs. In certain rooms where history still lingers faintly in the air. They are reminders of the battles fought. The nights survived. The storms endured when I did not think I would see morning. They are etched into me. But they no longer define me. They are not labels stamped across my identity. They are evidence. Evidence of survival. Evidence of endurance. Evidence of the strength that rose when I believed I had none left. Scars are not signs of defectiveness. They are proof of healing. Of a wound that closed. Of a body, or a spirit, that refused to remain open forever. I am not the fire that burned me. I am the tree that kept growing. The rings inside me tell a story not of destruction, but of persistence. Of seasons survived. Of roots deepened. Of light sought even after long winters. And as the old bark falls away, as the self-blame thins, I stand more fully in who I am becoming. Not perfect. Not finished. But real. Alive. Awake. And still growing. I have learned something that once felt impossible to believe: I was never too broken to heal. I was never too damaged to change. Those sentences once felt like poetry meant for other people, beautiful, but not applicable to me. For years, I treated transformation as a luxury reserved for the untouched. I believed growth belonged to the stable, the unscarred, the emotionally intact. I did not see that within me, buried beneath sedimented doubt and inherited shame, , was a capacity for renewal far greater than I had allowed myself to imagine. It had always been there. Not extinguished. Just covered. Covered by years of self-criticism. Covered by the echoes of manipulation. Covered by the fatigue of survival. But beneath that weight, something resilient had been waiting. Healing was not easy. It was not cinematic. It was not swift. It did not sweep in like a miracle and rearrange everything overnight. It demanded time, long, patient stretches of it. It demanded effort when I would have preferred avoidance. It demanded humility, the kind that requires you to admit where you were wrong, where you were wounded, where you were afraid. It required relentless dedication. To show up to therapy even when I felt exposed. To sit in silence when my instincts begged for distraction. To face truths that stung like antiseptic poured into an open wound. Healing required me to sit with discomfort long enough for it to transform. To tolerate the ache of growth. To keep moving when progress felt invisible, when change seemed microscopic, when doubt whispered that I was fooling myself.

And yet, something was shifting. Not in grand gestures. In repetition. In every honest conversation where I chose transparency over defensiveness. In every boundary held, even when my voice trembled. In every self-compassionate choice that replaced self-condemnation. In every moment, I chose to breathe instead of collapse. With each step, I felt myself becoming stronger. Not hardened. Strengthened. More confident, not loud, but grounded. More at peace, not because life had simplified, but because I no longer abandoned myself in it. The past did not vanish. It remains woven into the fabric of who I am. But it no longer controls me. It no longer dictates my reactions. It no longer scripts my worth. It no longer holds the pen to my identity. Doubt has not disappeared. But I have learned to walk through it without surrendering. To recognize it as weather, not climate. To understand that uncertainty does not invalidate progress. I am not who I was. That woman carried pain I no longer carry in the same way. She survived what she did not yet understand. She did the best she could with what she had. And I am not who I am becoming by accident. This is not passive evolution. This is intention. I am becoming her on purpose. The woman who chooses integrity over impulse. The woman who loves without abandoning herself. The woman who holds her boundaries like sacred ground. The woman who knows her worth without needing it validated by suffering. Becoming her is not effortless. It is deliberate. It is daily. It is the quiet, fierce commitment to align my actions with the truth I now know: I was never beyond repair. I was always capable of growth. And now, with eyes open and spine steady, I am walking toward the version of myself I once thought unreachable, not by accident, but by choice. Becoming her on purpose required more than intention; it required discipline, devotion, and something solid to grip when the ground beneath me trembled like shifting earth after a storm. It required calloused hands and a willing heart. Awakening had opened my eyes, yes, but staying awake demanded practice. It demanded rhythm. It demanded anchor. The kind of anchor that does not glitter or impress but holds fast when the current pulls hardest.

My sponsor's words became that anchor. They did not arrive wrapped in poetry or softened for comfort. They came plain, unadorned, almost stern, yet steady as a heartbeat beneath the ribs: ***"Nothing changes if nothing changes, and everything changes if everything changes!"*** At first, the words felt blunt. Almost too simple for the complexity of my unraveling, too clean for the tangled mess of trauma, betrayal, depression, and grief that had shaped my days. *"How could something so straightforward hold the weight of my chaos?"* And yet, simplicity can be sacred. Like water. Like breath. Like truth spoken without decoration. Over time, those words sank deeper. They moved from my ears to my chest, from my thoughts to my bones. I could hear them in the hush of early mornings when light spilled pale and golden across the floorboards, dust motes floating like quiet witnesses in the air. I could feel them in my pulse when I stood at crossroads, that subtle quickening in my veins when choice rose before me like an open gate. Emotionally, they felt like a firm hand at my back, not pushing, not dragging, but steady, reminding me that movement was mine to claim. They became a drumbeat. Low. Constant. Reliable. A cadence I could walk in rhythm with when doubt tried to throw me off balance. A sound beneath the noise. A pulse beneath the panic. And so, I changed. Not all at once. Not flawlessly. Not without resistance. But deliberately. I changed in the quiet ways first; the invisible shifts no one applauds. The pause before reacting. The breath taken instead of swallowed. The question asked instead of the accusation assumed. I changed the way I spoke to myself in the mirror, softening the edge of my internal voice. I changed the direction of my thoughts when they began circling old wounds like vultures. I changed the posture of my body; my shoulders no longer folded inward, and my chin no longer lowered in apology for existing. Each change felt small in isolation. But small things, repeated, become structure. Small choices become architecture. I began to notice the sensory texture of transformation. The way my chest felt less constricted when I chose honesty over avoidance.

The way my stomach settled when I declined something that did not align with my well-being. The way the air itself seemed lighter when I stopped carrying guilt that was never mine to hold. Even the emotional landscape shifted, less jagged, more navigable, as though the terrain within me was being slowly, lovingly restored. Change was not a lightning strike. It was erosion in reverse. Where once shame had worn me down grain by grain, now intention built me up, layer by patient layer. The mantra did not demand perfection. It demanded participation. If nothing changes, nothing changes. If everything changes, everything changes. That second line felt terrifying at first. *"Everything? Could I bear that much disruption? That much dismantling?"* But I began to understand that *"everything"* did not mean chaos. It meant commitment. It meant altering the roots, not just trimming the leaves. It meant refusing to live on autopilot. It meant choosing differently when the old way felt easier. So, I chose differently. When self-blame rose like muscle memory, I interrupted it. When guilt tried to tighten its grip around my throat, I loosened it. When fear whispered that growth was dangerous, I walked anyway. Deliberate. Measured. Awake. The rhythm steadied me. The drumbeat continued. And with every step taken in time with that truth, I felt something solid forming beneath my feet. Not the shifting ground of old narratives, but something firmer. Something earned. Becoming her on purpose was not a sudden rebirth. It was construction. It was excavation. It was laying new foundation where the old one had cracked. It was learning to trust that the earth beneath me, though once fractured, could hold. And now, when I stand at the edge of change, I no longer feel only fear. I feel the rhythm. I feel the anchor. I feel the quiet power of a woman who understands that transformation is not magic. It is movement. And I am moving. I worked incredibly hard to shift my thoughts, to challenge the reflex of self-blame that rose like muscle memory, automatic, well-practiced, almost elegant in its cruelty. It would surge up before I could catch it, a familiar tightening in my chest, a heat behind my eyes, the quiet verdict forming before evidence had even been weighed. It was as though my mind had grooves worn deep into it from years of repetition, tracks carved by shame and fear, and I had to take up the patient work of carving new paths with steady, trembling hands. Each time guilt flared, sharp and electric, I paused. I felt it fully, like holding a coal without closing my fist around it. Each time shame whispered, low, persuasive, intimate, I questioned it. *"Where did you come from? Whose voice are you wearing? Are you truth, or are you memory?"* The effort felt awkward at first, like learning to write with my non-dominant hand, letters shaky and uneven, movements slow and conscious. My thoughts resisted. They preferred the old shortcuts, the familiar descent into self-condemnation. But repetition strengthened new neural ground. With each interruption, each conscious redirection, I could almost feel something rewiring, subtle but real, like fresh roots pushing through soil long compacted. I altered my behaviors, too. Not dramatically at first. Quietly. Intentionally. I stopped shrinking to keep the peace. I stopped folding myself into smaller shapes to avoid conflict, no longer contorting my words or softening my truths to make others comfortable. For years, I had learned to make myself smaller, lower my voice, dim my presence, tuck in my needs like loose threads. That instinct still flickered when tension rose; I could feel it in my body, a tightening in my shoulders, a reflex to look down, smooth, and to placate. But I began choosing something different. I chose to remain. To feel my feet on the ground instead of mentally retreating. To breathe instead of apologizing for the air I took up. To speak, even when my voice quivered like a leaf in the wind. To occupy space as though I belonged there. There is a physical sensation to not shrinking. A subtle lift through the spine. A steadiness in the gaze. A warmth in the chest that feels like dignity reclaiming territory. Emotionally, it felt like stepping into sunlight after years of standing in shadow, uncomfortable at first, almost too bright, but undeniably life-giving. I reevaluated my relationships, holding them up to the light like fragile glass, turning them slowly to see where they caught the sun and where they fractured it. Some connections were draining me, siphoning energy I no longer had to spare.

I could feel it in my body after spending time with them, a heaviness behind my eyes, a fatigue that seeped into my bones, a subtle erosion of self-trust. Others felt different. They felt like shade in summer, steady, nourishing, quiet. Being with them did not require performance. I could exhale. I could laugh without measuring the sound. I could be silent without fearing misinterpretation. Those relationships felt like cool water on overheated skin, like soil rich enough to grow something lasting. Letting go of what depleted me hurt. Grief has a texture, a hollowing sensation in the ribs, a dull ache beneath the sternum. Even unhealthy attachments carry history, familiarity, and the illusion of safety. But I began to understand that familiarity is not the same as nourishment. Comfort is not the same as care. So I released what drained me, even when my hands trembled. And I leaned toward what fed me, even when it felt unfamiliar, toward kindness without agenda, toward respect without condition, toward love that did not require me to fracture myself to receive it. This was not just change. It was reclamation. Thought by thought. Choice by choice. Relationship by relationship. I was reshaping the landscape of my inner world and the ecosystem of my outer one. And slowly, almost imperceptibly, the woman I was becoming began to feel less like an effort, and more like a return. I learned to prioritize my own needs. There was a time when that sentence tasted bitter in my mouth, like I was swallowing something forbidden. It once felt selfish, indulgent, almost dangerous. Now it feels necessary. Like oxygen. Like water. Like the quiet instinct to pull your hand back from a flame. For so long, I had been fluent in tending to others, anticipating moods, softening edges, filling gaps before they were even named. I knew how to nourish, how to soothe, how to give until there was nothing left but bone and breath. But I had never turned that tenderness inward. I had treated myself like an afterthought, a footnote in the margins of everyone else's story. So I began tending to myself the way I once tended to others, carefully, attentively, without resentment. I rested when I was tired, not collapsing from exhaustion, but choosing rest before depletion hollowed me out. I let my body speak, and I listened. I felt the weight in my limbs, the dull ache behind my eyes, the subtle tremor in my nerves, and I honored it. Rest stopped being laziness. It became restoration. I asked for help when I was overwhelmed. That alone felt revolutionary. To let the words form in my throat, "*I can't do this alone right now*", felt like learning a new language. I could feel the vulnerability of it, the exposure, the old fear that needing would make me less worthy. But it didn't. It made me human. I spoke up when something felt wrong. Not explosively. Not defensively. But clearly. There is a different sound to clarity. It is not sharp. It is not chaotic. It lands with steadiness. My voice did not need to rise to be real. I did it not with apology, but with conviction. Not loudly, but firmly. Like placing a boundary stone in the earth and stepping back, knowing it belongs there. I began to value my worth as something intrinsic. Not something earned through endurance. Not something granted by approval. Not something contingent upon sacrifice. For years, I believed love was something you earned by suffering well. That value was proven by how much you could withstand. That goodness was measured by how small you could make yourself. But my worth was never meant to be bartered. It was there. Constant. Unconditional. Like a pulse beneath the skin. Like gravity holding everything in place, whether you acknowledge it or not. Emotionally, discovering that felt like uncovering a wellspring beneath dry ground, cool, steady water that had always existed, waiting for me to dig deep enough to find it. And perhaps most radically of all, I loved myself enough to say no. No to harmful situations. No to disrespect. No to conversations that tried to rewrite my reality. No to the subtle erasure of my experience. Even when my voice trembled. I remember the sensation of those first no's. My throat tight, as though words had to push through years of silence. My hands slightly shaking, fingers curling inward and then opening again. The air sharp in my lungs, cool and electric as I inhaled before speaking. But beneath the tremor was something solid, like bedrock beneath sand. A firmness I hadn't felt before. A quiet inner alignment. It did not roar. It did not announce itself. It simply held. Each no was not rejection. It was protection. It was the sound of a door closing gently but decisively. It was the scent of fresh air entering a room long sealed. It was the emotional sensation of standing upright after years of bending. Each no was not cruelty. It was care. It was the reclamation of my inner landscape, the refusal to let anyone redraw its borders without consent. It was me choosing to remain whole rather than fracture myself for the comfort of others.

And with each boundary set, each need honored, each clear and steady refusal, I felt myself anchoring deeper into my own life. Not as an accessory to someone else's story. But as the author of my own. It was alignment. Not defiance. Not rebellion for rebellion's sake. Alignment, the quiet, sacred act of bringing my inner truth and my outward life into the same line. For the first time, my no matched the tremor in my chest. My boundaries reflected what my body had been whispering for years. There was no more splitting myself in two to survive. No more smiling while shrinking. No more nodding while unraveling. Each boundary was not cruelty. It was care. It was the way a mother pulls a child back from traffic. The way a gardener fences what is fragile. The way skin forms over a wound to protect what is healing beneath. It was tenderness with teeth. Becoming her on purpose was not a single transformation. It was not a dramatic shedding of skin beneath a spotlight. It was a thousand small decisions made in moments no one else saw. Decisions made in kitchens at dusk. In parked cars before walking inside. In the quiet seconds between being triggered and reacting. In the space between an old habit and a new response. It was choosing growth over familiarity, even when familiarity felt warm and known, even when it carried the scent of nostalgia and the comfort of predictability. Growth often felt colder. Uncertain. Like stepping barefoot onto unfamiliar ground. But I stepped anyway. It was choosing health over habit. Breaking patterns that had once felt like instinct. Pausing instead of placating. Resting instead of overextending. Listening instead of defending. It was choosing truth over comfort. Truth does not always feel soft. Sometimes it tastes sharp in the mouth. Sometimes it tightens the throat before it frees it. But comfort built on self-abandonment is not comfort at all—it is slow erosion. And I had eroded enough. So I chose differently. Thought by thought. Choice by choice. Breath by breath. And with each change, subtle, private, uncelebrated, I felt something steady forming inside me. Not dramatic. Not loud. But strong. It was the sensation of a spine straightening after years of hunching. A subtle lifting through the sternum. A grounded weight in my feet. Emotionally, it felt like finding my center of gravity again, like the world could tilt and I would still remain upright. It was like roots deepening beneath soil no one else could see. Invisible work. Quiet growth. Drawing nourishment from pain once thought poisonous. Anchoring into myself so fully that the winds of accusation and doubt could no longer uproot me. And slowly, almost imperceptibly at first, I began to recognize her. A woman not reacting but responding. Not surviving but living. Not apologizing for existing but inhabiting her own life fully. Like a woman, finally, walking in rhythm with her own becoming. Not rushing. Not chasing. Just steady. Just aligned. Just here. And for the first time, that was enough. Those words, *"everything changes if everything changes"*, became more than a phrase murmured in passing. They became evidence. Living proof etched into the texture of my days. What once sounded like instruction began to feel like prophecy fulfilled. I could trace their truth in the subtle recalibration of my nervous system, in the steadier rhythm of my breath, in the quiet way my shoulders no longer carried the world as punishment. They serve now as a reminder of my strength and resilience, not the loud, defiant kind, but the enduring kind. The kind that survives winter. The kind that bends without breaking. They are a testament that even in the darkest seasons, when the air smells of damp earth and decay, when the sky feels permanently overcast, hope, healing, and transformation are not fantasies. They are seeds waiting beneath the frost. I am not defined by the darkness I endured. That darkness shaped me, yes. It carved its lessons into my bones. It introduced me to the raw edges of despair and the echo of my own breaking. But it does not name me. It does not get the final word. I am defined by the light I fought so fiercely to reclaim. By the nights I stayed when leaving would have been easier. By the mornings I rose again, eyes swollen but open.

By the boundaries I held when my voice trembled. By the apologies I offered without excuse. By the forgiveness I extended, first to others, and finally, trembling and tender, to myself. Each of those moments was a quiet revolution. Each was a brick laid in the rebuilding of a life once thought unsalvageable. I can still feel them in my body, the steadiness in my spine when I held a boundary, the warmth in my chest when I chose compassion over condemnation, the deep exhale that followed self-forgiveness like rain after drought. I am a testament to the resilience of the human spirit. Not because I never broke, but because I did and chose to mend. Not because I avoided despair, but because I walked through it and did not surrender my name to it. I am a testament to the power of healing, not as a miracle, but as a practice. A daily returning. A steady tending of wounds until scar tissue becomes strength. And I hold close the unwavering truth that even in the deepest despair, hope endures. Hope is not always radiant. Sometimes it is stubborn. Quiet. Almost invisible. Like a single green shoot pressing through cracked concrete. Like a fragile flower pushing its way through pavement that no one thought could yield. I can almost see it. Delicate petals brushing against rough edges. Roots threading through broken ground. Reaching toward light no one promised would come. There is something sacred in that image. Something defiant. Something holy in its refusal to remain buried. That bloom, that delicate, hard-won hope, is not naive. It knows the weight of winter. It knows the pressure of stone. It has felt the cold. And still, it rises. And that bloom, this life, this resilience, this reclaimed self, is worth fighting for. Not once. Not only in crisis. But every single day. When I look back now, I do so not with shame, but with pride. A quiet, grounded pride, the kind that does not need applause. It settles low in the chest like warm embers after a long night, steady and sustaining. It is not loud or boastful. It does not shout. It breathes. I am proud of the person I have become. A woman strong not because she was never broken, but because she gathered her scattered fragments with trembling hands and rebuilt herself piece by piece. I can almost see her kneeling among the ruins, dust in her lungs, grief on her skin, choosing not to curse the wreckage, but to begin again. Strength did not arrive polished. It arrived worn, calloused, learned through repetition. Resilient not because she avoided pain, but because she endured it, sat with it, tasted it, felt its sharp edges, and still chose growth. Resilience for me has not meant hardness. It has meant elasticity. The ability to bend under pressure without snapping. To absorb impact and still stand. Determined not because the road was smooth, but because she kept walking it when it was steep, uneven, and lonely. I remember the texture of that road, the grit beneath my feet, the ache in my calves, the moments when the horizon felt impossibly far away. And yet, step by deliberate step, I continued. Not dramatically. Not perfectly. But faithfully. I am proud of the choices I have made. The difficult ones that cost me comfort. The uncomfortable ones that exposed my vulnerability. The brave ones that required me to stand alone before I could stand supported. Each choice felt like a door closing and another cracking open. Each one reshaped the architecture of my life. They were not glamorous decisions. Some came with tears. Some came with shaking hands. Some came with grief for the version of myself I was leaving behind. But they were mine. And they have led me here. To a place of healing, not the kind that erases scars, but the kind that integrates them. To a place of liberation, where my breath feels fuller, my posture steadier, my voice my own. To a place of joy that feels earned and embodied. Joy now has weight to it. It is not fleeting or fragile. It settles into my body like sunlight warming skin after a long winter. I can feel it in the ease of my laughter, in the softness behind my eyes, in the way silence no longer frightens me. The journey was long. It wound through shadow and doubt. Through heartbreak and reckoning. Through nights that felt endless and mornings that demanded more than I thought I could give. It reshaped me. Refined me. Stripped away illusions and left something truer beneath. But I am here. Breathing. Standing. Awake. And I am blooming. Not suddenly. Not spectacularly. But steadily. Like that stubborn flower pushing through cracked concrete, petals brushing against rough edges, roots anchored in soil once thought barren. I am blooming in the very ground that once tried to bury me. And there is no greater pride than that.

And so, as this chapter gently comes to a close, I feel it in my body, the shift. It is not dramatic. Not seismic. It is subtler than that. A recalibration. A settling. Like the earth after tremors finally stilling beneath steady ground. This is not an ending heavy with grief. It is a threshold humming with possibility. I can feel it beneath my skin. There is excitement in my chest, a warm current beneath my ribs, like sunlight filtered through golden leaves. Anticipation tastes like fresh air after rain, clean, electric, alive. The scent of wet earth. The faint shimmer of light catching in puddles. Something in me inhales more deeply now. Something trusts the horizon. I know there will be challenges ahead. Life does not promise ease. Storms still gather. Winds still rise. Clouds will roll in without permission. But I am no longer bracing for destruction, no longer curling inward at the first rumble of thunder. I am standing in readiness. Rooted. Awake. Not armoured in denial but grounded in truth. The difference is not that storms have vanished. The difference is that I have changed. I am ready to face whatever comes my way, armed not with illusion, not with self-erasure, but with hard-earned knowledge: I am strong. I am capable. I am deserving of love, respect, and happiness. Not conditionally. Not once I prove myself. Not someday when I am *"better."* Now. There is a steadiness to those words when I say them. They no longer feel aspirational. They feel embodied. I can sense them in my posture, in the way my feet meet the ground, in the quiet certainty behind my gaze. I am Letitia. To say my name now feels like claiming territory. Not whispered. Not questioned. Stated. Whole. And I am healed, and in many ways, still healing. Healing is not a finish line crossed with confetti and applause. It is a rhythm.

A daily returning. A conscious tending. Like watering a garden that once lay barren. Like adjusting sails rather than abandoning the sea. It asks for attention. For humility. For presence. There are still tender places. There are still echoes that occasionally brush against my heart—old memories that drift through like faint music from another room. Sometimes they carry ache. Sometimes they carry grief. But they no longer define the landscape. They are weather passing through open sky. Temporary. Movable. Unable to eclipse the vastness of who I am becoming. The sky remains. And I remain. There is something profoundly freeing in that realization. The past may visit, but it does not reside. Pain may knock, but it no longer owns the house. And beneath it all, beneath the growth, the boundaries, the pride, the blooming, there is a truth that feels both simple and sacred: I am enough. Not because I have suffered. Not because I have endured. Not because I have transformed. But because I exist. And that is the quiet, revolutionary grace at the heart of this chapter's end and the next beginning. I stand at this threshold not as the woman who almost disappeared, but as the woman who chose to stay. And that choice, again and again, is the truest measure of my becoming. In the end, the question that once haunted me, whether I was truly to blame for everything wrong in other people's lives, has lost its grip. It used to echo like a shout inside a cavern, reverberating against stone walls, returning to me distorted and amplified until it felt like truth. Now, when it rises, it does so faintly. Distant. Like an old recording playing in another room. It no longer fills the chamber of my chest. It no longer dictates my worth. What matters now is not the accusation, but the accountability. There is a profound difference between the two. Accusation is heavy and indiscriminate, it seeks a scapegoat. Accountability is precise. Honest. Clean. It asks, "What *is mine?"* and equally, "*What is not?"* I have taken responsibility for my actions. I have made amends. I have worked, truly worked, to heal and to grow. Not in theory. Not in appearance. But in the quiet, daily labor of becoming someone aligned with her values.

There is humility in that. And there is freedom. I understand now that I am not defined by my past. The past informs me, shapes me, teaches me, it is etched into the grain of my story, but it does not imprison me. It is a chapter, not a cage. A teacher, not a jailer. The scars remain, yes, but they no longer bind my hands. I am not a victim of circumstance, tossed endlessly by forces beyond my control like driftwood in a merciless sea. I am a survivor. More than that, I am a warrior who has walked through fire and come out bearing light. I can feel that truth in my body. In the steadiness of my breath. In the strength of my stance. Fire did not consume me. It refined me. It burned away illusions. It stripped me down to what was essential and left something stronger in its place.

The darkness did not swallow me. It tempered me. It carved depth into my spirit. It etched compassion into my voice. It taught me resilience I never knew I possessed. Resilience is not hardness. It is forged softness that refuses to break. As I look toward the future, I feel that same excitement rising again, not frantic, not desperate, but steady and grounded. It hums beneath my ribs like a low current of electricity. It smells like possibility. It feels like open windows and sunlight warming bare floors. There is space ahead of me. Room to build. Room to breathe. Room to love in ways that are safe and reciprocal. Love that does not require shrinking. Love that does not barter respect. Love that mirrors back the wholeness I now recognize in myself. The horizon no longer feels threatening. It feels expansive. There is ground before me that has not yet been walked, stories not yet written, laughter not yet heard. The best is not behind me. It is unfolding. Like petals opening at dawn. Like light stretching across a quiet field. Like a path revealing itself step by deliberate step. And this time, I walk toward it not as someone searching for worth, not scanning the faces of others for validation, not bargaining for belonging, but as someone who already knows she carries it within. Worth is no longer something I chase. It is something I inhabit. And so I step forward, not frantic, not fearful, not fractured. But whole. Carrying light in hands once empty.

Chapter: Twenty-Four
Was it as bad as it seemed?

The best is unfolding... and yet sometimes, in the quiet spaces between breaths, I find myself looking back. Not with longing. Not with self-condemnation. But with curiosity. With the tender gaze of a woman who has survived her own storm and now studies the wreckage with steady hands. Looking now, years later, was it truly as bad as it seemed then? As I sit here today, older, steadier, sunlight resting gently across my skin like a blessing I no longer question, I am pulled back to that darkest night. The one that almost took everything from me. The one that stands in my memory like a jagged cliff dividing my life into before and after. I can still feel its texture. The air was heavy. Thick in my lungs, as though I were breathing through water. Each inhale scraped against my chest. Each exhale felt insufficient. The silence had a sound of its own, a hollow ringing that pressed against my ears, as if the world itself had stepped back and was holding its breath. There was a stillness in the room that felt unnatural. The kind of stillness that hums. That waits. The darkness did not simply surround me; it settled into me. It tasted metallic at the back of my tongue. It smelled faintly of stale air and sorrow. Emotionally, it felt like standing at the edge of an abyss with no visible ground below, only depth. Only drop. It is a night I will never forget. Not because of spectacle. Not because of drama. But because of rupture. It was the night something broke open—something terrifying and sacred all at once. The night that split my life into a before and an after. A fracture in time. A hinge upon which everything turned. Looking back now, across the chasm of years, across growth and healing and grace, I ask myself gently: *"Was it truly as bad as it seemed then?"* Memory is strange. It softens some edges and sharpens others. It rearranges light. But when I sit quietly and allow myself to feel into it, not intellectually, but bodily, I know this: it was as bad as it felt. Because pain is measured not by hindsight, but by capacity. In that moment, I was at the edge of my capacity. My nervous system was overwhelmed. My heart exhausted. My mind trapped in a narrative so tight it felt airtight.

To the woman I was then, the despair was absolute. The weight was crushing. The night was endless. And yet, from here, with distance, with the gentleness that healing grants, I can also see what that version of me could not. I can see how distorted my vision had become. How depression colored every shadow darker. How manipulation had warped my perception of self. I can see the layers. The context. The slow erosion that led to that brink. The answer, then, is not simple. It is layered. It is complex. It holds two truths at once: Yes, it was that bad, because I felt it that way. And no, it was not the whole truth, because the story did not end there. That night did not define me. It revealed me. It revealed the depth of my pain, yes, but also the depth of my will to live. It revealed how fragile and how fierce a human spirit can be at the same time. As I sit here now, sunlight warming my skin, I feel the contrast. The air today is light. Breath comes easily. Silence is not hollow, it is spacious. There is no ringing in my ears. Only the gentle hum of a life reclaimed. Still, I do not look back to dismiss that night. I look back to honor her, the woman standing there, trembling, overwhelmed, doing the only thing she knew how to do with the tools she had. I look back with compassion, not critique. And I understand now that the question itself, "*Was it truly that bad?* is less about judgment and more about integration. Because healing does not erase the darkness. It reframes it. And this exploration, this layered, complex reckoning, is not finished. It is something I will continue to unfold, carefully, honestly, within the pages of this book series. Not to relive the night. But to understand it. Not to reopen the wound. But to trace the scar and honor the strength that formed around it. Because that night, the night I decided to end my life, the darkness was absolute. It did not feel symbolic. It did not feel poetic. It felt physical. It pressed against me like a body with weight and intention. Like an inescapable, suffocating force bearing down on my chest, compressing my lungs until breath became labor. The pressure was crushing—dense, immovable—threatening to obliterate not just my hope, but my sense of self entirely. The room felt smaller than it was. The walls seemed to lean inward, tilting subtly as if conspiring to contain me. The air tasted metallic, sharp at the back of my tongue. My heartbeat pounded in my ears like distant thunder rolling across a storm-soaked sky, each beat heavy, insistent, impossible to ignore. There was a hum in the silence. A low, oppressive vibration that made everything feel sealed. Closed. Final. In that moment, it felt as though there was no way out. As though I were drowning in a sea of hopelessness and powerlessness, saltwater filling my mouth, burning my throat, my lungs searing as I fought for air I believed no longer existed. I could almost feel the drag of the current pulling me under, the disorienting spin of being  swallowed whole.

I was at the end of my rope. Truly. There is a texture to that kind of exhaustion. It is not dramatic. It is hollow. It is bone-deep. It feels like every internal resource has been spent. Like standing on ground that keeps giving way beneath your feet. It felt like there was no escape from the pain and suffering that had become my reality—no door, no window, no breath of relief. I believed, with the chilling certainty that only despair can manufacture, that I could not handle it anymore. That I was incapable. That I was too broken. That I had reached the outer edge of endurance. Despair has a way of masquerading as logic. It speaks calmly. Convincingly. It narrows your vision until annihilation looks like mercy. But it was a lie. A cruel, insidious lie that almost stole my life. My future. It almost robbed my children of their mother. I can feel the weight of that now in a way I could not then, the echo of small hands that would have reached for me and found only absence. The laughter that would have dimmed. The questions left unanswered. It almost robbed me of the beautiful, empowering life I now live, the steady mornings, the grounded joy, the hard-won peace that rests in my body like warmth. It almost stole my current husband from ever becoming my husband, almost erased the tenderness we now share, the quiet companionship, the safety of being loved without condition. It almost erased my son from ever existing. That truth lands differently. It reverberates in my chest. The idea that his laughter, his presence, his very being might never have come into this world because I believed a lie in a single devastating night, it humbles me. It undoes me. The darkness felt absolute. But it was not ultimate. It was vast, yes. Suffocating. Convincing. But it was not truth. It was a distortion born of untreated pain, accumulated trauma, and relentless internalized shame. It was a storm at full force, convincing me the sky would never clear. And yet; here I am. Breathing air that no longer tastes metallic. Standing in rooms that do not lean inward. Listening to a heartbeat that no longer sounds like thunder in a sealed chamber, but like life, steady and sure. That night did not take me. It almost did. But it didn't. And that thin, fragile line between almost and still here, that is sacred. It is the quiet miracle I carry with me. Not as a badge of shame. But as proof that even when darkness feels absolute, it is not the end of the story. It was a lie. And I am living evidence of the truth that survived it.

The magnitude of that nearly undoes me when I allow myself to fully feel it. When I pause long enough for the truth to settle, not just in my mind, but in my body, it rises like a swell in the chest. The emotional weight of what almost wasn't humbles me to my core. It is not a passing thought. It is a visceral awareness. A tremor beneath the ribs. A quiet ache that carries both grief and gratitude in the same breath. The truth? I only found it when it was almost too late. Snatched from the jaws of death by what felt like a thread of grace, a fragile, invisible lifeline thrown into the blackest hour. I can still sense it when I close my eyes: the thinness of that thread, the improbability of its strength. It did not blaze like a miracle. It did not descend like thunder. It was subtle. Barely there. And yet it held. I did not climb out because I was strong that night. That is a truth I honor now. I was not heroic. I was not fierce. I was exhausted. Fractured. Overwhelmed beyond reason. If strength had been the requirement, I would not have survived. I climbed out because something, somewhere, held me long enough for the light to break through. Whether it was grace, fate, love, instinct, divine mercy, I cannot name it fully. I only know that I was held. Suspended at the edge long enough for breath to return. For perspective to flicker. For life to whisper, almost inaudibly: "*Stay*". And now, as I look back across that chasm of years, what strikes me most is this: I had the power to change my circumstances all along. It was there. Quiet. Buried beneath layers of suffering. Beneath pain so loud it drowned out possibility. Beneath hopelessness and helplessness that felt permanent, like a climate I had been sentenced to inhabit forever. The power did not roar. It did not announce itself. It waited. I could have broken free from the shackles of despair sooner. I could have forged a new path, could have stepped away from toxicity, could have chosen healing before I reached the brink. That realization carries both sorrow and compassion. Because at the time, I was too blinded. Blinded by suffering. Blinded by pain. Blinded by hopelessness and helplessness that had wrapped around me like fog. Blinded by depression that distorted distance, depth, and direction.

Depression narrows the field of vision. It turns open rooms into cages. It turns unlocked doors into invisible walls. I believed I was trapped because I could not see the exit. I believed the cage was sealed because I could not find the handle. But the door was not locked. It was simply hidden. Hidden behind layers of belief that I was powerless. Hidden behind narratives that I was unworthy. Hidden behind exhaustion so deep it felt like destiny. And sometimes, survival is nothing more than finding the courage to reach for a door you cannot yet see. It is extending your hand into darkness, fingers brushing air, refusing to stop searching. It is trusting that possibility exists even when you cannot perceive it. It is believing—barely, shakily—that there might be a hinge somewhere in the wall. That is what I did. Not bravely. Not confidently. But instinctively. And that reaching, blind, desperate, trembling, became the beginning of everything. Now, when I stand in rooms filled with light, when I feel steadiness in my bones, when I witness the life that unfolded because I stayed, I understand something sacred: The power was never absent. It was obscured. And sometimes the difference between annihilation and transformation is not strength. It is the smallest flicker of willingness to reach. Even when you cannot yet see what you are reaching for. And sometimes, survival begins in the smallest, most ordinary moments. Not in grand revelations. Not in thunderclaps of clarity. But in the quiet, almost forgettable details that tether you to the present long enough for something inside you to keep breathing. I remember the woodchips on the windowsill. How they felt beneath my fingers. Rough. Splintered. Uneven. I would trace them absentmindedly, letting their coarse edges press into my skin. Tiny fragments, imperfect and raw. They scratched lightly against my fingertips, grounding me in sensation when my mind felt like it was dissolving into fog. They felt the way my despair felt. Jagged. Abrasive. Wearing me down slowly, grain by grain, until I hardly recognized myself. My thoughts had edges like that, sharp, splintered, catching on everything. My identity felt chipped away, eroded, reduced to fragments I could no longer assemble into something whole.

There is something hauntingly ordinary about that memory. The wood. The sill. The quiet tracing of texture. Nothing dramatic. Nothing cinematic. And yet, in that moment, those woodchips were real. Tangible. Solid in a way my hope was not. My fingers knew they were there. My skin registered their presence. It was something to feel when everything else felt unreal. Looking back now, across the vast chasm of years, growth, and grace, it is almost impossible to reconcile the woman I was that night with the woman I am today. The distance feels immense. Like standing on one side of a canyon and seeing, faintly, the outline of a figure across the divide. She is me. And yet she feels like someone else entirely. A character in a story I once lived through but can barely inhabit now. The night I decided to end my life feels like a story told about someone else. A distant echo carried across a landscape I barely recognize. The terrain has changed so drastically, new growth where there was once ash, open sky where there was once suffocating cloud, that the memory almost feels misplaced. And yet, I remember it with unsettling clarity. The texture of the air. Thick. Heavy. Pressing into my lungs as though breath required permission. The silence—not empty but vibrating. A low hum, like electricity running through walls. The way my body felt foreign to me, like I was inhabiting a shell rather than a self. In that moment, the darkness was absolute. Not metaphorical. Not poetic. Absolute. It was not simply the absence of light. It was the absence of perspective. The collapse of possibility. A narrowing so severe it felt like the world had shrunk to a single, suffocating point. And yet, even there, my fingers traced woodchips. Even there, something in me noticed texture. There is something profound in that. Something almost sacred. That in the midst of annihilating despair, I was still connected to the physical world. Still registering roughness. Still alive enough to feel splinters against skin.

Perhaps survival does not always begin with belief. Perhaps it begins with sensation. With a fingertip pressing into wood. With breath scraping through lungs. With the smallest awareness: "*I am still here.*" When I look back now, what unsettles me most is not only how close I came, but how quiet the beginning of my return was. It did not arrive with fireworks. It arrived in texture. In woodchips. In breath. In the simple, stubborn fact that my body had not yet given up. That woman on the other side of the chasm, she was fractured. Blinded. Overwhelmed. But she was still reaching. Still feeling. Still, somehow, alive. And in that small, ordinary act of tracing rough edges against my skin, survival had already begun, even if I did not yet know it. Hopelessness wrapped around me like a suffocating blanket pulled too tightly over my face. Not soft. Not comforting. Heavy. Airless. It pressed against my mouth and nose until every breath felt borrowed, strained through fabric thick with despair. Powerlessness settled deeper still, pressing against my chest like a crushing weight, an invisible stone placed squarely over my heart. It stole breath. It stole perspective. It narrowed my world until there seemed to be nothing beyond the walls of that night. There was, I believed with complete conviction, no way out. That belief did not feel dramatic. It felt logical. Final. As certain as gravity. And that was the lie. The insidious lie that almost cost me everything, my life, my potential, the future that had not yet had the chance to unfold. It almost took from my children their mother. Almost erased the quiet mornings, the bedtime laughter, the arms wrapped around me that I can feel now as memory and blessing. It almost stole from me the chance to become a wife to the loving husband I have now, a love that is steady, reciprocal, and safe. It almost erased my son from ever existing, his life unwritten because mine had ended too soon. It almost robbed me of the life I am living today. The air I breathe now. The sunlight warming my skin. The strength in my voice. The quiet pride in my becoming. It almost stole the very pen from my hand, the pen I write with now. The words flowing across these pages would have remained unwritten, dissolved into silence. The story would have ended mid-sentence. The lie was not that life was hard. Life was hard. Brutally so. The lie was that I had no choice. The belief in utter powerlessness. Hopelessness. Helplessness. The conviction that I was trapped, nothing more than a pawn in a game rigged against me. That my suffering was permanent. That the darkness was not weather but climate. That my only escape was disappearance. It was a narrative so complete it felt airtight. And I was wrong. Terribly, devastatingly wrong. But I did not see it then. In that moment, my perception was distorted by pain so loud it drowned out every alternative. Depression is not merely sadness; it is a narrowing of vision. It blurs the horizon. It erases exits. It convinces you that the cage is welded shut when, in truth, the door stands ajar. For me, the truth revealed itself only when it was almost too late. Not in triumph. Not in strength. Not in clarity. But by a thin line of grace. A thread of hope so fragile it felt like it might snap in my hands. So delicate I feared even breathing too hard would break it. It did not glow. It did not blaze. It was faint. Nearly invisible. But it was there. And I clung to it. Even when everything around me insisted there was nothing left to hold. I clung with trembling fingers. With breath that came uneven. With a heart that did not yet believe but refused to completely surrender. That thread did not promise certainty. It offered only possibility. A whisper instead of a guarantee. And sometimes, that is enough. Sometimes survival is nothing more than refusing to let go of the thinnest strand of light in a room that insists it is entirely dark. That night, I believed I was powerless. Today, I know the truth. The power was always there. Buried. Obscured. Muffled by suffering. But not gone. And that fragile thread, the one I almost didn't see, became the beginning of everything that followed.

The truth, the brutal, beautiful truth, arrived as I teetered on the precipice. Not with thunder. Not with blinding light. Not with some cinematic crescendo that split the sky in two. It came like a lifeline thrown just as my footing gave way. A quiet interruption in the freefall. A presence that did not demand attention but waited for recognition. It came softly. A whisper beneath the roar of despair. *"You have a choice."* Those words did not echo loudly. They did not silence the storm. They slipped in between the pounding of my heart and the ringing in my ears. They were barely audible beneath the heavy hum of hopelessness, but they were there. I can still feel the emotional shift of that moment. It was not explosive. It was not dramatic. It was subtle, a faint stirring beneath layers of numbness, like the first tremor of thaw beneath winter soil. Something beneath the frost was still alive. Something moved. The darkness did not vanish. It did not instantly loosen its grip or dissolve into light. The wounds did not close. The pain did not retreat. But something cracked. A door I thought was sealed shifted on its hinges. A window I believed was bricked shut let in the faintest draft of air. It was not enough to flood the room with light, but it was enough to remind me the room was not airtight. Choice. Such a simple word. Such a radical one. It had been there all along, buried beneath fear and pain. Beneath the story I had told myself that I was trapped. Beneath the conviction that I was powerless. Beneath the fog of depression that blurred every exit and distorted every possibility. Choice had not disappeared. It had been obscured. And in that whisper, *"you have a choice,"* I felt something return to me. Agency. Not loud or triumphant. But real. Dignity. The quiet recognition that I was not merely a victim of circumstance, not merely a pawn moved by forces outside myself. Possibility. Fragile. Flickering. But present. The woodchips on the windowsill were still rough beneath my fingers. Splintered. Uneven. Abrasive. My despair had not softened. The air was still heavy. My heart still pounded. But for the first time, I realized something extraordinary: I could lift my hand away. I was not fused to that windowsill. Not nailed to that moment. Not cemented into that room. My fingers could uncurl. My hand could rise. My body could move. That realization was microscopic and monumental all at once. It did not require strength. It required recognition. The smallest reorientation of belief: *"I am not as trapped as I think I am."* The power was not in conquering the darkness.

It was in choosing, even faintly, not to surrender to it. In that instant, I did not become healed. I did not become fearless. I did not become certain. But I became aware. Aware that the story I was telling myself was not the only story available. Aware that disappearance was not the only option. Aware that even in the narrowest corridor of despair, there remained a sliver of decision. And that sliver was enough. Because once you know you can lift your hand away, you are no longer entirely bound. Once you know there is a door, even if you cannot yet see the handle, you begin to turn toward it. That whisper did not save me in a blaze of glory. It invited me. And I, trembling, chose to listen. And that whisper, "*You have a choice*", did not vanish. It lingered. It hovered at the edge of my awareness like the faint glow before dawn, subtle but persistent. Even when despair surged again, even when the vortex of hopelessness spun me dizzy and breathless, that whisper remained. Not loud. Not triumphant. Just steady. All along, while I cowered in the shadows of despair, spun tight inside that suffocating spiral, convinced I was powerless and helpless, I possessed the very power I had been desperately searching for. I had been standing in the dark, pounding on what I believed was a locked door, palms raw, knuckles aching—not realizing the key was already in my pocket. I can see her now. That version of me. Curled inward. Shoulders folded toward her chest as if trying to make herself smaller. Breath shallow and uneven. Eyes dimmed by exhaustion, the light in them reduced to a faint flicker beneath layers of grief. The room around her felt cavernous and confining all at once. She believed the walls were real. She believed the locks were iron. She believed she was small. She did not know she was standing inside a story. She did not know the walls were perception. The locks, belief. The prison, constructed from years of accumulated doubt. And yet, beneath the rubble of despair, beneath the thick sediment of fear and self-doubt—something vital remained. The agency to change my circumstances.

The capacity to choose a different path. The control I craved. It was there all along. Dormant. Buried beneath layers of despair so thick they felt geological—strata laid down by years of fear, trauma, and distorted belief. Each layer compacted by repetition. Each doubt pressed deeper by silence. It felt ancient, immovable, like bedrock. But even beneath bedrock, seeds wait. Quiet as a seed beneath winter soil. Unseen. Uncelebrated. Hidden in darkness so complete it could easily be mistaken for death. But not dead. Never dead. Just waiting. That seed did not demand attention. It did not shout for recognition. It lay still beneath the frost of hopelessness, storing potential in silence. It did not care that I believed the winter was permanent. It did not argue with my despair. It simply endured. When I look back now, I do not see a woman devoid of power. I see a woman who had forgotten where she buried it. I see strength wrapped in exhaustion. I see courage disguised as collapse. I see resilience sleeping under snow. The whisper did not create my power. It revealed it. It brushed away just enough frost for me to sense the possibility that the ground beneath me was not barren after all. That something within me had survived the storm, intact and waiting. I had been searching for rescue from outside. But the rescue was internal. Not grand. Not immediate. But real. The key had always been there. And beneath the suffocating vortex, beneath the sediment of suffering, beneath the belief that I was nothing more than a victim of circumstance, my agency waited—quiet, patient, alive. Like a seed in winter. Like breath beneath water. Like light beneath the horizon, gathering itself for morning. The control I craved, the power I begged the universe for in whispered prayers and clenched-teeth desperation, was never external. It was not something someone else needed to grant me like permission. It was not hidden in another person's approval, not locked inside a relationship, not waiting at the end of someone else's apology. It was within me. My power had not vanished. It had been covered over, like embers smothered beneath thick ash, still warm, still alive, but dimmed from sight. If you had pressed your hand close enough, you might have felt the faint heat beneath the gray. But I could not see it. I believed the fire was gone. It took nearly losing my life to see it. That is the brutal irony. The bitter pill that scraped my throat on the way down, metallic and sharp.

The perspective shift required almost dying. I had to stand at the edge of annihilation to understand that I had never been as trapped as I believed. I had to feel the chill of oblivion brush against my skin, that cold, indifferent air grazing my arms like a final warning. I had to hear the deafening silence of what almost was, the silence of an erased future, the silence where my children's laughter would have been, the silence where my own breath would have stopped. It took a near-death experience to awaken me to this reality. To understand that I had been living in a state of false imprisonment. Trapped, yes, but trapped by my own perceptions. By beliefs that felt immovable, monumental, granite-solid, yet were, in truth, constructed from fear. Carefully layered. Repeated. Reinforced. Narratives spoken so often that they hardened into law inside my mind. The bars were not iron. The walls were not concrete. They were perception. Belief. Stories told and retold until they felt like scripture. And that is the brutal irony. The bitter pill that scraped against my throat when I swallowed it. The realization that the cage had no architect but fear. That the lock I rattled in desperation was fashioned from assumption. That the key I searched for in other hands had been resting in mine all along. The perspective shift required almost dying. It required standing at the edge of oblivion, feeling the cold exhale of it against my face, smelling the sterile scent of finality in the air, tasting the metallic edge of terror at the back of my tongue. It required hearing my own heartbeat pounding like a warning drum in the hollow chamber of my chest. It required emotionally feeling the rupture, the moment when despair no longer felt like relief but like theft. In that confrontation, something crystalline formed. Not comfort. Not immediate healing. Clarity. I saw that my "powerlessness" had been a story I believed because it felt safer than responsibility. Because if I was powerless, then I did not have to risk change. If I was trapped, then I did not have to test the door. But the door was never locked. It was hidden beneath the fog of my own fear.

And standing there, teetering between existence and absence, I understood something that rattled through my bones: I had mistaken exhaustion for incapacity. I had mistaken suffering for permanence. I had mistaken belief for truth. The prison dissolved the moment I saw it for what it was. Not a fortress. A mirage. And though the grief of that realization was sharp, grief for the years I spent crouched inside walls that were never real, it was also electrifying. Because if the cage was perception, then freedom was possible. If belief built the prison, belief could dismantle it. If fear had written the law, courage could revise it. I did not awaken to a life without pain. I awakened to the understanding that pain did not equal imprisonment. The chill of oblivion had brushed my skin. The silence of what almost was had roared in my ears. And from that edge, from that terrifying brink, I stepped back, not because the world changed, but because I did. The embers beneath the ash glowed. And this time, I saw them. I had built a cell from my own conclusions—stone by thought, bar by belief, mortar mixed from fear and fatigue. I mistook assumption for architecture. I mistook repetition for truth. And inside that structure, I paced like a prisoner, tracing the same mental perimeter over and over, convinced the walls were real because I could feel them pressing against me. It wasn't until I had faced the abyss, until I had come perilously close to losing everything, that the illusion began to fracture. Not gently. Not kindly. But with the sharp crack of truth splitting through denial. I remember standing there, breath thin in my lungs, my heartbeat pounding like distant thunder rolling across a dark horizon. The air felt tight, electric. My skin prickled with the chill of what almost was. In that suspended moment, between collapse and continuation, I glimpsed something radical. The cage had never been locked. I had simply believed it was. It took me nearly dying to see it. To grasp the simple, brutal truth of my own capacity. To understand that what I had labeled *"powerlessness"* was not an objective fact, but a conclusion, one I had drawn in the dim light of exhaustion and then accepted as law. I had been convinced my situation was hopeless. That I was at the mercy of forces beyond my control. That life was happening to me, and I had no say in the outcome. I saw myself as a leaf caught in a violent storm, flung in whatever direction the wind decided, destined only to endure, never to choose.

Emotionally, that belief felt heavy and metallic, like swallowing resignation and feeling it scrape all the way down. It tasted like surrender. Bitter. Final. It smelled like stale air in a room without windows, where breath grows thin, and possibility suffocates. It sounded like the low hum of inevitability, a drone that whispered, *"This is all there is."* And for a long time, I believed it. But as I slowly began to rebuild my life, brick by conscious brick, breath by deliberate breath, I realized something that both steadied and unsettled me. It had been a false narrative. A story perpetuated by my own fears, doubts, and limitations. A script I had memorized so thoroughly I could perform it without rehearsal. I had internalized the lines: I can't. I'm stuck. There's no way out. And

I spoke them fluently, convincingly, never pausing to ask who authored them in the first place. The realization was not triumphant. It was humbling. Because if the story was false, then I had been participating in my own confinement. Not maliciously. Not consciously. But faithfully. I had confused familiarity with inevitability. I had confused endurance with destiny. I had mistaken the echo of my fears for the voice of truth. And yet, there was something liberating in that discomfort. Because if the narrative had been constructed, it could be deconstructed. If the script had been memorized, it could be rewritten. If the storm had felt inescapable, perhaps it was because I had never realized I could step out of its path. As I rebuilt, brick by conscious brick, I felt the texture of choice returning to my hands. Rough. Real. Solid. Each decision carried weight. Each boundary laid like stone beneath my feet. It was not glamorous work. It was slow, deliberate construction. The smell of fresh mortar. The sound of new foundations settling. The emotional sensation of something steady forming where once there had only been chaos. The truth steadied me, even as it unsettled me: I had more agency than I had allowed myself to see. The storm had been real. The pain had been real. But I was never only a leaf. I had roots. And once I recognized them, once I felt them anchoring into something deeper than fear, I understood that endurance was not my only option.

I could choose. I could shift. I could step out of the narrative that had kept me small. The cell I built from conclusions began to crumble, not because someone rescued me, not because life suddenly softened, but because I dared to question the architecture. And in the dust of those falling walls, I felt something unfamiliar yet undeniable: Space. Air. Possibility. It was a story I had internalized and repeated until it sounded like truth, until its cadence matched my breathing, until its rhythm settled into my pulse. I wore it like skin. I spoke it without thinking. I defended it as though it were fact carved in stone rather than a narrative etched by fear. But the truth, the real truth, rose slowly, like dawn bleeding color into a night that had insisted it was permanent. I discovered that I had always had a choice. Not an easy one. Not a painless one. But a choice, nonetheless. Choice. The word itself felt sharp and electric in my mouth. Alive. It carried weight. It tasted different from resignation. It sounded different from surrender. It felt like cool water against a fevered brow. I had the power to say no, to the toxic patterns that looped like broken records through my relationships, their warped melodies repeating the same old harm. I had the power to say no to the negative self-talk that gnawed at my worth, that echoed in the hollow chambers of my mind like footsteps in an abandoned cathedral. I had the power to refuse the self-destructive behaviors that masqueraded as coping, those false comforts that soothed in the moment but hollowed me out over time. The power to interrupt the cycle. The power to step out of the familiar script and improvise something new. That realization did not feel soft. It did not feel gentle. It felt like standing at the edge of a cliff and realizing I could turn left or right. It was exhilarating. Terrifying. And equally intimidating. Because choice is freedom, but it is also responsibility. On one hand, the awareness thrilled me. It meant I was no longer merely reacting to life. I was no longer a passive character in someone else's story. I had agency. I could shape my destiny. I could redirect the course of my life. The current did not own me. The storm did not define me. I could turn the wheel. I could set a new course. I could plant myself in different soil and tend to what grew there. I could become gardener instead of weather. That realization carried a rush of oxygen through my lungs. It felt like wind filling sails I had forgotten I possessed. It smelled like fresh earth after rain. It sounded like possibility cracking open. But on the other hand, it stripped me of my hiding places. It meant I could no longer crouch beneath inevitability and call it fate. It meant I could no longer outsource responsibility to circumstance, to history, to other people's failures. It meant that healing was not something that would simply happen to me. It was something I would have to participate in. Deliberately. Repeatedly. Choice meant I had to show up. It meant I had to say no when it would be easier to stay silent. It meant I had to hold boundaries when my instinct was to fold. It meant I had to face discomfort instead of numbing it. Emotionally, that awareness felt like stepping into cold water—jarring, bracing, impossible to ignore. It woke something up in me that had been dormant beneath layers of learned helplessness. I could no longer say, *"There's nothing I can do."* Because there was. Even if it was small. Even if it was terrifying. Even if it required trembling hands and an unsteady voice. I had a choice. And with that choice came something heavier than blame and far more powerful than despair: authorship. I was no longer just the product of storms. I was the one holding the pen. The script that once felt sealed began to loosen in my hands. I could edit it. Rewrite it. Tear out pages that no longer serve me. Add chapters I had never imagined I would be brave enough to write. The realization did not make the path easy. But it made it mine. I could no longer blame only external forces for my unhappiness. I could no longer point outward and call that pointing truth. The storm had not been the only thing shaping my life; I had been steering, even when I claimed I wasn't. I could no longer cling to the strange comfort of powerlessness, the soft, suffocating blanket of *"there's nothing I can do."* If I had agency, then I also had responsibility. Responsibility for my healing. Responsibility for my growth. Responsibility for the choices I made moving forward. Responsibility meant I could no longer outsource the work of becoming. I could not hand my future to someone else and call it fate. I could not remain seated in the waiting room of my own life, hoping someone would come fix what hurt. It was daunting. Emotionally, it felt like standing at the base of a mountain I had just realized was mine to climb.

The peak disappeared into the mist. The air at the bottom was thin with anticipation. The incline looked unforgiving. No one could carry me. No one could strap me to their back and do the ascent on my behalf. The climb required my own legs. My own breath. My own resolve. My knees trembled at the thought. My palms felt damp. The ground beneath my boots seemed both solid and impossibly steep. I could almost hear the wind at higher altitudes, calling and warning all at once. And yet...Beneath the fear, beneath the weight of that realization, something else stirred. Determination. It rose quietly, like a current beneath still water. It felt like stepping into open air after years underground, lungs stinging, yes, but alive. It felt like emerging from a tunnel and realizing the sky is vast and uncontained. It felt like holding a blank map in trembling hands and understanding that the pen is yours. Not theirs. Not fate's. Yours. I was determined. Not because I felt fearless. Fear still brushed against my ribs, cool and persistent. Not because I felt ready. Readiness is often a myth; we wait for too long. I was determined because I had tasted what almost-not-living felt like. I had felt the metallic edge of surrender. I had stood at the brink where breath thins and the world narrows. I had brushed against the absence of everything I now cherish. And that taste, bitter, hollow, annihilating, was enough. I refused to return there. That refusal did not roar. It did not blaze like a bonfire. It settled into me like bedrock—dense, grounded, immovable. A steady resolve rising from somewhere deeper than doubt. Deeper than fear. Deeper even than despair. Yes, it was overwhelming. Yes, it required courage I had not yet fully embodied. But courage is not the absence of trembling. It is moving anyway. I was determined because now I knew something I could not unknow I was never as powerless as I believed. And once you see that, once the illusion cracks and light spills through, you cannot go back to pretending you don't. The woman who once believed she was trapped began, slowly, to see the faint outline of her own strength, like a figure emerging from fog at dawn. At first, it was only a silhouette. A suggestion. A shadow of something solid. But as the light grew, so did the clarity. She was not as small as she had imagined. Not as fragile. Not as doomed. The one who thought she was drowning—salt in her lungs, panic roaring in her ears like a storm tide, suddenly realized she could move her limbs. That her arms were not bound. That her legs were not weighted with chains. The water was still cold. The waves were still rough. But she was not as helpless as she had believed. She could kick. She could reach. She could turn her face toward air. The one who believed she was powerless began to feel something return to her body—quiet at first, like a distant drumbeat beneath the noise. A pulse. Steady. Undeniable. Agency does not always arrive with fireworks. Sometimes it returns like circulation to a numb limb: a tingling. A warmth. A reminder that life is still moving through you. I had always had a choice. Not an easy choice. Not a painless one. But a choice, nonetheless. It had been buried beneath fear, beneath narratives repeated so often they hardened into law. Beneath the belief that I was nothing more than a pawn on someone else's board. But it was there. Waiting. Like a key resting in a closed fist, forgotten only because I refused to open my hand. I just had to nearly lose everything to remember it. That is the part that humbles me still, the magnitude of what almost was. The children who might have grown without my presence. The love I might never have known. The chapters unwritten. The laughter unheard. The woman I would never have become. I stood on the edge of that absence and felt its chill brush against my skin. And in that cold, something awakened. Once remembered, I could not unknow it. The illusion shattered. The fog thinned. The story shifted. I was not a prisoner in a locked cell; I was someone standing in a room with the door ajar, too frightened to turn the handle. The key had been in my hand all along. Warm. Familiar. Mine. And this time, I did not hesitate. This time, I chose to use it. I felt it in my body, the click of metal turning, the subtle release of resistance, the rush of air as the door opened.

Emotionally, it felt like stepping into light after years of dimness. Like inhaling fully after breathing shallow for too long. Like reclaiming a name that had been taken from me. The woman who once believed she was trapped is not gone. She lives in my memory, in my scars, in my gratitude. But she is no longer cowering in shadow. She is standing. And she knows, now, that the power she begged the world for was always beating inside her own chest. And once you see that, you cannot go back to pretending you don't. So today, I share my story with you, not as a warning carved in cold stone, not as a monument to suffering, but as a lantern held gently in the dark. A small, steady flame cupped in open hands. I share it in the hope that you will not have to walk as far into the abyss as I did to discover your own strength. That you might glimpse your power before the ground gives way beneath your feet. Sitting here now, years removed from that precipice, bathed in the soft golden light of a new day, I feel the warmth of it resting on my skin. It settles across my shoulders like grace. The air smells clean, like morning after rain, like possibility rinsed free of ash. The quiet no longer rings hollow. It hums with life. With birdsong. With distant traffic. With the gentle rhythm of breath moving in and out of my lungs without resistance. Emotionally, the space around me feels open. Expansive. Not like a room closing in, but like a horizon stretching outward. And from this place, steady, grounded, clear, I can tell you with unwavering certainty and conviction: You do not need to die. You do not need to come within a hair's breadth of death, as I did, to find the strength to live. You do not have to endure the agonizing pain and torment of suicidal ideation to discover your resilience. You do not have to stand on the edge of annihilation to realize you matter. You do not have to feel the chill of oblivion at your back to understand that your life carries weight, meaning, consequence, beauty. You matter now. My mistake? It was my perception. I believed the situation was hopeless. I believed I was utterly powerless. I carried the unshakeable conviction that my circumstances were immutable, that I was a prisoner, shackled not only by my marriage, my depression, my trauma, but by myself.

I imagined the chains were iron. I imagined the lock was welded shut. I imagined there was no door. I was convinced I lacked the power to change my reality. That belief felt real. It tasted real, metallic and final on my tongue. It pressed against my chest like truth, heavy and immovable. It echoed in my mind with the authority of law. It shaped the way I breathed, the way I stood, the way I saw myself reflected in every surface. But it was not. It was a story. A story told so often it hardened into certainty. A narrative rehearsed until it sounded like fate. It had texture. Weight. Sound. But it did not have permanence. The truth was quieter. Softer. Less dramatic. And infinitely more powerful. The truth was that I was never as powerless as I believed. And neither are you. And I want to tell you, with the urgency of someone who has stood at the edge and felt the wind of oblivion against her skin, that you do not have to go through what I went through to see it. You do not have to fracture to awaken. You do not have to almost disappear to realize you want to stay. I was wrong. The truth is this: like me, you have a choice. A choice. And power. Not loud, cinematic power. Not the kind that roars and splits the sky. But the quiet, muscular kind that lives in your breath. The kind that steadies your spine. The kind that says, even in a whisper, "*no*". The power to say "no" to whatever is dragging you down. To whatever is gripping your ankles in that suffocating quicksand of despair. You can feel it sometimes, can't you? The way it pulls at your legs. The way it tugs, slow and persuasive. The way it whispers that sinking is easier than fighting. That stillness is simpler than struggle. That letting go would require less energy than climbing out. It lies. You can say no. You can reject the lies that murmur in your ear, telling you that you are powerless. Helpless. Beyond repair. You can interrupt that narrative mid-sentence. You can challenge it. You can refuse to let it narrate your life. You have the power to decide that you will no longer live in a state of darkness and despair. That you will no longer be ruled by your pain.

That you will no longer allow fear to dictate the boundaries of your life like barbed wire drawn too tight around your horizon. Like me, you get to decide, right here, right now, that you can no longer live this way. Feel that. Right here. Right now. It will not be easy. The work is real. The healing is layered, like sediment pressed down over years. It will demand courage when courage feels scarce. Honesty when honesty stings. Persistence when you are tired of trying. Like me, you will have to do the necessary work to claim that freedom. You will have to peel back the lies one careful layer at a time. Confront the wounds without flinching away. Sit with discomfort long enough to understand it. Choose again. And again. And again. Move toward light, even when you cannot yet see the sun. But hear this in your bones. The choice exists. Even if it feels small. Even if it feels fragile. Even if it feels impossible. A seed feels impossible beneath frozen ground. A heartbeat feels fragile in a silent room. A whisper feels insignificant against a storm. And yet, they endure. You do not need to nearly die to discover you want to live. You do not need to stand on the edge of annihilation to realize you matter. The strength you are searching for is not waiting at the edge of a cliff. It is not hidden in catastrophe. It is not reserved for your lowest hour. It is already inside you. Waiting. Not for perfection. Not for certainty. Not for fear to disappear. Just waiting to be claimed. The strength is already inside you. But choosing it, truly choosing it, comes with a caveat. This decision is not passive. It is not a gentle nod toward a better mindset while quietly continuing the same self-erasing patterns. It is not wishful thinking dressed up in pretty affirmations and whispered once in the mirror. It is not lighting a candle and hoping the dark will politely excuse itself. It is an active commitment. A deliberate, sometimes grueling devotion to the work required to achieve that freedom. Freedom is not handed to you like a gift wrapped in ease. It is built. Brick by conscious brick. Breath by steady breath. Boundary by trembling boundary. After my attempt, after that night when everything nearly ended, I did not awaken magically healed. There was no cinematic sunrise. No swelling music. No sudden, luminous transformation.

The air did not shimmer with clarity. My pain did not dissolve in a single epiphany. Instead, there were years. Years of relentless dedication to healing. To learning. To growing. Years of showing up to myself on mornings when the weight of memory pressed heavy against my ribs. Years of choosing discomfort over denial. Years of returning to the work when every instinct in me wanted to numb out, distract, disappear, or run. For the first time in my life, I truly faced my pain. I did not glance at it from a distance like something inconvenient on the horizon. I did not minimize it or rationalize it or package it into something more palatable. I did not dress it up in spiritual language or excuse it with logic. I felt it. Raw and visceral. I felt it in my chest like a burning ache, as though something inside me had been set alight and refused to go out. I felt it in my stomach, knotted, heavy, churning like a storm trapped beneath my skin. I felt it in my throat, where words once lodged like stones, thick and unspoken, scraping every time I tried to speak my truth. I allowed myself to sit with it. To taste its bitterness. To hear the echoes it left in the chambers of my mind. To feel the tremor in my hands when memories surfaced uninvited. It was not poetic in those moments. It was messy. There were tears that came without warning. Anger that rose hot and unfamiliar. Grief that smelled like dust and old rooms and things long buried. There were days when healing felt like dragging broken glass out of my own skin, one shard at a time. But something sacred was happening beneath the mess. Every time I stayed instead of escaping, I reclaimed a fragment of myself. Every time I told the truth, especially the truth that scared me, I loosened another chain. Every time I chose to feel instead of flee, I proved to myself that pain could be survived without annihilation. That is what choosing strength looks like. Not perfection. Not constant bravery. Not the absence of fear. But the willingness to remain present in your own becoming. Choosing your strength means stepping into the arena of your own life and refusing to look away.

It means deciding that your freedom is worth the discomfort of growth. It means understanding that healing is not a single revelation, but a thousand returns. And it is worth it. Because on the other side of that mess, on the other side of the tears and the trembling and the truth, is something solid. A self who can look in the mirror without flinching. A spine that does not collapse at the first gust of doubt. A heart that has been broken open and is stronger for it. Strength is already inside you. But when you choose it, when you commit to it with your whole body, your whole breath, your whole trembling honesty, it becomes more than potential. It becomes your life. I learned to understand its origins, where it began, how it was shaped, and what hands and histories molded it into the form it took inside me. I traced its mechanisms like a cartographer mapping unfamiliar terrain. I followed the patterns it repeated, the triggers that activated it, the subtle cues in my body, the tightening jaw, the shallow breath, the sudden drop in my stomach, which signalled it was rising again. I studied its insidious power. The way it crept in quietly, almost politely. The way it disguised itself as reason. The way it whispered in my own voice and convinced me it was truth. And slowly, so slowly it sometimes felt invisible, I began to loosen its grip. Pain that is faced loses its mystery. Pain that is understood loses its dominance. What once felt like an unnamed monster lurking in the dark began to take shape under scrutiny. And once it had shape, it could be approached. Questioned. Held up to the light. I confronted my demons one by one. Not with brute force. Not with self-hatred or denial. Not with the old reflex of punishing myself for having them in the first place. But with the quiet, steady strength of self-awareness. With acceptance. With compassion for the woman who had survived so much and blamed herself for all of it. Some days it felt like standing in a battlefield of memory, the air thick with smoke, armor discarded at my feet, choosing vulnerability instead of defence. Choosing to feel instead of fight. Choosing to soften instead of harden. Other days it felt like carefully untangling a knot that had been tightening for decades—fingers patient, breath measured, pulling gently at threads that had once felt fused together. Shame intertwined with trauma. Fear braided with love. Survival knotted with self-erasure. There were moments when the work was exhausting. When my chest ached from crying. When my body felt heavy with the weight of remembering. When the silence after a hard truth rang in my ears like a bell struck too sharply. But eventually, something shifted. The demons did not vanish in dramatic explosions. There were no thunderclaps, no cinematic defeats. Instead, they grew quieter. Smaller. Less authoritative. The shadows that once towered over me began to shrink under the light of understanding. Their edges softened. Their voices lost their echo. What once felt like law began to sound like suggestion. And suggestion can be challenged. One by one, I subdued them. Not because I destroyed them. But because I no longer fed them with denial and fear. I stopped nourishing them with secrecy. I stopped strengthening them with silence. I stopped believing everything they said. Freedom did not arrive as a single triumphant moment. It arrived in layers. In tears shed without apology. In truths spoken out loud for the first time. In boundaries held even when my voice trembled. In forgiveness extended to others, and to myself. In self-compassion practiced again and again, especially on the days I felt least deserving of it. Freedom arrived like dawn, incremental, subtle, and undeniable once fully risen. And that is the work. The decision to live is powerful. It is sacred. It is a turning point. But the commitment to heal—that is where transformation takes root. That is where the soil is turned. Where old debris is cleared. Where something new is planted. It is not easy. The work asks you to stay present when you would rather flee. To feel when you would rather numb. To look directly at what you once avoided. But it is possible. And it is worth it. Because on the other side of facing your pain is not a perfect life. It is a reclaimed one. And there is nothing more powerful than a life consciously reclaimed.

And that work, let me be honest, was not gentle. It was not bathed in soft lighting or accompanied by quiet, cinematic revelations. No violins were swelling in the background, no graceful montages of healing stitched neatly together. It was raw. It was gritty. It was often ugly in its honesty. It scraped against me. It demanded things from me I did not know I had to give. It was not easy. It took years. Years of dedication. Years of hard, unglamorous work. Years of perseverance when quitting would have been far simpler, far more seductive. There were mornings when the weight of continuing felt heavier than the weight of staying stuck. There were nights when exhaustion pressed into my bones and whispered, "*This is too much! Stop here! No more!*" Healing was not a straight path lined with encouragement and well-placed signposts. It was a long and winding road, uneven beneath my feet, gravel biting into my soles. It twisted unexpectedly, full of sharp turns and blind corners that forced me to slow down when I wanted to sprint away from the discomfort. Sometimes the ground felt solid. Other times, it shifted like loose sand, threatening to swallow my confidence whole. At times, it felt like walking through thick fog. The kind of fog that clings to your skin and seeps into your lungs. The kind that muffles sound and distorts distance. I could not see more than a step ahead. I had to trust the next breath. The next choice. The next inch of forward movement. The air felt damp with uncertainty, and emotionally, it carried a heaviness, like waiting for something unseen to emerge from the mist. There were moments of sheer terror. Moments when I felt as though I was drowning again, not in water this time, but in emotion.

Grief would surge unexpectedly, like a rogue wave crashing against the hull of my fragile boat, splintering the illusion that I had mastered the sea. I could taste it, briny and sharp, rising to the back of my throat. Shame would rise like saltwater in my mouth, stinging and bitter, coating my thoughts with accusation. Memories would surface without warning, cold and suffocating, like being pulled beneath icy depths where light barely penetrates. My body remembered what my mind tried to outrun. My hands would tremble. My heart would pound in my ears like a frantic drum. My breath would shorten, sharp and uneven. I would sit there, spine rigid, palms damp, convinced the tide would pull me under for good. Convinced this time, I would not resurface. Emotionally, it felt like standing at the mercy of a storm that had my name on it. And yet, here is the quiet truth that braided itself through those moments: The waves came. They rose. They crashed. And they receded. Every time. I was not as fragile as the storm wanted me to believe. There were days when healing felt less like growth and more like excavation. Digging through layers of sedimented pain. Uncovering things I had buried to survive. The work was not pretty. It was mud-streaked and tear-soaked. It required me to sit in rooms with my own history and not look away. It required me to feel what I had numbed, to name what I had minimized, to grieve what I had lost, not only the marriage, not only the years, but versions of myself that never had the chance to fully bloom. And still, I kept walking. Even when I could not see far ahead. Even when fear pressed cold fingers along my spine. Even when shame tried to convince me I was regressing rather than rebuilding. The fog did not mean I was lost. The storm did not mean I was failing. The trembling did not mean I was weak. It meant I was alive. It meant I was feeling. It meant I was healing in real time. There is something sacred about surviving your own emotional weather. About discovering that you can stand in the downpour and not dissolve. That you can be soaked in grief and still breathe. That you can taste shame and choose not to swallow it.

That work was not gentle. But it was transformative. Every wave that did not drown me strengthened the hull. Every memory faced without fleeing reinforced the spine of the woman I was becoming. Every trembling moment I endured without surrender became proof, not of fragility, but of resilience. Healing did not feel like floating toward the light. It felt like learning to swim in the dark. And I did. Stroke by trembling stroke. There were days when the pain felt like it would consume me whole, like standing too close to a fire that had once kept me warm but now threatened to devour everything in its path. My chest would tighten until breath felt rationed. My thoughts would spiral inward, tightening like a whirlpool pulling me toward its dark center. And in those moments, I would wonder, quietly, fearfully, if facing everything had been a mistake. Suppose I had disturbed something that would have been better left buried. The work required me to reopen wounds I had spent years trying to numb. Wounds I had carefully wrapped in distraction, obligation, performance. Wounds I had pressed down with silence and endurance. Healing demanded that I peel back those layers with trembling hands and look directly at what lay beneath. It asked me to sit in rooms, literal rooms with closed doors and folded tissues, and emotional rooms filled with memory, where the air felt thick with truth and accountability. The kind of air that clings to the back of your throat. The kind that smells faintly of something exposed. There was no escape hatch in those spaces. No softening the edges. No rewriting the narrative. No convenient villain to shoulder all the weight. Only truth. Unfiltered. Unflinching. It was a brutal, arduous trek. An agonizing journey. A painful voyage across a tempestuous, turbulent sea that threatened to capsize my fragile little boat countless times, more times than I care to remember. The sea was not metaphorical in those moments; it felt visceral. I could almost hear the wind howling through the hollow spaces of my chest, feel the deck tilt violently beneath my feet. The planks of my resolve would creak. The ropes of my composure would strain. I could taste the salt spray of old tears on my lips, familiar, sharp, persistent. Grief would roll in like storm clouds without warning. Shame would flash like lightning across my thoughts. Regret would rumble deep and low, like distant thunder that never quite moved on. There were nights when exhaustion settled into my bones like winter frost, slow, penetrating, merciless. It wasn't just physical fatigue. It was marrow-deep weariness. The kind that makes even hope feel heavy. I would lie awake staring into darkness, the quiet loud around me, and wonder if I had the strength to keep rowing. If my arms, already aching, could pull one more stroke against the current. And yet, even in the storm, something inside me kept reaching for the oars. It wasn't bravado. It wasn't certainty. It wasn't even optimism. It was something quieter. Instinct. A pulse of defiance. A refusal to surrender to the tide. Even when my hands shook. Even when the boat pitched wildly. Even when I felt small against the immensity of the sea, there was a part of me, ancient and stubborn, that would not let go. Healing was not graceful. It was messy and windburned and soaked through. It was mascara streaked down cheeks and voices cracking mid-sentence. It was admitting truths that scraped against pride. It was apologizing without knowing if forgiveness would come. It was sitting with discomfort long enough for it to teach me something instead of running from it. Sometimes healing looked like collapsing into tears on a kitchen floor. Sometimes it looked like sending a text I was terrified to send. Sometimes it looked like simply getting out of bed and choosing not to disappear. There was nothing elegant about it.

But there was something fierce. Every time the storm rose, and I did not abandon ship, something strengthened within me. Every wave that battered the hull and failed to break it reinforced the structure. Every night I survived without surrender became proof that I was more seaworthy than I had believed. The sea was wild. The voyage was brutal. But I was still rowing. And somewhere beyond the fog, beyond the wind and salt and sleepless nights, I began to sense, not see, not yet, but sense, a horizon. Faint. Uncertain. But real. Healing was not graceful. But it was mine. It was gritty. It was ugly crying on the bathroom floor. It was journaling through shaking hands. It was saying hard truths aloud and feeling them land in my chest like stones. It was learning to breathe through panic instead of running from it. It was choosing, again and again, not to turn back toward the darkness that had once felt familiar. It was terrifying. And it was transformative. Because every storm I survived proved something I had once believed impossible: I could endure the waves without surrendering to them. I could feel the pain without being destroyed by it. The sea was wild. But I was no longer helpless within it. It was gritty. Not cinematic grit. Not the kind that photographs well. The kind that clings under your fingernails and stings your eyes. It was ugly crying on the bathroom floor, cheek pressed against cool tile, the fluorescent light above me too harsh, too honest. It was sobbing without elegance, without restraint, shoulders shaking, throat raw, mascara streaked into something unrecognizable. The kind of crying that empties you and terrifies you at the same time. It was journaling through shaking hands. Ink blotting the page because my fingers wouldn't steady. Words scratched out, rewritten, circled, and underlined as if urgency alone could make them truer. The paper crinkling beneath my palm damp with tears. The smell of ink and paper and something metallic in the air, fear, maybe. Or release. It was saying hard truths aloud and feeling them land in my chest like stones. Not poetic truths. Not softened ones. The kind that reverberates when spoken. The kind that echoes back at you from the walls of a quiet room. I could feel each admission strike something inside me, heavy, undeniable.

My ribs felt tight around them. My heart would thud as if adjusting to a new gravity. It was learning to breathe through panic instead of running from it. Learning that the rush of adrenaline, the tightening throat, the spinning thoughts were not signs of imminent destruction, but signals. I would sit still while my pulse thundered in my ears. I would place a hand on my sternum and inhale slowly, deliberately, tasting the air like something earned. Breath in. Breath out. Again. Again. Again. Staying. It was choosing, again and again, not to turn back toward the darkness that had once felt familiar. The darkness had been predictable. It had been known. There is a strange comfort in what we know, even when it is painful. The shadows had wrapped around me like an old coat. Heavy. Worn. But familiar. Choosing light meant stepping into uncertainty.And that was terrifying. It was terrifying to say no when I once would have folded. Terrifying to speak when I once would have swallowed words. Terrifying to set boundaries and watch who stayed, and who did not. Terrifying to believe that I deserved more. And yet, it was transformative. Because every storm I survived proved something I had once believed impossible. I could endure the waves without surrendering to them. I could feel the pain without being destroyed by it. I could sit in grief without dissolving. I could taste shame without swallowing it whole. I could hear the old whispers without obeying them. Each wave that rose and fell without capsizing me rewrote something fundamental inside my nervous system. My body began to learn what my mind was still catching up to: I was not fragile glass. I was tempered steel. I bent. I shook. I trembled. But I did not shatter. The sea was wild. Its winds still rose. Its tides still shifted. There were still nights when the sky darkened without warning and I had to grip the rails of my resolve. But I was no longer helpless within it. I knew where the oars were. I knew how to steady my breath. I knew how to read the weather forming inside my own chest. The storms did not vanish. I changed. And that is the difference. Where once I felt like debris tossed by circumstance, I now felt like a sailor learning her craft. Scarred by salt and wind, yes, but seasoned. Alert. Capable. The sea was wild. But I was no longer lost in it. I was navigating. And for the first time, I trusted that even if the waves rose again, as they inevitably would, I had something stronger than fear guiding me. I had myself.

And yet, even after I learned to hold the oars, even after I found rhythm in my own strength, there were days, entire weeks even, when the darkness threatened to reclaim me. It did not vanish with dignity. It did not bow out because I had grown stronger. It circled. It watched. It waited for fatigue to thin my defenses. Sometimes it returned like a heavy fog rolling in from nowhere, dense, gray, swallowing the horizon I had worked so hard to see. One moment, the sky inside me would feel clear; the next, visibility would shrink to inches. The air would thicken. My limbs would grow heavy. Even sound seemed muffled, as if cotton had been packed between me and the world. My body would ache with exhaustion that sleep could not touch. Emotionally, it felt like gravity had intensified, like someone had quietly turned up the weight of the planet. My thoughts slowed. My chest felt compressed. The simple act of standing upright carried effort. There was a pull, subtle but persistent, urging me to lie down and surrender. Not dramatically. Not catastrophically. Just stop trying so hard. It was a painful journey. Not poetic pain. Real pain. The kind that drains color from the day. The kind that leaves your bones feeling hollowed and tired. The kind that hums low beneath your skin, constant and unrelenting. There were nights when I collapsed into bed and felt as though I had been fighting an invisible war all day. No applause. No witnesses. Just me and the battlefield of my own mind. My muscles tight. My jaw sore from clenching back tears I didn't even realize I was holding. My shoulders aching from carrying tension like armor. Overwhelmed. Exhausted. Raw. The sheets would feel cool against overheated skin. The room quiet except for the sound of my own uneven breath. And in that quiet, the weight of the day would settle over me like a damp blanket. But in the middle of that struggle, in the fog, in the heaviness, in the unglamorous fatigue, I discovered something profound. I was capable of sitting with my feelings. That may sound small. It was not. For years, my instinct had been to outrun discomfort. To numb it. To silence it.

To exile it like an enemy trespassing where it did not belong. I had treated sadness like a threat. Anxiety like a malfunction. Grief like a flaw. Now, I began to do something radical. I stayed. When sorrow rose like tidewater in my chest, I did not immediately reach for distraction. I let it crest. When panic fluttered beneath my ribs, I placed a hand there and breathed. When shame tried to whisper its old narrative, I listened, not to obey, but to understand. The sensations were vivid. Tears burning hot against cool air. Breath catching, sharp, and shallow before deepening. The metallic taste of fear dissolving slowly with each exhale. Emotionally, it felt like learning to sit across from my own shadow without flinching. Not numbing them. Not running from them. Not trying to exile them like enemies. But allowing them to exist. Allowing them to move through me like weather instead of trying to dam the sky. The darkness still came. But now, when it settled around me, I no longer mistook it for permanence. It was a visitor. Unwelcome, yes. But not sovereign. I had learned something storms do not teach you when you are drowning: Clouds pass. Waves crest and fall. Fog lifts.

And most importantly, I could remain steady long enough to see that happen. That steadiness did not mean I never shook. It meant I no longer collapsed at the first tremor.

The darkness could circle. But I was no longer prey. I was present. And in that presence, quiet, imperfect, hard-won, I found a strength that was not loud or flashy. It was simply enduring. And that endurance, more than anything, was proof that the woman holding the oars was still here. I could sit with my past demons. Not chained to them. Not fleeing from them. But seated across from them in the quiet of my own becoming. I could endure the pain without being swallowed whole. I could feel its heat rise in my chest, its chill settle along my spine, and remain. I could look directly at it, at the shame, the grief, the memories that once stole my breath, and say, with steadiness that surprised even me: "*You are a part of me, but you are not all of me.*" That sentence did not echo loudly. It rooted. It moved through me like a slow, grounding current, anchoring into places that had once trembled at the slightest shadow. That realization shifted something deep inside, like a tectonic plate adjusting beneath the surface of my life. Subtle at first. Then undeniable. The pain was no longer something to be banished or suppressed. It became something to be understood. When I stopped fighting it with fear, it lost some of its sharpest edges. It no longer lunged at me with the same ferocity. I began to recognize its patterns, the way it arrived on certain anniversaries, the way fatigue made it louder, the way certain tones of voice or certain silences could awaken it. I began to hear the messages beneath the noise. Pain was not just destruction. It was information. A signal flare rising from the body. A whisper from the nervous system. A reminder of where tenderness still needed tending. In time, those once-feared surges became unlikely allies and guides. They pointed toward boundaries that needed reinforcing. Toward wounds that still required care. Toward habits I no longer wanted to repeat. What once felt like sabotage began to feel like instruction. And I persevered. Through tears that blurred the edges of the day. Through doubt that crept in like evening chill. Through fatigue that felt bone-deep, marrow-heavy, as though even my skeleton had grown tired of carrying the weight of transformation. There were days when my reflection looked weary. When my voice sounded thinner than I wished. When progress felt invisible. And still, I persevered. Because in the process, I discovered something astonishing. A resilience I never knew I possessed. Not loud. Not defiant in a dramatic way. But steady. Quiet. Enduring. A strength that had been hidden beneath years of self-doubt, like bedrock beneath loose soil. It had always been there. I had simply never been still enough to feel it. I learned that I was capable of weathering the storm, not by pretending the storm wasn't raging, not by denying the thunder or dismissing the wind, but by staying anchored within it. By lowering my center of gravity. By gripping the oars and breathing through the surge. The storm could rage. I did not have to vanish. I persevered because I was hungry. Hungry for peace, the kind that hums softly in your chest instead of clenching it tight. Hungry for freedom, the kind that tastes like clean air after years of smoke. Hungry for a life that felt purposeful instead of merely survivable. Survival had been my baseline for so long that thriving felt almost mythical. But once I glimpsed even a flicker of something better, I could not unsee it. There were many times when I wanted to give up. Moments when the old voice returned, familiar and persuasive: "*This is too hard. You'll never fully heal.*" Moments when darkness felt seductive in its predictability. The known ache sometimes seemed easier than the uncertainty of growth. The shadows offered familiarity. The light demanded courage. But I didn't give up. Because I knew something I hadn't known before. I had a choice. A choice to keep moving forward. A choice to push through the pain instead of retreating into it.

A choice to continue even when progress felt microscopic, when the only evidence of growth was that I reacted a second later than I once would have. That I paused instead of lashed out. That I cried but did not collapse. Those shifts were almost invisible. But they were real. And slowly, incrementally, things began to change. It was not dramatic. There were no fireworks. No grand announcements. It was subtle. The way my shoulders sat a little lower. The way my breath moved more freely through my ribs. The way I recovered from setbacks a little faster.

The way the darkness lingered less long, spoke less loudly. The changes were quiet. But they accumulated. And one day, without fanfare, I realized something had shifted fundamentally.

The storm still existed, but it no longer defined the sky. The past still existed, but it no longer dictated the path. The pain still surfaced, but it no longer owned me. I was not healed in a single moment. I was becoming whole in a thousand small ones. And that, subtle, steady, hard-won, was everything. The darkness did not vanish overnight. It did not retreat in some dramatic sweep, nor did it apologize for how long it had lingered. It began, slowly, almost shyly, to recede. Like a tide pulling back from the shore after years of relentless crashing. I could feel the shift before I could see it. The air seemed less suffocating. The heaviness in my chest less constant. The silence less hostile. The water was still there. But it was no longer swallowing the land. And in its place, light began to seep in, thin at first, tentative, like dawn breaking through a narrow crack in the horizon. Not blazing. Not triumphant. Just a pale line of gold at the edge of a long night. The kind of light you almost miss if you are not paying attention. The kind that warms the skin before you consciously register the sun has risen. That light did not blind me. It revealed me. I began to see that I was not alone. The isolation that had once wrapped around me like a second skin began to loosen. I found stories, whispers at first, then voices, of others who had walked this path before me. Others who had faced their own storms and survived. Women and men who had stood at their own edges, who had tasted despair and chosen to remain. Their stories became lanterns along the road. Each testimony a small, steady flame. Each confession of survival a point of reference in the dark. When I felt unsure of my footing, I would hold their words close. I would imagine their hands gripping their own oars. I would remember that if they could cross their oceans, perhaps I could cross mine. I drew strength from them. Inspiration from their courage. Proof from their persistence. And just as their stories lit the path ahead of me, I began to understand that my story, raw and imperfect and hard-earned, could become a lantern for someone else. A small flame passed forward.

A quiet reassurance in the night: "*You are not alone here. I have walked this stretch of road. Keep going.*" Somewhere along the way, another truth emerged, subtle at first, then undeniable. I was not a victim. Yes, I had suffered. Yes, harm had been done. Yes, wounds had been inflicted that were not mine to earn. But I was not condemned to remain defined by them. Victimhood had once felt like the only narrative available to me, like the only lens through which my pain made sense. But as the light grew steadier, I realized something radical: suffering can shape you without owning you. It can mark you without imprisoning you. I had the power to choose my own path. To create my own unique destiny. Not in a grand, theatrical way, but in the quiet accumulation of daily decisions. In the boundaries I held. In the self-respect I cultivated. In the way, I refused to shrink back into old patterns just because they were familiar. I was not a prisoner of my circumstances. I was a pioneer. Charting new territory. There is something sacred about walking ground that no one in your lineage taught you to walk. About mapping a future that does not resemble your past. I felt it in my body, the way my spine straightened when I chose differently. The way my breath deepened when I stepped outside old roles. The way my heart steadied when I realized the map was in my hands. I was no longer retracing inherited pain. I was drafting possibility. A course filled with hope, promise, and possibility, not naive hope, not fragile promise, but hope tested by storm. Promise strengthened by fire. Possibility earned through endurance. And when I look back now, what stands out is not the pain. Not the suffering. Not even the depth of the darkness. Those things are part of the landscape, yes, but they are not the headline of my story. What defines me is my response. My choice to rise. My decision to endure when quitting would have been easier. My refusal to surrender to narratives that told me I was disposable.

It was not the storm that shaped me; it was the way I learned to stand in it. Feet planted. Breath steady. Eyes open. Storms come for everyone. But not everyone learns to anchor themselves in the gale. Because of that choice, because of that defiance, I emerged stronger. Not hardened. Not closed. But strengthened. Wiser, not cynical, but discerning. More resilient, not untouched by pain, but able to move through it without dissolving. I am not untouched by what happened to me. I am transformed by it. The darkness did not define my life. My decision to rise did. And that, quiet, unwavering, deliberate, that is the woman I have become. It was not the storm that defined me, but the way I chose to stand within it. And somewhere along that long, uneven road, between the fog and the oars, between the trembling and the steady breath, I learned one of the most important lessons of all: The power of forgiveness. Forgiveness was not an abstract virtue hanging framed on a wall. It was not a spiritual cliché whispered in soft tones. It was survival. It was oxygen. It became a crucial part of the process, as necessary as breath in a room that had once felt airless. Without it, I could feel the tightness in my chest return, subtle at first, then insistent. I could taste the metallic tang of resentment lingering at the back of my tongue, sharp and acidic. Bitterness had a texture, gritty, heavy, exhausting. It weighed on me like wet sand in my pockets, dragging at every step. Resentment is not loud. It is dense. It settles into the body like sediment. It tightens the jaw. It hardens the gaze. It narrows the heart. I carried it for a time, mistaking it for strength. Mistaking it for protection. But it was not armor, it was ballast, anchoring me to the very shore I was trying to leave. So I began with the hardest person to forgive. Myself. I forgave myself not out of self-indulgence, not to excuse my mistakes, not to bypass accountability, but because self-forgiveness was an essential step toward peace. And I was starving for peace. I hungered for it in my bones. I felt the ache for it in the quiet moments before sleep, when the day's distractions dissolved and memory sharpened its edges. I felt it in the early light of morning, when the world was still, and my thoughts were loudest. Peace was not luxury. It was necessity. Self-forgiveness became the key that unlocked a door I had been pressing against for years. A door swollen with shame and swollen with self-condemnation. For so long, I had stood on the other side of that threshold, insisting I did not deserve entry. Forgiving myself felt at first like trespassing into a room I had not earned. But as I turned that key, slowly, hesitantly, I felt something soften. The inner courtroom dissolved. The verdict of *"forever guilty"* lost its authority. I could look at my mistakes without flinching. I could acknowledge harm without annihilating myself. I could say, "*Yes, I faltered. Yes, I hurt. Yes, I failed in moments.*" And still believe that I was worthy of repair. Self-forgiveness did not erase the past. It released me from being permanently sentenced by it. And then, in time, I forgave others, not for their sake, but for mine. For my peace of mind. Their actions, their mistakes, the harm they caused, these were woven into my story like dark threads through a tapestry. To deny or ignore them would have been to deny parts of myself. I could not pretend the damage did not exist. I could not rewrite the fabric. But holding onto bitterness, clenching resentment like a weapon, only prolonged my suffering. It kept the wound open. It kept me tethered to the very pain I wanted to escape. It tied my present to their past actions in an endless loop. Forgiveness did not mean forgetting. It meant loosening my grip. It meant acknowledging what was done without allowing it to dictate who I would become. It meant refusing to let anger become the architect of my future. It meant saying, "*You hurt me. What you did mattered. But I will not carry you forward inside my nervous system forever.*" Letting go did not feel dramatic. There were no thunderclaps. No sudden light flooding the sky. It felt deliberate. It felt like unclenching a fist I had held tight for far too long. I could feel it physically, the way my shoulders dropped a fraction lower, the way my breath deepened into my belly instead of hovering high and shallow. Emotionally, it felt like setting down a weight I had mistaken for identity. Forgiveness was not weakness. It was reclamation. It was an act of self-compassion, a quiet but powerful step toward healing. It was choosing not to let the storm live inside me long after the clouds had moved on.

It was choosing softness where hardness had calcified. It was choosing freedom over familiar fury. In forgiving, I did not excuse. I released. And in releasing, I felt something I had been craving without fully naming. Space. Room to breathe. Room to grow. Room to become. Forgiveness did not change what happened. It changed what I carried. And that, more than anything, allowed me to keep walking forward, lighter than I had been in years. Forgiveness was not about condoning their behavior. It was not about pretending it didn't hurt. It was about liberating myself from the burden of carrying that hurt indefinitely. About setting down a weight, I had mistaken it for strength. I had thought endurance meant clenching my jaw and gripping the pain tightly, as if holding it proved I was righteous. But all that gripping had done was carve tension into my body, into my shoulders, into the hinge of my jaw, into the quiet spaces behind my eyes. Forgiveness was not surrender. It was release. It was opening my hands and realizing they had been clenched for years. And perhaps most importantly, I learned to love myself. Not in a glossy, mirror-affirmation kind of way. Not in a superficial, self-congratulatory performance that glossed over harm or rewrote history. This was something deeper. Something steadier. Less sparkle, more root. It was a deep and abiding acceptance of my imperfections, my vulnerabilities, my humanity. I began to see my flaws not as cracks to be concealed, but as the intricate threads in the tapestry of who I am. Threads of grief. Threads of resilience. Threads of mistakes that taught me what no comfort ever could. I could run my fingers across that tapestry and feel texture instead of shame. I learned to recognize my inherent worthiness of love and happiness, not because I was flawless, not because I had finally *"fixed"* myself, but because I am human. And being human is enough. Enough to deserve tenderness. Enough to deserve rest. Enough to deserve joy. I began to see myself as deserving of love, kindness, and compassion, the very things I had denied myself for so long. I had once rationed those things inwardly, offering them generously to others while withholding them from myself as if I had to earn them through suffering. That began to change. I could feel the emotional shift of it. The softening in my chest where armor had once lived. The easing of tension in my shoulders, as if invisible straps had finally been loosened. The warmth that slowly replaced the constant chill of self-criticism, a warmth that felt like sunlight after years of internal winter.

Self-criticism had once been my constant companion, whispering corrections, judgments, condemnations. Loving myself meant lowering its volume. Not silencing it completely but refusing to let it narrate my existence. This was not a sudden epiphany. There was no lightning bolt. No single revelation that split the sky and declared me whole. It was gradual. A slow unfolding, like petals opening in morning light. A culmination of countless small acts of self-kindness. The way I chose rest instead of punishment. The way I paused before tearing myself apart over a mistake. The way I spoke gently to the woman in the mirror when she looked tired instead of criticizing the lines around her eyes. It was a gentle choosing, day after day, to speak to myself differently. To sit with my mistakes without annihilating myself for them. To acknowledge harm without collapsing into self-hatred. To say, *"You are learning,"* instead of, *"You are failing."* It was offering myself the same grace I so freely extended to others. The same patience. The same understanding. The same belief that growth is possible. Forgiveness opened the door. Self-love taught me how to walk through it. And peace, real, steady peace, began to feel less like a distant dream shimmering on the horizon and more like something I could finally hold in my hands. Not fragile. Not fleeting. But solid. Breathable. Warm. Peace did not erase the past. It integrated it. It felt like standing in my own skin without flinching. Like inhabiting my life without bracing for impact. Like resting inside myself instead of constantly trying to escape. Forgiveness unburdened me. Self-love rebuilt me. And somewhere in that quiet reconstruction, I realized something extraordinary: I was no longer at war with myself. I was home. And as that peace began to settle into my bones, slowly, like warmth seeping into hands long held in winter, I could finally look back. Not with shame. Not with collapse. But with clarity. The past no longer loomed over me like a towering verdict. It lay behind me like terrain already crossed, scarred, yes, but mapped. I could trace its ridges and valleys without falling into them. I could remember without unraveling.

As I look back on my journey now, I am reminded of the profound importance of self-care and self-love. They were not indulgences. They were not spa days, or scented candles arranged for aesthetic comfort. They were lifelines. They were the rope thrown overboard when I was barely keeping my head above water. They were the oxygen mask placed over my own face first, awkward at first, guilt-laced, but necessary. Without them, I would have continued giving from an empty well, drawing from a reservoir long since drained. I had to learn, sometimes clumsily, sometimes stubbornly, to prioritize my own needs. It did not come naturally. At first, it felt selfish.

Wrong. Almost dangerous. My body had been trained to override its own signals. My heart had been trained to swallow its own ache. My spirit had been conditioned to endure. So I began again. I learned to take care of myself not only physically but also emotionally. To notice when my body was tired, not push through it. To feel when my heart was overwhelmed, not dismiss it. To listen when my spirit whispered, *"enough."* That whisper had been there all along. Soft. Persistent. Often ignored. Now, I began to treat it like sacred instruction. Enough. Enough giving. Enough explaining. Enough tolerating what eroded me. I had to learn to say no. That word tasted foreign at first, dry and unfamiliar on my tongue. It felt like speaking a new language without fluency. My voice trembled when I formed it. My palms would sweat. My chest would tighten. I could feel the old reflex urging me to retract it, to soften it, to apologize for it. But I did not. Over time, no grew steadier. It rooted itself in my spine. It carried weight without aggression. It sounded less like defiance and more like alignment. No became less about rejection and more about preservation. It became a quiet guardian standing at the threshold of my energy, no longer carrying the banner of shame or blame. I learned to set boundaries, not walls built from bitterness, not fortresses carved out of fear, but healthy edges drawn from self-respect. There is a difference. Walls isolate. Boundaries protect. Walls say, *"No one may enter."* Boundaries say, *"Enter kindly, or not at all."* Drawing those lines felt like tracing new borders on a map of my life. It felt deliberate. Intentional. Sometimes uncomfortable. But deeply right. And then something else began to change. I learned to surround myself with people who loved and supported me. Not people who thrived on chaos. Not people who sharpened their words into subtle weapons. Not people who drained me like slow leaks in a vessel. But people whose presence felt warm rather than depleting. People whose laughter softened the air. People whose words felt safe rather than sharp. People who listened without strategizing a rebuttal. Who celebrated my growth instead of resenting it. Their company felt different in my body. My shoulders did not rise defensively. My breath did not shorten. My nervous system did not brace for impact. Instead, there was ease. Safety. Space. Self-care began to look less like emergency response and more like daily devotion. Drinking water. Taking walks. Resting without justification. Turning off my phone when I needed quiet. Speaking up when something hurts. Letting tears fall without shaming them. Self-love became less about grand declarations and more about small, consistent choices. Choosing rest over performance. Choosing honesty over approval. Choosing alignment over obligation. Peace had opened the door. Self-care taught me how to stay inside the room. And as I stood there, feet planted on ground I had learned to protect. I realized something simple and extraordinary: Loving myself was not an act of rebellion. It was an act of return. Return to my body. Return to my voice. Return to the quiet authority that had always lived inside me. The woman who once survived on scraps of validation now nourished herself with intention. The woman who once whispered, *"I'm fine"* while breaking learned to say, *"I need,"* without apology. And that shift, steady, embodied, real, was not loud. But it was powerful. Because the peace that had once felt fragile was now supported by practice. By boundaries. By breath. By the sacred, daily act of choosing myself. Looking back on those difficult years now, I am struck by a realization that both steadies and humbles me:

I was never truly powerless. Even when I felt small. Even when I felt broken. Even when the darkness seemed absolute, thick as tar, swallowing light whole. Powerlessness had felt like a fact. It had lived in my chest like a verdict. But when I trace the years with gentler eyes, I see something else threaded through them, thin at first, almost invisible. Choice. I had the power to choose. Not always in sweeping, cinematic ways. Not with grand gestures or dramatic declarations. But in the smallest, quietest movements of will. The power to decide how I would respond to my circumstances. The power to shape my destiny, even if only one small decision at a time. A breath taken instead of held. A boundary spoken instead of swallowed. A phone call made instead of avoided. A day survived instead of surrendered. Choice did not roar. It whispered. And yet, those whispers accumulated. They formed a current beneath the chaos. Even when I felt as though the tide was dragging me under, there was a subtle muscle inside me still contracting, still reaching. I see it now. Even on the nights when despair pressed against my ribs and the air felt thin, I chose to stay one more hour. Even on the mornings when getting out of bed felt like climbing a mountain barefoot, I chose to swing my legs over the edge. Even when the voice inside me insisted I was too far gone, I chose, however faintly, to question it. Those were not glamorous acts. They were sacred ones. And I believe, deeply, fiercely, that this is true for anyone struggling with suicidal ideation, with feelings of hopelessness and despair. You have a choice. It may not feel like it. It may feel buried beneath exhaustion, beneath shame, beneath the suffocating weight of *"I can't."* But it is there. Sometimes it is no bigger than a flicker. Sometimes it trembles. Sometimes it feels almost ridiculous in its fragility. But it exists. A choice to say no to the negative narratives holding you back. A choice to challenge the voice that says, *"You are the problem."* A choice to refuse the lie that you are beyond repair. A choice to seek help. To pick up the phone. To send the message. To speak the truth aloud, even when your throat tightens. A choice to pursue healing and growth, not because it is easy, not because it is quick, but because you are worth the effort. A choice to reach for something different, even when your hands are shaking. Especially when your hands are shaking. Shaking hands still reach.

Trembling voices still speak. Exhausted hearts still beat. Choice does not require certainty. It requires willingness. One step. One breath. One refusal to disappear. Looking back, I see that I did not reclaim my life in a single moment. I reclaimed it in increments. In decisions so small they seemed almost insignificant at the time. But small decisions, repeated, become direction. Direction becomes momentum. Momentum becomes transformation. I was never truly powerless. And neither are you. Even in the depths of despair. Even in the quiet of your loneliest night. Even when the darkness feels like it has the final word. There is still a part of you capable of choosing. And sometimes, that is enough to begin.

And this is where the remembering becomes real. Not intellectual. Not theoretical. Not a quote pinned neatly to a wall. Real. *"You can't choose what life throws at you, but you can choose how to respond."* When I first heard those words, they sounded almost too simple. Almost dismissive of the complexity of trauma, of betrayal, of grief that claws at your ribs. I wanted something more profound. More dramatic. Something that matched the scale of what I had survived. But over time, those words settled into me. They did not float lightly across the surface of my thoughts. They sank. Deep. Like truth carved into bone. Like something ancient and steady being etched beneath the noise. They speak of change. Of reclaiming authorship. Of understanding that we are no longer powerless, no longer passive victims tossed endlessly by circumstance like driftwood in a merciless sea. Yes, people will still hurt us. Yes, we will still make mistakes. Yes, pain will still find us. Yes, we will still get triggered. Healing does not make life sterile. It does not wrap the world in foam. Life does not suddenly soften because we have done the work. The winds still rise. The storms still form. The unexpected still crashes against us. But now, we get to choose what we do with it. That choice is everything. It is the difference between reaction and response. Between reenactment and evolution. Between being swept away and standing, even trembling, on our own two feet. When pain arrives now, I feel it. I do not pretend it isn't there. I notice how it lands in my body, the tightening in my chest, as though invisible fingers have drawn a cord too tight. The warmth rising to my face, flushing through skin like a warning flare.

The tremor beneath my breath, subtle but unmistakable, like the first ripple before a wave breaks. Emotionally, I feel the old reflexes stir. The urge to shrink. To apologize for existing. To lash out in defence. To retreat into silence. They rise like ghosts of muscle memory, familiar and fast. But now, something else rises too. A pause. A breath that stretches a fraction longer than it once did. A widening of space between stimulus and response. And in that pause, choice. It feels almost invisible from the outside. But inside, it is seismic. A hinge turning. A current shifting direction. A hand reaching for the oars before the wave crests. In that pause, I can ask: *"What is actually happening here? What do I need? What would align with who I am becoming?"* Sometimes, I still stumble. Sometimes I respond imperfectly. But even in imperfection, the awareness remains. The choice remains. Choice is not about controlling life. It is about directing yourself. It is about remembering that you are not the storm. You are the one standing within it. It is about understanding that triggers are not commands. Pain is not prophecy. Emotion is not destiny. That pause is sacred. It is where the old story loosens its grip. It is where the inherited script can be rewritten. It is where the woman I once was meets the woman I am becoming, and they speak to one another gently. The remembering becomes real when it moves from theory to embodiment. When you feel it in your nervous system. When your shoulders drop instead of being tense. When your voice steadies instead of fractures. When you respond from alignment instead of survival. You can't choose what life throws at you. But you can choose how to stand. You can choose whether to absorb the blow and collapse or absorb it and recalibrate. You can choose whether to let pain define you or inform you. And that choice, repeated over time, becomes power. Not loud power. Not domineering power. But grounded power. The kind that feels like standing in your own body without flinching. The kind that says: Life may still throw its stones. But I decide what I build with them. And in that remembering, something extraordinary happens. You stop waiting for life to change. You begin changing your life. And this is where it deepens. Because once you understand the power of the pause—once you feel that sacred space between hurt and reaction, you begin to see how much agency has always been waiting there. We get to choose whether the hurt becomes another wound that festers or a lesson that refines us. Hurt will come. It will land sharp and hot. It will sting. But it does not get to decide what it becomes inside us. Left unattended, pain can sour. It can swell and pulse beneath the surface, infecting the very places that once tried to protect us. But tended with honesty, with curiosity, with courage, it becomes something else. It becomes refinement. Fire that tempers rather than destroys. We get to decide whether the trigger becomes a weapon against ourselves or a signal pointing toward something that still needs care. Triggers used to feel like proof that I was broken. Now, they feel like flares in the night sky. Signals. Indicators. Not verdicts. When my chest tightens, when my breath shortens, when old panic stirs, I ask: "*What is this protecting? What still aches here?"* The trigger is no longer a whip. It is a whisper. It is an invitation to tend the places still tender. We get to choose to let our experiences empower us, to become tools for growth rather than forces that destroy us.

Experiences can harden us. They can calcify into armor so thick that nothing soft can reach us. Or they can shape us. Sharpen discernment. Strengthen boundaries. Deepen empathy. Pain can carve us hollow, or it can carve us open. We get to choose boundaries. And boundaries are not cruelty. They are clarity. To say *"no."* That word once trembled in my mouth like something forbidden. Now it feels clean. Grounded. A line drawn not in anger, but in self-respect. To say *"yes."* When something aligns. When it nourishes. When it expands rather than contracts, my spirit. To say *"Maybe."* To grant myself time. Space. Reflection. To say *"Later"* or *"Not now."* To resist urgency. To refuse to be rushed into self-betrayal. To say, *"Not my responsibility."* And mean it. To finally separate what belongs to me from what does not. To set down burdens I once carried like inherited debts. And most importantly, to say, *"You do not get to treat me or talk to me that way!"* That sentence once felt impossible. Now it feels like a declaration of sovereignty. Not shouted. Not cruel. But firm. Anchored. A reclaiming of ground.

There is power in that. Power in walking away from relationships and friendships that are toxic, even when it aches. Even when your hands shake as you close the door. Even when the silence afterward feels unfamiliar and vast. Because sometimes what drains you disguises itself as loyalty. Sometimes what wounds you calls itself love. Sometimes what exhausts you insists it is normal. But your body knows. It knows the difference between warmth and depletion. Between safety and tension. Between nourishment and erosion. To recognize when something is draining rather than nourishing is an act of deep awareness. To honor yourself enough to step back is an act of courage. Stepping back can feel like loss. It can sting. It can echo. It can leave you standing in a quieter room than you are used to. But in that quiet, something else grows. Space. Breath. Integrity. We get to choose whether we remain in environments that diminish us, or whether we rise from them. We get to choose whether we betray ourselves to keep the peace or keep ourselves and risk discomfort. We get to choose ourselves. And that choice, repeated, becomes identity. Not the identity of someone hardened by pain, but someone shaped by it. Not someone who avoids hurt, but someone who refuses to let hurt dictate their worth. This is the quiet revolution. Not dramatic. Not explosive. But steady. It is the daily act of saying: I will not abandon myself again. And in that refusal, in that steady honoring of our own boundaries, something extraordinary happens. We stop surviving other people's storms. We begin building our own climate. One boundary. One *"no."* One brave walk away at a time. And beyond boundaries, beyond saying *"no"* and walking away, there is something even quieter and more powerful: We get to choose self-emotional regulation. That phrase once sounded clinical to me. Now it feels sacred. We get to sit with our feelings instead of being ruled by them. To remain in the room when emotion surges. To feel them fully, the heat of anger rising like fire beneath the skin, the ache of sadness spreading heavy and blue through the chest, the sting of disappointment sharp and quick behind the eyes. Anger has a temperature. Sadness has a weight. Disappointment has a taste, bitter, metallic, and lingering. For so long, I believed those sensations were threats. That if I allowed them too much space, they would consume me. But learning to regulate did not mean suppressing. It meant witnessing. It meant letting the wave crest without letting it carry me out to sea. To sit with emotion is to anchor while the current moves. It is important to notice the tightening in the jaw and soften it. To feel the pulse racing and breathe anyway. To say, *"I see you, anger. I see you, grief. I see you, fear."* Not as enemies, but as messengers. We get to analyze them. To understand them. To ask what they are trying to teach us. *"Is this anger protecting a boundary that was crossed? Is this sadness grieving something I never allowed myself to mourn? Is this disappointment revealing a longing I have not yet honored?"* Emotion becomes information. A compass rather than a command. And then, when they have spoken their truth, we get to release them. Not shove them down. Not pretend they never existed. But release them. Like a leaf caught in a gentle breeze, carried forward without clinging. Like rain that falls hard, nourishes the soil, and then passes, leaving the air clearer than before. Feelings are weather, not identity. They move. They shift. They do not define the sky.

Regulation is not numbness. It is mastery without domination. It is choosing to respond instead of react. To integrate instead of implode. And then there are mistakes. How long I lived beneath the crushing weight of mine. How tightly I wrapped them around my neck like evidence. As if each misstep were a verdict carved into stone. But we get to choose to see mistakes differently. Mistakes do not define us. They do not make us worthless. They are not verdicts on our humanity. They are indicators. Signals that something missed alignment. Evidence that we are human, still learning, still capable of growth. They are proof that we are alive and evolving. Only the inert do not err. Only the frozen do not stumble. Mistakes are footprints on the path of becoming. Some veer sideways. Some circle back. Some lead into brambles. But all of them mark movement. All of them mean we are walking. There is humility in recognizing error. There is strength in correcting course. There is grace in saying, *"I was wrong, and I am still worthy."* When I began to see mistakes not as proof of defectiveness but as invitations to refine, something softened again inside me. The inner critic lost its gavel. The courtroom dissolved. In its place, a workshop emerged. A place of shaping. Sanding. Adjusting. We are not statues carved once and for all. We are living sculptures. Chiseled by experience. Smoothed by insight. Strengthened by revision. To regulate emotion. To release rather than cling. To reframe mistakes as teachers instead of tyrants. These are not small choices. They are acts of profound self-leadership. And each time we choose them, we affirm something essential: We are not at the mercy of our storms. We are the stewards of our inner climate. And in that stewardship, in that steady tending, we become something extraordinary, not perfect, not flawless, but deeply, beautifully human. Still learning. Still growing. Still choosing. And that choice is freedom. You cannot choose how people treat you. That truth remains, stark and unvarnished. The world will still be the world. People will still act from their wounds, their fears, their unhealed places. Words will still be spoken that sting. Actions will still land hard against the ribs of your tenderness. But you can choose how you respond. And that is no small thing. You can choose dignity over destruction. Growth over stagnation. Boundaries over self-betrayal. Compassion over cruelty, especially toward yourself. Dignity is quiet. It does not need to shout. It is the steady lifting of your chin when someone attempts to diminish you. It is the calm refusal to mirror chaos. It is the decision not to let someone else's dysfunction dictate your character. Growth is not glamorous. It is incremental. It is choosing to pause instead of retaliating. To reflect instead of react. To ask, "*What is mine here? What is not?*" Boundaries are not barriers against love, they are guardians of it. They are the gentle but firm lines that say: "*I will not abandon myself to keep you comfortable.*" They are the architecture of self-respect. And compassion, especially toward yourself, may be the bravest choice of all. Because self-cruelty is often disguised as accountability. We tell ourselves we are being *"realistic," "responsible," "honest."* But sometimes we are simply repeating old punishments. And perhaps most healing of all. You can choose to forgive yourself. Not because you were perfect. But because you are human. Not because you never faltered. But because you are still here. Still breathing. Still learning. Still trying. Forgiveness is not a declaration that nothing went wrong. It is a declaration that wrongness does not get to define you forever. It is the softening of the inner voice that once sharpened every memory into a weapon. It is the choice to release yourself from a sentence that no longer serves your growth. In that stillness. In that breath between hurt and reaction. Lies your freedom. It is not loud. It is not theatrical. It is subtle. A fraction of a second where you feel the surge of emotion rise... and you do not immediately obey it. A sliver of space where you decide who you will be next. That breath is sovereignty. That pause is power. You may not control the storm. You may not command the wind or quiet the thunder. The rain may still fall hard. The sky may still darken without warning. But you can choose how you stand within it. You can plant your feet. You can steady your breath. You can lift your face to the rain instead of collapsing beneath it. Standing does not mean you are not afraid. It does not mean you do not tremble. It means you refuse to surrender your identity to the weather.

The storm may shape the landscape. But you decide the posture of your soul. And in choosing dignity. In choosing growth. In choosing boundaries. In choosing compassion. In choosing forgiveness. You reclaim authorship. You reclaim yourself. And that, more than any calm sky ever could, is what makes you free. I repeat this loudly, because it matters. Because whispering it would not do justice to the weight it carries. Just like me, you will need to do the work to achieve freedom. Freedom is not gifted. It is built. It is carved, breath by breath, choice by choice, from the dense rock of your own resistance. I am not promising you a quick or easy solution. There is no shining shortcut through this terrain. It was not easy for me. It was not short. And it will not be effortless for you either. Healing is not a soft breeze that drifts in while you sleep. It is more like learning to walk again after forgetting how to trust your own legs. Healing asks something of you. It asks honesty, the kind that burns a little when it first touches the skin. The kind that tastes sharp and metallic on the tongue because it cuts through illusion. It asks you to look at your life without filters, without carefully arranged narratives, and to say, "*This hurt. This shaped me. This is where I bled.*" It asks courage, not the loud, cinematic kind that arrives with applause, but the quiet kind. The kind that shows up in therapy rooms. In journals stained with tears. In conversations where your voice trembles, but you speak anyway. Courage that feels like standing barefoot on cold ground at dawn, unsure, exposed, but unwilling to retreat. It asks commitment. Not for a week. Not for a season. But for as long as it takes. Commitment that feels like returning to the mat after you fall. Like tending a garden you cannot yet see blooming. Like choosing, again and again, not to abandon yourself. You will need to confront your pain. Not circle it. Not outrun it. Not numb it into silence. You will need to face it head-on instead of turning away. To sit with it long enough that it stops being a faceless monster and begins to reveal its contours. To trace its edges. To feel where it lives in your body, the tightness in your chest, the knot in your stomach, the heat behind your eyes. To listen to its voice without letting it dictate your future. Pain has roots. It has patterns. It has a history. When you sit with it, truly sit with it, you begin to understand its language. You begin to see how it formed, where it took hold, and what it has been trying to protect you from. And in that understanding, something subtle shifts. The pain is no longer a tyrant. It becomes information. You will need to forgive yourself and others, not to excuse what happened, not to rewrite history, not to absolve harm, but for yours. Forgiveness is not about pretending it did not hurt. It is about refusing to let the hurt own you indefinitely. It is about setting down the stones you have been carrying in your pockets for so long that you forgot how heavy they are. Stones of resentment. Stones of anger. Stones of shame. You may not even realize how much they weigh until you loosen your grip and let one fall. And when you do, you will feel it. The subtle lift in your shoulders. The deeper breath that reaches places it hasn't touched in years. The way your spine straightens when you are no longer bowed under borrowed blame. This work will not be glamorous. It will not always feel rewarding. There will be days when you question why you started. Days when the old darkness feels closer than the new light. But every time you choose to face your pain instead of flee it, every time you choose forgiveness over bitterness, every time you choose honesty over denial, you are chiselling away at the walls that once confined you. Freedom is not a door that swings open all at once. It is a wall that thins. A weight that lightens. A breath that deepens. And one day, almost quietly, you will notice that you are no longer dragging stones behind you. You are walking. Unburdened. Forward. And most importantly, you will need to learn to love yourself. Not in a way that can be photographed or posted. Not in a way that performs wellness while neglecting truth. But deeply. Quietly. Rootedly. The kind of love that settles into your marrow and stays.

You will need to cultivate self-compassion as deliberately as one tends a fragile garden. To water it when it feels dry. To protect it when harsh winds of criticism blow through your mind. To speak to yourself gently when the world has not been gentle, when voices outside you have been sharp, and the voice inside you has learned to imitate their cruelty. There will be mornings when you look in the mirror and see only flaws. On those mornings, self-love will not feel like fireworks. It will feel like choosing not to flinch at your own reflection. It will feel like placing a steady hand over your own heart and saying, "*I am still here. I am still worthy. I am still enough.*" You will need to recognize your inherent worth, even when you feel unworthy. Especially then. Worth that does not rise and fall with productivity. Worth that does not evaporate when you make a mistake. Worth that does not depend on applause, validation, or perfection. You will need to anchor yourself in a sense of self that is not built on approval. Approval is wind, it shifts, it disappears, it changes direction without warning. But self-respect is stone. It is bedrock beneath your feet. When you know who you are, when you accept your humanity in all its flawed and luminous complexity, the ground no longer gives way so easily. That self-love will be the flame you return to in the darkest of times. Not a raging fire that blinds you. A steady flame. A candle cupped in your own hands. When grief comes, and it will. When disappointment presses heavy against your ribs. When pain arrives uninvited and tries to convince you that you are small again, that flame will still be there. Flickering perhaps, but alive. Because the darkness may visit again. Life does not stop testing us simply because we have healed. There will still be losses. Still be heartbreak. Still be moments when the air feels thin and the weight of it all presses down. But when you know your worth, when you care for yourself as fiercely as you care for others, you will not be extinguished. You will bend. You will ache. You may even weep on the bathroom floor again. But you will not disappear. You were never powerless. Even in your lowest moments, even when you believed the storm defined you, there was a pulse inside you that kept beating. A breath that kept returning. A small, stubborn ember that refused to go out. You were not empty. You were waiting. Waiting to remember your power. Waiting to see that the strength you searched for in others had been living quietly within you all along. Waiting to realize that your survival was not accidental, it was evidence. And that remembering begins the moment you decide you are worth the work. The moment you say, not with arrogance but with reverence, "*My life matters. My healing matters. I matter.*" From that decision, everything else grows. Not perfectly. Not instantly. But faithfully. And once you choose yourself, truly choose yourself, the path does not vanish when it becomes difficult. It remains beneath your feet. Because you are no longer walking it by accident. You are walking it awake. And most importantly, you will need to learn to love yourself. Not in a way that can be photographed or posted. Not in a way that performs wellness while neglecting truth. But deeply. Quietly. Rootedly. The kind of love that settles into your marrow and stays. You will need to cultivate self-compassion as deliberately as one tends a fragile garden. To water it when it feels dry. To protect it when harsh winds of criticism blow through your mind. To speak to yourself gently when the world has not been gentle, when voices outside you have been sharp, and the voice inside you has learned to imitate their cruelty. There will be mornings when you look in the mirror and see only flaws. On those mornings, self-love will not feel like fireworks. It will feel like choosing not to flinch at your own reflection. It will feel like placing a steady hand over your own heart and saying, "*I am still here. I am still worthy. I am still enough.*"

You will need to recognize your inherent worth, even when you feel unworthy. Especially then. Worth that does not rise and fall with productivity. Worth that does not evaporate when you make a mistake. Worth that does not depend on applause, validation, or perfection. You will need to anchor yourself in a sense of self that is not built on approval. Approval is wind, it shifts, it disappears, it changes direction without warning. But self-respect is stone. It is bedrock beneath your feet. When you know who you are, when you accept your humanity in all its flawed and luminous complexity, the ground no longer gives way so easily. That self-love will be the flame you return to in the darkest of times. Not a raging fire that blinds you. A steady flame. A candle cupped in your own hands. When grief comes, and it will. When disappointment presses heavy against your ribs. When pain arrives uninvited and tries to convince you that you are small again, that flame will still be there. Flickering perhaps, but alive. Because the darkness may visit again. Life does not stop testing us simply because we have healed. There will still be losses. Still be heartbreak. Still be moments when the air feels thin, and the weight of it all presses down. But when you know your worth, when you care for yourself as fiercely as you care for others, you will not be extinguished. You will bend. You will ache. You may even weep on the bathroom floor again. But you will not disappear. You were never powerless. Even in your lowest moments, even when you believed the storm defined you, there was a pulse inside you that kept beating. A breath that kept returning. A small, stubborn ember that refused to go out. You were not empty. You were waiting. Waiting to remember your power. Waiting to see that the strength you searched for in others had been living quietly within you all along. Waiting to realize that your survival was not accidental, it was evidence. And that remembering begins the moment you decide you are worth the work. The moment you say, not with arrogance but with reverence, "*My life matters. My healing matters. I matter.*" From that decision, everything else grows. Not perfectly. Not instantly. But faithfully. And once you choose yourself, truly choose yourself, the path does not vanish when it becomes difficult. It remains beneath your feet. Because you are no longer walking it by accident. You are walking it awake. But I also remember something else. Small glimmers. Tiny fractures in the darkness where light dared to enter. They did not arrive with trumpets or grand revelations. They slipped in quietly, like hairline cracks across a sealed room. A kind word from someone I did not expect, simple, almost casual, yet it landed against my bruised spirit like cool water on scorched skin. A moment of unexpected kindness that did not ask anything of me. It simply existed. And in that existence, it softened something rigid inside my chest. I remember the way sunlight once streamed through a window and warmed my face when I least deserved to feel warmth. I can still feel it, the gentle heat pressing against my closed eyelids, the faint scent of morning air drifting in, the hush of the room holding me. That light did not interrogate me. It did not ask if I had earned it. It just touched my skin and reminded me that warmth still existed. Even the simple act of getting out of bed when staying there felt easier, felt safer, was a rebellion. The texture of the floor beneath my feet. The heaviness in my limbs. The quiet thud of my heart insisting on another day. These were not dramatic victories. They were small acts of resistance. They may have looked insignificant from the outside. But inside, they were revolutions. Each one was a quiet refusal to surrender completely to despair. Each one was a flicker against the overwhelming tide that threatened to pull me under. When I brushed my teeth despite the fog. When I answered a message instead of isolating. When I chose to eat something nourishing instead of punishing myself. Each act whispered: "*I am still here.*" Those moments kept me going. They fueled something stubborn within me—a low, steady ember that refused to die. A determination to survive. To heal. To find my way back to the light, even if I had to crawl toward it on scraped hands and trembling knees. There were days when walking felt impossible, but crawling was still movement. And movement, no matter how slow, was hope in motion. And now, years later, I carry those memories with me like sacred artifacts. They are not loud. They do not glitter. But they are holy in their own way. I carry the lessons learned during that arduous journey. They are etched into my body, in the way my shoulders now relax instead of bracing. In the way my breath deepens instead of catches.

In the way my heart can hold both grief and gratitude without collapsing. They live in my emotional memory, a quiet archive of proof. They remind me of what I endured. And more importantly, what I overcame. They remind me that resilience is not a personality trait. It is a practice. That strength does not roar; sometimes it whispers, "*try again tomorrow*". They remind me of my capacity for love, even when I felt hollow. Of my ability to choose gentleness when I once chose self-destruction. Of the way hope can survive in the smallest of spaces. The terror was real. The despair was real. The nights that felt endless were real. But so were the glimmers. And in the end, it was not the darkness that defined me. It was my willingness to notice the light, however faint. To turn my face toward it. To move, inch by inch, in its direction. To believe, even when belief felt fragile, that the light was not mocking me. It was calling me. And I kept walking toward it.

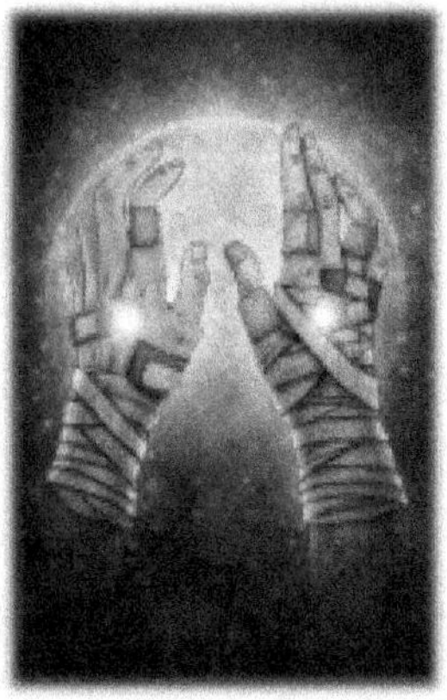

And so I carry the light forward, aware of the shadows that once shaped it. The light is different because of them. Softer. Truer. Earned. The scars remain. They are not loud. They do not demand attention. They do not ache the way they once did. But they are there, faint lines beneath the surface, subtle ridges in the landscape of my being, quiet testaments to a battle fought and won. If I trace them gently, emotionally, spiritually, I can still feel the history in them. Not as an open wound, but as texture. As memory woven into skin. They are reminders of the darkness I once inhabited. The place where hope felt impossible, and breath felt borrowed, like I was inhaling on credit, unsure if I deserved the next exhale. I remember how the air used to feel heavy in my lungs, how even sunlight seemed distant, filtered through layers of doubt. That world feels far away now, but it is not erased. It lives in the echo of who I was and who I chose to become. The scars are constant companions, not haunting, not accusing, but grounding. They anchor me in truth. They remind me of the preciousness of life. Of how fragile and miraculous it is to wake up and feel sheets beneath my fingertips. To inhale deeply and feel my ribs expand without fear. To step outside and let sunlight spill across my skin like quiet grace. These ordinary moments, once overlooked, now shimmer with significance. The scars remind me that I have stood at the edge and stepped back. They remind me to move through the world gently. They have deepened my compassion, first for myself. For the woman who once trembled. For the version of me who believed she was unworthy of staying. When I falter now, when I misstep or feel old fears flicker, I do not attack myself. I soften. I remember. I offer myself the tenderness I once withheld. And they have expanded my compassion for others. Because I know now how invisible battles can be. I know how someone can smile while their chest feels caved in. I know how silence can hide storms. So I move through the world aware that every person I pass may be carrying something heavy, something unspeakable. My pain has made me gentler. More patient. More willing to listen. Looking back, the pain is still there. Not sharp in the way it once was, no longer a blade, but present. It lives in memory, in lessons learned, in the quiet wisdom that only suffering can carve into the human spirit. It no longer grips me by the throat. It no longer defines the air I breathe. It does not dictate the rhythm of my days. It has transformed. What was once a crippling force has become a source of strength. What once threatened to break me has become a catalyst for growth. What once felt like proof of my weakness has revealed itself as evidence of my resilience, evidence of my capacity for healing, for endurance, for renewal. The darkness did not disappear. It changed shape. It became contrast, necessary for the light to be seen. And the woman who once believed she was shattered beyond repair now walks forward carrying both the memory of the night and the certainty of the dawn. Not untouched by pain. Not naïve to suffering.

But awake. Alive. And deeply, fiercely aware of the miracle it is to keep choosing the light. When I look back now, the night I almost ended my life feels distant. Almost unreal. Like a storm, I remember standing in, rain lashing my face, wind howling in my ears, lightning splitting the sky, though I am now safely on the other side, feet planted on steady ground.

I can still recall the scent of the air that night, metallic and charged, the way the darkness pressed in like a living thing. But I am no longer inside it. I am remembering it. And yet, its imprint remains. Not as trauma alone, but as testimony. It lives in me like the faint outline of a scar beneath warm skin. Not throbbing. Not raw. But present. It stands as proof of the resilience of the human spirit. Of the astonishing capacity we possess to heal, to stretch toward light, to grow even in the face of unimaginable darkness. It is a reminder that I have seen the abyss up close and still chose to step back. The scars will remain. Faint reminders etched into the architecture of my being. But they are not badges of shame. They are symbols of strength. Of perseverance. Of survival that refused to fold in on itself. They are quiet monuments to the woman who stood at the edge and did not disappear. They tell a different story now. They whisper that even in the deepest despair, when the night feels endless and the silence deafening, when breath feels thin and borrowed, hope still persists. Choice still persists. Light still persists. Sometimes not as a blaze. Sometimes only as a flicker. A pulse. A stubborn ember beneath ash. But it persists. The darkness may have shaped me. It carved lines into my heart. It deepened my understanding of suffering. It taught me the texture of grief and the weight of silence. It introduced me to the fragility of life in the most intimate way. But it did not claim me. It did not own me. It did not get the final word. And that, more than anything, is the miracle. Not that the storm never came. Not that the night was short. But that I am still here to tell it. Breathing. Choosing. Living. And carrying forward the quiet, radiant truth that even at the brink, especially at the brink, there is still something within us that longs for light. And that longing, however faint, is powerful enough to save a life.

My truest hope, rising like breath after everything that has been spoken, everything that has been survived, is that this book rests in your hands not as paper and ink alone, but as presence. A quiet companion. A steady warmth against your palms. Something you can return to when the world feels unbearably loud, voices clashing, expectations pressing in, or when it feels so silent that your own thoughts echo too sharply in the stillness. I hope it whispers to you in those in-between spaces. In the early morning light, when the house is hushed, and your thoughts feel tender. In the late hours when doubt grows louder, and the dark seems closer. I hope it feels like someone sitting beside you, not to fix you, not to rush you, but to remind you of what is still alive inside you. I hope it invites you to take hold of your life again. Gently at first. Like placing your hands on the reins after a long season of letting go. Like standing up after sitting in the shadows for too long. And then, with growing confidence. With steadier breath. With clearer eyes. I hope you pause at the crossroads where habit and fear have kept you circling, walking the same worn path until it feels like the only one that exists. I hope you feel the texture of that ground beneath your feet and realize you do not have to keep walking in circles. You can choose a different direction. One that bends toward healing. One that opens into freedom. One that belongs to you, not to your past, not to someone else's expectations, not to old narratives, but to you. You are not alone in this terrain. Even when the air feels thin with isolation. Even when silence convinces you that no one could possibly understand the weight you carry. You are not walking it by yourself. Others have stood where you stand. Others have trembled and still moved forward. Their footprints are in the soil beneath you, even if you cannot always see them. And you are not powerless. Beneath your fear, beneath the trembling and the doubt, there is a current moving, steady, persistent, alive. It runs through you like an underground river, quiet but strong. A force that has been there all along, even when you mistook it for weakness. It waits not to be created, but to be acknowledged.

You have the power to shape your life. Not all at once. Not perfectly. But choice by choice. Breath by breath. You can make decisions that honor your well-being. You can say yes to what nourishes you and no to what diminishes you. You can move toward happiness and peace not as distant, glowing ideals on a horizon you will never reach, but as lived experiences. Tangible. Embodied. Felt in the softening of your shoulders, in the steadiness of your heartbeat, in the quiet pride that rises when you know you chose yourself. The terrain may still be uneven. The path may still require courage. But you are not empty-handed. You carry strength. You carry agency. You carry possibility. And perhaps most importantly, you carry the capacity to choose a life that feels like yours. The message I carry for you, the one that hums beneath every chapter, that breathes between the lines, that lingers like a heartbeat under the skin of this story, is simple and unwavering: the power you are searching for is already inside you. Not somewhere distant. Not locked behind perfection. Not waiting for you to become someone else. Already. Inside you. Whatever darkness you are facing, whether it feels like a heavy fog pressing against your lungs or a storm that rattles the windows of your mind. Whatever weight you are carrying in your chest, on your shoulders, in your bones, it is not stronger than the part of you that wants to survive. The part that still inhales. The part that still hopes, even if hope feels like a faint pulse in the dark. The part that longs, quietly but persistently, to heal. To live. You are stronger than you think. Stronger than the stories that have whispered otherwise. Stronger than the verdicts handed down by fear. Stronger than the old narratives that have carved doubt into your memory like etchings in stone. Those stories may sound convincing. They may echo in your quietest hours. But they are not the whole truth of you. The path to healing is not short. It does not unfold like a straight line drawn neatly across a page. It winds. It climbs. It bends unexpectedly around corners you did not anticipate. It asks something of you, your honesty, your courage, your patience when you would rather be done. There will be moments when your legs ache from the climb. When your heart grows tired of hoping. When progress feels invisible, like walking through thick fog where you cannot see beyond the next step. The ground beneath you may feel unstable. You may question whether you are moving at all. But you are. Every step matters. Even the trembling ones. Every pause counts. Even the ones where you sit on the roadside and simply breathe. Every tear, every boundary held, every small act of choosing yourself, these are milestones, even if no one else sees them. It will not be easy. Healing rarely is. But it will be meaningful. The kind of meaning that settles into your muscles. The kind that reshapes how you carry yourself. The kind that changes the way your own name feels in your mouth. And one day, often without ceremony, without fanfare, you will look back. Perhaps while washing dishes. Perhaps while standing in sunlight. Perhaps in a quiet moment before sleep. And you will realize how far you have come. You will notice that what once consumed you now sits in the distance. That what once felt impossible now feels like terrain you have already crossed. That the version of you who once doubted everything has become someone who knows, deeply and quietly, that she can endure. And in that realization, you will feel it, not just as a thought, but as something embodied. Strength. Earned. Lived. Yours. Along the way, often without realizing it at first, you will begin to uncover reserves of strength that have been quietly waiting beneath the surface.

Strength that does not announce itself with bravado but reveals itself in endurance. In the way you keep showing up. In the way you breathe through moments that once would have undone you. You will surprise yourself. Again and again. Not because you suddenly become fearless, but because you learn how to move forward while still feeling afraid. You will come to see that shaping your own destiny does not require force or perfection. It does not demand that you conquer life or bend it to your will. It unfolds instead through persistence. Through awareness. Through the steady accumulation of small, deliberate choices. Choices made in kitchens and quiet rooms. Choices made when no one is watching. Choices that say, again and again, "*I am choosing myself today.*"

And slowly, something profound will shift. You will begin to understand, not intellectually, not as a motivational phrase, but as a felt truth that settles into your chest, that you are worthy of love, care, and compassion. Not because you earned it through suffering. Not because you fixed every flaw or smoothed every rough edge. But because you are human. Because you breathe. Because you feel. Because you exist. That understanding will not live only in your thoughts. It will live in your body. In the way your shoulders rest more easily. In the way your breath deepens without effort. In the way your nervous system learns, little by little, that it is safe to soften. You will begin to navigate the complexity of life with greater steadiness. When chaos swirls, when plans unravel, when pain resurfaces, when the world feels unpredictable, you will find meaning not by escaping the storm, but by standing within it without losing yourself. And from that steadiness, a different kind of peace will emerge. Not the brittle peace that depends on everything being perfect. Not the fragile calm that shatters at the first sign of trouble. But a peace that settles deeper. One that takes root not just in your mind, but in your body and spirit. A peace born of presence. Of grounding. Of kindness turned inward. A peace that knows you can survive discomfort, uncertainty, and change, and still remain intact. Once it takes hold, this peace becomes something you carry with you. Quiet. Enduring. Faithful. A companion that walks beside you through seasons of joy and seasons of sorrow alike. It does not shield you from life, but it steadies you within it. And it stays. Not as a destination you reach and leave behind, but as a way of being you grow into, one choice at a time, for the rest of your life. And so, in the stillness that follows everything I have laid bare, the storms, the breaking, the rebuilding, I stand here with you in that sacred quiet. The kind of quiet that hums beneath the surface of things. The kind that carries truth more gently than noise ever could. And I want to look at you, not as an idea, not as a reader turning pages, but as a living, breathing soul. A heart that beats. A chest that rises and falls. A human being who has felt things deeply. And I want to tell you this: You have the same power. The same capacity to choose. It is not reserved for the strong or the unscarred. Not for those who appear polished or unbroken. It is not something I was handed that you were denied. It lives in you already, steady and patient, like a pulse beneath your skin. Like a quiet ember beneath ash, waiting only for air. You can choose to say no. No to the lies that have wrapped themselves around your thoughts like thorned vines, tightening slowly, subtly, until you forgot what it felt like to think freely. No to the false narrative that has been scripting your inner dialogue, directing your reactions, convincing you that you are smaller, weaker, less worthy than you are. Those lies may feel familiar. They may echo in your chest. They may sound like your own voice in the quiet hours. They may taste like memory and feel like truth because you have repeated them for so long. But familiarity is not the same as truth. They are not your truth. And you have the authority to refuse them. You can choose to rise above your pain, not by pretending it does not exist, not by numbing it into silence, not by shrinking yourself to avoid feeling, but by stepping through it. By walking into it with eyes open and breath steady. By allowing the ache to move through your body without letting it define the shape of your future. You can face your fears. You can feel the tremor in your hands, the tightening in your throat, the rush of heat in your face, the way your heart pounds like a drum warning of danger, and still move forward. Courage does not mean the absence of sensation. It means movement despite it. You can emerge. Slowly. Imperfectly. Honestly. Into a brighter and more hopeful future. Not untouched by what happened. Not pretending it never hurt. But transformed by how you responded to it. Strengthened not by the absence of darkness, but by your refusal to let it swallow you whole. You are not defined by what wounded you. You are defined by what you choose next. And in that choice, made quietly, made bravely, made again and again, you begin to remember who you have always been.

Not powerless. Not broken. But capable. Alive. And far stronger than you were ever taught to believe. It will not be easy. There will be days when exhaustion settles into your bones like winter frost, when even lifting your head feels like an act of defiance. Days when your thoughts spiral inward, tightening like a storm funnel, pulling you toward doubt. Days when the temptation to give up feels almost reasonable, almost merciful, because continuing requires effort you are not sure you still possess. You may feel alone in those moments. As though the world has gone quiet around you. As though sound itself has withdrawn. As though you are standing in a vast, echoing space where your own breathing feels too loud and no one answers back. But you are not alone. Others have walked this path before you. Others have stumbled on the same uneven ground. They have wept until their throats were raw. They have doubted their strength. They have questioned whether the climb was worth it. And still, they kept going. Their stories are lanterns along the road. Soft lights flickering in the distance when night grows thick. They do not eliminate the darkness, but they mark the way. They remind you that forward is possible. That survival is possible. That transformation is possible. You can draw strength from them. You can borrow courage when yours feels thin and threadbare. You can lean on the knowledge that someone else once stood where you stand now and found a way through. Courage is not always something you must generate alone. Sometimes it is something you inherit, something passed quietly from one survivor to another. And in time, your own courage will grow. You have the power to create your unique destiny. Not as a grand declaration shouted into the sky, but as a steady practice. As the quiet turning of a wheel. As the decision to rise one more time than you fall. You are not a leaf condemned to drift wherever the current carries you. You are not debris at the mercy of the tide. You are a navigator standing at the helm. Even when the sea is rough. Even when the wind is unpredictable. Even when the sky darkens without warning, and the deck tilts beneath your feet. You can grip the wheel. You can adjust the sails. You can choose your direction.

You are not condemned to drift. You are capable of steering. And every small correction, every boundary set, every truth spoken, every moment you choose yourself, turns the vessel of your life ever so slightly toward safer waters. The ocean may not calm overnight. But you are no longer powerless within it. You are learning the currents. You are learning your strength. And you are moving, slowly, bravely, toward a horizon that is yours to claim. You can choose life. Not just once, in some grand, cinematic moment—but again and again, in the quiet folds of ordinary days. In the decision to rise when the sheets feel heavy. In the choice to step outside and let air fill your lungs. In the way you answer your own name when doubt calls it softly. Life is not only a heartbeat. It is a thousand small decisions to stay. You can choose love. Not the polished kind that looks effortless from a distance, but the brave, tender kind that exists even after fracture. The kind that trembles but still reaches. The kind that forgives itself for being human. You can choose to love others, yes, but also to love yourself when your reflection feels unfamiliar, when your history feels complicated. Love can be chosen in the tone of your inner voice, in the softness of your self-talk, in the patience you extend to your own becoming. You can choose freedom. Even if the cage door has only just begun to open. Even if your hands still remember the weight of the bars. Freedom does not always arrive as a wide, open field. Sometimes it begins as a crack in the wall. A hinge loosening. A breath taken without permission. You can step toward it, slowly, deliberately, until what once confined you becomes something you have outgrown. Not once. But again and again.

In small decisions that accumulate like droplets of water shaping stone. In boundaries whispered at first, then spoken clearly. In the refusal to shrink. In the courage to expand. Transformation rarely announces itself. It gathers quietly, through repetition, through choice. And I want to encourage you, deeply, fiercely, to make that choice. Choose to live, even when living feels heavy in your bones. Even when the day ahead looks long, and your strength feels thin. Choose it anyway. Choose to love, even when your heart carries hairline fractures from old betrayals. Even when vulnerability feels like standing barefoot on sharp ground. Choose it anyway. Choose to be free, even when your steps are hesitant. Even when you are unsure what freedom will require. Choose it anyway. Because, as I have learned, it is never too late. Never too late to change direction. Never too late to pivot toward light. Never too late to untangle yourself from a story that no longer fits. Never too late to begin again. Renewal does not demand perfection. It does not wait for you to be flawless or fearless. It asks only for willingness. A soft but resolute yes. A readiness to move, even if your legs tremble. And that willingness, that quiet decision to choose life, love, and freedom, is the beginning of everything. And it is never too late to discover this truth, no matter how many years have passed, no matter how far you feel you have wandered, that you have the power to choose. To choose. To decide. To create. Not a life dictated by fear. Not a life scripted by someone else's expectations. But a life that feels like yours when you wake inside it. A life that fits your breath. A life that echoes your own voice back to you without distortion. A life filled with hope that warms your skin like sunlight after a long, relentless winter. The kind of warmth that seeps slowly into numb fingers. That thaws what has been frozen. That reminds you that your body was always capable of feeling again. A life filled with promise that hums quietly in your chest, not loud, not frantic, but steady. Like a low, reassuring vibration beneath your ribs. Like a melody you almost forgot you knew. A subtle reminder that something within you is still alive and leaning forward. A life filled with possibility that stretches out before you like an open horizon. Wide. Unclaimed. The air crisp. The sky vast. The scent of something new carried on the wind. A landscape not yet defined by old mistakes or inherited shame, but waiting for your footprints. The choice is not always easy. It will not always feel inspiring. Sometimes it will feel heavy. Sometimes it will ask you to walk through discomfort. Sometimes it will require you to disappoint others in order to honor yourself. Sometimes it will mean saying no when you are used to saying yes. But it is yours. Yours to make in quiet moments. Yours to make when no one is watching. Yours to make when your hands shake but your heart knows. And that, more than anything, is your power. Not the power to control every storm. Not the power to rewrite the past. But the power to decide how you move forward. The power to respond. The power to shape what comes next. The power to say: this life is mine. And to live it accordingly. And so, after everything, the storms weathered, the salt still drying on your skin, the ashes sifted through trembling fingers, the light reclaimed from places you once thought it could never reach. I leave you with something simple, but not small. Not grand speeches. Not thunderous promises. But a series of choices. Quiet decisions made in the privacy of your own heart, where no one applauds and no one witnesses except the truest part of you. Choose life. Choose it when it feels fragile in your hands, like glass you're afraid to drop. Choose it when your breath feels heavy in your lungs and the morning light spills across the room too brightly for your tired eyes. Choose it when your body aches with memory and your mind whispers that it would be easier not to try. Choose it the way a seed chooses to split open in dark soil—cracking itself apart without proof of what waits above, trusting that somewhere beyond the pressure and the dirt, there is sun. Let life move through you, through your pulse, through your senses, through your trembling hands that have known both despair and defiance. Let it rise and fall with your breath. Because the fact that you are here, feeling, breathing, hoping, is not accidental. It is sacred. Choose love. Not only the love that arrives wrapped in warm embraces or spoken in gentle words from someone else's mouth. Choose the love you offer yourself in the quietest moments, when no one sees you struggle, when no one hears the conversation inside your mind.

Choose the love that tastes like patience when you make a mistake. The love that sounds like a softened inner voice instead of a sharp reprimand. The love that feels like wrapping your own weary shoulders in kindness instead of tightening them with criticism. Let love become the atmosphere you live in, not something you chase, not something you barter for, not a reward you wait to earn once you are flawless. Breathe it in. Let it warm the cold corners of your chest. Let it shift the texture of your days. Because the choices that shape a life are rarely dramatic. They are repetitive. Intentional. Tender. They are made in kitchens and quiet bedrooms and early mornings when the world is still hushed. And each time you choose life. Each time you choose love. You are not just surviving what was. You are building what will be. Choose hope. Even when it is small. Even when it flickers like a candle in a drafty room, its flame bowing and straightening, bowing and straightening, refusing to go out. Hope does not have to roar like thunder to be real. It does not need fireworks or certainty. Sometimes it is only a whisper brushing against your thoughts. A subtle warmth spreading in your chest. A tiny widening of the horizon in your mind where once there was only a wall. Choose it anyway. Feed it with small acts of courage. Protect it from the harsh winds of doubt. Cup your hands around it when the air feels cold and restless. Let it guide you forward when certainty is nowhere to be found, when the map has blurred and the path ahead seems unmarked. Hope is not naïve. It is brave. It is the quiet insistence that something better is possible, even when you cannot yet see it. Choose healing. Not as a destination you must sprint toward. Not as a finish line where you finally become "fixed." Choose it as a daily act. A tending. A returning. A slow stitching together of what has been torn. Healing may ache. It may taste like salt from tears that surprise you. It may sound like truths spoken through a shaking voice. It may feel like pressing gently on a bruise to understand its depth. But it is movement. It is growth. It is proof that you believe you are worth the effort. Healing is not glamorous. It is quiet. It is repetitive. It is the decision to show up for yourself when you would rather disappear. It is the soft but stubborn declaration: I am worth mending. Choose forgiveness. Not because what happened did not hurt. Not because it was acceptable. Not because you have forgotten the sting or erased the memory. But because carrying bitterness is like holding hot coals in your bare hands, waiting for someone else to burn. Forgiveness is the moment you decide to set them down. It is the unclenching of a fist you did not realize was tight. The easing of your jaw. The release of breath you have been holding for years. It is not approval. It is not surrender. It is liberation. It is freedom returning to your body. And when you choose hope, choose healing, choose forgiveness, you are not denying your pain. You are transforming your relationship with it. You are reclaiming your energy from the past. You are making space for something lighter, something steadier, something alive. These choices may feel small. But they are not small. They are sacred. And they will shape the landscape of your life in ways you cannot yet imagine. Choose self-care. Let it be practical. Tangible. Almost ordinary in its simplicity. Drink the water even when you forget you are thirsty. Feel it cool against your tongue, traveling through your body like a quiet act of restoration. Rest when you are tired, not only when you have earned it, not only when everything else is done, but when your muscles ache, and your eyelids grow heavy. Step outside and let the air touch your skin. Notice the temperature. The scent of rain or dust or morning light. Let the wind remind you that you are part of something breathing and alive. Notice when your heart whispers, "*enough*". It may not shout. It may not demand. It may arrive as a tightening in your chest, a weariness in your limbs, a subtle emotional ache. Listen to it. Honor it. Self-care is not indulgence. It is not weakness. It is the maintenance of the soul. It is tending to the inner garden so that nothing withers unnoticed. Choose self-love. Not the glossy version curated for applause. Not the performance of confidence. But the steady, grounded knowing that you are worthy simply because you exist. Not because you achieved. Not because you endured. Not because you were flawless. Because you are. Feel it in your bones. In the way your shoulders soften when you stop fighting yourself. In the slow exhale that follows when you release the need to prove your value. In the warmth that begins to replace the constant chill of self-doubt, the way sunlight gradually replaces frost on a winter morning. Love yourself as you would someone you are fiercely protective of. The way you would shield them from cruelty. The way you would speak up if they were mistreated. The way you would remind them, again and again, of their worth. Offer that same fierceness inward. Because you deserve that fierceness. You are worthy of it. Not someday. Not when you have healed completely. Not when you have proven yourself worthy through suffering or perfection. Now. You deserve it. And every time you choose life, love, hope, healing, forgiveness, self-care, and self-love—you are not merely surviving what tried to break you. You are not just enduring. You are becoming. Becoming someone who stands rooted in her own worth. Becoming someone who no longer negotiates her right to exist. Becoming someone who knows that healing is not about returning to

who you were—but about growing into who you were always meant to be. And that becoming is sacred.

Chapter Twenty-Five:
Volume One: Conclusion and Introduction to Volume Two

You are still here. And that matters more than you know. Not as a cliché. Not as a passing comfort. But as a profound, living truth. Your heart is still beating. Your lungs are still rising and falling. Your eyes are still moving across these words. That is not insignificant. That is not accidental. That is resilience in motion. That is quiet defiance against every storm that tried to silence you.

Dear Reader,

We have officially come to the end of Volume One. We stand now at the final chapter of our first section through darkness a place that once may have felt endless, like a night without a horizon, like a tunnel without a visible exit. And yet, here you are. You have walked through it. Page by page. Breath by breath. Word by word. Sometimes slowly. Sometimes hesitantly. But you walked. Well done. Truly, well done for reaching this point and enduring through all these pages. Some chapters may have felt heavy in your hands, as though the paper itself carried weight. Some words may have stirred memories like wind stirring ashes, lifting fragments you thought had long settled. Some passages may have pressed against tender places in your heart, places still warm with ache, still sensitive to touch. You may have felt your throat tighten. Your chest grown heavy. Your eyes sting with unshed tears. And yet, you stayed. You did not close the book at the first discomfort. You did not turn away from the places that mirrored your own hidden wounds. You allowed yourself to feel. To remember. To sit with what rose. Thank you. Thank you for walking this journey with me so far. For trusting these pages enough to let them meet you where you are. For showing up, even when it wasn't easy. As we conclude this volume, I want to pause, not rush forward, not push ahead, but pause. To acknowledge something important. The progress you have made. Even if it feels quiet. Even if it feels unseen. Even if no one else in your life knows the internal work you have been doing. You have shown courage simply by engaging with these words. By allowing yourself to reflect. By confronting emotions you may have spent years avoiding.

By letting truth brush against your defenses. The first steps toward healing are rarely loud. They are not accompanied by applause. They are often taken in silence, in the privacy of your own thoughts, in the stillness of your room, in the quiet decision to keep reading one more page. And you took them. That matters. You are still here. You are still reading. You are still willing. And that willingness, that quiet, stubborn presence, is the beginning of everything. As we draw the curtain on Volume One of this sacred journey together, taking our final bow before the next act of Volume Two begins, I want to pause in this soft, glowing space between endings and beginnings and extend my heartfelt gratitude to you. Truly. Thank you for your courage. Thank you for your open heart. Thank you for your willingness to step into the intricate labyrinth of your own life, the winding corridors of memory where old echoes linger. The shadowed rooms of grief where dust settles on unspoken sorrow, the hidden chambers of strength you may not have known were there. That kind of exploration is not casual. It is not easy. It requires bravery of the quietest and fiercest kind, the kind that does not shout, but endures. You walked those corridors. You opened those doors. You stood in rooms you once avoided and allowed yourself to feel what lived there.

Thank you for taking my story to heart. For allowing my vulnerability to sit beside your own, like two travellers resting on the same stone bench. For listening not only with your eyes as they moved across the page, but with your spirit, with the tender, intuitive part of you that recognizes truth when it hears it. Together, we have traversed hills and valleys. We have felt the chill of doubt creep under our skin, like cold wind slipping through seams we thought were sealed. We have also felt the warmth of resilience rising from within, like sunlight breaking through heavy clouds after a long storm. We have stood in places where shadowy whispers once seemed immovable, where fear felt anchored to the ground like iron. And yet, we have seen those whispers lose their grip. We have celebrated victories that were not always loud, but were profound, nonetheless. The victory of staying. The victory of choosing differently. The victory of seeing clearly what once felt distorted. We have ignited small but steady flames within our souls. Flames that flicker, yes. Flames that sometimes waver in uncertain wind. But flames that refuse to go out. They burn in the quiet determination to heal. They glow in the decision to love ourselves. They warm the spaces that once felt frozen by shame. And as the curtain falls on this first act, I hope you feel what I feel in this moment, not finality, but fullness. Not goodbye, but a breath before the next unfolding. A sense that something sacred has been honored here. That something real has shifted. You have not merely read these pages. You have participated in them. You have carried them inside you. And that, dear reader, is no small thing. Well done for sticking with me to the end of this Volume. Pause here. Truly pause. Let the pages settle in your hands, ears and soul. Let the silence after the final sentence stretch gently around you. Take a moment now. Feel the weight of what you've just completed, not just the physical weight of paper or words, but the emotional terrain you have crossed. Notice the steadiness in your breath. The way your lungs rise and fall without effort. The quiet rhythm of your pulse, steady and faithful beneath your skin. Sense, emotionally, the quiet strength that brought you here. It may not roar. It may not demand applause. It may simply sit within you like a deep, rooted tree, unseen beneath the soil, yet holding everything upright. That strength carried you through stories that may have stirred your own. Through memories that may have brushed against tender places.

Through shadows that once felt too heavy to name. The darkness did not swallow you. It may have brushed against your edges. It may have pressed close. It may have whispered old familiar doubts. But it did not claim you. You walked through it. Step by step. Page by page. Breath by breath. You did not look away. And that matters. If you close your eyes for a moment, you might sense it, the subtle shift inside. The faint but undeniable widening of space where constriction once lived. The emotional texture of resilience, no longer abstract but embodied. It feels like steadiness. Like warmth returning to fingers once numb. Like dawn seeping quietly across a horizon that once felt endless and dark. You walked through the night. And you are still here. Let that truth land gently in your chest. This is not the end of something. It is the threshold of something else. A doorway standing open. The beginning of a deeper unfolding. The first act of a story that continues—not defined by the darkness you survived, but by the light you are learning to carry. This is only the beginning. And you have already proven you can walk through the dark and keep going. You walked through it. And now, before we rush forward, pause. Let the momentum soften. Let the echo of everything you have just traveled settle gently into your bones. You walked through it. Not around it. Not numbed to it. Through it. And now, before we step into what comes next, pause. But do not linger too long in reflection, as though the past is a place you must camp in. This pause is not for dwelling. It is for honoring. Take a deep breath. Feel it fill your lungs slowly, deliberately. Let it press outward against your ribs. Notice how your chest expands, how space is made inside you. Feel the air as it enters, cool, almost silvery against the back of your throat. Notice how it leaves, warmer, softened by your body, carrying with it something unspoken. Release it slowly. Let your shoulders drop. Let your jaw unclench. If you need to, close this book for a moment. Let your fingers rest on its cover. Feel its texture beneath your palm. Feel the quiet hum of completion in your chest. Let your heart thrum with pride, not the loud, boastful kind, but the steady, grounded kind.

The kind that rises from effort. From endurance. From showing up when it would have been easier not to. You did not just read words. You embarked on something sacred. You stepped onto the most rewarding journey of all, an exploration into the intricate tapestry of who you are. A weaving of threads you may not have fully seen before. Threads of light and shadow. Wounds and wisdom. Pain and resilience. Shame and courage. All interlaced, crossing and recrossing, forming something complex and profoundly yours. You have traced the darker strands without tearing the fabric. You have noticed the glimmers of gold woven through places you once thought were ruined. As you reflect on the lessons and insights gained from Volume One, I encourage you to truly take pride in the work you've done so far. Not abstract pride. Not intellectual acknowledgment. Real pride. Feel it in your body. Notice where it lands. Maybe it settles as warmth in your chest. Maybe as a steadiness in your spine. Maybe as a quiet expansion behind your eyes. Let it register emotionally, the subtle shift from surviving to participating, from drifting to choosing. You stayed with the process. You allowed yourself to feel. You allowed yourself to consider new possibilities. That is not small. That is transformation in motion. You have already begun weaving a different story, not by erasing what was, but by meeting it with awareness. And awareness is the first light that enters any darkened room. Stand in that light for a moment. Breathe it in. You are not the same person who opened this volume. And that matters. Acknowledge the challenges you've faced. The nights that stretched long and thin, where silence felt heavier than sound. The truths that pressed against you like cold glass, clear, undeniable, and uncomfortable to hold. The memories that surfaced without invitation, rising like old photographs drifting up from the bottom of a dark lake. Do not rush past them. Name them. There were moments when your chest tightened as you read or listened. Moments when your throat burned with recognition. Moments when you had to pause because something inside you shifted. That matters. That is work.

Recognize the obstacles you've overcome, even the quiet internal ones no one else could see. The invisible negotiations. The arguments in your own mind. The times you almost closed the book, almost turned away from reflection, almost said, *"Not today."* And yet, you stayed. Celebrate your strengths. Celebrate your accomplishments. Even the small ones. Especially the small ones. The courage to keep reading when the words mirrored something tender inside you. The willingness to look inward when it would have been easier to blame outward. The strength to sit with discomfort instead of fleeing from it like a startled animal. These matter. They are not minor. They are monumental in ways only you can fully understand. They are tectonic shifts beneath the surface of your life, subtle, perhaps, but powerful enough to reshape the landscape over time. But I must also gently remind you. Our journey is far from over. In fact, we are just getting started. The ground beneath your feet may feel steadier now. You may sense a new balance in your breath, a new awareness in your posture. But ahead lies deeper terrain. Not darker for the sake of darkness, but deeper. More rooted. More revealing. The real work begins as we prepare to embark on the next phase of this journey, self-hate and the deep power it holds over us. We have touched the surface of darkness. Now we will begin to understand the roots. Roots that run quietly beneath behavior. Beneath reaction. Beneath identity. Roots that have shaped the way you speak to yourself in the quiet hours. Roots that have influenced the choices you've made, the love you've accepted, the limits you've believed about your own worth. We will not descend there to shame ourselves. We will not go there to reopen wounds without purpose. We will go there with lanterns in our hands. To uncover, with clarity and compassion, the hidden narratives that shaped us. To trace the origins of the voice that says, *"not enough."* To gently loosen its grip. To understand it so we can transform it. So breathe. Feel the quiet pride in your chest again, the steady rhythm of your own resilience. Let it anchor you. You have already proven you can walk through difficult terrain. And when you are ready, truly ready, turn the page. We are stepping into deeper waters. But you are no longer alone. And you are no longer powerless.

The Journey Ahead: Volume Two – Embracing the Next Step

You are no longer powerless. And yet, what lies ahead asks for even deeper courage. The kind that does not announce itself with fanfare but gathers quietly in the marrow. The kind that steadies your breath when your hands tremble. The kind that says, *"I am willing to see what I once avoided."* In **Volume Two**, we take our final journey through the value of shadows and darkness. Not to dwell there. Not to glorify suffering. But to understand it. To kneel beside it. To listen to what it has been trying to teach us beneath its harsh exterior. To extract its lessons like precious ore hidden in rough stone. To reclaim what it once stole from us, our worth, our voice, our softness, our strength. This Volume will be one of the most difficult journeys to travel. Let me say that with honesty. You may feel resistance rise in your chest as you approach it. You may sense a tightening in your shoulders, a subtle dread at the edge of awareness. That is natural. Because we will be taking a deep dive into the realm of self-hate, the quiet, corrosive voice that shapes so much of our internal world. The voice that disguises itself as truth. The voice that sounds like reason but tastes like rust. The voice that whispers in the early hours of the morning, when the house is still, and the world feels far away. The one that echoes in moments of failure, magnifying missteps into verdicts. It is not loud in the way anger is loud. It is quieter. More intimate. It speaks in your own cadence. It borrows your memories. It uses your history as evidence. It coils around your self-perception like smoke, subtle and suffocating. This will be deep work. Sacred work. Uncomfortable work. There may be moments when you feel exposed, like standing in a room with the lights turned on after years of dimness. There may be tears. There may be anger. There may be long silences where you sit with your journal open and your heart pounding, unsure where to begin. That, too, is part of the journey. We will begin with healing exercises, practical, intentional steps to anchor this exploration in action. Because insight without embodiment drifts away. Because awareness must be rooted in practice if it is to transform us. These exercises will not be abstract philosophies. They will be tangible. Grounded. Designed to steady you as you descend into places that once felt unsafe to visit. I will be providing journaling prompts and exercises throughout the book. Not as busywork. Not as something to complete and check off. But as mirrors. As lanterns.

As tools placed gently in your hands so you can excavate what has long lived beneath the surface. Think of them as shovels for the soul. As invitations to sit across from yourself and ask, *"Where did this voice begin? Whose words am I still carrying? What belief have I mistaken for fact?"* These pages will ask you to dig, not to punish yourself, but to understand yourself. To trace the roots of self-hate, not so you can shame them, but so you can loosen them. Uproot them. Replace them with something kinder. Truer. We are not going into the shadows to be consumed by them. We are going with light in our hands. And every word you write, every truth you face, every layer you peel back will be another act of reclamation. You are no longer powerless. And in Volume Two, you will begin to see just how powerful you have always been. This will be an exploration of ourselves within the shadow, not as fugitives running from it, but as seekers willing to enter it with a steady flame in our hands. We will not skim the surface. We will step inside. We will let our eyes adjust to the dimness. We will allow the air of those inner chambers to touch our skin, cool and honest, carrying the faint scent of old stories long stored away. We will look directly at what we hate about ourselves. Not flinching. Not disguising it. Not softening it prematurely. We will name it. Feel where it lives in the body, the tightness in the jaw, the sinking in the stomach, the heat behind the eyes, the subtle contraction in the chest. We will listen to the cadence of its voice. Is it sharp? Is it familiar? Does it sound like you, or like someone you once tried to survive? We will examine who created that hate, where it began, whose voices shaped it, and how it was reinforced over time like grooves worn into stone. We will trace its lineage through memory. Through childhood rooms. Through relationships. Through moments of humiliation or neglect. We will ask: *"When did this belief first take root? Who watered it? Who repeated it until it sounded like truth?"* And then we will ask the most important question, the one that changes everything: *"What is the truth about it?"* Because we cannot love what we refuse to understand. We cannot heal what we keep hidden in the dark. Hatred thrives in silence. It feeds on distortion. It grows stronger when left unnamed. But when brought gently into awareness, when examined with curiosity instead of condemnation, it begins to shift.

We need to first understand what we hate before we can begin to love and truly heal. This work will not be comfortable. It may feel like standing in front of a mirror without armor. It may stir grief. Anger. Resistance. You may taste old bitterness in your mouth. You may feel your pulse quicken as forgotten memories surface like objects rising from deep water. But remember, we are not entering this terrain to punish ourselves. We are entering it to reclaim ourselves. We will explore the complexities of our inner world. The hidden corridors. The silent wounds. The narratives that have quietly directed our lives from behind the curtain. The scripts we memorized without consent. The roles we performed without realizing we could step off the stage. We will confront the shadows and injuries that have held us back for so long, not with condemnation, but with curiosity and compassion. Not with a hammer, but with open hands. We will sit beside the parts of ourselves we once rejected and ask, gently: *"What were you protecting me from? What were you trying to survive?"* And as we do, something remarkable will begin to happen. The shadows will not disappear, but they will lose their terror. The self-hate will not evaporate overnight, but it will begin to unravel. And in its place, something steadier will emerge. Understanding. Context. Humanity. Because the truth is this: self-hate is rarely born from cruelty. It is born from pain. From misinterpretation. From adaptation. It is a shield that hardened over time. And shields, once necessary, can be set down. Volume Two is not about exposing yourself to shame. It is about liberating yourself from it. We are not walking into darkness to be consumed. We are walking in to gather what was left behind, to reclaim the parts of ourselves that were exiled, misunderstood, or silenced. This is sacred work. And you are ready for it. Not because you are fearless. But because you are willing. And willingness, more than anything, is the beginning of transformation. As we prepare to pivot toward the exploration that awaits in Volume Two, pause with me here, at this delicate, trembling edge. It is essential to recognize something with your whole being, not just your mind: this is not merely an ending. It is a threshold. You are not closing a door with finality echoing behind you. You are standing before a gateway, hand resting against its frame, feeling the cool grain of possibility beneath your fingertips. We stand before an expanse of possibility, a vast and untamed landscape stretching beyond the familiar terrain of survival.

The air here smells different. Sharper. Wilder. It carries the faint scent of rain and open earth. It leads into the profound wilderness of self-love, a wilderness not manicured or predictable, but alive. And like all wilderness, it is both beautiful and daunting. There will be thorns that catch at your sleeves. There will be uneven ground that tests your footing. There will be moments when the path disappears entirely, and you must trust your own internal compass. But there will also be breathtaking clearings you never imagined possible. Sunlight breaking through dense canopy. Still pools of water reflecting a sky you once thought unreachable. Silence that does not feel empty, but expansive. You will discover that the wilderness does not exist to defeat you; it exists to reveal you. Just as a seed buried beneath the earth must push through dark, compact soil to reach sunlight. So too, must we peel back the layers of our experiences, layer by layer, breath by breath, to reveal the powerful beings within us. The soil does not apologize for its weight. It presses. It confines. It feels cold and suffocating at times. Yet within that pressure, something sacred happens. The seed splits. Not in destruction, but in transformation. You are that seed. You are that becoming. You may not see the roots forming beneath the surface. You may not feel the slow stretch upward through resistance. But it is happening. Every tear you have shed. Every truth you have faced. Every boundary you have drawn. Every breath you have chosen to take instead of surrendering, these are roots anchoring you deeper. These are shoots reaching toward light. The darkness is not your final destination. It is the soil from which your truest self will rise. It is the place where strength germinates unseen. Where resilience gathers quietly. Where identity sheds what is false and prepares to unfold. And when you finally break through—when you feel the warmth of your own self-acceptance touch your face like sunlight after a long winter, you will understand something profound: the soil was never your enemy. It was your beginning. This is not the end of your story. It is the moment before emergence. The darkness is not your final destination. It is the soil. And now, in Volume Two, we begin to kneel in that soil, hands open, palms pressing into the cool, grainy earth, willing to feel what has long been buried there. We do not rush past it. We do not recoil from its dampness. We let it cling to our skin. We let it stain our fingers.

Because this is where truth has been waiting, beneath layers of silence, beneath roots of old belief, beneath the sediment of years. We will delve into the world of emotion, not skimming its surface like a stone skipping across water, but stepping into its currents. We will wade in until the water rises around our knees, our ribs, our throats. We will feel its temperature. Its pull. It's undertow. We will learn to recognize and understand the language of self-hate. Because self-hate speaks. It has a tone. A rhythm. A vocabulary that has shaped our internal dialogue for years. It has inflection. It knows exactly when to soften itself and when to strike. It whispers in certain moments, late at night, when the house is quiet, and the air feels thick. It shouts in others when we fail, when we are rejected, when we dare to try. It disguises itself as logic, as protection, as *"just being honest."* It dresses up as responsibility. As humility. As strength. It says, "*I'm only telling you the truth.*" And for so long, we believed it. But before we can learn to manage our emotions and feelings, we must first understand what they are. We must learn their textures. Their scents. Their weight. The heat of anger in the chest, sharp and rising, like sparks against dry wood. The ache of shame behind the eyes, hot and stinging, as if tears are always just beneath the surface. The tightness of anxiety in the stomach, coiled and restless, like a fist that will not unclench. The heavy, slow weight of sadness in the limbs, thick as wet wool draped across the shoulders, making even standing feel like effort. We must listen not only with our thoughts, but with our bodies. With the sixth sense, the emotional undercurrent that hums beneath every sensation. The part of us that feels before we understand. That reacts before we name. In this volume, we will not wage war against these emotions. We will study them. Sit with them. Ask them questions. We will turn toward what we once avoided and say, "*What are you trying to show me? Whose voice do you carry? When did you first arrive?*" Because we cannot heal what we refuse to touch. We cannot transform what we refuse to understand. So we kneel in the soil. We dig gently. We let the buried roots brush against our fingers.

And as uncomfortable as it may be, as raw as it may feel, remember this: nothing grows in untouched earth. And you, still becoming, still rising, are here to grow. Emotion has a language, and for many of us, we were never taught how to read it. We were handed the alphabet of performance instead, "*be good, be quiet, be strong*", but no one taught us how to translate the tremor in our hands, the heaviness in our chest, the sudden sting behind our eyes. We were told to silence emotion. Override it. Distrust it. To swallow tears before they formed. To smile through discomfort. To call sensitivity weakness and intuition exaggeration. And so we became fluent in suppression. But in this volume, we will begin to listen. Not to fix. Not to polish. Not to rush toward transformation. Healthy emotional self-regulation will be reserved for Volume Three, when we step fully into Self-love. But here, here we focus on awareness. On identification. On understanding what lives beneath the surface before we attempt to reshape it. We are not architects yet. We are archaeologists. We brush dust from ancient ruins. We kneel beside buried fragments. We whisper, "*Tell me who you are.*" We will learn to sit with the pulse of an emotion without immediately trying to tame it. To notice its shape. Its color. Its texture. The way anxiety hums like an electrical current beneath the skin. The way grief settles like fog in the lungs. The way anger can feel like wildfire—or like a steady, smoldering coal. We will learn that emotions are not enemies to conquer, but messengers to decode. We will also examine the role of trauma, anxiety, and stress in our lives—not as distant psychological terms, but as lived experiences. As nights spent hyper-alert. As shoulders that never quite relax. As hearts that learned to race before they learned to trust. Trauma is not just memory. It is imprint. It is the nervous system bracing for impact long after the danger has passed. It is the body remembering what the mind tries to forget. These patterns were not born from weakness. They were survival strategies. Brilliant, adaptive, life-saving responses that once protected us when we had no other tools. They were armor. They were shields. But what protected us then may now constrict us. What once kept us safe may now keep us small. So we will look gently at these strategies. We will trace their origins. We will thank them for how they carried us. And we will begin to ask whether they still serve us, or whether they are ready to be softened. We will begin developing strategies for coping with these challenges. Gentle strategies. Grounded strategies. Not dramatic overhauls, but steady practices. Tools that help us stay present instead of spiraling. Tools that help us pause instead of implode. A hand placed on the chest. A breath drawn slowly through the nose. A sentence spoken kindly to ourselves in the midst of chaos. Anchors in the storm. We are not trying to erase our emotional world. We are learning its dialect. We are tuning our ears to the subtle tremors beneath the noise. Because before healing becomes transformation, it must become awareness. Before love becomes practice, it must become understanding. And understanding begins here, kneeling in the soil, listening to the language our emotions have been speaking all along. But perhaps the most significant aspect of Volume Two will be this: we will face the deepest, darkest demons we have buried. Not with spectacle. Not with violence. Not with self-punishment masquerading as bravery. But courageously. Quietly. Intentionally. We will turn toward what we once avoided, the locked rooms within ourselves where dust has gathered thick, and the air feels stale with old shame. We will not kick down those doors. We will open them slowly. We will let our eyes adjust to the dimness. We will allow our breathing to steady. And then, together, we will step inside. We will face our inner critic, the one whose voice we may know better than our own. The one who speaks with unnerving familiarity. We will learn its tone. Is it sharp and cutting? Is it cold and clinical? Is it weary and disappointed? We will listen to its cadence, the rhythm of its accusations, the timing of its interruptions. We will notice its favourite phrases, the words it reaches for when we falter: "*not enough; too much; always; never; ...*" We will study it, not to obey it, not to silence it with force, but to understand it. Because when you understand a voice, you take away its mystery.

And when you take away its mystery, you take away much of its power. We will understand its language so that it no longer blindsides us in moments of vulnerability. So that when it rises in the early morning hours or slips into the quiet space after a mistake, we can say, "*Ah. I recognize you.*" Not as truth. Not as prophecy. But as a pattern. And slowly, deliberately, we will begin to dismantle the illusion self-hate has cast over us. The illusion that we are broken beyond repair. The illusion that we are fundamentally unworthy. The illusion that our flaws define the entirety of who we are. Self-hate is a shadow that distorts reflection. It bends the mirror. It warps proportion. It magnifies what is small and shrinks what is luminous. It convinces us that the scar is the whole body, that the mistake is the whole story, that the wound is the whole identity. In this volume, we will bring light to that distortion. Not harsh interrogation lights. Not exposure meant to humiliate. But steady, compassionate illumination. The kind that warms instead of scorches. The kind that reveals texture without condemning it. We will not shame ourselves for having believed the illusion. We will not berate ourselves for having internalized it. We will simply look at it, clear-eyed, grounded, awake. Because once you recognize an illusion for what it is, something subtle but irreversible happens. It begins to lose its grip. The spell weakens. The distortion flickers. And what waits beneath that illusion is not ugliness. It is not disgrace. It is not some hidden defect you were afraid to uncover. What waits beneath is truth. It is humanity. It is the tender architecture of a person who survived what they did not deserve and adapted in the only ways they knew how. Beneath the shadow is a self who has been waiting, not to be condemned, but to be understood. Not to be erased, but to be embraced. And in that understanding, something softer begins to rise. Something gentler than you have allowed yourself to believe possible. Not perfection. Not flawlessness. But compassion. And compassion is where self-hate begins to loosen its hold.

Volume Two: The Mirror We Avoid — Self-Hate

The illusion is cracking now. You have begun to see the shadow for what it is, not prophecy, not destiny, not identity, but distortion. A trick of light cast by old wounds. And so we step forward. Because there comes a point in every healing journey where the light is no longer enough. Where affirmations, though beautiful, feel like paper lanterns trembling in a storm. Where you can speak the words *"I am worthy"* and yet feel them fall flat against the inner walls of your chest, unable to take root. Where self-love sounds luminous in theory but hollow in the sternum, echoing instead of landing, like a bell rung in an empty cathedral. There is a point where something darker waits behind the ribs, arms folded, breath steady, whispering truths that do not feel kind. This is that place. Volume Two is not about loving ourselves more. It is about daring to meet the parts of us that do not. It is about standing before the mirror we avoid, the one we pass quickly in dim hallways, the one we refuse to linger in, and allowing our reflection to speak. Not the polished reflection. The raw one. The one that flinches. The one that winces. The one that tastes like shame at the back of the tongue and feels the familiar tightening in the throat. This is the mirror that does not flatter. It reveals. It shows the lines carved by years of self-criticism. The guarded eyes. The jaw set in quiet defence. The subtle shrinking we learned to perform. In this volume, we do not smash that mirror. We look into it. We let it show us the version of ourselves shaped by unkind voices, voices inherited, absorbed, rehearsed until they sounded like our own. We listen to the cadence of self-hate. The way it disguises itself as discipline. As realism. As *"just being honest."* We feel its texture, the way it burns in the chest, coils in the stomach, presses against the temples like a tightening band. We begin to understand its origin. *"Whose voice was it first? When did it move in? What did it promise to protect us from?* Because self-hate rarely begins as cruelty. It often begins as armor. As protection.

As an attempt to stay safe in environments that required shrinking to survive. But armor worn too long becomes a cage. And so, here, we do not attack ourselves. We study ourselves. We kneel in the soil of our shadow and sift through it gently, fingers brushing against roots we once thought were flaws. We learn the language of our inner critic, the rhythm of its accusations, the moments it grows loud, the situations that feed it. We learn to hear it without obeying it. We learn to feel shame without becoming it. We learn to separate fact from narrative, wound from identity, distortion from truth. Self-hate is a shadow that distorts reflection. It bends the glass. It elongates flaws. It shrinks strengths. It convinces us that our mistakes are definitions, that our pain is proof of defectiveness. But when light meets shadow, something remarkable happens. The distortion weakens. The illusion trembles. And beneath it, beneath the harsh glare and the critical voice, something else waits. Not ugliness. Not brokenness. But humanity. Tender. Complex. Imperfect. Alive. Volume Two is not comfortable. It is sacred. It is the wilderness where we finally turn toward the parts of ourselves that we have exiled. It is the excavation of old beliefs. The unlearning of inherited shame. The quiet dismantling of a narrative that told us we were unworthy. We do this not to condemn ourselves. But to understand. Because we cannot love what we refuse to see. And we cannot heal what we refuse to face. So we stand before the mirror. We breathe. We hold our own gaze a little longer than before. And instead of turning away, we stay. Not to punish ourselves. Not to prove anything. But to begin something deeper than affirmation. To begin truth. And truth, though it may tremble at first, is always the beginning of freedom. Self-hate is rarely born in isolation. It does not rise from the soul fully formed and venomous, as a storm conjured from clear sky. It is learned. It is absorbed. It is inherited like an heirloom no one remembers agreeing to carry, an antique necklace clasped around the small, tender neck of childhood, heavy with meaning we did not choose, mistaken for identity because we wore it for so long. It is the echo of old rooms. Rooms where the air smelled faintly of tension, sharp, metallic, like something burning just out of sight. Rooms where doors closed too hard, where silence followed mistakes like a verdict, where love felt conditional, and safety felt fragile. It is old faces, old tones of voice, old glances that lingered a second too long. It is the sound of comparison. The chill of disapproval. The way approval was rationed, measured, and withheld. It is the memory of being told, directly or indirectly, that you were too much. Too loud. Too sensitive. Too emotional. Or not enough. Not smart enough. Not grateful enough. Not worthy enough. Sometimes both at once, a dizzying paradox that left you spinning. Self-hate is the emotional bruise that formed long ago and was never allowed to heal. Press on it now, and you can still feel the tenderness beneath the skin. It is the internalization of someone else's frustration, someone else's unresolved wounds, someone else's inability to love well. It is taking their pain and swallowing it whole, letting it settle in the gut until it feels like your own truth. It is the sixth sense of shame, the felt knowing in the belly, the tightening in the throat, the heat behind the eyes, that whispers, "*There must be something wrong with me.*" And we believed it. Not because we were weak. But because we were human. We believed it because children do not question the air they breathe. We believed it because survival often means adapting—shrinking where needed, sharpening where required, softening ourselves into shapes that feel safer to love. We believed it because the nervous system remembers before the mind can reason. Because the body stores what the heart cannot process.

Because repetition becomes rhythm, and rhythm becomes identity. Over time, that borrowed voice became indistinguishable from our own. It began to narrate our choices. To color our reflections. To hum beneath our achievements and hiss beneath our failures. It showed up in mirrors, in relationships, in quiet moments before sleep. It tasted like bitterness on the back of the tongue. It sounded like certainty. It felt like truth. But it was never truth. It was adaptation. It was protection. It was pain that learned how to speak. And now, here, in this sacred turning, we are not here to destroy that voice. We are here to understand it. We are here to trace its origins with gentle hands. To ask whose words it once belonged to. To notice when it tightens in the chest or coils in the stomach. To recognize the old rooms it still carries inside its tone. Not to shame ourselves for having believed it, but to honor the younger versions of us who did what they had to do to survive. Self-hate was never proof that we are broken. It was proof that we were shaped. And what has been shaped can be reshaped. What has been learned can be unlearned. What was inherited does not have to be carried forever. We are not standing before this mirror to condemn the reflection. We are standing here to say, softly, steadily, "*I see where you came from. I understand why you formed. And I am ready to learn something truer now.*" In this volume, we will not bypass that truth. We will not rush to paint it in bright colors or drape it in premature positivity as though light alone can dissolve what was carved in shadow. We will sit with it. We will feel its texture, rough in some places, splintered in others, smooth where repetition has worn it down. We will hear its voice without flinching. We will trace its origins the way one traces the roots of an ancient tree, following them back through layers of soil, through memory, through the dim corridors of earlier years where the first seeds were planted. We will explore what it is we hate about ourselves, not vaguely, not abstractly, but specifically. The words. The accusations. The familiar refrains. We will ask who planted that hate. Whose tone does it carry? Whose disappointment does it echo? Whose fear does it mimic? We will hold those questions gently but firmly, like lanterns lowered into dark water. And then we will ask the most important question of all: "*What is the truth beneath it?*" Because before we can love ourselves fully, we must first understand what we have been taught to despise. Before we can build compassion, we must examine contempt.

Before we can cultivate tenderness, we must recognize the places where harshness took root. Before we can step into self-love, we must turn toward the mirror and not look away. This is not an easy threshold to cross. Standing before that mirror may feel like standing barefoot on cold stone. You may feel the tightening in your chest, the heat rising behind your eyes, the old reflex to turn your face, to dim the light, to distract yourself with anything softer. The mirror does not flatter. It reflects. And sometimes what it reflects is layered with distortion, shame smudged across the glass, old narratives fogging the surface, fingerprints of past voices pressed into the frame. But this threshold is sacred. Sacred because it asks for honesty without cruelty. Sacred because it invites us to look without annihilating ourselves. Sacred because on the other side of the mirror we avoid is not ugliness, it is clarity. And clarity does not scream. It arrives quietly. It feels like a steadying in the breath. A softening in the shoulders. A subtle rearranging inside the ribs where something once felt tight. Clarity reveals that what we called "broken" was often wounded. That what we labeled *"flawed"* was often frightened. That what we despised was often a survival strategy, wearing armor too long. And clarity, true clarity, is the beginning of freedom. It is the moment the illusion begins to thin. The moment the reflection stops being an enemy. The moment you realize the mirror was never meant to condemn you, but to show you what has been waiting, not to be judged, but to be understood. And over time, those external voices, sharp, dismissive, disappointed, cruel, stop sounding external at all. At first, they sting like cold wind against bare skin. You can feel the bite of them, sudden and bracing. You know exactly where they come from. You can see the face attached to the tone, hear the familiar cadence, recognize the posture, the raised eyebrow, the sigh. They arrive from outside of you, and though they hurt, they are clearly "*other*". But slowly, almost imperceptibly, they move closer. They stop knocking. They slip inside quietly. They take off their heavy boots at the door of your mind and leave no muddy footprints.

They sit down in the living room of your thoughts as if they have always belonged there. They rearrange the furniture. They soften their accent. They borrow your rhythm. They study the way you speak, the way you pause, the way you breathe. And then, gently, they begin to breathe when you breathe. Until one day, the voice that once said, *"You are not enough,"* no longer feels foreign. It does not echo from a memory. It rises from within. It sounds like your own reasoning. Your own logic. Your own conclusion. It feels natural. That is the most insidious part. Self-hate is rarely loud once it has taken root. It does not need to shout. It whispers in the quiet spaces, while you brush your teeth, while you replay a conversation, while you lie awake at night staring into darkness that feels thick and close. It hums beneath your pulse. It curls around your thoughts like smoke, subtle but suffocating. It tastes metallic at the back of the tongue. It feels like a tightening in the chest, a subtle drop in the stomach, a sixth-sense knowing that says, *"There must be something wrong with me."* And because it now sounds like you, you believe it. But self-hate is often not our voice. It is history speaking through us. It is the past disguised as personality. It is yesterday's wound wearing today's name. It is the echo of rooms where love felt conditional. The memory of eyes that scanned us for flaws. The residue of moments when we were too much, or not enough, or somehow both at once. It is someone else's frustration internalized. Someone else's fear absorbed. Someone else's limitation is mistaken for our identity. And when we do not question it, it hardens. It becomes doctrine. It becomes identity. It becomes the lens through which we interpret every mistake, every rejection, every imperfection. But here is the sacred turning: once you recognize that the voice is borrowed, something shifts. The air changes. The breath deepens. There is space, small at first, between the thought and the self. A pause. A flicker of awareness. A realization that what you have been calling *"me"* may, in fact, be memory. And in that space, the mirror begins to clear. Because if self-hate is history speaking through you, then it is not destiny. If it is the past disguised as personality, then it can be unmasked. If it is yesterday's wound wearing today's name, then it can be renamed. And that recognition, quiet, steady, undeniable, is the first crack in the illusion. The first breath of freedom. In the inner family, self-hate often appears not as a villain, but as a harsh protector. The critic standing guard at the gate of your heart, arms crossed, jaw tight, scanning the horizon for threat. You can almost see it there: shoulders squared, eyes narrowed, breath shallow but vigilant. It believes it is brave. It believes it is necessary. It believes that if it wounds you first, no one else can wound you worse. It believes that if it names your flaws loudly enough, the world will have nothing left to expose. It believes shame is armor, thick, impenetrable, forged in fire, and fitted carefully to your ribs. It believes self-rejection will prevent abandonment. "*If we reject ourselves first,* it reasons, *no one can surprise us with it.*" If we lower our own worth before someone else does, the fall will hurt less. This protector is not cruel in its own eyes. It is strategic. It is tired. It remembers what it felt like to be blindsided. To be laughed at. To be left. To be told, explicitly or subtly, that love could disappear without warning. So it stands at the gate with a weapon made of words. It lashes out pre-emptively. It sharpens criticism into a blade. It thinks it is saving you. But it does not realize it is perpetuating the very wound it is trying to prevent. It does not realize that every lash of its tongue lands not on an enemy, but on the tender child within, the one still learning how to feel safe in her own skin. The one who flinches when the voice rises. The one who absorbs each accusation like truth. The one who does not know this guard is misinformed. It does not realize that shame is not armor. It is acid. It corrodes slowly. It seeps into the joints of your identity. It tightens the throat. It hollows the chest. It teaches the inner child to hide, to shrink, to anticipate rejection before love has even had a chance to arrive. And yet, this harsh protector is not evil. It is afraid. It is loyal in the only way it knows how to be.

It is a part of you that once learned that attack was safer than exposure, that criticism was safer than vulnerability, that control was safer than trust. It is history dressed as authority. Pain masquerading as discipline. In this volume, we do not silence that voice. We do not banish it to the shadows. We do not shame it for existing. We do not declare war on it. We listen. Not to obey it. Not to agree with it. But to understand it. We will sit with it as one might sit across from a weary soldier who has been guarding the wrong door for too long. We will ask: "*What are you protecting? When did you first learn this was necessary? What are you afraid would happen if you laid your weapons down?*" Because beneath the critic's harshness is often grief. Beneath its certainty is fear. Beneath its rigidity is a longing to finally rest. And when we begin to see that, something softens. The gate does not vanish. But it opens. And the tender child within, the one who has been absorbing the blows, begins, at last, to feel seen. Because what we hate in ourselves is rarely random. It is not a flaw that appeared without origin. It is a map. A coded message written in the ink of memory. A signal flare burning against the night sky of our psyche, illuminating, again and again, the exact places where we were misunderstood, rejected, neglected, or shamed. Self-hate has coordinates. If we pause long enough, if we stop arguing with it and start listening, we can almost feel the map unfolding in the body. The tightness in the chest when we call ourselves *"too emotional."* The heat rising to the face when we feel *"too sensitive."* The sinking, hollow drop in the stomach when we believe we are *"too needy."* The subtle bracing of the shoulders when we anticipate being *"too much."* These sensations are not random storms. They are echoes. They are landmarks. What we hate is often what was never protected. What we reject is often what was never accepted. What we attack is often what was once attacked. The part of you labeled *"dramatic"* may have simply been expressive in a room that feared feeling. The part called *"clingy"* may have been longing for reassurance in an environment that withheld it. The part dismissed as *"weak"* may have been tender in a world that prized hardness. These were not defects. They were responses. They were adaptations. They were attempts to stay connected, to stay loved, to stay safe. And when we begin to see self-hate not as proof of our brokenness, but as evidence of our survival, something shifts. The air changes. The emotional temperature softens. The body exhales in a way it has not in years.

Because survival is not shameful. It is sacred. The harsh protector is no longer a monster pacing in the dark corridors of the mind. It becomes what it has always been: a frightened sentinel who learned the wrong strategy. A guard who mistook self-attack for safety. A loyal part who thought, "*If I wound us first, no one else will have the chance.*" And when we recognize that, compassion enters the room. The mirror we feared, the one we avoided, the one we rushed past, begins, slowly, to change. It no longer reflects a villain. It reflects a story. A layered, human, aching story. A history etched in muscle memory and nervous system responses. A child who adapted. A protector who overcorrected. A heart that endured. The reflection is no longer an enemy. It is a narrative waiting to be understood. And understanding, gentle, patient, curious understanding, is the first act of love we have ever truly offered ourselves. And so, standing before that mirror we once feared, the glass no longer warped by denial, no longer shrouded in avoidance, something deeper is asked of us. Not perfection. Not instant forgiveness. Not even immediate love. But curiosity. To heal, we must become curious about our own cruelty. Not ashamed of it. Not defensive against it. Curious. We must lean closer to the voice that cuts, the one that arrives sharp and certain, and ask, gently but bravely: "*Whose words are these? When did I first believe this? What did this part of me need that it did not receive?*" That question alone changes the air in the room. Because when you pause long enough, when you soften your jaw and unclench your fists, you can almost hear the layers beneath the criticism. The faint echo of an old room where your emotions felt like inconveniences. The sharp tone of someone disappointed. The heavy silence that followed your tears. The subtle withdrawal of affection that taught you to monitor yourself, to edit yourself, to shrink.

If you listen closely, you may even feel it before you hear it, the tightening in the chest, the subtle tremor in the belly, the familiar flush of heat rising to the face. The body remembers what the mind buried. It holds the emotional sediment of moments when you were too loud, too soft, too sensitive, too ambitious, too alive. Self-hate is not proof of brokenness. It is evidence of unprocessed pain. Pain that never had language. Pain that never had witness. Pain that lodged itself in the body like a splinter beneath the skin, too small to see, too deep to ignore. It is the sixth sense of shame, that felt knowing in the gut that whispers, "*Something is wrong with me.*" But that whisper was learned. It was planted. It was rehearsed in rooms where love was conditional or scarce. And when pain does not have space to move, it turns inward. It seeks an explanation. It finds the nearest target. Us. But when we become curious instead of condemning, something miraculous happens. The splinter begins to surface. The critic's voice loses its omnipotence. The mirror no longer feels like a tribunal, it becomes a window. And in that window, we do not see a monster. We see a human being who adapted. A nervous system that learned to survive. A child who did the best she could with what she was given. Curiosity is the first crack in the armor of self-hate. It is the moment the harsh protector feels seen rather than silenced. It is the beginning of translating cruelty into context. And context, held gently, bravely, is where compassion is born. And when we begin to separate our true voice from the echoes of the past, something subtle but undeniable shifts. The air feels different. Not dramatically, no thunderclap, no blinding revelation, but like a window cracked open in a room that has been closed for years. The critic, once booming like thunder in the skull, no longer fills the entire sky. Its voice, once omnipotent and unquestioned, becomes smaller. Human. Fallible. You can hear the strain in it now. The fear beneath the force. It is no longer God. It is a part. And that distinction changes everything. The inner child is no longer standing alone in the dark hallway of memory, arms wrapped around herself, bracing for another verdict. She is no longer the sole recipient of every internal lash. She feels presence beside her. Witness. Protection that is not cruel, but kind. The nervous system, long braced for impact, begins to exhale. You can feel it. Shoulders that have hovered near your ears for years begin to drop. The jaw unclenches. Breath deepens, not forced, not dramatic, but fuller. The body, which has been clenched like a fist, slowly opens. Fingers uncurl. The chest softens. The stomach, once tight with vigilance, loosens its grip. This is what happens when the past is named instead of obeyed. Healing requires honesty. And honesty is not always gentle. It is not curated. It is not polished. It does not flatter. It means standing in front of the mirror and resisting the urge to adjust the lighting. It means looking directly at the parts we avoid, the ones we tuck behind competence, humor, perfectionism, or silence. The parts we overcompensate for. The parts we disguise as strengths because we are terrified, they might be weaknesses. It means acknowledging the traits we secretly believe make us unlovable. The ones we criticize most harshly. The sensitivities we try to numb with busyness or distraction. The needs we pretend we do not have because needing once felt dangerous. It means admitting: "*I want reassurance. I want to be chosen. I want to be seen without earning it.*" It means allowing ourselves to feel the heat of shame in the cheeks, the drop in the stomach, the tremor in the hands, and staying. Not running. Not deflecting. Not punishing. Staying. Because the parts we hide are often the parts that were never held properly. The parts that learned to shrink because visibility came with risk. The parts that were told, directly or subtly, that they were inconvenient. And when we look at them now, not with contempt, but with clarity, the emotional climate shifts again. The hallway is no longer dark. The critic is no longer thunder. The body is no longer a battlefield. It becomes, slowly, a home. A place where even the most fragile parts are allowed to exist without being cross-examined. This is the sacred, unglamorous work of Volume Two. Not erasing the shadow. But learning to stand in it without turning against ourselves. And in that steadiness, in that brave, trembling honesty, freedom begins to take root. Volume Two is the descent into that shadow, not to drown in it, not to romanticize it, not to build a home there, but to reclaim what was buried beneath its weight.

We are not walking into darkness to be swallowed. We are walking in to retrieve ourselves. Because beneath self-hate is grief. And grief has a texture. It feels heavy in the chest, like damp wool pressed against the ribs. It sounds like the crack in your voice when you admit, finally, that something hurt. It tastes like salt on the lips from tears you once swallowed. Beneath the sharpness of self-criticism is sorrow, sorrow for the times you were misunderstood, for the love that felt conditional, for the moments when you reached out, and no one reached back. Beneath grief is unmet need. The need to be seen. To be soothed. To be reassured. To be chosen without audition. Unmet need hums quietly in the nervous system. It shows up as *"too sensitive," "too intense," "too much."* But it is not excess. It is hunger. A hunger that learned to disguise itself as self-disgust because it felt safer to blame yourself than to admit you were starving. And beneath unmet need. Is the part of you that has always been worthy of love. Not someday. Not once you improve. Not once you perform better. Not once you become easier, quieter, thinner, stronger, less emotional, more composed. Always. That worth was never revoked. It was only obscured, layered over by disappointment, by criticism, by the sediment of old stories repeated too often. It was buried, yes. But burial is not annihilation. Seeds are buried, too. We cannot heal what we refuse to see. We cannot free what we refuse to face. So here, in this volume, we turn toward the mirror we once avoided. We do not rush past it. We do not glance and recoil. We step closer instead of flinching away. We let our gaze rest, steady, breathing, on what we once judged too harshly to behold. The crease between the brows. The tenderness in the eyes. The places where shame once lived like a permanent resident. We look not to condemn. Not to criticize. Not to collect more evidence against ourselves. But to understand. And understanding changes the temperature of everything. When contempt meets curiosity, it softens. When shame meets compassion, it loosens. When avoidance meets presence, it begins to dissolve. In that quiet act of witnessing, of seeing ourselves fully and not turning away, something ancient begins to mend. Something older than the critic. Older than the wounds. Older than the stories we were handed. It is the remembering. The remembering that before the shadow, there was innocence. Before the armor, there was tenderness. Before the self-hate, there was simply a human heart trying to belong. Volume Two is not a punishment. It is a reclamation. And on the other side of this descent, we will not find perfection. We will find wholeness.

Preparing for the Next Phase

And now, as we stand at this threshold, having dared to look into the mirror and soften our gaze, there is a quiet pause before the next descent. It feels almost ceremonial. The air shifts. The light changes. You can sense it in the space around you, in the subtle stillness that comes just before something sacred begins. As you prepare to embark on this next phase of our journey, I want to remind you that it's okay to feel nervous or uncertain. Of course you do. Your body may feel it first: a tightening in the chest, a flutter in the stomach, a subtle tremor beneath the surface like the earth sensing an approaching storm. Your thoughts may whisper, *"Do I really want to go there?"* That hesitation is not weakness. It is the tremble of something sacred about to be touched. It is reverence. It is instinct recognizing depth. The work ahead will be challenging, yes. It may taste bitter at times, like medicine you know you need but would rather avoid. It may feel like walking barefoot across uneven ground, aware of every stone, every hidden thorn pressing into tender skin. There may be moments when old memories rise like dust shaken from forgotten rooms, when the air feels thick with truths long unspoken. There may be days when your emotional muscles ache, when vulnerability feels exposed and raw against the wind. But it will also be incredibly rewarding. There is a different kind of warmth waiting on the other side, a warmth that does not blaze dramatically but glows steadily, like embers banked deep within the hearth. A warmth that settles into the bones. A steady glow of self-understanding that no one can take from you. Because when you choose to step into this work, you are not stepping into darkness alone. You are stepping into reclamation.

You are stepping into the slow, deliberate recovery of parts of yourself that were buried beneath shame, beneath silence, beneath survival. Volume Two is not about tearing yourself apart. It is about learning how you were shaped. It is about tracing the lines of self-hate back to their origin and discovering that beneath them was always something softer, something human. So breathe. Feel your feet beneath you. Notice the rhythm of your heart. This is not a plunge. It is a passage. You are not being asked to be fearless. You are being invited to be honest. And honesty, though it may tremble, has always been the doorway to freedom. To get the most out of Volume Two, I encourage you to approach this next phase with an open mind and heart. Open like a window after a long winter, when stale air finally gives way to something crisp and alive. Open like soil ready to receive seed, dark, humble, willing to be broken open so that something new can take root. Feel that openness in your body: the gentle lift of your chest, the subtle unclenching of your jaw, the space that appears when you stop bracing for impact. Be willing to confront your fears, your doubts, your limitations, not as enemies to defeat, but as messengers carrying forgotten stories. They may not arrive politely. They may knock hard against your ribs. They may taste metallic on your tongue, sound sharp in your thoughts. But listen to them. Sit with them. Let them speak their truth without interruption. Ask them what they were protecting. Ask them when they were born. Notice what memories flicker behind them like old film, dim rooms, raised voices, silent disappointments. And trust, deeply, quietly, that you have the strength and resilience to overcome them. Not by crushing them. Not by silencing them. But by understanding them. You have already proven your strength simply by arriving here. By reading these words. By daring to stay present when turning away would have been easier. Your resilience is not theoretical. It is lived. It hums beneath your skin like a steady current. Remember, self-hate is not a destination; it is a journey. It is not a fixed identity carved in stone. It is a path we walk to understand the terrain of our inner world. Some stretches will feel rocky underfoot. Some will wind through dense forest where visibility is low. Some will open unexpectedly into clearings where the sky feels wide and forgiving. But it is movement. It is exploration. It is learning the language of your own landscape. And journeys require patience. They require kindness. They require compassion, not only toward others, but toward ourselves. Especially toward ourselves. Because the voice that has judged you the harshest will not soften through force. It will soften through gentleness. Through repetition. Through the quiet practice of staying. Approach this volume the way you would approach a wounded animal, slowly, respectfully, aware that sudden movements startle what has already been hurt. Approach yourself that way. There is nothing in you that cannot be met with understanding. And in that understanding, something profound begins to happen: What once felt like condemnation becomes context. What once felt like identity becomes story. And what once felt like permanent darkness begins, almost imperceptibly, to make room for light. As you close this book and prepare to begin Volume Two, take a deep breath. Not a shallow one taken out of habit, but a full, intentional breath. Feel the air enter cool against your nostrils, travel down your throat, and expand your lungs like sails catching wind after a long stillness. Let your chest rise. Let your ribs widen. Let your body register the space you are creating within yourself. As if you are clearing a room inside your soul for what is about to unfold. Hold that breath for a moment. Notice the quiet suspension. And then release it slowly. Feel the warmth of it as it leaves your lips. Notice the subtle softening in your shoulders. The slight unclenching in your jaw. The gentle settling in your spine. Your body knows when something meaningful has just occurred. Acknowledge the progress you've made so far. Not casually. Not as an afterthought. Really acknowledge it. Feel it land in your body. The hours you spent reflecting. The memories you allowed to surface. The truths you dared to face.

Let a quiet sense of pride settle into your chest, not loud, not boastful, but steady. Grounded. Earned. This is not arrogance. This is dignity reclaimed. You took the first steps toward your healing journey. And first steps are sacred. They are often the hardest. They require more courage than anyone sees from the outside. Let yourself feel that courage now. Let it warm you from within. And when you're ready, truly ready, pick-up Volume Two and let the journey continue. Do not rush. There is no race here. Healing unfolds in rhythm, not in haste. Begin when your spirit feels prepared to lean deeper. Remember, you are not alone on this path. Even in the quiet moments when it feels solitary, when the room is silent, and the work feels intensely personal, this journey is shared. Others have walked it. Others are walking it now. And I am walking alongside you in these pages. We are stepping into deeper waters. But you are no longer the person who first opened this book. You are steadier now. More aware. More awake. And that changes everything.

Setting Intentions

And before you turn the page, before you step fully into the deeper waters, pause here with me. As we stand on the cusp of this next phase, there is a hush in the air, like the stillness before dawn. The world has not yet brightened, yet something luminous is gathering at the horizon. You can feel it, even if you cannot yet see it. The light has not fully broken, but it is there, waiting, patient, inevitable. This is a sacred threshold. In this quiet space between what was and what will be, I encourage you to set intentions for what you wish to discover about yourself in the upcoming volumes. Not goals carved in stone. Not rigid expectations that tighten your chest. Intentions, soft but steady, like a compass resting gently in your palm. Intentions that breathe. Intentions that allow for unfolding. Close your eyes for a moment if you need to. Ask yourself gently, without judgment, without pressure: *"What are you hoping to heal? Is it the ache behind your ribs that never quite leaves, the one that flares unexpectedly when someone raises their voice? Is it the old belief that clings to you like smoke in your hair, lingering long after the fire has gone out? Is it the grief that tastes metallic at the back of your throat, rising when you least expect it? Is it the exhaustion that settles into your bones, heavy and familiar? Is it the tightness in your stomach when you dare to speak your truth?"* Let the question land in your body. Notice where it resonates. Notice what stirs. Perhaps you hope to uncover the origin of a fear that has shaped your choices. Perhaps you long to loosen the grip of shame. Perhaps you want to understand why certain words still wound you so deeply. Perhaps you simply want to feel at home within yourself again. There is no wrong answer here. Only honesty. Setting intentions is not about predicting who you will become. It is about honoring who you are right now. It is about saying, quietly but firmly: *"I am willing to look. I am willing to learn. I am willing to grow."* Intentions are promises made not to perfection, but to presence. So let your intention be gentle. Let it be curious. Let it be brave. Let it be as simple as: *"I want to understand myself more deeply."* Or as tender as: *"I want to treat myself with more kindness."* Or as fierce as: *"I am ready to confront what I have avoided."* Feel the emotional undercurrent of that choice. There is vulnerability there. And there is strength. You are not stepping into Volume Two blindly. You are stepping into it intentionally. With awareness. With breath. With a quiet steadiness that did not exist when this journey began. The dawn is gathering. When you are ready, turn the page, not as someone bracing for impact, but as someone choosing discovery. You are not entering darkness. You are entering understanding. And then ask yourself, softly but bravely: ***"What truths are you ready to confront?"*** The ones you have avoided because they sting like salt pressed into tender skin. The ones that tremble beneath your surface, vibrating quietly like a truth knocking from inside a locked room.

The ones your body already knows, the tightening in your throat when a memory surfaces, the heaviness that settles behind your sternum when certain names are spoken, the subtle clench in your stomach when an old belief rises uninvited. Let those truths come forward. Write them down. Do not rush the ink. Feel the pen resting between your fingers. Notice the faint resistance of paper beneath your hand. Hear the soft scratch as words take shape, fragile at first, then firmer. Each sentence is not merely language; it is courage made visible. Each word is a small lantern lowered into the dark. If tears come, let them. If your breath stutters, pause. This is not performance. This is pilgrimage. Give your intentions a physical home. A journal. A folded page slipped between chapters. A sheet tucked into a drawer like something sacred. Let them exist outside your mind so they no longer have to circle endlessly within it. When thoughts remain unspoken, they echo. When they are written, they anchor.

Each intention you name becomes a guiding star. Not one that demands perfection, but one that offers direction. When the waters of this next volume grow turbulent, when doubt pounds loudly against your ribs and the old voice tries to reclaim the microphone, you will have something steady to return to. You will be able to trace your own handwriting with your fingertips and remember the sound of your own resolve. Intentions are not rigid vows. They are invitations. They are compasses resting quietly in your palm. They are lanterns lit before the descent. They are seeds planted in soil that has already proven it can hold both darkness and growth. And perhaps most importantly, they are whispers to your future self: *"I am willing. I am ready to see. I am ready to become."* So pause here. Breathe again. Feel the air cool as it enters and warm as it leaves. Notice the subtle hum of anticipation in your chest, the sixth sense of something sacred unfolding. You are not stepping into Volume Two blindly. You are stepping into it with intention. And that changes everything.

CLOSING WITH EMPOWERMENT

And now, dear reader, as your fingers rest on the final pages of Volume One, perhaps feeling the faint texture of paper beneath your touch, perhaps hearing the soft whisper as you prepare to close the cover, pause. Let the air settle around you. Let your breath move slowly in and out, cool as it enters, warm as it leaves. Feel the steady rise and fall of your chest, the quiet rhythm that has carried you through every chapter. This closure does not signify an end. It is not a door slamming shut in darkness. It is a powerful juncture in the larger journey of self-exploration and healing, a threshold. A sacred pause between what has been unearthed and what is waiting to be revealed. Like standing at the edge of a forest at dusk, aware that deeper paths lie ahead, but no longer afraid of the shadows because you have already learned how to walk among them. Take a moment to honor yourself. Truly. Feel the quiet pulse of pride beneath your ribs. Notice the subtle warmth that spreads through your chest when you allow yourself to acknowledge what you have done here. Acknowledge the dedication it took to stay with these pages. The vulnerability required to let the words land in your body. The courage it demanded to see parts of yourself reflected in ink and not turn away. You have not simply read this volume; you have walked through it. You have carried its weight. You have let it stir what was dormant. You have allowed memory, grief, resilience, and truth to breathe beside you. Some passages may have tasted bitter. Some chapters may have felt heavy in your hands. Some sentences may have brushed against tender places you did not know were still raw. And yet, you stayed. You kept turning pages. You kept breathing. You kept choosing to remain present. That matters. Feel it now—the steadiness in your spine. The groundedness in your feet. The emotional shift that may be subtle but undeniable. You are not who you were when you began these pages. Something has softened. Something has strengthened. Something has awakened. This is empowerment, not loud, not theatrical, but embodied.

It is the felt sense that you can face yourself and not collapse. That you can look at your past and not be consumed by it. That you can acknowledge your pain without surrendering to it. As you close this volume, do not rush away from this moment. Let it register. Let the silence around you hold what has been spoken. Let your body absorb what your mind has learned. This is not an ending. It is a gathering of strength. Ahead lies deeper work. More honesty. More tenderness. More courage. But you do not step toward it as the person who once felt powerless. You step toward it as someone who has already walked through fire and discovered that she does not burn as easily as she once feared. Carry that knowing with you. You are still here. You have endured. You have chosen to look inward. And that, more than anything, is proof of your power. Remember: you are not alone. Even if the room around you feels impossibly still, so quiet you can hear the faint hum of electricity in the walls, the soft ticking of a clock marking time, even if the world outside your window moves on unaware, traffic sighing past, birds calling into indifferent sky, there is a thread connecting us in this shared pursuit of truth and wholeness. It is not visible, but you can feel it if you grow still enough. A subtle warmth in the chest. A recognition. A knowing that someone else has stood where you stand and chosen not to turn away. Together, we will continue to delve deeper into the realms of self-love and understanding. Not as a concept polished and framed on a wall, but as something lived, felt in the body, tasted in the quiet after tears, heard in the gentler tone of your own inner voice. Together, we will step into the next layer, the next unveiling. Like lifting a veil from a mirror that once reflected only distortion and discovering clarity beneath. The path may not always be easy. There will be days when the wind feels sharp against your skin, when it cuts cold and carries the old echoes back to your ears. Days when familiar doubts attempt to reclaim their seat at the table of your mind. When shame tries to whisper in your own cadence. When fatigue settles into your bones, you question whether the climb is worth it. But this path, this deliberate, courageous turning toward yourself, is undoubtedly worth traveling. Because every step forward, no matter how small, is a reclaiming. Every tear shed is not weakness but release, saltwater washing something ancient from the shore of your heart. Every insight gained is a lantern lit in a corridor that was once dark. Every boundary drawn is a stake placed firmly in the ground that says, "*This is where I begin.*" This journey is not about becoming someone else. It is about coming home. And you, dear reader. with your trembling hands, your resilient heart, your history, and your hope, you are worth every step. Worth the discomfort. Worth the tears. Worth the slow, sacred unfolding. The wind may rise. The road may bend. But you are not walking alone. And you are worth the walk.

Conclusion

And so, here we are. Let's take a deep breath together, slowly now, feel the air enter cool against the inside of your nostrils, travel downward, steady and life-giving. Feel it expand your chest like a sail catching wind. Let it press gently against your ribs. Let your shoulders soften. Let the quiet beneath your thoughts grow wider, like a lake settling after stones have stopped skipping across its surface. Hold it for a moment. And then release. Let's gently close this chapter, not with finality, not with the sharp sound of something ending, but with reverence. With the tenderness of placing something sacred back on an altar. This is not a goodbye. It is a bow. A pause. A hand resting over your own heart in acknowledgment of how far you have come. And then, hand in hand across these pages, let's step forward into the next stage of our journey together. The best is yet to come. Not because the road will suddenly smooth itself into perfection. Not because the sky will stretch endlessly blue without storm. But because you are no longer walking it asleep. You are walking it awake. Aware of your breath. Aware of your choices. Aware of the quiet power that hums beneath your skin. You are willing now. Brave in ways that are not loud but rooted. Grounded. Intentional. You feel differently. You see differently. You carry yourself differently. And that changes everything. I am deeply honoured to be part of your journey. To sit beside you in these pages. To witness your courage as you turn toward what once frightened you. To walk with you into the hidden corridors of your heart, the locked rooms you once avoided, the quiet chambers where memory and meaning intertwine.

The thresholds where light and shadow meet and refuse to cancel one another out. There is sacred work ahead of us. Work that asks for honesty, the kind that tastes raw but cleanses. Work that asks for tenderness, the kind that feels like warm hands around something fragile. Work that will prepare the soil of your inner world for something extraordinary to take root. We are not chasing perfection. We are cultivating wholeness. And as you sit here now, breathing, present, alive, feel the emotional truth of this moment settle into your bones: You are not who you were when you began. You are not finished becoming. And you are ready. Close this volume gently. Feel the weight of it in your hands. Feel the weight of your own growth inside your chest. Then, when you are ready, turn the page. The next chapter is not waiting for a different version of you. It is waiting for this one. But before you turn the page, before the paper lifts and the next chapter inhales, I want to leave you with one final question, one not meant to be solved quickly, but carried. Held. Tended. A question to tuck into your pocket like a small, glowing ember you can warm your hands around when the night feels long: ***"What is the greatest***

gift you can give yourself on this journey of self-discovery and self-love? Is it the gift of forgiveness? The gift of self-acceptance? Or the gift of self-compassion?" Pause. Do not rush past it. Feel the weight of those words settle into your chest. Notice what happens in your body. *"Does something tighten behind your ribs? Does your throat constrict? Does your stomach dip gently, as though recognizing something long unnamed? Or does something soften, like a muscle that has been clenched for years, finally allowed to loosen?"* Listen for what whispers back. Perhaps forgiveness rises first, tasting like salt and release, like unclenching a fist that has been gripping regret. Perhaps self-acceptance hovers quietly, like standing before a mirror and not flinching. Perhaps self-compassion moves through you like warmth, like placing your own hand over your heart and choosing kindness instead of critique. Whatever your answer is, I encourage you to give that gift to yourself freely. Without conditions. Without waiting until you *"deserve"* it. Without postponing it for a future, more perfected version of you. Offer it to yourself the way sunlight offers warmth, without asking if the ground has earned it. The way rain offers nourishment, even to cracked and hardened soil. The way breath offers life, again and again, without judgment, without tally. Let it be simple. Let it be sacred. Because the greatest transformation does not come from striving harder. It comes from loving deeper. From choosing, in quiet and ordinary moments, to treat yourself as someone worthy of tenderness. Carry this question with you. Let it glow softly beneath your days. Return to it when you falter. Return to it when you triumph. Return to it when you are unsure which direction to walk. And when you are ready, truly ready, turn the page not as someone searching for worth, but as someone remembering it. The ember is already lit. Remember this, let it echo gently against the walls of your ribs until it no longer feels foreign: You are deserving of love, care, and respect, not just from others, but from yourself as well. Not as a reward. Not as something earned through endurance. Not as a prize for perfection. But as a birthright. Let that truth settle into your bones the way warmth settles into sunlit stone. Let it move through you like a quiet current beneath your skin.

Let it become the soft, steady hum beneath your steps, the rhythm your body returns to when doubt tries to rise. Feel it in the way your shoulders drop when you stop fighting yourself. Feel it in the breath that deepens when you stop bracing for criticism. Emotionally, let it land like something long-awaited, finally arriving home. And know this: The next journey, into self-hate, is not a detour. It is not a setback. It is not proof that you are failing at love. It is preparation. It is the sacred clearing before the temple. The final stretch of forest before the clearing opens wide. It is the soil that must be turned before seeds can truly take root. We must walk through the shadow to understand the light, not to dwell there, but to see its contours. To know where it bends and where it thins. We must listen to the critic, not to obey it, but to understand its origin. To hear the fear beneath its volume. To trace the wound beneath its accusation. We must face the mirror, not the polished version, but the honest one, before we can fully embrace what it reflects. Because self-love that bypasses self-hate is fragile. But self-love born from understanding? That is rooted. That is unshakeable. So as this page closes, do not mistake it for an ending. Feel the shift instead, the subtle widening in your chest, the sense of something gathering just beyond the horizon. The air before a new chapter always carries a certain electricity. A tremble. A promise. The page is closing, but the journey is unfolding. And you are not the same person who began it. You are steadier. More aware. More willing. You have walked through darkness and not disappeared. You have touched truth and not turned away. And now you stand at the threshold, not naïve, not untouched, but ready. Ready to kneel in the soil. Ready to meet the shadow. Ready to reclaim what was once misnamed as broken. The mirror is waiting. And this time, you will not look away. As we come to the end of this volume, I want to pause here with you, truly pause. Not rushing ahead. Not turning the page yet. Just resting in the quiet between these words. Feel it. The stillness. The space where breath deepens and something unspoken lingers, warm and present. I want to thank you again for walking this journey with me so far. Not casually. Not as a polite closing line. But with sincerity that settles low in the chest. Truly. It has been an honour, one I feel in my bones, and a privilege to share my insights, my wisdom, and my guidance with you. These were not simply ideas placed on paper. They were lived. Wrestled with. Wept over. Forged in fire and carried carefully into these pages.

I do not take lightly the fact that you have allowed my story to sit beside yours. That you have let it breathe in the same space as your memories. That you have held these pages in your hands, felt their weight, heard their soft turning, and allowed their words to echo in the quiet corners of your mind. Perhaps even in your heart. There is something sacred about that exchange. Story meeting story. Wound meeting wound. Light meeting light. You did not simply read. You engaged. You reflected. You felt. And that matters more than you know. As we stand here at this gentle threshold, I find myself looking forward, not hurriedly, but with a steady, sincere anticipation—to continuing this journey with you in the volumes to come. There is more to uncover. More to understand. More to soften. More to reclaim. And I am grateful, deeply grateful, that you are here. The path ahead will ask for courage again. It will ask for honesty. It will ask for tenderness toward places long misunderstood. But you have already proven something essential: You are willing. And willingness is where transformation begins. So for now, let this moment land. Let gratitude settle like a warm shawl around your shoulders. Let the quiet hum of connection remind you that this journey, though deeply personal, is not solitary. We will continue. Together. If you listen closely right now, truly listen, you might notice the subtle rhythm of your breath moving in and out like a tide that has never abandoned you. You might feel the steady pulse beneath your skin, steady and faithful, a quiet reminder that life is still choosing you with every beat. And somewhere deeper than thought, beneath the noise, beneath the analysis, there is a soft knowing: you have already grown simply by staying. Simply by reading. Simply by being willing to feel. Growth is not always dramatic. Sometimes it is this, breath by breath, page by page, tear by tear. As you step forward from here, remember to be gentle with yourself. Not just in theory. Not as a phrase you nod at and forget. But in the texture of your days. In the way you speak to yourself when you stumble. In the tone that rises in your inner voice when you make a mistake.

Let that tone soften. Let it sound more like a hand resting on your shoulder than a gavel striking a verdict. Be gentle in the way you hold your own flaws. In the way you respond to your fatigue. In the way you honor your limits. When your body whispers that it is tired, listen. When your heart says, *"This is too much,"* pause. When your spirit quietly breathes, *"Enough,"* believe it. Trust in the wisdom and guidance that are always available to you, the quiet intuition that hums beneath the surface of your thoughts, like a low, steady current beneath restless waves. That inner compass has never truly left you. It may have been drowned out by noise. It may have been doubted. It may have been silenced by fear. But it remains. It lives in the subtle tightening when something is not right. In the warmth that spreads through your chest when something aligns. In the emotional resonance that feels like truth settling into place. Cultivate the love, care, and respect that you deserve the way one tends a garden—patiently, intentionally, hands in the soil. Feel the earth beneath your fingers. Notice the slow work of roots forming beneath the surface where no one can see. Some days you will water. Some days you will prune. Some days you will simply wait. Growth does not rush. It unfolds. You are on a journey of forgiveness. Of self-discovery. Of self-love. These are not abstract destinations; they are living practices. They are daily decisions. They are small choices made in ordinary moments, choosing rest instead of punishment, honesty instead of avoidance, compassion instead of condemnation. And yes, you can create the life you desire. Not all at once. Not perfectly. Not without missteps. But deliberately. Deliberately choosing what you feed your mind. Deliberately choosing who you allow into your emotional space. Deliberately choosing to respond instead of react. Deliberately choosing to try again when you fall. You are not rebuilding overnight. You are becoming, layer by layer, breath by breath. There will still be challenges. There will still be days when old doubts tap at the door. But you are not who you were. You are more aware. More anchored. More capable of standing in the storm without mistaking it for yourself. And as you move forward from this place, carry this with you like a steady flame cupped in your palms: you are not behind. You are not too late. You are not too damaged. You are in motion.

Keep tending. Keep choosing. Keep listening. Keep becoming. The journey continues, and so do you. The journey of self-love is a lifelong path. It is not a destination marked by fireworks and finality, no grand crescendo where trumpets sound, and the work is declared complete. It is a trail walked daily, sometimes barefoot over rough terrain, feeling every sharp stone press against tender skin; sometimes beneath warm sunlight that kisses your shoulders and reminds you that growth can feel gentle too. Some days it smells like rain-soaked earth and renewal. Other days it tastes like salt from tears you didn't know you were still carrying. But it is a path, nonetheless. A living one. It is a journey that requires patience, the kind that does not rush a seed to bloom. It requires kindness, the kind that places a steady hand over your own trembling one. It requires compassion, especially toward the one person who will walk with you through every season of your life: yourself. You are the only companion guaranteed from first breath to last exhale. The only witness to every thought, every fear, every quiet triumph. And so the way you speak to yourself matters. The way you hold yourself matters. The way you forgive yourself matters. As we move toward the shadow of self-hate, I want to encourage you, again and again, like a heartbeat you can return to, to be gentle with yourself. The work ahead will stir old memories, old sensations, old emotional echoes that have long slept beneath the surface. They may rise suddenly. You may feel tightness in your chest, as though something is pressing against your ribs. A lump in your throat that makes words feel heavy. A heaviness in your stomach, like gravity has intensified. Emotionally, you may feel the sixth sense of it, a familiar ache, a subtle dread, a whisper of shame trying to reassert its place. Let it come. Let it teach. Do not mistake its arrival for failure. It is simply history asking to be understood. Trust in the wisdom and guidance that are always available to you, even when they whisper instead of shout. Your intuition does not need volume to be true. It may come as a subtle shift in your breath. A softening in your shoulders. A quiet knowing that settles behind your sternum. Listen for it. It is steady. It has been with you all along. And above all, cultivate the love, care, and respect that you deserve. Not as a reward for progress. Not as something earned through perfection. Not as a distant prize waiting at the end of healing. Now. You are deserving of love, care, and respect, not just from others, but from yourself as well. Let that truth land in you like warm sunlight after winter. Let it settle into your bones. Let it root itself in your spine.

Let it become the foundation beneath everything that follows, the ground you stand on when doubt tries to shake you. Because the work ahead will ask you to look at what you once avoided. And when you do, you will need something steady beneath your feet. Let that steadiness be this: you are worthy, even here. Even in the shadow. Even before the transformation. We are only just beginning. And this beginning is sacred. As you gently close this book, feeling the weight of it resting in your palms, hearing the soft whisper of pages meeting like a quiet exhale, perhaps even catching the faint scent of paper and ink lingering in the air, pause. Do not rush this moment. Let the quiet gather around you like twilight settling over a landscape. Let your breath move slowly in and out, steady and alive, cool as it enters, warm as it leaves. Feel your chest rise. Feel your shoulders soften. Feel the simple, sacred fact that you are here. There is something holy about this pause. I want to leave you with a final thought to carry, not loudly, not urgently, but like a low, steady hum beneath the surface of your days. A question that does not demand an answer immediately, but invites one gently: ***"What is the next step on your journey of self-love?"*** Not the entire staircase. Not the summit. Just the next step. Is it to practice greater self-awareness, to notice your thoughts as they pass through you like weather across the sky, without immediately believing every cloud that drifts overhead? To observe the inner critic without surrendering to it? To say, softly, *"Ah, there you are,"* instead of *"You must be right."* Is it to cultivate more self-acceptance, to soften toward the parts of you that feel rough, unfinished, imperfect? The edges you've tried to sand down. The traits you've labeled as flaws. To sit with them instead of pushing them away. To feel the warmth of your own humanity rather than the chill of judgment. Is it to develop a deeper sense of self-compassion, to speak to yourself with the gentleness you would offer someone you cherish? To change the tone of your inner voice from sharp to steady. From cutting to kind. To let your words land in your own chest like balm instead of blades. Notice what stirs as you consider these questions. Does your chest tighten slightly at one of them? Does your stomach flutter? Does something inside you lean forward with quiet recognition? That is your inner compass speaking. Not in thunder. Not in fireworks. But in sensation. In subtle knowing. In the sixth sense of truth, the emotional resonance that hums beneath language. There is no right answer. Only the one that feels alive in you. Your next step may be small. It may look ordinary from the outside. But within you, it may be revolutionary. It may be the first time you choose not to criticize yourself for a mistake. The first time you say no without apology. The first time you rest without guilt. The first time you allow yourself to be enough, exactly as you are. Whatever it is, let it be yours. Hold it gently. Like a seed in your palm. And remember, this is not the end of anything. It is a continuation. A widening. A deepening. The journey of self-love does not close with a cover. It continues in the way you wake tomorrow. In the way you breathe. In the way you choose to meet yourself. You are still here. You are still becoming. And the next step, however quiet, however trembling, is waiting for you. Whatever it is, the next step that stirred when you asked the question. I encourage you to take it with courage, kindness, and compassion. Not force. Not perfection. Not urgency. Courage to look honestly at what rises within you, even when it trembles. Kindness to hold yourself the way you would cradle something fragile and living. Compassion to remember that growth is not linear, and healing is not a race with a finish line and cheering crowds. It is a pilgrimage. Your healing journey is uniquely yours. It has its own rhythm, sometimes a steady heartbeat, sometimes a hesitant pulse. It has its own seasons. There will be winters when everything feels dormant and quiet, when progress seems buried beneath frozen ground. There will be springs when insight breaks through like green shoots pushing stubbornly toward light. There will be summers of warmth and expansion. And there will be autumns of shedding, old beliefs falling like leaves around your feet. It is okay to take your time. It is okay to pause. It is okay to feel uncertain.

Uncertainty is not a sign that you are failing. It is often the sensation of standing at the edge of something new. The path through self-hate that awaits in the next volume may feel dark at times, heavy, confronting, raw. It may feel like stepping into a room you once locked and swore never to open again. The air might seem thick at first. Your chest may tighten. Old emotions may stir like wind moving through forgotten corridors of memory, lifting dust from shelves you thought were cleared. Let that be part of the process. Notice the sensations without judging them. The heat rising in your face. The ache behind your eyes. The heaviness in your stomach. The emotional undertow that whispers, *"This is too much."* These are not signs that you are broken. They are signs that you are touching something real. Healing is not the absence of discomfort. It is the willingness to stay present with it. There may be days when the shadow feels louder than the light. When self-doubt echoes in the hollow spaces of your ribs. When the old critic clears its throat and tries to reclaim authority. On those days, do not rush yourself toward brightness. Do not demand instant clarity. Sit. Breathe. Place your hand over your heart if you need to. Feel the warmth of your own skin beneath your palm. You are not meant to conquer yourself. You are meant to understand yourself. Let the darkness teach you where the wounds are. Let it show you where tenderness is required. Let it reveal what was once silenced. And when it feels heavy, when the work tastes bitter, and your throat tightens around unspoken truths, remember this: you are walking this path with intention now. You are not stumbling blindly. You are choosing to enter the shadow so that you may one day stand in the light without flinching. That choice alone is powerful. Be gentle with yourself as you step forward. Move like someone carrying something sacred, because you are. You are carrying your own becoming. And becoming, as you are learning, is not rushed. It is nurtured. Take the step. However small. However trembling. Take it knowing that you are allowed to move at the speed of your own healing. Use this question, "*your next step*", as a compass for the next leg of your journey. Hold it the way a traveler holds a small brass instrument in trembling hands, watching the needle steady itself. Especially when the terrain grows uneven. Especially when the fog thickens, and the path feels swallowed by shadow. In those moments, return to it. Feel it in your chest. Let it orient you when your thoughts scatter like leaves in a restless wind. Do not compare your progress to someone else's highlight reel, the polished snapshots, the curated triumphs, the filtered smiles. You are not walking their road. You are walking yours. Your healing has its own scent, its own texture, its own pace. Do not measure your worth against someone else's timeline as though growth were a race marked by finish lines and applause. Healing is not a competition; it is a reclamation. A slow gathering of what was scattered. A careful return to yourself. Instead, focus on your growth. Your progress. Your transformation. Notice the subtle shifts in how you speak to yourself, the way the inner voice softens, even slightly. The way criticism hesitates before striking. The way compassion lingers a breath longer than it used to. These are not small things. They are tectonic movements beneath the surface of your life. Pay attention to the victories no one else sees. The quiet morning when you choose to get out of bed even though the weight feels heavy. The moment you pause instead of react. The evening you sit with discomfort instead of numbing it. The conversation where you say "no" and feel your pulse steady afterward. The tear you allow to fall without shame. The boundary you hold even when your voice trembles. These are sacred acts of courage. Each time you choose awareness over avoidance, you are lighting a candle in a once-dark room. Each time you choose compassion over criticism, you are loosening an old knot inside your chest. Each time you choose truth over fear, you are stepping out from behind a mask that was never meant to fit. As you move forward, let your next step be intentional. Not rushed. Not reactive. Chosen. Feel it in your body before you take it. Let it align with the quiet knowing that hums beneath your ribs. Let it be yours. And trust this deeply: even when the darkness feels thick around you, even when the wind howls and the old echoes rise, you are not walking in circles. You are not regressing. You are not lost. You are still moving. Toward clarity. Toward wholeness. Toward light. The light may not yet flood the horizon.

It may appear only as a faint silver line where night meets morning. But you are facing it now. And every step, however small, however hesitant, is a step in its direction. As you carry that final question with you into the quiet after these pages, into the stillness that follows turning the last sheet, let me offer you one more image to hold gently in your hands. Think of your life as a fire. Not a wildfire raging out of control. Not destruction. But a living flame. A breathing, responsive presence. A hearth-fire. One that shifts with the wind, brightens with attention, softens when left untended. It leans toward what you feed it. When you add kindling, carefully, intentionally, you can hear it crackle. A steady pop and whisper of heat. You can feel its warmth brush your skin, thawing places that once felt cold. You can smell the faint trace of smoke curling upward, rising like memory into open air. There is something ancient and grounding about it. Something alive. The same is true for you. Your thoughts are a fire. When you feed that flame with negativity and fear, when you replay old wounds, rehearse old shame, retell the same painful stories as if they are prophecy, your past continues to define your present. The fire grows in that direction. It licks at the dry wood of memory. It consumes the oxygen of the now with yesterday's smoke. The air thickens. The warmth turns harsh. The light flickers erratically, casting distorted shadows across the walls of your mind. But here is the sacred truth: you choose the kindling. You decide what you place on those embers. If you feed your inner fire with awareness instead of avoidance. With compassion instead of condemnation. With truth instead of distortion. The flame changes. It steadies. It warms instead of burns. It illuminates instead of blinds. You may still hear it crackle, but now it is the sound of growth. The sound of transformation. The sound of old wood giving way to new light. The warmth against your skin no longer feels like threat; it feels like life. Like possibility. Like presence. When you choose to speak to yourself differently, you are adding dry, clean wood. When you choose to set a boundary, you are adjusting the logs so the flame can breathe. When you choose to forgive yourself, you are clearing the ash that once smothered the glow. And slowly, the smoke begins to lift. The present becomes visible again. You can see your hands. Your breath. The room around you. The fire of your life was never meant to be fueled by fear alone. It was meant to be tended. Honored. Protected. Fed with intention. As you step into what comes next, remember this: you are not at the mercy of the flame. You are its keeper. You are not the smoke of your past. You are the one who decides what burns now. And when you choose carefully, when you add patience, honesty, courage, kindness, you do not merely survive the fire. You are warmed by it. Lit by it. Guided forward by its steady, living glow. But something extraordinary happens when you begin to change the kindling. When your hands, once trembling, once feeding the flame with old splinters of shame and fear, reach instead for different wood. When you begin placing love on the embers. Worth. Acceptance. When you offer the fire truth instead of distortion, gentleness instead of self-punishment. The quality of the flame changes. When you turn toward your demons of self-hate, not with weapons drawn, not with fists clenched, not with a sword of self-correction, but with compassion, kindness, and curiosity, another fire begins to rise. A steadier one. A warmer one. Not the frantic blaze of survival, but the hearth-fire of home. It does not roar. It glows. The inner fire of peace and serenity begins to take shape. You feel it first in your chest—a quiet warmth spreading slowly, like sunlight touching cold stone. Your breath deepens without you forcing it. Your shoulders lower. The tight band around your ribs loosens. Emotionally, something unclenches. The constant bracing softens. The vigilance eases. You notice that your thoughts are no longer sparks flying wildly in every direction. They move more slowly. More intentionally. The smoke of yesterday does not choke the air quite so fiercely. There is space now. Space to choose. Space to respond instead of react. Space to let the past cool into ash instead of reigniting it again and again. So be careful which inner fire you tend to. Because you are always tending one. Every thought is kindling. Every belief is fuel. Every story you repeat is another log placed on the flame.

Feed it resentment, and it will scorch you from the inside out. Feed it fear, and it will burn hot but leave you empty. Feed it self-hate, and it will consume the very oxygen you need to breathe. But feed it love, real love, not performance. Feed it truth, steady and compassionate. Feed it forgiveness, awareness, and worth, and watch what happens. The fire becomes sustaining instead of destructive. Illuminating instead of blinding. Warming instead of wounding.And that warmth, soft, steady, alive, becomes your companion. You will still face the wind. Storms will still come. There will be nights when the dark presses close and old embers try to flare. But when you know how to tend your fire, you are no longer afraid of the night. You carry light within you. And that is the quiet miracle of this journey. Not that the darkness disappears. But that you learn how to keep the flame. Remember, the goal of this journey is not to become perfect. Perfection is cold. Perfection is brittle. It gleams like glass, smooth, untouchable, and easily shattered by the slightest tremor. It smells sterile. It sounds hollow. It demands performance and punishes humanity. The goal is not that. The goal is to become whole. To gather the scattered pieces of yourself, the jagged fragments, the softened edges, the parts you once hid in drawers labeled "*too much*" or "*not enough*" and hold them without flinching. To feel their weight in your palms. To trace their texture with compassion instead of critique. To understand that wholeness is not the absence of cracks, but the sacred art of embracing them. To become whole is to sit with your contradictions without needing to resolve them. To allow the quiet part of you and the fierce part of you to share the same breath. To welcome both your tenderness and your strength. Your wounds and your wisdom. Your fear and your courage. It is to embrace your imperfections, not as flaws to erase, but as fingerprints of your humanity. Your quirks. Your uneven rhythms. Your beautifully human contradictions. The laugh that comes too loud. The tears that arrive too quickly. The dreams that still feel fragile in your chest. To love yourself exactly as you are, not once you have fixed everything, not once you have polished every rough edge, not once you are flawless, but now.

Now, with the scars still visible. Now, with the doubts still occasionally whispering. Now, with the healing still in motion. Because love is not a reward for completion. It is the soil in which completion grows. So take a deep breath, dear reader. Let it enter cool through your nose. Feel it expand your lungs, stretching gently against your ribs. Let your chest rise. Let your shoulders soften. Hear the steady rhythm of your heartbeat, alive, persistent, faithful. Feel the quiet hum of being here. Being breathing. Being becoming. Get ready to embark on the next phase of our journey together. Not with urgency. Not with pressure. But with willingness. The best is not behind you. Not because the past did not matter, it did. It shaped you. It strengthened you. It taught you. But the past is no longer the ceiling of your life. The best is yet to come. Not because the road will be easy. Not because there will be no more shadows. But because you are walking it differently now. Awake. Aware. Whole in progress. And that changes everything. And so, with that steady flame now glowing within you, not roaring, not consuming, but warm and alive, we step forward.

Volume Two: The Journey Continues...

Breathe deeply. Feel the air cool against your nostrils as it enters, crisp and clean. Let it travel down into your lungs, expanding your chest, stretching gently against your ribs. Feel the quiet weight of your own aliveness. Let the breath settle into the hidden spaces inside you, the spaces that once held doubt, that now hold possibility. Close this book with pride. Feel its weight in your hands. The subtle texture of the cover beneath your fingers. Hear the soft, grounding thud of its spine meeting its pages, a sound not of ending, but of completion. Like the closing of a sacred chapter, you did not just read but lived through. There is strength in that sound. There is honour in having stayed. In having felt. In having turned each page instead of turning away. You did not rush through this. You walked it. And when you feel ready, truly ready, reach for the next volume. Not out of pressure. Not out of fear. Not because you *"should."* But from that quiet courage rising within you. From that inner knowing that does not shout, but whispers steadily: "*There is more for me to uncover.*" Embrace the journey that lies ahead, for within its pages is a treasure trove of wisdom waiting to be unearthed. Not glittering gold that dazzles and fades. Something far more enduring and valuable. Truth. Clarity. Understanding. The kind of insight that does not simply inform the mind but reshapes the heart. The kind that hums softly through your nervous system and steadies your breath. The kind that says, without drama or spectacle, "*You are ready.*" Your journey to healing and self-love awaits. It waits patiently, like a path just beyond the treeline. Quiet. Certain. Neither chasing you nor abandoning you. Simply there. You may feel anticipation flutter in your chest like a small bird taking flight. Perhaps a flicker of nervousness. Perhaps even resistance that tightens your stomach or stiffens your shoulders. All of it is welcome. All of it belongs. All of it is part of the unfolding. You are not stepping into darkness unarmed. You are stepping in with awareness. With intention. With a flame already lit.

With gratitude and anticipation,

Letitia Swanepoel

Embrace the pages that follow in Volume Two. Let your fingers trace them. Let your breath move with them. Let the words meet you where you are, raw, ready, human. And let us walk this path of transformation together, step by step,

shadow by shadow, flame by flame.

END OF VOLUME ONE – A Sacred Pause

And so, here we stand. At the quiet edge of what once felt like an endless night, an expanse so vast it seemed it would never loosen its grip. The horizon that once held only shadow now holds something softer. Something breathing. Take a breath with me, slow, deliberate. Draw it in as though you are reclaiming oxygen after years beneath water. Feel the air enter your body, cool and alive against your skin, brushing the inner walls of your nostrils before filling your lungs. Feel your ribs widen like ancient wooden doors opening to morning light. Let your shoulders soften, dropping the armor they have carried for far too long. Notice your heartbeat. It is steady. It is faithful. It is still here. And so are you. Volume One was not simply a collection of pages bound together by ink and spine. It was a descent. A confrontation. A remembering. It was the echo of footsteps spiraling down into caverns long avoided—the sound of your own courage reverberating against stone walls of memory. It was the scent of old grief stirred from corners you once sealed shut. It was the weight of truth resting in your palms, heavy yet strangely grounding. It was the texture of vulnerability beneath your fingertips. The quiet tremor in your chest when recognition landed. The sixth sense, the emotional knowing—that something buried was finally being acknowledged. We walked through darkness, not to glorify it, not to drown in it, but to see it clearly. To name it. To survive it consciously. We did not rush through. We did not pretend the shadows were light. We let our eyes adjust. We felt the cool dampness of old wounds in the air.

We listened to the drip of memory in the silence. We allowed the ache to rise and fall like breath. And you did not turn away. You stood in rooms you once avoided. You touched the edges of pain you once numbed. You let words land in places that had not been visited in years. Some passages may have tasted bitter. Some truths may have stung like salt against tender skin. Some reflections may have felt like standing before a mirror in harsh light, seeing what you had long blurred. And yet, you stayed. That staying is not small. It is seismic. The darkness did not swallow you. The silence did not erase you. The old narratives did not get the final word. You walked through them. Breath by breath. Page by page. Pulse by pulse. Volume One was the awakening. The moment when you stopped sleepwalking through inherited beliefs. The moment you began to question the voice that said you were broken beyond repair. The moment you sensed, perhaps faintly at first, that your existence was not the harm, it was the beginning of healing. Feel that. Feel the subtle shift beneath your sternum. The slight widening in your chest. The way your breath no longer feels borrowed but owned. There may still be scars. There may still be echoes. But there is also awareness. There is choice. There is presence. And presence is power. Pause here. Let the quiet settle around you like dusk settling over water. Let the pride, not loud, not boastful, but grounded, register in your body. You have done something sacred. You have dared to look inward instead of away. You have chosen honesty over avoidance. You have chosen consciousness over collapse. You are not who you were when you began this volume.You are more aware. More attuned. More awake to your own inner landscape. This is not the end of healing. It is the end of pretending you are powerless within it. The storms may still gather. The winds may still rise. But now you know something the darkness once tried to hide from you: You can stand in it. You can feel without being erased. You can grieve without being consumed. You can remember without disappearing. And staying, staying when your past once convinced you to vanish, is one of the most radical acts of self-love imaginable. So close this volume gently when you are ready. Feel the faint texture of the cover beneath your fingertips. Hear the soft whisper of pages meeting. Let that sound echo not as an ending, but as a sacred pause between movements of a larger symphony. This is a threshold.

Behind you lies what you have faced. Before you lies what, you are ready to understand. Rest here for a moment. Let the light and shadow settle evenly within you. Let the air feel different in your lungs. You are still here. And that is not ordinary. It is miraculous. Volume One ends not with finality, but with reverence. You have begun. And beginning, truly beginning, is the bravest step of all.nYou did not turn away. Some of these chapters may have felt heavy in your hands, as though the paper itself carried gravity, as though each page held its own weather system, dense with unspoken years. You may have felt that weight settle into your palms, into your wrists, into the quiet space behind your sternum. Some sentences may have pressed against bruised places you thought had already healed, tender spots beneath the skin of your story. Places that flinched at the slightest touch. Words can be like fingertips tracing scars you forgot were still sensitive. They can awaken nerves long numbed. Some memories may have surfaced like old ghosts rising from deep water, slow at first, then sudden and breath-stealing. The kind that leaves salt at the back of your throat. The kind that blurs the edges of the room for a moment. You may have felt your chest tighten as if bracing for impact. Your eyes sting, not only with tears, but with recognition. Your pulse quicken, echoing in your ears like a drumbeat calling you back into the body. You may have felt anger, hot and electric beneath the skin. Grief, heavy and tidal. Recognition, a sharp, almost sacred click of truth landing. Relief, a subtle loosening, like a knot finally beginning to give. And yet, you stayed.nYou did not slam the book shut. You did not retreat into distraction. You did not exile yourself from the discomfort. You remained. That matters more than you realize. That is not passive. That is courage in its rawest form. The darkness did not swallow you. It may have pressed close. It may have whispered in familiar tones. But it did not consume you. The shame did not silence you. It may have tried to crawl back into your mouth and seal it shut.

But you kept breathing. The old narratives did not win. They may have roared like storms trying to reclaim the sky. They may have risen up, indignant at being questioned. But they did not take you with them. They may have howled.

They may have accused. They may have tried to drag you backward into the rooms where they were born. But you walked through them. Step by trembling step. Breath by breath. Heartbeat by steady heartbeat. You walked through the echo chambers of your own history and did not collapse beneath the sound. You let the past rise without letting it rewrite you. You felt the heat of it. The chill of it. The ache of it. And you did not disappear. That staying, through tightening chest and stinging eyes, through anger and grief and recognition, is a sacred act. It is the moment the narrative begins to shift. Not loudly. Not theatrically. But internally, where it matters most. You are not the darkness you walked through. You are the one who walked. And that distinction changes everything. This is a sacred pause. Not an ending. Not a retreat. Not the dimming of a flame. But a moment to feel the quiet after courage, the kind of quiet that follows thunder. The kind that hums softly in the air once the storm has passed, when the ground is still damp, and the sky is clearing. A moment to sense the subtle warmth of resilience in your bones, like embers glowing beneath ash. Not blazing. Not demanding attention. But steady. Alive. Enduring. This is the exhale after holding your breath for years. A moment to honour the emotional truth you have faced, the truths that tasted bitter at first, that scraped against your pride, that trembled in your hands like fragile glass. You did not shatter beneath them. You held them. You examined them. You allowed them to exist without turning away. That is strength of the deepest kind. Not the loud kind. The rooted kind. A moment to feel, physically, the way your body carries what you have survived. The softened shoulders. The steadier breath. The pulse that no longer races quite as wildly at the sound of old echoes. There is a subtle recalibration happening within you. A reordering. A remembering. You stood at the edge of your own night. At the brink where shadows once felt endless. At the threshold where silence felt suffocating. At the place where fear once whispered that there was no way forward. And you did not disappear. You did not dissolve into the dark. You did not surrender your name. You did not let the night claim your voice. You are still here. Feel the weight of that. Feel the miracle of that. Your breath is moving through you right now. Your heart is steady beneath your ribs. There is warmth in your hands. Light in your eyes. A consciousness that has walked through fire and come back carrying its own spark. This pause is sacred because it marks something profound: You have crossed terrain that once terrified you. You have faced what once defined you. You have stepped through shadow and remained intact. You are not who you were when you began these pages. Something has shifted, perhaps subtly, perhaps invisibly to the outside world, but undeniably within. A widening. A deepening. A strengthening of roots beneath the surface. So stand here for a moment longer. In the quiet after courage. In the warmth after weather. In the stillness that follows survival. You are still here. And that is not small. It is everything. Volume One was about waking up. Waking up inside the fog, when everything felt muffled and distant, as though life were happening behind thick glass, your own reflection blurred and unreachable. When sound arrived dulled, like voices carried through water. When even your own thoughts felt foreign, echoing in a room you could not quite locate. Waking up inside the storm, rain lashing against the fragile windows of your certainty. Wind howling through the corridors of memory, the ground unsteady beneath your feet as if the earth itself had decided to shift. Waking up soaked, breathless, disoriented, yet conscious. Aware. No longer sleepwalking through the thunder. Waking up inside the belief that you were broken beyond repair, like a cracked vessel no one could mend. And daring, trembling but brave, to question it. Daring to run your fingers along the fracture and whisper, "*What if this is not ruin? What if this is history?*" Daring to challenge the verdict that had once felt carved into bone. And now; something is different. Maybe it's subtle. Maybe it doesn't arrive with fireworks or thunderclaps splitting the sky. Maybe it is not dramatic at all. Maybe it is only a quiet shift in your chest, a softening where there was once a fist.

A little more space in your breath, as if your lungs have finally remembered how to expand fully. A small but steady widening where once there was constriction. Maybe it is the way your shoulders no longer live up near your ears. Maybe it is the way your jaw unclenches without you forcing it. Maybe it is the way silence no longer feels like accusation. A little less panic when old thoughts knock at the door like uninvited guests. You can hear them. The familiar rhythm of self-doubt tapping against the glass. The old narratives clearing their throats. The whisper that once sounded like truth. But you do not immediately hand them the keys. You pause. You notice the sound of the knock. You feel the reflex in your body, the tightening, the quickened pulse, the instinct to comply. And then, space. In that space lives something new. Discernment. Choice. A steadier voice that says, "*I hear you, but you do not own this house anymore.*" Volume One was the awakening. The moment your eyes adjusted to the dim light and realized you were not as lost as you thought. It was the slow return of sensation, the taste of truth on your tongue, the scent of memory stirred in the air, the hum of your own heartbeat beneath layers of noise. And now, standing here, you are no longer asleep inside the storm. You are awake within it. You are aware of the wind without believing it defines you. You are aware of the fog without mistaking it for your identity. You are aware of the old belief that you were broken—and you are no longer convinced by it. Something has shifted. It may be quiet. It may be tender. It may still feel fragile in your hands. But it is real. You can hear the old thoughts, but you no longer bow to them. You can feel the storm, but you are no longer convinced it will swallow you whole. You can stand inside your own life now, not as a victim of its weather, but as a witness to your own resilience. And that shift, however subtle, is the beginning of something powerful. Not noise. Not spectacle. But sovereignty. You were wounded. You were misled. You were overwhelmed. Your nervous system was flooded, like a river after relentless rain, carrying debris that was never yours to hold. Your heart was exhausted, beating faithfully through storms that did not pause to ask whether you had strength left to give. Your body bore tension like armor, shoulders tight, jaw clenched, breath shallow and cautious. You survived in ways that made sense at the time. You adapted. You endured. You coped the only way you knew how. But you were never unworthy. And that realization, however fragile, however new, is sacred. It is like the first thin ray of dawn slipping beneath a door you thought was sealed. It is subtle, but it changes the temperature of the room. It changes the way the air feels in your lungs. It changes the way your name sounds inside your own mind. Pause here. Feel the weight of what you've survived. Let it settle into your muscles, into your bones, not as burden, but as evidence. Evidence that you endured nights that felt endless. Evidence that you carried grief without collapsing entirely. Evidence that you kept breathing when breath felt borrowed. Feel the strength it took to look inward instead of away. To sit with discomfort instead of numbing it. To allow tears instead of swallowing them. To face truths that stung like salt on open skin and stay present anyway. Feel the quiet pride that does not boast, does not need applause, but knows. It hums softly beneath your ribs like a steady drumbeat. Not loud. Not dramatic. But constant. Grounded. Alive. You stood at the edge of your own unraveling and chose to remain. You questioned the story that once defined you. You examined the shadow instead of running from it. You began separating your voice from the echoes of the past. That is no small thing. Volume One was not about becoming perfect. It was about becoming aware. It was about waking up inside the fog and realizing that even in confusion, even in despair, there was still a part of you watching, noticing, surviving. A part that refused to vanish. That part is still here. You are still here. And as you stand in this sacred pause, let yourself feel it, not just intellectually, but physically. The steadiness of your breath. The warmth in your chest. The subtle release in your shoulders. The space that now exists where once there was only constriction. You did not escape your story. You reclaimed it. The darkness shaped you, yes. But it did not claim you. And in that truth, in that lived, embodied, breath-filled truth, there is something extraordinary. There is hope. Not loud hope. Not naïve hope. But the kind that has been tested.

The kind that has walked through fire and come out carrying embers instead of ashes. Let this be your sacred pause. Not the end. Not the retreat. But the quiet moment between inhale and exhale where you realize: You survived the night. You are learning the language of your own worth. And you are stronger than the story that once tried to erase you. You were wounded. You were misled. You were overwhelmed. Your nervous system was flooded, like a river after relentless rain, carrying debris that was never yours to hold. Your heart was exhausted, beating faithfully through storms that did not pause to ask whether you had strength left to give. Your body bore tension like armor, shoulders tight, jaw clenched, breath shallow and cautious. You survived in ways that made sense at the time. You adapted. You endured. You coped the only way you knew how.nBut you were never unworthy. And that realization, however fragile, however new, is sacred. It is like the first thin ray of dawn slipping beneath a door you thought was sealed. It is subtle, but it changes the temperature of the room. It changes the way the air feels in your lungs. It changes the way your name sounds inside your own mind. Pause here. Feel the weight of what you've survived. Let it settle into your muscles, into your bones, not as burden, but as evidence. Evidence that you endured nights that felt endless. Evidence that you carried grief without collapsing entirely. Evidence that you kept breathing when breath felt borrowed. Feel the strength it took to look inward instead of away. To sit with discomfort instead of numbing it. To allow tears instead of swallowing them. To face truths that stung like salt on open skin and stay present anyway. Feel the quiet pride that does not boast, does not need applause, but knows. It hums softly beneath your ribs like a steady drumbeat. Not loud. Not dramatic. But constant. Grounded. Alive. You stood at the edge of your own unraveling and chose to remain. You questioned the story that once defined you. You examined the shadow instead of running from it. You began separating your voice from the echoes of the past. That is no small thing. Volume One was not about becoming perfect. It was about becoming aware. It was about waking up inside the fog and realizing that even in confusion, even in despair, there was still a part of you watching, noticing, surviving. A part that refused to vanish. That part is still here. You are still here. And as you stand in this sacred pause, let yourself feel it, not just intellectually, but physically. The steadiness of your breath. The warmth in your chest. The subtle release in your shoulders. The space that now exists where once there was only constriction. You did not escape your story. You reclaimed it. The darkness shaped you, yes. But it did not claim you. And in that truth, in that lived, embodied, breath-filled truth, there is something extraordinary. There is hope. Not loud hope. Not naïve hope. But the kind that has been tested. The kind that has walked through fire and come out carrying embers instead of ashes. Let this be your sacred pause. Not the end. Not the retreat. But the quiet moment between inhale and exhale where you realize: You survived the night. You are learning the language of your own worth. And you are stronger than the story that once tried to erase you. You were wounded. You were misled. You were overwhelmed. Your nervous system was flooded like a river after relentless rain, carrying debris that was never yours to hold. Your heart was exhausted, beating faithfully through storms that did not pause to ask whether you had strength left to give. Your body bore tension like armor, shoulders tight, jaw clenched, breath shallow and cautious. You survived in ways that made sense at the time. You adapted. You endured. You coped the only way you knew how. But you were never unworthy. And that realization, however fragile, however new, is sacred. It is like the first thin ray of dawn slipping beneath a door you thought was sealed. It is subtle, but it changes the temperature of the room. It changes the way the air feels in your lungs. It changes the way your name sounds inside your own mind. Pause here. Feel the weight of what you've survived.

Let it settle into your muscles, into your bones, not as burden, but as evidence. Evidence that you endured nights that felt endless. Evidence that you carried grief without collapsing entirely. Evidence that you kept breathing when breath felt borrowed. Feel the strength it took to look inward instead of away. To sit with discomfort instead of numbing it. To allow tears instead of swallowing them. To face truths that stung like salt on open skin and stay present anyway. Feel the quiet pride that does not boast, does not need applause, but knows. It hums softly beneath your ribs like a steady drumbeat. Not loud. Not dramatic. But constant. Grounded. Alive. You stood at the edge of your own unraveling and chose to remain. You questioned the story that once defined you. You examined the shadow instead of running from it. You began separating your voice from the echoes of the past. That is no small thing. Volume One was not about becoming perfect. It was about becoming aware. It was about waking up inside the fog and realizing that even in confusion, even in despair, there was still a part of you watching, noticing, surviving. A part that refused to vanish. That part is still here. You are still here. And as you stand in this sacred pause, let yourself feel it, not just intellectually, but physically. The steadiness of your breath. The warmth in your chest. The subtle release in your shoulders. The space that now exists where once there was only constriction. You did not escape your story. You reclaimed it. The darkness shaped you, yes. But it did not claim you. And in that truth, in that lived, embodied, breath-filled truth, there is something extraordinary. There is hope. Not loud hope. Not naïve hope. But the kind that has been tested. The kind that has walked through fire and come out carrying embers instead of ashes. Let this be your sacred pause. Not the end. Not the retreat. But the quiet moment between inhale and exhale where you realize: You survived the night. You are learning the language of your own worth. And you are stronger than the story that once tried to erase you. You can feel it, can't you? The difference in your body. The way your breath lingers a second longer before leaving you, no longer rushed, no longer fleeing. The way your lungs expand more fully, as if there is finally space enough inside you to hold air without panic. The way your thoughts no longer arrive like unquestioned commanders barking orders, but like passing weather systems, clouds drifting across a wide sky you now recognize as yours. They move through. They shift. They dissolve. The way your emotions, even the heavy ones, have texture now instead of total control.

Grief feels like a deep tide, not a drowning. Anger feels like heat that rises and falls, not a wildfire consuming everything in its path. Sadness feels like rain on a windowpane, steady, sometimes relentless, but not permanent. You can feel them without becoming them. You can notice them without surrendering your entire identity to their presence. Something inside you has widened. And that widening is not small. The next volume will take us deeper, into the shadow of self-hate, into the mirror we once avoided, into rooms that may feel dim at first, where old echoes still linger in the corners like dust unsettled by new light. There may be moments when the air feels thick again. When you sense the old narratives stirring, whispering their familiar accusations. When your body remembers before your mind does. But you are not stepping into that darkness unarmed. You are stepping in awake. And that changes everything. Awake means you can hear the critic and recognize its tone. Awake means you can feel the tightening in your chest and pause instead of collapsing. Awake means you understand that what rises is not always truth, it is memory, it is conditioning, it is protection dressed as punishment. You are not entering the shadow to be consumed by it. You are entering it to understand it. So close this book gently. Feel its weight in your hands, the solidness of it, the grounded reality of pages that carried you through confession and confrontation. Notice the texture of the cover beneath your fingertips. Hear the soft sound of paper meeting paper, that quiet, sacred thud of completion. Let that sound register in your body, not as an ending, but as a milestone. A marker in the terrain of your becoming. Proof that you stayed. That you faced. That you walked through. You have begun. And beginning, truly beginning, is the hardest part. Beginning requires courage before confidence. Faith before certainty. A step before you can see the full path. You took that step. You kept turning pages even when the words pressed against bruised places. You kept breathing even when the memories stirred. Well done. Truly. Rest here for a moment. Let your nervous system soften like soil after rain. Let your jaw unclench. Let your shoulders lower. Let pride, not loud, not boastful, but steady and grounded—settle warmly in your chest. Feel it like a small ember glowing beneath your ribs. It does not need to flare. It only needs to exist. You survived the descent. Now, when you are ready, we go deeper. Not because you are broken. But because you are brave.

Dear reader or listener, I leave you now with this poem:

A Declaration from the Edge

I speak now as one who has stood with her hand on the cold handle of the last door.
I have felt the grain of it beneath my palm, splintered wood and iron chill,
the air metallic in my mouth, the silence thick as winter breath.
I have walked the hallway where light thins, where sound folds inward,
where even your own name echoes as if it belongs to someone already gone.
I have stood at the lip of the abyss. I have tasted its promise, bitter as rust at the back of the tongue.
I have heard its whisper, not loud, not dramatic, but smooth and reasonable, like logic sharpened by exhaustion.
I have felt the wind of it pulling at my ribs from the inside.
And I tell you this: the abyss is not silent. It breathes. It waits. It studies your weariness and calls it surrender.
That night, the darkness was not only around me, it was under my skin.
My bones felt hollowed by grief. My chest burned with shame.
The room smelled of endings. The world narrowed to a single unbearable thought:
"Maybe I am the wound. Maybe I am the harm. Maybe the world would breathe easier without me."
But there, at the edge, something older than despair stirred.
Not loud. Not heroic. Not thunder and angels and blinding light. Just a pulse.
A small, defiant rhythm beneath my ribs. It said, "*No.*"
Not a scream. Not a battle cry. A whisper that refused to die.
I did not survive because I was fearless. I survived because somewhere inside the wreckage a seed refused burial.
I have stood in that place where annihilation masquerades as mercy.
Where shame dresses itself as responsibility.
Where self-hate calls itself protection.
I have learned what it means to mistake exhaustion for weakness.
To mistake illness for identity. To believe the lie that I was the poison.
But I was never the poison. I was wounded. Flooded. Overwhelmed.
A nervous system braced too long. A heart bent beneath inherited storms.
And wounds, when tended, can mend. Surviving death was not a miracle in bright colors.
It was waking to the sterile scent of antiseptic, the weight of breath re-entering my lungs,
the tremor of being returned to a body that still wanted to live.
It was terror. It was disorientation. It was the unbearable clarity of what I had almost taken from myself.
But it was also this: a rupture in the old story.
A crack in the illusion that I was beyond repair.
Surviving death meant I could no longer pretend I was powerless.
It meant the lie lost its authority. It meant the cage door, once invisible, stood open, and I could choose.
Choose to stay. Choose to fight. Choose to gather the shattered pieces not to recreate who I had been,
but to become someone truer.
I learned to sit with my demons without handing them the throne.
I learned that self-hate was not my voice it was history speaking through me.
I learned that the harsh protector inside was a frightened sentinel, trying to keep me safe with the wrong weapon.
I learned to forgive myself. To lay down hot coals of bitterness that burned only my own hands.

To speak gently to the child within who once believed she had to disappear to make things right.
I learned to be okay, not because the past vanished, but because it no longer ruled me.
Okay means breathing without flinching.
Okay means feeling pain without becoming it.
Okay means waking in the morning and choosing life again.
Surviving death did not make me perfect. It made me honest. It made me awake.
It made me understand that standing at the edge is not proof of weakness.
It is proof of how long you have been carrying too much. And so I declare this, to you who stand there now,
to you who feel the wind of that abyss against your skin,
to you who are deep in the thick soil of healing and wonder if the sun will ever find you:
You are not the wound. You are not the curse.
You are not the problem to be erased.
The voice telling you otherwise is not your truest voice.
It is memory. It is pain. It is protection gone rigid. There is a pulse inside you that has not given up.
You may barely hear it. You may barely feel it. But it is there.
You are still here. And that matters more than you know.
The door of death is not your destiny. It is a threshold that can be stepped back from.
The abyss is not the end of your story.
It is the place where false narratives lose their grip and truth begins to whisper.
If you are standing on the edge, hold on one more breath.
If you are deep in healing, keep tending the wound. The darkness is soil. Not a grave.
And you, you are the seed that knows how to rise.

Till we meet again

Till we meet again within the pages of Volume Two, carry this with you like a quiet ember cupped in your hands, warm, steady, alive. Not a roaring flame demanding attention, but a small, faithful glow that hums against your palms when the air turns cold. Guard it gently. Feed it with patience. Shield it from the winds of self-criticism that once blew so freely through your inner world. Be gentle with yourself. Not only in the dramatic crescendos of pain or breakthrough, but in the ordinary, almost invisible moments that shape your days. In the kitchen light at dusk, when you replay a conversation and wince. In the quiet morning, when the mirror catches you off guard. In the small missteps that once would have spiraled into self-reproach. Be gentle in the way you speak to yourself when you make a mistake. Notice the tone. Does it sting? Does it bruise? Let it soften. Let your words land like hands resting lightly on a shoulder rather than a gavel striking wood. You are not on trial. You are learning. Be gentle when old memories brush against your skin like a sudden chill—when something in the air smells like yesterday, and your body tenses before your mind understands why. When your chest tightens unexpectedly. When your throat thickens with something unspoken. That is not weakness. That is history moving through tissue and breath. Place your hand there. Feel the warmth of your own touch spreading slowly beneath your palm. Let your body register that you are here now. That you are safe in this moment. Be gentle with your exhaustion. With the heaviness that sometimes settles into your bones like evening fog. Rest without guilt.

Pause without apology. You have carried storms. You have walked through nights that stretched longer than they should have. Of course you are tired. Of course your nervous system sometimes hums with leftover thunder. Treat that tenderness not as inconvenience, but as sacred terrain. Let your inner voice soften its edges. Let it sound less like a judge delivering a verdict and more like a steady companion walking beside you on uneven ground. Imagine its cadence changing, less sharp, less hurried, less absolute. More curious. More kind. More willing to understand. When your thoughts begin to spiral, when they whirl like leaves caught in a restless wind, slow your breath. Feel it move in and out. Cool as it enters your nostrils. Warm as it leaves. Let it remind you that you are not your thoughts. They are weather. You are the sky. They may pass through you, but they do not own you. Listen to your breath the way you would listen to waves against a shoreline that has weathered storms before and still remains. That shoreline is you. Eroded in places, perhaps. Reshaped. But still here. Still standing. Carry yourself the way you would carry someone you fiercely love—aware of their fragility, aware of their strength. Protect your own humanness. Honor your own growth. Speak to your own heart with the reverence you once reserved only for others. And when doubt returns, as it sometimes will, do not panic. Do not declare the journey undone. Simply return to the ember. Cup it again in your hands. Remember what you survived. Remember what you learned. Remember that gentleness is not weakness, it is wisdom earned through fire. Until we meet again in Volume Two, let kindness be the atmosphere you breathe. Let softness be the ground beneath your steps. Let your own presence be a safe place to land. You have come this far. Walk gently now. Be compassionate. Remember that healing is not silent. It is not tidy. It stirs the sediment at the bottom of the lake. It loosens what has long been packed down. It awakens old sensations that rise unexpectedly in the body—an ache behind the ribs, a tightening in the throat, a heaviness settling into the limbs like dusk settling over water. It reopens doors you once closed just to survive. It brings back old narratives that once felt absolute, carved into stone, unquestionable. But listen closely: *"If something aches, it does not mean you are failing. If something feels heavy, it does not mean you are weak."* It means you are alive. It means you are processing. It means you are growing. Growth has weight. Transformation has texture. Sometimes it tastes like salt at the edge of your lips.

Sometimes it sounds like your own breath catching as truth lands in your chest. Sometimes it feels like standing barefoot on uneven ground, aware of every stone, every shift beneath your feet. Be compassionate with that. Look after yourself as if you are tending something sacred. Eat when you are hungry not only for food, but for rest, for beauty, for silence. Rest when you are tired, not only when your body gives out, but when your spirit feels thin. Step outside and let the air touch your face. Feel it cool against your skin, warm against your cheeks, alive against your lungs. Notice the light, how it moves across walls, how it spills across the earth whether you feel ready for it or not. Notice the sound of the world continuing. A bird calling. A car passing. Leaves shifting in wind. Life is moving. You are still part of it. Notice your own heartbeat, faithful and steady beneath it all. It does not rush to condemn you. It does not question your worth. It simply keeps time. It keeps you here. Tend to your inner fire with care. Do not throw harsh words onto it like dry wood soaked in gasoline. Feed it warmth. Feed it gentleness. Feed it truth, not the sharp, distorted truth of shame, but the grounded truth of your humanity. Feed it courage. Feed it rest. Feed it compassion. You are always tending a fire. Choose what you place into it. And until we meet again in Volume Two, hold yourself the way you would hold someone you love deeply, cradled close, aware of their fragility and their strength. With patience when they falter. With tenderness when they tremble. With quiet respect for the journey they have walked. Wrap your own shoulders in that care. Let it settle into your bones. Let it become the atmosphere you breathe. You are worth that care. Not because you have healed completely. Not because you have proven anything. Not because you never struggle. But because you are here. Always. Till we meet again...

Surviving Death
Echoes of the Abyss
A Memoir of Despair and Discovery
ISBN: 978-1-0492-3375-8
Surviving Death is not a story about dying.
It is a story about what happens when you don't.
It is about the quiet deaths no one sees —
the slow erosion of self beneath expectation.
The belief that your existence is the wound,
the crushing weight of thinking your absence
might bring relief. This book delves into my
personal reckoning with a suicide attempt,
and the complicated, disorienting reality of
surviving it. Not as spectacle. Not as shock.
But as truth. Volume One walks directly into the
darker shadow of my suicide story. Tracing the
invisible threads that led me there. It examines
depression not as a mood, but as an architecture.
A slow construction.
A narrowing corridor of thought. It offers a stark
and unfiltered look at what suicidal ideation
really is. How it forms, how it distorts perception,
how it convinces you that disappearance is mercy.
It is about a child who learned to fragment in order to endure.
About the inner family we build when safety is uncertain.
About memory that refuses to dissolve. About love that was
imperfect, and pain that was real. This book does not promise
easy healing. It does not romanticize survival. Instead, it walks into
the shadowed rooms — the ones where shame grows roots in
silence, where identity fractures to survive impact, where the mind
turns against its own existence — and it stays long enough for
breath to return. Blending poetic memoir with psychological
excavation. Surviving Death is a journey through the invisible
mechanics of despair, the complexity of family, and the radical
act of choosing to remain. This is for the ones who believed they
were the problem. For the ones who survived their own darkness.
For the ones still learning how to live after the quietest kind of dying.
You are not weak for having reached the edge.
You are not broken for having fallen. You are still here.
And that matters.
By Letitia Swanepoel

'[;

bh

www.ingramcontent.com/pod-product-compliance
Lightning Source LLC
LaVergne TN
LVHW081958200926
848481LV00010B/2760
* 9 7 8 1 0 4 9 2 3 3 7 4 1 *